4000
champagnes

To my beloved wife, Sara
To my children, Stella and Henrik.

Richard Juhlin

4000
champagnes

Flammarion

Contents

Preface

Richard does not simply speak about wine, he speaks the language of wine in the way others speak Swedish or French—and, what is more, with a light Champagne accent! And he does not, as one might believe, simply stare at the glass of wine standing in front of him. He plunges into it, studying it from within, like an actor getting under the skin of his role. Ostensibly a wine journalist, Richard is in fact a kind of medium, a hypersensitive transmitter, with an artist's knack for making the unconscious visible. When we first met on my estate in Reims, and then again at Gamla Stan, the old town of Stockholm, where we gazed out over a breathtaking expanse of water, it struck me that this young expert, in addition to having undeniable charm and an impressive CV, was able to understand a wine from the inside. Since that time he has devoted himself to thorough studies, emerging uplifted or discouraged from his various explorations. His knowledge of the Champagne region is the fruit of countless journeys undertaken in every season. Knowing the region, its vineyards, and its history like the back of his hand, his experiences in our winelands exude all the freshness of a young love that has since consolidated into an enduring yet still fiery passion. For three hundred years now, the ageless wines of Champagne have been bewitching successive generations. What is in store for the future?

Time has become as precious as Iranian caviar, and culture is receding before the age of zapping. But wine is a time-consuming affair; the time required for its creation and the time needed to learn how to enjoy it. How can we convince our contemporaries to turn their backs on the exhilaration of speed and start enjoying the pleasures of years past once again? Long live Bacchus! Long live Richard!

It is not only his carefully chosen words, his wealth of knowledge, and the almost physical symbiosis between wine and man that arouses our envy and joy in equal measure; it is also the youthfulness, the authenticity of his tone. I have a dream that one day later generations will produce voices like his—voices that will broadcast the beauties of Champagne to the world at large, and sing of the delicious flavor of its wine.

Prince Alain de Polignac
Reims, February 14, 2002

Swedish and crazy about Champagne

I have been asked so often why I chose to take such a keen interest in Champagne that I have now thought long and hard about it myself. As a teenager, I was keen to communicate my taste impressions, and from my mother's side I have inherited an interest in fragrances—whatever their source. I owe my passion for wine to my father, though. My maternal grandfather and he shared a common fondness for classical music, sport, geography, and wine. I saw for myself how close they seemed when sitting and talking of some inaccessible and dreamy wine, all the while sipping a rather more affordable Ockfener Bockstein Kabinett. At the tender age of ten, I took a journey of initiation through the ravishing wine valley of the Moselle, savoring its delicious sweet wines, which I adored immediately. It was surely this that made me understand just how awful the taste of a Vino Tinto, Kir, or Beyaz could be.

When, as an adolescent, I began hesitantly to enter the adult world, I was just as dependent as my friends on alcohol's simultaneously inebriating and liberating effect, but I soon discovered that it was worth spending a little extra to enjoy a more palatable wine. The filmmaker Hannes Holm and I were great friends at high school. One St. John's Day, which we were celebrating in the Stockholm archipelago, a movie producer, eager to impress us, ordered some genuine Champagne. We enjoyed it so much that Hannes and I completely forgot the producer and, inspired by the Champagne, sunk into philosophical meditation. I was hooked.

Several years after this, and with this unspoken passion for Champagne still bubbling away in my subconscious, I rented a house in Brittany with some friends. My parents, sister and her companion soon joined us with a bottle of Pommery in hand. They were all breathless after a trip through Champagne on the way to Brittany, and gave a fascinating and vivid description of the rows of bottles in the chalky cellars and the birth of the bubbles. On my way back from my holiday, I decided to stop off at Reims. This visit, and the train trip through the cellars at Piper-Heidsieck, were never going to do anything but heighten my interest. Back home, and with my enthusiasm rekindled, I threw myself into the few books I could find about Champagne and discovered my talent for tasting.

Today I am one of those happy few who are lucky enough to be able to turn what was a hobby into a career. Together with a group of equally committed collaborators, I am head of the Juhlin Champagne Company, whose activities center for the most part on Champagne.

When I look out of the window and gaze on the tentative February sunlight glinting on the still leafless trees, I feel my nostrils quivering and my desire reawakening. It is a longing for spring and for a youthful, brightly sparkling vintage Champagne enjoyed out on the terrace. Will spring ever come? Will it be sufficiently warm in this country of mine to sit outside and slake my thirst with a Blanc de Blancs? For the moment, we'll have to bide our time—but we can always savor a glass of Champagne. A bottle of Bonnaire this evening, perhaps. For a fine Champagne is a bit like drinking spring! Yes, a Champagne can be so many things. It can be an imposing monument, or charming and airy, penetrating in its intensity, or elegant and subtly sensual—or just a let-down. In can be sensational in its youth, yet deep and thought-provoking when properly aged, for the very best Champagnes can live as long as a human being. It is a drink produced by driven individuals and enjoyed by equally passionate people. I have been forcibly struck to find that people who make good wine are both agreeable and enthusiastic. Though perhaps it is not that odd, since the less spiritual ones—those deprived of the subtlety of intuition necessary to any creative process—tend instead to rely on technology.

There are of course exceptions, and it is in these cases that my humility and objectivity are really put to the test. I recall, for example, one visit to a wine-grower who appeared completely indifferent to me as a person, to my passion for this beverage, and even to his own wines. He hardly knew how the principal *cuvées* were composed, and just as little about the blending of the grape varieties. In a room with a sickening smell, cigarette in hand, he took out some cheap Duralex glasses and filled them to the brim with what turned out to be a marvelous Champagne. On another visit, I was extremely well received by the most charming winemaking family imaginable. After an enriching conversation ranging over the things that make life important, we wandered round their property exploring the winemaking plant and the remarkably neat cellars. So, in these perfect conditions, I was at last on the point of tasting a Champagne that had been produced according to the rules of the art, incorporating some particularly costly details designed to improve its quality. Yet in the end, I was served up a wine of infinite drabness. The exception that proves the rule, perhaps.

Many people think that my enthusiasm for the French lifestyle means that in the long term I will settle in France and produce a wine of my own. I have always loved the Mediterranean, the Alps, the apple orchards of Normandy, the sunsets of Brittany, and the scented limestone breeze of Champagne, but it is in Sweden that I feel most at home. My roots are here. I adore returning to France to experience life, to rediscover it, to breathe it in with all my senses, but I really believe that I can do it better and with more passion as a visitor than as a resident.

In 1997, my love of France and its Champagne—as well as my passion as a taster—earned me the honor of being made Chevalier of the Coteaux de Champagne. In 2001, I had the pleasure of publishing *Champagne, la grande dégustation,* which told of the great tasting session that saw 1959 Billecart-Salmon proclaimed as the greatest Champagne of the twentieth century. This volume was awarded the title of "Best Book on French Wine" at the gathering of the Salon du Livre Gourmand in Périgueux.

For an earlier tome devoted to tasting 3,000 Champagnes (published in Swedish), I had set my sights on finding a first-rate photographer capable of sharing my passion for the region, and of doing justice to the bottles of Champagne and the bubbles within. Sometimes, I believe in fate. How could it be otherwise when I tell you the curious story of how Pål Allan's and my paths crossed? In my search for someone who might work in the style I had in mind, I pored through every cookbook; indeed every book illustrated with photographs. In a fabulously beautiful book entitled *Modern Asian Cuisine* I finally found what I was looking for. Pål Allan shot the ingredients of Asian cooking in a unique way, and in such extraordinary close-up that they appeared to float in mid-air, like planets in space or cells in the human body. The only problem was that Pål Allan lived in New York, most likely an American of Scandinavian origin. Time passed, and I had more or less given up hope of finding a suitable cover illustration. However, at the last moment, just as the finishing touches were being put to the text, an amazing thing happened. I received what I at first mistook for a poison-pen letter written by an articulate young woman. The final lines of this missive outlined exactly why its author had taken against me to such a degree: her husband had stopped going to bed with her and had begun going to bed with my book on Champagne instead! This, she reckoned, gave her the right to summon me in secret to their house to celebrate her husband's birthday. She went on to introduce herself and her husband—a photographer by trade, a purebred Swede by the name of…Pål Allan! A couple of weeks later, I found myself hiding in a built-in cupboard until a rather perplexed Pål opened it: now he understood why the table was laid with three Champagne glasses! A few hours later and Pål had accepted the project. Since then we have worked together in a close collaboration that I hope manages to convey all the harmony of the many diverse elements that go to make up a truly great Champagne *cuvée*.

CHAMPAGNES AND THE NOBEL PRIZE

Being Swedish, I was of course extremely interested in the Champagne served at the Nobel Prize presentations that take place every year in Stockholm. At this annual banquet, 300 bottles of Champagne are served to 1,100 distinguished guests. After in-depth research, I am now able to reveal the complete list of Champagnes served at this occasion, a list that is all the more interesting since it reflects the "tastes of the day" throughout the different eras. Several brands that feature at the beginning of the list have long-since disappeared. Equally worthy of note is that Veuve Clicquot, the largest Champagne brand represented in Sweden until it was overtaken by Moët & Chandon, has not once been served at a Nobel Prize banquet! Louis Roederer, who remained in second place for many years

and who became the supplier for the royal court on May 9, 1951, appears several times in the list. Curiously, Krug appears for several years in a row in the first half of the 1970s, but then not afterward. Mumm is featured ten times and Moët fourteen times. Pommery seems practically to have acquired a warrant to appear at this gala dinner, reigning supreme with twenty entries in the list. Until 1961, Champagne was served mainly with dessert, but occasionally with dishes as surprising as lamb fillet. The Champagne that is served today is drier, and goes best with the starter.

Here are the Champagnes that have been served at the Nobel Prize dinner since 1901:

1901	Crème de Bouzy Extra Dry
1902	Mumm Crémant de Cramant, Desbordes Brut
1903	Mumm Crémant de Cramant, Dumigny Sec
1904	Mumm Crémant de Cramant, Dumigny Sec
1905	Mumm Crémant de Cramant, Dumigny Sec
1906	Mumm Crémant de Cramant, Pol Roger Demi-Sec
1908	Louis Roederer Carte Blanche
1909	Charles Heidsieck Extra Dry
1910	Charles Heidsieck Extra Dry
1911	Charles Heidsieck Millésimé 1900
1912	Charles Heidsieck Millésimé 1904, Goût Américain
1913	Charles Heidsieck Millésimé 1904, Goût Américain
1921	Georges Goulet Sec
1922	Ayala Goût Américain
1925	Pommery Goût Américain
1926	Georges Goulet Extra Sweet
1927	Dumigny Goût Américain
1928	Dumigny Goût Américain
1929	Bollinger Extra Dry
1930	Mumm Cordon Rouge
1931	Louis Roederer Grand Vin Sec
1932	Louis Roederer Grand Vin Sec
1933	Louis Roederer Grand Vin Sec
1934	Louis Roederer Grand Vin Sec, Pommery Sec
1935	Louis Roederer Grand Vin Sec, Pol Roger Millésime 1926
1936	Louis Roederer Grand Vin Sec, Pol Roger Brut
1937	Louis Roederer Grand Vin Sec, Pol Roger Brut
1938	Louis Roederer Grand Vin Sec, Pol Roger Brut
1950	Perrier-Jouët Brut
1953	Deutz Brut
1954	Heidsieck & Monopole Brut
1955	Eugène Barbier Brut
1956	Lanson Brut
1957	Lanson Brut
1959	Moët & Chandon Brut Impérial
1960	Moët & Chandon Brut Impérial
1961	Pommery Brut Royal
1962	Pommery Brut Royal
1963	Pommery Brut Royal
1964	Pommery Brut Royal
1965	Pommery Brut Royal
1966	Pommery Brut Royal
1967	Pommery Brut Royal
1968	Pommery Brut Royal
1969	Krug Private Cuvée
1970	Krug Private Cuvée
1971	Krug Private Cuvée
1972	Krug Private Cuvée
1973	Krug Private Cuvée
1974	Krug Private Cuvée
1975	Krug Private Cuvée
1976	Pommery Brut Royal
1977	Pommery Brut Royal
1978	Pommery Brut Royal
1979	Mumm Cordon Rouge
1980	Mumm Cordon Rouge
1981	Mumm Cordon Rouge
1982	Mumm Cordon Rouge
1983	Pommery Brut Royal
1984	Moët & Chandon Brut Impérial
1985	Moët & Chandon Brut Impérial
1986	Moët & Chandon Brut Impérial
1987	Moët & Chandon Brut Impérial
1988	Moët & Chandon Brut Impérial
1989	Moët & Chandon Brut Impérial
1990	Moët & Chandon Brut Impérial
1991	Moët & Chandon Brut Impérial
1992	Moët & Chandon Brut Impérial
1993	Moët & Chandon Millésime 1988
1994	Moët & Chandon Cuvée Anniversaire Millésime 1983
1995	Taittinger Millésimé 1989
1996	Pommery Millésimé 1990
1997	Pommery Millésimé 1991
1998	Pommery Millésimé 1991
1999	Pommery Millésimé 1992
2000	Pommery Millésimé 1992
2001	Louise Pommery Millésimé 1989
2002	Dom Pérignon Millésimé 1993
2003	Dom Pérignon Millésimé 1993

Everything you want to know about Champagne

1

The party wine

"Champagne…" Isn't the word on its own enough to create that tingling feeling of hope? For three centuries now Champagne has been synonymous with luxury, frivolity, elegance, and glamor. Few victories, few festivals can now be celebrated without a precious bottle or two. For the majority of people, Champagne is a celebratory drink, but not many bother to ask themselves whether they are drinking a fine Champagne or a bottle of cheap fizz—for them any wine with bubbles is "Champagne." This misconception is so prevalent that even the most serious wine-taster can forsake his or her critical faculties when a Champagne glass is put into their hands, abandoning the age-old rituals of tasting. Attitudes are changing, however, and today very few journalists, enologists, or wine waiters would question the superiority of Champagne over other sparkling wines. In my opinion, Champagne constitutes one of France's greatest gifts to the civilized world.

Annual global production of sparkling wine is nearly two billion bottles, but only 250 million of these contain genuine Champagne. The name Champagne can only be used to refer to wine produced in a relatively small area in the north of France—nowhere else. The unique character of this region is due to a series of circumstances that has made it the best place in the world for the production of sparkling wines. Natural effervescence in wine results from a temperate climate. But it was only at the beginning of the eighteenth century that winemakers gradually began to understand how to control a second fermentation, which today produces approximately 47 million pretty bubbles in each bottle.

The monk Dom Pérignon, often called the father of Champagne, is just one figure among many who developed the process that is nowadays called the *méthode champenoise*. The same method is used throughout the world, with varying degrees of success, but its results are never as good as in Champagne. The triumphant march of Champagne started with the creation of Champagne houses at the end of the eighteenth century, and continued through to the recent millennium celebrations.

One of the great plus points of Champagne is that it is a fantastic wine for every occasion. Besides its natural role as a celebratory wine, it can also be drunk to break the ice at gatherings and is both an ideal aperitif and a fine accompaniment to various dishes. Champagne is a magical wine blessed with everything one could possibly wish for: beauty in its youth, a blooming maturity, and, finally, a capacity for aging into a complex blend that can become even more captivating with the years.

A miracle of nature at dawn.

Champagne has all the elements necessary to maintain one's passion for life. In most countries, Champagne has remained the prerogative of the wealthiest in society, but changes are afoot, and it is gradually becoming more democratic, a tendency that is accelerating more quickly than one would ever have believed possible. Champagne will never be dirt cheap, but in fact, in comparison to average disposable incomes, the price of a bottle is lower today than ever before.

Perhaps, reading this book, you will become an ambassador for Champagne among your friends, and so increase the number of connoisseurs of what is an incomparable wine....

CHAMPAGNE-LOVERS YESTERDAY AND TODAY

There have been countless Champagne-lovers throughout history, the supreme example perhaps being Winston Churchill, who drank a bottle of Pol-Roger a day. He contended that Champagne improved one's mood, steeled one's courage, excited the imagination, and kept the mind keen. Champagne, he stipulated, should be "cool, dry, and free." Unlike most of us, though, Churchill did not have to pay for his. He had met Madame Odette Pol-Roger at a buffet in 1944, after which Pol-Roger became his daily tipple. Specially bottled in pints, the Champagne followed him faithfully wherever he went. Churchill quaffed some of the greatest vintages of the time: 1928, 1934, 1943, and 1945. On tasting a bottle of 1947 in the early 1950s, he acclaimed it as the finest Champagne he had ever drunk in the post-war period, and ordered sufficient stocks to last until his death. No less than 20,000 bottles were set aside for him! After he died, a black band was added to Pol-Roger labels. Champagne is still delivered to the British prime-minister's residence at 10 Downing Street, London, even today.

Churchill's brother-in-law, Christopher Soames, also loved Pol-Roger. Sent to Rhodesia to supervise the transition of the country to independence, he was asked when peace was going to be restored. In exactly 30 days, he replied, since he only had 30 bottles of Pol-Roger left.

Long before Churchill, however, other famous people had voiced their adoration of Champagne. Madame de Pompadour declared: "Champagne is the only wine that leaves a woman with her beauty after drinking it." And there must have been a fair number of guests at the masked ball in the Hôtel de Ville in 1739 when no less than 1,800 bottles were consumed! Alexandre Dumas kept a glass of Champagne next to his quill and inkwell for inspiration. When Tannhäuser flopped in Paris, Richard Wagner (also a friend of Monsieur and Madame Chandon) wrote that his reconciliation with France was thanks to Champagne alone; it had restored his *joie de vivre*.

Ernest Hemingway was not only keen on strong alcohol, he also appreciated Champagne: "The only expensive wine I can drink is a good, dry Champagne." Marlene Dietrich was another great Champagne lover, who on tour would always have a glass to hand. "It makes you think it's Sunday and that happiness cannot be far away." Obviously her weekdays must have been rather different from most of ours. Coco Chanel would drink Champagne on only two occasions: when she was in love and when she wasn't. This kind of reasoning reminds us of Lily Bollinger, who supposedly confessed: "I drink Champagne when I'm merry and when I'm low. Sometimes, I drink it alone. When I have company, I consider it obligatory. I sip a little when I'm hungry. If not, I don't touch it—unless of course I'm thirsty."

Madonna is a fan of Amour de Deutz. Marilyn Monroe, however, preferred Piper-Heidsieck, a firm which seems to have inextricably bound its destiny to Hollywood; today it supports most of the major movie festivals. If one really wanted to splash out, one would have to take a leaf out of Michael Jackson's book, who on his birthday paid the incredible sum of 1.2 million dollars for two bottles of Champagne that were delivered in an oak case gilded in pure gold. Yes, the list of celebrities who love Champagne, of real or fictitious figures who celebrated their happiest hours with Champagne glass in hand, is endless. For more than two hundred years, countless opera-goers have listened to Don Giovanni singing the praises of Champagne to Mozart's music, and who can imagine the opening scene of Verdi's *La Traviata* without Champagne? In *My Darling Clementine*, director John Ford included a character who, though in the heart of the American West, drinks nothing but Champagne. Alfred Hitchcock was an unrepentant lover of the wine, a fondness often reflected in his films. But the best-known example from the film world is James Bond, who started by drinking Comtes de Champagne, went on to Bollinger R. D., and moved on to Dom Pérignon in later films in the series. My favorite scene is in *The Man with the Golden Gun* when, lounging on a now famous sandy beach in Thailand, Scaramanga fires a revolver and uncorks a "Dompa" served by the bizarre dwarf Nic-Nac. George Lazenby was less fortunate in *On Her Majesty's Secret Service*: he ordered a "Dom Pérignon 1957," a year that was never produced! Since Timothy Dalton and Pierce Brosnan have played the part, 007 has reverted to drinking "Bolly:" the producers were keen to give Bond an exclusively British profile and Dom Pérignon was considered too American.

After the Second World War, Champagne even managed to make its mark in the world of sport. Countless victories are celebrated with Champagne and certain sporting events positively swim in fizz. Champagne and strawberries are pretty much de rigueur at Wimbledon. The larger Champagne houses even

My "Juhlin glasses" at the Millennium Tasting.

sponsor sports events, such as the America's Cup sailing race, as well as major golfing tournaments and automobile competitions. In motor sports, we have become accustomed to seeing the winners spray themselves and their supporters with magnums of Moët & Chandon. Interestingly, Moët & Chandon used to sponsor FI races, but the firm later took the decision to withdraw, as the publicity it gained seemed to be as negative as it was positive. However, since Grand Prix organizers have the means of buying it themselves, the podium is still showered with floods of Moët & Chandon.

Champagne and the motor car have gone hand in hand for a long time now. At the beginning of the twentieth century, automobile competitions were organized that served Champagne before, during, and after the race, and the link became even closer when, on October 12, 1936, the winner of the American Vanderbilt Cup was awarded a jeroboam of 1926 Moët & Chandon as a prize.

The custom of launching ships by breaking a bottle of Champagne onto the hull seems to have started in France in the eighteenth century. At the beginning, this was a combination of the

Christian tradition of blessing newly built boats, and the pagan ritual of offering drinks to the gods. The English quickly adopted the tradition, inventing the idea that if a ship were launched without the taste of wine it would soon swallow blood instead. This notion gains added poignancy when one recalls the *Titanic* disaster: the bottle intended to launch the ship had simply refused to break.

Champagne at weddings has become commonplace in most countries, but in many places the great moment for Champagne is Christmas. Ultimately, midnight on New Year's Eve is the only celebration where one focuses on a single moment demanding a solemn toast. The nature of this wine, with its column of beaded bubbles, its frothy beauty, and the agreeable way it goes straight to the head, makes it well-nigh compulsory.

As you see, if you want to crack open a bottle of Champagne, any excuse will do. The common denominator on all occasions at which corks fly is merrymaking. Indeed the French have met with such success marketing Champagne as the preeminent symbol of party-time and of gaiety generally that today it has become an obvious choice.

A history of Champagne

Archaeological excavations indicate that wine has been made for more than 7,000 years. Five thousand year-old presses found in Egypt constitute undeniable proof of its production in very ancient times. Progress in winemaking techniques and the use of present-day varieties, however, seems unquestionably to have commenced in the Caucasus, an area covering what is today eastern Turkey, northern Iraq, Azerbaijan and Georgia. Starting from the Caucasus, vine cultivation then extended to Palestine, Syria, Egypt, and Mesopotamia, from there soon reached the Mediterranean basin and later northern Central Europe. The majority of these ancient wines were probably medium dry and would have been turned into vinegar the following spring.

Before embarking on the history of Champagne, it should be noted that not just any sparkling wine is a Champagne. Burgundy, Rioja, and Moselle wines all originate in strictly defined geographical areas, and the same very much applies to Champagne. Yet the word "Champagne" has three different meanings: Champagne (the province), the Champagne wineland, and Champagne (the wine itself). *Champagne* in French means, more or less, "open countryside," and it is a good description of this area in the middle of a vast agricultural center that has rolling hills stretching as far as the eye can see. The province of Champagne covers no less than four *départements*: Ardennes, Marne, Aube, and Haute-Marne. From north to south it measures 320 kilometers (178 miles) and east to west 150 kilometers (83 miles), corresponding approximately to the area of Belgium.

Before Roman colonization, Champagne formed part of Gaul. It is even claimed that the Gauls cultivated the vine here, though the more commonly held view is that it was the Romans who first planted vines in the region. Indeed, significant archaeological finds of winemaking artifacts have reinforced the theory that the Romans were cultivating the vine in Champagne fifty years after the birth of Christ. The oldest documentary evidence of wine production in Champagne dates from 800 CE when an archbishop of Reims wrote a letter to the bishop of Laon, in which he recommended the wines of Épernay and the especially tonic wines of Mailly.

The history of Champagne is marked above all by the frequency and bloodiness of its battles. No other region in France has been so touched by war, plunder, and mayhem. Franks, Goths, Burgundians, and Vandals all figure significantly, but

For sheer visual pleasure: one of the fine bas-reliefs in the Pommery cellars.

Attila the Hun takes the prize as the worst of them all. In the year 451, on the Catalaunic Fields, one of the most murderous battles in human history took place. It concluded with Attila being forced to beat a retreat and flee from Western Europe. The role of Champagne as a theater of conflict did not cease there, however. In the Middle Ages, Épernay was fired and ransacked on no less than twenty-five occasions, while during the First and Second World Wars the city once more found itself in the eye of the storm.

The area's central position in France and in Europe, however, brought more positive effects. The proximity of Paris did much to advance the reputation of its wines, while the first crowning of a king of France at Reims, that of Clovis in 496, helped make the city into a cultural center. By the ninth century, the "wines of the mountain" and "wines of the river" were already seen as distinct. The most famous villages were Bouzy and Verzenay on the uplands and Aÿ lower down in the Marne valley. Gradually, a vin de Champagne *appellation* began to be sold. With Louis XIV's declaration that "Champagne is the only conceivable beverage," the reputation of the wine reached its apogee; all those with the wherewithal to do so would follow the recommendations of the Sun King unquestioningly. Curiously enough, at that time Champagne was a rather pale red wine, and sixteenth-century descriptions testify to a wine whose notes recall a rosé. Acidity was probably too high compared to the concentration of the wine, and we would surely have found it too sour today. It would have had the aroma of peaches, a flavor that reemerges in present-day Rosé des Riceys, a practically unique still rosé from Aube. It is likely that the wine's year played an even more crucial role than it does today as regards its quality. The chilly climate of Champagne made harvests a hazardous enterprise that guaranteed a profit only in the hottest years. (Even today, the major Burgundy Pinots are pale and lack concentration in approximately one year out of three.)

With its south-facing slopes, Aÿ enjoyed the most glowing reputation among the Champagne villages, at a time when Louis XII himself owned vineyards in this inner sanctum of Champagne. It is also at Aÿ that the oldest Champagne house can be found. The Gosset family has been producing still wines since 1584. But the first actually to sell Champagne were Ruinard in 1729. Yet great wine-producers in the sixteenth and seventeenth centuries did not come from Aÿ. It was in 1543 that a noble, Pierre Brulart, created a firm in the *grand cru* village of Sillery, marking the onset of a highly successful venture. In 1621, his son Nicholas obtained the title Baron de Sillery, by which time the family was already the greatest landowner in the region. All the wines were sold under the Sillery name, although the base for their finest products often came from the sunny slopes of Verzenay, on the hillside just below where the celebrated Moulin de Verzenay stands today. Hardly had Dom Pérignon succeeded in making white wine from black grapes than the Marquis de Sillery followed his example. His firm thus managed to conserve its supremacy in the area—until the French Revolution when, along with many other aristocrats, the last marquis was guillotined. The village of Sillery still possesses a quite unjustified status as a *grand cru* vintage, often being confused with the far superior Verzenay.

DOM PÉRIGNON

A Benedictine monk who lived and worked in the abbey of Hautvillers, close to Épernay, Dom Pierre Pérignon (1638–1715) is probably the most famous personality in the whole history of wine. I have lost count of the number of times I have been asked at tastings whether it was Dom Pérignon who actually "invented" Champagne—I have always had to say "No." On the other hand, it was indeed he who originated the method by which Champagne is made, by assembling still wines and letting them ferment a second time, and finally sealing them with a cork and stopper wire. The myth that has arisen around Dom Pérignon was partly concocted by Moët & Chandon at the beginning of the 1900s. This was when they purchased the Mercier *droit d'appellation*. Moët & Chandon took over the abbey where Dom Pérignon had officiated, turning it into a popular museum. In 1936, they launched their first prestige Champagne, which cleverly bore the name of the venerable monk. It met with overnight success.

The whole region has profited from the myth of Champagne being the creation of one man, but the truth is very different. The transformation of a still wine into a sparkling one was not a sudden brainwave, but the end-result of a lengthy process. Wines from cold climates have been fermented since the dawn of time—whether intentionally or not. All late-harvested wines find it hard to complete fermentation before the first cold snap arrives. The yeast, responsible for transforming the sugar into alcohol, slows to a halt, postponing fermentation at the moment of bottling. When the temperature outside rises again with the return of spring, carbon dioxide forms and produces the "disastrous" fizz.

There are quotations in the Bible that show that the wine drank 2,000 years ago was actually sparkling. Proverbs 23:31 talks about "…wine…when it sparkles in the cup," while in Saint Matthew's gospel 9:17 one reads: "Neither do men put new wine into old bottles; else the bottles break, and the wine runneth out, and the bottles perish; they put new wine into new bottles, and both are preserved."

The famous monk has his statue in front of the estate of Moët & Chandon in Épernay.

DOM PERIGNON
1638 – 1715
CELLERIER DE L'ABBAYE D'HAUTVILLERS
DONT LE CLOITRE ET LES GRANDS VIGNOBLES
SONT LA PROPRIETE DE LA MAISON
MOËT & CHANDON

In 1531 the monks of Saint-Hilaire in the south of France painstakingly produced an effervescent wine by the method known today as "natural." Such wines can be found today under the name Blanquette de Limoux. However, there is good reason to believe that it was the English who were responsible for the first effervescent Champagne wines. The French had encountered problems in making the bottle stoppers airtight, since they did not use cork, and the bottling glass employed was too fragile to withstand the pressure from the wine. The English had been using cork for 130 years before the French, and in the British Isles all cask-shipped wines were bottled and fitted with cork bungs. Only in 1685 did the French turn to the material. In a document penned by Christopher Merret and dating from 1662, one reads that the English added sugar to still wines from Champagne and stopped them with cork to make them sparkling! These records date from six years before Dom Pérignon's arrival at the abbey of Hautvillers. In other words, it was—as in so many things—the English who were the first to make real Champagne. So while certainly one of the first people to attempt to create a *pétillant* Champagne wine, Dom Pérignon was far from being alone in his endeavor. He was, nevertheless, a winemaker of the highest order, celebrated in his own lifetime.

At the outset, Dom Pérignon had looked on the tendency of a wine to fizz as a problem but, paradoxically, his striving for perfection actually increased the risk of making the wine gassy. In his unrelenting quest for quality, Dom Pérignon left nothing to chance. His meticulous approach began with the vine. Very soon he understood the advantages of low output, of pruning the vine-plants hard, and of tending them attentively throughout the year. And, above all, he used grapes from old vines, making for higher concentration and superior quality. He also ushered in a revolution in the way the gathering of the grapes was carried out: before his time, harvesting intentionally took place during the hottest autumn afternoons under a blazing sun, so as to obtain fruit of the deepest possible color. Dom Pérignon reckoned, however, that grapes were better when picked in fog or when the ground is still dewy—in practice on far cooler days. In this way, the wine gained in freshness and elegance. Moreover, more grapes could be picked, since they fell free of the shoots more readily.

The grapes would then be transported, with the utmost caution, in large openwork baskets weighing 100 kilos (221 pounds) called "mannequins." Just as a present-day Champagne house would, Dom Pérignon set up his presses as close as he possibly could to the vines. He believed that the more quickly a grape was pressed, the more likely the wine would be clear and of good quality. He pondered over not only *when* it was best to press the grapes, but also *how* this should be done. He was the inventor of the traditional "vertical" Champagne press,

which is still unbeatable today for ensuring rapid but careful pressing. With his concern for quality, our monk would quickly have noticed that it was the first pressing of the grape that yielded the most delicate juice.

Dom Pérignon was probably the first to separate the wines in three pressings, an enduring practice that is widespread throughout Champagne nowadays. Following the first fermentation, the wine was twice poured from one barrel to another. It was then clarified using a fish-skin filter. Thanks to this novel approach and various experiments, Dom Pérignon was the first to create a white wine from black grapes. Moreover, he was also the first to stop white Chardonnays losing their color, since before him they tended to go yellow after a few months. The wines he made were lighter in color and superior to all those produced before him in the region.

Beyond all these advances, however, it is possible that the famous monk's most significant contribution to the development of Champagne was in fact the *cuvée*, that is the "*assemblage*," or the blending of the various varieties. Until a few years ago, his method of blending was still so much the benchmark in the world of viticulture that anyone contending that a mono-*cru* Champagne could possibly measure up to a blended wine would have been thought of as incompetent.

For the most part, Dom Pérignon's grapes would have grown in villages near Hautvillers. He could identify the source of each grape with awesome accuracy, and was a past master in the art of blending grapes originating from various villages. Then—as today—it was a question of balancing powerful wines with sour, almost green, basic wines, so as to attain a perfectly harmonious Champagne.

Since Dom Pérignon picked his grapes in such cool climatic conditions, the acidity of the wine was high and the tendency to fizz was even greater than previously. To prevent the naturally effervescent wine exploding out of the bottle, he scoured the land for stronger glass, as well as for improved methods to prevent the wine from escaping. Soon "English glass" was being used. The majority of the glassmakers who began to manufacture this new, stronger type of glass worked in the forest of Argonne, a wooded area that also supplied the region with oak for making barrels. Unfortunately, no cork-oaks were grown there, though, so Dom Pérignon traveled as far as Spain in his search for an efficient stopper, and was soon convinced of the supremacy of the cork.

As the demand for effervescent wines grew greater and greater, Dom Pérignon—like many other winemakers—started to sell his product; but in the beginning sparkling Champagne wine was greeted halfheartedly. Henceforth though, adroit winemakers could choose either to avoid producing bubbles, or to encourage them. Dom Pérignon was, of course, in the vanguard of the advocates of fizz. He probably created his earliest sparkling wines around 1690, yet it was more than 100 years before this new wine was to become popular in France.

It must be conceded that, however much the monk of Hautvillers might have done in contributing to winemaking, he was far from alone in his discoveries. Another monk, Dom Oudard, worked in a similar fashion at his abbey at Pierry, but, since this abbey was less known and the Chardonnay vine he had at his disposal was less esteemed than the noble Pinot, his task proved much more difficult. If he had not been hampered by these restraints, perhaps Dom Oudard would have been regarded as the "father of Champagne" instead.

THE BEGINNINGS OF THE CHAMPAGNE TRADE

The law prohibiting the transport of wine in bottles was only revoked in 1728, bringing in its wake the creation of the first Champagne house. Ruinart was the earliest, founded in 1729, followed by several world-famous names: Chanoine in 1730, Forneaux (today Taittinger) in 1734, Moët in 1743, Vander-Veken (now called Abelé) in 1757, Lanson et Dubois in 1760, Clicquot in 1772, Heidsieck in 1785, and Jacquesson in 1798.

In the mid 1730s, *pétillant* wines had tightened their grip on Paris night-life, which was soon drowning in Champagne: any gathering worthy of the name had to begin with the noise of an exploding cork. Until the beginning of the nineteenth century, Champagne invariably had sediment in the bottom of the bottle. In 1918, Veuve Clicquot, assisted by her consummate winemaker Antoine Müller, hit on the brilliant idea of laying the bottles upside down on wooden racks (*pupitre*), so that the lees or sediment would remain in contact with the cork. This process is known as *remuage* or riddling. The sediment could then—with a deft maneuver—be removed, and the wine stoppered with a fresh cork. This operation is still practiced today and is called *dégorgement*—disgorging.

At the beginning of the nineteenth century, a French chemist by the name of M. François invented an instrument called the densimeter for gauging the sugar level after fermentation. This device was a step forward, since it was essential to obtain an exact measure of the quantity of yeast and sugar necessary for second, bottle-based fermentation. Of prime importance in preventing bottles exploding, the process also created tiny, delicate bubbles in the Champagne. Although the instrument was cheap and handy, it was many years before this system of measurement was used in earnest. For a long time bottle breakage represented a real stumbling-block; in 1828, 80 percent of bottles still exploded, to the point that workers in the cellars were forced to wear protective iron masks.

Napoleon had a keen interest in wine in general and in Champagne in particular, and many makers courted his approbation. Jacquesson, awarded a medal by the emperor for the beauty and the richness of his cellars, was considered his second favorite firm after Moët & Chandon. Napoleon formed a friendship with Jean-Rémy Moët, who was also mayor of Épernay. Their mutual admiration seems to have known no bounds. Jean-Rémy built two houses for Napoleon on Avenue de Champagne, while the emperor repaid his steadfast efforts during the Russo-Prussian occupation of Épernay in 1814 by raising him to the rank of Chevalier de la Légion d'Honneur. Without this relationship to Napoleon, Moët & Chandon would surely never have acquired the status it enjoys today. Some claim that Napoleon was in the habit of making a detour through Champagne before major battles to stock up on this invigorating beverage. There was at least one exception to this rule, however—he did not stop there on his way to Waterloo!

During the Prussian occupation of 1814, the invaders downed enormous quantities of Champagne from Reims and Épernay. Yet even this pilfering had a silver lining. The Russians soon developed a taste for the sparkling beverage and news of its quality spread to their native land. M. Bohne, Veuve Clicquot's agent, reported that in Russia the wine was regarded as a nectar, and that rosé Champagne had gained unheard-of popularity there. Along with other Champagne house agents of the time, agents from Clicquot and Roederer would visit the battlefields immediately after the end of an engagement. In this way, Louis Roederer inspired an interest in his products in Russia, most importantly in the tsar himself. It was the Russian sovereign who ordered a specially designed Champagne bottle manufactured out of authentic clear crystal. But the "Cristal" that Alexander II drank was immeasurably sweeter than the prestige Champagne of the same name that ensures the renown of the Roederer house today.

On the other hand, Bollinger and Krug, whose foundation dates back to 1843, turned to the British market—with great success. About the middle of the nineteenth century, 40 percent of all the Champagne produced was exported to the British Isles, and it was firms catering to the English that enjoyed the reputation for the very best Champagne. The English preferred older, riper, and more especially drier Champagnes than the French. As opposed to the French, who often drank it at dessert, the English saw Champagne as an aperitif. Bollinger, Clicquot, Pommery, and Ayala launched a "*très sec* 1865," while in its turn in 1874 Pommery created a wine that has since become legendary: it was the first dry Champagne and labeled "*extra dry*, reserved for England."

As for the Swedes, they suffered—then as now—from a sweet tooth. Traveling through Champagne, I have encountered wine-growers who refuse even to sell their produce in Sweden, since dry Champagne is so much out of favor there. In the mid-nineteenth century, a Champagne was being exported to Sweden and Norway containing 30 grams of sugar per liter (1 oz. per 34 fl. oz.). The Russians called for 20 grams, the Germans 17, the French 15; before 1874, the English were satisfied with only 12. Unquestionably we have the English to thank for the fact that we are able to drink dry Champagne today.

Thanks to technical advances in the second half of the nineteenth century, sales of Champagne increased dramatically in this period. It should be remembered that the majority of these were made by only a handful of Champagne houses. At that time, the size of a company was the determining factor in being able to turn these new techniques to their advantage. The majority of the more prosperous houses had been founded by German immigrants, such as Bollinger, Heidsieck, Krug, Delbeck, Deutz, and Mumm. Their knowledge of foreign languages facilitated exports, and they prospered at the expense of their colleagues who spoke only French. Thereafter, Charles Heidsieck—"Champagne Charlie"—and Mumm made serious inroads into the North American market. Mumm even managed to convince Americans to make no real distinction between table wines and vin de Champagne, though not everyone was persuaded: a great many people today still remain attached to this distinction.

PHYLLOXERA

Just when the Champagne industry was beginning to flourish, a dark cloud appeared on the horizon in the form of a parasitic plant-louse called phylloxera. This little yellow louse brought more devastation to the vineyards of Champagne than any manmade disaster of the past. Though so small it can only be observed under a microscope, it is capable of destroying entire vineyards. When it attacks the roots of the plant it leaves behind a poisonous secretion that infects the wound, preventing it from closing up. Phylloxera was first discovered on wild vines in the Mississippi by an American entomologist in 1854. The plant louse had existed long before that, of course, but, since American wild vines were resistant to the plague, its finding aroused little concern.

It was only in 1863, when phylloxera crossed the Atlantic for the first time, that a problem was acknowledged. From a ship moored in the port of Marseilles, the louse gradually spread through vineyards around Nîmes in Provence, and traveled from there to infect all of Europe. Owing to the fact that European vines presented no resistance to infection by the louse, there was untold destruction. Practically every major wine-growing region was affected: the Bordeaux area and Portugal (except Colares) in 1869, Beaujolais and the valley of the Rhône by 1870, Burgundy by 1878, and Italy by 1888. The devastation extended beyond the frontiers Europe, to California in 1873, Australia and South Africa in 1874, and Algeria in 1887. The only renowned vineyards initially saved

lay in northern areas: in the valley of the Rhine, the Moselle, and in Champagne itself. It was thought the louse would be unable to survive in such a cold climate, but in 1890 that hope was dashed when it was discovered in a vineyard lying on the western fringes of the valley of the Marne. In an effort to halt the louse's progress, Moët & Chandon bought up the vineyard concerned and burned every vine. But two years later, a few stocks were found to have been attacked again; they too were immediately burned. By 1894, by which time the infestation had reached epidemic proportions, the ineffectual "scorched-earth policy" was abandoned. Instead, experiments were made with various insecticides. Some appeared to stave off the louse, but they proved at the same time almost as dangerous for humans.

The Champagne region was lucky in that phylloxera propagated more slowly under its cool skies than elsewhere in France. Salvation eventually came from the United States and Canada, where more robust, wild vines proved resistant to attack. The main problem was that the quality of such varieties was too poor to adorn the slopes at Montrachet or Aÿ. But eventually it was demonstrated that American vines could be employed as rootstocks, onto which European cuttings could be grafted; this resulted in a range of more resistant plants that produced grapes of European taste. Almost every *Vitis vinifera* plant in the world was thus uprooted and restocked. The almost unanimous view today is that the potential quality of the vines was higher prior to the phylloxera attack. Some claim as well that the increase in output that has resulted from the grafted vines has been a determining factor in the shorter lifespan of the vines. It is certainly true that anyone fortunate enough to have savored a Bollinger Vieilles Vignes Françaises from non-grafted stocks, or a Romanée Conti from a vintage before the phylloxera years, would without a doubt wish that the dreaded creature had never crossed the Atlantic.

REVOLT IN CHAMPAGNE

At the beginning of the twentieth century, several events of major importance took place which greatly affected the present-day shape of the wine-growing Champagne region and which came to a head in the so-called Champagne revolt of 1911. As the region of Aube is geographically and geologically closer to Chablis than the rest of Champagne, the right of the area to be integrated into Champagne proper was hotly debated—and with some reason. Spearheaded by Aube vine-growers, one side claimed that incorporation into the region was inescapable, since in former times Troyes had been the capital of the entire Champagne province. The other camp pointed to discrepancies in quality, and also noted that Champagne the province was not to be confused with the wine

known as Champagne. At that time, the 20,000 hectares (50,000 acres) of the region were predominantly planted with Arbanne, Petit Meslier vines, and with a Beaujolais variety, Gamay. Output was high, and very few producers in the Aube expended much effort on improving grape quality. In a nutshell, Aube grapes were of such low quality that no Champagne house would even entertain the notion of using them in a vintage. The Aube wine-growers tried to turn to Burgundy as well, but neither Burgundy nor Champagne was keen to welcome Aube into their wine-producing area.

Competition between the two opposing groups of Aube and Champagne became so intense that the government had to intervene. On December 17, 1908, it made a decision about which type of vine would be permitted to be made into Champagne, and which areas would be allowed to sport the *appellation* Champagne. They were confined to two *départements*: Marne (all the *communes* around Reims and Épernay, including thirty-five *communes* around Vitry-le-François) and Aisne, with eighty-two communes ringing Château-Thierry and Soissons. Naturally enough, the Aube growers were enraged at finding themselves so comprehensively excluded. Worse still, the whole area had recently suffered several years of poor harvest. Moreover, and despite Draconian regulations, the majority of producers in the valley of the Marne used grapes from the south of France, something that infuriated Aube *vignerons* still more.

The Champagne region was a tinderbox, ready to explode at any moment. In February 1911, the law further tightened the screw, threatening severe penalties for anyone discovered using vines from Aube or from other areas of France in their Champagnes. The fuse was now lit. Wine-growers from all over Aube met at Troyes, organizing massive and angry demonstrations. The Senate, sensing that worse things might follow if the situation continued as it was, opted to repeal the law—if only temporarily. But the decision came too late. At two o'clock in the morning on the night of April 11, 1911, the inhabitants of Aube smashed down the doors to the cellars of a winemaker in Cumières, and of another in Damery. By dawn, an army of growers 5,000 strong had reached Aÿ, where producers suspected of using southern French grape varieties saw their cellars, barrels, and bottles laid waste. As the streets ran with wine, the authorities slept on, and by the time the police arrived from Épernay they had little to do other than record the damage.

With the cellars destroyed, the rioters moved on to the Aÿ producers' homes, which met a similar fate. Bollinger was one of the rare firms to be spared. Madame Lily Bollinger is supposed to have learned later that the rebels had decided between themselves to lower their banners as a mark of respect when passing in front of Bollinger. The government declared the area

a war zone, and 40,000 soldiers were dispatched to maintain order. A further government diktat resulted in a new classification of sparkling wines, which were now divided into four categories:

> Champagne (as before)
> Champagne *deuxième zone* (Aube, Seine-et-Marne)
> Sparkling wines (the rest of France)
> *Vin gazéifié* (obtained by addition of carbon dioxide)

In practice, the new classification made it possible for winegrowers from Aube to produce Champagne, a right they would never have obtained without their violent revolt. In 1927, the law was overhauled once again. The category "second zone" was removed from the list, and Aube was finally incorporated in the Champagne region.

I will perhaps spark off a fresh revolt in Champagne by proposing a return to the "second zone" for grapes from Aube. My opinion is that, whatever happens, their quality will never attain that of grapes from the heart of Champagne, and this should be made clear on labels.

THE TWENTIETH CENTURY

In the years known subsequently as the Belle Époque, well-heeled people—blissfully unaware both of the revolt in Champagne and of phylloxera—consumed Champagne as never before. The Belle Époque really started about the time of the World's Fair of 1889, when France was entering the industrial era and great changes were afoot. Gustave Eiffel had just completed building the impressive 300-meter-(984-feet)-high tower that was to bear his name. The Eiffel Tower was a symbol of a belief in the future; it housed four restaurants, where naturally Champagne flowed freely.

Also for the World's Fair, Eugène Mercier built the largest barrel ever constructed, with a capacity corresponding to 200,000 bottles. The barrel had to be drawn by twenty-four white oxen and took three weeks to reach Paris. Houses had to be leveled and roads laid so that it could reach the World's Fair. At this exhibition Mercier also showed the first advertising film ever to be produced; the subject, inevitably, was the Mercier Champagne house itself. While the exhibition was on, staggering quantities of Champagne were drunk, and news of its euphoric properties began to reach all four corners of the world.

Meanwhile, Maxim's restaurant became the most *à la mode* hangout for the Paris upper crust, where caviar, lobster, and oysters were served accompanied by Champagne, which remained a relatively sugary wine. Social life was increasingly significant for the French, and for the privileged few, regular appearance in high society became a must. If one had money, then that definitely had to be flaunted. By the beginning of the twentieth century, the French were consuming four times as much Champagne as they had in the middle of the nineteenth century.

The Perrier-Jouët Champagne house has carefully preserved the memory of these salad days before the Great War. The museum opposite its wine-stores at Épernay exhibits furniture and objects from the Art Nouveau period. The same house also markets a prestige Champagne with the telling name of "Belle Époque." Dating from the beginning of the century, the bottle is decorated with an anemone originally painted by the artist Émile Gallé who, along with Daum and Tiffany, was to become one of the greatest master glass-makers of the time. Nobody would have dreamed then that this bottle would become a real symbol of the era.

The outbreak of the First World War in 1914 sparked a long series of difficult years for the people living in the Champagne region. Shortly after the evacuation of Épernay and Château-Thierry, on September 7, 1914, German troops entered France by way of the Marne valley. Only a few kilometers of marching would bring them to the strategically important Seine river, from where they could head toward Paris. Reims was occupied for ten days before the French turned the situation round in what became the most heroic encounter of their history: the First Battle of the Marne. Fortunately then, the Germans never made it as far as the Seine.

The frontline now crossed through Champagne and the war raged on. As wave after wave of attack followed, at the beginning of October 1914 Champagne was retaken by the Allies. In spite of the hostilities, in 1914 and 1915 a few hardy souls managed to blaze a trail to the vineyards and take in a tiny but superb harvest—though in 1914 more than twenty children perished in the attempt. Maurice Pol Roger was then mayor of Épernay and, although the Germans threatened to fire his city and have him executed, he stood as firm as an oak. His 1914 vintage thereafter became his own favorite Champagne, the one chosen for truly special occasions. Once, however, in 1914, he had been disappointed to find the wine too green, so he asked his *maître de chai* to disgorge a large number of bottles in advance so as to obtain a more mature vintage. In May 1994, in the presence of the current owner of the firm, Christian Pol Roger, I had the extraordinary honor of drinking a bottle of this late-disgorged 1914 Champagne. Never before have I had the sensation of drinking such an historic wine. The fact that the Champagne was truly superb, with a coffee aroma and high sugar content, only added to my pleasure.

After the First World War, Reims concentrated its efforts on rapidly rebuilding the city. The export market remained elusive. The Germans were bankrupt after the war, while in Russia the tsar's family, which had been one of the region's most important customers, had lost power after the October Revolution. Americans were entering the era of Prohibition, and the Scandinavians were edging in the same direction, with ration books for alcohol. Moreover, the rigors of the Champagne climate were to preclude a single good year before 1926.

By the mid-1920s, to add to the problems caused by the devastating effects of phylloxera and of the First World War, the distant rumblings of the Great Depression could be heard. By 1927, sales of Champagne on the domestic market had decreased by half. In 1929 in New York came the infamous Wall Street Crash, kindling a slump on a global scale. The most calamitous year of the Depression, 1934, nevertheless produced a marvelous vintage that is still drinkable today—if you are lucky enough to unearth a bottle.

In an effort to survive the global Depression, many Champagne houses concealed their *grands vins* behind ordinary labels, so as to avoid the loss of prestige represented by selling off such excellent Champagne so cheaply. Winemakers had recourse to all kinds of expedients in order to survive, and it was not unusual for them to offload their produce in Paris, at very low cost, as still wine. These still wines very quickly became popular. It is heartrending to think of an extraordinary wine such as the 1928 vintage being sold off as still wine. Many wine-growers were unhappy at having to sell produce that could have been turned into truly great Champagnes in this way, but, without the technical knowledge necessary to make up effervescent wine on their own, during the Depression they joined forces in cooperatives. In fact, it is primarily due to the size of the domestic market that Champagne houses were able to survive at all.

During the Second World War, the president of Moët & Chandon, Robert-Jean de Vogüé, mooted a revolutionary proposal. He suggested multiplying the price of grapes tenfold so as to guarantee both higher quality and the future livelihood of vine-growers. Vogüë's idea was not well received by other firms, but they were later forced to admit that de Vogüé's radical notion had saved the Champagne industry. He also set up the *Comité Interprofessionnel du Vin de Champagne* (*C.I.V.C.*), which was formed in 1941 with the backing of the Germans.

When German tanks rolled into France in 1940, wine-producers were far better prepared than they had been at the time of the Great War. Hitler had already been strutting around the international scene for some time, and there had been enough time to erect false walls behind which large stores of Champagne bottles could be hidden from the Germans. The Germans drank vast quantities of Champagne in Reims

CHAMPAGNE SALES

(in bottles per year)

1850	7 million
1880	20 million
1900	32 million
1920	14 million
1940	25 million
1960	50 million
1980	176 million
1996	256 million
1999	327 million

and Épernay, but, following French capitulation, Hitler put a halt to the plundering. He ordered production to continue as normal, and for Germany to be supplied with Champagne of the highest class. A vine-grower from the Rhine valley, a certain Herr Klaebisch, thus became the "Führer" of Champagne. Sales to private individuals were prohibited, and around 350,000 bottles a week were sent on to German troops on the various fronts. Unfortunately for the fighting Germans, the bottles were often sent in the wrong direction, and the quality of the Champagne was as bad as it could be. Moreover, as no new plantings took place during the war, the aging vines yielded poor harvests.

One day in the autumn of 1942, Robert-Jean de Voguë was summoned by the "Führer" to be summarily informed that the Gestapo had condemned him to death. Happily, the execution order was never carried out, but for the rest of the war de Voguë was forced to languish in various concentration camps. Champagne-producers also had to exercise the utmost caution in their resistance to the Germans, since Himmler had threatened to blow up all the Champagne cellars so as to give the German sekt industry an advantage when hostilities eventually ended. However, General Patton's army moved in on August 28, 1944, and as soon as the Germans left Champagne all the cellars' dummy walls were torn down. There was an unexpectedly large quantity of Champagne saved for posterity.

After the end of the war, pessimism was rife concerning the future of Champagne. The financial state of the Champagne houses was not good, and there was a dearth of product, partly due to the intrigues of the Germans. Practically the whole of Europe was flirting with Socialism, and the royal courts that had provided an ever-faithful market were disappearing. The only people who could afford Champagne in large quantities were the newly wealthy Americans.

Things were indeed looking bleak, but soon the doubters had to eat their words. Thanks to fantastic vintages in 1943, 1945, 1947, 1949, 1952, 1953, and 1955, sales of Champagne doubled in twelve years. Over the following ten years they doubled again. In 1976, 153 million bottles were sold, and in 1999 about 327 million. Patently, something dramatic had happened. The most important factor was that after the war industrialized countries soon succeeded in putting their economies back on an even keel. Like most other luxury products, Champagne had been "democratized," and it was now a drink for (almost) everyone.

CHAMPAGNE TODAY

Today the media are instrumental in spreading the delights of Champagne. Champagne's producers should also be grateful to the blanket publicity afforded the region at every conceivable opportunity by Moët & Chandon. They succeed in presenting Champagne as a necessity whenever a party or a note of luxury is called for. The image that James Bond films have given Dom Pérignon and Bollinger R. D. outstrips all attempts made by other producers to improve the consumer profile of their product. If you want to create an impression with a wine in a restaurant, then a magnum of Dom Pérignon, Cristal, Krug, or even the new Hollywood favorite, Belle Époque, is an obvious choice.

A good many people brighten things up with the occasional bottle. Lavish? Over the top? For sure, but not particularly expensive if you compare it to the price of a few beers in a restaurant. Why not treat yourself to what is a value-for-money luxury product if you know how to appreciate the qualities of a wine? Champagne is also the ideal drink to offer guests, as pretty much everyone feels honored when presented with something really special. In fact, in difference in price between Champagne and other alcoholic drinks is often less that you might think.

Let us take a look at what has happened within Champagne since the Second World War. Unfortunately for quality, yields have sky-rocketed, vineyards have increased in size, and, as techniques have improved, production too has soared. By the beginning of the 1960s, most Champagne houses had replaced expensive oak barrels with stainless-steel vats. *Remuage* and *dégorgement* were automated. More and more houses began to use a higher proportion of Chardonnay grapes in their *cuvées*, a trend that persists today. Whether it was the *cuvées* or the customers' palate that changed first depends rather on your point of view. But it is certain that the growers had suddenly gained the technical know-how to make Champagne themselves. In 1950 only 2.4 million bottles were sold directly by growers; this has risen to 70 million today. Such developments

Recently disgorged bottles in Anselme Selosse's cellar.

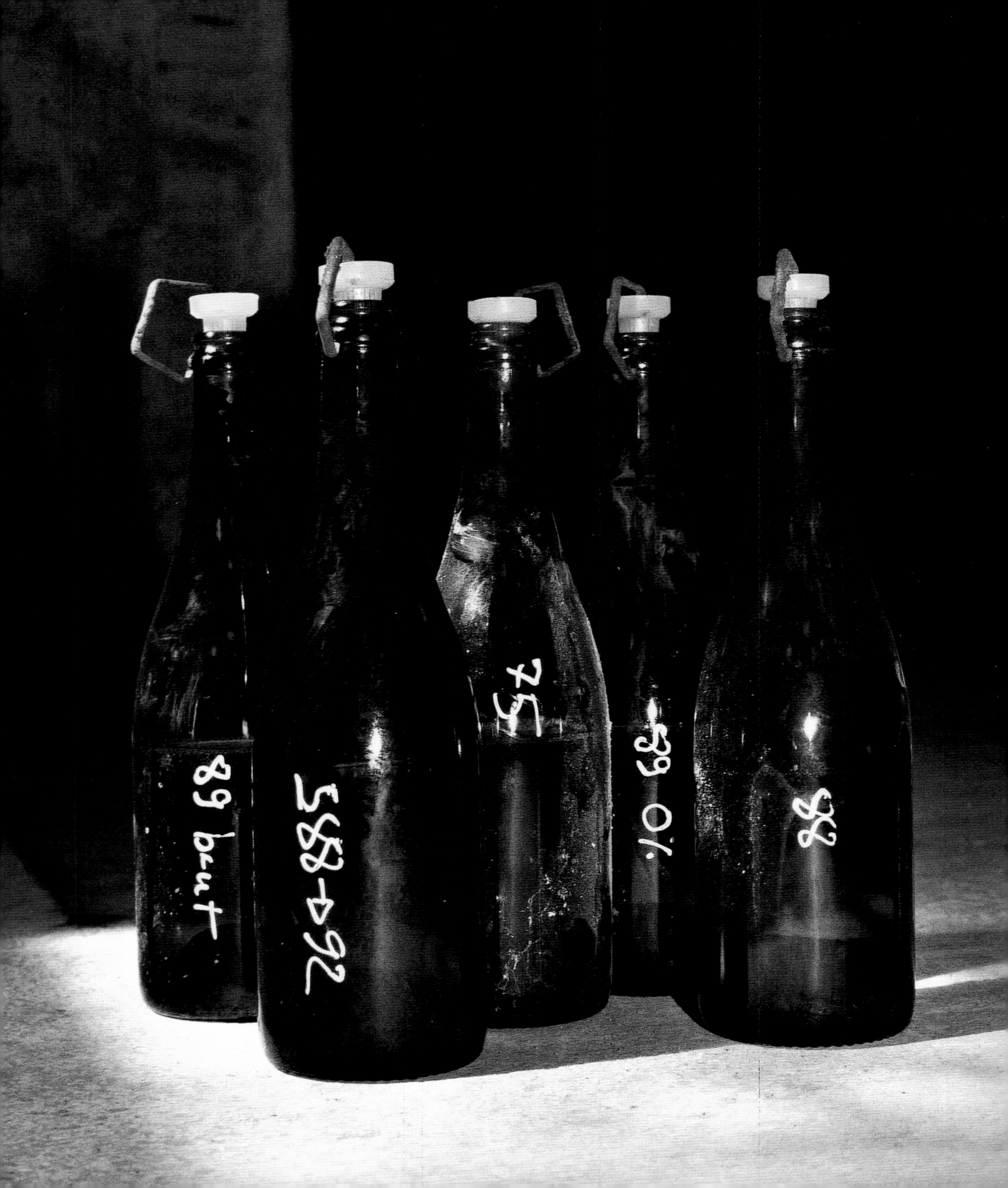
89 brut
75
88

are both good and bad. Well-established houses do not always have access to the best grapes, something that can lower quality; on the other hand, there are now many up-and-coming growers making pure mono-*cru* Champagnes of high quality at extremely competitive prices.

Tastes are more varied today, and the consumer is no longer dependent on just eighteen Champagne houses, as was the case before the war. The importance of the cooperative system is tremendous. Today many wine-producing villages have formed into cooperatives involving a sizable percentage of the population. As for the Champagne houses themselves, the bigger ones have become even larger, as they are forever buying one another out and continually forging new business alliances. Moët-Hennessy is today part of the L.V.M.H. conglomerate, while Veuve Clicquot, Ruinart, Krug, Mercier, and Canard-Duchêne are parts of a group controlling almost 50 percent of the entire export market. Another important merger concern is the Vranken group, whose stable includes Heidsieck & Monopole, Charles Lafitte, Charbaut, Demoiselle, Sacotte, Germain, Pommery, and Barancourt. Perrier-Jouët and Mumm are today owned by Allied Domecq. Charles Heidsieck, Piper-Heidsieck, and F. Bonnet belong to Rémy-Cointreau. Another constantly expanding group is B.C.C., spearheaded by Bruno Paillard. The firms under its umbrella include Chanoine, Boizel, De Venoge, Abel Lepitre, Philipponnat, and Alexandre Bonnet. Laurent-Perrier has taken the initiative to form a group comprising respected names such as De Castellane, Joseph Perrier, Delamotte, and Salon.

Among the major houses to remain independent, we have Bollinger, Pol Roger, Taittinger, and Louis Roederer. The fact that they have been able to do this is due in major part to their manageable size. Up until a couple of years ago, Louis Roederer was the world's most profitable wine company, thanks mainly to the large number of vineyards it owns. Another important factor is the amazing success of their Champagne Cristal, a wine that today makes up a significant part of the firm's total production, with each bottle costing a tidy sum. Roederer is also owner of the Deutz Champagne house, which is, nonetheless, allowed a free hand to cultivate a brand style under the watchful eye of Fabrice Rosset.

At the beginning of the 1990s, Champagne was affected by the recession and sales dropped. Then came, as everyone must be all too aware, the somewhat overblown junkets of the millennium. Though every sales record was beaten, Millennium Eve did not quite live up to its billing. There were those who predicted that Champagne would run out, and many built up significant stocks that they later found hard to offload. Moët & Chandon in particular experienced post-party blues, and had to wait almost a year before receiving fresh orders from its American agent. However, I remain persuaded that the hysteria surrounding the millennium will—in the long term—have proven a boon for the Champagne industry. I am thinking specifically of the unique occasion it afforded us—all those who work with this sublime beverage—to promote our activities, as well as the wine and region of Champagne. No one could have escaped the media frenzy concerning the noble bubble: suddenly talk of Dom Pérignon, the *méthode champenoise*, the various types of Champagne glass, and the passion of Winston Churchill for his favorite tipple was on everybody's lips. It is this sort of discussion that leads to greater knowledge of the subject, and in turn a demand for higher standards by the consumer.

THE FUTURE OF CHAMPAGNE

Worldwide, more and more Champagne is being drunk. However, fifty years ago the region accounted for 30 percent of global consumption of sparkling wine, against a mere 13 percent today. Currently the two largest producers of sparkling wine are Spanish: Freixenet and Codorníu. Should the Champagne industry be worried about these developments? Not really, since the market for sparkling wine is still expanding, and there ought to be room for both the simpler varieties and authentic Champagne. The main competition, quality-wise, has come from the U.S.A., where Champagne houses, thanks to their know-how, have started up some highly successful companies.

In the 1970s, the chill wind of competition awoke many a producer from its slumbers. The *C.I.V.C.* spotted the danger at an early stage and in recent times has made great strides in improving average quality levels in Champagne. The latest legislation banning a third pressing has meant that today even the most modest Champagnes possess an elegance and stylistic purity that no other sparkling wine can match. Fifteen years ago, very few wine buffs had anything good to say about growers' Champagne, but the best of these deserves to be treated with the utmost respect today. Established Champagne houses that fail to take seriously competition from the best growers in the *grand cru* villages could be in for an unpleasant surprise.

In the next century, many winemakers will probably return to fermenting in oak barrels, since it is easier to attract the attention of wine writers by quality rather than quantity. The development of Champagne lies largely in the hands of consumers. If they show that they demand quality Champagne with an individual personality, then producers will have to supply it. It is also gratifying to note that finally more and more wine-growers in the area are becoming ecologically aware and aiming for a more biodynamic approach to cultivation.

The celebrated widow herself, Madame Veuve Clicquot.

Growing areas and grape varieties

How did Champagne become so famous? How can the prices shown on the labels that adorn the bottles of the finest Champagnes be justified? Is there any real difference between Champagne and an ordinary sparkling wine? These are the kind of questions I am often asked at tastings and lectures. I'd like to take this opportunity of replying from my own special Nordic perspective.

We Scandinavians are proud of our new potatoes and our strawberries. Personally, I have always thought that there was something special about freshly picked Swedish fruits and vegetables, but thought that might be more for sentimental reasons than for scientific ones. One day, however, as part of a magnificent meal eaten on the terrace of a restaurant in Liguria, overlooking the Mediterranean, we were served strawberries that had been freshly picked from the restaurant garden and they gave me food for thought. I had considered that these Swedish delicacies were special mainly because they were foods that were unusually fresh. And here I was, being served strawberries as if I were at home, yet these strawberries were not nearly as good. How could that be?

The explanation lies in the fact that fruits and vegetables are most delicious when cultivated in the northernmost part of the northern hemisphere or the southernmost part of the southern hemisphere. It is hard for potatoes, as well as strawberries and apples, to survive our harsh climate, but during the long ripening process complicated chemical combinations develop that give fruits and vegetables are particularly subtle, fresh, and balanced flavor. A really ripe strawberry, cultivated in Sweden, has the same sugar content as a strawberry from Italy, but the acidity is higher in the Swedish one. The combination of sweetness and acidity encourage the development of subtle and complex aromas. This is where the initial explanation lies for the freshness and elegance that can be found in Swedish strawberries (in those years when they can ripen without suffering from excessive rainfall). This phenomenon is even more applicable to grapes destined for vinification after fermentation.

All of the numerous grape varieties used by man to make wine require unique conditions as regards climate and soil. Some of them do particularly well in a warm climate, while others manage to set fruit, even though they are cultivated in regions situated farther north, such as Champagne or Moselle. Champagne is the northernmost *A.O.C.* (*Appellation d'Origine Contrôlée*); the climate here is such that only a few grape varieties can tolerate it.

A bunch of ripe Pinot Noir grapes covered in bloom and dew.

When creating a sparkling wine, the ripe grapes that are used must have attained a degree of acidity that would be completely unsuitable for making a still wine. The Chardonnay grape harvested in Champagne would be considered unripe in Burgundy, for example, while grape-growers in Champagne would regard the Burgundy grape as too ripe for their purposes.

A balance is constantly being sought between acidity and sugar content, but the criteria used vary depending on the wine that is to be made. In a climate barely warmer than that of Champagne, the wines soon become heavy and unbalanced in comparison with the original. Even Champagne itself has suffered from excessive heat in certain years. The years 1947, 1959, 1976, 1989, and 2003 produced a grape with a potential alcohol content one or two degrees higher than average. The acidity was too low and the wines had to rely on their high alcohol content and their richness in extraction in order to maintain their quality. The fact that Champagnes produced in these years are not heavy is basically down to the unique character of the region's calcareous soil. It may be reassuring to note this fact in view of global warming, which in the short term may also affect the Champagne region.

The lowest average annual temperature of 10.6°C (51°F) for this region forces the roots of the vines to grow down deep in search of water and nutrients. At this depth, the vine absorbs a large quantity of minerals, which give Champagne its unique finesse. It is also interesting to note that the average outside temperature is identical to that found inside the wine cellars of Champagne in Roman times. The wine develops best in a temperature similar to that in which the vine grew.

In view of the fact that artificial irrigation is prohibited—for a number of reasons—in Champagne as elsewhere in France, the quantity of rain needed at the right moment is crucial in this region. The annual precipitation of 662 mm (26 in.) situates it between Burgundy, which is drier, and the Bordeaux region, which is wetter. Champagne is reasonably well irrigated naturally, thanks to a large network of rivers and canals in the area. The river Marne, the main source of irrigation in the region, also reflects the sun's rays onto the southern slopes of its valley, and so makes its own contribution to equalizing the annual temperature. It has a beneficial cooling effect in summer and to some extent prevents the vineyards from getting too cold in wintertime.

THE SOIL

There are numerous places on earth that match the description of the climatic conditions that are needed to cultivate high quality grape vines. The production of superior wines requires that such climatic conditions are combined with the appropriate soil type. The geology of Champagne is absolutely unique, and represents a determining factor in the difference that exists between Champagne and other sparkling wines. It may be easier to understand the importance of the soil if the qualitative variations that exist in the region are examined.

The département of the Aube in the south, where the Kimmeridge clay replaces chalk, never attains the heights of perfection in terms of grape quality that are characteristic of the *grand cru* villages. And it is not really necessary to go as far as the Aube to understand how vital the differences in soil types are. Numerous villages huddle together, benefiting from a similar climate and and yet producing grapes with very different characteristics.

Although a large belt of chalk extends from the white cliffs of Dover over hundreds of miles toward eastern Europe, no place in the world, other than Champagne, has such a high concentration of a superficial layer of belemnite and micraster marls. Belemnite is found mainly on the upper slopes and micraster lower down. Belemnite (*Belemnita quadrata*) takes its name from the belemnite fossils, similar creatures to octopus and squid, that inhabited the sea that covered the Parisian Basin. When this sea retreated it left innumerable fossils behind. This particular fossil is rich in lime and eventually turns into chalk. Opinions are divided as to the superiority of belemnite chalk over that formed from micraster. In my opinion, one gets top quality Champagnes more easily from the special minerals absorbed by grapes grown in belemnite-rich soils. Most of the *grand cru* villages have been built on belemnite chalk, just as some of the best *premiers crus* have benefited considerably from the remains of this cephalopod. This type of chalk releases more limestone, giving the grapes a higher acidity, reacts positively on the plant's photosynthesis, and prevents chlorosis, which can cause the vine leaves to turn yellow. Belemnite-rich chalk also provides excellent drainage, and this greatly benefits the vines, since they don't like living with wet feet. Furthermore, all types of chalk are capable of maintaining a constant temperature throughout the year. Since the roots of the vine penetrate deep into the soil in their search for water, the mineral content of the grapes is very high, giving a quality Champagne its distinctive chalky flavor.

It is easy to confuse limestone with chalk. All chalks are limestone, but only one type of limestone is chalk. Chalky soil is of a very particular type and gives the Champagne vine its unique ability to produce ripe grapes with a high level of acidity. The chalkiness of the soil has only one disadvantage, since it limits the iron and magnesium content that the vine needs in order to prevent chlorosis.

This natural chalk pit at Mareuil shows clearly what the magical soil of Champagne looks like beneath the surface.

Apart from the exceptional properties of the soil, the region benefits from suitable topography. The long, low, rounded hills known as the Falaises de Champagne are also very suitable for the production of sparkling wines of great quality. Geologically, the province is divided into three regions:

• *La Champagne humide* (Wet Champagne) is formed by the eastern part of this ancient inland sea that has become the Parisian Basin. This inland sea dried up about 70 million years ago, leaving a layer of clay behind it. The region extends from the Ardennes at the Franco-Belgian frontier to Burgundy in the southeast. The soil is very fertile and is particularly suitable for market gardening. But *La Champagne humide* is completely unsuitable for producing great sparkling wine; these require a poor soil.

• Immediately to the west of *La Champagne humide* lies a narrow geological strip known as *La Champagne pouilleuse* (Flea-bitten Champagne), where the depth of the layers of chalk, covered by poor clay, means that the soil is incapable of retaining rainwater around the roots of the vine. Here again, the conditions are unsuitable for viticulture.

• The only region authorized to cultivate the noble grape varieties destined for making Champagne is that known as *La Champagne viticole*, "wine-producing Champagne." During the Tertiary Era, about 30 million years ago, a fold formed in the centre of the Parisian Basin. This fold caused the sea bed to be raised upward. Twenty million years later, a new fold caused the soil to rise again by about 500 feet, producing quite a sheer chain of chalk hills. Over time, these hills have become rounded and covered with a thin layer of soil; this is only a few inches thick and consists of sand, marl, clay, lignite, and chalk gravel. To be able to benefit fully from its advantages, this layer of soil needs to be constantly renewed through fertilization. It is gradually becoming exhausted and large pieces can even break away from the slopes during heavy rain.

Beneath the forests of the Montagne de Reims lies the black gold of the Champagne district, the *Cendres Noires* (black cinders). This earth is black, moist, and particularly rich in sulfur and iron. It has been carefully nurtured by the grape-growers for hundreds of years, to the point where today it consists mainly of soil brought in from elsewhere. Some people who are concerned about the environmental protection of the region are beginning to worry and ask whether the black gold will last for much longer. A century or two, perhaps. It would seem to be impossible to renew quickly what nature has created over the course of millions of years. But it still happens—in rare instances—that city mud, garbage from Paris, is used as fertilizer. This blue mixture, which is harmful to the environment, owes much of its color to the Parisians' plastic garbage bags. This unhealthy practice dates from the 1960s and 1970s, before people became ecologically aware, and remains a cause

of shame for the Champagne region. Unfortunately, it has even affected serious vine-growers, who have to clean their vines of all sorts of detritus that the rain and wind cause to circulate from one vineyard to the next. All this demands effort from a great deal of hard-working people who are trying to preserve nature's heritage.

Along with the influence of the soil, the choice of grape variety is also a decisive factor in obtaining a good result. It has been proven throughout the world that Pinot Noir and Chardonnay grapes are the most suitable for creating sparkling wines. Their structure and aromas are of unmatched quality. These grape varieties have been cultivated for a very long time in Champagne, thus making it possible to choose with great care clones that are adapted to the region.

Pinot Noir is a variety of grape that mutates easily. For centuries, unique local varieties have been created, thus contributing to increasing considerably the variety in terms of flavor and quality. As in all the other great wine regions, different types of yeast fungi have become acclimatized to certain locations, and have left their mark on the grapes in most of the vineyards. The unique conditions for cultivating vines in Champagne have made it possible to create a single type of sparkling wine that attains perfection. The height of the hills, their gradient and the soil, combined with a propitious climate has been nature's gift to the human race.

All of these opportunities offered by the Champagne district have been enhanced by the people who labor in the region, who work hard to obtain the finest quality. Every self-respecting grape-grower is faced with the choice of producing in quantity or producing high quality. Most of those given the chance to make a very great wine would obviously choose quality. It is not by chance that the *méthode champenoise* was born in this locality. Any vine-grower who wants to imitate it throughout the world is free to try. The problem is that the procedure is costly and the qualitative benefit is not very great outside of the Champagne region. Furthermore, the know-how handed down through the generations is lacking elsewhere. This is the particular knowledge and expertise that is indispensable for the creation of the most prestigious of all sparkling wines.

THE THREE GREAT GRAPE VARIETIES

The grape is the fruit that is the most extensively cultivated throughout the world. More than 23 million acres of the planet are covered with vines. Of the grapes produced, 71 percent are destined for wine-making, 27 percent for the table, and 2 percent end up as raisins. Almost three-quarters of all the world's vineyards are in Europe, and the number of grape varieties can be counted in the thousands.

For making Champagne, just three varieties of grape are normally used: Pinot Noir, Pinot Meunier, and Chardonnay. In Champagne, 38 percent of the vineyards grow Pinot Noir, 35 percent Pinot Meunier, and 27 percent Chardonnay. In the *grand cru* villages, the expensive Chardonnay is the most common. In the Aube, Pinot Noir is the variety that is most frequently grown, whereas Pinot Meunier is predominant in the Aisne and Seine-et-Marne départements. Even if most Champagnes are the result of a blend of grapes, the character of the various varieties should make itself felt. Good Blancs de Blancs and Blancs de Noirs should naturally express the character of the grapes of different origins.

Pinot Noir: Pinot Noir is at the same time a nightmare for the grape-grower and paradise for the wine-drinker. The grape is very difficult to grow, but can result in a fantastic wine. The compact bunches of Pinot Noir grapes are very prone to rot. Leaf-curl virus was also a serious problem until it became possible to check whether a plant had been attacked by a virus of any sort. This grape is not only difficult to grow and sensitive, it also has to be kept away from any contact with the skin if the wine is to retain its white color. The must, however, is darker than that produced by Chardonnay.

Unlike Cabernet Sauvignon, a grape that is successfully cultivated throughout the world, the finest Pinot Noir can only be grown in Burgundy and in Champagne. In Burgundy, this grape produces the best red wines in the world, with an inimitable bouquet that is rich in nuances and velvet, sugary, fruity flavor. Yet even in Burgundy, it can produce wines that are pale, insipid, and characterless. There are only a very few first-class Burgundies, made from the Pinot Noir grape by just a few producers. Even though the Pinot Noir of Champagne never achieves the same power and depth as those of a red Burgundy, it nevertheless has a similar aroma. In Champagne, Pinot Noir is used mainly to give blends a firmness of structure and character.

Pinot Noir alone can never present the same elegance as Chardonnay, but it provides more weight and better depth. In its youth, Pinot Noir has a very fruity bouquet and a fairly mild though unbalanced flavor, but when it matures, it extends and softens the wine's length in the mouth. Champagnes made with Pinot Noir need time to develop their wonderful aromas and animal and vegetable notes. Even though Bollinger Vieilles Vignes Françaises is the best example of a Pinot Noir Champagne, excellent ones are also produced by wine-makers in Aÿ, Bouzy, Ambonnay, and Verzenay.

Pinot Noir is a vine that mutates easily, so that there are several hundred Pinot Noir clones in Champagne. The variety owes its genetic instability to the fact that it is one of the oldest vines. Much effort has been invested in the region in finding clones that are more frost-resistant, since frost remains a serious problem. Today, every village has its own clone, adapted to its own microclimate and its soil. The success of Pinot Noir in Champagne depends mainly on the limestone content of the soil in the region, as well as the fact that the grape's aroma develops mainly in a cool climate. The key to success for this grape variety is a long period in which the wine can mature without interference. I consider Pinot Noir to be the most exciting variety in the vine-growing world.

Pinot Meunier: Pinot Meunier is not often mentioned, but it is nevertheless used by most of the wine-makers in Champagne and is predominant in the Aisne and Seine-et-Marne départements. The variety was developed in the sixteenth century and is closely related to Pinot Noir. It can easily be distinguished from its ancestor, though, thanks to the downy leaves that look as if they are covered in flour—hence its name, which means "miller" in French.

Pinot Meunier is a very hardy variety of grape, the only one that ripens in very cold years. It is less sensitive to spring frosts than some others, which explains why it is so heavily cultivated in the frost-prone Marne valley. Furthermore, it yields 10 to 15 percent more fruit than Pinot Noir, which explains its great popularity.

Producers who use a lot of Pinot Meunier often praise the fruitiness of the grape. Wines made from Pinot Meunier reach maturity more quickly, and have a bouquet that is reminiscent of toast or fresh bread, as well as caramel and simple fruitiness. It also has an earthy flavor. On the other hand, wines blended from a mixture in which Pinot Meunier predominates do not age well. In a few of the old vintages of the great Champagne houses, one can still feel the vitality that remains in the characters of Pinot Noir and Chardonnay, but the Pinot Meunier element has collapsed, destroying the overall coherence of the *cuvée*. Pure Pinot Meunier Blanc de Noirs are rare and will only keep for ten years.

The great exceptions that prove the rule of Pinot Meunier's inability to age gracefully are Krug and José Michel. Krug's legendary 1953 vintage contains 30 percent Pinot Meunier, and well-matured bottles have retained all of their youthful vigor. The José Michel 1921, which contains nothing but Pinot Meunier, is one of the most magnificent Champagnes I have ever had the pleasure of drinking. It must be remembered, however, that the Pinot Meunier Krug uses was incorporated into other varieties during the course of long storage in bottle before the *dégorgement*. Furthermore, the Krug and José Michel grapes came from very old vines from the villages of Leuvrigny and Moussy. Neither brand uses malo-lactic fermentation, which is probably explained by the fact that Pinot Meunier has a high enough level of acidity for lengthy aging. The small 205-liter (54 gal.) oak vats also contribute to the way their Champagnes have withstood aging.

Louis Roederer has admitted that they would be happy to use Pinot Meunier if they were able to tame it in the way that Krug has managed, openly admitting that it is something they have not been able to do. The most important function of this grape is to contribute a mildness to Champagnes that are designed to be drunk young. Unlike its noble parent, Pinot Noir, Pinot Meunier produces, after only three years of aging, a sweet Champagne that is perfectly drinkable.

Chardonnay: this is the most elegant of the white wine grape-stocks in the world. Many producers all over the world dream of being able to copy the great Chardonnays of Burgundy, Chablis, and Champagne. In Australia and the United States, producers such as Leeuwin, Peter Michael, Mayacamas, and Kistler have created copies that are very similar to the original, but they have never attained the heights of the most prestigious French wines. The Raveneau and Dauvissat Chablis *grand cru* or the great Burgundies of Ramonet, Coche-Dury, Lafon, and Marc Colin combine the aromatic qualities of the grape-stock with an elegance derived from the soil that can only be matched by the Champagnes of Avize, Cramant, and Le Mesnil.

The origin of the Chardonnay stock is not clear. In some places, the grape is known as "Pinot Chardonnay," which incorrectly leads to the assumption that Chardonnay is related to Pinot Noir and Pinot Blanc. All of the *Vitis vinifera* varieties (in other words, all the wine-producing grapes of today) originate from wild vines, Green Muscat being their common ancestor. Chardonnay was probably one of the first new grape varieties developed from Muscat. It came to Europe from the Middle East.

Today, Chardonnay is a fashionable grape variety that is more and more heavily cultivated in France. The greatest increase in cultivation has been in Champagne, where growers consider it to be the king of grape varieties. The character of the grape is often mixed with the taste of oak; certain producers love to use new oak tuns in which to mature their Chardonnay. It is the New World producers, especially those in North America and Australia, who are most frequently responsible for offering Chardonnays with an exaggerated oak flavor. Some of these wines taste more strongly of planks and of pencils than of the fruit itself.

Chardonnay is nevertheless the variety that ages best in oak casks. Above all, it is a hardy and malleable grape. The special character of the grape is fairly attenuated but can be molded to perfection depending on the various climates and soils. The aroma of the grape is ample, buttery, and elegant, with fruity notes ranging from those of apple in cooler climates to a faint melon-y fragrance if the climate is too warm.

The Chardonnay plant is prone to wasting energy by developing its foliage at the expense of maturing the grape. In Champagne, this phenomenon is combated by severe pruning, and by planting the stocks in tightly packed rows. It is not unusual to find 7,500 plants to the hectare (about two-and-a-half acres) in the Côte des Blancs. The high quality of Chardonnay does not prevent a high yield. The grape is easy to cultivate and only has one disadvantage, which is—like Pinot Noir—it is very sensitive to frost. That is because it buds earlier than other varieties.

In Champagne, Chardonnay produces wines with an initially light body, high acidity, and a refined bouquet. When young, the bouquet is light and flowery, with evident touches of white blossom and Granny Smith apples. The flavor may be sharp and metallic with citrus notes and great mineral richness. Anyone who has been disappointed by the discreet revelation of a Blanc de Blancs should taste a mature Champagne made from Chardonnay. Though acrid in its youth, the wine eventually attains an incomparable richness and exuberance.

The citrus fragrances are riper and are completed by those of exotic fruits such as passion fruit, pineapple, and mango. The aroma becomes pleasantly toasted, with a hint of coffee as well. Since Chardonnay wines are high in acidity, they are long-lived. Anyone who has ever had the chance of tasting the old Salon vintages will know what I mean.

OTHER GRAPE VARIETIES

The *C.I.V.C.* and other official bodies only ever make veiled allusions to varieties other than the three classics of Champagne. It is certainly forbidden to cultivate them, but they can be used in making Champagne. Arbanne, Petit Meslier, Gamay, Fromenteau, and Pinot Blanc may enter into the composition of this drink with a worldwide reputation. Today, you will have to search long and hard to find a few vestiges of these vines, and those that remain will soon be replaced. A producer in Jouy-les-Reims, Aubry, is still making exciting Champagnes from varieties that are now neglected.

Arbanne: in the nineteenth century, Arbanne was an important variety in Aube. Its characteristically flowery bouquet could dominate an entire *cuvée*, even if only a small amount was used in the composition of the wine. The grape's sensitivity to mildew caused it to disappear more quickly from Champagne than Petit Meslier (see below). Arbanne is related to Chardonnay Blanc Musqué, which is still being grown by a nurseryman in Mâconnais. To my knowledge, only Moutard-Diligent at Buxeuil use Arbanne exclusively.

Chardonnay grapes ready for harvesting.

Petit Meslier: Petit Meslier is one of the most important of the less common secondary varieties. It is mainly cultivated in the Aube département but cultivation is dwindling fast. It is very sensitive to viruses and to gray rot. Furthermore, it comes into bud very early, at a time of year when spring frosts represent a serious threat to the harvest in the Aube. This variety does not always reach maturity in the heart of the Champagne region, and only ripens completely in hot years at the southern end of the Aube. The classic stocks grown in the Aube produce wines with a high percentage of alcohol in hot years and in the past they were lightened with more acid, lighter cultivars of Petit Meslier. If used on its own, this white grape produces acid wines with a fruity aroma that are reminiscent of Pinot Meunier. As soon as it comes on the market, I really want to try the Blanc de Blancs matured in oak vats that Jacquesson has made solely from Petit Meslier.

Pinot Blanc: Pinot Blanc was created from a combination of Pinot Gris and a Pinot Noir mutation. In Champagne and elsewhere in France, it has been confused with Chardonnay. Only by closely examining the foliage can one easily distinguish between these two varieties. Pinot Blanc has flat leaves, whereas those of Chardonnay are concave, and they are bare at the point where the stem joins the leaf. The Pinot Blanc that has managed to insinuate itself into certain vineyards in the Champagne region has done so without the knowledge of the grower. This grape is definitely inferior to Chardonnay, and produces neutral wines with a high alcohol content that age badly. Its high yield justifies its extensive cultivation in Alsace and certain parts of Germany.

Fromenteau: Fromenteau is a local *appellation* for a variation on Pinot Gris. Fromenteau has a generously fruity taste with a tropical note and it also has a generous body. The variety is mainly represented in the Aubry region of Champagne. Elsewhere, it is the main ingredient in the fat, rich wines produced in Alsace.

Gamay: this variety from the Aube was banned by law in 1927, but application of the law was delayed in order to allow vine-growers to replant their vineyards with noble varieties. It was not until 1952 that the use of this grape from Beaujolais was finally forbidden. Gamay has a light, raspberry taste in the wines of Champagne. It is a mystery to me why this variety continues to be cultivated, in view of the fact that special permission is required to do so and this permission is only granted if the vine-grower is more than ninety-five years old and the vines were planted prior to 1948!

THE ANNUAL LIFE-CYCLE OF THE VINE

The vine has a very regular annual life-cycle, regardless of the variety involved. It rests throughout the winter and gathers its strength before spring. The trunk is bare during this period and the sap takes refuge in the roots. It is not until the soil temperature exceeds 9°C (48°F) that the vine plant resumes its activity, generally in February or March. The active period of the plant lasts from 160 to 200 days, and it is customary to divide it into eleven stages:

Weeping: sap oozes from the wound created by pruning.

Budding: the rising sap causes the buds to emerge slowly. By late March, the buds will certainly have formed.

Leaf-sprouting: the first leaves appear in early April.

The show or emergence of the grape: the appearance of miniature bunches of grapes. The more of them there are, the richer the harvest will be.

Flowering: the flowering period, in late May, makes a stay in Champagne at this time unforgettable. In the evening, the vineyards produce delicious, exotic aromas that resemble those of passion fruit. Unfortunately, flowering doesn't last for more than three weeks.

Insemination: when the air temperature rises to over 20°C (68°F) and a light breeze is able to waft the pollen over the vineyards, pollination can take place. For pollination to be successful it needs to be completed within two or three days, since a longer period of pollination could prevent the grapes from forming.

Fruiting: immediately after pollination, in the summer months, the grape vine puts all its energy into forming the fruits. The grapes are still in their infancy: small, green, hard, acid, and devoid of sugar.

Ripening: in August, the fruits begin to ripen. They become softer and the Pinot grapes begin to turn blue-black in color. The chlorophyll disappears, the acidity diminishes, and the sugar content increases.

Bark toughening: at harvest-time, the branches and twigs begin to harden to enable them to withstand the coming winter. A very light bark now covers the shoot, which had previously been able to breathe and sweat.

Leaf drying: when the chlorophyll disappears from the leaves in the fall, they turn yellow and red. The vineyards are now unparalleled in their beauty.

Leaf-shedding: in early November, the leaves dry out and are easily shed in the wind. The sap decreases so that the plant can gather its strength and save itself for the effort of growth in the following year; the grape vine enters its hibernation phase.

The protective leaves ensure the plant stays cool under the burning summer sun.

Making Champagne

The *méthode champenoise* for making Champagne is a rather long and complicated one. To summarize the method in a few words, we could say that, after normal fermentation in a barrel or steel vat, the wine is then fermented a second time in the bottle. This is the technique used for creating a sparkling wine, in the course of which it may acquire certain aromatic advantages. But let us now start at the very beginning.

The work of the vine-grower lasts throughout the year. At very specific moments, he has to prune, fertilize, and spray his plantations. The fight against viruses, parasites, and fungi is never ending. The climate may also play tricks on him. A spring frost at the very moment of flowering could have a disastrous effect upon the entire harvest. The basic rule in wine-making is that the smaller the harvest the finer the quality of the grape. It is customary to measure the yield in hectolitres per hectare. Depending on the extent of the harvest, a maximum yield is set every year. When the harvest was exceptionally good in 1982, the region produced as much as eighty-six hectoliters per hectare. Nevertheless most of the makers of quality wines try to keep the yield to under fifty hectoliters per hectare.

Another important basic rule is that the older the vine, the higher the quality. These two rules place the vine-growers in a difficult position. They want to sell as much wine as possible, but since quantity and quality do not go together, they are forced to make a choice.

The average age of a vine plant in Champagne is around fifteen years. A vine that gets to be thirty years old, which is when quality is at its peak, would tend at this point to be replaced with a new plant by most producers. It is obviously very expensive to leave old, productive vines—which will have a highly developed root system—in the ground, since they take up a great deal of space in the vineyards, but there are those enthusiasts who currently harvest grapes grown on vines that are as ancient as sixty to eighty years old.

Diebolt, Moncuit, Pierre Peters, and Larmandier-Bernier specially separate the grapes from their old Chardonnay vines in order to make a luxury Champagne from them. Surprisingly, these Champagnes cost no more than vintage Champagnes produced by other firms. A real find!

The grape vine is most productive between ten and twenty-five years of age. Before that, most of its energy goes into producing grapes, diminishing the concentration of

Huge oak barrels in the Vilmart cellar at Rilly-la-Montagne.

flavor. Grapes from very old vines always contain much greater concentrate and far less water than younger plants.

The way the vines are laid out in the vineyard strongly affects the results. Before the phylloxera plague reached Europe, ungrafted vines in Champagne were planted "*en foule*" (in a crowd). This means that they were planted any-old-how, with five or six plant to the square meter. The yield on the surface was higher than it is today, but each plant actually produced far fewer grapes, so the quality was maintained. Bollinger still uses this method today for its ungrafted vines at Aÿ and Bouzy, which, for some inexplicable reason, have never been attacked by phylloxera. Why these particular plots of land have escaped remains a real mystery.

In addition to planting *en foule*, four pruning systems are permitted in Champagne: Chablis, Cordon, Guyot, and Vallée de la Marne.

The Chablis pruning system was developed for the Chablis variety, needless to say. Up to four branches are allowed on each vine—the fewer the branches, the greater the concentration of essence in the fruit. Anselme Selosse at Avize only leaves two thicker branches, but if you check out the vines at the large firms all around his, you will find vines with four thicker branches. All the Chardonnay plants in Champagne are pruned using the Chablis method.

The Cordon system is more frequently used for Pinot Noir. Only one main trunk is allowed.

The Guyot system is not allowed in the *grand cru* and *premier cru* villages, but is regularly used in the Aube on its three grape varieties.

The Vallée de la Marne system is only used for Pinot Meunier vines of inferior quality. The system has been adopted through almost the whole of the Aisne, due to its sensitivity to frost.

As in Burgundy, the Pinot Noir of Champagne is sensitive to gray rot, which must not be confused with noble rot, the mold that helps to create the sweet Sauternes dessert wines. Gray rot and noble rot are both caused by a fungal parasite called *Botrytis cinerea.* Gray rot has a moldy smell and is fortunately rare in Champagne. Since the grapes are picked by hand, bunches that are affected can be discarded immediately. If by accident, grapes damaged by gray rot fall into the Champagne presses, the flavor will not really be affected because only the grape skin is attacked. In Champagne, all contact is avoided with the grape skin in the production of white wines.

HARVESTING

Whichever the vineyard, the harvest is the high point of the year. Even though the old guard are wont to claim that things were different in their day, the harvest in Champagne still gives rise to impressive festivities. There are celebrations all over the region, at which there is always plenty to drink; these colorful and exuberant occasions have a certain exoticism about them to our Nordic eyes.

The *C.I.V.C.* decides on the date on which the harvesting will start by proclaiming the opening of the harvest, "*L'Ouverture des vendanges.*" Two different dates are set, one for the harvesting of the Pinot grapes and the other for Chardonnay. Once it was left up to nature to decide the date of the harvesting, which worked out at exactly one hundred days after the end of flowering. This date often coincides with the date determined by the *C.I.V.C.*

The date of the harvest naturally varies from one year to the next, but it is usually in mid-September. Champagne is the only region in France in which mechanical harvesting is prohibited, which means that each bunch of grapes has to be delicately hand-picked and deposited in a *mannequin* (wicker basket). Thousands of people arrive from all corners of France to help pick the grapes. Picking always starts at dawn to prevent spontaneous fermentation. Picking is avoided in full sunlight or in the rain. Each harvester is equipped with an *épinette*, an instrument that is somewhere between a pair of scissors and a pair of secateurs.

The date of the harvest is decided by the sugar content and acidity of the grapes. The grapes must have attained a sugar content that is high enough to produce 10 to 11 percent alcohol, while retaining enough acidity to ensure that the wine is balanced. The Germans measure the *oechsle* and the weight of the must, but in Champagne it is just the amount of acidity and sugar content that are measured.

Dom Pérignon, that ancient monk, always examined and handled the grapes to decide when it was time to harvest them. He also understood the advantages of harvesting in the cool weather and the benefit of transporting the grapes quickly to the press. His methods are still in use. All the harvesting operations are strictly divided and organized so that the content of the full baskets can be quickly loaded onto vehicles to be transported to the pressing plant.

PRESSING

It is vital that all the grapes are whole and in excellent condition when they reach the press. For this reason the pressing

The handsome wicker baskets known as "mannequins" have almost all been replaced by plastic containers.

facility is always located as close as possible to the vineyard. Many small growers send their grapes to be pressed in the huge cooperative facilities. The great Champagne houses still run their own presses to enable them to supervise all the handling stages as closely as possible.

At harvesting time, the pressing facilities bristle with inspectors from the *C.I.V.C.* who are there to check that the correct quantity of must is obtained from each pressing. In 1992, the law changed in relation to the volumes required from each pressing. The new legislation states that 2,550 liters (675 gal.) must be extracted from 4,000 kg (630 st.) of grapes.

The first pressing (*la cuvée*): this first pressing should produce 2,050 liters (542 gal.) of grape must. Unfortunately, the term *cuvée* is the same as that used in French to refer to the blend, and this can lead to confusion. The first pressing produces the purest and most delicate must from the grape pulp; there is not the slightest contact with the skin or seeds. This *cuvée* is stored for use in the blending process. Very few producers do more in the quest for quality. But Jacquesson and Vilmart, for example, go further. They have discovered that only part of the *cuvée* is of the very highest quality. This must is called *coeur de cuvée*, the "heart of the *cuvée*."

The second pressing (*première taille*): provides a further 500 liters (130 gal.) of grape juice. Very few Champagne houses admit to using anything but the first pressing in their wines, but in practice few are able to afford the luxury of just using the *cuvée*. Wines made from a second pressing are slightly more acrid and coarse. If the *première taille* from the two black Pinots grapes is used, there is risk that the Champagne will have a pinkish color.

The third pressing (*deuxième taille*): the third pressing was once used to make the numerous Champagnes destined to be sold in supermarkets, which were once the shame of the region. Under the new legislation, this third pressing has been banned from wine-making so as to prevent the production of such poor-quality Champagnes.

La rebêche: this is what remains after the last pressings. The process of pressing what are essentially dry grape skins produces a juice with a high tannin content, only to be used for distilling.

Many experiments using new types of presses have been carried out in the region, but the conclusion usually reached is that the type of old vertical press favored by Dom Pérignon, known as Le Coquard, remains the best. The Coquard press is always made of wood and may be round or square in shape. The grapes are pressed quickly and delicately under a large wooden board.

The other fairly common type of press is the modern horizontal press, which may be pneumatic or hydraulic. When it first appeared, it was the subject of much attention and enthusiasm, but it has fallen out of fashion in recent years.

OXIDATION AND SLUDGE REMOVAL

It is most important that the must is protected from excessive oxidation throughout the vinification process. Some winemakers claim that the wine can be "inoculated" against future oxidation by acidifying the must at an early stage. The very process of making wine involves oxidation, indicating that oxidation is not harmful in itself. What is decisive is the extent of the acidification of the wine and speed of oxidation that it can tolerate. A wine that is vinified in oak casks is subject to greater oxidation than a wine that is hermetically sealed inside a stainless steel vat.

The chemical effect of excessive oxidation is that the oxidizing enzymes attacking the phenols in the wine, giving it a brown color and a bitter, acrid flavor reminiscent of sherry. To protect the fresh must, about eight grams per hectoliter of sulfur dioxide has to be incorporated into it. The sulfite also helps kill the wild yeasts that might trigger uncontrolled fermentation. It is rare that the sulfur is detectable in the bouquet or the taste. The dose is too minute.

In order to remove any foreign matter in suspension, the must is decanted in a process known as *débourbage*, which may be natural or artificial. The artificial process consists of centrifuging, filtering, or precipitation using bentonite. Most Champagne makers use the natural method, in which sedimentation is caused by cooling the must to just above freezing point. There are many stages in wine-making, and removing the sludge or lees is the first one in making Champagne.

FERMENTATION

As soon as the must has been decanted into a vat, fermentation begins. It takes place thanks to the yeast that is found in that fine, waxy film that coats the surface of the grape and is called *pruine* in French. There are two categories of yeast: natural yeast and cultured yeast. One of the secrets of Moët & Chandon's "house-style" is the cultured yeast used for all of its production, which produces a bouquet of toast with notes of cream of mushroom soup.

Each village in Champagne may contain hundreds of varieties of wild yeast in the air. The yeasts are grown in the laboratory but all are originally found in the wild. The commonest type of yeast used in Champagne today is *Saccharomyces ellipsoideus*. All of the yeasts used to make Champagne are particularly well suited to fermentation at low temperature and high pressure in the bottle. The few Champagnes that are fermented with wild yeast are mainly wines from one single vineyard.

The argument advanced in favor of such a practice is that the characteristics of that vineyard are better emphasized through the use of a yeast taken from the skins of the grape that grow within it.

Yeast needs to be fed if it is to be able to convert the grape sugar into alcohol and carbon dioxide. It feeds on the must, which contains all of the proteins, vitamins, and minerals that the yeast needs. The 20 percent or so sugar content of a ripe Chardonnay grape is perfectly adequate for the yeast to start the process of conversion into alcohol and carbon dioxide. In reality, it is not the yeast cell itself that is behind the fermentation process, but rather twenty or more enzymes that are contained in this cell. Each enzyme has a special function during the complicated process of fermentation.

During the first normal fermentation—the alcoholic fermentation—the carbon dioxide that is formed is not used. The only concern is to increase the ethyl alcohol content and turn the grape juice into wine.

Two major factors in fermentation are time and temperature. Fermentation normally lasts ten days and takes place at a temperature of 18°C to 20°C (64–68°F), but a few winemakers ferment their wines at a lower temperature and thus enable the wine to retain more of its fruitiness. Billecart-Salmon is a pioneer of cold fermentation. Once again, Anselme Selosse proves to be the most extreme of the winemakers, leaving his wines to ferment for nearly two months.

The fermentation process is the stage that converts ordinary grape juice into the multi-faceted drink that is known as wine. Wine made from grapes is the only drink that can contain the aromas of all the other fruits in a single glass! Of course, it may be exciting to participate in a tasting of beers or whiskies, but the inexhaustible combinations of flavour that wine can produce cannot be found in any other drink. The aromatic constituents of a great wine may run into the hundreds and include acids, alcohols, aldehydes, esters and ketones. Anyone detecting an aroma with notes of apple or peach in a Champagne is not mistaken. The fifty elements that go to make up the scent of an apple may also be part of the complex composition of wine. Some aromas are present in lesser numbers. These include those of almond (benzaldehyde, acetone), hazelnut (diacetyl), honey (phenylacetic acid), peach (undecalactone), and banana (butyl acetate, butyl ethanoate).

Personally, I find it more appetizing to describe a wine as having the aroma of peach than of an undecalactone.

Malolactic fermentation: the advantages and disadvantages of malolactic fermentation (also know as malic acid fermentation) provoke controversy among winemakers. Whether they use it or not, they are convinced that theirs is the correct method. This controversial biological process consists in converting the tart malic acid into milder lactic acid.

Malolactic fermentation is activated if the fermentation vat is heated, and it is slowed down if sulfur is added to the wine at low temperature. The advantage of wines that have undergone malolactic fermentation is that they become milder and are more easily appreciated while young. Wines that have not undergone malolactic fermentation are more acrid and sharp when young but retain a high level of acidity for a very long time, which has a preservative effect.

Most Champagnes that are considered the best and the most suitable for laying down, such as Krug, Salon, and Selosse, will be considered aggressive in their infancy, but since they have not been subject to malolactic fermentation, their keeping qualities are considerably enhanced. On the other hand, there is no real point in avoiding such fermentation for a non-vintage light Champagne, as Lanson—for example—does. It should be added, nevertheless, that Piper-Heidsieck and Lanson produce vintage Champagnes that start life as a chrysalis but which, with time, develop into wonderful, colorful butterflies that are ready to take flight.

Malolactic fermentation is to some extent an unknown quantity. Certain enologists claim that it has always taken place, but it is still unclear as to when it actually happens in the life of a wine. It is clear, however, that this type of fermentation reduces the acidity of the wine. Ten grams of malic acid will convert into 6.7 grams (1/4 oz.) of lactic acid, the rest disappearing in the form of carbon dioxide. To summarize, malolactic fermentation has three separate effects on the quality of the wine: it reduces the acidity, stabilizes the bacteria, and alters the taste. More information about the position adopted by winemakers in relation to malolactic fermentation can be found in the section reserved for them.

When the wine has completed its first fermentation during the winter, double clarification is often the next step. The process of clarification consists of decanting the wine into a new vat, in which the wine separates out from the lees at the bottom. Some producers, who are very afraid that the wine will have too strong a character, filter their wine a second time. Fortunately, more and more of them are beginning to realize that this is unnecessary, and by doing so they lose many of the important aromatic components.

OAK BARRELS OR STAINLESS STEEL VATS?

Since the early 1960s, most of the vats in which Champagne is fermented have been made of stainless steel. Vats that are enameled, or made of glass and fiberglass are rarely used, while a tiny elite who are worried about quality—led by Bollinger and Krug—are still fermenting their wines in oak vats of all sizes. The standard size in Champagne is a 205-liter (54-gal.) vat known as a *pièce*. Most grape-growers on the Côte des Blancs who currently use oak vats buy them in Chablis; they hold 225 liters (59 gal.). Signature, the prestige Champagnes made by Jacquesson, is fermented in 1,000-liter (265-gal.) tuns, whereas a limited number of makers use demi-hogsheads holding 600 liters (160 gal.).

The great Champagne houses claim that quality has improved since the wines started to be fermented in the enormous stainless steel vats. Personally, I am charmed by Champagnes vinified in oak casks. It is obvious that the wine takes on a different dimension through its contact with the wood. The aromas are richer and the wine acquires greater strength. However, let it not be said that a Champagne of great class cannot be obtained from these stainless steel vats. Taittinger Comtes de Champagne, Roederer Cristal, Pol Roger Winston Churchill and Salon are all excellent examples of Champagnes fermented in stainless steel vats possessing a very pure fruitiness and an ubeatable elegance. The wines fermented in the oak casks used by Krug, Bollinger, and Jacques Selosse are unique in their depth and concentration.

Since Champagne is a wine that is so carefully blended and so fragile, it is important to safeguard its fruitiness from domination by the aromas of the oak. It is most unusual to use only new oak casks as they do in the United States and Australia. An oak cask used for Champagne is often so old that the tannin and vanillin of the oak will have disappeared long before use. In 1993 an enologist demonstrated, using chemical principles, that Krug Champagnes contained elements that were derived from the oak. Prior to this, chemists claimed that the oak flavor that can be detected quite easily in Krug Champagne was purely the product of the aeration from which the wine benefited when aged in these small old oaken casks.

Tannin and vanillin have a greater presence in Champagne fermented in oak vats rather than in stainless steel vats. Another notable difference is that Champagnes fermented in oak casks contain more glycerol, which renders the wine richer and more oily. Since the oak casks allow in small amounts of air, oxidation is quicker, which also increases the ester and aldehyde contents.

A few wine-waiters who are sensitive to oxidation mark down Bollinger and Krug Champagnes matured in oak casks as defective in blind tastings, since they reveal a soupçon of an aroma similar to that of sherry, which they believe is caused by excessive oxidation. I claim the opposite, namely that this note is a faint component that is perfectly natural in the character of the oxidation that is necessary for a classic Champagne. In any case, it is difficult to distinguish between the oak flavor and that of an old Chardonnay in Champagne—as it is in wines made from Chablis. Both contain an undernote of toast, hazelnut, and smoke that sometimes emanate from toasted bread and roasted coffee. Even the autolytic character, the aroma that develops in Champagnes that have remained in contact with their lees for a long time before the disgorgement process may easily be confused with the taste of oak.

Champagne houses whose concern for quality causes them to use oak casks rarely admit to using a few new casks to give the wine individuality. But without naming names, I can confirm that I have seen with my own eyes new oak casks containing wine within the cellars of several famous firms.

Anselme Selosse and the Vilmart winemakers do not hide the fact that they conduct experiments. Selosse claims that 50 percent new casks work well for Champagnes that are similar to Burgundies. He is also the first to have marketed a Champagne matured exclusively in new oak casks. Some of these wines require decanting before consumption, however.

The use of oak casks is much more risky than fermentation in stainless steel vats. The wines that are matured on a small scale in little oak casks sometimes present disconcerting variations in the bottle. They may sometimes, exceptionally, have been created under conditions of hygiene that leave something to be desired, resulting in a defective wine. Most of the large-scale producers find stainless steel vats a real blessing because it is almost impossible for anything to go wrong. The quality of the grapes and the abilities of the *chef de cave* (cellar master) in blending the grapes will have a far greater impact on the eventual taste of the Champagne.

BLENDING (*ASSEMBLAGE*)

Blending begins in March–April. This is one of the most difficult stages in the creation of Champagne. It is at this time that the cellar master imposes his style and the firm's mark on its Champagne. The wines whose fermentation has been completed are still, and most of them remain in separate vats, each originating from a particular village. The more sensitive the palate of the cellar master, the more he will be able to influence the wine. Krug is unique, having 4,000 small oak casks. If the cellar master is not happy with the contents of any of the casks, he merely rejects that particular wine.

The cellar master at Moët & Chandon, Monsieur Blanck, also has at his disposal an extraordinary mosaic of still wines originating from differents villages. His 800 great vats contain wines from 150 different villages. They may be of lesser quality than a Krug—but they are still pretty good!

The small winemakers have an easier life. They often separate out their best wines for making into prestige Champagnes, but they hardly ever have a problem knowing which wines need to be blended. Most of the time, all they have available are the grapes from one or two villages. Anselme Selosse, as usual, goes that extra mile, putting grapes from each plot of the *grand cru* village Avize into a different vat.

Krug still uses traditional winemaking implements.

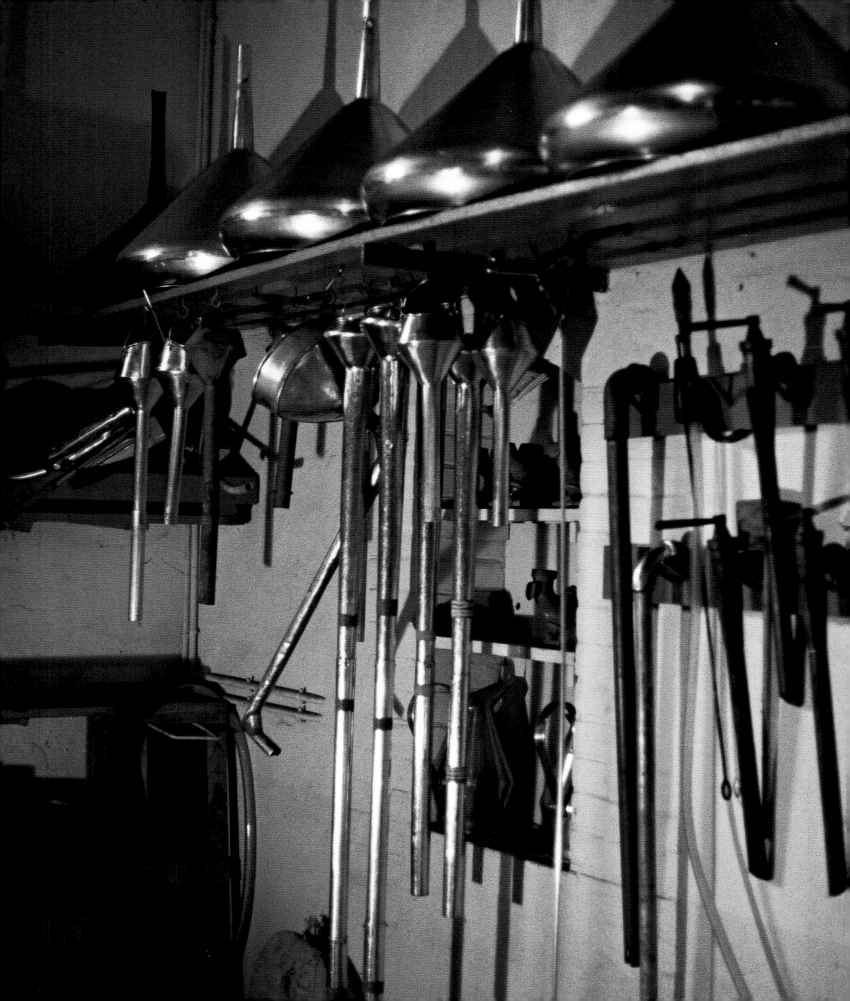

In view of the fact that basic material varies from one year to the next, one needs to have considerable knowledge and a great deal of experience to be able to produce a consistent Champagne that exemplifies the house-style of the firm. The cellar master will also have at his disposal a large quantity of wines reserved from previous years, which he will use to balance the taste. Krug keeps these reserved wines in stainless steel vats, because oxidation must be avoided at this stage of vinification. On the other hand, Louis Roederer, who ferments his wines in stainless steel vats, ages his reserve wines in large oak casks. Bollinger uses the most sophisticated method; its reserve wines are aged under light pressure in magnum bottles.

When the cellar master creates the *cuvée,* he needs to take various factors into account. Will the wine develop smoothly, so that the Pinot and Chardonnay are not at different stages of development? Should he try to keep to the house-style or follow the character of the vintage? What will the wine be like once it has become sparkling? Above all, he has to ask himself which wines will blend best together. It is not enough simply to assemble the best still wines. An unbalanced, immature wine can give nerve to a blend that is too heavy; a dull, neutral wine can serve as a bridge between the lighter and heavier wines in a *cuvée.* Some villages don't blend well together, even if individually the wines they offer are great.

The work of the cellar master is very similar to that of a chef who needs to know exactly how much of each ingredient he needs to use. Blending has become something of a sacred task since the days when Dom Pérignon began mixing grapes from different villages.

I am one of those who believes that unblended, single *cru* Champagnes can attain the same level of quality as blended wines, but it is true that a skilled cellar master can produce incredible miracles using fairly simple wines.

FOAMING

When the cellar master has decided how the still wines are to be assembled, they are blended in huge vats before being bottled. It is now that the Champagne acquires its knightly crest in the form of a snowy white foam.

During the first alcoholic fermentation, carbon dioxide forms and escapes into the air, but during the second fermentation the carbon dioxide is imprisoned in the bottle.

In view of the fact that the blend of still wines has already lost all its yeast content, the incorporation of sugar and additional yeast is now necessary. The sugar and yeast are diluted in wine and form a mixture that is known as the *liqueur de tirage.* The quantity of this liqueur is strictly calculated in relation to the amount of foam required. Generally, the recipe is 22 grams of sugar per liter of wine (about 1 ounce to 1 quart of wine). This increases the alcohol content to around 1.2 percent.

Once this solution has been added, the wine is bottled and provisionally corked using a capsule or a real cork. The interior of the capsule is covered in plastic to protect the wine against

SUGAR CONTENT OF CHAMPAGNE

Extra Brut	0–6 grams per liter
Brut	0–15 grams per liter
Sec	17–35 grams per liter
Demi-Sec	33–50 grams per liter
Doux (sweet)	more than 50 grams per liter

the possibility of rust. The bottles are then taken down to cellars where the temperature is 10–12°C and are laid horizontally (on racks) piled one on top of the other to an impressive height. This is an unforgettable sight which you will see if you visit the cellars of the great houses: those interminable vistas of rows of shelving filled with bottles.

This whole process has taken an enormous length of time to develop. Even though the English were adding sugar as long ago as 1662, it was not until 1801 that Chaptal was able to prove the effects of various different additions of sugar. In 1857 the role of yeast in the fermentation was totally mastered, thanks to Louis Pasteur's discoveries.

The expression *liqueur de tirage* was used for the first time by Professor Robinet, a native of Épernay, in 1877. It was probably not until the 1880s that sugar and yeast began to be added. Until then, the bubbles had been the result of an extended first fermentation; there was no second fermentation as there is today.

AGING

According to law, non-vintage Champagne has to rest in this way.

Fermentation only lasts for two weeks. During this period, the bottles are shaken by hand many times. This stage is called *poignetage.* It is very rare today for bottles to explode while the foam is forming, but in the old days, before the exact quantities of yeast and sugar required were known, many reputable makers lost half their annual production in this way.

During fermentation, a deposit forms that is called the lees. It consists of dead yeast cells and particles of undesirable chemicals. This deposit imbues the wine with its own aroma and is called the autolytic character, a very important element

A good "riddler" can turn thousands of bottles in a few hours.

in the production of Champagne. Autolysis has numerous positive effects. For example, a reduction enzyme is released that prevents oxidation and has a preservative effect on the Champagne for as long as it is in contact with this deposit. Furthermore, the amino acids increase in number, giving the Champagne this breadlike fragrance and aroma of acacia that is so often found in newly disgorged Champagnes. A manno-protein known as MP 32 also develops. Certain nutrients originating from the yeast are absorbed, producing a yeast-like and fungal, while preventing the triggering of a third fermentation after the administration of the dosage. The best example of a Champagne with an autolytic character is probably the Bollinger R. D. prestige Champagne, which is only disgorged after eight to twelve years.

After the racking stage, the bottles are placed, with the stopper facing downward, in large crates known as *pupitres* ("desks"). At first, the bottles are angled at 45°. The opening in which they are secured is designed in such a way as to turn them gradually until they are at a 90° angle. A *remueur* ("riddler") uses a swift gesture to turn the bottles one-eighth of a turn to detach any deposit from the sides of the bottle. This is the *remuage*, much of which is performed today with the help of machines called gyropalettes. These computerized machines can perform an average of one complete riddling cycle in eight days, whereas turning the bottles manually would take eight weeks. This saves a lot of time, but the charm of a craftsman practicing a traditional art has been lost. From the point of view of quality, I see no disadvantage in the gyropalettes, except that not all the bottles are riddled in the same way. With a gyropalette, the bottles that are nearest to the center move less than those that are on the periphery.

At the end of the *remuage*, the bottles are now standing upside-down and are ready to lose their lees, but numerous winemakers prefer to let the wine age further "*sur pointes*," or "on tiptoe," so as to be able to open a well-kept, really old bottle immediately when asked for one.

Moët & Chandon are trying to revolutionize the concept of *remuage* by using yeast capsules that don't form deposits in the bottle—these are called *billes* (marbles). Unfortunately, the technique has not proven to be entirely satisfactory.

DISGORGEMENT (*DÉGORGEMENT*)

The last important stage in the creation of Champagne is called the disgorgement. Nowadays, the tip of the stopper is frozen by plunging it into a brine bath at a temperature of −28°C. The deposit is thus half-frozen and viscous and can easily be expelled by means of a swift, mechanical movement. The name of this method is "*dégorgement à la glace*." It dates from 1884 and was invented by a Belgian, Armand Walfart.

A few makers still disgorge their Champagne by hand, a technique known as "*à la volée*." The deposit is expelled with a swift, precise movement; at the same time the bottle is turned upright. This technique requires years of training, if the wine obtained is to be completely yeast-free without losing half the contents of the bottle! The firm of Salon au Mesnil performs the *dégorgement* in this way, so as to be able to check and aerate the wine. Dom Pérignon himself used to practice disgorgement on his bottles, which were buried upside-down in sand.

The volume of the wine lost in the *dégorgement* process is adjusted by adding more wine and a little sugar. The quantity of sugar varies depending on the type of Champagne that the maker wants to obtain. This sugary solution is known as the *liqueur d'expedition* or the dosage. Some makers use aged wines for their dosage so as to obtain a riper flavor, but others are content to add a few drops of wine from the same pressing.

Until 1960, a small quantity of Cognac was used for the *liqueur d'expedition*. Since this is now illegal, I have promised not to snitch on those who still use it. Some makers have their own secret recipe. A small winemaker in Aÿ told me that he even used honey in his mixture!

THE ROLE OF THE CORK

After this final addition of wine, the bottle must be corked. The role of cork is crucial in the aging process. At the beginning of the last century, all Champagne corks were manufactured from a single block, but the high cost of cork caused Champagne-makers to resort to corks made of several layers bonded together. The upper part is made of synthetic cork and the lower parts of two or three slices of natural cork. The part that is in direct contact with the wine is always of the highest quality. The length and quality of the cork may be the most important reasons why Champagne is able to age for several decades. All of the aged Champagnes that have been given a good grade in the part of the book dedicated to discussing Champagne-makers have corks in a perfect state of preservation. It is very interesting to compare the length of a 1938 cork with one made in 1979. The former is almost twice as long and cut from one piece of cork!

When the final cork is fitted, the bottle is shaken again so that the additional dosage is well mixed in with the wine already in the bottle. The cork is held in place by a wire cage known as the *muselet*.

CHAMPAGNE LABELS

Once the cork is in place, the label must be affixed, manually or mechanically. The history of Champagne labels is not a long one. The bottles were once as naked as Adam and Eve. To be able to distinguish between the various *cuvées*, a wax seal was fixed to the cord that held the cork in place. In the mid-nineteenth century, bottles were often supplied with a small label discreetly glued to the base underneath. The information was sparing, but in the best of cases it specified the type and origin of the wine and, very rarely, the name of the maker. The first labels worthy of the name appeared in Champagne in 1820 and were based on a German model. Their use was quite a rare phenomenon for a while, and customers even had to pay extra to have their bottles labeled. At first, the word "Champagne" was never used on its own, but was often accompanied by the word "*pétillant,*" destined to specify the nature of the wine. Today labeling, which seems to be auto-matic, does not seem to me to be adequately valued. Is there a vineyard in the world whose labels can claim to be as beautiful as those on bottles of Champagne? On the other hand, the Champagne-makers could be accused of being too preoccu-pied with launching bottles in new shapes, and the labeling and packaging of all types of materials rather than concentrat-ing on what their bottles contain. But it must be admitted that a handsome label can make a wine more attractive!

After labeling, the bottles are stored for a short time at the maker's before being exported worldwide. The long and labo-rious process that first began among the vines many years ago has finally come to an end. Now all that there is left to do is to open the bottle and appreciate it!

HOW TO READ A LABEL

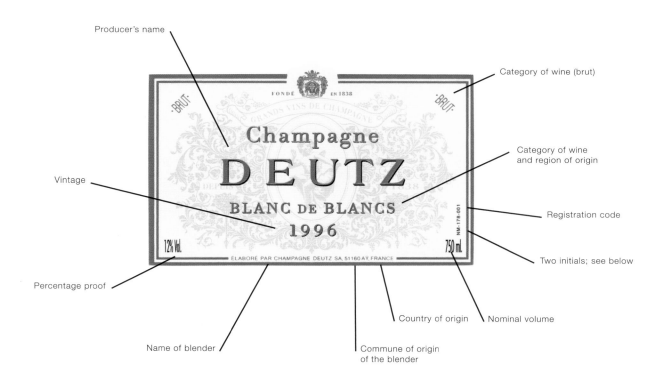

N-M : *Negociant-manipulant.* A Champagne firm that is authorized to buy in grapes for making Champagne.

R-M : *Recoltant-manipulant.* Vine-growers who only make and market Champagne from their own grapes.

C-M : *Cooperative-manipulant.* Group of Champagne grape-growers.

R-C : *Recoltant-cooperateur.* Vine-growers who remove their own bottles, bearing their own label, from the cooperative after it has made the wine.

M-A : *Marque d'acheteur.* A major buyer. For example, a hotel chain whose name features on the label even though the wine actually comes from a cooperative or Champagne house.

Buying, storing, tasting

The best way to buy Champagne is buy directly from the producer. The wine is then guaranteed to be in perfect condition. It is usually even possible to taste the wine before buying. Unlike their German counterparts, the winemakers of Champagne do not appear to get annoyed if they are asked to open one bottle just to sell another single one. The mere fact that someone wants to buy their Champagne seems to be enough to satisfy them.

In Reims, as in Épernay, there are gourmet stores that will sell you Champagne—at an exorbitant price. Only Madame Salvatori, whose store is in the main square of Épernay, offers prices equivalent to those of the producers. With a little luck you can make great discoveries at La Cave d'Erlon, the Boutique Nominée, Delices Champenoises, and at La Vinocave, all four of which are located in the center of Reims. Only one store specializes in selling Champagnes from the growers: it is called Champagne Selection and is right opposite the cathedral.

Almost the only place that old Champagnes can still be found is in Britain. That is because the English have traditionally expressed a special affection for great, soft Champagnes which, when mature, are said to have the *goût anglais* (English taste). Many members of the British aristocracy filled their cellars with this type of Champagne over a century ago. In London, a loiterer can browse through the stock of various wine merchants and in a few hours find more old Champagnes than there are for sale anywhere else in the world. Old Champagnes are also relatively inexpensive when purchased in the auctions held by Sotheby's and Christie's, but in view of the fact that the quality of old Champagnes depends largely on the way in which the bottles have aged, buying without tasting can obviously be quite a risky business. Another problem is that the wines are sold by the case, and this can seriously affect the budget of most ordinary people.

If you are lucky enough to find an old Champagne in France or when you are on vacation somewhere, it is perfectly possible to bargain; often you will be able to get the price down in comparison to young Champagnes of the same brand that are being offered for sale. Many of my friends have told me, with a smile on their lips, how they bought—for instance—a Mumm 1979 at the same price as a Cordon Rouge, or a Comtes de Champagne 1966 at half the price of a 1995 of the same brand. The most incredible example of good fortune fell to the very knowledgeable expert, Håkan Nilsson, who comes from southern Sweden. While in Provence in the early 1990s, he managed to buy a case of Dom Pérignon 1975 at a country grocery store for 200 francs (around $25) a bottle.

The Billecart-Salmon wines that won the Millennium Tasting competition: the 1959 and the 1961.

BOTTLES LARGE AND SMALL

Nebuchadnezzar	20 bottles	15 liters
Balthazar	16 bottles	12 liters
Salmanazar	12 bottles	9 liters
Methuselah	8 bottles	6 liters
Rehoboam	6 bottles	4.5 liters
Jeroboam	4 bottles	3 liters
Magnum	2 bottles	1.5 liters
Bottle		75 centiliters
Half bottle		37.5 centiliters
Quarter bottle		18.8 centiliters

CHOOSING CHAMPAGNE

There are many people who ask themselves why Champagne has to be so expensive. The principal reasons are the rigorous rules for maintaining quality, as well as the costly *méthode champenoise* used to produce it. The cost of Champagne covers the price of the bottle, the cork, the grapes, the winemaking, and the aging; all these elements make it impossible to sell Champagne at less than a minimum of $10 per bottle. Most matters concerning wine are—obviously—a matter of taste, but when you consider the cost of a Château Petrus or a Romanée Conti, a vintage Krug for $100 represents a real bargain.

In most Champagne houses, vintage wine is often the best purchase one can make. For the price of a few dollars more it is currently possible to buy a 1998 Moët & Chandon and a 1996 Veuve Clicquot, both greatly superior to non-vintage Champagnes of the same brand. *Cuvée de prestige* Champagne is often slightly more refined and concentrated, but the question is whether the price is really worth the difference in quality.

I think that the less expensive Champagnes should be avoided. They often have an earthy flavor that makes them unpleasant to drink and are rarely worth what they cost. They often contain a high percentage of wine from the second pressing and are produced in Aisne or the Aube. The predominant grape in these Champagnes is Pinot Meunier. Most Champagnes sold in supermarkets in Europe match this description. The real bargains in this veritable jungle of Champagnes are the high-class Blancs de Blancs from the *grand cru* producers.

In Burgundy, wines from the producers are dearer than those bought from the wine merchants, but in Champagne the opposite is the case, since these well-financed firms are keen to support the theory that good Champagnes should be a blend and many people are prepared to pay more money for these blended wines. As producers become more prominent, they will soon learn how to charge more. That is why we, as price-conscious consumers, need to hurry up and buy these masterpieces at bargain prices. A few producers such as Selosse and Vilmart have already become cult Champagne-makers, which means that their wines have soared in price in Paris and in New York.

Whatever Champagne one chooses, it is important to ensure that it is in good condition. Never buy a bottle of Champagne that has been kept upright in the store. The cork can quickly dry out and the wine will be destroyed. Hold the Champagne up to the light to make sure that the wine is clear, and check that there are no deposits. If the Champagne is old, you need to smell the cork. If you notice the slightest odor of madeira, there is a considerable risk that the cork has let in a harmful amount of oxygen. The level of the contents will also be revealing: a noticeably low level is a warning that something is wrong.

If you are making your purchases in Champagne at the height of the summer, do not keep the Champagne for long in the overheated trunk of your car. If you can, take the wine to your hotel room (or wherever you are staying), and keep it there until you leave for home. It is preferable to keep it in its original packaging to prevent exposing the Champagne to intense light. Always keep the bottles lying flat throughout the return trip.

These few tips will help you to avoid the worst problems, but one defect remains that can only be discovered once the wine is served—a defect in the cork, which is occurring more and more often. Intensive research is constantly being conducted to discover the reason for these problems with the cork in certain wines. A satisfactory answer has still not been found. At any event, it has been clearly established that faults in the cork are due to trichloroanisol (2,4,6-TCA). This means that the wine has been attacked by a fungus that gives the wine a moldy, corky odor even at low concentrations. The substance probably originates from poor quality cork, and of clumsy treatment of cork that has been brought into contact with volatile chemicals. It is not impossible that the substance responsible in this case is PCP, a chemical spray which paradoxically is used to protect the cork oaks from the depredations of fungi. Another explanation is the possible use of chlorine.

STORING CHAMPAGNE

Champagne producers have ideal conditions for aging in their cold, dark, damp cellars; such conditions are difficult for Champagne-lovers to reproduce at home. But those of us who live in the Nordic countries can do so more easily than most, thanks to our cool climate. Many of us are lucky enough to own an underground larder or a food safe in the garden. Even though the temperature varies considerably between summer and winter, the cellar retains a relatively constant temperature. In fact it is more important to use a storage place with a consistent temperature than one that is very cold, as long as it never rises above 16°C (61°F) to 18°C (64°F). If you intend to allow your wine to age for a long time, the ideal temperature for storage is 10°C (50°F) to 12°C (54°F). If you live in an apartment, you can always store Champagne in the refrigerator for a short time. I would not recommended doing so for long, because some foreign aromas emanating from food could get into the bottle and destroy the wine completely. There is still the risk that the cork will dry out if you store the wine for more than six or seven years in the fridge. Even vibrations could precipitate a change in the wine, but research tends to show that their importance has been greatly exaggerated.

If you cannot afford to buy a costly wine chill-cabinet, you can always buy a second-hand refrigerator and use it exclusively for storing your Champagne. Champagne stored in this way retains its freshness and elegance for much longer than if it were being stored at room temperature. One of my friends matures his Champagnes more rapidly than normal by storing them in his larder. If you do not intend to store the bottle for more than two years, and you want to obtain a Champagne with a softer flavor and roundness, you can safely follow my friend's example.

Unfortunately, aging is not an exact science. Far too often I have drunk wines that were tired and lifeless, even though they had been aged in the most exemplary fashion; but I have also drunk fabulous wines which were appallingly badly aged. Wine is a living product and each bottle lives its own life, which makes it all the more fascinating.

If you are lucky enough to own a real wine cellar, you will get much more fun out of it if you organize it by region, type of wine, and vintage. To ensure you retain a good overview of the cellar contents, you should record everything in a notebook or on the computer.

When Champagne is to be aged, it is useful to know that a magnum matures more slowly than a bottle, and a half bottle more quickly. This is simply due to the fact that the relationship between the air and the wine in a magnum bottle is optimal for long and perfect aging. Too high a proportion of air in relation to the quantity of wine accelerates the aging process. Wines created in very large bottles such as the Jeroboam and the Methuselah age even more slowly—that is assuming they were subjected to a second fermentation in the bottle.

Here is a very special instance of conservation. In November, 1916, in the middle of the First World War, the ketch *Jönköping*, a ship about seventy feet long, encountered a German U22 submarine between Sweden and Finland. After checking the ship's log and ordering the ship's crew to board the submarine, the U-boat captain ordered the ship to be sunk by packing it with explosives. The 5,000 bottles of Champagne that the ketch was carrying only represented a minute proportion of the cargo. It was also carrying forty tons of Cognac in sixty-seven oak casks, as well as a large quantity of wines destined for the Bank of Finland.

Two Swedes, Peter Lindberg and Claes Bergvall, had long dreamed of taking possession of this treasure. Pessimists thought it would be impossible to locate such a tiny ship in the deep waters of the Finnish archipelago. Very few people imagined that the cargo would be drinkable, even in the unlikely event that it was still on board. After years of searching, in the summer of 1997 the ship was finally located. It was lying at a depth of sixty-four meters and the cargo appeared to be almost intact. The first bottle was uncorked at sea and the delighted divers immediately realized that this was an exceptional wine. The Germans had drunk copious amounts of it before they sank the ship, and numerous bottles had broken; nevertheless there remained several thousand bottles of 1907 Heidsieck & Co., American taste. I have drunk this rare wine several times and have always been just as surprised at its youth. For a particular reason, the water around the wreck was not very salty, and the temperature, according to the measurements taken by the divers, was as low as 2°C (35°F) rather than the 4°C (39°F) expected. These conditions, plus the darkness and immobility of the sea depths, created an environment in which the Champagne was able to retain its youth. It would have been different had it been stored at 10°C (50°F) in the cellars of Reims and Épernay.

The magnificent treasure discovered by Peter and Claes was worth its weight in gold. The question of ownership was obviously a particularly thorny legal question, as was the sale of the Champagne. Should the cargo all be brought to the surface at the same time? How could the wire cages, there to protect the cork but destroyed by rust, be replaced? How would the wine age when the corks would soon dry out?

Naturally, there was enormous interest when the wines were first auctioned, supported by the rather overly euphoric tasting notes made by Tom Stevenson. So the price was very high, somewhere between $2,000 and $3,000 a bottle. The price made it difficult to dispose of the stock of several thousand bottles, and a single buyer was sought. The Caviar House chain of luxury stores (which markets gourmet items and owns bars in all the major airports) decided to acquire a certain number, but it took time to clinch the deal and the price had dropped considerably by that time. Despite all this, not all the bottles were sold, and I am convinced that enophiles with patience may soon be able to acquire these exciting bottles for less than $500 each.

FOR HOW LONG SHOULD A CHAMPAGNE BE KEPT?

One crucial question is to decide the age at which a Champagne should be drunk. Here again, it is a matter of personal taste. Do you prefer a young, acidic Champagne, or one that is older with a golden color and bouquet of honey? The numerous tastings for beginners that I have directed in recent years have taught me that each style of Champagne has its fans. The average taste among most Europeans and Americans lies somewhere between the English taste and the French taste for younger wines.

The disgorgement process makes it harder to predict how a Champagne will age in comparison with other wines. Aging remains very slow as long as the wine is in contact with the yeast deposit. Carbon dioxide acts as a preservative, and ensures that very little oxygen comes into contact with the wine when it is first bottled. At the moment of disgorgement, the wine is exposed to a considerable amount of oxygen, which triggers the normal oxidation process. The disadvantage is that a prolonged aging of the wine during disgorging accelerates oxidation. Old Champagnes, dating from the start of the previous century and undergoing a delayed disgorgement, may taste like young, lively wines full of character, but only a few days after disgorging, such wines can become flat and oxidized. A bottle that has been "normally disgorged," on the other hand, is far superior to one that has been late disgorged on the first day, and will later resist the ravages of time more effectively. That is why Bollinger R. D. (Recently Disgorged) is better drunk one or two years after disgorging.

WHEN SHOULD VINTAGE
CHAMPAGNES BE CONSUMED?

Age of wine at time of disgorgement	Ideal moment of consumption after disgorgement
3 to 4 years	1 to 5 years
5 to 8 years	3 to 30 years (and even longer in certain cases)
10 to 15 years	1 to 5 years
15 to 20 years	6 months to 2 years
30 years	0 to 6 months
40 years	0 to 2 months
50 years	0 to 1 week
60 years	Immediately

A Champagne that has been aged for between one and four years, and has been disgorged, will not have had time to benefit from the character that results from the yeast deposit, and will not have great prospects for the future, despite its early disgorgement. The ideal age for disgorgement, if a Champagne is to be left to age, is generally five to eight years.

To complicate matters, certain older wines receive a shock when they are disgorged, but long afterward recover their vitality, usually when the remaining bottles have been drunk in the belief that they were already losing their quality.

A bottle of Pol Roger 1914, disgorged in 1944, was absolutely fabulous fifty years later. The reason is no doubt because the wine, despite its great age at the time of disgorgement, was still strong and had not yet reached maturity. So it is not time that counts, but the state of development of the Champagne at the moment of disgorgement.

OPENING AND SERVING A BOTTLE OF CHAMPAGNE

Of course there are different ways of serving a bottle of Champagne. At a party people may want to hear the noise made by the popping cork. But if you don't want to lose any of those precious drops, it is a good idea to take some advice.

Ensure that the bottle is at the right temperature (7–9°C (45–48°F)). A colder Champagne is practically flavorless, and one that is any warmer loses its freshness and its foam, even if the aromas are stronger and richer. Personally, I prefer Champagne served at 11–12°C (52–54°F), but do remember that it can warm up again very quickly at room temperature. That is why it is far better to serve the wine too cold rather than too warm, so that your guest can wait for the ideal tasting temperature to be reached, gradually familiarizing him- or herself with a wine that is at first rather closed. If it is not gulped down at high speed, it is advisable to top up your glass regularly with a few drops of really cold Champagne, thereby freshening up a gentle, aroma-rich Champagne with a lively mousse.

First wipe the bottle with a napkin and show the Champagne to all those who are going to drink it.

Remove the foil wrapper round the cork above the perforation. Remove the metal cage by turning the twisted wire six times, holding your thumb against the cork. Then hold the bottom of the bottle firmly, grasp the cork with the thumb of the other hand, keeping your fingers around the neck of the bottle. Hold the bottle at a 45-degree angle and turn the bottle, rather than the cork, while retaining pressure on the cork with your thumb. This will enable you to avoid spilling the wine when the cork starts to come away from the bottle. If the cork resists, as a last resort you can use pliers, which you should fix between the head of the cork and the mouth of the bottle. The risk that the cork will pop is greater if you turn the cork than if you turn the bottle.

Never open a bottle while pointing it at someone. Most eye injuries in France are caused by Champagne corks. I always wondered about the truth of this statistic, but I was finally convinced of it one day in 1999, when—in the company of a well-known presenter—I interviewed the head of the ophthalmology clinic at Épernay for an international television network.

Wipe the mouth of the bottle with a clean napkin or the bottom of the cork.

Pour a little into a glass and let the mousse subside. It will now be easier to pour out the right amount without losing any foam. Like beer, Champagne foams less if it is poured into a glass that already contains some of the liquid; it will then retain the carbon dioxide.

Fill the glass two-thirds full.

Return the bottle to the bucket or the refrigerator—with or without a stopper, depending on the quality and age of the Champagne.

You can serve Champagne elegantly using only one hand. The classic grip is with the thumb in the concave base of the bottle and the other fingers arranged in a fan-shape around the base of the bottle. If you have to serve with one hand, this is the only grip that can be used when serving a magnum. Turn the bottle slightly at the same time as you pour. The last few drops will then fall into the glass instead of ending up on the tablecloth.

A few more suggestions:

If you are using a napkin in the same way as a wine waiter in a restaurant, do not hide the label with it.

Never chill a glass of Champagne with ice before serving it. This could spoil the taste and mist up the glass.

Never use a Champagne swizzle stick or whisk. In thirty seconds you will have destroyed years of work.

Never return an empty bottle of Champagne neck down in the ice bucket. This gesture will be regarded as an insult to the producer.

If you do not have enough time to refrigerate the wine adequately, the quickest way to chill it is to use ice cubes and pass the bottle under a cold faucet. Some people claim that you should avoid the freezer, but ten minutes in the freezer have never spoiled the Champagnes I have drunk, as long as the wine's temperature does not drop lower than 5–6°C (41–43°F).

Probably the most daring way of opening a bottle of Champagne is to slice its top off with a saber! The history of this trick, known as "*le sabrage*," is rather obscure.

It probably began in the early nineteenth century. The French claim to have been the first to do it, of course. There is a story to the effect that Napoleon, having won a battle, distributed Champagne to his most brilliant soldiers, who were so moved by this gift that they decapitated the bottles with this theatrical gesture. Another tale centers around Madame Clicquot, who apparently loved the company of soldiers and would give them Champagne as a reward. On returning to the widow, the soldiers would hastily dismount and slice the tops off the bottles with their sabers to save time. Anyone who has ever practiced *sabrage*, however, will know that you cannot then drink from the bottle without risking finding yourself the owner of an extra-broad smile for the remainder of your days. Meanwhile these two legends are disadvantaged by the fact that the two central characters are the subjects of a variety of myths, mostly cultivated for publicity reasons.

A more plausible theory is that the practice originated among Russian cossacks. There were many Cossacks in Champagne and

Paris after the fall of Napoleon in 1814. An entire army was stationed in Reims, under the command of Prince Sergei Alexandrovitch Volkovsky, and it is possible that the troops would console themselves with freshly sabred sparkling wine.

A version of *sabrage* may also appear in the tradition of smashing one's glass after drinking a toast to the health of the tsar.

In fact, *sabrage* is easier than it looks. You just have to follow some guidelines.

First put the Champagne into the freezer for a while, but do not give it time to freeze. Take it out and remove the foil covering. Find the place where the two halves of the bottle are joined and turn it so that the joint is in the center of the bottle, pointing in the direction of your nose. Then remove the metal cage and hold the lower half of the bottle firmly in one hand and the saber in the other. Hold the bottle at a 45° angle, and place the blade on the bottle's body. Then use a smooth, sliding, horizontal stroke (the technique is similar to that used in a table-tennis backhand), starting from the stomach and moving straight ahead. Hit the edge of the mouth vertically with the saber and, if all goes well, the top of the bottle will smash in the shape of a crown around the flying cork. Thanks to the pressure in the bottle, there is little risk of shards of glass falling into the wine.

Serve the Champagne in the normal way and let it warm up in the glass.

I have explained *sabrage* as if it were an easy operation, but it must be emphasized that it can be dangerous if you are not very careful indeed. Always keep your distance from other people, and make sure that you do not perform this trick if you are in any way inebriated. I saw a skilled swordsman make a mess of it in the middle of a crowd. It all ended well that time, but it could easily have been a catastrophe.

Even if you follow all the instructions to the letter, some bottles are unbalanced, which means that they are liable to explode into a thousand pieces. I therefore strongly recommend opening Champagne in the traditional manner, even though it was at a *sabrage* competition that I met my wife, Sara.

GLASS, GOBLET, OR FLUTE

For a taster, the most important instrument, apart from his or her knowledge, is the glass. The importance of the glass can never be stressed enough. The few extra bills needed to buy a better quality Champagne will be wasted if you are not going to drink it from the right glasses.

In Champagne, tradition demands that the flute be used. The shape of the flute dates back to Roman times, but it is far from being the ideal glass. In the nineteenth century, most of the most beautiful flutes were made in Murano, Italy. They are still made there today, and are richly decorated with precious metals. It was not until the eighteenth century that Italian glasses first made their appearance in Champagne.

Before the technique of disgorging the wine was developed, the deposit remained in the bottle. Thanks to the shape of the glass, the deposit could be collected at the bottom.

The other typical Champagne glass is the goblet or shallow cup. It was first made in 1663 by Venetian glass-blowers who had settled in England. The Champagne goblet took its shape, according to legend, from the bust of Marie-Antoinette! Four Sèvres porcelain originals, the color of milk, decorated with discreet nipples and supported by three hinds, were made for the queen's temple-like château in Rambouillet. Only one of these has survived. After having been a huge success in England, the goblet crossed the Channel and became established on the continent.

When American movies were at the height of their popularity, the Champagne goblet was renamed the "Hollywood glass" in some countries. The shallow glass is still used in American films, although the shape of the glass is quite wrong for Champagne. Both the bouquet and the bubbles disappear due to the huge opening; an enormous area of wine is in contact with the air. At least the flute preserves the bubbles, although it diffuses the bouquet beyond the range of the nose of the taster. Most flutes are narrow and very tall. They concentrate the bouquet in their narrow opening, but the area of wine exposed is so limited that very little of the Champagne's aroma is released. Furthermore, it is very difficult to dip one's nose into the glass!

Ordinary wine glasses are good for tasting Champagne, in fact. They make it possible to capture the vitally important bouquet. One insoluble problem remains. No wine glass can retain the mousse for as long as a narrow flute. One therefore has to decide how important the mousse is compared to the aroma.

Whatever type of glass is used for drinking Champagne, I believe that it is important to use the same glass whenever tasting the drink, so as to have the same frame of reference. During the fifteen years in which I have been drinking Champagne, I have always been disappointed by the glasses I have been offered. Many glasses look attractive and are pleasant to hold, but very few of them are designed to enhance the subtle and essential characteristic of the wine: the bouquet.

I have long been preoccupied with designing a glass that would be suitable for tasting as well as for drinking. Thanks to a fruitful collaboration with the Reijmyre glassworks, my dream came true in time for the Millennium Tasting. Today, I own a whole series of glasses suitable for people who attach the greatest importance to the aroma. The Champagne glass was originally named "Perfect," but now all the glasses in the series are called "Juhlin."

When designing a Champagne glass, I started off by considering the most distinctive thing about Champagne in comparison to still wines—the bubbles. In order for the mousse to be lovely to look at, and so it could linger in the glass, the glass had to be quite tall. The common factor among all the best wine glasses is that the surface of the glass is greater than that of the opening, so that it can contribute to capturing the hundreds of thrilling aromas produced by the wine.

The very accentuated bouquet that you will discern when using the glass may be a shock for some people, but I think that most of you will consider my glasses to be the perfect instruments in the quest for enjoyment and a better knowledge of wines from all over the world.

The way in which the glass is treated is almost as important as its shape. Never wash your glasses with dishwasher liquid or rinsing liquid, because this can affect both the bouquet and the foam. Rinsing liquid polishes the interior of the glass to the point where carbon dioxide is no longer able to stick to irregularities in the glass, which is a requirement if there are to be bubbles. Always rinse the glasses by hand and wipe them with a clean and odorless linen kitchen towel.

Nor should you serve Champagne in glasses taken straight out of a cabinet: even in the cleanest kitchen, they will have picked up some dust. Ensure that your fingers are clean when you rinse your glasses. Smell the empty glasses to ensure that they are absolutely clean. That is particularly important if you are also preparing a meal. If you have been boning a salmon, for instance, let someone else rinse the glasses.

TASTING CHAMPAGNE

If you want to learn a little more about Champagne and get some sort of idea of what it has to offer, then going to a serious tasting is probably the best way to begin. The conditions for tasting that prevail for wines in general are exactly the same for Champagne.

First of all, the taster himself or herself must be in good condition. A cold can interfere with the tasting. The palate and tongue should not have been exposed to smoke, spicy food, or toothpaste, to confectionery, alcohol, or anything else that might affect the taste. No troublesome odor should disturb the atmosphere. Perfumes, food odors, and smoke are the most common distractions. The room temperature should be as normal as possible, i.e. 20 to 22°C (68–71°). Good lighting is indispensable so as to enable you to judge the color of the wine. The table should be covered with a white tablecloth, and since any serious appreciation requires intense concentration, the initial stage of the tasting should take place in silence. Even experienced

A discreet spittoon made by the Reijmyre glassworks.

tasters can be influenced by spontaneous comments from their colleagues about the wine. It is perfectly acceptable for one's own judgement of the wine to be affected by considering what other people have to say about it, but never before you have had a chance to form your own opinion. It is very rewarding to make tasting notes, and to catalog the wines according to one's own taste. For one thing, it helps one's concentration during the tasting if one is forced to formulate impressions for one's own record. Tasting notes are also an excellent way of jogging the memory.

Wine-tasting may in principle be divided into three main steps: appearance, nose, and taste.

Appearance: the appearance of a wine derives from its ability to absorb and reflect rays that are visible to the eye. The appearance alone may provide indications as to the type of Champagne that has been poured into the glass. If the Champagne is cloudy, with a matt surface and color, there is a good chance that it will be defective, affected by some sort of microbiological disease. A deposit that falls to the bottom of the glass is perfectly normal if the Champagne is very old. All great Champagnes have a luminous clarity and an intensity of color, regardless of shade and depth. These nuances of color are linked primarily to the grape variety and level of maturity.

A large quantity of Pinot and an advanced age produces darker colors. Consequently, a young Blanc de Blancs will be the palest wine you can find in Champagne.

Since there are two parameters to be taken into account, it may be very difficult to decide what type of Champagne you have in front of you by relying exclusively on the appearance.

An old Chardonnay is almost as dark as a *cuvée* of average age or a young Blanc de Noirs. Fortunately, to some extent, one can distinguish the shades of color of the grapes. Chardonnay grapes often produce a nuance ranging from a pale green to lemon yellow, while Pinot grapes may have reddish tones, like copper or bronze. Mature Champagnes are almost all golden with an amber luster, before oxidation eventually turns them brown.

The importance of the appearance of the mousse in the glass has been very much exaggerated. Chardonnay grapes do indeed often produce smaller bubbles, as do older Champagnes, which are naturally less abundantly foaming than young ones, but individual differences from one glass to another are also noticeable.

Most Champagnes that are produced today foam nicely, and it is only in the mouth that the quality can be judged. A good mousse must always consist of small, rapid, and continuous bubbles. A high-quality mousse should melt in the mouth like ice and burst against the palate like a firework, while assailing the tongue with little irritations that are the source of undeniable enjoyment. The worst mousse is one that is thick, like foaming toothpaste, and which deadens some of the gustatory sensations instead of increasing them.

The circle of bubbles that forms around the edge of the glass once the mousse has disappeared is called the "*cordon*." A Champagne with a very good mousse may even be accused of having bubbles that are too large. This is often because the wine contains air bubbles that are produced when the Champagne is poured. They can easily be gotten rid of by tapping the foot of the glass against the table once or twice. The reason small bubbles are preferred is not because they are more attractive, but because they produce a more pleasant and creamy sensation on the tongue.

The viscosity of the wine is also judged in a tasting. When you swill it around the glass, some of the wine moves very slowly around the sides of the glass and forms what are called "legs." These "legs" (*jambes*) or "tears" (*larmes*) as they are also called, may be formed by glycerol, sugar, or alcohol. The more of such components are present in the wine, the longer and more visible the "legs."

The nose: the nose provides the greatest number of indications as to the character of a wine.

During a tasting, the Champagne is poured into a glass that is left to rest on the table for a few moments, so that the sharpness of the carbon dioxide disappears. It is then time for the "first nose." Without swirling the glass, the nose is dipped in it and one carefully smells the intact aromas of the wine. The "second nose" is much stronger; this is preceded by a swirling of the glass so that the wine circulates round it. This is partly done so that the wine can oxygenate, and to remove any undesirable gases, but it is mainly to release the aromas of the wine. When inhaling the vapors, it is important not to do so violently or at too great a length. It is a good idea to move from one wine to another during a tasting, since the brain has the ability to accustom itself to odors. This also explains why people who live near a factory that emits nauseating odors do not move house. Their sense of smell becomes deadened after a certain time, so they no longer notice the odors.

The millions of nerve cells that we have in our noses can thus perceive thousands of smells, but to simplify things, we are accustomed to group them into eight main categories. All the smells can be classified in this way, but here I have selected the ones that appear in Champagne:

Aromas with animal notes: game, beef stew, raw beef, fish, crustaceans, oysters, the sea, cream.

Balsamic aromas: pine, resin, balsam poplar.

Empyreumatic aromas: any kind of smoke, burning and broiling, bread, hay, almond, walnut, coffee, wood, leather, marzipan, toffee, caramel, cakes.

Ether aromas: alcohol, acetone, vinegar, mercaptan, sulfur, yeast, oxidation, sherry, madeira, washing powder, glue.

Spicy aromas: any spice, but mainly vanilla, pepper, cinnamon, mint, ginger.

Floral aromas: any flower, but mainly honeysuckle, apple blossom, mayflower, acacia, lily-of-the-valley, jasmine, lime flower, rose, violet, and honey.

Fruity aromas: any fruit but mainly lemon, apple, apricot, peach, strawberry, raspberry, wild strawberry, cherry, gooseberry, lime, grapefruit, banana, mango, kiwi, passion fruit, grape, mandarin, orange, fig, date.

Mineral and vegetable aromas: chalk, limestone, mineral, flint, stone, greenery, fall leaves, mushroom, underground cellar, tea, cooked vegetable, bell pepper, broccoli, cauliflower, beet, green beans.

Another way of classifying the aromas is as follows:

Primary aromas: these come from the grape itself.

Secondary aromas: odors linked to fermentation.

Tertiary aromas: these aromas result from the vinification and aging processes.

When one smells a Champagne, one is confronted with a bouquet that is very rich in nuances and whose elegance and finesse are only matched in the best sweet Rieslings from Germany. Fruity and floral aromas should be found in abundance. The autolytic character should also be present in the aromas, evoking thoughts of bread and pastries. The characteristic earthy smell should also leave a note of chalk and mineral.

If, in addition, there are a quantity of toasted aromas, and notes of cream and honey, I am in seventh heaven.

It is important to give the wine time to develop in the glass so that you miss nothing. The discovery of an excess of notes that are similar to those of sherry is due to the presence of too many aldehydes, which indicates that the Champagne has lost its qualities. If, on the other hand, the wine has too faint a bouquet, it is no doubt because it is too young.

The taste: in view of the fact that the tastebuds can only distinguish between sweet, sour, salty, bitter and possibly *umami* (see glossary), as well as metallic notes, the sense of smell is the main instrument of what we call taste.

It is easy to understand how much we can "taste" through our nose when we think of how our sense of smell almost completely disappears with a cold.

We are used to distinguishing between the objective taste and the subjective taste. The objective taste is based on fact and what can be proven, whereas the subjective taste is based on an opinion. What we like or do not like depends on our capacity to become accustomed to new flavors. This process is called "accustomization." It is exactly what happens when we learn to educate our taste. In some countries and in certain sectors of the population, a child may grow up without ever being exposed to new taste experiences, and will thus retain an infantile sense of taste. This is a phenomenon that is widespread in the United States, and is no doubt one of the reasons why so few Americans like dry wines. As parents, we might believe that it would be good, for example, to teach our children to like fish; we might therefore give them little portions mixed with other foods at first to accustom them to this new taste. Accustomization in matters of wine-tasting causes the taster to develop a tolerance for acidity and acrid flavors that inexperienced wine-drinkers do not have. I have often talked to groups of novice wine-tasters about a creamy, sweet Champagne that they in fact consider far too acidic.

With taste, adaptation is another important phenomenon. This means that the olfactory memory, which is very strong, influences our perception of the next thing tasted. Normally, the taste experienced from contact with a new product lingers for a few minutes, but stays for much longer in the olfactory memory, thus influencing the appreciation of the next thing tasted. When we eat while drinking wine, our tongue and our memory will be influenced, and this modifies our appreciation of wine. It is due to this adaptation that a wine can suddenly be perceived as being acid or bitter, when a moment before we perceived it as being sweet.

When one tastes wine, it is important to swill it around the mouth while trying to inhale, in the same way that one swirls the wine around in the glass to release the dominant aromas. In this way certain components of the wine will become volatile and reach the taste cells through the back of the nose. It is also important to allow the wine to circulate throughout the mouth before swallowing it or spitting it out.

If you taste wines quite frequently or if you are faced with a large array of wines, you need to spit out the wines after tasting in order to ensure that you maintain your acuity.

New research shows that we do not only experience sweetness on the tip of the tongue, bitterness at the back of the tongue, and saltiness and acidity on the sides of the tongue. On the contrary, there are quantities of taste detectors dispersed all over the tongue, even if they are mainly concentrated on the above-mentioned parts. Furthermore, there are gustatory papillae on the palate, throat, and epiglottis. Each of these papillae possesses fifty or so epithelial cells that are designed to receive taste impressions. The tongue is also sensitive to contact, to temperature, to movement, and to consistency, and that is why the tongue is best able to appreciate the quality of the mousse.

Quality is obviously a hotly debated issue in the wine-producing world. It is subjective, of course, but some criteria are indispensable to improve the quality of wine. These are balance, symmetry, complexity, length, harmony, subtlety, potential for development, personality, and the capacity of wine to arouse interest. It is virtually impossible to define these concepts, since they are perceived so individually by every person.

When one judges the taste of a wine, one must not confine oneself to the aromas, but also take account of its structure. Numerous tasters may be blinded by the beauty of the aromas and fail to notice that the wine has no structure. Others could not care less about the aromas as long as the wine is well formed and balanced. Fortunately, good aromatic properties of a wine are usually accompanied by a good structure.

A pleasant wine must be composed according to the same principles that exist in any other form of art. A Chagall painting consists of contrasts and other elements combined in a harmonious composition. The colors, shapes, and light express feelings of harmony and of tension. A Mozart symphony is a whole entity. Even though the sound of each instrument can be distinguished and the dynamics, cadence, and rhythm can be followed, we also experience the harmony, making our enjoyment all the more profound. A great Champagne should be composed in exactly the same way in order for us to be able to derive the same enjoyment from it.

In order to be able to understand the whole, the various elements need to be analyzed. The interplay between the condensation, the concentration, the extension, and the expansion is just as important in wine as it is in a musical composition. Wine also needs to have a base around which it can balance the points and counterpoints, such as heaviness and lightness, hardness and softness, sweetness and acidity.

When one judges taste, one analyzes the internal relationship between opposites. One should try to sense whether the wine has a good "attack" as soon as one tastes it, before judging its "length" in the mouth, which is so important in an assessment of quality. A long aftertaste is always the mark of a great wine. The aromatic power of this length can sometimes be extended if the wine is of a high class. It is important to stress that it is not always the taste of the wine that resonates on the tongue. Sometimes certain acids can linger without dispensing any aromas. It is always an additional advantage if a wine that has good length also offers a completely new nuance in its aftertaste.

THE EFFECTS OF CHAMPAGNE

No one can be unaware that Champagne produces a very special kind of intoxication. Some people claim that Champagne gives them a headache, while others claim they can drink quantities of Champagne without feeling ill in any way. A common description of the effect of drinking Champagne is that one's head feels fine but one's legs don't follow suit. The way in which people react is very individual, but one can nevertheless detect a certain general pattern. The explanations are a mixture of the physiological and the psychological.

Since carbon dioxide accelerates the passage of alcohol into the bloodstream, intoxication is quicker than if one were drinking a still wine. When allied with a positive atmosphere and the fact that expectancy is high when one is about to drink Champagne, the result is that creativity and a desire to talk incessantly are increased. If one is also in a pleasant environment in which everyone is reacting in the same way, the feeling of well-being is reinforced. Alcohol in itself is a drug, an intoxicant which accentuates the state of mind a person was in when they started drinking. That is why it can be disastrous to drink in order to drown your sorrows.

The reason that some people get a hangover after drinking Champagne while others feel fine the next day is due to the fact that the enzymes in the liver, whose job it is to break down alcohol, recognize the drink of which it is a constituent. If the enzymes recognize the bond that retains the alcohol, their degree of activity increases, and the result is that one does not feel so bad. Personally, I have noted this phenomenon when, once or twice a year, I drink beer with my old soccer-playing pals. I get drunk much more easily and I have a much worse hangover after having drunk the equivalent amount of beer to the amount of Champagne I normally drink, even though the alcohol content of beer is much lower. In defense of Champagne, I feel I must add that this drink could almost be considered as beneficial, despite its alcohol content. Few drinks are as clean and mineral-rich as a true Champagne.

THE ART OF THE TASTER

Champagne can be drunk on any occasion. The most important thing, of course, is that the drinkers should obtain the greatest satisfaction from doing so. Whether one has something to celebrate, or whether one drinks the wine just for the pleasure, one should nevertheless grant the wine a few minutes of careful contemplation.

As mentioned, it is best to use an appropriate type of glass, and to avoid irritating odors such as cooking smells, smoke, flowers, and perfumes. If you are drinking Champagne on an ordinary day rather than as a special celebration, it makes sense to bring a more ordinary Champagne up from the cellar. As far as I am concerned, I reserve my less valuable Champagnes for drinking outdoors, shivering with cold, during the New Year celebrations. The best bottles only make their appearance at serious tastings, which are often supplemented by a well-thought-out meal at which Champagne takes pride of place.

A steady hand is required for pouring Champagne and balancing a tray covered with Champagne glasses.

Drinking Champagne outdoors in summer must be one of the greatest pleasures in life. It is a fact that it is hard to adequately judge all the characteristics of wine when the wind, the sun, and the smells of nature mingle with the bouquet of the wine. Obviously, Champagne that comes into contact with the sun does not have the same flavor. It is very rare to hear an expert evoke the phenomenon but, supported by the opinion of my closest friends, I dare to claim that a special bouquet is released from any Champagne that is exposed to the sun's rays. I can best describe this fragrance as being heavy, oily, with a petroleum note. This can affect wine to the extent that a Blanc de Blancs begins to taste like a Pinot Noir at maturity. A blind tasting outdoors thus requires a great deal of experience.

Vine-growers even stubbornly claim that moonlight can also change the bouquet of a wine. Personally, I confess that this "*goût de lune*," or "moon taste," escapes me.

I have often been in the position of watching a sunset in the company of my wife or of a friend, with a fantastic view laid out before us, while religiously drinking one of my favorite Champagnes. The sense of euphoria that one feels when the spectacle of nature reinforces the wonderful taste of Champagne is something that every true romantic ought to be able to experience.

Becoming a good taster takes time. Personally, I am convinced that being in good general physical condition is a great help, and not just to help one's concentration during tasting. Before the great Millennium Tasting, I lived like an ascetic, subjecting myself to very tough physical training that really paid off when I was faced with tasting 150 Champagnes under stressful conditions in only a few days. If you smoke, your sense of taste and smell will both deteriorate. You also need to think of how to develop your sense of smell generally. We are always surrounded by smells, some of which even register unconsciously on our psyche. By regularly smelling flowers, for example, while learning their names, it is possible to enrich one's vocabulary of odors and expand one's general knowledge. But there are no short-cuts to mastering the difficult art of wine-tasting. Good preparation, excellent concentration, a developed sense of smell, a good memory, an ability to express oneself well, a lively imagination, and an undeniable interest are the qualities required for becoming a great taster. In addition, one also needs a huge dose of knowledge and experience. Since all forms of art require training, the tastes of a wine connoisseur will change as he or she learns more about wine. The aromas that one found repulsive at the beginning may later on in his or her career become the favorite aromas of the taster.

Whether it is a question of wine, cuisine, music, the movies, literature, or painting, every consumer will get more out of the product if it contains a base of recognizable components. If one had to learn absolutely everything there was to know about

a product, one would probably tire of it very quickly; on the contrary, if one knows nothing at all about a product, it could provide you with too many surprises. That is why it is important to have a base of knowledge about wine to which one can refer when new nuances emerge and arouse interest. In a blind tasting, it is important—as soon as the appearance of the Champagne, its bouquet, and its flavor have been analyzed—to try and assemble the various impressions in such a way that you can formulate a theory about the wine. One should ask oneself about the age of the Champagne, when it was disgorged, whether the predominant grape variety is a Pinot or Chardonnay. Was the Champagne made by a large or small producer? Has the wine undergone malolactic fermentation? Has it aged in an oak cask? And no doubt the most important question of all: what is the level of quality of this Champagne?

After a few years of training and after having tasted a certain quantity of Champagnes, one often manages to guess right, which is naturally exciting and encouraging, and makes one want to know more of the secrets of this noble wine. I should emphasize that the process has nothing unique to Champagne about it; it is just as valid for tasting and learning about other types of wine.

THE MILLENNIUM TASTING

In 1997, I discovered that my cellar contained enough good bottles to enable me to organize a great tasting on the basis of a selection of my favorite wines. Like any writer about food and drink, I adore my work, and I cannot refrain from drinking wines in private, especially as over the course of years I have built up my own Champagne cellar. Each time I have had the opportunity of laying hands on another of the Champagnes on my list of the hundred finest, I have immediately taken advantage of it.

I was not in a hurry to organize this super-contest, which is why I continued for another year to collect wines for the purpose. My original idea was to organize a private tasting among close friends in the Swedish wine appreciation circle. But, during a meeting, someone remarked that our contest was too important to be limited to the national context. My associate at the time and I decided to initiate a program whose extent we could never have suspected at the time.

The first obstacle to overcome was the way in which the jury would be chosen. One option was to give it more publicity by inviting the superstars of the wine world, though there was a danger that might be to the detriment of the tasting's serious side. Another was to invite only the greatest connoisseurs, in order to make the results as significant as possible. As so often happens in Sweden, we chose a compromise by trying to interest a megastar of film and stage, so as to lighten the load of the hard work that the wine experts would have to put in.

With hindsight, I am very glad that we never managed to attract the movie star, who might subsequently have been used as an excuse to discredit the choices made by the jury during those three magical June days in Stockholm. In any case, the media coverage was more than adequate.

It was much easier to solve the problem of where we should hold the contest. In fact, we were all in agreement that this would be a wonderful opportunity to put Sweden on the international wine appreciation map. My associate and I had been childhood friends, raised a stone's throw away from Stockholm, and we were delighted to have the chance to show off the beauty of our city during the summer season.

We settled on the Villa Pauli as our location, which is well known for its high-class gastronomic gatherings, to which great chefs from abroad are invited. The participants at the tasting included Alain Passard, who had seen our invitation to the jury a few months previously when he had been invited to the villa to perform his culinary art.

But what about the Champagnes? How would they be chosen? We already had an impressive collection of wines, but of course it would be excellent if we could benefit from the cooperation of the Champagne houses. So I began by writing a letter to the biggest producers in the region, offering them a list of the wines that might qualify for the competition. Each producer was also offered the option of bringing over the wine of which he was proudest. The reaction of the big firms and of most of the winemakers was quite extraordinary. With a few rare exceptions, all of them dashed off to delve into the depths of their cellars and dig out the last bottles of the most sought-after vintages. Some bottles were so rare that it would be impossible today to stage a repeat of this historic competition.

In January, 1999, I traveled to Champagne to test out any Champagnes that would be appearing at the tasting with which I was unfamiliar. This is where I discovered some genuine treasures. A Pol Roger 1911 and a Veuve Clicquot 1955: two marvelous Champagnes. But the most important visit was to Billecart-Salmon. I then understood that I could fill a serious gap with two old vintages of this extraordinary Champagne. Antoine Billecart, whom I had previously met in 1988, considered long and hard before opting for a 1959 and a 1961. I realized while I was at Mareuil-sur-Aÿ that the forthcoming competition was being viewed as an event of outstanding importance.

When the bottles finally reached the Villa Pauli, all that remained was for us to cross our fingers and hope that all the members of the jury and the film crew would be present as expected, that the organization of the event into which so much planning had gone would meet our expectations, and that the weather would be fine. The international jury consisted of seven respected connoisseurs. Great Britain was represented by Serena Sutcliffe, head of the wines department of Sotheby's and the author of several books about Champagne, as well as her fellow countryman, Robert Joseph, founder of *Wine Magazine* in London. France was represented by Michel Dovaz, an expert enologist and author of several books on wine. From Denmark there was Jörgen Christian Krüff, chronicler of the Danish magazine *Vinbladet*, and from Sweden Josephine Nordlind, a sommelier who at the time of the competition was working at the Villa Pauli, as well as Anders Röttorp, famous enologist and correspondent for *Dagens Industri*—and your humble servant.

We used my scale of 1 through 100, and took into consideration only the potential points, so as not to put the youngest Champagnes at a disadvantage. The tasting of 150 wines dating from 1911 through 1990 was performed semi-blind. It was the jury's job just to assess the wines, and not to guess which Champagne was which.

The assessments of the jury in their totality constituted the list of prizewinners.

In the event, the winners surprised a lot of people, since some relatively unknown names topped the list and a few outsiders were the winners in certain categories. For example, the Paul Bara 1959 was considered the best Blanc de Noirs. We—the fortunate members of the jury of this gold-standard wine-tasting contest—were very much aware that we were writing an important page in the history of wine. I felt as if I were in a trance during those three days, and I completely collapsed a few days later. On the other hand, I was conscious of having participated in something that hardly anyone will get the chance to experience. I had fulfilled one of my greatest dreams.

THE TEN FINEST CHAMPAGNES
OF THE MILLENNIUM TASTING

1	1959 Billecart-Salmon Cuvée N. F.	98.5
2	1961 Billecart-Salmon Cuvée N. F.	97.7
3	1952 Gosset	97.7
4	1964 Dom Pérignon	97.3
5	1961 Dom Pérignon	97.0
6	1959 Pol Roger Blanc de Chardonnay	96.9
7	1979 Dom Ruinart	96.9
8	1961 Krug Collection	96.9
9	1979 De Venoge Des Princes	96.4
10	1959 Paul Bara	96.2

The various Champagnes

Every Champagne-maker tries to produce a complete range of Champagnes in different styles and in different price brackets. The most frequent assortment on offer generally consists of a non-vintage Champagne, a pink Champagne, a vintage Champagne, and a *cuvée de prestige* Champagne, but many firms also sell a Blanc de Blancs, a Blanc de Noirs, an undosed Champagne, a sweet Champagne, a crémant, a late-disgorged Champagne, as well as still wines and other drinks. The products on offer depend on the resources of the firm, its locality, its vineyards and the house-style. Some producers maintain the same level of quality throughout the range, while others can make a grandiose, *cuvée de prestige* Champagne at the same time as producing a non-vintage Champagne that is the equivalent of a cheap sparkling wine.

In this section I have introduced the various wines and then chosen a few of each type to recommend. I have not taken vintage or price into account. For a more detailed description, see the section devoted to the producers.

NON-VINTAGE CHAMPAGNE

The law states that non-vintage Champagne must be sold—at the very earliest—one year after it is made, and that it must have an alcohol content of at least 10 percent. This non-vintage Champagne is almost always the simplest Champagne made by the firm. It is never vintage, should be easy to drink, and should reflect the house-style. When there is a series of average years, the quality will become poorer, especially among producers of non-vintage Champagne, while among those who have large quantities of wines in reserve at their disposal, the level of quality will remain relatively constant. On the other hand, there are very few producers who did not produce an unusually good standard *cuvée* after the three quality years of 1988, 1989, 1990. More recently we have noticed a few marvelous non-vintage Champagnes, especially in 1995 and 1996. This last *cuvée* was so exceptional that it was very difficult to differentiate between the various houses in terms of quality. Subsequent *cuvées* also exhibited the same tendency.

A Champagne producer usually uses the first and second pressing to make his non-vintage Champagne and uses a higher dosage in his vintage wines. The role of Pinot Meunier is also frequently more prominent in non-vintage Champagne, both because the quality is inferior, and also because the grapes ripen faster and non-vintage Champagne is sold for earlier consumption. Most non-vintage Champagnes will nevertheless

Numerous stone markers indicating the ownership of the land are set in vineyards in Champagne.

improve if they are aged for a few years after *dégorgement.* Maturing in bottles gives the wine aromas of bread and honey while eliminating the more prominent acids, those that are "greener" due to the youth of the Champagne.

Firms that have the means to do so age their non-vintage Champagnes for four or five years instead of the more normal two or three years, and always produce a better class of Champagne.

For most producers, the non-vintage Champagne is the most important of their wines because it accounts for an average of 80 percent of their production. That is why some producers put a lot of effort into improving the quality of their simplest wine by vinifying part of the wine in oak casks, or by adding a lot of older reserve wines and using only the *cuvée.* Krug Grande Cuvée is indisputably the most simple wine made by the firm and it is not even vintage, so it must be classified as a non-vintage Champagne. Yet in price and quality the Grande Cuvée is often superior to Dom Pérignon and to Belle Epoque, so it is difficult not to agree with Krug when it claims that this wine is a multi-vintage *cuvée de prestige.*

The best wines: Bollinger, Charles Heidsieck Mis en Cave, De Sousa Caudalies, Henriot, Leclerc-Briant "Les Authentiques," Roederer Brut Premier and Selosse Extra Brut, Gosset Grande Réserve, Moët les Sarments d'Aÿ.

SWEET CHAMPAGNE

Very few demi-sec, sec, or sweet Champagnes are well made today. Furthermore, almost all the producers use their worst wines as the basis for the sweetest types. The grape juice is often taken from the second pressing, and contains a large proportion of Pinot Meunier. The sugar camouflages the characteristics of the wine and overpowers the more subtle aromas. I must admit, however, that my earliest enthusiastic encounters with the sparkling drink usually involved sweet Champagnes. But it didn't take me many months before my palate started to prefer the more classic, dry Champagnes, and today it has become hard for me to enjoy a glass of demi-sec or sec. Nevertheless, as an aperitif or to accompany certain desserts, these wines will certainly fulfill their function.

A new fashion has emerged, first started by Veuve Clicquot with its Rich Réserve, in which a sweet, high-quality vintage wine is created, designed to accompany duck foie gras, marinated salmon, or even a dessert.

The best wines: Delamotte, Deutz, Philipponnat Sublime, Selosse Exquise, and Veuve Clicquot Rich Réserve.

VINTAGE CHAMPAGNE

The first vintage Champagnes were probably made in the middle of the eighteenth century. Under the rules of the *Comité Interprofessional du Vin de Champagne* (*C.I.V.C.*), all the grape juice must come from one and the same years, and this must then be indicated on the label. The alcohol content must be at least 11 percent, and the wine cannot be sold until three years after it has been bottled. Furthermore, the producer must not sell more than 80 percent of the harvest under the label of vintage Champagne. This is to guarantee that there will be reserve wines available for use during the next harvest, and to enable the vintage Champagne to be of a higher quality. Certain less scrupulous firms sell Champagnes from poorer years such as 1974, 1977, 1984, 1987, and 1991 under a vintage label, whereas in fact the idea is that only the best years should be able to produce vintage Champagnes. Bollinger underlines the notion that this Champagne should only be produced in the best years, by calling its vintage Champagne Grande Année.

Before the introduction of *cuvée de prestige* Champagne, vintage Champagne was the best wine that a firm had to offer. Even today, vintage Champagne tends to be a very good buy because the quality is noticeably better than that of non-vintage Champagnes, and the price is much lower than that of a *cuvée de prestige* Champagne.

Almost all of the producers of renowned Champagnes market their vintage Champagnes at the age of about five or seven years, which means there is a good chance that it will benefit from extended aging.

If you find a reasonably priced vintage Champagne that you enjoy drinking, it is a good idea to buy a few bottles of it. Then you can create a little reserve for yourself, which will enable you to follow its pleasant development in the course of subsequent years.

Most vintage Champagnes are the result of a blend of Pinot and Chardonnay grapes. Until the 1980s, most of them consisted of 60 to 70 percent of Pinot Noir. Today, the tendency is to create lighter and more elegant wines, and a percentage of Chardonnay as high as 60 percent is not rare. In the transitional period between the vintage wines of 1985 and 1988, Chardonnay grapes appear to have predominated for the first time in vintage Champagnes. Krug and Bollinger are still really majestic wines, thanks to the significant presence of Chardonnay, and they become powerfully mellow with age. Billecart-Salmon, Roederer, Perrier-Jouët, and Clicquot have also spoiled us with fabulous vintage wines over the years.

The best wines: Billecart-Salmon, Bollinger, Clicquot, Gosset, Henriot, Krug, Perrier-Jouët, Pol Roger, and Roederer.

A glass of Louis Roederer Brut Premier to sharpen the appetite.

BLANC DE BLANCS

Blanc de Blancs is an expression that means "white wine made from white grapes." Until 1980, a Blanc de Blancs could contain some Chardonnay, Arbane, Petit Meslier, and Pinot Blanc varieties, but now all Blancs de Blancs can only be based on the noble Chardonnay grape. It is, of course, always possible to produce a Blanc de Blancs from grapes other than Chardonnay if you do what Jacquesson has done and ask for special dispensation, in its case for its own Petit Meslier Blanc de Blancs. In other regions, a Blanc de Blancs can contain any variety of white grapes.

The Blanc de Blancs is represented in all the regions of Champagne—the Aube, Sézanne, Montagne de Reims, and the Marne Valley. The fabulous and elegant Champagnes produced on the Côte des Blancs have no equivalent elsewhere in the wine world. No other wine can develop such noble, elegant, and deceptive aromas as a Blanc de Blancs from Avize, Cramant, or Le Mesnil.

Many critics often find these wines rather light and acidic, but few wines gain so much complexity with age as these rare beauties. A young Blanc de Blancs is always extremely pale, with a greenish coloring. The nose may be closed and slightly flowery The taste contains a touch of citrus or appley fruit, with an acerbic, heady acidity. The aftertaste in the mouth can feel swift and immature as well, but even in its youth one can detect the purity of the wine and its mineral elegance. After the wine has been aerated, one can detect the aromas of butter and toast that will develop wonderfully with age.

In their middle years the best Blancs de Blancs Champagnes contain a profusion of ripe exotic fruits; mango, peach, and apricot predominate over the lemony scents, which are now ripe. The feeling in the mouth is creamy and yet fresh at one and the same time.

When fully mature, a Blanc de Blancs will adopt a golden appearance with an incredibly full nose, a symphony of roasted coffee beans, toast, and walnuts. For me, the nutty aroma of an old Champagne by a producer such as Charlemagne, Pierre Peters, or Salon represents the dizzy Olympian heights in terms of bouquet.

A few rare producers refuse to make a Blanc de Blancs, because they want to reserve their best Chardonnay grapes for use in their *cuvée de prestige* Champagnes. Perrier-Jouët is one example, although an exception was made in the case of a Belle Epoque. This was a Champagne that they produced for the new millennium, which was destined for the American market. Otherwise, the tendency is for a producer to make a Blanc de Blancs in order to be able to claim to offer a complete range of Champagnes.

Blanc de Blancs has been produced throughout the long history of Champagne, but the first Blanc de Blancs to be sold commercially was the Salon 1911, which was a huge success at Maxim's in Paris. The Salon version is still one of the best Champagnes. Its style is classic, sober, and acidulated, with a wonderful walnut aroma. Taittinger Comtes de Champagne should be considered the best in the slightly sweeter, exotic, and mild style. Krug Clos du Mesnil dominates the third style,which is less conservative than Salon but more seriously vinous than the charming Comtes de Champagne.

In addition to these great Blanc de Blancs, there are many producers in the *grand cru* villages of the Côte des Blancs who are trying to get in on the act, and a smaller number who reach the heights in certain years. These include Selosse and Diebolt. Many of the great houses produce very good and sometimes magnificent Blancs de Blancs, in particular Pol Roger, Deutz, Billecart-Salmon, Roederer, and Ruinart, who are able to offer the same combination of purity and complexity as the finest growers.

The best wines : non-vintage Blanc de Blancs: A. Robert, B. Schmitte, Charlemagne, De Sousa, Henriot, Legras, Selosse, Sugot-Feneuil, and Turgy.

Vintage Blanc de Blancs: Billecart-Salmon, Bonnaire, Charlemagne, Diebolt, Launois, Legras, Pierre Peters, Pol Roger, Selosse, Sugot-Feneuil, and Roederer.

Prestige Blanc de Blancs: Amour de Deutz, Diebolt Fleur de Passion, Des Princes, Dom Ruinart, Krug Clos du Mesnil, Mesnillésime, Peters Cuvée Spéciale, Salon, Selosse "N," and Taittinger Comtes de Champagne.

BLANC DE NOIRS

This type of Champagne is much less frequently encountered than the Blanc de Blancs, although in actual fact far more black grapes than white are grown in the region. A Blanc de Noirs may be produced from Pinot Meunier or from Pinot Noir grapes, or it may contain both these varieties. However, it is very rare for a producer to use the name Blanc de Noirs on the label, even if the wine contains no Chardonnay. Unfortunately, far too few producers of Pinot villages currently make their best wines in this style. Instead, a first-class Pinot Noir tends to be blended with a Chardonnay from the same village, as they have been told for years that their Pinot Champagnes are heavy and unbalanced.

Of course, a Blanc de Noirs cannot measure up to a Blanc de Blancs when it comes to finesse and elegance but, like the great wines, they have an important role to play. That is because few Blancs de Noirs are suitable as an aperitif, but they absolutely cry out to be drunk alongside food. The Aÿ Blanc de Noirs is incomparable, with a character that is similar to that of a Burgundy and its velvety fruitiness. Producers such as Fliniaux and Pierre Laurain come close to the strength and inimitable richness of the Bollinger Vieilles Vignes Françaises in their wines. The aromas may vary between animal and vegetable notes, but they are always underpinned by a heavy, dark fruitiness.

As the wine ages, smoky notes appear, along with flavors of honey, honeysuckle, caramel, and mushroom. Leather, fish, and cheese have also been invoked as comparisons to describe the fragrance of the greatest Blanc de Noirs.

The *grand cru* villages of Verzy, Verzenay, Bouzy, Ambonnay, and Mailly are also capable of creating first-class Pinot Champagnes. The example of Bernard Hattes of Verzenay clearly shows the firmness and aggression that numerous Blancs de Noirs can display in their youth.

Many people are led to believe that a Champagne made from Pinot has a short life-span due to its low acidity in comparison with a Blanc de Blancs, but behind this simple, candy-like fruitiness there lies a quantity of extracts that are yet to develop, and that require more time than a Blanc de Blancs in order to mellow. Wine made from Pinot can then maintain itself at its peak as long as an average quality Blanc de Blancs would do. It is not the easiest thing in the world, however, to appreciate the qualities of an old Blanc de Noirs, since the aromas—with their animal and vegetable notes—may be too prominent for some people's tastes.

The best wines: Bollinger Vieilles Vignes Françaises, Fliniaux, Jacquesson Blanc de Noirs d'Aÿ, P. Bara, and P. Laurain.

CUVEES DE PRESTIGE

The *cuvées de prestige* are always the most expensive wines produced by a firm, and they must always represent the quintessence of what a producer has to offer. A typical *cuvée de prestige* is always blended from the best *grand cru* grapes from the slopes that enjoy the best exposure. The oldest vines are used; their yield is lower and the wine is vinified more ambitiously.

Some producers use oak casks, and most only make *cuvée de prestige* Champagnes in the very best years. Some practice *dégorgement à la volee,* or use real cork for the fermentation in the cellar. The aging time is longer than it is for vintage wines, and the presentation is as luxurious as possible, involving decorated wooden crates or cartons with specially designed bottles, whose shape is very often reminiscent of the eighteenth-century bottles that Dom Pérignon and his contemporaries might have used. The Moët & Chandon 1921 Dom Pérignon must be regarded as the first *cuvée de prestige* Champagne; it was launched in 1936. The Roederer Cristal was apparently

sold even earlier to the Russian tsar, but was not sold commercially until the 1950s, the first vintage being 1945. The first Taittinger Comtes de Champagne vintage was 1952.

In 1961, Bollinger took the decision to begin marketing its late-disgorged wines—which had originally been made in the 1950s—under the R. D. (Recently Disgorged) *appellation.* The 1959, Dom Ruinart became the second *cuvée de prestige* Champagne to be made solely from Chardonnay grapes. The Perrier-Jouët 1964 Belle Epoque was launched on the occasion of Duke Ellington's seventieth birthday. Designed by the artist Emile Gallé (1846–1904), it was decorated with beautiful white anemones. Today, this is the *cuvée de prestige* Champagne that is most rapidly gaining ground. The most recent successful launch of a prestige Champagne by a leading firm is the Pol Roger Winston Churchill, of which the first vintage—the 1975—was only sold in magnums.

There are no special rules governing the making of prestige Champagnes. Some producers make non-vintage *cuvées de prestige*; these include Krug Grande Cuvée, Laurent-Perrier Grand Siècle, Perrier-Jouët Blason de France, Alfred Gratien Cuvée Paradis, and Cattier Clos de Moulin.

A large number of firms produce marvelous prestige Champagnes but, apart from Krug Millésime et Collection, Bollinger Vieilles Vignes and the wines I have listed under the Blanc de Blancs heading, here are the best Champagnes:

The best wines: non-vintage prestige Champagnes: Clos de Moulin, Grand Siècle, Krug Grande Cuvee, L'Exclusive Ruinart, Réserve Charlie and Selosse Substance.

Prestige Champagne: Belle Epoque, Vilmart Cœur de Cuvee, Billecart-Salmon Grande Cuvée, Clos des Goisses, Cristal, Diamant Bleu, Dom Pérignon, Joséphine, La Grande Dame, P. R., Winston Churchill, Signature, and William Deutz.

SPECIAL CLUB

Moët & Chandon was the first to produce a *cuvée de prestige*, with its Dom Pérignon 1921; Roederer Cristal 1945 followed. However, it was not until the mid-1960s that the concept of prestige Champagnes became established. Today, almost all the Champagne houses produce a *cuvée de prestige*.

In other wine-making regions, each wine-maker will generally set aside a barrel or two of his best wine to be enjoyed by himself or his friends. This still happens, even though it is becoming more and more common to vinify this cream of the crop separately and sell a small number of bottles at astronomical prices. The consumer pays not only for the quality, but also for the rarity of the wine. Unfortunately, today these exceptional wines are sometimes offered when a journal of enology or a wine writer with a world-class reputation is supposed to be writing about a table wine. Fortunately, Champagne is pretty much free from such abuses. Occasionally it may happen that fraud is committed when wines that have reached maturity are sent out when it is supposed to be a non-vintage Champagne that is being assessed. Obviously a Champagne that has been aged for a few years after disgorgement will almost always be more impressive than a newly disgorged Champagne.

Ever since the *cuvée de prestige* Champagnes first made their appearance, there has been a constant debate as to whether they are worth the price. In view of the fact that the grapes are chosen so rigorously and the whole vinification process is so costly, I do actually believe that their price is justified. However, it is quite another matter as to whether, from the point of view of its actual taste, the wine deserves to be sold at such a high price. For example, I would rather buy two and a half bottles of Clicquot Millésime than a bottle of La Grande Dame. At the same time, though, it is wonderful to be able to offer oneself this additional luxury of purchasing the very finest wines from time to time. So, while the value of these prestige Champagnes produced by some leading firms is debatable, one can be pretty certain that the *cuvées de prestige* produced by the wine-makers are worth the money.

Most of these *cuvées de prestige des vignerons* cost $10 or more than vintage Champagne, and the difference in quality is obvious. Prestige Champagnes from the growers are always produced from grapes that have been grown in the best spots and have come from the older vines. The care taken in harvesting is even greater. Furthermore, the wine is allowed to remain in contact with the yeast for longer, in order to increase its autolytic character. All this for a mere $10!

For many years, the smaller growers looked enviously at the *cuvées de prestige* made by the great Champagne houses, before understanding that it was possible to imitate the concept. The main problem was in working out how they would be able to afford to design a bottle that would bear witness to the exceptional character of the wine it contained. On the initiative of Michel Gimonnet of Cuis, a few wine-makers met to discuss the matter. The solution was provided by the formation of the Club de Viticulteurs Champenois, an association of the main wine-growers, each of whose members had to submit his prestige Champagne for the approval of a jury before it could be sold as Special Club.

In view of the fact that a large number of wine-makers joined the club, the wholesale price of the extravagant bottle could be reduced. The idea is that all the bottles of Special Club must be identical, as must the label, although it must contain the particular information concerning vintage, the wine-producer,

and his village of origin. In the early 1980s, the shape of the bottle and the shape and color of the label were changed—for the better, in my opinion. The shape of the bottle is similar to that of La Grande Dame, with an attractive discreet, green, white, and gold label. Special Club has very recently become available in a magnum. The idea is also that this bottle will be a guarantee of quality and enjoyment, but for people to be able to appreciate it, it is necessary for there to be a sufficient number of club members, since each wine-maker only produces one or two thousand bottles.

It is not always easy nowadays to get all these various wine-makers to cooperate, and disputes have been frequent over the years. Some members only want to allow growers from the *grand cru* villages to join the club, for example, while others feel that this is unfair discrimination. Furthermore, some wine-makers have become famous to such a point that they have resigned from the club in order to market their own-brand prestige Champagne. The best examples of this are Pierre Peters' Cuvée Speciale, Guy Charlemagne's Mesnillésime, "N" by Selosse, and Prestige by Bonnaire.

These four Champagnes are inimitable from a quality point of view, and that's a fact, but I must nevertheless admit that I tremble with joy as soon as I spot a Special Club. Naturally, the quality is variable within this club, but bad wines under this label simply do not exist. Furthermore, this is a unique way in which one can contemplate the diversity of Champagne and the character of the territory when vinification is optimal. All the wines produced and sold in this unique bottle share the attributes of being creamy, concentrated, and rich. It has happened that, during a blind tasting, I have guessed that we are drinking a Special Club, but I have been uncertain as to the blend of grape varieties and where they were grown. These wines are far from being neutral in style, which is an attractive property, and one that I often encounter in the wines of the great Champagne houses of the region. The old vines and small harvest produce a concentrated essence that is always thick and saturated with nectar.

The best of these are generally the Chardonnay wines from the *grand cru* growers, since they can balance the power of the wine with a sufficiently large quantity of acid in order to be able to produce a splendid taste sensation. I would advise you to buy all such wines you may come across and let them age for five years or even more after buying. My preferences are for Bonnaire (last vintage, 1990) and Launois, which is made from 50 percent Cramant and 50 percent Mesnil, a magnificent mixture don't you think? Other great bottles are the Champagnes of Sugot-Feneuil, Larmandier, Larmandier-Bernier, and the simply brilliant Pinot Champagnes by Paul Bara and Bernard Hatté.

Few bottles are as attractive as those of Taittinger Comtes de Champagne, which so eloquently reflect the contents.

The current members of the Club are: Paul Bara, Bouzy; H, Beaufort, Bouzy; Yves Beautrait, Louvois; Roland Champion, Chouilly; Charlier, Montigny; Marc Chauvet, Rilly-la-Montagne; Gaston Chiquet, Dizy; Jean-Paul Deville, Verzy; Forget-Chemin, Ludes; François-Delage, Ludes; Gérard Fresnet, Verzy; Gimonnet, Cuis; François Gonet, Le Mesnil; Philippe Gonet, Le Mesnil; Michel Gonet, Avize; Vincent Gonet, Epernay; Henri Goutorbe, Aÿ; Grongnet, Etoges; Bernard Hatté, Verzenay; Marc Hébrart, Mareuil-sur-Aÿ; Hervieux-Dumez, Sacy; André Jacquart, Le Mesnil; Pierre Lallement, Verzy; Lamiable, Tours-sur-Marne; Larmandier, Cramant; Larmandier-Bernier, Vertus; Lassalle, Chigny-les-Roses; Launois, Le Mesnil; Margaine, Villers-Marméry; José Michel, Moussy; Nomine Renard, Villevenard; Charles Orban, Troissy; Pertois-Moriset, Le Mesnil; Michel, Pithois, Verzenay; Quénardel, Verzenay; Sugot-Feneuil, Cramant.

LATE-DISGORGED CHAMPAGNES

The wine-makers of Champagne have always set aside old vintages that they allow to age "*sur pointes,*" or "on tiptoe," until the *dégorgement.* This means that the bottles are stored upside-down, the top resting in the hollowed-out bottom of a bottle below, so as not to disturb the lees. On special occasions, the old bottles are taken out, disgorged, and enjoyed immediately without being recorked. When, in 1961, Bollinger decided to sell its 1952, 1953, and 1955 vintages and disgorge them just before they left the cellar, they granted us consumers a privilege that up until then had been reserved for those who made wine.

As I have already explained, extended contact with the yeast deposit produces a special bread-like flavor which is called the autolytic character. I have also stressed the advantages and disadvantages of late disgorgement. But clearly Bollinger is entering another dimension with its R. D. wines. R. D. stands for Recently Disgorged, and has been registered as a trademark. The other producers were forced to give their late-disgorged wines a different name. There is a group of producers today who occasionally sell an old vintage that they disgorge late, but there are very few makers who sell this category of Champagne on a regular basis.

In most of the restaurants of the region, it has become quite a regular occurrence to be offered a few old, recently disgorged wines at affordable prices. The Royal Champagne restaurant stands in a magnificent position, on top of a hill overlooking the beautiful vineyards of the *premier cru* village of Champillon. Here one can sometimes find a newly disgorged Henriot bottle. I have personally had the great pleasure of coming across an example of the 1959 of this same absolutely fabulous wine, and Mats Hanzon, a wine fanatic, telephoned me from the restaurant, having been moved to tears after drinking what he described as a magical 1955. The Roederer 1979 is quite widely available in the region, as are bottles from the 1970s of Clos des Goisses, a monumental wine, and the frailer Grand Blanc. At Les Berceaux, a restaurant in Épernay, I had the great pleasure of being able to drink a few delicious magnums of Moët & Chandon 1964 and Dom Pérignon 1971.

Moët & Chandon is the owner of the Royal Champagne restaurant, and it has been very generous as regards providing wine for the cellar there. I had the opportunity in a single evening of sharing a few incredible wines with traveling companions who were just as generous. There is nothing more to be said about a Moët & Chandon 1952, 1928, 1921, and a fabulously fresh 1914. How lucky I am to have such crazy friends!

Laurent-Perrier Millésime Rare is a newly disgorged Champagne that is relatively inexpensive and that I would like to find in stores that sell Champagne. Bruno Paillard is marketing a series of late-disgorged vintages that are liked by many. Some of the Krug Collection vintages are late-disgorged wines. Another exceptional Champagne is the Jacquesson D. T. ("*dégorgement tardif,*" or "late-disgorged"). It has a very pronounced autolytic character of bread, and is very reminiscent of the substantial R. D. Champagnes by Bollinger, although the grape variety used is generally the Chardonnay from Avize. In any case, Jacquesson sells its D. T. at a much later age than Bollinger. In January, 2002, Bollinger R. D.1990 and Jacquesson D. T. 1985 went on sale. A newcomer to the late-disgorged Champagnes is the Dom Pérignon Œnothèque, and this is also one of the best. To summarize, the late-disgorged Champagnes will be sure to offer you a young, particularly fresh Champagne with ancient aromas.

The Millennium Tasting proved that the most impressive wines are those from bottles that were disgorged in the normal way and have not been recently disgorged.

It is only then that the complete maturity of the bottle manifests itself, in an exuberance of aromas that are reminiscent of honey, chocolate, walnut, molasses, and caramel, in an oily, thick structure supported by the most harmonious of bubbles.

The best wines: Bollinger R.D., Jacquesson D.T., Dom Pérignon Œnothèque.

UNDOSED CHAMPAGNES

Examples of unsweetened Champagnes have existed ever since the English demanded dryer Champagnes in the late nineteenth century. Laurent-Perrier has dominated this field ever since it brought out its Grand Vin sans Sucre in 1893. Today, it produces the most popular extra-dry Champagne, the Laurent-Perrier Ultra Brut. Piper-Heidsieck also brought out a non-dosé Champagne called Brut Sauvage, and the contribution to this category by Besserat de Bellefons is known as Brut Intégral. Most young Champagnes that have not been dosed are too acidic. Very old Champagnes do not require dosing, since maturity in itself forms sweet, soft flavors. That is why it is surprising that the Champagne houses that specialize in producing very dry Champagnes do not age their wines for longer to make them more balanced.

The Jacquesson D. T. that I mentioned under the heading "Late-Disgorged Champagnes," is, thanks to its age, the best non-dosé Champagne that can be found sold over the counter. De Venoge will soon be launching a few mature, late-disgorged, non-dosé Champagnes that are very much in the the spirit of the quest for quality that is the hallmark of the management of this house.

The more conventional, unsweetened vintage wines in this category include the extraordinary Jacques Selosse's Extra Brut, which is in a class of its own.

The following are some of the names under which unsweetened Champagnes might be sold: Extra Brut, Sans Sucre, Ultra Brut, Brut Sauvage, Sans Liqueur, Non-Dosé.

The best wine: Selosse Extra Brut.

SLIGHTLY SPARKLING CHAMPAGNES

Champagne has recently lost the right to use the name crémant, which was used to describe a Champagne that was only slightly sparkling. The Crémant d'Alsace, the Crémant de Bourgogne and the Crémant de Loire have all been allowed to retain the name for those of their wines that contain a normal mousse. It's no wonder that Champagne-makers are indignant at no longer having the right to use this *appellation*, which actually originated in Champagne.

Some producers still make a less effervescent Champagne with a pressure of 3.6 atmospheres instead of the normal pressure of 6 atmospheres. These wines do not keep for as long as their more sparkling counterparts, but the gentle, creamy foam can be appreciated as being very delicate, and it melts like butter in the mouth. Cramant, a village in Chardonnay, once had a tradition of making Crémant de Cramant. Mumm still makes a similar wine, but calls it Mumm de Cramant. Chauvet is the only maker to produce a pink crémant, which happens to be a very good one. As for vintage wines, Alfred Gratien is the best, and very few pople know the fact that this is a slightly sparkling wine.

Best wine: Alfred Gratien Millésime.

ROSÉ CHAMPAGNE

Rosé Champagne (*Champagne rosé*) became popular in the early nineteenth century. The British and the Russians were particularly fond of this romantic drink. Clicquot, which made its first rosé Champagne in 1977, must be considered the firm that pioneered pink Champagne, but for more than a century this drink was not really taken seriously, even by the makers themselves.

Rosé Champagne used to have the reputation of being a drink that was more suitable for women than for men, and one that men would only drink on their wedding day, if at all. Even today, pink Champagne is still more than anything a Champagne for a wedding celebration.

Until the 1970s, very few producers made rosé Champagne, and very few of them produced a vintage product. It is very rare for English wine salerooms to auction vintages that predate 1970. The prestige rosé Champagne is, above all, a 1980s phenomenon.

Since the juice of Pinot grapes is colorless, the pink color has to come from the grape skin. In other parts of France, rosé wines have to get their coloration from maceration of the skins which produces the pigmentation. This can happen at different phases of the vinification, but the coloration must never be produced by adding red wine to white wine—except in one region: Champagne!

It is traditional to use 8 percent through 20 percent red wine, usually a Bouzy Rouge still wine, or one from another village-producer of red wine. This is added to the *liqueur de tirage* (see glossary). Although this method has been severely criticized, most of the best rosé Champagnes are made in this way, and, in a blind tasting, it is practically impossible to notice any difference between these blended pink Champagnes and macerated wines. In the best cases, one might find that there are more raspberry and strawberry aromas in a rosé Champagne that has been made by maceration of the grape skins, since these aromas originate mainly from the skins of Pinot Noir grapes. Producers who do not add red wine but who use the so-called *saignée* method claim that their wine ages better, but tastings have never persuaded me of this. On the other hand, a rosé Champagne to which red wine has been added will take longer to become harmonious, because the red wine has to become integrated into the rest of the wine.

That is why one should wait a year or two after the launch of a rosé Champagne before opening a bottle that has been produced using this method. In practice this means that you should take this precaution with more than 95 percent of all rosé Champagnes!

Rosé Champagnes are currently made in colorways ranging from palest pink to darkest red. They often have a reddish-blue tinge when young, turning almost orange at 12–15 years and amber after 20 years. At 40 years, they look very much like an old "white" Champagne. Rosé Champagne is often more costly to produce, which means that the price will be a few dollars higher than that of non-vintage Champagne. In the majority of cases, the quality of a pink Champagne is slightly inferior.

The Champagnes made by growers from the best Pinot villages may often attain their peak as a rosé. Since one looks for aromas of raspberry and strawberry in the skins of a Pinot grape, as much Pinot Noir as possible needs to be used in a rosé Champagne. If one has Pinot Noir grapes from Aÿ available, whose aroma is similar to a Chambolle-Musigny, it is perfectly possible to make pink Champagne that is tasty and delicious. In terms of their concentration and the grape's aroma, wine-makers such as Pierre Laurain and Fliniaux generally produce the best prestige rosé Champagnes. Once again, I have to mention the wine produced by Bernard Hatté from Verzenay as a splendid example of a first-class Pinot in a style that is different from that of Pinot from Aÿ, persuasive and with an aroma of leather. Its pink Champagne is more spicy, with aromas of apple and plum, along with hints of red berries.

A few rosé luxury Champagnes are actually superior to the best rosés made by the growers. The problem is that they cost four times as much! Krug Rosé and Jacquesson Signature Rosé are the heavyweights; these have an extra finesse from their oak casks. The Cuvée William Deutz Rosé is very similar to the Pierre Laurain Rosé, having an aristocratic distinction that the small Champagne-makers can never achieve.

I have included two other favorites, not because they are typical rosé Champagnes but because these are really great Champagnes. It would be impossible to name them as being pink in a "true" blind tasting. Cristal Rosé and Belle Epoque Rosé are both masterpieces of sensuality, with the "white" aromas of walnuts, flowers, and honey. Dom Pérignon Rosé and Taittinger Comtes de Champagne Rosé are indisputably wonderful Champagnes that will develop superbly over the years. Dom Ruinart Rosé is the best proof possible that one can make a resplendent rosé Champagne in which the Chardonnay is totally predominant.

The best wines: Non-vintage rosé Champagnes: Bernard Hatté, Billecart-Salmon, Blason de France, Clouet, Fliniaux, Gosset Grand Rosé, Krug, Paul Bara, and Pierre Laurain.

Vintage rosé Champagnes: Belle Epoque Rosé, Billecart-Salmon Elisabeth, Gosset Grand Millésimé Rosé, Cristal Rosé, Cuvée William Deutz Rosé, Dom Ruinart Rosé, La Grande Dame Rosé, Roederer Rosé, Signature Rosé, and Taittinger Comtes de Champagne Rosé.

OLD CHAMPAGNE

The huge capacity for aging is one of the factors that distinguishes Champagne from the wines of other regions. If you visit the big houses as a tourist, you will be taught that Champagne is a fresh drink that cannot withstand aging after disgorgement. Once you have got to know growers better, you will soon discover that—the moment they have something they want to celebrate—they bring out Champagnes that are forty or fifty years old.

Most of them drink their old, recently disgorged bottles without dosage, since they prefer to drink Champagne that has been aged in the English style, i.e. for several years after disgorgement.

The richness revealed by an old Champagne that is normally disgorged shows that there is nothing like it. The bouquet has developed and is rich and fruity, thanks to the large quantity of esters and aldehydes that form when there is a minimum amount of oxygen between the cork and the wine. Dosage itself plays an important role in the development of new aromas during long aging in the bottle after disgorgement. The process is called "the Maillard reaction," and it means that the sugar is reacting with the amino acids in the wine, producing a toasted flavor, similar to that of honey and vanilla. There may still be an element of risk involved in buying a very old Champagne, but if the cork has held out and the aging has been performed correctly, you will be in for an exceptional enological experience. Champagnes that have aged perfectly have an exotic bouquet of honey, with notes of coffee and chocolate. The taste easily becomes caramelized and rich, with a heightened sensation of sweetness. The quantity of sugar has not increased, but esters and aldehydes provide the aromas of various types of candy. The complexity increases, and these Champagnes become very reminiscent of old white Burgundies. The best Champagnes made in the 1960s are marvelous today.

If you want to taste even older Champagnes, you will have to wait until two or three bottles out of ten have become maderized and lost their effervescence. However, I have drunk several fantastic Champagnes dating from the 1940s and 1950s, whose foam was invisible to the eye but very much in evidence on the tongue. If the wine contains a reserve of carbon dioxide you will be in for a great gastronomic moment.

To prevent frostbite, primitive stoves are still placed among the vines to keep them warm.

Wines and spirits of the Champagne region

E ven if still wines have been made in the region for even longer than the sparkling wines, the *appellation* Coteaux Champenois only appeared in 1974. In 1927, still wines from Champagne were called "*Vin originaire de la Champagne viticole.*" In 1953, this denomination was changed to "*Vin nature de la Champagne.*"

Three types of wine are made under this *appellation*: rosé, white, and red. The rosé, which is rare, is pale, light and acidulated; the white is slightly superior, and the red is excellent. The problem with trying to produce still wines in Champagne is due to the cold climate. The grapes contain too little sugar and are too acidic. There is even greater dependence on warm years than in Burgundy if ripe Pinot Noir and Chardonnay grapes are to be obtained. The best post-war years were 1947, 1959, 1976, 1989, 1990, and 1996. The Champagne houses make very few interesting still wines. Growers who have small, high-quality plots at their disposal—at Avize for white, and at Bouzy, Aÿ, Ambonnay, Cumières, and Mareuil-sur-Aÿ for red—make the most interesting wines.

RED WINES

In warmest years, the best wine-makers in the *grand cru* villages make a red wine that is reminiscent of a good Burgundy, nothing more. The aromas may be of a very high class but, except in very rare cases, the structure cannot be compared to that of a normal *premier cru* Burgundy. Raspberry, cherry, strawberry, and spices from the tropics predominate in the typical aromas of the grape. The taste is light, acidic, and elegant. I recently drank a Bouzy Rouge 1989 by Georges Vesselle to accompany a Scania chicken cooked in herbs—a fantastic culinary marriage! All the diners were convinced that I had brought out a great Bur-

gundy for them, which proves the high standard of the still wines classified under this *appellation*. Bollinger makes one of the best red wines in the region. La Côte aux Enfants is made from grapes from a south-facing slope in Aÿ. Small, new oak casks are used and only wines from good years are sold. It is in Aÿ, in fact, where two of the best red wines of the region are made. Gosset-Brabant produces the most impressive wine and Gatinois offers a variation on the same wine, but with a little more elegance and a little more acidity.

Otherwise, it is Bouzy that is best known for its red wines. Personally, I find that Bouzy Rouge is, on average, of lower quality than the wines of Cumières and Ambonnay, but the three producers in Bouzy—Georges Vesselle, Andre Clouet, and Paul Bara—are among the elite. The king of red wine at Cumières answers to the name of René Geoffroy, and has been very sucessful since 1990. At Ambonnay, Secondé-Prévoteau has supplied Roederer with grapes for its Cristal for several generations, and for a time made an exemplary Ambonnay Rouge. Unfortunately, it is very rare to get the opportunity of drinking the red wines of the region. However, there are exceptions. The parents of the Clouet family were born in 1946 and 1953, so a small reserve of red wine from those years has been set aside for them. The grapes came from a *clos* vineyard just behind their house in Bouzy. It must be said that, in general, I have developed a taste for youth when it comes to red wines, and I will happily drink my Clos de la Roche or Hermitage at only five years old. That is why I was very surprised to be just as fascinated by the fantastic way in which these wines have developed over the years. These are the only two still wines in Champagne to have given me goosebumps. Of course, once again it is the insurmountable acidity that is present here; this is what keeps the sparkling wines

Rows of small oak casks of Burgundy at Selosse in Avize.

alive for so long, and which at the same time is able to develop a complexity of a type that is rarely encountered. I recommend that you let your Bouzy Rouge mature, even if the makers themselves prefer the lightness of cherry and raspberry in young wines.

The best wines: Bollinger La Côte aux Enfants (Aÿ), Clouet (Bouzy), Gatinois (Aÿ), Georges Vesselle Cuvée Veronique-Sylvie (Bouzy), Gosset-Brabant (Aÿ), Paul Bara (Bouzy), René Coutier Rouge (Ambonnay), and Secondé-Prévoteau (Ambonnay).

WHITE WINES

Although white wines are used as the basis for the fantastic Chardonnay Champagnes, there is nothing exciting about this type of wine. The Laurent-Perrier, which has been such a commercial success, is a good example of the lightness and acidity that these wines often have. The bouquet smells like the striking surface of a box of matches. If you find any fruitiness, it will be that of a lemon, and an unripe one at that. One of the reasons why so few still white wines are of any quality is, of course, that the best wines are destined to be used for Champagne. The still wines from Avize made by Selosse and Jacquesson when tasted straight from the oak barrels are reminiscent of a young Corton-Charlemagne or a Chablis Grand Cru. The best white wine from Champagne that is sold commercially is Saran by Moët & Chandon, which is made from grapes that would otherwise be used to make Dom Pérignon.

In fact, the flavor is reminiscent of a "Dom" that has been diluted and become flat. The best is the exceptional white wine from Clos des Goisses, but that is not commercially available.

ROSE DES RICEYS

Although the Rosé des Riceys is a still a rosé, it is not included in the Coteaux Champenois *appellation*, having its own denomination. Louis XIV, the Sun King, made this wine famous, and the tradition has been maintained. In this little village in the Aube, the wine-producers put all their energy into the creation of a first-class rosé wine. Along with Tavel from the Rhône Valley, the rosé wines from this location are considered to be the best in the world. Even though it is a rosé, this pride of the Aube ages well. The relatively dark appearance takes on an orange coloration, and the aromas of strawberry and peach then become more chocolaty and minty. The taste may be very interesting and full, and the impression on the tongue is always mild. Alexandre Bonnet makes the most expensive and best wines in the village.

The best wines: A. Bonnet, Devaux, Morel.

RATAFIA

Ratafia is a fortified wine and thus has a high alcohol content. It is made from unfermented grape juice originating from the three grape varieties grown in the region, to which 90 degree proof alcohol is added. The French drink ratafia as an aperitif, or as a digestif after the meal. Ratafia is a sweet, strong, pale brown drink with the fragrance of raisins. The grapes used in making it are subject to the same quality control as for Champagne grapes. Since grape juice is sweet already, no additional sugar is necessary, but most of the makers of ratafia add a little all the same. The alcohol content is around 20 percent, but the drink does not give the impression of being that strong. Very few producers use the first pressing for their ratafia, but most of the best makers use Pinot Noir, which provides a milder and more grape-like flavor than Chardonnay. Once the alcohol has been added—a process known as *mutage*—ratafia is aged in casks or vats for about a year. Ratafia aged in casks takes on the flavor of an oxidated sherry, which is well-suited to the purpose for which this wine is made. I have drunk so little of it that it is hard for me to give an opinion as to the quality of the main ratafias, but it is mostly made by the largest distillery in the region, Goyard at Aÿ. In 1976, Jacques Selosse made a ratafia for his own consumption which was absolutely fabulous!

SPIRITS AND BRANDIES

Since Cognac is the name of a region in its own right and not of a type of wine, the name cannot be used in Champagne. The wine created in the Champagne region on the same principles as Cognac is called Marc de Champagne. The alcohol is always produced from the grape skin. Ordinary Marc is made from the remains of grapes that have been completely pressed and which are fermented and distilled to obtain an alcohol content greater than 40 percent.

Marc de Champagne, on the other hand, is made from wine that was destined to be made into Champagne but which has failed to meet the quality requirements; to this is added residues from clarification and *débourbage*. Everything must be recovered and ought to be drinkable, but the question remains as to whether that is really the case. Apart from a few Marcs de Bourgogne and an old Cognac, I do not like any form of spirits, and so I am not best placed to judge the spirituous liquors of the region. The pleasantest Marcs de Champagne that I have had the opportunity of tasting (though I only had a couple of sips), came from the Comte de Dampierre and Pierre Peters.

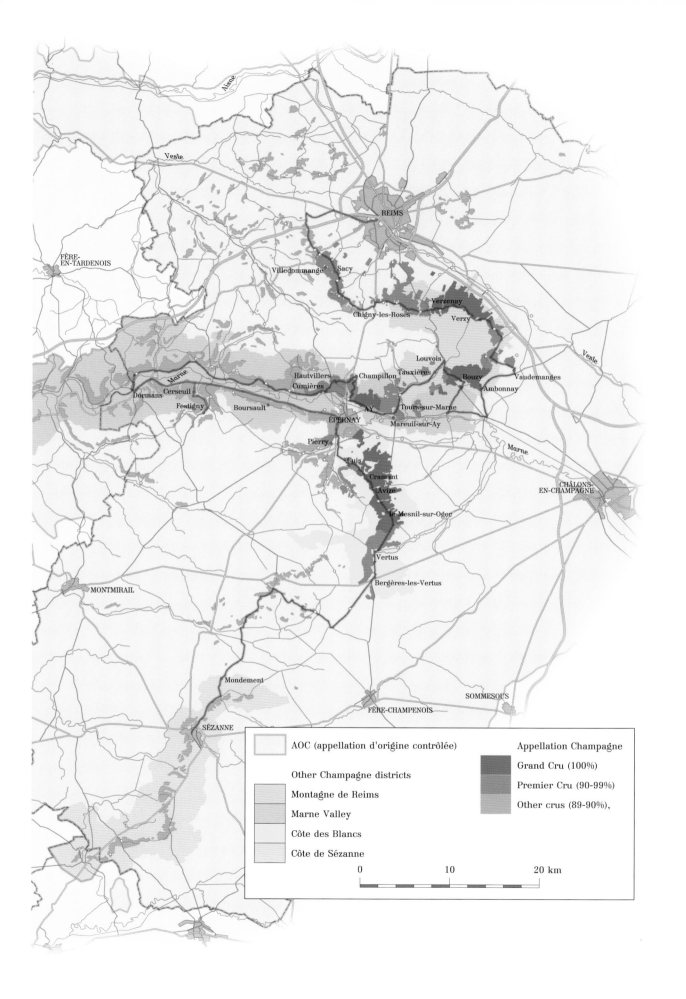

Vesle

Aisne

REIMS

FÈRE-
EN-TARDENOIS

Villedommange Sacy

Chigny-les-Roses

Verzenay

Verzy

Louvois

Vaudemanges

Vesle

Champillon Tauxières

Bouzy

Hautvillers

Cumières

Ambonnay

Marne

Dormans

Cerseuil

Festigny

Boursault

AY

Tours-sur-Marne

ÉPERNAY

Mareuil-sur-Ay

Marne

Pierry

Cuis

CHÂLONS-
EN-CHAMPAGNE

Cramant

Avize

le-Mesnil-sur-Oger

Vertus

Bergères-les-Vertus

MONTMIRAIL

Mondement

SOMMESOUS

FÈRE-CHAMPENOIS

SÉZANNE

AOC (appellation d'origine contrôlée)

Appellation Champagne

Other Champagne districts

Grand Cru (100%)

Montagne de Reims

Premier Cru (90-99%)

Marne Valley

Other crus (89-90%),

Côte des Blancs

Côte de Sézanne

0   10   20 km

Champagne and gastronomy

In France, Champagne is usually drunk with dessert, whereas elsewhere in the world it is generally enjoyed as an aperitif. Champagne does, of course, make the perfect aperitif, with its appetite-sharpening acids and its fast-working, refreshing effect, but as an accompaniment to food it can produce even more pleasure. The French are, of course, the world champions where cuisine is concerned; their pre-eminence is due to long tradition, expertise, and the finest raw ingredients. Each province has its own specialties, and these often have a worldwide reputation themselves, but within France itself, Champagne is not considered to be one of the great culinary regions. Most of the restaurants serve dishes that originate from other parts of France. Yet the local cuisine is rich and varied. The surrounding rivers are full of fish, and the Ardennes forests north of Reims are one of the few regions of western Europe that are still full of furred and feathered game; here one can find fallow deer, red deer, and the game birds that find their way into many local dishes. Dishes based on lamb and pork are more common than those based on beef. In Champagne, soups and salads of all kinds are very popular. Their main ingredients are potatoes, beans, lentils, and other vegetables. Fish is cooked in every imaginable way, with wine being an obligatory ingredient.

The region's most important contribution to French food is in the form of cheeses. It is a real pleasure to tour Champagne buying cheeses straight from the farm. It is preferable to avoid the characterless factory-made cheeses if you want to taste something special. The best-known cheeses of the region are the Bries, of which the most famous is Brie de Meaux—the most delicate and creamy of them all. If you ever find yourself in Champagne faced with a varied cheese board, allow yourself to be tempted by the Arrigny, Boursault, Caprice des Dieux, Chaumont, Chaource, Explorateur, or Maroilles.

The Champagne region is also famous for its patisseries, and especially its fruit cakes. For anyone with a sweet tooth, I recommend a visit to the extravagant chocolatiers and patisseries of Reims. Just be sure not to bring out the chocolate truffles while you are drinking Champagne, something that some French people are unfortunately inclined to do. If, contrary to all good sense, you insist on drinking Champagne with dessert, it is preferable to choose a sweet Champagne. Sugar is dry Champagne's worst enemy, which gains an unmistakably acidic taste if drunk with dessert. In my opinion, fresh strawberries are the only dessert that goes well with Champagne. Even so, I would rather choose a German Riesling Spätlese to accompany these delicate summer berries.

Champagnes on ice at Les Crayères restaurant.

PERFECT HARMONY

When combining wine with food, the rule has always been that the heavier and stronger the flavor of the dish, the heavier and stronger the wine should be, and vice versa. It is very fashionable today to make exceptions to the rule in the spirit of experimentation, but analyses prove that certain substances do react negatively when entering into contact with others. One example is the salty seawater in crustaceans, which reacts with the tannin in red wine. White wines with meat are often a more acceptable choice, but they can have difficulty competing with the powerful flavors and seasonings of some sauces.

However you choose to construct a meal, it is important to consider the balance between food and drink. This can be achieved by choosing a wine that perhaps contributes something the food lacks, or by choosing a wine that contains flavors similar to those that already exist in the food. A game dish could, for example, be accompanied by a red wine whose aromas have animal notes, while a nutty-flavored dish of caviar could be teamed with a Champagne that already has a walnut note. Restauranteurs throughout the world are constantly seeking new combinations in which balance is the prime consideration, whether that is attained through a wine that complements or matches the food.

It is the very importance of these aromas that is often forgotten in the North American school of the science of taste. Tim Hanni, who has become a world authority in this field, concerns himself almost entirely with our basic tastes. The most controversial aspect is, no doubt, his consideration of *umami* as a basic taste. It is clear that *umami* genuinely exists, and that it is an important component in the combination of food and wine. The word, which is of Japanese origin, means something like "subtle and fragrant." From a purely scientific point of view, *umami* is the sodium salt in glutamic acid, which is simply an amino acid. The full name of this salt is monosodium glutamate, or MSG. The real taste of *umami* is rich in sweet, creamy aromas. The foods that are richest in *umami* are fatty fish, the finest caviar, hard cheeses, rich meat stock, and tender meats. If I have correctly tasted this flavor, it is in raw foods that I have found this creamy sugar that is close to caramel, but without the direct sensation of sugar. Not long ago, I had the good fortune to eat one of the most delicious Iranian caviars which had notes of licorice, the sea, walnuts, and caramel—was this *umami*? The combination of wine with *umami* may often prove to be unsuccessful, leaving a metallic, bitter aftertaste. One can try and neutralize the effect by adding a suitable raw food. Salt and acid are often the ingredients to be used in such a case.

Tim Hanni's teaching consists entirely in creating harmony between the food and wine in such a way that no flavor conflicts with any other. I think I have mentioned, however, that many fine wines lose their definition and purity when they are combined with food in this way. If I buy a Chablis *grand cru* and, on the basis of his principles, I balance it with a dish that has lots of acidic and salty flavors, I shall indeed have a pleasant, mild, and harmonious flavor in the mouth, but those subtle little notes that will help me to recognize the vintage and the maker will be blotted out.

Personally, I take care to ensure that what I eat does not contain an excess of the basic tastes that could anesthetize my taste buds. I always begin by choosing the wine, and then the dish, which should be of suitable mildness. My severest critic would accuse me of using too much salt as a means of attenuating the acidity of the wine. It is true that this is a way of reducing it, but I want to taste the acidity in my Champagne, which I consider to be balanced at the start. Salt really has an anesthetizing effect if it not used with caution.

Of course there is a lot of truth in Tim Hanni's doctrine. For example, it is striking to note how much a sweet Champagne can be perceived as being dry, elegant, and balanced when it accompanies a sweet dessert. The wine therefore needs to be sweet if it is to meet up with the sugar in the food. Another observation is that an acidic wine should also be confronted with acidity in a dish. It is also indisputable that saltiness will make a wine taste sweeter. Hanni has also identified the enemies of wine in a remarkable way. The most difficult foods are vinegar, citrus, tropical fruits, grapes, cranberries, fresh asparagus, sorrel, Jerusalem artichokes, globe artichokes, rhubarb, salt, strong spices, and eggs. Here again, it is possible to overcome the difficulty by cooking these foods in the right way, using a bridge to the taste, and choosing the wine carefully. The egg poses an interesting problem because, not only is it rich in *umami* and sulfur, but also because the yolk has such a fatty consistency that the taste buds are coated with it, thus preventing one from tasting the wine. It is amusing to note that the high acidity of Champagne neutralizes sulfur, and the foam cleans the tongue in such a way that raw egg yolk and Champagne can form the alliance of a pleasant contrast. I know of nothing better than to drink Champagne with Iranian caviar accompanied by soft-boiled quail's eggs prepared by Alain Passard.

Many people consider that Champagne will go with any sort of food, without homing in on a particular dish. It is quite true that Champagne is suited to a particularly large number of dishes, but this wine can attain heavenly heights if it is combined with the dishes that really suit it. The bubbles and the acidity cut violently through sauces that are rich in cream and butter, as well as purées, eggs, and other greasy, bland foods. Vegetable and fish dishes, as well as seafoods, are enhanced by an elegant Champagne, while the drink can also cleanse the mouth after certain slightly stronger flavors. But beware of foods that are too acidic. Citrus and vinaigrette dressing, if taken with Champagne, will produce an overall impression of excessive acidity, just as hot dishes that are too highly spiced can have a catastrophic effect on most wines.

As an accompaniment to meat, I tend to avoid Champagne in preference to red wine. However, a classic combination that I would recommend is a Clos des Goisses with fillet of beef.

OYSTERS, TRUFFLES, FOIE GRAS...
AND JAPANESE CUISINE

One can certainly combine Champagne with relatively simple and inexpensive dishes, but I find that one can also indulge in slightly more exotic foods when one has occasion to open a bottle of Champagne. Oysters and Champagne is one of the most classic of combinations, as is Champagne and Russian caviar. It is important in such a case to choose a young, dry, light Chardonnay Champagne which will be able to better contend with the flavor of seawater. Oysters will become milder if oven-baked in a gratin with a cream sauce or mild cheese sauce. As for Russian and Iranian caviar, avoid Sevuga because it is too salty. Beluga is better because it is milder, or try the much rarer Oscietra with its nutty flavor. Serve the caviar with Russian blinis (yeast-raised dollar pancakes) with sour cream or crème fraîche (avoid slices of lemon!).

All the crustaceans go well with Champagne, but the question is whether lobster and Champagne go well together. Salmon and flatfish in a wine sauce accompanied by a Champagne *de cuvée* of average age also make a good marriage. Even lightly smoked fish go well with a Champagne that has aromas of toast: a Blanc de Blancs, for example. Sauces that are going to be consumed with Champagne should be based on clear broth, such as fish broth or chicken broth, to which butter, or light or heavy cream are added. An acid-rich wine should complete the picture, Champagne for preference.

Truffles are delicious with a Pinot-based Champagne, with its light animal and vegetable notes. Asparagus is generally considered a difficult partner for wine, but Champagne is an obvious exception. A dish of asparagus, served with a hollandaise sauce or sprinkled with grated parmesan and accompanied by a well-blended *cuvée* Champagne, will give you the impression that you are drinking the spring. Avoid asparagus in a vinegar dressing, however. As always, a well-aged balsamic vinegar is the exception that proves the rule.

The subtle flavors of Japanese cuisine go very well with this sparkling drink, and the great chef from Champagne, Gérard Boyer—who has just left the Les Crayères restaurant—is one of the pioneers in the use of curry powder and ginger, which are a great success in his culinary creations. But do watch out for

Asian dishes containing *wasabi* (horseradish paste), a lot of soy sauce, or strong spices.

A Blanc de Noirs is perfect with poultry. Pinot Champagnes and pink Champagnes are the only ones that go well with hard cheeses and soft cheeses with washed rinds.

Personally, I find that the supreme combination is that of an old Champagne with foie gras. The sweet, toffee-like aromas in a completely mature Champagne are a much more sophisticated choice for foie gras than a Sauternes or a heavy Alsatian Gewürztraminer. The acids in Champagne contribute to reducing the powerful flavors that fatty foie gras can have. A terrine of duck liver is even better, since the broiled and toasted notes from cooking might easily predominate. Duck and goose liver are appallingly expensive, but there are cheaper alternatives—goose pâté, for instance, or duck mousse with a few slices of real foie gras in it. You can accompany the duck liver with something sweet, such as, for example, jello made with Sauternes, or mango or fig purée, but do so with caution or the wine may taste acidic and bitter. I tasted most of the old Champagnes that are described in the chapter of the book devoted to producers on their own first; it was only later that I accompanied them with a substantial morsel of duck foie gras.

If you want to choose a theme for a Champagne dinner, let me suggest a subtle variation—a pink dinner. Serve only rosé Champagne, first to accompany a lobster appetizer, then with a pink salmon entrée, ending with strawberries or a raspberry soufflé. Ensure that the candles, napkins, and tablecloth are pink, and decorate the table with lots of pink roses. You couldn't host a more romantic dinner.

A more simple alternative is an outdoor picnic featuring Champagne, consisting of a chicken salad, or toast with fish roe and crème fraîche.

The classification of Champagnes

Based on their own criteria, all of the important wine-growing regions classify or list the differences between vineyards in terms of quality. Sometimes the producer is considered more important, and sometimes the method used for making the wine, but generally it is the geography that is the principal criterion used to establish the classification. In Champagne, the origin of the grapes is taking on an increasing importance for the consumer. Producers therefore have to concentrate their efforts on buying grapes that are highest on the scale of quality.

THE SYSTEM OF *CRUS*

Since vineyards in Champagne sell most of their grapes to the big houses, the system of classification in Champagne is based on the price of the grapes. The system was introduced in 1919 and is called "the scale of *crus*." It is based on the fact that all of the vineyards are placed on the scale of *crus* at somewhere between 80 percent and 100 percent. The word "*cru*," incidentally, comes from the infinitive *croître* (to grow), and indicates the location in which the vines grow.

Nowadays, there is a free market, but in the past the *C.I.V.C.*, in agreement with the growers and Champagne houses, fixed the price per kilogram of grapes for the current year. For grapes from *crus* classified at 100 percent, the producers would have to pay a high price. The prices would then reduce in proportion to the percentage classification, so as the status of the *cru* diminished, the price would drop.

When the *cru* system was first introduced, the scale went from 50 percent through 100 percent. In recent years there have been numerous calls to make the scale a wider one. The critics of the system claim that there is not enough of a price difference between, for example, grapes from a simple Pinot Meunier from the Marne valley and a *grand cru* Chardonnay. Another problem that arises with the scale is that the system only takes account of the *cru* of origin, but not of the exact location within a particular holding.

In 1985, certain vine-growing villages were reclassified. Five new vine-growing villages were awarded the title of *grands crus*, in addition to the twelve original *crus*. Many saw their status improve, and none were declassified. The result is that, even today, certain vine-growing villages are overestimated, while others ought to be higher up the scale. Among the vine-growing villages classified as *premier cru*, there are some whose level of quality deserves *grand cru* status. Personally, I consider that the scale of *crus* adopted for the wines of Burgundy is fairer, because it judges each vineyard in isolation.

A magnificent Belle Epoque door at the firm of Perrier-Jouët

GRAND CRU

In Burgundy, it goes without saying that the most prized and costly wines come from the *grand crus*. What is not as well known is that Champagne has a similar system, with vine-growing villages that are classified as *grand cru* and *premier cru*. I maintain that the difference between a Champagne from Aÿ and one from Verzenay is just as great as that between a Chambertin and a Musigny.

Numerous Champagne producers rightly stress the importance of having *grand cru* wines. The reason the *grand cru* system isn't better known is that the major houses have always promted *cuvées* from a mosaic of villages, with lowly ranked areas included. The small firms and growers who have had access to first class grapes have not had the same PR machinery behind them as the giants such as Moët, Mumm, Clicquot, Pommery, and Lanson, among others. On the other hand, these companies never miss an opportunity to trumpet the fact that they only use grapes that are classified as *grand cru* for their best Champagnes.

The best producers in the *grand cru* villages make classic Champagnes with the wonderful tastes of the *terroir*. The prices of these *grand cru* Champagnes purchased directly from the producers cannot be compared with those that are paid for, say, *grand cru* Burgundies. So by buying from them you will be getting a bargain.

Certain villages produce grapes of a very different quality to the rest. My favorites are Aÿ and Verzenay for black grapes, and Avize, Cramant, and Le Mesnil for Chardonnay. These grapes have a special sparkle, whether they are used for producing classic, *cuvée de prestige* Champagnes for one of the big houses, or more modestly for a mono-*cru* Champagne made by growers.

The quality of the raw materials is crucial for obtaining a Champagne of the finest quality. Fortunately, more and more consumers are starting to realize the importance of these *grand cru* Champagnes. This has caused a certain amount of consciousness-raising among the larger producers who are now using this information in their publicity material. Of course, such wines are very rare, since there are only a total of 324 vine-growing villages that produce Champagne, and a mere seventeen of them have been classified as *grand cru*.

Grand cru **villages 100%:** Ambonnay, Avize, Aÿ, Beaumont-sur-Vesle, Bouzy, Chouilly (1985), Cramant, Louvois, Mailly, Le Mesnil-sur-Oger (1985), Oger (1985), Oiry (1985), Puisieulx, Sillery, Tours-sur-Marne, Verzenay, and Verzy (1985).

It is interesting to note that the grapes for Tours-sur-Marne Chardonnay are only classified at 90 percent, and the rare grapes of Chouilly are rated no higher than 95 percent on the scale of *cru*s.

PREMIER CRU

The *premier cru* villages are those that have obtained between 90 percent and 99 percent on the scale of *cru*s. If the *premier cru* grapes from Chouilly and Tours-sur-Marne are included among the *grand crus*. There are forty-three *premier cru* villages, but in fact the true figure of *premier cru* is forty-one. Some *premier cru* villages exceed some of the *grand cru* villages in quality, so it is a good idea to be well informed about the characteristics and reputation of each of the villages. Even if the village has been correctly classified, certain small plots may be capable of producing Champagne whose quality is actually that of a *grand cru*. At Mareuil-sur-Aÿ, the Clos des Goisses produces grapes of the very finest quality, and ought absolutely to be granted the status of a *grand cru*. Some of my other favorite *premier cru* villages include: Cuis, Dizy, Grauves, Trépail, Vertus, Chigny-les-Roses, Rilly-la-Montagne, Avenay, Champillon, and Cumières.

Premier cru **villages:**
99%: Mareuil-sur-Aÿ and Tauxières.
95%: Bergères-les-Vertus (white grapes only), Billy-le-Grand, Bissueil, Chouilly (black grapes only), Cuis (white grapes only), Dizy, Grauves (white grapes only), Trépail, Vaudemanges, Vertus, Villeneuve-Renneville, Villers-Marméry, and Voipreux.
94%: Chigny-les-Roses, Ludes, Montbré, Rilly-la-Montagne, Taissy, and Trois-Puits.
93%: Avenay, Champillon, Cumières, Hautvillers, Mutigny.
90%: Bergères-les-Vertus (black grapes only), Bezannes, Chaméry, Coligny (white grapes only), Cuis (black grapes only), Écueil, Étrechy (white grapes only), Grauves (black grapes only), Jouy-les-Reims, Les Mesneux, Pargny-les-Reims, Pierry, Sacy, Tours-sur-Marne (white grapes only), Villedommange, Villers-Allerand, and Villers-aux-Nœuds.

UNCLASSIFIED VILLAGES

Only a tiny part of the area in which Champagne vineyards are cultivated include the vine-growing villages that are classified as *grand cru* and *premier cru*. A substantial part of the production of Champagne consists solely of grapes that fall between 80 percent and 89 percent on the scale of *cru*s and are thus called "unclassified." All the regions on the periphery of Champagne, such as the Aube, Sézanne, and the Aisne, only have vine-growing villages in this category. There are very few villages lower down the scale whose wines are special, but there are a few exceptions such as Bethon, Daméry, Urville, Leuvrigny, Mancy, Montgenost, and Les Riceys.

The principal role of these unclassified vineyards is to act as "diffusers of taste" in the Champagne *cuvées*. These relatively

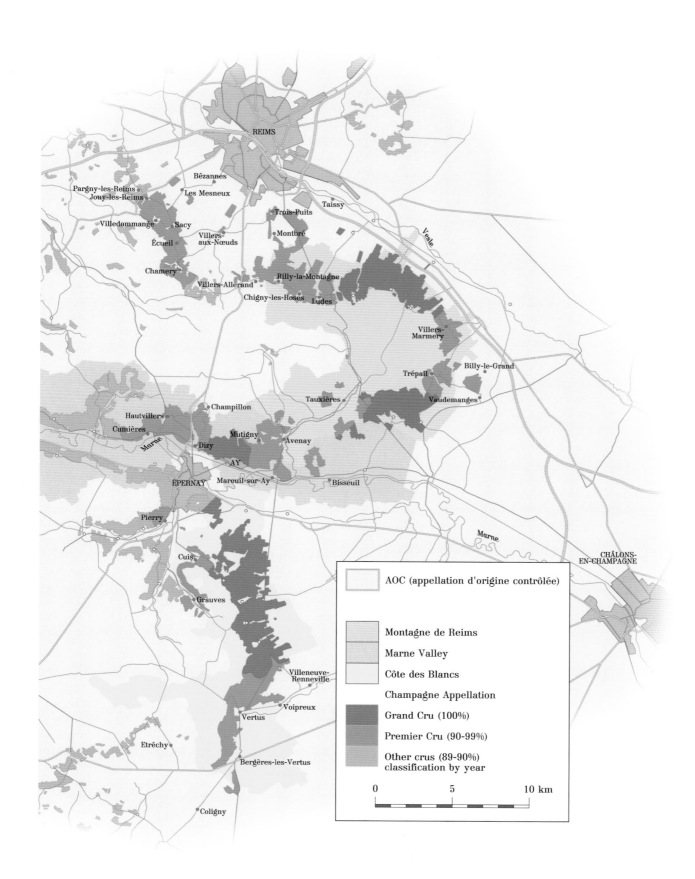

REIMS

Bézannes

Pargny-les-Reims
Jouy-les-Reims

Les Mesneux

Taissy

Trois-Puits

Villedommange   Sacy

Montbré

Villers-
aux-Nœuds

Écueil

Chamery

Rilly-la-Montagne

Villers-Allerand

Chigny-les-Roses   Ludes

Villers-
Marmery

Billy-le-Grand

Trépail

Vaudemanges

Tauxières

Champillon

Hautvillers

Cumières

Mutigny

Dizy

Avenay

AY

ÉPERNAY   Mareuil-sur-Ay

Bisseuil

Marne

Marne

Veele

CHÂLONS-
EN-CHAMPAGNE

Pierry

Cuis

Grauves

Villeneuve-
Renneville

Voipreux

Vertus

Etréchy

Bergères-les-Vertus

Coligny

AOC (appellation d'origine contrôlée)

Montagne de Reims

Marne Valley

Côte des Blancs

Champagne Appellation

Grand Cru (100%)

Premier Cru (90-99%)

Other crus (89-90%)
classification by year

0   5   10 km

neutral wines can balance extreme wines whose characteristics are highly differentiated, thereby contributing to the creation of a harmonious ensemble. The non-vintage *cuvées* of the big Champagne houses are often constituted using hundreds of unclassified wines.

Unclassified vine-growing villages, 80% to 89%:

89%: Coulommes-la-Montagne, Daméry, Moussy, Sermiers, Venteuil, and Vrigny.

88%: Chavot-Courcourt, Épernay, Mancy, Monthelon, and Reims.

87%: Allemant (84% Pinot), Barbonne-Fayel (85% Pinot), Bethon (84% Pinot), Broyes (85% Pinot), Celle-sous-Chante-merle (85% Pinot), Chantemerle (85% Pinot), Courmas, Fontaine-Denis (84% Pinot), Montgenost (84% Pinot), Nogent l'Abbesse, Saint-Thierry, Saudoy (85% Pinot), Sézanne (85% Pinot), Thil, Trigny (85% Pinot), Vindey, Villenauxe-la-Grande (85% Pinot), and Villers-Franqueux.

86%: Binson-Orquigny, Bouilly, Branscourt, Brouillet, Brugny-Vaudancourt, Courthiézy, Crugny, Cuisles, Faverolles, Hourges, Lagéry, Lhéry, Montigny-sur-Vesle, Reuil, Sainte-Euphraise, Saint-Martin d'Ablois, Savigny-sur-Ardres, Serzy et Prin, Soulières, Traméry, Treslon, Unchair, Vandeuil, Vandière, Vauciennes, Verneuil, Villers-sous-Châtillon, Vinay, and Vin-celles.

85%: Barzy-sur-Marne, Bassu, Bassuet, Baye, Beaunay, Celles-sur-Ource, Cernay-les-Reims, Coizard-Joches, Congy, Cormoyeux, Courjeonnet, Etoges, Férébrianges, Fleury-la-Rivière, Germigny, Givry-les-Loisy, Gueux, Janvry, Loisy-en-Brie, Mondement, Ormes, Oyes, Passy-sur-Marne, Prouilly, Romery, Saint-Lumier, Talussaint-Prix, Trelou-sur-Marne, Vert-Toulon, Villevenard and Vitry-en-Perthois.

84%: Baslieux-sous-Châtillon, Belval-sous-Châtillon, Berru, Boursault, Broussy-le-Grand, Cerseuil, Châlons-sur-Vesle, Champvoisy, Chenay, Cuchery, Festigny, Hermonville, Jonchry-sur-Vesle, Jonquery, Leuvrigny, Mardeuil, Mareuil-le-Port, Marfaux, Merfy, Mesnil-le-Hutier, Montigny-sur-Vesle, Morangis, Moslins, Nesle-le-Repons, Neuville-aux-Larris, Œuilly, Olizy-Violaine, Passy-Griny, Pevy, Port-à-Binson, Pontfaverger-Moronvilliers, Pouillon, Pourcy, Prouilly, Sainte-Gemme, Selles, and Villers-Franqueux.

83%: Bligny, Breuil, Brimont, Cauroy-les-Hermonville, Celles-les-Conde, Chambrécy, Champlat-Boujacourt, Chapelle-Monthodon, Chaumuzy, Chavenay, Châtillon-sur-Marne, Cormicy, Connigis, Courcelles-Sapicourt, Courthiezy, Crézancy, Dormans, Igny-Conblizy, Poilly, Reuilly-Sauvigny, Rosnay, Saint-Agnan, Sarcy, Soilly, Try, Vassieux, and Vassy.

82%: Arcis-le-Ponsart, Aubilly, Bergères-sous-Montmirail, Bouleuse, Cortagnon, Courville, Méry-Prémecy, Nanteuil-la-Forêt, Orbais-l'Abbaye, Romigny, Saint-Gilles, and Ville-en-Tardenois.

81%: Châlons-sur-Vesle.

80%: All the remaining vine-growing villages in the départements of the Marne and the Aube. The villages to remember for their quality in this category are Avirey-Lingey, Balnot-sur-Laignes, Bar-sur-Seine, Bligny, Buxeuil, Charly-sur-Marne, Château-Thierry, Columbe-le-Sec, Fontette, Gyé-sur-Seine, Les Riceys, Urville, and Ville-sur-Arce.

CHAMPAGNE HOUSES, GROWERS, AND COOPERATIVES

In most of the vine-growing regions of France, each grower makes wine from their own grapes. In Champagne, ever since the time of Dom Pérignon, the concept of blends has dominated production in this region. The big Champagne firms have always had the ability to make Champagne from a large number of grapes coming from numerous vineyards in a variety of vine-growing villages.

Things are different today. Cooperatives and growers who make their own wine represent a growing sector of the annual production. It is becoming more and more crucial for the big firms to own their own vineyards, or at least to have long-term contracts with producers to ensure that their needs in terms of grapes are covered.

There is no such thing as a Champagne house that is totally self-sufficient, one which is able to produce all the grapes that it uses. If you want to find out the origin of the grapes for a particular Champagne, you need to know how to read a Champagne bottle label. At the bottom right-hand corner of the label you will usually find one combination of the following letters, accompanied by a producer number: N.-M. (Négociant-Manipulant) indicates that it is a Champagne house, R.-M. are the intials of grower-producers (Récoltant-Manipulant) and C.-M. (Coopérative-Manipulant) indicate that the Champagne has been produced by a cooperative.

In total there are 19,000 growers in Champagne, of whom only 5,091 sell Champagne under their own label. What this figure does not reveal is that most of the growers do not make their Champagne themselves but have the vinification performed by one of the cooperatives. The true figure for growers who make the wine themselves is only 2,200. It is true that 5,419 producers in total claim make their own Champagne, but less than half of them—2,500 in fact—actually do. In this book, I have chosen not to name the producers who sell wine under their own label that actually comes from a cooperative, and who are listed

An unusual advertisement on the road from Reims to Montagne-de-Reims.

on the label as R.-C. (Récoltant-Coopérateur), because these wines are identical to those sold by the cooperative in question.

Assuming that the producers in a district make an average of four different Champagnes each, this would result in 10,000 different Champagnes a year! Add to this all the successive vintages that have been produced over the years, and it's easy to see why one can never claim to be totally knowledgeable in this sphere. To complicate matters further, several names may be recorded for the same wine under the heading "la marque propre de l'acheteur" (the "Buyer's Own Brand") or under a subsidiary name within the same Champagne house. One extreme example of this is Marne & Champagne in Épernay, who produce fifteen or so *cuvées* under 200 different names. In total, there are 12,000 registered trademarks for Champagne. It will therefore be no surprise if I get complaints from some readers who will be disappointed that they did not find the brand of Champagne that they drink mentioned in my book.

Champagne houses: the difference between a Champagne house and a grower is that the house has the right to make Champagne using grapes bought in from all over the region. Despite the fact that the big houses only own 12 percent of the vineyards, they account for 66 percent of all sales. The Champagne houses have always had a dominant position in this field. There are currently 280 houses of different sizes. The ten largest, who account for about 50 percent of sales, created the "Syndicat des Grandes Marques de Champagne" in 1964, in an attempt to safeguard the special status of the houses. Membership of this syndicate does not mean much nowadays because some of these firms produce mediocre Champagnes, and many of the very biggest names are absent from the list.

The original members were Ayala, Billecart-Salmon, Bollinger, Clicquot, Delbeck, Deutz, Heidsieck & Co. Monopole, Charles Heidsieck, Irroy, Krug, Lanson, Masse, Moët & Chandon, Montebello, Mumm, Perrier-Jouët, Joseph Perrier, Piper-Heidsieck,

Pol Roger, Pommery, Prieur, Roederer, Ruinart, Salon, and Taittinger. This syndicate was dissolved in 1997, despite numerous attempts to regroup and reintroduce members' rules.

The growers: as I have already indicated, the growers are much more of a force to be reckoned with these days, since, with the aid of new techniques, they are becoming capable of producing better wines than ever before. Some of them own land in communes whose grapes lack the qualities required for separate vinification, while other produce outstanding wines.

Today, 5,091 growers sell Champagne, of whom 2,200 make their own Champagne from their own grapes. The latter use the initials R.-M., and the wines produced by a cooperative use the initials R.-C. Apart from these two categories, there is another variation, whereby several growers create a company in order to make and sell Champagne under several names. S.-R. (Société de Recoltants) are the initials that distinguish this rare variation.

The cooperatives: the number of cooperatives in Champagne has increased considerably in recent years. Currently, there are forty-eight cooperatives; village wine-growers have grouped together within these to help each other with the vinification of their grapes. Formerly, they sold almost all of their grapes to the big Champagne houses, but they now have the opportunity of becoming a Récoltant-Manipulant, or of getting help from their neighbors in a cooperative.

There are four categories of cooperative: the "*cooperatives de pressoir*" who merely press other growers' grapes; cooperatives that press grapes and make still wines; "*cooperatives sur lattes,*" which press the grapes, vinify still wines, and make sparkling wines that are then sold under someone else's label; and the "*cooperatives de vente,*" who make Champagne and sell it under their own name. Their labels always feature the initials C.-M. (Coopérative-Manipulant).

There are now several high-tech cooperatives that produce pure and original Champagnes, but few reach the level of quality of the individual vine-growers. The resources exist, but only a very small number of cooperatives dare to concentrate on a prestigious Champagne obtained from carefully selected grapes or one that uses sophisticated vinification methods. It often comes down to the fact that members of the cooperative cannot agree when it is a matter of deciding who harvests the best grapes.

The Mailly cooperative is a well-established, model cooperative, which definitely produces a better Champagne than that of any individual grower in the village. The Avize and Le Mesnil cooperatives do not enjoy a reputation of excellence in their respective villages but, thanks to the impeccable raw materials available to them, they are able to produce tasty Champagnes at all price ranges.

It is mainly in the villages in which Pinot Meunier predominates that the cooperatives have considerably improved the quality of the wines. Beaumont des Crayères in Mardeuil and H. Blin in Vincelles have made substantial contributions to the progress of these villages. The fact that an increasing number of vine-growers are joining cooperatives also facilitates the task of those of us who want to taste the wines produced by different wine-makers.

It is thus becoming simpler to classify the growers and get an idea of their production. However, there is an added complication, because numerous members of cooperatives also sell Champagne from the cooperative under their own R.-C. (Récoltant-Coopérateur) wine-maker labels.

The "Marque d'Acheteur" (M.A.) indicates a major buyer, such as a hotel chain or department store, which will use its own name on the label, even though the wine is produced entirely by a cooperative or a Champagne house. In Great Britain the major department stores insist on selling their "own Champagne" but, so as not to mislead the consumer, it is now compulsory to show the producer number along with the initials, M.A.

Some Champagne houses specialize in the production of M.A. Champagnes. Other houses are too proud to do so, and too careful of their reputation to allow a label other than their own to be displayed on their wines. If one is lucky, a great Champagne-maker may be hidden under the label. More than one fancy restaurant in France serves a Legras de Chouilly, for example, as its own Champagne, under the restaurant's name.

The letters N.-D. (Négociant-Distributeur) rarely appear on the labels of Champagne bottles, but they indicate that the Champagne has been sold by a company that does not actually produce the wine. Against all these special producers, I have made a note of these initials.

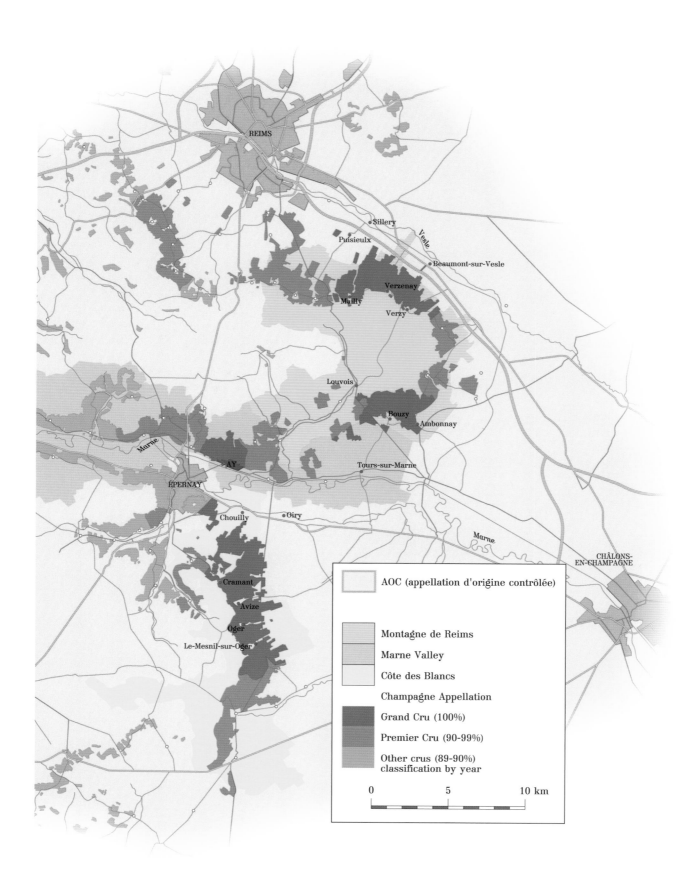

AOC (appellation d'origine contrôlée)

Montagne de Reims

Marne Valley

Côte des Blancs

Champagne Appellation

Grand Cru (100%)

Premier Cru (90-99%)

Other crus (89-90%)
classification by year

0   5   10 km

Champagne vintages

In all the northernmost grape-growing regions, the quality of the vintages is more variable than in milder climates. In Champagne, the problem has been solved by mixing vintages so as to rebalance the wine. In the years in which the grapes ripen to perfection, vintage Champagne is produced. These wines have to represent the style of the producer and the year in which the grapes were harvested.

There is no definite guidelines as to how to achieve a perfect year. The style of the vintage is influenced a by a whole complicated series of factors in which temperature, sunshine, and precipitation all play an important part. What determines the quality of the wine is mainly the way in which the all these factors come together in the course of the year. The various characteristics of the vintages are a favorite subject of conversation for Champagne-lovers. Some prefer the richer vintages, such as those of 1947, 1959, 1976, 1989, 1990, and 1996, whereas others tend to favor the more elegant and subtle vintages, such as those of the years 1966, 1969, 1971, 1979, 1985, 1988, 1995, and 1998. Whichever is chosen, the different vintages have a richness of variation that merely serves to increase the wine buff's fascination with the subject.

It is an arduous task to establish a classification of vintages on the basis of their overall qualities, since certain vintages are generous when young but others require several years in which to reach their zenith. Remember that the following classification of vintages is very general. The vintages that were rated very highly are those whose wines are destined for longevity and that reach a very high maximum level. Several vintages that have not gotten a very good grade may be fine to drink right now because they are at their best. It might be a good idea to check carefully how these various wines were rated in the chapter devoted to assessments that you will find later on in this book.

1900 ****	1949 *****	1980 **
1904 ****	1950 *	1981 ****
1906 ****	1951 **	1982 *****
1907 **	1952 ****	1983 ***
1911 ****	1953 ****	1985 ****
1914 *****	1954 ***	1986 ***
1915 ****	1955 *****	1987 **
1919 ****	1958 ***	1988 *****
1921 *****	1959 *****	1989 ****
1923 ***	1961 *****	1990 *****
1926 ***	1962 ***	1991 **
1928 *****	1964 *****	1992 **
1929 ****	1965 *	1993 ***
1932 **	1966 *****	1994 ***
1933 ***	1967 *	1995 ****
1934 ****	1969 ****	1996 *****
1937 ****	1970 **	1997 ***
1938 ****	1971 ****	1998 ****
1941 ***	1973 ***	1999 ****
1942 **	1974 *	2000 ***
1943 ****	1975 ****	2001 *
1944 **	1976 *****	2002 ****
1945 ****	1977 *	2003 ***
1947 *****	1978 ***	
1948 ***	1979 *****	

An impressive view of the Pommery enothèque.

***** = A perfect vintage of its type
**** = Exceptional vintage
*** = A good year for Champagne with reliable wines
** = A simple vintage, with few good Champagnes
* = A really poor vintage, to be avoided

THE NINETEENTH CENTURY

1874: this was the greatest year of the nineteenth century as far as Champagne is concerned. The other good years whose reputation is recorded for posterity are: 1804, 1811, 1825, 1834, 1846, 1858, 1862, 1870, 1880, 1884, 1892, 1898, and 1899.

THE TWENTIETH CENTURY

1900: A great harvest of high quality. Often compared with the 1899 vintage, which was easier to store.

1904: An abundant harvest of wines that have a reputation for elegant style and good keeping qualities.

1906: A normal harvest and average quality. The wines had better keeping qualities than expected.

1907: A normal harvest that produced fairly simple wines, with a light body and high acidity level. It is this very acidity level allied with the perfect storage conditions that prevail at the bottom of the ocean, that produced the famous and greatly appreciated Champagne made in 1907 by Heidsieck & Co., one that is so fresh that it was still dancing like a teenager when opened.

1911: A vintage some of whose wines are still lively. Magnums of Pol Roger and Pommery taste more as though they date from the 1970s.

1914 : A major vintage, although it was harvested in the midst of the First World War. The bite of the young wines took a long time to attenuate, but they have maintained their strength. The Pol Roger is legendary, as is the Moët & Chandon with its caramelized notes.

1915: A well-thought-of vintage which nevertheless did not have the keeping qualities of the 1914 vintage. De Castellane remains a wine that has retained all of its magnificence.

1919: At first it was believed that this was not a particularly good vintage, but the wines had marked acidity and extreme longevity, even though they are a little light.

1921: All over Europe, this was one of the great vintages for white wines. In Champagne, the 1928 vintage has received more praise, but the quality of the 1921 vintage was superb and the bottles continue to be viable today. The Dom Pérignon of that year was the very first of the *cuvée de prestige* Champagnes. Personally, with a few exceptions, I prefer this vintage to the renowned 1928.

1923: A little-known vintage with a very small harvest. Originally, the wines had elegance and bite. Some of the Champagnes from the more famous houses may still have a spark of life—if any bottles remain. The Roederer is fantastic!

1926: A vintage that has almost completely fallen into oblivion, eclipsed by the 1928 vintage. A bottle of Krug 1926, drunk in 1994, naturally lacked much of its mousse, but was not dissimilar to a noble Château d'Yquem of the 1920s in its mildness and caramelized aromas.

1928: The vintage of the century for many people. Many wine buffs agree that a Krug made in that year is the most perfect Champagne that ever existed. A Champagne that is seventy-six years old is always something of a gamble, and unfortunately I admit that I am no longer as excited by this vintage as I was initially. Of course, there are still some excellent examples, and the acidity is still impressive, but most of the wines have been corroded by an excessive maderization, unlike the delicate 1921 vintages. A major exception remains my greatest Champagne experience, the luminous and magical Pol Roger Grauves.

1929: A very good vintage that is frequently forgotten in comparison to the 1928, but which is often more delicious with its mellow mildness and smoothness spiked with a hint of orange. Bollinger is the model.

1933: Of little interest today, but I have been told that it was good during the first years of its life.

1934: Elegant and long-lived wines that can still be fantastic today. The Pol Roger 1934 is magic.

1937: Very great and rich wines that can produce intense sensations if they have been correctly stored. As is often the case, my number one is Krug.

1938: A great harvest producing acidulated wines which at first had the reputation of being good without being particularly exceptional. You can imagine my surprise when a 1938

The famous Castellane water tower at Épernay.

Krug Champagne came second out of all those I had drunk hitherto, even though it was more than half a century old.

1941: A vintage that is rarely found and often neglected. And yet the bottles I have drunk had a feeling of spring about them. The Pommery is exceptional.

1943: A good vintage that produced powerful wines which were a little too robust. A few good examples are left today. José Michel at Moussy is the most outstanding memory I have of this wartime vintage.

1944: A minute quantity of Champagne was produced during this war year. That is why I was very surprised recently to drink a really superb Mailly 1944.

1945: The great vintage at the end of the Second World War. If you want to experience the grandeur of a vintage which elsewhere is manifestly tired, direct your attentions to Bollinger, Roederer, or Clicquot. Furthermore, 1945 was the year when Roederer Cristal was launched.

1947: All the claret lovers will have heard of the famous 1947 Cheval-Blanc. Although they did not attain quite this level, the Champagnes of this vintage are known for their mildness, the richness of their essence, and their strength. Despite a fairly low level of acidity, these wines have aged very well. Salon and Launois of Le Mesnil are the most brilliant.

1948: A year that is little known in comparison with the 1947 and 1949 vintages, but good for Côte des Blancs.

1949: These wines are almost as rich as those of 1947, of comparable longevity and even better acidity. Cristal and Krug are monuments in the history of Champagne.

1951: A terrible year otherwise, but Salon demonstrates its magnificence and vitality.

1952: Balanced wines with good longevity, but unfortunately their relative youth is the main merit of this vintage. Some 1952 wines are amazingly young, even though this does not make them into impressive Champagnes. This was the year when Taittinger Comtes de Champagne made its first appearance. The 1952 Gosset obtained third place in the Millennium Tasting (see page 66).

1953: The situation is the exact opposite to the wines of 1952. Many of the 1953 wines have become slightly maderized and have lost their freshness. The bottles that are still lively

nevertheless produce a sensual and delicious sensation. Salon, Clos des Goisses, and Diebolt are stunning.

1954: A vintage of whose existence few people were aware before Henriot surprised us with a magnum that contains the fragrances of spring when we tasted it at the Millennium Tasting. One of the 100 points awarded by the Danish representative, Jörgen Krüff.

1955: A fantastic vintage that continues to offer us privileged moments. Fine, acidic, perfectly harmonious wines, with a pleasantly toasted bouquet. Clos des Goisses, Cristal, and Billecart-Salmon won my very rarely given 99 points.

1958: There is a very small number of survivors in the Côte des Blancs from the 1958 vintage. I personally have only found a single bottle.

1959: An abundant harvest of Champagnes that often exceed an alcohol content of 13 percent due to the heat wave. The wines showed remarkable aging qualities, despite their lack of acidity. The power and concentration are masterly, whether the predominant variety is Chardonnay or Pinot Noir. A marvelous vintage. Numerous prestige Champagnes were launched in 1959, including Dom Ruinart and Pol Roger Blanc de Chardonnay. This was by far the best vintage of our Millennium Tasting. A Billecart-Salmon 1959 came top!

1961: Just as the 1961 wines of Bordeaux have become so famous, the Champagnes of 1961 are more expensive than those of 1959, 1964, and 1966, although their quality is no better. In 1961, Krug was colossal, and many consider that the Dom Pérignon of that year is the best Champagne they have ever tasted. The 1961 Billecart-Salmon won second place in the Millennium Tasting.

1962: A year that is often underestimated in Champagne circles, but which produced great, rich, and smooth Champagnes. My only note of reproach would be that they lack a certain amount of bite. Diamant Bleu, Dom Pérignon Œnothèque, and Dom Pérignon Rosé are for me the masterpeices of this vintage.

1964: A wonderful vintage, often compared to the 1966. The wines of 1964 today, with rare exceptions, have a perfume of chocolate, mint, bergamot, and fresh bread, allied to a full flavor that is caramelized and concentrated at its peak. If you want to try an old Champagne without taking risks, the 1964 wines are the best guarantee. It was in this vintage that the prestigious Perrier-Jouët Champagne, decorated with Art Nouveau flowers, made its appearance. Dom Pérignon is my first choice, but closely followed by Cristal and Diamant Bleu.

1966: Frost and hail limited the harvest and reduced to a bare minimum a vintage of which nothing much was expected. The great blends are vibrant, full of the aromas of exotic fruits and with an elegant structure. The valuable Blancs de Blancs are of a rare elegance, and the great names of Pinot have produced very powerful Champagnes with vegetable notes. One merely has to think of Bollinger 1966, whose bouquet is reminiscent of a great La Tâche.

1969: After numerous difficulties, a meager harvest of acidic grapes at first produced simple and trenchant wines. Today, the best of them have blossomed, offering a remarkable grandeur and a superior elegance. Salon, Comtes de Champagne, and Jacquesson Blanc de Blancs are the best.

1970: A potentially good vintage, but overproduction slightly spoiled the quality. A mediocre year, with lots of tired and faded Champagnes. The one monumental exception is Bollinger Vieilles Vignes Françaises.

1971: A difficult year for the vines, with a meager harvest on September 18. The wines were rather patchy, normally elegant and light, but rendered fragile through lack of acidity. Note that the Comtes de Champagne Rosé 1971 is probably the best pink Champagne known to this day.

1973: Another particularly hot summer, which produced a late harvest toward the end of September. The wines considered to be ephemeral luxuries have surprised us by their remarkably good aging. As for 1971, some examples are tired already, but 1973 still offers more roundness and richness, with particularly successful Blanc de Blancs. Peters, Belle Epoque, and Dom Pérignon with its walnut scents clearly stand out from the crowd.

1974: A cold and rainy year produced a wet harvest on September 28. The wines were poor and diluted; only Vertus and Aube produced grapes worthy of the name. Roederer Cristal is the number one from this lean year. One can often smell distinct notes of tea leaves and grass in the wines of 1974.

1975: The experts disagree profoundly over this vintage. Some claim that 1975 was a model year for storage. Others maintain that the wines need to be drunk in the prime of their youth in order to preserve their attractive fruitiness. Personally, I find that they lack charm, but I admit that they keep perfectly and are well balanced. The Pinot Noir generally faired better than the Chardonnay, highlighting the little miracles—Winston Churchill, La Grande Dame, and Bollinger R. D. 1975.

1976: A large harvest of sun-gorged grapes produced very rich and slightly thick Champagnes that are reminiscent of the 1947 and 1959 vintages, without however attaining quite the excellence of those years. There is often an earthy and smoky aftertaste that emerges from beneath the smooth structure. This is the best developed vintage of the last five years, and today it is one of those that I prefer to savor in the evening at home, drinking gulp after gulp of the smooth and mellow liquid. Cristal, Billecart-Salmon, and Salon are all exquisite wines that have managed to avoid the heaviness of that very hot year. The best-tasting remains the Des Princes and the inimitable Comtes de Champagne.

1977: A catastrophic year with abundant rainfall and mildewed grapes. The fact that Cristal was so delicious is a miracle in itself.

1978: During my most recent travels, I met more and more vine-growers who praised the merits of their 1978 Champagnes. These Champagnes have the gift of developing and have reserved happy surprises for us. As far as I am concerned, I am both under the spell of their juvenile, floral freshness and troubled by their narrow, rigid structure. The Clos des Goisses is definitely the most concentrated wine of the vintage. Furthermore, it is a vintage that unequivocally illustrates the fact that the qualities of the vintages of Champagne and Burgundy are quite dissimilar. There is no counterpart to the Richebourg 1978 in Champagne.

1979: A wonderful classic vintage with incredibly elegant wines supported by good concentration. If one considers the weather conditions during 1979, there is almost nothing that would enable one to forecast a great vintage. Most of the 1979 wines are now delicious to drink, with their subtle notes of toast and hazelnut. Only time will tell us whether they will develop further as they age. For many years, the Krug 1979 was the most complex Champagne I had ever tasted, and the Clos du Mesnil is even better.

1980: There was barely enough sugar in the grapes to achieve an alcohol level of 8 percent, which meant that the wines had to be excessively chaptalized. Some producers with south-facing slopes who harvested in early November nevertheless produced grapes of fairly good quality. Comte Dampierre Blanc de Blancs, Dom Pérignon, Clos des Goisses, and Bonnaire are some of the best Champagnes of 1980, after the Clos du Mesnil, which is clearly superior to all the others.

1981: A year about which little has been said but which proved to be much better than it seemed at the time. Since there had been a succession of meager years, hardly any reserve wines were left. Everyone hoped for an abundant harvest but it was not to be. The 1981 Champagnes are aristocratic, elegant, and slow to ripen, with a very feminine balance for the Pinot Noir, and even eventually for the Chardonnay, which was initially of modest quality. Unfortunately, many wines of this vintage with promising potential were used to produce non-vintage Champagne. Look out for Champagnes of that year in which Pinot from Aÿ or Chardonnay from Mesnil and Cramant predominate. Clos du Mesnil, Bollinger Vieilles Vignes Françaises, and Krug stand out in this vintage.

1982: Finally, the long-awaited year, with a massive harvest (295 million bottles). The vines of Côte des Blancs were so heavily laden with grapes that they collapsed under the weight. This overproduction was harmful, because too many of the 1982 vintages were far less resistant to the ravages of time than was forecast. Above all, 1982 was the year of Chardonnay. If one can find a *grand cru* Champagne from this vintage, one can practically be assured of its exoticism. In 1993, at a major tasting of 1982 wines at which all the great names were represented, the overall winners included many Blanc de Blancs. Krug and Bollinger Vieilles Vignes Françaises were the only exceptions. Krug's Clos du Mesnil won, but Jacques Selosse and Krug 1982 ran it a close second.

1983: The record of 295 million bottles in 1982 seemed impossible to beat, and yet in 1983 the colossal figure of 300 million bottles was achieved. There had not been two consecutive years combining quality and quantity in this way since 1957 and 1958. The wines may have had a higher level of acidity than those of 1982, but a goodly number of them matured with an alarming speed, and most had to be drunk before the smoky notes of dryness became too prominent. The fresh wines from 1983 are without doubt the Billecart-Salmon Blanc de Blancs and Krug Clos du Mesnil.

1985: One of my favorite vintages of all, but unfortunately the development of the wines began to slow down two or three years ago. Will the wines emerge from this tunnel? And if they do, when will it happen? Only time will tell. During the winter, the temperature dropped as low as –25°C (–13°F), damaging 10 percent of the vines. An Indian summer in September–October saved a small harvest that proved to be of exceptional quality. Pinot and Chardonnay are both perfectly balanced. Clos du Mesnil was awarded 99 points.

1986: A harsh winter was followed by late budding. It rained at the beginning of the harvest, but growers who held their nerve and waited for warmer weather harvested rich and fully ripe grapes. An average vintage but with one "superstar:" the paradoxically acidic and marvelously rich Jacques Selosse 1986.

1987: Those who chose to make a 1987 vintage were merely bowing to economic considerations. The wines are rather thin and coarse. Louise Pommery, on the other hand, is a delight.

1988: The amazing three-year run of vintages that began in 1988 has no equivalent in the history of Champagne. If one had to choose between the three years, it would be a matter of style rather than quality. The most classic is the 1988, whose conservative and harmonious style is reminiscent of the 1985, 1979, and 1966 vintages. Pinot Noir surpassed itself that year. Krug is of an incomparable finesse, and Cristal Rosé is, in my opinion, the best rosé Champagne of all time.

1989: The year 1989 immediately distinguished itself as the most generous and developed of vintages. The weather conditions were reminiscent of the years 1947, 1959, and 1976. Consequently, the wines obtained are high in alcohol content, low in acidity, mellow, and rich in aromatic essences. I can easily imagine that the public would feel particularly enthusiastic about the Champagnes of 1989. It's a wonderful vintage to drink now. And there's plenty of it to choose from.

1990: For a long time, the Champagnes of 1990 were tenser than those of 1989, but more ample than those of 1988. The 1988 vintage may be a classic one, but 1990 is really special too. I am too young to have known the wines of 1928 in the prime of their youth, but I can imagine that they had the same dense and impressive structure, allied to magnificent aromas. The wines are so rich in aromatic essences that you can almost chew them. At about ten years of age, many of the 1990 Champagnes have matured, taking on notes of honey with an aftertaste of saffron that has confused more than one expert at blind tastings. It would be really exciting to be able to monitor this famous trilogy of years in their voyage through time. For the moment, the only Champagne that is awarded 99 points is Krug Clos du Mesnil. Hardly surprising.

1991: The Pinot grapes harvested were of decent quality, but they were used to make non-vintage Champagnes rather than vintage ones. Stick to the famous names whose wines are fruity and pure to derive the most benefit from a tasting. Vilmart, Clos des Goisses, and Billecart-Salmon are the most successful.

The magnificent Bollinger headquarters at Aÿ.

1992: A lean year with wines that were low in acidity and alcohol. Here again, there were just a few wines of vintage quality. The 97 points obtained by Bollinger Vieilles Vignes should be considered to be the exception that proves the rule. Vilmart Coeur de Cuvée is also a feast.

1993: Heavy rainfall destroyed any hope of a good harvest. The vine-growers began to lose patience. These were three consecutive years without wines of vintage quality. Since the quality was decent, however, with high acidity, most wine-makers decided to go for broke and make vintage wines. I do not have a single 1993 in my cellar. But I wouldn't say no to a Vilmart Coeur de Cuvée or a Winston Churchill.

1994: A mild winter and a normal spring, with an unusually large number of local hailstorms. I remember the wonderful summer that broke all heat records. In Champagne, everything seemed to be going well until the harvest, which once again was ruined by the rain. A large proportion of the grapes were attacked by gray rot. The inspection records of Champagne in casks—monitored by Jacques Selosse and Krug, among others—show that good wines were produced in the region in 1994 all the same. The real winner for that year remains Roederer, which took the first four places in my top ten.

1995: At last, a great vintage. Attractive wines with a delicious and generous fruitiness with a well-dosed character of caramel. With their low alcohol content, the wines have been classified by some as being ephemeral. I adore vintages that are pleasant even now and which I believe will age well. Many years will pass before the marathon vintages of 1996 will overtake these wonderful jewels. Bollinger Grande Année is sublime, Cristal and Cristal Rosé irresistible, and others will follow.

1996: Probably one of the great vintages of all time. Such acidity, allied to such a high alcohol potential, had not been seen since 1928, which should guarantee an unusual longevity. Just as in 1990, there are a few examples of wines produced from grapes on the point of overripeness with low acidity. They are full and ample. Otherwise, most of the wines of 1996 are very young, with a mordant acidity and monumental power. I am extremely impressed by the producers of *grand crus*, and especially Diebolt's Fleur de Passion. The Dom Pérignon is magnificent, as is the Cuvée William Deutz Rosé, Cristal, Bollinger, and the monumental Bollinger Vieilles Vignes.

1997: The history of wine is full of these forgotten vintages, eclipsed by previous outstanding years. It is not easy for the wines of 1997 to follow on from the delicious 1995 and magical 1996. However, all the technical constituents would lead one to forecast a good vintage, and most of the producers brought out a vintage Champagne that year. The wines are full of charm but need to be drunk relatively young. The two prestige wines from Vilmart are in a class of their own.

1998: The 1998 harvest is the most abundant ever experienced by the region. Each appellation managed to attain the maximum permitted limit of 10,400 kg of grapes per hectare (51640 st. per 2 1/2 acres). The vine-growers were also authorized to harvest another 2,600 kg (410 st.), destined to be used as reserves for Champagne and known as *blocage*. So this represents a total of 330 million bottles of Champagne. The *blocage* system (which allows excess production to be authorized in order to meet demand) proved to be an indispensable tool for maintaining price stability during the 1990s. The year 1998 may possibly not have been an exceptional one, but this does not prevent us from waiting impatiently and excitedly for the pleasures that these wines will assuredly procure for us in future. Most of the firms considered that wine was good enough to make a vintage. I had the immense pleasure of tasting still Veuve Clicquot base wines with the cellar master, Jacques Peters, who asked me if I thought that this raw material would do justice to the Grande Dame. With the range of choices at his disposal, I thought it certainly would. Furthermore, this vintage, while being good as a general rule, does not present itself as being extraordinary, although this ought to be a criterion for producing a vintage.

1999: Whatever the quality of the wines, it was established in advance that this vintage would be historic and very much in demand. Who would have thought it! The idea of toasting the New Year with a sparkling wine made from the grapes of the last harvest of the previous millennium! Fortunately, the caprices of the weather spared the vine-growers of Champagne. Just as in 1982, we witnessed a happy marriage between quantity and quality. As far as the style is concerned, many people mention an intermediate mix between the 1982 vintage and the generous wines of 1989. The grapes were perfectly ripe and the only slight shadow cast over the picture was a slight deficiency in malic acid. In the 1989 vintage, only the wines of the highest standard were scrupulously carefully vinified and chosen, and this will probably be the case for 1999 too. The managers at Bollinger claim that 1999 is a very uneven vintage where the qualitative difference between *grand cru* and *premier cru* and the other villages is more obvious than usual. The wine year of 1999 began with quite a mild winter with a record amount of sunshine. The first days of March were rainy, but in late March, the sun came out and warmed the land and the fine weather lasted into the first ten days of April. These conditions led to premature budding. A few nights of frost caused difficulties for some growers before the heat returned at the end of the month.

May was beautiful and dry, despite a few violent hailstorms that caused devastation over a small area. Flowering occurred in late June under good conditions, and a large quantity of grapes formed. July was very variable. Late summer was pleasantly hot and sunny. The grapes ripened in plenty of time, and the harvesting took place in excellent conditions. In Côte des Blancs, harvesting began on September 14. It took two weeks, and this year the grapes were abundant and well-balanced. In the Marne Valley, harvesting began on September 16. The potential alcohol level was very high, rising in some cases to 12.5 percent, which produced a Champagne containing more than 13 percent alcohol after the second fermentation. The grapes were completely healthy, with no insect pests or rot. In the Montagne de Reims, the harvest did not begin until September 18. The grapes were not quite as high in alcohol as those in the Marne Valley. The Verzy and Verzenay harvests came close to record levels. The most abundant harvest reached 12,000 kilograms per hectare, more than 1,000 kg being put aside as reserve quality. The wines are rounded and promising.

2000: A warm, damp winter was followed by a spring that was just as wet. The warm weather held back until May and produced a rapid flowering on around June 14. There were serious signs of chlorosis and mould. June and August were warm and dry. But if, like me, you spent your July vacation in Champagne, you will know from experience that it was cold and rainy. The weather was almost as bad as in Sweden, with constant rain and hailstorms in places. It all seemed hopeless, but the good weather came back in time for the harvest and saved a considerable number of grapes which remained healthy. Harvesting began on September 11 and ended in early October. The Chardonnay and Pinot Meunier proved more resistant than the delicate Pinot Noir. The vintage would be made since the magic number had been achieved. The quality does not seem to be remarkable for the moment. No doubt we shall have to wait for many years for the presently unremarkable wines of the year 2000, but the fruity taste is pleasant in the first few examples that we have been given to taste.

2001: Since Champagne lies so far to the north, the region is more exposed than other wine-growing areas to bad weather. The year 2001 was one that had problems of levels. Until the second two weeks of July, the levels were almost identical to those of the year 1982, with heavy, abundant, and healthy bunches of grapes. That is when the skies opened and heavy showers poured down continuously for weeks at a time. Harvesting began on September 25 in the pouring rain. Unfortunately, the vines were seriously damaged by rot, and both quantity and quality suffered, eventually resulting in a mediocre wine. Let us hope that no vintage was made that year. On the other hand, the non-vintage Champagnes from the leading firms will be of good quality because the moldy grapes were discarded.

2002: With a few delightful exceptions, this vintage will not leave its mark on history.

2003: This vintage will be one of the most important ever for Champagne. That is because of the extreme heat that affected the region that year, something that will no doubt become a more frequent occurrence when climate change becomes established. The grapes were much too sweet, however, and the level of acidity much too low. And yet there are similarities with the years 1976 and 1959 which produced remarkable vintages. The question is whether the porous soil and vinification will be able to correct this lack of acidity and still contribute sufficient elegance to the essence-rich appearance of this wine. Let us hope so for our grandchildren's sakes!

Sparkling wine worldwide

Bubbly— but not Champagne

No region other than Champagne benefits from the truly exceptional conditions that enable it to produce sparkling wine of such quality. Such favorable conditions being so rare, the number of producers around the world who aim to produce sparkling wine is lower than those producing still wine. Over the last ten years, however, production has grown by leaps and bounds, and is clearly heading in the right direction. At the time I wrote my first book, I was far from thinking that outside the Champagne region it might one day be possible to make sparkling wines as outstanding as those that are now produced by the Roederer Estate in California, in particular the *curvée de prestige* L'Ermitage vintages of 1991 and 1993. Even in regions where, until now, anything and everything containing bubbles has verged on the catastrophic, one can discover bottles worthy of the name of Champagne.

The best sparkling wines from beyond the borders of Champagne are produced with same type of vines and following exactly the same winemaking processes as are followed in that region. The handful of still wines to which Champagne-making processes have been applied and which are aged with yeast deposits for as long as a prestige Champagne can, in rare cases, reach a quality level comparable to a basic Champagne. Such special sparkling wines have proven extremely costly to manufacture, however. In some places the wine can be left to ferment in little oak casks with only a small proportion of the harvest set aside for the precious product. One should not therefore be too surprised to see the price of such wines attaining levels close to that of a true vintage Champagne. The market for these wines remains minuscule, however, since few buyers are really convinced that these wines represent good value for money.

Areas that enjoy soil favorable to Champagne seldom benefit from a suitable climate—and vice versa. If the soil in the Franciacorta region of Italy, for instance, is full of minerals, the climate on the other hand is too hot to produce grapes with a sufficiently high level of acidity. The New Zealand climate is similar to that in Champagne, but the soil is far from ideal. If some of the best sparkling wines are produced in the subtropical climate of California, it is above all because it has benefited from the exported know-how of the Champagne houses. Sparkling winemakers on every continent should ask themselves whether it is really worthwhile struggling to produce something resembling Champagne, or whether they might be better advised to employ local varieties of grapes that make for more characterful wines. For example, the finest German sparkling (sekt) wines are all made from Riesling. They do not necessarily put one in mind of Champagne, but nevertheless they remain very good sparkling wines, with a characteristic aroma and elegant freshness.

The majority of sparkling wines have the same pressure as Champagne, namely six times atmospheric. In French these are termed *pétillant*, while they are known in Portuguese as *espumante*, *spumante* in Italian, and *espumoso* in Spanish. For wines with pressure 3.6 times atmospheric there is a single French term: *crémant*. Between 2.5 and 3.5, wine is classified as semi-sparkling, which is *spritzig* in German, *spritsigt* or *pärlande* in Swedish and, more poetically, in Italian, as *frizzante*. In French, wines with a still lower pressure are called *perlant* or *perlé*. The English speak of *prickle*, the Germans *perlwein*, the Spanish of *vino de Aguja*. The Italians keep plowing their furrow and have christened it *frizzantino*.

THE *MÉTHODE CHAMPENOISE* IS NOT ALONE

Until very recently, makers were allowed to mention on the bottle label that the *méthode champenoise* had been applied. Unfortunately, the use of this expression is now prohibited. In addition to the Champagne method proper, there exist many other ways of producing sparkling wine. None of these results in bubbles that have the same delicacy and long-lasting quality, nor can they ever dream of attaining the autolytic character of the *méthode champenoise*.

Cuvée close or the *méthode Charmat*
The method that bears his name was invented by Eugène Charmat in 1907. It consists of adding sugar and yeast to the wine to cause a second fermentation in a stainless-steel tank. The wine is subsequently pressure filtered directly into the bottle, together with added dosage. As the whole process lasts only about a fortnight, one can easily understand why it is such a popular method. The results are superior to those attained by the carbonation or gasification method, but fall well short of those obtained with the *méthode champenoise*.

Currently, the Charmat method is more commonly employed to introduce bubbles into still wine. Italy's sweet Asti Spumante is produced using this method, since in that case the point is to keep the sugar level up, while forgoing autolytic character and bringing out the savors of the grape. The Russians often use an alternative to this process, the so-called "Russian" or "continuous" method, in which an interconnecting series of pressurized tanks are used. The wine and a predetermined quantity of sugar and yeast are poured into a tank, where the mixture is left to ferment. During the fermentation process, the mix flows between the tanks, allowing the dead yeast cells to settle out. It is a complicated method that does not display any obvious advantages.

The *méthode rurale*
Also dubbed the *méthode ancestrale*, this method is the precursor of the *méthode champenoise*. In 1531, monks at the Saint-Hilaire abbey were already employing this method to produce a sparkling wine, the Blanquette de Limoux. At the time, the wine began to ferment a second time in the barrel after the winter, since it had remained in contact with the lees. Nowadays, the wine is bottled before the end of fermentation, so that a thin layer of foam forms. In point of fact, the wine does not ferment a "second" time at all, since this bottle fermentation is just a continuation of the first. Today Blanquette de Limoux is still the only wine produced in accordance with this principle. Since it is neither filtered nor disgorged, it runs the risk of stalling halfway through the process.

Transfer method
Yeast and a solution of sugar are added to the bottled wine (*prise de mousse*), bringing about a second fermentation. However, instead of putting the wine through the stages of *remuage* and disgorging, it is conveyed to a tank, where the sediment is allowed to sink. Then the clear wine is filtered prior to being bottled under pressure. This method, a cross between the *rurale* and Charmat methods, is used chiefly in the United States. The transfer method has also long been employed in Champagne itself, though it is soon to be outlawed there. The reason for the use of such a method in Champagne is that the size of certain bottles makes handling them difficult at the *prise de mousse* stage. This is particularly the case with the 25-centiliter bottles served on aircraft, where the contents are first fermented in bottles of normal size. Transfer is also used for jeroboams and other outsized bottles. It should, however, be noted that certain producers specialize in second fermentation in large bottles, among them Pommery, Veuve Clicquot, and Henriot.

The *méthode dioise*
This is a derivation of the "*rurale*" method and is only used to make the Rhône valley sparkling Muscat wine, Clairette de Die. The wine ferments for four months before being filtered.

The *méthode gaillacoise*
This method is used solely in Gaillac in southwest France and is yet another variation on the *ancestrale*. Here, the extra fermentation is in truth only a continuation of first fermentation, and no extra sugar or yeast is added.

The carbonation or gasification method

This is the simplest and least expensive way of getting bubbles into a wine. Carbon dioxide is pumped into a large tank full of wine. Bottling is performed under pressure. The big, fizzy bubbles the method creates may be acceptable for mineral water and sodas, but are totally unsuitable for sparkling wines.

FRENCH SPARKLING WINES

Though it is true that Blanquette de Limoux, which appeared in 1531, was indeed the first sparkling wine of its kind, it was only around 1820 that the more sophisticated production methods invented in Champagne extended to the rest of France. Of the two billion bottles of sparkling wine produced each year in the world, the French are responsible for one quarter. Sparkling wines exist under fifty-two different names. Unfortunately, the majority of French producers make their sparkling wines from their worse grapes. Their approach seems to be that, if a wine is barely drinkable, then a blast of carbon dioxide will mask it. The truth is, however, that carbon dioxide tends to underline, instead of camouflage, impurities in a wine. This pitfall may be avoided by serving the wine very cold so that the taste is almost imperceptible. Another problem is the quantity of sulfur heaped into such mediocre products, something that only renders them more tart and unpalatable.

Loire

Even in the Loire, where excellent *crémants* are made from Chenin Blanc, many of the best producers only turn to sparkling wine in years when they consider the grapes too poor for good, bubble-free wine.

Gaston Huet of Vouvray, a maker of some of the finest sweet wines in the world, claims that poor years are the only ones when the grapes reach a high enough level of acidity to make them suitable for sparkling wine. Whatever the truth of this, it would be interesting to see just how good a sparkling wine made from a good year of *meilleurs coteaux* grapes might be. In 1979 Huet produced hardly any still wine at all, so all the grapes that usually end up in his fabulous *moelleux* were used for a sparkling wine that turned out to be the best ever made from Chenin Blanc. Normally, this grape is unmanageable insofar as it is far too aromatic to leave space for an autolytic character. Moreover, its marked aroma prevents the formation of mature types following *dégorgement*.

Sparkling wines from the Vouvray and Saumur districts are very popular, and Saumur is the greatest sparkling wine *appellation* in France after Champagne. For a small outlay one can purchase a light, fresh wine with a soupçon of the elegance of Champagne. Far too often, however, the grape leaves a rubbery aftertaste that becomes increasingly penetrating in even slightly older wines. Marc Bredif's sparkling wines are probably the closest thing to Champagne that is produced in the area, with a satisfactory autolytic character and a fine mineral aroma.

The best sparkling wine from the Loire — *Trésor*—is not made solely from Chenin Blanc but includes 30 percent Chardonnay. The oak-barrel-fermented wine made by Bouvet-Ladubay is so good that it could easily be mistaken for a basic Champagne. Taittinger, which has an interest in Bouvet-Ladubay, are by no means the only Champagne house to dip a toe in Crémant de Loire. The Saumur firm Gratien & Meyer belongs to Seydoux, who also own the Alfred Gratien house in Épernay, best characterized as a hobby. The wines produced in the Loire valley are pale imitations of Gratien's Champagne. All in all, approximately 25 million bottles of Crémant de Loire are produced each year, and the region is one of the first after Champagne.

Burgundy

Apart obviously from Champagne, this is the only region of France to produce better sparkling wines—from time to time —than the Loire. What is lost in terms of climate and soil is compensated for by the quality of the grapes. Of course, both Aligoté and Pinot Blanc are used very occasionally, but most of the Burgundy Crémants produced each year contain only Pinot Noir and Chardonnay. Alas, the majority of the sparkling wines here are manufactured by cooperatives, which tend to place quantity above quality. One of the main problems is that the overall impression is undermined by the marked earthy character of most Crémant de Bourgogne, with the addition of bubbles not being regarded seriously enough by producers.

One of the foremost producers is probably Simonnet-Febvre in Chablis, whose Crémant de Bourgogne Blanc ranks on a par with the products of the poorer growers of Aube. Another producer making fine, Champagne-like wines is Cave de Bailly, which is based south of Auxerre, near Chablis. Chablis stands on the same soil, rich in belemnite chalk, as nearby Aube, so it is not particularly surprising to find that their wines share certain common characteristics.

The principal representative of the Mâconnais is Henry Mugnier, Charnay. Another particularly pleasant wine is the Ruban Mauve, made almost exclusively from Pinot Noir of the Côte Chalonnaise. The wine comes from a tiny field, the Domaine Déliance, and is extremely difficult to come by. On a very different scale are the sparkling wines of Kriter; they turn out upward of 15 million bottles per annum, more than any Champagne house, except for the colossal Moët & Chandon. Another important sparkling wine player in the region is André Delorme.

It is a crying shame that Burgundy, with all its fantastic whites and reds, seems unable to produce better sparkling wines from its Pinot Noir or Chardonnay. The problem lies in the fact that, even if a sparkling Montrachet were strong and deep enough, its power would remain unbalanced, and it would be practically impossible to make a sparkling wine out of it. This is because the second fermentation would attain an alcohol level in the vicinity of 15 percent. Even if one succeeded in spite of these obstacles, the wine would prove far too expensive relative to its quality.

Personally, were I to be given a free hand to produce a sparkling Burgundy, I would rather go for Chablis *premier cru*, such as Montée de Tonnerre, a glorious combination of fruity characteristics with an unashamedly limestone edge. I would be happiest with one of the lighter years, with a high acidity level, and I would vinify a quarter of the wine only in oak barrels. Half of these barrels would be brand new. The harvest would take place early, and malolactic fermentation of any kind would be avoided; I would leave the wine in contact with the yeast for half a dozen years in a cellar at a temperature of 9°C (48°F). I would then wait a further four years before unveiling the fruits of my labors. Perhaps this might give Raveneau, Dauvissat, Michel, or Droin an idea or two….

Alsace

The third region authorized to employ the term "*crémant*" is Alsace, and in 1976 it gained its very own *appellation*, "Crémant d'Alsace." Although almost all the wines with this *appellation* are made according to the Champagne method, the quality is demonstrably inferior to both Burgundy and Loire *crémant*s. The majority of Alsace sparkling wines are made from the insipid Pinot Blanc. Alas, it is rare to find a pure Riesling in these *pétillant*s. More and more Chardonnay vines are being planted for production of Crémant d'Alsace, so perhaps there is an exciting bubbly future to look forward to in this wine district. Meanwhile, the most surprising wine in the area today is a Crémant d'Alsace Rosé made from Pinot Noir. Just as in Burgundy, the majority of sparkling wines here are made by cooperatives.

OTHER REGIONS OF FRANCE

The Jura and Savoy produce very good sparkling wines from local grape varieties. Seyssel Mousseaux, a fresh, *méthode champenois* wine, contains Roussette, Molette, Jacquère, Clairette, and Chenin Blanc.

In the southwest, where the first sparkling wines were produced in the fourteenth century, several domains still produce Blanquette de Limoux. Roger Antech's *cuvée* Saint-Laurent is a pleasant light wine, reminiscent of Seyssel Mousseaux. The Limoux cooperative, numbering some 360 members, uses primarily a local *cépage*, Mauzac, but also small quantities of

Chenin Blanc and Chardonnay. In Gaillac, an area close to Limoux, Mauzac also appears in sparkling wine, though there the result is not so favorable.

The least French sparkling wine produced in France, if I may put it like that, is the Clairette de Die, made from Mauzac grapes. This Rhône valley offshoot of the sparkling wine river is redolent of a Spumante and has something of the taste of Asti elderflower. The main producers in the region are Buffardel Frères and Achard-Vincent.

Recommended producers: Bouvet-Ladubay (Loire), Huet (Loire), Simonnet-Febvre (Chablis), Cave Bailly (Chablis), Domaine Deliance (Côte Chalonnaise), Henri Mugnier (Mâconnais), Roger Antech (Limoux).

THE SPARKLING WINES OF ITALY

Italy produces about as much sparkling wine annually as Champagne, but very few of the country's winemakers place sparkling wine at the top of their range. Yet Italy has more *appellations* for sparkling wine than any other nation. Spumante, as the Italians call their bubbly, is a party tipple for which less effort is expended than for the more "serious" reds. The great majority of Italy's sparkling wines are made using the Charmat method. The country's most famous sparkling wine, Asti Spumante from Piemonte, is often sugary, always musky, and with a scent of elderflower. The Muscat grape often leaves a pippy aftertaste. Personally, I am not one of those who confess to enjoying this exceedingly sweet wine. Lambrusco and Prosecco are two further horrors that this otherwise marvelous nation has on its conscience.

The wines from Trentino-Alto-Adidge in northernmost Italy can, on the other hand, be much more rewarding. The Trentino producer Ferrari is one of the most intriguing sparkling winemakers outside Champagne. Their Ferrari Brut is fine but expensive and not quite up to Champagne quality. Neither the vintage nor the réserve Giulio Ferrari Riserva has much to offer above and beyond the standard wine.

Italy's best sparkling wine—Franciacorta—is made in Lombardy, around Lake Iseo. The district, a D.O.C.G., is the only one where the *méthode champenoise* must be used in the production of all sparkling wine. Cà del Bosco produce well-structured and mineral-rich sparkling wines that are among the best outside Champagne. The most refined is the *curvée de prestige* Annamaria Clementi. Winemaker Maurizio Zanella cut his teeth at Moët & Chandon and utilizes oak barrels for his reserve wines. Apart from Pinot Noir and Chardonnay, the rather flat Pinot Blanc grape is often used. The main rival to Cà del Bosco is its neighbor, Bellavista, which produces a fine rosé and good, supple, vintage sparkling wine.

Umbria is an interesting wineland, containing an example (and the most elegant to date) of a sparkling wine combining Pinot Noir and Chardonnay in equal measure that is called Lungarotti. For reasons that must be obvious, nothing of interest in terms of sparkling wine haunts the pretty slopes of Tuscany. The only wine of the type of any note is Antinori Millesimato.

My opinion is that all these wines should be chilled slightly more than Champagne prior to drinking, as otherwise they have a tendency to become heavy.

Recommended producers: Cà del Bosco (Franciacorta), Bellavista (Franciacorta), Antinori (Tuscany), Lungarotti (Umbria), as well as Ferrari (Trentino).

SPANISH SPARKLING WINES

Spanish wines that have gone through the Champagne method are termed Cava, and the one thing they have in common is that they do not improve with laying down. The mature tones that a Cava develops with age are earthy and smoky, and the sad truth is that the wine's natural development unfortunately creates an aroma that tends to bring to mind a corked wine. For several years I thought that Spanish corks must be of particularly poor quality, but having tasted a great many Cavas of various ages, I am now of the opinion that the corky taste is inevitable in older wines. The Spanish climate is really far too warm to make sparkling wine, but despite this Cavas are popular in many parts of the world. Could this be due to the attractive bottles and the low price?

It is thought that the first sparkling wine from Spain was produced in 1862, and, from 1974 on, in volume terms at least, Spanish production has been viewed positively. The gigantic Freixenet company, which turns out 80 million bottles a year, has done a roaring trade with its Cordon Negro. This is presented in a lovely black bottle, though sadly the wine is by no means as enjoyable as its packaging. This is a syrupy wine that suffers from a repulsive chemically odor: half hair treatment half burnt plastic.

I have met with many serious-minded Spanish winemakers, but unfortunately they are faced with an intractable foe—the climate! Modern vinification techniques may keep the grape must fresher and fruitier than previously, but Spanish sparkling wines still possess that unwelcome earthy bouquet and taste, allied to a robust, raw, rather oily fruitiness.

In Catalonia, which totally dominates the Cava industry, the commonest grape is Parellada, although Macabeo and Xarel-Lo are also exploited. Many firms are experimenting with Chardonnay, and that may trim back its earthy character, but the warm climate still gives, at best, a "tutti-frutti" aroma.

Codorníu—the world's biggest producer of sparkling wine with (if you can credit it) 120 million bottles a year—also make an unpretentious but palatable Anna de Codorníu from a blend of local varieties and Chardonnay. However, the country's two heavy hitters, Codorníu and Freixenet, have to surrender to Segura Viudas when it comes to quality. This is the only producer in the country to have succeeded in making rich, complex wines, that have a hint of lemon. The autolytic character is unmistakable in all their wines, but at its best in the Reserva Heredad Brut.

Recommended producers: Segura Viudas.

GERMAN SPARKLING WINES

As I have said, Germany has been a preponderant influence on Champagne production. Among the best-known figures in Champagne who have German roots one might list Joseph Bollinger, Frederick Delbeck, William Deutz, Pierre Gelderman, Florens-Louis Heidsieck, Charles Koch, Johann-Josef Krug, Jean-Baptiste Lanson, Philipp Mumm, Louis Roederer, and Pierre Taittinger. The first German sparkling wines were probably made around the end of the eighteenth century; it was already realized at that time that competing with France in terms of quality was going to be impossible.

For this reason—and in the belief that this might produce more powerful wines—for a long period foreign grapes were added to the mixture. Regrettably, the Germans seemed to have had an inferiority complex about the low alcohol level of their sublime wines. Now, at last, they have begun to deal with this problem of alien varieties in sparkling wine.

Today almost all German sekt is actually made from grapes cultivated in Germany. Dreadful blends such as Henkell Trocken have given German sekt an undeserved reputation. Of course, most of the country's sparkling wines taste like sweet cider, but quality producers making sekt purely from Riesling grapes market a wine that may not show much resemblance to Champagne, but which is most enjoyable anyway.

Ten- to fifteen-year-old sekt wines from Rheingau Fürst von Metternich develop aromas all their own: petroleum with a touch of toffee and honeysuckle. The wines retain their freshness throughout aging, thanks to a high acid level in the Riesling. The much-vaunted Deinhard Lila usually turns out with an elderflower flavor, but they also produce a wonderful but absurdly expensive sparkling wine under the label of the famous Bernkasteler Doctor. Even though the wine is a far cry from Champagne, it is one of the best sparkling wines I have tasted outside Champagne.

One of my favorite wines of any type, the Eiswein, with its very fresh acidity and its sweetish, fruity taste, also exists as a sparkling wine. I have not yet had an opportunity to taste this rare and expensive wine, unfortunately. Kurt Schales, of the Rheinhasse, is the pioneer in this new production.

Recommended producers: Deinhard, Fürst von Metternich.

SPARKLING WINES FROM AUSTRIA AND EASTERN EUROPE

The Austrians should follow the German lead and use Riesling in their sparkling wines. Today, they are made mostly from Welschriesling and Grüner Veltliner, but neither of these grape varieties possesses the acidity level required for decent sparkling wines. Schlumberger is the biggest and best sekt house in Austria, and is one of the few producers to use the classic Champagne method to produce their wines.

Before the Russian Revolution, vast quantities of genuine Champagne were drunk in the country, and the tsar's fondness for sweet Champagne inspired many Russian winemaking districts to begin producing a sparkling wine called Shampanskoye. Then, as now, rivers of sweet, flat, mediocre tipple was produced, which Russians appeared to enjoy immeasurably. These wines' misleading reputation for quality might be explained by the fact that they were often served in conjunction with Russian caviar.

The Crimean peninsula is the site of some of Russia's finest vineyards, and Abrau Durso is judged by most observers to be the country's finest sparkling wine, as well as being one of the few to be made using the *méthode champenoise*. Georgia is the other important wine-producing region, but unfortunately it turns out unprepossessing, unpalatable wines. About as much sparkling wine is made in the former Soviet Union as is produced in Champagne, but the quality is hardly comparable. Even the Slovenian pear-flavored Zlata Radgonska Penina and Backarska Vodika make more of an impression than any sparkling wine from Russia that I've ever drunk.

SPARKLING WINES OF BRITAIN

The U.K. is without question one of the countries whose soil and climate—in certain places—would appear to bear the most similarities with Champagne. Personally speaking, I have always believed that it should be possible to produce very good sparkling wines on south-facing slopes in Wales or Sussex, for example. The climate of these regions is not unlike Champagne, and a very hot year should give fully ripened fruit with an exemplary acidity level, allowing the production of a very elegant sparkling wine. It would seem, however, that one is at the borderline here as regards temperature. I have the utmost respect for my British counterparts, and I took their word for it when they affirmed that Nyetimber was a wine of the

highest quality. Both times I have blind tasted this wine, however, I have described it as a simple sparkling wine, without finesse. Two explanations come to mind: either the judgment of these enologists has been swayed by economic forces, or the British are as patriotic about their wine as they are about their football teams—which are all too often hyped up, only to get knocked out of tournaments early on. British wine may well hold a surprise or two in store for us in the future, however. It should be remembered that sparkling wine was first produced in Britain only in 1976, and that it takes time to weed out the vins and aging varieties. For the moment, though, it looks more like "much ado about nothing." Still, the last few years have been pretty hot and seem promising....

AMERICAN SPARKLING WINES

About half of the states of the U.S.A. are home to a producer of sparkling wine, the most exotic example perhabs being Tedeschi Vineyard on Hawaii. After California, New York is the state that produces most sparkling wine. The first American semi-sparkling wine was produced in 1842 by Nicholas Longworth near Cincinnati, but it took a long time for sparkling wines to make inroads into the States. Moët & Chandon were roundly criticised when they established Domaine Chandon in Napa Valley. The French were frightened of the competition that the United States would bring in the long term, since they had already showed their mettle by producing rivals to red Bordeaux. The United States had, moreover, shamelessly abused the Champagne name: every other sparkling wine from California had previously emblazoned the term in capital letters on the label. As a matter of fact, this sleight of hand remains totally legal, since it is controlled by American legislation and no agreement to outlaw the practice between France and the United States has ever been ratified. Fortunately, most reputable producers have abandoned this silly practice.

It was the Chandon domain and a good American producer, Schramsberg, who instilled dynamism in the Californian sparkling wine market. In the 1980s, French know-how invaded the country, and several Champagne houses established themselves in the region. Piper-Sonoma started the ball rolling in 1980, followed by Maison Deutz in 1981, Roederer Estate in 1982, Mumm Napa Valley in 1985, and Taittinger's Domaine Carneros in 1987. Clicquot, Bollinger, Laurent-Perrier, and Pommery have interests in large American concerns.

Today, the lion's share of Californian producers strive to imitate Champagne, and without doubt it is the American copies that come closest to the real thing. Moët & Chandon's special variety of yeast is in common use, and the method of vinification is almost identical to that in Champagne. In order to recreate the original as closely as possible, the grapes are picked only partially ripe so that the acidity level holds up. This is a hard trick to pull off, however. Lately many disadvantages to this approach have been discovered, even when sugar and acidity levels appear to be satisfactory, since underripe grapes lack the qualities that confer complexity and depth on a wine. Moreover, if the harvest is held too early, the level of maltic acid in the grapes (relative to the same level of acidity as fruit in Champagne) is much too high. In consequence, those wines that are sufficiently acidic are at the same time too green and insufficiently ripe. It seems that the only means of attaining reasonable results is to use almost ripe grapes that have been entirely or partially grown in the cool.

The harvest usually takes place in the chilliest hours of the night. In addition to this precaution, during the winemaking process it is crucial to curtail oxidation, and to take care that fermentation also occurs in the coolest possible environment. The Chardonnay grapes that grow in California can easily become heavy, so only the most temperate zones of the state are suitable for sparkling wine. Anderson Valley and Potter Valley seem to present the most favorable conditions, and the Roederer Estate in Anderson Valley makes the most Champagne-like sparkling wines. They are not just like a French wine, they do actually resemble Louis Roederer Brut Premier very closely. Only a slightly strained chocolate tone—which emerges when the glass warms up—betrays the wine's place of origin. In recent years, the wines of this estate have improved still more, and the Ermitage *cuvée de prestige* vintage is truly exceptional, exotically fruity with an eminently Champagne elegance.

Other European wine companies have also followed in French footsteps: the Chianti producer Antinori works with Bollinger, and the two Spanish giants Cordoniu and Freixenet of course own land in the area too.

Apart from Roederer Estate, two local firms produce a fine sparkling wine. Forrest Tancer at Iron Horse is very proud of its dry and tartly acid wines. Both the vintage wines and the Blanc de Blancs are neat and elegant. The other wholly American competitor to the Roederer Estate is the pioneering house of Schramsberg in Napa Valley. Their wines are more controversial than the other top-flight wines, as they are much fuller and more powerful. They call themselves the "American Krug," and employ in-oak fermentation and a lengthy maturing period before *dégorgement.* As with many American producers, they use brandy in the dosage. Schramsberg's Cuvée de Pinot is a great sparkling wine in years when the acidity is high enough, but I for one have yet to detect any similarities with Krug.

One unusual, intriguing, and tasty wine, is the sparkling Sauvignon Cabernet by a producer with Swedish roots, Sjoeblooms Estate. This has cedar flavors and a true autolytic character. Washington State and Oregon have not for the moment produced any remarkable sparkling wines, although objectively speaking, the conditions there appear superior to those in California. On the other hand, certain properties on the East Coast seem promising, in particular the sleek, sparkling wines of Fingers Lake, together with some other auspicious-looking projects near Charlottesville, Virginia, where the still wines tend to lack body. I would also advise you to keep an eye on wines coming out of the Kluge Estate, home of Patricia Kluge. She is someone determined to produce the best sparkling wine on the continent.

Recommended producers: Roederer Estate, Iron Horse, Schramsberg.

AUSTRALIAN AND NEW ZEALAND SPARKLING WINES

In the northern zones of New Zealand's South Island and in eastern parts of the North, the climate should be practically ideal for the production of sparkling wine. The grapes grown there naturally show a high level of acidity and fine balance. As New Zealand is such a young winemaking country, many potentially exceptional winemakers are still feeling their way. Only over the last twenty years have classic grape varieties been planted, and it was not before 1988, when Deutz and Montana started to work in tandem, that the unquestionable potential of the country was finally taken seriously.

The star player among New Zealand wines is Cloudy Bay Pelorus. This wine is exotic, acidulous, and fruity, with an agreeably roasted character. The French Champagne house Veuve Clicquot is one of the joint owners of the domain, but it keeps a low profile. In 1980, a man from Champagne named Daniel Le Brun set up a much-vaunted estate famous for its production of the best sparkling wines, the only ones to bear comparison with Champagne. Unfortunately I have not yet had the opportunity of tasting these. They make superb Chardonnay wines—comparable to Burgundies—at the Morton estate, and the sparkling wines augur well too. With the exception of Pelorus, the best results have been achieved by producers using a lot of Chardonnay in their *cuvées.*

Compared to New Zealand, Australia has come a lot further in wine production. The earliest sparkling wine in Australia was made in 1843. Just as in the United States, several Champagne houses have interests in Australia. Bollinger's cooperation with the legendary winemaker Brian Croser at Petaluma is a highly successful venture. Today Petaluma produces, together with Pelorus, the best sparkling wines in the Southern Hemisphere. Moët & Chandon produce more effective wines in Australia than in the United States; one example is its rich and intensely fruity Green Point. Seaview too produces excellent sparkling wines in a more traditional and tempered style. Those after a rich and powerful oak-style "New World" wine should absolutely taste one of the staggering vintages of Yalumba. The first sparkling wine to be made in Australia using the traditional *méthode champenois* was Seppelt's Great Western Show Champagne. It is generally known as Australia's Bollinger R. D. as it kept on the lees for at least ten years.

Tasmania, with its cool climate, might also prove favorable area for producing sparkling wines, or at least that was Roederer's opinion when setting up Jansz, though the estate was later dropped in 1994.

Recommended producers: Pelorus (New Zealand), Morton Estate (New Zealand), Seaview (Australia), Petaluma (Australia), Green Point (Australia).

OTHER SPARKLING WINES

A respectable amount of sparkling wine is made in a number of unexpected countries around the world.

Canada's cool climate would seem adapted to sparkling wines, but so far no really thrilling dry wines have emerged. The great masters of sweet wines, Château des Charmes and Inniskillin, are, however, making great strides with their experiments in sparkling wine.

Moët & Chandon are very active in South America, and wines under the appellation "M. Chandon" are made in both Brazil and Argentina. One wonders how many brows have furrowed on drinking a "M. Chandon" in the belief that it is genuine Champagne....

South Africa is another wine-growing country that is worthy of interest; it has been producing sparkling wines since 1929. The first sparkling wine produced according to the Champagne method appeared only in 1971, when Simonsig brought out its Kaapse Vonkel wine. In South Africa sealed tanks are employed for the most part in producing sparkling wines. The wine called Cape Classique is a simple fruity wine, but one which is constantly improving. In my own country, Pongrácz, a Bergkelder wine with a bready character and abundant foam, is much appreciated. Unfortunately, once in the glass this wine tends to become heavy, and it has to be drunk well chilled. Another highly regarded wine is Cape Cuvée, produced by Twee Jongegezellen for Mumm. This is a wine I not yet been lucky enough to find. All in all, it should be borne in mind that advances in wine production in South Africa appear to be very much on the cards.

The most famous winemaker in Spain, Miguel Torres, has just launched a palatable sparkling wine from Chile, while it is Concha y Torro that are the leading Spanish producers.

The most interesting wine from the Rest of the World must definitely be Omar Khayham (formerly Marquise de Pompadour), which is made in India. With the help of the Champagne house Piper-Heidsieck, they have produced a fresh and well-balanced sparkling wine from Ugni Blanc, Pinot Blanc, and Chardonnay grapes. The torrid climate in the Maharashtra area outside Bombay makes for a tough opponent that is countered with hi-tech and French know-how. The grapes are picked at night to avoid the effects of the boiling-hot sun.

Sparkling wine is even being made up in the far north of Europe, in Scandinavian countries, although most is made from low-quality grapes bought in from southern climes. Some are fruit wines made from apples or elderflower.

A list of various other countries producing sparkling wine worthy of mention might include: The Netherlands, Luxembourg, Hungary, Romania, Bulgaria, Czech Republic, Greece, Portugal, Switzerland, Malta, Turkey, Israel, Mexico, Colombia, Peru, Bolivia, Venezuela, Kenya, Zimbabwe, China, and Japan.

THE TWENTY BEST SPARKLING WINES

1. Roederer Estate L'Ermitage, California	11. Iron Horse Sonoma Green Valley, California
2. Roederer Estate Anderson Valley Brut, California	12. Schramsberg Napa Valley Brut, California
3. Iron Horse Blanc de Blancs, California	13. Bellavista Brut, Italy
4. Schramsberg Blanc de Noirs, California	14. Petaluma Croser Brut, Australia
5. Iron Horse Vrais Amis, California	15. Tresor, Loire
6. Bernkasteler Doctor Sekt, Moselle	16. Roederer Estate Rosé, California
7. Annamaria Clementi Brut, Italy	17. Ruban Mauve Cremant de Bourgogne
8. Kluge Estate Brut, Virginia	18. Simonnet-Febre Blanc de Blancs, Chablis
9. Pelorus, New Zealand	19. Cuvée Saint Laurent, Limoux
10. Ca del Bosco Brut, Italy	20. Cave Bailly Blanc de Noirs, Burgundy

Champagne winelands

Towns and villages of the Champagne region

In this part of the book, I provide detailed descriptions of the various villages and vine-growing areas. It also incorporates a classification of each village on the vintage scale, describes the surface area of the vineyards, how the various varieties are distributed, as well as their geographical position. You will also find information on the number of growers making their own product in each village and, in certain cases, on those best able to bring out the character of the growths in their wines. These villages are arranged, not according to their place on the vintage scale or geographical position, but in alphabetical order. It may well be that a large number of readers will be satisfied to flick through this section of the book, preferring to consult it like a dictionary in order to glean something about a producer or the village he comes from. It is absolutely fine if you want to proceed in that way, but if you really want to become an expert and understand why wines can taste so different, this part of the book is essential reading. The importance of *encépagement* for top-flight French wines can never be stressed enough, particularly at a time when the wine-growing world is going through a move to standardization and internationalization that has resulted in the production of fruity, over-explosive wines with exaggerated oaky notes, and excessively marked by the sorts of characteristics demanded by larger wine-producers. A true Champagne-lover must be able to grasp distinctions between Champagnes of great class originating from neighboring villages such as Avize, Cramant, and Le Mesnil. And if tasting remains the best means of gaining all-round knowledge, the task is made easier if you know in advance that most connoisseurs discover fruity and dominant apple aromas in the wines of Avize, find the wines of Cramant to be creamy, fat, and have a milky-toffee taste, while those of Le Mesnil are stony, mineral, full of nuances, and of impressive complexity. In other words, the following pages, which may appear somewhat arid, are well worth trying to absorb.

Few Champagne houses have vines on the doorstep as they do here at Jacquesson in Dizy.

Ambonnay | 100 %

Ambonnay is one of the largest *grand cru* villages, with 383 hectares under vine.

Today many growers are members of the village cooperative, although this does not prevent them from retailing their own Champagne in small quantities. Some of the best vineyards in the village are owned by R. Coutier, H. Billiot, Soutiran-Pelletier; there are also great *maisons* like Moët, Clicquot, Mumm, and Taittinger. It is above all the *cuvées* that make the greatness of Ambonnay. Their sweetish, oily, but slightly neutral taste is something of an intermediary between, for example, highly aromatic Pinot d'Aÿ and Chardonnay d'Avize, consummately elegant and acidic. In itself Ambonnay seldom reaches the level of the pure Blancs de Noirs at Aÿ and Verzenay. Following the example of Sillery and Bouzy, the wines of Ambonnay gain much when left in contact with the oak barrels. Unfortunately, today there is only one winemaker utilizing oak. Anyone harboring doubts as to whether oak barrels impart greater complexity to Pinot wines should sample Krug's Ambonnay. Geographically and geologically, Ambonnay is an eastward prolongation of the Bouzy vineyard. The best slopes face southeast and are located to the northwest of this picturesque village with narrow streets. As in the Bouzy vineyards, quality varies widely. The best grapes are picked at an altitude of from 150 to 180 meters (492 to 590 ft.). Unfortunately for us Champagne amateurs, too many of these grapes are used to make the still red wine, Ambonnay Rouge. Area under vine: 80% PN, 20% CH.

Arconville | 80%

A winegrowing village of fifty hectares located ten kilometers to the south of Bar-sur-Aube.
Area under vine: 90% PN, 5% PM, 5% CH.

Avenay | 93%

As with many other villages in the Marne valley, the land hereabouts has acquired its name from the nearby village of Avenay. The quality is that of a very superior *premier cru*, especially along the belt of southern slopes planted at an altitude between 140 and 180 meters (459 and 590 ft.). The resemblance to the round and velvety Vin d'Avenay is striking. It is an important village for Bollinger, Gosset, Mumm, Henriot, Philipponnat, and Pommery.
Area under vine: 73% PN, 15% PM, 12% CH.

Avirey-Lingey | 80%

This village is situated in the southwest of the region of Aube to the northwest of Les Riceys.
Area under vine: 90% PN, 10% CH.

Avize | 100%

The Avize slopes are planted entirely with Chardonnay. The grapes from the steep slopes provide better and more delicate wines, but, in blending, the slightly more robust specimens from the relatively flat terrain lower down in the village hold their own. Essentially, Avize produces rather more powerful wines than the slightly more fragrant ones from Cramant or Le Mesnil. The village does not abound in outstanding, first-class growers in the same way as those villages. Besides the extraordinary Anselme Selosse, the best wines in the village are made by the larger houses. Jacquesson D. T. is a pure Avize product, testifying to the powerful style of the village in its highly concentrated form. The nutty and roasted aromas are not to be found among its neighbors, leaning more to chocolate, leather, and truffles, and improving with age. One often finds a high percentage of Avize Chardonnay in famous prestige Champagnes produced by the larger houses. The acreage is 455 hectares (1124 acres) and supplies a touch more than 1 million bottles per year.
Area under vine: 100% CH

Aÿ | 100%

Aÿ—pronounced [Ai]—was already well known in the region long before effervescent wines were made here. Innumerable kings and popes expressed a preference for the vin d'Aÿ. Today the town, with its 14,000 inhabitants, houses nineteen more-or-less celebrated Champagne houses and about fifty growers producing wine. The vineyards are located on the steep slopes of the Bois de Charlefontaine, a village on the banks of the Marne. The best plots are sheltered from the wind, just above the town, and benefit from maximum exposure to the sun. It includes several areas providing a base for the wines by Bollinger, Deutz, Gosset, Krug, Fliniaux, and Laurain. Anselme Selosse, the expert in Chardonnay, has access to the plots close to the Côte des Enfants belonging to Bollinger, from which it produces a Blanc de Noirs fermented in oak barrels. The Aÿ Pinot Noir is an inimitable combination of purity in aroma, richness in taste, and velvety structure.
Area under vine: 86% PN, 4% PM, 10% CH.

Bagneux-la-Fosse | 80%

Five growers and several *maisons* share the 129 hectares (319 acres) of this village.
Area under vine: 99% PN, 1% CH.

Balnot-sur-Laignes | 80%

This village lies thirty-four kilometers (twenty-one miles) southeast of Bar-sur-Aube (80 percent on the vintage scale), where the majority of the inhabitants are involved to a greater or lesser extent with the Gremillet Champagne house.
Area under vine: 90% PN, 10% CH.

Bar-sur-Aube | 80%

A town of 7,000 inhabitants located 200 kilometers (120 miles) to the southeast of Paris and fifty-two kilometers (thirty-two miles) east of Troyes. The town stands on the right bank of the Aube and can be viewed from the magnificent wooded hills thereabouts. The medieval town contains many curiosities, such as the church of Saint Maclou, as well as many charming small stone dwellings.
Area under vine: 75% PN, 17% PM, 8% CH.

Bar-sur-Seine | 80%

All the growers of the village work under the umbrella of the Union Auboise cooperative (Devaux). Bar-sur-Seine is the second-largest town in Aube.
Area under vine: 68% PN, 3% PM, 29% CH.

Beaumont-sur-Vesle | 00%

The twenty-eight hectares of cultivable surface of this village are on the plain and do not deserve the status of a *grand cru*. The wines here are lightweight. The village borders on the least suitable, larger plots under cultivation at Verzenay, a fact that it has turned to its advantage —as Sillery and Puisieulx have done too. Today, the terrain is mostly cultivated by growers who sell their grapes on to larger houses. There are only three producers in the village: a pretty modest number.
Area under vine: 95% PN, 5% CH.

Bergères-les-Vertus | 95%

[95% CH, 90% PN]
This village forms the southern tip of the Côte des Blancs. Just as at Vertus, part of the soil is too rich and fertile, giving slightly coarse and fruitier wines. A surprisingly high percentage of Pinot Noir (5 percent) is grown here, just as at Vertus. There are no well-known producers here, but the grapes are used by several respectable houses.
Area under vine: 5% PN, 95% CH.

Bethon | 5%

[85% PN, 87% CH]
A village of high classification in the district of Sézanne. Considered by many as the best of the region. Almost entirely dominated by the Le Brun de Neuville cooperative.
Area under vine: 20% PN, 80% CH.

Bezannes | 90%

[90%, revaluated in 1985]
A little-known village standing two kilometers southwest of Reims. Twelve wretched hectares (thirty acres) furnishing Chardonnay alone and sold to Champagne houses.
Area under vine: 100% CH.

Billy-le Grand | 95%

Billy-le-Grand ("Billy the Great") sounds more like a cowboy in a Western than the name of a Champagne village. Curiously, in this village on the Montagne de Reims, they grow mostly Chardonnay. The wine produced there is regarded as reminiscent of that from the nearby village of Vaudemanges. Personally, I have never tasted Champagne from Billy-le-Grand.
Area under vine: 25% PN, 75% CH.

Bisseuil | 95%

Bisseuil lies to the east of Mareuil-sur-Aÿ and Avenay. An unjustly forgotten village that is redolent more of Hautvillers or Cumières than Aÿ or Bouzy, though geographically speaking these are closer. Rich, not especially complex, fruity wines are produced here; these can best be savored in Champagnes by Chauvet and Tours-sur-Marne. They contain a very high percentage of Pinot Noir coming from the best slopes at Bisseuil. Like Charbaut, even Bollinger has some vineyards there. Analyses made in the barrel show that the acidity of Bisseuil wine appears less noticeable than for villages close by. The precocious mature style of the Chauvet makes me skeptical as to its suitability for aging.
Area under vine: 80% PN, 20% CH.

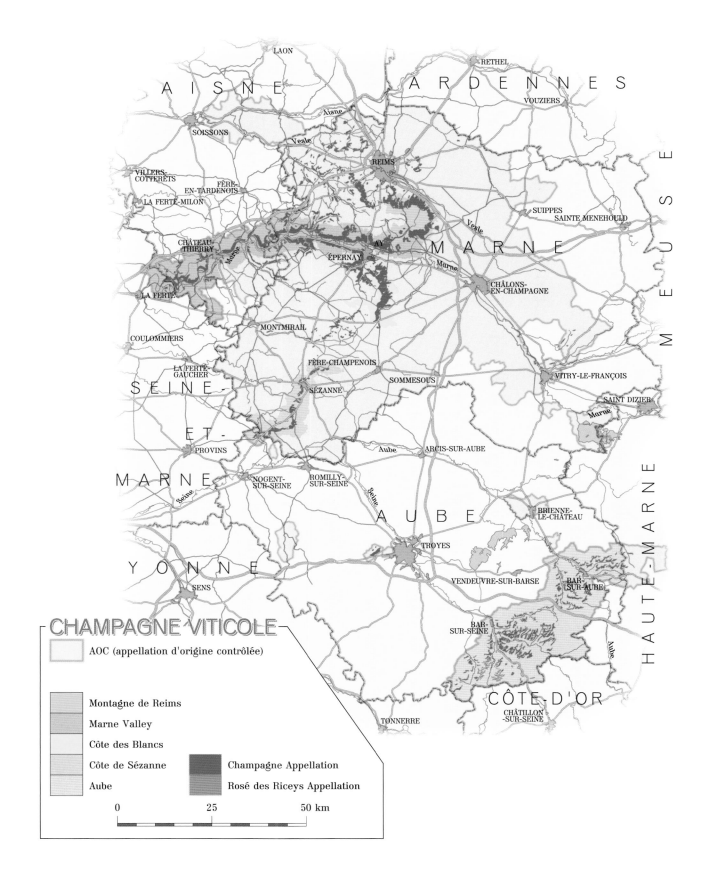

CHAMPAGNE VITICOLE

AOC (appellation d'origine contrôlée)

Montagne de Reims
Marne Valley
Côte des Blancs
Côte de Sézanne
Aube

Champagne Appellation
Rosé des Riceys Appellation

0   25   50 km

Bligny | 80%

A village in Aube known for being the setting for some of the finest châteaux in Champagne.
Area under vine: 81% PN, 5% PM,14% CH.

Bouilly | 86%

Two growers alone produce 60,000 bottles out of fifty hectares (124 acres) under vine.
Area under vine: 18% PN, 72% PM, 10% CH.

Boursault | 84%

The *commune* of Boursault is best known for the beautiful Château de Boursault, a fairy-tale castle very like the château at Ussé in the Loire Valley. The domain was formerly the property of the Veuve (widow) Clicquot and is today the Champagne house of the same name.
Area under vine: 26% PN, 67% PM, 7% CH.

Bouzy | 100%

Bouzy, with its 380 hectares (940 acres), is one of the best-known Champagne villages. It owes its reputation partly to a still red wine produced by growers such as Paul Bara, Clouet, and Georges Vesselle, which can recall anything from a slightly insipid Beaujolais to a magnificent Burgundy. The variable quality in this village is even more apparent in the grapes used in sparkling wines. The reason is to be found in both the geological conditions and the declivity of the terrain. The cultivable area is divided into three bands. The one farther north and highest up produces excellent *grand cru* grapes that furnish wines with a juicy fruitiness and great depth. The central zone gives wines with peachy aromas, but they lack the concentration obtained from the topmost vineyards. The vineyards on the plain around the village tend to the tasteless; they are fragrant with a slack structure and lack vigor. Even if Bouzy is an overrated village, it is nonetheless *grande classe*. Virtually all the greatest Champagne houses own or purchase grapes from the southern slopes of this village for their *cuvées de prestige*.
Area under vine: 88% PN, 1% PM, 11% CH.

Breuil, Le | 83%

Le Breuil shelters within its borders one of the greatest concerns in the west of the Marne valley, Jean Moutardier. As with the majority of villages in Aisne, it grows the extremely sturdy Meunier grape. Le Breuil is located on a tributary of the Marne called Surmelin.
Area under vine: 10% PN, 87% PM, 3% CH.

Brouillet | 85%

The total area of the *commune* is 430 hectares (1060 acres), but only seventy hectares (170 acres) are under vine. The village stands twenty-two kilometers (fourteen miles) from Reims and is home to four producers.
Area under vine: 20% PN, 60% PM, 20% CH.

Buxeuil | 80%

Buxeuil, with its fine stone-built church, is situated in the very heart of Aube. There are nine producing growers in the village, as well as a Champagne house.
Area under vine: 90% PN, 1% PM, 9% CH.

Celles-sur-Ource | 85%

An important village in Aube with fifty producers. It is to be found twenty-nine kilometers (eighteen miles) southeast of Bar-sur-Aube.
Area under vine: 85% PN, 10% PM, 5% CH.

Cerseuil

The village is not classified and possesses no vineyards, but it does have two Champagne houses, with S. A. Dehours the most famous, belonging to the Frey group.

Châlons-en-Champagne | 98%

Châlons-en-Champagne used to be an important town in Champagne. Today, there are only two Champagne houses there, and even the nearest vineyard stands rather far away. The history of Châlons is particularly rich, and there are many Roman remains in the city. In the Middle Ages, Châlons was the capital of Champagne. Today, minds are focused on things other than bubbly drinks—mainly on the flourishing food industry. The price of Champagne may be slightly lower here than in the more touristy cities of Épernay and Reims. The restaurants are undoubtedly cheaper and of high quality. A visit to Hôtel d'Angleterre is a must!

Chamery | 90%

Chamery stands to the west of the heartlands of the Montagne de Reims. This side of the Nationale 51 trunk-road does not produce great wine. The reason is that there is not enough sunlight to make the grapes as rich in extract as those that are grown on the east side of the road. During the 1985

reclassification, Chamery rosé from 88 percent to 90 percent. A convincing argument for the diversity of Champagne is that fifty-two producers work out of this relatively little-known village.
Area under vine: 27% PN, 55% PM, 18% CH.

Champillon | 93%

The village is known especially for its first-class restaurant, the Royal Champagne. It is located on the summit of a hill, with sublimely beautiful vineyards stretching out below at its feet. On several occasions traveling around the region, my intrepid companions and I treated ourselves to a bottle of Champagne while getting our breath back amid all the vines. The panoramic view over Épernay and the ocean of vines offers much food for thought. In this place, more than in any other, one feels part of a whole. The vines are planted at altitudes of from 120 to 250 meters (394 to 820 ft.). The grapes are exposed south–southeast and are generally among the fastest maturing in all Champagne. Their quality reaches the level of a very great *premier cru*. Alas, growers stubbornly persist in cultivating far too much Pinot Meunier. The best plots are the property of Louis Roederer (Pinot Noir), though Mercier and Oudinot also have vineyards here. Many firms purchase grapes from the forty-eight growers in the village.
Area under vine: 45% PN, 47% PM, 8% CH.

Charly-sur-Marne | 80%

Lying thirteen kilometers (8 miles) to the southeast of Château-Thierry to the west of the Marne Valley.
Area under vine: 5% PN, 85% PM, 10% CH.

Château-Thierry | 80%

Château-Thierry is the county town of the western Marne valley, halfway between Paris and Reims. Its 16,000 inhabitants therefore find themselves cut off from the main Champagne region. The city still has remains from the Roman era; it suffered much in the two World Wars.
Area under vine: 14% PN, 78% PM, 8% CH.

Châtillon-sur-Marne | 83%

Located eighteen kilometers to the northwest of Épernay, thirteen growers tend an acreage under vine of 250 hectares (618 acres).
Area under vine: 20% PN, 60% PM, 20% CH.

Chaumuzy | 83%

Eighteen kilometers (eleven miles) to the north of Épernay, the village covers seventy-seven hectares. Beside the local cooperative, there are fifteen growers cultivating solely Pinot Meunier.
Area under vine: 1% PN, 98% PM, 1% CH.

Chavot | 88%

Located to the south of Pierry. From the first-class restaurant "La Briqueterie" in Vinay just outside Épernay, one can gaze on the splendid stone church of Chavot, which stands rather surprisingly among the vineyards. The church is known for miles around, but the Champagnes of the village have a lower profile.
Area under vine: 5% PN, 65% PM, 30% CH.

Chenay | 84%

No satisfactory vineyard exists north of Reims. As there is a ceaseless push to produce more Champagne, the agricultural zone is continually expanding. A hundred years ago, villages located north of Reims produced negligible volumes, but quantities have since shot up dramatically. The notoriety of Chenay is due to Comte Audoin de Dampierre, a charismatic figure who possesses an estate and Champagne house there.

Chigny-les-Roses | 94%

The splendid rose gardens gave this village its current name at the beginning of the last century; it was previously known simply as Chigny. This is one of the best *premier cru* villages where, moreover, there are many talented growers. Its situation on the northern slopes of the Montagne de Reims should mean it has perfect growing conditions for Pinot grapes alone. But in my opinion, Chigny-les-Roses is the only village where Pinot and Chardonnay display the same high quality. Neither the white nor the black grapes reach *grand cru* level, but readily achieve a relatively high *premier cru* status. This affords growers the potential to produce good vintages, although these will be mono-*cru* Champagnes. The wines can never be as powerful and rich as those from the nearby village of Mailly. As regards balance and charm, though, Chigny is seldom exceeded.
Area under vine: 20% PN, 65% PM, 15% CH.

Chouilly | 100%

[100% CH, 95% PN]
It should be noted that Chouilly is one of the villages to have different classes of vintage for Pinot Noir and Chardonnay. In truth, this is of limited importance, since the proportion of Pinot grown here is no more than 2 percent. The best sites in the village are on the edges of Cramant, and many growers own land

in both villages. A narrow strip on the southern slope of the Butte de Saran is of very high quality and supplies grapes resembling those of Cramant. But in Chouilly, quality remains highly variable. Most of the 498 hectares (1230 acres) in the village stand on the plain, making for rather ordinary Chardonnay. In my opinion, Chouilly is a notch below Avize, Cramant, Oger, and Le Mesnil. Many Chouilly wines show clear almond notes. Only exceptionally do Champagnes from this village possess the character of roasted notes or walnut. They are generally rougher and have more body than their more famous neighbors. The village contains sixty-eight producing growers, and several Champagne houses are proud to own land at Chouilly. Pol Roger, Moët, and Roederer all use a significant percentage of Chouilly grapes. Area under vine: 2% PN, 98% CH.

Coligny | 90%

[90% CH, 87% PN]
This little-known village lies in the southwest of the Côte des Blancs. The vineyards, for the most part, are located on the plain, and should never have been raised to *premier cru* level in 1985. Area under vine: 10% PN, 90% CH.

Colombé-le-Sec | 80%

Situated eight kilometers (five miles) to the northeast of Bar-sur-Aube with an area of 120 hectares (297 acres). Area under vine: 80% PN, 10% PM, 10% CH.

Courteron | 80%

[93% PN, 1% PM, 6% CH]
This village in Aube has twenty-four growers over sixty-seven hectares (166 acres).

Cramant | 100%

Cramant is perhaps the most beautiful village in the Côte des Blancs. It lies in rolling country with marvelous views over the Château de Saran, the prestigious estate of Moët. The village itself is surrounded by a sea of Chardonnay vines. Exposure is to the southeast. The plots immediately to the south of the village towards Avize, like those on the slopes down from the Château de Saran at Chouilly, supply some of the finest Champagne grapes. The wines enjoy a bouquet that is exceeded only at Le Mesnil and exude a marvelous caramely taste. Among the merits of this village, one of the most noteworthy is the even quality of its wines. It is no rare thing to encounter a poor Champagne at Le Mesnil, but, to date, I have never drunk a poor wine

from Cramant. The wine there matures earlier than in the nearby villages, but it also preserves its high quality for a long time. In addition to Diebolt, Bonnaire, Lilbert, and Sugot-Feneuil, and some others, the greater Champagne houses also possess the highest-rated plots at Cramant. The vineyards of Perrier-Jouët all enjoy a fine reputation, but Moët, Taittinger, Clicquot, Laurent-Perrier, Pol Roger, Oudinot, Mercier, Pommery, and Mumm also own sizeable plots under vine. Area under vine: 100% CH

Cuchery | 84%

[13% PN, 83% PM, 4% CH]
This village in the Marne valley is very much dominated by Meunier and supports no less than ninety-one growers over a large surface area of 137 hectares (339 acres).

Cuis | 95%

This excellent *premier cru* village lies northwest of Cramant. Bollinger's réserve proves that the best plots can produce wines of a great elegance. The best vines are to be found planted at an altitude of from 160 to 200 meters (525 to 656 ft.). Generally it can be said that the wines of Cuis are a little more powerful than those in Cramant, but with a less refined bouquet. Bollinger owns the best sites, with Pol Roger and Moët not far behind. Among the smaller producers here are Larmandier and Gimonnet. Area under vine: 1% PN, 9% PM, 90% CH.

Cumières | 93%

The village is extremely famous for its red Coteaux Champenois which, in my opinion, frequently outranks Bouzy Rouge. Cumières could very well have become a *grand cru*, if the percentage of Pinot Meunier were lower. Its south-facing slopes give the fastest maturing grapes in all Champagne. Pascal Leclerc from Leclerc-Briant at Épernay is one winemaker who appreciates the greatness of Cumières. Today he produces three fantastic Vins de Clos, imbued with the splendid personality of this village. The best grapes grow at altitudes ranging generally between 50 and 150 meters (164 and 492 ft.), and give fruity and well-structured wines that can outperform many a *grand cru* Champagne. In addition to Leclerc-Briant, the houses with vineyards here include Joseph Perrier, Moët, and Roederer. Area under vine: 47% PN, 39% PM, 14% CH.

Damery | 89%

Damery should absolutely be classified as a *premier cru*. The village has suffered, as has its neighbor Cumières, from the fact that such a significant part of its vine-growing area is occupied by Pinot Meunier. Some of the 352 hectares (870 acres) are located on steep slopes giving rise to very vigorous Pinot grapes that mature well in the sun. Damery is in fact a significant Champagne village embracing ninety-two growers and eleven Champagne houses. Area under vine: 19% PN, 72% PM, 9% CH.

Dizy | 95%

This tipsy-sounding village is located in the heart of the Marne valley. Bordering on Aÿ, the king of Pinot, it shows a singular resemblance to it in character. The vines grow at an altitude from 100 to 200 meters (328 to 656 ft.) and are exposed southwest. The sites near Aÿ are those with the best grapes. One of my favorite *premier cru* villages.
Area under vine: 29% PN, 41% PM, 30% CH.

Écueil | 90%

This Pinot village is located seven kilometers to the southwest of Reims. Interesting for its historic past.
Area under vine: 85% PN, 5% PM, 10% CH.

Épernay | 88%

Practically everyone living in Épernay has some link to the Champagne industry. The town boasts twenty-five Champagne houses with Moët, Pol Roger, Perrier-Jouët, and Mercier being the best known. The majority are located along the imposing Avenue de Champagne, and Moët & Chandon stands close to the town obelisk. The fact is that Épernay can be proud of the vineyards that lie immediately outside the town, which get 88 percent on the vintage scale. These 222 hectares (549 acres) are owned by the Champagne houses and twenty-six producing growers.

Etoges | 85%

Located twenty-five kilometers (sixteen miles) to the south of Épernay, Etoges contains eighty-six hectares (212 acres) of vineyard.
Area under vine: 7% PN, 72% PM, 21% CH.

Etréchy | 90%

Situated thirty kilometers (nineteen miles) south of Épernay outside Côte des Blancs. It is the smallest of the *premier cru* villages. No Champagnes are produced with grapes solely from Etréchy.
Area under vine: 100% CH.

Festigny | 84%

I am truly nonplussed as to why wine writers systematically seem to forget this village. In style it is entirely reminiscent of its neighbor, Leuvrigny.
Area under vine: 4% PN, 95% PM, 1% CH.

Fontette | 80%

Fontette lies in the middle of Aube and features only two producers: a minor grower and a *maison*, Cristian Senez.
Area under vine: 80% PN, 20% CH.

Grauves | 95%

[95% CH, 90% PN /PM]
A very good village located to the west of Avize. The best slopes lie at an altitude of 220 meters (722 ft.), exposed eastwards. The village has a reputation for the heaviest wines of Chardonnay and most full-bodied of all the Côte des Blancs. The most significant landowner is Bollinger, which uses Chardonnay grapes best adapted to the virile style of its wines. Other houses with land at Grauves include Moët and Pol Roger. My best Champagne ever is from Grauves.
Area under vine: 1% PN, 15% PM, 84% CH.

Gueux | 85%

[8% PN, 89% PM, 3% CH]
With its automobile racetrack and glorious golf course, Gueux has space for only eighteen hectares of vineyards shared between nine growers at Petite Montagne.

Gyé-sur-Seine | 84%

A village close to Buxeuil in the south of Aube. There are 202 hectares (499 acres) here, mostly Pinot. Four Champagne houses account for two-thirds of the 350,000 bottles the village produces each year. The remainder falls to sixteen grower-producers.
Area under vine: 94% PN, 2% PM, 4% CH.

Hautvillers | 93%

To the northeast of Cumières stands Hautvillers, in some ways

the cradle of Champagne. The pretty monastery where Dom Pérignon lived is still there and bestows a particularly historical atmosphere on the village. The vineyards spread over slopes around the village in various directions, and their quality is variable. Obviously enough, its fame derives from the wine of Dom Pérignon, though in fact his wines were made with grapes from many villages. I have tasted the still wines of Hautvillers in cask on several occasions, but never a Champagne solely from Hautvillers. The wines are not on a par with those from Cumières and Dizy.
Area under vine: 34% PN, 53% PM, 13% CH.

Janvry | 85%

Janvry is located north of Petite Montagne. A village where eight growers and two cooperatives divide the thirty-five hectares (eighty-seven acres) between them.
Area under vine: 20% PN, 75% PM, 5% CH.

Jouy-les-Reims | 90%

These south-facing slopes beside Villedommange obtained *premier cru* status in 1985.
Area under vine: 23% PN, 68% PM, 9% CH.

Landreville | 80%

A village in Aube dominated by the Dufour family.
Area under vine: 80% PN, 20% CH.

Leuvrigny | 84%

The charm of this magical village on a shady bank of the Marne has been incorporated as a significant element in the majestic Krug Champagnes. The very special clone that grows there indisputably gives a Pinot Meunier wine with a unique nose and excellent aging capacity. The flavor of the grapes in this village strongly recalls apricot and violet. Because of the northern exposure of the vineyards, the grapes mature more slowly. For this reason, acidity is higher and aging potential can improve. It should be pointed out, however, that the grapes that Krug uses are ruthlessly selected and come from very old vines. The special oak-barrel treatment, and the fact that malolactic fermentation is avoided, contributes much to its peerless qualities. Other still wines that I have been able to taste from this village have not had the same exceptional character.
Area under vine: 8% PN, 90% PM, 2% CH.

Louvois | 100%

The vineyards of Louvois are located in a sizable clearing, which is a rarity. It is astonishing to stare out on rows of vine along the slopes on the edge of the woods. The village is remote and, although classified *grand cru*, its wines are not particularly well known. During work on this book, the majority of people with whom I discussed the subject agreed that this village should not be classified *grand cru*. That may be true, but the tasting of the still wines impressed me a lot. From the geological point of view, Louvois and Bouzy arise from the same folding of the earth's crust. Louvois lies at the westernmost point of the Bois des Dames. Today, eighteen winemakers cultivate vines over the village's forty-one hectares. The Champagne houses owning most land here are Bollinger, Clicquot, Roederer, and Laurent-Perrier.
Area under vine: 90% PN, 10% CH.

Ludes | 94%

This village lies on a relatively flat stretch of land between Mailly and Chigny-les-Roses. Passing down the Route du Champagne, one suddenly comes across a huge, frightful concrete cube standing improbably among the vineyards: it is this village's new Canard-Duchêne plant for the Montagne de Reims. The vineyards mainly face north. The wines reach on average *premier cru* level and many *cuvées* attain body and character.
Area under vine: 30% PN, 50% PM, 20% CH.

Mailly | 100%

The village of Mailly clearly deserves its *grand cru* status. It should be stressed, however, that at first glance conditions do not appear especially good. Immense vineyards stretch over the plain, but, instead of being entirely dependent on the rays of the sun, the plants are heated by a warm air current that accelerates the maturing of the grapes. The village's plantations face in all directions except west. The mesoclimate and other conditions mean that the best sites in the *commune* are located on the north and south slopes. The prime sites in the village are situated just below the Mailly cooperative and are the property of its members. Some claim that Mailly has the potential to pose a serious threat to Verzenay for top spot on the Montagne de Reims. My opinion is that Mailly lacks that indefinable something to be a truly great wine. Nevertheless Mailly wines are highly reliable, well structured, and early on develop a chocolate aroma typical of *grande classe* Pinot Noir. The village grows a considerable quantity of Chardonnay, which was elevated to *grand cru* status in 1972.
Area under vine: 89% PN, 4% PM, 7% CH.

Mancy | 88%

Mancy is a beautifully situated village that nestles high up on the hills between Chavot and Grauves, with a fine view over the Côte des Blancs. The vineyards there should be replanted with as much Chardonnay as possible. With a higher percentage of white wine grapes, the village would almost certainly have been rewarded with *premier cru* status in 1985.
Area under vine: 5% PN, 55% PM, 40% CH.

Mardeuil | 84%

I do not know the wines of Mardeuil very well, but am familiar with all the slopes, as I have often gone jogging through the countryside west of Épernay. In 1985, the village passed from 82 to 84 percent in the classification. Today the predominant force in the village is the Beaumont des Crayères cooperative.
Area under vine: 30% PN, 60% PM, 10% CH.

Mareuil-sur-Aÿ | 99%

Mareuil-sur-Aÿ is located immediately to the east of Aÿ. This picturesque village of 1,200 inhabitants, who all almost work in wine, enjoys a splendid position near the Marne. The village is known especially for the exceptional site of Clos des Goisses, owned entirely by Philipponnat. Undeniably, Mareuil should belong to the *grand cru* villages. Most of the vineyards reach almost same quality as those of Aÿ. In their youth, what may distinguish a Mareuil wine from an Aÿ wine is a hawthorn-like flowery bouquet. On aging, the wines become practically impossible to tell apart. Due to its very steep slopes close to the river, Clos des Goisses has the highest average temperature of all Champagne vineyards, which means its wine has potentially the highest alcohol content.
Area under vine: 82% PN, 9% PM, 9% CH.

Merfy | 84%

Located seven kilometers (four miles) to the northeast of Reims on the southern slopes of the massif of Saint-Thierry. The hills of Merfy were originally planted by the Romans, and the cultivated area used today was first divided up by monks from the local monastery 1,300 years ago.
Area under vine: 30% PN, 45% PM, 25% CH.

Merrey-sur-Arce | 80%

Six growers produce 150,000 bottles from 116 hectares (288 acres).
Area under vine: 85% PN, 10% PM, 5% CH.

Mesneaux, Les | 90%

Lying close by Reims on a piece of flat terrain. Does not deserve its *premier cru* status. The majority of the vineyards are owned by Mercier.
Area under vine: 50% PM, 50% CH.

Mesnil-sur-Oger, Le | 100%

For more than forty years, Le Mesnil missed *grand cru* status by a single ridiculous point. This changed only in 1985, although for a long time the village had been regarded as the best of all. The grapes growing along the belt at between 160 and 220 meters (525 and 722 ft.) high provide the most elegant Champagnes the world has ever known. The village produces a very special Chardonnay clone that imparts a penetrating bouquet, even if its presence in the pressing is brief. The wines of Mesnil are often understated and acidulous when young, only to subsequently explode sensationally into a delicious rainbow of flavors. At maturity, aromas of nut and coffee, in combination with a cheeky flavor of exotic fruits, form the major ingredient of Champagnes from this village. But there are also Champagnes of poor quality at Mesnil, demonstrating the extent to which the mesoclimate can vary within the limits of the village. The zones enjoying the highest reputations are Chétillon, Musettes, Jutées, Cocugneux, Champ d'Alouettes and—above all—Clos du Mesnil, which was once owned by Julien Tarin. This unique enclosed field, which stands right in the middle of the village, was bought in 1971 by Krug, who immediately began new plantings. Only in 1979, however, did the Krug brothers reckon that the wine had attained a high enough quality to be marketed. From a historical viewpoint, it is Salon, also a mono-*cru* Champagne, that has conferred worldwide fame on the village. The area under vine today is 432 hectares (1067 acres), distributed between forty growers and a few houses that managed to buy up some of the very expensive land in time. Krug, Clicquot, Salon, and Moët are among those happy few.
Area under vine: 100% CH.

Montbré | 94%

The vineyards lie on the plain, which means that top-quality viniculture is not possible. The village contains no producers.
Area under vine: 30% PN, 40% PM, 30% CH.

Montgenost | 85%

[85% PN/PM, 87% CH]
Along with Bethon, this is the main village in Sézanne. The

Chardonnay grapes possess a mineral richness close to Chablis that clearly makes them worthy of interest.
Area under vine: 6% PN, 3% PM, 91% CH.

Montgueux | 80%

[12% PN, 1% PM, 87% CH]
The Chardonnay from this village in Aube was for a long time much vaunted by Charles Heidsieck and Veuve Clicquot's wine-makers. It has a particularly fruity style, with none of the heaviness that characterizes the majority of Aube Champagnes. Alexander L. is the rising star among the seventy-four growers in the village. The total surface area under cultivation is 189 hectares (467 acres).

Moslins | 83%

The village is located eight kilometers (five miles) from Éper-nay and has just one grower. Only fifteen hectares (thirty-seven acres) are planted, with an equal percentage of all three type of vines.

Moussy | 89%

Standing seven kilometers (5 miles) to the south of Épernay and with 133 hectares (329 acres) under vine, this village is home to the marvelous José Michel.
Area under vine: 4% PN, 76% PM, 20% CH.

Mutigny | 93%

Fantastic slopes lie just down from the village. Unfortunately for Mutigny they belong to Mareuil-sur-Aÿ. The seventy-five hectares (185 acres) within the limits of Mutigny attain the lower reaches of a *premier cru*. This village highlights the superiority of Pinot Noir over other varieties on the northern banks of the Marne.
Area under vine: 65% PN, 30% PM, 5% CH.

Neuville-aux-Larris | 84%

Located to the north of the Marne valley and to the west of the forest of Reims. The plantations lie north of a tributary of the Marne called Belval. During the classification of 1945 the village received 81 percent, which was upgraded to 84 percent. This is another village that has contributed to Pinot Meunier being, for a long time, the most extensively grown vine in Champagne.
Area under vine: 5% PN, 90% PM, 5% CH.

Neuville-sur-Seine | 80%

One of the main localities in Aube. Nearly all the grapes in this relatively flat landscape belong to the Clérambault cooperative.
Area under vine: 90% PN, 5% PM, 5% CH.

Œuilly | 84%

Œuilly lies ten kilometers (6 miles) west of Épernay in the valley of the Marne. It is home to twelve growers and a cooperative.
Area under vine: 40% PN, 55% PM, 5% CH.

Oger | 100%

Quite rightly Oger obtained its *grand cru* status in 1985, gaining the crucial 1 percent that it had been missing. The village stands on belemnite chalk.

Oiry | 100%

Admittedly, the village itself is located far from the main artery of the Côte des Blancs, but the plantations belonging to the village grow near Cramant and Chouilly. I have found myself in the company of a grower at this "crossroads of the three king-doms," who feels annoyed that his older vines and best grapes grew on the Oiry side, making them less valuable. The quality of the grapes on the lower slopes of the Butte de Saran is very high. Most of the eighty-nine hectares (220 acres) of vineyards at Oiry lie on the lower slopes. The key explanation for the quality being lower than at Avize or Cramant is the dearth of belemnite chalk. There is, on the other hand, a broad band of micraster chalk. The village's optimum sites lie at an altitude of 150 meters (492 ft.) and belong to Pol Roger and Larmandier. Prior to 1985, Oiry was merely a *premier cru*.
Area under vine: 100% CH.

Pargny-les-Reims | 90%

Unexpectedly raised to the status of *premier cru* in 1985, this little village with its pleasant restaurant, Le Pargny, is located just north of Jouy-les-Reims. Clos des Chaulins de Médot is found in the village.
Area under vine: 14% PN, 82% PM, 4% CH.

Pierry | 90%

The monk Dom Oudart, a contemporary of Dom Pérignon's, lived in this village just outside Épernay. Today, it is perhaps known most especially for the Château de la Marquetterie, owned by Taittinger. The view from Pierry's vineyards is breathtaking. Behind you lies a forest rich in birds and game, while on the left you can see Épernay and Champillon. At your feet lies Pierry itself, with Taittinger's imposing château and, on the other side of the road, the glorious stone church of Chavot. Away on the horizon, the heart of the Côte des Blancs can be glimpsed with the pearls of Cramant and Avize. The Pierry vineyards lie on a chalky soil mixed with flint. Several winemakers from the larger houses affirm that the wines from Pierry display clear flinty notes.

Area under vine: 20% PN, 65% PM, 15% CH.

Pouillon | 84%

A relatively unknown village eleven kilometers (nine miles) to the north of Reims. The surface area of the *commune* is 277 hectares (685 acres), of which forty-nine are planted with the vine. This village produces 143,000 bottles per year from twenty-one growers and a cooperative.

Area under vine: 10% PN, 82% PM, 8% CH.

Prouilly | 85%

The majority of the 130 hectares (321 acres) of this village belong to various Champagne houses. There are no grower-producers here—all the growers belong to the local cooperative.

Area under vine: 20% PN, 75% PM, 5% CH.

Puisieulx | 100%

It is a mystery how this tongue-twister of a village has become a member of the exclusive *grand cru* club. Puisieulx bathes in the reflected glory of Sillery's reputation, which in turn became famous thanks to the grapes grown at Verzenay. Puisieulx is, at eighteen hectares (forty-five acres), the smallest *grand cru* village. It lies to the east of Reims on the plain north of the Montagne de Reims. The vine grows on a singularly pebbly soil, low in chalk. Most of the land under vine belongs to Moët, and there is no producer among the 300 inhabitants of the village. Puisieulx presents perhaps the prime example of the injustice of the system of Champagne growth rankings.

Area under vine: 60% PN, 9% PM, 31% CH.

Reims | 88%

Reims has forty-nine hectares (121 acres) of vineyard of its own, but it is not really for this reason that the city has become famous as an epicenter of Champagne. It is home to fifteen of the best-known Champagne houses, the majority of which have Gallo-Roman chalk cellars where millions of bottles are aged. The city has had a very rich history, and today attracts tourists by offering a wealth of activities. Throughout everything, though, the presence of the bubbling wine can be felt. In Reims, one can drift into any old bar and be sure of being able to get a glass of Champagne produced by an established house. Reims is meant to compete with Épernay for the title "capital of Champagne," but, with houses like Krug, Roederer, Taittinger, Clicquot, Heidsieck, Mumm, Lanson, and Pommery established here, the only choice for me is Reims.

Area under vine: 31% PN, 38% PM, 31% CH.

Reuil | 86%

This village, located twelve kilometers (seven and a half miles) north of Épernay, houses sixty-one producers cultivating 151 hectares (373 acres).

Area under vine: 25% PN, 70% PM, 5% CH.

Riceys, Les | 80%

Without doubt, Les Riceys is the best-known village in Aube. The main reason is that the village features the largest cultivated surface in all Champagne. Several innovative winemakers have set up here, attracted by the famous rosé des Riceys and, in their wake, a large number of quality Champagnes are being made. The fact that wine journalist Tom Stevenson, with others, have drawn attention to several growers in this village has enhanced their status. In Paris and London, Bonnet, Horiot, Gallimard, and Laurenti have become cult figures. I would venture to say that the fuss around this village is rather overdone, though I agree that it is the most important and interesting village in Aube. And the rosé wine is, along with Tavel from the Rhône valley, the best in the world. Les Riceys is the only Champagne *commune* to have earned the right to three different appellations: Champagne, rosé des Riceys and *coteaux champenois*. What few people realize is that Les Riceys comprises three small villages permitted to use the appellation (Haut, Haut-Rive, and Bas).

Area under vine: 96% PN, 2% PM, 2% CH.

Rilly-la-Montagne | 94%

The best vines grow at an altitude of 140 to 200 meters (459 to 656 ft.). The wines are very reminiscent of those from the nearby village of Chigny-les-Roses. Even in Rilly, the Chardonnay is of an unexpectedly high quality. The village swarms with interesting-sounding winemakers.

Area under vine: 40% PN, 30% PM, 30% CH.

Romery | 85%

During the reclassification of 1985, Romery, located northwest of Hautvillers, moved up from 83 to 85 percent. One half of the surface under vine is the property of the Champagne houses, while the other half belongs to the growers, who sell most of their harvest on.
Area under vine: 20% PN, 60% PM, 20% CH.

Sacy | 90%

There isn't a single grower producing truly great quality grapes at Petite Montagne. Sacy, however, enjoys—together with its neighbor, Villedommange—the best reputation. The big firm Mercier owns the majority of the vineyards, as in Mesneaux.

Saint-Martin-d'Ablois | 86%

Situated at the westernmost point of the strip of land including Pierry and Vinay.
Area under vine: 5% PN, 85% PM, 10% CH.

Saulchery | 80%

A small village in Aisne located ten kilometers (six miles) from Château-Thierry. Sixteen growers over 110 hectares (272 acres).
Area under vine: 3% PN, 95% PM, 2% CH.

Sept-Saulx

The village is located outside the Champagne-growing region, but possesses one of the most agreeable restaurants in the area, the "Cheval Blanc."

Sermiers | 89%

One hundred and fifty-seven hectares (432 acres) shared between fourteen growers and a cooperative.
Area under vine: 20% PN, 75% PM, 5% CH.

Serzy-et-Prin | 86%

There are seven growers and a cooperative. Half of the 736 hectares (1819 acres) in the village is worked by various Champagne houses.
Area under vine: 5% PN, 93% PM, 2% CH.

Sillery | 100%

At the beginning of this book I mentioned the Marquis de Sillery, who made his famous wines in the sixteenth century. Since all the marquis's wine was sold under the Sillery name, the village enjoyed an undeserved reputation that in truth should belong to Verzenay. Today covering some ninety-four hectares (232 acres), the vineyards of Sillery are located on the plain to the north of the Montagne de Reims, on soil that is susceptible to frost. Conditions for viniculture are far from ideal. Nevertheless many large houses own vineyards in the village. One should never forget that several prestige Champagne firms use large quantities of wine from the least inspiring *grand cru* villages, so that they can still market the wine as being produced solely from *grand cru* grapes. Taking account of the remorseless increase in certain super-Champagnes at the moment, one is probably justified in wondering if this has not been mirrored in recent years by the proportion of inferior quality *grand cru*. Ruinart is proud of its Dom Ruinart Blanc de Blancs, which contains a significant amount of Chardonnay grapes from Sillery. The village is better known for its Pinot Noir. Usually Sillery wines lack concentration and character, but a tasting of an oak-aged Lanson Sillery at Jacquesson's convinced me that Pinot Noir of the first order does indeed exist there.
Area under vine: 48% PN, 8% PM, 44% CH.

Taissy | 94%

Apart from a south-facing slope called Mont Ferré, most of the village's vineyards are located on the plain. An overrated village where the major landowners are Moët & Chandon.
Area under vine: 23% PN, 45% PM, 32% CH.

Tauxières | 99%

One of the two villages that only need one single point to achieve *grand cru* status. But, in contrast to Mareuil-sur-Aÿ, Tauxières is ranked too high. Its wines only attain the level of a *premier cru* and are used especially in *cuvées*. Bollinger has the oldest vines and all the best slopes in the village. Moët and Mercier have land near the road.
Area under vine: 80% PN, 5% PM, 15% CH.

Tours-sur-Marne | 100%

[100% PN, 90% CH]
Because of the many enjoyable times I have spent there, this village occupies a very special place in my heart. It is not too big yet it contains everything that makes the heart of Champagne beat: the Marne, the vineyards, the growers, and two well-known Champagne houses. The atmosphere in the village is unhurried

and relaxed. On the other hand, the grapes produced here do not make the heart beat faster…. The best slopes, those facing the south, give at best a wine reminiscent of that produced on the fringes of Bouzy. The aroma can be fragrant and simply fruity. The structure is often satisfactory, but one is entitled to expect more of a *grand cru*. It should be noted that Chardonnay grapes from this village do not enjoy *grand cru* status.
Area under vine: 60% PN, 40% CH.

Trépail | 95%

Trépail stands to the northeast, an extension of Bouzy and Ambonnay. The village has much in common with its neighbors. The best southeast-facing plots lie at 160 to 200 meters (525 to 656 ft.). As in Bouzy, one has to bear in mind where the grapes come from within the village. It certainly deserves to be better known.
Area under vine: 13% PN, 87% CH.

Trigny | 84%

Thirty-eight growers produce no less than 600,000 bottles from 168 hectares (415 acres) of grape vines.
Area under vine: 25% PN, 69% PM, 6% CH.

Trois-Puits | 94%

Today Trois-Puits lies practically in the suburbs of Reims. The vines grow on flat ground near built-up areas. Quality is regarded as mediocre.
Area under vine: 45% PN, 45% PM, 10% CH.

Urville | 80%

Urville, the site of the famous firm of Drappier, lies ten kilometers (six miles) from Bar-sur-Aube.
Area under vine: 70% PN, 20% PM, 10% CH.

Vandières | 86%

Vandières is situated twenty kilometers (twelve and a half miles) northwest of Épernay. I have never tasted wines from this village, and have neither read nor heard of anyone who has—although it apparently finds room for fifty producers!
Area under vine: 8% PN, 85% PM, 7% CH.

Vaudemange | 95%

The celebrated Reims firm George Goulet has its headquarters here. With Billy-le-Grand, Vaudemange forms the easternmost point of the Montagne de Reims. This is yet another village bent on growing grapes other than those for which it is best suited. Vaudemange should be a village teeming with Pinot! Today Mumm owns the majority of the Pinot vines.
Area under vine: 20% PN, 80% CH.

Venteuil | 89%

The village jumped from 85 to 89 percent on the vintage scale in 1985. Some south-facing slopes deserve their *premier cru* status, but the level overall in most of the village is only average. Venteuil borders on Damery on the Marne's north bank.
Area under vine: 35% PN, 55% PM, 10% CH.

Vert-Toulon | 85%

Located southwest of Côte des Blancs and twenty kilometers (twelve and a half miles) north of Sézanne. Almost all the thirty growers in the village make their wine at the Grappe d'Or cooperative.
Area under vine: 10% PN, 14% PM, 76% CH.

Vertus | 95%

In terms of area, Vertus is the largest of all *premier cru* villages. It is also the southernmost of all the high quality ones. From a historical point of view it is better known (curiously) for its Pinot grapes than for its Chardonnay. My many tastings at the barrel of Vertus Pinot Noir have failed to impress me, in spite of the fact that the vines originate from Beaune stocks that predate phylloxera. To my mind the Chardonnay grapes are much more appealing. Though they certainly do not reach the class of *grand cru* villages, they have a rich and fruity style and belong to the elite of the second division. Many famous Champagne houses buy grapes from this village, and a fairly significant number of them own vineyards there. With twenty-two hectares (fifty-four acres) each, Duval-Leroy and Louis Roederer are the major landowners in the area. Moët, and Larmandier also have significant holdings. Few growers make Champagne entirely from Vertus grapes, and the majority are *cuvées* from various Chardonnay villages in the surrounding area.
Area under vine: 12% PN, 88% CH.

Verzenay | 100%

As I've already mentioned, Puisieulx, Sillery, and Beaumont-sur-Vesle obtained their *grand cru* status thanks to their proximity to Verzenay. The 420 hectares (1038 acres) in the village provide the blackest grapes in all Champagne. How the northern slopes in one of the most northerly wine-growing villages in the world produces such rich, peppery, and virile Pinot wines is one of the great mysteries of viniculture. The majority of the northern sites in the village actually lie more to the northeast, and thus enjoy the sun's rays for a substantial part of the day. Just as in Mailly, the vineyards are caressed locally by a warm air current. Some of the most illustrious vineyards belong to Bollinger, Mumm, Roederer, and Heidsieck and Monopole, and are located below the historic Moulin de Verzenay. Even the Chardonnay grapes cultivated in the village have enjoyed *grand cru* status since 1972. Unfortunately more and more growers produce mixed Champagnes instead of concentrating solely on doing what they do best, Pinot Noir! Jean-Paul Morel even produces a village Blanc de Blancs. As a Pinot village, Verzenay is definitely the genuine star of the Montagne de Reims. Admittedly, the wines of the village never acquire the soft, aromatic opulence of Champagnes from Aÿ, but they gain greater weight with age, and are extremely important as bases for great vintages, such as Bollinger R. D. and Roederer Cristal, for example. Verzenay Champagnes betray a very strong and individual fragrance. Pepper and iron notes mix with the aroma of the grape. It is persistently long and hard for many years before it settles down to utter perfection. Tastings at the barrel of Bollinger and Krug are simply majestic.
Area under vine: 90% PN, 10% CH.

Verzy | 100%

The terrain of Verzy is made up of belemnite chalk and two varieties of micraster chalk. Verzy's plantations form an extension of the famous vineyards at Verzenay on the northern slopes of Montagne de Reims. The best exposed slopes are those at an altitude of from 150 to 200 meters (492 to 565 ft.). Oddly enough, Verzy was formerly a Chardonnay village. It is today famous for its peppery, virile Pinot wines. With those of Verzenay, the Pinot Noir grapes here form the base for the finest Champagne vintages. A stony and gunpowder edge can be detected in the aftertaste, just as at Verzenay. Here 105 hectares (260 acres) furnish 800,000 bottles a year. I have also tasted some marvelously structured still Verzy wines, produced by Bollinger and Jacquesson. But the most staggering, which I still recall, is a particularly fabulous tasting at the barrel of a Krug that just exploded in the mouth.
Area under vine: 80% PN, 20% CH.

Villedommange | 90%

Along with Sacy, this is the best Petite Montagne village. The vines are set at altitudes of from 115 to 240 meters (377 to 787 ft.), and are scattered all around the village. Clicquot and Oudinot are the great landowners here.
Area under vine: 30% PN, 65% Pinot Mercier, 5% CH.

Villeneuve-Renneville | 95%

The village lies on the plain to the east of the main region of the Côte des Blancs. The wines from here are very pure and elegant, but they hardly justify their high classification. A narrow strip that extends to the low Mesnil hills provides the best Chardonnay grapes in the village. There is no actual producer here, however.
Area under vine: 100% CH.

Villers-Allerand | 90%

In spite of its northerly situation, the village's vineyards are exposed to sunlight every day for enough hours to ensure maturity for the grapes. Thirty-eight percent of the annual production of 50,000 bottles is supplied to Champagne houses, with the remaining 31,000 being sold by two families: Prévot and Stroebel. The Champagne they sell is a Blanc de Noirs, composed primarily of Pinot Meunier.
Area under vine: 27% PN, 55% PM, 18% CH.

Villers-aux-Nœuds | 90%

Another village outside the heartland. Re-evaluated in 1985.

Villers-Marmery | 95%

Located between Verzy and Trépail on the slopes of the Montagne de Reims. The special grape clone that grows here has aroused fierce debate. Having discussed the matter over with several wine-producers, I get the impression that Villers-Marmery wines are either loved or loathed. One interesting detail is that Deutz uses from 5 to 10 percent of Villers-Marmery Chardonnay in its excellent Blanc de Blancs. Clearly the wines possess great personality, a high degree of potential alcohol, and fine acidity.
Area under vine: 5% PN, 95% CH.

Villers-sous-Châtillon | 86%

The village's classification was upped in 1971 from 83 to 85 percent. In 1976, it went up to 86 percent, which is where it remains today. Even if the growing area does extend westward for dozens of kilometers, it lies beyond the borders of the core region as far as quality is concerned. The soil is primarily composed of clay, sandstone, and soft limestone. The terrain is all too prone to frost, with the result that growers here have opted for Pinot Meunier over the nobler varieties of vine. They can manage to turn out almost a million bottles a year from the village's twenty hectares (fifty acres). A startlingly high output!
Area under vine: 4% PN, 95% PM, 1% CH.

Ville-sur-Arce | 80%

To the east of Bar-sur-Seine there is a branch of the Seine called the Arce. The only Champagne village of recognized quality adorning its banks is this one. The arable area is significant, and nearly 500,000 bottles are produced from 192 hectares (474 acres).
Area under vine: 93% PN, 3% PM, 4% CH.

Villevenard | 85%

Annual production of half a million bottles from 120 hectares (297 acres).
Area under vine: 3% PN, 70% PM, 27% CH.

Vinay | 86%

Geologically almost identical to Pierry, but with a greater area under vine and too high an output. The village is prized primarily for its marvellous restaurant La Briqueterie and its incomparable *terrine de foie de canard*.
Area under vine: 11% PN, 71% PM, 18% CH.

Vincelles | 86%

Located halfway between Château-Thierry and Épernay along the Marne valley. On relatively flat terrain the grapes cultivated here create charming wines intended to be drunk young.
Area under vine: 30% PN, 55% PM, 15% CH.

Voipreux | 95%

A little-known village located outside the Côte des Blancs. Several slopes border on Vertus and Villeneuve-Renneville and provide very fine Chardonnay grapes, though it is not as outstanding as its classification might imply.
Area under vine: 100% CH.

Vrigny | 89%

Eight kilometers (five miles) from Reims with twenty-four growers over eighty-three hectares (205 acres).
Area under vine: 20% PN, 40% PM, 40% CH.

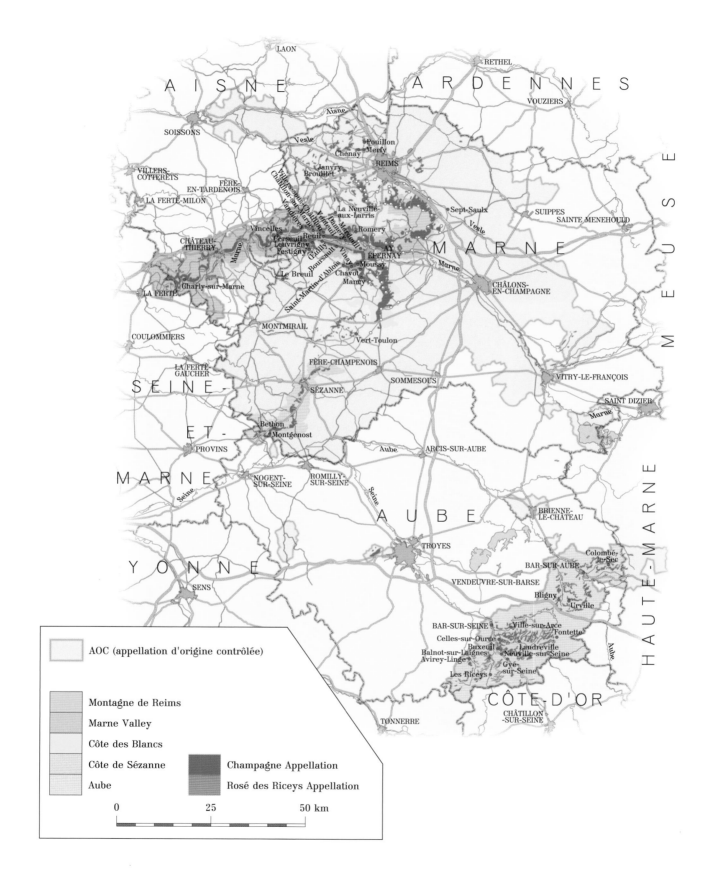

AOC (appellation d'origine contrôlée)

Montagne de Reims

Marne Valley

Côte des Blancs

Côte de Sézanne

Aube

Champagne Appellation

Rosé des Riceys Appellation

0   25   50 km

4000
Champagnes

4

Rating Champagne

In this section of the book, I have attempted to rate with great care the most important wine-producing villages, wine-makers, and wines in Champagne. As with the villages, the producers are classified alphabetically, so that the reader can find the required wine as quickly as possible. Under each producer's name, the wines are ranked in order from the non-vintage to the *curvée de prestige* Champagne.

Vintages are listed from the youngest to the oldest wine.

The specific quality of each producer is rather difficult to evaluate, since the range of products from some of them can be somewhat uneven. In contrast there are other winemakers producing fantastic non-vintage Champagnes who have never been able to release a vintage. Furthermore, historical factors play a role here. Some of the most famous houses make poor Champagne today, while conversely there are brilliant new producers who constitute the rising stars of the Champagne firmament. In spite of the obstacles standing in the way of classifications of this kind, with the experience of almost twenty years' tasting I have ventured to award stars to each producer. These are meant to take account of the weight and import of the historical background.

I employ a scale ranging from one to five stars for the most famous producers in the region.

To avoid making too many enemies, I have chosen not actually to allot one or even two stars, and to begin with the three highest marks.

My obviously subjective judgment is based on a concerted battery of tastings that I carried out between 1987 and 2004, and represents the most exhaustive evaluation of Champagne ever undertaken. The vintage and the occasional non-vintage but year-dated Champagnes will be awarded two marks: one for the quality of the wine at the time of the last tasting to date, and another for the quality when it reaches its optimum level.

Non-vintage Champagnes have only one mark, based on the quality of the wine when it is delivered for sale. However, certain non-vintage wines improve so much with laying down that if you drink such wines at their best you will certainly find the mark awarded here too low.

The year that a wine will reach its full bloom is generally also indicated in these type of listings, but since a Champagne's age of maturity is a very subjective question, depending on taste, I have refrained from making such an assessment.

If very marked differences between the two marks (tasting and potential) are noted, then the wine obviously requires more rather than less time in the cellar. The individual consumer can then determine by experience the stage of aging that best suits his or her personal preferences.

I have chosen to employ the Juhlin scale, which goes up to 100 points, because I believe that a scale should have as broad a range as possible. A wine that gives no pleasure at all should not, in my opinion, receive a single point. This is why I start with zero points. It should be added, however, that all Champagne, unless it is actually defective, will be of a quality such as to afford drinking pleasure. Fifty points is average for any non-vintage Champagne.

The average in this category in my book lies above this mid-point, owing to the fact that I have concentrated on the best known of the 5,419 producers. If I had had the opportunity of tasting every single wine, I am sure that the average would have edged down closer to fifty points.

One hundred points should be given to a wine that represents perfection in Champagne form—and to nothing

else. For a long time I believed that I would never give such a mark. Some people have claimed that the handful of Champagnes to which I have awarded ninety-nine points were so outstanding that they deserved 100, but I wanted to avoid finding myself faced one day with a wine tasting better than all those I had drunk hitherto, and with no mark high enough to give it! At the time of the great Millennium Tasting sessions, this actually happened; off the record I will tell you that some tasters had to give 101 points. After having written my book *Three Thousand Champagnes*, I encountered a perfect Champagne (or rather a perfect bottle) that indeed deserved 100 points. Deep down, I hope that in the future I will never meet a wine that is even better. Then I too might be obliged to exceed the upper limit of my scale.

As 4,000 Champagnes is a pretty daunting number of wines, in this volume I have chosen to describe only those Champagnes that score more than eighty points.

Those wishing to look at all my comments and the notes taken during tastings, and to follow my current activities in the field, can find the relevant information on my website: www.champagneclub.com

My points system is not divided into subsections that cover all the various aspects of a wine, but reflects instead an overall judgment on its general quality. I am well aware of the fact that some of my readers, familiar with Robert Parker or the Winespectator scale, would snub wines earning less than eighty points and would certainly look down on a sixty-six-pointer. This is a mistake! If the product concerned is a non-vintage Champagne from the fringes of the region, the wine-maker might have performed his job perfectly well within the constraints of his situation, and the wine may well be delicious if consumed in optimum conditions.

Having presented the wine-producers, I then provide a summary of the finest wines from each year and each decade, as well as a list of the 100 best Champagnes, without regard to category.

I can only repeat that these judgments are mine and mine alone; that they are eminently subjective: a wine is a living being that varies from bottle to bottle. Points are a necessary evil that enable one to gain a rough idea of the quality of a wine; beyond that the description of the personality and style of each Champagne can provide valuable information about the wines. I hope that this will prove an effective aid for readers trying to make their way through the "Champagne jungle."

Remember, too, that marks and rankings are not designed to reflect the pleasure of drinking an unpretentious Champagne while gazing over a local vineyard and/or in good company. In fact, these are precisely the factors I have deliberately tried to exclude from my judgment on the wines. Above all, it is your personal taste that counts the most; my marks should by no means be considered as universally valid.

KEY TO SYMBOLS

*****	An unimpeachable world-class producer across the entire range of his output
****	A fantastic producer with some world-beating wines
***	A very good producer one should keep an eye on
N-M	*Négociant-manipulant.* A Champagne house with a license to purchase grapes.
R-M	*Recoltant-manipulant.* A grower who produces his own Champagne.
C-M	*Cooperative-manipulant.* Cooperative.
R-C	*Recoltant-cooperateur.* A grower who puts his own label on a wine produced by a cooperative.
N-D	*Négociant-détaillant.* Champagne made with grapes from a grower and sold under his own label, but made by a Champagne house that also ensures its distribution
98%	Classification of the villages on the official 100-point *cru* scale
69	Mark given at the most recent tasting
JULY 2002	Date of the most recent tasting
(87)	Maximum potential points
(>)	The wine has reached its peak and will from now on decline steadily
(50% PN, 20% PM, 30% CH)	Grape proportions. In some non-vintage wines the approximate composition of the wine varies a great deal from year to year. Moreover, it should be understood that few winemakers attach much importance to this factor, so indications here may differ considerably from publication to publication.
PN	Pinot Noir
PM	Pinot Meunier
CH	Chardonnay

Tasting notes

ABELÉ*** N-M
50, rue de Sillery
51100 Reims
03 26 87 79 80
Production: 400,000

When Téodore Vander-Veken founded the firm in 1757 he laid the foundations for the fifth Champagne house in history. Abelé stayed within the family until 1828, when Auguste de Brimont took over and began an experimental partnership with Antoine Müller, Clicquot's innovative *chef de caves*. After a short-lived move to Ludes, the Champagne house is now back in Reims. José Ferrer Sala, of the Spanish branch of Freixenet, was so delighted by Abelé's wines at a tasting that he bought the company in 1985. Abelé's wines are marked by a purity and lightness that closely resembles Henriot. *Degorgé à la glace* was invented in Abelé's cellars. At present, Hervé Ruin is the winemaker.

- ABELÉ BRUT   74
  (60% PN, 13% PM, 27% CH)
- ABELÉ EXTRA DRY   84
  (From the 1940s)
  Hervé at Le Vigneron is probably the only one who still has something like this left: rich, old Champagne with Tokay-like style. The flavors of dates, figs, raisins, and honey are all discernible in this richly sweetened, dessert-y wine.
- ABELÉ ROSÉ   67
  (100% PN)
- 1998 SOIRÉES PARISIENNES   84, FEB 2004 (87)
  Initial fierce acidity. Fine, individual strength, metallic purity, and slowly evolving beauty. Still, there are already subtle signs of maturity with suggestions of cream, nuts, and toasted bread, together with a youthful floral character and citrus.
- 1997 SOIRÉES PARISIENNES   83, MAY 2003 (83)
  (30% PN, 70% CH)
  A typically charming '97. A delightful springtime luncheon wine that invigorates and radiates sun and mellowness. The fruit is supple and exotic with youthful vitality. This is not something to keep for the cellar, with its low alcohol content and low acidity. On the other hand, there can be very few people who wouldn't agree that this Champagne tastes good.
- 1996 ABELÉ   80, JAN 2004 (85)
  (24% PN, 29% PM, 47% CH)
  For once, rather undeveloped and miserly in the nose. There is a mineral character that borders on soil and stone. Weak toastiness and a few green notes with a suggestion of lime peel. Medium bodied and young.
- 1990 SOIRÉES PARISIENNES   87, JUNE 2003 (87)
  (30% PN, 70% CH)

A most refreshing and beautifully floral aperitif Champagne, with fresh notes of apple and citrus. Can surely tolerate long storage, but probably exhibits its greatest charm as a youthful, spring-like appetizer.

- 1988, SOIRÉES PARISIENNES   84, MAY 1998 (87)
  (35% PN, 25% PM, 40% CH)
  Very elegant and young, with nice acidity and cogency. Fine, crispy finish. I wonder how it tastes today?
- 1986 ABELÉ   84, AUG 1999 (86)
  (60% PN, 40% CH)
  Many 1986 wines are in a pleasant phase of development, with notes of caramel and exotic fruit. The refreshing house-style will help keep the wine alive for a long time to come. Should be mature now.
- 1985 ABELÉ   70, MAR 1994 (82)
  (60% PN, 40% CH)
  The nose is less developed than in the delightful Abelé Brut. Steely acidity and a slightly thicker body suggest that the '85 will develop well. At the moment, though, I prefer the nonvintage.
- 1982 ABELÉ   88, OCT 2002 (88)
  (60% PN, 40% CH)
  Big and beautifully developed bouquet of roasted coffee, gun-smoke, orchid, and nougat. Medium-bodied, handsomely accomplished palate with vintage-typical buttery fruit and a sweet, delicious finish.
- 1966 ABELÉ   93, JAN 2003 (93)
  (60% PN, 40% CH)
  Brilliantly flowery nose and elegant, sensual flavor—as so often in this perfect vintage.
- 1964 ABELÉ
  (60% PN, 40% CH)
- 1983 ABELÉ BLANC DE BLANCS   88, JUN 2003 (88)
  (100% CH)
  The latest bottle at Royal Champagne was a delightful, newly disgorged beauty, full of delicately toasted and lightly bready notes, and producing a soft, refreshing feeling in the mouth.
- 1990, SOURIRE DE REIMS   85, MAY 2003 (86)
  (25% PN, 75% CH)
  Bouquet of malt, cacao, and green tea. Soft, somewhat curt but pleasant taste with a muted vanilla note and a generous fruitiness reminiscent of strawberries, wild strawberries, and gooseberry. Fine and decidedly personal.
- 1986, SOURIRE DE REIMS   85, APR 2003 (85)
  (25% PN, 75% CH)
  An enormously expensive bottle decorated with a golden plastic angel. The Champagne almost feels like a Blanc de Blancs in the nose, with flowery and gamy tones. The flavor is well balanced, with a fine, mineral-rich Champagne character.

- 1983 ABELÉ REPAS   80, JAN 2003 (80)
  (100% CH)
  At one time this must have been a fine Champagne but, in common with other '83s, the wine has acquired an all too oxidative and muddy character. Most of Abelés wines should be drunk relatively young.
- 1976 ABELÉ IMPERIAL CLUB   83, FEB 2003 (83)
  (40% PN, 60% CH)
  Dry and long, but lacks any interesting fruit aromas.
- 1975 ABELÉ IMPERIAL CLUB   85, JAN 2000 (85)
  (40% PN, 60% CH)
  Light, sparkling, and appetizingly youthful. Unfortunately, this is not enough; a few taste layers are missing as well as a dollop of concentration. Short and dry aftertaste.

ADNOT, ROBERT R-M
33 rue Vertus
51130 Bergères-les-Vertus
03 26 52 16 57
Colin at Vertus has purchased a stock of this producer's older vintages from Bergères-les-Vertus, which were already disgorged and therefore not allowed to bear the Colin label. Production has been discontinued.

- ROBERT ADNOT BLANC DE BLANCS   64
  (100% CH)
- 1977 ROBERT ADNOT BLANC DE BLANCS   75, DEC 2003 (75)
  (100% CH)
- 1975 ROBERT ADNOT BLANC DE BLANCS   88, DEC 2003 (88)
  (100% CH)
  The finest wine in the collection of older vintages that Colin purchased from Adnot. This is a classically grand and walnut-y smelling Blanc de Blancs in the tradition of Salon. Besides the nutty tone there is grain, browned butter, dried fruit, and a slightly coarse, mineral character. Moreover, the chewable palate is almost like Finnish rye bread. Lengthy aftertaste with a waft of sea-splashed winds.
- 1973 ROBERT ADNOT BLANC DE BLANCS
  (100% CH)
- 1971 ROBERT ADNOT BLANC DE BLANCS
  (100% CH)
- 1970 ROBERT ADNOT BLANC DE BLANCS   80, DEC 2003 (80)
  (100% CH)
  Broad, smoky, and mature nose with elements of petroleum. Rich, slightly rough flavor that still has its youth. Somewhat featureless.

AGRAPART *** R-M
57, avenue Jean-Jaurès
51190 Avize
03 26 57 51 38
Production: 65,000
Agrapart owns ten hectares in Avize, Cramant, Oger, and Oiry, and produces storable wines vinified in oak barrels of varying sizes. The wines are a bit rustic, but rich in extracts.

- AGRAPART BRUT   75
  (100% CH)
- AGRAPART RÉSERVE   77
  (100% CH)

- CUVÉE DE DEMOISELLES ROSÉ   73
  (7% PN, 93% CH)

- 1996 AGRAPART   83, JUN 2003 (87)
  (100% CH)
  Grand and accomplished with a note of ripe fruit. Acids are present but they are well camouflaged. Agrapart really makes appetizing and expressive Champagnes in a bold style.
- 1995 AGRAPART   86, JAN 2004 (88)
  (100% CH)
  Sublime nose with floral accents of hawthorn and lily. Very creamy and fat as well. Round, caramel-rich, very tasty palate that is unfortunately a tad too brief.
- 1988 AGRAPART   80, MAR 1997 (87)
  (100% CH)
  The '88 has a fine nose—of bakery products—and a vinous, powerful flavor that has great potential for the future.
- 1985 AGRAPART   87, MAY 2003 (87)
  (100% CH)
  A monumental, masculine wine loaded with unripe extracts that give a slightly bitter aftertaste. It has almost the structure of a Pinot, which makes it suitable to drink with food.

ALEXANDRE L. N-M
7, chemin du Coteau
10300 Montgueux
33 25 74 84 83
Production: 60,000
Jacques Lassaignes's sons have decided to make high-class wines from Montgueux. For a long time now, Chardonnay from this village in Aube has been praised by the winemakers at Charles Heidsieck and Veuve Clicquot. It clearly has a special fruity style without the clumsiness that characterizes several of Aube's Champagnes. The young brothers, led by Emmanuel, are very serious, and produce well-made wines that only partly undergo malolactic fermentation. Experiments with aged oak barrels from Bordeaux have been started.

- ALEXANDRE L. BRUT   70
  (100% CH)
- ALEXANDRE L. ROSÉ   53
  (20% PN, 80% CH)
- 1995 ALEXANDRE L.   81, APR 2003 (82)
  (100% CH)
  This has much more depth than the nonvintage Champagne. Fine, deep yellow color; pliant mousse of tiny, delicate bubbles. Interesting, generous bouquet with elements of mint, honey, and sweet pastry bread. Rounded and fine on the palate with a stable, harmonious spine.
- LE COUTET   75
  (100% CH)

ARISTON N-M
4, Grande Rue
51170 Brouillet
03 26 97 43 46
Production: 80,000
Five generations of Aristons have made wine in this area since 1794. Remi Ariston is the winemaker today and has run the company since 1964. Ariston presides over ten hectares of unusually old vines, most of them over thirty-five years old.

- ARISTON ASPASIE BLANC DE BLANCS   78
  (100% CH)

ARNOULD, MICHEL *** R-M
28, rue de Mailly
51360 Verzenay
03 26 49 40 06
Production: 80,000
Patrick Arnould is onto something big. He still sells grapes to
Bollinger, but today he keeps the best ones for his own
Champagnes. He exchanges grapes with Bonnaire in Cramant and
will soon be making vintage wines of the highest class. Today, he
and his father Michel control twelve hectares of some of the
blackest grapes Champagne can produce. The house-style is highly
sophisticated; it is unexpectedly elegant considering its origins.
- M. ARNOULD BRUT   70
  (100% PN)
- M. ARNOULD CARTE D'OR   83
  (50% PN, 50% CH)
  Patrick's pride and joy, but half of the wine comes from Bonnaire
  in Cramant. A voluptuous wine with a sensual, soft nose, and
  caressing flavor. Always from a good vintage.
- M. ARNOULD CUVÉE 2000   81, JAN 2003 (87)
  (85% PN, 15% CH)
  A powerful, yet simultaneously balanced *cuvée* made for the
  millennium, which should be stored for many years to come.
  Firm, bready foundation and an uplifting acidity that carries the
  wine into the future.
- M. ARNOULD CUVÉE RÉSERVE   72
  (67% PN, 33% CH)
- M. ARNOULD ROSÉ   70
  (100% PN)
- M. ARNOULD CUVÉE PRESTIGE   79
  (100% PN)

ARNOULT, JEAN N-M
100, Grande Rue
10110 Celles-sur-Ource
03 25 38 56 49
Production: 150,000
When the firm was started in 1919 by Jean Arnoult, it became the
Aube district's first Champagne house. Today it is run by Alain
Cheurlin, who aims for quality. Other wines: Carte Noir Brut,
Rosé, Brut Prestige.
- JEAN ARNOULT BRUT RÉSERVE   48
  (80% PN, 10% PM, 10% CH)

ASSAILLY-LECLAIRE R-M
6, rue de Lombardie
51190 Avize
03 26 57 51 20
Production: 25,000
Pure Avize Grand Cru Chardonnay.
- ASSAILLY-LECLAIRE BLANC DE BLANCS   71
  (100% PN)

AUBRY, L.*** R-M
6, Grande Rue
51390 Jouy-les-Reims
03 26 49 20 07
Production: 100,000
In the heart of Petit Montagne de Reims, twin brothers Pierre and
Philippe Aubry have shouldered a legacy dating from 1790, with
16.5 hectares from 60 individual locations. Today, Pierre holds a
national diploma in enology and Philippe in biology; they run this
small company in a highly innovative way. The yield is low and
only "*coeur de cuvée*" is used for the vintage wines. The grapes are
divided into five classes according to their quality, and a
considerable amount is vinified in old, traditional 205-liter oak
barrels. The most remarkable thing about Aubry is that, through
almost archaeological searching for old plant varieties, they have
succeeded in making a brilliant Champagne out of three forgotten
grape types: Pinot Gris, Arbanne, and Petit Meslier. Furthermore,
many grapevines are planted "*en foule,*" as they were before
phylloxera.
- AUBRY CLASSIC   74
  (30% PN, 40% PM, 30% CH)
- AUBRY ROSÉ   66
  (22% PN, 18% PM, 60% CH)
- 1998 AUBRY CUVÉE MANNERSTRÖM   82, NOV 2003 (84)
  (5% PN, 15% PM, 10% CH, 30% PINOT GRIS, 30% PETIT MESLIER,
  10% ARBANNE)
- 1996 AUBRY   83, JUL 2003 (87)
  (30% PN, 70% CH)
  Totally vinified in oak barrels. Selosse-like bouquet: I can clearly
  discern that the wine has not gone through malolactic
  fermentation. Perhaps a slightly pungent nose as yet, and a
  thoroughly immature, tart palate, but it also has a large portion
  of elegance. Wait a long time before opening this promising
  wine.
- 1996 AUBRY CUVÉE MANNERSTRÖM   83, AUG 2003 (87)
  (30% PN, 70% CH)
  The wine is identical to a 1996 Aubry.
- 1995 AUBRY BLANC DE BLANCS   78, MAR 2001 (81)
  (100% CH)
  So, this is how a Chardonnay from Jouy tastes? Very distinctive
  and striking character with a certain creamy butteriness. What is
  most clear is the relationship with a really fine Sancerre! Notes of
  flint, currant leaves, and gooseberries are unexpected and
  interesting. The wine went well with a mushroom risotto.
- 1996 AUBRY SABLÉ ROSÉ   81, APR 2001 (87)
  (25% PN, 25% PM, 50% CH)
  Aubry's '96s really improve by keeping to give them a rounder
  and more easily accessible character. This Champagne, with a
  barely noticeable color, has a fine creaminess in its elegantly
  bready, big-house-like bouquet. The palate is oh-so-young and
  steely sharp. What should we expect in the future?

- 1998 AUBRY LE NOMBRE D'OR   82, NOV 2003 (84)
(5% PN, 15% PM, 10% CH, 30% PINOT GRIS, 30% PETIT MESLIER, 10% ARBANNE)
Youthful, elegant, passion-fruity bouquet; it does not have an especially eccentric or provocative style this time. Lengthy, medium-bodied palate, where licorice and dried fruit become more evident after decanting.
- 1997 AUBRY LE NOMBRE D'OR   84, SEP 2002 (85)
(60% PINOT GRIS, 20% PETIT MESLIER, 20% ARBANNE)
Basically characterized by the vintage's charming, refreshing lightness. Sophisticated and ice-cream-like with clear notes of plum, melon, pineapple, and vanilla. Softly melting and slightly short palate with a pleasant sweetness. Impossible to trace, grapewise.
- 1996 AUBRY LE NOMBRE D'OR   84, NOV 2001 (87)
(60% PINOT GRIS, 20% PETIT MESLIER, 20% ARBANNE)
Magnificent, rich Champagne with a tendency towards raisin, banana, and plum, which exposes the strange grape content. The taste is decidedly more classic, with elements of grape and apple braided into a very full-bodied Champagne with razor-sharp tartness. Not as elegant as the '95, presumably because it contains so much Pinot Gris.
- 1995 AUBRY DE HUMBERT   87, MAY 2003 (89)
(33% PN, 33% PM, 34% CH)
Grand, characterful bouquet of first-class ripe grapes. Deliciously concentrated palate of exotic fruit such as mango, pineapple, and litchi, as well as a remarkably lengthy, sweet aftertaste. It feels as though the wine is made of grapes from old grapevines.
- 1995 AUBRY LE NOMBRE D'OR   87, MAY 2003 (89)
(33% PINOT GRIS, 33% PETIT MESLIER, 34% ARBANNE)
Sensational wine with irresistible charm. Polished and big-house-influenced yeast character. Cake-like and chocolaty aromas. Mellow, dark, and at the same time elegant fruit and a smooth, smiling finish. Truly a fascinating wine made from unusual grapes. How Pinot Gris, Petit Meslier, and Arbanne can produce such classic elegance is beyond me.

AUTREAU DE CHAMPILLON R-M

15, rue Renet Bandet
51160 Champillon
03 26 59 46 00
Production: 150,000

During the fifteen years that I have traveled around and visited producers in Champagne I have always been struck by the commitment that the growers show to their wine. It is very rare that one gets an impression of carelessness or ignorance. Sadly I have to say that Autreau is an exception to that rule. Despite their impressive twenty-one hectares in Champillon, Aÿ, Dizy, and Chouilly, in my opinion they produce sweet and unstructured Champagnes. These have, however, recently improved slightly.

- AUTREAU BRUT   48
(40% PN, 50% PM, 10% CH)
- AUTREAU RÉSERVE   51
(50% PN, 50% CH)
- 1988 AUTREAU   66, MAY 1994 (66)
(66% PN, 34% CH)
- 1997 CUVÉE LES PERLES DE LA DHUY   82, JUN 2003 (83)
(10% PN, 90% CH)

Not as sweet as earlier vintages. Now it has a fine freshness and an oily Chardonnay character where toffee is a noticeable element. Unfortunately, there is a weak bitterness in the finish that somewhat diminishes the impression.
- 1996 CUVÉE LES PERLES DE LA DHUY   83, JAN 2003 (86)
(100% CH)
One hundred percent Chouilly. I hadn't been tempted to try anything new from here because I was so disappointed on a visit in May 1994. All the more pleasant to discover that the '96 far surpassed all the wines I had previously tried from Autreau. The dosage feels, if anything, low, and the acidity is truly fierce, almost raw. The wine is very pure and promising.
- 1988 CUVÉE LES PERLES DE LA DHUY   72, MAY 1994 (75)
(5% PN, 95% CH)
- 1982 CUVÉE LES PERLES DE LA DHUY   79, JUL 1990 (81)
(5% PN, 95% CH)
The same aromas as the '88 but with a faint, pleasant nuance of toasted bread that makes this wine more interesting and fresh.

AYALA *** N-M

2, boulevard du Nord
51160 Aÿ
03 26 55 15 44
Production: 800,000

When Edmond de Ayala, the son of a Colombian diplomat, married into Aÿ society in 1860, he started up a Champagne house that quickly became one of the most popular. The firm's best market was England, and it still owns the Château de Mareuil and the Champagne house Montebello. Their own vineyards are in Mareuil-sur-Aÿ, but 80 percent are bought in from grapes rated 95 percent on the *cru* scale. For a long time the house was run by the former president of the C.I.V.C., the legendary J.-M. Ducellier, but in 1996 his son Alain took the helm. Thierry Budin has left Perrier-Jouët for Ayala and Château La Lagune in Bordeaux. Nicolas Klym is now the winemaker. The house-style has always been influenced by Pinot, and the wines have a fine roundness. The Blanc de Blancs are something of a disappointment, but the vintage wine is always dependable.

- AYALA BRUT   73
(75% PN, 25% CH)
- AYALA DEMI-SEC   50
(50% PN, 40% PM, 10% CH)
- AYALA ROSÉ   67
(55% PN, 20% PM, 25% CH)
- 1998 AYALA   83, FEB 2004 (86)
(80% PN, 20% CH)
A dark, slightly old-fashioned Champagne with touches of red and a full-bodied character that demands to be drunk with food. Big, tasty gulps of licorice, leather, red apples, and meat. However, it is somewhat one-dimensional.
- 1996 AYALA   83, MAR 2004 (87)
(80% PN, 20% CH)
This wine exhibits a generous, open attitude. The nose is richly composed with licorice and ripe fruit mixed up in a spicy register. Sweet and soft, like a toffee on the palate. I haven't been so excited by a vintage from Ayala for a long time. Fine Aÿ-weightiness and beautifully finished chocolaty flavor. Juicy and grand in its dimensions.
- 1995 AYALA   84, SEP 2003 (85)
(70% PN, 30% CH)

An impetuous Champagne that shamelessly throws itself about. Uncompromisingly old fashioned and rustic. Expressive Pinot with herby, spicy notes. Herbal tea and peppery mint chocolate sound a little quirky, but that is the aromatic image I want to convey.

- 1993 AYALA   82, SEP 2003 (84)
(80% PN, 20% CH)

Dense and robust with a fine Pinot Noir fruit at the base. One might think the wine will develop handsomely, but it feels as if there is not much space for such development. Honey notes and windfall fruit have already revealed themselves; shades of chocolate together with purple plums appear when aired.

- 1990 AYALA   77, JAN 2002 (81)
(70% PN, 30% CH)

Ayala have pulled off a decent piece of workmanship, but no more. This rich and relatively mature '90 has a sweet fruit reminiscent of the 1989 vintage.

- 1989 AYALA   81, JUL 1995 (86)
(75% PN, 25% CH)

A fruity, Pinot-dominated Champagne, bursting with life and with a smooth, long aftertaste.

- 1985 AYALA   81, DEC 1996 (85)
(70% PN, 30% CH)

Great weight and meaty Pinot aromas flow through this well-built '85.

- 1983 AYALA   83, MAR 2000 (83)
(75% PN, 25% CH)

Pleasant citrus tone that lifts up this mature wine. Otherwise, nothing much to wax lyrical about. Perhaps I should add that Chardonnay is more noticeable this year.

- 1982 AYALA   88, NOV 2002 (88)
(75% PN, 25% CH)

Typically generous, fruity Ayala nose with a rich and nutty flavor. Dark chocolate and tobacco appear when aired. A delightfully rich and voluptuous Champagne that has certain similarities with its famous neighbor on the other side of the hill.

- 1979 AYALA   87, AUG 1996 (88)
(75% PN, 25% CH)

An intense, fruity wine, with a pleasant butterscotch finish.

- 1975 AYALA   91, APR 1996 (91)
(75% PN, 25% CH)

Very lively and fiery, with clear Pinot aromas and a powerful aftertaste.

- 1973 AYALA   84, JUN 1997 (84)
(75% PN, 25% CH)

On its way to the grave, but still enjoyable nevertheless.

- 1964 AYALA   95, NOV 2001 (95)
(75% PN, 25% CH)

A wonderful, classic '64! Deep golden color and minimal bubbles, which never stop streaming upward out of the glass. A broad, mature nose with a wide spectrum of lovely aromas, such as toffee, mint chocolate, honey, and dried fruit. A wonderfully sweet caress on the palate with a romantic, ultra-long aftertaste of butterscotch.

- 1961 AYALA   92, JUL 1995 (92)
(75% PN, 25% CH)

Rather light and lively thirty-three-year-old. Slightly vegetable nose, with elements of licorice, tobacco, tar, and leather. Rich, dry, masculine, and long Champagne with some severe acidity. One of the last years that Ayala used oak barrels.

- 1959 AYALA   93, OCT 2001 (93)
(75% PN, 25% CH)

Apart from a strange, plastic-like nuance in the aroma, this is a classic Krug-like wine with glorious toffee tastes and a perfect balance. Somewhat lighter than expected, considering the vintage. I guessed that it was a '55.

- 1945 AYALA
(75% PN, 25% CH)

- 1943 AYALA   92, JAN 2003 (92)
(75% PN, 25% CH)

This faintly pearly half bottle was dark and slightly dim. Heavy scent of hardwood, Italian cantuccini, and dried apricots. Fleshy palate with an aromatic profile identical to the nose. Long and compact with a dry twist.

- 1941 AYALA   90, OCT 2001 (90)
(75% PN, 25% CH)

At the height of World War II Ayala succeeded in producing this fascinating wine. Now, at the age of sixty, its bubbles are a thing of the past. Despite this, the wine holds its own in the glass and is surprisingly free of any hint of maderization. Instead, one finds dried roses and a bouquet reminiscent of teak oil.

- 1928 AYALA
(75% PN, 25% CH)

- 1923 AYALA
(75% PN, 25% CH)

- 1998 AYALA BLANC DE BLANCS   84, FEB 2004 (87)
(100% CH)

Fine green color, beautiful mousse, and a handsomely composed floral bouquet. Pleasant plumpness mid-taste and a note of lime in the finish.

- 1996 AYALA BLANC DE BLANCS   85, DEC 2003 (87)
(100% CH)

Well-rounded and richly ample with a layer of fat fruit. One of this wine's richest vintages. It will be interesting to see which branch of the tree of life this wine is going to pick—it seems to become more toasted with time, as my latest bottle exuded coffee and toast.

- 1992 AYALA BLANC DE BLANCS   79, SEP 2002 (79)
(100% CH)

- 1990 AYALA BLANC DE BLANCS   76, AUG 1999 (78)
(100% CH)

- 1988 AYALA BLANC DE BLANCS   67, MAR 1995 (71)
(100% CH)

- 1985 AYALA BLANC DE BLANCS   83, MAR 1998 (83)
(100% CH)

Massively roasted and already fully matured Chardonnay. Delightfully enjoyable but hardly elegant.

- 1982 AYALA BLANC DE BLANCS   66, JUL 1989 (70)
(100% CH)

- 1979 AYALA BLANC DE BLANCS   78
(100% CH)

- 1975 AYALA BLANC DE BLANCS   84, MAR 2000 (84)
(100% CH)

Ever a vigorous Chardonnay, though lacking the refinement of the truly great ones. Robust, fleshy, and tolerably fat. Excellent with breast of pigeon in a morel sauce: not normally something I would recommend with a Blanc de Blancs!

- 1997 PERLE D'AYALA   87, DEC 2003 (89)
(20% PN, 80% CH)

A floral, headstrong Champagne with a hint of the same Sauvignon Blanc notes that one finds in a Pavillion Blanc from Château Margaux. It also has a touch of oak barrel that is suggestive of a white Burgundy. Thierry Budin believes the tone comes from cellar-aging with real corks, or from dosage from oak barrels. Mint is another note that causes me to stop and reflect.

- 1996 PERLE D'AYALA   84, DEC 2001 (88)
  (80% PN, 20% CH)

A balanced mix of grapes from Aÿ, Mareuil-sur-Aÿ, Chouilly, Mesnil, and Cramant. Lighter and definitely purer than the usual vintage Champagne of the same year. Otherwise, the piquant spiciness and licorice notes are easily recognizable. Just a few points more and yet double the price of the 1996 Ayala.

- 1993 AYALA GRANDE CUVÉE   85, SEP 2003 (85)
  (30% PN, 70% CH)

Not in any way an old or aged Champagne, but I still give it no extra points for great potential. In my opinion its youthful merits are fine as they are; the wine may become more trivial when it is older. Its floral refinements and crispy gooseberry notes are lovely today and stand in harmony with the sweet hints of butterscotch toffee.

- 1990 AYALA GRANDE CUVÉE   85, JUL 2002 (88)
  (30% PN, 70% CH)

Refined and ever youthful, with a completely lovely appearance and expression. The nose shifts vigorously in the glass—from flowery, citrus influences to buttery and exotic, with shades of roasted almonds.

- 1988 AYALA GRANDE CUVÉE   84, JUL 1995 (89)
  (30% PN, 70% CH)

A most delicate Champagne with notes of white chocolate and jasmine. Light and stylish.

BANCHET-LEGRAS R-M
8, rue Pont
51530 Chouilly
03 26 55 41 53
Production: 60,000

I have never visited this small grower, but have often tasted his Champagnes in restaurants in Épernay. I've never come across a single Champagne producer outside of Chouilly who knows of this firm's existence.

- BANCHET-LEGRAS BLANC DE BLANCS   70
  (100% CH)

BARANCOURT N-M
B.P. 3
51150 Bouzy
03 26 53 33 40
Production: 800,000

In 1966 a trio of winemakers from Bouzy joined together to form Barancourt. Twelve years later, Brice, Martin, and Tritant bought a vineyard in Cramant in order to make *cuvées* from *grand cru* grapes. For many years, Barancourt has been seen as a producer of good, storable wines, but despite my passion for that style, I've never been convinced about this company's greatness. Certainly the wines do have a personal style, with their vegetable aromas, but they don't come close to greatness. In 1994 Barancourt was taken over by the Vranken group, and today their grapes come from ten different villages, including a couple of places in Aube.

- BARANCOURT BRUT   67
  (50% PN, 10% PM, 40% CH)
- BARANCOURT BOUZY BRUT   56
  (80% PN, 20% CH)
- BARANCOURT CRAMANT BLANC DE BLANCS   68
  (100% CH)
- BARANCOURT ROSÉ   70
  (40% PN, 60% CH)
- 1985 BARANCOURT BOUZY BRUT   79, APR 1995 (79)
  (90% PN, 10% CH)
- 1979 BARANCOURT   84, APR 2000 (85)
  (90% PN, 10% CH)

Still retains a little undeveloped extract and a youthful, pumped-up, muscular body. Somewhat coarse, with some special, almost atypical currant and grass flavors. Impressive strength, good with meat.

- 1971 BARANCOURT   88, MAR 2004 (88)
  (80% PN, 20% CH)

Very fleshy, textbook, Pinot-influenced Champagne. The lightness and elegance of this vintage are hardly noticed. Vegetables, meat, and mushroom aromas dominated the impressions of my tasting group—I agree.

- CUVÉE FONDATEURS   80
  (80% PN, 20% CH)

Bouzy only. Weak, musky nose lifted up by vegetable aromas, a fine mousse and a promising structure. Worth storing for a while.

- CUVÉE FONDATEURS ROSÉ   83
  (95% PN, 5% CH)

Almost a Rosé de Noirs. A very rich and full-bodied food Champagne, perfectly suited to a good assortment of cheeses. Strongly imprinted with Bouzy's *terroir* character.

- 1988 CUVÉE FONDATEURS   82, MAY 1995 (87)
  (80% PN, 20% CH)

The vegetable and animal tones return here, but are now backed up by much-needed creaminess and a crispy fruit that makes this the firm's very best wine.

- 1983 CUVÉE FONDATEURS   78, SEP 1993 (79)
  (50% PN, 50% CH)

BARA, PAUL **** R-M
4, rue Yvonnet
51150 Bouzy
03 26 57 00 50
Production: 90,000

Paul Bara is a living legend in Champagne. He took over the firm as a teenager sixty years ago and remembers every vintage in perfect detail. He belongs to the sixth generation to run the company since it was founded in 1833. Many major Champagne houses have approached Bara over the years to try to buy the thirty exceptional locations he controls in the village. The average age of the vines is around twenty-five years, but those that produce the vintage wines are closer to forty. The butterfly-collecting legend is, together with Camille Savès and André Clouet, the most quality-obsessed grower in Bouzy. Only the first pressing is used, the wines are aged for at least four years in the cold cellar, and the yield is maintained at the lowest possible level. Despite the traditional methods, Bara's wines have a very elegant fruitiness, which is unique in Bouzy. It is incomprehensible that he is best known for his red wine when his Champagne is of world class. His '59 was hailed as the best Blanc de Noirs at the Millennium Tasting.

- PAUL BARA BRUT   80
(80% PN, 20% CH)
It's a lovely, life-enhancing experience to drink a glass of the rich, fruity Pinot Champagne. When it is young, aromas of green apples dominate, but with time a rich chocolate flavor takes over.

- PAUL BARA ROSÉ   84
(90% PN, 10% CH)
A very masculine and well-built rosé Champagne with Burgundy-like form and a unified aroma. Suitable for aging.

- 1995 PAUL BARA   83, MAY 2003 (89)
(100% PN)
Vigorous, charming, and youthful. It incorporates a deliciously ingratiating candy tone that successfully takes charge of the crispy gooseberry fruit. Other discernible notes, here at the beginning of this wine's life, are currant leaves, cream, and early summer flowers. The Champagne will naturally increase in fullness with maturity.

- 1993 PAUL BARA   85, FEB 2004 (88)
(90% PN, 10% CH)
Young, light, and stony in an unusually restrained style. The fruit that stands out is similar to yellow apples and equally yellow plums. Nice aging.

- 1990 PAUL BARA   86, APR 2000 (92)
(100% PN)
Unexpected creaminess and an elegant bouquet. Bara's wines always appear lighter and more Chardonnay-influenced than they really are. In time, the grape and original earthiness will come to the fore with more clarity. At ten years of age the wine is creamy and charmingly exotic. Only the peppery aftertaste convinces me that I am drinking a Blanc de Noirs.

- 1989 PAUL BARA   86, APR 1998 (92)
(100% PN)
A dark yellow Blanc de Noirs with outstandingly tight, honeyed nose and massive buttery candy flavor. Focused and concentrated without being clumsy. The wine has a special sweet complexity which only old vines and a warm year can give.

- 1961 PAUL BARA   93, AUG 1999 (93)
(100% PN)
Delighted with his success at the Millennium Tasting, Paul Bara brought out this pale, youthful '61. I must admit that I was a little disappointed in the wine's vigor, but just as pleasantly surprised by its subtlety and elegance. Minerals, clean sheets, and unlit cigars were aromas that spontaneously came to mind.

- 1959 PAUL BARA   97, JUN 1999 (97)
(100% PN)
I asked Paul Bara which of the vintages he has produced during his lifetime he was most satisfied with. "Come here and I'll show you," he said, and he fetched a normally disgorged half bottle of this peerless wine. The mousse was weak and the color glowed amber. In the nose I was met by an indescribably wonderful wave of sensations: mint chocolate, rum, peaches, wood, and honey. The flavor was even more impressive, if that's possible, with an Yquem-like structure and sweetness. The flavor was exceptionally deep, uniting mint chocolate with rum liqueur. When Pinot Noir tastes like this, even the most confirmed Chardonnay lover can't fail to be converted. Winner in the Pinot Noir class at the Millennium Tasting.

- 1994 PAUL BARA SPECIAL CLUB   80, NOV 1999 (85)
(70% PN, 30% CH)

A fine '94 and quite a rich and accomplished wine, with lots of flavor of yellow apples and a pleasant taste of gooseberry. Special Club from Bara is usually quite a bit heftier and more muscular.

- 1993 COMTESSE MARIE DE FRANCE   85, JAN 2004 (90)
(100% PN)
Paul Bara always seems to produce a concentrated wine to put in this prestige bottle. This demonstrates great fleshiness and the classic Pinot spectrum. Already there are very mature aromas but, speaking from experience, I would like to recommend storing the wine for several years in order to extract the wonderful secondary aromas that always seem to drop straight into one's lap. One of the district's foremost and most reliable Blanc de Noirs!

- 1991 COMTESSE MARIE DE FRANCE   85, JUN 2002 (88)
(100% PN)
Sensationally polished and floral multifaceted Champagne with an almost feminine elegance, despite its grape composition. Litchi, orange blossoms, and tomato-plant leaves were aromas that confronted me in the nose. The flavor is compact and youthful with a great integral ability to transform stylishly with time.

- 1990 COMTESSE MARIE DE FRANCE   86, MAR 2003 (92)
(100% PN)
A blunt, unbelievably gamy and naughty wine that only those with an erotic bent will appreciate at the moment. The wine divided a tasting group with the importer Vindirekt into two distinct camps at Riche in May 2000. I am convinced that in time this will become a great Burgundy-like mealtime Champagne, even if today some think that the wine is a little too pushy.

- 1990 PAUL BARA SPECIAL CLUB   85, MAR 2001 (93)
(67% PN, 33% CH)
Rich in minerals, finesse, and elegance, with a dormant creaminess under the surface. Early days yet.

- 1989 COMTESSE MARIE DE FRANCE   87, JUN 2003 (89)
(100% PN)
Cloudberry and sun-ripened plums, backed up by honey, molasses, and shades of oyster shell. These are the most important ingredients in this compact, integrated, mellow Blanc de Noirs. Considering how long Bara's wines usually last, and despite the current impression of full maturity, aging might be an interesting proposition.

- 1989 PAUL BARA SPECIAL CLUB   85, APR 1998 (90)
(70% PN, 30% CH)
What the wine gains in elegance it loses in concentration, with the addition of Chardonnay. The nose is closed but has an extra dimension of jasmine. Very good attack but a shorter aftertaste than the vintage wines.

- 1988 COMTESSE MARIE DE FRANCE   92, NOV 2003 (94)
(100% PN)
Soft and balanced, with a lovely focused fruit. A really elegant wine to show those who doubt that Bouzy grapes can make it on their own without the Chardonnay from Côte des Blancs. Unbelievably sensual and bright in personality. Honeysuckle and mandarin as well as pineapple and coconut can be discerned. In many ways, the wine acts like a white Burgundy.

- 1986 PAUL BARA SPECIAL CLUB   85, MAR 2003 (85)
(70% PN, 30% CH)
Most of the '86s have seen better days, as has this one. The wine is not just tired and oxidized, but has also acquired a

homogeneous, accentuated ripe plumminess that is too dominant. The color is deep and intense, the mousse a model of buoyancy. The entire wine will surely stay cohesive for many years to come. Large bottle variation.

• 1985 COMTESSE MARIE DE FRANCE   85, APR 1995 (91)
(100% PN)

An incredibly elegant and delicate '85. A typical Champagne nose with elements of toasted bread, chestnuts, and lemon peel. The wine leaves a pared-down, crystal-clear impression on the palate, with its balanced, restrained aftertaste.

• 1983 COMTESSE MARIE DE FRANCE   85, JAN 2003 (85)
(100% PN)

A strangely perfumed wine with an exaggerated nose of banana and blackcurrants. The flavor is of a much higher class with its pure, slightly one-dimensional hazelnut aroma. It has become weightier of late.

• 1982 COMTESSE MARIE DE FRANCE   94, OCT 2003 (94)
(100% PN)

Totally wonderful with its extreme butterscotchy style. Almost like a fleshy, highly explosive, heavy Blanc de Blancs—but when aired it is still too spicy, gamy, and licorice-laden to be one of them. As a tasting leader, it seldom occurs to me that participants are going to be led down the wrong path, but here I knew they were never going to find the Blanc de Noirs in such a fat, ingratiating, and toffee-like gem. Outstanding, but with a mousse that was slightly too weak and a "nuance" slightly too defective to enable it to belong to the legendary greats. Still, a truly fantastic Champagne.

• 1978 PAUL BARA SPECIAL CLUB   90, MAY 1996 (90)
(100% PN)

Rich and mellow, with ripe plum flavors and good length, especially considering the vintage.

BARDOUX R-M

5, rue Saint Vincent
51390 Villedommange
03 26 49 23 15
Production: 25,000

The Bardoux family has produced wine ever since Pierre Bardoux first broke ground in 1684. They have been producing their own Champagne since 1929. Pascal Bardoux, educated in Beaune, is the winemaker today.

• PASCAL BARDOUX BRUT   53
(15% PN, 65% PM, 20% CH)

• PASCAL BARDOUX RÉSERVE   61
(20% PN, 40% PM, 40% CH)

BARDY PÈRE & FILS R-M

3, rue d'Oiry
51190 Le Mesnil-sur-Oger
03 26 57 57 59
Production: 60,000

Unfortunately, Monsieur Bardy no longer makes vintage wines from his six hectares full of twenty-five-year-old vines.

• BARDY CUVÉE RÉSERVE   75
(100% CH)

• BARDY BLANC DE BLANCS   65
(100% CH)

BARNAUT, E.*** R-M

2, rue Gambetta
51150 Bouzy
03 26 57 01 54
Production: 70,000

The property was founded in 1874 and covers twelve hectares in Bouzy. Philippe Secondé is always the last in the village to harvest his grapes and he handpicks the ripest. The wines are stored for at least five years before being sold. The first prestige Champagne, Cuvée Edmond, was produced for the company's 125th anniversary. It contains a splash of Pinot Meunier, which Philippe obtained from the Marne Valley.

• E. BARNAUT EXTRA BRUT   80
(90% PN, 10% CH)

A multi-vintage made from older wines. Incredibly tight and focused. The color is red-brown and the aromas almost meaty.

• E. BARNAUT GRANDE RÉSERVE   71
(80% PN, 20% CH)

• E. BARNAUT BLANC DE NOIRS   79
(100% PN)

• E. BARNAUT CUVÉE DOUCEUR SEC   55
(66% PN, 34% CH)

• E. BARNAUT ROSÉ   79
(100% PN)

• 1995 E. BARNAUT   86, FEB 2004 (90)
(50% PN, 50% CH)

Lighter and more influenced by Chardonnay than expected. Somewhat floral and appley, with a beautifully toasted, nuanced palate. A slender-limbed gem!

• 1990 E. BARNAUT   76, MAY 1997 (86)
(50% PN, 50% CH)

Unexpectedly elegant nose of apple and almonds. The flavor is acidic and medium-bodied, with interesting mineral tones. The origin is, as usual, much easier to trace after a moment's breathing.

• E. BARNAUT CUVÉE EDMOND   87
(40% PN, 20% PM, 40% CH)

The grower's nonvintage prestige Champagne has a very fine bouquet of cinnamon, freshly baked bread, and mint. The taste is rich, but youthfully undeveloped, and full of some bitter extract. Fine storability potential. Reminiscent of Cuvée Juline from Georges Vesselle.

BARNIER, ROGER N-M

1, rue du Marais de Saint-Gond,
51270 Villevenard
03 26 52 82 77
Production: 50,000

The house was founded in 1932. Frédéric Berthelot owns seven hectares.

• ROGER BARNIER CARTE NOIRE   48
(20% PN, 40% PM, 40% CH)

• ROGER BARNIER EXQUISE   67
(40% PM, 60% CH)

• ROGER BARNIER ROSÉ   50
(50% PN, 5% PM, 45% CH)

• ROGER BARNIER   73, OCT 1997 (76)
(45% PN, 5% PM, 50% CH)

BARON ALBERT N-M
Grand-Porteron,
02310 Charly-sur-Marne
03 23 82 02 65
Production: 500,000

The Baron family has lived in Charly since 1677. Today Claude, Gilbert, and Gervais make Champagne from their thirty-two hectares. The average age of the vineyards is as much as thirty-five years. The wine doesn't go through malolactic fermentation in order to maintain its freshness. In the firm's best wines they use a small number of oak barrels to give weight and vanilla aromas.

- BARON ALBERT CARTE D'OR   52
  (35% PN, 35% PM, 30% CH)
- JEAN DE LA FONTAINE SEC   51
  (5% PN, 45% PM, 50% CH)
- BARON ALBERT ROSÉ   62
  (5% PN, 50% PM, 45% CH)
- JEAN DE LA FONTAINE ROSÉ   62
  (5% PN, 50% PM, 45% CH)
- 1996 JEAN DE LA FONTAINE   79, JAN 2003 (83)
  (5% PN, 45% PM, 50% CH)
  A prestige wine with 15 percent oak-barrel-fermented wine from seven villages. Smart, youthful image with high acidity. There's a certain plumpness in the taste; it has a crisp, sparkling mousse and a lovely finish of vanilla aromas.
- 1995 BARON ALBERT   62, MAY 2003 (63)
- 1996 LA PRÉFÉRENCE DE BARON ALBERT   76, JUN 2003 (79)
  (5% PN, 30% PM, 65% CH)

BAUCHET R-M
rue de la Crayère
51150 Bisseuil
03 26 58 92 12
Production: 36,5000

This relatively unknown property produces quite a healthy quantity of wine from its thirty-seven hectares, of which twenty-five lie in Aube. In fact, this is one of the largest growers in Champagne. The foremost grapes come from Bisseuil and Grauves. The firm was founded in 1920 by Félicien Bauchet. At the helm today is Laurent Bauchet, leading a workforce of twenty-seven.

- BAUCHET BRUT SÉLECTION   66
  (50% PN, 50% CH)
- BAUCHET BRUT RÉSERVE   66
  (40% PN, 60% CH)
- BAUCHET ROSÉ   61
  (10% PN, 90% CH)
- BAUCHET LE PREMIER JOUR   79
  (50% PN, 50% CH)

BAUDRY, P. N-M
51390 Pargny-les-Reims

Located in Pargny-les-Reims, this is a sub-brand of Charles de Cazanove in Reims.

- BAUDRY CHADELIES   40
  (35% PN, 60% PM, 5% CH)
- PRINCESSE DE BAUDRY   49
  (50% PN, 40% PM, 10% CH)
- BAUDRY MALHERBE   60
  (50% PN, 50% PM)

BAUGET-JOUETTE N-M
60, rue Chaude-Ruelle
51200 Épernay
03 26 54 44 05
Production: 200,000

Up until quite recently, it was rare to find a grower's Champagne in Épernay. The work began in 1822 with grapes from fifteen hectares in Mancy, Monthelon, Grauves, Damery, Venteuil, and Hautvillers. Their wines have received a great deal of attention in the international press in recent years. Traditional methods are used. The firm's style is made up of uncomplicated, bready Champagnes for the broader public. The *cuvée de prestige* doesn't cost any more than nonvintage Champagnes from the major houses.

- BAUGET-JOUETTE CARTE BLANCHE   54
  (20% PN, 40% PM, 40% CH)
- BAUGET-JOUETTE GRANDE RÉSERVE   60
  (20% PN, 20% PM, 60% CH)
- BAUGET-JOUETTE ROSÉ   62
  (80% PN, 20% CH)
- 1990 BAUGET-JOUETTE   78, JUL 1995 (81)
  (30% PN, 70% CH)
  A 1990 that has developed a touch too early, with buttery and creamy nose and taste.
- 1990 BAUGET-JOUETTE BLANC DE BLANCS   78, JUL 1995 (84)
  (100% CH)
  Somewhat more restrained and elegant than the blended '90. Short aftertaste.
- CUVÉE JOUETTE   81
  (30% PN, 70% CH)
  Fine, mineral-rich nose and a delicate, stony taste with hints of digestive biscuit. Can develop!
- BAUGET-JOUETTE CUVÉE 2000   79, OCT 2001 (81)
  (30% PN, 70% CH)
  Young, unusually fresh with elastic, uncomplicated fruit and fine Chardonnay character. The first apple aromas slide into melon and citrus in the relatively dry aftertaste.

BEAUFORT, ANDRÉ R-M
1, rue de Vaudemanges
51150 Ambonnay
03 26 57 01 50
Production: 25,000

André Beaufort founded his company in Ambonnay in 1933. Today Jacques Beaufort owns seven hectares planted with 65 percent Pinot Noir. This grower is among the select group that sells older vintages. He really makes personal wines.

- ANDRÉ BEAUFORT BRUT   47
  (66% PN, 34% CH)
- 1990 ANDRÉ BEAUFORT   78, OCT 1997 (85)
  (66% PN, 34% CH)
  Strong nose of dill and meat stew. Quite heavy and cumbersome without food to help it along. Fine structure.
- 1989 ANDRÉ BEAUFORT   80, OCT 2001 (80)
  (65% PN, 35% CH)
  Deeply yellow, almost golden in color, with fine, tiny bubbles. Bouquet rich with fruit. Notes of vanilla, flowers, and heavy Pinot character, with a palate of roasted apples and the warmth of this vintage. Red beets, meat stew, and blueberries in the nose.

Very round and full-bodied taste of blueberries, as in an
Australian Shiraz.

- 1987 ANDRÉ BEAUFORT   82, OCT 1997 (82)
(66% PN, 34% CH)
Totally different from the others. Creamy aroma of melted butter,
peach, banana, and chewing gum. Soft, exotic Chardonnay on
the palate.
- 1986 ANDRÉ BEAUFORT   66, OCT 1997 (66)
(66% PN, 34% CH)
- 1985 ANDRÉ BEAUFORT DEMI-SEC
(66% PN, 34% CH)

BEAUFORT, CLAUDE R-M
16, boulevard des Bermonts
51150 Ambonnay
03 26 57 01 32
Production: 40,000
Today, Claude is the mayor of Ambonnay, and his daughter is
married to Ambonnay's most prominent grower, R. H. Coutier.

- CLAUDE BEAUFORT CUVÉE RÉSERVE   65
(15% PN, 85% CH)
- CLAUDE BEAUFORT BLANC DE BLANCS   65
(100% CH)
- CLAUDE BEAUFORT ROSÉ   63
(50% PN, 50% CH)
- 1988 CLAUDE BEAUFORT   75, DEC 1998 (82)
(35% PN, 65% CH)
Big, somewhat musty scent of cheese and boiled vegetables.
Makes a considerably fresher impression on the palate, where
Chardonnay plays the most noticeable role.

BEAUFORT, C. R-M
5, rue des Neigettes
51380 Trépail
03 26 57 05 63
Production: 40,000
Yet another grower from the Beaufort family of Bouzy. The family
have been growers in Trépail for five generations. Today Arnaud
Beaufort is at the helm. Malolactic fermentation is avoided.

- C. BEAUFORT BRUT RÉSERVE   65
(20% PN, 80% CH)

BEAUFORT, HERBERT R-M
32, rue de Tours
51150 Bouzy
03 26 57 01 34
Production: 140,000
Beaufort owns seventeen hectares in Bouzy and has a good
reputation for its range of Bouzy reds. This grower is known in
Sweden because the Monarque Bleu Club chose to invest in this
producer's nonvintage Champagne to drink as the clock struck
twelve on New Year's Eve 2000. It would be interesting to hear just
how this normally disgorged Bouzy tasted then.

- H. BEAUFORT CARTE BLANCHE   69
(70% PN, 30% CH)
- H. BEAUFORT CARTE D'OR   74
(100% PN)
- LE MONARQUE BLEU   69
(70% PN, 30% CH)

- H. BEAUFORT ROSÉ   70
(100% PN)
- 1981 H. BEAUFORT   82, JUL 1990 (87)
(80% PN, 20% CH)
The color is brilliant and the nose is full of apple blossom and
hawthorn. The flavor is long and impressive.
- 1998 H. BEAUFORT CUVÉE LA FAVORITE   83, MAY 2003 (88)
A really fine, deliciously flavor-packed Champagne with great
power and unctuous depth. But it also possesses a straight-backed
elegance as a base at the same time as the concentrated palate
accentuates ingratiating aromas of strawberry and toffee.

BEAUMET N-M
3, rue Malakoff
51200 Épernay
03 26 59 50 10
Production: 1,500,000
Beaumet was founded in 1878 in Pierry. Today the company is
owned by Jacques Trouillard and is situated together with Oudinot
and Jeanmaire in the beautiful "Parc Malakoff." Beaumet owns
more than eighty hectares spread across Champagne, and about
half the grapes are bought in. For many years Swedes have been
acquainted with Beaumet's wines, as Couronne d'Or is made by
this Épernay company. The winemaker Denis Colombier also
makes Oudinot and Jeanmaire.

- COURONNE D'OR   50
(40% PN, 30% PM, 30% CH)
- MARQUIS D'AUVIGNE   50
(40% PN, 30% PM, 30% CH)
- COURONNE D'ARGENT   25
(40% PN, 30% PM, 30% CH)
- BEAUMET ROSÉ   50
(70% PN, 30% PM)
- 1994 BEAUMET GRAND CRU   68, MAY 2001 (70)
(60% PN, 40% CH)
- 1990 BEAUMET GRAND CRU   66, NOV 2003 (66)
(60% PN, 40% CH)
- 1989 BEAUMET GRAND CRU
(60% PN, 40% CH)
- 1985 CUVÉE MALAKOFF   83, JUL 1999 (85)
(100% CH)
Rich and full bodied with a smoky tone. Butterscotch soft
aftertaste. Other than that, though, somewhat one-dimensional.
- 1982 CUVÉE MALAKOFF   85, JUN 1999 (88)
(100% CH)
Large, impressive, buttery Blanc de Blancs with a lovely mature
style.
- 1982 CUVÉE MALAKOFF ROSÉ   80, JUN 1995 (81)
(100% PN)
A well-kept but insignificant, fruity '82 without complexity.
- 1995 BEAUMET MILLENNIUM CUVÉE   73, JUL 2001 (75)
(60% PN, 40% CH)
The bottle I happened to taste was full of the same scent of
children's glue that earlier denoted Laurent-Perrier. The wine
was soft and medium bodied with a fine sweetness and a
clear almond note that sat as firm as a rock in the mouth
after swallowing.

BEAUTRAIT, YVES R-M
4, rue des Cavaliers
51150 Louvois
03 26 57 03 38
Production: 65,000
This grower owns 16.5 hectares in Bouzy, Louvois, Tauxières, and Tours-sur-Marne. Beautrait's cellars are clinically clean and the equipment is highly modern, unusual given the relatively minor level of production.

- YVES BEAUTRAIT BRUT   76
  (75% PN, 25% CH)
- 1983 YVES BEAUTRAIT SPECIAL CLUB   76, JUN 1989 (80)
  (60% PN, 40% CH)
  Made completely from Bouzy grapes. The nose isn't as complete as the nonvintage Champagne, but in the mouth it has a concentrated, long, Pinot flavor.

BECKER N-M
51100 Reims
A company that belongs to the past. It's all the more fun when one finds bottles from such a house.

- 1964 BECKER MEMORIAL CUVÉE

BEERENS, ALBERT R-M
10200 Bar-sur-Aube
Production: 35,000
A small grower from Aube who uses over six hectares planted with 80 percent Pinot Noir and 20 percent Chardonnay. The producer makes only two Champagnes: a rosé and a white.

- ALBERT BEERENS BRUT   54
  (90% PN, 10% CH)

BENARD, ROGER R-M
25, rue Louis Lange
51530 Moslins
03 26 59 49 69
I ran into this wine on the island of Gran Canaria: it was the house Champagne at my hotel in Puerto Rico. Not exactly the place I would have expected to run into a Champagne I'd never heard of before. Go to the Hotel El Greco if you'd like to try this grower's products.

- ROGER BENARD BRUT   51
  (33% PN, 33% PM, 34% CH)

BERGÈRE, ALAIN R-M
81, Grand Rue
51270 Étoges
03 23 70 29 82
Production: 70,000

- ALAIN BERGÈRE RÉSERVE BRUT   68
  (25% PN, 50% PM, 25% CH)

BERGERONEAUX, FRANÇOIS R-M
10, rue Aurore
51390 Villedommange
03 26 49 24 18
Production: 15,000
According to many, this is one of the best growers in Petit Montagnem.

- PHILIPPE BERGERONEAUX BRUT   65
  (30% PN, 50% PM, 20% CH)

BERTHELOT, PAUL R-M
889, avenue du Général-Leclerc
51530 Dizy
03 26 55 23 83
Production: 150,000
The Berthelot family owns twenty hectares in the Marne valley. Other wines: Rosé, Brut.

- PAUL BERTHELOT BRUT RÉSERVE   69
  (30% PN, 40% PM, 30% CH)
- 1983 BERTHELOT CUVÉE DU CENTENAIRE   84, OCT 2001 (84)
  (60% PN, 40% CH)
  A rustic, prestige wine from Dizy, full of ripe notes and rich fullness. Absolutely brilliant as an accompaniment to a cheese platter. I was served this wine blind and didn't come anywhere near with my guess of a 1985 Vilmart.

BERTRAND, GILBERT R-M
5, ruelle des Godats
51500 Chamery
03 26 97 63 19
Production: 80,000
The grower utilizes more than 9.5 hectares in Eceuil, Chamery, Villedommanges, and Montbré with equal quantities of the three grape types. The grower makes five *cuvées* in which Chardonnay is sometimes fermented in oak barrels. No wine is put through malolactic fermentation. The winemaker today is Didier Bertrand.

- GILBERT BERTRAND BRUT   50
  (20% PN, 60% PM, 20% CH)

BESSERAT DE BELLEFON N-M
19, avenue de Champagne
51200 Épernay
03 26 78 50 50
Production: 1,300,000
Founded in Aÿ in 1843. Bought by Pernod-Ricard in 1971. Today housed at Marne et Champagne. Marie-Laurence Mora is responsible for keeping the quality at Besserat to an acceptable level. Vincent Malherbe is the man behind the *cuvées*. The purchased grapes come from 110 communes. The wines are vinified in ultra-modern style and filtered so hard that the aging potential is minimal. The firm has a good reputation in France for their fruity crémant wines, but they should be drunk young. They have no vineyards of their own and only 14 percent of production is exported. Other brands: de Monterat, de Vauzelle.

- CUVÉE DES MOINES   67
  (45% PN, 35% PM, 20% CH)
- GRANDE TRADITION   75
  (35% PN, 25% PM, 40% CH)
- CUVÉE DES MOINES ROSÉ   61
  (60% PN, 20% PM, 20% CH)
- 1996 BESSERAT DE BELLEFON   79, APR 2003 (84)
  (25% PN, 15% PM, 60% CH)
  A lovely wine with stylish grace and elegance. Faint, pure, and handsomely compounded bouquet. Acidity dominate over a creamy, tempering layer of taste. Fine Chardonnay character reigns over the red-wine grapes.
- 1990 BESSERAT DE BELLEFON   84, MAR 2003 (84)
  (25% PN, 15% PM, 60% CH)

A handsome, piquant toasted note has crept in and draped itself around the floral, fruity core. Long, intense, fruity, sparkling taste. A refreshing '90 that is going to develop greater depth in the future. Despite this, my personal taste begs me to drink this Champagne again soon.

- 1989 BESSERAT DE BELLEFON   80, AUG 1997 (82)
(25% PN, 14% PM, 61% CH)
Discreet, flowery, and young on the nose. Correct, but rather charmless in the mouth.
- 1985 BESSERAT DE BELLEFON   79, OCT 2001 (79)
(25% PN, 15% PM, 60% CH)
- 1982 BESSERAT DE BELLEFON   85, NOV 2001 (85)
(50% PN, 50% CH)
A voluptuous wine with a delightful coffee bouquet. Somewhat less impressive on the palate, but still very good with its fine mineral, orange, chocolaty notes. Completely mature and not too expensive.
- 1975 BESSERAT DE BELLEFON   84, JAN 2000 (84)
(25% PN, 25% PM, 50% CH)
Besserat's wines are not made for storage. This twenty-five year old, however, suffers no signs of aging. Appearance, nose, and palate all exhibit youthful vitality and energy. The only problem is that the wine is insipid and lacks concentration.
- 1982 BESSERAT DE BELLEFON ROSÉ   86, APR 2002 (86)
(50% PN, 50% CH)
A smiling wine with an uplifting, light, summery character. The bouquet possesses the vintage's plumpness combined with a real dollop of coffee aroma and puffs of wind from a raspberry patch. Constant on the palate is a fat, buttery keynote, around which a refreshing lightness dances gracefully.
- 1964 BESSERAT DE BELLEFON ROSÉ   89, MAR 2004 (89)
(50% PN, 50% CH)
Impressive toffee note and big, leathery fruit. Delicate but piquant mousse, and a chocolaty basic flavor. Most agreeable mealtime Champagne.
- GRANDE CUVÉE BESSERAT DE BELLEFON   67
(40% PN, 60% CH)
- 1996 GRANDE TRADITION   85, SEP 2003 (88)
Almost metallic bouquet with beautiful floral elements. Fine mineral character and tight fruit. Tartly restrained, promising a prestige cuvée.
- 1979 BRUT INTÉGRAL   84, DEC 2003 (84)
(50% PN, 50% CH)
Still a perky wine with a middle-aged appearance. The bouquet, however, is mature, with notes of tea, coffee, vegetables, bread, and damp wood. It is fascinating that the bouquet is so mellow and evolved when the unsweetened flavor is sharp, raw, tart, and as dry as a stick. There is a malty feeling here, together with a sea-saltiness reminiscent of shellfish—with which it should go well.
- 1977 BRUT INTÉGRAL   75, DEC 2003 (75)
(50% PN, 50% CH)
- 1975 BRUT INTÉGRAL   88, DEC 1995 (88)
(50% PN, 50% CH)
Dry, long, and rather forceful in a stiff, slightly charmless manner. I drank this wine, unfortunately, as an aperitif.

BÉRAT, JACQUES R-M
8, rue Saint Roch
51480 Boursault
03 26 58 42 45
Production: 100,000
The Bérat family have cultivated grapes in Champagne since the eighteenth century, but only in 1950 did Jacques Bérat begin to sell his own Champagne. The firm's twelve hectares are in Oeuilly and Boursault, and the current owners are Isabelle and Vincent Bérat. Other wines: Vintage, Carte Perle, Carte Blanche.
- JACQUES BÉRAT SPECIAL CUVÉE   59
(50% PN, 25% PM, 25% CH)
- JACQUES BÉRAT ROSÉ   60
(5% PN, 95% CH)

BICHOIT N-M
51100 Reims
This firm disappeared a long time ago.
- 1955 BICHOIT   92, OCT 2001 (92)
What a little tidbit; this flirty wine is irresistible! Deliciously and easily drunk, sweet, refreshing, and full of strawberries, bergamot, and peppermint candy cane aroma—both in the nose and palate.

BILLECART-SALMON ***** N-M
40, rue Carnot
51160 Mareuil-sur-Aÿ
03 26 52 60 22
Production: 600,000
It's a real pleasure for any wine enthusiast to visit this small, well-run house in Mareuil-sur-Aÿ. The firm, which is very much "in" at the moment, makes elegant, sporty wines that work perfectly with "nouvelle cuisine." The company was founded in 1818 and has always concentrated on quality Champagne in quite a light style. Billecart has a very innovative attitude towards winemaking. They are pioneers of cold stabilization, which entails sinking the wine's temperature to 5°C for two days and then adding dried yeast to the fermentation, which takes place in stainless-steel vats for three weeks. The slow fermentation is made possible by keeping the vat's temperature at around 12°C. The wine must then be heated up to 18°C so that the malolactic fermentation can take place.

Since 1998 the winemaker François Domi has performed several successful experiments with oak barrels from Louis Jadot in Burgundy. Another exciting event to look forward to is the arrival of the upcoming clos wine, Clos Saint Hillaire—a grand Blanc de Noirs made from fifty-year-old vines in Mareüil-sur-Aÿ. The philosophy of the house is to avoid oxidation at all costs: the flavor should come from the grape itself as far as possible, and not from secondary aromas from the vinification.

Billecart buy in 95 percent of their grapes from twenty-three top-rated vineyards, and their own grapes are Pinot Noir from the village. They have contracts with many respected growers from *grand cru* villages Avize, Cramant, and Le Mesnil. The house's refreshing, fruity, and elegant style led me for many years to believe that Billecart's Champagnes should be consumed young. However, their greatness lies in the fact that, despite their early and direct charm, they develop in an incomparably beautiful way in the cellar. That this little house, up until today, would make the entire world's two foremost Champagnes is something I cannot completely agree with, but I am convinced that the '59 would have won the

Millennium Tasting even with a different jury. Simply a fantastic Champagne with no difficult aromas. The fun thing is that the house has produced several other wines that maintain the same high standard. See to it that you buy Billecart-Salmon before they become as expensive as Krug!

• BILLECART-SALMON BRUT   81
(35% PN, 30% PM, 35% CH)
This is the creation of the son, Antoine Billecart. I claim this to be the best nonvintage Champagne of the extremely fruity school. The nose is lively and as fresh as a spring morning, the flavor is light and citrus-fresh with a long, balanced aftertaste of Granny Smith apples. Softer, sweeter, and more creamy recently.

• BILLECART-SALMON BLANC DE BLANCS   86
(100% CH)
A new and exciting wine in Billecart's captivating collection. Probably an excellent wine to store. It reminds me personally of Jacquesson's now-extinct nonvintage Chardonnay. Perhaps slightly less spicy and a tad purer. Definitely not in the same league as the vintage wines, but still a very respectable and affordable wine.

• BILLECART-SALMON DEMI-SEC   60
(35% PN, 30% PM, 35% CH)

• BILLECART-SALMON ROSÉ   86
(40% PN, 20% PM, 40% CH)
As opposed to many other wine writers, I do not believe that this wine should be drunk in its infancy! After five or six years more years in the bottle, the salmon-pink color gains an orange tone. The elegant, fruity nose gets deeper and nuttier, the flavor more serious and prolonged. A half bottle—with a cork as straight as a rod—at the Tour d'Argent restaurant in Paris in 1993 was outstanding.

• 1997 BILLECART-SALMON CUVÉE N. F.   89, APR 2004 (93)
(60% PN, 40% CH)
A very easily drunk, delightfully good, charming wine with a mellow silhouette. The aromas are nice and delicious with a rich, sweet, vanilla-packed layer and a juicy layer of lusciously ripe and supple fruit. Less tart than usual. I would be surprised if this wine stands up to long storage, but one never knows with Billecart-Salmon.

• 1996 BILLECART-SALMON CUVÉE N. F.   89, JUN 2004 (95)
(60% PN, 40% CH)
The fruit is certainly luxuriantly sun-ripened and the wealth of tastes is fantastic, but this is still a young, unfinished wine that must be stored for a very long time in order to peak. Notes of vanilla, winter apples, plum compote, and redcurrants appear at the end—exuding greatness and French bakery smells.

• 1995 BILLECART-SALMON CUVÉE N. F.   88, AUG 2003 (92)
(60% PN, 40% CH)
A very difficult wine to judge—as yet, it doesn't promise very much. Balance is not present yet and the Pinot Noir dominates a little too outlandishly. Young, Gosset-like tones of red apple peel and purple coneflower can also be discerned. I would never have given such high future points if I had not been fooled so many times before by Billecart's potential development. This is the voice of experience speaking, isn't it?

• 1991 BILLECART-BALMON CUVÉE N. F.   85, FEB 2000 (89)
(60% PN, 40% CH)
This Champagne is unusually soft and packed with exotic buttery fruit and licorice. Less tight and elegant than usual and with a certain lack of depth. At the same time the wine is very good and easy to drink. Billecart-Salmon is always a sure thing.

• 1990 BILLECART-SALMON CUVÉE N. F.   93, APR 2004 (96)
(60% PN, 40% CH)
A very youthful and wonderfully refreshing wine. Extraordinary nose of lemon peel, kiwi, and white chocolate. Exemplary balance and finesse. The wine is really refreshing despite its exotic richness.

• 1989 BILLECART-SALMON CUVÉE N. F.   90, FEB 2003 (92)
(60% PN, 40% CH)
A wonderful balance, freshness, and charm. Sophisticated and almost impossible to tell apart from the '88.

• 1988 BILLECART-SALMON CUVÉE N. F.   94, NOV 2003 (95)
(60% PN, 40% CH)
A masterpiece of balance! The wine dances forth like a beautiful fairy on a misty midsummer's meadow at dawn. Beautiful impressions whirl up with unsurpassable lightness and precision. The wine has always been beautiful and balanced with buoyant floral and citrus notes. At the age of fifteen the spaces were filled in with delicious layers of coffee, toffee, crème brûlée, and chocolate nut. The time-released beauties that Billecart makes are simply amazing!

• 1986 BILLECART-SALMON CUVÉE N. F.   90, AVR 2004 (90)
(60% PN, 40% CH)
A buttery, slightly muffled, high-class nose of vanilla. Multidimensional and harmoniously balanced flavor.

• 1985 BILLECART-SALMON CUVÉE N. F.   92, FEB 1999 (94)
(40% PN, 60% CH)
N. F. has always had a brilliant golden color with an extremely fine mousse—a symphonic masterpiece in a relatively light style. An aristocratic nose, full of finesse, and a feminine Chardonnay flavor wrapped around the backbone of a first-class Pinot Noir.

• 1983 BILLECART-SALMON CUVÉE N. F.   92, FEB 2004 (92)
(45% PN, 55% CH)
The '83 is beginning to show its age. The nose is fully mature, toasted, and soft. The flavor is less rich than other vintages. Drink now. I recently had a lovely bottle at Lucas Carton in Paris.

• 1982 BILLECART-SALMON CUVÉE N. F.   95, AVR 2004 (95)
(60% PN, 40% CH)
A wine that has proven to be even better than I had predicted. Toasted, slightly nutty, with a peacock's tail of tastes wrapped in silk.

• 1979 BILLECART-SALMON CUVÉE N. F.   95, MAY 2001 (96)
(60% PN, 40% CH)
Only tasted twice from a magnum. Young, slowly evolving, delightful bouquet. Like a painting by Monet with its summery, mild, colorful complexity. The flavor begins bubbly fresh and resounds with a slight nod toward roasted coffee.

• 1978 BILLECART-SALMON CUVÉE N. F.   93, MAY 2001 (93)
(60% PN, 40% CH)
It is not often that I praise '78s, but I am going to here. The wine is actually even richer than the heavenly '79, with its thick layer of concentrated fruit, toffee, treacle, honey, and vanilla. A little elegance disappears when aired, and this somewhat lowers the points given.

• 1976 BILLECART-SALMON CUVÉE N. F.   95, OCT 1999 (96)
(50% PN, 50% CH)
Billecart-Salmon's elegant house-style combined with a rich vintage is an assured success. One of the vintage's absolute

foremost and refreshing Champagnes. The wine has such a rich, citrus-fresh, lime-dominated fruit that it positively explodes in the mouth. The color is surprisingly light and the mousse is utterly creamy. All of this is wrapped in a cloth of the softest candy.

- 1975 BILLECART-SALMON CUVÉE N. F.   94, NOV 2003 (94)
(60% PN, 40% CH)
Initially they probably went for a light, fruity approach. Today this wine has some lovely secondary aromas that bear up the charming apple element. Layers of chocolate and vanilla fill a wine that has become very complex.

- 1971 BILLECART-SALMON CUVÉE N. F.   95, MAY 2003 (95)
(60% PN, 40% CH)
It is never pleasant when one is forced to send back a corked bottle in a restaurant, and even worse when the bottle is one of the last remaining magnums of a vintage. This happened to me and a group that visited Alain Passard's three-star restaurant in Paris. How much nicer it was when I could confirm that I had been right to do so—the next magnum was completely different, with a depth of character reminiscent of most things autumnal: mushrooms, leaf bonfires, wet bark, dampness, and windfall fruit. Medium bodied and serious, lacking the extra layer of fruit usually associated with Billecart.

- 1966 BILLECART-SALMON CUVÉE N. F.   96, MAR 2000 (96)
(60% PN, 40% CH)
Not really the same bite as the '59 and the '61. This wine is milder, with a fine undertone of mineral, along the lines of the company's other '66s. I tasted two bottles on the same day—one was more nutty and toasted, the other was filled with dried fruits and dry toffee flavor. The level of quality was the same.

- 1961 BILLECART-SALMON CUVÉE N. F.   98, JAN 1999 (98)
(60% PN, 40% CH)
One of the most elegant and harmonious '61s I have tasted. There is an exquisite toasted Chardonnay note in the nose, but above all an exotic, almost tropical impression dominates. Not as monumental as the '59, but just as enjoyable, with its d'Yquem-like finish and essence of taste. Not unlike a well-preserved '49 with its concentrated fruity sweetness. "A potential winner," I wrote in my notes. The wine was voted second-best Champagne in history at the Millennium Tasting.

- 1959 BILLECART-SALMON CUVÉE N. F.   99, JUN 1999 (99)
(60% PN, 40% CH)
It was very easy to find this '59 at a blind tasting with Antoine Billecart. No other vintage has such force. I find it hard to imagine anything better than a typical, monumental '59, perfectly combined with Billecart's uniquely subtle and mineral-rich, fresh house-style. Absolutely perfect Champagne in its category, with a smoky, honey-soft, extremely long taste of walnut, orange blossom, and honey. Afterward, I heard that Antoine's brother did not want Billecart-Salmon to contribute just any old bottle to the Millennium Tasting. You can guess what happened. It won!

- 1955 BILLECART-SALMON CUVÉE N. F.   99, MAR 2000 (99)
(60% PN, 40% CH)
Antoine asked me which wine was highest on my Billecart-Salmon wish list. He got a special look in his eye when, without thinking, I answered "the '55." A few seconds later he said, "It was supposed to be a surprise, but it's just as well that you find out now. I have already prepared a '55 for this evening's dinner at

Royal Champagne." I am not going to tell you what I did—you will have to ask him—but I showed my appreciation in a most un-Swedish fashion. Ahaa! you're thinking. That's why he gave it ninety-nine points. Not at all! The truth is, I always take a step backward into my mental tasting room and peel away all irrelevant factors when I judge wine. Actually, the '55 was even more elegant and deeper than either the '59 or the '61. The house-style is astonishingly constant, with a Grand Siècle-like note of newly laundered sheets and browned butter as an extra bonus. It goes to prove that Cuvée N. F. Billecart is one of history's absolute foremost Champagnes.

- 1997 BILLECART-SALMON BLANC DE BLANCS   92, MAY 2003 (93)
(100% CH)
Wonderfully thirst-quenching, sublime Champagne with great youthful, sorbet-like freshness. Light and flighty as a spring breeze. Antoine Billecart is rightly proud of this drinkable, sensual creation.

- 1996 BILLECART-SALMON BLANC DE BLANCS   90, JUN 2004 (96)
(100% CH)
With stony acidic Chardonnay from Le Mesnil as a base, fruit from Avize as well as creaminess from Chouilly and Cramant, this young, crystal-clear '96 has everything needed for a really great Blanc de Blancs. When freshly poured there are notes of egg toddy, but they are quickly transformed when aired, winding up closer to Sabayon, with roasted almonds and lemon cream supported by, naturally, a blast-wave of white flowers.

- 1995 BILLECART-SALMON BLANC DE BLANCS   94, JUN 2003 (95)
(100% CH)
Because the Chardonnay was harvested a few days before the black grapes, it managed to escape the damaging rain that hit the Pinot. This is especially noticeable with Billecart, whose N. F. this time is clearly not as good as the Blanc de Blancs. The bouquet is youthful and light, the palate exemplary, pure, and elegant with a big mineral portion.

- 1990 BILLECART-SALMON BLANC DE BLANCS   95, AUG 2003 (96)
(100% CH)
Billecart has really created some magnificent wines for this vintage. This Blanc de Blancs is no exception. The elegance shines through and the wine has everything a good Champagne should have. Tons of mineral, citrus fruit, and an exemplary, velvet-soft mousse. A fantastic bouquet of nut toffee appears when the glass has been left to stand for twenty minutes.

- 1989 BILLECART-SALMON BLANC DE BLANCS   91, JAN 2003 (93)
(100% CH)
"This wine is a clear favorite among many other firms. Billecart's reputation in Champagne is untouchable. So far I'm a little disappointed myself with what is a pure but somewhat shy wine. Give this steely, grassy, and mineral-rich wine plenty of years in the cellar." I wrote this two years ago. It's already happened—the wine is as nutty and as buttery as can be.

- 1988 BILLECART-SALMON BLANC DE BLANCS   93, AVR 2004 (94)
(100% CH)
The first time I tasted this wine it was served far too cold. At the right temperature the wine exudes subtle aromas of grass, hawthorn, hay, and minerals. A wine to keep for a while.

- 1986 BILLECART-SALMON BLANC DE BLANCS   77, JAN 1997 (84)
(100% CH)
Perhaps rather on the light side for my taste, but otherwise definitely pure and elegant.

- 1985 BILLECART-SALMON BLANC DE BLANCS   70, MAR 1993 (85)
(100% CH)

From the best villages in Côte des Blancs only. A pure style, and fruity, but a touch naked and impersonal. Probably much better than I understood it to be then.

- 1983 BILLECART SALMON BLANC DE BLANCS   93, APR 2003 (94)
(100% CH)

"Almost watery in color, with ample mousse. Elements of hay and grass in the nose. Thin taste with acidity." This is what I wrote in 1990. Knowing now that Billecart's wines develop in an unexpectedly phenomenal fashion, I couldn't resist this wine when it reappeared, despite having given it only eighty points for potential development. Most of the '83s are tired, and almost all have a smokiness and an element of desiccation reminiscent of cork. When slowly developing celebrities like Salon stand on the brink of decline, it is astonishingly refreshing to sink your teeth into this magnificently tart, youthful wine. The bouquet is sublime, with roasted coffee beans and flowers in wonderful harmony. The taste is sensual and bitingly fresh.

- 1976 BILLECART-SALMON BLANC DE BLANCS   94, JAN 2004 (94)
(100% CH)

The wine's normally rather shy style fits very well with the richness of the vintage.

- 1973 BILLECART-SALMON BLANC DE BLANCS   94, JUN 1999 (94)
(100% CH)

At the age of seventeen it was still very youthful, with a light green hue in the faint golden color. The mousse was superb, the nose a discreet chocolaty affair, backed up by lime and white flowers. The flavor wasn't completely developed, but very fine and rich in minerals. Today it is completely mature and elegantly nutty.

- 1966 BILLECART-SALMON BLANC DE BLANCS   98, MAR 2000 (98)
(100% CH)

An unusual wine journey in a Champagne glass. Initially almost painfully characterized by stony mineral, a note that confusingly resembles cork. When I, Antoine Billecart, and a few good friends tasted three of the house's '66s, we were all slightly puzzled in the beginning about the cork tone in all of the wines. We deduced that this must be due to reduction in conjunction with the vintage's strongly fossil character. When this Blanc de Blancs opened up we found ourselves transported to Alsace. The deep yellow color, the intensely petroleum and lime-scented beverage carried my thoughts to an uncontrollably good 1971 Clos St.-Hune. After half an hour the wine carried us onward to Burgundy, with its increasingly grape-typical Montrachet-like aromas from high-class soil. When we were down to our last drops my points had risen from ninety-five to an astonishing ninety-eight. We were now back in Champagne with a strong Mesnil imprint. Nut, coffee, lime, acacia, and chalk were strong flavors, but an embarrassingly poor description of what the wine actually expressed. Thank you for an unforgettable journey.

- 1974 BILLECART-SALMON ROSÉ   91, MAY 2001 (91)
(35% PN, 35% PM, 30% CH)

A sensationally good wine for this vintage—weak mousse, pale yellowish color, and a floral bouquet with strains of caramel custard and orange blossom. Long, silky-smooth aftertaste.

- 1973 BILLECART-SALMON ROSÉ   88, JUN 2000 (88)
(35% PN, 35% PM, 30% CH)

Heavier and decidedly more gloomy and aged than the '74.

Figs, dates, and Tokay compete for scent supremacy. Fat, vintage-typical palate that flows merrily down the throat.

- 1969 BILLECART-SALMON ROSÉ   94, JUN 2000 (94)
(35% PN, 35% PM, 30% CH)

Brilliant, multifaceted wine with classic structure and superb balance. The aromas are very similar to those found in a Dom Pérignon from the 1960s. The style is somewhat lighter, with a buoyantly fresh, uplifting evanescence.

- 1966 BILLECART-SALMON ROSÉ   94, MAR 2000 (94)
(35% PN, 35% PM, 30% CH)

Finally I get to meet this deliciously butterscotchy wine: a renowned charmer. The color was very light and just as salmon-pink as the name implies. The mousse sparkled abundantly and accentuated a stony mineral character that initially reminded me of a taste from a Verzenay cask. But in the end, after playing hard to get, the Champagne proved an easy catch. Wonderfully easy to drink, with an irresistibly sweet and sexy finish.

- 1990 BILLECART-SALMON GRANDE CUVÉE   91, DEC 2001 (95)
(40% PN, 60% CH)

Difficult to distinguish from the N. F. of the same year. Dazzlingly intense fruit with gobbets of youth. One layer of taste is like green gooseberries, another more reminiscent of exotic passion fruit. All this rather cold fruit is masterfully braided together with strains of vanilla.

- 1989 BILLECART-SALMON GRANDE CUVÉE   92, JAN 2003 (94)
(40% PN, 60% CH)

More Pinot in the bouquet than usual, which lends a slightly disturbing Gosset-like note of raisin and plum. The wine—as never before—is seductive, with a fine, mineral-rich cleanness and a velvety-soft creamy flavor. The latest bottle I tasted displayed the firm's unfailing elegance and had a magnificently toasted nose.

- 1988 BILLECART-SALMON GRANDE CUVÉE   96, FEB 2004 (96)
(40% PN, 60% CH)

A very beautiful and harmonious Champagne that is clean and clear like spring water. The fruit is, as usual, very fresh. It is supported nicely by a discreet buttery flavor and a lovely nuance of toasted bread. This has strengthened with time, and everything is supported by an incredibly beautiful element of vanilla pralines.

- 1982 BILLECART-SALMON GRANDE CUVÉE   96, JAN 2004 (96)
(20% PN, 80% CH)

One of the fattest and richest '82s ever; despite this, it naturally exhibits great freshness and incomparably elegant and rich gradation. Nut toffee is the strongest note in this gigantic, easily drunk wine. There is much reminiscent here of Pol Roger's mythical Blanc de Chardonnay from the same year.

- 1995 BILLECART-SALMON LE CLOS ST HILLAIRE   91, JUN 2004 (95)
(100% PN)

In 1964 vines were planted on this single hectare beside the house in Mareuil-sur-Aÿ. The character of this unique, oak-barrel-aged Blanc de Noirs lies somewhere between its neighbor, Clos des Goisses, and the Bollinger Vieilles Vignes Français (VVF) produced from pre-phylloxera vines in Aÿ and Bouzy. The biggest difference, perhaps, is that the wine is completely devoid of dosage, which can prove to be a good decision in the long run but one that makes the wine a bit difficult to appreciate now when entering the market. With its price of several hundred dollars and its small production of 3,500–7,500 bottles a year, the wine will soon become a cult item and much in demand. After having tasted this fantastic wine directly from the barrel, I was—despite my high points—slightly disappointed by my first meeting with this youthful, powerfully explosive Champagne. The color is considerably lighter than Bollinger VVF, and the heavy nose is characterized by plum, dried apricots, chocolate, and leather, with a grassy undertone also found in Clos des Goisses. The oak from Alliers isn't especially dominant and the wine feels soft, despite its lack of sugar, due to the rich fruit. Store and wait and see. It wouldn't surprise me if everything is set up now for a great '96.

- 1997 BILLECART-SALMON ROSÉ CUVÉE ELISABETH 89, MAR 2004 (92)
(55% PN, 45% CH)
A genuinely delicious wine packed with charm and early summer warmth. Pale, beautiful color. Incomparably caressing, fruity fragrance of summer berries, early summer flowers and a smooth vanilla note that can also be found in the sophisticatedly supple, balanced, as well as fairly delicate taste. A wine that does not need as much storing as we are used to with Champagnes from this exceptional house.

- 1995 BILLECART-SALMON ROSÉ CUVÉE ELISABETH 90, JAN 2003 (93)
(44% PN, 56% CH)
A grand, utterly seductive '95 with "white" Champagne flavors, spiced with a dash of raspberry scent. This has refinement, balance, and potential.

- 1991 BILLECART-SALMON ROSÉ CUVÉE ELISABETH 87, OCT 2000 (90)
(55% PN, 45% CH)
Brilliant Billecart! How one can get a '91 to be so sensually seductive is a mystery. The taste is incredibly well put together. A handsome wine, to enjoy during all of its phases of development.

- 1990 BILLECART-SALMON ROSÉ CUVÉE ELISABETH 91, OCT 2000 (94)
(45% PN, 55% CH)
A great rosé Champagne with marvellous crispy aromas of fruit and minerals. Perfect length and balance. Drink now, or enjoy when fully mature in ten years or so.

- 1989 BILLECART-SALMON ROSÉ CUVÉE ELISABETH 91, SEP 2003 (93)
(45% PN, 55% CH)
Billecart is one of the masters when it comes to rosé Champagnes. Great elegance, good grip, and the vintage's richness are all there without taking over. A very exciting wine to follow in the future.

- 1988 BILLECART-SALMON ROSÉ CUVÉE ELISABETH 95, OCT 2003 (95)
(45% PN, 55% CH)
What a superb debut wine! As beautifully salmon-pink as the successful nonvintage. Full of refinement, berry-like aroma and an unexpected sweet and rich vanilla taste; the fruit is so intense that it perfectly supports the sweetness. Nowadays completely mature, with Billecart's fantastic butterscotchiness and hints of nougat. A dream to gulp down. Winner in Paris 2003 of the rosé category in the "Spectacle du Monde" comprehensive tasting.

- BILLECART-SALMON 150 ANNIVERSARY CUVÉE 87, MAR 2004 (87)
(60% PN, 40% CH)
It is always fantastically exciting when one finds one of these old rarities. Unfortunately, the wine was slightly corroded by the tooth of time and incorrect handling. Still, a weak vein of mousse elevated this rather demanding, dark wine. Exciting notes of red

wine, spices, old wood, ashes, and mushrooms combined with roasted almonds, toffee, and golden syrup.

- BILLECART-SALMON 150 ANNIVERSARY CUVÉE SEC 86, MAR 2004 (86)
(60% PN, 40% CH)
Basically a great '60s wine, with a heavenly nose of oranges, butterscotch, and aged Sauternes. Slightly gooey in taste, but a perfect accompaniment to duck-liver crème brûlée. One of the best sweet Champagnes I have tasted. Younger and bubblier than the dry version of this same wine.

BILLIARD, G. N-M
78, rue de Général de Gaulle
51530 Pierry
03 26 54 02 96
Production: 80,000
The house was founded in 1935 and controls two hectares in Pierry. Eighty-five percent of the grapes are bought in, and this producer is one of few that doesn't have reserve wines. Other wines: Blanc de Blancs, Rosé, Vintage.

- G. BILLIARD CACHET ROUGE   25
(40% PN, 40% PM, 20% CH)

BILLION, F. *** R-M
4, rue des Lombards
51190 Le Mesnil-sur-Oger
03 26 57 51 24
Production: 80,000
Robert Billion was previously responsible for wines at Salon, but still found time to make a small amount of Champagne under his own name. Even today, Billion still sells grapes to Salon and has some similarities of style. The smokiness and nut aromas are very broad, but Billion lacks the elegance that the very best producers in Le Mesnil have in common. A. Robert and F. Billion lead the heavier, oak-barrel-fermented Mesnil school.

- F. BILLION BRUT   75
(100% CH)
- F. BILLION VINESIME   73
(100% CH)
- 1989 F. BILLION   83, APR 1997 (86)
(100% CH)
Both the vintage and the producer usually produce fat wines, but this one retains its balance. If there's anyone who doubts that asparagus and Champagne can work together, I can recommend this wine, which goes up a few gears when alongside "the golden treasure of spring."

- 1988 F. BILLION   80, DEC 1994 (84)
(100% CH)
A wealth of tastes and very friendly. Packed with exotic Chardonnay fruit and buttery charm, but it is aging too quickly.

- 1985 F. BILLION   90, AUG 1999 (92)
(100% CH)
A rustic version of Salon's aromas. Dark yellow color, oaky nose backed up by butter and honey. Vinous as a white Burgundy. Impressively old-fashioned.

BILLIOT, HENRI *** R-M
Place de la Fontaine
51150 Ambonnay
03 26 57 00 14
Production: 45,000

The minimal number of bottles that annually leave Billiot's cellars are bought almost exclusively by committed fans in Britain. His wines are so rare that I had never come across one before I managed to arrange a visit to the property in 1994. It was with mounting excitement that I opened the gate to the vineyard itself. How was this cult figure among winemakers going to look? Had the pressures of fame gone to his head, as they had with so many of Burgundy's minor demonic growers? No. It was with great relief that I found that he, like Selosse, Peters, and Diebolt, had kept his feet firmly on the ground. M. Billiot is a very unassuming and modest person, who was dressed in his worn jeans and knitted sweater throughout our visit. When you've just come from one of the major houses with their slim, Armani-clad, business-minded directors, it's wonderful to meet a real wine farmer in the true sense of the phrase. The British believe that he ferments his wines in oak barrels. Can this misunderstanding originate from the fact that Billiot prefers to speak German with his guests? They also believe that his two-hectare-large vineyards contain only Pinot Noir. He is very proud of his Chardonnay plants and uses most of their fruit in his *cuvée de prestige*, Cuvée Laetitia, which is named after his daughter.

Billiot's greatness depends chiefly upon his hard work in the vineyard. Old vines and low yield is the recipe for success. Despite the high quality, Billiot's Champagnes are hardly for beginners, as malolactic fermentation has not been used. The concentration and richness that lies under the surface can be hard to appreciate in the wine's youth. All of his wines demand at least a further five years in the bottle to mature properly.

- H. BILLIOT TRADITION   70
  (70% PN, 30% CH)
- H. BILLIOT CUVÉE DE RÉSERVE   79
  (90% PN, 10% CH)
- H. BILLIOT CUVÉE DE RÉSERVE ROSÉ   78
  (100% PN)
- 1975 H. BILLIOT
  (100% PN)
- 1959 H. BILLIOT   90, APR 1995 (92)
  (100% PN)
  Once again recently disgorged and youthful, but filled with power and aromas typical of the grape. Heroically built without finesse. It would be fun to try again.
- H. BILLIOT CUVÉE LAETITIA   85
  (40% PN, 60% CH)
  According to the winemaker, there are a number of secrets in this *cuvée*. It is a blend of nine different vintages, but he strongly denies that oak barrels are involved at all. The color is a deep greenish-yellow and the nose is buttery and mature. The flavor is fruity and sweet in a positive way, unified and with a long aftertaste of honey. Nineteen eighty-two is the dominant vintage in my mouth. Sure, this is a damn good Champagne, but I would rather have seen a *cuvée de prestige* made entirely out of Pinot grapes. Later versions have been slipperier, younger, and even more homogeneously concentrated, with an impressively unreleased density. The amount of reserve wine has been reduced.

BINET N-M
31, rue de Reims
51500 Rilly-la-Montagne
03 26 03 49 18
Production: 300,000

Founder Léon Binet's great gift to the world was cold disgorging (*dégorgement à la glace*). He was head of the house from 1849 to 1893. The house was almost completely destroyed by German bombs during World War I; in order to be able to continue, Binet linked up with Piper-Heidsieck. After World War II it was Germain's turn to take over Binet. Until quite recently both Germain and Binet were owned by the Frey group. In 1999 Vranken took control over Germain. Hervé Ladouche is the cellar master for Binet.

- BINET BRUT ELITE   62
  (40% PN, 20% PM, 40% CH)
- BINET SÉLECTION   79
  (60% PN, 40% CH)
- 1961 BINET   87, NOV 2001 (87)
  (60% PN, 40% CH)
  A very tight and powerfully built Champagne that is perfectly suited to a heartening winter dinner in front of the fireplace. The taste is dry, smoky, and gamy.
- 1945 BINET
  (60% PN, 40% CH)
- 1988 BINET BLANC DE BLANCS   78, APR 1995 (83)
  (100% CH)
  The character of this Champagne is definitely influenced by grapes from the Marne Valley and Montagne de Reims. I don't find any finesse or freshness, but the flavor is robust and rich with a long finish.
- 1979 BINET BLANC DE BLANCS   84, APR 1996 (84)
  (100% CH)
  Beautifully green, shimmering with a yellow base. A fine stream of small bubbles. Faint nose, decent length. Delicious.

BLIARD-MORISET R-M
2, rue Grand Mont
51190 Le Mesnil-sur-Oger
03 26 57 53 42
Production: 20,000

This grower owns six hectares in Le Mesnil, which are divided up into ten plots.

- BLIARD-MORISET RÉSERVE   68
  (100% CH)

BLONDEL N-M
B.P. 12
51500 Ludes
03 26 03 43 92
Production: 35,000

A very well-run house that owns ten hectares (50 percent Pinot Noir and 50 percent Chardonnay) in the village and makes highly enjoyable and tasty Champagnes in a public-pleasing style.

- BLONDEL CARTE D'OR   64
  (75% PN, 25% CH)
- BLONDEL ROSÉ   74
  (80% PN, 20% CH)
- 1996 BLONDEL VIEUX MILLÉSIME   82, NOV 2003 (83)
  (100% CH)

The best thing about this Champagne—which for some unfathomable reason is sold as an old vintage—is the rounded medium palate, with a volume and fleshiness that is impressive. The entire wine breathes honey and yellow flowers, with an aftertaste reminiscent of certain Easter-lily-scented wines from Lasalle in Chigny-les-Roses. Otherwise, rather rustic in personality.

- 1992 BLONDEL VIEUX MILLÉSIME   76, OCT 2001 (77)
  (100% CH)
- 1985 BLONDEL VIEUX MILLÉSIME   85, AUG 1997 (85)
  (50% PN, 50% CH)
  Wonderful nose of digestive biscuits. Long, mature taste, full of dried fruit.
- 1999 BLONDEL BLANC DE BLANCS   78, NOV 2003 (82)
  (100% CH)
  Fantastically low price on a par with the house's nonvintage Champagnes. On the other hand, about the same quality as the best of these. An uncomplicated and well-rounded Champagne with a mellow feeling and strong pear scents both in taste and fragrance. The wine is like a young rooster that is let out of the cage too early. A slight soda-pop and Popsicle-like feeling when the Champagne is drunk well chilled. Already, just a year after launching, the wine is becoming more concentrated and interesting. Honey notes and this vintage's oiliness are becoming more evident.
- 1993 BLONDEL BLANC DE BLANCS   75, OCT 2001 (79)
  (100% CH)
- 1990 BLONDEL BLANC DE BLANCS   80, AUG 1995 (84)
  (100% CH)
  Tones of vanilla and butterscotch dominate this round, rich, and delicious Blanc de Blancs.
- BLONDEL CUVÉE 2000   70, AUG 2003 (73)
  (55% PN, 45% CH)

BOIZEL *** NM
46, avenue de Champagne
51200 Épernay
03 26 55 21 51
Production: 3,000,000

Boizel still has eleven bottles from 1834, the year when the firm was founded in Épernay. This treasure house is unique in Champagne, with several undisgorged wines from the nineteenth century. The cellars lie under the Avenue de Champagne, by the house where Christian Pol-Roger lives.

   Boizel has always been better known abroad than home in France. Evelyne Roques-Boizel is president of the company today, but all her decisions are made together with her very likeable husband. Chanoine and Bruno Paillard are now shareholders in the noble Champagne house. Boizel buys grapes from fifty different villages, which are then blended by Pascal Vautier, the enologist on the nineteen-man staff. Boizel are best known for their low prices, but I think the quality deserves better. Both the Chardonnay and the *cuvée de prestige* Joyau de France are of very high class in their respective categories, and a few of the older chanterelle-scented vintages are truly great.

- BOIZEL BRUT   63
  (55% PN, 15% PM, 30% CH)
- BOIZEL CHARDONNAY   78
  (100% CH)
- BOIZEL ROSÉ   72
  (50% PN, 40% PM, 10% CH)

- 1996 BOIZEL   78, JAN 2002 (85)
  (50% PN, 10% PM, 40% CH)
  Very promising and truly youthful, with rough and tough malic acidity; stylistically actually the same as Lanson. Classic structure and bitingly robust acidity with a nascent breadiness and underlying nutty tone.
- 1990 BOIZEL   81, JAN 1999 (86)
  (60% PN, 10% PM, 30% CH)
  Heavy, rich, meaty, and bready scent with a thus-far repressed undertone of chocolate. Healthy, potent, and vigorous taste. A real powerhouse with a meaty structure.
- 1990 BOIZEL CUVÉE SOIS BOIS   86, JAN 1999 (90)
  (50% PN, 50% CH)
  Fifteen thousand bottles containing wine from Chouilly, Mesnil, Oger, Vertus, Cuis, Aÿ, Mailly, Mareuil, and Tauxières stored and fermented in old Meursault barrels. A completely different depth and structure from the usual vintage. Multifaceted aroma that slowly spreads in the glass. Soft Gosset-like taste with profound depth.
- 1989 BOIZEL   81, JAN 1999 (86)
  (60% PN, 10% PM, 30% CH)
  Too much sulfur in the aroma, but also an enjoyable flowery tone. A bit lighter and more elegant than the '90.
- 1988 BOIZEL   73, APR 1995 (81)
  (60% PN, 10% PM, 30% CH)
  Slightly vigorous, extrovert Champagne with spiced aromas and rich, slightly licorice-like taste. Development hard to judge!
- 1976 BOIZEL   85, FEB 1996 (85)
  (60% PN, 10% PM, 30% CH)
  Rich, chocolate flavor and a fine, nutty bouquet.
- 1971 BOIZEL   88, MAR 2000 (88)
  (61% PN, 9% PM, 30% CH)
  Nineteen seventy-one is a vintage of which I become more and more enamored. Boizel's vintage wine often has a harshness that is difficult to smooth down. There is nothing of the sort in this vintage. Instead, the wine is characterized by an unusually buttery softness and several silky-smooth layers of taste—all of them reminiscent of various sweets and candies.
- 1961 BOIZEL   95, JUN 1999 (95)
  (65% PN, 35% CH)
  Produced completely in oak. Very light and sparkling green nuance to the color. Vintage-typical, with its obvious truffle tone supported by toasted and balsamic aromatic nuances. Newly disgorged, the taste is very tight and biting, but the interesting tones of maturity—evocative of tar and tobacco—reestablish order.
- 1955 BOIZEL   92, OCT 2001 (92)
  (65% PN, 5% PM, 30% CH)
  An intellectually very good—if not great—wine. Still, I get a bookish feeling: it is a wine more of carefully encouraged nods than lustful shouts, like a Bordeaux compared to the more charming, romantic wines from Burgundy. Dry, tight, finely structured, and long.
- 1945 BOIZEL   94, JUN 1999 (94)
  (65% PN, 35% CH)
  Boizel's best wine ever! Lightly golden, intense color. The aroma is chock-full of freshly picked chanterelle mushrooms and autumn forest. I love the scent, but apparently, according to Evelyne, it is usually much less evident in the legendary '45.

The mousse is soft and perfect. The wine's concentration and oily structure are outstanding. Even the taste is marked by a delicate mushroom aroma.

- 1991 JOYAU DE FRANCE   82, DEC 2001 (84)

(65% PN, 35% CH)

I never get really excited by '91s! There is certainly nothing wrong with this wine, but a prestige *cuvée* from such a good house as Boizel should impart greater pleasure. The clearest notes are vanilla and bread. A certain imbalance appears on the palate.

- 1989 JOYAU DE CHARDONNAY   84, JAN 1999 (91)

(100% CH)

Only 12,000 bottles produced. The grapes come from high-class villages such as Vertus, Oger, and Mesnil. Gloriously complex and delicate scent with acacia tones. Very youthful and undeveloped taste. Very likely to be a pretty bauble in ten years or so.

- 1989 JOYAU DE FRANCE   85, NOV 2003 (88)

(65% PN, 35% CH)

Expressive aroma that with its gamy bent reminds one of certain grower's white Burgundies from Chassagne-Montrachet. Big, developable, and tight taste. Development not as impressive as I had predicted.

- 1988 JOYAU DE FRANCE   88, MAR 2003 (91)

(65% PN, 35% CH)

A pure *grand cru* Champagne of high class. Incredibly tight and promising with a Belle Époque-like spectrum of aromas where coffee, lime, and minerals set the tone. The taste is almost hard, but concentrated.

- 1982 JOYAU DE FRANCE   92, JAN 1999 (92)

(65% PN, 35% CH)

Unexpectedly youthful and weak aroma. A weak coating of caramel and crème brûlée. Elegant and fresh, full-bodied '82 with fine, intact acidity. There is also a smoky backbone and a long aftertaste of fine Chardonnay.

BOLLINGER ***** N-M

16, rue Jules Lobet
51160 Aÿ
03 26 53 33 66
Production: 1,300,000

Joseph Bollinger was the German from Würtemberg who founded this ancient house in 1829. The French called him simply "Jacques." The firm's large estates in the best Pinot villages were bought by his sons Georges and Joseph, and in 1918 it was time for the next Jacques to take over the property. He became the mayor of Aÿ, but died during the German occupation at the age of forty-seven. The most colorful person in the history of the house is his widow, Lily Bollinger, who kept a watchful eye on every bunch of grapes by cycling through the vineyards regularly. Her rigorous demands for quality still run through the house to this day. Now Bollinger is run by Ghislain de Montgolfier and Michel Villedey, who control over 144 hectares, providing 70 percent of the grape supply. The winemaker today is the highly regarded Gérard Liot.

     Besides the house's exceptional vineyards, they also use very expensive vinification methods. All the vintage wines are fermented in small, aged oak barrels and are never filtered. Malolactic fermentation—which would probably take place very late in the process—is not encouraged either. The reserve wines are stored at low pressure in magnums. Unfortunately the handcrafted Champagnes created by Bollinger vary from bottle to bottle. Nowadays it's not at all unusual to come across charmless Bollinger bottles that lack fruit. However, when everything works, they have few superiors. Bollinger make the heaviest and most full-bodied Champagnes of any house, and their wines always have a smoky and hazelnut-y complexity that is very hard to beat. The vintage wines are among the very best, but the question is whether the rare and fantastic Vieilles Vignes Françaises, made with grapes from non-grafted Pinot vines, can reach even greater heights.

- BOLLINGER SPÉCIAL CUVÉE   82

(60% PN, 15% PM, 25% CH)

Yet again, one of my absolute favorites among nonvintage Champagnes. Since the beginning of the 1990s the wine has only been four years old when it enters the market and is vinified in steel vats. Even so, it's fascinating to see how much 12 percent old reserve wines, vinified in oak barrels and stored in magnums, do to lift the product. The oakish, smoky, and deep Bollinger style develops after a couple of years in the bottle.

- 1996 BOLLINGER GRANDE ANNÉE   94, MAR 2004 (96)

(70% PN, 30% CH)

In many respects the wine is reminiscent of the critically acclaimed '90 with its exotically rich fruit and a timbre somewhat less masculine than in the more classic vintages. Nor does one find the Krug-like elegance that the '95 displays. But that could very well prove to be compensated for with the fantastically high acidity. A magnificent, powerful wine in all respects, which breathes more and more greatness every time I open a new bottle.

- 1995 BOLLINGER GRANDE ANNÉE   95, MAR 2004 (96)

(61% PN, 39% CH)

I chose 1990 R. D. (Recently Disgorged) and Grande Année 1995 to accompany all dishes when I tested a ten-course menu at a top restaurant. It was hardly surprising that both shone as beautiful stars alongside the glittering dishes. The hugely fleshy '90 better suited the truffle risotto and veal sweetbread on small potato pancakes à la Georges Blanc, but this incomparably gorgeous and subtle '95 shone both on its own and with the other eight dishes. The wine is wonderfully direct from the start, with a seldom-seen, lemony-elegant fruit of superb Chardonnay combined with a Krug-like oaky complexity. This is hardly the most monumental vintage that Bollinger has ever made, but absolutely one of the most enjoyable and sophisticated.

- 1992 BOLLINGER GRANDE ANNÉE   92, MAR 2004 (92)

(70% PN, 30% CH)

It is fair to ask if it is right for Bollinger to come out with a '92. Obviously one should be restrictive in launching vintages. Bollinger defends the '92 by stating how incredibly selective they were at harvest, something absolutely noticeable. The wine is mature and has developed relatively early. The house-style is distinct with its smoky, masculine Pinot Noir. There are also notes of mango and apricots, elements discernible even in the '90. Does this mean there is going to be a change of direction within the otherwise narrow and traditional framework?

- 1990 BOLLINGER GRANDE ANNÉE   92, JUN 2003 (94)

(69% PN, 31% CH)

A wonderfully good and heavy wine, with a much richer fruit and Chardonnay character than usual. The nuttiness typical of Bollinger is toned down to leave space for a wave of sweet and pleasure-filled fruity flavors. Superb length.

- 1988 BOLLINGER GRANDE ANNÉE 93, NOV 2003 (94)
(75% PN, 25% CH)

I always get a tingling sensation in my stomach when I hear that a new vintage Bollinger has come onto the market. The '88 is classical and promising but, as yet, drinking it is still like eating the turkey long before Christmas.

- 1985 BOLLINGER GRANDE ANNÉE 92, JUN 1997 (95)
(65% PN, 35% CH)

This is what Bollinger is all about. The color is deep and the concentrated, glycerol-rich Champagne forms clear "legs" along the edge of the glass. The nose combines weight with complexity. Biscuits, hazelnuts, chocolate, and toasted bread, together with a faint element of oyster shell. The life-bearing malic acidity is restrained and fine, and elevates this powerfully chewy wine to greatness.

- 1983 BOLLINGER 92, JAN 2003 (92)
(70% PN, 30% CH)

This wine was fantastic when newly introduced onto the market, but it has lost fruitiness, and the nuttiness shines without sweetness.

- 1982 BOLLINGER 93, OCT 2003 (93)
(70% PN, 30% CH)

Certain bottles are already showing signs of age, while others resemble the successful R. D. version (the same as the vintage wine, but stored a few more years in contact with the yeast). Whether or not this is due to the date of disgorging, I don't know. At its best it is round and rich with a good aftertaste.

- 1979 BOLLINGER 93, DEC 2003 (93)
(70% PN, 30% CH)

Elegant and nutty with a much weaker body, but better fruit than the R. D. from the same vintage.

- 1976 BOLLINGER 87, OCT 1998 (87)
(50% PN, 50% CH)

Completely mature at the tender age of twelve. Buttery and rich, but the flesh is a little loose and baggy.

- 1975 BOLLINGER 94, MAY 2003 (94)
(70% PN, 30% CH)

Just as big, bold, nutty, and full of chocolate as one might expect after having tasted R. D. on thirty or more occasions.

- 1973 BOLLINGER 92, MAR 2003 (92)
(75% PN, 25% CH)

Considering the full development of the '73 R. D., I was afraid that this wine would have seen its best days. Actually they're very similar to one another, and only a tone of hay and toffee separates them.

- 1970 BOLLINGER 93, MAR 2003 (93)
(70% PN, 30% CH)

The flavor is full of berries and surrounded by a veil of oak character. Its bouquet is delightful and stimulating, with strong elements of my favorite flower, the honeysuckle.

- 1969 BOLLINGER 95, SEP 1998 (95)
(70% PN, 30% CH)

A classic Bollinger!

- 1966 BOLLINGER 97, JUN 2002 (97)
(75% PN, 25% CH)

Momentous, almost statesmanlike vintage. At that time there were grapes from the non-grafted vines from Aÿ and Bouzy in the vintage wine, something that is actually quite noticeable. The wine expresses Aÿ Pinot at its very best. In the glass, orange color

and gamy, vegetable, and toasty aromas hit you. The nose actually resembles a mature La Tâche from D. R. C. The attack is enormous, despite the wine's meaty structure and rich fruit. The aftertaste accelerates in the mouth and it takes a long, long while before one is left with just the popcorn aroma lingering on the palate.

- 1964 BOLLINGER 96, JAN 2003 (96)
(75% PN, 25% CH)

The '64 is a touch less generous and a tad drier than the '66. The wine is packed with dry, exciting notes of tar, cacao, tobacco, and truffles. Fabulously long aftertaste. All twelve bottles that I have drunk have been good, but none was as magical as the first.

- 1962 BOLLINGER 95, DEC 1998 (95)
(75% PN, 25% CH)

A wonderfully pleasurable wine filled with sweet aromas. Because I am also of the same vintage, I think it is fun that Bollinger is the only Champagne house that has reached the ninety-five point mark for the 1962. The scent is reminiscent of the aroma from a French patisserie on a summer morning. Plenty of vanilla, almond, and Danish pastry. The taste is less classic than the best Bollinger vintages of the '60s, but it is just as easy to appreciate.

- 1961 BOLLINGER 90 JAN 2003 (90)
(75% PN, 25% CH)

Few nuances, but there's good stringency and earth-cellar aromas, along with a powder-dry barrel character. Slightly lacking in fruit. Very young, light color.

- 1959 BOLLINGER 97, OCT 1999 (97)
(75% PN, 25% CH)

A majestic Champagne with unbelievable dimensions.

- 1955 BOLLINGER
(75% PN, 25% CH)

- 1953 BOLLINGER 94, AUG 1994 (94)
(75% PN, 25% CH)

Not a bubbly Champagne exactly, but definitely a great wine. The '53 is an amber-colored drink with faint reservoirs of carbon dioxide. The nose is dominated by oak and dried roses, with a unique, red-wine-like bouquet. This is a very well-built and muscular Champagne with huge dimensions. The dry, Cognac-like aftertaste lasted for an entire three minutes!

- 1952 BOLLINGER 80, DEC 1996 (80)
(75% PN, 25% CH)

Despite a high level and total lack of sediment, the two bottles I tasted had long since passed their peak. Surprisingly strong oxidation for this vintage.

- 1949 BOLLINGER
(70% PN, 30% CH)

- 1947 BOLLINGER 80, APR 1996 (80)
(75% PN, 25% CH)

Only tasted in a half bottle. No mousse to speak of and a clear maderized tone that is disturbing. Otherwise a remarkably well-structured wine that would certainly have reached the ninety-five-point mark in a magnum.

- 1945 BOLLINGER 99, NOV 2000 (99)
(75% PN, 25% CH)

It's not often that '45s are as brilliant as this. Bollinger have made a refined wine with teasing aromas and a romantic bouquet. It's easy to swallow this caress of a wine, with its smooth fruit and lively freshness. One of my three winners at the Millennium Tasting. Extraordinarily forceful with exciting, gamy notes.

- 1929 BOLLINGER   97, MAR 2003 (97)
(80% PN, 20% CH)
Weak mousse, brilliant golden luster, and a multifaceted scent.
Medium-bodied homogenous nectar with tones of apricot and
peach and a long, honeyed finish.

- 1928 BOLLINGER   97, APR 2003 (97)
(75% PN, 25% CH)
This is one of history's most legendary Champagnes. I don't really
know what to say. The bouquet of the first bottle I tasted was
frankly quite unpleasant. Honestly, hints of death and decay were
evident—or penicillin, if one wants to be more polite. The taste,
on the other hand, was heavenly, with a vigor and dimension that
I've rarely experienced. The vitality of the next bottle was not as
monumental. Here the bouquet was most delicious, with a slight
note of digestive biscuit and cream. The flavor was extremely
long, creamy, and caressing. More Chardonnay-like than usual,
and actually more like a '29 in its soft, soothing manner.

- 1923 BOLLINGER
(75% PN, 25% CH)

- 1914 BOLLINGER   98, MAR 2002 (98)
(75% PN, 25% CH)
One of the most impressive Champagnes I've come across. The
color is still light and the mousse weak. The bouquet is hardly
grand with its bready, chocolaty, slightly smoky preamble. On the
other hand, the accelerating, stony, and immeasurably vigorous
and dryly stringent palate is out of this world.

- 1971 BOLLINGER CHOUILLY RÉSERVE   96, JAN 1996 (96)
(100% CH)
Bollinger, as you may know, stores its reserve wines in magnums
under a slight pressure. I have, on a few occasions, had the
pleasure of tasting a few of these faintly sparkling, Burgundy-like
beauties. Because it is doubtful that Bollinger itself considers
these to be Champagnes, I have chosen to write only about my
favorite among these odd curiosities. The wine was perfect, at the
age of twenty-five, with a style that is in many ways reminiscent
of a Chablis *grand cru* from Dauvissat or Raveneau. The bouquet
is exotically floral with elements of lanolin, wet wool, popcorn,
and smoke. The taste is fantastically complex with superb acidity,
clarity, faintly tingly mousse, and a forceful exit.

- 1996 BOLLINGER ROSÉ   89, DEC 2002 (94)
It took a few minutes in the glass before the note of a sauna,
along with smoke and a mushroomy aroma, revealed their origin.
Only just before, the wine had seemed like a juicy, creamy, softly
Chardonnay-dominated charmer. This wine will hardly be
described like this in a few years but, as newly launched on the
market, it sings a singularly popular tune.

- 1995 BOLLINGER ROSÉ   85, JUN 2002 (89)
(70% PN, 30% CH)
It is strange how much worse Bollinger's vintage wine often
becomes when you add the local red wine. It is possible that time
will afford this wine a little harmony and finesse. For the
moment, however, it is slightly coarse and unbalanced in
comparison to the white '95.

- 1990 BOLLINGER ROSÉ   88, JUN 1999 (92)
(71% PN, 29% CH)
Greatly reminds one of its base wine, the white '90 Grande
Année. The color is relatively pale and the wine has a handsome
nuance of cream alongside the intensely evolved windfall-fruit-
like characteristic taste.

- 1988 BOLLINGER ROSÉ   88, NOV 2003 (91)
(74% PN, 26% CH)
Very good house-style, light orange color. A "Bolly" nose and a
dry classic palate, strongly characterized by ripe grapes.

- 1985 BOLLINGER ROSÉ   73, JUL 1993 (78)
(68% PN, 32% CH)

- 1983 BOLLINGER ROSÉ   89, NOV 2002 (89)
(70% PN, 30% CH)
Totally devoid of signs of fatigue. Handsome appearance and a
fine, dry feeling both in the mouth and via olfactory clues.
Mineral and slightly aged nutshell, with a gamy undertone and
faint cellar note. Lighter than expected, with a fine, perky mousse
and nutty complexity.

- 1982 BOLLINGER ROSÉ   68, JUN 1988 (75)
(70% PN, 30% CH)

- 1976 BOLLINGER ROSÉ   90, OCT 2003 (90)
(60% PN, 40% CH)
Fat, rich, and fruity, with a butterscotchy, luxurious finish.
Completely mature.

- 1975 BOLLINGER ROSÉ   95, SEP 2000 (95)
(75% PN, 25% CH)
Wonderfully first-rate, appetizing wine! The mousse is weak in
the glass but fine on the palate. The color is rather aged. The
bouquet is audaciously, ingratiatingly delicious, with a creaminess
and vanilla tone that I hardly expected. Also beneath this array of
sweet aromas are Bollinger's nutty vitality and beautiful notes of
forest mushrooms.

- 1973 BOLLINGER ROSÉ   84, SEP 1996 (84)
(75% PN, 25% CH)
Oaky and leaden-footed rosé Champagne without elegance.
However, a good, full-bodied Champagne with food.

- 1996 VIEILLES VIGNES FRANÇAISES   97, NOV 2003 (99)
(100% PN)
Just as expected: a monumental wine experience! The wine
belongs to the select few that behave with such evident, obvious
authority that commentary and comparison feel superfluous.
Still, to me the '90 is its closest cousin, with its vigor and velvety,
young creaminess. Deep golden hue with extremely small bubbles
that slowly make their way up through the glass. The bouquet is
mute, tight, and powerful, like a distant rumbling thunderstorm.
The palate is met by an oily, creamy essence of dark fruit and
licorice. Long and wide as an American highway. A complete
Champagne in its make-up. Drink it soon or wait ten years for
the next phase. There's a great risk that it'll go hide in a tunnel
for a few years—the second bottle I opened six months after
launching already showed signs of heading into that tunnel.

- 1992 VIEILLES VIGNES FRANÇAISES   95, MAR 2004 (97)
(100% PN)
Unparalleled, superior wine for this vintage. Dazzlingly apple-
flavored, youthful bouquet with a palate that can be likened to a
shock wave of great and obvious authority. So rich and
concentrated, with a fruity sweetness and grapiness that is better
than most. I wish all wine-lovers could taste this heroic beverage
once in their life.

- 1990 BOLLINGER R. D.   93, MAR 2004 (94)
(69% PN, 31% CH)
More mute and more potent than the exotic Grande Année of
the same year. The wine has acquired R. D. character by this
time and it is difficult to predict how long it will be on top.

What further complicates the matter is that this R. D. wine is going to be disgorged several times, which makes it almost impossible to predict the development of the bottle one is about to drink. One guess is that this wine is going to peak two years after disgorging into a normal bottle, and three to four years after disgorging into a magnum. The wine itself has a pronounced house-character, with great masculine fleshiness and mushroom notes combined with dark chocolate and windfall fruit.

- 1990 VIEILLES VIGNES FRANÇAISES   96, MAR 2003 (98)
(100% PN)
Naturally already a fantastic Champagne, but undeveloped, evasive, and so far just a bit short in the aftertaste in comparison to the heavenly '89. An extremely interesting wine to follow in the future.

- 1989 VIEILLES VIGNES FRANÇAISES   98, MAY 2003 (98)
(100% PN)
As usual, almost perfect. So far the wine is Yquem-like, with its enormously sweet, concentrated, exotic fruit. Only when aired does there appear a magnificent, secondary aroma of cèpe mushrooms.

- 1988 BOLLINGER R. D.   93, MAR 2004 (94)
(75% PN, 25% CH)
Classic Bollinger style is evident here, with hazelnut, bread, mushrooms, and smoke. The wine, on the other hand, has hardly benefited from its late disgorging. This wine will be exciting to see when it reaches its peak. Beautifully delicious and nutty in a magnum.

- 1988 VIEILLES VIGNES FRANÇAISES   94, NOV 2003 (97)
(100% PN)
When first introduced onto the market it was unusually raw and abrupt. At the time I missed the creamy complexity that previous vintages had shown in their infancy. One year later it was all there: the creaminess, the power, and the tons of fruit. A giant!

- 1986 VIEILLES VIGNES FRANÇAISES   93, FEB 1999 (94)
(100% PN)
Champagne's greatest rarity is made of grapes from ungrafted pre-phylloxera stocks in Aÿ and Bouzy. No other Champagne can display such richness. The '86 may not be one of the greatest vintages, but here too there is an intractable power that lifts it over its competitors. The color is always dark, with elements of mahogany; and the nose is astonishingly broad, with layers of fruit and vegetable aromas. The wine is compact, with a strict finish. Store!

- 1985 BOLLINGER R. D.   95, MAR 2004 (95)
(65% PN, 35% CH)
Surprisingly little true R. D. character, yet with a delicate flowery bouquet that hints at more Chardonnay than is actually the case. A fresh, fruity flavor, rich in nuances, with a stifled, underlying power that reveals its origin in the end. Creamy and beautifully elusive in the magnum, with extreme depth. Since the autumn of 2003, more gamy and mushroomy.

- 1985 VIEILLES VIGNES FRANÇAISES   96, MAR 2003 (98)
(100% PN)
One of the rare Champagnes in this book that has received ninety-eight points. It is always difficult to describe in words the great Champagnes, so let me instead say that this Champagne is close to perfection, with its deep golden color, outstandingly mature, multifaceted bouquet, and shocking attack. The acidity is wrapped up in an incomprehensibly rich and elegant fruit. A masterpiece!

- 1982 BOLLINGER R. D.   94, JAN 2003 (94)
(70% PN, 30% CH)
R. D. (Recently Disgorged) is the same as the vintage wine, but stored a few more years in contact with the yeast. The '82 has a more vigorous fruit than the normally disgorged wine. In this vintage the rich autolytic character and muscular build come in very handy.

- 1982 VIEILLES VIGNES FRANÇAISES   93, OCT 2000 (96)
(100% PN)
A brilliant color, like red gold. Undeveloped, compact nose. Full of minerals, cold and deep, packed with exciting aromas. The yogurt that you sometimes find in red Burgundies is a very clear element here. Cream, olives, iron, tar, figs, and orange are other clearly discernible nuances. At first the flavor is as harsh as a red Hermitage, but goes on to develop a toasty, wonderful complexity. Don't touch it for ten years!

- 1981 BOLLINGER R. D.   88, SEP 2003 (89)
(70% PN, 30% CH)
This is a wine that Bollinger has tried to get rid of several times. The wine has always been tart, hard, and tight. Unfortunately, this is still the case, even though the autolytic character has thoroughly enriched this thin wine. The high acidity will hold the wine alive far longer than usual after disgorging. Classic R. D. fragrance of raw mushroom.

- 1981 VIEILLES VIGNES FRANÇAISES   96, FEB 1999 (97)
(100% PN)
A wonder of delicacy. That a Blanc de Noirs can be so elegant and multifaceted astonished an entire tasting group in November 1993. The nose is only of medium scope, but has a lovely romantic, flowery style. Alongside the flowers there is a broad spectrum of all the treasures of the bakery, as well as white chocolate, marzipan, lilies, and lime.

- 1980 VIEILLES VIGNES FRANÇAISES   95, FEB 1999 (95)
(100% PN)
These wines are always in a dimension of their own. The scent is incredibly weighty, but somewhat limited in scope. The taste is ingratiatingly full-bodied and unbeatably concentrated. Unfortunately the aftertaste is a bit shorter than usual.

- 1979 BOLLINGER R. D.
(70% PN, 30% CH)

- 1976 BOLLINGER R. D.   93, JAN 2003 (93)
(50% PN, 50% CH)
A touch lighter than expected, considering the house and the vintage. The hazelnut aromas and smoke tones are weaker than usual. The '76 relies instead upon a polished citrus fruitiness. Unusually short aftertaste. Delightful in a magnum!

- 1975 BOLLINGER R. D.   95, JAN 2003 (95)
(70% PN, 30% CH)
For several years the best Champagne I'd drunk. The critics are unanimous—this is a great vintage for Bollinger. Some bottles with the Année Rare label have been too young and closed. The wine is best appreciated two or three years after being disgorged, when its classic hazelnut tones and rich flavor of truffles, cheese, and chocolate appear more clearly in the relatively hard and acidic wine. The aftertaste is majestic, with layers of nut and leather aromas.

- 1975 BOLLINGER R. D. ANNÉE RARE   92, MAR 1994 (95)
(70% PN, 30% CH)

The same wine as the R. D., but stored for a few more years. This one was too young! Such bottle variations, of course, depend on the date of disgorgement.

- 1975 VIEILLES VIGNES FRANÇAISES   95, FEB 1999 (96)
  (100% PN)
  Still quite young, With a strong nose, considerable length, and a gorgeous Pinot flavor. Very good indeed.

- 1973 BOLLINGER R. D.   93, SEP 2003 (93)
  (75% PN, 25% CH)
  Broad, tannin-rich Champagne with a musky and gamy nose. Bollinger's characteristic "sauna tone" (from the oak barrels) takes center-stage. A mature, slightly abrupt power-pack that has charm. Very elegant and honeysuckle-scented with severe acidity—if you are allowed, as I was, to drink a magnum directly from the house.

- 1973 BOLLINGER R. D. ANNÉE RARE   92, MAR 1994 (92)
  (75% PN, 25% CH)
  Same impressions as the R. D.

- 1973 VIEILLES VIGNES FRANÇAISES   91, FEB 1999 (91)
  (100% PN)
  This has to be the mightiest Champagne I've ever drunk. The nose was amazingly broad, but I wonder if it wasn't *too* overwhelming. The Champagne as a whole resembles a great red Burgundy. Boiled vegetables, paprika, green beans, red beet, fish, raw meat, and gun-smoke. The gigantic flavor runs along the same lines, with extra tones of cauliflower, lavender, basil, tar, and duck liver. The richest and most idiosyncratic Champagne I've tasted, but hardly worth the exorbitant price.

- 1970 BOLLINGER R. D.   94, MAR 2003 (94)
  (70% PN, 30% CH)
  This is *the* wine of the vintage. The flavor is somewhat less concentrated than both the '73 and '75, but the nose is among the most exquisite I have experienced. Never before has honeysuckle dominated a wine so clearly. The house's typical hazelnut aroma is also a faithful companion here. A wine to lose yourself in. Actually still holding up!

- 1970 BOLLINGER R. D. ANNÉE RARE   94, MAR 1994 (94)
  (70% PN, 30% CH)
  Same impressions as the R. D.

- 1970 VIEILLES VIGNES FRANÇAISES   98, JUN 1999 (98)
  (100% PN)
  After having read both Sutcliffe and Broadbent's judgments on this wine, I was extremely surprised by its character. Along with my British colleagues I was impressed by the wine's concentration, but the aromas were very different from those I'd noted in other vintages of this pre-phylloxera wine. The aromas were fruity and creamy, like a Cramant Blanc de Blancs. The nose was tactful and the flavor fat and full of exotic mango aromas. The wine's concentration and length confirm that the label isn't on the wrong bottle. One of the finest bottles of Champagne to be found!

- 1969 BOLLINGER R. D.   96, JUN 1999 (96)
  (70% PN, 30% CH)
  A beautiful golden color and a sensual spectrum in the nose, where flower and fruit aromas are more prominent than usual. Paradoxically fresh and mature at the same time. There is a faint vegetable element in the refined flavor of exotic fruits and popcorn.

- 1969 VIEILLES VIGNES FRANÇAISES   96, JUN 1999 (96)
  (100% PN)

A fantastic vintage and one of the greatest Champagnes I have ever tasted. I managed to get a bottle from the last remaining case the producer had. This is also unique for being the first vintage of Vieilles Vignes Françaises. A very dark golden-reddish color, perfect mousse, and a magnificent bouquet. There are none of the '73's vegetable tones, but instead this '69 is dominated by sweet licorice, dark chocolate, tobacco, apricot, and peach. The texture is oily and fat, but the acidity is impressive under the benign surface. A disappointment at the Millennium Tasting at Villa Pauli.

- 1966 BOLLINGER R. D.   95, DEC 2001 (95)
  (75% PN, 25% CH)
  Disgorged in 1999 and opened two years later. Lighter and much younger in demeanor than the usual vintage Champagne. Delicious and very elegant bouquet of mushrooms, Valhrona chocolate, Autumn Fire, and duck liver. Slim and tall.

- 1964 BOLLINGER R. D.   95, MAR 2000 (96)
  (75% PN, 25% CH)
  Tasted when recently disgorged in a magnum. It was still a young Champagne with enormous integral power, but of course the date of disgorgement was decisive.

- 1961 BOLLINGER R. D.   84, NOV 1993 (84)
  (75% PN, 25% CH)
  Red wine notes that are reminiscent of a heavy Barolo. A weak mousse and somewhat dried-up fruit. Meaty and vinous. Disgorged in 1972, so other examples, disgorged more recently, may be considerably better.

BONNAIRE **** R-M
120, rue d'Épernay, B. P. 5
51530 Cramant
03 26 57 50 85
Production: 200,000

The largest individual producer in Cramant was originally called Bonnaire-Bouquemont, and for three decades Bonnaire has provided us with some of the creamiest Chardonnay wines the world has ever seen. A few years ago Jean-Louis Bonnaire moved his office and reception down to the ultra-modern plant in the middle of the village's vine rows. He owns a few of Cramant's best locations, and the grapes from here are always used in the vintage wine or the Special Club. These wines in particular are among the area's real charmers, if they are given about ten years in the cellar. Malolactic fermentation is used, and thus the wines gain a buttery, mature character in their youth, but the acidity is always very high, lifting the wines up to an exotic wealth in their middle age and a splendid nutty fullness when mature. Bonnaire make textbook Cramant for the sensualist. My private cellar is full of bottles from Bonnaire.

- BONNAIRE TRADITION   72
  (30% PN, 30% PM, 40% CH)

- BONNAIRE CREMANT DE CRAMANT   79
  (100% CH)

- BONNAIRE SÉLECTION   83
  (100% CH)
  A blend from 1984 and 1985, which in its light and ingratiating style is one of Monsieur Bonnaire's personal favorites.

- BONNAIRE VARIANCE   82
  (100% CH)

A new, brilliant nonvintage Champagne from oak barrels. Fairly oxidative style with aromas of plums, bananas, and windfall apples. Still, it is very good, ample, and filled with toasted oak. Immediately mature.

- 2000/1999 BONNAIRE   82, MAY 2003 (90)
(100% CH)

It is of course difficult at this early stage to judge a wine for future points, but the foundation seems fine. Already evident is a fine nuttiness, together with an exemplary silky mousse that beautifully elevates the melted butter.

- 1999/1998 BONNAIRE   85, MAY 2003 (90)
(100% CH)

This wine—not yet on the market—has much to gain from swimming with the yeast for a few years to come. Despite this, it is exceedingly enjoyable, and it's interesting to see the purity in fruit uplifted at this early stage. Passion-fruit aromas are strongest, combined with a gooseberry-like, early summer, butterfly-light tone.

- BONNAIRE BLANC DE BLANCS   79
(100% CH)
- BONNAIRE BLANC DE BLANCS NON DOSÉ   76
(100% CH)
- BONNAIRE ROSÉ   68
(10% PN, 90% CH)
- 1997 BONNAIRE   89, JUL 2003 (90)
(100% CH)

It is always difficult to predict how a vintage wine from Bonnaire is going to develop. This '97 is seductively ingratiating and complete in its appearance, giving the impression that it should not be stored. However, I am convinced that storage would only make the wine better. Already evident is complete mellowness and a fluffy creaminess. The fruit is rosy-red, with a clear note of wild strawberries and ripe, sweet strawberries.

- 1997 BONNAIRE SOIS BOIS   91, MAY 2003 (93)
(100% CH)

Not as seductive and well-integrated as the '95, but still beautifully exotic and peach-drenched. I am truly fascinated by this oak-barrel-fermented wine, which Jean-Louis makes for private consumption.

- 1995 BONNAIRE   91, JUN 2003 (93)
(100% CH)

An incomparably complex, multifaceted wine with enormous potential and direct charm. Meringue, sweet citrus, crème brûlée, and vanilla are strong aromas in this tart, superbly structured wine.

- 1995 BONNAIRE SOIS BOIS   93, MAY 2003 (95)
(100% CH)

Unbelievably delicious Burgundy with a Chassagne-like concentration and vinosity. Oily, fat, and buttery with a beautiful toasted oakiness. Great Chardonnay from the best villages can really absorb the oak character in a most satisfactory manner.

- 1994 BONNAIRE SOIS BOIS   84, SEP 1999 (89)
(100% CH)

A wine solely from Cramant fermented to the full in new oak barrels. In other words, a Selosse from Cramant. The wine seems surprisingly rich in minerals and, just as surprising, slightly oaky. Notes of newly cut wood, vanilla, and coconut are present, but only as highlights to this harmonious, Chablis-like Champagne.

- 1993 BONNAIRE   81, SEP 1999 (89)
(100% CH)

A vintage from Bonnaire that seems a little stingy and surly when first encountered. I am otherwise not the least bit worried about this child's future. Rest assured, the creaminess will come.

- 1992 BONNAIRE   82, MAR 1999 (86)
(100% CH)

Not yet out on the market. The wine will of course be better after longer contact with the yeast sediment.

- 1992 BONNAIRE BLANC DE NOIRS BOUZY   88, JUN 2003 (88)
(100% PN)

Love has encouraged Bonnaire to work with the black grapes of Bouzy, where his wife owns land. This Blanc de Noirs will be very good in a few years, but naturally feels a little clumsy in comparison with the Blanc de Blancs.

- 1991 BONNAIRE   87, APR 2003 (89)
(100% CH)

Tart and smart today, but less plump than the '92. A promising wine that is among the better ones from this vintage.

- 1989 BONNAIRE   84, JUN 1997 (91)
(100% CH)

A wine more typical of the vintage than the house. The nose is heavy and exotic with elements of saffron and petunia. The flavor is deep and spicy.

- 1988/1989 BONNAIRE   89, JUN 2003 (90)
(100% CH)

For many years a classically lemony-fresh, flowery, and delicately mineral-toned Chardonnay, this has now become fat and honey-saturated. An experimental wine in a clear bottle with '89 as its dominant other half.

- 1988 BONNAIRE   92, NOV 2003 (93)
(100% CH)

A textbook Bonnaire. Impossible to miss in a blind tasting. Light color, ultra-fine mousse, buttery nose of toffee, white flowers, and wild strawberries. Long, tight, and creamy flavor.

- 1987 BONNAIRE   88, JUL 2003 (88)
(100% CH)

Perhaps Bonnaire's greatest asset is that he has always succeeded in harvesting fully ripe grapes from his southerly slopes in Cramant. The '87 is one of the top wines of the vintage.

- 1986 BONNAIRE   92, MAY 1999 (93)
(100% CH)

A little less restrained than the '87. The wine is full of sun-ripened fruit and a whiff of toasty aromas. An incredible attack and yet, paradoxically, soft and buttery.

- 1985 BONNAIRE   92, JUL 2003 (92)
(100% CH)

Nineteen eighty-five is a special vintage for Bonnaire. The wines contain less of the toffee aroma, but display a fascinating, baffling spectrum in the nose and have a more restrained form. An intellectual wine.

- 1983 BONNAIRE   94, NOV 1993 (94)
(100% CH)

Bonnaire's '83 and '82 are among the most enjoyable and generous Champagnes one can find. The grower's answer to the Comtes de Champagne. Astoundingly rich, exotic, and creamy.

- 1982 BONNAIRE   94, MAR 2003 (94)
(100% CH)

The '82 is, if possible, even greater, with its mango-dominated fruit and toasty nose. A frequent winner in blind tastings.

• 1975 BONNAIRE   96, MAY 2003 (96)
(100% CH)
For many years a discreet wine that has changed drastically for the better. It's true that I have never tasted this wine in a magnum before, something that can raise the points even higher. Now the wine is vibratingly elastic, toasted, snortingly vital, and creamily rich, like a really warm 1964 or 1976 vintage. Marvelous!

• 1974 BONNAIRE   89, MAY 2003 (89)
(100% CH)
A wonderful nose of butter and Salon-like depth. Fat initially, then a little thin and dried out in the finish, with tones of tea leaves and fine sherry. Loses it in the glass.

• 1973 BONNAIRE   94, MAY 1999 (94)
(100% CH)
This is a Bonnaire in full maturity. The color is dark, the nose incredibly broad with smoky, deep, Salon-like aromas. Massive nutty fullness and a rich body.

• 1971 BONNAIRE   91, NOV 1993 (91)
(100% CH)
More restrained than the '73, with delicious young acidity and a very long citrus flavor. The maturity is only hinted at in the faintly smoky nose.

• 1959 BONNAIRE   94, MAY 2000 (94)
(100% CH)
The Bonnaire family's own favorite vintage, and of course my expectations were gigantic when it was finally decanted. I had succeeded in getting M. Bonnaire to release a bottle for our auction at Christie's in New York during the autumn of 1999. Of course it was I who made the successful bid on the bottle. At first glance, the bottle appeared to be wrongly labeled, but a look at the cork dispelled all such thoughts, as did the forceful, smoky bouquet with its gamy notes and tar-like overtones. The palate was, to be honest, slightly disappointing: Cramant's butteriness had vanished into thin air and the notes I described from the bouquet had taken over. On the other hand, length and mousse were extremely impressive.

• 1998 BONNAIRE CUVÉE PRESTIGE   88, DEC 2003 (92)
(100% CH)
Toasted oaky notes can be found here, even though the wine is entirely made in steel tanks. Not so buttery yet, but instead smokily complex and stuffed with mineral and young fruit— pear, kiwi, cherimoya, and papaya. Hard acidity and a fine, clean attack. Storage will surely bring this wine closer to its relatives in Cramant.

• 1997 BONNAIRE CUVÉE PRESTIGE   89, JUL 2003 (91)
(100% CH)
Already a great culinary pleasure. In every way a perfect summer wine, best enjoyed out of doors with its mellowness, sweet citrus creaminess, and summery, smiling character. I know, having drunk the wine with good friends by the exquisitely beautiful Lake Garda.

• 1996 BONNAIRE CUVÉE PRESTIGE   91, JUL 2003 (94)
(100% CH)
A thoroughly unreleased Bonnaire with bound nose and tart, undeveloped palate. Polished fruit with a hint of bread, lemon, and fresh pineapple. For the moment green, apple-flavored, and

full of minerals. It began to show its creaminess around the year 2000.

• 1990 BONNAIRE SPECIAL CLUB   94, MAR 2003 (95)
(100% CH)
As expected, Bonnaire have succeeded well with this marvelous vintage. A fabulous Champagne that is extremely fat and chewy. Buttery, exotic, and loaded with saffron.

• 1989 BONNAIRE SPECIAL CLUB   93, JUL 2003 (93)
(100% CH)
Full of incredibly sweet, charming fruit. Fat flavor with honey tones, creamy palate, and toffee finish. A real charmer at the moment!

• 1988 BONNAIRE SPECIAL CLUB   89, OCT 1997 (93)
(100% CH)
Harvested from some of the village's best locations. Always very similar to the vintage wine, but less developed after six or seven years. After that the Special Club unfailingly exhibits a somewhat greater concentration of similar aromas.

• 1985 BONNAIRE SPECIAL CLUB   95, MAY 2003 (95)
(100% CH)
I love this Champagne in the young phase it's going through right now. There is a refinement lacking in the ultra-generous '82. Restrained, elegant, and withdrawn, with a Montrachet-like tone of nut and a crystal-clear mineral flavor. Certain bottles have a decided maturity.

• 1983 BONNAIRE SPECIAL CLUB   93, JUN 1997 (93)
(100% CH)
Almost identical to the usual '83, last time I tasted it.

• 1982 BONNAIRE SPECIAL CLUB   94, APR 1997 (94)
(100% CH)
Even softer and more concentrated, but less acidity.

• 1981 BONNAIRE SPECIAL CLUB   95, MAY 2003 (95)
(100% CH)
A sensation, which I fell head-over-heels for. Supremely elegant, and a broad nose of toasted bread and Dom Pérignon-like explosive fruit. Extraordinary balance and a delicate flavor that reminded me of the '85. One of this vintage's absolute finest Champagnes.

• 1980 BONNAIRE SPECIAL CLUB   90, NOV 1993 (90)
(100% CH)
A bastard child. Dark and smoky tones: it's incredible that oak barrels weren't used. Awesome power—this wine demands food.

• 1976 BONNAIRE SPECIAL CLUB   92, MAY 1997 (92)
(100% CH)
A most reliable wine with good extracts and concentration. Full-bodied palate of lemon and butterscotch.

BONNET, ALEXANDRE N-M
138, rue de Général de Gaulle
10340 Les Riceys
03 25 29 30 93
Production: 650,000
Bonnet is for me the only producer in the village who almost deserves his cult status. It would be interesting to see what this house could achieve with Pinot grapes from Aÿ or Verzenay. Their Rosé des Riceys has a seductive nose, and the owner's Coteaux Champenois is Aube's best. The Champagnes are also influenced by an intense grape aroma that lifts them above the wines of his neighbors. Owned by Bruno Paillard.

- A. BONNET BRUT   66
  (100% PN)
- A. BONNET BRUT PRESTIGE   66
  (70% PN, 30% CH)
- A. BONNET GRANDE RÉSERVE   70
  (55% PN, 15% PM, 30% CH)
- A. BONNET ROSÉ   70
  (100% PN)
- 1993 A. BONNET BLANC DE BLANCS   70, MAR 2000 (75)
  (100% CH)
- 1990 A. BONNET BLANC DE BLANCS   75, JAN 2003 (75)
  (100% CH)
- 1993 MADIGRAL   81, MAR 2000 (80)
  (50% PN, 50% CH)

Bonnet's prestige *cuvée* is made of equal parts Chardonnay from Grauves and Pinot Noir from Les Riceys. Excitingly intense, personal bouquet with notes of duck liver, figs, and toffee. The flavor is balsamic-round, and I suspect that the Champagne's greatest merit is its relative youthfulness.

BONNET, FERDINAND N-M

12, allée du Vignoble
51055 Reims
03 26 84 44 15
Production: 1,000,000

Stephane Lefebvre runs this recently established house that has its roots in Oger. The original firm's ten high-class hectares are retained, but 90 percent of the grapes are bought in. Rémy-Cointreau took over management in 1988. (See also F. Bonnet in the *grand cru* village Oger.)

- F. BONNET BRUT PRESTIGE   66
  (70% PN, 30% CH)
- F. BONNET CUVÉE ERIKS   67
  (32% PN, 50% PM, 18% CH)
- F. BONNET HÉRITAGE BRUT   67
  (32% PN, 50% PM, 18% CH)
- F. BONNET PRINCESSE BRUT   67
  (32% PN, 50% PM, 18% CH)
- 1996 F. BONNET   81, SEP 2003 (85)

Not so ingratiating just yet. Is this a sleeping beauty? At the moment a tad raw, with its hard, acidic appearance. Green-drenched nuances of fine Chardonnay in the hue.

- 1989 F. BONNET   78, DEC 1998 (81)
  (70% PN, 30% CH)

Big, slightly rustic, and a developed, bready nose. The taste is ordinary, soft, and powerful.

BONNET, F. N-M

1, rue de Mesnil
51190 Oger
03 26 57 52 43

This well-run house, presently owned by the Rémy-Cointreau group, has close connections with Charles Heidsieck. The house was founded in 1922 by Ferdinand Bonnet and owns ten hectares in Oger, Avize, and Vertus. The house is well known in connoisseur circles, and those Champagnes I have tasted have left me wanting to try more.

- F. BONNET CRÉMANT   68
  (10% PN, 90% CH)

- 1983 F. BONNET SÉLECTION   85, JUL 1990 (90)
  (100% CH)

Surprisingly dark color. An almost erotic nose, with smoky and spicy perfumed tones. The same aromas return in the mouth.

- 1982 F. BONNET SÉLECTION   83, JUL 1992 (88)
  (100% CH)

The wine doesn't have the same stringency and romantic tension as the '83, but it is a classic multi-*cru* Blanc de Blancs with juicy fruit and fine breadiness.

- 1976 F. BONNET SÉLECTION   94, NOV 2003 (94)
  (100% CH)

A fantastically sophisticated Champagne with a complex, modulated bouquet of floral, toasted, buttery, butterscotchy, vanilla-like, balsamic parts. Mineral-full, almost smoky palate with bunches of nutty, smoky richness that envelope this stony package in a perfect way.

BONVILLE, ED **** R-M

3, rue du Gué
51190 Oger
03 26 57 53 19
Production: 40,000

The Bonville family has always used oak barrels, both in Avize and in Oger, and all the wines are still fermented in oak barrels. Malolactic fermentation is only performed in exceptional cases, which affords even the nonvintage Champagnes good storability. Madame Bonville is one of Champagne's most elegant ladies. She administers her seven hectares exceedingly well. For those of you who have always wondered how a Bollinger Blanc de Blancs would taste if one was ever produced, I can recommend these nutty wines. The method of vinification is identical to the great model in Aÿ. Madame Bonville also provides Bollinger with a great deal of its Chardonnay. In the Millennium tasting, the '59 came in at a fantastic thirteenth place, and thus is the foremost grower's Champagne of all time! Unfortunately, the company is slowly being dissolved, as there is no one to take over after Madame Bonville.

- ED BONVILLE BLANC DE BLANCS   79
  (100% CH)
- 1993 ED BONVILLE   79, OCT 2002 (86)
  (100% CH)

Sadly, Madame Bonville's last vintage. Hereafter, we will have to hunt for these grapes in Grand Siècle and Bollinger Grande Année. Oh, her wines were so young! If you find a bottle somewhere, it is probably best to store it relatively warm for anything to happen. In about ten years or so this is going to be a rich, buoyant wine with real authority.

- 1976 ED BONVILLE   91, OCT 2002 (91)
  (100% CH)

It is hardly surprising that Bonville made a good wine this warm year. Considering how exceptional the '59 was, one might have guessed that the normally rigid, acidic wines from this area would be helped once again by the weather gods, giving this a pleasing, naturally warm fruity-sweetness. The wine is fleshy and rich, with substantial width across the shoulders—unusual for a Blanc de Blancs.

- 1970 ED BONVILLE   84, OCT 2002 (87)
  (100% CH)

Tasted newly disgorged at "Madame's," the wine was boisterously young when freshly poured. Only at the end did the wine display why many growers in Côte de Blancs consider 1970 to be a good, storable vintage. Such is rarely the case when the wines have been on the market a while.

- 1959 ED BONVILLE   97, JUN 1999 (97)
  (100% CH)

  Lightly nutty, with a hint of smoke and dominated by an aroma of coffee. Something as unusual as a Bollinger-like Chardonnay. Creamy taste with an element of gooseberries. Lovely finish with a taste of digestive biscuit.

- 1928 ED BONVILLE   92, MAY 2001 (92)
  (100% CH)

  Madame Bonville promised me in London that I could taste the '28 the next time I came to visit Oger. To be on the safe side she opened two bottles of this legendary vintage. I was doubly thrilled when I learned that this was also the year of her birth. The bouquet was interesting with notes of petroleum, cellar, coffee, and brioche. The acidity is a spike on the palate, the taste rather young. The mousse is rather faint and the depth of taste could be greater.

- 1985 ED BONVILLE SPECIAL CLUB   89, OCT 2002 (91)
  (100% CH)

  Expansively generous with a sweetness of fruit that is unusual in Bonville's wine. Decidedly fatter and totally different than the 1979. Which is better is a matter of choice.

- 1982 ED BONVILLE SPECIAL CLUB   85, OCT 2002 (85)
  (100% CH)

  I was somewhat disappointed in this newly disgorged wine, with its oxidative secondary note of overripe apples, licorice, and tar. The more I drank, the more I appreciated this gunpowder-fragrant, dry Champagne. The fruit should have been more generous.

- 1979 ED BONVILLE SPECIAL CLUB   91, MAY 2001 (91)
  (100% CH)

  Classic Blanc de Blancs possessing the vintage's elegance and nutty tones. Restrained and relatively lightweight with delicious mineral notes, acidity, and a long, biscuity aftertaste.

BONVILLE, FRANCK *** R-M

9, rue Pasteur
51190 Avize
03 26 57 52 30
Production: 130,000

The firm was founded in 1947, and today Franck Bonville makes very rich, nutty Champagnes in the English style. His '83 was mistaken for a Krug Grande Cuvée in a big blind tasting in Stockholm in 1992. Personally I think that Bonville and De Sousa are the only growers in Avize who come close to Selosse.

- F. BONVILLE SÉLECTION   79
  (100% CH)

- 1998 F. BONVILLE   83, FEB 2003 (88)
  (100% CH)

  Both the '98 and the '96 are dominated by an aroma that I learned early on, but one that has fallen into oblivion because so many wines from this village lack this aroma. We called the note "Avize apples." It is an aroma that one never finds in Champagnes from the neighboring villages, and that otherwise comes closest to young Pinot Noir. It is undeniably fascinating to see how the other attributes of Côte des Blancs—such as high acidity, purity, microscopic bubbles, and the blackboard-chalky-like stoniness—are as clear as can be. Very buoyant, early summery, and promising.

- 1996 F. BONVILLE   85, MAY 2003 (89)
  (100% CH)

  Fascinatingly clear apple aroma that totally subdues the grape's citrus notes. Classic purity, attack, and mineral elegance. Brilliantly buoyant and uplifting.

- 1990 F. BONVILLE   84, SEP 1999 (87)
  (100% CH)

  Somewhat too rich and fat to be regarded as a classic Blanc de Blancs. The wine is oxidative and full bodied with a distinct impression of oak barrel. The taste is soft as honey and potent.

- 1985 F. BONVILLE   68, DEC 1993 (68)
  (100% CH)

- 1983 F. BONVILLE   90, AUG 1992 (90)
  (100% CH)

  The oak character takes one's thoughts to Bollinger or Krug. Smoky, broad Champagne with a lovely depth and classic oxidative style. Drink within a couple of years.

- 1976 F. BONVILLE   91, MAY 2001 (91)
  (100% CH)

  Big, very delicious, well-dressed Champagne, like all the '76s from Avize. Nut toffee, honey, and chocolate envelope the sweet, powerful, buttery fruit. Impressive!

BOUCHÉ PÈRE & FILS N-M

10, rue Général de Gaulle
51530 Pierry
03 26 54 12 44
Production: 600,000

Established in 1945. Today run by Pierre and José Bouché. The firm owns thirty-five hectares of vineyards in ten villages, of which four are *grand cru* (Chouilly, Verzy, Verzenay, and Puisieulx), and exports half of its production. Bouché use only the first pressing in all their wines.

- BOUCHÉ BRUT RÉSERVE   70
  (30% PN, 20% PM, 50% CH)

- BOUCHÉ BLANC DE BLANCS   70
  (100% CH)

- BOUCHÉ ROSÉ   67
  (60% PN, 30% PM, 10% CH)

- 1990 BOUCHÉ   82, MAY 2001 (84)
  (55% PN, 45% CH)

  Soft and balanced, approachable Champagne with a somewhat simple, apple-flavored fundamental tone. Appears slightly too sweet and superficial, despite the use of fine grape material from *grand cru* villages.

- 1988 BOUCHÉ   74, AUG 1995 (82)
  (35% PN, 20% PM, 45% CH)

  A pure *grand cru* Champagne, marked by heavy Pinot from Montagne de Reims. Meaty and dark aromas.

- BOUCHÉ "2000"   77, MAY 2000 (82)
  (50% PN, 50% CH)

  Contains wine from the vintages '93, '94, and '95. Very pleasant floral bouquet, with elements of pear. Elegant, mild, and delicate flavors with a supple finish; capable of development.

BOUCHER, GILLES R-M
10, rue Pasteur
51160 Champillon
03 26 59 46 64
Production: 50,000

A grower since 1806 and Champagne-maker since 1991. Today's owner, Sylvain Baucher, uses five hectares in Champillon.

• BOUCHER CARTE BLANCHE	62
(50% PN, 50% CH)	

BOULARD, RAYMOND N-M
rue Tambour
51480 La Neuville-aux-Larris
03 26 58 12 08
Production: 90,000

Raymond Boulard is one of the newest companies in Champagne, having first seen the light of day in 1952. The house is still wholly under the control of the Boulard family, owning vineyards in seven villages: Neuville-aux-Larris, Cuchery, Belval, Paradis, Hermonville, and Cauroy-les-Hermonville. All of them are low-ranked villages north of Reims or on the outskirts of the Marne valley. The only high-ranking vineyards owned by the firm lie in the *grand cru* village of Mailly. The *cuvée de prestige* is disgorged *à la volée*, and the average age of the vines is thirty-five.

• CUVÉE TRADITION SYMPHONIE	51
(20% PN, 30% PM, 50% CH)	
• RAYMOND BOULARD MAILLY GRAND CRU	76
(90% PN, 10% CH)	
• RAYMOND BOULARD RÉSERVE	51
(25% PN, 50% PM, 25% CH)	
• RAYMOND BOULARD BLANC DE BLANCS	54
(100% CH)	
• RAYMOND BOULARD ROSÉ SAIGNÉE	52
(50% PN, 50% PM)	
• 1998 RAYMOND BOULARD	84, DEC 2003 (87)
(30% PN, 20% PM, 50% CH)	

Made completely in barrels, like Burgundy with *bâtonnage*. The grapes come from thirty-year-old vines and are harvested late. The wine is delightful, with deep notes of bread, honey, and juicy red apples, concurrent with a certain floral, beautiful mineral character. Complex and modulated without any prevalent oaky notes.

• 1986 L'ANNÉE DE LA COMÈTE	80, MAY 1995 (80)
(25% PN, 25% PM, 50% CH)	

Fortunately the contents were far more stylish than the bottle. The firm's *cuvée de prestige*, which received the Guide Hachette's medal of honor, the "*Coupe de Coeur*" in 1995, is made from grapes that come from very old vines. At the age of nine it is already fully mature. Without being either particularly concentrated or refined, it's very good, with a broad nose of banana, dried fruit, leather, and honey. The flavor is as soft and mature as Champagne from the 1970s, but it finishes abruptly in the mouth. Drink now!

BOURDELOIS, RAYMOND R-M
737, avenue du Général Leclerc
51530 Dizy
03 26 55 23 34
Production: 30,000

Raymond Bourdelois has found a niche: he alone makes a Blanc de Blancs from Dizy. The Champagne is more of a curiosity than a great wine. The grower presides over six hectares in Dizy and Cumières.

• RAYMOND BOURDELOIS BRUT	41
(70% PN, 30% CH)	
• RAYMOND BOURDELOIS BLANC DE BLANCS	60
(100% CH)	

BOUTILLEZ-GUER R-M
38, rue Pasteur
51380 Villers-Marmery
03 26 97 91 38
Production: 80,000

The grower blends Chardonnay from Villers-Marmery and Pinot Noir from Verzenay.

• BOUTILLEZ-GUER BRUT	55
(30% PN, 70% CH)	
• BOUTILLEZ-GUER BLANC DE BLANCS	54
(100% CH)	

BOUY, LAURENT R-M
7, rue l'Eglise
51380 Verzy
03 26 97 93 23
Production: 20,000

One of the few producers to make a Blanc de Blancs from Verzy. Four and a half hectares planted with twenty-five-year-old vines. Modern vinification.

• LAURENT BOUY BLANC DE BLANCS	70
(100% CH)	

BOVIÈRE-PERINET R-M
18, rue Chanzy
51360 Verzenay
03 26 49 80 96
Production: 120,000

This grower owns three hectares in Verzenay, all of which are planted with Pinot Noir. Other wines: Brut, Réserve, Cuvée Spéciale.

• BOVIÈRE-PERINET ROSÉ	66
(100% PN)	

BRICE *** N-M
3, rue Yvonnet
51150 Bouzy
03 26 52 06 60
Production: 100,000

Jean-Paul Brice founded this company as recently as 1994, after previously having been one of the trio behind Barancourt. Michel Joly is *chef de caves* and has set *terroir* Champagnes as his top priority. Very good value for money.

• BRICE TRADITION	50
(45% PN, 5% PM, 50% CH)	

- BRICE AŸ   83
(90% PN, 10% CH)
The purity of the aromas is striking, even if I miss the maturity that gives Aÿ Pinot its characteristic weight. Definitely worth storing.

- BRICE BOUZY   80
(80% PN, 20% CH)
Surprisingly light, with a deliciously pure and fruity bouquet and a crystal-clear flavor that reminds me of green apples.

- BRICE CRAMANT   74
(100% CH)

- BRICE VERZENAY   83
(75% PN, 25% CH)
Rich creamy style as well as fine *terroir* character. Considerable length in the stony aftertaste.

BRICOUT *** N-M
29, rempart du Midi
51190 Avize
03 26 53 30 00
Production: 2,800,000
In 1820 the young German Charles Koch came to Avize and started his operations. His three sons began working with Arthur Bricout, a former winemaker for De Venoge in Épernay. The company never grew to be as big as had been hoped, and it was only in 1966, when Andreas Kupferberg renovated the firm's premises, that Bricout established itself as a famous house. Today it's the largest company in Avize. Almost all the grapes are bought in, and the vinification methods are extremely modern. In 1998 Bricout was sold to Delbeck. The winemaker is Philippe Pomi. The company have had a lot of problems recently and we can only hope they are able to solve them.

- BRICOUT CUVÉE PRESTIGE   61
(60% PN, 40% CH)

- BRICOUT CUVÉE RÉSERVE   38
(30% PN, 30% PM, 40% CH)

- BRICOUT ROSÉ   60
(20% PN, 80% CH)

- 1997 BRICOUT   75, JAN 2003 (77)
(40% PN, 25% PM, 35% CH)

- 1992 BRICOUT   81, JAN 2003 (82)
(100% CH)
Fine color. Faint, almost nonexistent bouquet. The palate, luckily, is several grades better. With the vintage's mellowness as a recurrent theme, the taster is carried toward a pleasant, biscuit-flavored finish, passing on the way a section of refreshing lemoniness.

- 1990 BRICOUT   82, MAR 2000 (85)
(100% CH)
The same wine with normal dosage. Strangely, the wine seems lighter and less toasted. The toasted note is missed, especially in the taste, which instead is floral and slightly bready.

- 1990 BRICOUT NON DOSÉ   82, MAR 2000 (86)
(100% CH)
House-typical Champagne with light toasted notes and a good helping of biscuit-like aroma. Fine explosive flavor and a tight structure. The grand house-style makes the wine feel like a *cuvée*.

- 1986 BRICOUT   70, MAY 1996 (73)
(60% PN, 40% CH)

- 1985 BRICOUT   80, MAR 2000 (80)
(100% CH)
Develops a little too quickly. Already a distinct oxide note. Should this mineral-rich wine already be like this?

- 1982 BRICOUT   81, FEB 2003 (81)
(100% CH)
A rather flat, somewhat overripe '82 with dosage that is too high and a few oxidative elements. Round and amenable if you're lucky.

- CUVÉE ARTHUR BRICOUT   83
(30% PN, 70% CH)
Pinot from Bouzy, Aÿ, and Verzenay, as well as Chardonnay from Avize, Cramant, and Chouilly. Despite the fine grapes, this is a shy, discreet wine that trusts to a refreshing, thirst-quenching, springtime radiance. All elements of the bouquet are young and floral, and the palate is fresh and short—for the time being.

- 1990 ARTHUR BRICOUT   83, MAR 2000 (88)
(30% PN, 70% CH)
Ten to 15 percent new casks: this fact is actually noticeable. A faint tone from the cask is discernible, together with green, youthfully delicate, tingly fruit. Excellent, very youthful acidity. Pure of style, developable, Chardonnay-dominated prestige Champagne.

- 1985 ARTHUR BRICOUT   85, MAR 2000 (87)
(40% PN, 60% CH)
In the space of just a few years, Bricout's *cuvée de prestige* have had three different names. Cuvée Elegance, Charles Koch, and now Arthur Bricout. Obviously, they're not satisfied with the sales of their *cuvée de prestige*. The '85 has a toasty nose that almost forces itself upon you, and which many of my colleagues perceive as burned rubber. I connect the nose with toasted bread that has stayed in the toaster a tad too long. This wine is undeniably good, but perhaps one expects a greater wealth of nuances in a *cuvée de prestige*.

- 1982 ARTHUR BRICOUT   87, MAR 2000 (87)
(30% PN, 70% CH)
This prestige *cuvée* is always made only of *grand cru* grapes. Very grand, developed, honey bouquet, with hints of paraffin and beeswax. Medium-bodied, concentrated, accomplished, and mature taste.

BROCHET-HERVIEUX R-M
28, rue de Villers-aux-Noeuds
51500 Écueil
03 26 49 74 10
Production: 60,000
Founded in 1945. The grower has access to 9.4 hectares of Pinot Noir and 1.6 hectares of Chardonnay from Écueil. The owners are Vincent and Alain Brochet.

- BROCHET-HERVIEUX EXTRA BRUT   61
(60% PN, 40% CH)

- 1991 BROCHET-HERVIEUX   70, OCT 2001 (73)
(60% PN, 40% CH)

- 1989 BROCHET-HERVIEUX   68, JUL 1995 (75)
(60% PN, 40% CH)

- 1986 BROCHET-HERVIEUX   82, MAY 2002 (82)
(60% PN, 40% CH)
An extremely rich, very fruit-driven Champagne that more than amply fills all the gaps in one's mouth. Juicy, exotic taste

reminiscent of dried pineapple, papaya, and treacle. One glass is enough, and—if eating—beware of dishes that demand tart, refined wines. Instead, choose something stronger, which will pick up some of the sweetness of the Champagne.

- 1983 BROCHET-HERVIEUX SPECIAL CLUB   68, JUL 1990 (75)
(60% PN, 40% CH)

BRUN, ALBERT LE N-M

93, avenue de Paris
51016 Châlons-en-Champagne
03 26 68 18 68
Production: 300,000
This house is one of only two that remain in what was once an important Champagne town. The Le Brun family has held the reins ever since it began in 1860 in Avize. The cellars they own today are the ones for which Napoleon rewarded Jacquesson. The winemaker is Françoise Le Brun.

- A. LE BRUN RESERVÉE   52
(65% PN, 35% CH)
- A. LE BRUN BLANC DE BLANCS   81
(100% CH)
  Without doubt the company's best wine. A pure Avize Champagne with a scent of ripe apples. Perhaps the resemblance to apple cider is too great.
- 1986 VIEILLE FRANCE   72, JUL 1990 (77)
(54% PN, 46% CH)
- 1983 A. LE BRUN RESERVÉE   69, JUL 1990 (74)
(41% PN, 59% CH)
- 1983 VIEILLE FRANCE   73, JUL 1990 (80)
(54% PN, 46% CH)
  Very weak but rather elegant nose. Rather more restrained than the '86, but shorter in growth.
- 1986 VIEILLE FRANCE ROSÉ   70, JUL 1990 (73)
(80% PN, 20% CH)

BRUN, ED. N-M

14, rue Marcel Mailly
51160 Aÿ
03 26 55 20 11
Production: 250,000
This house, founded in 1898, was among the first I ever visited. Ed. Brun uses 5 percent oak barrels and the grapes come from twenty-three villages, with Aÿ being the most important. The house is garnering more and more attention.

- ED. BRUN CUVÉE DE RÉSERVE   61
(95% PN, 5% CH)
- ED. BRUN CUVÉE SPÉCIALE   50
(60% PN, 38% PM, 2% CH)
- ED. BRUN BLANC DE BLANCS   63
(100% CH)
- ED. BRUN ROSÉ   60
(50% PN, 25% PM, 25% CH)
- 1997 ED. BRUN   70, MAR 2003 (73)
- 1988 ED. BRUN   69, JAN 1997 (83)
(60% PN, 40% CH)
  Completely closed nose. Well-structured and rich Champagne with a smoky undertone that could develop well.
- 1982 ED. BRUN   61, JUL 1988 (73)
(70% PN, 30% CH)

- 1971 ED. BRUN   88, MAR 1988 (88)
(80% PN, 20% CH)
  Not a great Champagne, but an enjoyable wine that was best when freshly poured, before it collapsed in the glass. At first a seductive nose of honey and butterscotch. Soft, honeyed flavor without much acidity or mousse.

BRUN, RENÉ N-M

4, place de la Libération
51160 Aÿ
03 26 55 21 24
Production: 200,000
The Brun family have grown vines in Aÿ for at least five generations, and house status was achieved in 1941. The proportion of Chardonnay grapes is surprisingly high, thus removing some of the village character from the wines. Other wines: Blanc de Blancs.

- RENÉ BRUN BRUT   48
(60% PN, 40% CH)
- RENÉ BRUN ROSÉ   39
(60% PN, 40% CH)
- 1985 RENÉ BRUN   70, JUN 1992 (76)
(40% PN, 60% CH)

BRUN, ROGER R-M

1, rue Henri IV
51160 Aÿ
03 26 55 45 50
Production: 35,000
Roger Brun runs this eighteen-hectare property together with his daughter Caroline. Like many other growers, this private production comprises only a small amount of the large volume of grapes that he is responsible for. All the wines of Aÿ used by Piper-Heidsieck pass through the hands of Roger Brun.

- ROGER BRUN ROSÉ   71
(41% PN, 37% PM, 22% CH)
- ROGER BRUN BRUT RÉSERVE   54
(33% PN, 40% PM, 27% CH)

BUNEL, ERIC R-M

32, rue Michel Letellier
51150 Louvois
03 26 57 03 06
Production: 38,000
The grower uses more than 6.5 hectares in Louvois and makes modern wines in a fruity style. The vintage wine always contains 50 percent Pinot Noir and 50 percent Chardonnay.

- 1994 ERIC BUNEL   75, JAN 2002 (80)
(70% PN, 30% CH)
  Youthful, as yet a little aggressive in appearance. The fruit is idiosyncratic, if somewhat immature. Present are notes of tender spring vegetables and gooseberry as well as white currants. Fresh, hard taste; good potential for development.
- 1992 ERIC BUNEL   80, JAN 2002 (80)
(70% PN, 30% CH)
  It's hard to believe that this wine comes from the same man as the '94. Here the wine is much darker in color. The nose is completely different, with hints of honey and almond combined with a coarse, substantial, and rounded taste.

BUSIN, JACQUES R-M

33, rue Thiers
51360 Verzenay
03 26 49 40 36
Production: 100,000

A grower who is always much appreciated in French wine guides. Other wines: Carte d'Or, Rosé.

* J. BUSIN BRUT RÉSERVE   50
  (75% PN, 25% CH)
* 1988 J. BUSIN   81, AUG 1994 (83)
  (90% PN, 10% CH)
  A strong nose of tequila and burned sugar. The flavor is very rich, with a compact fat structure and burned, buttery aromas. Where is the acidity?

B.O.B.

Many Champagne names bear the designation M-A (*marque-auxiliaire*), which means that anyone can obtain their own brand, but another Champagne producer is behind the label. Marne & Champagne, Duval-Leroy, Martel, Feuillate, etc. are really big players in this market. Because these "Buyer's Own Brand" can come from anyone, with great variance in quality, I have only listed some of the most common or most exciting that I have encountered in my career. It is usually in this category that you will find the names that you tell me I have forgotten to include in my book. I would not recommend buying any of the wines in this category. M-A is equivalent to a warning light for me, even if—particularly among the oldies—there can be a few goodies.

* LECHÈRE   70
* TAILLEVENT BRUT   38
  (100% CH)
* 1985 EUGENE LAROCHE   78, SEP 2003 (78)
* 1981 LENOTRE ROSÉ   87, APR 2003 (87)
  A really impetuous rosé with ripe notes that resemble old red Burgundy. Cheese, truffles, red beets, farmyard smells, and bouillon can be noticed. Round, fleshy taste with good mousse and gamy features.
* 1969 BARON DONAT
* 1966 BARON DONAT   85, JAN 2003 (85)
  Delicate and refreshing, with coffee notes, mineral, and resin in the nose. Light but unfortunately slightly short aftertaste.
* 1964 BARON DONAT   84, SEP 2002 (84)
  Heavy and forceful with rustic notes. Lengthy, oxidative aftertaste.
* 1961 BARON DONAT   87, FEB 1995 (87)
  Absolutely not a great wine, but in perfect condition and with the lovely chocolate tones of aged Champagne in both nose and flavor.
* 1947 BORDIER   89, SEP 2002 (89)
  One of the foremost Champagnes I have encountered using other labels. Reddish color, super-concentrated and intense, as well as a long, butterscotchy finish.
* 1985 TAILLEVENT BLANC DE BLANCS   50, FEB 1993 (60)
  (100% CH)

CAILLEZ-LEMAIRE R-M

25, rue Pierre Curie
51500 Damery
03 26 58 41 85
Production: 55,000

The firm was founded in 1942 by Raymond Caillez; today it is run by Henry Caillez. He owns six hectares planted with Pinot Noir, Chardonnay, and the dominant grape, Pinot Meunier.

* CAILLEZ-LEMAIRE ROSÉ   67
  (100% PN)

CALLOT & FILS R-M

31, avenue Jean-Jaurès
51190 Avize
03 26 57 51 57
Production: 40,000

You will find Callot on the main street in Avize, opposite Michel Gonet. My fleeting acquaintance with this grower's Champagne took place on the island of Jersey in 1992. The Callots have been growers since 1784! The size of the vineyard is five hectares.

* PIERRE CALLOT BLANC DE BLANCS   61
  (100% CH)
* PIERRE CALLOT GRANDE RÉSERVE   74
  (100% CH)
* PIERRE CALLOT NON DOSÉ   65
  (100% CH)
* 1989 PIERRE CALLOT   80, JAN 2003 (80)
  (100% CH)
  This one has developed a little too quickly. The wine is certainly good, fleshy, and honey-saturated, but I perceive a certain exaggerated oxide note, together with leather and tar.

CANARD-DUCHÊNE N-M

1, rue Edmond Canard
51500 Ludes
03 26 61 10 96
Production: 4,000,000

Canard-Duchêne, founded in 1868 by Victor Canard, is owned today by the powerful Louis Vuitton Group; before that it was owned by Clicquot. Canard-Duchêne's vineyards can only supply 5 percent of their annual production. The rest is purchased, 40 percent of the grapes coming from simple plots in Aube. The firm is definitely one of many that invest in quantity rather than quality. Local talent Jean-Jacques Lasalle is winemaker on the property.

* CANARD-DUCHÊNE BRUT   68
  (40% PN, 35% PM, 25% CH)
* CANARD-DUCHÊNE ROSÉ   46
  (46% PN, 34% PM, 20% CH)
* CANARD-DUCHÊNE DEMI-SEC   48
  (35% PN, 25% PM, 40% CH)
* 1991 CANARD-DUCHÊNE   77, JUL 2002 (78)
  (42% PN, 28% PM, 30% CH)
* 1990 CANARD-DUCHÊNE   77, OCT 1996 (84)
  (46% PN, 24% PM, 30% CH)
  An extremely personal and fragrant Champagne that hides a great deal of beauty behind its exotic, fruity façade.
* 1988 CANARD-DUCHÊNE   79, DEC 1994 (84)
  (44% PN, 22% PM, 34% CH)

The vintage wine is in a quite different class to the nonvintage Champagne, with its lush Pinot nose and charming, rich fruit.

• 1976 CANARD-DUCHÊNE   83, FEB 1996 (83)
(33% PN, 33% PM, 34% CH)
Creamy and delectable, but already showing age.

• 1975 CANARD-DUCHÊNE   81, FEB 1996 (81)
(33% PN, 33% PM, 34% CH)
Very faint bouquet. Pedestrian taste with a pleasant undertone of chocolate.

• 1955 CANARD-DUCHÊNE
(44% PN, 22% PM, 34% CH)

• 1962 CANARD-DUCHÊNE BLANC DE BLANCS   91, NOV 2002 (91)
(100% CH)
Faint mousse, beautiful walnut bouquet with elements of browned butter. Supple and harmonic, quietly aged. Good acidity that appears distinctly in the aftertaste.

• 1969 CANARD-DUCHÊNE ROSÉ   90, DEC 2003 (90)
(65% PN, 7% PM, 28% CH)
A perfectly preserved rosé Champagne that I'd like to show Michael Broadbent, who persistently claims that you can't store rosé Champagne. Beautiful orange color and fine, tiny bubbles. The bouquet is sweet and butterscotchy, with a fine note of cherry and raspberry. The palate is met with a sweet, intense, colorfully oily fruit, a faint hint of the cellar, and a long aftertaste of orange chocolate. Balanced and refreshing, but a tad too sweet for the purist.

• CHARLES VII   84
(61% PN, 39% CH)
A very elegant Champagne of true refinement and class, but which needs a better backbone if it is to develop into something great.

• CHARLES VII BLANC DE NOIRS   86
(73% PN, 27% PM)
Big, heavy, mature, and impressively mellow. Honey-saturated and oily with a somewhat faint mousse and a sweet, rich style reminiscent of 1989. Somewhat one-dimensional, even though it is imposingly rich.

• CHARLES VII ROSÉ   81
(65% PN, 7% PM, 28% CH)
Considering how good the Blanc de Noirs variety of this wine is, this rosé Champagne must be considered a failure. Meaty and rustic with a certain bitterness in the finish.

CARLINI, JEAN-YVES DE R-M
13, rue de Mailly
51360 Verzenay
03 26 49 43 91
Production: 50,000

I am incredibly grateful to all the people who bring me new Champagnes. I had been trying to make contact with this grower—to no avail—when two strangers residing near me in Lidingö, Sweden, contacted me and asked if I would like to taste a Champagne that they had fallen in love with during a trip to the region. They had been using my book *2000 Champagnes* as a guide and wondered if I hadn't missed this big-shot. The grower has six hectares planted with Pinot and Chardonnay in Verzenay, Ludes, and Mailly.

• CARLINI BLANC DE NOIRS   76
(100% PN)

CASTELLANE, DE *** N-M
57, rue de Verdun
51204 Épernay
03 26 51 19 19
Production: 3,200,000

The noble Vicomte de Castellane founded his house in 1895. Today, the house is probably best known for its strange water tower below the Avenue de Champagne. They also have a wine museum as well as a butterfly house with species from all over the world. Despite being an old butterfly collector, I haven't yet had time to pay a visit. Previously, the Champagne was fermented in all kinds of containers, including big oak barrels, creating a personal (though not terribly hygienic) style. Since Laurent-Perrier took over in 1985 the vinification and the wines have been modernized, leading to greater purity but less personality in the Champagnes.

Patrick Dubois is the winemaker. The firm's wines bear not only the name de Castellane but are also sold under the names Maxim and Ettore Bugatti. When I was last in Épernay the man in charge took me down to the cellar and let the corks fly like mad. I think we tasted twelve vintages to as early as 1915, the oldest wine they have left. Most of the wines we tasted were magnums. Not only that: we actually tasted two magnums of each to see if newly disgorged or normally disgorged bottles were preferable. Champagne experts like things like that! What struck me at this tasting was how well the wines held up structurally and aromatically. The condition of the mousse wasn't as good, however. This explains why I have never been particularly impressed by de Castellane's older wines in restaurants and from private cellars. In other words, always check if an older bottle comes directly from the house or not.

De Castellane gained thirty-first place at the Millennium Tasting, which is nothing to be ashamed of for a company that is more often mentioned for its water tower than for its wines.

• DE CASTELLANE BRUT CROIX ROUGE   69
(40% PN, 30% PM, 30% CH)

• DE CASTELLANE TRADITION   69
(40% PN, 25% PM, 35% CH)

• DE CASTELLANE MAXIM'S   69
(40% PN, 25% PM, 35% CH)

• DE CASTELLANE CHARDONNAY BRUT   74
(100% CH)

• DE CASTELLANE ROSÉ   50
(60% PN, 40% CH)

• 1995 DE CASTELLANE   85, JUL 2002 (87)
(65% PN, 35% CH)
Classic and vintage-typical. Moët-like aroma spectrum of freshly baked bread, yeast, and orange chocolate. Good elasticity and attack as well as a long, flavorful summing-up. Already tolerably mature.

• 1992 DE CASTELLANE   73, JUN 2002 (74)
(60% PN, 40% CH)
A vintage that has never been marketed—a good decision, I think. The wine lacks acidity and feels slightly flat. The aromas are ripe with a vegetal undertone.

• 1991 DE CASTELLANE   81, AUG 2001 (84)
(60% PN, 40% CH)
There is a green, slightly immature note here, of currant leaf, grass, and elderberry. This is cleverly masked by a handsomely composed dosage, which in turn lends notes of pineapple, orange, and passion fruit. A refreshing Champagne that would be

suitable to enjoy with good friends gathered under the summer arbor, or lying in your hammock, listening to the radio, outside a little country cottage.

- 1990 DE CASTELLANE   85, FEB 1999 (88)
(60% PN, 40% CH)

It is striking how often Champagnes from Épernay are reminiscent of each other, even though the grape selection varies quite a bit from house to house. In this case the resemblance to Moët is striking. Rich autolytic scent of freshly baked bread, mushroom cream, and sweet, exotic fruit. Soft, sociable, and smile-inducing taste.

- 1989 DE CASTELLANE   80, AUG 1997 (82)
(53% PN, 7% PM, 40% CH)

Well-made commercial blend, very soft and fruity. Quite mature.

- 1985 DE CASTELLANE   81, JAN 1999 (83)
(60% PN, 40% CH)

Lots of Pinot character and noticeable almond tone weakly supported by toasted aromas. Tight and fairly short taste.

- 1983 DE CASTELLANE   79, JUN 1997 (79)
(60% PN, 40% CH)

Mature but flat, featureless vintage Champagne.

- 1979 DE CASTELLANE   92, JUL 2002 (92)
(60% PN, 40% CH)

What a goody! Sweet, butterscotchy general impression. Refined, with a floral elegance and flighty finesse. The taste is dominated by those—for the vintage—typical aromas of hazelnut and peach. Intensity could have been greater.

- 1976 DE CASTELLANE   89, OCT 2003 (89)
(60% PN, 40% CH)

A typical, good '76 that still seems to lack the ability to stand out from the crowd. Fine vitality and buttery maturity with a nice, smooth vanilla tone of honey and bready notes. Long aftertaste that follows the same theme.

- 1975 DE CASTELLANE   87, JUN 2003 (87)
(60% PN, 40% CH)

A robust, solid Champagne that definitely will hold up for a long time to come. Slightly dull and dry perhaps, but well made and suitable to serve with heavy dishes.

- 1970 DE CASTELLANE   91, JAN 1999 (91)
(60% PN, 40% CH)

Much healthier and more buoyant than the magnum without dosage. Sensationally good and harmonious taste with the acidity playing an unexpectedly strong role considering the vintage. Long, soft taste of plum and blackberry.

- 1970 DE CASTELLANE D. T.   84, APR 2002 (84)
(60% PN, 40% CH)

The supremely modest Hervé Augustin took me down into the house's holiest cellar to conduct one of the most ambitious tastings I have experienced. Most of the wines were served from magnums, a large portion of them as both newly disgorged and disgorged "á la volée," without dosing. Strangely enough, it was this, the newly disgorged Champagne, that was more developed and oxidative. The vintners explained the rare phenomenon by the dosage also having received a touch of sulfuric preservative, thus counteracting the oxidation.

- 1969 DE CASTELLANE
(60% PN, 40% CH)

- 1964 DE CASTELLANE   91, JUL 2002 (91)
(60% PN, 40% CH)

Alert and in top condition. Relatively faint nose but with a delightful hint of peppermint and newly baked vanilla buns. The aromas are also there in the taste, where the wine reveals a certain lack of concentration and length, despite its elegant vitality.

- 1964 DE CASTELLANE D. T.   91, JAN 1999 (91)
(60% PN, 40% CH)

Big, stately Pinot aroma leaning towards truffles and beets. The attack is initially good, but the aftertaste is somewhat too oxidative, despite the bright color and healthy mousse.

- 1962 DE CASTELLANE   88, NOV 2000 (88)
(50% PN, 25% PM, 25% CH)

Tasted on three occasions from magnums. As young as a wine from the '80s every time. The aromas are faint and flowery and the wine a little too light and lacking in concentration, but the aromas are lovely, with a fine note of nougat.

- 1959 DE CASTELLANE   92, JAN 1999 (92)
(60% PN, 40% CH)

Unfortunately Castellane used corks that were too short during these years; the result is that certain potentially fantastic wines such as this have been robbed of their life-sustaining bubbles. Otherwise this is a typical, alcohol-rich nectar from the "super year," 1959.

- 1955 DE CASTELLANE   96, JUL 2002 (96)
(60% PN, 40% CH)

Dark color bordering on mahogany. Hardly noticeable mousse, but still—yet again—a wonderful wine with crème brûlée, toffee, and vanilla notes. Thought-provoking depth and concentrated taste with notes of treacle, honey, fig, and aged oak.

- 1953 DE CASTELLANE   69, DEC 2003 (69)
(60% PN, 40% CH)

- 1919 DE CASTELLANE
(60% PN, 40% CH)

- 1915 DE CASTELLANE   93, JAN 1999 (93)
(60% PN, 40% CH)

De Castellane's oldest remaining bottle. Hervé Augustin had never before tasted a Champagne that was this old, but he ordered the *chef de cave* to remove the cork on that unforgettable Tuesday morning. A weak hissing sound was heard, but there was no mousse to be found by eye or mouth. The scent was Krug-like and toffee-toned with a strong note of crème brûlée. The treacly, liqueur-like taste was built around the same aromas as the scent. Thanks!

- 1989 DE CASTELLANE BLANC DE BLANCS   83, FEB 1999 (87)
(100% CH)

A charming Chardonnay, where the softness is palpable and the juicy fruitiness a clear reflection of the vintage's typical character. Such Champagne tends to disappear quickly from the glass.

- 1986 DE CASTELLANE BLANC DE BLANCS   76, NOV 1994 (76)
(100% CH)

- 1981 DE CASTELLANE BLANC DE BLANCS   89, JAN 1999 (91)
(100% CH)

Wonderful toasted scent with hazelnut as the strongest ingredient. Even the young and healthy taste has a magnificent backbone of hazelnut aroma and lemon. Very subtle Champagne from the leading Chardonnay villages.

- 1980 DE CASTELLANE BLANC DE BLANCS   80, OCT 1997 (80)
(100% CH)

A delicate but much too faint nose and crispy palate.

- 1976 DE CASTELLANE BLANC DE BLANCS   94, JUN 2001 (94)
(100% CH)

Only tasted on one occasion under perfect circumstances: in Champagne, from a magnum, normally disgorged with an integrated dosage and bottle maturity. Wonderfully butterscotchy, coffee-drenched nose and an impressively rich, ripe, nutty taste, full of tropical fruit. Brilliantly enjoyable. Undoubtedly much less spectacular in a normally stored bottle.

- 1971 DE CASTELLANE BLANC DE BLANCS   96, NOV 2000 (96)
(100% CH)
Completely unparalleled, this was a magnum opened for me and my travel companions, the SAS Wine Club, at an unplanned Sunday visit to Castellane. There is a depth here found only among the greatest wines. Petroleum and lime notes carried me to Riesling from Alsace, but the nuttiness drew me in the other direction to Burgundy. Tartness and a honey tone in the finish, and the super-soft mousse, brought me home again to its true origin in Champagne.

- 1970 DE CASTELLANE BLANC DE BLANCS   89, MAR 2000 (89)
(100% CH)
A difficult vintage, but the vintners "under the water tower" succeeded very well. Definitely still a buoyant wine with layers of mature flavor. The most dominant taste layer is composed of leather-like aromas, which would be totally uninteresting and unclean in themselves, had they not been backed up by a pleasant fruitiness reminiscent of grapefruit and pineapple.

- 1966 DE CASTELLANE BLANC DE BLANCS   94, JAN 2000 (94)
(100% CH)
Beautiful scent of white flowers, citrus, and perfume. There is also a somewhat paradoxical tone of violet. Soft, focused, long, rich taste with a tail of the purest vanilla. One of Castellane's best Champagnes ever.

- 1961 DE CASTELLANE BLANC DE BLANCS   87, MAY 1999 (87)
(100% CH)
The scent is very well put-together and delicious. The wine tastes a bit short and dried-out in the mouth. The aromas are otherwise rich and developed.

- 1952 DE CASTELLANE BLANC DE BLANCS
(100% CH)

- 1975 DE CASTELLANE ROSÉ   87, NOV 2003 (87)
(60% PN, 20% PM, 20% CH)
Orange color. Intense bouquet of tar, vegetable stock, and meat. Dry and smoky palate with fine fleshiness and good length.

- 1974 DE CASTELLANE ROSÉ   87, MAR 2000 (87)
(60% PN, 20% PM, 20% CH)
A very rare wine from an even more unusual vintage. The wine is light and delicate with a pale pink color and a flighty bouquet of frozen strawberries and lilac. The freshness and elegance are grand. The body, however, is slightly too slender.

- CUVÉE COMMODORE   92
(70% PN, 30% CH)
This lovely Champagne is unfortunately not made any longer. My bottle was from the 1960s and had an impressive bouquet of various aromatic sweets. The wine was both full bodied and soft, right in line with a later vintage of this underestimated prestige Champagne.

- 1991 CUVÉE COMMODORE   85, JUL 2002 (87)
(70% PN, 30% CH)
Good concentration of grapes from good villages. Still, it is difficult to disregard the vintage's negative influence. The wine will never be as complex as the usual vintage from a good year, such as a '95.

- 1991 CUVÉE FLORENS DE CASTELLANE   83, JUL 2002 (84)
(10% PN, 90% CH)
Pale, delicately grassy, and mineral bouquet with the beginnings of a toffee aroma. Buoyant, light palate and stony, fairly long taste. Slightly too sulfurous.

- 1990 CUVÉE COMMODORE   83, MAY 2000 (85)
(70% PN, 30% CH)
Deeply golden yellow with a mature bouquet. Already there are hints of dates, raisins, straw, and figs. Even the flavor has the unusual note of straw, backed up by corn and Pinot Noir. Hardly one of the more memorable '90s.

- 1989 CUVÉE COMMODORE   90, SEP 2003 (91)
(70% PN, 30% CH)
Nearly identical to the Dom Pérignon-like '88, but with an even higher concentration of extract and an additional candy tone. Impressive!

- 1989 CUVÉE FLORENS DE CASTELLANE   92, MAY 2003 (92)
(5% PN, 95% CH)
This is, to say the least, an enjoyable, Meursault-like wine that I have tasted at five different occasions in magnum, but never in a regular bottle. Brioche, white blossoms, and orange are prominent and characteristic fragrances.

- 1988 CUVÉE COMMODORE   84, JAN 1995 (89)
(70% PN, 30% CH)
This is where the firm shows a new face; this appeals to me far more than the other wines. A Dom Pérignon-like nose with a wide spectrum of bread and cocoa aromas. Concentrated, chocolate-filled taste with good body. Very enjoyable now, but will develop even more.

- 1988 CUVÉE FLORENS DE CASTELLANE   82, JAN 1999 (87)
(10% PN, 90% CH)
Extremely flowery and easy to drink, as are most of the Chardonnay Champagnes from Castellane. Soft, balanced, with perhaps a slightly impersonal taste. I prefer Commodore, the house's other and noticeably richer prestige Champagne.

- 1986 CUVÉE FLORENS DE CASTELLANE   77, JAN 1995 (77)
(10% PN, 90% CH)

- 1982 CUVÉE FLORENS DE CASTELLANE   92, AUG 2000 (92)
(10% PN, 90% CH)
A delightful, easily drunk, not easy to spit out wine with a pleasing character. No one alive could dislike this mellow, caressing wine. At the same time as the vanilla-tasting plumpness seduces, the impression is lightened by flowery, lemony aromas. The aftertaste is rather short and the amount of extract could be greater, but the pleasure element is fantastic.

- 1981 CUVÉE COMMODORE D. T.   91, JUL 2002 (91)
(65% PN, 35% CH)
Despite the wine having been disgorged on the spot and lacking dosage, the wine revealed itself to be mature and soft. The nose is reminiscent of coffee and cacao, with a weak mushroom note. I expect its normally disgorged twin to be really round and powerful.

- 1979 CUVÉE COMMODORE   92, MAY 1999 (92)
(75% PN, 25% CH)
As it should be, this year's wine is more elegant than usual. Fine notes of toasted bread combine nicely with a slender fruit that hints of peach and mango. Long, refreshing, medium-bodied taste that does justice to the steep price tag.

- 1976 CUVÉE COMMODORE   91, OCT 2003 (91)
(75% PN, 25% CH)

Somewhat richer and rounder than a usual '76, with strong chocolaty notes. It feels as though they wanted to cast this prestige *cuvée* in the same mold as the bottle. Never mind—it tastes how it looks. In other words, there is no misrepresentation here.

- 1975 CUVÉE COMMODORE   91, FEB 1996 (91)
(75% PN, 25% CH)
A magnificent Champagne, with a lovely nutty bouquet and a full, awesome taste of dark chocolate.

- 1974 CUVÉE COMMODORE   87, DEC 2002 (87)
(75% PN, 25% CH)
De Castellane has for some reason succeeded with this otherwise extremely weak year. Big, generous, soft Champagne with a slightly abrupt finish. Otherwise quite yummy!

- 1964 CUVÉE COMMODORE   87, OCT 2003 (87)
(75% PN, 25% CH)
The nose promises more than the palate has the energy to fulfill. Present here is a large portion of warmth and sweetness, together with dark, saturated, Yuletide notes. Chocolate is, as usual, a dominating feature of this prestige bubbly. Unfortunately, the wine finishes slightly pinched and bitter.

- 1961 CUVÉE COMMODORE   87, JUN 2002 (87)
(75% PN, 25% CH)
Dark, tiresome amber color, with notes of tea, molasses, wool, and dates. It has seen better days.

CASTELNAU, DE N-M

18, rue de Reims
51200 Épernay
03 26 51 63 09
Production: 80,000
Champagne de Castelnau was first produced in 1916, in honor of General de Castelnau, one of the leaders involved in the Battle of Marne. After a long period in the wings, Sylvain Batteux moved the Champagne house center-stage, and now has a portfolio of three low-price wines. All the grapes are bought in.

- CASTELNAU BRUT   51
(33% PN, 34% PM, 33% CH)
- CASTELNAU EXTRA QUALITY   50
(33% PN, 34% PM, 33% CH)
- CASTELNAU CHARDONNAY   67
(100% CH)

CATTIER *** N-M

6, rue Dom Pérignon
51500 Chigny-les-Roses
03 26 03 42 11
Production: 600,000
The family owned the vineyard in Chigny as early as 1763. In the beginning they sold almost the entire harvest to the big houses, but little by little they have established themselves as an independent, respected Champagne house. Today, the firm is run by Jean-Louis and Jean-Jacques, who have taken over from their father (also called—not surprisingly—Jean). Nowadays Cattier exports as much as 55 percent of their total production. They are, to a great extent, self-supporting when it comes to grapes. The house-style is made up of charming, well-made, reliable wines. Because they sell their wines at a very affordable price, it is nice that Cattier is represented in Sweden. Clos du Moulin is one of Champagne's best-kept secrets.

- CATTIER BRUT ANTIQUE   67
(35% PN, 40% PM, 25% CH)
- CATTIER BLANC DE BLANCS   74
(100% CH)
- CATTIER ROSÉ BRUT   56
(50% PN, 40% PM, 10% CH)
- 1998 CATTIER   84, APR 2003 (85)
(35% PN, 30% PM, 35% CH)
A delightfully fine-tasting, youthful, harmlessly naïve, and energetic wine. Beautiful floral bouquet, with clear notes of passion fruit, vanilla, crème brûlée, and spring flowers. Soft, balanced mousse and elastic, young, pleasant fruit. One of the rare Champagnes that doesn't need storing.

- 1996 CATTIER   83, SEP 2003 (86)
(35% PN, 30% PM, 35% CH)
Brilliantly well-structured, balanced wine, where all three grape types come together from the outset to make an interesting, harmonious unit. Already, as a newly released baby, it has a polished plumpness and a soft, almost chewable dark fruit. Acidity and elasticity play second fiddle but are absolutely present.

- 1996 CATTIER RENAISSANCE   81, MAY 2000 (86)
(33% PN, 33% PM, 34% CH)
An extremely fresh wine with masses of refreshing pear and apple aromas. Dry and fine with high acidity and a slightly soapy undertone. Hard, unripe aftertaste. To be placed in the cellar.

- 1995 CATTIER   79, APR 2002 (84)
(35% PN, 30% PM, 35% CH)
Faintly vintage-typical, delicious nose of vanilla, biscuits, digestive biscuit, mint, and dried pineapple. Light, supple Champagne that asks for high dosage; the vintage character is particularly well suited to combining with a rich dosage.

- 1993 CATTIER   80, MAY 2000 (83)
(35% PN, 30% PM, 35% CH)
Light and enjoyable party bubbly with a fine autolytic scent of digestive biscuit. Pure, unpretentious, and short taste. I enjoyed it in the same way I would an American TV detective show: it was entertaining for a while, but totally erased from the memory banks the day after.

- 1993 CUVÉE RENAISSANCE   80, MAR 2000 (84)
(40% PN, 20% PM, 40% CH)
Younger than the usual '93. The bouquet is perfumed and sharply floral. High acidity and fine abundance of nuance around the base of mashed apples.

- 1990 CATTIER   87, SEP 2002 (88)
(35% PN, 30% PM, 35% CH)
Big and muscular, but with perhaps too much ripe fruit and too little acidity for time to treat this creation nicely. Plum, fig, windfall fruit, and sweetened berries are my aromatic associations, together with a pleasant, bready note that is always present in Cattier's Champagnes.

- 1989 CATTIER   70, FEB 1995 (79)
(35% PN, 30% PM, 35% CH)
- 1989 CUVÉE RENAISSANCE   74, MAY 1997 (82)
(37% PN, 30% PM, 33% CH)
As usual, a well-made and appealing wine with rich, smooth fruit. The aromatic spectrum is dominated by red apples, plums, and toffee.

- 1988 CATTIER   75, NOV 1994 (79)
(35% PN, 30% PM, 35% CH)

- 1988 CUVÉE RENAISSANCE   80, NOV 1994 (88)
(40% PN, 20% PM, 40% CH)
The wines made under this label are very similar to Clos du
Moulin. A honeyed creaminess is already present. Balanced, pure
acidity.
- 1985 CATTIER   80, AUG 1994 (87)
(35% PN, 30% PM, 35% CH)
I've never really found a unified style in Cattier's vintage wines.
This example could just as easily have come from Clicquot or
Venoge. A classic toasty nose, vintage-typical orange fruit, a
complex, nervy flavor and a harmonious, uplifting finish.
- 1983 CUVÉE RENAISSANCE   87, JUN 1993 (87)
(33% PN, 33% PM, 34% CH)
A deep yellow, developed, gorgeous Champagne for early
consumption. The nose is like a tropical rainforest with all its
exotic flowers. Acacia honey dominates the creamy and soft
flavor. It dies in the glass, so drink it now.
- 1982 CATTIER   75, APR 1992 (85)
(35% PN, 30% PM, 35% CH)
A wine where the nose is far more developed than the flavor. In
1992 the acidity was still hard. The mineral-rich aftertaste is
promising.
- 1975 CATTIER   85, MAR 2000 (85)
(30% PN, 35% PM, 35% CH)
Youthful appearance, great honey-saturated nose with hints of
bouillon. Heady taste of morels and nutmeg. Long aftertaste, but
oxidized licorice spine.
- CLOS DU MOULIN   90
(50% PN, 50% CH)
One of the few Champagnes that are allowed to put the Clos
sign on their labels. The vineyard covers 2.2 hectares and was
once owned by Allart de Maisonneuve, an officer in the army of
Louis XV. Jean Cattier bought the land in 1951. The old mill
that gave the place its name burned down, but the name stuck.
The *cuvée* is a blend of three vintages, and it has an average age
of seven or eight years when it comes onto the market. Without
doubt it's the firm's finest wine, combining the honey and cream
aromas typical of the house with a mineral freshness. The mousse
is something I rarely comment on as the differences these days
are relatively small, but the velvet-smooth firework displays
performed by the bubbles in Clos du Moulin and Laurent
Perrier's Grand Siècle are unique. Develops well in the bottle
from three to ten years.
- CLOS DU MOULIN (1996/95/93)   83, APR 2003 (87)
(50% PN, 50% CH)
Rather undeveloped Champagne, with a scent of red apples,
cinnamon, plums, and echinacea. Taut, neutral, and original
where the acidity rests far forward in the palate. Should have
more potential than I realized.
- CLOS DU MOULIN (1995/93/90)   87, JUL 2002 (90)
(50% PN, 50% CH)
Very harmonious and true to its origin: basically a classic Clos du
Moulin. Vanilla, apple, honey, and raisin, embedded in one of
the creamiest, most delicious carbonated cushions to be found.
- CLOS DU MOULIN (1993/90/89)   85, MAR 2000 (90)
(50% PN, 50% CH)
Still somewhat perfumed and enclosed in apple scents.
Surprisingly already present are a velvety soft mousse and supple
honey taste. A pure edition of this fascinating Clos wine.

- CLOS DU MOULIN (1990/89/88)   89, MAR 2000 (93)
(50% PN, 50% CH)
This elegant and well-balanced wine carries my thoughts to yet
another great nonvintage *cuvée* made in the same fashion: Grand
Siècle. Beneath the fleeting, modulated blanket of scents lies a
chocolaty undertone waiting to be set free. Perfect balance
between the wine's creaminess and its refreshingly tart fruit.
- CLOS DU MOULIN (1989/88/86)   92, DEC 2003 (92)
(50% PN, 50% CH)
Only 11,000 bottles of this handsome *cuvée* have been made,
which is probably the reason why I had never tasted this wine
before. I was very impressed when I finally got a glass. Totally
evolved, with a lovely coffee nose, combining the buttery rich
style of a '89 and the even more dominatingly classic, restrained,
nutty, and tart side of a '88. A very sophisticated, fragrant wine
that is perhaps a bit too short to be considered a big-shot.
- CLOS DU MOULIN (1988/86/85)   87, MAR 2000 (87)
(50% PN, 50% CH)
Tons of acacia honey in the nose, but a much-too-developed and
simplistic Champagne, with an oxidative tone of leather and
licorice.
- CLOS DU MOULIN (1986/85/83)   90, MAR 2000 (90)
(50% PN, 50% CH)
A deliciously buttery version, with the honey tone strongly
present in the wings. Highly enjoyable, almost seductive, but
lacking the depth found in other versions of Clos du Moulin.
- CLOS DU MOULIN (1985/83/82)   93, MAR 2000 (94)
(50% PN, 50% CH)
The foremost Clos du Moulin I have tasted! A wonderful wine
with heaps of Chardonnay notes. Pure bouquet of the most
delightful nut chocolate, toasted bread, and grain. Perfect balance
and great depth in its lemony-fresh flavor.
- CLOS DU MOULIN (1983/82/80)   90, MAR 2000 (90)
(50% PN, 50% CH)
Fatter and rounder than other blends, containing perhaps the
finest and tiniest bubbles as well. The flavor has more than a hint
of chocolate mousse.
- CLOS DU MOULIN (1982/80/79)   92, MAR 2000 (92)
(50% PN, 50% CH)
A typical '82 with a great buttery and exotic depth. Honey yet
again, accompanied now by peach and apricot in the chorus.
Thanks to the slow process of maturity, the wine has developed
an impressive length and full, creamy aftertaste.

CAZALS, CLAUDE **** R-M
28, rue du Grand Mont
51190 Le Mesnil-sur-Oger
03 26 57 52 26
Production: 100,000
One of Le Mesnil's better-known producers. The lovely Delphine
Cazals, married to Olivier Bonville of the firm Franck Bonville,
produces clear, pure, fast-maturing, toasted Champagnes in a
somewhat light style. She has access to grapes from Le Mesnil and
Oger and sells most of them to Bollinger, Roederer, and Deutz.
She convinced her family, at last, to make a prestige *cuvée* of Clos
Cazals, the walled vineyard that you see to your right when you
enter Oger from the north. The vines were planted in 1947 and
the vineyard is all of 3.5 hectares, but, due to rigorous culling, she
only makes 2,000 bottles of this future cult wine.

- C. CAZALS VIVE EXTRA BRUT   75
  (100% CH)
  Powder-dry, lively, and sharp, with pure apple aromas, citrus, and mineral. Handsome and sophisticated through and through.
- C. CAZALS BLANC DE BLANCS   73
  (100% CH)
  Unexpectedly dark color. Open, toasty, and slightly fleshy nose, with an appealingly rich and fruity flavor. The first glass always tastes better than the last. Low acidity. Fresher at the most recent tasting.
- 1996 C. CAZALS   86, DEC 2003 (90)
  (100% CH)
  Big, developed, honey nose and a fleshy, round taste with delicious, creamy, elegant notes. Long aftertaste with clear notes of maturity.
- 1995 C. CAZALS   88, APR 2003 (92)
  (100% CH)
  What wines this grower turns up! Handsome, fat, polished, buttery, complex, modern, grand, and delightfully delicious. Fine *terroir* character backed up by a rich, concentrated fruit. Cazals is establishing itself as one of Champagne's most interesting growers.
- 1990 C. CAZALS   84, JAN 1997 (90)
  (100% CH)
  An extremely focused and floral Blanc de Blancs. Pure and village-typical.
- 1988 C. CAZALS   84, JAN 1997 (85)
  (100% CH)
  Surprisingly toasty character. A little artificial, and looser than the '90.
- 1985 C. CAZALS   83, DEC 1992 (84)
  (100% CH)
  Another developed wine with an immediate charm. Surprisingly complete for an '85.
- 1959 C. CAZALS   95, SEP 2003 (95)
  (100% CH)
  A majestic wine with superb elasticity and intact, light character. The fruit is sweet like a perfect '47, and the power is never intrusive or demanding, despite the heat of this year. Aromas tend toward vanilla, apricot, orange, peach, mango, and coconut. Extremely long and impressive.
- 1997 CLOS CAZALS   87, DEC 2003 (91)
  (100% CH)
  Superbly beautiful wine with brilliant, sparkling elements and minimal, lively bubbles. Very exotic nose of melon, honey, passion fruit, flowers, and nougat. Rich, deep taste with unexpected traces of red fruits like wild strawberries, red apples, and raspberries. Flirtatious and elegant. Two thousand bottles to divide amongst the world.
- 1996 CLOS CAZALS NON DOSÉ   84, DEC 2003 (92)
  (100% CH)
  Only 2,000 bottles made of this wine. Tasted without dosage at the producer's; this wine, of course, is too young and ascetic. Still, it evinces an incredible balance, with fine, delicate aromas.
- 1995 CLOS CAZALS   92, FEB 2003 (94)
  (100% CH)
  What a debut! Claude Cazals is hardly the only grower in the *grand cru* villages to have access to an exceptionally good location that makes extraordinarily concentrated wine. On the other hand, he is one of the few that has a walled enclosure, a real "*clos*" in the true meaning of the word. I am convinced that this will become a wine sought after by connoisseurs. The wine is radiantly lively, gracious, and first-rate. The bouquet is creamy and discernible with a nice finesse of mineral and citrus backed up by an intense petroleum note. The taste is keen and concentrated with a fine freshness. The finish is rounder than expected considering the mineral elements found here.

CAZANOVE, DE *** N-M

1, rue des Cotelles
51200 Épernay
03 26 59 57 40
Production: 3,000,000

Founded in 1811 by Charles Gabriel de Cazanove in Avize, the house was further developed by his son, Charles Nicolas, a leading botanist who took up the fight against the phylloxera grape louse. But not until the end of the 1970s did the firm get its first break. Today it produces very easily drunk, accessible, modern Champagnes at low prices (Cuvée Stradivarius being the only exception). Their nonvintage Champagne always places high in blind-tastings. Talented Olivier Piazza is winemaker there at the moment.

- CUVÉE CAZANOVA   74
  (50% PN, 20% PM, 30% CH)
- DE CAZANOVE BRUT AZUR PREMIER CRU   76
  (30% PN, 10% PM, 60% CH)
- DE CAZANOVE GRAND APPARAT   80
  (30% PN, 10% PM, 60% CH)
  First-rate, buttery, saffron-saturated Champagne made in a different style than De Cazanove's other wines. More vinous, serious, and demanding, but on the same level of quality as the others. A storable mealtime Champagne.
- DE CAZANOVE DEMI-SEC   50
  (50% PN, 20% PM, 30% CH)
- DE CAZANOVE ROSÉ   68
  (5% PN, 95% CH)
- 1996 DE CAZANOVE BRUT AZUR   81, OCT 2003 (84)
  (20% PN, 80% CH)
  The wine is soft and accessible, like a '95, with notes of cinnamon buns, vanilla, and ripe red Katy apples. The mousse is fine and supple with a charming creaminess. The aftertaste masks a harder acidity than one might expect after such a cashmere-soft opening. Aromatically rather short and faint.
- 1993 DE CAZANOVE BRUT AZUR   75, JUN 1999 (81)
  (20% PN, 80% CH)
  Apple-flavored, slightly cheesy nose. Soft, generous, summery fruitiness with an uncomplicated twist.
- 1989 DE CAZANOVE BRUT AZUR   76, FEB 1997 (79)
  (20% PN, 80% CH)
- 1995 STRADIVARIUS   87, MAY 2003 (88)
  (30% PN, 70% CH)
  Many '95s are presently irresistible purveyors of pleasure. Stradivarius is always ready to display its expansiveness, even now. The way the dosage meets the deliciously rich and youthful lush fruit is irresistible. Together they impart a popsicle-like caramel character that refreshes during the hottest of summer days—or has us longing for that summer vacation during the darkest winter months.

- 1990 STRADIVARIUS   89, MAY 2003 (89)
  (30% PN, 70% CH)
  The wine smells and tastes like a smooth, polished Blanc de Blancs, with its abundance of citrus notes and polished elegance. Completely mature and very exotic at the beginning of 2003.
- 1989 STRADIVARIUS   80, MAR 1997 (86)
  (33% PN, 67% CH)
  A luxurious nose of sweet grapes; a medium-bodied, bold taste that would have been happier with a lower dosage.
- 1985 STRADIVARIUS   80, MAY 1995 (84)
  (30% PN, 70% CH)
  After having been impressed time after time by Brut Azur, I had great expectations of this luxury Champagne. I found a very fine mineral tone and a discreet toasty tone in the nose. However, the taste was too lacking in concentration and simplistically lemony to elevate it to among the greats.
- DE CAZANOVE GRANDE RÉSERVE 2000   79, JUL 2000 (83)
  (20% PN, 10% PM, 70% CH)
  Very young bouquet of elderberry, hawthorn, and pear. A pure, refreshing, dry, and sublime summer aperitif.
- 1992 DE CAZANOVE BRUT AZUR 2000   83, JUN 1999 (88)
  (20% PN, 80% CH)
  Only made in magnums. Refreshing, buoyant, and promising, with precisely those elements that impart handsomely toasted aromas at storage. The fruit is reminiscent of mango and peach.

CHAMPION, ROLAND R-M
51530 Chouilly
03 26 55 40 30
Production: 90,000
This grower owns fifteen hectares in Chouilly and a dash of Pinot Noir in Verneuil, which is used in the rosé.
- 1990 ROLAND CHAMPION SPECIAL CLUB   89, DEC 2002 (89)
  (100% CH)
  Big, powerful bouquet of honey and saffron that passes into butterscotch and chocolate after one hour in the glass. Fleshy and concentrated with a mature sweetness, but without the finesse and refinement that one finds in Bonnaire and Sugot-Feneuil's closely related Champagnes. On all counts, a very pleasant new acquaintance.

CHANOINE N-M
avenue de Champagne
51100 Reims
03 26 36 61 60
Production: 600,000
The house was founded in 1730 in Reims and is the second oldest Champagne house. Philippe Baijot, who is one of the district's tallest and humblest gentlemen, makes a house Champagne that he sells at a very low price. All three grapes are used in the firm's *cuvées.*

     He works closely with Bruno Paillard and has just built an ultra-modern facility with temperature-controlled cellars above ground. Chanoine will certainly gain more attention in the future. The Tsarine wines are a real bargain.
- CHANOINE BRUT   73
  (70% PN, 15% PM, 15% CH)
- CHANOINE BRUT ROSÉ   69
  (35% PN, 10% PM, 55% CH)

- 1991 CHANOINE   73, MAY 2000 (74)
  (50% PN, 20% PM, 30% CH)
- 1988 CHANOINE   80, APR 1996 (85)
  (50% PN, 20% PM, 30% CH)
  I must have misjudged this wine when I first tasted it. The last time I tasted this Champagne it still had an excess of almond aromas, but the fruit felt a great deal richer than at the first tasting.
- 1973 CHANOINE   92, APR 1996 (92)
  Good-looking, enjoyable, mature Champagne with plenty of chocolate tones and exotic fruit.
- CHANOINE TSARINE   82
  (35% PN, 15% PM, 50% CH)
  The first *cuvée* of this prestige Champagne is made up of wine from the '94 and '95 vintages. Even this wine is very reminiscent of Moët, this time of their vintage wine. Once again, Chanoine succeeds in making a very affordable Champagne with good chances of fine development with aging. The wine has a clean and delicate lightness combined with a bready, biscuit-like complexity. The Champagne has a pleasant sweetness in its finish and a large dose of finesse.
- 1995 CHANOINE TSARINE   83, OCT 2003 (85)
  (35% PN, 15% PM, 50% CH)
  More floral and taut than the red-labeled, nonvintage variety of the same wine. The potential is, however, better here, despite a shorter aftertaste. Great elegance and finesse. It need hardly be said that the price is among the lowest of the prestige *cuvées.*

CHARBAUT *** N-M
17, avenue de Champagne
51205 Épernay
03 26 54 37 55
Production: 1,200,000
André Charbaut founded his house as late as 1948. When he died in 1986 the firm was taken over by the commercially minded sons, Guy and René. In 1995 Charbaut became part of the Vranken-Lafitte empire, and in future the wines will be made by enologist Dominique Pichart, who is responsible for all the concern's wines. Charbaut had a very good reputation during the 1960s and 1970s, but in the 1980s only the *cuvée de prestige* Certificate received regular praise.
- CHARBAUT BRUT   58
  (60% PN, 20% PM, 20% CH)
- CHARBAUT BLANC DE BLANCS.   69
  (100% CH)
- 1985 CHARBAUT   70, NOV 1992 (78)
  (50% PN, 50% CH)
- 1966 CHARBAUT   93, JUN 2002 (93)
  (50% PN, 50% CH)
  A real charmer with exotic fruit and toffee aromas. Hints of warm vanilla rolls and dried roses dominate after a time in the glass. Exceedingly rich, voluptuous Champagne that has woken up on the right side of the bed.
- 1959 CHARBAUT   94, DEC 2001 (94)
  (50% PN, 50% CH)
  Some of my wine friends from Skåne, Sweden, found this treasure at Guy Charbaut in Mareuil-sur-Aÿ. They came to my home on a rare free Friday night during the winter of 2001 and uncorked this magnificent wine, full of grilled, burned aromas.

The structure is monumental and the aromas exceedingly interesting.

- 1990 CHARBAUT TÊTE DE CUVÉE   77, FEB 2004 (77)
  (100% CH)
- 1985 CHARBAUT CERTIFICATE   83, APR 2003 (83)
  (100% CH)

Today a completely mature and rather rustic, coarse Blanc de Blancs, but still with a certain complexity and good walnut aroma.

- 1982 CHARBAUT CERTIFICATE   90, JUL 2000 (90)
  (100% CH)

A critically praised *cuvée de prestige* that is really good. It has a smoky complexity together with the soft, exotic fruit, and vanilla taste.

- 1979 CHARBAUT CERTIFICATE   87, JUL 2000 (87)
  (100% CH)

I often prefer the '79 to the '82 but, despite a delightful toasted tone in the nose, the '79 doesn't quite hit the heights. The wine is quite simply not concentrated enough to be great.

- 1976 CHARBAUT CERTIFICATE   93, JAN 2000 (93)
  (100% CH)

Oh, so delicious! A superbly genuine Champagne that carries one's thoughts to a Comtes from the same year. Extremely refreshing aroma of apple, pineapple, and sweet lemon cake. It's truly a pity that, since 1982, this wine has fallen from the ranks of the elite.

- 1973 CHARBAUT CERTIFICATE   89, JAN 2003 (89)
  (100% CH)

The wine has a very distinct, flagrant, perfumed bouquet. Sweet, soft, completely mature palate. A perfect wine with duck liver!

- 1971 CHARBAUT CERTIFICATE   92, JAN 2000 (92)
  (100% CH)

Blanc de Blancs from '71 are a sure buy today. This juicy if somewhat sweet wine is no exception. Certificate is redolent of exotic fruit. The taste fills the mouth with a sunny wealth of pineapple and mango. A smiling wine, difficult to resist.

- 1982 CHARBAUT CERTIFICATE ROSÉ   90, JAN 2000 (90)
  (60% PN, 40% CH)

Grand bouquet of Burgundian proportions. Very soft, round taste—unstoppably drinkable. I think we should hurry along and drink up these goodies—acidity is probably a little too low to ensure cellar storage.

CHARBAUT, GUY R-M
12, rue Pont
51160 Mareuil-sur-Aÿ
03 26 52 60 59
Production: 120,000

When Vranken bought the name Charbaut in Épernay, Guy started his family business—together with a small hotel—in Mareuil in 1995. Guy is said to be a kind soul, generous both with his own time and his old vintage wines. The better the friendship, the older the wines.

- GUY CHARBAUT CUVÉE 2000   66
  (50% PN, 10% PM, 40% CH)

CHARLEMAGNE, GUY **** R-M
4, rue de la Brèche d'Oger
51190 Le Mesnil-sur-Oger
03 26 57 52 98
Production: 130,000

This elegant firm was founded in 1892. Guy Charlemagne and his son, Philippe, make some of the purest Champagnes on the market, and the Le Mesnil character is, if possible, even more tangible than in wines from the neighboring Salon. Besides eight hectares in Le Mesnil they own two in Oger, four in Sézanne, and eight in Cuis. The average age of the vines is an impressive thirty, and in the vintage wines there are grapes from three locations: Vaucherot, Aillerand, and Masonière. They have recently begun using small oak barrels for some 20 percent of the harvest. The prestige wine Mesnillésime is a super-concentrated wine, where half of the wine has been through malolactic fermentation in steel tanks, while the other half is fermented in oak casks with the malic acidity intact. This is a grower to watch with the greatest respect in the future.

- CUVÉE MARIE JUSTINE   79
  (100% CH)
- GUY CHARLEMAGNE BRUT EXTRA   75
  (50% PN, 50% CH)
- GUY CHARLEMAGNE BLANC DE BLANCS   82
  (100% CH)

This Champagne, which is aged for three years, is made from grapes from Oger and Le Mesnil. It's one of the most elegant nonvintage Champagnes I've ever had! The nose is incredibly pure and flowery, like a Chablis *grand cru* from Louis Michel. The flavor is also romantically light and multifaceted—the perfect aperitif on an early summer evening.

- GUY CHARLEMAGNE ROSÉ   60
  (20% PN, 80% CH)
- 1995 GUY CHARLEMAGNE   81, MAY 1999 (89)
  (100% CH)

Store for heaps of years! Pure as few are, but with a stature and strictness that will take some time to soften, to round off the edges. Buying magnums will test your patience to an even higher degree.

- 1992 GUY CHARLEMAGNE   78, SEP 1997 (85)
  (100% CH)

Youthfully light and flowery. It may be pure and balanced, but I miss the customary concentration.

- 1990 GUY CHARLEMAGNE   90, FEB 2002 (92)
  (100% CH)

At the age of eight years, still very bound and tight, but after twenty minutes in the glass one could perceive its origin and its high quality. A stony wine with fine depth. At the age of eleven in magnum, this classic Champagne was village-typical with a beautiful autumn fragrance and great complexity.

- 1985 GUY CHARLEMAGNE   89, JUN 2000 (91)
  (100% CH)

Vegetal and strongly imprinted by the flinty soil. Smoky, dry and distinctive, high-class connoisseur bubbly.

- 1982 GUY CHARLEMAGNE   90, JUN 2001 (90)
  (100% CH)

Once again, diamond-clear seductive tones of jasmine, yellow roses, and lily of the valley. The flavor is full of toffee and is very reminiscent of Chardonnay from Cramant.

• 1979 GUY CHARLEMAGNE   93, JUN 2001 (93)
(100% CH)
All the wines from this property are light, with a rare crystal
clarity. The '79 is a delicate, feminine wine, full of innumerable
aromas. Lime, white roses, and toasted bread are the front-
runners. A sensual lightweight.

• 1976 GUY CHARLEMAGNE   93, JUN 2001 (93)
(100% CH)
A perfect reflection of this grower, the village, and the vintage.
The Champagne tasted exactly as I had expected. Pure, elegant
fruit with a stony *terroir* character from Mesnil, combined with
the vintage's fat, buttery warmth and richness.

• 1999 MESNILLÉSIME   83, JUN 2001 (94)
(100% CH)
Tasted long before the wine came onto the market and years
before the autolytic character had developed to its fullest. Still, it's
remarkable how well integrated the oak note already is, and how
village-typical the pure Champagne is. I'll be back.

• 1996 MESNILLÉSIME   91, SEP 2003 (94)
(100% CH)
A fantastic wine with crystal-clear nuances and a magnificent
depth just lurking around the corner. Spontaneously, I think of
the absolutely finest steel-tank-fermented wines from Puligny-
Montrachet. The oaky influence is markedly weaker than
previous vintages of this exceedingly interesting wine. Its
seductively floral essence can be likened to the most beautiful
scent that the perfume-makers of Grasse might dream of creating.
Fatter and more influenced by the oak in 2003.

• 1995 MESNILLÉSIME   92, MAY 2003 (94)
(100% CH)
Half of the wine is fermented in oak barrels without malolactic
fermentation; the other half has undergone malolactic
fermentation in steel tanks to create a wine that Philippe
Charlemagne makes only for himself. On the other hand, he
doesn't seem too dejected when someone else shares his passion
for this rarity. We Swedes bag 25 percent of the approximately
ten to fifteen thousand bottles that are made during a select
number of vintages. Presently, the '95 can be considered a little
light and floral, but give it a couple of years in the cellar and this
flowery, mountain-stream-pure Champagne will completely
change character.

• 1990 MESNILLÉSIME   94, SEP 2003 (95)
(100% CH)
The '90's nose is slightly closed, and personally I prefer the
similar Pierre Peters Cuvée Spéciale from this year. However, the
flavor is superb, packed with layers of intense Chardonnay
experiences. A little Salon in the making. The wine has become a
little nutty with aging.

• 1988 MESNILLÉSIME   94, NOV 2003 (95)
(100% CH)
This was my favorite Champagne of this vintage before Salon
and Krug released their '88s. Despite only 0.4 percent sugar
content, we have here an astonishingly honeyed wine with the
broad spectrum of aromas that only Le Mesnil grapes can give.
The oak barrel provides yet another dimension in the fantastically
concentrated flavor. The wine contains everything, and offers a
whole lot of that already.

CHARLEMAGNE, ROBERT *** R-M
avenue Eugène Guillaume
51190 Le Mesnil-sur-Oger
03 26 57 51 02
Production: 35,000
Guy Charlemagne's cousin owns 4.3 hectares in the village, divided
between thirty-six locations.

• R. CHARLEMAGNE BLANC DE BLANCS   62
(100% CH)

• R. CHARLEMAGNE ROSÉ   56
(15% PN, 85% CH)

• 1993 R. CHARLEMAGNE   83, NOV 1998 (88)
(100% CH)
This little grower has a very constant and admired style. His
polished, elegant public style is actually reminiscent of the
blended Chardonnay wines of the fine Champagne houses. Sweet,
appealing fruit backed up by biscuit aromas and soft acidity.

• 1989 R. CHARLEMAGNE   85, AUG 1995 (91)
(100% CH)
An extraordinarily sophisticated Champagne where the lightness
and finesse are intertwined in outstanding fashion. The wine's
aromatic spectrum is dominated by nutty toffee, peppermint
candy, mandarin oranges, and grapefruit. The family resemblance
to the famous cousin is marked.

CHARLES-LAFITTE N-M
Champ-Rouen
51150 Tours-sur-Marne
03 26 53 33 40
Production: 1,600,000
In 1983, Paul François Vranken took over the firm, which is
regarded as Demoiselle's second company. Dominique Pichart—
responsible for the blending—considers Lafitte to be a classic
mixed Champagne, but uses their best grapes in Heidsieck and
Demoiselle. The company recently moved from Vertus to Tours-
sur-Marne.

• CHARLES-LAFITTE BRUT   50
(40% PN, 20% PM, 40% CH)

• CHARLES-LAFITTE GRAND PRESTIGE   79
(100% CH)

• CHARLES-LAFITTE ROSÉ   42
(40% PN, 60% CH)

• 1985 CHARLES-LAFITTE ORQUEIL   90, JUN 2002 (90)
(50% PN, 50% CH)
Mumm evidently had difficulty selling its '85 Rene Lalou but, as
so many times before, the business genius Vranken swooped in and
bought the remaining surplus and relabeled them under the name
above. Because of the fantastically low price, this is now quite a
find. Very creamy and soft with a scent of dark chocolate candy.

CHARLIER, JACKIE *** R-M
4, rue Pervenches
51700 Châtillon-sur-Marne
03 26 58 35 18
Production: 100,000
The grapes come from Châtillon, Montigny, Jonquery, and
Oeuilly. All the wines ferment and are stored in large oak barrels
and go through malolactic fermentation. The rosé wine is made
using the Saignée method.

- J. CHARLIER CARTE NOIRE 72
(20% PN, 60% PM, 20% CH)
- J. CHARLIER ROSÉ 76
(30% PN, 70% PM)
- 1990 J. CHARLIER 85, MAY 1996 (88)
(30% PN, 40% PM, 30% CH)
Juicier, purer, and more classical than the extravagant '89 Special
Club. The wine is filled with fine nutty and leathery tones.
- 1996 J. CHARLIER SPECIAL CLUB 82, JAN 2002 (87)
(20% PN, 30% PM, 50% CH)
An impudent wine with considerable weight and smoky oakiness.
As yet, slightly aggressive and rambunctious with fine acidic
structure and fruity concentration. Tasty and personal
Champagne that would be fun to have in the cellar.
- 1989 J. CHARLIER SPECIAL CLUB 84, JUN 1996 (86)
(20% PN, 30% PM, 50% CH)
Wow, what concentration and oily weight! The first gulps slip down
much more easily than the last, when the Champagne becomes
almost too much of a good thing. There's a slight lack of elegance,
but this honey- and toffee-filled wine is certainly impressive.

CHARPENTIER, J. R-M
88, rue de Reuil
51700 Villers-sous-Châtillon
03 26 58 05 78
Production: 90,000
Pinot Meunier fills most of the property's ten hectares. The
location is extremely beautiful, lying at the foot of the village's
magnificent papal statue.
- CHARPENTIER TRADITION 54
(100% PN)
- CHARPENTIER BRUT PRESTIGE 71
(60% PN, 20% PM, 20% CH)
- CHARPENTIER BRUT RÉSERVE 52
(20% PN, 80% PM)
- CHARPENTIER ROSÉ 50
(10% PN, 80% PM, 10% CH)
- 1996 CHARPENTIER 82, DEC 2002 (85)
(50% PN, 50% CH)
Things are happening here! Many similarities with Bollinger and
perhaps even more with Clouet in a somewhat less distinguished
guise. Powerful and expansive bouquet of ripe apples, mushrooms,
and plum. Evolved taste with few but nevertheless integrated
notes that make up an ample, fleshy completeness.
- 1994 CHARPENTIER 71, AUG 2001 (75)
(50% PN, 50% CH)

CHARTOGNE-TAILLET R-M
37, Grande Rue
51220 Merfy
03 26 03 10 17
Production: 100,000
Already in the 1500s, Fiacre Taillet was a wine-grower in the small
village of Merfy. Today, Chartogne-Taillet is still a family business.
Philippe and Elisabeth Chartogne run a quality-controlled
property with access to very old grapevines—even a little pre-
phylloxera rootstock. Philippe was educated in Burgundy and has a
strong faith in the recipe: low yield equals high quality. The grapes
come from eleven hectares in Merfy, Chenay, and Saint Thierry.

- CHARTOGNE-TAILLET BRUT 60
(50% PN, 10% PM, 40% CH)
- CHARTOGNE-TAILLET ROSÉ 60
(50% PN, 10% PM, 40% CH)
- 1996 CHARTOGNE-TAILLET 75, SEP 2003 (78)
(60% PN, 40% CH)
- 1995 CHARTOGNE-TAILLET 67, SEP 2003 (67)
(60% PN, 40% CH)
- 1996 CHARTOGNE-TAILLET FIACRE 85, APR 2003 (89)
(40% PN, 60% CH)
A selection of the oldest grapevines with a high percentage of
pre-phylloxera vines. A brilliantly refreshing, elastic, potent wine
with a deliciously concentrated young fruit. Truly genuine *terroir*
character is, of course, missing but this deficiency is well
compensated for by its tart, rich, fruity cannonade.

CHASSENAY D'ARCE C-M
10110 Ville-sur-Arce
03 25 38 30 70
Production: 750,000
This large cooperative was founded in 1956. Today, 160 members
till the land in twelve communes in Aube, producing strong,
Pinot-dominated Champagne on 320 hectares. Thirty percent is
exported to Belgium and England. Other brands: Martivey,
Montaubret, and Armanville.
- CHASSENAY D'ARCE SÉLECTION 49
(88% PN, 12% CH)
- CHASSENAY D'ARCE BRUT PRIVILÈGE 51
(60% PN, 40% CH)
- CHASSENAY D'ARCE ROSÉ 52
(90% PN, 10% CH)

CHASSEY, GUY DE R-M
1, rue Vieille
51150 Louvois
03 26 57 03 32
Production: 40,000
In 1993, when Guy de Chassey passed away, his two daughters
took over the firm. This grower is one of the few to make expressly
Louvois Champagne.
- GUY DE CHASSEY BRUT DE BRUT 68
(65% PN, 35% CH)
- GUY DE CHASSEY BRUT GRAND CRU 76
(95% PN, 5% CH)
- GUY DE CHASSEY RESERVÉE 75
(35% PN, 65% CH)
- 1990 GUY DE CHASSEY 80, JUL 1998 (86)
(50% PN, 50% CH)
Forty-year-old vines! Closed on the nose. Wonderful unreleased
intrinsic power.

CHAUVET N-M
41, avenue de Champagne
51150 Tours-sur-Marne
03 26 58 92 37
Production: 80,000
The company was started in 1848 by Constant Harlin, who at the
time used grapes from Bouzy. Later on he bought the Croix Saint
Jacques domain in Tours-sur-Marne, which had belonged to the

Archbishop of Reims, and today the house and wine plant are run by the Chauvet family. The name of Chauvet came from Harlin's nephew, Auguste, who successfully marketed the wines in Paris. In 1946 his daughter Jeanine Chauvet took over, and together with her husband Jean she keeps a loving eye on their two sons Arnaud and Jean-François as they run operations.

Stepping into the family's living room is like moving back in time a hundred years. The walls are filled with stuffed animals, with everything from herons to wild boars. As the Chauvet family collects antique Champagne glasses, all the drinks are served in different kinds of glasses. Madame Chauvet was very disappointed when I asked to use the same glass for all the Champagnes. She also had problems understanding my request for a spittoon at ten o'clock in the morning. She maintains that a little Champagne before lunch every day prolongs life, and when you see this incredibly well-preserved, stylish elderly lady, you may ask yourself if she has a point.

The firm owns many fine vineyards, with an average *cru* status of 98 percent. Four hectares in Bouzy, Ambonnay, and Verzenay, and five in Bisseuil. Despite its tiny size, this company has a good reputation, and I too am delighted by its charming and personal wines. Those of you who believe that Frenchmen are boring and introverted should pay a visit to the house of Chauvet.

- CHAUVET BRUT   70
  (65% PN, 35% CH)
- HARLIN BRUT   65
  (65% PN, 35% CH)
- CHAUVET BLANC DE BLANCS   79
  (100% CH)
- CHAUVET GRAND ROSÉ   80
  (15% PN, 85% CH)
  Still a *crémant* Champagne, although the term is tragically banned today. This is truly a great rosé, despite the high proportion of Chardonnay. The color is salmon-pink, the nose contains all the fruits of the summer, and the flavor is an unmistakable buttery Chardonnay.
- 1989 HARLIN   74, APR 2001 (75)
  (15% PN, 85% CH)
- 1985 CHAUVET   79, MAY 1995 (84)
  (15% PN, 85% CH)
  Unusually this wine is dominated by Chardonnay from Verzenay. A great personality with a faintly cheesy nose. The flavor will probably be integrated in a few years' time, but today the Verzenay wine is undeveloped and hard. The aftertaste promises good things with its wealth of minerals.
- 1985 HARLIN   84, MAY 2001 (84)
  (15% PN, 85% CH)
  A new release of Chauvet to Paris. Round, soft, chocolaty, pleasantly smiling style. Relatively uncomplicated.

CHÂTEAU DE BLIGNY R-M

Lorin Frère
10200 Bar-sur-Aube
03 25 27 40 11
Production: 300,000
Makes one of the two château-named Champagnes. The other is Château de Boursault. The Marquis de Dampierre founded the firm at the end of the 1800s, and today the large, thirty-hectare property is part of Rapeneau's comprehensive stable.

- CHÂTEAU DE BLIGNY BRUT   59
  (50% PN, 50% CH)
- 1982 CHÂTEAU DE BLIGNY BLANC DE BLANCS   70, MAY 2001 (78)
  (100% CH)

CHÂTEAU DE BOURSAULT N-M

51480 Boursault
03 26 58 42 21
Production: 60,000
The second of two Champagnes named after a château, this independent company was once owned by Veuve Clicquot. Château de Boursault doesn't make vintage wines, and in fact probably has the smallest production of any house, even though the proportions of the building itself are impressive. Today run by Harald Fringhian.

- CHÂTEAU DE BOURSAULT BRUT   65
  (50% PN, 37% PM, 13% CH)
- CHÂTEAU DE BOURSAULT ROSÉ   63
  (50% PN, 37% PM, 13% CH)

CHÂTEAU VILLERS PESSENET R-M

51700 Villers-sous-Châtillon
Production: 50,000
The elegant, mustachioed man who previously ran the Royal Champagne restaurant has found his dream château high up in the rolling hills of the Marne Valley. Château Villers was built in 1914 and bought by Pessenet in 1985. In January 2001, the slightly chintzy hotel and accompanying restaurant were opened, totally renovated—they possess enormous potential and one of the best locations in Champagne. Of course the house drink is Champagne, but it is not particularly exciting.

- CHÂTEAU VILLERS PESSENET   35
  (100% PM)

CHEURLIN, ARNAUD DE R-M

58, Grande Rue
10110 Celles-sur-Ource
03 25 38 53 90
Production: 45,000
Mr. and Mrs. Eisenträger-Cheurlin own six hectares in Aube.

- ARNAUD DE CHEURLIN PRESTIGE   68
  (50% PN, 50% CH)
- ARNAUD DE CHEURLIN RÉSERVE   59
  (70% PN, 30% CH)

CHEURLIN, RICHARD R-M

18, rue des Huguenots
10110 Celles-sur-Ource
03 25 38 55 04
Production: 40,000
The grower pronounces his name almost as the French pronounce mine. The Cheurlin family originally come from Landreville but have settled in Celles-sur-Ource in force—at least four producers bear this name. Richard is the most famous and he produces two Champagnes from all three varieties.

- RICHARD CHEURLIN BRUT   55
  (50% PN, 30% PM, 20% CH)

CHIQUET, GASTON *** R-M

912, avenue du Général Leclerc
51530 Dizy
03 26 55 22 02
Production: 120,000

Nicolas Chiquet planted his first vines in 1746, and since then eight generations have tilled Dizy's soil. Gaston Chiquet registered the company in 1935 and expanded the property with land in Aÿ, Cumières, and Hautvillers. The current owner, Claude Chiquet, controls more than twenty-two hectares, which he runs together with his two sons. They are best known for making the only Blanc de Blancs from the Pinot village of Aÿ.

- GASTON CHIQUET TRADITION BRUT   66
  (20% PN, 45% PM, 35% CH)
- GASTON CHIQUET BLANC DE BLANCS D'AŸ   78
  (100% CH)
- 1997 GASTON CHIQUET   82, NOV 2003 (85)
  (60% PN, 40% CH)

This is one of those classically constructed wines possessing a slightly neutral style that can excel with age, if everything goes well. If not, it may stay neutral and suave without ever coming into full bloom. Today it has a tight, fine concentration with a smidgen of coffee and bready aromas, both in the nose and the palate. Wait and see where this wine will go.

- 1996 GASTON CHIQUET   84, FEB 2004 (87)
  (60% PN, 40% CH)

Dazzlingly big and magnificent with weight and fullness. Evolved fruit and unobtrusive embedded acidity. Round and harmonious finish with apple-pie notes throughout.

- 1995 GASTON CHIQUET   82, NOV 2003 (84)
  (60% PN, 40% CH)

Intensely characterized by ripe Pinot from the Marne Valley, with hints of plum, licorice, red apple peel, and the health-food favorite, purple coneflower. Calm and well balanced with good fruit, a soft, fleshy plumpness, and a juicy, simultaneously smooth mousse. Not really my cup of tea, but the wine is very well made.

- 1989 GASTON CHIQUET   70, DEC 1994 (78)
  (60% PN, 40% CH)
- 1959 GASTON CHIQUET   93, JUL 1999 (93)
  (20% PN, 45% PM, 35% CH)

The '59s are always something extra. The mousse was weak, but the wine's tremendous richness kept all the elements together for several hours in the glass. Here are heaps of heavy figs and plum fruits, elements of molasses and tar. Certain lack of finesse.

- 1990 GASTON CHIQUET SPECIAL CLUB   82, MAR 1999 (86)
  (30% PN, 70% CH)

A soft and fruity Champagne with a light undertone of bread and an impressively full, buttery aroma. The taste is less impressive with its somewhat unpolished style.

- 1989 GASTON CHIQUET SPECIAL CLUB   80, JUN 1994 (85)
  (30% PN, 70% CH)

An agreeable wine with a bready nose and a clear whiff of digestive biscuit. The flavor is medium bodied and charming with a fruity pineapple finish on the palate.

- 1988 GASTON CHIQUET BLANC DE BLANCS D'AŸ   85, FEB 1998 (91)
  (100% CH)

The company's pride and joy. In really good years they bottle a handful of magnums. They're at least nine years old when they go on sale. Superb elegance and lovely Chardonnay aromas.

- 1982 GASTON CHIQUET BLANC DE BLANCS D'AŸ   89, JUN 1999 (91)
  (100% CH)

The '82 is very lively and shares the paradoxical character of the nonvintage version. Once again the nose speaks of ripe Chardonnay, but the roundness and full nature whispers of its true origins.

- 1970 GASTON CHIQUET BLANC DE BLANCS D'AŸ   92, MAY 2003 (92)
  (100% CH)

Drunk newly disgorged "*à la minute*," without additional sugar, of course. A deep, greenish color. A medium-broad nose of coffee and toasted bread. The flavor is very elegant and rich in minerals, with the classic Chardonnay tones of hazelnuts and lime. This could easily have been a Blanc de Blancs from one of the major plantations in Côte des Blancs.

- 1985 GASTON CHIQUET JUBILÉE   80, JUL 1999 (83)
  (30% PN, 70% CH)

A relative disappointment with exaggerated rustic fruit. The make-up of this full-bodied and decidedly food-requiring Champagne is fine. Purple coneflowers, red apples, and raisins are my strongest associations.

CLÉRAMBAULT C-M

Grande Rue
10250 Neuville-sur-Seine
03 25 38 38 60
Production: 150,000

As with most cooperatives, this one started off supplying the major houses with grape juice, but now the best grapes go to their own Champagne production. Clérambault get consistently good reviews in the French press.

- CLÉRAMBAULT TRADITION   48
  (100% PN)
- CLÉRAMBAULT CARTE NOIRE   52
  (60% PN, 20% PM, 20% CH)
- CLÉRAMBAULT ROSÉ   22
  (100% PN)
- 1985 CLÉRAMBAULT BLANC DE BLANCS   69, FEB 1995 (73)
  (100% CH)
- 1985 CLÉRAMBAULT ROSÉ   70, FEB 1995 (70)
  (100% PN)

CLICQUOT, VICTOR N-M

51100 Reims

One of the ancient relics that still turns up now and then. The house no longer exists.

- 1959 VICTOR CLICQUOT   75, APR 2003 (75)
- 1942 VICTOR CLICQUOT   91, OCT 2001 (91)

Sweet bouquet of apricot and peach. Very fine, butterscotchy note with an uncomplicated construction and slightly curt aftertaste. Completely perfectly aged, evolved Champagne from a not particularly remarkable year.

CLOS DE LA CHAPELLE C-M

rue de Reims
51390 Villedommange
03 26 49 26 76
Production: 280,000

Since 1948, twenty-three independent winegrowers on the western side of Reims's hills have joined together under the beautiful name of Clos de la Chapelle. The wines are always made up of a mix of the three grape types, with Pinot Meunier dominating. Acreage: fifty hectares.

- CLOS DE LA CHAPELLE TRADITION   66
  (13% PN, 75% PM, 12% CH)
- CLOS DE LA CHAPELLE ROSÉ   53
  (13% PN, 72% PM, 15% CH)
- CLOS DE LA CHAPELLE PRIVILÈGE   61
  (15% PN, 65% PM, 20% CH)
- 1997 CLOS DE LA CHAPELLE PRESTIGE   67, SEP 2003 (69)
  (30% PN, 25% PM, 45% CH)

CLOUET, ANDRÉ **** R-M

8, rue Gambetta
51150 Bouzy
03 26 57 00 82
Production: 65,000

Pierre and Françoise Santz-Clouet own nine hectares in Bouzy and Ambonnay. Young and full of ideas, their son Jean-François is striving toward Bollinger in style and quality. Sometimes he succeeds. These wines have rapidly enjoyed great success in Sweden, mostly due to the embarrassingly low prices that importer Vindirekt has been keeping these past years. These rare vintage wines come from old vines right next to Bollinger's ungrafted vines in Bouzy. They can be enjoyed at Bar å Vin in Stockholm, Sweden. The labels look old-fashioned—either you love them or hate them. The wines, on the other hand, are hard to dislike.

- CLOUET BRUT   75
  (60% PN, 40% CH)
- CLOUET GRANDE RÉSERVE   75
  (100% PN)
- CLOUET SILVER BRUT   82
  (100% PN)
  A tremendously powerful Champagne with a gorgeously hideous label. The mature reserve wines give weight and softness and round off the completely dry aftertaste. Bollinger-like.
- CLOUET GRAND CRU ROSÉ   84
  (100% PN)
  Almost the color of red wine, with a heavy nose of almonds, smoke, nuts, and honey. Tight and chewy with amazing concentration. One of the most full-bodied rosés that I know of. Unfortunately the wine has been sold a little too early, which gives rise to a slightly unripe appearance.
- 1998 CLOUET   87, DEC 2003 (91)
  (50% PN, 50% CH)
  A floral, beautifully vague Champagne that needs many years to develop correct village-typical weight and oiliness. Still, wonderfully good and appley-fresh; now it has also acquired passion-fruit tones—a pleasant new addition.
- 1997 CLOUET   81, JUN 2002 (84)
  (50% PN, 50% CH)
  Not much better than the nonvintage wines. More Chardonnay and a fresh, almost flowery style. None of its usual concentration or vigor. Skip this vintage.
- 1996 CLOUET   88, DEC 2003 (93)
  (70% PN, 30% CH)
  I have never before encountered a wine from Clouet with such youthful acidity. There is of course an undertone of vanilla, full, fleshy body, and rich apple aroma. But it is still the wine's tart

dryness and reserved intensity that leaves the greatest impression so far in this wine's young life. According to Jean-François, this wine was a mistake—too much Pinot Noir. A pleasant mistake in my opinion.

- 1996 CLOUET (SPECIAL BOTTLE)   85, NOV 2001 (92)
  (50% PN, 50% CH)
  To be honest, I discern very little difference between this wine—with more Chardonnay and made in a special bottle—and the wine above. I think I must taste them side by side.
- 1995 CLOUET   85, NOV 2000 (90)
  (50% PN, 50% CH)
  Very young and dazzlingly apple-flavored, with Clouet's house-style strongly accented. Already enjoyable, of course, but I am waiting for the rich aroma of almond that will soon appear.
- 1994 CLOUET   85, NOV 1998 (88)
  (50% PN, 50% CH)
  Unfortunately the demand for Clouet's vintage Champagne is extreme, which leads to its earlier release than the nonvintage ones. One wouldn't expect much yet of a 1994, but it is already classic and complex.
- 1993 CLOUET   84, MAY 1998 (89)
  (50% PN, 50% CH)
  More closed and heavier than the fruity '94. High acidity and a fine Pinot aroma.
- 1990 CLOUET   93, OCT 2003 (93)
  (50% PN, 50% CH)
  A truly popular bubbly that has converted the entire Swedish wine elite. The wine possesses a cannonade of rich fruit and nutty tastes. Superbly balanced with tons of honey in the aftertaste.
- 1989 CLOUET   89, AUG 1997 (90)
  (50% PN, 50% CH)
  Very ripe and powerful Champagne, with bready aromas and a meaty finish.
- 1986 CLOUET   84, APR 1996 (86)
  (50% PN, 50% CH)
  Bushy, developed nose of mature fruit. Sadly, this impressive '86 is a bit short.
- 1977/1976 CLOUET   87, DEC 2003 (87)
  (100% PN)
  At the time, this wine was classed as nonvintage. The family has a few bottles left today, which they kindly let me taste. Decidedly poorer and sweeter than the pure '76, with a medium body and a stony keynote coupled with butterscotch and honey.
- 1976 CLOUET   93, MAY 2000 (93)
  (100% PN)
  Heaps of muscle and sun-ripened fruit leaning toward dates and figs. Big, smoky, and impressively powerful taste. Jean-François Clouet considers this to be his best wine ever. Personally, I'm a bit more taken by the finesse of his '69, but he managed to pull out a perfect and impressive bottle just in time for the Millennium Tasting.
- 1973 CLOUET   92, OCT 1998 (92)
  (100% PN)
  Tasted together with Jean-François Clouet (also born in 1973) during the recording of a TV show in his cellar. When we eventually finished our lines we discovered that we were partaking of a soft, mature, and easy-to-drink Blanc de Noirs. It is true that one could sense smoke and vegetable tones in the aroma, but the overall impression was soft and accommodating.

• 1969 CLOUET   94, NOV 1998 (94)
(100% PN)

The first old Clouet I have tasted that was not newly disgorged. The '69 strengthens my conviction that the best Champagnes are older, normally disgorged bottles that have lain undisturbed in the producers' cellars. The aroma is fantastically complex and well interwoven. The dominant tones are coffee and marzipan. The taste is somewhat lighter and less fascinating, but utterly delectable. The aromatic spectrum is reminiscent of 1964 Krug.

• 1961 CLOUET   92, APR 1997 (94)
(100% PN)

Jean-François, born in 1973, doesn't usually like older Champagnes, but even he was forced to bow to this lively power-pack. Personally I'd prefer to wait for the maturity that comes from a few more years in the bottle.

• 1959 CLOUET   90, DEC 2003 (90)
(100% PN)

Big and smoky, of course, but I had expected greater dimensions and more gamy energy. Fish, tar, sea, and smoke are words that appropriately describe the medium-bodied, bubblingly fresh, mineral-propelled taste.

• CLOUET CUVÉE 1911 (91/90/89)   91, OCT 2003 (93)
(100% PN)

A prestige *cuvée* made with exactly the same label that was used in 1911. The idea is that only 1,911 bottles will be produced every year under that name. The first version is a blending of 25 percent 1991, 25 percent 1989, and 50 percent 1990. The grapes are selected from places within Bouzy that give a great deal of mineral and elegance. The color is light. The fruit is intensely fresh and surprisingly light and Chardonnay-like. With storage, this wine will certainly remind one of Cristal, as opposed to the vintage wines, which more resemble Bollinger, their grape-blending notwithstanding.

CLOUET, PAUL *** R-M
10, rue Jeanne d'Arc
51150 Bouzy
03 26 57 07 31
Production: 45,000

A property owned by Marie Therese Bonnaire, who is married to the famous winemaker in Cramant! It is he who makes those classic Bouzy Champagnes in his modern headquarters in Cramant. Definitely a name to remember. The Chardonnay comes from Chouilly.

• PAUL CLOUET SELÉCTION   63
(40% PN, 20% PM, 40% CH)

• PAUL CLOUET GRAND CRU   69
(80% PN, 20% CH)

• PAUL CLOUET ROSÉ   60
(33% PN, 33% PM, 34% CH)

• 1994 PAUL CLOUET   70, JUN 1997 (80)
(80% PN, 20% CH)

A pure fruit in this young and undeveloped wine. A plum aroma and meaty structure with a somewhat short aftertaste.

• 1993 PAUL CLOUET   85, OCT 2003 (87)
(80% PN, 20% CH)

Wow, what dense, mighty power! The wine is creamy and smooth with lots of plum and chocolate aromas.

• 1992 PAUL CLOUET   88, DEC 2003 (88)
(80% PN, 20% CH)

Bonnaire has succeeded, even with this weak year, in making a buttery, rounded, plum-saturated, fat Bouzy Champagne. The wine is increasingly filled with aromas reminiscent of Christmas.

• 1998 PAUL CLOUET PRESTIGE   84, DEC 2003 (88)
(66% PN, 34% CH)

Tight, floral, light, buttery bouquet. Clear, pure, promising taste, with handsome acidity and buttery fruit. The wine will naturally feel much heavier when the first wave of maturity sets in.

• 1996 PAUL CLOUET SOIS BOIS   87, DEC 2003 (92)
(66% PN, 34% CH)

For the first time, Jean-Louis Bonnaire has fermented Bouzy-Pinot in small oak barrels. The result is a big, round wine with heaps of sweet fruit and tons of layered tastes. A real "layer upon layer" wine, with nutty complexity and leathery aromas together with barrel and butter toffee. Extremely fleshy, toasted, oaky, and heavy. A mealtime wine that needs decanting in order to bring out the ripeness and immensity. I predict good acidity and a long life.

COLIN R-M
48, avenue Louis Lenoir
51130 Vertus
03 26 58 86 32
Production: 55,000

Today, Philippe Colin has access to twelve hectares in Vertus, Bergères-les-Vertus, Cramant, Oiry, Dormans, Reuil, Venteuil, Fossoy, and Sézanne. Pierre Radet founded the property in 1890. Only 3,000 bottles are exported to Germany and England. Every year a large portion of the grapes are bought by Lanson.

• COLIN BLANCHE DE CASTILLE   60
(100% CH)

• COLIN ALLIANCE   65
(20% PN, 80% CH)

• COLIN BLANC DE BLANCS   58
(100% CH)

A certain butteriness in the nose gives a lift to what is rather a rustic wine.

• 1997 COLIN   75, OCT 2003 (85)
(100% CH)

A very distinctive wine—I really don't know if I am correct in giving the high future points that I do. Today, this is an extremely stingy, acidic affair, almost completely devoid of fruit. But the acidity is high enough to carry it far into the future. Then, when it finally matures, new discreet acacia notes will appear and make the wine beautiful. As I have previously stated, there is no other wine in the world that increases its concentration and richness with long storing as Champagne does. Something for our grandchildren to experience.

• 1985 COLIN   83, FEB 2003 (84)
(100% CH)

Big, developed, buttery nose that borders on the rancid. Slightly cheesy and straw-smelling, but also surprisingly fresh with fine acidity and mousse. Rich mid-palate leaning towards peach, and a short, dry aftertaste of grass as well dried fruit.

• 1997 COLIN PRESTIGE CRAMANT   84, DEC 2003 (86)
(100% CH)

Colin was correct when he decided to vinify his best grapes from Cramant separately. I await with excitement a vintage with more substance and potential, as there is nothing wrong with the purity and elegance. Rather apple-propelled aroma with good mineral and a hint of citrus.

COLLARD-CHADELLE R-M

51700 Villers-sous-Châtillon
Production: 60,000

The firm was founded in 1970 by Daniel and Françoise Collard. The thirty-year-old vines, spread over 8.5 hectares, are largely planted with Pinot Meunier. A small portion of the production is stored in large oak barrels.

- 1986 COLLARD-CHADELLE   66, SEP 2003 (66)
  (40% PN, 40% PM, 20% CH)

COLLARD, JEAN R-M

51480 Reuil
03 26 58 32 29
Production: 20,000

The grower has ten hectares in Reuil and the surrounding area, planted with all three grape types. The wines are not put through malolactic fermentation.

- JEAN COLLARD CARTE D'OR   60
  (80% PM, 20% CH)

COLLARD, RENÉ R-M

18, Grande Rue
51480 Reuil
03 26 58 32 01
Production: 60,000

An odd grower, much appreciated in France for its oxidative Champagnes made in oak barrels with only Pinot Meunier as the raw material. Actually, this style should suit English people better.

- 1976 RENÉ COLLARD   81, MAR 2000 (81)
  (100% PM)

  The structure is much better than with the oxidized '69. This is a composed, creamy and smiling wine. Both the bouquet and the palate have more than a touch of pleasant vanilla aroma. Unfortunately, this wine doesn't stand up for long in the glass.

- 1969 RENÉ COLLARD   66, MAR 2000 (>)
  (100% PM)

- 1985 RENÉ COLLARD ROSÉ   80, MAR 2000 (80)
  (100% PM)

  Surprisingly light color. Nutty bouquet with shades of smoke. Refreshingly balanced and relatively long. Completely mature at fifteen years of age.

COLLET, RAOUL C-M

34, rue Jeanson
51160 Aÿ
03 26 55 15 88
Production: 3,000,000

The best known of the two Aÿ cooperatives was founded in 1921 in Dizy. The company's present name came about when director Raoul Collet died in 1960. The cooperative has 400 members who work more than 600 hectares. The cooperative collaborates with Clérambault in Aube and gets its grapes from there, which explains the simplicity of certain *cuvées*.

- RAOUL COLLET CARTE NOIRE   57
  (40% PN, 60% CH)

- RAOUL COLLET CARTE ROUGE   62
  (75% PN, 25% CH)

- RAOUL COLLET ROSÉ   60
  (100% PN)

- 1995 RAOUL COLLET   79, NOV 2003 (82)
  (50% PN, 50% CH)

  A rather grand, accomplished, impressive nose with lots of grape sweetness and a smidgen of Aÿ character. Slightly too much dosage takes all the peaks away and smoothes out any nuances. Otherwise the wine is good and rounded, with low acidity.

- 1993 RAOUL COLLET   82, NOV 2002 (85)
  (50% PN, 50% CH)

  Round, fine fruit, and clean grapey character. Impressive and fleshy, with a simultaneously fruit-propelled taste featuring apple, red beet, and plum. Nice, sweet, rather long aftertaste.

- 1988 RAOUL COLLET   80, OCT 1997 (84)
  (80% PN, 20% CH)

  Here we are dealing with a pure Aÿ Champagne. The most obvious aromas are leather, plums and licorice.

COLLON R-M

27, Grande Rue
10110 Landreville
03 25 38 31 51
Production: 80,000

Right in the heart of Côtes des Bar we find this eight-hectare property. The vineyards are comprised of 80 percent Pinot Noir; the rest is Chardonnay. Only the *cuvée* is used and the wines are fermented in steel tanks. No vintage wines are made on the property. Instead, all of the three nonvintage wines are a mix of the three latest years.

- COLLON RÉSERVE BRUT   55
  (70% PN, 30% CH)

COMTE DE LANTAGE N-M

20, rue Chapelle
51700 Cerseuil
03 26 51 11 39
Production: 150,000

Victor Mandois founded the firm at the end of the 1800s. After being a grower for several generations, they received house status in 1987. The house owns ten hectares in Cerseuil. The vintage wine lies three years on the yeast before disgorging.

- COMTE DE LANTAGE RÉSERVE   59
  (20% PN, 25% PM, 55% CH)

- COMTE DE LANTAGE DEMI-SEC   43
  (20% PN, 25% PM, 55% CH)

- COMTE DE LANTAGE GRAND CRU 2000   84
  (100% CH)

  Very exotic and rather sweet. At the same time palatable, with its notes of passion fruit, pineapple, and sweet grapefruit. No particularly noteworthy length, but still rich in taste with a thoroughly rounded tutti-fruttiness.

CONTET N-M

23, rue Jean Moulin
51200 Épernay
03 26 51 06 33

The firm is now owned by Martel and has the same address. The brand no longer exists.

- CONTET BRUT   70

COOP. DE BLÉMOND C-M

route de Cramant
51530 Cuis
03 26 59 78 30
Production: 80,000

This is a relatively small cooperative that has over forty hectares in Cuis, Cramant, Chouilly, and several small villages outside Côte des Blancs. Today the cooperative is run by Christian Deliege.

• BLÉMOND BRUT	50
(40% PN, 40% PM, 20% CH)	
• BLÉMOND SÉLECTION GRANDE RÉSERVE	56
(30% PN, 30% PM, 40% CH)	

COOP. DE LEUVRIGNY C-M

51700 Leuvrigny
03 26 58 30 75

The cooperative is best known for selling its best grapes to Krug; today it makes no wines of its own.

• COOP. DE LEUVRIGNY BRUT	65
(100% PM)	

COOP. DES ANCIENS DE LA VITICULTURE D'AVIZE C-M

Lycée Viticole
51190 Avize
03 26 57 79 79
Production: 130,000

Monsieur Anglade started this cooperative in 1952, together with the students at the enology school in Avize. The Champagne that is sold today is made by the students and is sold under three names: Sanger, Louise Puisard, and Vaubécourt. Sanger is the cooperative's top brand, and only the *cuvée* is used. The grapes come from thirty-five villages and the wines are always technically correct. Other wines: Sanger Brut, Vaubécourt, Louise Puisard, Millésime.

• SANGER BLANC DE BLANCS	68
(100% CH)	
• SANGER ROSÉ	61
(10% PN, 90% CH)	

COOP. ESTERLIN C-M

25, avenue de Champagne
51200 Épernay
03 26 59 71 52
Production: 1,200,000

Mancy's cooperative was formed in 1948 and has recently moved to Épernay. Today, 145 members harvest from 140 hectares. The house is run by Michel Plantagenet.

• ESTERLIN BRUT SÉLECTION	52
(10% PN, 30% PM, 60% CH)	
• ESTERLIN BLANC DE BLANCS	50
(100% CH)	
• ESTERLIN ROSÉ	53
(25% PN, 55% PM, 20% CH)	
• ESTERLIN ELZÉVIA	84, JAN 2003 (88)
(100% CH)	

A nonvintage prestige *cuvée* made of Chardonnay from the best villages. There must be a lot of wine from 1996 in this mix because the palate is so incredibly acidic in relation to the otherwise generous and sweet fruit layers. The nose is aristocratic and well defined, with hints of citrus, white peach, crème brûlée, and an intimation of mint toffee. A very promising prestige wine from this house, in a style reminiscent of its grand neighbors in Épernay.

COOP. MAILLY GRAND CRU *** C-M

28, rue de la Libération
51500 Mailly
03 26 49 41 10
Production: 450,000

Today, seventy members in the cooperative share as many hectares in a very professional and successful manner. The clever winemaker is now Hervé Dantan. Cooperative Mailly is absolutely up there among the best, and best known, of the cooperatives in the district. Their marketing is well organized and aggressive. It is therefore not surprising that they've approached the Swedish Wine Monopoly with their Blanc de Noirs, actually the first of its kind in our country.

• MAILLY BRUT RÉSERVE	69
(80% PN, 20% CH)	
• MAILLY EXTRA BRUT	78
• MAILLY BLANC DE NOIRS	78
(100% PN)	
(75% PN, 25% CH)	
• MAILLY ROSÉ	73
(90% PN, 10% CH)	
• 1997 MAILLY	82, SEP 2003 (84)
(90% PN, 10% CH)	

Even such a fleshy and gamy food Champagne as this is transformed—this year—into a summer wind, with refreshing and cooling elements. Notes like pineapple, dried citrus, and yellow roses can actually be discerned, despite the fact that we are dealing with an almost pure Pinot Champagne. Later, its heritage will most likely fight its way up to the surface.

• 1996 MAILLY	82, SEP 2003 (84)
(90% PN, 10% CH)	

Good weight, but a little waxy and jammy, with plum and fig aromas. A snobbish, rustic Champagne that will stand up to the destructive processes of nature.

• 1995 MAILLY	82, MAY 2000 (87)
(90% PN, 10% CH)	

Expansive scent of baked goods and exotic flowers, with a fine attack and underlying softness. Full bodied, with an appealingly mature grape character and a fine potential for development. For the time being it is slightly too appley and one-dimensional.

• 1990 MAILLY	82, OCT 1999 (87)
(75% PN, 25% CH)	

Superb freshness and vivacity. This "*vin de garde*"—wine for laying down—has got a good lingering aftertaste and a great structure.

• 1989 MAILLY	86, OCT 1997 (89)
(75% PN, 25% CH)	

Surprisingly even better than the '90. Balanced, fresh, and full of ripe fruit aromas. Nice nose of chocolate and coffee beans.

• 1988 MAILLY	81, MAR 2000 (85)
(75% PN, 25% CH)	

I found dried fruit in this vintage Champagne, which tends to lift the house-typical aroma of licorice and chocolate.

- 1944 MAILLY   91, OCT 2003 (91)
(100% PN)

An incredible wartime find! Somehow this wine wound up in my possession and expectations were low, as the wine level was very low. All the more fun when the wine proved itself to be completely sound and very good. Vital golden color, deep nose of cinnamon stick, wax, and cacao. The taste is like an oily essence of honey, orange blossom, and dried fruit. Long and very fleshy.

- CUVÉE DE ÉCHANSONS   89
(75% PN, 25% CH)

Always a blend of two vintages. Many wine journalists often complain that the wine is oxidative, but I got quite another impression. The color shone and there was a fine mousse, the nose was creamy soft with elements of mushroom cream and leather. The aromas returned in the soft, enjoyable flavor.

- 1996 CUVÉE DE ÉCHANSONS   84, SEP 2003 (87)
(75% PN, 25% CH)

Rather soft due to the rich, ripe fruit. Sleeping for the moment—the nose is bound and it hasn't really found its equilibrium yet. Tart and probably made for a long life.

- 1996 MAILLY LA TERRE   86, NOV 2003 (89)
(70% PN, 30% CH)

Big, ripe appley nose with fine grape character. Very restrained acidity with real power and extremely good future prospects.

- 1996 CUVÉE L'INTEMPORELLE   85, SEP 2003 (88)
(40% PN, 60% CH)

Unexpectedly creamy and elegant where the fruit is finely balanced by a classic Champagne character. Fine, acidic, and mineral-saturated aftertaste.

- 1995 CUVÉE DE ÉCHANSONS   85, SEP 2003 (88)
(75% PN, 25% CH)

Fine balance, hints of butter, mint, and ripe apples in vanilla sauce. Creamy and sophisticated with a chocolate undertone. Should reach its peak somewhere around 2008.

- 1992 MAILLY MILLENNIUM   76, JUN 1999 (83)
(60% PN, 40% CH)

Surprisingly acidic and underdeveloped for a fast-maturing '92, with a relatively large dose of Chardonnay tones.

- 1983 CUVÉE 60EME ANNIVERSAIRE   87, SEP 1997 (87)
(60% PN, 40% CH)

A lovely Champagne with elements of roasted almonds and chestnuts. The mature flavor is full and well balanced.

COOP. MESNIL, LE *** C-M

11, rue Charpentier Laurain
51190 Le Mesnil-sur-Oger
03 26 57 53 23
Production: 100,000

This cooperative had every chance of becoming something a little bit special, but careless grape handling and a yield that is far too high have led to inferior wines. Some growers in the village have their labels marked with the letters R.-C. (Récolteur-Coopérateur). Such a Champagne is made by the cooperative in the village under various labels.

- CHRISTIAN ROBINET   67
(100% CH)

- DESHAUTELS   25
(100% CH)

- LE MESNIL   73
(100% CH)

- MICHEL POYET   67
(100% CH)

- 1989 MICHEL ROCOURT   82, JAN 1999 (83)
(100% CH)

One of the earliest developed Champagnes from Le Mesnil that I have ever tasted. Already, at nine years of age, the color is very deep, and the nose breathes honey, oak, coffee, and almond. The initial taste is fairly uncomplicated and straightforward; the mid-palate is splendid with its powerfully developed notes of coffee and almond biscuit. The aftertaste is uncomplicated and somewhat bitter.

- 1988 JEAN-PIERRE LAUNOIS   79, MAY 1995 (84)
(100% CH)

The best Champagne from the cooperative that I've tasted. Powerfully vinous nose and hard malic acidity.

- 1985 DESHAUTELS   40, JUN 1995 (>)
(100% CH)

- 1998 MESNIL SÉLECTION BLANC DE BLANCS   85, OCT 2003 (89)
(100% CH)

An extremely pleasant and focused Blanc de Blancs, which is soft and fresh at the same time. Nothing of the village's inaccessibility is found here, only a mellow, vintage character that has been given free scope. Both the nose and palate are harmonious, with light, sweet, nutty notes and elements of tropical sun-ripe pineapple.

- 1995 MESNIL SÉLECTION BLANC DE BLANCS   86, SEP 2003 (88)
(100% CH)

Surprisingly soft, developed Champagne from the cooperative in Le Mesnil. There is, of course, nothing of the classic nutty complexity that old Champagnes from this *grand cru* often have. Instead, it is ripe, supple, with exotically juicy fruit and notes of mint.

- 1990 MESNIL SÉLECTION BLANC DE BLANCS   85, OCT 2001 (86)
(100% CH)

Developed and impressive, with a big, palatable fruit compote in which fresh fruit is accompanied by windfall fruit and oxide notes. Acidity is high so the wine will surely hold for several decades—but it won't get much better.

COOP. PANNIER C-M

23, rue Roger Catillon
02400 Château-Thierry
03 23 69 51 30
Production: 1,900,000

The largest firm in Aisnes today was founded in 1899 by Louis-Eugène Pannier in Dizy, but was moved to Château-Thierry in 1937. The house became a cooperative in 1971 and expanded rapidly. Today, 230 growers are involved in the care of 415 hectares in forty nearby villages. I still think that Pannier is a relatively low-performing cooperative in relation to its reputation, even if a change for the better can be discerned. The winemaker at Pannier is Philippe Dupuis.

- PANNIER TRADITION   79
(19% PN, 40% PM, 41% CH)

- PANNIER ROSÉ   49
(17% PN, 61% PM, 22% CH)

- 1996 PANNIER   82, SEP 2003 (84)
(20% PN, 46% PM, 34% CH)

Handsome, exotic, with a slightly bready, modulated nose. The palate is fleshy and supple with a peach-saturated fruitiness supported by orange aromas and vintage-typical strong acidity under the mellow surface. The general impression is only tainted by a much-too-short aftertaste.

- 1995 PANNIER   78, SEP 2003 (79)
  (20% PN, 46% PM, 34% CH)
- 1990 PANNIER   85, OCT 2001 (86)
  (20% PN, 46% PM, 34% CH)
  The young vintage wines from Pannier have impressed me. The '90 is pure and fruity with toasty aromas and a soft, well-balanced, big house-style.
- 1988 PANNIER   77, OCT 1995 (84)
  (20% PN, 46% PM, 34% CH)
  Bready and faintly toasty, with impressive class and structure despite the high proportion of Pinot Meunier.
- 1981 PANNIER   80, FEB 2003 (80)
  (20% PN, 46% PM, 34% CH)
  Seldom do '81s feel old, but here we have a rather gloomy affair with notes of wet wool, cheese, and hay. Luckily enough, a sweet bready note holds the wine together.
- LOUIS-EUGÈNE PANNIER   84
  (22% PN, 38% PM, 40% CH)
  Reminiscent of how Laurent-Perrier—until quite recently—could taste, with a decided note of amaretto. Overpowering, rich, mealtime Champagne.
- LOUIS-EUGÈNE PANNIER ROSÉ   84
  (27% PN, 34% PM, 39% CH)
  Deliciously fruit-saturated, summer-smelling wine, with a sunny luster and charming appearance. The nose is perky and full of berries: raspberry, cherry, and wild strawberry. The taste is medium bodied, harmonious, and heavily pumped up with crispy fruit.
- 1995 EGÉRIE   79, OCT 2001 (82)
  (25% PN, 33% PM, 42% CH)
  Mildly pleasant toasted note in the nose. Refreshing, rather simple mixed fruit in the mid-palate. Everything is fine so far. Unfortunately, I cannot disregard the note of cardboard box that turns up in the aftertaste; to my delight this was even noticed by the house's pleasant importer.
- 1990 EGÉRIE   69, NOV 1999 (69)
  (25% PN, 33% PM, 42% CH)
- 1988 EGÉRIE   80, OCT 1995 (84)
  (25% PN, 33% PM, 42% CH)
  Steely and ascetic, but with a superb attack and fresh acidity. The clear aftertaste hints at oranges. The company has obviously gone in for raising its quality with this vintage.
- 1985 EGÉRIE   78, JAN 1995 (83)
  (25% PN, 33% PM, 42% CH)
  Good weight and backbone, unlike their nonvintage prestige *cuvée*. Even so, it fails to match the 1985 vintage Champagnes from the better houses.

COOP. SOCIÉTÉ CHAMPENOISE D'EXPLOITATION VINICOLE C-M
51016 Châlons-en-Champagne
03 26 68 18 68
One of Champagne's lesser-known cooperatives.
- CHENEVAUX PREMIER   53

COOP. UNION CHAMPAGNE *** C-M
7, rue Pasteur
51190 Avize
03 26 57 94 22
Production: 4,000,000
Established in 1966. The Avize cooperative is perhaps the best in Champagne. The grapes come from eleven subsidiary cooperatives that only use *premier cru* and *grand cru* grapes from the villages of Mesnil, Avize, Bergeres, Vertus, Oger, Cramant, Cumieres, Bouzy, Aÿ, and Ambonnay. Twelve hundred growers share 1000 hectares, and six million bottles are sold as still wines to the larger houses. Furthermore, almost three million bottles are sold under other names of group members. The cooperative's wines are ingredients in, for example, Taittinger Comtes de Champagne, Grand Siècle, and Dom Pérignon. Their own wines are sold under several names: St Gall, Pierre Vaudon, and Orpale. Forty percent of the Champagne is exported. The head winemaker is Alain Coharde.
- BERNARD CUGNART   68
  (100% CH)
- PIERRE VAUDON BRUT   55
  (70% PN, 30% CH)
- SAINT GALL SÉLECTION   68
  (33% PN, 67% CH)
- ST GALL PREMIER CRU   73
  (33% PN, 67% CH)
- ST GALL BLANC DE BLANCS   75
  (100% CH)
- ST GALL EXTRA BRUT BLANC DE BLANCS   76
  (100% CH)
- ST GALL EXTRA BRUT GRAND CRU   79
  (100% CH)
- ST GALL ROSÉ   55
  (15% PN, 85% CH)
- ST GALL ROSÉ PREMIER CRU   63
  (15% PN, 85% CH)
- 1998 ST GALL PREMIER CRU BLANC DE BLANCS   85, DEC 2003 (87)
  (100% CH)
  The nose is met by lilies of the valley, hawthorn, and vanilla in a fresh, uplifting version. The mouth gets its share with a pleasant caress of creaminess and softness. A large portion of mineral besides, and an intimation of smokiness.
- 1996 PIERRE VAUDON   80, SEP 2003 (82)
  Because my memory of the wine is rather hazy, I'll quote my own notes from *Wine International*'s Champagne Tasting in September 2003: "Neutral big-house style. Hint of artificial notes, but structure is still good and there's hope for a long life to come."
- 1995 ST GALL PREMIER CRU BLANC DE BLANCS   84, JAN 2003 (87)
  (100% CH)
  Fresh and clear as a bell, as are all wines from this model cooperative. A superb aperitif or a perfect partner to authentic whitefish roe. Well built, classic, and elegant, without being ingratiating.

- 1995 ORPALE   90, DEC 2003 (92)
(100% CH)

Yet again, a brilliant prestige wine from the cooperative in Avize! This Champagne's whole appearance exudes class and refinement—a polished elegance and harmony that I usually associate with the big Champagne houses' prestige *cuvées*. The nose is concentrated and complex, almost like a Dom Pérignon Blanc de Blancs—if one existed. Toasted, fine aromas of bread and coffee are beautifully braided together with citrus notes in a creamy, simultaneously acidic attire.

- 1990 ORPALE   89, MAY 2003 (90)
(100% CH)

Brilliantly handsome '90 with everything in the right place. Clean attack and creamy, long aftertaste with a balanced, toasted finish. Exotic, sensational bouquet tightened up by the scent of clean, sun-dried sheets.

- 1985 ORPALE   91, SEP 2003 (91)
(100% CH)

One of the best cooperative Champagnes I've ever drunk. The wine is creamy-soft and is rich in minerals and elegance. Oranges and tangerines are aromas that can clearly be detected.

- 1983 ORPALE   85, MAR 2000 (85)
(100% CH)

Toasted, rich, and full-bodied. There is, unfortunately, something indefinably mushy about many of these '83s nowadays. Very good, but a tad simplistic.

- 1980 ORPALE   91, MAY 2003 (91)
(100% CH)

Highly reminiscent of Dampierre's '80. Light and delicate with small, tasty pyrotechnics of acacia and mint chocolate. Exceedingly light and immediately enjoyable.

COOP. VINCENT D'ASTRÉE C-M

rue Léon Bourgeois
51530 Pierry
03 26 54 03 23
Production: 100,000

The Pierry cooperative was founded in 1956 and today boasts 140 members with a cultivated area of sixty hectares. Other wines: Cuvée Jean Gabin.

- VINCENT D'ASTRÉE BRUT   52
(80% PM, 20% CH)
- VINCENT D'ASTRÉE CUVÉE RÉSERVE   55
(40% PN, 60% CH)
- VINCENT D'ASTRÉE ROSÉ   69
(50% PN, 50% CH)

COOP. VINICOLE D'AMBONNAY C-M

boulevard des Bermonts
51150 Ambonnay
03 26 57 01 46
Production: 400,000

Most of the growers in the village are members of the cooperative Vinicole d'Ambonnay that sells its Champagnes under the names Saint-Reol and Elégance. Today the cooperative is run by Marcel Billiot, the brother of Henri. Other wines: Elégance, Rosé, Blanc de Blancs, Prestige d'Argent.

- SAINT-REOL BRUT   49
(80% PN, 20% CH)
- 1990 SAINT-REOL   90, JAN 2003 (91)
(80% PN, 20% CH)

A sensational magnum from the cooperative in Ambonnay, which I—a little disrespectfully—had chosen as a "midnight bubbly" for New Year's Eve. Unfortunately, most of this superb wine was consumed outside at -15°C, accompanied by gunpowder-smelling fireworks. Of course I know that a weighty Pinot-dominated grower's Champagne—ten years old or more— is the most wonderfully tasting bubbly water for these dubious drinking occasions, but I had no idea that it would be this good. Hardly surprising, the wine was even better when we came in from the cold. What a dazzlingly aromatic display of color! Tons of ripe, Burgundy-like grapiness with gamy characteristics and truffley sensuality. The magnum freshness is so good that I suspect it will be of an even higher quality in a few years' time.

- 1988 OUIRET-PATUR   82, OCT 1997 (86)
(50% PN, 50% CH)

Focused and well-structured Champagne with fine mousse, fruity nose, and a rich, fleshy palate.

- 1985 CUVÉE ELEGANCE   86, SEP 2003 (86)
(80% PN, 20% CH)

A very exciting wine that impresses with its big, massive style. As soon as one finds the expected heavy, gamy aromas from the high-class Pinot Noir, there appears a light and charming side, where distinct notes of nougat, mango, and vanilla dance forth caressingly on the palate.

COOP. VINICOLE DE MARDEUIL C-M

64, rue de la Liberté
51530 Mardeuil
03 26 55 29 40
Production: 350,000

This wine is better known under the name Beaumont des Crayères. The second wine is called Charles Leprince. In Sweden, we have become acquainted with the low-price wine Cuvée de Réserve. The firm was started in 1955 and now has 210 members, with eighty hectares in Mardeuil, Cumières, Verneuil, and Vauciennes. The cooperative's cellar master J.-P. Bertus has a very good reputation. He keeps a stern eye on his members and aims for perfectly ripe grapes from some relatively old vines. The firm has really pulled its socks up recently, but although they make very reasonably priced wines, I am not particularly impressed with their handiwork.

- BEAUMONT DES CRAYÈRES GRAND PRESTIGE   78
(40% PN, 20% PM, 40% CH)
- BEAUMONT DES CRAYÈRES GRANDE RÉSERVE   70
(60% PN, 15% PM, 25% CH)
- BEAUMONT DES CRAYÈRES GRAND ROSÉ   50
(35% PN, 40% PM, 25% CH)
- 1996 BEAUMONT DES CRAYÈRES   78, APR 2003 (83)

Stringent acidity and a rich, apple-like fruit may transform this wine into something much more exciting in the future. At the moment it feels a tad unbalanced, tart, and over-refined, with a certain lack of personality.

- 1995 BEAUMONT DES CRAYÈRES FLEUR DE PRESTIGE 74, MAY 2000 (78)
(40% PN, 10% PM, 50% CH)
- 1997 BEAUMONT DES CRAYÈRES FLEUR DE ROSÉ 76, MAY 2003 (79)
(25% PN, 25% PM, 50% CH)

- 1995 BEAUMONT DES CRAYÈRES FLEUR DE ROSÉ   58, JAN 2002 (60)
  (25% PN, 25% PM, 50% CH)
- 1995 BEAUMONT DES CRAYÈRES NUIT D'OR   87, NOV 2002 (88)
  (30% PN, 70% CH)
  Somewhat lighter and more charming than the '90, with fine, elegant cold fruitiness. Popsicle with a taste of pineapple and passion fruit. This cooperative goes from strength to strength and must be classed among the absolute top in this category.
- 1995 NOSTALGIE   86, SEP 2003 (88)
  (30% PN, 70% CH)
  Very clean and delicious with great breadiness and a fine aroma of dried fruits. Tolerably fleshy taste with great depth and perfect balance. The finish is sophisticated and comfortably fruity.
- 1992 NOSTALGIE   75, MAY 2000 (78)
  (30% PN, 70% CH)
- 1990 BEAUMONT DES CRAYÈRES NUIT D'OR   88, OCT 2001 (88)
  (30% PN, 70% CH)
  A prestige Champagne from that famous year, with rich, exotic fruit and a honey-soft appearance. Big and impressive with a fine personality of ripe Chardonnay grapes from old vines. Bouquet of vanilla and butterscotch as well as a long taste of pineapple.
- 1987 NOSTALGIE   80, APR 1997 (84)
  (30% PN, 70% CH)
  It was an odd decision to produce a *cuvée de prestige* in this mediocre year. The nose is well made and concentrated with good attack.

COPINET, JACQUES R-M
11, rue Ormeau
51260 Montgenost
03 25 80 49 14
Production: 80,000
- JACQUES COPINET BRUT   51
  (100% CH)
- COPINET ROSÉ   51
  (20% PN, 80% CH)
- 1992 COPINET   67, OCT 2001 (67)
  (100% CH)

COULON, ROGER R-M
12, rue Vigne du Roy
51390 Vrigny
03 25 03 61 65
Production: 65,000
The grower has over ten hectares in Vrigny with all three grape types. His foremost Chardonnay ferments in oak barrels. The vintage wine is the only one that does not go through malolactic fermentation. The rosé is made by allowing the grape skins to macerate.
- ROGER COULON   65
  (50% PN, 20% PM, 30% CH)

COURTOIS-CAMUS R-M
270, rue du 8 mai 1945
51530 Cramant
03 26 57 91 18
Production: 8,000
The owner, who possesses probably the largest hands in Champagne, met me in his villa during a spontaneous visit in April 1996. Unfortunately, production is too modest for vintage Champagne. They own only two hectares, spread out in twenty-two small plots. The company is well worth a visit, not least to feel the firmest handshake in the region.
- COURTOIS-CAMUS TRADITION   74
  (100% CH)
- COURTOIS-CAMUS CARTE ROUGE   70
  (100% CH)

COUTIER, RENÉ-HENRI **** R-M
7, rue Henri III
51150 Ambonnay
03 26 57 02 55
Production: 25,000
This model firm was founded in 1880. Coutier own seven hectares in the village but sell 80 percent to the cooperative. Malolactic fermentation is used on half of the still wine. The father of the present owner was the man who first planted Chardonnay in Ambonnay, back in 1946. Coutier is now the uncrowned king of Ambonnay.
- R. H. COUTIER BRUT   74
  (60% PN, 40% CH)
- R. H. COUTIER BRUT VINTAGE   84, DEC 2003 (87)
  (100% PN)
  I had no idea that you could name a wine "Vintage" when it has been blended from two different vintages; it is certainly not a "vintage" in the true meaning of the word. The first edition of this wine consists of two equal portions of '95 and '96, creating a soft, pleasant appearance without any real distinction. Shorter and more buttery than the vintage wines, but fine for those of you who have patience.
- CUVÉE HENRI III   75
  (100% PN)
- R. H. COUTIER BLANC DE BLANCS DE AMBONNAY   77
  (100% CH)
- R. H. COUTIER ROSÉ   78
  (50% PN, 50% CH)
- 1996 R. H. COUTIER   88, DEC 2003 (93)
  At the moment, the wine is vanilla-ish and ingratiatingly buttery in a delightful and unexpected way, with a large portion of acidity under the surface. The deep, gamy characteristics need more time to take shape. What a fantastic winemaker Coutier is! His wines are the only ones from the Pinot-growers that continually have the same elegance as the wines from the largest growers.
- 1996 R. H. COUTIER OEIL DE PERDRIX   87, JAN 2002 (93)
  (100% PN)
  "Oeil de Perdrix" means "partridge eye," and alludes to the faintly reddish, macerated color of the wine. Here, Coutier has succeeded in making the most impressive wine I have ever tasted in this very odd category. Powerful bouquet with strong elements of apple peel and petroleum. Fleshy and crispy with exceptional balance. Actually reminiscent of a '92 Bollinger Vieilles Vignes.

• 1995 R. H. COUTIER   89, MAR 2003 (92)
(100% PN)

This brilliant grower has, yet again, hit upon an amazingly delicious wine. For once this is a pure Blanc de Noirs, which suits well the velvety smooth and deliciously creamy vintage. Toffee and cream envelop the classically rich red fruit, and, as yet, the dark gamy and smoky notes can only be hinted at under the softly inviting blanket. Fashionably pedigreed Pinot Noir.

• 1994 R. H. COUTIER   83, SEP 2002 (85)
(100% PN)

Coutier never just throws things together. The '94 is very good and devoid of the emptiness that characterizes so many Champagnes from this vintage. As always, both gravity and elegance are present. I discern smells reminiscent of licorice, yellow apple peel, and the creaminess of a suckling calf.

• 1990 R. H. COUTIER   90, SEP 2001 (93)
(75% PN, 25% CH)

A wine that is personal and hard to judge. It has fresh acidity and youthful fruit, with clear elements of melon, kiwi, and Alexander pear. Very elegant.

• 1988 R. H. COUTIER   90, AUG 1995 (94)
(75% PN, 25% CH)

Colossally elegant and sophisticated. The wine's aromas resemble Roederer's Cristal from the same year. Nuts and butterscotch back up the pure fruit.

• 1982 R. H. COUTIER   86, MAY 1998 (88)
(60% PN, 40% CH)

Very creamy, buttery, and easily drunk. Somewhat diluted due to a high yield. Like a wishy-washy Cristal.

• 1978 R. H. COUTIER   88, MAY 1998 (90)
(75% PN, 25% CH)

A harmonious Champagne with a complete, elegant nose of nuts, marzipan, and brioche. Unfortunately somewhat short.

• 1964 R. H. COUTIER   95, JUL 1995 (95)
(100% PN)

Wonderfully golden and lively. A magnificent wine with a dark nose of cigars, brioche, treacle, chanterelle mushrooms, plums, truffles, and rotten wood. The flavor is exceptionally tight and concentrated, with an accelerating aftertaste. Like a great Bordeaux wine in its tones of cigars and leather.

CUPERLY N-M
2, rue de l'Ancienne Eglise
51380 Verzy
03 26 70 23 90
Production: 300,000

The house of Cuperly was founded in 1845. In those days they sold mostly still wines and spirits. We are now on to the fourth generation of Cuperly, with Gérard at the rudder and a considerable production of Champagne. Even this house has joined the trend of vinifying some of the wine in small oak barrels. Malolactic fermentation is consistently avoided. A large portion of the wine comes from their home village of Verzy, and they have more than ten hectares of vineyards at their disposal.

• CUPERLY CHARLES D'EMBRUN   60
(40% PN, 20% PM, 40% CH)

• CUPERLY DEMI-SEC   40
(60% PN, 40% CH)

• CUPERLY ROSÉ   66
(50% PN, 50% CH)

• 1994 CUPERLY   72, SEP 2003 (74)
(20% PN, 80% CH)

• CUPERLY PRESTIGE   69
(70% PN, 30% CH)

DAMPIERRE, COMTE AUDOIN DE **** N-M
5, Grande Rue
51140 Chenay
03 26 03 11 13
Production: 90,000

Counts from the Dampierre family have lived in Chenay for more than 700 years. Champagne production started as late as 1980, and the house run by the present Count is one of the newest in Champagne. He lives, together with his wife and dogs, in a lovely mansion in this charming village. Count Audoin has no vineyards of his own but instead buys in all his grapes from *premier* and *grand cru* villages. They are vinified in Avize, where they are stored for at least four years. I get the impression that Champagne production is a passionate hobby for the Count. He loves good Champagne and classic cars, and the connection between these outwardly separate things is something he exploits regularly. He has produced a Champagne set for Aston Martin, and usually poses in front of his house with his private collection of sports cars and a glass of Champagne in his hand. I'll never forget a ride in his black Alvis from 1935. Audoin makes me think of Roger Moore in the old TV series *The Persuaders*. Luckily the impression of frivolity and luxuriousness is not just an image. His Champagnes are wines worthy of counts and barons with their aristocratic style. And the Count himself is one of the most charismatic and light-hearted people in all of Champagne.

• CUVÉE DES AMBASSADEURS   77
(50% PN, 50% CH)

• DAMPIERRE GRANDE CUVÉE   74
(50% PN, 50% CH)

• DAMPIERRE OEIL DE PERDRIX   72
(12% PN, 88% CH)

• DAMPIERRE BLANC DE BLANCS   78
(100% CH)

• DAMPIERRE DEMI-SEC   65
(50% PN, 50% CH)

• 1995 DAMPIERRE GRANDE ANNÉE   84, NOV 2003 (86)
(65% PN, 35% CH)

An excellent wine with immediate, irresistible charm. All vintage wines from the Count have a resplendent, pumped-up Pinot character, but the question is this: will the '95 be even more luxurious than previous vintages? The wine is full of soft fruit and sweet caramel taste. Lately, however, I have been less impressed.

• 1991 DAMPIERRE GRANDE ANNÉE   83, MAY 2001 (85)
(65% PN, 35% CH)

The Count's wines are always flattering creators of happiness without being ingratiating. Most '91s have a hollowness that cannot be filled even by the process of aging. This wine is an exception. Harmony, polished fruit, and balance characterize this Champagne.

• 1990 DAMPIERRE GRANDE ANNÉE   88, SEP 2003 (88)
(70% PN, 30% CH)

Big, impressive, elegant, fruity, Pinot-dominated wine with a promising structure. Developing a little quicker than expected.

- 1988 DAMPIERRE GRANDE ANNÉE   89, JUL 2003 (90)
(70% PN, 30% CH)
Lovely Pinot bursting in the nose with clear elements of leather, mushrooms, and plums. The vanilla flavor that seems to be one of the company's trademarks is present on the palate, in harmony with the Roederer-like fruit.

- 1979 DAMPIERRE GRANDE ANNÉE   92, MAY 2001 (93)
(50% PN, 50% CH)
The good Count invited me in to enjoy one of two remaining magnum bottles kept in his private cellar. It is an absolute delight and an occasion for intellectual exercise of a rare kind to dine with the Count in his tasteful, ocher-yellow dining room. The wine itself was seductively good and feminine, a wine that tastes best when the glass is almost empty. Springtime floral and youthful, full of modulated perfume-like aromas and delicate tastes of the finest Chardonnay.

- 1988 DAMPIERRE ROSÉ   87, OCT 2003 (88)
(12% PN, 88% CH)
Wonderful, complex bouquet with toasted coffee as a base. The beautiful, sweet, Burgundy bouquet is reminiscent of the Dom Ruinart Rosé of the same year. Unfortunately, the taste falters slightly and the finesse is less pronounced. But still, good and creamy.

- 1985 DAMPIERRE ROSÉ   90, JAN 2001 (90)
(12% PN, 88% CH)
A completely perfect New Year's Champagne, which I drank while watching the always-funny TV-sketch "Dinner For One." The palate is full of sun-ripened summer berries and smiling warmth. Strongly reminiscent of a Charles Heidsieck Rosé of the same vintage. Fantastically charming and easily drunk.

- 1996 DAMPIERRE FAMILY RESERVE   85, SEP 2003 (89)
(100% CH)
Promisingly floral Chardonnay with grapefruit, lemon, and lilies in the nose. Hard acidity and a fine, caressing mousse. It takes its time to develop enough complexity.

- 1995 DAMPIERRE PRESTIGE GRAND CRU   88, FEB 2003 (91)
(100% CH)
Wonderfully polished and beautifully sophisticated, with sweet fruit and a Pol Roger caramel tone. Fine development in the glass and a buttery grape character. Mineral-characterized aftertaste that will be prolonged with aging.

- 1990 DAMPIERRE FAMILY RESERVE   91, SEP 2003 (92)
(100% CH)
The Count makes only 7,000 bottles of this model Blancs de Blancs. The vineyards are identical to those used in *prestige grand cru*, but the blend is composed somewhat differently. The color has more than a touch of green; the sparkling mousse unwinds beautifully up in the glass. There is nothing of the vintage's overripe character. Instead, the wine is handsomely floral with strains of linden, petroleum, and lime. Impressive, provocative intensity, despite the Champagne being light and gracious.

- 1990 DAMPIERRE PRESTIGE GRAND CRU   87, JUL 2003 (89)
(100% CH)
My points are surprisingly mean considering how good this wine usually is, and even more so considering how good the Family Reserve was from this vintage. Neither can I plead a too short and flighty meeting with this Champagne, because I—thoroughly out of character—drank the bottle almost entirely by myself. We had brought the bottle along for our Walpurgis Night supper, when my wife Sara suddenly took ill—so what could I do?! The wine felt slightly over-refined and impersonal, with a rich, pineapple-like fruit and a tad too much sweetness. Indeed, it was good and delicious, but surely ambitions must have been higher.

- 1985 DAMPIERRE PRESTIGE GRAND CRU   91, JAN 2003 (92)
(100% CH)
The cork is fastened with string instead of with a wire hood. What won't people do to be different? A classical, crispy, well-balanced Blanc de Blancs with all the aristocratic posture you might expect from the Count's top wine.

- 1980 DAMPIERRE PRESTIGE GRAND CRU   91, MAR 2003 (91)
(100% CH)
A wine made from equal proportions of Avize, Cramant, and Le Mesnil. One of the best Champagnes I've drunk from this forgotten vintage. A classical nose in which petroleum and citrus fruits struggle for supremacy. The nuts and toasty aromas are toned down but are present in the wings. The flavor is very fresh and flowery in its fat, almost oily viscosity.

DAUBY, GUY *** R-M
22, rue Jeanson
51160 Aÿ
03 26 54 96 49
Production: 40,000
Despite its insignificant size, this is still a highly regarded firm in Aÿ. Guy Dauby founded it in 1951. Today, the property is managed by Francine Dauby. Vineyard size is eight hectares.

- GUY DAUBY BRUT   78
(80% PN, 20% CH)
- GUY DAUBY ROSÉ   67
(90% PN, 10% CH)
- 1992 GUY DAUBY   78, MAR 2000 (82)
(70% PN, 30% CH)
Relatively developed and charming '92 with an aroma of sun-ripened plums, almonds, and a rustic, raisiny aftertaste.

- 1990 GUY DAUBY PRESTIGE   86, JUL 2001 (87)
(80% PN, 20% CH)
Mature and richly honey-saturated grower's Champagne with much more exotic fruitiness and juicy-sweet generosity than origin and grape composition hint at. Peachy taste and a clearly defined scent of honeysuckle and licorice. Vintage-typical.

DAUVERGNE, HUBERT R-M
33, rue de Tours
51150 Bouzy
03 26 57 00 56
Production: 45,000
Fernand Dauvergne started the business in 1860. Eighty-seven percent of the 6.5 hectares are planted with Pinot Noir. Other wines: Fine Fleur de Bouzy, Cuvée Saphir.

- HUBERT DAUVERGNE BRUT   69
(87% PN, 13% CH)
- HUBERT DAUVERGNE ELÉGANCE ROSÉ   76
(50% PN, 50% CH)

DEHOURS, S. A. N-M
2, rue Chapelle
51700 Cerseuil
03 26 52 71 75
Production: 1,000,000
The house was founded in 1930 by L. Ludovic. The man at the helm today is Jérôme Dehours.

- DEHOURS BRUT   50
  (33% PN, 33% PM, 34% CH)
- DEHOURS GRANDE RÉSERVE   65
  (33% PN, 33% PM, 34% CH)
- 1995 DEHOURS   81, JAN 2002 (84)
  (40% PN, 20% PM, 40% CH)
  A big, appetizing Champagne with vintage-typical accessibility and exoticism. Deep golden color and great aromatic intensity. The scent contains notes of hard bread, mint, smoke, and yellow apples. The taste is fleshy and food-oriented with a fine alleviating fruity-sweetness.

DELAMOTTE * N-M**
7, rue de la Brèche d'Oger
51190 Le Mesnil-sur-Oger
03 26 57 51 65
Production: 300,000
This neighbor of Salon was founded as far back as 1760, and although closely linked with Lanson for a period it was taken over by the Nonancourt family in 1949. Since Laurent-Perrier bought Salon in 1989, Delamotte has functioned as Salon's second label. Delamotte owns five hectares in Le Mesnil and has access to Salon's vineyards during those years when Salon isn't produced. Didier Dupond runs both firms with feeling and enthusiasm. Delamotte buys in 75 percent of its grapes, mostly from *premier cru* villages.

- DELAMOTTE BRUT   68
  (30% PN, 20% PM, 50% CH)
- CUVÉE NOBIS   78
  (100% CH)
- NICOLAS LOUIS DELAMOTTE   75
  (100% CH)
- DELAMOTTE BLANC DE BLANCS   77
  (100% CH)
- DELAMOTTE ROSÉ   65
  (100% PN)
- 1976 DELAMOTTE   88, JAN 2003 (88)
  (25% PN, 75% CH)
  A well-structured '76 that has nevertheless reached its peak. The wine completely paled in comparison to the Salon, but it still has a charming, toasted bouquet with elements of biscuits and bread.
- 1997 DELAMOTTE BLANC DE BLANCS   84, OCT 2003 (86)
  (100% CH)
  It seems as though Delamotte has become more and more concerned about preserving the original character of the home village of Le Mesnil in its wine. The village's aromatic fingerprint is clearly etched—both in nose and palate—in the '97. The mineral notes are beautifully woven together with the vintage-typical elements of brioche, vanilla, and tropical fruit. As usual, there is a note of pineapple. This same note never appears in its more serious and vinous brother, Salon.
- 1996 DELAMOTTE BLANC DE BLANCS   88, JUL 2003 (92)
  (100% CH)

Deep greenish-yellow color and lovely mousse. Crispy, attractive scents with notes of lime and lemon, thoroughly supported by a tough mineral character. Bound, steely, and beautifully potent with a soft, sweet finish. In my opinion, one of Delamotte's finest Champagnes ever.

- 1995 DELAMOTTE BLANC DE BLANCS   82, APR 2003 (85)
  (100% CH)
  A nice, easily drunk, juicy wine from Mesnil, Avize, and Oger. Perfumed and floral with a refreshing, pure taste. A deliciously sophisticated taste-layer of grapefruit and blood orange is also present.
- 1993 DELAMOTTE BLANC DE BLANCS   82, MAR 2002 (84)
  (100% CH)
  A crystal-clear feeling is conveyed here, both visually and orally. The bouquet is fresh and floral with strains of acacia and orange-blossom. The taste is mellow and pleasant with good finesse and a slightly shy mineral character.
- 1990 DELAMOTTE BLANC DE BLANCS   85, MAY 2003 (87)
  (100% CH)
  A big vintage for Delamotte, with better concentration and greater depth than usual. Good toasted notes in a magnum.
- 1985 DELAMOTTE BLANC DE BLANCS   84, JAN 2003 (84)
  (100% CH)
  A fine nose of elegantly youthful Chardonnay. Once again, a nice hint of pineapple and rhubarb.
- 1982 DELAMOTTE BLANC DE BLANCS   83, MAY 2001 (83)
  (100% CH)
  Smell of reduction that was aired out in five minutes. Light, youthful, and house-typical. The wine is made of grapes that were not properly concentrated, due to a yield that was too high—a common occurrence in 1982. Slightly lacks concentration, but clean, with a handsome toffee note in the background.
- 1976 DELAMOTTE BLANC DE BLANCS   90, JAN 2003 (90)
  (100% CH)
  Somewhat cleaner than the Brut, with a fresh citrus note left intact. This rich vintage suits very well what is normally a rather light wine. The muscle that is sometimes missing with Delamotte is present here.
- 1976 DELAMOTTE BLANC DE BLANCS NON DOSÉ 87, AUG 1999 (87)
  (100% CH)
  The La Reine Blanche restaurant in Vertus serves this special, bone-dry Champagne. The bouquet is characterized by aged butter, smoke, and walnut. The flavor is tight and delicious, but the aftertaste is shorter and less harmonious than it would have been with a well-balanced sugar additive.
- 1990 DELAMOTTE DEMI-SEC   78, JUL 1997 (83)
  (100% CH)
  Sensationally good sweetened Champagne. Elegant, citrus-fresh flavor. One of the best that I have tasted in this category.
- 1993 CUVÉE NOBIS   82, MAR 2002 (84)
  (100% CH)
  Identical to the Delamotte Blanc de Blancs, carrying the label of the exclusive Swedish restaurant and bar, Operakällaren.

DELAUNOIS, ANDRÉ R-M

18, rue Chigny
51500 Rilly-la-Montagne
03 26 03 48 85
Production: 55,000
Today's owners, Alain Toullec and Eric Chanez, have more than eight hectares planted with equal amounts of the three different grapes. The family property was founded in 1925.

- ANDRÉ DELAUNOIS BRUT   50
(33% PN, 33% PM, 34% CH)

DELBECK *** N-M

39, rue du Général Sarrail
51100 Reims
03 26 77 58 00
Production: 350,000
An historic house, founded in 1832, which quickly acquired a grand reputation when its owner, Félix-Désiré Delbeck, married widow Ponsardin's niece. For several years Delbeck was the official Champagne supplier to the French royal family. In the beginning of the 1960s the firm was closed for thirty years, only to be reopened in 1993, directed by Bruno Paillard. The company is, to a great extent, self-reliant when it comes to grapes. In 1995 the house was taken over by Pierre Martin, who previously worked for Barancourt. They also now own Bricout in Avize, as well as Waris & Chenayer. The office is still in Reims, but the wines are made in Avize.

- DELBECK BRUT HÉRITAGE   65
(70% PN, 30% CH)
- DELBECK AŸ GRAND CRU   80
(80% PN, 20% CH)
Freshly decanted, the wine is refreshing and surprisingly lightweight, with a faint smell of gooseberries. When the wine has aired for a bit and become more buoyant, Aÿ's plump, powerful character appears. The fleshiness is almost severe, and the aromas are characterized more by power than finesse. A fine, beefy wine suitable with fowl.
- DELBECK BOUZY GRAND CRU   85
(80% PN, 20% CH)
The bouquet makes one think of a vigorous Pol Roger. A deliciously sophisticated Champagne with surprisingly elegant fruit, creamy mousse, and a deep taste of butterscotch. The aftertaste is more reminiscent of a Bollinger with its gunpowder-stained aroma. With ten years' storage, this wine will clear the 90-point mark.
- DELBECK CRAMANT GRAND CRU   78
(100% CH)
- DELBECK DEMI-SEC   49
(70% PN, 30% CH)
- DELBECK ROSÉ   61
(90% PN, 10% CH)
- 1996 DELBECK   85, JUN 2003 (89)
(70% PN, 30% CH)
Most of the grapes come from Avize, Chouilly, Ambonnay, and Bouzy. Big, spicy nose of cinnamon and cumin with strongly toasted, creamy elements. Fleshy taste with a long, spicy finish way at the back of the tongue. Handsome and polished.
- 1990 DELBECK   85, MAR 2000 (91)
(70% PN, 30% CH)

Fantastically good rip and tear, fully noted, in the peppery and youthfully tart Pinot fruit that is the spine here. A fascinating balancing act, as the lemony aroma from the Chardonnay is nevertheless expressed, despite its insignificant share. Very potent!

- 1988 DELBECK   83, AUG 1997 (88)
(70% PN, 30% CH)
Restrained, meaty, and dry. Rather fishy on the nose at the moment. Good future.
- 1985 DELBECK   70, OCT 1993 (75)
(70% PN, 30% CH)
- 1953 DELBECK   84, SEP 2002 (84)
(70% PN, 30% CH)
Surely there are sounder bottles than this slightly decrepit, yet still-good wine. Windfall fruit, apple sauce, moss, and forest are aromas hard to miss. Oxidative notes both in the nose and palate. Still, I have to be impressed by this once-great Champagne.
- 1949 DELBECK   86, DEC 2003 (86)
(70% PN, 30% CH)
Unfortunately, the wine I tasted that day was completely still. Despite this, it was still light and creamy with beautiful vintage-typical characteristics. It's not the first time that I have encountered a delicious '49 lacking mousse. Reminiscent of a Chablis.
- 1945 DELBECK   94, JUN 1997 (94)
(70% PN, 30% CH)
An incredibly concentrated, viscous wine. Despite a total lack of mousse, the wine is fresh and free from sherry notes. Instead, a heavy, buttery bouquet is present, together with a compact taste of leather, cacao, and dried fruit.
- 1943 DELBECK
(70% PN, 30% CH)
- 1996 DELBECK ORIGINES   84, DEC 2002 (91)
(66% PN, 34% CH)
As yet, closed and slightly affected by sulfurous notes that, with time, will become beautifully toasted. The wine is mixed with equal amounts of Aÿ, Bouzy, and Cramant grapes and is only made in the magnum. Store for a long time if you are looking for the total experience with this fine wine.
- 1995 DELBECK ORIGINES   85, JUN 2002 (90)
(70% PN, 30% CH)
This is the second vintage of this prestige wine after its debut year of 1985. Only grapes from Aÿ, Bouzy, and Cramant are used. Floral and stylishly clean with an underlying toasted note and a newness that promises big things.

DELPORTE, YVES R-M

12, rue de la Haie du Bois
51150 Tours-sur-Marne
03 26 58 91 26
Production: 56,000
This grower makes loose and rustic wines from three fine villages: Tours-sur-Marne, Bisseuil, and Bouzy. The average age of the wines is only fifteen. Other wines: Brut, Vintage.

- YVES DELPORTE BLANC DE BLANCS   46
(100% CH)
- YVES DELPORTE DEMI-SEC   23
(75% PN, 25% CH)
- YVES DELPORTE ROSÉ   30
(80% PN, 20% CH)

DEMETS, MARIE N-M
10250 Gyé-sur-Seine
03 25 38 23 30
Production: 100,000
The house owns nine hectares planted with Pinot Noir.
- MARIE DEMETS   58
  (100% PN)

DEMOISELLE N-M
42, avenue de Champagne
51200 Épernay
03 26 53 33 20
Production: 2,500,000
Paul-François Vranken, an ambitious businessman from Belgium, owns one of Champagne's most powerful groups. In 1976 he formed Vranken-Lafitte and today owns Demoiselle, Charles Lafitte, Sacotte, Heidsieck, Barancourt, Germain, and Charbaut. Both Demoiselle and Charles Lafitte use a great number of grapes from Aube and Sézanne, but in Demoiselle you will also find some Chardonnay from Avize and Cramant. The company's headquarters in Épernay look more like an advertising agency than a Champagne house. There is no doubt that Monsieur Vranken is more interested in quantity than quality, even though they sometimes go hand in hand. Thanks to the extremely skilful enologist Dominique Pichart, who creates all the *cuvées*, all the wines are well made. Demoiselle has improved considerably recently, as Vranken puts his best Pinot Noir into Heidsieck and the best Chardonnay into Demoiselle. However, one drawback is the firm's confusing attempt to get their nonvintage Champagne to look like a *cuvée de prestige*.
- DEMOISELLE BRUT "TÊTE DE CUVÉE"   74
  (15% PN, 85% CH)
- DEMOISELLE GRANDE CUVÉE   69
  (30% PN, 70% CH)
- DEMOISELLE ROSÉ   40
  (15% PN, 85% CH)
- 1996 DEMOISELLE   83, SEP 2003 (85)
  (30% PN, 70% CH)
  Made in a clear prestige bottle with an appetizing appearance. Toasted, almost slightly coarse burned smell. Citrus-dominated keynote with smoky, slightly hard elements. Medium-bodied, supple resonance.
- 1990 DEMOISELLE   86, SEP 2003 (88)
  (30% PN, 70% CH)
  A beautiful bouquet of summer flowers, seasoned with vanilla and nut toffee. A refreshing, floral, fairly sweet, and easily drunk Champagne with a smiling, sunny warmth.
- 1979 DEMOISELLE   89, JAN 2003 (89)
  (20% PN, 80% CH)
  Perfectly brilliant light color. Big scent of hard peppermint candy, dark chocolate, vanilla, coconut, and sweet toffees. Possibly a trifle too sweet and ingratiating. On the other hand, enormously enjoyable with its delicious, Comtes-like buttery taste. Aftertaste of saffron and vanilla.
- DEMOISELLE CUVÉE 21   83, JAN 2004 (86)
  (20% PN, 80% CH)
  Summery, charming; a Champagne to sip under the arbor. Buttery, mellow, and easily drunk, with a modern touch. Clean and proper, albeit a little bit neutral.

DENOIS, ALFRED R-M
151, rue Henri Martin
51480 Cumières
03 26 55 55 63
Production: 40,000
A grower with a good reputation, even outside of Champagne. The firm was established in 1967 by Alfred Denois and is run today by Agnes Francis.
- DENOIS CARTE BLANCHE   75
  (25% PN, 50% PM, 25% CH)
- DENOIS CRÉMANT ROSÉ   75
  (50% PN, 25% PM, 25% CH)

DERVIN, MICHEL N-M
51480 Cuchery
A producer of Champagnes reminiscent of the big commercial houses.
- MICHEL DERVIN BRUT   60
- MICHEL DERVIN ROSÉ   43

DESAUTELS-ROINARD R-M
1, rue de Mesnil
51190 Oger
03 26 57 53 75
Production: 30,000
A small grower that consistently declines to answer my requests for information.
- DESHAUTELS-ROINARD RÉSERVE   35
  (100% CH)
- DESHAUTELS-ROINARD CUVÉE PRESTIGE   60
  (100% CH)

DESBORDES-AMIAUD R-M
2, rue de Villers aux Noeuds
51500 Écueil
03 26 49 77 58
Production: 60,000
Madame Christine Desbordes runs the firm together with her daughter Elodie. They have nine hectares in Écueil and the surrounding area.
- 1986 DESBORDES-AMIAUD   80, FEB 1999 (80)
  (60% PN, 40% CH)
  The nose is truly pleasant and flattering. One finds here a distinct note of orange chocolate blanketed in a honey aroma. The taste is as round and soft as a down pillow, but simple and notably short.

DESMOULINS, A. N-M
44, avenue Foch
51201 Épernay
03 26 54 24 24
Production: 95,000
Founded in 1908 by Albert Desmoulins and still a family business. Almost all wines are sold via mail order.
- DESMOULINS ROSÉ   65
  (100% PN)
- 1988 DESMOULINS   76, MAY 1997 (81)
  (100% CH)
  Unexpectedly vinous and powerful for a Blanc de Blancs. The fruity nose is quite bushy; the flavor is focused but one-dimensional.

DETHUNE, PAUL *** R-M

2, rue du Moulin
51150 Ambonnay
03 26 57 01 88
Production: 30,000

This Ambonnay domain is among the most beautiful and well looked-after in the whole of Champagne. Every flower in the garden is perfectly pruned and immaculate. The freshly polished façade of the house is half-covered by a gorgeous ivy, which stylishly follows the changing colors of the seasons. Inside, in the tasting room, everything is just as perfectly handled. It's a pleasure to sit in front of the fireplace with the shy Madame Dethune, who makes the wines now. That the excellent care that goes into the property is the work of a woman is perhaps no surprise, although when it comes to the wines I'm less overwhelmed. Dethune is the only producer in Ambonnay to ferment and store their wines in oak barrels, but I managed to detect oak tones only in the *cuvée de prestige*. The wines are often dry and restrained and lack that dimension that the cask should have given them.

- PAUL DETHUNE BRUT   60
  (100% PN)
- PAUL DETHUNE ROSÉ   50
  (100% PN)
- 1997 PAUL DETHUNE   79, JAN 2002 (84)
  (50% PN, 50% CH)
  Youthful Champagne with gamy notes and elastic fruit. I have a feeling that the wine is going to mature relatively quickly and suddenly. Notes of almond, honey, and toffee under the surface.
- 1990 PAUL DETHUNE   85, OCT 1997 (90)
  (50% PN, 50% CH)
  Lovely nose of vanilla, butterscotch, and hazelnut. Marvelous, fat texture on the palate with a sweet, mature taste of honey.
- PRINCESSE DETHUNE   87
  (100% PN)
  Only after twenty minutes in the glass does a hint of oak appear, in the guise of a weak nutty tone. The wine has astounding lightness and elegance, and those who guess at a Blanc de Blancs in a blind tasting need feel no shame. Worth storing for decades.

DEUTZ **** N-M

16, rue Jeanson
51160 Aÿ
03 26 56 94 00
Production: 1,000,000

In 1838 two Germans, William Deutz and Pierre Glederman, founded this distinguished firm in Aÿ. Deutz was hit hard during the Champagne Uprising of 1911. The house has been run since the 1970s by André Lallier, who has made large investments in other wine districts. Notable among these properties are Delas in the Rhône Valley, Maison Deutz in California, as well as another site producing sparkling wine in the Loire Valley. In 1993, Louis Roederer gained a majority stockholding in Deutz. Nowadays the firm is ably run by the very likeable Fabrice Rosset. The winemaker is the extremely keen Odilon de Varine. Seventy-five percent of the grapes are bought from *grand cru* and *premier cru* villages. Deutz themselves own land in five villages.

       The property is among the most beautiful in Champagne, and even the wines are very distinguished. The style is laid-back, elegant, and sophisticated, with a medium body, crystal-clear fruit, and an exemplary mousse. All the wines are good, but the Cuvée William Deutz Rosé is something special. Recently Deutz launched *Amour de Deutz*, a new ultra-sophisticated prestige Champagne. It has sold like hot cakes since Madonna took a liking to it—they say that there is always a chilled bottle ready wherever she goes. Unfortunately she seems to like candy just as much; according to reports when she was last in Stockholm, she happily consumes it together with Champagne.

- DEUTZ BRUT CLASSIC   80
  (38% PN, 32% PM, 30% CH)
  The Champagne is always of a high quality, but has previously been sold too early. If you put the wine aside for a few years in the cellar, a fine, bready note will develop, which will tone down the exaggerated apple-like fruit. I tasted a couple of bottles at the beginning of 2001 that already had a classic maturity. Very good, exuberant, and complex at the moment. I hope this tendency continues.
- DEUTZ DEMI-SEC   52
  (38% PN, 32% PM, 30% CH)
- 1996 DEUTZ   86, JAN 2004 (90)
  (60% PN, 10% PM, 30% CH)
  Fine structure and powerful acidity. House-typical clarity and crispy apple aroma cuts like a knife through the medium-bodied wine. The other aromas are many but discreet—among them biscuits, dough, vanilla, and seaside notes. It is exactly these seaside notes, combined with high acidity, that make this wine a perfect partner for sushi.
- 1995 DEUTZ   85, SEP 2003 (88)
  (60% PN, 10% PM, 30% CH)
  It feels like Deutz vintage wine has finally found its true self. Classic, irresistible style, without forgetting its past. Everything is in its place in a totally satisfying way. Mature Pinot Noir and sublime, crispy fruit in lovely harmony. Somewhat less impressive when last tasted.
- 1993 DEUTZ   80, JAN 2002 (86)
  (60% PN, 10% PM, 30% CH)
  Well-made Champagne, cast in the same mold as the reliable and balanced nonvintage Champagne Classic, in a somewhat embellished dressing. Attractively formed, with primarily bready tones around a stable backbone, as well as soft, voluptuous tastes of dried fruit.
- 1990 DEUTZ   83, JUL 1997 (88)
  (40% PN, 30% PM, 30% CH)
  Incredibly fruity and rich, with a relaxed charm so typical of this house. Good balance and harmony.
- 1988 DEUTZ   77, FEB 1995 (86)
  (45% PN, 20% PM, 35% CH)
  A wine in the laid-back, polished Deutz style. Young and soft at the same time.
- 1985 DEUTZ   83, JUL 1991 (86)
  (40% PN, 25% PM, 35% CH)
  This chocolaty Champagne has developed early, with a broad, ripe fruit in the flavor. Only the length will be improved by a few years in the cellar.
- 1982 DEUTZ   86, SEP 2001 (86)
  (40% PN, 25% PM, 35% CH)
  A relative disappointment, where the only positive tones were those of freshly baked bread. Still quite youthful.
- 1976 DEUTZ   87, MAR 1999 (88)
  (50% PN, 10% PM, 40% CH)

Disgorged in September 1998. Spunky, youthful, and a bit neutral. The aftertaste is somewhat demanding, with its bitterness and alcohol-rich power.

- 1975 DEUTZ   88, JAN 2003 (88)

(40% PN, 25% PM, 35% CH)

Very fresh and well preserved, but not very unusual, with slightly exaggerated Pinot Meunier aroma and a short aftertaste. Considerably more austere in magnum.

- 1973 DEUTZ   86, JAN 2000 (86)

(40% PN, 25% PM, 35% CH)

It might as well be said. Since Cuvée William and the ultra-sophisticated Blanc de Blancs turned up, Deutz's regular vintage wine has had difficulty impressing me. Actually, I am often disturbed by the high proportion of Pinot Meunier in these wines. This, in certain cases, gives a slightly mushy impression. I am sorry to sound so negative—I have such high expectations of everything done by this brilliant house.

- 1970 DEUTZ   82, DEC 2002 (82)

(40% PN, 25% PM, 35% CH)

Only tasted in a half bottle, which is exceedingly risky with this mature vintage. Big nose of dark chocolate and brown sugar. Unfortunately, rather sleepy, flat taste. Has seen its best days.

- 1966 DEUTZ   93, AUG 2002 (93)

(50% PN, 20% PM, 30% CH)

I am extremely impressed, despite having only tasted this wine in a half bottle. Chocolaty and rich, with a compact nuttiness and an undertone of mushroom. Perfect with duck liver, and most likely even better in magnum.

- 1953 DEUTZ

(50% PN, 20% PM, 30% CH)

- 1996 DEUTZ BLANC DE BLANCS   88, MAR 2004 (93)

(100% CH)

An unexpectedly fat and approachable Champagne with big, soft fruit and impressive taste-layers. Every now and then you come across a '96 that seizes upon the high sugar content instead of the usual biting acidity. This wine is one of the best examples of this phenomenon. One of the foremost vintages yet of this ever-stylish wine. Certain bottles have, on the other hand, been less mature, and the acidity has been too intrusive and intense.

- 1995 DEUTZ BLANC DE BLANCS   90, MAY 2003 (93)

(100% CH)

A wonderfully appealing wine, already thoroughly endowed with an elegant note of butterscotch. Perfect Chardonnay with white flowers, hawthorns, citrus, and a light note of hazelnut. Soft, harmonious summer fizz.

- 1993 DEUTZ BLANC DE BLANCS   85, JAN 2004 (89)

(100% CH)

Ultra-elegant with a clean and refreshing mineral taste. The vintage's lack of weight is compensated for by its life-preserving acidity. I appreciate that the wine must be at least fifteen years old before it comes close to its full potential.

- 1990 DEUTZ BLANC DE BLANCS   89, FEB 2003 (91)

(100% CH)

Deutz Blanc de Blancs reminds me of Pol Roger's Chardonnay wine. Both are ultra-sophisticated and aristocratic, but lack that character that a really great wine needs. The '90 is typical of its vintage, with a tight structure and a collected inner power.

- 1989 DEUTZ BLANC DE BLANCS   92, FEB 2003 (92)

(100% CH)

For once this feels like a grower's Champagne of the highest class from Le Mesnil. The wine is clearly influenced by the village's *terroir* character, with smoky and mineral-rich undertones and a fat, concentrated, acidic flavor, which is an advantage in my view. Aging a bit too fast.

- 1988 DEUTZ BLANC DE BLANCS   88, DEC 2002 (92)

(100% CH)

Light green/yellow color and fine, microscopic mousse. A textbook Blanc de Blancs with superb finesse and overflowing with young acidity. A delicate and faintly toasty tone complements the floweriness. Pure, dry, and long.

- 1985 DEUTZ BLANC DE BLANCS   93, JAN 2003 (94)

(100% CH)

When I first encountered this wine in 1990, I was incredibly impressed by its abundance of finesse. Only the future can tell whether it is presently in a slightly weaker phase, or should have been enjoyed when very young. Fortunately, it has become lovely with aging.

- 1982 DEUTZ BLANC DE BLANCS   93, MAR 2003 (93)

(100% CH)

Tranquil Blanc de Blancs with an underlying sweet, evolved fruit. Deutz Blanc de Blancs is always easily placed in blind tastings: the vintage character plays a subordinate roll to the dominant house-style. Incredibly creamy and delicious in a magnum.

- 1979 DEUTZ BLANC DE BLANCS   90, FEB 2003 (90)

(100% CH)

Featherlight Champagne with great bottle variation. I like certain really young bottles better when the refinement and stony keynote appear more clearly.

- 1975 DEUTZ BLANC DE BLANCS   92, JAN 1996 (92)

(100% CH)

Lighter and weaker in the nose than expected. However, all is forgiven when the citrus-crispy flavor is as delicate and never-ending as it is here.

- 1973 DEUTZ BLANC DE BLANCS   88, AUG 2000 (88)

(100% CH)

Tighter and more stringent than most '73s. More strongly influenced by the house-style, with its low dosage and pronounced mineral character. Somewhat too short and one-dimensionally mature to excite my spoiled palate.

- 1993 DEUTZ DEMI-SEC   70, MAY 1999 (70)

(60% PN, 40% CH)

- 1990 DEUTZ DEMI-SEC   78, NOV 2003 (79)

(40% PN, 30% PM, 30% CH)

- 1996 DEUTZ ROSÉ   84, MAY 2003 (91)

(100% PN)

This wine was completely voted down at two comprehensive rosé tastings that took place during "Champagne Days" in Gothenburg and Stockholm in May 2001. The wine is simply far too young still. However, I am convinced that the fruit is sufficiently rich to pad out today's extremely tough acidity in the future.

- 1993 DEUTZ ROSÉ   85, MAY 1999 (89)

(100% PN)

This wine has the big, sumptuous fruit of ripe Pinot Noir. It is difficult to predict exactly how it will develop, but it is fantastically rich, almost juice-like in its sweet, concentrated, soft, strawberry-exuding style.

- 1990 DEUTZ ROSÉ   83, SEP 1997 (90)

(100% PN)

Contains 14 percent red wine from Bouzy. A smooth nose of cream and butterscotch. Softly delicate, laid-back, rich, and fruity flavor of good length.

• 1988 DEUTZ ROSÉ   82, MAR 1995 (87)
(100% PN)
The firm has a well-deserved reputation for its rosé Champagnes. The '88 has a lovely Pinot character and a fresh, bubbling liveliness.

• 1985 DEUTZ ROSÉ   89, MAR 2001 (90)
(80% PN, 20% CH)
A pale orange color and a delicate, multifaceted nose containing elements of cream. The palate is lined with delicate, smooth sensations. Creamy, elegant, and developed.

• 1981 DEUTZ ROSÉ   88, FEB 1997 (88)
(100% PN)
Big, bold, and elegant all at the same time, with a lightness that is typical of this vintage. The aromatic spectrum includes tones of orange, lemon, and Aÿ Pinot.

• 1975 DEUTZ ROSÉ   89, AUG 1996 (89)
(80% PN, 20% CH)
Meaty and mature, with a smoky nose that reminds one of an old-fashioned butcher's shop. A sweet, mature fruit flavor that edges toward plums and sun-ripened tomatoes. Good, with plenty of personality.

• 1997 AMOUR DE DEUTZ   85, NOV 2003 (91)
(100% CH)
This is one of the least evolved '97s I have ever encountered. An unruly acidity makes me suspect that parts of the wine have not gone through malolactic fermentation. The winemaker Odilon has, at all costs, tried to avoid the vintage's flaccid, good-natured, and unstructured character. The nose consists of creamy, almost clinically mellow elements of newly washed sheets, which become more apparent the longer the wine is aired. Otherwise, this young greenish-yellow wine is dominated by fruity aromas. Most obvious are cherimoya, papaya, banana, and grapefruit. Incredibly acidic finish, just like a great '96.

• 1996 CUVÉE WILLIAM DEUTZ   89, DEC 2003 (94)
(55% PN, 10% PM, 35% CH)
Already seductively creamy and deep, with delightful notes from Aÿ that with time will become more gamy and sexy. Long, creamy, uniform taste. The wine benefits from airing and the last glass is—at the moment—much better than the first. During the autumn of 2003, the fruit of this high-class Pinot Noir began to make itself known, like a rumbling thunderstorm in the distance.

• 1995 AMOUR DE DEUTZ   92, MAR 2003 (95)
(100% CH)
For the time being less developed than the usual Blanc de Blancs, with a shy, delicate, clear bouquet. The wine is most impressive in the mouth, with its fantastic concentration of grapes from old vines. I think that all but the most hard-core connoisseurs will be disappointed today, but be patient and let the aromas lift the heavy lid that covers the surface. This will happen, but when?

• 1995 CUVÉE WILLIAM DEUTZ   92, NOV 2003 (94)
(55% PN, 10% PM, 35% CH)
For a long time, a very discreet and floral version of this famous wine. The Champagne felt enticingly light and citrus-crispy, completely devoid of the big kettledrums from Aÿ. The purebred fruit that is compressed by the youthful acidity has just begun to show its muscle. An elegant, creamy, and long-lived Champagne made by the clever Odilon.

• 1993 AMOUR DE DEUTZ   87, JAN 2003 (92)
(100% CH)
The vineyards used are the same as for the usual Blanc de Blancs: 60 percent Mesnil, 35 percent Avize, and 5 percent Villers-Marmery. It is primarily the choice of individual grapes from old vines that justifies the high price. Despite high acidity there is a grand, concentrated creaminess that can only come from old vines or from a truly great year, something that 1993 hardly was. Only 15,000 bottles were produced of this greenish-yellow wine with its sparkling, bubbly mousse. The nose is very distinct: white flowers, lime, and a nascent nuttiness. Super-refreshing and creamy, with elegant fruit and streaks of vanilla.

• 1990 CUVÉE WILLIAM DEUTZ   94, JAN 2004 (94)
(55% PN, 10% PM, 35% CH)
William Deutz is a Champagne that impresses me more and more. The '90 combines a fabulously elegant lime note with a deep, chocolaty Pinot aroma. This is the height of elegance among Pinot-dominated Champagnes, even though the nose is rather bound. An evolved bouquet of mint-chocolate appeared in 2003.

• 1988 CUVÉE WILLIAM DEUTZ   93, NOV 2003 (95)
(50% PN, 10% PM, 40% CH)
A wonderfully balanced Champagne that makes me sing the praises of this blend. Slender Aÿ Pinot that is uplifted by a citrus-fresh, mineral-rich Chardonnay finish. Takes a long time in the glass to show its best sides, and several years of extra aging are recommended.

• 1985 CUVÉE WILLIAM DEUTZ   91, NOV 2001 (93)
(62% PN, 8% PM, 30% CH)
Brilliant appearance, classical Champagne nose and flavor, but somewhat impersonal in its medium-bodied, polished style.

• 1982 CUVÉE WILLIAM DEUTZ   86, AUG 1993 (90)
(62% PN, 8% PM, 30% CH)
Copper-colored, clear, and brightly shining with a stylish cordon. A delicate, mineral-rich nose with faint ripe tones. Medium-bodied, elegant flavor of young Pinot. A touch short.

• 1979 CUVÉE WILLIAM DEUTZ   90, MAR 2003 (90)
(62% PN, 8% PM, 30% CH)
Delightfully rich vanilla aroma that dominates the entire wine. Today the wine is rather oxidative, with notes of raisin, mushroom, and leather in best Aÿ style.

• 1976 CUVÉE GEORGES MATHIEU   90, JUL 1995 (90)
(60% PN, 15% PM, 25% CH)
The wine avoids the fatness of the vintage and is instead stylish and pure. However, personality and length are missing here.

• 1975 CUVÉE WILLIAM DEUTZ   94, JUN 1998 (94)
(60% PN, 10% PM, 30% CH)
More developed than most other '75s, but still showing superbly high quality. The wine is very similar to Bollinger, with its nutty richness and mushroom aromas. Aÿ Pinot also provides a concentrated, impressive aftertaste.

• 1975 DEUTZ Aÿ   95, NOV 2001 (96)
(100% PN)
"Too good to be sold!" claims Deutz's winemaker. The most striking thing is that this wine is so incredibly elegant for a Pinot Noir. There is a superb multifaceted and toasty nose, with strong acidity and a light, buttery, Chardonnay-like character. A masterwork that reflects Deutz more than Aÿ.

- 1973 CUVÉE WILLIAM DEUTZ   90, SEP 1996 (>)
(60% PN, 10% PM, 30% CH)

Definitely a high-flier with an early peak. When I tasted the Champagne it was beginning to go downhill, but still achieved an impressive ninety points. Balance, charm, and chocolate aromas still delightful.

- 1971 CUVÉE WILLIAM DEUTZ   94, FEB 1999 (94)
(62% PN, 8% PM, 30% CH)

Several years ago I condemned this quickly aging wine. Now I know that it was the aging and not the wine that was the problem. Today, properly aged bottles are extremely clean and sublime, with a fine note of vanilla.

- 1961 CUVÉE WILLIAM DEUTZ   94, OCT 1997 (94)
(60% PN, 10% PM, 30% CH)

Old-fashioned, oaky, and heavy. A food Champagne that was perfectly suited to duck liver. Apparently the first vintages of this *cuvée de prestige* were made in a more full-bodied style than today's.

- 1996 CUVÉE WILLIAM DEUTZ ROSÉ   93, DEC 2003 (96)
(75% PN, 25% CH)

Many of us have waited for a new vintage of this favorite wine. When it finally arrived, the Champagne fulfilled all our expectations. The color is very light, with salmon-pink and yellowish hints. The nose is tight and impressive, with layers of toffee, leather, honey, lilies, white chocolate, and exotic fruit. The taste is excellent: naturally sweet, creamy, and possessing a caressing structure. The length is impressive—and underneath all this we know that the acidity is present, keeping the wine alive for a long time to come.

- 1990 CUVÉE WILLIAM DEUTZ ROSÉ   93, NOV 2001 (96)
(75% PN, 25% CH)

A colossal concentrated nectar of the highest class. Possessed of an outstanding softness and an exotic fruit reminiscent of sweet pears and passion fruit. Clear similarities with the rich '89 Cristal Rose. Surprisingly enough, William Deutz is even a bit lighter in color.

- 1988 CUVÉE WILLIAM DEUTZ ROSÉ   97, MAR 2004 (97)
(100% PN)

Once again, this wine takes its place among the truly greats. What latitude, depth, and elegance! The silkiness is incredible and caresses the tongue in the most delightful way. The fruit explosion is beautiful and intense, with deep red floral notes, like a Richebourg from DRC. All along, the vintage's lovely, nutty keynote is present, like an orchestra of string instruments in the background.

- 1985 CUVÉE WILLIAM DEUTZ ROSÉ   94, JUN 1999 (97)
(100% PN)

This prestige rosé is without doubt the crown jewel of Deutz's assortment. Both the '82 and the '85 are magnificent romantic wines that make me cry with happiness. The '85 doesn't really have the same concentration as the '82, but it has more restrained acidity. The nose is lush, with a gorgeous tone of Aÿ Pinot. Leather, cheese, and chocolate are aromas that give the strawberry tone greater nuances, and the flavor is incredibly long.

- 1982 CUVÉE WILLIAM DEUTZ ROSÉ   96, MAY 1998 (96)
(100% PN)

Absolutely one of the best rosé Champagnes I've ever drunk. Only *grand cru* grapes have been used, with Aÿ dominant. Deep red color, tremendously broad nose of ripe berries, leather, and

nougat. The flavor is fat and concentrated and contains an explosion of sweet fruits. Extremely well balanced.

- DEUTZ ANNIVERSAIRE   90, MAY 2001 (90)
(70% PN, 10% PM, 20% CH)

Jubilee *cuvée* with wine from 1979, 1981, and 1982. Delicate and refined Champagne with a taste of lemon licorice. Initially, however, a great disappointment considering the high price. Today though, ten years later, the fresh finesse has combined with deep mature notes of chocolate and honey.

DEVAUX, A. C-M

Domaine de Villeneuve
10110 Bar-sur-Seine
03 25 38 30 65
Production: 3,500,000

The whole thing started in 1967 when the area's eleven cooperatives merged, and now Devaux has 800 member-growers who together control 1,400 hectares in Côte des Bar. This is now the leading company in the Aube district. The winemaker is Claude Thibault, and everything is impeccably run in this model cooperative. The modern facilities where they make the wine are clinically clean, the production methods are very serious, with a large amount of reserve wines stored in large oak barrels *à la* Roederer. All the wines are well stored and handled in a traditional manner, and the firm will surely improve as they gain access to more grapes from Côte des Blancs. My only complaint is the high prices.

- DEVAUX CUVÉE D   73
(66% PN, 34% CH)
- DEVAUX GRANDE RÉSERVE   74
(75% PN, 25% CH)
- DEVAUX BLANC DE NOIRS   78
(100% PN)
- DEVAUX ROSÉ   61
(75% PN, 25% CH)
- 1990 DEVAUX   78, NOV 2001 (78)
(100% CH)
- 1990 DISTINCTION   85, MAR 2000 (85)
(50% PN, 50% CH)

Obvious notes of wood and vanilla. Full-bodied and complex, but marks lowered by a somewhat coarse mousse.

- 1988 DISTINCTION   84, MAR 2003 (84)
(50% PN, 50% CH)

Vanilla and oak again as well as a pleasant toasted biscuit-like note in the nose. The truth be told, I prefer the scent of the '88 to the '90, but the taste is not as long or complex.

- 1990 DISTINCTION ROSÉ   84, MAR 2002 (85)
(60% PN, 40% CH)

Grand, heavy bouquet of windfall fruit and butter. Initially fat with a radiantly fresh, fruity finish. Aube's relative clumsiness is masterfully erased here.

- 1988 DISTINCTION ROSÉ   87, MAR 2000 (87)
(60% PN, 40% CH)

A masterful wine from the big cooperative in Aube. Handsome, mature color bordering on orange. Yummy strawberry caramel scent that lapses into chocolate when in the glass. Elegant and creamy taste with minimal bubbles and grand house-style leaning toward Pol Roger.

DEVAVRY, BERTRAND R-M

43, rue Pasteur
51160 Champillon
03 26 59 46 21
Production: 80,000
Same firm as Méa-Devavry, which is the baby of Jean-Louip
Devavry's wife. The property has nine hectares in total.

- BERTRAND DEVAVRY BRUT   67
  (20% PN, 20% PM, 60% CH)

DIEBOLT-VALLOIS**** R-M

84, rue Neuve
51530 Cramant
03 26 57 54 92
Production: 70,000
Jacques Diebolt and his family are some of the nicest people I've
met in Champagne, and the fact that they produce Chardonnay
wines of world class doesn't hurt either. Several producers in the
village make supremely enjoyable Champagnes, but personally I
think Diebolt gives the *cru* another dimension, especially with
those wines that haven't gone through malolactic fermentation, and
which were harvested from the sixty-five-year-old vines in Les
Pimonts or Les Buzons. There is a thought-provoking depth
reminiscent of Le Mesnil, combined with Cramant's creamy
structure. Unfortunately, the demand for Diebolt's wines is so great
that they are forced to sell the Champagne far too early. Diebolt
was an unknown name before the firm was awarded Champagne
Producer of the Year in 1992 by the magazine *Gault Millau*, but
since then the connoisseurs of the world have fought over their
bottles. Jacques's most recent inventions are Fleur de Passion from
1995 and 1996, two of the foremost young Champagnes I have
tasted, and the '53 and '61 are already legendary. Terribly close to
five stars because everything Diebolt does is perfect in its way.

- DIEBOLT BLANC DE BLANCS   78
  (100% CH)
- 1996 DIEBOLT   84, MAY 2002 (90)
  (100% CH)
  This one is truly snatched from the cradle, but it will change
  enormously with a few years of aging. How quickly that will take
  place is, however, difficult to predict.
- 1995 DIEBOLT   85, MAY 2001 (91)
  (100% CH)
  Before one has tasted Diebolt's Fleur de Passion, this feels like an
  unbeatable classic Chardonnay. The aromas are unusually round
  and exotically developed, coupled with a refreshingly bracing,
  clean-mountain-stream acidity.
- 1993/1992 DIEBOLT   84, MAR 2000 (89)
  (100% CH)
  Cramant and Cuis. Surprisingly grand wine with more vigor and
  less elegance than expected. Fatty fruit and a uniformly long,
  vinous taste.
- 1990 DIEBOLT   93, DEC 2003 (93)
  (100% CH)
  It's not far to Perrier-Jouët's best plots in Cramant. The
  Champagne is very much like Belle Époque, with its
  characteristic vanilla and biscuit notes. The wine's fruit leans
  toward peach, mandarin, and mango. The concentration is
  somewhat less than a prestige wine, but the aromas are extremely
  charming, with a clear note of saffron.

- 1989 DIEBOLT   91, JAN 2003 (93)
  (100% CH)
  Harvested from the old vines and vinified without malolactic
  fermentation. An incredibly fine wine reminiscent of a few of the
  best '85s from Le Mesnil. The nose is multifaceted and furtive.
  Petroleum, toasted coffee, walnut, and pure mineral notes. A
  brilliant Blanc de Blancs with an enormous attack. I must admit,
  though, that I've become less impressed with this wine through
  the years.
- 1988 DIEBOLT   83, MAY 1994 (90)
  (100% CH)
  Pure, fine nose of white flowers, cherries, Williams pears, and
  almonds. Once again, similar to Le Mesnil with its deep,
  authoritative style. Undeveloped, pure, and vigorous flavor. We'll
  meet again sometime this century.
- 1985 DIEBOLT   93, DEC 2003 (93)
  (100% CH)
  A *grand cru* Blanc de Blancs from 1985 always provides a
  wonderful experience, with its toasty aromas and clear, brioche-
  like subtleties. Diebolt have made a classic '85.
- 1985 DIEBOLT CUIS   90, DEC 2003 (91)
  (100% CH)
  Since Jacques Diebolt has bought up the entire family stock of
  Guy Vallois's older undisgorged vintages, he has the right to label
  them Diebolt-Vallois. This wine is actually made by Vallois and
  comes from Cuis. The difference is that Jacques has disgorged the
  bottles and added a small dosage of three grams of sugar. For the
  time being, the wine is almost identical, with the same attributes
  of cream and passion fruit as the aromatic guiding stars. The
  aftertaste of this deep and elegant Champagne exudes summery
  feelings of strawberry and whipped cream.
- 1983 DIEBOLT   94, DEC 2000 (94)
  (100% CH)
  What a winner! A wine with equal parts Cuis and Cramant.
  Completely wonderful breakfast Champagne that needs no coffee
  or toast and lemon marmalade. All of these are present, in excess,
  in this magnificent Champagne. Both Jacques Diebolt and I were
  surprised by the high acidity and pure elegance this wine
  conveys.
- 1982 DIEBOLT   92, DEC 2003 (92)
  (100% CH)
  The '82 is richer and bushier than the balanced '85. I enjoyed
  this freshly disgorged bottle tremendously in the company of the
  Diebolt family.
- 1982 DIEBOLT CUIS   80, DEC 2003 (80)
  (100% CH)
  The least exciting of the wines purchased from their relative, Guy
  Vallois in Cuis. Good color, acidity, structure, and mousse, but
  the praise stops there. Oxidative aromas of malt, tea, licorice,
  earth, and raisins. It must be said that many, including Jacques
  Diebolt, are considerably more captivated than I am by this wine.
- 1979 DIEBOLT CUIS   90, DEC 2003 (90)
  (100% CH)
  One of the vintages that Jacques has bought from Guy Vallois—
  in other words, a pure Cuis disgorged by Diebolt during 2003
  and dosed with three grams of sugar. Up until now, the wine has
  behaved completely differently on the occasions I have tasted it.
  The first time, elegance and floweriness were the focus and the
  points were way over 90. The second time, the Champagne was

unattractive and slightly clumsy, with certain coarse mature notes, despite a medium-deep color and good mousse. The trilogy of '85, '79, and '76 is fascinating because the wines are still undisgorged and they truly allow the taster to see how individual bottles develop after this much contact with the yeast residue.

- 1976 DIEBOLT CUIS   93, DEC 2003 (93)
(100% CH)
This is a great wine that comes from Guy Vallois in Cuis, but which has been disgorged and dosed by Jacques Diebolt and thus carries his name—that's how strange the laws in Champagne are. The wine is deliciously butterscotchy and exotically rich with tons of browned butter and créme-brûlée tones. Big and impressive, as you would expect from this warm year.

- 1973 DIEBOLT   92, JUN 2001 (93)
(100% CH)
One of the last three bottles from the cellar of the Diebolt family. Slight caramel tones are found in this fine and buttery Blanc de Blancs.

- 1973 DIEBOLT CUIS   94, DEC 2003 (94)
(100% CH)
What depth! A pure Cuis wine from Guy Vallois, disgorged and dosed by Diebolt. Unfortunately the number of bottles left is limited. But those who get to taste this rare wine will have a powerful experience—notes of forest mushrooms, mocha, cacao, nuts, and tart fruit acting in perfect harmony. The wine has a rare attack and explosive intensity, actually a little reminiscent of Diebolt's really old wines from '61 and '53.

- 1961 DIEBOLT   97, DEC 2003 (97)
(100% CH)
I've been present several times when a producer has opened a new bottle of the same vintage because he wasn't satisfied with the first. Jacques, on the other hand, is the only one I know who opens a new bottle in order to show how bad the wine can be! At its best the '61 has a fantastic, almost Pinot-like nose of truffles, decaying autumn leaves, barrels, and boiled vegetables, while the other he opened was more like mushroom soup. The structure was impressive in both, however.

- 1953 DIEBOLT   97, JUN 2003 (97)
(100% CH)
One of the best Champagnes I have tasted. Drunk newly disgorged, undosed, in Diebolt's cellar. The wine was made in oak barrels without malolactic fermentation. The color was brilliantly, beautifully golden. The bubbles continued to wind their way up the glass two hours after the wine was poured. The nose was given the maximum numbers of points! The entire wine was like a grand symphony by Sibelius—full of sadness, joy, nature, and romance. The freshness and playful ease, combined with the wine's length, were exceptional, but the nose's complexity was probably the most impressive part of the Champagne: coffee, treacle, bergamot oil, brioche, walnuts, limes, and passion fruit were the clearest aromas. A disappointment at the Millennium Tasting. Large bottle variation.

- DIEBOLT PRESTIGE WEDDING CUVÉE   88, MAY 2001 (94)
(100% CH)
This wine was made for the Diebolt son's future wedding from the vintages of 1982, 1983, 1985, and 1986. I hope he waits a while yet before tying the knot, so that the delightful but undeveloped wine has time to show off its best side. However, my judgment is only of interest to the Diebolt family themselves, as the 100 bottles produced will never go on sale.

- DIEBOLT PRESTIGE (90/91)   87, MAR 2000 (94)
(100% CH)
1990/91 buttery nose. Bitingly fresh, youthful, fruity acidity. Wait at least ten years before you take on this uncut diamond.

- 1990 DIEBOLT PRESTIGE   94, DEC 2003 (94)
(100% CH)
A pure '90 harvested from one location—Les Pietons—from sixty-five-year-old vines. Colossal concentration of amazingly sweet, saffron-scented fruit. Yellow plums are there to be found in both nose and flavor. This wine is partially vinified in oak barrels.

- 1999 DIEBOLT FLEUR DE PASSION   87, JUN 2003 (96)
(100% CH)
It is incredibly difficult to judge what will happen with this embryo. A somewhat piercing sulfuric tone meets the nose initially because the wine hasn't undergone malolactic fermentation. Big, round, exotic fruit, and eminent purity. Mineral finesse.

- 1998 DIEBOLT FLEUR DE PASSION   93, DEC 2003 (95)
(100% CH)
Surprising style that differs completely from other vintages of this wine. It is extremely easily drunk, even though it still has a few years before being released onto the market. Lightly roasted, smiling Dom Pérignon-ish flavor with a large dollop of passion fruit. Very good and charming.

- 1997 DIEBOLT FLEUR DE PASSION   90, JUN 2003 (94)
(100% CH)
Slightly greener nose than usual. Mild, harmonic palate that still feels a tad neutral. The weakest Passion yet. Nevertheless, a first-class, concentrated, and delightful wine.

- 1996 DIEBOLT FLEUR DE PASSION   92, APR 2004 (96)
(100% CH)
A wine that Jacques has made in his most passionate way. This is supreme Champagne with purity, oak aroma, and power. Which one is more supreme, the '95 or the'96, I leave for the future to decide. Today the oaky '95 is more impressive, but the elegance in this wine is difficult to beat.

- 1995 DIEBOLT FLEUR DE PASSION   93, DEC 2003 (95)
(100% CH)
A new super-wine is born. Jacques Diebolt has put his heart and soul into the 3,000 bottles that are sold under this label. The philosophy is to copy earlier generation's methods of craftsmanship: only the oldest vines, no malolactic fermentation, storage and fermentation in small oak barrels, lengthy maturation in the bottle. The result is astonishing. Vintages '95, '96, '97, and '98 are all exceptional wines, with a concentrated Chardonnay flavor that one only finds with Clos du Mesnil, Selosse "N" and a number of *grand cru* wines from Burgundy.

DOMI, PIERRE R-M

8, Grande Rue
51190 Grauves
03 26 59 71 03
Production: 80,000
Pierre Domi Champagne was established in the great year—for wine—of 1947. For half a century they have been making robust Blanc de Blancs from Grauves. Today the dosage is often a little too high. In the simplest wines there is also Pinot Meunier from the neighboring villages of Monthelon and Mancy.

- PIERRE DOMI TRADITION   65
(30% PM, 70% CH)

- PIERRE DOMI CUVÉE SPÉCIALE 84
  (100% CH)

This concentrated and honey-saturated prestige Champagne comes from a specific location on the steepest slope of Grauves. The sweet grapes come from fifty-year-old vines in a place called Le Rouvelles. This is always nonvintage Champagne that has a minimum of five years of cellar storage. My only objection to it is the unnecessarily high dosage.

- PIERRE DOMI EXTRA DRY 57
  (100% CH)

- PIERRE DOMI GRANDE RÉSERVE 65
  (40% PN, 60% CH)

- PIERRE DOMI BLANC DE BLANCS 73
  (100% CH)

- PIERRE DOMI DEMI-SEC 40
  (100% CH)

DOUQUET-JEANMAIRE R-M

44, chemin du Moulin
51130 Vertus
03 26 52 16 50
Production: 100,000

The same origins as Jeanmaire in Épernay. The grower owns thirteen hectares of Chardonnay in Vertus and has specialized in producing vintage wines during those years when no one else does. The older vintages remain in contact with the yeast for up to twenty years. This is an initiative worthy of praise, although the wines are more interesting as curios than a source of any great pleasure. The prices are reasonable, so if you see an older vintage, snap it up.

- DOUQUET-JEANMAIRE BLANC DE BLANCS 64
  (100% CH)

- 1989 DOUQUET-JEANMAIRE 81, NOV 1998 (82)
  (100% CH)

Unfortunately this grower is one of few that sells older Champagnes, even though these don't improve much in the process. This '89 is soft and creamy, but you should drink it within the next few years.

- 1982 DOUQUET-JEANMAIRE 81, DEC 1996 (81)
  (100% CH)

Dark, developed color, and a delightfully exotic nose. Sadly the aftertaste contains some oxidation tones.

- 1977 DOUQUET-JEANMAIRE 70, MAY 1994 (70)
  (100% CH)

- 1974 DOUQUET-JEANMAIRE 85, JAN 1993 (86)
  (100% CH)

Strong autolytic character, with hazelnut and wood aromas. The flavor is also surprisingly full of extracts and is concentrated. Vertus produced the best grapes in this mediocre year.

- 1970 DOUQUET-JEANMAIRE 65, APR 1994 (>)
  (100% CH)

DOYARD-MAHÉ R-M

Le Moulin d'Argensole
51130 Vertus
03 26 52 23 85
Production: 20,000

- DOYARD-MAHÉ CARTE D'OR 49
  (100% CH)

DOYARD, ROBERT R-M

61, avenue de Bammental
51130 Vertus
03 26 52 14 74
Production: 50,000

Yannick Doyard is the fourth generation after Maurice Doyard, who was one of the founders of the C.I.V.C. Doyard is one of the few who make a Vertus Rouge.

- ROBERT DOYARD EXTRA BRUT 72
  (100% CH)

- ROBERT DOYARD BLANC DE BLANCS 72
  (100% CH)

- ROBERT DOYARD DEMI-SEC 50
  (100% CH)

- ROBERT DOYARD CUVÉE VENDÉMIAIRE 84, SEP 2002 (87)
  (100% CH)

A real rarity, with wine from the vintages '93, '94, and '95 fermented in oak barrels. Fleshy and rich, with a nice smell of petroleum, diesel fumes, and the hard crust on newly baked white bread. Somewhat less finesse in the taste, but still a pleasant harmony between mineral, fruit, and barrel.

- 1996 ROBERT DOYARD OEIL DE PERDRIX 73, AUG 2003 (76)
  (67% PN, 33% CH)

- 1995 ROBERT DOYARD COLLECTION BLANC DE BLANCS
  (100% CH) 82, JUN 2002 (84)

Six thousand five hundred bottles produced. Only Chardonnay from the best plots in Côte des Blancs. A fourth of the wine is fermented in oak barrels. Both the nose and palate are fine and evolved, with a developed, round appearance. A little rustic, perhaps, but pleasant and juicy.

DRAPPIER N-M

Grande Rue
10200 Urville
03 25 27 40 15
Production: 600,000

One wonders if Drappier would have the same position today if President de Gaulle hadn't been enamored of Drappier Champagne. This quality-conscious firm was founded in 1808. Today, André Drappier maintains their fine reputation with good support from his enologist son Michel. Drappier extracts a surprisingly low yield from their forty hectares in Aube and seventeen in Marne. The firm cold-ferments the must in order to avoid secondary aromas from the fermentation process. They also add small amounts of sulfur to keep the wine as natural as possible.

In 1991 Drappier bought a cellar in Reims where their vintage and prestige *cuvées* are now stored. This investment might seem a little strange when they already have fantastic cellars from the 1100s, built by the Cistercians of Clairvaux Abbey. But the cellars in Urville are actually too warm. A specialty of Drappier's is the giant *primat* bottle (36 liters). Another specialty is the storage of old reserve wines with super dosage in big glass demijohns. Drappier's wines are very rich and well made. We can expect more positive surprises from Drappier with the experimental and knowledgeable Michel at the helm.

- DRAPPIER CARTE D'OR 57
  (90% PN, 5% PM, 5% CH)

- DRAPPIER BRUT NATURE 72
  (100% PN)

- DRAPPIER EXTRA BRUT   62
  (90% PN, 5% PM, 5% CH)
- DRAPPIER BLANC DE BLANCS   75
  (100% CH)
- ROSÉ VAL DES DEMOISELLES   50
  (100% PN)
- 1999 DRAPPIER EXCEPTION   79, OCT 2003 (84)
  (65% PN, 5% PM, 30% CH)

A round, rich Champagne that completely avoids Aube's usual clumsiness in its make-up. Lots of honey, a little almond, and nut-toffee tone. Pleasant and harmonious with fine, pure acidity.

- 1990 CHARLES DE GAULLE   75, MAR 2000 (76)
  (75% PN, 25% CH)
- 1990 DRAPPIER   80, MAR 2000 (82)
  (90% PN, 3% PM, 7% CH)

Despite the fact that the grapes come almost exclusively from Aube, there is a classic breadiness and cake-like autolytic bouquet. As so often happens, the taste does not really live up to the expectation that the bouquet promises. Good fruit, but rather short.

- 1983 DRAPPIER   83, NOV 1999 (83)
  (90% PN, 3% PM, 7% CH)

Vigorous, fresh, and thirst quenching, with a green, unexpectedly young color, and a mellow, creamy mousse. Well made and approachable to the highest possible degree.

- 1979 DRAPPIER   83, MAY 2001 (83)
  (90% PN, 3% PM, 7% CH)

Totally evolved and enjoyable with great depth of fruit and mellowness. Somewhat rounder than the similar '78 and characterized, as usual, by dried fruits.

- 1978 DRAPPIER   82, NOV 2000 (82)
  (90% PN, 3% PM, 7% CH)

Refreshing and harmonious Champagne with notes of malt, bread, and honey. The flavor is mellow, warm, rich, and first-rate. I am convinced that most people like this even more than I do. My perhaps snobbish objection is that I miss finesse and tartness. Never mind me; try it yourself if the occasion presents itself. The wine belongs to a collection of older vintages released for the Millennium.

- 1970 DRAPPIER   75, MAY 2000 (75)
  (90% PN, 3% PM, 7% CH)
- 1969 DRAPPIER   87, OCT 2001 (87)
  (90% PN, 3% PM, 7% CH)

Considering how poorly the '70 has survived the destructive ravages of time, the '69 must be considered a sensationally vital and elegant wine. The freshness is better than in any other vintage from Drappier, and the truffle-like, citrus aromas are completely new additions.

- 1959 DRAPPIER   92, NOV 2003 (92)
  (90% PN, 3% PM, 7% CH)

A truly surprising wine. Not that I am surprised by the high quality—no. It's more that the wine is so refreshing and tart, and the alcohol is not especially pronounced. Nevertheless, there are layers of dried fruits and vanilla flavors here. The refreshing bouquet also has a slightly heavier note of dried hay as well as a smoky undertone. Truly a handsome newly disgorged wine! The highest-ranked Champagne with its 98 points that I have ever seen in *Wine Spectator*. It is also my highest-ranked wine from Aube.

- 1990 DRAPPIER BLANC DE BLANCS   78, MAR 2000 (81)
  (100% CH)

Fifty percent from Cramant and 50 percent from Urville. Round and fruity with an Aube imprint. The grape character is good, but I miss *terroir*.

- 1996 GRANDE SANDRÉE   85, DEC 2003 (88)
  (55% PN, 45% CH)

Personal and good. Honeysuckle and fig nose. Softly flirtatious palate with sweet notes and low acidity. Feels almost like a '95 in its creamy sweet, evolved style. Impressively fleshy and sweet. How is this youthfully vigorous wine going to develop?

- 1995 GRANDE SANDRÉE   85, SEP 2003 (85)
  (55% PN, 45% CH)

What a youthful little looker! Delicate mineral tones, crispy lime finish, and a floral, developable bouquet. For the moment lacking a little fat and length. Still, I'd prefer to drink this wine while it is still in spring attire. The wine is always made from grapes from seventy-year-old vines.

- 1989 GRANDE SANDRÉE   78, MAR 2000 (78)
  (55% PN, 45% CH)
- 1988 GRANDE SANDRÉE   75, APR 1995 (78)
  (55% PN, 45% CH)
- 1982 GRANDE SANDRÉE   77, APR 1999 (77)
  (55% PN, 45% CH)
- 1996 GRANDE SANDRÉE ROSÉ   79, MAY 2003 (85)
  (100% PN)

At the moment the wine lacks the complexity and harmony that only time can give. Today it smells like currant juice and tastes like raspberry soda with a whole lot of undeveloped extract. Store for another four to five years.

- 1990 GRANDE SANDRÉE ROSÉ   87, MAY 2000 (88)
  (100% PN)

There have been 3,000 bottles made of this, perhaps Aube's foremost Champagne. Drappier extracts a first-class Pinot Noir from the chalk-rich gravel of Grand Sandrée's steep slopes in Urville. The pale, modest color of the rosé is made from skin contact. No other wine in Aube has such mineral elegance as this chalky Champagne. Superb finesse in the bouquet, with a discreet note of raspberry. As light and beautiful as a ballet dancer.

DRIANT, E. R-M
12, rue Marie-Coquebert
51160 Aÿ
03 26 54 27 16
Production: 60,000
Founded in 1920 by Émile Driant. The firm owns only twenty hectares in Mareuil-sur-Aÿ, but buys grapes from Aÿ and Côte des Blancs.

- E. DRIANT BRUT   65
  (60% PN, 40% CH)

DUBOIS PÈRE & FILS R-M
Les Almanachs
Route d'Arty
51480 Venteuil
03 26 58 48 37
Production: 70,000
One of the few growers in Venteuil who have always stored all their wines in oak barrels. They use more than seven hectares in

the Marne valley. During the Champagne Uprising of 1991, Edmond Dubois was heavily involved as an advocate of growers' rights and traditions—in the area he was known as the "Champagne Savior." During World War I, Venteuil was completely destroyed and the small company had to fight hard to get back on its feet. Traditional methods of vinification are still adhered to as homage to their famous founder.

- CLAUDE DUBOIS   66
  (40% PN, 50% PM, 10% CH)
- DUBOIS CUVÉE DU RÉDEMPTEUR   72
  (33% PN, 34% PM, 33% CH)

DUBOIS, GÉRARD *** R-M
67, rue Ernest Vallé
51190 Avize
03 26 57 58 60
Production: 30,000
Paul Dubois started the business in 1930 in Avize. Today's owner Gérard has access to six hectares in Côte des Blancs.

- GÉRARD DUBOIS RÉSERVE   73
  (100% CH)
- 1985 GÉRARD DUBOIS   88, AUG 1997 (89)
  (100% CH)
  Fleshy Blanc de Blancs, with mature aromas and rich fruit.
- 1981 GÉRARD DUBOIS   88, AUG 1997 (88)
  (100% CH)
  Mature, clean, and creamy. A nice nutty, dry, classic aftertaste.

DUBRINCE, LOUIS N-D
51390 Villedommange
Production: 60,000
The Lallement family has long been established in the region. The wine has been sold to Jacquart in Reims for several years, and now the new generation have begun to produce wine under their own label at Jacquart. Today, young Myriam and Nicolas, twenty-four and twenty-two years of age respectively, run the company. The family owns fifty hectares in six villages.

- LOUIS DUBRINCE BRUT   67
  (20% PN, 50% PM, 30% CH)

DUFOUR, ROBERT R-M
4, rue de la Croix Malot
10110 Landreville
03 25 29 66 19
Production: 110,000
This grower has over ten hectares in Landreville and the surrounding area planted with 80 percent Pinot Noir and 20 percent Chardonnay. The vines are twenty years old. Two of this grower's five *cuvées* are Blanc de Blancs.

- R. DUFOUR SÉLECTION   50
  (50% PN, 50% CH)
- R. DUFOUR BLANC DE BLANCS   25
  (100% CH)

DUMANGIN-RAFFLIN R-M
42, rue Georges Legros
51500 Chigny-les-Roses
03 26 03 48 21
Production: 20,000
The grower has more than four hectares in Chigny-les-Roses. Half the production is sold to Champagne houses in Épernay. The vines average twenty-three years old.

- DUMANGIN-RAFFLIN BRUT   53
  (25% PN, 50% PM, 25% CH)
- DUMANGIN-RAFFLIN ROSÉ   49
  (30% PN, 45% PM, 25% CH)

DUMANGIN, JACKY R-M
3, rue de Rilly
51500 Chigny-les-Roses
03 26 03 46 34
Production: 100,000
This is recognized as the foremost of all the confusing Dumangins. The Dumangin family have been growers in the village since the beginning of the last century. Jacky Dumangin has more than 5.2 hectares in Montagne de Reims. The firm's other brand is Olivier Walsham (sold in Switzerland).

- DUMANGIN BRUT   70
  (25% PN, 50% PM, 25% CH)
- DUMANGIN EXTRA BRUT   67
  (25% PN, 50% PM, 25% CH)
- DUMANGIN GRANDE RÉSERVE   65
  (25% PN, 50% PM, 25% CH)
- DUMANGIN BLANC DE BLANCS   68
  (100% CH)
- DUMANGIN ROSÉ   58
  (40% PN, 10% PM, 50% CH)
- OLIVIER WALSHAM ROSÉ   59
  (40% PN, 13% PM, 47% CH)
- 1997 DUMANGIN   72, JUN 2003 (73)
  (47% PN, 53% CH)
- 1995 DUMANGIN   79, MAR 2004 (79)
  (42% PN, 58% CH)
- 1995 OLIVIER WALSHAM   77, OCT 2003 (79)
  (42% PN, 58% CH)
- 1994 DUMANGIN   79, NOV 2003 (81)
  (46% PN, 54% CH)
  Generous, bready bouquet with a plentiful portion of warmth and fruit. The taste is surprisingly compact and contained, with a surprisingly hard finish at the end. Neutral, fruity spectrum of tastes.
- 1992 DUMANGIN   75, OCT 1998 (80)
  (47% PN, 53% CH)
  Unusually stringent considering this usually mellow vintage. Rich, one-dimensional fruit and an as-yet rather short taste.
- 1991 DUMANGIN   81, MAR 1996 (86)
  (47% PN, 53% CH)
  A superb '91! The nose is delightfully perfumed and flowery and the citrus flavor is long and crispy.

DUMONT, DANIEL *** R-M

11, rue Gambetta
51500 Rilly-la-Montagne
03 26 03 40 67
Production: 50,000

Daniel Dumont is one of Champagne's twenty-five "*pépinières*," who sell 200,000 selected, grafted vines every year to the growers in the area. He combines his plant farm with a quality-minded Champagne production. In his nine-degree, churchlike cellar, the Champagnes are stored for at least five years before being sold. Dumont owns ten hectares in seven villages: Sézanne, Villers-Allerand, Villers-Marmery, Ludes, Rilly-la-Montagne, Chigny-les-Roses, and Dormans. He produces medium-bodied and well-made wines in a style that is similar to many of the big houses.

- D. DUMONT TRADITION   61
  (33% PN, 33% PM, 34% CH)
- D. DUMONT GRANDE RÉSERVE   64
  (40% PN, 30% PM, 30% CH)
- D. DUMONT ROSÉ   63
  (40% PN, 30% PM, 30% CH)
- 1992 D. DUMONT   79, OCT 2001 (79)
  (40% PN, 30% PM, 30% CH)
- 1990 D. DUMONT   86, NOV 2001 (89)
  (40% PN, 30% PM, 30% CH)
- 1970 D. DUMONT   80, APR 1995 (83)
  (40% PN, 30% PM, 30% CH)

  This is the oldest wine in Dumont's "wine archives," but at the age of twenty-five it was still very young and fresh. Otherwise the wine's quality is by no means impressive. The nose is a trifle mean, with a weak bready element and a steely, hard, and somewhat thin flavor. Above all, the aftertaste is too short.
- 1989 CUVÉE D'EXCELLENCE   83, APR 1995 (87)
  (50% PN, 50% CH)

  A typical '89! Sweet and rich nose of honey and red fruits, with a generous, rich, creamy and mature flavor of strawberries.

DUVAL-LEROY *** N-M

69, avenue de Bammental
51130 Vertus
03 26 52 10 75
Production: 5,000,000

A large percentage of the bottles that the firm sells go under other names or labels ordered by the buyer. Duval-Leroy is in fact the largest player in this market. In Sweden, we've become acquainted with their affordably priced nonvintage Blanc de Blancs. The company harvests from forty-eight villages and uses all the grapes from the second pressing. All year long, thirty-five people take care of the 150-hectare vineyard. They are probably one of the firms that buy the "*taille*" cheaply from more conscientious producers. The company, which was founded in 1859, is something of a mixed bag today—some of the worst Champagnes I've drunk are second-labeled Duval-Leroy wines. On the other hand, those Champagnes that carry Duval-Leroy's own name certainly maintain a good standard. The present owners, with female president Carol Duval-Leroy and winemaker Hérve Jestin, are very serious. They are presently going through a process of modernization, aiming for higher quality. The latest vintages have been brilliant.

- DUVAL-LEROY TRADITION   55
  (25% PN, 60% PM, 15% CH)
- E. MICHEL BRUT   24
- P. VERTAY BRUT   30
- VEUVE MORANT   19
- DUVAL-LEROY FLEUR DE CHAMPAGNE   71
  (35% PN, 65% CH)
- DUVAL-LEROY PREMIER CRU   74
  (30% PN, 70% CH)
- DUVAL-LEROY BLANC DE BLANCS   74
  (100% CH)
- DUVAL-LEROY DEMI-SEC   58
  (50% PN, 20% PM, 30% CH)
- DUVAL-LEROY ROSÉ SAIGNÉE   76
  (100% PN)
- 1995 DUVAL-LEROY FLEUR DE CHAMPAGNE   83, JUN 2002 (86)
  (20% PN, 80% CH)

  The wine comes from six *grand cru* villages and one *premier cru*. Despite this, the wine is often very timid in character. Gentle, mild, and short taste of good but slightly anxious Chardonnay.
- 1992 DUVAL-LEROY FLEUR DE CHAMPAGNE   71, DEC 1998 (73)
  (25% PN, 75% CH)
- 1990 DUVAL-LEROY FLEUR DE CHAMPAGNE   83, NOV 1998 (85)
  (25% PN, 75% CH)

  Like all vintage wines from Duval-Leroy, this is strongly characterized by fine Chardonnay. The '90 is a very harmonic and well-balanced wine that hardly needs to be stored for any time at all. The aroma is clearly bready, with an element of fine grape sweetness. The taste and the mousse are soft and pleasing, the aftertaste somewhat short.
- 1988 DUVAL-LEROY FLEUR DE CHAMPAGNE   80, FEB 1997 (84)
  (100% CH)

  A little sweet, but a pleasing almond flavor and good grape character.
- 1986 DUVAL-LEROY FLEUR DE CHAMPAGNE   68, NOV 1993 (75)
  (30% PN, 70% CH)
- 1985 DUVAL-LEROY FLEUR DE CHAMPAGNE   84, AUG 1999 (87)
  (10% PN, 90% CH)

  Typically well-balanced '85 with a handsome spectrum of refreshing taste nuances. Still very young with a distinctly chalky mid-palate. Dry and storable.
- 1955 DUVAL-LEROY FLEUR DE CHAMPAGNE   83, OCT 2003 (83)
  (30% PN, 70% CH)

  Many were completely captivated by this Sauternes-like wine, and almost as many thought that the lack of bubbles and distinct oxide notes rendered the wine defective at a tasting—Swedish Taste—in Gothenburg, Sweden. I give this wine a passing grade as a dessert wine or as a companion to a dish of duck liver, but the sweetness is still too strong and its age is showing. I must confess, though, this is a good, honey-saturated rarity.
- 1996 DUVAL-LEROY BLANC DE BLANCS   82, SEP 2003 (84)
  (100% CH)

  Big, slightly smoky, spicy scent reminiscent of Avize from Jacquesson. Fat and rich, relatively developed '96. Stronger, but less sophisticated than usual.
- 1995 DUVAL-LEROY BLANC DE BLANCS   83, DEC 2001 (86)
  (100% CH)

  Tranquil and impressively pure with good acidity and usual shy style. Fine citrus tone and balance. Rather mild, short aftertaste with a pleasant apple note.

• 1993 DUVAL-LEROY BLANC DE BLANCS   83, NOV 1998 (85)
(100% CH)

An impressive, clear '93, with a somewhat neutral style, but with very appetizing aromas of pear and grapefruit. Light and playful aperitif with fine softness and invigorating acidity. Markedly softer and less storable than most of the grower Champagnes in Côte des Blancs.

• 1990 DUVAL-LEROY BLANC DE BLANCS   73, FEB 1996 (86)
(100% CH)

Vintage-typical and restrained. Not a particularly big personality but a good example of a Chardonnay *cuvée.*

• 1995 DUVAL-LEROY FEMME   85, OCT 2003 (89)
(11% PN, 89% CH)

The same considerate style that characterizes all of Duval-Leroy's wines, but with a reliable concentration of luxurious fruit that most likely will give delightful toasted aromas at the age of fifteen years. Truly elegant, luxurious Champagne, which one is tempted to drink much too young.

• 1990 DUVAL-LEROY CUVÉE DES ROYS   87, OCT 2003 (90)
(5% PN, 95% CH)

An undeveloped, restrained, storable Champagne with a somewhat dry and acidic taste. The scent is at this point rather weak and cold, but the aromas that develop when the Champagne airs out a bit in the glass remind me of a Blanc de Blancs. An exciting wine to follow into the future.

• 1990 DUVAL-LEROY FEMME   93, MAY 2002 (93)
(11% PN, 89% CH)

This much-talked-about firm finally hit the bull's-eye! A sterling Champagne, reminiscent of Taittinger's sweet nut-toffee-influenced style. Truly impressive, grandiose bouquet, and an incredibly delicious taste with big, inviting depth.

• 1986 DUVAL-LEROY CUVÉE DES ROYS   82, FEB 1997 (87)
(5% PN, 95% CH)

Duval-Leroy has succeeded in making a striking, broad, prestige Champagne with buttery overtones and impressive, ripe fruit. The aftertaste is clean with a pleasant note of lime.

• 1985 DUVAL-LEROY CUVÉE DES ROYS   92, NOV 2001 (93)
(5% PN, 95% CH)

A magnificent wine with a fantastically beautiful toasted scent of toast, coffee, and nuts. Sensually caressing fruit and velvety-smooth mousse. My absolute favorite Champagne from Duval-Leroy.

• DUVAL-LEROY PARIS MILLENNIUM   85, MAY 2002 (87)

A truly elegant charmer packaged in a luxurious bottle illustrated with the most famous buildings of Paris, stylishly and tastefully done in gold. The entire wine feels luxurious, with high-class Chardonnay in the driver's seat.

EGLY-OURIET **** R-M

15, rue de Trépail
51150 Ambonnay
03 26 57 00 70
Production: 68,000

Egly-Ouriet makes one of Robert Parker's favorite Champagnes. The company started out in 1930 and today Michel Egly owns six hectares in Ambonnay, half a hectare in Bouzy, and half in Verzenay. The vines are over thirty-two years old on average, and those used for the prestige wine are more than fifty-six years old.

• EGLY-OURIET TRADITION   80
(70% PN, 30% CH)

A copy of Bollinger's nonvintage Champagne. Chocolate, hazelnut and ripe apples; a broad, masculine fleshiness and vigor.

• EGLY-OURIET ROSÉ   73
(80% PN, 20% CH)

• 1998 EGLY-OURIET   90, NOV 2003 (93)
(60% PN, 40% CH)

Super concentrated power and superb tart finesse. A brilliant grower's wine that, with all the clarity one could want, exhibits Ambonnay's greatness and beauty. One of the most interesting growers in Champagne has done it again.

• 1989 EGLY-OURIET   83, MAY 1996 (88)
(60% PN, 40% CH)

This Champagne is already highly developed and bold, and the meaty and sweet Pinot aromas link together in perfect harmony. Several tasters guessed an older vintage from Bollinger, which I couldn't understand as the wine had none of the nutty and smoked aromas found there.

• EGLY-OURIET BLANC DE NOIRS   86
(100% PN)

Grapes from Pinot vines cultivated in 1946 give the wine an extra weight and concentration. The fruit is rich, soft, and dense, and the potential for cellar storage is huge.

ELLNER, CHARLES N-M

6, rue Côte-Legris
51207 Épernay
03 26 55 60 25
Production: 1,000,000

Founded by Charles Emile Ellner. Received house status in 1972. The firm specializes in "Buyer's Own Brand" under different labels. The house has fifty-four hectares at its disposal in fifteen villages, all planted with 55 percent Chardonnay. Winemaker Jacques Ellner makes round, fruity *cuvées* in which the reserve wines in oak barrels are very influential.

• CHARLES ELLNER RÉSERVE PREMIER CRU   71
(40% PN, 30% PM, 30% CH)

• ELLNER CARTE D'OR   67
(10% PN, 90% CH)

• MARQUIS D'ESTRAND   50
(40% PN, 30% PM, 30% CH)

• PHILIPPE D'ALBERTCOURT BRUT   65
(40% PN, 30% PM, 30% CH)

• CHARLES ELLNER BLANC DE BLANCS   67
(100% CH)

• CHARLES ELLNER DEMI-SEC   51
(40% PN, 30% PM, 30% CH)

• CHARLES ELLNER SEC   57
(40% PN, 30% PM, 30% CH)

• CHARLES ELLNER ROSÉ   64
(50% PN, 50% PM)

• 1995 CHARLES ELLNER BLANC DE BLANCS   84, OCT 2003 (85)
(100% CH)

Big, developed Champagne with notes of wet wool, honey, marzipan, dried fruit, and vanilla. Fat taste that unfortunately is a little too short. Not as sweet as some of the firm's Champagnes. Hard to believe that only Chardonnay has been added to this *cuvée,* as the wine is already so fleshy and honey-saturated.

• 1995 CHARLES ELLNER PRESTIGE   79, MAR 2004 (79)
(40% PN, 60% CH)

PERRIER-JOUËT BELLE ÉPOQUE ROSÉ
1989

PERRIER-JOUËT BELLE ÉPOQUE
1985

HEIDSIECK DRY MONOPOLE
1966

PHILIPPONNAT CLOS DES GOISSES
1975

BOIZEL BRUT
1961

JOSEPH PERRIER CUVÉE ROYALE
1979

PIERRE PETERS BLANC DE BLANCS
1988

WILLIAM DEUTZ ROSÉ BRUT
1990

PERRIER-JOUET BLASON DE FRANCE
1966

SALON
1949

VEUVE CLICQUOT PONSARDIN
1959

LANSON
1959

POL ROGER EXTRA CUVÉE DE RÉSERVE BRUT
1990

VEUVE CLICQUOT GRANDE DAME
1990

LAUNOIS FRÈRES
1964

ERNEST IROY CARTE D'OR
1943

JACQUESSON
1969

LARMANDIER-BERNIER CRAMANT
1990

PAUL BARA BRUT
1959

AYALA BRUT
1964

DE CASTELLANE CUVÉE ROYALE
BLANC DE BLANCS 1966

DE CASTELLANE BRUT
1970

GOSSET GRAND MILLÉSIME
1985

DELBECK BRUT EXRA RÉSERVE
1943

• 1993 CHARLES ELLNER SÉDUCTION   85, SEP 2003 (85)
(25% PN, 75% CH)
Fine nut-toffee nose with notes of lemon and cream. Delicate harmonious palate with a fine, mellow mousse and evolved sweet finish. Sensationally good '93 with delicious big-house style.

• 1990 CHARLES ELLNER SÉDUCTION   67, APR 2003 (67)
(25% PN, 75% CH)

• 1989 CHARLES ELLNER PRESTIGE   87, SEP 2003 (87)
(25% PN, 75% CH)
Deep golden color and slowly rising mousse. Intensely vinous bouquet full of honey and almond. Fleshy and round with sweet notes.

FAGOT, MICHEL R-M
6, rue de Chigny
51500 Rilly-la-Montagne
03 26 03 40 03
Production: 90,000
Adrien Fagot founded this property in 1910. Today's owner, Michel Fagot, utilizes more than sixteen hectares.

• MICHEL FAGOT TRADITION   60
(20% PN, 40% PM, 40% CH)

• 1985 MICHEL FAGOT   82, JAN 2001 (82)
(50% PN, 50% CH)
Certainly impressively powerful and heavy with fine Pinot character, but I am still not completely enchanted; the wine is slightly too rustic and difficult to drink without food.

• 1983 MICHEL FAGOT   84, FEB 2000 (84)
(50% PN, 50% CH)
More vigorous and austere than the '85, which is extremely unusual. Fine smoky, gamy keynote with dry fruit and a long aftertaste of gunpowder.

FALLET, MICHEL R-M
56, rue Pasteur
51190 Avize
03 26 57 51 97
Production: 30,000
One of the chefs at Boyer recommended this producer, about whom I had known nothing. At first I thought it was strange that I had missed Fallet, but when it became apparent that the gate didn't have a sign I began to understand why. The wines are only sold direct to customers who knock on the door. The elderly widow Fallet runs what is now a rather run-down property. However, there is plenty of potential, with seventy-five-year-old vines in excellent locations.

• MICHEL FALLET BRUT   45
(100% CH)

• MICHEL FALLET EXTRA BRUT   65
(100% CH)

FAŸE, SERGE R-M
51150 Louvois
03 26 57 81 66
A rarely experienced acquaintance from this little-known *grand cru* village.

• 1998 LE LOUVRE   70, MAY 2003 (76)
(88% PN, 12% CH)

FEUILLATTE, NICOLAS *** C-M
B.P. 210
51530 Chouilly
03 26 59 55 50
Production: 16,000,000
The French-American businessman Nicolas Feuillatte founded this firm together with the Centre Vinicole de la Champagne in Chouilly in 1971. Today he is constantly on the move, working as an ambassador for the cooperative's Champagnes. *Chef de cave* is the talented Jean-Pierre Vincent. Two hundred gigantic fermentation tanks of stainless steel tower over the ultra-modern wine plant, which has a production capacity of sixteen million bottles. The plant is used by eighty-five sub-cooperatives. The grapes from the various cooperatives come from 130 *crus* and are all blended in the giant tanks. Every stage in the Champagne-making process is automated, and the cellars contain some thirty-three million bottles. Those wines that are released under the name of Nicolas Feuillatte (2.8 million bottles) contain *premier* and *grand cru* grapes only.

• NICOLAS FEUILLATTE RÉSERVE PARTICULIÈRE   53
(50% PN, 30% PM, 20% CH)

• NICOLAS FEUILLATTE BLANC DE BLANCS   50
(100% CH)

• NICOLAS FEUILLATTE ROSÉ   48
(60% PN, 30% PM, 10% CH)

• 1996 NICOLAS FEUILLATTE   81, SEP 2003 (82)
(40% PN, 40% PM, 20% CH)
Mellow and honed Champagne that lacks the acidity common to this vintage. The scent is rich and good, with elements of honeysuckle and jasmine. Fat; with the risk of imminent flabbiness, the wine subsides, resting on the palate.

• 1990 NICOLAS FEUILLATTE   84, MAY 2002 (84)
(40% PN, 40% PM, 20% CH)
A lovely, fruity wine with plenty of immediate charm and toasty aromas. There's also an explosive, juicy flavor of peach. The Chardonnay grapes must be top class.

• 1985 NICOLAS FEUILLATTE   86, AUG 1997 (87)
(50% PN, 25% PM, 25% CH)
Sensational bready nose and a long, slightly monotonous taste of honey.

• 1982 NICOLAS FEUILLATTE   80, DEC 1993 (84)
(50% PN, 25% PM, 25% CH)
Light and lively. An exciting nose of hawthorn, redcurrants and blackcurrants, and orange marmalade. Good, dry, mineral-rich and medium-bodied flavor with an aftertaste that is a touch too short.

• 1979 NICOLAS FEUILLATTE   86, NOV 1997 (86)
(50% PN, 25% PM, 25% CH)
Light and elegant with a scent that reminds me of a white burgundy. Creamy and tasty. Many tasters—at a tasting at Edsbacka Krog arranged by Scandinavian Airlines for 70 people—allocated this Champagne much higher points than I did.

• 1975 NICOLAS FEUILLATTE   82, NOV 1997 (82)
(50% PN, 25% PM, 25% CH)
More heavy and gamy than the '79. Smoky and robust. Went well with veal and morel sauce.

• 1995 NICOLAS FEUILLATTE CHOUILLY   80, AUG 2003 (83)
(100% CH)

An admirable initiative from Feuillatte, with pure mono-*cru* Champagnes from several different villages, all vinified in the same clean, somewhat expressionless, slightly neutral way. Chouilly is reminiscent of Cramant, which is only natural, but Cramant is a touch more complex and slightly more buttery. The impression is polished, fresh, and good, without being particularly grand.

- 1995 NICOLAS FEUILLATTE CRAMANT   82, AUG 2003 (84)
(100% CH)
Exceedingly pleasant and precise wine with nice citrus and complex buttery aromas. On the down side, it is a little thin and lacking in extract. However, this village is seldom disappointing!

- 1995 NICOLAS FEUILLATTE MESNIL   81, SEP 2003 (83)
(100% CH)
I had expected more from this wine. I might be wrong, but it feels as if there isn't much room for development here. This creature is lively and handsome, but the tasty aromas feel a little too developed and open to be really good. Figs, dried apricots, and bananas can be discerned, along with repressed, fresh Chardonnay.

- 1993 NICOLAS FEUILLATTE BLANC DE BLANCS   80, MAY 2001 (81)
(100% CH)
An ingratiating and popular Champagne with aromas reminiscent of licorice, melon, tutti-frutti, and newly unwrapped toffee-wrappers. Brisk performance on the palate with elastic tartness. Not enough concentration, though.

- 1992 NICOLAS FEUILLATTE BLANC DE BLANCS   75, OCT 1998 (79)
(100% CH)
Nice ripe nose braided together with biscuit-like, lingering aromas. Aftertaste of green apples.

- 1996 NICOLAS FEUILLATTE AŸ   79, FEB 2004 (84)
(100% PN)
The mellowness and plumpness of this wine camouflage the underlying acidity, convincing you to drink up all your bottles straight away. I want to save mine in order to get rid of the gingerbread notes, the slightly unpolished apple tones, and other teething troubles. Should be a great experience in a few years.

- 1995 NICOLAS FEUILLATTE VERZY   83, AUG 2003 (85)
(100% PN)
Probably the most impressive of the vineyard Champagnes from Feuillatte. Delicious bouquet of vanilla and young, potent, red fruit, with a fine ring of fresh apples and biscuits. A little fleshier and more dense than the wines made from Chardonnay. Modern, polished style, of course.

- 1992 NICOLAS FEUILLATTE ROSÉ   62, OCT 1997 (62)
(60% PN, 30% PM, 10% CH)

- 1995 NICOLAS FEUILLATTE CUVÉE SPÉCIALE   82, SEP 2003 (84)
(40% PN, 20% PM, 40% CH)
Both delicious and sophisticated. Excellent density with an underlying note of butterscotch. Big, fat, charming fruit leaning toward both citrus and the exotic.

- 1995 PALMES D'OR   87, SEP 2003 (88)
(40% PN, 60% CH)
What an exotic nose! Peach, orchid, and roses. Ripe fruit from sweet grapes gives this wine a very good, evolved taste. The entire wine radiates generosity and luxuriousness. Probably won't get any better than it is now, but the decided apple note may mean I am proved wrong.

- 1992 PALMES D'OR   84, JAN 2003 (85)
(40% PN, 60% CH)

Brilliantly yellow Champagne with a nose of lemon peel, fresh croissant, and mango. Round, rich palate of pears, grapefruit, and candy. Soft and ready to open as soon as the occasion presents itself.

- 1990 NICOLAS FEUILLATTE CUVÉE SPÉCIALE   83, AUG 1999 (87)
(40% PN, 20% PM, 40% CH)
A delightful fireworks of fragrance filled with pineapple, grape and saffron. It feels almost like a Blanc de Blancs with its elegant elasticity and fruity taste. Very good future prospects. The latest bottles that I have tasted have exhibited completely different spicy and bready sides—therefore slightly difficult to judge.

- 1990 PALMES D'OR   86, MAY 2001 (89)
(40% PN, 60% CH)
A big wine that only gets fatter and fatter with time. The nose still has some delicious floweriness and the taste a few greenish elements.

- 1988 NICOLAS FEUILLATTE CUVÉE SPÉCIALE   78, JUN 1997 (84)
(40% PN, 20% PM, 40% CH)
Not much to get excited about. Has stringency and potential, but at the age of nine it felt a bit unbalanced.

- 1985 PALMES D'OR   90, JUL 1997 (90)
(40% PN, 60% CH)
A lovely Champagne, classically built and bursting with vitality. Even so, I can't help thinking it's reached its peak.

- 1997 PALMES D'OR ROSÉ   84, FEB 2004 (87)
This new prestige rosé—very dark in color—exhibits a Burgundy-like aromatic personality. Present is a gaminess and a rather sweet, fruity side with a dash of ripe berries. Fleshy and soft with good vigor and depth. Manages decanting very well!

FLEURY
10250 Courteron
Production: 180,000

- FLEURY BRUT   56
(100% PN)
- FLEURY ROSÉ   62
(100% PN)
- 1996 FLEURY   80, OCT 2003 (82)
(80% PN, 20% CH)
It's nice to find a vintage that adds a little tartness to normally one-dimensional, flat wines. Soft and pleasant, with pineapple and banana as well as elastic, biting acidity.

- 1995 FLEURY   72, SEP 2003 (73)
(80% PN, 20% CH)

FLINIAUX, RICHARD *** N-M
12, rue Léon Roulot
51160 Aÿ
03 26 55 17 17
Production: 85,000
Fliniaux is one of the Champagne houses closest to my heart. A better Pinot Noir producer is hard to find. James Richard, who has had a great deal of success in the German-speaking countries, now runs the company in the same uncompromising spirit as Roland and Regis had done. They own four hectares in Aÿ, which constitutes 25 percent of production needs. Most of the grapes that are bought in come from Aÿ. No oak barrels are used, but the richness in Fliniaux's wines is reminiscent of Bollinger. The Champagne is not for acidic fetishists, or those who are seeking

elegance in their wines. Fliniaux's greatness is built on power and a wealth of flavors—which is just as it should be from this little town.

- FLINIAUX BLANC DE BLANCS   56
  (100% CH)
- FLINIAUX CARTE NOIR BRUT   80
  (80% PN, 20% CH)
  The same foundation wine as its predecessor, but stored longer. A massive yet charming wine, with a broad meaty nose of leather and hazelnut. Rich, round, fruit taste of raisins, plums, and banana.
- FLINIAUX CUVÉE DE RÉSERVE   75
  (80% PN, 20% CH)
- FLINIAUX CUVÉE TENDRESSE   73
  (80% PN, 20% CH)
- FLINIAUX ROSÉ   88
  (100% PN)
  A textbook rosé that expresses a lot of the character of the soil, together with the grape's wonderful strawberry aroma. The dark color puts many people off, but just close your eyes and let yourself be washed away by the incredibly rich grape character.
- 1985 FLINIAUX   90, JUL 1995 (90)
  (100% PN)
  Massive gunpowder scent in this Aÿ Champagne, with good attack and a superb length.
- FLINIAUX 1983/1982   82, JUL 1990 (85)
  (100% PN)
  1982/1983. The rounder and softer vintage of 1982 dominates the wine with a vengeance. For once the structure is loose, even though the aroma of chocolate and banana is overwhelming.
- 1982 FLINIAUX   83, MAY 1995 (83)
  (100% PN)
  Fat, round, mature, and gutsy. Drink up!
- 1979 FLINIAUX   92, JAN 2002 (92)
  (100% PN)
  Once one of my favorites, which I regularly placed ahead of '79 Bollinger R. D. at blind tastings. Some bottles are losing it, but most are at their peak. If you're lucky you'll experience an outstandingly rich wine with an exotic nose of honeysuckle, honey, hazelnut, mushroom, and chocolate toffee. All these tones recur in the palate in a luxurious, soft package.
- 1988 FLINIAUX ROSÉ   90, JUL 1993 (93)
  (100% PN)
  Somewhat lighter in color than the nonvintage variety. More restrained and younger, but with even more potential. The last glass was a symphony of the Pinot grape's various incarnations, where the aftertaste reverberated like a singer's voice in a cathedral.
- 1983 FLINIAUX CUVÉE PRESTIGE   85, FEB 1994 (89)
  (100% PN)
  Fliniaux's wines resemble La Grande Dame with their generous, soft, and chocolaty Pinot aromas. The '83 isn't as magnificent as the '79, but has better acidity and a teasing resistance, along with a tone of roasted chestnuts.

FOREZ, GUY DE R-M
32, rue du Général Leclerc
10340 Les Riceys
03 25 29 98 73
Production: 20,000
This firm started out in 1987, founded by Roland Spagnesi and now run by Sylvie Wenner. Besides Champagne they make a respected Rosé des Riceys from their eight hectares.
- GUY DE FOREZ BRUT   53
  (80% PN, 20% CH)

FORGET-BRIMONT N-M
51500 Ludes
03 26 61 10 45
Production: 100,000
Eugène Forget began selling Champagne in 1920. The current owner, Michel Forget, runs eight hectares in Ludes, Chigny, Mailly, and Verzenay.
- FORGET-BRIMONT CARTE BLANCHE   55
  (60% PN, 20% PM, 20% CH)
- FORGET-BRIMONT EXTRA BRUT   56
  (60% PN, 20% PM, 20% CH)
- FORGET-BRIMONT DEMI-SEC   39
  (60% PN, 20% PM, 20% CH)
- FORGET-BRIMONT ROSÉ   50
  (75% PN, 12% PM, 13% CH)

FREMIERES N-M
51000 Châlons-en-Champagne
One of the many houses that disappeared from Châlons a long time ago.
- 1943 FREMIERES   87, DEC 2000 (87)
  A well-preserved treasure of war from a long-dead house in Châlons-sur-Marne. Judging by the style, it is clearly Chardonnay influenced. Pale color, perky appearance and performance, with a nose reminiscent of fine, dry sherry and straw. Medium bodied and dry.

FRESNET-JUILLET *** R-M
10, rue de Beaumont
51380 Verzy
03 26 97 93 40
Production: 75,000
The firm was started in 1954 by Gerard Fresnet, once the Mayor of Verzy. The vineyards cover nine hectares in Mailly and Verzy, which are planted with 75 percent Pinot Noir grapes and 25 percent Chardonnay.
- FRESNET-JUILLET BRUT   55
  (80% PN, 20% CH)
- FRESNET-JUILLET ROSÉ   51
  (50% PN, 50% CH)
- 1995 FRESNET-JUILLET   83, APR 1999 (90)
  (100% PN)
  A brilliantly lucid and shimmering Champagne, full of youthful vigor and *joie de vivre*. The fruit is fresh and intense. I am convinced that most of the '95s will be drunk far too early because they are so good right from the start. It is difficult so early on to notice any great amount of grape character in this lemony, refreshing wine. The dominating tone, both in scent and

taste, is passion fruit, which is hardly something one commonly finds in Champagnes made from Pinot Noir.

- 1994 FRESNET-JUILLET SPECIAL CLUB   83, APR 1999 (88)
  (50% PN, 50% CH)
  An exemplary purity and seductively soft mousse. Chalky mineral, passion fruit, and an intimation of butter toffee can be discerned right now in this wine's uncomplicated youth.
- 1993 FRESNET-JUILLET CUVÉE EMILIE   80, APR 1999 (84)
  (40% PN, 60% CH)
  All of Fresnet-Juillet's wines are unusually light and elegant, considering the extraction. The note of passion fruit exists here again, together with the beginnings of a mature tone.

FUENTÉ, BARON N-M
02310 Charly-sur-Marne
32 38 01 97
Production: 650,000
The house was founded in 1961. Today they have twenty-five hectares around Charly and purchase the rest of their grapes from neighboring villages. Sixty percent of their production is from Pinot Meunier and processed organically. The quality is very high, particularly considering the limitations of being so removed at the outer edges of the Champagne region.

- BARON FUENTÉ TRADITION   74
  (70% PM, 30% CH)
- BARON FUENTÉ GRANDE RÉSERVE   68
  (10% PN, 60% PM, 30% CH)
- ESPRIT DE BARON FUENTÉ   54
  (33% PN, 33% PM, 34% CH)
- BARON FUENTÉ CUVÉE AMPELOS   77
  (100% PM)
- BARON FUENTÉ ROSÉ DOLORÈS   55
  (20% PN, 40% PM, 40% CH)
- 1996 BARON FUENTÉ GRAND MILLÉSIME   75, JAN 2003 (77)
  (20% PN, 30% PM, 50% CH)
- 1995 BARON FUENTÉ GRAND MILLÉSIME   76, SEP 2003 (76)
  (20% PN, 30% PM, 50% CH)

FURDYNA, MICHEL R-M
13, rue du Trot
10110 Celles-sur-Ource
03 25 38 54 20
Production: 60,000
Started by the owner of the same name in 1974, this company's vineyards lie in Celles-sur-Ource, Loches-sur-Ource, Neuville, and Landreville.

- MICHEL FURDYNA CARTE BLANCHE   49
  (85% PN, 5% PM, 10% CH)
- MICHEL FURDYNA RÉSERVE   58
  (100% PN)
- MICHEL FURDYNA ROSÉ   62
  (100% PN)
- 1988 MICHEL FURDYNA CUVÉE PRESTIGE   80, MAR 1996 (83)
  (66% PN, 34% CH)
  A lovely flowery nose with elements of lime and mint. Creamy, voluptuous flavor that lacks a little acidity.

GAIDOZ-FORGET R-M
1, rue Carnot
51500 Ludes
03 26 61 13 03
Production: 65,000
This nine-hectare grower in the heart of Montagne de Reims is attracting more and more attention with his fruity and complex Champagnes. M. Gaidoiz-Forget has more than nine hectares at his disposal. Other wines: Quintessence.

- GAIDOZ-FORGET CARTE D'OR   65
  (25% PN, 50% PM, 25% CH)
- GAIDOZ-FORGET RÉSERVE   68
  (25% PN, 50% PM, 25% CH)
- GAIDOZ-FORGET ROSÉ   59
  (30% PN, 70% PM)

GALLIMARD R-M
18, rue du Magny
10340 Les Riceys
03 25 29 32 44
Production: 75,000
Today, this grower is represented at many of France's best restaurants. The firm made a rather mediocre impression on me in March, 2000. Strangest of all was that Gallimard himself liked his odd rosé. I thought it was a poor bottle.

- GALLIMARD BRUT   65
  (100% PN)
- GALLIMARD ROSÉ   30
  (100% PN)
- 1996 GALLIMARD   77, MAR 2002 (77)
  (100% PN)
- 1998 GALLIMARD PRESTIGE   59, DEC 2002 (59)
  (65% PN, 35% CH)
- 1990 GALLIMARD PRESTIGE   80, MAR 2000 (80)
  (100% PN)

GARDET *** N-M
13, rue Georges Legros
50500 Chigny-les-Roses
03 26 03 42 03
Production: 1,000,000
Charles Gardet founded the house in 1895 in Épernay, but his son George moved it to Chigny, where it is now run by Pierre Gardet. Gardet has no vineyards of its own, but instead has to buy in all its grapes. Many wine journalists are very enthusiastic about the quality of Gardet's Champagnes, but to call them "mini-Krugs" is going a bit too far, I think. There are no oak barrels or any other special vinification methods. Gardet's wines are quite simply well made and good, but the company is certainly not in the top league.

- GARDET BRUT   70
  (45% PN, 45% PM, 10% CH)
- GARDET SPECIAL   75
  (33% PN, 33% PM, 34% CH)
- GARDET ROSÉ   75
  (50% PN, 50% PM)
- 1997 GARDET   82, JUL 2003 (83)
  (50% PN, 50% CH)
  Broad, fat, and lightly strewn with chocolate aroma. Neutral, but still relatively fine tasting. Low acidity and unified mellow taste.

Also known by the name Delcave under Lorenzo Fassola's direction in Perugia.

• 1996 CHARLES GARDET   84, DEC 2002 (89)
(67% PN, 33% CH)

The usual vintage wine, now in a new bottle and with a somewhat smaller amount of Chardonnay. A good example of the vintage's ability to camouflage high acidity under a blanket of generous, sun-ripened, appley fruit. The wine is juicy, potent, and rich, but needs time in the cellar to develop its intrinsic complexity.

• 1990 GARDET   81, NOV 1999 (83)
(50% PN, 50% CH)

Gardet, a very reliable producer, has made a rather good and very affordable wine. But shouldn't this '90 be fresher and better? The wine is mellow, pleasant, and one-dimensional.

• 1988 GARDET   81, SEP 1998 (88)
(50% PN, 50% CH)

Shy, almost undetectable though coherent nose. Sober, focused, undeveloped, tight, potent taste. Best after the year 2020!

• 1985 GARDET   80, JAN 1995 (87)
(50% PN, 50% CH)

A promising but undeveloped Champagne in January 1995. It reminded me a lot of the '83, but with a somewhat less developed nose.

• 1983 GARDET   83, JUL 1993 (88)
(50% PN, 50% CH)

Superior to the '82! A very fine rosé nose combined with the smell of a good bakery. Crystal-clear, pure flavor with perfectly pure acidity and a fruit that lays the foundation for a great future.

• 1982 GARDET   85, MAY 2003 (85)
(50% PN, 50% CH)

The wine was completely unbalanced when young and newly disgorged. Today, it is harmonious, with a fine creaminess, newness, and an appealing vanilla tone. However, it has none of the more monumental constructions.

• 1979 GARDET   92, JUL 1993 (92)
(50% PN, 50% CH)

This lovely '79 is a textbook Champagne for the vintage. Mature, golden color, a brilliant Pinot nose with leather, hazelnuts, and honey. A fruity revelation in the mouth with a perfectly balanced finish of walnuts. Buy one if you see one!

• 1976 GARDET   86, APR 1993 (88)
(50% PN, 50% CH)

Unexpectedly light color for a seventeen year old. An extremely broad, wonderful, sweet, exotic nose with elements of bread, chocolate, and mint. It feels a little clumsy in the mouth, as do many '76s. The acidity is a trifle too low but it may end up developing like the '59s.

• 1995 GARDET BLANC DE BLANCS   74, SEP 2003 (75)
(100% CH)

GARNOTEL, ADAM N-M

17, rue de Chigny
51500 Rilly-la-Montagne
03 26 03 40 22
Production: 300,000

When you take the "Champagne Road" through Rilly, it's easy to drive straight into Adam's well-signposted plant. It's much harder to find an open door or a person who can show you a few bottles. Only on my third attempt did I succeed. The firm, founded in 1899 by Louis Adam, has expanded considerably since the end of the 1970s. Other wines: Rosé.

• DANIEL ADAM BRUT   61
(30% PN, 40% PM, 30% CH)

• 1990 CUVÉE LOUIS-ADAM   85, JUL 1997 (89)
(30% PN, 70% CH)

The company's new *cuvée de prestige* is tight and focused, with a concentrated, undeveloped fruit and a creamy feel. It resembles the Special Club from Côte des Blancs.

GATINOIS **** R-M

7, rue Marcel Mailly
51160 Aÿ
03 26 55 14 26
Production: 30,000

The man who runs Gatinois today, Pierre Cheval, reserves his greatest pride for his red wine from Aÿ. Together with Bollinger, Gosset-Brabant, and Gotourbe, he is alone in making an Aÿ rouge. The Gatinois family have been winemakers in Aÿ since 1696 and own twenty-nine pieces of land in Aÿ with a total area of seven hectares. Half of the harvest is sold annually to the neighbors, Bollinger. Gatinois produces classic Aÿ Champagne that takes many years to reach full maturity.

• GATINOIS TRADITION BRUT   76
(90% PN, 10% CH)

• GATINOIS RÉSERVE   80
(90% PN, 10% CH)

A blend of three vintages. A very red color, massively sweet nose of honey, banana, and raisins. A broad, complex taste of mature Pinot grapes and strawberries.

• GATINOIS ROSÉ   82
(100% PN)

A delicate Aÿ rosé that contains a wide spectrum of flowery and spicy aromas and a long, elegant, balanced flavor.

• 1992 GATINOIS   87, MAR 2004 (88)
(100% PN)

A creamy Vieilles-Vignes-like item packed with baby-fat. Very generous Aÿ Pinot. Exquisite, nearly unbelievably concentrated when one considers the vintage. Pierre Cheval is beginning to stand out more and more as one of the district's foremost winemakers.

• 1991 GATINOIS   87, MAR 2004 (87)
(100% PN)

Very deep and impressive mealtime Champagne. Brilliant winemaking considering the vintage. Round and fat with village-typical nutty notes.

• 1990 GATINOIS   89, OCT 1997 (94)
(90% PN, 10% CH)

Almost bronze in color. Magnificently long taste and a fine, heavy bouquet of honeysuckle and honey.

• 1989 GATINOIS   86, APR 1996 (90)
(100% PN)

Extremely deep color, more orange than copper. A sweet, honeyed nose that is typical of the vintage. The flavor is strong and full of character.

• 1985 GATINOIS   89, MAR 2000 (91)
(90% PN, 10% CH)

A grand, gamy wine with fine basic freshness. The bouquet breathes smoke, truffles and hazelnuts. As usual, very similar to a Bollinger of the same vintage, but lacking the sophistication of its famous neighbor in Aÿ.

- 1983 GATINOIS   81, APR 1995 (85)
  (100% PN)
  Pierre Cheval's favorite vintage. Light color, faint nose of vegetable bouillon and stewed meat. An oily, gamy flavor with good acidity, thanks to the malolactic fermentation being left out this year.

GAUTHIER, ROGER R-M
8, rue Bacchus
51150 Ambonnay
03 26 57 01 94
Production: 20,000
This grower only owns grapes in his home village of Ambonnay. The grapes are either pressed by a cooperative or he does it himself.

- ROGER GAUTHIER ROSÉ   65
  (100% PN)
- 1993 GAUTHIER SPÉCIALE   79, APR 2003 (82)
  Light, bready, almost smoky and slightly coarse scent. Good, thundering taste, with notes of licorice and newly baked bread. The entire wine imparts a rather robust and simultaneously genuine impression.

GENET, MICHEL R-M
22, rue des Partelaines
51530 Chouilly
03 26 55 40 51
Production: 40,000
Right next to Legras there is a medium-sized villa where Michel Genet lives and makes Champagne. Other wines: Brut, J.-B. Fleuriot.

- MICHEL GENET BLANC DE BLANCS   65
  (100% CH)
- 1995 MICHEL GENET   70, MAY 2001 (73)
  (100% CH)
- 1990 MICHEL GENET   81, JAN 1997 (86)
  (100% CH)
  Genet's wines are always perfectly pure but slightly thin and too tactful. In this vintage the weather helped him to fill the empty spaces with an exotic richness.
- 1986 MICHEL GENET   73, APR 1993 (85)
  (100% CH)
  A shining revelation. Faint but pleasant nose of hawthorn and citrus fruits. The flavor is powder-dry, with exciting mineral tones. The aftertaste is a little short, however.

GEOFFROY, RENÉ *** R-M
150, rue Bois des Jots
51480 Cumières
03 26 55 32 31
Production: 100,000
The Geoffroy family were winemakers as long ago as the seventeenth century and have kept the property within the family since then. Besides Cumières they own vineyards in Damery, Hautvillers, and Dizy. They aim for the highest possible quality and ferment the wines in oak barrels for their Cuvée Sélectionnée

and Brut Prestige. The wines don't go through malolactic fermentation, which gives them the nerve and aging potential that most Cumières Champagnes lack. When you talk to the well-educated young Jean-Baptiste Geoffroy, you understand that this is a family that cares passionately about wine.

- GEOFFROY BRUT   77
  (34% PN, 66% CH)
- GEOFFROY CARTE BLANCHE BRUT   50
  (50% PN, 50% PM)
- GEOFFROY CUVÉE DE RÉSERVE BRUT   75
  (50% PN, 40% PM, 10% CH)
- GEOFFROY CUVÉE SÉLECTIONNÉE BRUT   80
  (66% PN, 34% CH)
  Vinified in oak barrels and always from one vintage only. It lies for five years in contact with the yeast and develops a thoroughly full autolytic character. The nose is weak but impressively complex, and the flavor expresses a cannonade of ripe fruit aromas. This Champagne will probably cope extremely well with a few years in the cellar.
- GEOFFROY PRESTIGE   75
  (33% PN, 67% CH)
- GEOFFROY ROSÉ   60
  (60% PN, 40% PM)
- 1996 GEOFFROY   85, AUG 2003 (91)
  (60% PN, 40% CH)
  This first vintage Champagne from Geoffroy is eagerly awaited. Oak barrels, of course! No malolactic fermentation or cork during the period of storage. At first the nose is rather bound and timid, but underneath the surface lies a sleeping monster that shows itself like a mini-Bollinger when aired. Acidic, hard, and beautifully animal taste. Big style, containing lots of fine tones of cider apples and Williams pears. Should keep for a long time— to open on an autumn evening in five to six years' time, accompanied by a newly shot peasant and freshly picked forest mushrooms.
- 1979 GEOFFROY   92, MAY 1994 (92)
  (70% PN, 30% CH)
  Naturally they save some bottles of their best vintages to open on suitable occasions. I considered it an honor when I was asked to share this wonderful '79 with the family in May, 1994. The color was almost bronze, the nose was delightfully broad and impressive, with elements of coffee and leather, and the flavor reminded me of an old Burgundy with clear aromas of boiled vegetables and earth. An extremely long and smoky aftertaste. Good storage potential.

GEORGETON-RAFFLIN R-M
25, rue Victor Hugo
51500 Ludes
03 26 61 13 14
Production: 7,000
Not one of the more prominent growers in the region.

- GEORGETON-RAFFLIN BRUT   39
  (33% PN, 33% PM, 34% CH)
- GEORGETON-RAFFLIN DEMI-SEC   26
  (33% PN, 33% PM, 34% CH)
- GEORGETON-RAFFLIN ROSÉ   46
  (33% PN, 33% PM, 34% CH)

GERMAIN, H. N-M
Ch. de Rilly
51500 Rilly-la-Montagne
03 26 03 49 18
Production: 1,600,000

Germain was founded in Ludes in 1898 but moved to Rilly and has strong links to Binet today. Recently deceased Henri-Louis Germain was honored with the new *cuvée de prestige* Champagne, Cuvée Président. Henri-Louis was for many years president of the town's sporting pride and joy, the Reims football team. Since 1999 the company has been owned by Vranken.

- GERMAIN TÊTE DE CUVÉE   55
  (50% PN, 35% PM, 15% CH)
- GERMAIN ROSÉ   50
  (10% PN, 10% PM, 80% CH)
- 1990 GERMAIN   82, MAR 1999 (86)
  (60% PN, 40% CH)
  A sweet, fruity, generous Champagne with clear tones of gooseberry, mango, and passion fruit in both nose and flavor. However, my fiancée was decidedly less positive when we drank this wine at the Moulin de Mougins outside Cannes.
- 1988 GERMAIN   70, MAY 1995 (79)
  (60% PN, 15% PM, 25% CH)
- 1986 GERMAIN PRÉSIDENT   80, APR 1995 (86)
  (20% PN, 80% CH)
  It's as if the prestige *cuvées* of Binet and Germain have exchanged labels. The wine has Binet's slightly more restrained Chardonnay style. The nose is Sauternes-like and the flavor is restrained, with hints of ginger, gingerbread, and strawberries.
- 1979 GERMAIN BLANC DE BLANCS   88, MAR 1996 (88)
  (100% CH)
  Yet one more step up from Binet's '79. Timid and refreshingly beautiful wine.
- 1983 CUVÉE VENUS   87, JAN 2003 (87)
  (60% PN, 40% CH)
  A really good wine from Germain. Fully evolved, of course, but without that boring, earthy, dried-up sign of aging that so many '83s are forced to carry around. Fine, delicate mousse and a beautifully subtle nose braided together with mineral and nougat. Light, smoky taste with flinty, clean resonance.
- 1979 CUVÉE VENUS   89, JAN 1996 (89)
  (60% PN, 40% CH)
  Lighter and more refined than the fleshy '76. Bready, shallow, and finely polished.
- 1976 CUVÉE VENUS   89, JAN 1996 (89)
  (60% PN, 40% CH)
  Just as good as the '79, but made in a fat style, of course, as this year should be.
- 1971 CUVÉE VENUS   87, JUL 1995 (87)
  (60% PN, 40% CH)
  Very well-kept *cuvée de prestige* with the fine acidity of the vintage and a mature nose of gorgonzola and Danish pastries.

GIMONNET, PIERRE **** R-M
1, rue de la République
51530 Cuis
03 26 59 78 70
Production: 165,000

When you travel through the Côte des Blancs you can see Gimonnet's house just by the road. It's easy to drop in spontaneously and maybe even have an improvised tasting. Gimonnet owns twenty-six hectares of Chardonnay in Cuis, Chouilly, and Cramant. The firm creates very well-made, low-priced Blanc de Blancs. He owns two plots in Cramant with vines planted in 1911! Unfortunately, Didier and Olivier Gimonnet don't like mono-*cru* Champagne, which means that their Special Club is derived from this Cramant wine—but lightened up by tart, fresh Cuis. Gimonnet know exactly what they want to do with their Champagnes, and they love young, fresh Champagne that has gone through malolactic fermentation. Just in time for the Millennium, they introduced their finest wine—Gimonnet Collection—but only in magnum, of course. Larmandier in Cramant is made by Gimonnet, and a few wines are identical, even if Larmandier Special Club is richer in style, with 100 percent Cramant. The price is far lower than the big companies' nonvintage Champagnes, despite the quality being higher.

- GIMONNET MAXI-BRUT OENOPHILE   79
  (100% CH)
- GIMONNET BLANC DE BLANCS   75
  (100% CH)
- 1998 GIMONNET   84, APR 2003 (88)
  (100% CH)
  Big and expressive Blanc de Blancs with the usual mineral clarity and lime-fresh vigor. A truly energetic summer wine with great depth. The grower himself wants it to be drunk at once, but I advise waiting a few years so it can grow into itself.
- 1997 GIMONNET GASTRONOME   79, AUG 2001 (85)
  (100% CH)
  Thirty-seven percent Cramant, 33 percent Chouilly, and 30 percent grapes from the home village of Cuis. A classic Gimonnet with austere acidity, dryness, chalky notes, dashes of lemon, and a faint but delicious undertone of egg-based baked goods. Already delicious as a refreshing aperitif, and probably really good on all occasions after 2008.
- 1996 GIMONNET FLEURON   84, DEC 2003 (90)
  (100% CH)
  Fresh and clean as alpine air. Clear in its dry, mineral-characterized expression. Long and acidic aftertaste that will be even longer if you are patient. Peach and dried apricot in the mid-palate before the draught sets in.
- 1996 GIMONNET GASTRONOME   86, SEP 2001 (92)
  (100% CH)
  Twenty-eight percent Cramant, 22 percent Chouilly, and 50 percent Cuis. This is a shining example of Gimonnet's winemaking and displays the greatness of this vintage. Crunchingly dry with stony elegance and lush, as-yet-subdued citrus fruit. Opens beautifully in the glass.
- 1995 GIMONNET   80, NOV 2000 (87)
  (100% CH)
  Taut, dry, and extremely youthful. Green apples and hawthorn lead the otherwise timid notes. Store for many years.

- 1995 GIMONNET FLEURON   83, SEP 2003 (87)
(100% CH)

Forty-two percent Cramant, 18 percent Chouilly, and 40 percent Cuis. Clearly immature and slightly straggling as yet. For the moment the wine suffers from its low dosage, which in the future will surely be an advantage. One-dimensional and strongly characterized by Cuis's stony expression.

- 1993 GIMONNET   81, NOV 1998 (84)
(100% CH)

Fascinating flowery scents of acacia and hawthorn. All in all the youthful phase that the wine currently finds itself in is very charming. The three extra potential points that I gave it will be a long time coming. Drink it now, or wait ten years.

- 1992 GIMONNET   78, NOV 1998 (80)
(100% CH)

Round and relatively mature with an exaggerated malolactic, somewhat milky character. The fruit is thoroughly satisfying.

- 1990 GIMONNET FLEURON   84, NOV 1998 (89)
(100% CH)

Well-structured and rich Champagne strongly marked by the wonderful vintage character that so many '90s can claim.

- 1989 GIMONNET   83, FEB 1996 (87)
(100% CH)

A Champagne that already displays a broad spectrum of sun-ripened tastes. Lemon, butter, and pineapple are there in both nose and flavor. An extra plus-mark for the long, creamy aftertaste.

- 1988 GIMONNET   74, MAR 1994 (83)
(100% CH)

The '88 doesn't really have the body of the '89, but the acidity is higher, which should give it an equally long life. Nor is the fruit as expansive and exotic as the '89.

- 1986 GIMONNET   83, MAR 2000 (83)
(100% CH)

Mature and buttery. Definitely a very vintage-typical Champagne that lacks buoyancy. Easily imbibed and as tame as a Swede. The more '86s I taste, the more surprised I feel at how well Selosse succeeded with this fairly average year.

- 1985 GIMONNET   69, MAR 1994 (75)
(100% CH)

- 1982 GIMONNET   90, MAY 1993 (91)
(100% CH)

A wine of exceptional quality. The nose makes me think of Taittinger Comtes de Champagne from the same year. Butterscotch, vanilla, and meadow flowers are blended with passion fruit and citrus aromas. The flavor is extremely pleasing, with a soft, delicate, honeyed aftertaste.

- 1979 GIMONNET   96, OCT 2002 (96)
(100% CH)

Oh my gosh! Certain similarities with a celebrity like Krug Clos du Mesnil from the same vintage. Honey, lanolin, cotton, and roasted chestnuts can be discerned, along with a rich, oily, almost petroleum-like keynote. Initially there is a wonderfully fat weight in the mouth before the fresh acidity and the nutty resonance take over. A great wine!

- 1961 GIMONNET   91, MAY 2002 (91)
(100% CH)

Well-preserved, nutty, rich Champagne with fresh acidity and intact citrus notes. It's always a joy to drink a beautifully aged

Blanc de Blancs from the foremost growers. At this point in time there are many similarities to Salon.

- 1996 GIMONNET SPECIAL CLUB   82, NOV 2000 (94)
(100% CH)

An embryonic, incredibly difficult wine to judge. Underneath the tartness and the green, almost grassy bouquet is something big, decidedly aristocratic, and with a petroleum fragrance. Wait at least fifteen years before you lap up this winner.

- 1995 GIMONNET COLLECTION   84, MAR 2001 (90)
(100% CH)

Stonier and in all ways meaner when compared with the sumptuously perfect '90. The 40 percent Cuis could explain this. The wine is youthful, dry, and clinically clean. Store.

- 1990 GIMONNET COLLECTION   90, FEB 2002 (93)
(100% CH)

An incredibly good wine that's only been made in a magnum for the Millennium. Present is a fantastic acidity and freshness backed up by a mature fruit that tastes of lime, ginger, and sweet lemon. A hint of vanilla and meringue are discerned. Very near 94 points. One of the freshest and most uplifting '90s in the area; the 89 percent grapes from Cramant may be an explanation as to why I think this wine is better than the '95.

- 1989 GIMONNET COLLECTION   90, JUL 2001 (92)
(100% CH)

I actually guessed at an '82 before I tasted this lush and surprisingly evolved wine from a magnum. Honey and almond notes carry the sweet nectar along to a worthy finish. Incredibly delicious and refreshingly balanced Champagne, enjoyed in the summer warmth of Liguria.

GIRAUD, HENRI R-M

71, boulevard Charles de Gaulle
51160 Aÿ
03 26 55 18 55
Production: 70,000

I discovered this grower in a Finnish women's magazine. The Aÿ grower doesn't give any details about his wines, but will happily sell a few bottles to anyone who knocks on his door. Close to three stars.

- HENRI GIRAUD BRUT RÉSERVE   77
(100% PN)

- HENRI GIRAUD ROSÉ   30
(100% PN)

- 1995 HENRI GIRAUD FÛT DE CHÊNE   87, JUL 2004 (87)
(70% PN, 30% CH)

A very good, fleshy Champagne from Aÿ with oak character and an abundance of extract. Unfortunately the wine doesn't keep at all in the glass and the deliberate oxidative character becomes much too exaggerated.

- 1993 HENRI GIRAUD FÛT DE CHÊNE   85, MAY 2000 (89)
(70% PN, 30% CH)

One hundred percent oak, 100 percent Aÿ. The Champagne doesn't feel completely integrated yet. Good concentration, refreshing acidity, and a long enjoyable palate. Oaky bouquet.

- 1991 HENRI GIRAUD   69, APR 1996 (73)
(50% PN, 50% CH)

GOBILLARD N-M

Château de Pierry
51530 Pierry
03 26 54 05 11
Production: 150,000

The Gobillard family have been winemakers in Pierry since 1836, but the house wasn't started up until 1941. His widow and his son, Jean-Paul, who is now in charge of the firm, have followed founder Paul Gobillard. Other wines: Réserve, Cuvée Régence.

* GOBILLARD CARTE BLANCHE BRUT   60
  (75% PN, 25% CH)
* GOBILLARD CARTE RÉSERVE   63
  (70% PN, 30% CH)
* GOBILLARD ROSÉ   49
  (90% PN, 10% CH)
* 1982 PAUL GOBILLARD   73, OCT 2000 (76)
  (40% PN, 60% CH)

GOBILLARD, J. M. N-M

38, rue de l'Eglise
51160 Hautvillers
03 26 51 00 24
Production: 250,000

The Gobillard Family settled in Hautvillers in 1945. Today, Thierry Gobillard runs the company. The vineyard consists of twenty-five hectares, and 30 percent of the grapes are bought. Lately, they have been experimenting with oak barrels for certain wines.

* J. M. GOBILLARD TRADITION   59
  (35% PN, 35% PM, 30% CH)
* J. M. GOBILLARD GRANDE RÉSERVE   64
  (25% PN, 25% PM, 50% CH)
* J. M. GOBILLARD BLANC DE BLANCS   64
  (100% CH)
* J. M. GOBILLARD ROSÉ   61
  (60% PN, 40% CH)
* 1999 GOBILLARD CUVÉE PRESTIGE   69, AUG 2003 (75)
  (40% PN, 60% CH)
* 1998 GOBILLARD PRIVILÈGE DES MOINES FÛT DE CHÊNE
  (30% PN, 70% CH)   82, AUG 2003 (85)
  A new prestige wine completely in line with the latest trends. The wine has been given a fine, buttery, supple character after two years in oak barrels from Puligny-Montrachet. The result: A really good and well-structured wine.
* 1997 J. M. GOBILLARD PRESTIGE   72, NOV 2002 (76)
  (40% PN, 60% CH)
* 1999 GOBILLARD CUVÉE PRESTIGE ROSÉ 71, AUG 2003 (76)
  (40% PN, 60% CH)

GODMÉ PÈRE & FILS R-M

11, rue Werle
51360 Verzenay
03 26 49 41 88
Production: 90,000

Hugues Godmé's grandfather began the business in 1935, and today Hugues owns ten hectares in Verzenay.

* GODMÉ BRUT RÉSERVE   71
  (100% PN)
  Very light and elegant, considering its origins. A pure, fine apricot aroma is handsomely combined with fresh acidity.

GODMÉ, HUGUES R-M

10, rue de Verzy
51360 Verzenay
03 26 49 48 70
Production: 85,000

The grower owns 11.5 hectares in Verzenay, Verzy, Beaumont-sur-Vesle, Villers-Marmery, and Villdommange. A minimal amount of the wines are aged in oak barrels.

* H. GODMÉ BRUT   25
  (100% PN)
* 1986 H. GODMÉ   60, JUL 1992 (69)
  (100% PN)

GODMÉ, SERGE R-M

1, rue Roger
51160 Aÿ
03 26 55 43 93
Production: 60,000

This Godmé shouldn't be confused with Bertrand Godmé in Verzenay.

* SERGE GODMÉ BRUT   39
  (80% PN, 20% CH)

GOERG, PAUL C-M

4, place du Mont Chenil
51130 Vertus
03 26 52 15 31
Production: 600,000

Paul Goerg is the brand from the La Goutte d'Or cooperative, which owns 115 hectares in Vertus, Chouilly, and Mesnil. La Goutte d'Or has for many years supplied the major houses with first-class "*vin clair*" Chardonnay. In 1982 they decided to launch their own label, using only *premier* and *grand cru* Chardonnay, and only the first pressing is considered good enough to fill Goerg's bottles. The nonvintage Champagne is first sold after three or four years and the vintage after at least five. Other wines: Rosé, Brut Absolut, Cuvée du Centenaire.

* PAUL GOERG BRUT TRADITION   68
  (40% PN, 60% CH)
* PAUL GOERG BLANC DE BLANCS   71
  (100% CH)
* 1996 PAUL GOERG   78, MAR 2003 (83)
  (100% CH)
  Packed solid with fruit and extract, but for the moment still a tad unstructured and heavy-footed. It strikes one as a bit like a painting where someone has thrown together a bunch of beautiful colors without thinking of the balance. We'll see if the

high acidity has the energy to carry the wine on to greatness via a slowly corrective development.

- 1995 PAUL GOERG   78, OCT 2001 (78)
(100% CH)
- 1990 PAUL GOERG   80, OCT 1997 (85)
(100% CH)

The wine combines power and elegance in a most satisfying fashion.

- 1988 PAUL GOERG   74, APR 1995 (82)
(100% CH)

This wine is made in the same style as their nonvintage Blanc de Blancs, but with greater concentration and better length.

GONET SULCOVA R-M

13, rue Henri Martin
51200 Épernay
03 26 54 37 63
Production: 120,000

This grower works in what is perhaps Épernay's most run-down building. Eighty percent of the fifteen hectares they own are full of Chardonnay. They own vineyards in Épernay, Oger, Le Mesnil, Vertus, Barbonne Fayel, Montgueux, and Loches-sur-Ource. The man in charge is Vincent Gonet, and of course he is related to everyone else of the same name in Côte des Blancs.

- GONET SULCOVA BLANC DE BLANCS   59
(100% CH)
- GONET SULCOVA ROSÉ   58
(100% PN)
- 1998 GONET SULCOVA GRAND CRU   80, SEP 2002 (83)
(100% CH)

You can hardly go wrong with grapes from Oger and Le Mesnil. The vintage's easy accessibility and direct charm are well highlighted in this clean, mellow wine. Under the smile lies a layer of cooler mineral character that tightens up the overall picture.

- 1989 GONET SULCOVA   80, SEP 2001 (80)
(100% CH)

In my opinion, a bit too fat and low in acidity. Gigantic almond and honey aromas fill the palate and nose. Sweet, rich taste that goes well with goat cheese and truffle honey.

- 1995 GONET SULCOVA SPECIAL CLUB   84, JUL 2002 (86)
(100% CH)

A concentrated prestige wine from fifty-five-year-old vines that is actually really explosive in its expression, with burned, bready notes and a suggestion of white chocolate. Perhaps a bit one-sided and rustic in appearance, but still fascinating in its straight, frank style.

GONET, FRANÇOIS R-M

1, rue du Stade
51190 Le Mesnil-sur-Oger
03 26 57 53 71
Production: 30,000

François is the brother of the more famous Philippe Gonet and owns eleven hectares in Le Mesnil, Cramant, and Monteux. Fifty thousand bottles are sold "*sur-lattes*" annually, and those under his own label are among the village's more basic wines. The company is just as proud of its property in Loire, Domaine de Cathyanne. Other wines: Vintage, Special Club.

- F. GONET BRUT   53
(50% PN, 50% CH)
- F. GONET RÉSERVE   58
(50% PN, 50% CH)
- F. GONET DEMI-SEC   33
(50% PN, 50% CH)
- F. GONET ROSÉ   48
(20% PN, 40% PM, 40% CH)

GONET, MICHEL *** R-M

196, avenue Jean-Jaurès
51190 Avize
03 26 57 50 56
Production: 300,000

One of Champagne's biggest growers in terms of volume, and one of the most colorful personalities in the region. Michel Gonet, who is a keen huntsman, controls forty hectares in Avize, Le Mesnil, Vindey, Montgueux, Oger, and Fravaux. Eighty percent of the ground is planted with Chardonnay, and three-quarters of production is exported to English-speaking countries, where his dubiously named Champagne Marquis de Sade is a big hit. Michel Gonet makes quite a few commercial, uncomplicated wines, but all his vintage Champagnes have a good reputation. Since 1986, the Gonet family has owned Château Lesparre, a huge domain of 180 hectares in Graves de Vayres.

- MICHEL GONET BRUT   59
(50% PN, 50% CH)
- MARQUIS DE SADE   68
(100% CH)
- MICHEL GONET BLANC DE BLANCS GRAND CRU   70
(100% CH)
- MICHEL GONET RÉSERVE BLANC DE BLANCS   69
(100% CH)
- MICHEL GONET ROSÉ   45
(100% PN)
- 1996 MICHEL GONET   77, MAY 2003 (82)
(20% PN, 80% CH)

Very personal and intensely perfumed scent; I also detected, beside the floral notes, licorice and boiled meat. Decidedly elastic, Mesnil-like palate, carrying the imprints of the grower.

- 1996 MICHEL GONET RÉSERVE   79, FEB 2002 (80)
(30% PN, 70% CH)

Grapes from Vindey, Fravaux, and Montgueux are included, something you really notice. The wine completely misled me at a pleasant little private tasting in my home with ten Blanc de Blancs from *grand cru* villages. I was careless enough to think that this was one of them. The wine stood out as strange and oxidative in comparison to the others. Fully evolved with notes of mushroom, licorice, and hyacinth. Considerably nicer by itself than tasted alongside elegant beauties from Avize, Cramant, and Le Mesnil.

- 1994 MICHEL GONET   80, NOV 2003 (83)
(100% CH)

A slightly strange vintage that still needs a few years to develop something exciting. Maybe the acidity and the somewhat skinny body will get some muscles by then, but I doubt it. Gonet always makes Blanc de Blancs that are more powerful than elegant. This time the real power is missing. The overall picture is brightened by good clarity and acidity.

- 1993 MICHEL GONET   82, APR 2000 (85)
(100% CH)
Very broad, almost big-house-influenced bouquet, with hints of newly baked bread and biscuits. Ample, lemony-fresh flavor with undertones of mandarin and spices. Good structure and a low dosage worthy of praise.

- 1988 MARQUIS DE SADE   73, JUL 1996 (83)
(100% CH)
A concentrated, rich Champagne with good vinosity but without the charm or elegance that one has the right to demand from Avize.

- 1982 MICHEL GONET   85, JAN 2002 (85)
(100% CH)
Rich and fat '82 lacking greater finesse. Buttery finish with an undertone of mushrooms.

- 1976 MICHEL GONET   93, FEB 2003 (93)
(100% CH)
The '76 is a great wine full of manly power, richness, and spice. One of the vintage's stars, with its oily fruit and remarkable smokiness.

- 1990 MICHEL GONET   84, JUL 2003 (87)
(100% CH)
Big and brusque with smoky, warm notes as well as a nascent maturity. Many—above all those who have never tasted the grower's fatty-sweet '76—believe that the wine has reached its peak, but I'm convinced that it will become more harmonious and polished in five years or so.

- 1992 MICHEL GONET ROSÉ   59, SEP 1997 (61)
(100% PN)

- 1998 MICHEL GONET PRESTIGE   78, MAR 2004 (84)
(100% CH)
Something of a disappointment to me. Personally I find it a bit too coarse, earthy, rustic, and disobligingly dry for the time being. However, I know how well Gonet's wines develop with time, and clearly there is enough *terroir* and extract present to create a fine future harmony.

- 1996 MICHEL GONET PRESTIGE   84, OCT 2003 (88)
(100% CH)
Grapes from Oger and Le Mesnil here too. Classic purity and smoky, almost flinty complexity, with big, evolved fruit and beautiful underlying acidity. A real tidbit in a few years.

GONET, PHILIPPE *** R-M
6, route de Vertus
51190 Le Mesnil-sur-Oger
03 26 57 53 47
Production: 150,000
This Gonet is of course a relative of Michel Gonet in Avize. The family business has been around for six generations, since 1820, and has one of the most impressive collections of old vintages in all of Champagne. Of Gonet's nineteen hectares, six lie in Oger and the rest in Le Mesnil. Today the property is run by Chantal Brégeon Gonet and her brother Pierre Gonet. Candidate for four stars.

- P. GONET ARTIST BOTTLE   75
(100% CH)

- P. GONET RÉSERVE   56
(50% PN, 50% CH)

- P. GONET BLANC DE BLANCS   68
(100% CH)

- P. GONET ROSÉ   63
(5% PN, 95% CH)

- 1998 P. GONET   84, JUN 2003 (88)
(100% CH)
Brilliant evidence that wines from Mesnil and Oger must be given lots of time. The wine has superb potential, but for the moment it is a biting, unripe experience with purity and lots of minerality. The biscuit-like finish gives a hint of what our children will experience. Ninety-eight percent Mesnil and 2 percent Oger.

- 1996 P. GONET   85, SEP 2003 (89)
(100% CH)
Hide this wine away deep in the cellar and forget where you've stored it for the time being. It's good already, sure, but the true reward won't be for a while. A big, well-structured, storable wine to surprise friends with in ten or so years.

- 1995 P. GONET   84, JUN 2003 (86)
(100% CH)
Buttery and evolved with a rich milk-chocolate-like sensation in the mouth. Not really classic or village-typical. Lacks a little bite, which is unusual for this producer.

- 1990 P. GONET   82, FEB 1997 (88)
(100% CH)
A rich, vintage-typical wine, with a clear aroma of saffron and a long aftertaste.

- 1988 P. GONET   75, JUL 1995 (85)
(100% CH)
Pure, elegant, crisp, full of mineral, and bone dry.

- 1975 P. GONET   96, OCT 2002 (96)
(100% CH)
Oh, so beautiful! I had hardly counted on this wine being the very best I've tasted from this grower. Neighboring Salon, for example, had skipped the '75. The apogee of finesse is now exhibited to those few who go down into Gonet's cellar and taste this hidden treasure. The wine is reminiscent of a '66 and '79 from Launois and a '73 from Pierre Peters. The entire wine exudes Le Mesnil.

- 1966 P. GONET   91, JUN 2003 (91)
(100% CH)
Slightly tired appearance and mousse. Still classic and beautiful; nutty, dry, and almost salty, with a buttery depth that only wines from Mesnil acquire.

- 1945 P. Gonet
(100% CH)

- P. GONET ROY SOLEIL   84, DEC 2003 (88)
(100% CH)
This new prestige *cuvée* from Mesnil has spent eight months in new 600-liter Burgundy barrels. Because the barrels are so large, the oak influence is smaller, but the wine is probably quite characterized by this treatment. As usual with such barreled wine, decanting is recommended. The first version is made of the young vintages 2000 and 2001. The acidity is very high and the fruit extremely promising.

- 1998 P. GONET SPECIAL CLUB   85, JUL 2003 (91)
(100% CH)
Big, dry, and powerful Blanc de Blancs with all the concentration one has a right to expect from a Club bottle. Fine mineral notes play faintly in the background.

- 1996 P. GONET SPECIAL CLUB   88, SEP 2003 (92)
(100% CH)

Textbook Champagne from Le Mesnil! Incredibly focused and balanced with luxurious fat and concentrated fruit. The high acidity is in no way troubling because it is enveloped in so much wonderful stuff.

- 1995 P. GONET SPECIAL CLUB   85, FEB 2002 (88)
(100% CH)

Rarely do I happily prefer a '96 over a '95 of the same wine, as I have in this case. This wine is very good, but gets nowhere near the next year's vintage, even in the beginning. Polished, fine, and medium-bodied, with notes of red citrus in the stony finish.

- 1990 P. GONET SPECIAL CLUB D. T.   91, JUN 2003 (92)
(100% CH)

Keeps together brilliantly but not evolved as yet. Toffee notes and exotic fruit set the tone. A delight to follow!

- 1989 P. GONET SPECIAL CLUB   80, JUL 1995 (88)
(100% CH)

Made from sixty-six-year-old vines in Les Hauts Jardins. So fat and chewy that it almost feels clumsy.

- 1988 P. GONET SPECIAL CLUB   88, MAY 2002 (92)
(100% CH)

Incredibly concentrated and rich Champagne with tones of red fruit, almonds, and beeswax. A deceptive impression of maturity.

- 1988 P. GONET SPECIAL CLUB D. T.   93, JUN 2003 (93)
(100% CH)

Newly disgorged and without dosage, this wine is totally evolved and beautiful at the age of fifteen. Salon-like nuttiness and austere elegance of browned butter and oysters.

- 1976 P. GONET SPECIAL CLUB   89, OCT 2002 (89)
(100% CH)

This '76—as an un-dosaged cellar-baby—is slightly oxidative and corpulent, without the finesse that has made the village famous. Probably more enjoyable when newly disgorged. Why not in a magnum?

GOSSET **** N-M

69, rue Jules Blondeau
51160 Aÿ
03 26 56 99 56
Production: 900,000

Ruinart might be the oldest Champagne-producing firm, but Gosset made still wines much earlier. Pierre Gosset sold his "*vin d'Aÿ*" as a *négociant* as early as 1584. Today the family owns twelve hectares in the villages of Aÿ, Bouzy, Mareuil, and Rilly, all filled with Pinot Noir. This is only enough for 20 percent of their needs, but the village character is clearly noted in their vintage wines. Gosset is one of the true traditionalists of the region, with labeling and disgorging done by hand. For a short time they store their vintage wines in oak barrels, imparting a hint of oak character into the wine. The wines are always fleshy and rich, with a large element of Aÿ Pinot and high-class Chardonnay. The winemaker is the clever Jean-Pierre Mareignier. In 1994, after more than 400 years of family ownership, Gosset was sold to the family group Renaud-Cointreau, which owns Cognac Pierre Frapin Grande Champagne. As Gosset is known and appreciated by initiated wine-lovers the world over, they can increase their international presence while still keeping their high quality. The distinct *cuvées* are served at the finest restaurants. The vintage wines are especially enjoyable with the ethereal '52 as a milestone—it won third prize at the Millennium Tasting! One of the absolute foremost houses in the Champagne region.

- GOSSET BRUT EXCELLENCE   80
(42% PN, 9% PM, 49% CH)

Less mighty and concentrated than the Grande Réserve, but more enjoyable in large amounts. The wine is rich in Pinot fruit and chocolate aromas. The dosage is unnecessarily high in both of Gosset's nonvintage Champagnes.

- GOSSET GRANDE RÉSERVE   83
(40% PN, 12% PM, 48% CH)

A fat, oily Champagne with tons of mature apples and a meaty Pinot taste. Only in the mineral-rich finish does one notice the Chardonnay grapes. Wonderfully rich nonvintage Champagne that is always among the best.

- GOSSET BRUT (1966-BASE)   92, JUN 2001 (92)
(40% PN, 10% PM, 50% CH)

Jean-Pierre Mareignier, cellar man at Gosset, has at his disposal a very interesting cellar, where chaos and disorder reign after a recent move. This wine came from the exciting surprise section of the cellar. After meticulously checking the cork and the flavor, we found that this was a nonvintage Champagne with 1966 at its core. The wine itself is a wonderful example of how well the foremost nonvintage Champagnes can develop under perfect conditions. Nineteen sixty-six was, it is true, an exceptional year, and one must remember that oak barrels were still used in the majority of cases. I have become sufficiently convinced to hide away a few of Gosset's nonvintage Champagnes in the darkest corner of my cellar.

- GOSSET GRANDE ROSÉ   88
(40% PN, 14% PM, 46% CH)

Big and powerful, like all of Gosset's wines. Somewhat rustic and one-dimensional, with grower-like aromas when it first came on the market. The bouquet evokes thoughts of red-apple-peelings and plums. Today the wine is very big and harmonious, with a big dollop of freshness and elegance. The sensation is very round and compact to the palate, with an aftertaste of the juiciest apples.

- 1983 GOSSET   88, DEC 2003 (88)
(60% PN, 40% CH)

Vigorously Pinot-dominated taste and fine fatty structure. Most of the tasters found an apple flavor. Personally, I feel that plum, raisin, and red beets are comparisons that more aptly describe this fleshy Champagne.

- 1979 GOSSET   93, JAN 2003 (93)
(34% PN, 5% PM, 61% CH)

Today, a classic Champagne that well represents both the vintage and the house. Perfect balance, a compound and seductive bouquet, as well as a lovely, nutty finish.

- 1978 GOSSET   91, JAN 2002 (91)
(34% PN, 5% PM, 61% CH)

I knew that Gosset's rich, rounded style would perfectly suit this slightly thin vintage. I usually find a hollowness in the mid-palate with most of the '78s, but not this time. The nose is really good, with a Krug-like complexity of spices, wood, honey, duck liver, and nut toffee. The taste isn't really of the same class, even if it holds together in an excellent manner.

- 1976 GOSSET   95, JAN 2003 (95)
(50% PN, 50% CH)

Amazing acidity in an almost oily, chewable wine. Marvelous aromas of tea, apricot, and honey.

- 1975 GOSSET   93, JUN 2001 (93)
(60% PN, 40% CH)

The '75 is wonderful today. At the age of thirteen it still retained its youth, but one could detect a hint of the chocolate aromas to come. Massive, rich, fat fruit with a long, dry, and stringent aftertaste. The stringency is still there like a unified spine, even if the wine has become nutty and honey-saturated.

- **1973 GOSSET**   93, APR 2002 (93)
(60% PN, 40% CH)
Typical oxidative Gosset style, with hints of purple coneflower, red apples, honey, and truffles, both in the scent and the taste. The structure is masculine and fleshy and the vigor unmistakable. Tasted newly disgorged and without dosage. When newly disgorged the wine seems beautifully floral.

- **1971 GOSSET**   93, NOV 1996 (93)
(60% PN, 40% CH)
The '71 has almost become a creature of myth. I didn't think it was all that wonderful. However, this is a muscular '71 with a smoky Pinot character *à la* Bollinger.

- **1970 GOSSET**   94, JUN 2001 (94)
(40% PN, 60% CH)
A fantastic '70 with deep color, superb acidity, and buttery notes of mature Chardonnay. The low yield has arranged a concentrated, complete drink full of aromas. I've written in my notebook: crème brûlée, coffee, chanterelle, and nougat.

- **1966 GOSSET**   88, JAN 2001 (88)
(40% PN, 60% CH)
Taking into account that the wine was still in good condition, eighty-eight points are a disappointment. Refreshing mousse and impressive structure. Unfortunately, the wine, with its vegetal, gamy, rather demanding aroma, was one-dimensional and slightly lacking in charm.

- **1964 GOSSET**   92, JUN 1999 (95)
(34% PN, 66% CH)
A newly disgorged magnum without added sugar, which accounts for the span between the points assigned at this tasting and the potential points. Extremely youthful and delicate Gosset. Subtle flowery scent of hawthorn, lilies, and digestive biscuits. Even the taste is pure and filled with a mineral-rich finesse. Dosage and a few more years in the bottle after being disgorged are needed to allow the wine to round off some of its sharp edges.

- **1961 GOSSET**   94, MAY 2001 (94)
(60% PN, 40% CH)
Bright and smooth, with strawberry, raspberry, and red plum notes at the center. More elegance than strength, despite the red-wine-like soft aromas.

- **1959 GOSSET**   95, JAN 2003 (95)
(60% PN, 40% CH)
The '59 Gosset is as good as it sounds. Muscular and round at the same time, with a delightful attacking hazelnut flavor and a smooth aftertaste of honey.

- **1952 GOSSET**   99, JUN 2001 (99)
(60% PN, 40% CH)
A delightful wine with wonderful complexity and toasty notes. Youthful, with a long and lively toffee flavor. Incredibly intense and well balanced with a nutty keynote. Wine doesn't get much better than this. A giant that took third place at the Millennium Tasting. My former colleague favorite Champagne—it actually made him cry on a rainy day in Aÿ.

- **1996 GOSSET GRAND MILLÉSIME**   90, FEB 2004 (93)
(38% PN, 62% CH)

Already a grand and concentrated, oily, full-bodied wine. The flavor is a fine balancing act between softness and freshness. Nuts, toffee, and honey are already recognizable aromas in this compact, youthful, passion-fruit-tasting wine.

- **1995 GOSSET CÉLEBRIS**   88, OCT 2003 (94)
(54% PN, 46% CH)
Mild, delicious, and surprisingly mellow. I usually recognize Champagnes that have not gone through malolactic fermentation straightaway, by their bouquet. There is nothing here of the usual prickliness that denotes these types of wine in their youth. Ten percent oak is a rather nice spice here. Fine development through the years.

- **1993 GOSSET GRAND MILLÉSIME**   89, MAY 2003 (90)
(46% PN, 54% CH)
There is a definite similarity to the Chardonnay-dominated tastes in Célebris. The wine is very floral and fresh, without the oxidative plumpness that we've become accustomed to with Gosset's Champagnes. Suddenly completely evolved in the summer of 2003.

- **1990 GOSSET CÉLEBRIS**   91, FEB 2003 (94)
(34% PN, 66% CH)
The same style as '88, but even more concentrated and with a greater depth. The character bears resemblance to Krug, Gratien, and Salon. The apple tang is bitingly fresh and the oak character evident. According to many judges, this is one of the best Champagnes Gosset has ever produced. Despite that, this Champagne was one of the weakest at the Millennium Tasting.

- **1989 GOSSET GRAND MILLÉSIME**   90, JAN 2003 (90)
(34% PN, 66% CH)
Almost chewable and viscous with a developed, reddish color. The nose is heavy and overwhelming, with notes of fig and windfall fruit. Completely evolved now.

- **1988 GOSSET CÉLEBRIS**   91, NOV 2003 (94)
(34% PN, 66% CH)
Lighter and more delicate than usual, with an appetizing, flowery nose and an exquisite, crispy lime flavor. This is the first vintage of this remarkable wine. Incredibly slow development curve—a candidate for decanting.

- **1985 GOSSET GRAND MILLÉSIME**   92, FEB 2002 (94)
(38% PN, 62% CH)
One of the most classic Champagnes from Gosset that I've tasted. A wine in perfect equilibrium, with an impeccable appearance and a refined spectrum in the nose—of white flowers, nectar, passion fruit, mango, and a faint barrel tone. The wine hasn't gone through the malolactic fermentation, which gives a frisky bite to the pure, flowery, and fruity aromas.

- **1983 GOSSET CUVÉE SUZANNE**   82, APR 1996 (85)
(60% PN, 40% CH)
Sadly too sweet, but enjoyably round and almost robust in large amounts. Undeniably rich and impressive.

- **1983 GOSSET GRAND MILLÉSIME**   82, AUG 1997 (85)
(60% PN, 40% CH)
A big, powerful wine that many would surely deem mature. Personally, the overwhelmingly sweet, oxidative fruit is slightly unbalanced at present. The wine is reminiscent of the solid '83.

- **1982 GOSSET GRAND MILLÉSIMÉ GREEN LABEL**   84, MAY 1991 (89)
(55% PN, 7% PM, 38% CH)
A weak, nutty, and stylish Champagne for the aesthete. Lighter and more restrained than the "Red Label."

- 1982 GOSSET GRAND MILLÉSIMÉ RED LABEL   89, MAY 1994 (89)
(60% PN, 40% CH)
A mature Pinot style. The home ground of Aÿ has certainly left its
mark on this round and overflowing, full-bodied, plum-like flavor.

- 1979 GOSSET GRAND MILLÉSIMÉ   80, JAN 2002 (80)
(60% PN, 40% CH)
I was very disappointed when I took this seemingly perfect
Champagne to celebrate New Year's Eve 2002. It was the
unclean, slightly musty smell that muddled the impression.
Otherwise the taste was round and good with notes of figs,
truffles, raisins, and red apples. The color is medium-deep and
the mousse is relatively spirited, which should assure delicious
Champagne.

- 1975 GOSSET GRAND MILLÉSIMÉ   91, JAN 2002 (92)
(60% PN, 40% CH)
Two days after being really disappointed by the '79, I opened
this—on paper—weaker wine with a few friends. This is just how
unpredictable the wine world is: this oldie was as spry as the '79
was tired. I actually believe that this wine can develop even more
from its vigorous youthful plateau. It still has a few un-evolved,
slightly hard extracts, and is reminiscent of Deutz from the same
year. Unmistakable deep Aÿ-Pinot with streaks of tar and
honeysuckle. Long, fruity aftertaste with high level of acidity
and a certain hardness in the finish.

- 1998 GOSSET CÉLEBRIS ROSÉ   89, OCT 2003 (94)
(39% PN, 61% CH)
Already a full-fledged luxury rosé with juicy fruit, plumpness,
and vinous complexity. Enormously fresh and aromatic, with
Gosset's apple notes handsomely intertwined with strawberry-
fragrant Pinot and butter-caressing Chardonnay.

- 1990 GOSSET GRAND MILLÉSIMÉ ROSÉ   90, MAR 2003 (92)
(18% PN, 82% CH)
This light wine has an aroma of oak-fermented Chardonnay that
hasn't gone through malolactic fermentation. The resemblance to
Selosse Rosé is striking. It has a fine attack and plenty of
personality and richness.

- 1988 GOSSET GRAND MILLÉSIMÉ ROSÉ   83, NOV 1994 (88)
(18% PN, 82% CH)
Sixty percent of the wine has been vinified in oak barrels,
which hardly makes a difference. Here the elegant Chardonnay is
the mark of distinction. So far the excellent nose of strawberry,
cream, and mineral is rather discreet. The flavor is more
impressive with deep, thought-provoking, and elegantly nutty
Chardonnay.

- 1985 GOSSET GRAND MILLÉSIME ROSÉ   93, JAN 2003 (94)
(18% PN, 82% CH)
Sensational, outstanding, unique Champagne with a ripe orange
color and amazingly multifaceted nose. The dominant tones are
mint chocolate and forest mushrooms. The flavor is creamy and
tremendously buttery.

- 1982 GOSSET GRAND MILLÉSIME ROSÉ   88, JAN 2004 (88)
(12% PN, 88% CH)
A reputable rosé made in contemporary fashion. Light, beautiful
color, bubbling mousse, fine mineral character leaning toward the
lighter side. A laid-back wine that really doesn't make much noise
but that lately has become richer and better.

- 1986 GOSSET CUVÉE LIBERTÉ   84
Nonvintage anniversary wine with high dosage to suit the
American palate. Nice looks and a pleasant toffee and mint-

smelling bouquet. Unfortunately the wine doesn't hold very well
in the glass and must be considered a disappointment.

- GOSSET LA TOUR EIFFEL
(60% PN, 40% CH)

- 1983 GOSSET LA TOUR EIFFEL   87, JAN 2002 (87)
(60% PN, 40% CH)
This beautiful label and—today—nutty, dry Champagne was
made for the 100th Anniversary of the completion of the Eiffel
Tower, celebrated in 1989. It is a well-preserved '83 with a young
appearance and nice mousse. The nose exudes hazelnut and
chocolate but the taste is somewhat dried out, as is the case with
so many Champagnes from this overrated year.

- GOSSET CUVÉE LIBERTÉ ROSÉ   1986 83, JAN 2003 (83)
A clear glass bottle that was made to celebrate the birthday of the
Statue of Liberty. The base wine is from the end of the '70s and
the beginning of the '80s. Light orange color. Smoky and simple,
oxidative note. Light taste without any greater dimensions.

GOSSET-BRABANT *** R-M
23, boulevard du Maréchal-de-Lattre-de-Tassigny
51160 Aÿ
03 26 55 17 42
Production: 50,000
Strangely enough, many growers in Côte des Blancs praise this
grower who is Bollinger's neighbor. The family have been
winegrowers in Aÿ since 1584. Gosset-Brabant is one of the few
who make Aÿ rouge. They only make 1,500 bottles of this treasure,
which I consider to be one of the district's foremost red wines.

- GOSSET-BRABANT TRADITION   70
(70% PN, 10% PM, 20% CH)

- GOSSET-BRABANT RÉSERVE   77
(75% PN, 5% PM, 20% CH)

- GOSSET-BRABANT ROSÉ   51
(74% PN, 8% PM, 18% CH)

- 1997 CUVÉE GABRIEL SPECIAL CLUB   88, FEB 2004 (90)
(70% PN, 30% CH)
This is the first time I have seen a Special Club bottle with an
additional name. Is this allowed? No matter what, the wine is
wonderfully enjoyable. Creamy and harmonious with a
luxuriously concentrated feeling; only wines made with grapes
from old vines from the foremost villages can convey this feeling.

- 1995 CUVÉE GABRIEL   89, OCT 2001 (93)
(70% PN, 30% CH)
Personally, I think the brothers have succeeded in making an
extremely good wine. The recipe is pure Aÿ without malolactic
fermentation. At the moment, the wine is smartly youthful with
certain Roederer basic characteristics and an enormous crispy
finesse. Promising and exceptionally well made.

- 1990 CUVÉE GABRIEL   83, MAR 2000 (83)
(70% PN, 30% CH)
Truly a pumped-up, generous wine with heaps of maturity, honey
flavors, and a decided taste-build-up of red fruits. The wine is
slightly one-dimensional despite a pleasant dash of honeysuckle. Fine
concentration, but should a '90 be mature before its tenth birthday?

- 1989 CUVÉE GABRIEL   74, JUL 1995 (83)
(70% PN, 30% CH)
The nose is creamy and full of sweet plums. A good initial taste,
but the length is insufficient.

GOULET, GEORGE *** N-M
1, avenue de Paris
51100 Reims
03 26 66 44 88
Production: 1,500,000
A firm with a complicated history. François André Goulet started
the business in 1834, and in 1960 the house was taken over by Abel
Lepitre, who let the well-respected name fade away. Today most of
the operation has moved to Vaudemanges, where Luc Chaudron is
determined to elevate Goulet's name to the top echelons once again
(Goulet was a supplier to the Swedish Royal Family for many
years). Less than 10 percent of production—100,000 bottles—are
sold under the Goulet name, with most marketed under the
"Buyer's Own Brand," or as Chaudron & Fils. The company makes
some lovely, soft, Pinot-based Champagnes of great quality.

- G. GOULET BRUT   76
(66% PN, 34% CH)
- G. GOULET ROSÉ   75
(70% PN, 30% CH)
- 1988 G. GOULET   80, NOV 1994 (86)
(66% PN, 34% CH)
In the nose I found mostly Chardonnay tones like flowers and
cream. The flavor, on the other hand, is dominated by the
characteristic house aroma of soft Pinot Noir. Long, almond
aftertaste.
- 1985 VEUVE G. GOULET   80, NOV 1994 (89)
(50% PN, 50% CH)
Young, undeveloped Champagne, which holds much of interest
within it. Fine bakery tones in the nose and good attack in the
mouth, but the aftertaste needs a few more years in order to
develop a satisfactory length.
- 1982 G. GOULET   87, DEC 1999 (87)
(66% PN, 34% CH)
This wine caused a sensation around a Christmas table
dominated by women at the home of one of my best friends.
Most waxed lyrical about this ingratiating, milk-chocolaty tasting
and syrupy-smelling Champagne. Personally, I was carried along
by the hedonistic atmosphere, but the wine has too high a dosage
and the aftertaste is too short.
- 1979 G. GOULET   89, MAR 2000 (89)
(66% PN, 34% CH)
Mature, yeasty, newly baked character with a stable backbone of
distinguished Pinot Noir. With time in the glass, one can divine
the vintage's hazelnut aroma. Massive, gastronomically directed
taste with a finely tart and spicy twist.
- 1976 G. GOULET   88, MAY 2000 (88)
(66% PN, 34% CH)
Extravagantly fat and rich in alcohol. Clearly impressive, but I
missed tartness—perhaps because I drank this rather demanding
Champagne on its own, out of doors, in the sun of a fair May
day; it is probably better with food.
- 1975 G. GOULET   88, JAN 2000 (88)
(66% PN, 34% CH)
Austere and dry. Lively bouquet with an oaky undertone.
Charming is a word that seems alien here; serious and stringent
are more suitable epithets for this well-made, still youthful,
distinguished Champagne.
- 1973 G. GOULET   89, OCT 1996 (89)
(60% PN, 40% CH)

Full, big, fruity and mature on the palate. Chocolaty nose. Drink
at once.
- 1970 G. GOULET   86, APR 2000 (86)
(66% PN, 34% CH)
Far too few '70s have shown themselves capable of withstanding
storage. Most are on the way down. Even Goulet's version has
seen better days, but personally I think that this—bordering on
overripe, aldehyde-rich wine—still exhibits a distinguished and
tranquil charm.
- 1942 G. GOULET
(66% PN, 34% CH)
- 1928 G. GOULET   90, MAY 2001 (90)
(66% PN, 34% CH)
Normally the acidity is very noticeable in the '28s, but here the
entire wine felt very syrupy, sweet, and mellow. Like a
harmonious dessert wine from Loire, this peach-tasting nectar
scurried down our welcoming throats. Hardly noticeable mousse,
fine youthful pure color, and completely devoid of sherry aromas.
- 1926 G. GOULET   84, DEC 2002 (84)
(66% PN, 34% CH)
Old, noble appearance, with the same edge of orange as an older
German *Beerenauslese*. Smells and tastes of old Tokay. No mousse,
but good acidity and fine dark, burned aromas. Like an elderly
gentleman in a bowler.
- 1904 HENRY GOULET
(70% PN, 30% CH)
- 1982 G. GOULET BLANC DE BLANCS   78, DEC 1996 (78)
(100% CH)
- 1973 G. GOULET BLANC DE BLANCS   79, SEP 1997 (79)
(100% CH)
- 1976 G. GOULET CUVÉE DU CENTENAIRE   91, JAN 2002 (91)
(66% PN, 34% CH)
Better freshness and more bubbling mousse than with the usual
'76. Whether that depends on the bottle variation, or whether
this *cuvée* actually is a somewhat better wine, I will leave unsaid.
Very light color and simultaneously—strangely enough—a
powerful bouquet of Brussels sprouts and other boiled vegetables
combined with smoked, candy-like aromas. Great complexity and
weight. Fine character of mature Pinot Noir with a magnificent
fleshiness and balance.

GOUTORBE, H.*** R-M
9, bis rue Jeanson
51160 Aÿ
03 26 55 21 70
Production: 120,000
Henri and his son René Goutorge are known for their Aÿ rouge, but
they also make fine Champagne. The firm belongs among the few
that sell older vintages. Most of the wines have a fine plumpness,
and if you are lucky you may discern lovely notes of summer's most
delicious floral fragrances, such as jasmine and honeysuckle.

- H. GOUTORBE BRUT   75
(65% PN, 5% PM, 30% CH)
- H. GOUTORBE PRESTIGE   77
(65% PN, 5% PM, 30% CH)
- H. GOUTORBE BLANC DE BLANCS   65
(100% CH)
- H. GOUTORBE ROSÉ   61
(100% PN)

- 1998 H. GOUTORBE 82, FEB 2004 (84)
(66% PN, 34% CH)

Highly personal style with lots of yellow plums mixed into the whole. A certain floweriness with acridness and perfume. Fine, concentrated taste that could have been longer.

- 1996 H. GOUTORBE 83, SEP 2003 (86)
(66% PN, 34% CH)

More mellow than expected, but it's probably dumb to expect a tart wine from Goutorbe. What I mean is, these wines are usually fat, oily, and slightly flat, with windfall fruit aromas. That's why '96 is a good year for Goutorbe. The nose is village-typical, but it also has a buttery film over the windfall fruit and purple coneflower notes.

- 1995 H. GOUTORBE 81, APR 2003 (83)
(66% PN, 34% CH)

Developed, rather sweet, and slightly raisiny. To be frank, I had expected more from this normally reliable grower. Soft, round, and unusually rustic.

- 1994 H. GOUTORBE 77, SEP 2001 (79)
(67% PN, 33% CH)

- 1983 H. GOUTORBE 90, SEP 1996 (90)
(66% PN, 34% CH)

A sensual Champagne with a lovely nose of honeysuckle, oyster shell, and leather. The flavor may not be quite so sensational, but is rich enough to take it up to the magic ninety-point mark.

- 1982 H. GOUTORBE 86, JAN 2003 (86)
(66% PN, 34% CH)

A supreme nose of honeysuckle and a sweet, mature, honeyed flavor with elements of plum.

- 1976 H. GOUTORBE 86, MAY 1996 (86)
(66% PN, 34% CH)

This oldie was still on sale in May, 1996. Rather recently disgorged and very well kept, it's a good example of the house-style. There's power beneath the elegant surface, and the mineral tones are very clear.

- 1989 H. GOUTORBE SPECIAL CLUB 84, FEB 2003 (84)
(50% PN, 50% CH)

A pure Aÿ Champagne with golden color and scent of roses, plums, and cream. Fresh, rich taste that's very fleshy and clearly best suited to substantial meals. Somewhat blunt.

- 1988 H. GOUTORBE SPECIAL CLUB 85, JUL 1995 (89)
(70% PN, 30% CH)

Incredibly rich, round, and accessible, creamy and sweet.

- 1987 H. GOUTORBE SPECIAL CLUB 80, APR 1996 (82)
(66% PN, 34% CH)

An elegant and focused '87 with a fine tone of brioche and vanilla. Somewhat hollow and green with a pleasant vanilla tone returning in the aftertaste.

GRATIEN, ALFRED **** N-M

30, rue Maurice Cerveaux
51200 Épernay
03 26 54 38 20
Production: 175,000

Founded in 1864 in Épernay, this is one of the most traditional Champagne houses. All wines are fermented in small oak barrels and the reserve wines are stored in large oak *foudres* (vats). Malolactic fermentation is also avoided. The chief reason Gratien does not make wines as great as Bollinger or Krug is that the grapes purchased from outside are not always of the highest class. Pinot Meunier also makes up a surprisingly large proportion of the grape content. The wines made by Jean Pierre Jaeger are, on the other hand, very good: true Champagnes for the cellar, full of youthful acidity. The '55 is historic, but the house refused to release any of their three last bottles for the Millennium Tasting.

- A. GRATIEN BRUT 78
(12% PN, 44% PM, 44% CH)

- A. GRATIEN CUVÉE LINGSTRÖM 78
(12% PN, 44% PM, 44% CH)

- A. GRATIEN CLASSIC RÉSERVE 76
(10% PN, 45% PM, 45% CH)

- A. GRATIEN ROSÉ 67
(20% PN, 20% PM, 60% CH)

- 1996 A. GRATIEN 90, SEP 2003 (94)

One of the absolute foremost vintages ever from Gratien. Simply a wonderfully, beautifully braided composition. A real work of art with oily, accessible, modern fruit with buttery elements. Fresh acidity under a layer of vanilla-propelled aromas. Elegant and as sophisticated as an Italian sports car. However, I was somewhat less impressed at my latest tasting.

- 1991 A. GRATIEN 85, JAN 2003 (89)
(21% PN, 7% PM, 72% CH)

More developed and creamy than the almost aggressive '90. It takes many years, of course, before the wine takes on its final form. Personally, I think there is enough baby-fat and fruity sweetness here for the level of enjoyment to be satisfying already.

- 1990 A. GRATIEN 89, JAN 2003 (94)
(15% PN, 20% PM, 65% CH)

A classic Gratien! This means that the acidity is raw and sharp as a knife, which in turn means that at least ten years of additional storage are recommended. Those who can bear to wait long enough will experience an impressive Champagne with a colossal depth.

- 1989 A. GRATIEN 87, MAR 2003 (90)
(10% PN, 30% PM, 60% CH)

In recent years this wine has begun to take on a floral profile, with its own particularly perfumed fragrance. Acidic and probably long-lived. It's difficult to predict where this wine will go in the future.

- 1988 A. GRATIEN 88, JAN 2004 (93)
(16% PN, 26% PM, 58% CH)

Initially bound, but when aired the wine exhibits delicious chocolate aromas. Dry, clean, acidic with an extremely long, ringing aftertaste. Slightly strange and medicinal when I tasted my way through the forty-five best '88s in November 2003.

- 1985 A. GRATIEN 85, OCT 1997 (88)
(30% PN, 40% PM, 30% CH)

Lovely floral bouquet with minty undertones. A strange wine when it was released, but today it is creamy and very elegant.

- 1983 A. GRATIEN 94, FEB 2004 (94)
(40% PN, 20% PM, 40% CH)

This wonderful wine has similarities to Bollinger's delightful '83, but Gratien has shown that it can keep even better. Today, this fresh creature is classically nutty, with a piquant scent of fresh mushrooms and orchids. Substantial, toasted-oaky taste, balanced palate with good attack, and a sublime finish of nut toffee. The Swedish Wine Monopoly's oldest Champagne must be the perfect drink to ring in the New Year!

- 1982 A. GRATIEN   86, NOV 1998 (91)
(40% PN, 20% PM, 40% CH)
The toasty aromas border on burned rubber and are slightly exaggerated. The taste is undeveloped, but very promising.
- 1979 A. GRATIEN   91, MAR 2003 (91)
(22% PN, 22% PM, 56% CH)
Already in April 1990 this wine was completely mature, with a delightful combination of exotic fruit and toasted aromas. Actually, a bit on the way out: the acidity is softening and the fruit is beginning to subside. Certain bottles still render great pleasure. Uneven.
- 1976 A. GRATIEN   87, SEP 1992 (87)
(22% PN, 39% PM, 39% CH)
Rather one-dimensional, like many '76s. Weak nose, but with heavy, meaty tones. Hard finish to an initially creamy-smooth taste.
- 1973 A. GRATIEN   90, APR 2004 (90)
(22% PN, 39% PM, 39% CH)
Despite having tasted a well-seasoned magnum, the wine was somewhat sluggish and on its way down. The color was deep and clear. Both the scent and taste were dominated by marzipan. The wine was rich and full bodied, but lacked Gratien's refreshing acidity. The Champagne's greatest asset was the long aftertaste of walnut.
- 1970 A. GRATIEN   95, DEC 1998 (96)
(100% CH)
In certain years Gratien reserves a special batch of the best Chardonnay wines from Mesnil and Cramant for their own use. To be honest I didn't believe it was possible to create a Blanc de Blancs this impressive from such a Pinot vintage. The aroma is broad and rich with nuance, yet still somewhat bound. The wine has an enormously dense and concentrated structure, with a fantastically long aftertaste of browned butter and walnut in the best Salon style.
- 1969 A. GRATIEN   93, DEC 2003 (93)
(22% PN, 39% PM, 39% CH)
You could actually buy this Champagne at the Swedish Wine Monopoly at the end of the 1980s. At that time it was one of my greatest wine experiences, but when I drank it in March 1994 my impressions were of a lower key. The nose is mature and bready, the taste fresh and elegant. The aftertaste gives this wine its high class, lasting for several minutes. Drink within the next few years.
- 1966 A. GRATIEN
(30% PN, 30% PM, 40% CH)
- 1964 A. GRATIEN   94, MAY 1992 (94)
(100% CH)
Not the conventional '64, but a special *cuvée* that is offered freshly disgorged on grand occasions at Gratien. Aromas typical of the vintage: coffee, mint, biscuits, vanilla, dwarf banana, honeysuckle, and cream. Almost the perfect nose. The taste is a little too steely and light.
- 1959 A. GRATIEN   91, OCT 1999 (91)
(27% PN, 38% PM, 35% CH)
This should be a fantastic wine. I was disappointed, despite having tasted a well-preserved magnum. The wine is certainly impressive in all its potency but, to be honest, it's unbalanced. The alcohol content is too high and the impenetrable Champagne is actually difficult to drink. One of the strongest and most vinous Champagnes I have come across.

- 1955 A. GRATIEN   98, OCT 1997 (98)
(100% CH)
Only Mesnil and Cramant. An absolutely fantastic Champagne with extraordinary mousse and green-yellow color. Excellent flowery bouquet with hits of lime, wet rocks, and brioche. Perfect balance and as close to perfection you can get. One of the few really great wines missing in the Millennium Tasting.
- 1953 A. GRATIEN   82, JUN 2000 (82)
(40% PN, 25% PM, 35% CH)
Aged amber color of good clarity. Lovely nose of dried fruits, mocha, and banana. Full-bodied taste with hints of old wood and unfortunately a large dose of Madeira in the aftertaste.
- 1969 A. GRATIEN BLANC DE BLANCS   93, OCT 1997 (93)
(100% CH)
Astonishingly fresh and youthful, but at the same time blessed with old aromas of mushrooms, almonds, and honey. A bit thin and bony in the aftertaste.
- A. GRATIEN CUVÉE PARADIS   86
(15% PN, 10% PM, 75% CH)
Gratien's new prestige Champagne is not one of the greatest. Still bound in the nose, but when aired, vanilla, honeysuckle, and violet appear. The taste is light and elegant, not at all house-typical, but delicate. Recently more mature and concentrated, with very good length. Store it yourself and the wine will break the 90-point barrier.
- A. GRATIEN CUVÉE PARADIS ROSÉ   84
(18% PN, 17% PM, 65% CH)
Another true disappointment with slightly minty, discreet, and elegant nose, unexpectedly weak, delicate taste with no direct rosé character. Rather like the white variety.
- 1985 A. GRATIEN CUVÉE PARADIS   82, NOV 1995 (88)
(15% PN, 10% PM, 75% CH)
As far as I know this is the only vintage variety of this wine—Prestige is now a nonvintage prestige Champagne. Slightly thin and acidic with candy notes and a pleasant mint taste. Store!
- A. GRATIEN CUVÉE DU MILLÈNAIRE   85, MAY 2001 (89)
(18% PN, 21% PM, 61% CH)
For the moment still a closed Champagne that is highly reminiscent of Cuvée Paradis, and which imparts more in the mouth than in the nose. The nose is slightly medicinal and the palate fleshy, with a big helping of mature, high-class Chardonnay grapes. Big, young fruit, and fine acidity. Don't drink before 2010.

GREMILLET, J.M. N-M
1, chemin des Fleurs Sauvages
10110 Balnot-sur-Laignes
03 25 29 37 91
Production: 100,000
Extremely low prices are the trademark of this Aube house, which owns twelve hectares in the area. Other wines: Brut Sélection, Brut Prestige.
- GREMILLET GRANDE RÉSERVE   40
(50% PN, 50% CH)
- GREMILLET ROSÉ   50
(100% PN)
- 1989 GREMILLET CHARDONNAY   60, AUG 1997 (65)
(100% CH)

GRONGNET R-M

41, Grande Rue
51270 Étoges
03 26 59 30 50
Production: 80,000

One of the privileged members of Special Club. The darling of the village.

- 1996 GRONGNET SPECIAL CLUB   87, MAR 2004 (89)
  (45% PN, 22% PM, 33% CH)
  Very round and oily with high concentration and a typical spectrum of aromas for members of the grower's prestige club. Yet another worthy member of Special Club, despite the fact that this is not one of the foremost villages. Delightfully rich aftertaste of pure acacia honey.

GUIBORAT R-M

Boîte Postale 11
51530 Cramant
03 26 57 54 08
Production: 10,000

This "*recoltant-manipulant*" sells the greater part of its grapes to Laurent-Perrier. The vintage wines come from old vines in the high-class vineyard of Le Mont-Aigu. Considering how exceptional the '58 was, one should take every chance to drink a Guiborat, even though the young wines that I have tasted have been supremely ordinary.

- GUIBORAT BLANC DE BLANCS   65
  (100% CH)
- 1994 GUIBORAT   70, FEB 1998 (79)
  (100% CH)
- 1958 GUIBORAT   94, OCT 1998 (94)
  (100% CH)
  I myself was almost as surprised as a couple of restaurateurs in Reims, when I succeeded in hitting the bull's eye on both the village and the vintage, despite never having tasted a '58 before. On further consideration it seems less strange, because the style was something between a 1955 and a 1959. Furthermore, Cramant is one of the easiest villages to find in blind tastings. In any case, the Champagne was wonderful, with its distinct coffee aroma and rich, Diebolt-like creamy fruit. Low yield and storage in small oak barrels have also left their signature.

HAMM, E. N-M

16, rue Nicolas Philipponnat
51160 Aÿ
03 26 55 44 19
Production: 250,000

Émile Hamm started as a grower in Aÿ at the beginning of this century and received house status in 1930. The firm owns 3.5 hectares in Aÿ and buys in 90 percent of its grape supplies.

- E. HAMM BRUT   53
  (35% PN, 35% PM, 30% CH)
- E. HAMM RÉSERVE IER CRU   68
  (40% PN, 20% PM, 40% CH)
- E. HAMM BRUT ROSÉ   66
  (60% PN, 40% CH)
- 1987 E. HAMM   71, MAR 1995 (75)
  (50% PN, 50% CH)

HATTÉ, BERNARD **** R-M

1, rue de la Petit Fontaine
51360 Verzenay
03 26 49 40 90
Production: 40,000

Bernard Hatté is definitely one of Champagne's best growers. Sadly the Hatté family have recently been influenced by their enologist, who prefers lighter Champagnes with a higher Chardonnay content, vinified in sterile conditions in stainless-steel vats. Hatté was one of the last growers in the village to use oak barrels, but on the advice of the enologist they were replaced by steel tanks after the harvest of 1985. Hatté has the lowest yield in the village and makes storable wines with biting acidity and a youthful harshness.

- B. HATTÉ BRUT   78
  (70% PN, 30% CH)
- B. HATTÉ CARTE D'OR   78
  (50% PN, 30% PM, 20% CH)
- B. HATTÉ RÉSERVE   78
  (50% PN, 30% PM, 20% CH)
- B. HATTÉ ROSÉ   84
  (100% PN)
  It's always exciting to see how this rosé stands against the best Aÿ rosés. The nose is almost Burgundy-like, with plums, raspberries, and strawberries. The flavor is a little less generous, with green apples and licorice candies that sneak in among the red fruits.
- 1996 B. HATTÉ SPECIAL CLUB   88, JUN 2002 (93)
  (50% PN, 50% CH)
  Incredibly clean in style, full of youthful acidity and fresh apple aromas. Simultaneously, there is dark richness that will, with time, become reminiscent of gamy, plum-like red wines. For the moment, this aspect is only noticeable as a dormant layer of taste.
- 1990 B. HATTÉ SPECIAL CLUB   90, MAY 2003 (92)
  (50% PN, 50% CH)
  Fleshy, distinctly fishy, and fruity. Magnificent acidity.
- 1989 B. HATTÉ SPECIAL CLUB   88, FEB 2003 (91)
  (50% PN, 50% CH)
  Unfortunately much too much Chardonnay now, but still a very fine wine with a mineral nose and an initially fat, round taste that has a young, abrasive, peppery finish. Now there is a vital, vibrating, fresh note of ruby grapefruit under the fat surface.
- 1988 B. HATTÉ SPECIAL CLUB   75, JUN 1993 (90)
  (40% PN, 60% CH)
  Light color, exemplary mousse, and closed nose. Very long, undeveloped flavor with a slightly sour extract. Should go down in the cellar for at least ten years!
- 1985 B. HATTÉ SPECIAL CLUB   90, MAR 1993 (94)
  (100% PN)
  The last vintage using oak barrels and exclusively Pinot Noir. A "Rambo Champagne," which is almost chewable in its wealth of extracts. Dark color, a hugely broad nose of cellars, nut biscuits, and bitter chocolate. The Champagne feels almost like a red wine with its tannic finish and corpulent structure. One of the most powerful Champagne I've ever tasted. An almost indestructible wine that can be stored for decades.

HATTÉ, LUDOVIC R-M

8, rue Thiers
51360 Verzenay
03 26 49 43 94
Production: 20,000
One of many Hattés in Verzenay. Unfortunately he's following the village trend of using more and more Chardonnay.

- 1990 LUDOVIC HATTÉ   69, APR 1995 (76)
  (60% PN, 40% CH)

HEIDSIECK & MONOPOLE **** N-M

17, avenue de Champagne
51200 Épernay
03 26 59 50 50
Production: 1,500,000
This important label became part of the Canadian Seagram Group in 1972. But later, in October 1996, the house was taken over by the Vranken Group. The former Reims house owns 112 first-class hectares in Verzenay, Bouzy, Verzy, and Ambonnay, to name a few. They even owned the mill in Verzenay and the vineyards that belonged to it. In the beginning the company—founded in 1834—was called Hiedsieck & Co. It took its present name in 1923, when it was situated in Reims. In recent years the firm has been recognized for its 1907s, which have been lying at the bottom of the Gulf of Finland since 1916. This good but hardly exceptional Champagne has quickly achieved cult status. The bottles sell for astronomical sums, despite the fact that this is the world's commonest old Champagne. The house has been in a deep rut since the fantastic 1960s, when both the vintage wine and the Diamant Bleu belonged to the extreme elite. Under Vranken's protection, large amounts of money are now invested to restore its reputation. With Dominique Pichart as *chef de cave*, things actually look very promising.

- HEIDSIECK & MONOPOLE BLUE TOP   75
  (35% PN, 32% PM, 33% CH)
- HEIDSIECK EXTRA DRY   73
  (70% PN, 10% PM, 20% CH)
- HEIDSIECK & MONOPOLE RED TOP   50
  (35% PN, 32% PM, 33% CH)
- 1996 HEIDSIECK & MONOPOLE   85, JUL 2003 (88)
  (70% PN, 30% CH)
  Oh my gosh!—this one's crackling with vigor and big, somewhat bushy aromas. A delicious, expressive wine with fine nerve and a long future. The wine is full of warm fruit and honey aromas. The acid attack is rounded off and converted into a mellow, chocolaty sensation, with nut toffee and almond in the aftertaste.
- 1982 HEIDSIECK & MONOPOLE   70, DEC 1991 (79)
  (67% PN, 33% CH)
- 1979 HEIDSIECK & MONOPOLE   82, OCT 1996 (82)
  (67% PN, 33% CH)
  Despite its toasty aromas this was a weak, watery vintage at a time when the firm had entered a rut. Are they on their way up and out of it?
- 1975 HEIDSIECK & MONOPOLE   90, FEB 1996 (90)
  (67% PN, 33% CH)
  Lighter and less concentrated than Diamant Bleu from the same year. The wine is fresher than the '73 but displays much the same aromatic spectrum.

- 1973 HEIDSIECK & MONOPOLE   88, JUN 2003 (88)
  (67% PN, 33% CH)
  Chocolate, nut, and honey are the first things I associate with the flavor and nose of this smooth, mature wine. That perfect stringency may be missing, but the aromatic spectrum is extremely enjoyable.
- 1971 HEIDSIECK & MONOPOLE   93, MAY 2001 (93)
  (70% PN, 30% CH)
  Wow, what power! A mega-wine in magnum. Relatively newly disgorged, of course, and direct from the house to our auction at Sotheby's in London in 2000. Numbingly big, smoky, masculine, snorting nose. Massive, sweet taste with layers of vanilla, peach, and nougat. Not for weaklings.
- 1969 HEIDSIECK & MONOPOLE   94, JUL 1995 (94)
  (67% PN, 33% CH)
  An old, mature Champagne in its element. Filled with enjoyable toffee and mint chocolate aromas, as well as a sensual, melting, long aftertaste of honey.
- 1966 HEIDSIECK & MONOPOLE   94, FEB 2003 (94)
  (70% PN, 20% PM, 10% CH)
  A brilliantly pale-orange color and sparkling mousse. The Champagne makes a slightly more lively and fruity impression than the '64, with tones of mango, orange, and chocolate in the flavor. The delightful nose is dominated by orchids, roasted coffee beans, and butter melting in the frying pan. Unfortunately maderized at the Millennium Tasting.
- 1964 HEIDSIECK & MONOPOLE   95, APR 1995 (95)
  (67% PN, 33% CH)
  The same deep orangey color. The mousse is a bit tired, but there's a more masculine power in the vinous flavor. The nose is also older than the '66, with a Krug-like mint-chocolate tone that I have a weakness for.
- 1962 HEIDSIECK & MONOPOLE   78, JUN 2002 (>)
  (60% PN, 10% PM, 30% CH)
- 1961 HEIDSIECK & MONOPOLE   95, AUG 2000 (95)
  (67% PN, 33% CH)
  Regardless of the vintage, this wine is always extremely reliable. Typical of the vintage are the tobacco and tar tones, handsomely braided with the house's characteristic chocolate and Pinot aromas. The nose is dry and I have the feeling that the wine wants to flirt but does not really dare to. The finish firmly reconnects to gentlemanly correctness. Classic!
- 1959 HEIDSIECK & MONOPOLE
  (75% PN, 25% CH)
- 1955 HEIDSIECK & MONOPOLE   95, APR 2003 (95)
  (67% PN, 33% CH)
  When the wine was poured I detected some impurity in the nose, but this was soon aired out and along came the old majestic wine with a carpet of fine white mousse. Great depth and dark aromas that are as thrilling as a Hitchcock movie.
- 1952 HEIDSIECK & MONOPOLE   95, DEC 1998 (95)
  (75% PN, 25% CH)
  Very youthful and light with perfect attack and bubbles. Tantalizing and seductive aroma of peppermints and nut candy. Long, enviably vigorous, medium-bodied taste with great finesse.
- 1949 HEIDSIECK & MONOPOLE   94, JUL 2001 (94)
  (70% PN, 5% PM, 25% CH)
  A pure essence of everything this house stands for. Vinous Pinot Noir, rich, chocolaty maturity, and an explosion of dried sweet

fruit. The aftertaste is syrupy fat and surprisingly smoky at the same time.

- 1947 HEIDSIECK & MONOPOLE   88, JAN 2003 (88)
(70% PN, 5% PM, 25% CH)

Legendary reputation that was reinforced even more when a writer for *Decanter* magazine pronounced this wine its greatest sensation that year. It might be that he got a hold of a better bottle than I did, because despite a clearly noticeable mousse and normal color, this oldie couldn't keep itself upright after a short time in the glass. Vintage-typical richness and vigor, with aromas of tarred rope, malt, plums, and fiery intensity. An historic wine that has recently begun its inevitable journey to the grave.

- 1945 HEIDSIECK & MONOPOLE
(70% PN, 5% PM, 25% CH)

- 1929 HEIDSIECK & MONOPOLE   95, NOV 1999 (95)
(75% PN, 25% CH)

What exquisite Champagnes have come from this house through the years! Whether a '49, '52, or '29, it doesn't seem to matter. They all share freshness and honey-soft richness in perfect harmony with one another. The deep orange color with a sparklingly rich mousse is another sign of these real keepers.

- 1923 HEIDSIECK & MONOPOLE
(67% PN, 33% CH)

- 1921 HEIDSIECK & CO.   96, DEC 1996 (96)
(75% PN, 25% CH)

Richer than the 1919, with a dense aftertaste of dry cacao. As so often, the wine is borne up by a wonderful Pinot aroma.

- 1919 HEIDSIECK & CO.   94, MAY 1996 (94)
(70% PN, 30% CH)

A vintage that had been totally unknown to me, but this magnum was an unforgettable experience. A powerful mousse, medium-deep color, and wonderfully assembled bouquet of dried roses, orange, coffee, mint chocolate, and wood. The flavor was light and fresh, and dominated by apricot, peach, and dark chocolate.

- 1907 HEIDSIECK & CO. GOUT AMERICAIN   89, MAR 2004 (89)
(70% PN, 30% CH)

The world's most famous Champagne, but also one of the most common prewar Champagnes. In other words, this is the Champagne that has lain on the bottom of the Baltic Sea since the ship *Jönköping* went down in 1916! Probably a rather ordinary wine that, under exceptional and perfect slow-storage conditions, has become fantastically idiosyncratic and interesting. The cold water has apparently had a preserving effect on the semi-sweet Champagne that was bound for the Russian army's officers. The color is incredibly light, and the entire wine comports itself as if it was born in the 1970s. The nose is dominated by apple and banana, but there is also a deeper side, with notes of tar and petroleum. The wine does not taste as sweet as it probably is; it is very enjoyable. The greatest part of the pleasure is, of course, intellectual, emotional, and historical. The wine has degenerated slightly in recent times.

- 1979 HEIDSIECK & MONOPOLE ROSÉ   87, OCT 2003 (87)
(50% PN, 20% PM, 30% CH)

It's odd that I was forty-one years old before I saw a bottle of Hiedsieck & Monopole Rosé for the first time. It must be a long time since they made a vintage rosé. Maybe this '79 was the last vintage of this rare wine. No matter what, this twenty-four-year-old wine is in good health, with a medium-deep, slightly dull, murky color; big, sweet, delicious nose; and a rich, somewhat

fruitless taste. The bouquet hints at cacao and nougat, with strains of tar and dried rose petals. The taste is robust and red-wine-like, with a dry finish. Perfect with pheasant mousse!

- 1976 HEIDSIECK & MONOPOLE ROSÉ   88, OCT 2003 (88)
(50% PN, 20% PM, 30% CH)

Somewhat fatter and nicer than the '79, with a large helping of warmth and potent Pinot Noir sturdiness. Keeps well in the glass and feels very homogeneous.

- DIAMANT BLANC   85
(100% CH)

Surely it is right to make this young wine a vintage Champagne from now on. With its stony, undeveloped character, this wine actually craves storage. The price is the same as Diamant Bleu and Diamant Rosé, which flatters this far from fantastic Blanc de Blancs. The base comes from Oger and demands lengthier storage than any other *grand cru*.

- 1995 DIAMANT BLEU   87, AUG 2003 (91)
(50% PN, 50% CH)

Handsomely polished and modern Champagne that many gladly drink too young. The future seems safe, considering how the '82 has developed. Nice, biscuity note in the aftertaste.

- 1989 DIAMANT BLEU   92, APR 2003 (93)
(50% PN, 50% CH)

Many have been skeptical about the famous diamond after the change in ownership. Therefore it was with great happiness that I could conclude that the '89 was very pleasing to my palate. The scent is sumptuous, filled of honey and hazelnut. The vintage's generous style marks the taste emphatically. Do not store for too long, as this will be mature very soon.

- 1985 DIAMANT BLEU   84, OCT 2000 (86)
(50% PN, 50% CH)

It takes a few minutes in the glass before the notes of dill and beef stew are aired out and substituted by a mineral-rich Chardonnay aroma. The last time I tasted this Champagne I was hit by how fat it had become. There were actually a few clumsy characteristics that my mind associated with the New World.

- 1982 DIAMANT BLEU   93, JAN 2003 (93)
(50% PN, 50% CH)

Beautiful fruit and more bready aroma than the '79, but I must admit that for many years I didn't like the Diamant Bleu with its stony finish. Today the nose is full of wet wool, bitter chocolate, and cellar notes. The taste is rich and bready. Delicious every time. Surprising finish.

- 1979 DIAMANT BLEU   88, MAY 2003 (88)
(50% PN, 50% CH)

You can really chew on the stony mineral flavor. Both the nose and the flavor lack a generosity of fruit and allow the minerals to take over. Verzenay dominates the impression emphatically.

- 1976 DIAMANT BLEU   95, MAY 2001 (95)
(50% PN, 50% CH)

One of the best '76s and clearly more homogeneous today than the '79. The wine is grand and aristocratic, with a sophisticated, buttery tone from the vintage adding a touch of charm to an otherwise rather barren wine.

- 1975 DIAMANT BLEU   95, MAY 2001 (95)
(50% PN, 50% CH)

The first year with the new bottle. Today, an incredibly rich and fat Champagne with a warmth and sweetness reminiscent of 1976. Very good.

- 1973 DIAMANT BLEU   92, JAN 2000 (92)
(50% PN, 50% CH)

A wine full of stony notes, handsomely interwoven with layers of buttery taste. Slightly stingy bouquet and a certain lack of length in an otherwise magnificently complicated wine.

- 1969 DIAMANT BLEU   94, MAR 2004 (94)
(50% PN, 50% CH)

Superbly fresh and fleshy prestige Champagne with good bite and a strictly stony demeanor. Perhaps a little sweetness, warmth, and generosity is missing, but I still let myself be seduced by this wine's cold charm.

- 1964 DIAMANT BLEU   98, JAN 2003 (98)
(50% PN, 50% CH)

This wine, the subject of many a myth and rumor, is a legend that lives up to expectations. I've heard that it's best in magnums, but considering the freshness it displayed from an ordinary bottle, I wonder. Diamant Bleu is lighter and more elegant than the vintage wine, but they have in common a mint-chocolate aroma and an improbable mineral finesse.

- 1962 DIAMANT BLEU   96, OCT 2000 (96)
(50% PN, 50% CH)

Disgorged in November 1969 and stored until 1998 in Heidsieck's own cellar. Tasted on two occasions. Fantastically clean with an aroma of acacia, just like a newly disgorged Dom Pérignon. Actually, there is an amount of undeveloped extract that makes itself known in the stonily imprinted Verzenay aftertaste. Paradoxically, a delicate wine with tremendous power. The next bottle was a mature and sterling symphony with kettledrums and rumbling bass.

- 1961 DIAMANT BLEU
(50% PN, 50% CH)

- 1988 DIAMANT ROSÉ   92, APR 2003 (92)
(50% PN, 50% CH)

Completely evolved, deliciously smoky, and radiantly enjoyable with its beautiful, unexpected mix of licorice, orange liqueur, cloudberry, and strawberry flavors. An individual, brilliant prestige rosé that we gladly embrace.

- 1982 DIAMANT ROSÉ   83, APR 1990 (89)
(75% PN, 25% CH)

Only 15,000 bottles were made of this prestige rosé. It had an intensely beautiful salmon color and a sophisticated, slightly restrained nose. With time in the glass this rare and expensive Champagne produced aromas of toffee, nuts, and strawberry.

HEIDSIECK, CHARLES **** N-M

4, boulevard Henri Vasnier
51100 Reims
03 26 84 43 50
Production: 3,000,000

Charles Hiedsieck may be both the best and most famous of the three Hiedsieck houses, but it was the last of the three out of the starting gates. It was sixty-six years after Florens-Louis Hiedsieck had first laid the foundation for the Hiedsieck clan that Charles-Camille Heidsieck founded the house in 1851. In 1857, Charles-Camille made his first trip to America. There he was quickly dubbed "Champagne Charlie," and grew to be so well known that his name appeared in music hall songs performed around the country.

     For a while Charles Heidsieck was owned by Henriot, but it was sold in 1985 to the Rémy-Cointreau Group. Daniel

Thibault was *chef de caves* here, and at Piper-Hiedsieck, before his premature death in February 2002—he is missed by the entire wine world. Before the incomparable Thibault came onto the scene, Heidsieck owned no vineyards of their own. Today they own thirty hectares in Ambonnay, Bouzy, and Oger. The nonvintage Champagne Brut Resérve Mis en Cave is among the best on the market, and the vintage wine is always a joy to follow. The decision to close down Champagne Charlie and to substitute the prestige Champagne with Blanc de Millénaires has been praised by many. I, however, have my reservations about this, as the firm derived its fine reputation from its mature, Pinot-influenced style. All the wines are beautifully toasted. It won't be an easy task for Daniel Thibault's successor to fill the space left by this legendary winemaker.

- CHARLES HEIDSIECK BRUT   73
(40% PN, 40% PM, 20% CH)

- CHARLES HEIDSIECK BRUT RÉSERVE   81
(40% PN, 35% PM, 25% CH)

From a hundred or so villages and 40 percent reserve wines from eight vintages, Daniel Thibault produced one of the very best nonvintage Champagnes produced by a large house. With a couple of years extra storage in the bottle it develops a high-class nose of toasted bread, vanilla, and a long complex fruitiness with a smooth aftertaste of toffee.

- CHARLES HEIDSIECK MIS EN CAVE 1998   86, MAR 2004 (90)
(40% PN, 35% PM, 25% CH)

There's no question: Charles Heidsieck has established itself at the absolute top of Champagne with its fantastic string of "*mis en cave*" wines. This wine, with a base from the slightly thin but charming vintage 1997, is as yet rather too young to make us totally goggle-eyed, but wait six months more and hold on for a fantastic ride! The fruit is luxuriant and exotic, with notes of pineapple, mango, and peach. Charles Heidsieck's mark of nobility—the extremely roasted, almost toasted oak style—is not yet so apparent, but surely there is already a hint of nut, brioche, oyster shell, coffee, and gun smoke. The time will come to polish the aromatic building blocks into beautiful, rounded shapes, in the same way that sea and time create the shapes of Brittany's round and beautiful cliff formations. Why not travel there next year and bring a bottle of "Charles" along?

- CHARLES HEIDSIECK MIS EN CAVE 1997   86, OCT 2002 (89)
(40% PN, 35% PM, 25% CH)

This wine often has a slightly earthy and reductive note that can be aired out. Of course, Thibault had cranked up the toasted and burned notes fantastically. Getting so much coffee, toasted bread, and gunpowder in a nonvintage Champagne is exceptional. Most impressive is that he basically succeeded in doing this every time. The fruit might be slightly low-key in the nose, but it comes along beautifully on the palate.

- CHARLES HEIDSIECK MIS EN CAVE 1996   88, MAY 2003 (90)
(33% PN, 33% PM, 34% CH)

For the moment the wine seems a little thinner than usual, but I am convinced it is because the Champagne is too young. Under the surface there is an orange-tasting fruit and nascent notes of coffee and toasted bread. Forget your bottles for a few years. Oh my gosh—half a year later the warmth had appeared!

- CHARLES HEIDSIECK MIS EN CAVE 1995   86, SEP 2003 (87)
(40% PN, 35% PM, 25% CH)

Still a bit too young, but at least as good in the long run as all of Charles's nonvintage Champagnes. Very storable, with a long, concentrated taste.

- CHARLES HEIDSIECK MIS EN CAVE 1993   79, OCT 2000 (84)
(40% PN, 35% PM, 25% CH)

The "*mis en cave*" concept is a brilliant business idea and an exciting opportunity for us Champagne freaks to follow the development of a nonvintage Champagne from a large house. Personally, I think that it would have been enough with just the date of disgorgement, something that I am very keen to see on all Champagnes! The 1993 designation is not indicative of the vintage, but rather the year that the wine was put away in Heidsieck's cellar. Consequently the base wine in this Champagne comes from 1992, with a large portion of older reserve wines. In March '99 it was flowery, pure, and buttery.

- CHARLES HEIDSIECK MIS EN CAVE 1992   81, OCT 2000 (86)
(40% PN, 35% PM, 25% CH)

Unusually toasted already. Might that be because of the reserve wine from 1990? Deliciously developed, classically toasted, and buttery taste.

- CHARLES HEIDSIECK MIS EN CAVE 1990   83, OCT 2000 (88)
(40% PN, 35% PM, 25% CH)

The base vintage is 1989. Tested alongside the '93 version, this one has definitely had time to build a greater level of complexity—as a result of longer contact with the yeast, as well as its greater age. The house-typical glorious aroma of toasted coffee beans can already be discerned. It is certain to be even better in ten years or so.

- RESERVE CHARLIE MIS EN CAVE 1990   90, OCT 2001 (93)
(34% PN, 33% PM, 33% CH)

An expensive prestige Champagne from Charles Heidsieck's enoteque. A super-sophisticated Daniel Thibault wine with tons of delicious toasted layers, vital fruit, and a smart, youthful, peppery attack. Daniel exhibits his entire opus and strengthens my conviction that it is possible to get a very long way in terms of complexity by mixing several vintages. Delightful contrast between youthful snarling vigor and mellow butterscotchy maturity. Already very good in May 2001. Most likely totally exceptional with additional storage. Here I've given a potential rating because the *cuvée* is a one-time phenomenon that doesn't exist in other versions, as is usually the case with nonvintage Champagnes.

- 1995 CHARLES HEIDSIECK   91, SEP 2003 (94)
(70% PN, 30% CH)

It's great to start in on a new vintage of this wine. The wine is one of the best from this vintage and Thibault created a masterpiece. The fruit is massive and dazzling, with a yummy, mouth-filling, bready keynote. Vanilla, coffee, and toast are also clear aromas. Balanced, fresh, and evolved.

- 1990 CHARLES HEIDSIECK   89, FEB 2004 (91)
(70% PN, 30% CH)

Much lighter than normal, but as soon as I put my nose in the glass I felt at home. This is a very good Champagne, typical of the house, with tones of coffee and orange chocolate. Rather quick to develop and somewhat more characterized by Chardonnay than usual: something that we should get used to, because Daniel Thibault had a clear preference for the delicious green grape variety. Recently entered a weak phase where the dosage feels intrusive.

- 1989 CHARLES HEIDSIECK   88, MAR 2003 (88)
(70% PN, 30% CH)

Lots of coffee and toasted bread in the nose, as usual. A rich, pleasurable, orangey fruit and a long, generous aftertaste.

- 1985 CHARLES HEIDSIECK   89, JAN 2003 (89)
(70% PN, 30% CH)

Open and generous Heidsieck, with a more typical, big-house style. Broad, toasty, and orange-fruity. Slightly overdeveloped already and a touch sweet.

- 1983 CHARLES HEIDSIECK   88, APR 2000 (89)
(60% PN, 40% CH)

Distinctly toasted bouquet, like all '83s from this house. Bready and orange-sated, rich taste with a corpulent structure and smoky finish. Good acidity.

- 1982 CHARLES HEIDSIECK   90, DEC 1999 (90)
(60% PN, 5% PM, 35% CH)

Drier than the '85, with a good, fit-to-burst, chewable fruit and house-typical bread aroma. Wonderful nose, with a slightly shorter resonance.

- 1981 CHARLES HEIDSIECK   93, MAY 2000 (93)
(75% PN, 25% CH)

Beautiful, multifaceted bouquet leaning toward orange-chocolate and coffee. The taste actually explodes in the mouth. Fantastic, sensational development through the years!

- 1979 CHARLES HEIDSIECK   92, JAN 2000 (92)
(65% PN, 35% CH)

Just like the '82, this is extremely delicious Champagne with a thorough aromatic spectrum and perfect balance—and, unfortunately, a surprisingly short aftertaste. I'm afraid to say this appears to be a part of the house-style. The wines are quite reminiscent of the toasty and broad Champagnes from Perrier-Jouët, but in a more vigorous incarnation. The greatest similarity is otherwise with neighboring Veuve Clicquot who, in contrast, have better length in their wines. Back to this fine '79. The bouquet is wonderfully complicated with a great depth of fruit, a sweet, bready, biscuity side and a clear note of nut chocolate. The flavor is supremely refreshing, elegant and fruity, but short.

- 1979 CHARLES HEIDSIECK OENOTÈQUE   88, JAN 2003 (91)
(65% PN, 35% CH)

Newly disgorged direct from the house's beautiful cellar collection. A very youthful twenty-two-year-old that isn't at all as expressive as its normally disgorged twin. Intensely sparkling, brilliant young color. Vegetal freshness mixed with fishy notes. A lively wine with good structure and a short aftertaste. Only 1,500 bottles are sold under this label.

- 1976 CHARLES HEIDSIECK   94, JAN 2000 (94)
(65% PN, 35% CH)

Popular winner at tastings among my friends. Powerful and very good with its bready, toasted aromas in the nose and its thick meaty taste. The finish with its burst of vanilla is especially enjoyable.

- 1975 CHARLES HEIDSIECK   91, FEB 2003 (91)
(75% PN, 25% CH)

Straw-yellow color, brioche nose, and a rich, well-structured flavor with elements of peach. Somewhat one dimensional.

- 1973 CHARLES HEIDSIECK   88, MAY 2000 (88)
(75% PN, 25% CH)

Hardly a great '73, or even one of the house's more memorable vintages. Uniform mature bouquet with hints of the cellar and a great portion of chocolate aroma. One-dimensional, fine flavor that keeps well in the glass, despite notes of maturity.

- 1971 CHARLES HEIDSIECK   90, OCT 2000 (90)
(65% PN, 35% CH)

A typical Charles! Toasty house-notes and chalky Champagne cellar-tone are the two foundation stones here. The fruit is pure and the finish has a nice, sweet tail. In style, reminiscent of a '79 and a '66—only the cocoa fragrance is slightly less intensive.

• 1970 CHARLES HEIDSIECK   88, MAR 2002 (88)
(55% PN, 45% CH)
Well-preserved, rich Champagne lacking those common signs of tiredness that so often characterize this vintage. The coffee notes are less dominating than usual; the wine trusts instead to a more chocolate-saturated, raisiny character, which is well-suited to veal sweetbread, goose liver, or some such.

• 1969 CHARLES HEIDSIECK   94, JAN 2002 (94)
(75% PN, 25% CH)
What a magical nose! So sweet and charming, with all the flowers and fruits of the garden. The flavor is also magnificent, although not quite so outstanding. Unfortunately the dosage is a little high and there's a somewhat short aftertaste.

• 1966 CHARLES HEIDSIECK   94, JAN 2002 (94)
(75% PN, 25% CH)
For those who don't know what dry cacao smells like, I can recommend a sniff of this Champagne. Golden, fresh color with a virile mousse. The full-bodied, dry taste is a little withdrawn at first, but with some time in the glass a lovely length develops, with aromas of cacao, mandarin, and orange.

• 1964 CHARLES HEIDSIECK   94, DEC 1996 (94)
(75% PN, 25% CH)
Not as elegant as the '66, but boldly expansive and rich with a fat, buttery bottom.

• 1962 CHARLES HEIDSIECK   84, JUN 2002 (84)
(75% PN, 25% CH)
Super-perky and reductive. Slightly strange nose that certain tasters distinctly disliked. For me personally, Finnish tar pastilles, asphalt, green peppers, as well as burned rubber came to mind. Chalky, thin Champagne with notes of gunpowder and tart, slightly sour, weak grapefruit fruitiness.

• 1961 CHARLES HEIDSIECK   94, JUN 2002 (94)
(75% PN, 25% CH)
This wine brought Charles extremely close to entering the 95-point club. The house has made lots of wines of approximately this same quality without ever really hitting the bull's-eye. Nose and taste of sweet, apricot marmalade with brioche. Fresh and rich at the same time.

• 1959 CHARLES HEIDSIECK
(75% PN, 25% CH)

• 1955 CHARLES HEIDSIECK   84, FEB 1995 (>)
(75% PN, 25% CH)
A weak pop! Mousse that is hardly visible, broad chocolate nose with weakly oxidized elements of overripe apple. Good, rich, and united flavor. On the way out, but still a pleasure to drink.

• 1953 CHARLES HEIDSIECK   90, JAN 2002 (90)
(75% PN, 25% CH)
Plenty of life and mousse, but a surprisingly weak nose. The divine flavor of old tarred sea timbers inspires forgiveness.

• 1952 CHARLES HEIDSIECK   93, JAN 2003 (93)
(67% PN, 33% CH)
Enchanting Champagne with a nose of dark chocolate and vanilla. The taste is elastic and youthful with a long, fine-balanced taste full of sweetness and caramelized elements. However, these fine-limbed '52s is never really grow into themselves.

• 1949 CHARLES HEIDSIECK   94, JUN 1999 (94)
(75% PN, 25% CH)
Extremely light and youthful. Long and shockingly fresh. A mineral note bordering on the cellar is the only clue that this wine is more than twenty years old.

• 1947 CHARLES HEIDSIECK   88, JUN 2000 (88)
(75% PN, 25% CH)
A wine of legendary reputation that surely must be fantastic in very well-aged bottles. My bottle looked fine, but had too little mousse and too many notes of aging. Still, clearly enjoyable and rich, but another example that proves Charles Heidsieck's wines are not among the most storable.

• 1945 CHARLES HEIDSIECK   77, MAR 2003 (77)
(67% PN, 33% CH)

• 1943 CHARLES HEIDSIECK
(67% PN, 33% CH)

• 1941 CHARLES HEIDSIECK   94, JUN 2001 (94)
(75% PN, 25% CH)
A superb Champagne that we drank together with Gosset's top staff at the Royal Champagne restaurant. Orange color and viscous, Sauternes-like character with elegance intact. A powerful, sweet wine that melted the goose liver down to a silky consistency. Jean-Perrier Mareignier just smiled.

• 1937 CHARLES HEIDSIECK
(75% PN, 25% CH)

• 1983 CHARLES HEIDSIECK BLANC DE BLANCS   90, MAR 1997 (90)
(100% CH)
A sensational Champagne with an overwhelming toasted nose. My colleagues were two decades out when they guessed wrong at a blind tasting in Cannes in 1996. The flavor was lighter and younger, without the many nuances that would take it up among the greats.

• 1982 CHARLES HEIDSIECK BLANC DE BLANCS   92, JAN 2003 (92)
(100% CH)
Powerful and rich, with toasted nose and a fine taste of mature grapes. In a brilliantly beautiful state of development at the moment.

• 1981 CHARLES HEIDSIECK BLANC DE BLANCS   94, JAN 2003 (94)
(100% CH)
Straw color, sparklingly lively, characteristic vintage-typical hawthorn nose, and slightly unpolished taste. For the moment, completely wonderful, with a nose of mint toffee, mango, vanilla, sweet butter toffee, and acacia honey. Butterscotchy and elegant, with fine fatness and beautiful freshness. Fantastic development.

• 1976 CHARLES HEIDSIECK BLANC DE BLANCS   91, OCT 2002 (91)
(100% CH)
Sulfur-yellow in color with a lively mousse. Mature, heavy, and oily. The Chardonnay fills the senses, although citrus tones do the groundwork.

• 1971 CHARLES HEIDSIECK BLANC DE BLANCS
(100% CH)

• 1969 CHARLES HEIDSIECK BLANC DE BLANCS   94, DEC 2002 (94)
(100% CH)
Superbly multifaceted and teasing, flowery nose, quite without any toasted undertones. A flavor that is a nectar that melts in the mouth, with lively citrus tones wrapped up in a smooth chocolate veil.

• 1961 CHARLES HEIDSIECK BLANC DE BLANCS   91, APR 1997 (>)
(100% CH)

A way past its peak with aromas of overripe apples and raisins. Even so, a muscular Blanc de Blancs with a pure finish and magnificent butteriness.

- 1996 CHARLES HEIDSIECK ROSÉ   70, JAN 2003 (79)
(70% PN, 30% CH)
- 1985 CHARLES HEIDSIECK ROSÉ   88, JAN 2003 (88)
(70% PN, 30% CH)

Huge overripe rosé with a loose bready style. A generous, soft, round, and pleasurable flavor that gives a far sweeter impression than the '83. At the moment, a fine coffee note.

- 1983 CHARLES HEIDSIECK ROSÉ   66, JUN 1992 (76)
(65% PN, 15% PM, 20% CH)
- 1982 CHARLES HEIDSIECK ROSÉ   70, JUN 1990 (78)
(70% PN, 5% PM, 25% CH)
- 1976 CHARLES HEIDSIECK ROSÉ   85, NOV 1995 (85)
(75% PN, 25% CH)

A rich, full-flavored wine, long and clean on the finish. Mellow, fine nose.

- 1969 CHARLES HEIDSIECK ROSÉ   93, JUN 2002 (93)
(75% PN, 25% CH)

Youthful, deliciously vital Champagne with a nose of gooseberries, wild strawberries, strawberries, and caramel. Butterscotchy, creamy taste with a fine mousse and an air of romance. Light, easily drunk summer Champagne, to gather together around.

- 1966 CHARLES HEIDSIECK ROSÉ   83, JUN 2002 (83)
(75% PN, 25% CH)

Robust, red-wine-like with slightly bitter tannins and forest elements. Rustic, food-oriented Champagne. Where is the charm?

- 1961 CHARLES HEIDSIECK ROSÉ   87, DEC 1999 (87)
(75% PN, 25% CH)

Completely still and with a rather dull, unclear color. Despite this, clearly better than the cheery '55 from Ruinart that stood beside it. Clicquot-like bready, red-wine-like scent. Masculine food Champagne made with very mature and high-class Pinot Noir grapes. Healthier examples than the one I tasted should be very good.

- 1990 BLANC DE MILLÉNAIRES   93, DEC 2001 (95)
(100% CH)

The foremost vintage so far of this acclaimed prestige Champagne. The scent is clear as a bell with Grand Siècle's beautiful note of sun-dried, newly laundered sheets, along with more than a dash of famous coffee-roasting house. Clean, focused, lemony-fresh, and sporty taste. A Ferrari of the wine world!

- 1985 BLANC DE MILLÉNAIRES   87, JUN 2001 (89)
(100% CH)

I must admit a certain disappointment with this light, citrus-fruity, toasted wine. I'm longing for Champagne Charlie! But it's good, nevertheless, isn't it?!

- 1985 CHAMPAGNE CHARLIE   93, OCT 2003 (93)
(45% PN, 55% CH)

For a long time, a bound and delicate Champagne. The wine finally found itself during 2003 and passed into the classic nutty, biscuity, and toasted phase that is so typical of Charles. Present also is a floral lightness and a beautiful, dancing sensation all the way through. The wine is a big pleasure today, and I can really recommend it.

- 1983 BLANC DE MILLÉNAIRES   91, JUN 2003 (91)
(100% CH)

Heidsieck's new *cuvée de prestige* is a constant winner at blind tastings all over the world. I'm less impressed by the deep yellow drink with its fine but rather miserly classical nose and buttery Chardonnay flavor. Clean and attractive, like a well-produced American West Coast rock album.

- 1983 CHAMPAGNE CHARLIE   94, APR 2000 (94)
(50% PN, 50% CH)

What a fantastic bouquet! Super-elegant, flowery undertone of the finest Chardonnay. Those tones, however, must be content to play second fiddle, because the Dom Pérignon-like coffee-roasting house aroma is so extremely pronounced. This is, for sure, a conscious house-style, and one would have to look far and wide to find something stronger than here in the company's '83s. The flavor is slightly smoky, lemony-fresh, and peppery in the finish. One of the vintage's most distinguished Champagnes.

- 1981 CHAMPAGNE CHARLIE   93, JAN 2003 (93)
(50% PN, 50% CH)

The name Champagne Charlie didn't go down so well in the English-speaking world, so Charles Heidsieck decided to discontinue this lovely Champagne. Juicy, exotic, and well-balanced, with a good grip and long aftertaste of mango.

- 1981 LA ROYALE   92, JAN 1999 (92)
(52% PN, 48% CH)

The notorious Hong Kong bottle! Beware all wine journalists who come to Charles Heidsieck's tastings. As a little blind extra number, there is always a special bottle that shows up—from the batch that was sent to Hong Kong, left in the heat, and then sent back. I do understand the house's desire to play tricks on us. It's just that those who are in the know always take the circumstances into account when trying to identify a wine at a blind tasting. When with a Champagne producer one tends to assume that all of the wines will taste more youthful than they usually do—and not the opposite. This wine has matured extremely quickly and has a color and aroma that resemble a '53 taken direct from the cellar. As luck would have it, I avoided embarrassing myself because the waiter was clumsy enough to let the label show. This wine demonstrates above all something that few people in Champagne understand, namely how good certain Champagnes can be when they are allowed to mature quickly.

- 1979 CHAMPAGNE CHARLIE   93, JAN 2003 (94)
(50% PN, 5% PM, 45% CH)

The '79 is made in the same juicy exotic style, but based on an even better backbone of Pinot grapes. Delightfully enjoyable. My mouth waters when I think back to that delicious mango flavor. Young and toasty in magnum.

- 1973 LA ROYALE   90, MAY 1996 (92)
(75% PN, 25% CH)

Powerful and exceptionally potent for a vintage that sees most wines now beginning to near their end. The nose is classical and bready and the flavor acidic and tough, with an afterthought of cacao.

- 1970 LA ROYALE   92, APR 1999 (92)
(60% PN, 40% CH)

All of the bottles I have tasted were disgorged in August 1998. A wine in exemplary condition. The cork sits like a rock and the mousse bubbles forth with vigor. Big aroma of coffee, mushrooms, tea, and toast. The velvety nougat-like flavor is very good, if a bit impersonal and short.

- 1966 LA ROYALE   96, JAN 2003 (96)
(75% PN, 25% CH)

This must be one of the best Champagnes Charles Heidsieck has ever made. The nose is filled with breakfast aromas, like toast, coffee, butter, and some exotic fruit marmalade. The flavor is very elegant and refreshing, with a strong tone of peach.

- 1961 LA ROYALE   92, MAR 2004 (92)
(75% PN, 25% CH)
Slightly muddy and musky, but very exciting with notes of tar, autumn forest, truffle, and earth cellar. Prepare a mushroom dish and enjoy a rainy evening.

- 1955 LA ROYALE   93, JUN 2002 (93)
(75% PN, 25% CH)
A wine that should be better than this. I found a few too many cellar notes and missed the fruit intensity. The color was deep and the mousse is well preserved. The nose is big with clearly defined notes of cacao and tobacco. The same notes come again in the long, oxidative taste.

- CHARLES HEIDSIECK 140 ANNIVERSARY CUVÉE   94, NOV 2002 (95)
A clean '79 made only in magnum. An enormous depth, both in the nose and palate. Lush, generous fruit tending toward orange and peach. Handsomely toasted, of course, but that's not enough to describe the palette of tastes that it offers. This wine shows with obvious authority what a wonderful and often underestimated house this is.

- CHARLES HEIDSIECK ROYAL JUBILEE   90, NOV 2002 (90)
An anniversary Champagne with base wine from 1971. Rather light color and lively mousse. Very weak, creamy nose completely without the toasted keynote one expects of Charles Heidsieck. Balanced, medium-bodied taste with a certain sweetness in the mid-palate as well as a dry, sophisticated finish.

HENIN, PASCAL R-M
22, rue Jules Lobel
51160 Aÿ
03 26 54 61 50
Production: 8,000
The tiny but well-run Aÿ house was founded in 1920. Pascal Henin owns vineyards in Chouilly and Aÿ that he blends in equal proportions in all his wines.

- PASCAL HENIN BRUT   70
(50% PN, 50% CH)
- PASCAL HENIN ROSÉ   70
(50% PN, 50% CH)
Deep red with a mighty nose. Aÿ Pinot is in there, screaming for attention, along with additional aromas of wine gums and raspberry.

- 1990 PASCAL HENIN   87, FEB 1997 (88)
(50% PN, 50% CH)
Amazingly impressive beside Krug Grande Cuvée. Shares weight and an aroma normally found in Bollinger, but sadly looses some freshness when aired. Exceptionally affordable.

HENRIET-BAZIN R-M
9, rue Dom Pérignon
51380 Villers-Marmery
03 26 97 96 81
Production: 60,000
The firm owns six hectares in Villers-Marmery, Verzy, and Verzenay. It is owned by Daniel Henriet and Marie-Noëlle Henriet.

- D. HENRIET-BAZIN BLANC DE BLANCS   72
(100% CH)

- D. HENRIET-BAZIN ROSÉ   68
(100% PN)
- 1991 D. HENRIET-BAZIN   75, OCT 2001 (75)
(50% PN, 50% CH)

HENRIET, MICHEL R-M
12, rue du Paradis
51360 Verzenay
03 26 49 40 42
Production: 30,000
The grower owns three hectares in Verzenay and uses modern methods. Michel belongs to the fourth generation of vintners in the *grand cru* village of Verzenay. In their fifteen-meter-deep chalk cellar lie bottles that are made of 80 percent Pinot Noir and 20 percent Chardonnay.

- MICHEL HENRIET TRADITION   70
(100% PN)
- MICHEL HENRIET GRANDE RÉSERVE   73
(100% PN)
- 1993 MICHEL HENRIET CARTE D'OR   84, DEC 2002 (87)
(80% PN, 20% CH)
Initially bound bouquet that comes thundering along like an imminent thunderstorm. Big, plump taste of red beets, crayfish stock, orchids, licorice, and a mature finish of honey. A rambunctious, fleshy, duck-liver wine.

- 1989 MICHEL HENRIET CARTE D'OR   76, JUL 1997 (82)
(100% PN)
Blanc de Noirs from Verzenay. The color is so red that it could easily be mistaken for a rosé. The nose has hints of almonds and heavy fruit. Heavy and a tad rustic.

HENRIOT **** N-M
3 place des Droits de l'Homme
51100 Reims
03 26 89 53 00
Production: 1,000,000
Joseph Henriot is one of Champagne's most powerful men. After having been the boss of Veuve Clicquot for many years, he returned to Henriot in 1994. Today the firm is run by his modest and extremely competent son, Stanislau Henriot. The Henriot family were established as growers in Champagne by 1640; they started their own Champagne house in 1808. The firm's strength has always been the high-class vineyards they owned in Côte des Blancs. Today they only own twenty-five hectares of vineyards in Chouilly, Avize, and Épernay. The total proportion of Chardonnay obtained from the firm's fine contracts with growers is more than 20 percent; it dominates the house-style with its clean, elegant, fresh citrus fruit. The Henriot family has always had strong ties with Charles Heidsieck, and still shares offices and wineries. With Clicquot, on the other hand, they share a cellar. The firm's biggest export market is Switzerland, where Henriot's dry, classic, slightly discreet Champagnes are a great success. The firm did well at the Millennium Tasting. Personally, I like these elegant classics more and more.

- HENRIOT SOUVERAIN BRUT   83
(55% PN, 45% CH)
It's wonderful to avoid Pinot Meunier in a large firm's nonvintage Champagne. The nose is classically bready. The large portion of Chardonnay sticks out in the delicate, light taste. The house-style

is marked. Very fine and evolved of late, thanks to up to seven-year-old reserve wines.

- HENRIOT BLANC DE BLANCS   85
(100% CH)
Through the years, a highly regarded wine. It's only now, in the beginning of the new century, that I've fallen for this elegant, storable beauty. The wine has a wonderful note of white flowers, vanilla, lightly perfumed honey, and lime peel. All of this clad in a silky, buttery, dusky dress.

- 1996 HENRIOT   86, SEP 2003 (91)
(50% PN, 50% CH)
Classically fine, creamy, and fruity nose. I get a feeling that the '96 is somewhat softer than the '95. Packed with delicious fruit.

- 1995 HENRIOT   90, DEC 2003 (92)
(45% PN, 55% CH)
I like this classic Champagne very much. Certainly the wine is, from start to finish, a touch too discreet, but this textbook concoction possesses a rarely seen elegance among blended Champagnes. The Champagne exhibits a sophisticated depth of autolytic aromas and a crystal-clear, lemony-fresh, Chardonnay palate. Handsome and distinguished, like a lighter version of the great vintages from Veuve Clicquot.

- 1990 HENRIOT   88, MAY 2002 (91)
(50% PN, 50% CH)
A beautiful construction with a stable foundation and an imaginative façade. Henriot's superb vineyards in Côte des Blancs are clearly noticeable in the ultra-sophisticated, lime-saturated taste. The nose needs a few years extra storage in order to bloom fully.

- 1989 HENRIOT   82, FEB 1997 (86)
(55% PN, 45% CH)
Henriot has made a light and elegant '89 with a discreet, floral bouquet. The mineral and citrus taste is appetizing. The wine has probably grown in strength and breadth with age.

- 1988 HENRIOT   80, FEB 1997 (86)
(55% PN, 45% CH)
A restrained and elegant Champagne with signs of maturity in the nose and a pure, agreeable flavor.

- 1985 HENRIOT   88, MAR 2003 (90)
(55% PN, 45% CH)
Strangely enough, only tasted in jeroboam. Purchased straight from the house, fully disgorged, noticed for its autolytic character but also because the cork was almost impossible to remove. Ten men worked for almost as many minutes with muscle power, slip-joint pliers, and a pair of pincers before a good old corkscrew rescued us from our precarious situation. Now, on to the wine, which was very delicious: youthful appearance, finely toasted with a dash of gunpowder and an underlying Moët-like fruit. Springtime-ish, balanced palate with an element of passion fruit and chalk. Probably somewhat poorer in a regular bottle.

- 1983 HENRIOT   87, NOV 2001 (87)
(50% PN, 50% CH)
The wines from 1983 are today often slightly coarse, with a hint of dehydration and nuttiness that borders on cork notes—something even this wine suffers from a little. Otherwise it's classically made and richer than usual, with a nougat tone that backs up the mineral notes.

- 1982 HENRIOT   82, OCT 2002 (>)
(50% PN, 50% CH)

This was once a young and delightful, chalky Champagne, with honey tones in the scent, though rather weak and thin. The wine is beginning to oxidize. Drink up!

- 1979 HENRIOT   94, OCT 2002 (95)
(50% PN, 50% CH)
Yet another exceptional wine from Henriot. Weaker nose and hardly as enchantingly beautiful as a Blanc de Blancs from the same year; on the other hand, there is more depth and room in this than in that other beauty. The wine is—at least if you get to taste it at Henriot, as I did—very young and develops quickly in the glass. Delightful weight and fruit concentration that is unusual for this classic vintage that normally smells so beautifully of hazelnuts.

- 1976 HENRIOT   96, OCT 2001 (96)
(50% PN, 50% CH)
Wonderful aroma with toasted bread and nougat tones that are as clear as a bell. Fabulously elegant taste with a higher than usual concentration of all of the glorious tones that are usually found in the house's wines. The aftertaste is like the out-of-this-world vanilla sauce that Gérard Boyer spoiled us with.

- 1975 HENRIOT   95, MAY 2002 (95)
(67% PN, 33% CH)
I insanely misjudged this wine previously! It is nothing less than a total bull's-eye! Velvety smooth, classic, and seductive at the same time, with a wonderful richness and citrus-fresh fruitiness. As usual, filled with chalky notes and elegance. Also beautifully backed up by a wonderfully rich vanilla aroma.

- 1973 HENRIOT   81, AUG 1996 (81)
(50% PN, 50% CH)
Surprisingly loose and clumsy. The house-style has gone with the wind. Instead, the wine is generous and chocolate-saturated, with an unclean, earthy secondary tone. Most likely could be much better.

- 1971 HENRIOT   78, JUN 2003 (>)
(50% PN, 50% CH)

- 1969 HENRIOT   93, MAY 2003 (93)
(51% PN, 49% CH)
Purebred, minerally Champagne with a gracious posture. Fine floweriness and fruit, with passion fruit as the strongest point of difference. Extremely lively and youthful with a small body and tons of life-preserving acidity.

- 1964 HENRIOT   93, FEB 2003 (93)
(51% PN, 49% CH)
A newly disgorged variety direct from the house (July 1998). The structure is light and luscious with a rather ordinary length. A delightful but somewhat overdominant nose of mushroom forest has crept into the elegant and strongly Chardonnay-like wine. This has been tasted more than ten times with brilliant consistency.

- 1962 HENRIOT   90, DEC 2002 (90)
(51% PN, 49% CH)
Fantastically fresh and floral with youthful charm. Unexpectedly light and short but with a discreetly beautiful smile that carries the wine over the ninety-point line.

- 1959 HENRIOT   99, JUN 2003 (99)
(51% PN, 49% CH)
Henriot considers the '59 to be their foremost Champagne. It's a monumental wine of gigantic dimensions. Unfortunately, the first bottle I tasted was completely devoid of mousse, as well

as possessing too much aldehyde. Bottle number two was exceedingly mature with a wonderful toffee aroma and butterscotchy structure. Luckily enough I'll soon be able to taste a bottle direct from Reims; my mouth is watering already.

Now it's happened! A newly disgorged magnum was elegance personified. Everything was present in a thick, viscous nectar with acacia-like fresh floweriness. Very reminiscent of both a '55 and a '59 Billecart N. F.

- **1955 HENRIOT**   97, OCT 2002 (97)
(50% PN, 50% CH)
A complete jewel with perfect balance. Considerably lighter than the '59 with an otherwise similar taste profile. The nose is elusively restrained, with a clear note of whipped cream together with a fragile, butterscotchy surface and monumental, truffle-like notes of maturity. The taste is sweet and exotic with a resoundingly pure and fresh finish.

- **1954 HENRIOT**   96, JUN 1999 (96)
(50% PN, 50% CH)
I thought I had misread a fax from Henriot that listed what they considered to be their best vintages when I saw that 1954 was included. After having tasted a newly disgorged magnum I understood what they meant. From the glass flowed a completely fantastic, pure, and uniquely flowery perfume. Playfully twirling bubbles supported the elegant and youthful flavors of crisp yellow plums and peaches.

- **1979 HENRIOT BLANC DE BLANCS**   96, OCT 2002 (96)
(100% CH)
Henriot's Blanc de Blancs are usually vintage-less, but here they have picked a pure '76 out of their hat. It is simply an exceptionally good and sexy wine. The nose makes me euphoric with its toasted and classic creamy butterscotch elegance. Lighter and shorter than the usual vintage Champagne, but with a finesse and grace that makes me long for the next bottle.

- **1998 HENRIOT ROSÉ**   87, JAN 2004 (90)
(52% PN, 48% CH)
Exceedingly homogeneous and faithful to its luxurious and unmistakably elegant house-style. Lovely apricot color, and exceptional mousse that creates the most beautiful string of pearls in the glass. Handsome nose with a purebred floweriness; vanilla bun note and fresh appley-ness as well as strawberries and whipped cream. Not at all rich or obvious; just so ingeniously precise and architecturally perfect.

- **1996 HENRIOT ROSÉ**   83, JAN 2003 (88)
(52% PN, 48% CH)
Light, undeveloped, shy Champagne with high acidity and good structure. For the time being the nose is casually floral, with notes of eucalyptus, melon, and anisette pastilles. After a while in the glass, a certain breadiness and a clear note of orange blossom appear. Fresh, promising taste.

- **1993 HENRIOT ROSÉ**   84, OCT 2001 (87)
(52% PN, 48% CH)
Clear as a bell and light, this is house-typical Champagne with fine mineral taste, uplifting acidity, and a chalky character, like the most elegant Chardonnay.

- **1990 HENRIOT ROSÉ**   89, JAN 2003 (90)
(57% PN, 43% CH)
Beautiful and well-built Champagne with a bit more heft than in earlier vintages. Rich, evolved, fat, with creamy fruit. A delightful symphony in a fluffy style.

- **1988 HENRIOT ROSÉ**   81, FEB 1997 (87)
(52% PN, 48% CH)
A pure and well-made rosé with good red and blackcurrant tones and excellent mineral riches.

- **1985 HENRIOT ROSÉ**   86, DEC 2001 (87)
(52% PN, 48% CH)
Pale color and weak, tranquil, relatively young aromas with a floral hint. Softly harmonic taste with finesse, class, and elegance. A discreet wine that demands subtle company, and which should be enjoyed in great gulps.

- **1976 HENRIOT ROSÉ**   93, MAR 2001 (93)
(55% PN, 45% CH)
This is the kind of exuberantly good, uncomplicated wine that you want all your friends to taste. Sweet, nectar-like essence, with tons of different candy notes and a thick, massive, fruity richness. Uniform and voluptuous. Healthy color and mousse.

- **1989 LES ENCHANTELEURS**   91, APR 2004 (94)
(40% PN, 60% CH)
Tasted newly disgorged before the wine had gone onto the market. That's why it was not so strange to detect a slightly restrained, unevolved characteristic about this—in all other ways—classic, house-typical Champagne. Vanilla, peach, lemon, rolls, bread, and mineral clothed in a fat, balanced exterior. Beautiful and developable. Highly reminiscent of Henriot's delightful '76s.

- **1988 LES ENCHANTELEURS**   94, NOV 2003 (96)
(45% PN, 55% CH)
Initially weak, but beautiful nose of white flowers, acacia, toffee, and vanilla. Light to medium-bodied taste with fine freshness, breeding, and elegance. Today its strength is just beginning to appear. Incredibly splendid! Totally brilliant recently, with an increased fattiness and buttery concentration of all the vanilla aromas and beautifully floral perfume. This is a sort of Champagne of Champagnes—a more classic, typical representative of this type of wine does not exist.

- **1985 LES ENCHANTELEURS**   85, JAN 1999 (88)
(45% PN, 55% CH)
The firm's new *cuvée de prestige* is identical to Cuvée Baccarat. Their efforts to make a light and discreet Champagne are fully rewarded in this wine. Slightly thin and nondescript but with a flowery elegance.

- **1983 CUVÉE BACCARAT**   89, JUN 2002 (89)
(45% PN, 55% CH)
Both the '83 and the '85 lack concentration. The wines are light, bordering on the brittle. The color is light with hues of green. A weak, smoky, mature tone is noticeable in the flowery nose. The flavor is also flowery rather than fruity. A frail vanilla tone appears in the discreet aftertaste.

- **1982 CUVÉE BACCARAT**   91, FEB 2003 (91)
(45% PN, 55% CH)
A somewhat broader and meatier nose than usual, but otherwise the same laid-back, balanced, big-house-style that we've come to expect. A classic Champagne character all the way, but a touch impersonal.

- **1981 BARON PHILIPPE DE ROTHSCHILD**   88, JAN 2001 (88)
(50% PN, 50% CH)
The equal proportions of Pinot and Chardonnay give the wine balance. Baron Philippe is always a heavier and more full-bodied Champagne than Baccarat.

- 1981 CUVÉE BACCARAT   91, OCT 2000 (92)
  (45% PN, 55% CH)
  The '81 is a textbook example of an elegant *cuvée* Champagne. It is smooth, generous, and easy to appreciate, with its bouquet of mature Chardonnay and exemplary soft mousse. The flavor is woven together with veils of exotic fruit.

- 1979 BARON PHILIPPE DE ROTHSCHILD   96, JUL 2003 (96)
  (50% PN, 50% CH)
  The Baron's own Champagne from 1979 is similar to the '81 for the most part. The fruit may be a touch richer in this wine. Previously this wine appeared clumsy and low in acidity. Today we know better. The concentration is magnificent, almost like a '76; at the same time the wine enters with a new floral and citrus-fresh Chardonnay side. Completely wonderful!

- 1979 CUVÉE BACCARAT   90, AUG 1996 (90)
  (40% PN, 60% CH)
  Elegant and charming Champagne. The lovely balanced taste is full of vanilla. A classic that is probably even better than I thought in 1996.

- 1976 CUVÉE BACCARAT   96, OCT 2002 (96)
  (40% PN, 60% CH)
  I found a normally disgorged bottle in a small wine shop in central Paris. The price was ridiculously low and the wine was wonderful. Relatively dark and developed in color. The nose had more maturity than Les Enchanteleurs in magnum, but the scent was still floral and completely packed with sensual, vanilla-drenched fruit.

- 1976 LES ENCHANTELEURS   97, OCT 2002 (97)
  (40% PN, 60% CH)
  Together with the '55, the best Champagne that I tasted during an extremely comprehensive vertical tasting by Henriot in October 2002. This magnum contains the exact same wine as Baccarat, but because Taittinger owns Baccarat Crystal, this label was used. It took a while for the nose of this light, incredibly fat wine to blossom fully. When that happened, a fantastically beautiful, sensual symphony was played for the olfactory glands. The taste is extremely intense and vintage-typically butterscotchy and sweet, with the house's finely refreshing, citrus-clad spine as a counterbalance and interest-catcher.

- 1975 BARON PHILIPPE DE ROTHSCHILD   93, DEC 2003 (93)
  (50% PN, 50% CH)
  This rich, honey-saturated wine is very reminiscent of the '73. In other words: big and powerful with notes of mature, slightly oxidative dried fruit and the same fleshiness and almond aromas. A big and impressive wine, though Baron Philippe de Rothschild is never particularly refined or house-typical, unlike the other wines in Henriot's graceful portfolio.

- 1973 BARON PHILIPPE DE ROTHSCHILD   93, FEB 2002 (93)
  (50% PN, 50% CH)
  Completely evolved purebred horse with class, charm, and respect. Fat and extremely concentrated, with vintage-typical maturity and oxidative aromas. Raisins, almonds, plums, and intense honey-saturation.

- 1969 BARON PHILIPPE DE ROTHSCHILD   93, FEB 2003 (93)
  (50% PN, 50% CH)
  A truly monstrous wine with its almost obese dimensions. Tons of heavy, sweet, toffee-ish scent. Oily, concentrated, demanding taste with a fruitiness bordering on the overripe. Impressive, but not as elegant as I had expected from Henriot. Pinot grapes dominate completely.

- 1983 CUVÉE BACCARAT ROSÉ   84, FEB 1997 (87)
  (60% PN, 40% CH)
  Slender-limbed and sophisticated bread aroma and a hint of spring flowers in the nose. Medium-bodied, restrained flavor with fine mineral tones.

- HENRIOT WEDDING CUVÉE   90, JAN 2003 (90)
  (50% PN, 50% CH)
  A cuvée from the 1970s made for Prince Andrew's and Sarah Ferguson's wedding in 1986. Completely evolved today, with tons of deep, sweet signs of maturity combined with the house's classic style and elegantly light construction.

HENRY DE LAVAL R-M
51480 Damery
A grower that stopped selling their own Champagne long ago.
- 1953 HENRY DE LAVAL BLANC DE BLANCS   92, OCT 2001 (92)
  (100% CH)
  It's not every day that one runs into a Blanc de Blancs from Damery. Approaching its fiftieth birthday, this brilliant '53 was radiantly vital and intimate. Big nose of tar, anise, fennel, and green peppers. A somewhat tannin-generated abrasive taste, with elastic acidity and Marne Valley *terroir* character.

HERARD, PAUL N-M
31, Grande Rue
10250 Neuville-sur-Seine
03 25 38 20 14
Production: 180,000
The Herard family have been growers in Aube for generations, but the house was only founded in 1925. Their reputation today is fairly good.
- PAUL HERARD RÉSERVE   58
  (75% PN, 25% CH)
- PAUL HERARD BLANC DE NOIRS   52
  (100% PN)

HERBERT, DIDIER *** R-M
51500 Rilly-la-Montagne
03 26 03 41 53
Production: 65,000
The grower has more than six hectares with twenty-year-old vines in Rilly, Mailly, and Verzenay. The malolactic fermentation is sometimes blocked and the proportion of oak barrels is great. This clever grower will soon launch an oak-barrel-aged *grand cru* from Verzenay and Mailly. Already his Blanc de Blancs are made from 100 percent Burgundy barrels.
- 1997 PLATINIUM   89, JAN 2004 (90)
  (35% PN, 65% CH)
  An explosive Champagne with barrel-like character, big muscles, tough apple acidity, and exotic, Vilmart-like concentration.

HÉBRART, MARC *** R-M
18, rue du Pont
51160 Mareuil-sur-Aÿ
03 26 52 60 75
Production: 80,000
Marc Hébrart and his son Jean-Paul are the most famous growers in the village. Besides Pinot grapes from Mareuil, they have access to Chardonnay from Chouilly and Oiry, with an average of twenty-eight-year-old stocks. It's always a joy to visit Jean-Paul at this beautiful property by the Marne River. He belongs to the new type of well-educated, quality-concerned vintners—a grower to keep your eyes on. Jean-Paul has found love in Cramant, and the object of his happiness is Isabelle Diebolt. What a *cuvée*!

* HÉBRART RÉSERVE   69
  (80% PN, 20% CH)
* SÉLECTION JEAN-PAUL HÉBRART   75
  (70% PN, 30% CH)
* SÉLECTION MARC HÉBRART   76
  (70% PN, 30% CH)
* HÉBRART BLANC DE BLANCS   76
  (100% CH)
* HÉBRART ROSÉ   78
  (70% PN, 30% CH)
* 1998 HÉBRART SPECIAL CLUB   83, DEC 2003 (88)
  (60% PN, 40% CH)

All Chardonnay from Oiry and Chouilly, as well as Pinot Noir from their home village of Mareuil-sur-Aÿ. Probably just as good as the beautifully airy and finely built '97, but slightly harder today, despite the fine honey note that hovers over the fruit. Nice malic acidity that livens up the taste buds.

* 1997 HÉBRART SPECIAL CLUB   85, DEC 2002 (87)
  (60% PN, 40% CH)

I became quite enamored of this crystal-clear, stylish Champagne when it was sneaked into a blind tasting that I led. The wine is more discreet than expected, with fine, chalky elegance and a polished finish. The weak nose is sophisticatedly constructed and floral, with clear notes of hawthorn and marigolds. The taste is slightly fuzzy, aromatically speaking, but it hits the bull's-eye in the structure department.

* 1996 HÉBRART PRESTIGE   84, DEC 2003 (88)
  (60% PN, 40% CH)

Delightful combination of freshness and snobbishly plump Pinot Noir. The acidity cuts through as clearly as sunshine on a bright winter's day. Long; it will be exciting to follow this one into the next decade.

* 1995 HÉBRART PRESTIGE   84, OCT 2001 (87)
  (60% PN, 40% CH)

The relative from Diebolt that married into the family really pulled it off this time—this is a juicy, powerful Champagne, strongly imprinted by mature Pinot grapes. Under the big, direct gamy and bready nose, I catch a whiff of lake vegetation and moist summer nights. Good grip, structure, and fine, youthful acidity.

* 1990 HÉBRART SPECIAL CLUB   78, MAR 2000 (83)
  (50% PN, 50% CH)

Deep, almost orange color. A broad nose of vanilla and ripe apples. A rich young flavor of Swedish cheesecake and apple peel.

* 1989 HÉBRART PRESTIGE   70, APR 1995 (79)
  (60% PN, 40% CH)

HÉRARD & FLUTEAU N-M
route Nationale
10250 Gyé-sur-Seine
03 25 38 20 02
Production: 70,000
Founded by Georges Fluteau and Émile Hérard in 1935, the firm owns five hectares in Aube and buys in most of its grapes. The current manager is Bernard Fluteau. Other wines: Cuvée Réservée, Rosé.

* 1995 G. FLUTEAU PRESTIGE   69, OCT 2001 (70)
  (100% CH)

HORIOT PÈRE & FILS R-M
11, rue Cure Bas
10340 Les Riceys
03 25 29 32 21
Production: 40,000
The grower only uses grapes from his home village of Les Riceys.

* HORIOT BRUT   50
  (50% PN, 50% CH)

HOSTOMME R-M
5, rue de l'Allée
51530 Chouilly
03 26 55 40 79
Production: 140,000
The Hostomme family has produced *grand cru* Champagne for three generations. They are the principal owner of Chouilly's rare Pinot Noir vines, and even make a Blanc de Noirs with mostly Chouilly Pinot.

* HOSTOMME GRANDE RÉSERVE   68
  (100% CH)
* HOSTOMME BLANC DE BLANCS   66
  (100% CH)
* HOSTOMME ROSÉ   53
  (50% PN, 50% CH)
* HOSTOMME BLANC DE NOIRS   60
  (80% PN, 20% PM)
* 1989 HOSTOMME   70, JUL 1995 (80)
  (100% CH)

Unexpectedly light, with weak, creamy tones and a certain elegance.

HUSSON R-M
2, rue Jules Lobet
51160 Aÿ
03 26 55 43 05
Production: 50,000
Unfortunately they have stopped making their own wines.

* HUSSON BRUT   55
  (70% PN, 30% CH)
* HUSSON ROSÉ   65
  (100% PN)

H. BLIN C-M
5, rue de Verdun
51700 Vincelles
03 26 58 20 04
Production: 630,000
This Marne cooperative was formed in Vincelles in 1947. The 105

members control more than 110 hectares, and today 30 percent of the harvest is exported. The grapes come from ten villages in the Marne Valley. I've been positively surprised by Blin's charming Champagnes. They're no classics, but they do offer a lot for your money with their mature, personal style. In all the wines I found aromas of orange-chocolate and nougat. Tony Rasselet is *chef du cave*.

- H. BLIN TRADITION   51
  (5% PN, 77% PM, 18% CH)
- H. BLIN BRUT RÉSERVE   68
  (5% PN, 75% PM, 20% CH)
- H. BLIN CHARDONNAY   65
  (100% CH)
- H. BLIN DEMI-SEC   40
  (5% PN, 95% PM)
- H. BLIN ROSÉ   50
  (20% PN, 62% PM, 18% CH)
- 1998 H. BLIN   73, SEP 2003 (76)
  (50% PN, 50% CH)
- 1990 H. BLIN   83, NOV 1998 (85)
  (50% PN, 50% CH)
  The chocolate-orange note is backed up by an impressive structure. The finest Champagne I have tasted from Blin.
- 1988 H. BLIN   79, SEP 2003 (79)
  (50% PN, 50% CH)
- 1986 H. BLIN   78, OCT 2001 (78)
  (20% PN, 30% PM, 50% CH)
- 1979 H. BLIN   83, FEB 1996 (83)
  (70% PN, 30% CH)
  Golden yellow, toasted, and a fine, long, butterscotchy finishing twist.

IRROY *** N-M
44, boulevard Lundy
51100 Reims
03 26 88 37 27
Production: 500,000

Taittinger's second house was founded in 1820. Originally one of the great labels—today virtually invisible. The stars denote past glory.

- 1959 IRROY   94, APR 2002 (94)
  (70% PN, 30% CH)
  A fully packed, energetic powerhouse with every characteristic of this great vintage. Big, smoky nose and a massively masculine taste of great dimensions. An impressive mealtime Champagne.
- 1945 IRROY
  (70% PN, 30% CH)
- 1943 IRROY   94, AUG 1997 (94)
  (70% PN, 30% CH)
  For a long time this was the only Champagne from this house that I had tasted; the Irroy '43 is judged by many to be the best Champagne from this vintage! It is still majestic with its irrepressible energy, lively mousse, and fiery finish. The wine is marked by oak aromas and heavy Pinot Noir. The nose is Krug-like, with scents of honey and nuts, and the full flavor is dominated by cacao aromas.
- 1941 IRROY
  (70% PN, 30% CH)
- 1928 IRROY   95, JAN 1999 (95)
  (70% PN, 30% CH)

As long as the storage has been good, this '28 is a remarkable and aristocratic Champagne. The strength is huge and the taste is like nectar. Some bottles, however, have been completely ruined.

- 1953 IRROY BLANC DE BLANCS   90, MAR 2003 (90)
  (100% CH)
  I wasn't aware that Irroy made Blanc de Blancs—until this perfect, swirling '53 was presented to me at the formidable restaurant, Swedish Taste, in Gothenburg, Sweden. Fresh as a spring morning, this wine brought life to the olfactory organ with its elastic, floral bouquet. Perky, tiny, spunky bubbles ripped into my taste buds as a supple toffee note calmed the impression superbly. After thirty minutes in the glass the nose changed into a piquant pear grappa aroma.
- 1964 IRROY ROSÉ   94, OCT 2003 (94)
  (70% PN, 30% CH)
  I had no great expectations for this wine because the '61 was so weak. Imagine my joy when my nose was met by newly shaved white truffle, railway, smoke, boiled vegetables, and heavy, exotic collections of orchids. Dark and masculine with a surprising energy and attack, the mousse in no way plays out its roll as taste conveyor. Long and serious with an aftertaste of dark, unsweetened, bitter chocolate.
- 1961 IRROY ROSÉ   81, FEB 2001 (81)
  (70% PN, 30% CH)
  Much too much oxidation in the nose. Rich, fleshy taste of plums, raisins, old raspberry juice, and sherry. Still has a hint of mousse. This has seen its best days ages ago.
- 1970 IRROY MARIE ANTOINETTE   93, APR 2003 (93)
  (70% PN, 30% CH)
  A homogeneous, totally brilliant '70. The wine is highly reminiscent of a nice '66, with its fine acidity and strong smell of honeysuckle. There is also a plumpness and a butterscotchiness that makes one think of Cristal. Velvety finish of toffee and honey.
- 1966 IRROY MARIE ANTOINETTE   96, AUG 1999 (96)
  (66% PN, 34% CH)
  Simply wonderful! An utterly irresistible '66 with perfect elegance and style. The bouquet is clean and flowery with a pronounced tone of orange and nougat. The flavor combines strength and freshness in a way that reminds one of a beautifully toasted Dom Pérignon of the same vintage.
- 1962 IRROY MARIE ANTOINETTE   94, JUN 1999 (94)
  (70% PN, 30% CH)
  This is the first time I have happened across a bottle this young from the once so-famous house Irroy. Marie Antoinette is the name of this prestige Champagne. The famous woman lived in Château d'Irroy in 1786. The wine itself is impressive with a magnificent depth. As with all great '62s, this lady lives by a unified, soft, concentrated fruit. There are many similarities with Krug's nutty and treacle-soft '62.

IVERNEL N-M
6, rue Jules Lobet
51160 Aÿ
03 26 55 21 10
Production: 85,000

Since 1989 this historic house has been owned by Gosset, which in practice looks upon Ivernel as its second label. The Ivernel family has lived in Aÿ since the fifteenth century, but didn't start their

Champagne house until 1955. All the grapes are bought in from outside, and Ivernel have specialized in supplying France's top restaurants. In Sweden, master chef Paul Bocuse's own Champagne is identical to Ivernel Brut Réserve.

- PAUL BOCUSE BRUT   72
  (30% PN, 30% PM, 40% CH)
- IVERNEL BRUT RÉSERVE   72
  (30% PN, 30% PM, 40% CH)
- IVERNEL ROSÉ   51
  (20% PN, 80% CH)
- 1989 IVERNEL   76, AUG 1995 (80)
  (45% PN, 12% PM, 43% CH)
  Round and powerful. Just as might be expected, considering the vintage and the producer. The '89 is hardly one for the cellar, though.

JACKOWIACK-RONDEAU R-M
26, rue Saint-Martin
51390 Pargny-les-Reims
03 26 49 20 25
Production: 50,000

This grower of Polish descent owns six hectares in Jouy-les-Reims and their home village of Pargny-les-Reims, planted with 30 percent Pinot Noir, 55 percent Pinot Meunier, and 15 percent Chardonnay. The average age of the stocks is twenty-five years old and the oldest is thirty-eight. Their philosophy is to harvest late and to take only completely ripe grapes. They are particularly careful with the Prestige Champagne Cuvée d'Or, which has a very ripe and round taste. The nonvintage Champagne gets its supple style from storing for five and a half years before going on the market. A good producer and an excellent representative of its home village.

- JACKOWIACK-RONDEAU BRUT   70
  (30% PN, 55% PM, 15% CH)
- JACKOWIACK-RONDEAU EXTRA DRY   67
  (30% PN, 55% PM, 15% CH)
- CUVÉE D'OR   80
  (45% PN, 10% PM, 45% CH)
  A prestige Champagne made from extremely ripe grapes from southern slopes, and then stored for a long time in the grower's cellar. Deep yellow color, unctuous, dense structure, and soft, evolved, sweet taste slightly reminiscent of a good *vendage tardive* from Alsace. Naturally oxidative taste with heaps of dried apricots, pineapples, raisins, and papaya, as well as honey and leather.
- JACKOWIAK-RONDEAU ROSÉ   70
  (30% PN, 55% PM, 15% CH)

JACQUART *** C-M
5, rue Gosset
51100 Reims
03 26 07 88 40
Production: 9,000,000

Today this is one of the largest Champagne producers, despite the fact that the cooperative is only thirty-five years old. When Robert Quantinet originally collected together a group of growers they produced 100,000 bottles. Today that figure is up to nine million every year, and the cooperative, with more than 600 members, controls over 1,000 hectares from 64 villages in Marne. Just like

Reims' other cooperative, Palmer, they use the new 8,000-kilo presses at their ultra-modern plant. These well-made wines have a good name among critics. The quality of the grapes is good with an average rating of 96 percent on the *cru* scale. The winemaker is Richard Dailly.

- JACQUART BRUT SÉLECTION   58
  (35% PN, 15% PM, 50% CH)
- JACQUART MOSAÏQUE   63
  (35% PN, 15% PM, 50% CH)
- JACQUART TRADITION   64
  (33% PN, 33% PM, 34% CH)
- JACQUART DEMI-SEC   49
  (35% PN, 15% PM, 50% CH)
- JACQUART ROSÉ   51
  (45% PN, 15% PM, 40% CH)
- 1997 JACQUART MOSAÏQUE   81, SEP 2003 (82)
  (38% PN, 12% PM, 50% CH)
  Big, bready, deep nose with house-typical character. Perhaps surprisingly big and powerful considering the vintage. Already a certain butterscotchy maturity.
- 1996 JACQUART MOSAÏQUE   85, FEB 2004 (87)
  (38% PN, 12% PM, 50% CH)
  More toasted and exotic than usual, with peach and pineapple as star billing. For the time being the fruity base holds back the bready notes, but they are there if you pay careful attention. Nice acidity and good bite. Certain bottles are extremely toasted in a way that makes you think of Charles Heidsieck.
- 1992 JACQUART MOSAÏQUE   75, JAN 2002 (76)
  (50% PN, 50% CH)
- 1990 JACQUART MOSAÏQUE   85, MAR 2000 (85)
  (50% PN, 10% PM, 40% CH)
  All these Champagnes share a nectar-like, chewable, exotic taste. The wine is made from ripe grapes, but develops too quickly.
- 1990 JACQUART MOSAÏQUE   78, FEB 1997 (82)
  (50% PN, 50% CH)
  A rounded wine made for early consumption, already including aromas of peach, apricot, and chocolate.
- 1990 RITZ   78, FEB 1997 (82)
  (50% PN, 50% CH)
  This seems to be exactly the same wine as the 1990 Jacquart. The fruit is generous, with concentration that brings chocolate pudding to mind.
- 1987 JACQUART MOSAÏQUE   85, MAR 2002 (85)
  (50% PN, 50% CH)
  Pleasant scent of apricot marmalade and Fazer's green jelly balls from Finland. Superbly refreshing and deliciously fruity, with notes of honey and apricot in the taste. It is a delight to drink this uncomplicated wine.
- 1983 JACQUART   81, DEC 2002 (81)
  (50% PN, 50% CH)
  Unfortunately this fleshy, bready wine is on its way out! Fruit is now missing and the wine is only kept alive through its toasted aromas and caramelization.
- 1978 JACQUART   78, MAY 2001 (78)
  (50% PN, 50% CH)
- 1997 JACQUART BLANC DE BLANCS   84, NOV 2003 (85)
  (100% CH)
  Great! Fun that this wine seems to have stabilized its style over the years. Nowadays, it's always soft and balanced, with fine

toasted strains of coffee and chocolate. Good, soft, citrus-influenced fruit and a mild finish.

- 1996 JACQUART BLANC DE BLANCS   83, NOV 2003 (86)
(100% CH)

For the moment dry, toasted, slightly bready, and a tad sharp, with good potential. A hint of sulfur and ripping acidity. This is how I experienced the wine the last time I tasted it; the strange thing is, the first bottle I tasted was soft and mature.

- 1995 JACQUART BLANC DE BLANCS   70, MAR 2000 (70)
(100% CH)

- 1992 JACQUART BLANC DE BLANCS   83, OCT 1997 (84)
(100% CH)

Charming and mature, but without any potential.

- 1998 MOSAÏQUE ROSÉ   73, MAY 2003 (76)
(45% PN, 15% PM, 40% CH)

- 1986 MOSAÏQUE ROSÉ   78, APR 1997 (80)
(45% PN, 15% PM, 40% CH)

As with so many '86s, this wine felt a little loose. There are elements of cheese and other mature tones; the flavor has popular appeal but lacks complexity and length.

- CUVÉE NOMINÉE   80, JUL 2001 (84)
(50% PN, 50% CH)

Contains grapes from 1996 as well as a little reserve wine. Rather undeveloped and neutral for the moment. Perhaps a little over-refined and overworked. I'd rather see a more generous fruit, but the acidity is fine, which is promising. The future is difficult to judge.

- JACQUART CUVÉE RENOMÉE   84, DEC 2002 (84)
(50% PN, 50% CH)

The predecessor of Cuvée Nominée, with base wine from 1982. Big and generous and ingratiatingly sweet and exotic. The wine tastes like a rather sweet peach pie. The nose even has some interesting notes of duck liver and butterscotch. The taste is round and good, if somewhat short.

- 1990 CUVÉE NOMINÉE   89, SEP 2001 (89)
(50% PN, 50% CH)

A prestige wine with base wines from ten different *grand cru* vineyards. Here freshness combines with a strong chocolaty base in exemplary fashion. Superb balance and a nice fruit, leaning toward the exotic. Best of all is the very long separate aftertaste of cacao and vanilla bean.

- 1988 CUVÉE NOMINÉE   85, MAR 2000 (87)
(40% PN, 60% CH)

Cheese and chocolate in the nose. Soft taste filled with exotic fruit and the ever-recurring note of chocolate.

- 1986 CUVÉE NOMINÉE   83, MAY 1997 (83)
(60% PN, 40% CH)

Fully developed at the age of ten. Enjoyable, round, and full of honeyed fruit with exotic overtones. The wine is oxidative and gives a Pinot-dominated impression.

- 1985 CUVÉE NOMINÉE   78, NOV 1994 (85)
(40% PN, 60% CH)

When many firms make their *cuvée de prestige*, they strain so hard to make a soft and refined wine that they tend to remove some of the wine's character. Cuvée Nominée is just such a *cuvée de prestige*. Very sophisticated style with a smooth mousse and weak, delicate peach aromas, and discreet breadiness in the nose.

- 1985 CUVÉE NOMINÉE ROSÉ   87, SEP 1998 (87)
(50% PN, 50% CH)

A beautiful, delicious wine with charming aromas and creamy structure. Already completely evolved at the age of twelve.

- 1990 CUVÉE NOMINÉE MILLENNIUM   89, NOV 2001 (90)
(50% PN, 50% CH)

The standard Nominée in a magnum bottle for the Millennium. Somewhat stricter and a tad more elegant than the regular bottle.

JACQUART, ANDRÉ *** R-M
6, avenue de la République
51190 Le Mesnil-sur-Oger
03 26 57 52 29
Production: 100,000

André Jacquart is one of the growers who is moving up in the world, and can soon be expected to demand sky-high prices. At their command they have seven hectares in Aube and the Marne valley, but it's their eleven hectares in Le Mesnil that are making them famous.

- ANDRÉ JACQUART BRUT   49
(30% PN, 30% PM, 40% CH)

- ANDRÉ JACQUART BLANC DE BLANCS   75
(100% CH)

- ANDRÉ JACQUART ROSÉ   54
(15% PN, 85% CH)

- 1997 ANDRÉ JACQUART   83, SEP 2003 (86)
(100% CH)

Clean, sound, and softer than usual. Thick, captivating fruit that leans toward pineapple and papaya. A good, straight throw.

- 1993 ANDRÉ JACQUART   80, OCT 1998 (86)
(100% CH)

Extremely clean Mesnil style with intractable acidity and tons of mineral. Light but long and chalky aftertaste. Should be stored quite a while to reach its full potential.

- 1990 ANDRÉ JACQUART   85, FEB 2001 (91)
(100% CH)

Exceptionally clean and youthfully tight Champagne, completely characteristic of its place of origin. Vintage character is conspicuously absent. Despite its respectable age it continues to produce flowery tones, and even the palate experiences the knife-sharp acidity.

- 1989 ANDRÉ JACQUART   77, JUN 1995 (86)
(100% CH)

Tough and unexpectedly light, with high acidity and a strong mineral tone.

- 1985 ANDRÉ JACQUART   87, JUN 1993 (92)
(100% CH)

This is where André Jacquart displays their greatness, with a classic Blanc de Blancs in a mature style. An almost exotic nose of mango and peach; funnily enough the toasty elements only arrive in the flavor.

- 1989 ANDRÉ JACQUART SPECIAL CLUB   80, MAY 1996 (89)
(100% CH)

As usual, superior concentration and roundness in the Special Club when compared to the ordinary nonvintage Champagne. Identical aromas.

- 1986 ANDRÉ JACQUART SPECIAL CLUB   81, JUL 1995 (83)
(100% CH)

Mature and rounded with a creamy flavor.

JACQUESSON & FILS **** N-M
68, rue du Colonel Fabien
51530 Dizy
03 26 55 68 11
Production: 350,000

Jacquesson—founded in 1798 in Châlons-sur-Marne—was one of the first Champagne houses. It didn't take them long to become a famous firm. Their reputation wasn't hurt either when Napoleon, visiting the company, bestowed a gold medal on Jacquesson in recognition of their beautiful cellar. America became their foremost export market; recently old Jacquesson bottles were found aboard a wreck named the *Niantic*, a ship forgotten after it sank during the Great San Francisco Fire of 1851. The first bottle was opened with great ceremony; the disappointment must have been enormous when they took their first gulp of seawater!

By 1867 Jacquesson had already sold one million bottles, but after Adolphe Jacquesson's death a sharp decline set in. Leon de Tassigny took over in 1920 and bought the fine vineyards they own today in Avize, Aÿ, Dizy, and Hautvillers. Still, the quality didn't reach the level of the 1800s. For a long time the company played second fiddle, until Jean Chiquet bought the noble house in Dizy in 1974. Today, the company is run by his two determined sons: Laurent (vintner) and Jean-Hervé (businessman). When I first met Jean-Hervé in 1990, he told me that they were aiming for the very top. All new investments were made with quality in mind. The second pressing was sold, the proportion of reserve wine and oak barrels was increased, a greater amount of *grand cru* grapes was bought in. Today, this costly venture is beginning to bear fruit. The nonvintage Champagne Perfection is brilliant, and has now been given a number to differentiate it from the other blends. Prestige Champagne Signature and Signature Rosé are now among the best every year. Moreover, they have some of the oldest commercially available Champagnes in their D. T. series. In the future, several exciting mono-*cru* wines will be launched, so keep your eyes open. The Chiquet brothers won't give up until they reach the absolute top. Jacquesson is one of the most interesting houses today, giving fantastically good value for money.

- JACQUESSON CUVÉE 728   82, DEC 2003 (86)
(27% PN, 37% PM, 36% CH)
Jacquesson have become masters of creating new, interesting *cuvées* and concepts. The nonvintage Champagne Perfection has changed its look, and now appears under the blend name 728. A full 68 percent of the wine comes from the year 2000 and the rest is reserve wine. The proportion of oak barrel and *grand cru* vineyards is very high in this unfiltered and faintly dosed wine. As usual, Avize, Aÿ, and Dizy make up the base of this very interesting *cuvée*. For the moment there are tons of young pear-scented fruit and green apple notes. These will become more complex in time, and the present high-class Chardonnay will come to be even more creamy. Wood notes, forest, spices, chocolate, and a hint of fino sherry parallel the fruitiness.

- JACQUESSON PERFECTION   81
(33% PN, 35% PM, 32% CH)
One of the secrets of this Champagne's dramatic increase in quality at the beginning of the 1990s is that one quarter of it is vinified in oak barrels. Compare this with Bollinger, which previously made an oak-influenced, nonvintage Champagne (today only 12 percent is vinified in oak barrels). Another explanation is that the Chardonnay comes from the *grand cru*

village of Avize. The Champagne combines seriousness with charm in a wonderful way. The fruity nose is backed up by a creamy Chardonnay aroma. The taste is perfectly balanced with a nutty oak note in the finish. Sometimes too young and pear-scented. If you have patience, even the—initially—green bottles will achieve wonderful complexity. In other words, store the bottles for a few extra years to be on the safe side.

- JACQUESSON BLANC DE BLANCS   78
(100% CH)

- JACQUESSON PERFECTION ROSÉ   77
(31% PN, 36% PM, 33% CH)

- 1990 PERFECTION   80, FEB 1997 (84)
(40% PN, 20% PM, 40% CH)
In my opinion this wine is far too similar to the nonvintage Perfection. The Meunier grapes make their presence felt and the fruit is accessible and quite ordinary. A disappointment in a way.

- 1988 PERFECTION   80, OCT 1994 (84)
(40% PN, 20% PM, 40% CH)
This Champagne is among those species threatened with extinction. Vintage Perfection is no longer sold, but is now part of the house's nonvintage Champagne of the same name. The '88 has a great deal of the firm's typical spiciness in the nose, while the flavor is young, balanced, and fruity.

- 1987 PERFECTION   75, JUL 1995 (83)
(40% PN, 20% PM, 40% CH)
A wine the brothers regret they never sold. Surprisingly fresh and storable.

- 1986 PERFECTION   78, MAY 1994 (80)
(40% PN, 20% PM, 40% CH)
Much more developed and ingratiatingly vanilla-like than the more restrained '88. The flavor is uplifting with its tones of lemon and pineapple. This ready-to-drink wine is lighter and less concentrated than either the '85 or '88.

- 1985 PERFECTION   74, JUL 1992 (84)
(40% PN, 20% PM, 40% CH)
Impersonal and neutral, but with a promising structure.

- 1979 PERFECTION   92, OCT 1997 (93)
(35% PN, 36% PM, 29% CH)
Superb elegance and rich in glycerol. Clean and lingering on the palate.

- 1966 PERFECTION   89, OCT 1997 (89)
(32% PN, 36% PM, 32% CH)
Deep golden color, nose of leather, truffles, Sauternes, and roasted almonds. A bit tired, despite its youthful appearance. Several of us thought the aftertaste suggested figs.

- 1964 JACQUESSON PERFECTION   92, JAN 2002 (92)
(40% PN, 25% PM, 35% CH)
The Chiquet Brothers have never wanted to open a bottle of this wine from their cellar for me—not because the wonderful brothers are stingy, but because the bottles they have left display a dull and oxidized character, despite having lain undisgorged in Dizy. When I encountered a normally disgorged British bottle, my expectations were low. It's on these occasions one delights in being surprised. Of course the wine was mature—already one foot in the grave—but what a buttery richness and truffley bouquet! As usual, the house-style was distinct and full of personality.

- 1953 PERFECTION   94, APR 1996 (94)
(40% PN, 25% PM, 35% CH

Pale color and a shy, multifaceted, flowery nose. A super-elegant flavor, similar to that of the '69. Kiwi and melon work together with a layer of creamy butteriness.

- 1952 PERFECTION   92, APR 1996 (92)

(40% PN, 25% PM, 35% CH)

Quite light, fine mousse and wonderfully toasty nose of nut, coffee, and bread. Poorer taste but impressive young acidity.

- 1928 PERFECTION   95, OCT 1997 (95)

(40% PN, 25% PM, 35% CH)

The two bottles I had the honor to drink were unfortunately without mousse. The structure and the honeyed taste are majestic. This d'Yquem-copy is probably one of the greatest Champagnes ever made.

- 1995 JACQUESSON BLANC DE BLANCS   88, SEP 2003 (91)

(100% CH)

The masterful brothers in Aÿ are acquiring a drier taste, which displays itself here with all the clarity one would wish for. Bone dry, tart, but also amply fleshy with a slightly rustic, individual bushiness. Besides the oaky notes and usual appley aromas, oxidative nose with hints of malt and grain.

- 1995 JACQUESSON LES CORNE-BAUTRAY DIZY BLANC DE BLANCS

(100% CH)   87, OCT 2002 (92)

The Chiquet Brothers have made only 750 bottles from this exceptional plot that has vines planted in the great year of 1959. It is striking to see how well the house-style is retained with all the bottles that have passed through Jacquesson's cellar. As always, the house's special spicy, appley-fresh style is evident. The acidity is impressive, as are the mineral notes. The nose is beautiful and personal, with hints of dwarf banana, tobacco, smoked meat, and yellow roses. The taste is, as yet, somewhat short.

- 1993 JACQUESSON BLANC DE BLANCS   87, JUN 2003 (89)

(100% CH)

Initially a slightly exposed structure. Weak but fine, subtle aromas. This could be a wine that holds some pleasant surprises for the future. Classic *terroir* character. Suddenly more spicy, evolved, and house-typical than grape-typical!

- 1990 JACQUESSON BLANC DE BLANCS   93, APR 2004 (93)

(100% CH)

Their first vintage Blanc de Blancs was released in October 1994, replacing the much-praised nonvintage version with a lot of fuss and bother. I don't know if this remarkable vintage was the reason for the huge jump in quality, but it is clear that this is a much broader and richer Champagne. The mousse melts in the mouth like the finest caviar, the nose is rich in bread aromas and Granny Smith apples, the flavor is soft and harmonious with a long, buttery, burgundy-like aftertaste.

- 1985 JACQUESSON BLANC DE BLANCS   92, JUN 2002 (95)

(100% CH)

The Chiquet brothers made only 200 magnums of this wonderful wine. It's easy to be fooled by the wine's charming qualities now, but the '85 needs at least five more years in the bottle before it reaches its full maturity. Already we have a completely wonderful, buttery and classical Blanc de Blancs with Signature-like aromas and an astonishing length.

- 1996 JACQUESSON BLANC DE NOIRS D'AŸ   88, AUG 1999 (97)

(100% PN)

An exceptional wine, which shows absolutely plainly that the fanatically quality-conscious Chiquet Brothers are on the right track with their investment in mono-*cru* Champagnes. I see

distinct similarities with the heavenly Champagne Deutz made in Aÿ in 1975. In other words, the gamy flavors are toned down in favor of a mineral-sparkling chalky finesse. I blind-tasted the wine, but had no difficulty recognizing Jacquesson's personal chocolaty barrel tone. Those that claim that great Champagne must always contain Chardonnay should taste this absolutely brilliant wine.

- 1974/1973 DÉGORGEMENT TARDIF   85, JUL 1995 (85)

(100% CH)

1974/1973 An experimental wine containing 85 percent of 1974 grapes. The Champagne has the scent of a landscape on a summer's night, when the dew hits the vineyards and meadows. The nose resembles tea and wet hay but, with time, hints of Sauternes arrive. The flavor is light and appetizing.

- 1995 SIGNATURE   90, OCT 2003 (93)

(55% PN, 45% CH)

This time the Pinot Noir comes from Aÿ and Sillery, and the Chardonnay mainly from Avize mixed with 15 percent Chouilly. Young, focused, and delicious, with classic aromas. Big success at our wedding.

- 1993 SIGNATURE   90, MAY 2003 (93)

(60% PN, 40% CH)

Signature is a really suitable name for a *cuvée de prestige* that has one of the most distinct personalities around today: the style is unmistakable and unlike any other. Chocolate, oak, smoke, spices, ginger, cardamom, and green apples. Everything is there! The taste has a nascent creaminess, despite the dosage being so low. A very successful '93.

- 1990 SIGNATURE   95, OCT 2002 (96)

(54% PN, 46% CH)

A highly successful Champagne, where finesse and richness go hand in hand in excellent fashion. Hazelnut, white chocolate, honey, licorice, and a hint of oak are found in this refreshing and clearly youthful taste. Brilliant winemaking!

- 1990 SIGNATURE NON DOSÉ   90, JUN 1999 (94)

(54% PN, 46% CH)

The grapes come from Mailly, Dizy, Aÿ, and Avize. This is a wonderful wine that combines the power of the '89 with a good deal of the finesse of the '88. The nose is dominated by honey and licorice and the flavor is tremendously focused.

- 1989 SIGNATURE   93, MAY 2003 (93)

(50% PN, 50% CH)

An unmistakable Signature in which maturity has arrived more quickly than expected. The bouquet is broad and elegant with elements of coffee and red fruit. The flavor is puffed-up and soft as honey, with a pleasant burst of almond aromas.

- 1989 SIGNATURE NON DOSÉ   91, APR 1999 (92)

(50% PN, 50% CH)

The richest Signature I've tasted. I'm not fully convinced of its longevity, but it's a delightful *cuvée de prestige* with excellent roundness and a sweet finish.

- 1988 SIGNATURE   93, NOV 2003 (95)

(50% PN, 50% CH)

Jacquesson use their very best grapes in their Signature and let them ferment in large oak barrels that hold seventy-five hectoliters. At the pressing they do something unique. They aren't satisfied with just using the *cuvée* but take only the best part, the "*coeur de cuvée.*" All the Chardonnay comes from Avize, while the Pinot grapes come from Aÿ with a small amount from

Dizy. The '88 is just as much a classic as the '85. It combines the power of the Pinot grapes with the buttery, soft Avize Chardonnay in a fantastic manner. The awesomely long aftertaste is worth a chapter all to itself.

- 1988 SIGNATURE NON DOSÉ   93, MAR 2003 (95)
(50% PN, 50% CH)
Every time I taste the '88 I become more and more impressed. The wine has outstanding elegance and clear similarities with 1969 D. T. The nose is full of lilies, nut chocolate, and cream. The flavor is like a symphony by Mozart.

- 1985 DÉGORGEMENT TARDIF   87, APR 1999 (88)
(40% PN, 20% PM, 40% CH)
The same wine as Perfection. Unexpectedly young and undeveloped. Those who are used to '75 D. T. will certainly be displeased with this correct—but rather lacking in charm—wine.

- 1985 SIGNATURE   93, JUL 2002 (93)
(50% PN, 50% CH)
A gorgeous Champagne! It flashes and sparks in golden hues, and the nose has a complete spectrum of tones. Sometimes it's dominated by the fruity and exotic elements; sometimes the deeper aromas of Brazil nuts, smoke, licorice, and wood take over. The acidity is very high and will keep this Champagne alive for at least another thirty years, although it has probably already reached its peak. Unfortunately some bottle variation.

- 1985 SIGNATURE NON DOSÉ   84, OCT 2002 (84)
(50% PN, 50% CH)
Refreshing and lively but with oxidative sherry notes and a certain bitterness. Licorice, cheese, and hay reminiscent of '85 D. T. I definitely prefer the normally disgorged variety of this Signature.

- 1983 SIGNATURE   92, MAR 1998 (92)
(50% PN, 50% CH)
The same craftsmanlike personality as the '88 and '85. The nose has a more developed biscuitiness with elements of orchid. The oak is more noticeable than in other vintages, and the acidity is still very lively.

- 1982 SIGNATURE   80, FEB 1998 (>)
(50% PN, 50% CH)
When I first tasted the '82 in 1990 I was very impressed. However, it hasn't developed as expected, but has instead taken on some odd berry aromas and tones of gingerbread and sherry.

- 1981 SIGNATURE   90, JUL 1995 (90)
(50% PN, 50% CH)
Despite the oak aromas it's a more delicate wine than the other Signature vintages. The nose is pleasantly romantic, with hawthorn and honeysuckle. The flavor is as fresh as a mountain stream, with plenty of mineral tones.

- 1978 DÉGORGEMENT TARDIF   91, FEB 1998 (91)
(100% CH)
This wine has never been available on the market, which is a shame. It has a wonderful autolytic character that is in perfect harmony with the fruity flavor.

- 1976 DÉGORGEMENT TARDIF   93, FEB 1998 (93)
(100% CH)
Similar to the '75 with a slightly fatter character and greater richness. Fully mature but plenty of life left in it yet.

- 1975 DÉGORGEMENT TARDIF   93, FEB 2003 (93)
In 1997 Jacquesson was still selling this Champagne, which is disgorged on demand. As with all recently disgorged

Champagnes, there is a great deal of bottle variation. I've drunk the '75 on around forty occasions, and on five of them it was too old and sherry-like, while just as often it's been too young and closed in the nose. Usually it's tasted best around fifteen months after being disgorged, when the wine has recovered from the shock of being re-corked so late in life. The mousse should always be ultra-fine. At its best the nose is superbly toasty and buttery, with a great autolytic character that is often confused with oak character. The flavor can contain such diverse notes as truffles, goat cheese, Port, butter, and dried fruit. The aftertaste is extremely long. A very controversial wine with a style you either love or hate.

- 1973 DÉGORGEMENT TARDIF   93, JUN 2002 (94)
(100% CH)
This wine gives a much younger impression than the blended '73 or '75. The color is a light green/yellow, the mousse is almost aggressive, and the nose is like a firework display of flower aromas. When aired in the glass the sun-ripened dwarf bananas come out, together with fresh-cut hay. The flavor is surprisingly light. Very elegant and youthful.

- 1973 DÉGORGEMENT TARDIF   93, APR 1995 (93)
(50% PN, 50% CH)
A lot like the '75, despite its high Pinot content. A nose of banana, honey, and lemon, while the flavor has even more tones of newly melted butter than the '75, if that's possible. Sometimes there's a faint sherry tone in the very long aftertaste.

- 1970 DÉGORGEMENT TARDIF
(50% PN, 50% CH)

- 1969 DÉGORGEMENT TARDIF   98, JUN 2001 (98)
(100% CH)
Initially, Jacquesson was very disappointed with this vintage and decided to use it as "*liqueur d'expédition*" for the nonvintage Champagne. Many years later they discovered that it had changed dramatically. Unfortunately, only a few bottles were left. Today, both the brothers rank the '69 as the best Champagne Jacquesson has made since the war. I've had the honor of tasting this rarity five times newly disgorged. The color is light greenish-yellow and the nose is indescribably elegant. Yellow roses, Lilies of the Valley, and lime reoccur in the nose and palate together with a faintly toasted element. The oily aftertaste is among the longest I've ever experienced. A superb Blanc de Blancs possessing unique finesse!

- 1961 DÉGORGEMENT TARDIF   94, FEB 1998 (94)
(40% PN, 25% PM, 35% CH)
Majestic and impressive wine of great weight. Plenty of truffle aromas and vigor. A Champagne for a classic meal!

- 1995 SIGNATURE ROSÉ   93, DEC 2003 (95)
(59% PN, 41% CH)
So far the finest and most subtle vintage of this delightful Champagne! Exactly the same beautiful aromatic profile as before, but with an extra-refined, floral, mineral finesse. Brilliantly "white" in character, but with a superb creaminess despite the wine being very dry. Crispy freshness and clarity with spicy, gamy, barrel notes swirling together with the red-berry aromas in an exquisite dance.

- 1993 SIGNATURE ROSÉ   92, NOV 2002 (94)
(63% PN, 37% CH)
Pinot from Aÿ and Mailly as well Chardonnay from Avize. Slightly more than 1,000 bottles of this superbly elegant prestige *cuvée* were produced this year. Totally, irresistibly seductive with

its light, pleasant color and creamy summer bouquet. As I acquaint myself with this delicate, direct hit, I find myself in an arbor surrounded by fresh raspberries, strawberries, and whipping cream, mixed with the scent of flowers and bountiful nature.

- 1990 SIGNATURE ROSÉ   92, JUN 2001 (95)
  (54% PN, 46% CH)
  When I tasted this wine for the first time the brothers hadn't decided what dosage they were going to use. I can guarantee that, whatever they decide, this will be a "hit." A wonderful rosé nose and a deep, oak-influenced, focused flavor.
- 1989 SIGNATURE ROSÉ   92, APR 2003 (93)
  (54% PN, 46% CH)
  Jacquesson's latest newcomer on the market is a total success! It goes straight into the "top ten" of my best rosé Champagnes. Almost all top rosés have a considerable element of velvety soft Aÿ Pinot, but exceedingly few are also vinified in *oak* barrels. The result is an extraordinary hedonistic experience. This rosé is more full and has a lower acidity than the white Signature. The nose is reminiscent of Cristal Rosé—hazelnuts and candy drowned in strawberry liqueur. The palate is covered with a layer of soft red fruit. The aftertaste is phenomenal!
- JACQUESSON MEMOIRES DU 20ÈME SIÈCLE   88, OCT 2003 (92)
  (33% PN, 33% PM, 34% CH)
  A totally fantastic idea, whereby twenty-two older vintages, going back to 1915, contribute to the reserve wine, which in turn lends a fine, chocolaty tone of maturity. The main element, however, is the regular nonvintage Champagne with its notes of apple and spice. Undoubtedly very storable. Most remarkable is the pronounced house-style and how ridiculously cheap the wine is in comparison to the counterpart produced by Moët, *Ésprit du Siècle*, which costs $17,000 per bottle.

JACQUINOT N-M

36, rue Maurice Cerveaux
51200 Épernay
03 26 54 36 81
Production: 150,000
This house was founded by Monsieur Jacquinot in 1947; Jacques Jacquinot owns it today. The house owns sixteen hectares of land.

- 1985 JACQUINOT   77, MAY 2001 (77)
  (50% PN, 50% CH)
- 1978 JACQUINOT   85, OCT 2003 (85)
  (50% PN, 50% CH)
  An exceedingly lively, vital golden oldie that's at the apex of its life without making a fuss about it. The wine will simply not get any better than this, despite perfect timing and storage. Lively, floral bouquet with mature notes of chocolate and dried fruit. Refreshing and delicious, but much too short and one-dimensional.
- 1976 JACQUINOT   90, FEB 2003 (90)
  (50% PN, 50% CH)
  An almost unctuous, almond-packed essence that screams for foie gras! Very luxuriant, delicious, and impressive. A vintage and a wine that leaves no one untouched. I was lucky to open my bottle in the company of a few Americans who really appreciated its fat, sweet, and powerful style.
- 1975 JACQUINOT   70, MAR 2003 (70)
  (50% PN, 50% CH)
- 1964 JACQUINOT   88, FEB 2003 (88)
  (50% PN, 50% CH)

A typical toffee, chocolate-scented '64; medium-bodied with a round, fine taste. Voluptuous and homogeneous, but lacking greater depth. The aftertaste is relatively short.

JANOT-MARCHWICKI R-C

4, rue du Bac
51220 Pouillon
03 26 03 10 62
Production: 6,000
The grower, who started business in 1992, has a beautifully situated property ten kilometers from Reims in Massif St. Thierry. The wines are made by the local cooperative and the grower has more than 3.5 hectares at his disposal. Some of the wines are stored in oak barrels.

- JANOT-MARCHWICKI BRUT   45
  (25% PN, 45% PM, 30% CH)

JARDIN, RENÉ *** R-M

B. P. 8
51190 Le Mesnil-sur-Oger
03 26 57 50 26
Production: 130,000
Louis Jardin founded the company in 1889; today the pure Mesnil Champagnes are made by Madame Jardin. The wines are an exceedingly nice combination of vigor, personality, and steely acidity.

- JARDIN PRESTIGE   76
  (100% CH)
- JARDIN BLANC DE BLANCS   70
  (100% CH)
- 1996 JARDIN   91, JAN 2004 (94)
  (100% CH)
  So wonderfully balanced and paradoxically light, deep, concentrated, evolved, and youthful—all at the same time. The oldest vines the grower has at his disposal have created here a sublime wine with clear similarities to Clos du Mesnil *sans* barrel. An underlying nuttiness is the main theme, together with the oily fruit and elastically elegant layers of sensation that the palate is subjected to. Magnificent!
- 1990 JARDIN   79, FEB 1997 (86)
  (100% CH)
  A clear tone of saffron has crept into many of Le Mesnil's '90s, a trend that is illustrated nowhere better than in this Champagne. The flavor is rich and a touch rustic.
- 1988 JARDIN   76, AUG 1995 (84)
  (100% CH)
  Once again burned, smoked, and aromatic, carrying tones of bacon. Very long.
- 1985 JARDIN   83, JUL 1995 (87)
  (100% CH)
  Beautiful developed color. A nose of meat stew that is also found in Pierre Moncuit's wines. The flavor is much better. Rich, buttery, and long.
- 1996 JARDIN MILLÉSIME RARE   88, SEP 2003 (91)
  (100% CH)
  A delightfully elegant, concentrated wine that has a polished appearance reminiscent of Billecart-Salmon Blanc de Blancs. Mellow and elegant, with a beautifully creamy scent devoid of spice and rawness. Orange blossom and juicy grapes with a pleasant oiliness.

JARRY, ANDRÉ R-M

25, Grande Rue
51260 Bethon
03 26 80 48 04
Production: 50,000

Jarry owns twelve hectares of Chardonnay vineyards in Sézanne and makes a widely-praised *cuvée de prestige* from forty-year-old vines that I have yet to taste.

- ANDRÉ JARRY BRUT   66
  (100% CH)

JEANMAIRE N-M

12, rue Godard-Roger
51200 Épernay
03 26 59 50 10
Production: 1,500,000

Today Jeanmaire is owned by Trouillard and shares facilities with Oudinot. The house was founded in 1933 by André Jeanmaire. The Trouillard concern began to concentrate on Jeanmaire and Beaumet in 1982; both have become popular, low-price Champagnes in Sweden. Jeanmaire buy in more than half of their grapes and use some thirty-seven *crus* from 296 hectares in their *cuvées*. Chouilly, Cramant, Les Riceys, and Oiry are the villages where the firm owns its largest vineyards. The winemaker Denis Colombier also makes Oudinot and Beaumet.

- JEANMAIRE BRUT   63
  (40% PN, 30% PM, 30% CH)
- JEANMAIRE BRUT PREMIER CRU   71
  (90% PN, 10% CH)
- JEANMAIRE TERROIRS D'OR   67
  (100% CH)
- JEANMAIRE BLANC DE BLANCS   64
  (100% CH)
- JEANMAIRE DEMI-SEC
  (40% PN, 30% PM, 30% CH)
- JEANMAIRE BLANC DE NOIRS   79
  (100% PN)
- 1995 JEANMAIRE MILLENNIUM BLANC DE BLANCS
  (100% CH)   77, MAR 1999 (84)
  Young elderberry-fresh Champagne with notes of hawthorn and green apples. Harmonic and youthful aftertaste with a glorious acidity.
- JEANMAIRE ROSÉ   45
  (70% PN, 30% PM)
- 1996 JEANMAIRE   84, DEC 2002 (88)
  (60% PN, 40% CH)
  "Awesome nose," as my children say. White Bordeaux is actually what first comes to mind having plunged my nose in the glass. Impressively big and nutty. I don't recognize the house-style at all; this one has real, barrel-like vinous notes. Complex and impressive.
- 1995 JEANMAIRE   75, FEB 2004 (75)
  (60% PN, 40% CH)
- 1989 JEANMAIRE   77, OCT 1999 (79)
  (60% PN, 40% CH)
- 1988 JEANMAIRE   68, MAY 1995 (77)
  (60% PN, 40% CH)
- 1979 JEANMAIRE   90, FEB 2003 (90)
  (60% PN, 40% CH)

This must be among the most enjoyable creations to come out of Jeanmaire's cellar. Superbly delicious and well balanced, with classic nutty notes, biscuity nose, and caressingly seductive aged sweetness. Hardly monumental, but still totally wonderful as a drinking experience.

- 1981 JEANMAIRE ROSÉ   90, JUN 2000 (90)
  (100% PN)
  This was tasted on a fantastic summer evening at the home of Jan and Ulla Naliwajko. A sensationally good, romantic wine. The color is very pale, and pressure from the mousse very strong. Much about this elegant and enjoyably tasty wine is actually quite reminiscent of Cristal Rosé. The bouquet has cheesy overtones paired with overripe strawberries. The palate has a lightness and pedigree that few wines from this house possess.
- 1995 ELYSÉE   74, MAY 2000 (77)
  (100% CH)
- 1990 ELYSÉE   83, JUN 2002 (83)
  (100% CH)
  Fresh nose of lemon peel, young on the palate, with aromas of crispbread and mineral. Ages fast.
- 1989 ELYSÉE   90, JUN 2003 (90)
  (100% CH)
  What impressive richness! Incredibly powerful and viscous, like treacle or toffee. Tons of sweet aromas and a great depth. Once past puberty, the wine will be reminiscent of some of the great Chardonnay wines from 1976. Coconut, honey, and dark chocolate-toffee are already discernible. This house's foremost Champagne ever?
- 1985 ELYSÉE   84, MAY 2001 (85)
  (100% CH)
  Exceedingly ingratiating Chardonnay overtones are found in this prestige bubbly. A creamy nose with vanilla and butterscotch. The same enveloping soft style meets the taste buds and leads to a slender finish.
- 1976 ELYSÉE   90, MAY 2001 (90)
  (100% CH)
  The grapes come from Avize, Chouilly, and Cramant. Sensationally good and well kept. Deeply shimmering green, indecent nose of goat cheese, truffles, forest, and port wine. The Champagne is oily and concentrated, with a typical autolytic Chardonnay aroma not unlike Jacquesson D. T.
- 1982 ELYSÉE ROSÉ   75, JUL 1998 (80)
  (100% PN)
  A *grand cru* rosé aged in the company's darkest cellar for at least seven years. Despite that I was not impressed by this Champagne. Very light color and delicate, small bubbles. The taste is dominated by mineral tones. Medium length.
- JEANMAIRE CUVÉE MILLENIUM   78, JUN 2002 (82)
  (20% PN, 80% CH)
  Fresh and exotic scent with notes of pineapple and banana. The taste is also exotic and has a healthy balance. Clearly a very young Millennium wine.

JEEPER N-M

8, rue Georges Clemenceau
51480 Damery
03 26 58 41 23
Production: 400,000

M. Goutorbe, who is of course related to the Aÿ brothers, runs this house. His father, who was handicapped, always used to drive around in a Jeep, which explains the somewhat unlikely company name. Dom Grossard is the name of the monk who took over from Dom Pérignon in Hautvillers.

- JEEPER DUCALE   50
  (20% PN, 40% PM, 40% CH)
- JEEPER GRANDE RÉSERVE   62
  (100% CH)
- JEEPER ROSÉ   39
  (90% PN, 10% CH)
- 1991 JEEPER   66, MAY 1996 (70)
  (100% CH)
- 1989 DOM GROSSARD   74, MAY 1996 (80)
  (40% PN, 60% CH)

Grapes from the vicinity of Damery. The wine resembles Piper Brut Sauvage, with the nose dominated by crispbread, dark chocolate, and licorice. The flavor has a nice element of cocoa.

JOSSELIN, JEAN R-M

4, rue de Vannes
10250 Gyé-sur-Seine
03 25 38 21 48
Production: 80,000

An Aube producer who, in my opinion, seems to have a hard time summoning any elegance whatsoever out of this area's rich earth. The grower has more than ten hectares in Gyé-sur-Seine and the surrounding area. The vines are young and the wines are treated in a modern fashion. Their portfolio is big, with all of six different *cuvées.*

- JEAN JOSSELIN BLANC DE BLANCS   45
  (100% CH)
- JEAN JOSSELIN BLANC DE NOIRS   50
  (100% PN)

JUGET-BRUNET R-M

5, rue Roulot
51160 Aÿ
03 26 55 20 67
Production: 30,000

The firm run today by Michel Baudette was founded in 1927 by Lucien Juget. It encompasses 4.3 hectares, planted with Pinot Noir and Chardonnay in roughly equal portions.

- JUGET-BRUNET TRADITION   71
  (80% PN, 20% CH)
- JUGET-BRUNET ROSÉ   71
  (50% PN, 50% CH)
- 1996 JUGET-BRUNET   82, JAN 2002 (87)
  (50% PN, 50% CH)

What a wonderful year 1996 has proven to be! Here is yet one more example of this vintage's grandeur, where rich fruit is combined with enormous acidity. Store really long and it could become really good.

JUILLET-LALLEMENT R-M

30, rue Carnot
51380 Verzy
03 26 97 91 09
Production: 35,000

The firm was founded by Arthur Lallement in 1930 and is run today by Pierre Lallement. The grower owns four hectares in Verzy.

- 1990 JUILLET-LALLEMENT SPECIAL CLUB   86, JAN 2002 (88)
  (40% PN, 60% CH)
  Fat and creamy with elastic acidity, good body, and exotic aromas, with an undertone of game. A delicious wine from a small, unknown grower.
- 1989 JUILLET-LALLEMENT SPECIAL CLUB   85, MAR 1999 (87)
  (40% PN, 60% CH)

KRUG ***** N-M

5, rue Coquebert
51100 Reims
03 26 84 44 20
Production: 500,000

For me, Krug is more than a Champagne. It is a word that stands for artistry, tradition, craftsmanship, and moments of pure pleasure. The Krug family has used the same methods since the house was founded in 1843 by Johann-Joseph Krug from Mainz. It is hardly likely that the Krug philosophy will be abandoned in the foreseeable future, since it has brought so much success. Put simply, that philosophy means that all the wines are fermented *cru* by *cru* in well-aged 205-liter barrels from the Argonne and central-east France. The wines are seldom filtered: they undergo just two rackings, by gravity, from cask to cask. Nor do they induce a malolactic fermentation, which is one of the reasons for Krug's fantastic aging potential. None of the wines is disgorged before it is six years old, and the reserve wines are stored in stainless-steel tanks from the Swedish company Alfa Laval. The firm's least costly wine, Grande Cuvée, is made from fifty or so wines from ten different vintages. Naturally the raw materials are also of the very highest class. Twenty hectares in Aÿ, Le Mesnil, and Trépail are owned by the house, but above all it is the network of prestigious contracts with some of the region's best growers that answers for the quality, as the growers consider it an honor to supply Krug with grapes.

Johann-Joseph Krug, the founder, learned his Champagne craft at Jacquesson and, when he regarded himself as qualified after nine years there, he set off to Reims to start his own house. After Joseph's death his son Paul took over and built the powerful Krug dynasty, followed as he was by Joseph Krug II in 1910 and Joseph's nephew, Jean Seydoux, in 1924. It was he, together with Paul Krug II, who created the famous *cuvées,* and it was only in 1962 that the legendary Henri Krug took over. Today the wines are made by Eric Lebel and Henri Krug. Henri Krug leads the company, together with his more business-minded brother Rémi. They work undisturbed and independently, despite the fact that the firm is owned by LVMH. All Krug's wines are small masterworks, and although Grande Cuvée may be lighter and fresher than its predecessor, Private Cuvée, after a few extra years in the cellar it outshines the competitors' vintage Champagnes. Clos du Mesnil is a newcomer that combines the best Blanc de Blancs while simultaneously distinguishing the wine with the house's own distinct style. For me, Krug Clos du Mesnil is the best wine in the world! Vintage Krug competes with today's Clos du Mesnil, but if we go backward in time, it is without doubt the best Champagne. If the opportunity arises, never miss the chance to drink a Krug!

- KRUG GRANDE CUVÉE   95
(50% PN, 15% PM, 35% CH)

Krug's nonvintage wine costs about $150. They themselves would rather call it a "multi-vintage." Strangely enough, this exceptional wine is one of the Champagnes I've drunk on the greatest number of occasions—more than ninety times, in fact. Almost every time, some new element is revealed. Because it's been blended from ten different vintages and forty-seven different wines from twenty-five *crus*, variation is understandable. However, I have only missed spotting it on one occasion at a blind tasting, proving that its basic character is unique. The extremely tough acidity, together with the heavy, rich Krug aromas, are the foremost clues. Always check how straight the cork is in order to decipher when it was disgorged. When young, the acidity can be too hard. When middle aged and older, the Grand Cuvée has a fabulously complex nose and palate, dominated by nuts and honey. The aftertaste is always long and majestic, like a great symphony. The best bottles deserve even higher points than I've given here.

- KRUG PRIVATE CUVÉE   96
(55% PN, 20% PM, 25% CH)

I drank a magnum from the 1950s in September 1995, and was astonished at how youthful and fresh the Champagne was. The nose is restrained, but the taste is very deep and has a classic Pinot character. Always majestic.

- KRUG ROSÉ   95
(55% PN, 20% PM, 25% CH)

Krug Rosé is a relatively new product from the Krug brothers. Their aim was to make a wine with a proper house-style, where the color was the only clue that it was a rosé. The color is an extremely light salmon-pink, and the nose is definitely Krug! Their unmistakable symphony of full, complex aromas is backed up by a whiff of raspberry. The taste is tremendously austere and acidic, but less generous than a Grande Cuvée and definitely a wine to store.

- 1990 KRUG   95, JUN 2004 (98)
(40% PN, 23% PM, 37% CH)

I don't know how many years I've waited to try this much-talked-about wine. Now, at the age of fourteen years, Krug finally feels the 1990 is ready to meet the public. You don't have to be an Einstein to figure out that the vintage and the house's character would marry in perfect fashion. The wine is already monumental, with a style that lies somewhere between the acidly classic '88 and the generous, honey-tasting '89. To be honest, the acidity is high, but the fruit is so rich that the acidity is beautifully enveloped. Warmly toasted, almost burned, smoky aromas are present, together with notes of orchids, vanilla, and dried fruit—making one think of an older Krug of warmer years. Wait at least another ten years if you want to see this wine at its pinnacle!

- 1989 KRUG   96, MAY 2003 (97)
(47% PN, 24% PM, 29% CH)

A most voluptuous, honey-saturated Krug. Already richly evolved. Butterscotchy, with a long aftertaste. Less classical than the '88, but just as good for the moment.

- 1988 KRUG   97, DEC 2003 (98)
(50% PN, 18% PM, 32% CH)

It's that time again! How do they do it? Together with Rémi Krug I first tasted this '88 beside the unbelievably good '89 and could hardly believe my taste buds when they sent the message that the '88 was even better. At Krug they themselves compare the wine with the '81, the '55, and the '61. Personally, I compare it to the '66 and the ultra elegant '79. The finesse is unbeatable and the acidity very noticeable. This is a wine that is going to be enjoyed by our grandchildren. Most people probably discourage immediate consumption of this young wine, but I am of a different opinion. I believe that a little bit of the subtle feeling of "tears of joy" disappears when the wine matures. I hope this explains the unusually stingy point differential between today's points and the potential maximum rating.

- 1985 KRUG   92, JAN 2002 (95)
(48% PN, 22% PM, 30% CH)

Vintage Krug is the yardstick against which all vintage Champagnes are measured. They began selling the '85 in 1994. These majestic wines always require long bottle storage, but the '85 was surprisingly accessible from the start, with its wonderful, elusive nose of smoke, cream, honey, nuts, peaches, and vanilla. The oak character doesn't stand out; rather, it is the elegant, velvety soft fruit—particularly Pinot Meunier from Leuvrigny—that is noticeable. Very long aftertaste of vanilla. During the last year of the 1990s the wine hit a clear rut that it still hasn't recovered from. I'm not going to drink my bottles until 2010.

- 1982 KRUG   96, MAY 2003 (98)
(54% PN, 16% PM, 30% CH)

Krug '82 will soon join the ranks of the legendary wines. It has all the bricks needed to build a mighty castle. The fruit is enormous, the acidity, the concentration, the house's barrel tones: all are present and correct. The '82, along with the '89, is the most full-bodied wine to come from the property since 1976, but has a far greater elegance than that vintage. The nose's spectrum embraces nuts, coffee, butter, sun-dried sheets, toffee-wrappers, orchids, vanilla, balsam poplars, and oranges. Most of these aromas are found once again in the explosive taste.

- 1981 KRUG   95, FEB 2004 (96)
(31% PN, 19% PM, 50% CH)

This wine probably lacks the qualities needed to become legendary and achieve longevity, but at the age of eleven it was a sensual wine experience. A 1985 Le Montrachet from Drouhin felt clumsy compared to this elegant bottle of Krug. The fruit is rich, elusive, and exciting, and the bouquet is multifaceted, with elements of apple pastry and custard, coffee, honey, and white chocolate.

- 1979 KRUG   97, JAN 2002 (97)
(36% PN, 28% PM, 36% CH)

Although this wine will probably live long, it will never be better than it was in 1990. Then there was a life and a glass development that was an unmatchable pleasure. First a closed but top-class nose, which opened up after ten minutes into a Montrachet-like depth of the loveliest of wine aromas. It has a classically well-balanced structure, with a long, nutty aftertaste that is close to perfection. Later bottles have shown an even greater richness of taste, but some of the elegance has been lost.

- 1976 KRUG   95, JUN 2003 (95)
(42% PN, 26% PM, 32% CH)

Loads of Krug aromas and voluptuousness, gigantic body, and warm fruit. Even so, this is the vintage that has constantly failed to impress me. The vanilla aroma is a little exaggerated, and the elegance is greater in Cristal and Salon—to take two examples—this year.

- 1975 KRUG   94, MAY 1998 (95)
(50% PN, 20% PM, 30% CH)
This marvelous Champagne is truly classic and will last a very long time. Deep nutty flavor and great length.

- 1973 KRUG   95, MAR 2003 (95)
(51% PN, 16% PM, 33% CH)
A wonderfully accessible Champagne that fills the room with its euphoric bouquet of honey, peach, and apricot. The taste is concentrated and developed, with an expansive fruit and silky-smooth structure. The '73 is made in the same style as the '79 and '66. A classic Krug!

- 1971 KRUG   96, MAR 2003 (96)
(47% PN, 14% PM, 39% CH)
This is what Krug is all about! Mature and exotic; the nose of the '71 is unbeatable. The taste lacks the right concentration and length to take the score up to 100 points, but the nose is perfect, as is the aromatic breadth in the taste. The innumerable aromas are honeysuckle, honey, cakes, strawberry jam, boiled vegetables, popcorn—the list is as long as you care to make it. Unusually, the taste hints more at Chardonnay than Pinot Noir.

- 1969 KRUG   96, DEC 2002 (96)
(50% PN, 13% PM, 37% CH)
Youthful and tart, with the same feeling and spectrum of aromas as Collection. A rather lean Krug perhaps, but still incredibly beautiful and purebred.

- 1966 KRUG   98, JAN 2003 (98)
(48% PN, 21% PM, 31% CH)
One of the most elegant vintages from Krug that I'm aware of. Lots of unmistakable Krug aromas in the bouquet, with a richer fruit and floweriness than usual. The taste is like a gentle brush of deep, mature, exotic fruits. Very fresh acidity; unbeatable long, elegant taste, with all the most enjoyable tones that can be found in a Champagne. The '66 is a lot like the '79.

- 1964 KRUG   95, AUG 2003 (95)
(53% PN, 20% PM, 27% CH)
Yet another legendary vintage that many select as the best ever to come from the property. However, despite its greatness, I contend that this is no more than a normal Krug. At the age of thirty it's still very youthful and acidic. The oak tones have a delightful nerve and are supported by the aroma of a bakery in the morning. The mid-palate is more impressive than the aftertaste, which is dominated by ripe apple and vanilla.

- 1962 KRUG   95, APR 2000 (95)
(36% PN, 28% PM, 36% CH)
An even richer wine than the '64 and '66, although lacking their elegance. The '62 probably reached its peak in the early 1980s. The nose is so strong that you feel it in the room when the wine is poured. It holds the scents of the traveling carnival: popcorn, cotton candy, and vanilla ice cream. In the mouth the Champagne expresses an oily weight and an incredible explosion of riches. Lots of Krug tastes, but slightly bottom-heavy compared with other vintages.

- 1961 KRUG   98, JUN 2000 (98)
(53% PN, 12% PM, 35% CH)

One of history's most heroic Champagnes! While those of us in our forties see our waistlines expanding, this '61 has just finished building up its body. Even though I prefer the aromatic merits of the '38, the '61 is the grandest monument to the craft. The color is still light, with touches of bronze and copper. The nose has one side with all the oaky, toasted aromas from the barrel, and another with fascinating tones from the sea and the forest. The superb taste is also on the dark, masculine side, with truffles, duck liver, mushroom, earth cellar, wood, and fish. The fruit is by no means ingratiating, but the depth and breath of the wine are amazing. The aftertaste is actually one of the longest I've ever experienced!

- 1959 KRUG   97, MAY 1998 (97)
(50% PN, 15% PM, 35% CH)
Krug have deliberately made a more acidic and drier wine than usual, as the character of this vintage is so heavy and rich in itself. This is undeniably one of the giants of the history of wine. A gigantic nose of freshly baked bread, apple pie, and vanilla. The taste has elements of that wonderful mint -chocolate tone that vintage Krug gains with age. Extremely fat, oily, majestic, Burgundy-like structure. Fantastic!

- 1955 KRUG   95, JUN 1997 (97)
(50% PN, 20% PM, 30% CH)
A legend that still has a way to go before peaking! The acidity is amazing and the mousse almost aggressive. I'm still waiting for the mint-chocolate tone that will pop up in ten years or so, but otherwise the wine is quite complete.

- 1953 KRUG   96, SEP 1995 (96)
(35% PN, 30% PM, 35% CH)
One wonders how Pinot Meunier can survive for so long. Incredibly fresh and acidic on the palate, with a colossal, meaty richness. Superb!

- 1952 KRUG
(43% PN, 19% PM, 38% CH)

- 1949 KRUG   96, OCT 1998 (96)
(47% PN, 18% PM, 35% CH)
The nose is somewhat weak, if not exceedingly refined. On the other hand, the nectar-like, relatively mild, playful taste is a masterpiece. Fresh and succulent peach-and-honey taste with remarkable length.

- 1947 KRUG   94, SEP 1994 (94)
(43% PN, 15% PM, 42% CH)
A legendary wine that was in fact not as good as expected. The wine was in perfect condition, with a light color and highly active mousse, and the nose was closed but opened in the glass, which is highly impressive for a forty-seven-year-old wine. A typical Krug nose of nutty complexity with aging tones of tar and wood. An extreme attack and length; a dry, austere taste, slightly lacking in fruit, but with lovely tones of cocoa and wood.

- 1945 KRUG   90, OCT 1997 (90)
(42% PN, 16% PM, 42% CH)
This legendary wine was a huge disappointment for me. Good structure and nice acidity. Refreshing but charmless and pointless.

- 1943 KRUG   95, JUN 1999 (95)
(56% PN, 12% PM, 32% CH)
Unexpectedly weak but collected scent. Majestically deep and seriously eternal taste. Meaty and well preserved.

- 1938 KRUG   99, MAR 1994 (99)
(57% PN, 16% PM, 27% CH)

A year that is almost completely forgotten, but which produced the most delicious Champagne I have ever drunk. It was a shock of the positive kind when the cork flew off at great speed, and I saw the bubbling drink with its clear, middle-aged color. The nose cannot be described with words, but it was very like the 1945 Mouton Rothschild, with its tremendously rich tone of mint chocolate. There were also layers of fruit and minerals, and the wine was chewy and huge, with a divinely minty, bready, and nectar-like basic taste. The finish was majestic, with a clear tone of truffles and aged wood, alongside the mint chocolate. Is the '28 even better?

- 1937 KRUG   94, JAN 1999 (94)
(49% PN, 19% PM, 32% CH)
A deep golden color, active mousse, and a thought-provoking bouquet. Unified taste of peach and chocolate.

- 1928 KRUG
(70% PN, 8% PM, 22% CH)

- 1926 KRUG   95, NOV 1994 (95)
(55% PN, 20% PM, 25% CH)
Orange-brown, with only a thin line of bubbles. A developed mint-chocolate aroma in less sophisticated style than the '38, but with a greater dessert character. Chocolate, rum, and honey in the nose. The taste is a revelation of sweet Yquem-like style, with layers of toffee, caramel, and dried fruit. Probably even better twenty to thirty years ago.

- 1920 KRUG

- 1990 KRUG CLOS DU MESNIL   96, NOV 2003 (98)
(100% CH)
I have harbored enormous expectations for this wine. The foremost vintage in recent years combined with—in my opinion—the world's foremost vineyard. I was initially disappointed when the wine exhibited a relatively coarse side, with oxidative notes of maturity akin to the Salon of the same vintage. After a while, clear and unexpected aromas of papaya and melon arose. This wave was followed by a spicy breeze, laden with juniper elements. The oxide note disappeared and the taste suddenly felt keenly acidity and slightly one-dimensional. After fifteen minutes in the glass the wine finally found itself. Suddenly, it became incredibly subtle and multifaceted, just as it headed into its last and—in my opinion—best phase: the "Selosse Phase!" Never before have I found a wine with a scent reminiscent of the 1986 Selosse that I had six years ago. The last sips were like rekindling an old love in a new body. The fascinating wine journey on which this Champagne will take you will be shortened the longer you wait before opening a bottle. On the other hand, those who are patient will drink a significantly better wine. One year after launching, the wine is much more stable and now totally in its "Selosse Phase."

- 1989 KRUG CLOS DU MESNIL   97, MAR 2003 (98)
(100% CH)
Is there a better wine in this world than Clos de Mesnil? I doubt it. The '89 is one of the richest and most delicious vintages ever. At the same time, the vineyard's elegant expression shines through clearly.

- 1988 KRUG CLOS DU MESNIL   97, NOV 2003 (99)
(100% CH)
A miracle of finesse; mountain-stream-pure art when at its most subtle. Despite being only two points shy of absolute ripeness, I warn you that the wine is still very young and illusive. That I am

delighted to the point of hearing angels sing is due to the delicate, subtle, spring-like beauty. Are birches more beautiful in bud or when they have just burst into leaf?

- 1986 KRUG CLOS DU MESNIL   94, MAR 2003 (96)
(100% CH)
Extremely youthful with tooth-meltingly-high apple acidity. In spite of an arrow-straight cork, one had to wait an hour before the Champagne whispered hints regarding who had made it and where the grapes had come from. A discreet Clos du Mesnil that seems to be the least spectacular vintage to date. Even so, I would not be surprised if it shines as brightly as its siblings a decade from now.

- 1985 KRUG CLOS DU MESNIL   96, JAN 2003 (99)
(100% CH)
The height of elegance! The '85 reminds me of the '79, but I wonder if this wine doesn't reach even greater peaks. What balance and indescribable finesse! Sadly it's rare these days that I become so awestruck by a wine that I go through an almost religious experience. This wonderful, lime-fruity Champagne with its polished butteriness and sparkling clarity succeeded in inducing that feeling three days in a row during a tour with Henri Krug in November, 1995.

- 1983 KRUG CLOS DU MESNIL   93, MAR 1996 (96)
(100% CH)
The 1.87-hectare Clos du Mesnil vineyard, in the heart of the village, is a location that sums up all that Le Mesnil's Champagne stands for. In Krug's hands this is the essence of Chardonnay. The '83 has a little way to go before it is fully mature: the color has a clear green gleam, the nose is young, finely balanced, and flowery, with lily of the valley, freesia, and white lilies clearly discernible. There is also a complex, creamy side filled with toasty aromas, young fruit, and damp wool. The taste is long and dry, with massive elegance and feminine frivolity.

- 1982 KRUG CLOS DU MESNIL   99, DEC 2003 (99)
(100% CH)
The wine of the vintage. More Krug-like than Mesnil-like. The color is reminiscent of a big, white, toasted, oak-barrel Burgundy—even the scent points in that direction. It has an oriental, spicy nose. Toffee, honey, coffee, linden, cream, butterscotch, sun-ripened oranges: it's got everything! Enveloped in a Corton-Charlemagne-like fat, nutty, enormous taste. The acidity is incredibly high but it hides beneath a layer of sweet fruit. One of my winners at the Millennium Tasting.

- 1981 KRUG CLOS DU MESNIL   95, JUN 1999 (97)
(100% CH)
In 1981, 12,793 bottles were made of a discreet and developable Clos du Mesnil. Discreet nose, pale color, and delicate citrus taste. Wonderful at the Millennium Tasting. Height of elegance.

- 1981 KRUG COLLECTION   96, AUG 2002 (96)
(31% PN, 19% PM, 50% CH)
This wine is so pure in style that one is dumbfounded. On the other hand, it's difficult to sense any difference between Collection and the usual vintage.

- 1980 KRUG CLOS DU MESNIL   97, MAR 1999 (97)
(100% CH)
I can hardly believe that it's true. Honestly, can a wine from this relatively simple vintage really be this good? Yes—at least my first bottle was fantastic. The similarities with the fabulous '79 were many. The aroma spectrum was basically identical to the legend.

Only the cleanness of the '79 surpassed this sensational wine. I just have to taste them together!

- 1979 KRUG CLOS DU MESNIL   99, JAN 2004 (99)
  (100% CH)
  A perfect Blanc de Blancs and a "decent" first try by the Krug family. The nose lives more on finesse than richness. Juicy Cox's Orange apples, Cointreau, and acacia honey raise high expectations for the taste, and they are triumphantly met. There is a wonderfully exotic richness that reminds me of Taittinger Comtes de Champagne, but with an aftertaste even richer in glycerol honey sweetness. One of the true milestones of wine history.
- 1979 KRUG COLLECTION   97, FEB 2003 (97)
  (36% PN, 28% PM, 36% CH)
  It still has the Montrachet-like elegance, like a young 1979 Krug. A fantastic masterpiece of absolute world class.
- 1976 KRUG COLLECTION   96, FEB 2004 (96)
  (42% PN, 26% PM, 32% CH)
  David Peppercorn and Serena Sutcliffe graciously treated me to this mammoth wine as an aperitif in their beautiful London home. After a brilliant and sophisticatedly elegant '81 from the same house, our senses were numbed by this bombshell. There is so much incredible taste packed into each gulp that you are dumbfounded. But I must point out that purity, elegance, and polish are somewhat lacking. Still, many consider this to be the foremost Champagne they've ever tasted.
- 1973 KRUG COLLECTION   95, OCT 1996 (95)
  (51% PN, 16% PM, 33% CH)
  A bit younger than the vintage; otherwise identical.
- 1971 KRUG COLLECTION   94, FEB 1997 (96)
  (47% PN, 14% PM, 39% CH)
  Despite being the exact same wine as the vintage wine, Collection feels lighter.
- 1969 KRUG COLLECTION   96, SEP 1995 (96)
  (50% PN, 13% PM, 37% CH)
  "Collection" merely means that the Champagne has been stored in Krug's cellars much longer than usual. Disgorged after six or seven years, the '69 is smoky and tough and is reminiscent of the austere 1969 Bollinger R. D. Beautiful and ultra-sophisticated.
- 1966 KRUG COLLECTION   98, JUN 1999 (98)
  (48% PN, 21% PM, 31% CH)
  It can't get much better than this. Extremely delicate, nutty, complex, and fabulously refreshing.
- 1964 KRUG COLLECTION   95, SEP 2002 (95)
  (53% PN, 20% PM, 27% CH)
  Identical to well-kept bottles of the normal vintage.
- 1962 KRUG COLLECTION   95, MAR 2003 (95)
  (36% PN, 28% PM, 36% CH)
  Identical to the straight vintage wine.
- 1961 KRUG COLLECTION   98, JAN 2003 (98)
  (53% PN, 12% PM, 35% CH)
  Here we go again! Pale, euphoric perfume with orchid, orange, and oriental spice flavors. Not as soft as the Krug vintage, yet it is really vigorous. Incredibly good! Belongs in the world of the divine.
- 1959 KRUG COLLECTION   98, JAN 1999 (98)
  (50% PN, 15% PM, 35% CH)
  Wine can hardly get better than this! One is treated here to a smorgasbord of sweets and an explosive wave of momentous power.

- 1952 KRUG COLLECTION   92, FEB 1997 (92)
  (43% PN, 19% PM, 38% CH)
  Despite the fact that the wine was in prime condition, it was a great disappointment and one of the wines I've tasted that gave least value for money. The '52 is slender and fine, with a faint nose of burned butter and oak. The flavor is very acidic and vigorous, but lacks both charm and depth.
- 1949 KRUG COLLECTION   98, JUN 1999 (98)
  (47% PN, 18% PM, 35% CH)
  Weak mousse, but a light, creamy, and super-concentrated Chardonnay, judging by the aromatic spectrum. Immensely fat with tones of butterscotch and lemon. Superb.
- 1938 KRUG COLLECTION   98, JAN 2003 (98)
  (57% PN, 16% PM, 27% CH)
  A magnum that was disgorged in September 1983 and enjoyed at the Millennium Tasting. Developed very slowly in the glass. Weak mousse, but a matchless charm and complex bouquet of nut toffee, and a resoundingly clean and long aftertaste. It tasted best of all ten hours after the tasting!
- 1928 KRUG COLLECTION   98, JUN 1999 (98)
  (70% PN, 8% PM, 22% CH)
  One of the most sought-after and legendary Champagnes that has been made. Deep, vegetal, and grand nutty scent. Warm, forceful, and majestic taste. Actually, nothing less than a scandal that it did not even place among the 100 foremost Champagnes at the Millennium Tasting.

LABBÉ, MICHEL R-M
24, rue du Gluten
51500 Chamery
03 26 97 65 89
Production: 30,000
The grower has more than ten hectares in Chamery and surrounding areas. *Chef de cave* today is Didier Labbé. The vineyards are planted with 70 percent Pinot Noir, 5 percent Pinot Meunier, and 25 percent Chardonnay. The wines don't go through malolactic fermentation—according to Didier, there's no need because the cellars are so cold!

- MICHEL LABBÉ CARTE BLANCHE   56
  (70% PN, 15% PM, 15% CH)
- MICHEL LABBÉ ROSÉ   51
  (50% PN, 50% PM)

LAGACHE-LECOURT R-M
29, rue du Maréchal Juin
51530 Chavot
03 26 54 86 79
Production: 60,000
The company owns vineyards in Chavot, Épernay, Mousy, and Vinay. Other wines: Rosé, Cuvée Chambecy.

- LAGACHE SÉLECTION   60
  (30% PN, 40% PM, 30% CH)
- LAGACHE BLANC DE BLANCS   46
  (100% CH)

LAGACHE, GILBERT R-M
rue de la Marquetterie
51200 Pierry
03 26 54 03 12
Production: 95,000
Despite its relatively limited production, 15 percent is exported to England. Claude Lagache is the name of the winemaker, who primarily has access to grapes from Chouilly. The wines are stored up to five years, which lends a fine, mature note.

• LAGACHE BRUT	68
(10% PN, 40% PM, 50% CH)	
• LAGACHE GRANDE RÉSERVE	71
(100% CH)	
• LAGACHE ROSÉ	56
(10% PM, 90% CH)	
• 1995 LAGACHE GRAND CRU	81, JAN 2001 (84)
(25% PN, 75% CH)	

The Chardonnay grapes come from Chouilly. Fine roundness and maturity. Delightful fruity tones and a bready side note. When aired: aromas of nuts, vanilla, and brioche. An exciting surprise.

LALLEMENT-DEVILLE R-M
28, rue Irénée Goss
51380 Verzy
03 26 97 95 50
Production: 50,000
The grower has access to more than five hectares in Verzy and utilizes modern vinification methods.

• LALLEMENT-DEVILLE BRUT	71
(100% PN)	
• LALLEMENT-DEVILLE ROSÉ	71
(100% PN)	
• 1990 LALLEMENT-DEVILLE VERZY BLANC DE BLANCS	
(100% CH)	76, MAR 1999 (77)
• 1991 DOM BASLE	76, MAR 2000 (78)
(66% PN, 34% CH)	

This vintage wine from Lallement-Deville carries the name of yet another monk to keep track of. The wine is already mature, which should hardly be taken as a sign of quality. The color is deep and the nose is grand but one-dimensional. I am searching for finesse even in the taste.

LALLEMENT, JEAN R-M
1, rue Moët & Chandon
51360 Verzenay
03 26 49 43 52
Production: 20000
Jean-Luc and his parents, Jean and Louisette Lallement, love straightforward, unaffected, dry, rich wines. They have ample opportunities to make these wines from their 4.5 hectares in Verzy, Verzenay, and Ludes. Eighty percent of the land is covered with Pinot Noir, and 20 percent is sown with Chardonnay. The average age of the vines is twenty-six years old. The wines, which are very clean and dry, have at most only three grams of sugar added.

• JEAN LALLEMENT BRUT	68
(80% PN, 20% CH)	
• JEAN LALLEMENT RÉSERVE	80
(80% PN, 20% CH)	

Clean and dry with a fine, slowly evolving, chocolaty Pinot Noir. Compact, acid, focused, and developable. Actually, a pure '96 when I tasted the wine—thus higher points than expected.

LAMIABLE *** N-M
8, rue de Conde
51150 Tours-sur-Marne
03 26 58 92 69
Production: 70,000
The house was founded in 1950 by Pierre Lamiable and is one of the few in Tours-sur-Marne. Five percent of the grapes are bought in and the rest come from the company's six hectares. Other wines: Extra Brut, Vintage, Rosé.

• LAMIABLE GRAND CRU BRUT	75
(75% PN, 25% CH)	
• LAMIABLE DEMI-SEC	49
(75% PN, 25% CH)	
• 1992 LAMIABLE SPECIAL CLUB	81, JAN 2002 (82)
(50% PN, 50% CH)	

A completely mature and suitably rounded-off Champagne with clear evidence of malolactic fermentation. Fat and buttery without any greater complexity.

• 1989 LAMIABLE SPECIAL CLUB	84, MAY 1999 (87)
(50% PN, 50% CH)	

A most reliable and affordable Champagne. Not as elegant as the '88, but with more meat on the bone. The bouquet is somewhat overblown, and characterized by a raisiny Pinot Noir. Fat and buttery taste that I at least regarded as "difficult to spit out."

• 1988 LAMIABLE SPECIAL CLUB	80, MAY 1996 (87)
(50% PN, 50% CH)	

Creamy and buttery, like so many Special Club Champagnes from various villages. The finish is a little short and diluted, however. Otherwise a fine and elegant Champagne, rich in minerals.

• LAMIABLE CUVÉE 2000	87, OCT 2001 (90)
(100% PN)	

Jean-Pierre Lamiable made only 3,000 bottles of this pure '95. The wine comes from fifty-year-old stocks in Tours-sur-Marne. The relatively dark wine radiates strength, with red-wine notes of blueberry, currants, and leather. Very vinous and concentrated in the mouth, with a deep gamy flavor and an exciting finish reminiscent of truffles. A brilliant wine from this forgotten *grand cru*.

LANCELOT-PIENNE R-M
1, allé de la Forêt
51530 Cramant
03 26 57 55 74
Production: 100,000
This firm, which was founded in 1870, is one of two with the knight's name of Lancelot. The *cuvée de prestige* is called *Table Ronde*, in homage to the "Knights of the Round Table." Other wines: Brut, Rosé.

• LANCELOT-PIENNE SÉLECTION	43
(15% PN, 50% PM, 35% CH)	
• LANCELOT-PIENNE TABLE RONDE	85
(40% PN, 60% CH)	
• LANCELOT BLANC DE BLANCS	69
(100% CH)	

LANCELOT-ROYER R-M
540, rue Général de Gaulle
51530 Cramant
03 26 57 51 41
Production: 30,000
This generous producer holds property not only in Cramant, but also in Avize, Oger, and Chouilly. The average age of the vines is twenty-five years and the reserve wines are stored in oak barrels.

- LANCELOT-ROYER   78, JUL 1997 (84)
  (100% CH)
  1989/90 Medium bodied and honey scented, with good roundness and exotic fruit.
- LANCELOT-ROYER EXTRA DRY CHEVALIER   70
  (100% CH)
- LANCELOT-ROYER BLANC DE BLANCS   66
  (100% CH)
- 1983 LANCELOT-ROYER   76, APR 1996 (82)
  (100% CH)
  The flavor is harmonious with a fine citrus tone, but the gamy style of the nose is demanding.
- 1982 LANCELOT-ROYER   82, APR 1996 (84)
  (100% CH)
  Unusually developed '82 with a unified flavor of cream and licorice.
- 1969 LANCELOT-ROYER   81, APR 1996 (>)
  (100% CH)
  A wine that is on its last legs. English oxidative flavor with leather and licorice saltiness.

LANDRAGIN R-M
14, rue Chanzy
51360 Verzenay
03 26 49 48 01
The Landragin family have been growers here in Verzenay since 1772, and they sold their first-class grapes to the major houses for many years. At the end of the 1960s, Dominique Landragin decided to make a Champagne of his own from his twenty-five hectares in Verzenay, Sillery, Beaumont-sur-Vesle, and Tauxières. The Champagne has been made by J.-P. Morel for the past several years as Landragin himself now lives in Australia, which makes the firm's future extremely uncertain.

- LANDRAGIN BRUT   70
  (80% PN, 20% CH)
- 1973 LANDRAGIN   85, FEB 2002 (85)
  (80% PN, 20% CH)
  Powerful and evolved in vintage-typical fashion with oxide notes. Raisins, almonds, plums, and mulled wine bombard the senses in a rich, somewhat indelicate package. A round, sweet Champagne that will hardly get any better.

LANG-BIÉMONT N-M
Les Ormissets
51530 Oiry
03 26 55 43 43
Production: 500,000
A married couple began selling Lang-Biémont Champagne in 1875, and today the very modern property is run by *chef de cave* Lionel Chaudron. Lang-Biémont buy in grapes from a widespread area, but the basic ingredient is Chardonnay from Oiry. Other wines: Carte d'Or, Rosé, Exception, Cuvée III.

- LANG-BIÉMONT RÉSERVÉE   61
  (10% PN, 90% CH)
- 1981 LANG-BIÉMONT   88, MAR 2000 (88)
  (100% CH)
  A featherlight Champagne with a very delicate touch. Light, sparkling and as thirst-quenching as a spring rain. Floral and youthful through and through.
- 1986 LANG-BIÉMONT BLANC DE BLANCS   80, JAN 1995 (85)
  (100% CH)
  A well-made wine with good depth and a high acidity that carries the grapefruit aromas on to a neat finish.

LANSON *** N-M
12, boulevard Lundy
51100 Reims
03 26 78 50 50
Production: 6,700,000
Lanson was founded in 1760 by François Delamotte; it was one of the first Champagne houses. François's son Nicolas-Louis, who was a knight in the Maltese Order, took over in 1798 and decided to use the Maltese Cross as the company's symbol. The name Lanson didn't appear until 1837, and it wasn't until twenty years later that the firm moved to the present address in Reims. After a brief period in the Louis Vuitton group, Lanson ended up as part of Marne & Champagne in 1990.

    The Champagne house, much appreciated by the Swedish royal family, doesn't own its own vineyards, but instead buys its grapes from sixty different villages. They avoid using malolactic fermentation, making the nonvintage wines a little sour and green when young. I've had in-depth discussions with the heads of Lanson—including the serious winemaker, Jean-Paul Gandon—and I must admit that I'm impressed by their solid determination to retain the house-style at any cost. It is no secret that I recommend malolactic fermentation for all blended nonvintage Champagnes that are aimed at direct consumption. We are, on the other hand, in total agreement that the "Parkerization" that has affected all the red-wine producers of the world should be avoided in Champagne. It would be most unfortunate if the Champagne houses took into consideration my own or Tom Stevenson's opinions when they make their wines. The region's diversity must be preserved, and obviously there is a large following for Lanson Black Label. Even the vintage wine is markedly acidic during its first few years on the market, but actually develops very well with age. Old vintages of Lanson are sure bets and value for money. If you have the patience, put the latest vintage down in the cellar for ten years or so—then open and enjoy the bready, yet still-fresh Champagne. Wines from the 1950s and 1960s are, to say the least, brilliant.

- LANSON BLACK LABEL   64
  (50% PN, 15% PM, 35% CH)

- LANSON DEMI-SEC   59
(50% PN, 15% PM, 35% CH)
- LANSON ROSÉ   56
(53% PN, 15% PM, 32% CH)
- 1996 LANSON   85, SEP 2003 (90)
The name alone sounds acidic, like an unripe gooseberry. Both the vintage and the house are known for their hard acidity—and so it proves in reality. The wine is exceptionally acidic and dentally corrosive, but at the same time exceedingly promising. It exhibits clearly what I've always said about Lanson's Champagnes: in their infancy they are extremely tough, but in time will become exceptionally enjoyable and acquire a nutty depth. Already, just one year after launching, its more aggressive sides have been toned down, creating a much more pleasant "big picture."
- 1995 LANSON   80, JAN 2002 (87)
(53% PN, 47% CH)
Hardly more accessible than usual, despite the vintage generally being so generous and capital. At the moment, youthfully undeveloped with a slightly prickly sulfuric note. Refreshing apple tone that demands lengthy storage before all its niceties reveal themselves.
- 1994 LANSON   82, SEP 2000 (88)
(53% PN, 47% CH)
A truly successful wine from this unremarkable year. An unusually great richness and complexity is present here in the nose. The flavor is understandably very young and still tart. Considering the development of previous vintages, I am convinced that the patient have a very fine wine to look forward to.
- 1993 LANSON   76, SEP 1999 (86)
(51% PN, 49% CH)
A young and typical Lanson with noticeable aromas of apple sauce, almond, and honey. Sharp acidity and relatively long aftertaste. Good structure and marked autolytic character. Store this one!
- 1990 LANSON   82, JUN 2001 (88)
(50% PN, 50% CH)
Drinking this wine now is like getting up at dawn on a Sunday. It's too early. There is hard acidity that burn in the stomach, but don't be surprised if great complexity and fine, toasty aromas turn up and take over in a few years.
- 1989 LANSON   78, JUN 2001 (83)
(56% PN, 44% CH)
Few know that this is in fact a *grand cru* Champagne. The grapes come from Verzenay, Aÿ, Bouzy, Oger, Chouilly, and Cramant. With acidity at 5.5 grams it is far softer than the '85, which has 7 grams of malic acid. Rounded and pleasant, but it loses it all disturbingly fast in the glass.
- 1988 LANSON   82, JUN 2003 (86)
(51% PN, 49% CH)
Surprisingly soft, candy-influenced Champagne with a creamy openness in the nose and a somewhat short finish. Deceptive behavior, it seems, as the wine will most likely change dramatically in the future, as so many wines from Lanson do.
- 1985 LANSON   83, JAN 2002 (87)
(50% PN, 50% CH)
For the time being a very difficult, sharp Champagne, where the malic acid is much too intrusive. The nose, on the other hand, is handsome and refreshing, with a nascent breadiness. This embryo should eventually grow into something big.

- 1983 LANSON   75, FEB 1989 (81)
(50% PN, 50% CH)
Unexpectedly developed bready nose, but that ungenerous house-style reappears in the taste and the malic acid is intrusive again.
- 1982 LANSON   94, JAN 2003 (94)
(50% PN, 50% CH)
White Burgundy with bubbles! That's how several of us described this brilliant wine, which swept the board against the somewhat pale bottle of 1990 Dom Pérignon that I'd chosen alongside this wine to accompany my newly caught turbot with tarragon sauce. Completely fresh and buoyant, without a sharp edge in sight. At the same time lightly toasted and warmly buttery, with a delightful range of exciting aromas. Long and seductively focused with a lingering note of chestnuts and almond macaroons.
- 1981 LANSON   91, JUN 2001 (91)
(54% PN, 46% CH)
1981 is a lovely vintage for Lanson. Few have succeeded so well in making such classical Champagnes with a solid backbone and faint toasted aromas.
- 1980 LANSON   80, FEB 2000 (83)
(50% PN, 50% CH)
Fresh and creamy nose. Hard, sour, and somewhat short flavor.
- 1979 LANSON   91, MAR 2003 (91)
(50% PN, 50% CH)
The '79 has all the advantages of the vintage. A particularly elegant wine with a round Pinot nose and well-built structure. The malic acid is well integrated with this wine. Long and thin as a supermodel.
- 1976 LANSON   91, MAR 2003 (91)
(46% PN, 54% CH)
Relatively mature color, incredibly toasty, almost burned character. Impressive with its dill, licorice, and brioche. Slightly heavy in the rump, with a structure resembling the '59 but without that year's purity. Young and elegant in magnum.
- 1975 LANSON   92, MAR 2002 (92)
(55% PN, 45% CH)
Aside from the horrible bottle design, this Champagne creates a lovely overall impression. Mature, full of chocolate, and a fresh, long flavor.
- 1971 LANSON   90, NOV 1995 (90)
(50% PN, 50% CH)
Pure and honeyed. Light to medium bodied with a charming apple character that reminds me of Cox's Orange apples.
- 1969 LANSON   70, MAR 1999 (>)
(50% PN, 50% CH)
- 1966 LANSON   92, JAN 2003 (92)
(50% PN, 50% CH)
Considering how exceptionally good the '61 and the '59 from Lanson are, this is a comparative disappointment. Sure, it is a well-built and rich wine with a strong aroma of windfall fruit and almonds. However, I miss a touch of finesse; though, on the other hand, I am impressed by the strength, which is exceptional for the vintage.
- 1964 LANSON   95, AUG 2000 (95)
(50% PN, 50% CH)
What wonderful wines Lanson made once upon a time! Krug-like, nutty, and incredibly deep. Such giants are sometimes lacking in sweetness and fruit. Not this '64. A delightful, exotic

richness is present here, with pleasant flavors reminiscent of vanilla and milk chocolate.

- 1961 LANSON   96, JAN 2001 (96)
(50% PN, 50% CH)
Extraordinarily pale and clear considering its age. A superbly well-composed Champagne, with a gorgeous bouquet of mint chocolate and tremendous depth, not unlike Krug. The '59, '55, and '61 from Lanson are definitely in a class of their own.
- 1959 LANSON   96, JAN 2002 (96)
(50% PN, 50% CH)
Probably the greatest Lanson I have tasted. The wine is almost heroic in its dimensions, and amazingly vital in its color and mousse. The nose opens slowly to reveal all the colors of the rainbow. The Champagne is very masculine, with nuances of juniper and Havana cigars. The wine is astoundingly heavy and full bodied, with the same aromas as the nose. The finish is a textbook example of the vintage: very dry and tough, fiery and rich in tannin. Lovely at the Millennium Tasting. Certain bottles breathe—strangely enough—young, floral Chardonnay.
- 1955 LANSON   95, NOV 2003 (95)
(50% PN, 50% CH)
It was hardly surprising to discover that Lanson made a super wine in 1955. The entire wine exudes harmony and coconut. One taster thought this was the most luxurious piña colada he'd ever drunk. Despite a classic aridness and a laid-back style, it's the sweet aromas of vanilla, cacao, and coconut that dominant. Lighter than the '59 but just as irresistible. Big bottle variation.
- 1945 LANSON
(50% PN, 50% CH)
- 1943 LANSON   87, DEC 2002 (87)
(50% PN, 50% CH)
I'm convinced that this wine is really good in a regular bottle. Because, despite sixty years in a half bottle, the acidity is buoyant and you can still detect a streak of mousse. Even the color is pale and the wine breathes iron, blood, smoke, and tar. The palate is replete with apple tones and honey in the lingering note.
- 1937 LANSON
(55% PN, 45% CH)
- 1928 LANSON   90, OCT 2001 (90)
(55% PN, 45% CH)
Totally vigorous and extraordinarily buoyant, with a young, unadorned appearance. Mineral and citrus integrated with a soft mousse is not exactly what you'd expect from such an old wine, but this was exactly what was proffered. The aftertaste suggests age, with a slowly evolving dark note of wood and burned sugar. Slightly lighter and less complex than expected, which explains the relatively low points for such a fresh oldie from one of the greatest vintages.
- 1921 LANSON   96, OCT 2001 (96)
(50% PN, 50% CH)
Absolutely, irresistibly delicious, handsome, and good! Light color, lively mousse, creamy feeling, and a strongly vanilla-ish balanced taste. Long, feminine finish with citrus and nut toffee.
- 1892 LANSON   87, APR 2001 (87)
(50% PN, 50% CH)
A bottle that had, until recently, lain immured and forgotten in the cellar of an English university. The vintage was impossible to decipher from cork and label remnants. However, I sincerely agree that the vintage has been correctly identified, as the

thickness of the glass, the depth of the cavity, and all other bottle details were identical to an 1892 Pol Roger. Furthermore, the wine was incredibly like that wine. Deep, sherry-like, thought-provoking dark bouquet, with elements of wood varnish, cognac, tobacco, date, figs, and tar.

- 1994 LANSON BLANC DE BLANCS   84, DEC 2001 (87)
(100% CH)
A very successful vintage for Lanson, which shows they are heading in the right direction. A buttery and refreshing, lime-tasting Champagne with great authority and weight.
- 1990 LANSON BLANC DE BLANCS   90, JAN 2002 (93)
(100% CH)
An astonishing wine with a wonderfully fresh aperitif quality. The balance between freshness and sweet ripe fruit is perfect. The vintage's rich character fits the house's ascetic style like a hand in a glove. Among the best Champagnes I've tasted from Lanson.
- 1989 LANSON BLANC DE BLANCS   86, MAR 2003 (88)
(100% CH)
The firm's new *cuvée de prestige* is made from equal portions of Chouilly, Cramant, and Avize grapes. A textbook appearance and an attractive nose of biscuits and lemon. The flavor is relatively basic and impersonal.
- 1983 LANSON BLANC DE BLANCS   85, FEB 1995 (89)
(100% CH)
The wine's 12.7% alcohol content is extremely unusual! The wine also has an extraordinary power for a Blanc de Blancs. The nose is marked by petroleum and overripe lemons, with a weak toasty element. In the mouth the company's apple tang comes in handy in an otherwise rather mature wine. Somewhat one-dimensional grapefruit taste.
- 1995 NOBLE CUVÉE   85, SEP 2003 (89)
(100% CH)
This is actually the same wine that was previously called Blanc de Blancs under the Noble Cuvée label. A creamy, exciting Champagne from Lanson, with substantial acidity and delightful aromas of lemon cupcake, honey, and sweet citrus.
- 1989 NOBLE CUVÉE   84, JUN 2002 (88)
(40% PN, 60% CH)
Light and subtle aroma with tones of first-rate Chardonnay. A slightly discordant finish at this point. It will surely come right within a few years when the wine's hard youthfulness softens.
- 1988 NOBLE CUVÉE   86, NOV 2003 (90)
(40% PN, 60% CH)
A pure *grand cru* Champagne from Avize, Cramant, Chouilly, Verzenay, and Ambonnay. Austere and concentrated, with a promising aromatic spectrum. Store for many years to come!
- 1985 NOBLE CUVÉE   83, MAR 1995 (88)
(40% PN, 60% CH)
I have only drunk one glass of this wine. It seemed to be much more restrained than the '80, but with more of a mineral accent and less generous fruit.
- 1981 LANSON CUVÉE 225   92, MAY 1996 (93)
(45% PN, 55% CH)
A brilliant Lanson! Everything's gone right here. The wine has a classic Champagne character, full of minerals, toasted bread, and delicious, citrus-influenced fruit. The harmonies in the flavor are also outstanding.
- 1981 NOBLE CUVÉE   90, MAY 1997 (90)
(20% PN, 80% CH)

Classically toasted, beautiful, and honey-saturated, with balanced fruit and a long aftertaste.

- 1980 NOBLE CUVÉE   86, JUN 1989 (87)
(20% PN, 80% CH)
The color was a deep yellow and the nose was filled by mature Chardonnay, but with a perceptible element of eggnog. Richly peach-like, soft, and medium-long taste.

- 1990 LANSON MILLENNIUM CUVÉE   86, MAY 1999 (92)
(50% PN, 50% CH)
Exactly the same wine as the usual vintage, but in magnum, and with longer yeast contact. The autolytic character is rather prominent, and the entire wine exudes depth and concentration.

LARMANDIER **** N-M

B. P. 4
51530 Cramant
03 26 57 52 19
Production: 100,000

The Larmandier family have been leading winegrowers in Cramant for several generations. It was only in 1978 that they received house status, through Dominique Larmandier. Today the firm is closely linked with Gimonnet in Cuis. The house owns eight hectares in five *crus* in Côte des Blancs.

- LARMANDIER BLANC DE BLANCS   77
(100% CH)
- 1982 LARMANDIER   79, JUL 1992 (>)
(100% CH)
- 1990 LARMANDIER SPECIAL CLUB   84, JAN 1998 (84)
(100% CH)
A wine that surprised me with its dark, developed color and oxidative character. Should this Cramant-based Champagne really develop this quickly? The aroma is already full of chocolate and licorice tones. The wine's pleasing creaminess allows me to forgive a lack of acidity. Does it vary from bottle to bottle?

- 1989 LARMANDIER SPECIAL CLUB   83, MAR 1996 (91)
(100% CH)
A surprising nose of beef stew and cheese, which I've only previously found in Champagnes from Le Mesnil. The wine is hardly charming but has a good structure.

- 1988 LARMANDIER SPECIAL CLUB   90, MAR 1996 (93)
(100% CH)
Much richer and sweeter than the '89. The wine gives a juicy impression that is irresistible.

LARMANDIER-BERNIER **** R-M

43, rue du 28 Août
51130 Vertus
03 26 52 13 24
Production: 85,000

The firm owns 9.5 hectares in Bergères-lès-Vertus, Chouilly, Cramant, and Vertus. Pierre Larmandier, who also chairs the young winemakers' association, makes some of the purest Chardonnay Champagnes around today. This relaxed and intellectual thirty-five-year-old works in tandem with his mother, who took over after her husband died. With his father's death coming so suddenly, it took time before Pierre felt ready to take on the controlling role in the company, and he speaks openly of the differing tastes he and his mother have. Pierre loves acidic, restrained Champagnes, while his mother enjoys more

accessible, fruity wines. Fortunately Pierre's taste is taking over more and more. The family has owned a few hectares of extremely old Chardonnay vines in Cramant for a long time, and during the 1990 harvest Pierre decided to make an exclusive Champagne from these eighty-year-old vines alone. The result is a Champagne that will be legendary well into the 2000s. All his wines gain from keeping for ten years—or maybe even more in a good cellar!

- LARMANDIER-BERNIER TRADITION   69
(20% PN, 80% CH)
- LARMANDIER-BERNIER VERTUS TERROIR NON DOSÉ   70
(100% CH)
- LARMANDIER-BERNIER BLANC DE BLANCS   76
(100% CH)
- LARMANDIER-BERNIER ROSÉ   56
(100% PN)
- 1989 LARMANDIER-BERNIER   84, AUG 1997 (87)
(100% CH)
Always refreshing, with an almost Chablis-like nose. Dry and clean mid-palate, fresh attack and an acidic finish.

- 1998 LARMANDIER-BERNIER VIEILLES VIGNES CRAMANT
(100% CH)   88, JUN 2003 (94)
A wonderful wine that shines from the get-go. Here we encounter a lively, witty beauty combined with an unexpected depth. Looks are faithful to their heritage, but the nose is actually a bit Bollinger-like, with intense notes of ripe apples side by side with the citrus-oriented fruit aromas. This must be due to the old vines that give the wine such exceptional concentration. The wine is long, balanced, pleasant, and aristocratically built.

- 1997 LARMANDIER-BERNIER SPECIAL CLUB   83, MAR 2003 (85)
(100% CH)
The wine tired disquietingly in the glass, but what an entrance! Handsome, generous Champagne with great roundness. Mineral notes and buttery Chardonnay. Both the nose and the taste are impressively big, but the aftertaste is somewhat short.

- 1996 LARMANDIER-BERNIER SPECIAL CLUB   87, OCT 2003 (92)
(100% CH)
Well-balanced, creamy, and sophisticated, like a great vintage from Bonnaire. Brilliant aromatic clarity and well-composed, harmonious structure. Considerably finer than Vieilles Vignes Cramant for the time being.

- 1996 LARMANDIER-BERNIER VIEILLES VIGNES CRAMANT
(100% CH)   83, MAY 2002 (91)
I don't know if this is a passing phenomenon, but for the moment I'm more impressed by the Special Club from this year. The old vines in Cramant have resulted here in an impressively powerful wine with high concentration and richness. I personally think that the scent is a little too oxidative and coarse in all its power. Difficult to judge this wine's future.

- 1995 LARMANDIER-BERNIER SPECIAL CLUB   84, MAY 2002 (87)
(100% CH)
Big, buttery bouquet with a saturated appearance. Round and good in a rather uncomplicated fashion. I had probably expected more elegance and definition from this well-balanced vintage.

- 1995 LARMANDIER-BERNIER VIEILLES VIGNES CRAMANT
(100% CH)   84, NOV 2000 (90)
I have waited a long time for this wine. It's possible that it will become even better than predicted, but it is extremely bound in the nose and difficult to judge. The palate has nicely polished fruit and creaminess with a floral bouquet. Tight finish.

- 1990 LARMANDIER-BERNIER SPECIAL CLUB   82, MAY 2002 (85)
(100% CH)
Completely evolved, powerful '90 with a big whiff of licorice toffee, plum, and whipped cream. Sufficient roundness and creaminess but a somewhat rustic appearance.

- 1990 LARMANDIER-BERNIER VIEILLES VIGNES CRAMANT
(100% CH)   91, MAY 2001 (94)
I believe that all the great wines in the world have something in common: a superior intensity in the nose that comes from their unique soil. This Cramant Champagne is such a wine. The nose is incredibly elusive, with an explosive, indescribable floweriness. Even though it is a little shy now, it's lying there under the surface, waiting to explode in all its beauty. The flavor is extremely long, tight, and focused. Buy all the bottles you can get your hands on and put them away for your grandchildren!

- 1988 LARMANDIER-BERNIER SPECIAL CLUB   80, NOV 1994 (89)
(100% CH)
Almost exclusively Cramant grapes in the *cuvée*. Very similar to the '88 Bonnaire, with its butterscotch nose and Chablis-like Chardonnay fruit.

- 1979 LARMANDIER-BERNIER SPECIAL CLUB   91, AUG 1996 (91)
(100% CH)
A crisp wine, with citrus flavors and nutty nuances. Dry, classic finish.

- 1975 LARMANDIER-BERNIER SPECIAL CLUB   93, NOV 1995 (94)
(100% CH)
It's always a pleasure to drink an older Blanc de Blancs straight from the producer himself. The '75 is the firm's first vintage, and it resisted for many years before it eventually found itself. Today it is a wonderfully harmonious Champagne, so classical and restrained, with all of Chardonnay's mature tones like coffee, toasted bread, butterscotch, and popcorn. Perfectly pure acidity, like a great Salon.

LARMANDIER, GUY *** R-M
30, rue du Général Koenig
51130 Vertus
03 26 52 12 41
Production: 65,000
This small company, which was started in Vertus in 1977, has built up a good reputation since Robert Parker boosted their wines. Personally, I think that Côte des Blancs has a great number of more interesting growers, and every wine I've tasted from this property has been well-made but a bit closed in the nose. Guy Larmandier, who left Larmandier in Cramant, is most proud of his four hectares in Cramant, besides his three hectares in Vertus, half a hectare in Cuis, and two in Chouilly. The wines are put through malolactic fermentation and cold stabilization. The vines in Cramant are almost thirty years old and should give more exciting Champagnes than they do today. The vintage wine always comes from two Cramant locations: Gros Mont and Fond du Bateaux.

- GUY LARMANDIER CRAMANT   70
(100% CH)
- GUY LARMANDIER PREMIER CRU   68
(5% PN, 95% CH)
- GUY LARMANDIER PERLÉ   63
(100% CH)
- GUY LARMANDIER ROSÉ   57
(20% PN, 80% CH)

- 1997 GUY LARMANDIER CRAMANT GRAND CRU   85, MAR 2004 (87)
(100% CH)
An incredibly thick, oily Champagne full of creamy, honey-saturated aromas. The level of acidity is a little too low and rather one-dimensional, but it's nevertheless very delicious.

- 1992 GUY LARMANDIER CRAMANT GRAND CRU   79, JUL 1997 (83)
(100% CH)
One of the better Champagnes from this vintage. The wine is already showing a friendly attitude, with a rich nose of apple and pear. The flavor is a touch too sweet—there is already enough fruit to go around.

- 1989 GUY LARMANDIER CRAMANT GRAND CRU   81, APR 1995 (87)
(100% CH)
Very pale color, faint nose with elements of cream candies and white flowers. Creamy, sweet flavor with good purity.

- 1982 GUY LARMANDIER CRAMANT GRAND CRU   84, APR 1995 (87)
(100% CH)
Once again a shy, closed nose. Those tones that one can make out are high class, and the flavor is restrained, full of finesse, but not that generous for an '82.

LASSALLE-HANIN R-M
2, rue des Vignes
51500 Chigny-les-Roses
03 26 03 40 96
Production: 30,000
Lassalle-Hanin is a far less successful wine house than their famous "cousin," J. Lassalle.

- LASSALLE-HANIN RÉSERVE   50
(33% PN, 33% PM, 34% CH)
- LASSALLE-HANIN BLANC DE BLANCS   60
(100% CH)
- LASSALLE-HANIN ROSÉ   48
(50% PN, 30% PM, 20% CH)
- 1989 LASSALLE-HANIN   82, OCT 1997 (83)
(50% PN, 50% CH)
Only 2,000 bottles produced of this Champagne. Rounded, honeyed, and creamy.

- 1988 LASSALLE-HANIN   86, OCT 1997 (90)
(50% PN, 50% CH)
Superb biscuit-like and minty *cuvée de prestige*. Concentrated and with an oriental richness.

LASSALLE, J. *** R-M
rue des Châtagniers
51500 Chigny-les-Roses
03 26 03 42 19
Production: 100,000
This little gem, like so many others, is run by a stylish widow and her daughter. Their Champagnes are characterized by broad, ripe, exotic fruit. They have few critics and the wines are exceedingly drinkable. The Chardonnay wine is among the very best outside of Côte des Blancs. The grower has had unprecedented success in the U.S.A.

- LASSALLE BRUT   75
(60% PN, 40% CH)
- LASSALLE ROSÉ   70
(70% PN, 30% CH)
- 1996 LASSALLE BLANC DE BLANCS   87, JUN 2003 (90)
(100% CH)

- 1988 LASSALLE BLANC DE BLANCS   79, OCT 1997 (84)
(100% CH)

Still a bit sharp and unpolished. Aromas of grapefruit, grass, gooseberry, and mineral. Rather long acidic aftertaste.

- 1987 LASSALLE BLANC DE BLANCS   80, AUG 1996 (83)
(100% CH)

A big, bold nose of daffodils, nectar, and honey meets the taster. The flavor is soft and pleasant, but lacks the finesse of a Blanc de Blancs from Côte des Blancs.

- 1985 LASSALLE BLANC DE BLANCS   84, AUG 2001 (84)
(100% CH)

This Champagne has a very open nose of mature exotic Chardonnay and daffodils. The structure is almost oily, the flavor is rich and creamy, and the dosage is just a touch high. The overall impression is more one-dimensional than Special Club.

- 1982 LASSALLE BLANC DE BLANCS   84, AUG 2001 (84)
(100% CH)

Amazingly similar to the '85. Here too one discovers the highly personal nose of daffodils. The richness is the same.

- 1995 LASSALLE SPECIAL CLUB   86, SEP 2003 (88)
(40% PN, 60% CH)

You can tell that the wine is made from high-class grapes from old vines, and that the yield is low. The wine is very concentrated and expressive without any extra finesse.

- 1993 CUVÉE ANGÉLINE   84, SEP 2003 (85)
(60% PN, 40% CH)

Rather simple nose, but at the same time charming in an uncomplicated way—just like a really good pop song. Sweets and fruity desserts mixed with vanilla. Soft and smiling.

- 1992 LASSALLE SPECIAL CLUB   80, OCT 1997 (82)
(40% PN, 60% CH)

Very creamy and ripe as always. The wine lacks aging potential but it is quite charming anyhow.

- 1989 CUVÉE ANGÉLINE   86, OCT 2001 (86)
(60% PN, 40% CH)

A real "candy Champagne": high dosage packed with sweet aromas from sun-bathed grapes. Vanilla, treacle, and hard candy together with dried pineapple and a creamy mousse.

- 1989 LASSALLE SPECIAL CLUB   92, FEB 2003 (92)
(40% PN, 60% CH)

Lassalle has attracted a lot of attention in the wine press recently. This rich wine has popular appeal, a lovely buttery Chardonnay nose, and a fat, full Pinot sweetness. Very creamy and great richness.

- 1988 CUVÉE ANGÉLINE   79, OCT 1997 (83)
(60% PN, 40% CH)

Softer than the Blanc de Blancs. A fruity nose of plums and dough. Medium-bodied, clean taste.

- 1987 CUVÉE ANGÉLINE   75, JAN 1997 (80)
(60% PN, 40% CH)

This may be a very good '87, but it's hardly a great wine. The nose hints at vanilla and fresh bread and the flavor plays a similar tune.

- 1985 CUVÉE ANGELINE   50, APR 1993 (>)
(60% PN, 40% CH)

- 1985 LASSALLE SPECIAL CLUB   88, OCT 1992 (91)
(40% PN, 60% CH)

I wonder if this isn't the best Lassalle I've tasted. It's odd that the '85 Cuvée Angeline constantly flops while at the same time they did so well with Special Club. The nose is typical for the firm, with all kinds of pastries and white chocolate. The citrus aroma is stronger than usual and adds yet another dimension. The flavor is marked by an expansive exotic fruitiness and perfect balance.

- 1982 CUVÉE ANGELINE   87, APR 1993 (89)
(60% PN, 40% CH)

A lovely Champagne even when it was released, but perhaps more for the reveler than the analyst. White chocolate, vanilla, butter, honey, and toffee are there in both flavor and nose. Despite the fact there is more Pinot in the composition, it is Chardonnay that dominates proceedings. The acidity is a little too low for the wine to enjoy a really long life.

- 1982 LASSALLE SPECIAL CLUB   89, AUG 1996 (89)
(40% PN, 60% CH)

Lassalle made a luscious and ripe '82 with great complexity. Fully mature today.

LAUNOIS PÈRE & FILS **** R-M

2, avenue Eugene Guillaume
51190 Le Mesnil-sur-Oger
03 26 57 50 15
Production: 180,000

The firm was founded in 1872 and owns twenty-one hectares, most of which lie in Le Mesnil. Bernard Launois has recently set up a fantastic wine museum on his property. Few winemakers in Champagne have such a well-stocked cellar full of old vintages as Bernard. Even fewer are as generous and willing to share as this connoisseur of life. Since 1970, he has owned vineyards in Avize, Oger, and Cramant. Launois's finest wine, Special Club, is a blend of equal parts of Le Mesnil (Les Chetillons) and Cramant (Les Justices).

- LAUNOIS BRUT   77
(100% CH)
- LAUNOIS CUVÉE CAROLINE   78
(100% CH)
- LAUNOIS CUVÉE CLEMENCE   77
(100% CH)
- LAUNOIS MESNIL SABLÉ   79
(100% CH)
- LAUNOIS OEIL DE PERDRIX   58
(100% PN)
- CUVÉE ERIK LALLERSTEDT BLANC DE BLANCS   80
(100% CH)

The same wine as Launois Réserve Blanc de Blancs in, as yet, a slightly young edition. Store a few years to get that delightfully buttery complexity that I know Erik loves.

- LAUNOIS RÉSERVE BLANC DE BLANCS   83
(100% CH)

A powerful Blanc de Blancs with fierce attack and good length as well as a delightful almond aroma. In a big competition at a wine fair in Stockholm in 2003 (in which most of the best nonvintage Champagnes featured), this was the winner. Wonderfully rich and oily with a beautifully exotic quality.

- LAUNOIS ROSÉ   48
(20% PN, 80% CH)
- 1997 LAUNOIS   84, DEC 2003 (88)
(100% CH)

As usual with such young examples from Launois, I find sulfur in the nose. Otherwise pear and apple dominate, backed up by fine strains of brioche and nougat. Soft and pleasant on the palate but without much concentration.

- 1996 LAUNOIS   87, APR 2004 (92)
(100% CH)

It's hardly surprising that Launois has made a really tremendous wine this year. I was a little worried after the dry and stony '95, but here the ascetic, tart, *terroir* character is charmingly uplifted by a generous, sun-ripened fruitiness. The citrus notes are mature and there's even an element of passion fruit and mandarin orange, just as there are in most of the vintages of neighboring Pierre Peters's wines. Handsomely sophisticated finish with toffee and long acidity.

- 1995 LAUNOIS   83, FEB 2002 (89)
(100% CH)

Stony, tough, even a little thin as yet. Rest assured, the Champagne will one day be great. As regards concentration and complexity, Le Mesnil, like no other, has the ability to expand.

- 1993 LAUNOIS SEVERINE   75, JAN 2002 (81)
(100% CH)

The nose is really developed, with a weak undertone of mint chocolate and steak tartare. Fleshy, with a clear green appley palate and fine purity. Finishes much too abruptly for a wine from Launois.

- 1992 LAUNOIS   80, JAN 1999 (87)
(100% CH)

Launois doesn't make simple wines. Don't be surprised if this '92 becomes a winner at tastings in ten years' time. Le Mesnil's pedigree and unbending tartness are already present.

- 1990 LAUNOIS   90, FEB 2003 (94)
(100% CH)

Plenty of toffee and saffron aromas, but also a steely, acidic finesse that is typical of this unbeatable village.

- 1988 LAUNOIS   94, NOV 2003 (95)
(100% CH)

A classic Mesnil Champagne that is at its best in magnums. The wine already has a typical village perfume that is wonderful. At fifteen years of age, a beautifully toasted Dom Ruinart-like bouquet had appeared. Fantastically complex and softly enjoyable. A big performer at the 1988 Tasting.

- 1988 LAUNOIS SABLÉ   86, APR 1996 (91)
(100% CH)

Faintly sparkling, a broad meaty nose with notes of roasted chestnuts and citrus fruits. A delicate mousse and extremely purebred young flavor.

- 1985 LAUNOIS   90, MAY 1998 (92)
(100% CH)

A wine with a tightly focused style, closed and stringent, but with a long, acidic, and developable aftertaste.

- 1985 LAUNOIS SABLÉ   91, JUL 1997 (92)
(100% CH)

Packed with so much mineral that it feels like chalk in the mouth. Won't mature for many years to come. Today, suddenly open and approachable. Classic.

- 1982 LAUNOIS   88, JUL 1991 (91)
(100% CH)

Extremely fine, small bubbles that create gorgeous pearl necklaces in the glass. Subtle nose of mineral and newly baked bread. I have an obvious weakness for Blanc de Blancs of this caliber.

- 1979 LAUNOIS   94, JUL 1997 (94)
(100% CH)

Great freshness on the nose, with a bouquet of freshly cut hay. Wonderful taste of walnuts.

- 1975 LAUNOIS   89, APR 1992 (89)
(100% CH)

A brutal Blanc de Blancs that steams ahead with deep chocolate aromas and a corpulent body.

- 1971 LAUNOIS   92, APR 1992 (94)
(100% CH)

Tasted together with the '75, this vintage was lighter and its bouquet more refined. A typical example of how easily older Blanc de Blancs can taste as if they have been aged in oak.

- 1969 LAUNOIS CRÉMANT   89, MAR 2003 (89)
(100% CH)

Apparently you have to be careful about storing Crémant wines for too long. The mousse dies too quickly and hastens decline. This wine is basically fantastic, with a Salon-like bouquet and palate of walnut and old butter. The acidity is biting, but the color is exaggeratedly dark. Some oxide notes creep in when the bubbles disappear.

- 1966 LAUNOIS   96, JAN 2002 (97)
(100% CH)

What a magical Champagne! The wine has an elusive, refined nose that I've only previously encountered in 1985 Krug Clos de Mesnil. The feminine elegance returns in the buttery, eternal flavor.

- 1964 LAUNOIS   96, JUN 1999 (96)
(100% CH)

Shared first place with the 1943 Krug at a comprehensive tasting of mature Champagnes that took place in the Stockholm archipelago in June 1998. It was just as wonderful one year later at the Millennium Tasting. Somewhat sweeter than the finesse-laden '66.

- 1964 LAUNOIS CRÉMANT   89, SEP 2003 (89)
(100% CH)

Originally the same wine as the lovely '64, but with half the pressure and somewhat weaker autolytic character. A former colleague and I took a bottle apiece home. His had a weak but noticeable mousse; mine was completely flat but still healthy and buoyantly Mesnil-like. The aromas are austere and classic, as should be the case with such a soloist. I've tasted several completely exhausted bottles, so it's hardly a wine I can recommend, despite high points.

- 1952 LAUNOIS   88, DEC 2003 (88)
(100% CH)

It's rare to be offered a murky, half-empty bottle of old Champagne by a grower, but this is exactly what happened at Launois in 2003. In their museum they have a *pupitre* with undisgorged '52s, all with low wine levels. A perfect bottle should be wonderful, as the butterscotchy aromas were exceedingly lovely and the acidity markedly low. Unfortunately, in this version there is a little too much yeast aroma and the mousse is too weak.

- 1947 LAUNOIS   97, APR 1996 (97)
(100% CH)

What a gem! Not as elegant as the '66 but much richer, with a youthful nose of peppermint candy, passion fruit, and a magically concentrated nectar-like flavor. A wine for everyone to love.

- 1932 LAUNOIS   92, APR 1996 (92)
(100% CH)

Leather, meat, and truffles in the nose. When in the mouth, it's dominated by old butter and licorice aromas.

- 1999 LAUNOIS SPECIAL CLUB   81, NOV 2003 (91)
(100% CH)

The first bottle of this wine was a big disappointment, with its earthy notes and a prominent dollop of sulfur. The next bottle also had an irritating amount of sulfur, but was much cleaner and honeyed. It feels too soon to predict where this wine is heading. At Launois in Mesnil they wax lyrical about this wine. I suppose the prickly sulfuric notes will become toasty with time.

- 1996 LAUNOIS SPECIAL CLUB   91, DEC 2003 (94)
(100% CH)
Fantastic Mesnil character in the nose with notes of chalk, flint, and wet stones. There is also a beautiful fruitiness, with strains of lime and passion-fruit juice. Handsomely concentrated, with complex taste layers and stringency. Fine attack and a remarkably rich mid-palate of sweet, mature grapes. The acidity is, of course, enormous.

- 1995 LAUNOIS SPECIAL CLUB   88, SEP 2003 (90)
(100% CH)
Much richer and more developed than the pure '95 from Mesnil, which is released alongside this Mesnil/Cramant-Cuvée. The old vines lend a buttery, fat and delicious fullness that carries the reluctant Mesnil character to great heights.

- 1994 LAUNOIS SPECIAL CLUB   91, SEP 2003 (92)
(100% CH)
This fantastic grower goes from strength to strength; this is the first '94 to pass my ninety-point barrier. This prestige Champagne always combines Mesnil's austere, deep finesse with Cramant's rich, buttery style in an amazing way. Fantastic acidity, depth, and Dom Pérignon-like scents of roasted coffee.

- 1990 LAUNOIS SPECIAL CLUB   91, MAR 2003 (94)
(100% CH)
More characterized by Mesnil than the '88. Brilliantly focused and developable. Recently, spectacularly fat and creamy. The vintage's foremost Champagne according to the jury at the Millennium Tasting.

- 1988 LAUNOIS SPECIAL CLUB   93, APR 1996 (95)
(100% CH)
Bonnaire's favorite Champagne, and I understand him! Cramant shines brightly in this wonderful solo piece.

- 1986 LAUNOIS SPECIAL CLUB   83, MAY 1998 (83)
(100% CH)
Very highly developed personal style. Big cheesy scent and round taste that reminds me of a high-class Riesling from Alsace. A slightly tired aftertaste of raisin.

- 1985 LAUNOIS SPECIAL CLUB   80, APR 1992 (93)
(100% CH)
A closed package of minerals; it literally feels like drinking chalk soil. The wine has not gone through malolactic fermentation and has very high acidity. Today also rich and classic.

- 1982 LAUNOIS SPECIAL CLUB   91, MAY 1998 (92)
(100% CH)
Surprisingly stingy aroma. Rich, lightly smoky taste.

- 1981 LAUNOIS SPECIAL CLUB   94, JUN 1997 (95)
(100% CH)
Several '81s are beginning to show previously unimagined qualities, with a flowery elegance common to them all. Launois's example is among the most beautiful, with its shining green/yellow color, ultra-elegant nose, and exotic fruit flavor.

- 1979 LAUNOIS SPECIAL CLUB   96, MAY 1998 (97)
(100% CH)

A masterpiece of finesse. Uplifting as a springtime walk in a beech forest in bloom. Perfect balance. Le Mesnil at its best.

- 1978 LAUNOIS SPECIAL CLUB   89, MAY 1998 (90)
(100% CH)
The aroma is nearly identical to 1978 Dom Pérignon. Fruity, clean, and light Champagne with a mineral finish.

- 1986 LAUNOIS CUVÉE 2000   84, MAR 2000 (84)
(100% CH)
Greenish color, with completely ripe—if not overripe—aromas. Toasted and fine, with a somewhat one-dimensional taste.

LAUNOIS, LEON R-M
3, ruelle de L'Arquebuse
51190 Le Mesnil-sur-Oger
03 26 57 50 28
Production: 100,000
Launois controls eighteen hectares of first-class vineyards in Le Mesnil, and claims in all seriousness that all wines in Le Mesnil taste the same—it seems a miracle that they make such good Champagne! Other wines: Rosé, Cuvée Perlée.

- LEON LAUNOIS BLANC DE BLANCS   75
(100% CH)
- 1992 LEON LAUNOIS   70, FEB 1997 (73)
(100% CH)
- 1978 LEON LAUNOIS   89, SEP 2003 (89)
(100% CH)
Probably nothing special in a regular bottle, but with the slow development of Mesnil in magnums stored in a cellar, this wine is excellent. The color is deep with splashes of red. Despite the developed color, the mousse is perfect and the nose exudes class. There are notes of tea, orchids, browned butter, and tobacco. The taste is fresh but there is the addition of a layer of dried fruit as well as aromas of the combined bouquet of old warm wood and the metallic, almost rusty notes of railway tracks.

- 1989 LEON LAUNOIS CUVÉE PRESTIGE   82, APR 1995 (90)
(100% CH)
Slightly closed in the nose, but with pure Le Mesnil tones in the flavor. Dry and fine, and very promising.

LAURAIN, PIERRE**** R-M
2, rue Roger Sondag
51160 Aÿ
03 26 55 18 90
Production: 60,000
After having sold Collery to Germain, Alain Collery continued under the name of Pierre Laurain. Today he has a wine museum and a popular restaurant in the middle of town, while at the same time he takes good care of his exceptional properties in Aÿ and Mareuil-sur-Aÿ. When Collery was sold, he kept a store of older vintages in order to be able to sell fully mature wines to us Collery fans.

- COLLERY BRUT   67
(70% PN, 20% PM, 10% CH)
- PIERRE LAURAIN BRUT   69
(70% PN, 20% PM, 10% CH)
- COLLERY BLANC DE BLANCS   66
(100% CH)
- PIERRE LAURAIN DEMI-SEC   52
(100% PN)

- COLLERY ROSÉ   88
(100% PN)
The same wine as Pierre Laurain Rosé.

- PIERRE LAURAIN ROSÉ   89
(100% PN)
(Previously Collery Rosé.) One of the best rosé Champagnes in existence. Aÿ Pinot gives the most Burgundy-like aromas in all of Champagne, and no rosé Champagne shows this more clearly. The color is dark and clear, the nose screams out Pinot aromas, with all the gamy notes, cheeses, spices, and strawberry-like fruit aromas that one would expect. The flavor is compact, with a deep, juicy, Pinot aroma and exquisite length.

- 1989 PIERRE LAURAIN   70, MAR 1993 (84)
(20% PN, 80% CH)
A slightly strange wine, which was hard to judge when young. A strong, rank bouquet of mushrooms and boiled vegetables. A sharp attack with highly concentrated vegetable power. Not a wine for beginners.

- 1985 PIERRE LAURAIN   91, OCT 1997 (94)
(100% PN)
(Previously Solange Collery.) A pure Aÿ Blanc de Noirs, with a good deal of bottle variation. Some are full of vegetables, while others have a roasted nose and an astonishingly young flavor. The greatest wines are dominated by leather, mushroom, truffles, and hazelnut.

- 1981 PIERRE LAURAIN   96, SEP 2002 (96)
(90% PN, 10% CH)
A Champagne made in the Bollinger style, with smoky complexity, a full nutty aroma, and vigorous fruit. Perfect with fowl and game. Has developed into a grandiose, magically truffle-scented masterpiece.

- 1985 SOLANGE COLLERY   91, JUN 1995 (94)
(100% PN)
The same wine as 1985 Pierre Laurain.

- 1981 COLLERY HERBILLON   92, AUG 1997 (92)
(90% PN, 10% CH)
The same wine as 1981 Pierre Laurain.

- 1980 COLLERY HERBILLON   90, APR 1993 (90)
(100% PN)
Not as restrained and massive as the '81, but with a seductive nose of honey and chocolate. The flavor is medium bodied with a creamy finish.

- 1976 COLLERY SPECIAL CLUB   93, OCT 1995 (93)
(100% PN)
Fleshy and awesome in its volume. Marvelous with rabbit in rosemary-flavored gravy.

- 1973 COLLERY HERBILLON   90, SEP 1988 (90)
(90% PN, 10% CH)
Drunk when I was a beginner in this field, but it will be a while before I forget the incredible power or the velvety aftertaste of licorice.

- 1971 COLLERY SPECIAL CLUB   90, APR 2000 (90)
(100% PN)
Incredibly light color and an astounding elegance. Tentative bouquet initially before the creamy softness makes its entrance. Harmoniously beautiful and expressive wine that today must be considered a rarity.

LAURENT-PERRIER **** N-M
32, avenue de Champagne
51150 Tours-sur-Marne
03 26 58 91 22
Production: 6,500,000

Laurent-Perrier is the biggest success story since World War II. The family firm was on the verge of going under in the early 1950s, but is now among the largest and most respected companies in all of Champagne. The house was founded by Monsieur Laurent, a cooper from Chigny-les-Roses. His son married Mathilde Perrier, a stubbornly ambitious woman who really established the house. World War I strained to the limit the house's chances of survival, as several of the appointed heirs were killed. Marie-Louise de Nonancourt bought the firm just as World War II broke out, and her son, whom she had groomed to run the company, was killed in that war. Her other son, Bernard, survived despite playing a leading role in the Resistance, and later returned home to take over the business.

     This genius of a businessman, Bernard de Nonancourt, set out to capture new export markets. He began in West Africa, supplying his agents with fresh, recently disgorged Champagne that could cope with the tropical heat. Back home he specialized in *coteaux champenois*, producing more still white wine than anyone else in Champagne. Today, Laurent-Perrier is part of a holding company that controls several other famous wine-producers in France, including the Champagne houses Salon, Delamotte, Lemoine, and De Castellane. Laurent-Perrier themselves own only 100 hectares but have contracts with growers covering around 800 hectares. The firm is known for its clinically clean plants, where oxidation is avoided at all costs.

     Alain Terrier, the company's head enologist, is a man widely praised for his fruity and elegant *cuvées*. The nonvintage is finally beginning to lose its note of children's glue; the rosé Ultra Brut and the vintage wine are all faithful old servants. The house's real trump card is Grand Siècle—a wine that beautifully carpets even the most fastidious palate. A wonderfully complex, world-class Champagne.

- LAURENT-PERRIER BRUT   79
(40% PN, 15% PM, 45% CH)

- LAURENT-PERRIER CRÉMANT BRUT   59
(33% PN, 33% PM, 34% CH)

- LAURENT-PERRIER ULTRA BRUT   85
(60% PN, 40% CH)
Laurent-Perrier is a pioneer of completely dry Champagnes. The wine needs several years in the bottle to round off the slight green-appley tones and develop its chocolate bouquet. Delightful maturity at the beginning of the 2000s.

- LAURENT-PERRIER ROSÉ BRUT   78
(100% PN)

- 1995 LAURENT-PERRIER   85, MAR 2004 (89)
(50% PN, 50% CH)
I served this very good wine blind to my wife Sara—she immediately thought of almonds and children's white glue. In other words, exactly the same aromas that have previously bothered me in some of Laurent-Perrier's wines. The strange thing is, I didn't perceive this toned-down '95 as having anything of that almond taste. Instead, I think that the clinical note of newly washed sheets is clearly present, together with a young and juicy fresh fruit. Bready and balanced straight through with an aftertaste of licorice.

- 1993 LAURENT-PERRIER   85, SEP 2003 (87)
(50% PN, 50% CH)
Alain Terrier is back on track again! The lovely note of freshly laundered sheets together with a pure, acidic character of Granny Smith apples is present despite the relatively weak vintage. Truly fine winemaking.

- 1990 LAURENT-PERRIER   84, MAY 1999 (90)
(50% PN, 50% CH)
I have finally found a connection between Laurent-Perrier's vintage wine and Grand Siècle. In this wonderfully rich vintage there is an intense fruitiness backed up by an apple-fresh crispiness. The scent even shares Grand Siècle's unmistakable tone of sun-dried sheets.

- 1988 LAURENT-PERRIER   82, MAY 1999 (86)
(47% PN, 53% CH)
Laurent-Perrier produces relatively little vintage Champagne and the wine follows the house style more than the year. Often the vintage wine is like a slightly richer version of the nonvintage Champagne.

- 1985 LAURENT-PERRIER   80, NOV 1994 (87)
(50% PN, 50% CH)
The aromas follow the firm's usual pattern, but the concentration and abundance of extract are very high, which paves the way for a great future. The nose has elements of mint, apples, and cinnamon. The flavor is pleasant and harmonious.

- 1982 LAURENT-PERRIER   76, JUL 1993 (82)
(60% PN, 40% CH)
An impersonal and surprisingly thin '82. Correct but tame and a trifle toasty.

- 1981 LAURENT-PERRIER   84, JUN 1999 (84)
(75% PN, 25% CH)
Completely evolved and in perfect shape, but still hardly a Champagne to write poems about. The medium-bodied taste is a little too sweet and neutral, leaning toward Amaretto.

- 1979 LAURENT-PERRIER   89, JAN 2003 (89)
(75% PN, 25% CH)
This vintage almost never disappoints me. Laurent-Perrier's contribution isn't one of the stars that shine the brightest, but the Champagne is at its peak right now, with a lovely vintage-typical nose of nuts, honey, and honeysuckle. The flavor is toffee-like and fresh at the same time.

- 1978 LAURENT-PERRIER   83, SEP 2003 (83)
(75% PN, 25% CH)
A mighty wine with low acidity, chocolate aromas, and an excess of Amaretto flavor.

- 1976 LAURENT-PERRIER   84, JAN 1997 (>)
(75% PN, 25% CH)
Probably good if you buy the wine directly from the house. Normally disgorged bottles are a little tired, if still quite good with their spicy, vanilla taste and smooth roundness.

- 1975 LAURENT-PERRIER   89, APR 2003 (89)
(75% PN, 25% CH)
Classic structure and vigor. Good, slightly severe Champagne—but still I miss the twinkle.

- 1970 LAURENT-PERRIER   90, MAR 2004 (90)
(75% PN, 25% CH)
Only tasted in magnum, and naturally very refreshing. Light color and superbly gushing mousse. Intense, pure nose, with cool segments and intact floweriness. Richer, more substantial taste with bready notes, meatiness, warmth, and a finish reminiscent of apple cobbler.

- 1966 LAURENT-PERRIER   89, NOV 1998 (>)
(75% PN, 25% CH)
Newly poured, this oldie imparts a delightfully all-encompassing bouquet, dominated by butter toffee and buttered paper. The palate is soft, rich, and oxidative. After ten minutes in the glass the acidic influence is inexorable—the wine is dead on the spot.

- 1964 LAURENT-PERRIER   70, AUG 1995 (>)
(75% PN, 25% CH)

- 1961 LAURENT-PERRIER   86, DEC 1999 (86)
(75% PN, 25% CH)
This Champagne displays a harmonious oneness filled with chocolate, but there's a lack of freshness. The wine probably reached its peak in the early eighties.

- 1959 LAURENT-PERRIER ROSÉ   92, NOV 2001 (94)
(100% PN)
Disgorged in June 1998. Only produced as a magnum and never available on the commercial market. Incomprehensibly youthful in every aspect. I decanted the wine in a carafe as an encore after a very comprehensive vertical tasting of Clos des Goisses. The forty-year-old wine continued to bubble like raspberry soda and was very bound in the nose. Only the aftertaste had a smoky and oaky undertone that revealed a glimpse of a certain maturity. Exactly the same impression at the Millennium Tasting at Villa Pauli.

- GRAND SIÈCLE   93
(45% PN, 55% CH)
Laurent-Perrier's flagship wine is made from three vintages that, since blending, have been stored for five to six years in the firm's cellar with real corks. This luxurious Champagne was first introduced in 1957; if you have the patience, keep the wine for four or five years, so that you can experience the wonderful vanilla flavor that Grand Siècle develops with time. The mousse is worth a chapter in itself: no other Champagne has a more delicate mousse than Grand Siècle. The refined and balanced fruit aromas harmonize perfectly with each other, together with an element of newly washed sheets.

- GRAND SIÈCLE (1996/95/93)   93, MAR 2004 (96)
(45% PN, 55% CH)
Bull's eye! Alain Terrier has captured all of the distinctly acidic character of the '96s, with additional smiling charm from the pure, feminine '93, as well as the creamily beautiful '95. Exquisite harmony and balance. Handsome toasted notes, crackling aromas and mousse, refreshing attack, and a strong imprint on the palate that remains some few hours later in the glass. A big Grand Siècle!

- GRAND SIÈCLE (1993/90/88)   92, OCT 2003 (94)
(45% PN, 55% CH)
At present, this is the Grand Siècle dominating the market. For the time being it is difficult to find any special vintage character, something that takes a few years to develop. Still, this is a classic Grand Siècle with brilliant finesse, elegance, and breeding. The freshness is grand but never overbearing, the breadiness easily discernible but never dominating. The aftertaste is also impressively long, considering the youth and fleeting quality of the wine. Store a few years and welcome an even more enjoyable wine.

- GRAND SIÈCLE (1990/88/85)   93, NOV 2003 (95)
(45% PN, 55% CH)

Surely one of the finest Grand Siècles ever made. Already present is the long, soft, vanilla-dominated aftertaste. The finesse and complexity are unmistakable, even if the fruit is still quite youthful.

- GRAND SIÈCLE (1988/85/82)   90, JAN 1999 (93)
(45% PN, 55% CH)
Not really as complete as the '90-base, but still possessing a radiant vitality and lightly toasted character. More developed in the nose than in the palate. Classic, pure Grand Siècle.

- GRAND SIÈCLE (1985/82/81)   91, MAR 2003 (93)
(45% PN, 55% CH)
The first of eight wines in an unbelievable vertical tasting with Alain Terrier. All the wines were newly disgorged and completely free from dosage. They were, as well, all from magnums. This wine with 1985 as a base stood out as relatively light and youthful—distinctly toasted and elegant. Bouquet of lilies, acacia, and white roses. Some green flavors in the palate, reminiscent of asparagus. Will surely become less noticeable with bottle maturity and added sugar.

- GRAND SIÈCLE (1982/79/78)   92, OCT 2003 (92)
(45% PN, 55% CH)
A rather severe, ascetic Grand Siècle with notes of metal, fish, and mineral. After a while, a wave of vanilla and cleanliness waft over you as the wine shows its more generous side. The wine is not bestowing its broadest smile upon you, but surely you will smile if you get the chance to taste this distinctive, interesting wine.

- GRAND SIÈCLE (1979/78/76)   91, MAR 2000 (95)
(45% PN, 55% CH)
This wine changed considerably in the glass. Every time we refilled our glasses, the green, vegetal aromas came back. After half an hour in the glass, the wine acted the way a classic '79 should. I have previously noticed that pure '79s suffer without dosage, taking on a slightly anorectic appearance.

- GRAND SIÈCLE (1978/76/75)   93, MAR 2000 (93)
(45% PN, 55% CH)
This one stuck out considerably with its scent of mandarins, bird cherry tree, and fruitcake. Quite reminiscent of a 1978 Dom Pérignon. Here, the fat vintage of 1976 has succeeded in filling in all the gaps that the '78s usually have. Handsome proof of what one can achieve by blending Champagne vintages.

- GRAND SIÈCLE (1976/75/73)   96, OCT 2003 (96)
(45% PN, 55% CH)
Considerably deeper in color than earlier wines in the tasting. Wonderful, voluptuous bouquet of candied fruits and brioche. Alain Terrier's personal favorite, which is not so surprising when one considers his place of origin: Bordeaux. This is the most robust and vinous Grand Siècle ever made. I am also transported by the wine's glycerol richness and chewable, exotic taste of mango and papaya.

- GRAND SIÈCLE (1975/73/70)   96, OCT 2003 (97)
(45% PN, 55% CH)
A gargantuan wine with wonderful aromas of crème brûlée. Supple, finesse-rich essence with minimal creamy bubbles and tons of butter-toffee aroma. My favorite among these beauties, with a decided note of honeysuckle and exceptional mousse.

- GRAND SIÈCLE (1973/70/69)   93, MAR 2000 (93)
(45% PN, 55% CH)
Yet another silky-smooth, caressing wine with hints of coffee in the nose. Somewhat one-dimensional, if still a great hedonistic pleasure. The wine almost behaves like a Blanc de Blancs.

- GRAND SIÈCLE (1970/69/66)   85, MAR 2000 (85)
(45% PN, 55% CH)
A powerful Champagne with typical '70s tone; in other words, exaggerated oxidative tone and slightly clumsy fruit. The flavors are reminiscent of truffle broth, mushroom stew, licorice, and earthy soil. It seems almost impertinent to dismiss this wine as the worst Grand Siècle I have tasted, as Alain Terrier was kind enough to open this third-from-last bottle in the cellar for me.

- GRAND SIÈCLE (1955/53/52)   96, OCT 2003 (96)
(45% PN, 55% CH)
The premier edition of Grand Siècle! With 1955 as a base, it's hard to lose. The wine is truly faithful to the vintage, with a silky-smooth surface that embraces the entire experience. This is a poetic wine that conceals a great deal of beauty under its mildly elusive creaminess. Not completely unexpectedly, the wine reaches its crescendo in a colorful firework-display of coffee and lemon taste sensations.

- 1990 GRAND SIÈCLE   92, MAY 2003 (95)
(58% PN, 42% CH)
Wonderfully rich and pure, classically constructed with fantastic elegance. It contains a little extra touch of everything wonderful that's found in the nonvintage version.

- 1988 GRAND SIÈCLE   94, NOV 2003 (95)
(48% PN, 52% CH)
It seems as if Laurent-Perrier has buckled under pressure, abandoning the firm's conviction about the superiority of nonvintage wines. The isolated case of the 1985 Grand Siècle was immediately followed by the '88. This is a sumptuous, aristocratic Champagne, which does, however, need storing for a few years in order to do it justice. More Pinot weight than in the *cuvée*. Fantastically rich and toasted at the end of 2003.

- 1985 GRAND SIÈCLE   92, JUN 2003 (94)
(58% PN, 42% CH)
On the American market, Grand Siècle is always a vintage Champagne, and in Europe this '85 is the first example. The wine is very much like the nonvintage version, with flowers and vanilla as its leading notes. However, there is a greater weight in the '85 that bodes well for the future.

- 1976 LAURENT-PERRIER MILLÉSIMÉ RARE   94, APR 2000 (95)
(100% CH)
Only made in magnum and not to be confused with the pinot-dominated and simpler Champagne of the same name in a regular bottle. Brilliant at The Millennium Tasting at Villa Pauli. Somewhat more human on a few later occasions. Deliciously discreet toasted and fruity elegance, with Grand Siècles elusive bouquet of newly washed linen, dried in the sun and wind.

- 1976 LAURENT-PERRIER MILLÉSIMÉ RARE   92, JAN 1999 (92)
(75% PN, 25% CH)
As the Rare wines are always disgorged after a very long time, they have grown in complexity. The autolytic character really helps this '76. The bread aromas from the yeast smooth out the almond tones in a positive fashion.

- 1975 LAURENT-PERRIER MILLÉSIMÉ RARE   86, DEC 1992 (89)
(75% PN, 25% CH)
Just as with so many '75s, the nose is more developed than the palate. Light chocolate dominates the voluptuous bouquet. The excellent attack in the initial taste is of the highest class, but the wine needed a few more years before it developed length in the aftertaste.

- 1973 LAURENT-PERRIER MILLÉSIMÉ RARE   89, MAR 2000 (89)
(75% PN, 25% CH)
The nose is very similar to the '75, with milk chocolate playing the leading role. The flavor is softer and more homogeneous. Smoke and earth cellar give character to the sweet, soft whole.
- 1969 LAURENT-PERRIER MILLÉSIMÉ RARE   85, AUG 1993 (>)
(75% PN, 25% CH)
Sadly it's already going downhill! Toward the end of the 1980s I gave this wine very high marks, but a couple of years ago maderization began to creep in.
- 1966 LAURENT-PERRIER MILLÉSIMÉ RARE
(75% PN, 25% CH)
- 1959 GRAND SIÈCLE
(50% PN, 50% CH)
- 1959 LAURENT-PERRIER MILLÉSIMÉ RARE
(75% PN, 25% CH)
- 1990 GRAND SIÈCLE ALEXANDRA ROSÉ   85, MAY 2001 (89)
(80% PN, 20% CH)
I just hope that it is only the Swedish market that has suffered the cork problem so prevalent here. I have, together with the wine importer Vinunic, opened a dozen bottles where almost every other bottle was corked. When everything is as it should be, you usually find a quiet spectrum of pure aromas spiced with a light note of currants. For the time being I definitely prefer the white version of Grand Siècle.
- 1988 GRAND SIÈCLE ALEXANDRA ROSÉ   85, APR 2001 (86)
(80% PN, 20% CH)
A much too bony prestige wine at much too high a price. The fruit is fine but slightly weak. Instead, the wine is dominated by sea scents such as seaweed, sea breezes, oyster shells, and fishy Pinot Noir. Fine, dry mineral tone.
- 1985 GRAND SIÈCLE ALEXANDRA ROSÉ   90, OCT 1997 (92)
(80% PN, 20% CH)
A lovely orangey-fruity and toasty rosé Champagne, which would grace the finest dinner tables. The color is appetizingly light and the flavor delightfully sophisticated. This elegant Champagne is very like its white sister.
- 1982 GRAND SIÈCLE ALEXANDRA ROSÉ   88, MAY 2003 (89)
(80% PN, 20% CH)
An extremely elegant and delicate prestige rosé that does, however, lack impact and weight at its base. The wine feels so shy that one wonders if whether this flower bud will ever burst open into full bloom.
- LAURENT-PERRIER SILVER JUBILÉE 1977   86, NOV 2001 (86)
(75% PN, 25% CH)
As did many other big houses, Laurent-Perrier introduced a special *cuvée* for Queen Elizabeth II in 1977, to commemorate her twenty-five years on the British throne. The wine is, of course, from previous '70s vintages. Fine appearance and mousse. Individual bouquet of windfall fruit and cherry stones, akin to certain Italian red wines. Mature and slightly mushy, but still full-bodied flavor of ripe apples and almond.
- 1990 GRAND SIÈCLE LUMIERE DU MILLÉNAIRE   92, MAY 2001 (95)
(58% PN, 42% CH)
The same wine as 1990 Grand Siècle, but luxuriously packaged for the Millennium. The price tag is automatically heavily inflated.
- 1975 LAURENT-PERRIER WEDDING CUVÉE BLANC DE BLANCS
(100% CH)   94, MAY 1997 (94)

Laurent-Perrier joined Veuve Clicquot in making a special *cuvée* for the wedding of Prince Charles and Lady Diana Spencer in Britain in 1981. The nose, full of clean sheets and a polished, big-house-style, is clear if a touch shy. The flavor is a firework-display of fruit, with a delayed action in the mouth. Fantastic!

LAURENTI PÈRE & FILS R-M
rue de la Contrescarpe
10340 Les Riceys
03 25 29 32 32
Production: 100,000
This family firm is now run by Dominique and Bruno Laurenti. The fourteen hectares they control are planted with 90 percent Pinot Noir and 10 percent Chardonnay. Other wines: Grande Cuvée.
- LAURENTI ROSÉ   60
(100% PN)

LE BRUN DE NEUVILLE C-M
route de Chantemerle
51260 Bethon
03 26 80 48 43
Production: 400,000
In 1963 the cooperative "La Crayère" was formed, and changed to its present name ten years later. Most of the firm's Champagnes are dominated almost completely by Chardonnay.
- LE BRUN DE NEUVILLE SÉLECTION   65
(30% PN, 70% CH)
- LE BRUN DE NEUVILLE BLANC DE BLANCS   52
(100% CH)
- LE BRUN DE NEUVILLE ROSÉ   52
(20% PN, 80% CH)
- 1995 LE BRUN DE NEUVILLE   85, NOV 2003 (85)
(100% CH)
Considering the low points received by the '88, the wine was shockingly good! We're dealing with a luxuriant beauty full of buttery richness and Burgundy-like merits. Actually, it's unusual to encounter such a syrupy, fat Champagne that hasn't become unbalanced. Both the nose and the palate exude sensual pleasure!
- 1988 LE BRUN DE NEUVILLE   48, MAY 1996 (48)
(8% PN, 92% CH)
- CUVÉE DU ROI CLOVIS   83
(50% PN, 50% CH)
The firm's *cuvée de prestige* is their best wine, as indeed it should be. A multi-vintage wine with delightfully mature Chardonnay fruit and roundness. Not to be stored.
- LEBRUN DE NEUVILLE LADY DE N   81
(100% CH)
An agreeable Champagne that still doesn't come up to the level of the usual vintage wine's class, despite the prestige label. Concentrated and focused with a somewhat tempered nose. Fine structure, but neutral spectrum of aromas.

LEBIS, A. R-M
11, rue Jean Baptiste Morizet
51190 Le Mesnil-sur-Oger
- A. LEBIS BLANC DE BLANCS   50
(100% CH)

LECLAIRE-GASPARD R-M

51190 Avize
03 26 52 88 65
Production: 20,000

The grower has more than three hectares in Avize and Cramant and the same amount in the Marne Valley. Only Chardonnay is used in their *cuvées*, and the black grapes are sold to the big Champagne houses. The vines average the advanced age of thirty years. Modern vinification.

• LECLAIRE-GASPARD GRANDE RÉSERVE   70
  (100% CH)

LECLAIRE, ERNEST ALFRED R-M

24, rue Pasteur
51190 Avize
03 26 52 88 65
Production: 30,000

The wine I tasted was specially made for the Millennium. The grower only makes vintage Champagnes from Chardonnay. Ernest Alfred Leclaire founded the company in 1878, and today it is run by Reynald Leclaire-Thiefaine. They have six hectares of property.

• ERNEST ALFRED LECLAIRE MIS EN CAVE 1974   46, JUN 2001 (46)
  (100% CH)

LECLERC-BRIANT **** N-M

67, rue Chaude-Ruelle
51204 Épernay
03 26 54 45 33
Production: 250,000

Lucien Leclerc made his first bottles of Champagne in 1872, and since 1978 the grandson, Pascal Leclerc-Briant, has been at the tiller, overseeing thirty hectares of classic property. They have vineyards in six villages, of which Cumières produces the majority of the grapes. It's in Cumières that Leclerc-Briant make three fantastic Clos wines in a series called "Les Authentiques." Better examples of the importance of the soil are hard to find, and the laughably low prices don't hurt either. All three—Les Crayères, Chèvres Pierreuses, and Clos des Champions—are among the best nonvintage wines Champagne has to offer. Pascal Leclerc, one of the region's most innovative winemakers, grows his crop biodynamically and is a leading light in teaching visitors about Champagne's unique conditions. In summary, Leclerc-Briant is a pioneering house with extremely interesting wines of a complex, expressive nature.

• LECLERC-BRIANT BRUT RESÉRVE   74
  (70% PN, 30% CH)
• LECLERC-BRIANT EXTRA BRUT   69
  (70% PN, 30% PM)
• LECLERC-BRIANT CHÈVRES PIERREUSES   86
  (55% PN, 5% PM, 40% CH)
  The tiny 5 percent Pinot Meunier comes from some of the oldest vines I've seen in Champagne—around 100 years old! This is my favorite of the three wines. The nose is a masterpiece, where goat cheese, minerals, and yellow roses compete for the upper hand. It has a perfect balance in the mouth with its appetizing acidity, lime and lemon tones, and long taste of honey.
• LECLERC-BRIANT CLOS DES CHAMPIONS   85
  (70% PN, 30% CH)
  This is one of three Clos wines in the fantastic Les Authentiques series. The wines are sold together at a ridiculously low price. All

three are harvested from old vines, with an average age of thirty. Clos des Champions is a walled-in area with an extremely warm microclimate. This wine is the richest of the three, with a sensual nose full of white flowers and exotic fruit. A good initial attack and citrus tones. Long, fat aftertaste of mature Pinot.

• LECLERC-BRIANT LES CRAYÈRES   83
  (90% PN, 10% PM)
  With this wine you fully realize the soil's importance. This plot has received its name from the mineral-rich chalky earth. If the truth be told, the wine exhibits the same aromas as a Blanc de Blancs from the Côte des Blancs, despite being a Blanc de Noirs! The wine is the lightest of the three, the nose cold, fresh, and floral with a large portion of lime aroma. The taste continues along in the same discreet vein. When aired and warmed up, the character of the blue grapes becomes more pronounced. This is the aperitif of the Les Authentiques trilogy.
• LECLERC-BRIANT BLANC DE BLANCS   79
  (100% CH)
• LECLERC-BRIANT BLANC DE NOIRS   69
  (70% PN, 30% PM)
• LECLERC-BRIANT DEMI-SEC   55
  (70% PN, 30% PM)
• 1978 LECLERC-BRIANT BRUT ZERO   92, APR 2003 (92)
  (75% PN, 25% CH)
  Fantastic nose and palate of tea, bergamot, mint, garden cress, tar, smoke, sauna, marigolds, and smoked meat. Tobacco is the keynote in the stick-dry finish. A fascinating, substantial wine.
• 1973 LECLERC-BRIANT   84, FEB 2003 (84)
  (75% PN, 25% CH)
  A bottle that I received from Pascal Leclerc, so I know had been perfectly stored. Still, the wine was rapidly going downhill— almost completely devoid of mousse and with a muddy, sherry-drenched nose. The taste was a decidedly more pleasant experience, with notes of cigar, iron, and just overripe strawberries, as well as an impressive fleshiness.
• 1995 LECLERC-BRIANT RUBIS DE NOIRS ROSÉ   83, JAN 2001 (88)
  (100% PN)
  Very young, dark, and focused. Unbalanced for the time being because the tannin needs to be softened around the edges. Store!
• 1990 LECLERC-BRIANT RUBIS DE NOIRS ROSÉ   83, MAY 1999 (89)
  (100% PN)
  Pascal Leclerc received a warning saying that this would be the last time he would be allowed to sell such a red and tannic rosé Champagne. Enormously powerful, with a red-wine-like structure. Fantastically exciting culinary Champagne, which is, presumably, something that should be hidden deep inside the cellar's deepest cranny. As near to a sparkling red wine as one can come.
• 1989 LECLERC-BRIANT RUBIS DE NOIRS ROSÉ   82, JUL 2001 (83)
  (100% PN)
  Juicy, focused, sophisticated, and tasty, but lacking any meaningful potential. Buttery finish.
• 1996 LECLERC-BRIANT DIVINE   85, APR 2003 (89)
  (50% PN, 50% CH)
  Big and muscular, like a purebred horse full of energy and evident authority. Powerful nose with gamy elements under the sweet, ripe-strawberry tone. Fleshy, round, and sturdy wine that demands food of a substantial nature.
• 1995 LECLERC-BRIANT DIVINE   84, NOV 2003 (86)
  (50% PN, 50% CH)

Somewhat more appley and rounder than usual, without that extra richness. Delicious and inoffensive, with a weak honey note and a sweet fruitiness reminiscent of juicy red apples and sugary plums.

- 1990 LECLERC-BRIANT CUVÉE DU SOLSTICE   87, AUG 2001 (93)
  (50% PN, 50% CH)
  A honey-drenched and powerful '90 with a distinct impression of Pinot Noir. There is great depth here and lots of extract, which will most likely impart notes of gunpowder smoke and meat. Actually, this is the same wine as Divine, but is sold together with a Millennium wristwatch and is therefore horribly expensive in comparison to the '89.
- 1990 LECLERC-BRIANT DIVINE   88, NOV 2001 (93)
  (50% PN, 50% CH)
  The same wine as Cuvée du Solstice for a much better price.
- 1989 LECLERC-BRIANT DIVINE   88, JAN 2000 (93)
  (50% PN, 50% CH)
  A gigantically scrumptious and super-fresh '89 with a beautiful citrus spectrum blended with an aroma of raspberries from first-class Pinot Noir grapes. Fresh and soft with considerable length. Explicit aroma of passion fruit.
- 1988 LECLERC-BRIANT CUVÉE CLOVIS   87, JAN 2001 (93)
  (75% PN, 25% CH)
  A very dense wine, strongly marked by high-class Chardonnay. Focused and young-tasting, bearing notes of white currants, butter pears, and butter toffee. Astonishing length. For the time being lacking toasted notes.
- 1988 LECLERC-BRIANT DIVINE   87, MAY 2001 (89)
  (50% PN, 50% CH)
  Perhaps not as close to the gods as the name suggests, but very rich and enjoyable with a lovely Pinot structure and substantial fruity nose, where plum and sweet red licorice-sticks are present. The color is deep and suggests a greater content of Pinot than is actually the case.
- 1985 LECLERC-BRIANT CUVÉE LIBERTÉ   87, MAY 1999 (93)
  (75% PN, 25% CH)
  A wonderful series of vintages of Cumières-based Champagne, only produced in magnum bottles for different jubilees. The '85 is, of course, still too young but very promising. The scent is reminiscent of boiled mutton and has certain similarities to Ramonets's white Burgundies of the same vintage. The young taste is focused and developable.
- 1982 LECLERC-BRIANT CUVÉE LIBERTÉ   94, JUN 1999 (94)
  (75% PN, 25% CH)
  One week I tasted an undeveloped and promising magnum. Imagine my surprise when, the following weekend, I drank a similar magnum which was the pure essence of coffee aroma. That is—or will become—a fantastic roasted and rich Champagne. If you should be lucky enough to run across this wine you would be well advised to let it mature for a few years to be on the safe side.
- 1981 LECLERC-BRIANT CUVÉE LIBERTÉ   90, JUN 1999 (93)
  (75% PN, 25% CH)
  More classic than the '80 and lighter than the '82. Strong characteristics of a first-class, elegant Pinot Noir with smoky complexity.
- 1980 LECLERC-BRIANT CUVÉE LIBERTÉ   90, JUN 1999 (92)
  (75% PN, 25% CH)
  Vigorous and bubbling, with an aroma of fruity sweets and a personal, exotic, refreshing style.

LEFÈVRE, JEAN R-M
26, rue du Général de Gaulle
51150 Bouzy
03 26 57 06 58
Production: 60,000

- JEAN LEFÈVRE BRUT   60
  (80% PN, 20% CH)

LEFÈVRE-CHAUFFERT R-M
51400 Sept-Saulx
Once a firm of good repute that no longer exists.

- 1973 LEFÈVRE-CHAUFFERT   87, AUG 1995 (87)
  This producer was an unknown entity for me when I was confronted with this well-kept '73. The nose was closed with a gamy touch. The flavor is polished and stylish, with an undertone of vanilla.

LEFÈVRE, ETIENNE R-M
rue de Verzenay
51380 Verzy
03 26 97 96 99
Production: 30,000

A spur-of-the-moment visit took me to the door of this skillful winemaker in Verzy. He sells well-made, mature Champagnes at low prices, and if you follow the "Champagne Route," it's easy to pop in and enjoy a tasting and an uplifting chat with the Lefèvre family.

- E. LEFÈVRE BRUT   67
  (80% PN, 20% CH)
- E. LEFÈVRE RÉSERVE   71
  (80% PN, 20% CH)
- E. LEFÈVRE DEMI-SEC   46
  (80% PN, 20% CH)
- E. LEFÈVRE ROSÉ   70
  (90% PN, 10% CH)
- 1985 E. LEFÈVRE   75, JUL 1992 (85)
  (80% PN, 20% CH)
  Lefèvre makes vintage wines only in very good years, with equal amounts of Verzy and Verzenay. The nose is a bit basic, with a splash of caramel in the musty apple aroma. The flavor is far more fascinating and homogeneous, with an oily structure and the aroma of pistachio nuts.

LÉGLAPART, DAVID **** R-M
10, rue de la Mairie
51380 Trépail
03 26 57 07 01
Production: 8,000

David Léglapart is a biodynamic artist who works according to the Selosse Method. His bone-dry, refreshing wines have a bite and sting like few others. The wines are stored in oak barrels for fifteen months and are never filtered. The prestige *cuvées* come from secluded plots in Trépail that were planted by David's grandfather in 1946. It's going to be very interesting to follow David's journey to the top.

- 2000 DAVID LÉGLAPART ARTISTE   85, JUN 2003 (90)
  (100% CH)
  Brilliant vinification and Selosse influence. Very refreshing and young, with stylish, deep complexity straight through. Not too

dreadfully oaky. What will happen if we leave these rare wines in a forgotten corner of the cellar for a few years?

- 2000 DAVID LÉGLAPART L'APÔTRE   85, JUN 2003 (91)
(100% CH)

An un-dosaged wine from old vines. It feels less evolved, drier, slightly more metallic, and purer than Artiste—strangely enough. Old vines usually give a sweeter and rounder impression. Store and see.

LEGRAS & HAAS **** N-M

9, Grande Rue
51530 Chouilly
03 26 54 92 90
Production: 40,000

François Legras is the former winemaker at R. & L. Legras; he has broken away and started his own house with his German wife Brigitte, née Haas. Together with their sons Rémi and Olivier, they work more than fourteen hectares in Chouilly. They actually produce up to 400,000 bottles for the big Champagne houses. Even if they don't want to compare themselves to their famous neighbors of the same name, the similarities are striking. The style is very clean, with crystal-clear acidity and elegant fruit. A small house to keep your eye on in the future.

- LEGRAS & HAAS TRADITION   67
(30% PN, 10% PM, 60% CH)
- LEGRAS & HAAS BLANC DE BLANCS   79
(100% CH)
- LEGRAS & HAAS ROSÉ   55
(100% PN)
- 1996 LEGRAS & HAAS   87, JAN 2004 (89)
(100% CH)

A big, juicy, and rather unexpectedly evolved '96, with clear influences from the big houses. Slightly toasted undertone and a soft, bready style, with juicy toffee notes and a rich pineappley fruitiness. Rather fleshy and mature now.

- 1995 LEGRAS & HAAS   84, JUN 2001 (91)
(100% CH)

Same purity as nonvintage Blanc de Blancs. Now with a developed almondy note in the mid-palate. Delightful, with so much stringency and mineral presence.

- 1996 LEGRAS & HAAS CUVÉE 2000   84, MAR 2000 (94)
(30% PN, 70% CH)

Seventy-year-old vines, 2,000 bottles. Recognize the concept? Pinot from Aÿ and Chardonnay from Chouilly. Such exceptional blended Champagnes from small producers is extremely unusual. Here, Legras & Haas has succeeded in making a fantastic wine reminiscent of a prematurely released La Grande Dame. Fantastic mousse. Bound and fabulously delicate bouquet of a springtime garden's every flower. Slightly prickly malic acidic tone for the time being. For the lucky few who succeeded in acquiring one of these sweet bottles, wait until 2010 to drink it.

LEGRAS, R. & L. **** N-M

10, rue des Partelaines
51530 Chouilly
03 26 54 50 79
Production: 250,000

House status was achieved in 1973. This impeccably run firm now owns twenty-one hectares in Chouilly's finest vineyards. Monsieur Barbier, who is a big man in more ways than one, runs his company with a successful mixture of modern and traditional vinification methods. Even though the wines go through malolactic fermentation, they retain a very high degree of life-giving acidity for decades. Legras is the house Champagne at many of France's three-star restaurants, and must be counted among the top producers in all of Champagne.

- LEGRAS BLANC DE BLANCS   83
(100% CH)

One of the very best nonvintage Champagnes! The nose is an olfactory pleasure of the highest class. The stringency and purity are striking, as are the crisp aromas of Granny Smith apples. The flavor is fresh and clear as a mountain stream, and is dominated by citrus and minerals. The long aftertaste puts many a vintage Champagne in the shade.

- 1995 LEGRAS PRÉSIDENCE   86, SEP 2003 (90)
(100% CH)

Floral, elegant nose. Fine mineral character, creamy palate, and brilliant purity. Drink with thoughtful care!

- 1992 LEGRAS PRÉSIDENCE   84, SEP 2002 (87)
(100% CH)

Unexpectedly full bodied and rustic, full of ripe fruit. Naturally backed up by buoyant acidity.

- 1990 LEGRAS PRÉSIDENCE   91, JUN 2003 (93)
(100% CH)

Interestingly meaty—beef-stew-like—with notes of iodine. Pungently fresh Burgundy-like flavor, with impressive concentration and brilliant acidity.

- 1989 LEGRAS PRÉSIDENCE   90, MAR 2000 (92)
(100% CH)

The company style surfaces here in all its glory. Few match its restraint and elegance, both of which are supported by a sun-ripe richness from the vintage.

- 1985 LEGRAS PRÉSIDENCE   86, APR 1992 (93)
(100% CH)

Much lighter than the '89, but with a greater wealth of nuances. Extremely light in color, with glowing shades of green. A faint buttery nose with layers of flower aromas. Feminine, delicate, and harmonious flavor with a faint element of hazelnuts; this will only grow with time.

- 1979 LEGRAS PRÉSIDENCE   92, AUG 1996 (92)
(100% CH)

Lovely toasted nose. Creamy and refreshingly balanced, like all good Chardonnay.

- 1990 CUVÉE ST VINCENT   86, JUL 2001 (90)
(100% CH)

A lovely young, vigorous, citrus nose, fresh and attractive with plenty of potential. Feels a tad too thin and short to be something truly great.

- 1988 CUVÉE ST VINCENT   92, NOV 2003 (94)
(100% CH)

Tremendously elegant and sophisticated, with superb creaminess and smooth acidity. Feminine and graceful. Can still be stored for a long time.

DIEBOLT-VALLOIS
1953

LAURENT-PERRIER GRAND SIÈCLE
1990

LAURENT-PERRIER ROSÉ BRUT
1959

GUY CHARLEMANGNE MESNILLÉSIME
1990

LOUIS ROEDERER BRUT
1928

LOUIS ROEDERER BRUT
1949

LOUIS ROEDERER CRISTAL
1964

LOUIS ROEDERER CRISTAL ROSÉ
1988

POL ROGER BLANCS DE CHARDONNAY
1959

P.R.
1988

POL ROGER BRUT
1914

POL ROGER GRAUVES
1928

KRUG CLOS DU MESNIL
1979

KRUG
1982

KRUG COLLECTION
1928

KRUG COLLECTION
1966

HEIDSIECK DIAMANT BLEU
1964

CHARLES HEIDSIECK
1949

CHARLES HEIDSIECK ROYAL
1966

CHARLES HEIDSIECK CHARLIE
1979

PHILIPPONNAT CLOS DES GOISSES
1955

JACQUES SELOSSE GRAND CRU
1986

VEUVE CLICQUOT GRANDE DAME
1988

TAITTINGER COMTES DE CHAMPAGNE
1976

• 1983 CUVÉE ST VINCENT   92, JAN 2003 (92)
(100% CH)

In certain years the grapes from the very oldest vines in the
village are separated for this *cuvée de prestige*. The '83 has a
mature green color, a broad, complex nose, and a honey-scented
and long flavor.

• 1975 CUVÉE ST VINCENT   92, JUL 1997 (92)
(100% CH)

This wine really reminds me of Salon, with its classic bouquet of
walnuts and steely taste.

• 1969 CUVÉE ST VINCENT   95, JUN 1998 (95)
(100% CH)

There's always something special about normally disgorged
Champagnes that are stored in the producer's cellar. During a visit
to the firm at Easter 1992, Monsieur Barbier chose this expensive,
oak-fermented specimen from his cellar. The color was a fierce
gold, and the mousse was sparse but consistent. The nose was
wonderful, with its Salon-like aroma of walnut. There was also an
exotic element that verged on petroleum and sensual perfume.
Another layer of aromas appeared to be smoky, oaky, and tar-
scented. The freshness and length were seriously impressive.

• 1959 CUVÉE ST VINCENT   96, JUN 1998 (96)
(100% CH)

Delighted by my correct analysis of his '69, Monsieur Barbier
sent a runner off to fetch something even older. Nineteen fifty-
nine is a legendary vintage that was strongly influenced by a very
warm summer. The elegance and freshness weren't so tangible as
in the '69, but the power and weight were magnificent. Nor does
top-class Chardonnay ever feel clumsy. Legras's example exhibited
a remarkably broad, aromatic spectrum, with clearly definable
tones of chocolate, nuts, vanilla, coffee, and honeysuckle.

LEHERLE, RAYMOND C-M

3, rue des Marais de St-Gond
51130 Vert-Toulon
03 26 52 26 94
Production: 100,000

The firm's wines are made partially by the village cooperative:
hence the low prices. Leherle also sells grapes to Moët and
Clicquot. Similarities with the semi-sweet "Yellow Widow" can't be
missed.

• RAYMOND LEHERLE BRUT   66
(34% PN, 33% PM, 33% CH)

• RAYMOND LEHERLE ROSÉ   67
(34% PN, 33% PM, 33% CH)

LEMAIRE, R. C. R-M

57, rue Glacière
51700 Villers-sous-Châtillon
03 26 58 30 18
Production: 66,000

A family property founded in 1945 by Roger Constant Lemaire;
today it is run by his son-in-law, Gilles. The domain comprises ten
hectares in Cumières, Reuil, Binson-Orquigny, Leuvrigny, and
Hautvillers.

• LEMAIRE ROSÉ   45
(50% PN, 50% PM)

I'm almost happy that for once I can give a rating of under fifty
points. It proves that my senses haven't been deadened by all the

American assessments that place mediocre wines around the
ninety-point level. The wine is actually quite dismal and would
have difficulty holding its own against many sparkling wines
outside of Champagne. The entire structure is messy and there is
clear bitterness despite a rather distinct fruit.

LENIQUE, MICHEL R-M

20, rue du Général de Gaulle
51530 Pierry
03 26 54 03 65
Production: 70,000

Michel Lenique is a business-minded grower that was very active
around the Millennium. He has become very popular by selling
vines to private buyers, who later get Champagne produced from
their own vines. In other words, this is an attempt to push the
primeur concept even further. The company has been a family
concern since its founding in 1768. The vineyards are planted with
5.4 hectares of Chardonnay, three hectares of Pinot Meunier and
only 0.5 hectares of Pinot Noir.

• MICHEL LENIQUE SÉLECTION   70
(5% PN, 45% PM, 50% CH)

• MICHEL LENIQUE BLANC DE BLANCS   72
(100% CH)

LENOBLE, A. R. *** N-M

35, rue Paul Douce
51480 Damery
03 26 58 42 60
Production: 300,000

Lenoble was started in 1920 by Armand-Raphaël Graser, but the
house was destroyed in the World War I. Leon de Tassigny from
Jacquesson fixed up some buildings in Damery for his friend
Armand-Raphaël. Today the firm is run by Jean-Marie Malassagne,
who controls eighteen hectares in Chouilly and Bisseuil. Fifty
percent of their grapes are bought in. The amount of oak barrels
used is increasing every year.

• LENOBLE RÉSERVE   45
(33% PN, 33% PM, 34% CH)

• LENOBLE BLANC DE BLANCS   60
(100% CH)

• LENOBLE ROSÉ   54
(15% PN, 85% CH)

• 1995 LENOBLE   80, FEB 2002 (85)
(60% PN, 40% CH)

Young and promising, with crispy acidity and a distinct character
of elegant Chardonnay. The toasted and bready notes will have to
wait a bit longer. Fine purity and balance.

• 1992 LENOBLE   85, FEB 2002 (85)
(60% PN, 40% CH)

What a delicious wine! Handsomely toasted, impressively bready
and round, with a good concentration of tastes and rich fruit.
Polished and incredibly drinkable.

• 1990 LENOBLE   75, SEP 1998 (82)
(60% PN, 40% CH)

Packed with rustic fruit that will keep this Champagne vibrant
for at least a couple of decades to come. A bit blunt and edgy at
this point.

• 1988 LENOBLE   67, AUG 1995 (80)
(60% PN, 40% CH)

When Champagne bursts with life and vigor like this '88, you expect young, flowery aromas. Here it is accompanied instead by the restrained, acidic flavor of a sweaty, slightly moldy touch.

- **1979 LENOBLE**   90, OCT 2002 (90)
(60% PN, 40% CH)

I succeeded in getting the last magnum of this sensational wine at the restaurant Le Chardonnay in Reims. I imagine the wine is less impressive in a regular bottle. In magnum the color is very light. The nose is a lot like a 1964 Moët & Chandon in magnum, with its seductive notes of nougat, coffee, and kiwi. Refreshing taste, with a hint of exotic fruit, peach peel, and slightly undeveloped chalky notes. The aftertaste is austere and a touch bitter, with a clear note of ruby grapefruit.

- **1995 LENOBLE BLANC DE BLANCS**   84, OCT 2003 (88)
(100% CH)

Extremely delicious Champagne with a distinct gamy nose and a wild whiff of the sea together with burned, toasted elements. Stony and chalky palate, with enough fruity sweetness to avoid being mean and ascetic. An idiosyncratic, connoisseur's wine of a very high standard.

- **1992 LENOBLE BLANC DE NOIRS**   80, SEP 2002 (83)
(100% PN)

Pure Pinot Noir from Bisseuil. A harmonious wine with fine focused fruitiness leaning toward plum. When aired, the Champagne is more sea-splashed and licorice-influenced. The structure is faultless and the future looks bright. Nice fruity ripeness this early on.

- **1998 LENOBLE BLANC DE NOIRS**   79, FEB 2004 (83)
(100% PN)

Rather austere and full of mineral. At the same time there is a hint of the vintage's floweriness, together with plum and apple-peel notes. Deep color tending toward terracotta, and fine mousse. Slightly less concentrated than one might have cause to expect, considering that this is a pure Pinot from Bisseuil.

- **1990 GENTILHOMME**   87, FEB 2003 (88)
(100% CH)

Absolutely not grape-typical! Deep, difficult-to-define nutty notes reminiscent of Krug Grande Cuvée are present. Certainly it is creamy and delicious, but I can't help being fascinated by its personal character.

- **1988 GENTILHOMME**   86, AUG 1997 (90)
(100% CH)

A stylish Blanc de Blancs from Côte des Blancs. Absolutely pure and very elegant, with aromas of lime and butterscotch.

LEPITRE, ABEL N-M

13, rue du Pont
51160 Mareuil-sur-Aÿ
03 26 56 93 11
Production: 500,000

Founded in 1924 in Ludes. Abel Lepitre was a relatively poor young man who succeeded thanks to his knowledge and stubbornness, selling 100,000 bottles as early as 1939. Hitler put a stop to this young man's success, and Abel Lepitre died a tragic death in one of the Nazi concentration camps. Fortunately, Abel's son was also ambitious. He managed to get the firm to expand still further by buying a grand house with its own chalk cellar in Reims in 1955.

In 1960, Abel Lepitre ceased to be an independent Champagne house when it merged with two others of similar size.

Today Abel Lepitre is closely linked to Philipponnat, which is run by the same man, Charles Philipponnat. This company is hard to get a grip on as they often change the name of their *cuvées*. They lack any vineyards of their own and have few permanent contracts with growers. This means that the quality has been quite inconsistent over the years, but with Paul Couvreur and then Guy de Saint Victor and Charles Philipponnat at the helm, the company has found a style all its own. In reality, the firm is Philipponnat's second brand.

- **ABEL LEPITRE BRUT**   68
(60% PN, 15% PM, 25% CH)
- **ABEL LEPITRE CUVÉE 134**   75
(100% CH)
- **ABEL LEPITRE ROSÉ**   66
(60% PN, 15% PM, 25% CH)
- **1997 ABEL LEPITRE**   78, DEC 2001 (83)
(60% PN, 40% CH)

Mild scent of lactic acid, a lot like yogurt. Round and polished taste that is refreshingly balanced at the same time. I found notes of yellow apples, wet wool, and vanilla buns.

- **1990 ABEL LEPITRE RÉSERVE C.**   81, JUL 1995 (90)
(100% CH)

A sparkling, youthful Champagne full of hawthorn and gooseberry aromas, with a perfectly pure, vigorous aftertaste of grapefruit.

- **1988 ABEL LEPITRE**   70, JUL 1995 (83)
(60% PN, 40% CH)

A lot like the nonvintage Champagne, with a slightly acrid, flowery nose backed up by gunpowder smoke and oyster shell. Young, medium-bodied, and restrained flavor.

- **1985 ABEL LEPITRE CUVÉE RÉSERVÉE**   78, JUL 1995 (82)
(35% PN, 65% CH)

Surprisingly developed '85 with an oxidative nose of sweet licorice. The flavor is creamy and good—if somewhat artificial.

- **1959 ABEL LEPITRE**
(35% PN, 65% CH)
- **1955 ABEL LEPITRE**
(35% PN, 65% CH)
- **1953 ABEL LEPITRE**
(35% PN, 65% CH)
- **1983 ABEL LEPITRE BLANC DE BLANCS**   80, JUL 1990 (88)
(100% CH)

Intensely perfumed and hawthorn-scented. Very vigorous and fresh. A joker in the pack.

- **1979 ABEL LEPITRE BLANC DE BLANCS**   88, JUN 2003 (88)
(100% CH)

Still a lightweight, with fine floral notes and a dash of lemon peel. Short, mineral-saturated, and metallic, but with impressive freshness and vitality.

- **1973 ABEL LEPITRE BLANC DE BLANCS**   88, DEC 2001 (88)
(100% CH)

Hardly a lecture on balance at the university of equilibrium, but nonetheless a good mouthful of buttery rich Chardonnay. Just getting close to the glass one is met by a heavenly scent of fresh Danish pastry.

- **1964 ABEL LEPITRE BLANC DE BLANCS**   87, JAN 2002 (87)
(100% CH)

Delightfully warm with rich buttery Chardonnay in both the nose and palate. The mousse is hardly visible, and the infirmities of old age are noticeable in the dull aftertaste. Otherwise still enjoyably delicious Champagne.

- 1988 ABEL LEPITRE ROSÉ   81, JUL 1995 (89)
(70% PN, 30% CH)
A real surprise, with a lovely tight structure and a sensual nose of peach and vanilla. Balanced and full of nuances.
- 1970 PRINCE A. DE BOURBON PARME
(35% PN, 65% CH)
- 1953 PRINCE A. DE BOURBON PARME
(35% PN, 65% CH)

LEPITRE, MAURICE R-M
26, rue de Reims
51500 Rilly-la-Montagne
03 26 03 40 27
Production: 40,000
Maurice Lepitre started his company in 1905, and today his creation owns seven hectares in Rilly-la-Montagne. M. and Mme Millex are very proud of their chalk cellar. Other wines: Cuvée Rilly, Vintage.

- MAURICE LEPITRE BRUT   60
(33% PN, 33% PM, 34% CH)
- CUVÉE HÉRITAGE   81
(100% CH)
Clear grape character, if somewhat more full bodied than its equivalent from Côte des Blancs. The fruit is in harmony with tropical elements.
- MAURICE LEPITRE ROSÉ   57
(33% PN, 33% PM, 34% CH)

LEPREUX-PENET R-M
18, rue de Villers
51380 Verzy
03 26 97 95 52
Production: 50,000
The grower has more than seven hectares in Verzy and Verzenay, planted with twenty-five-year-old Chardonnay and Pinot Noir vines. Malolactic fermentation is used.

- JEAN-BAPTISTE LEPREUX   68
(80% PN, 20% CH)
- JEAN-BAPTISTE LEPREUX   55
(80% PN, 20% CH)

LEROUX, FRED R-M
4, rue du Moulin
51500 Chigny-les-Roses
03 26 03 42 35
Production: 25,000
Strong connections with Ed Brun in Aÿ. The vintage is made in old oak casks only.

- FRED LEROUX CARTE D'ARGENT   64
(60% PM, 40% CH)
- FRED LEROUX CARTE D'OR   67
(20% PN, 40% PM, 40% CH)
- FRED LEROUX ROSÉ   61
(25% PN, 40% PM, 35% CH)
- 1992 FRED LEROUX   79, OCT 1997 (84)
(50% PN, 50% CH)

Very good considering the weak vintage. Good structure and a nice oaky taste.

- 1988 FRED LEROUX   82, OCT 1997 (86)
(50% PN, 50% CH)
Woody, acidic, dry, and storable. Very good value for money.
- 1975 FRED LEROUX   89, SEP 2001 (89)
(50% PN, 50% CH)
I bought the last case of this chewable Champagne. This is a wine for all to like, with delightful chocolaty aromas.

LEROUX, HILAIRE R-M
12, rue Georges Legros
51500 Chigny-les-Roses
03 26 03 42 01
Production: 60,000
Patrice Leroux makes Champagnes that do not go through malolactic fermentation. That fact keeps them fresh for a really long time.

- LEROUX CARTE BLEU   65
(33% PN, 33% PM, 34% CH)
- LEROUX BRUT   82
(70% PN, 10% PM, 20% CH)
A fantastically well-preserved magnum from the 1950s that—yet again—shows how well nonvintage Champagne stores in large bottles. Lively mousse, clear copper color, and a medium-bodied apple, plum, iron, and leather palate. Somewhat short and arid finish that brings down the score a bit.
- LEROUX CARTE ROUGE   80
(33% PN, 33% PM, 34% CH)
I'm very impressed by this wine's masculine power. A subdued, focused personality with severe Pinot Noir. A real keeper.
- LEROUX ROSÉ   81
(60% PN, 20% PM, 20% CH)
Light orange, exotic nose of herbs and flowers. Sold at the great age of ten years!
- 1989 LEROUX   80, OCT 1997 (82)
(30% PN, 10% PM, 60% CH)
Very opulent on the nose, but still with a tough, youthful acidity that bodes for a long life.
- 1955 LEROUX   88, OCT 1997 (90)
(20% PN, 50% PM, 30% CH)
Extremely fresh, light color and a bit closed at first. Opens up nicely in the glass, with aromas of nougat and tar. Would have been even better if normally disgorged.

LILBERT **** R-M
223, rue du Moutier
51530 Cramant
03 26 57 50 16
Production: 30,000
Georges Lilbert is the man who makes the toughest wines in all of Cramant. His vineyards lie in Chouilly and Cramant, the yield is low, and the wines are stored for at least five years before being sold. The fact is that the wines are so hard and acidic that the 1964 is the only fully matured wine I have ever drank from Lilbert.

- LILBERT BRUT PERLE   77
(100% CH)
- LILBERT BLANC DE BLANCS   80
(100% CH)

Wonderfully fine, fruity bouquet dominated by apple and honey. Stringent, almost hard, developable flavor in which the soil leaves some clear fingerprints.

- 1990 LILBERT   86, FEB 1997 (93)
  (100% CH)

Sweeter than I usually perceive Lilbert's otherwise bone-dry Champagnes to be. The fruit is rich and village-typical, with a little extra fatness.

- 1989 LILBERT   87, JUL 1997 (88)
  (100% CH)

Surprisingly ripe, deep, and rich. Great vinosity.

- 1985 LILBERT   87, MAY 1994 (93)
  (100% CH)

Broad and exquisite Cramant nose, where petroleum and nuts together build a symphony. The flavor is far more restrained, with plenty of potential.

- 1983 LILBERT   86, FEB 1997 (88)
  (100% CH)

Undeveloped and with a longer life than most '83s. Very fresh and flowery, with only a faint smoky undertone hinting at the wine's considerable age.

- 1982 LILBERT   89, MAY 1994 (93)
  (100% CH)

A heavy, smoky, masculine nose that doesn't soft-soap you. The palate is met by a sensational attack, where the hard, acidic, mineral taste whispers of wonderful future possibilities.

- 1964 LILBERT   95, FEB 1997 (95)
  (100% CH)

It was a great honor to share this pearl with Monsieur Lilbert in his cellar. Despite a complete lack of dosage, the wine gave off a very sweet scent and a velvet-smooth, concentrated, rich, exotic flavor. There were also tones of mushroom, truffles, tar, and smoke, like those to be found in certain '61s.

- 1990 LILBERT "CUVÉE 2000"   86, AUG 2000 (93)
  (100% CH)

The same wine as an ordinary '90, but with a later disgorgement. Compact, as yet undelivered greatness. Made for aging.

LOCRET-LACHAUD R-M

40, rue Saint Vincent
51160 Hautvillers
03 26 59 40 20
Production: 100,000

A company that came into being only recently, but this family of growers have worked in Champagne since 1620. That even predates their neighbor Dom Pérignon! Eric and Philippe Locret make fruity and pure Champagnes from their thirteen hectares. Other wines: Abbatiale.

- LOCRET-LACHAUD BRUT   63
  (40% PN, 20% PM, 40% CH)
- LOCRET-LACHAUD DEMI-SEC   32
  (33% PN, 33% PM, 34% CH)
- LOCRET-LACHAUD ROSÉ   56
  (33% PN, 33% PM, 34% CH)

LORIN, MICHEL R-M

24, Grande Rue
51700 Le Mesnil-sur-Oger
03 26 57 54 13

After Michel's death, the grower's grapes have been turned over to the cooperative.

- MICHEL LORIN BLANC DE BLANCS   19
  (100% CH)

LORIOT, MICHEL N-M

13, rue de Bel Air
51700 Festigny
03 26 58 34 01
Production: 300,000

Founded in 1931 after having supplied Moët with grapes since the turn of the century. Today they control fourteen hectares in Festigny and three neighboring villages.

- M. LORIOT CARTE BLANCHE   58
  (100% PM)
- M. LORIOT ROSÉ   54
  (100% PM)
- 1989 M. LORIOT   76, OCT 1997 (81)
  (100% PM)

An intense scent of violets and mint. Dry, well-balanced palate with a dry, mineral finish.

- 1995 LE LORIOT   80, APR 2002 (85)
  (100% PM)

I was incredibly proud when I succeeded in targeting this wine blind at a private dinner. I'm finally learning how the elusive Pinot Meunier grape actually tastes; few wines do it better than this one. The nose is big and rich like a dry Moët, with freshly baked bread, diesel exhaust, and mushroom cream. The taste is simple, dry, acidic, and undeveloped.

- 1990 LE LORIOT   78, AUG 1995 (86)
  (100% PM)

The firm's prestige wine boasts my favorite bird on the label—the golden oriole. The Champagne itself is impressive, with a nose of hay and vanilla. The flavor is concentrated and citrus fresh. An excellent Pinot Meunier.

LOSSY, DE N-M

51100 Reims

Suddenly, two bottles of this finely aged Champagne (from an extinct house) turned up on the market.

- 1928 DE LOSSY
- 1921 DE LOSSY

LOUVET, YVES R-M

21, rue du Poncet
51150 Tauxières
03 26 57 03 27
Production: 35,000

This producer owns 6.5 hectares in Bouzy and Tauxières. Other wines: Sélection.

- YVES LOUVET BRUT   69
  (75% PN, 25% CH)
- YVES LOUVET RÉSERVE   72
  (75% PN, 25% CH)

- 1978 MANDOIS SPECIAL CLUB   87, APR 2002 (87)
(50% PN, 50% CH)

Rich and nutty with an amber-like color. Tones of tea, spruce forest, and apricot. Rather short aftertaste and old character.

MANSARD-BAILLET *** N-M

14, rue Chaude-Ruelle
51200 Épernay
03 26 54 18 55
Production: 2,000,000

M. Mansard is a relaxed man who runs one of Champagne's fastest-growing houses. He owns seventeen hectares in Marne, covering a third of his needs. Today he uses grapes from some twenty-five villages in his blends and creates well-balanced wines in a typical Épernay style. Malolactic fermentation is used in all wines except for Tradition.

- MANSARD-BAILLET PREMIER CRU   69
(15% PN, 15% PM, 70% CH)
- MANSARD-BAILLET BRUT   66
(25% PN, 25% PM, 50% CH)
- MANSARD-BAILLET DEMI-SEC   51
(25% PN, 25% PM, 50% CH)
- MANSARD-BAILLET ROSÉ   79
(65% PN, 35% PM)
- 1992 MANSARD-BAILLET BLANC DE BLANCS   80, OCT 2001 (80)
(100% CH)

Very creamy and butter-toffee-ish Chardonnay. Smack-dab in the middle there's a taste of uplifting acidity and pearling mousse.

- CUVÉE DES SACRES   88, MAY 1995 (90)
(40% PN, 60% CH)

A *cuvée de prestige* in a limited edition and only in magnums. The blend is made from the vintages of '85, '86 and '87. A lovely Champagne with Dom Pérignon overtones. Less toasty, but the same gorgeous, delicate fruit and sophisticated style.

- DU TRIOMPHE   64
(15% PN, 15% PM, 70% CH)
- 1989 TRADITION DE MANSARD   85, MAY 1995 (90)
(10% PN, 90% CH)

The grapes originate from Mareuil, Chouilly, Oger, Le Mesnil, Avize, and Cramant. A lovely rich Chardonnay fruit. Superbly mature already.

- 1988 CUVÉE DES SACRES   82, MAY 1995 (88)
(30% PN, 70% CH)

The grapes come from Mareuil, Cumières, Chouilly, Vertus, and Le Mesnil. Surprisingly it's the Pinot character that makes itself known here. Dark, tight, and oily. Extremely packed and rich with aromas from dark berries. Not as elegant as the nonvintage Cuvée des Sacres.

MARGAINE *** R-M

3, avenue de Champagne
51380 Villers-Marmery
03 26 97 92 13
Production: 64,000

All the wines produced by the company are mono-*cru* Champagnes. They own seven hectares.

- MARGAINE TRADITIONELLE   67
(12% PN, 88% CH)
- MARGAINE ROSÉ   64
(18% PN, 82% CH)

- 1989 MARGAINE SPECIAL CLUB   70, JUL 1995 (86)
(100% CH)

The wine hasn't gone through malolactic fermentation and is undeveloped and hard. The flavor is restrained but very long. Hide somewhere in the cellar!

MARGUET-BONNERAVE *** R-M

14, rue de Bouzy
51150 Ambonnay
03 26 57 01 08
Production: 120,000

This family property was founded in 1905 by the Bonnerave brothers. The family today owns more than thirteen hectares in the *grand cru* villages of Ambonnay, Bouzy, and Mailly. It's worth noting that slightly more than half of the grapes are Chardonnay. Benôit, who has married into Launois in Le Mesnil, is the young driving force and brains behind this producer.

The reserve wines are stored in oak barrels and the grower makes rosé from a third of their grapes: most unusual. The grower also sets a good example by stating the date of disgorgement on the back of their labels.

- MARGUET-BONNERAVE TRADITION   77
(70% PN, 30% CH)
- MARGUET-BONNERAVE RÉSERVE   78
(60% PN, 40% CH)
- MARGUET-BONNERAVE ROSÉ   69
(85% PN, 15% CH)
- 1999 MARGUET-BONNERAVE ROSÉ   82, FEB 2004 (87)
(100% PN)

A fresh, luxuriant wine suffering from teething problems, where a certain angular quality is discernible. As yet not fully integrated, with lots of peel aromas. However, fine attack and richness of extract that is promising.

- MARGUET-BONNERAVE ANCIENS VINTAGES (97/98)
(50% PN, 50% CH)   84, JAN 2004 (87)

Lively and floral with creamy purity and sophisticated structure. Thought the wine would be heavier.

- MARGUET-BONNERAVE ANCIENS VINTAGES (96/97)
(50% PN, 50% CH)   87, DEC 2003 (90)

What a bull's-eye by Benôit! Exceedingly sophisticated and sensually good. There is a buttery surface that embraces all the other parts. The freshly baked-bread notes, the nuttiness, the sweetly intense as well as classically juicy fruit—all have a protective membrane of fat butter-toffee covering them.

- MARGUET-BONNERAVE ANCIENS VINTAGES (95/96)
(50% PN, 50% CH)   84, JAN 2002 (87)

Vintages 1995–1996. This is the first time I've found a bottle with two different vintages on the label, and that's not all that is surprising about this wine. I question how they can call a 1996 an "old vintage" at five years of age. Whatever; the Champagne itself is very good and balanced. Wines from Ambonnay are seldom powerful when young, but often have—as in this case—a radiant elegance and aristocratic stature not unlike vintage wines from the big houses.

- 1998 MARGUET-BONNERAVE   84, MAR 2004 (87)
(75% PN, 25% CH)

Once again, a creamy, polished, and very well-made Pinot-wine from this producer. Plum, red beets, licorice, and dark chocolate are the other aromas that make themselves known.

- YVES LOUVET BLANC DE BLANCS   70
  (100% CH)
- YVES LOUVET ROSÉ   59
  (80% PN, 20% CH)
- 1991 YVES LOUVET M   73, OCT 1997 (78)
  (75% PN, 25% CH)

MAITRE-GEOFFROY R-M
116, rue G. Poittevin
51480 Cumières
03 26 55 29 87
Production: 80,000
This grower owns ten hectares in Cumières and Hautvillers, which are planted with equal amounts of all three grape types. Modern vinification for all four *cuvées*.

- 1964 MAITRE-GEOFFROY   94, DEC 2000 (94)
  (80% PN, 20% CH)
  I had the pleasure of enjoying this old magnum at the home of a colleague the day before Christmas Eve. After all the Christmas stress that we at Champagne Club are always caught up in, it felt like balm for the soul to be able to enjoy this powerful and oily, concentrated goose-liver wine. The wine is full of sun-ripened notes of textbook Pinot Noir. Undertones of tar, mushroom, and redcurrants are all found here, but most noticeable of all is the intensely sweet taste of honey.

MALLOL-GANTOIS R-M
51530 Cramant
Production: 25,000
A small, little-known grower in delightful Cramant, who unfortunately represents the coarse, slightly impure style that certain growers have.

- MALLOL-GANTOIS BLANC DE BLANCS   51
  (100% CH)
  A blunt, coarse Blanc de Blancs that should be enjoyed as soon as opening from a well-chilled bottle. The longer the wine stands in the glass, the coarser the aromas become. Initially there is a little honey, wild strawberries, and citrus, but the aromas are soon drenched in clumsy notes of "cooking smells and well-drilling," according to one of my pupils.

MALOT, J. C. R-M
5, route d'Hermonville
51140 Trigny
03 26 03 11 81
Production: 60,000
Wines not tasted, but this grower has a good reputation in France.

- 1992 VIEILLE RÉSERVE BLANC DE BLANCS   61, JAN 2003 (61)
  (100% CH)

MANDOIS, H. *** N-M
66, rue de Général de Gaulle
51530 Pierry
03 26 54 03 18
Production: 300,000
A pleasant new acquaintance for me from Pierry. Victor Mandois was the name of the man who, after several years as a grower, received house status. Today, they have access to more than thirty-five hectares in twelve villages. The house-style is comprised of

refreshing, slightly exotic, and popsicle-like Champagne. I only discovered that their Special Club could be so good the day before turning in this manuscript to the publisher.

- MANDOIS ROSÉ   68
  (30% PN, 70% CH)
- MANDOIS CUVÉE RÉSERVE   55
  (34% PN, 33% PM, 33% CH)
- 1999 MANDOIS   76, JUN 2003 (79)
  (70% PN, 30% CH)
- 1990 MANDOIS   60, AUG 1995 (62)
  (50% PN, 50% CH)
- 1998 MANDOIS BLANC DE BLANCS   76, JUN 2003 (78)
  (100% CH)
- 1995 MANDOIS BLANC DE BLANCS   80, FEB 2000 (83)
  (100% CH)
  Delicious and easily drunk Chardonnay with a tropical-fruity basic quality. Pineapple and grape harmonize nicely with a certain chalky mineral tone.
- 1993 MANDOIS BLANC DE BLANCS   81, SEP 1998 (84)
  (100% CH)
  I really like the exotically fruity style that seems to be Mandois's theme tune. Once again the aromas remind one of the most delicious tutti-frutti ice cream. Passion fruit, pineapple, and grape are the most obvious to me. Fizzy and good in its own piquant way.
- 1990 MANDOIS BLANC DE BLANCS   82, JUL 1995 (89)
  (100% CH)
  Aromas of peach peel and passion fruit can be traced in the relatively closed and tight nose. Medium-bodied, faintly buttery revelation, with good potential and an exciting, Burgundy-like aftertaste.
- 1996 CUVÉE VICTOR MANDOIS   87, JUN 2003 (89)
  (50% PN, 50% CH)
  Thirty percent oak barrels, and the whole wine is made of grapes from old Chardonnay vines in Pierry. A real "deluxe popsicle," where the tropical coconut and pineapple taste is substantiated with grand concentration and a deeper, more vinous, nutty tone. A good prestige Champagne that shows why Taittinger uses old vines in Pierry for their Comtes de Champagne.
- 1983 MANDOIS SPECIAL CLUB   93, JAN 2003 (93)
  (50% PN, 50% CH)
  I was taken aback when I stuck my nose into the glass and was met by a mature Clos du Mesnil-like bouquet. A completely brilliant, sensational wine with several wonderful taste layers and surfaces. Supple and packed with fruit, with a juicy, exotic undertone. Vanilla, treacle, chocolate, and apple cake are associations that all the tasters made.
- 1981 MANDOIS SPECIAL CLUB   93, MAR 2002 (93)
  (50% PN, 50% CH)
  Very much like the '83 but lacking its superbly layered beauty. More homogeneous, with an even more evolved, mature, high-class aftertaste.
- 1979 MANDOIS SPECIAL CLUB   87, MAR 2002 (87)
  (50% PN, 50% CH)
  Surprisingly enough, the worst of the old Club bottles. The acidity is good and the mousse is still very lively. The nose is like a poorer variety of a 1979 René Lalou, with slightly impure notes of bark and rubber as well as a fine hazelnut aroma. Somewhat lighter than the '81 and the '83.

- 1996 MARGUET-BONNERAVE   85, JAN 2004 (89)
  (75% PN, 25% CH)

  Perhaps a little mute and bound, but otherwise a delicious, fully packed Champagne with rounded edges. Distinct chocolate, licorice, and milk-toffee tones. Fluffy feeling on the palate—anything but aggressive.

MARIE-STUART N-M
8, place de la République
51100 Reims
03 26 47 92 26
Production: 1,700,000

The Scottish queen Mary Stuart, who was very popular in Reims during the sixteenth century, gave her name to this house in 1919. Today the company is a very commercial operation that has gone in strongly for "Buyer's Own Brand" wines, and has specialized in world-record bottle sizes. Both the largest and smallest Champagne bottles in the world come from this house, which has no vineyards of its own. Owned by Alain Thienot since 1994. Today Laurent Fedou makes all the Champagne in the group.

- MARIE-STUART BRUT TRADITION   40
  (50% PN, 25% PM, 25% CH)
- MARIE-STUART ROSÉ   39
  (40% PN, 20% PM, 40% CH)
- 1988 MARIE-STUART   70, AUG 1995 (70)
  (10% PN, 90% CH)
- CUVÉE DE LA REINE   76
  (10% PN, 90% CH)

MARNE & CHAMPAGNE N-M
22, rue Maurice Cerveaux
51200 Épernay
03 26 78 50 50
Production: 11,000,000

Moët & Chandon is often—and somewhat unfairly—given the label "Coca-Cola Champagne." This description fits Marne & Champagne (a member of the Lanson Group) far better. The firm was founded in 1933 by Gaston Burtin, a man far more interested in business than Champagne. Today the company is the second largest in Champagne, despite the fact that they shy away from all forms of advertising. Paul Messin has chosen to buy the cheapest available grapes in order to produce as much wine as possible as cheaply as possible. The company now leads the market in "Buyer's Own Brands." I've come across any number of Champagnes with a buyer's label stating that have been produced by Marne & Champagne. Although I was impressed by the low price at first, I'm always extremely disappointed by the quality. The different labels are very confusing; there are in total 200 different names from this house! Gautier, Eugéne Clicquot, Pol Gessner, Colligny, Leprince-Royer, Delacoste, Geissman, Pol Albert, and Giesler are all production-line Champagnes from the Marne & Champagne science-fiction-style industrial complex. The firm's giant steel tanks have a capacity of 200,000 hectoliters of wine! The foremost Champagne from the house is Alfred Rothschild. The wines are not particularly special, but the firm does have a role to play—it uses grapes and juice no one else wants and makes neutral but very affordable Champagnes. Vincent Malherbe is the winemaker responsible for the quality of the wines.

- A. ROTHSCHILD BRUT   61
  (35% PN, 25% PM, 40% CH)
- EUGÈNE CLICQUOT BRUT   35
  (40% PN, 40% PM, 20% CH)
- POL GESSNER BRUT   29
  (40% PN, 40% PM, 20% CH)
- ROGER PERROY BRUT   29
  (40% PN, 40% PM, 20% CH)
- A. ROTHSCHILD BLANC DE BLANCS   68
  (100% CH)
- GAUTIER ROSÉ   32
  (45% PN, 35% PM, 20% CH)
- 1996 A. ROTHSCHILD   75, APR 2003 (79)
- 1990 GEISMANN   82, JUL 2001 (82)
  (10% PN, 25% PM, 65% CH)

  Completely ripe and generously bready with nutty elements and a warm sweetness. A smiling and uncomplicated wine.
- 1989 A. ROTHSCHILD   73, JUL 1996 (76)
  (10% PN, 25% PM, 65% CH)
- 1989 GEISMANN   74, OCT 1998 (76)
  (10% PN, 25% PM, 65% CH)
- 1986 A. ROTHSCHILD   79, APR 1994 (80)
  (35% PN, 10% PM, 55% CH)

  Mildness, maturity, marzipan—three *Ms* that describe this wine very well.
- 1976 A. ROTHSCHILD   88, NOV 1995 (88)
  (50% PN, 50% CH)

  Luscious and spicy, with several layers of candy and fruit cream.
- 1966 A. ROTHSCHILD   82, DEC 2002 (82)
  (50% PN, 50% CH)

  Absolutely on its way downhill—clear signs of aging have put a half nelson on this wine. Still, it remains rather good, with butterscotchy and chocolaty round and sweet aromas.
- 1938 GAUTHIER
  (60% PN, 10% PM, 30% CH)
- 1961 GIESLER BLANC DE BLANCS   89, OCT 2000 (89)
  (100% CH)

  Grand bouquet of mocha and toffee. Alert, energetic, and relatively toasty palate with good fruit and a velvety smooth finish of fudge, browned butter and tar. The '61s go from strength to strength.
- 1989 A. ROTHSCHILD ROSÉ   60, MAY 1997 (68)
  (25% PN, 40% PM, 35% CH)
- 1988 GRAND TRIANON   85, MAR 1997 (86)
  (40% PN, 60% CH)

  Fantastically close to 1988 Moët & Chandon. Perhaps a touch lighter, but an almost identical nose of freshly baked bread and chocolate orange. Enjoyable for a wide audience.
- 1973 GRAND TRIANON   83, JAN 2000 (83)
  (40% PN, 60% CH)

  Perhaps a little too dull and ripe now. Still, a chocolaty, rich wine with clear culinary merits. The mousse remained, at least in the bottle I enjoyed. One of my co-tasters thought the wine tasted of sherry and that it was done for.

MARNIQUET, J.-P. R-M
8, rue des Crayères
51480 Venteuil
03 26 58 48 99
Production: 110,000
This grower has more than seven hectares in Venteuil, planted with 50 percent Pinot Noir, 15 percent Pinot Meunier, and 35 percent Chardonnay. The vines average twenty-five years in age. The wines are not put through malolactic fermentation.
- J-P MARNIQUET BRUT   58
  (15% PN, 50% PM, 35% CH)
- J-P MARNIQUET ROSÉ   55
  (5% PN, 5% PM, 90% CH)

MARTEL & CIE, G. H. N-M
23, rue Jean-Moulin
51201 Épernay
03 26 51 06 33
Production: 2,000,000
In total, eight million bottles in the group. Founded in 1869 by a grower from Avenay. When the firm's owner died in 1979, the house was taken over by Rapeneau. Today Martel is Rapeneau's first brand, and Francine Rapeneau runs the house.
      This house has 150 hectares, making it a substantial house. Because 80 percent is sold under "BOB" labels, they are not often seen on the market. Other wines: Crémant, Cuvée Henry Leopold.
- MARTEL CARTE D'OR   67
  (70% PN, 30% CH)
- MARTEL BLANC DE BLANCS   70
  (100% CH)
- MARTEL DEMI-SEC   40
  (70% PN, 30% CH)
- MARTEL ROSÉ   56
  (80% PN, 20% CH)
- 1996 MARTEL CUVÉE VICTOIRE   82, NOV 2002 (84)
  (50% PN, 50% CH)
  Big, impressive, slightly rustic style. The nose is generous, with several layers of bready notes—everything from cookies to newly baked bread. The taste is expansive and generously developed. Acidity is also present and the dosage is well structured. The only thing you can object to is that the yeasty taste so typical of Épernay is slightly too short and pedestrian.
- 1995 MARTEL CUVÉE VICTOIRE   78, APR 2001 (81)
  (66% PN, 34% CH)
  Yeasty, big-house nose that resembles the big guys in Épernay. Rather sweet, relatively neutral taste that is certainly quite delicious, but lacks elasticity.

MARTIN, LOUIS R-M
3, rue Ambonnay
51150 Bouzy
03 26 57 01 27
Production: 100,000
Madame Francine Rapeneau runs this firm today, which Louis Martin founded in 1864. They have ten hectares.
- LOUIS MARTIN GRAND CRU BRUT   54
  (70% PN, 30% CH)

- 1996 LOUIS MARTIN BLANC DE BLANCS   77, OCT 2002 (79)
  (100% CH)

MARTIN, PAUL R-M
355, rue Bois Jots
51480 Cumières
A grower that I have failed to get in touch with during work on this book.
- PAUL MARTIN BRUT   30

MASSÉ N-M
48, rue de Courlancy
51100 Reims
03 26 47 61 31
Production: 700,000
Founded in 1853 in Rilly-la-Montagne. A label you often find in Denmark, actually. A low-priced Champagne that in practice is Lanson's second wine, although the company was one of the exclusive members of the "Syndicat des Grandes Marques." Other wines: Vintage.
- MASSÉ BRUT   45
  (45% PN, 20% PM, 35% CH)
- BARON EDOUARD   53
  (45% PN, 35% PM, 20% CH)
- CUVÉE HENRY MASSÉ   53
  (40% PN, 20% PM, 40% CH)

MATHIEU, SERGE R-M
route d'Avirey à Lingey
10340 Avirey-Lingey
03 25 29 32 58
Production: 90,000
Serge Mathieu is one of Aube's most-praised producers. He owns nine hectares around Avirey-Lingey. A very serious winemaker who would be even better using grapes from Marne.
- SERGE MATHIEU TRADITION   47
  (90% PN, 10% CH)
- SERGE MATHIEU CUVÉE SELECT   66
  (50% PN, 50% CH)
- SERGE MATHIEU PRESTIGE   48
  (75% PN, 25% CH)
- SERGE MATHIEU BLANC DE NOIRS   62
  (100% PN)
- SERGE MATHIEU ROSÉ   55
  (100% PN)
- 1989 SERGE MATHIEU   64, AUG 1995 (75)
  (75% PN, 25% CH)
- 1988 SERGE MATHIEU   66, NOV 1994 (75)
  (75% PN, 25% CH)

MAZET, PASCAL R-M
8, rue des Carrières
51500 Chigny-les-Roses
03 26 03 41 13
Production: 50,000
Pascal is an elegant, mustachioed gentleman who works together with several of the big houses while making his own quality-conscious wines. His oldest vines were planted in 1954 and the others are about twenty-five years old. He works more than three hectares in Chigny and

Ambonnay. Half of the grapes are Pinot Meunier. Pascal is known for his low yield—in certain *cuvées* as little as fifteen hectoliters per hectare.

• PASCAL MAZET BRUT RÉSERVE   75
  (20% PN, 50% PM, 30% CH)

MÉA, GUY R-M
1, rue de l'Eglise
51150 Louvois
03 26 57 03 42
Production: 65,000
Guy Méa's Champagne first saw the light of day in 1953. The wines are stored for three years in the cellar before they go on sale. The vineyards cover 8.5 hectares, divided among the villages of Ludes, Tauxières, Bouzy, and Louvois. Other wines: Rosé, Prestige.

• GUY MÉA BRUT   71
  (70% PN, 30% CH)

MÉA-DEVAVRY R-M
43, rue Pasteur
51160 Champillon
03 26 59 46 21
Production: 80,000
This domain was planted in 1945 by Bertrand Devavry. At the helm today: Jean-Loup Devavry. The vineyards cover nine hectares.

• 1992 MÉA-DEVAVRY   74, SEP 2001 (75)
  (20% PN, 20% PM, 60% CH)

MÉDOT N-M
30, rue Werlé
51100 Reims
03 26 47 46 15
Production: 250,000
A small house in Reims that was founded in 1897 by Jules Pascal. The firm has stayed in the family and is now run by Philippe Guidon; it is best known for producing one of the area's few *clos* Champagnes, Clos des Chaulins. The hillsides are covered with vines that were planted in 1927. From 0.8 hectares they produce about 8,000 bottles.

• MÉDOT BRUT   67
  (33% PN, 33% PM, 34% CH)
• MÉDOT MILLENNIUM CUVÉE 2000   60, AUG 2003 (65)
• MÉDOT BLANC DE BLANCS   66
  (100% CH)
• MÉDOT ROSÉ   56
  (50% PN, 50% PM)
• 1991 MÉDOT   68, OCT 2001 (69)
  (50% PN, 50% PM)
• 1989 MÉDOT   68, AUG 1995 (69)
  (50% PN, 50% PM)
• CLOS DES CHAULINS   79
  (90% PN, 5% PM, 5% CH)

MENU, GILLES R-M
1, rue Jobert
51500 Chigny-les-Roses
03 26 03 43 35
Production: 30,000
This grower has more than five hectares in Chigny-les-Roses.

• GILLES MENU BRUT   66
  (25% PN, 50% PM, 25% CH)
• GILLES MENU GRANDE RÉSERVE   68
  (25% PN, 50% PM, 25% CH)
• GILLES MENU ROSÉ   60
  (25% PN, 25% PM, 50% CH)

MERCIER *** N-M
75, avenue de Champagne
51200 Épernay
03 26 51 22 00
Production: 6,000,000
Eugène Mercier is one of the most important people in the history of Champagne. In 1858 he began his work in Épernay, digging eighteen kilometers of cellar, which he showed off to celebrities. They even say that a car rally sped off from here! Eugène Mercier was a very PR-conscious Champagne entrepreneur. He had the world's largest oak barrel built, which was pulled by twenty-four white oxen to the World's Fair in Paris in 1889. He also made an advertising film about Champagne for the World's Fair that received much attention. In 1970 Mercier merged with Moët & Chandon. Even today, Mercier is very careful about its marketing. A tourist train runs through the cellars, carrying an enormous number of visitors each year. Mercier is definitely a great house to visit for any beginner. They buy basic grapes and use a lot of wine from the second pressing in their *cuvées*. Moët & Chandon concentrate more on exports, while Mercier maintain an interest almost exclusively in the domestic market. Their vintage wines can be really good and are all good value. The house-style is well maintained by *chef de cave* Alain Parenthoen, even if the three stars are mostly historical.

• MERCIER BRUT   50
• MERCIER DEMI-SEC   40
  (55% PN, 45% PM)
• MERCIER ROSÉ   55
  (50% PN, 50% PM)
• 1995 MERCIER   81, MAR 2003 (85)
  (45% PN, 15% PM, 40% CH)
A Champagne that is easy to appreciate with its butterscotchy, slightly sweet image and passion-fruity, thirst-quenching basic taste. Breadiness *à la* Moët is also found here. On the other hand, fifteen grams of sugar is a little too much.
• 1990 MERCIER   81, AUG 1997 (86)
  (32% PN, 28% PM, 40% CH)
This vintage is a sure thing, whatever the name of the producer. Here Mercier have made a very enjoyable and easy-going Champagne.
• 1985 MERCIER   85, MAR 2000 (85)
  (45% PN, 15% PM, 40% CH)
This Champagne is already mature. The bouquet is expansive and vigorous with a spectrum of smoke, earth, dark bread, and mushroom. The taste, despite its flirtatious charm, is somewhat simpler. A little too sweet and short, with a metallic undertone.

An exotically fruity taste-build-up in the mid-palate elevates the points to a rather high level.

- 1982 MERCIER — 85, MAR 2000 (85)
(50% PN, 50% CH)
Here the cooperation with Moët & Chandon is very noticeable. The same nose of orange and mushroom cream, with a somewhat less clear, slightly rough taste.

- 1975 MERCIER — 86, MAR 2000 (88)
(45% PN, 15% PM, 40% CH)
Tasted at Mercier from a newly disgorged magnum. Fine, elegant acacia note gained from the autolytic process. Very young and smooth-skinned, with handsome notes of mandarin orange as a new personal attribute. Surely completely different in a seventy-five-centiliter bottle. In magnum hardly a typical Champagne from this vintage, yet still very enjoyable and sophisticated.

- 1966 MERCIER — 92, AUG 1995 (92)
(45% PN, 20% PM, 35% CH)
Lovely round and chocolaty '66 with good length.

- 1964 MERCIER — 93, MAR 2000 (93)
(35% PN, 20% PM, 45% CH)
Disgorged in 1972. Purchased at Tom Stevenson's Christie auction—that is to say, direct from the house. A wine in wonderful condition with a somewhat high dosage, but with the vintage's impressively rich merits. Very rich and long. The aroma is youthful and toasted with a hint of orange.

- 1962 MERCIER — 92, NOV 1993 (92)
(55% PN, 20% PM, 25% CH)
Just like Moët, Mercier have made a very good '62. Rather young color, rich mousse, and a large smoky nose with chocolate and hints of earth. Good weight, hard attack, and a mature, sweet aftertaste.

- 1961 MERCIER — 93, MAR 2000 (93)
(35% PN, 20% PM, 45% CH)
More gravity than Cuvée "M33," with even more integrated chocolate aroma. Very rich and pleasurable. The aroma is dominated by a pronounced forest scent. Like a freshly cut spruce forest. A masculine Champagne that is reminiscent of Krug's '61.

- 1955 MERCIER
(50% PN, 20% PM, 30% CH)

- 1942 MERCIER
(50% PN, 20% PM, 30% CH)

- 1941 MERCIER — 93, FEB 1999 (93)
(55% PN, 20% PM, 25% CH)
A wine purchased at Tom Stevenson's fantastic auction in October 1998, where all of the Champagnes came directly from the house's cellars. It was the first time I had come across this seldom-seen war vintage. The youthfulness was astonishing, to say the least. The color was pale yellow-green and the bubbles formed a tight and strong pillar in the middle of the glass. That the wine was disgorged in 1949 is a puzzle to me. The entire wine's aromatic spectrum and structure feels a bit too young and newly disgorged. Pure toasted and gunpowder-stained aroma and a medium-bodied focused and dry taste.

- 1966 MERCIER BLANC DE BLANCS — 92, AUG 1995 (92)
(100% CH)
A brilliant Champagne with a slender structure and delicate, ultra-refined fruit aromas. Also a touch of roasted coffee beans.

- MERCIER BULLE D'OR — 88
(40% PN, 60% CH)

Mercier's prestige Champagne, which I have been after for years. When I finally found an old bottle, it was at an Italian self-service shop in Terracina. Unfortunately the bottle had been standing upright for several years, which had caused the cork to dry out. The wine appeared complex and rich, but unfortunately the whole thing was ruined. The next bottle was much keener, with a fine nose of brioche.

- 1961 MERCIER CUVÉE "M 33" — 93, OCT 1998 (93)
(100% CH)
A very rare label that few know anything about today. This, Mercier's former prestige Champagne, follows the house-style well. Scent of roasted Brazilian coffee beans. Medium-bodied fruity taste.

- 1955 MERCIER CUVÉE "M 33" — 73, DEC 2003 (>)
(100% CH)

MÉRIC, DE *** N-M
17, rue Gambetta
51160 Aÿ
03 26 55 20 72
Production: 50,000
This family firm is one of my later discoveries. Christian and Patrick Besserat come from the family that owned Besserat de Bellefon, but in 1960 Christian left to start his own house in Aÿ. They still control more than fifteen hectares in the village, with an unusually high percentage of Chardonnay. Those grapes that are bought in come from the Côte des Blancs. Only the *cuvée* (first pressing) is used, and only the best of the first pressing goes into the *cuvée de prestige*. De Méric is one of the few producers to admit that they use cognac in their dosage. Today they use 50 percent oak barrels for their wines.

- DE MÉRIC BRUT — 78
(70% PN, 30% CH)

- DE MÉRIC GRANDE BLANC DE BLANCS SOIS BOIS — 75
(100% CH)

- DE MÉRIC GRANDE RÉSERVE SOIS BOIS — 81
(80% PN, 5% PM, 15% CH)
A brilliant, powerful nonvintage Champagne made in oak barrels. A truly gastronomic wine with incredible power and weight. Of course, a little elegance is lost along the way. The structure is compact and not easily demolished—the aromas are oaky, smoky, and dark, with a strong dominance of grilled meat.

- DE MÉRIC BLANC DE BLANCS — 76
(100% CH)

- DE MÉRIC ROSÉ — 72
(89% PN, 11% CH)

- 1996 DE MÉRIC — 84, APR 2004 (86)
(70% PN, 30% CH)
Powerful impression already in the nose, with strong red-wine characteristics. Red beets, apple peels, and cellar also come again on the palate. Fleshy, with good spine and a handsome finish.

- 1993 DE MÉRIC — 83, APR 2004 (83)
(70% PN, 30% CH)
Unexpected maturity with oxidative, fleshy character suitable for mealtimes. In comparison to a 1992 Lenoble, difficult to drink in a heated outdoor pool in the middle of winter. The gamy, licorice notes are clumsy in such circumstances. Powerful and rich, almost bordering on clumsiness.

- 1990 DE MÉRIC — 87, SEP 2003 (88)
(70% PN, 30% CH)

A wine that exudes weight, but for some probably a little clumsy. Personally, I'm impressed by this type of dark, masculine wine that rumbles like a titan over the tongue. The aftertaste is a little oaky, bordering on the abrasive. Take some game out of the freezer to keep this wine company.

- 1988 DE MÉRIC   76, MAR 1995 (84)
(70% PN, 30% CH)
A blend of Aÿ and Oger. Despite that, nothing out of the ordinary. The smoky house-style is combined here with a hint of green apples.
- 1969 BESSERAT   94, DEC 2002 (94)
(70% PN, 30% CH)
One of De Méric's earliest wines, at that time using the Besserat label. Decidedly idiosyncratic nose of gargantuan proportions. Partial aromas that shine brightly: mint chocolate, varnish, and birch bark. Exceptionally deep, fleshy Champagne intended for grand autumn suppers. Simply a super, fascinating wine experience!
- CATHÉRINE DE MÉDICIS   89
(50% PN, 50% CH)
The company's *cuvée de prestige* is made completely from the grapes of Aÿ. Always a blend of three vintages, with an average age of thirteen. A very mature and aromatic wine, in the English manner. Slightly exaggerated oxidative character, but gorgeous banana and chocolate aromas. The flavor is also magnificent and full of sweet, mature tones, but the aftertaste is devalued by an ounce of sherry tones.

MICHEL, GUY R-M
54, rue Leon Bourgeois
51530 Pierry
03 26 54 67 12
Production: 30,000
Vincent Michel is from the fifth generation of growers in this family. He owns more than twenty hectares in ten different villages. A small producer that makes all of ten different Champagnes!

- GUY MICHEL BRUT   50
(26% PN, 44% PM, 30% CH)
- GUY MICHEL ROSÉ   57
(100% PN)
- 1973 GUY MICHEL   75, JUL 1995 (75)
(10% PN, 75% PM, 15% CH)

MICHEL, JOSÉ **** R-M
14, rue Prélot
51530 Moussy
03 26 54 04 69
Production: 160,000
José Michel is one of my latest discoveries. On one single tour I was told on three separate occasions that the best truly old Champagnes ever made were pure Pinot Meunier Champagnes from José Michel. The winemakers at Deutz and Legras were unanimous. Although they themselves work with *grand cru* Chardonnay, they confirmed that the real cellar wines were Pinot Meunier. Could this really be true? Krug's wonderful older vintage wines are what I've always seen as the exception that proves the rule, but the fact is that José Michel's recipe is exactly the same. Extremely old vines, no malolactic fermentation, and fermentation in oak barrels. The grapes that make up Special Club come from vines planted in 1929!

The company has been owned by the family for four generations since 1847, and José himself started out in 1955. Today he controls twenty-one hectares in Moussy, Pierry, and Chavot. José's collection of normally disgorged older vintages is remarkable. There may only be four or five bottles of each vintage, but every year going back to 1912 is represented. The years 1914, 1928, 1947, and above all 1921 are his own favorites. I'll be back, José!

- JOSÉ MICHEL CARTE BLANCHE   74
(60% PN, 40% CH)
- JOSÉ MICHEL CUVÉE DU PÈRE HOUDART   84
(70% PM, 30% CH)
A mix of older vintages—in this case 1988, 1986, and 1985. Big and evolved; here you can clearly see how much quicker development takes place with still reserve wines than with sparkling wines. The wine is considerably older than a normal '85, with its rich chocolate, nutty presentation. Thick, rich, and fully packed but without any great finesse.
- JOSÉ MICHEL EXTRA BRUT   74
(60% PM, 40% CH)
- JOSÉ MICHEL BLANC DE BLANCS   79
(100% CH)
- JOSÉ MICHEL ROSÉ   72
(50% PN, 50% PM)
- 1996 JOSÉ MICHEL   86, JUN 2003 (91)
(30% PM, 70% CH)
Potential points given here are based on experience and knowledge about how José's wines develop with storage. Otherwise, this is hardly a Champagne that is peevish and youthfully unruly: quite the contrary! At the moment, the acidity is beautifully enveloped in a creamily soft fruit and an eiderdown quilt of snow-white mousse.
- 1993 JOSÉ MICHEL   80, SEP 2003 (85)
(30% PM, 70% CH)
You never know where José's wines are going. I suppose even this unruly wine will find itself in ten years or so.
- 1990 JOSÉ MICHEL   82, MAY 1998 (87)
(30% PM, 70% CH)
The grower's distinctive style is evident with tones of bark, violet, and thyme.
- 1989 JOSÉ MICHEL   89, AUG 1997 (91)
(30% PM, 70% CH)
A sensational wine with a wonderful nose of gunpowder smoke, toasted bread, and coffee. Resembles a top-class Pinot Noir; made me think of Cuvée Sir Winston Churchill.
- 1986 JOSÉ MICHEL   88, AUG 1997 (89)
(40% PM, 60% CH)
Suddenly a little Krug Grande Cuvée pops up. Nutty and deep, with fine honey and honeysuckle notes.
- 1983 JOSÉ MICHEL   80, MAY 2002 (>)
(30% PM, 70% CH)
A quickly developed vintage, with smoky, slightly coarse tones. One of Josés own favorites with its concentrated chocolate aroma. Aging too fast.
- 1982 JOSÉ MICHEL   90, OCT 2003 (93)
(70% PM, 30% CH)
An outstanding, broad nose of mushroom and meat grilled over a wood fire. A broad, tough, impressive, rasping flavor with great power. Cellar!
- 1973 JOSÉ MICHEL   90, JUN 1997 (93)
(50% PM, 50% CH)

An elegant, flowery nose with a strong perfumed tone of musk, violet, and dwarf banana. Fresh, steely, and well-structured flavor, with an extremely long and acidic aftertaste here too.

- 1965 JOSÉ MICHEL   93, JUN 1997 (93)
(100% PM)

Wow! A tremendous nose of lilac, plum, and violet. Initially fat and oily, once again with impressive acidity. A long, vinous flavor that resembles a great Chablis vinified in oak barrels.

- 1963 JOSÉ MICHEL
(100% PM)

- 1961 JOSÉ MICHEL   93, AUG 1997 (94)
(100% PM)

Much lighter and more elegant than the '59, with an irresistible peach nose. The mousse is youthful and delicious. The aftertaste will become even longer when the wine matures fully.

- 1959 JOSÉ MICHEL   95, AUG 1997 (95)
(100% PM)

Krug-like, with notes of tar, smoke, wood, tobacco, and dark foresty aromas. Grandiose.

- 1955 JOSÉ MICHEL   95, JUN 1997 (96)
(100% PM)

Youthful color with a beautiful golden hue. An extravagant, majestic, warm nose of smoke, nut, tar, nougat, and tobacco. The flavor is fruitier than the nose, with a perfect balance of freshness that typifies the vintage.

- 1952 JOSÉ MICHEL   94, MAY 1998 (94)
(100% PM)

Unbelievably exotic bouquet of tropical flowers, apricot cream, and passion fruit. Fabulous nectar abounding with natural sweetness. The bubbles are weak, but what a dessert! Like a German *Beerenauslese*.

- 1943 JOSÉ MICHEL   96, MAY 1998 (96)
(100% PM)

This wine from José's incredible archive was first thought to be a '42, until we took a look at the cork. Krug-like essence with an extravagant nutty complexity and butterscotch undertone. Very much like the '21, though somewhat less concentrated.

- 1921 JOSÉ MICHEL   97, JUN 1997 (97)
(100% PM)

Probably the best wine ever made from Pinot Meunier. A deep amber color, faint, prolonged mousse, a toffee-ish, gigantic Yquem-like nose and flavor that I've only faintly come across in 1926 Krug and 1914 Pol Roger. The depth was even greater here, even if the finesse was more tangible in Champagnes from Pol Roger. Sadly there are only four bottles left in José Michel's cellar. I hope he saves a couple for generations to come as archaeological milestones of the history of wine.

- 1998 JOSÉ MICHEL BLANC DE BLANCS   81, JUN 2003 (86)
(100% CH)

Pure and very young! Not as interesting as when Michel's grand and idiosyncratic Pinot Meunier grapes play the leading part. Still, a real keeper and absolutely well crafted.

- 1994 JOSÉ MICHEL BLANC DE BLANCS   76, NOV 1998 (79)
(100% CH)

- 1992 JOSÉ MICHEL CLOS DES PLANTS DE CHÊNES   87, FEB 2002 (88)
(100% CH)

Enormously concentrated for a '92, but also with finesse and a handsomely crafted structure. The wine feels as if it comes from Cramant, with its buttery, unctuously delicious style. Does José really use oak here? It doesn't feel like it.

- 1990 JOSÉ MICHEL CLOS DES PLANTS DE CHÊNES 88, AUG 2001 (90)
(100% CH)

This is a unique *clos* wine from Moussy. Exotically concentrated from a really low yield. Otherwise I miss the smoky complexity that has become Michel's signature.

- 1996 JOSÉ MICHEL SPECIAL CLUB   84, JUN 2003 (93)
(50% PM, 50% CH)

The seventy-year-old vines lend a fruit concentration and exoticism to the wine that differs from the usually almost identical regular '96. Store for the next generation.

- 1995 JOSÉ MICHEL SPECIAL CLUB   88, JUN 2003 (90)
(50% PM, 50% CH)

Creamy and usually evolved with chocolaty, long flavor. Not one of Michel's more memorable bottles, but still terribly delicious and full bodied.

- 1992 JOSÉ MICHEL SPECIAL CLUB   82, NOV 1998 (85)
(50% PM, 50% CH)

Big and well-built aroma of apple peel and violet. Massive flavor of pistachio. Always a very fleshy, tasty wine, regardless of vintage.

- 1990 JOSÉ MICHEL SPECIAL CLUB   87, MAY 1998 (92)
(50% PM, 50% CH)

It's amazing that all Club wines are like one another, whether they're made from Pinot or Chardonnay. The creaminess and concentration are reminiscent of Bonnaire in Cramant. Of course, there's a personal tone of spices and freesia, but the creamy, citrus-fresh Chardonnay dominates the overall impression.

- 1985 JOSÉ MICHEL SPECIAL CLUB   90, MAY 1998 (94)
(50% PM, 50% CH)

Both the aroma and taste are reminiscent of a red Hermitage. Clear elements of blackberry and smoked meats. High acidity and phenomenally long. One of Michel's best!

MIGNON & PIERREL N-M
24, rue Henri Dunant
51200 Épernay
03 26 51 93 39
Production: 200,000

An unknown Épernay house that has found its way to the Swedish Wine Monopoly. The company is actually best known for their horrible bottles in garish colors and floral patterns. Dominique Pierrel is winemaker. The wines are very accessible and moderately priced, with a clear keynote of mint candy.

- MIGNON & PIERREL BRUT PREMIER CRU   76
(40% PN, 60% CH)

- 1992 MIGNON & PIERREL   50, APR 2001 (50)
(100% CH)

- 1990 MIGNON & PIERREL   84, APR 2001 (84)
(100% CH)

The house's candy-like softness and minty style pop up again, but luckily without the toothpaste taste. Vintage-typical and powerfully evolved. Actually fades in the glass if you don't hurry up and drink it.

- 1988 MIGNON & PIERREL GRANDE CUVÉE   84, MAR 2001 (84)
(10% PN, 90% CH)

A medium-sized nose that is very delicate, with creamy Chardonnay tones in both nose and palate.

MIGNON, CHARLES N-M
1, avenue de Champagne
51200 Épernay
03 26 58 33 33
Production: 200,000
A new house that has a rather impressive address, hasn't it? The firm only uses wine from the first pressing. All the wines come from *grand cru* or *premier cru* villages. Bruno Mignon also sells other companies' Champagnes at reasonable prices.

• CHARLES MIGNON GRANDE RÉSERVE	58
(75% PN, 25% CH)	
• CHARLES MIGNON CUVÉE	75
(75% PN, 25% CH)	
• CHARLES MIGNON PRESTIGE ROSÉ	54
(75% PN, 25% CH)	

MIGNON, PIERRE R-M
51210 Le Breuil
03 26 59 22 03
Refuses to answer all fax and telephone queries. What are they afraid of?

• 1995 CUVÉE JACQUES CHIRAC	73, MAR 2004 (73)
(80% PN, 20% CH)	

MIGNON, YVES R-M
166, rue de Dizy
51480 Cumières
03 26 55 31 21
Has recently finished production and been incorporated into the cooperative.

• YVES MIGNON BRUT	73

MILAN, JEAN R-M
4, rue Avize
51190 Oger
03 26 57 50 09
Production: 80,000
Henry Milan is not the name of a football team, but rather of one of the few clever, visionary growers in Oger. Today run by Henri-Pol Milan, who owns five hectares. Just as Ed Bonville does, he uses a great many oak barrels—100 percent, in fact, for the *cuvées de prestige*. Jean Milan's Champagnes are all good, but who wouldn't miss having an Inzagi or Schevtjenko up front?

• CUVÉE JEAN CHARLES MILAN SÉLECTION	82
(100% CH)	

One of the firm's two prestige *cuvées*. Vinified exclusively in small oak barrels, it has a restrained, tight, buttery nose with orange and honey. Austerely well-balanced and concentrated Blanc de Blancs with good potential for the future.

• JEAN MILAN BLANC DE BLANCS	70
(100% CH)	
• CUVÉE JEAN CHARLES DEMI-SEC	45
(100% CH)	
• 1992 TERRES DE NOËL	78, MAY 1998 (80)
(100% CH)	

Light and ingratiating summer beverage with clear aperitif qualities. Grassy bouquet with notes of hawthorn. Polished and refreshing taste.

• 1990 TERRES DE NOËL	80, MAY 1998 (83)
(100% CH)	

From the firm's oldest vines comes this *cuvée de prestige* via more oak barrels. Lighter and fruitier style, less concentrated, and with a tingling flavor of yellow apples.

MOËT & CHANDON **** N-M
20, avenue de Champagne
51333 Épernay
03 26 51 20 00
Production: 26,000,000
The Moët family originally comes from Holland, but has been active in Champagne since the fifteenth century. The Champagne house was founded in 1743 by Claude Moët, but rose to fame under the leadership of Jean-Rémy at the beginning of the nineteenth century. Napoleon, who studied at the military academy in Brienne, became good friends with Jean-Rémy, who soon became the mayor of Épernay. It was the start of a fabulous success story! In order for Napoleon to have a suitable place to stay on his many visits to Champagne, Le Trianon Palace was built opposite Moët & Chandon on the Avenue de Champagne. Just before Napoleon was arrested and sent to Elba, he visited Moët to present Jean-Rémy with the French order of merit, the Légion d'Honneur.

Despite the defeat at Waterloo, Moët's Champagne increased in popularity. In 1832 the name was changed to Moët & Chandon and the company proved successful throughout the industrialized world. Millions of bottles were being sold at the beginning of the twentieth century, and since then production has steadily increased, apart from a brief hiatus early in the 1990s. Robert-Jean de Vogué was another strong man who ran the company in the 1930s, and was also the man behind the C.I.V.C. Today the house has over 553 hectares in forty-four villages, but this is still hardly enough. As all of 200 villages are used in the nonvintage cuvee, 75 percent of the grapes must be bought. As much as 82 percent of the entire production is exported.

Despite Moët achieving enormous success with their simple nonvintage Champagne, the step-up in quality for all of their vintage wines is gigantic. The standard vintage wine is very reliable and good. Dom Pérignon is, of course, the flagship. The first vintage of the world's most famous wine was 1921. A lesser-known fact is that all of Dom Pérignon's vintages up to 1943 actually were regular Moët vintages that—through transversage—were transferred to replicas of eighteenth-century bottles.

The '21 is without doubt the firm's greatest vintage Champagne. The greatest Dom Pérignon, on the other hand, is more difficult to pin down. Most would probably put their money on the '61, though personally I am very fond of the '64. The company's strength lies in the large number of *crus* they have access to in assembling their *cuvées*. If the wines were stored a little longer and the yield in their *grand cru* vineyards reduced, then they would be perfect. Up until the 1960s, Dom Pérignon was constantly one of the three foremost Champagnes—hands down. That can happen again!

• MOËT & CHANDON BRUT IMPERIAL	75
(50% PN, 40% PM, 10% CH)	
• MOËT & CHANDON BRUT PREMIER CRU	80
(33% PN, 33% PM, 34% CH)	

Wonderful house-style and charming aromas of tropical fruit and white flowers. Easy-to-drink, mature nonvintage Champagne made from *premier cru* vineyards.

- MOËT & CHANDON DRY IMPERIAL 54
  (33% PN, 33% PM, 34% CH)
- MOËT & CHANDON LES CHAMPS DU ROMONT 84
  (100% PM)

Grand cru Pinot Meunier is exceptionally unusual. Les Champs du Romont in Sillery is the largest *grand cru* vineyard for this grape type. All wines in this trilogy are just as faithful to their house as to their geographical origin—this wine especially, with its house-typical style. Bready and exotically fruity like an exceptional bottle of Brut Imperial. Now I understand exactly how much Pinot Meunier means to Moët & Chandon.

- MOËT & CHANDON LES SARMENTS D'AŸ 90
  (100% PN)

In 1798 Jean-Rémy bought the vineyard Les Sarments d'Aÿ, which gets to shine all on its own today. It will be very interesting to follow these wines through the years. I hope Moët will state the date of disgorgement and the vintage blends on the label, as I am utterly convinced that all these wines gain so much from storage. My points, for example, would be higher if I could state the potential future points. Most of all, the Blanc de Noirs gains from lying still for a few years in a good cellar. The wine first had a muffled nose, classic structure, and a somewhat short aftertaste. Now, a few years after launching, the wine is brilliant, with a Dom Pérignon bouquet and a fantastically fresh, delicious fruit.

- MOËT & CHANDON LES VIGNES DE SARAN 85
  (100% CH)

During the autumn of 2001 Moët launched Trilogie des Grands Crus from three different vineyards and from three different grape types. Only 15,000 bottles of each wine are made each year. The wines are nonvintage, but were based the first time on the 1996 harvest. All three are, in my opinion, a tad too sweet as well as youthfully bound in the nose. This Chardonnay wine is rich and fleshy, with a lovely aroma of sweet almonds straight through. Les Vignes de Saran is a very old vineyard that lies just beside the official castle of Saran in Chouilly. Promising!

- MOËT & CHANDON NECTAR 53
  (33% PN, 33% PM, 34% CH)
- MOËT & CHANDON DEMI-SEC 30
  (40% PN, 40% PM, 20% CH)
- MOËT & CHANDON ROSÉ 65
- 1998 MOËT & CHANDON 84, APR 2004 (88)
  (50% PN, 5% PM, 45% CH)

As usual, extremely charming with softly explosive exotic fruit right from the start. However, I am convinced that a few months more in the bottle will impart a more toasted, enjoyable tone to the wine. A good—if hardly grand—Moët.

- 1996 MOËT & CHANDON 88, NOV 2003 (92)
  (50% PN, 5% PM, 45% CH)

Totally brilliant through and through! The vintage's austere acidity is present as life insurance, but they haven't gripped the wine so severely that it is unable to shine now. The house-style is given free rein and the fruit is luxuriantly exotic. It was probably tempting to make the Champagne sweeter, as the acids acidity is so marked. Happily, though, Moët has given a thought to the future and made a perfectly balanced, developable Champagne instead of putting all their money on immediate charm.

- 1995 MOËT & CHANDON 86, MAY 2003 (89)
  (50% PN, 10% PM, 40% CH)

Already delightfully creamy. Dry and fine with an impressively exotic layer of tastes that will be even more apparent in a few years. Clearly an impressive wine already; perhaps even better than I had predicted.

- 1993 MOËT & CHANDON 85, OCT 2003 (87)
  (50% PN, 20% PM, 30% CH)

Sauternes-like aroma, according to many of my friends. Typical lovely bouquet and focused, toffee-like, and exotic taste. Long and generous. With this fine base wine, in my view it seems unnecessary to have such a high dosage. But truly a great '93.

- 1992 MOËT & CHANDON 87, MAR 2004 (87)
  (45% PN, 15% PM, 40% CH)

The nose is all right, but the flavor is much too thin and short. Moët & Chandon should, however, receive praise for such a low dosage in this weak year. Delightfully toasty and fatter in magnum.

- 1990 MOËT & CHANDON 90, MAY 2002 (90)
  (50% PN, 20% PM, 30% CH)

Moët's vintage wines are always of a relatively high class, without costing much more than the nonvintage wine. The '90 is more restrained and stricter than usual. The taste is both buttery and creamy, with a weak toasty tone and lemony complexity. Totally evolved today.

- 1988 MOËT & CHANDON 87, JUL 2001 (88)
  (50% PN, 20% PM, 30% CH)

Moët in a nutshell. Mature, charming nose of yeast, mushroom cream, orange, and toasted bread. Soft, weak toasty taste with a sweet, medium-long aftertaste. Good value for money.

- 1986 MOËT & CHANDON 81, MAY 2001 (81)
  (50% PN, 20% PM, 30% CH)

A lightweight when it was launched. With a couple of years in its favor it matured extremely quickly. Strong nose of smoke, mushrooms, and banana. Good soft flavor of exotic fruit and especially passion fruit.

- 1985 MOËT & CHANDON 89, JAN 2000 (89)
  (50% PN, 20% PM, 30% CH)

Much more storable and stricter than the charmer of '86. The nose is weak but Chardonnay-influenced. In the mouth you're met by a fat taste that stays on the palate. Less exotic than usual.

- 1983 MOËT & CHANDON 89, MAY 2001 (89)
  (50% PN, 20% PM, 30% CH)

A successful vintage for Moët; the wine has a lovely nose of liver paté and mushroom cream. The taste is very vigorous and vibrates with fruit.

- 1982 MOËT & CHANDON 87, MAY 2001 (87)
  (50% PN, 20% PM, 30% CH)

If someone was to ask me to describe Moët's house-style, I'd open a bottle of this Champagne—it screams Moët! Lately very sweet and butterscotchy.

- 1981 MOËT & CHANDON 85, NOV 1995 (85)
  (50% PN, 20% PM, 30% CH)

Very creamy, enjoyable nose. A distinctive, unexpectedly fleshy taste. Considering how fine and sensational most of the '81s have come to be during the last years, this wine could be a sensational long shot.

- 1980 MOËT & CHANDON
  (50% PN, 20% PM, 30% CH)
- 1978 MOËT & CHANDON 86, DEC 2002 (86)
  (50% PN, 20% PM, 30% CH)

During a trip with the SAS Wine Club, I bought a couple of recently disgorged bottles of this vintage. The wine is undoubtedly fresh and fruity, but lacks any great complexity and has a herbal finish of unripe grapes. The toasty nose is much better.

- 1976 MOËT & CHANDON   90, DEC 2000 (90)
(50% PN, 20% PM, 30% CH)
Porky and heavy. Maybe not especially elegant either. Still, this is an impressively warm and voluptuous wine. Honey, vanilla, and candied roasted almonds are discerned amongst the aromas.

- 1975 MOËT & CHANDON   93, MAR 2003 (93)
(50% PN, 20% PM, 30% CH)
This year there was very little difference in quality between Dom Pérignon and the vintage wine. Here we have a classical, compact structure with plenty of ballast, a sparkling mousse, and fresh acidity. The nose is seductive after a while in the glass, with notes of coffee, cream caramels, peach, and jasmine.

- 1973 MOËT & CHANDON   87, MAY 2001 (87)
(50% PN, 20% PM, 30% CH)
Luxuriant, mushroom-cream nose, typical of the Moët house, with soft acidity and mature, unified taste. Could be on its way out. Drink up!

- 1971 MOËT & CHANDON   93, DEC 2000 (93)
(50% PN, 20% PM, 30% CH)
The first bottle I tried was in poorer condition than the Silver Jubilee one I tasted from the same year. I was struck, however, by the similarity in structure and the lovely mango aroma, which was slightly disturbed by oxidation. Recently wonderfully delicious.

- 1970 MOËT & CHANDON   86, DEC 2000 (86)
(50% PN, 20% PM, 30% CH)
Beautiful straw color, medium large nose of currants, mango, and basil. Tastes like a rich Burgundy with fat, smoky Chardonnay. Very long indeed.

- 1969 MOËT & CHANDON   86, AUG 1998 (>)
(50% PN, 20% PM, 30% CH)
Fine reddish color and alert mousse. The Pinot Meunier part has completely collapsed! This means the wine is no longer a harmonious whole, even though the Chardonnay part is still full of vigor.

- 1966 MOËT & CHANDON   92, JAN 2001 (92)
(45% PN, 20% PM, 35% CH)
This wine holds its own at most kinds of tastings. By no means a great wine, but well kept and at its peak now. Very fine mousse despite the deep color. Unified, mature, toasty Champagne nose and very ingratiating taste of nectarines. Medium long.

- 1964 MOËT & CHANDON   95, DEC 2003 (95)
(50% PN, 10% PM, 40% CH)
This is almost a parody, with its exaggerated tones of roasted coffee. In a magnum, it is today a lovely Champagne, with its heavily refined nose, well-composed, tight taste, and very long toasty aftertaste.

- 1962 MOËT & CHANDON   93, DEC 2000 (93)
(40% PN, 5% PM, 55% CH)
The last year that oak barrels were used for the vintage wine. You immediately notice a completely different concentration and complexity in the wine. Almost artificial pear-soda-pop color and extremely lively mousse. Big exotic nose of sweat, cheeses, sea, smoke, and leather. A Meursault-like taste with a long aftertaste

of oak and nuts. Considerably younger than the Dom Pérignon from the same year.

- 1961 MOËT & CHANDON   94, MAY 2001 (94)
(40% PN, 5% PM, 55% CH)
"Only tasted once before: then slightly maderized and disobliging. Otherwise, the structure appeared promising—well-stored bottles can surely still offer a special treat for the Champagne lover." That's what I wrote in 1995. In June 1997 my hopes came true. A wonderful wine! And even better in magnum.

- 1959 MOËT & CHANDON   93, OCT 2003 (93)
(50% PN, 20% PM, 30% CH)
Volume and muscle characterizes this magnificent wine. I prefer the freshness the wine has in magnum. Signs of tiredness are detected in a regular bottle.

- 1955 MOËT & CHANDON   87, MAY 2003 (87)
(45% PN, 20% PM, 35% CH)
A well-kept and bubbling magnum was actually a disappointment for me because the vintage has previously provided so many big hits. The taste was a bit too sweet, mushy, and short. But this is an uncomplicated and enjoyable bag of candy.

- 1953 MOËT & CHANDON   95, JAN 2001 (95)
(45% PN, 20% PM, 35% CH)
An almost perfect Moët, with Dom Pérignon-like aromas. Here we find an overflow of candy, coffee, and honey tones, both in the aroma and in the harmonic, playfully teasing taste.

- 1952 MOËT & CHANDON   83, MAY 2001 (83)
(50% PN, 20% PM, 30% CH)
A newly disgorged bottle that we drank beside a 1914 Moët was light, clear, and perky, but too oxidized in the nose for my taste. In the mouth, the acidity keeps the wine alive and hints of coffee and citrus were discerned.

- 1949 MOËT & CHANDON
(45% PN, 20% PM, 35% CH)

- 1947 MOËT & CHANDON   94, AUG 1997 (94)
(45% PN, 20% PM, 35% CH)
The mousse is hardly visible but there's a spry yellow color and a pure chocolate nose. Magnificently full bodied, while the wine's viscosity is lifted up by fresh acidity and a long, buttery flavor.

- 1945 MOËT & CHANDON   85, OCT 1997 (>)
(45% PN, 20% PM, 35% CH)
This wine was wonderful for a couple of seconds before it rapidly died, like a fizzy sparkler in the glass.

- 1943 MOËT & CHANDON   90, APR 2000 (90)
(50% PN, 20% PM, 30% CH)
Fleshy, vigorous, mealtime Champagne. Perhaps not as clean and elegant any longer with its strongly aged woodiness. Instead, a historic drinking experience that proves how concentrated wines were at this time, thanks to the low yield.

- 1941 MOËT & CHANDON
(45% PN, 20% PM, 35% CH)

- 1928 MOËT & CHANDON   96, MAY 2001 (96)
(45% PN, 20% PM, 35% CH)
Disgorged in 1997 and enjoyed at a first-class restaurant in Champagne. Weak, minuscule bubbles that remain on the tongue. A grand and pumped-up super-wine that can be compared to a refreshing and masterfully made Sauternes.

- 1921 MOËT & CHANDON   98, MAR 2002 (98)
(45% PN, 20% PM, 35% CH)

The best vintage Moët of all time, just as Tom Stevenson predicted. One of the greats at the Millennium Tasting, with its incredible elegance and classic charm. The wine is identical to the '21 Dom Pérignon.

- 1919 MOËT & CHANDON
(45% PN, 20% PM, 35% CH)

- 1914 MOËT & CHANDON   97, JUN 2001 (97)
(45% PN, 20% PM, 35% CH)
Disgorged in 1997. A well-preserved masterpiece that, in an astonishing way, shows how constant Moët's house-style has been through the years. The nose is perfect, with an insolently youthful, perfumed fruit and a barrage of the most wonderful aromas a bakery can produce. The mousse, the balance, and the aromatic taste spectrum are also fabulous. With a somewhat greater weight, as well as better length, this Champagne would have been one of the best I have ever tasted. Considerably less vigorous when normally disgorged.

- 1911 MOËT & CHANDON   95, JAN 1999 (95)
(45% PN, 20% PM, 35% CH)
Disgorged 1997. Light and clear, youthful color. Fine, minuscule bubbles that disappear after some time in the glass. Muffled, sweet, personable aroma with a marzipan tone at the vanguard. The taste is truly impressive with its sweet, concentrated almond essence and stately length.

- 1904 MOËT & CHANDON   94, MAR 2004 (94)
(45% PN, 20% PM, 35% CH)
There was an incredible difference between the first heavenly glass and the flat sludge that finished the bottle. My high points only apply to the beautiful first meeting with this elusive 100-year-old, which took us by storm with its toffee nose and deep, intense emotional drama. It was like a last passionate greeting that etched itself in our memory before the wine was blown away from this world and into the history books.

- 1998 MOËT & CHANDON ROSÉ   85, APR 2004 (88)
(55% PN, 5% PM, 40% CH)
A deliciously fragrant, finely floral '98 with handsome berry notes of frozen strawberries and fresh raspberries, together with a house-typical breadiness. Juicy and refreshing, with a luxurious, early summer, smiling charm. Richly delicious and very difficult to spit out—for those of us who occasionally must spit out.

- 1996 MOËT & CHANDON ROSÉ   86, MAR 2003 (90)
(55% PN, 5% PM, 40% CH)
Somewhat lighter and more delicate in color than earlier vintages. Slightly sweeter and softer overall impression than the white '96. Fine, soft fruit, with appley notes and a dash of strawberry. Bready base that is not the slightest bit toasted yet—but it will be, that's a sure bet. Yes, there it is—handsomely toasted and classic, just a few months after release.

- 1995 MOËT & CHANDON ROSÉ   91, JUN 2002 (92)
(62% PN, 10% PM, 28% CH)
Heavenly, voluptuous, sensationally good wine. So luxuriant and Burgundy-like that it takes one's breath away. Moët always makes vintage wine that is relatively ripe and easily drunk all at once. Very rarely have these modern wine-crafters created such an irresistibly rich and sensual fruity-sweet "layer-upon-layer creation" as here. Take your hat off to the giant of Épernay. The wine is remarkably similar to young vintages from Ponsot in Morey-Saint-Denis.

- 1993 MOËT & CHANDON ROSÉ   82, OCT 2000 (86)
(62% PN, 10% PM, 28% CH)

Rich, utterly beguiling, yummy rosé. Surprisingly full bodied and sweet concentration. Might possibly lack a bit of elegance and purity.

- 1992 MOËT & CHANDON ROSÉ   80, MAY 2002 (81)
(47% PN, 22% PM, 31% CH)
The 92s never reach greatness, and this rosé is no exception. There is a range of aromas, including apricot, roses, and passion fruit. A rather full but short flavor.

- 1990 MOËT & CHANDON ROSÉ   89, MAY 2002 (90)
(47% PN, 22% PM, 31% CH)
A successful wine that combines the house-style with the vintage's stringency in an excellent way. Pure, clear fruit and good balance. Highly reminiscent of the white '90.

- 1988 MOËT & CHANDON ROSÉ   81, DEC 2000 (81)
(60% PN, 15% PM, 25% CH)
Deep color, developed, cheesy style with candy and raspberry. Deep, ripe and blunt Pinot taste.

- 1986 MOËT & CHANDON ROSÉ   85, MAR 2003 (85)
(47% PN, 22% PM, 31% CH)
Evolved, bready, and not easily put down, with a pleasant modest fruit and a rather short aftertaste—but still really delightful to drink! The wine becomes more and more Burgundy-like with every year that passes.

- 1985 MOËT & CHANDON ROSÉ   81, MAY 2001 (81)
(60% PN, 15% PM, 25% CH)
The color was tremendously developed and orange, but the nose and taste showed more restraint. Unusually delicate rosé from the firm, with mineral character.

- 1983 MOËT & CHANDON ROSÉ   88, APR 1999 (88)
(60% PN, 15% PM, 25% CH)
Sensationally fine Champagne with heavenly, juicy fruit and an uplifting roasted character.

- 1982 MOËT & CHANDON ROSÉ   88, MAY 1999 (88)
(60% PN, 15% PM, 25% CH)
Difficult to spit out because so good; a truly intense, "Moët-like" Champagne that seduces with its strong bready and toasted nose and its fruity-sweet and mellow, easily imbibed appearance. I was surprised that some tasters in my company regarded this charmer as demanding, with notes of cabbage, fish, and sulfur.

- 1981 MOËT & CHANDON ROSÉ   65, JUN 1990 (70)
(60% PN, 15% PM, 25% CH)

- 1978 MOËT & CHANDON ROSÉ   88, JUN 2000 (88)
(60% PN, 15% PM, 25% CH)
A wine that didn't impress me at all previously. Today, this is a lovely, mature Champagne with a delightful, Burgundy-like Pinot aroma. The taste actually retains a youthful undertone of gooseberry.

- 1970 MOËT & CHANDON ROSÉ   82, MAR 2000 (82)
(60% PN, 15% PM, 25% CH)
Not particularly special. Rather earthy, basic character and flat personality with low acidity. Big, red fruit with a darkly crimson color. A weak vintage.

- 1969 MOËT & CHANDON ROSÉ   93, OCT 2000 (93)
(60% PN, 15% PM, 25% CH)
In all respects a seductively beautiful wine. A little short and slightly lacking in concentration, it is true, but so sumptuous and summery-fragrant, with buttery flavors of vanilla ice cream and strawberry jam, that all is forgiven.

- 1966 MOËT & CHANDON ROSÉ   88, JUN 2000 (88)
(60% PN, 15% PM, 25% CH)

Rich, nearly meaty Champagne, with a scent of cellar and Fanta. Solidly aged and a slightly parched taste.

- 1961 MOËT & CHANDON ROSÉ   86, DEC 2002 (86)
(60% PN, 15% PM, 25% CH)
Tasted beside the '55, this wine felt gloomier and somewhat less vigorous; neither was there any mousse to speak of. My English friends usually decant their old rosé Champagnes, and in this case I think that it would have liberated the Champagne from a few indistinct aromas, and better set off the vegetal Burgundy elegance that actually was there.
- 1959 MOËT & CHANDON ROSÉ   94, DEC 2003 (94)
(60% PN, 15% PM, 25% CH)
An incredibly homogeneous, rich rosé! Monumental and aristocratic. The nose is mute and still impressive in all its weight and Burgundy-like presentation. There are layers of sweet fruit and compact toffee tastes, at the same time as the dark depth beckons from its gamy side, its tobacco notes, and its indecent taste of Gruyère.
- 1955 MOËT & CHANDON ROSÉ   85, JUL 2003 (85)
(60% PN, 15% PM, 25% CH)
Hardly any mousse at all, and a dark, compact color that is identical to an old red Burgundy. Even the nose and palate head in that direction, with a strongly gamy imprint mixed with red-beet aromas and leather. Sweetly concentrated finish and a smidgen of tannin. Very interesting.
- 1996 DOM PÉRIGNON   94, FEB 2004 (96)
(50% PN, 50% CH)
When I tasted this wine for the first time it was together with Tom Stevenson at its world premier at the Mandarin Oriental Hotel in London. Both of us were surprised by the openness and direct charm that this classic, unmistakable Dom Pérignon exhibited. The acidity was there, under the blanket of sweet, rich aromas created by a rather high dosage and ripe grapes. The nose is heavenly with its elements of peach, lemon, and lime, together with vanilla, chocolate creams, and coffee beans. The taste is caressingly soft and very rich. Wonderful on the spot, but surely a wine to follow through life's every phase. Geoffroy is a genius!
- 1995 DOM PÉRIGNON   94, APR 2004 (95)
(48% PN, 52% CH)
Here is a soft, charming, sensual, and classic Dom Pérignon. The wine carpets the palate with the softest silky texture you can desire. This supple, complex wine runs down your throat with the greatest ease, trailing a fresh aftertaste. The aromatic palette is the same as usual, with its exotic fruit and breakfast-y notes, as well as an unusually strong dash of vanilla that is a distinguishing feature of the vintage.
- 1993 DOM PÉRIGNON   90, APR 2003 (93)
(45% PN, 55% CH)
Minty and elegant with an underlying exotic fleshiness. Fine mineral note and stringency. Delicious, sweet finish. It would be fun to taste beside the somewhat weaker '92. The coffee notes and richness began to appear at nine years of age.
- 1992 DOM PÉRIGNON   90, JUN 2003 (90)
(40% PN, 60% CH)
A vintage that is impossible to perform tricks with, yet Richard Geoffroy has succeeded in capturing one's attention with this easily imbibed, balanced, and superbly enjoyable Dom Pérignon. The fruit is delicious and the taste is unmistakable. The lack of vitality and depth is the only thing that reveals the vintage.

- 1990 DOM PÉRIGNON   94, OCT 2003 (96)
(42% PN, 58% CH)
Very youthful and elegant with typical Dom Pérignon finesse. It will be a pleasure to follow the internal development of the '88 and '90. A great debut for Richard Geoffroy! Toasty coffee aromas in magnum, and like a great Chablis *grand cru* in regular bottle.
- 1990 DOM PÉRIGNON OENOTÈQUE   90, FEB 2004 (96)
(42% PN, 58% CH)
During a big Gala night full of celebrities in London in 2004, several bottles exhibited problems with their corks and a mineral-laden introversion that few of us had expected. The finer specimens had an exciting nose—sea water, oyster shell, minerals, and spices. The taste was dry, anorectic, and clear as a bell, but will become seductive again in its next phase of life.
- 1988 DOM PÉRIGNON   94, NOV 2003 (95)
(55% PN, 45% CH)
Dom Pérignon is probably the world's most famous Champagne, and the '88 is an outstanding example of how beautiful this wine can be. Its notes are pure, like a brilliant diamond, and the nose is very fine. Toast, coffee beans, and fresh orangey fruit come to mind. The taste is also brilliant with clear, sharp, uplifting aromas of fruit and nuts. An ultra-sophisticated, rather light Dom Pérignon.
- 1988 DOM PÉRIGNON OENOTÈQUE   91, JAN 2003 (93)
(55% PN, 45% CH)
For several years I've run into late disgorged versions of older vintages of Dom Pérignon, with half the dosage and a few years of bottle aging after disgorging. The date of disgorging has, in exemplary fashion, been stated on the back of the label. Now Richard Geoffroy has tired of the constant questions about these wines and decided to check the release of these Champagnes himself—in order to make sure that they are absolutely at their peak when the customer enjoys the wine. The label is impressive, with a black background and classic "Dom" shape. The wines are a kind of Dom Pérignon R. D. Personally, I think that Dom Pérignon—with its toasted, reductive style—is better suited as a late disgorged wine than Bollinger's oxidative, beefy Champagnes. The autolytic mushroom-smelling character is never very intrusive with Dom Pérignon. Strangely enough, this wine tasted slightly coarser than the normally disgorged version.
- 1985 DOM PÉRIGNON   93, JUN 2003 (94)
(40% PN, 60% CH)
I was more impressed with this wine when it was launched than I am today. "Dom's" lovely coffee tones are there already, but the exhaust-fume note and mushroom aroma are toned down. The flavor is delicate and fruitily elegant, with a sophisticated smoothness and long aftertaste that reminds me of toffee and oranges.
- 1985 DOM PÉRIGNON OENOTÈQUE   94, MAY 2002 (95)
(40% PN, 60% CH)
A fabulously beautiful Champagne with floral notes and elusive bouquet. Velvety smooth and buttery, like the finest white Burgundy. Clearly better than the normal '85.
- 1983 DOM PÉRIGNON   88, JUN 2002 (90)
(50% PN, 50% CH)
A typical Dom Pérignon style! The wine has a style similar to many others, but once you have it in your glass there is no doubt as to the origin. The '83 has more orchid, mushroom

cream, and diesel fumes than the '85, but fewer toasty tones. The Champagne is easy to drink and juicy, rather like chewing a sweet peach.

- 1982 DOM PÉRIGNON   90, APR 1998 (92)
(40% PN, 60% CH)
Tasted a score of times since May 1988, this wine is easy to identify at blind tastings. It was developed relatively slowly and has an even quality from bottle to bottle. The complex nose has a perfect balance between the Pinot and the Chardonnay. Exhaust fumes, mushroom cream, orchid, and orange are some of the most obvious aromas in this medium-bodied Champagne.

- 1980 DOM PÉRIGNON   90, MAY 2002 (90)
(60% PN, 40% CH)
One of the best from 1980. Light, but very well developed in its toasty style. Sea and shellfish, along with mint chocolate, are present in the wide spectrum of aromas. Fresh and crisp, but somewhat too hollow to be seen as a great Dom Pérignon.

- 1980 DOM PÉRIGNON OENOTÈQUE   91, MAY 2002 (91)
(60% PN, 40% CH)
The long time in contact with the yeast has filled in a few of the holes that can be found in the usual featherlight '80. More beefy and toasted.

- 1978 DOM PÉRIGNON   93, MAY 2002 (93)
(50% PN, 50% CH)
Fruitier than the '80 but without its restrained elegance. An aroma of mushroom cream and bread-like taste, with well-rounded edges.

- 1978 DOM PÉRIGNON OENOTÈQUE   93, MAY 2002 (93)
(50% PN, 50% CH)
A brilliantly rich wine thanks to the increased concentration from the autolytic character. Actually reminiscent of the '76, which it was not at all like before.

- 1976 DOM PÉRIGNON   96, APR 2004 (96)
(50% PN, 50% CH)
A wine that has impressed me very little in the past, with its vintage-typical, slightly burned, warm character. That's why it was it was such a great surprise that I liked the '76 best of all among sixteen vintages at a gargantuan dinner featuring wines from Moët in December 2000. This bottle had a sensual floweriness that distinguishes the foremost '76s, as well as a stately, long, sweet finish. Grandiose! It should perhaps be pointed out that the wine was served blind.

- 1976 DOM PÉRIGNON OENOTÈQUE   96, FEB 2004 (96)
(50% PN, 50% CH)
Fabulously chewy and powerful with an indestructible power and a layered richness. Multifaceted nose with an elusive, almost flowery undertone and beautifully nutty, toasted, and honeysuckle elements. An embracing richness is combined with a fleshy, soft sensation in the mouth. The twist exudes ruby grapefruit and coffee-flavored candy.

- 1975 DOM PÉRIGNON   94, MAY 2003 (94)
(50% PN, 50% CH)
A pure Dom Pérignon with everything in its rightful place. Perhaps this wine lacks charm compared to some other vintages, and I go against the grain in preferring the '73.

- 1975 DOM PÉRIGNON OENOTÈQUE   93, MAY 2002 (94)
(50% PN, 50% CH)
Slightly neutral and weak in the nose. Incredibly compact and focused on the palate. Long and intense.

- 1973 DOM PÉRIGNON   96, MAY 2002 (96)
(50% PN, 50% CH)
The last of the truly great "Doms"? The '73 is a remarkable wine with a lovely walnut bouquet interweaved with coffee and nougat aromas. The aftertaste is oily and packed with walnut aromas. Not quite as concentrated as the "Doms" of the 1960s, but just as enjoyable aromatically, and elegant too.

- 1973 DOM PÉRIGNON OENOTÈQUE   96, MAY 2002 (96)
(50% PN, 50% CH)
Heavenly in its appearance with an almost Blanc de Blancs finesse and floweriness. One of the most classic toasted and elegant vintages of this super-wine. The aftertaste of walnut is present as usual.

- 1971 DOM PÉRIGNON   94, AUG 2001 (94)
(50% PN, 50% CH)
All the older vintages of Dom Pérignon develop a clear tone of roasted coffee beans. The '71 is full of such aromas. The taste is slightly thinner than the '73 and without its walnut tones, but the aftertaste is actually longer.

- 1970 DOM PÉRIGNON   90, DEC 2000 (90)
(50% PN, 50% CH)
Relatively weak nose with slightly toasted elements. The taste is fruity and good, but the wine hardly holds up its label. Big bottle variation, where certain bottles have a strongly toasted bouquet.

- 1969 DOM PÉRIGNON   96, JUN 2003 (96)
(50% PN, 50% CH)
The last vintage in oak barrels. Lighter than many of the old vintages of Dom Pérignon I have tasted, with a sensual acacia honey nose and the usual hint of coffee. It dances in the mouth. Almost Blanc de Blancs in style. Long, pure aftertaste.

- 1966 DOM PÉRIGNON   96, APR 2004 (96)
(50% PN, 50% CH)
A completely wonderful wine that almost reduced a good friend of mine to tears. It is full of life and vigor. Similarities to Krug '66 are many. The nose is elusive and appetizing with lots of fruit aromas from apricot and peach to mango. Weak tones of chocolate, nuts, oak, and coffee are there too, of course. In the mouth one can perceive the finest marmalade and small uplifting bubbles. Majestic aftertaste.

- 1966 DOM PÉRIGNON OENOTÈQUE   93, MAY 2002 (95)
(50% PN, 50% CH)
Slightly younger and more straggling than the normally disgorged variety. Store for a couple more years in order to increase the concentration and density.

- 1964 DOM PÉRIGNON   98, APR 2004 (98)
(50% PN, 50% CH)
Believe it or not, but the '64 may even be a touch sharper than the '66. The winner of a tasting with twelve of the best vintages from Dom Pérignon, Krug, and Bollinger. This wine combined the big nutty tones of age with young acidity and fresh attack. The wine has every-thing, where the butterscotch taste is separated from the fruit and nut aromas. This butterscotch taste remains all the way and makes up the entire, exceptionally long, aftertaste. One of my three winners at the big Millennium Tasting at Villa Pauli. Since then, never really as impressive.

- 1964 DOM PÉRIGNON OENOTÈQUE   95, MAY 2002 (96)
(50% PN, 50% CH)
As wonderful and complex as can be, but without impressing as much as the usual mint-chocolate-scented, rather uneven '64.

- 1962 DOM PÉRIGNON   95, JAN 2004 (95)
(50% PN, 50% CH)
One of the best '62s, although only marginally better than Moët's ordinary vintage Champagne. Actually less concentrated and with a shorter aftertaste. On the plus side, a silky-smooth fruit that is always outstanding in Dom Pérignon.

- 1962 DOM PÉRIGNON OENOTÈQUE   96, MAY 2002 (96)
(50% PN, 50% CH)
A wine that really benefits from handling, according to the "Oenotèque concept." The shape is round and vintage-typically rich, but the wine is vigorous and orange-sated as usual, with a taste of apricot marmalade. Brilliant!

- 1961 DOM PÉRIGNON   98, MAY 2002 (98)
(50% PN, 50% CH)
The only Champagne given six stars by Michael Broadbent in his book on vintage wines, where the maximum is five stars! Very fleshy and toasted, with a long, oaky aftertaste that has several nuances; coffee, as usual, is the most distinct. One of the jury's real favorites at the Millennium Tasting.

- 1959 DOM PÉRIGNON   94, MAY 2002 (94)
(50% PN, 50% CH)
Totally overshadowed by '59 Cristal at a recent big tasting. Incredibly viscous with its lively mousse. A heavy, nutty nose and a long taste of almond. The same points even with a totally different gun-smoke-smelling, youthful character when newly disgorged.

- 1959 DOM PÉRIGNON OENOTÈQUE   95, MAY 2002 (95)
(50% PN, 50% CH)
Rather big bottle variation with some light and undeveloped young examples and a number of powerful vintage-typical monumental bottles, which I prefer.

- 1955 DOM PÉRIGNON   95, MAY 2002 (95)
(50% PN, 50% CH)
More full bodied and rich than any other Dom Pérignon vintage. Some of the refinements have been lost in this compact, unified wine. The wine's fruitiness is overshadowed by the dark, deep, cellar aromas, the smokiness, and the almond taste.

- 1952 DOM PÉRIGNON   95, NOV 1998 (95)
(50% PN, 50% CH)
A deep golden color with a healthy mousse. A very idiosyncratic Dom Pérignon, without the usual fruit and roast bonanza. Instead the wine is dominated by truffles, leather, meat, and tar.

- 1943 DOM PÉRIGNON   94, MAR 1996 (94)
(50% PN, 50% CH)
Apparently the same wine as the Coronation Cuvée. Here it held up better in the glass, though. A wonderful base flavor and a lovely, luxurious feel in the mouth.

- 1993 DOM PÉRIGNON ROSÉ   92, APR 2004 (94)
(63% PN, 37% CH)
Already caressingly beautiful with subtle coffee aromas braided with soft red fruit and stylish berry scents. Deliciously rounded and slender without being ingratiating. Yet another masterpiece of elegance and balance from Richard Geoffroy.

- 1992 DOM PÉRIGNON ROSÉ   87, JAN 2003 (90)
(58% PN, 42% CH)
So far, it's the taste that is the attraction of this famous wine. The nose is simple and floral while the taste has an exotic richness and a delightful Burgundy-like round character.

- 1990 DOM PÉRIGNON ROSÉ   94, MAY 2003 (96)
(50% PN, 50% CH)
Superbly euphoric nose, as languorous and silky as a guitar solo by Carlos Santana. As usual, Richard Geoffroy—like his predecessor—has succeeded in creating a wine that has seductive suppleness, complexity, and concentration in one and the same wine. In that sense, Dom Pérignon has a greatness that no other wines can really match, excepting La Tâche in Burgundy. Besides wonderful structure there are layers of red and exotic fruit, with blood orange as the guiding star. All these fruits are sensitively braided together with all the classically toasted fireworks. I noticed with interest—when this wine was served blind—that it wasn't at all popular with the novices: they couldn't see past the stables and outhouse in the nose. How differently people can perceive things!

- 1988 DOM PÉRIGNON ROSÉ   96, MAR 2004 (97)
(60% PN, 40% CH)
Oh my goodness! A fantastic rosé wine with the same delightful Aÿ aroma as the '85. Moët's bready, mushroomy, yeasty note is certainly recognizable and hogs a big part of the picture. There is also a *terroir*-propelled elegance and a La Tâche-like silkiness on the tongue that only the truly great wines can mobilize.

- 1986 DOM PÉRIGNON ROSÉ   93, DEC 1998 (94)
(60% PN, 40% CH)
One of this vintage's foremost Champagnes. As always, seductively soft and exotic with a wonderful bouquet of roasted coffee beans, nougat, and orange chocolate. A wine that can be compared to the kiss of an angel.

- 1985 DOM PÉRIGNON ROSÉ   96, MAY 2002 (97)
(50% PN, 50% CH)
A marvelous wine with a nose marked by the extraordinary Aÿ Pinot. Moët & Chandon have succeeded in the art of making a wine with a powerful Pinot nose and at the same time a buttery, elegant Chardonnay texture. One of the best rosé Champagnes I've tasted.

- 1982 DOM PÉRIGNON ROSÉ   91, OCT 1997 (93)
(40% PN, 60% CH)
Dom Pérignon Rosé is always amazingly expensive and seldom worth the money. The '82 has an orange color, an elegant fruity nose, and a powerful taste of orange toffee, leaving quite a definite impression on the palate.

- 1980 DOM PÉRIGNON ROSÉ   90, OCT 1997 (92)
(65% PN, 35% CH)
Very reminiscent of the '82, with a lovely orange bouquet and a classic taste.

- 1978 DOM PÉRIGNON ROSÉ   89, SEP 2000 (89)
(60% PN, 40% CH)
Dark red color, cheesy nose, concentrated, fruity, long taste. Sweeter and more full bodied than the white "Dom." Certainly more vinous, but less elegant. Spend your money elsewhere.

- 1975 DOM PÉRIGNON ROSÉ   93, MAR 1995 (93)
(60% PN, 40% CH)
Extremely dark red color, mousse almost foaming. The nose is unexpectedly fruity and young, with a broad spectrum of orange, strawberry, plum, black, and redcurrant notes. At first the taste was young and full of strawberry. It was only in the acceleratingly fat aftertaste that the wine's greatness shone through.

- 1973 DOM PÉRIGNON ROSÉ   95, MAR 2003 (95)
(60% PN, 40% CH)
Superbly elegant, light-footed Champagne with charismatic grace and inviting charm. One of the lighter but also more classic

vintages of this super-wine. The luscious fruitiness exudes newly picked raspberries, and the bready notes are magnificently balanced. A wine that should be enjoyed in great gulps!

- 1971 DOM PÉRIGNON ROSÉ   95, MAY 2002 (95)
(60% PN, 40% CH)

What can one say? Certain vintages of this precious commodity are simply fantastic. The color has the same deep red appearance. The mousse bubbles up in a sensational way. The entire wine exudes seriousness and sumptuous vinosity. This has everything required of a really big red Burgundy. The spice, the coffee aromas, the smokiness, and the massive vegetal tones in the fruit call to mind red beets; the aftertaste is reminiscent of the finest bitter chocolate. All of this is an unusually clear expression of first-class Pinot Noir.

- 1969 DOM PÉRIGNON ROSÉ   96, MAY 2002 (96)
(60% PN, 40% CH)

Not as rich as the '62, but composed more like the '71. Both the bouquet and flavor are very reminiscent of high-class red Burgundy. Leather, truffles, red beet, raspberry, and chocolate are just a few of the wonderful things one can associate with this precious nectar.

- 1966 DOM PÉRIGNON ROSÉ   96, MAR 2000 (96)
(60% PN, 40% CH)

A super-elegant and light vintage in comparison with the '62 and the '71. Fabulous and euphoria-inducing with nuances of meringue, tea, and roses, together with the rich, mature, Burgundy-like Pinot aroma. A true winner of a Champagne.

- 1962 DOM PÉRIGNON ROSÉ   96, MAR 2000 (96)
(60% PN, 40% CH)

Well, well, I finally ran into the best Champagne from the year of my birth. A completely divine Champagne that for pleasure alone received ninety-seven points, but which I knocked down a notch because, if one wants to be fussy, it is perhaps a little too generous and round with a certain lack of acidity. All vintages of this very great wine are dark in color, yet the '62 has a somewhat lighter tone with hints of orange. The bouquet is overwhelming with its plumpness and extremely rich caramel-toffee character. The taste, with its treacly, layer-upon-layer concoction of goodies, is almost chewable. This bottle is as historical as it is delicious—it was the premier vintage for pink Dom Pérignon.

- 1959 DOM PÉRIGNON ROSÉ   96, MAR 2003 (96)
(60% PN, 40% CH)

All the books on wine that I have describe the wine served at the Shah of Iran's birthday party as the premier vintage of Dom Pérignon Rosé, 1962. And yet, amazingly, I ran into a bottle of '59! One is seldom able to drink wines that weren't made, but this appears to be such a wine! I was forced to check with Richard Geoffroy, who smiled mischievously and said: "Hmm, so you've found one of those? We made a few experimental bottles." Whatever—the wine was enormously concentrated and full of alcohol with a weight and length that crushed everything in its path. Absolutely the most powerful vintage of this wine, but lacking the ethereal sensuality of the best ones.

- MOËT & CHANDON AMERICAN INDEPENDENCE   84, JAN 2001 (84)
(50% PN, 20% PM, 30% CH)

Champagne made for the Bicentennial, 1776–1976. Too sweet, but charming and fresh, with notes of almonds and ripe apples.

- MOËT & CHANDON SILVER JUBILEE 1977   92, JAN 2003 (92)
(50% PN, 20% PM, 30% CH)

This jubilee bottle is actually a pure '71, with a clear nose of newly washed sheets that have dried in the wind. The dominant element in both the nose and the medium-bodied flavor is mango.

- 1983 MOËT & CHANDON ANNIVERSARY CUVÉE   83, OCT 1993 (89)
(60% PN, 40% CH)

A special blend from Moët's vineyards, according to Moët themselves. For me it is confusingly similar to the ordinary '83 in a later-disgorged guise.

- 1943 MOËT & CHANDON CORONATION CUVÉE   94, SEP 1996 (>)
(50% PN, 50% CH)

This special cuvée was made in honor of the coronation of the British Queen Elizabeth II in 1953, and gave myself and my companions a truly historic experience. The color was deep and the nose oxidized quickly in the glass, but the fresh, majestic flavor was wonderful.

MONCUIT-BIGEX, ALAIN R-M
5, avenue Gare
51190 Le Mesnil-sur-Oger
03 26 57 52 71
The firm was recently disbanded but the bottles are still in circulation.
- ALAIN MONCUIT-BIGEX   70
(100% CH)

MONCUIT, PIERRE *** R-M
11, rue Persault Maheu
51190 Le Mesnil-sur-Oger
03 26 57 52 65
Production: 125,000

Nicole Moncuit runs this well-respected domain, which owns twenty hectares in Le Mesnil, including a share of Les Chétillon's old vines. Moncuit is often mentioned in the same breath as greats like Selosse, Diebolt, and Peters, which is something I have trouble understanding. For a long time Moncuit's wines were remarkable: when young they were more closed and sharp than most, only to suddenly develop some very odd tones of maturity. The nose became perfumed and the flavor gained a strange tone of lingonberry, which isn't what you would expect from Le Mesnil. To be honest, I think that the hygiene conditions at Moncuit left something to be desired. I've noticed the same strange lingonberry aroma in their *cuverie*, and seen a few things there that don't belong near fermentation tanks. However, there is little doubt that the grapes are fantastic, proved by a big lift in the 1990s. The nonvintage Champagne is particularly delicious now, and with the '96 on the market, they are now playing among the big boys—and rapidly approaching four stars.

- CUVÉE HUGUES DE COULMET   60
(100% CH)
- P. MONCUIT CUVÉE DELOS   78
(100% CH)
- 1988 P. MONCUIT VIEILLES VIGNES   81, MAY 1994 (81)
(100% CH)

For the first time Moncuit separated their oldest vines in Les Chétillons for use in the *cuvée de prestige*. The nose is closed for half an hour in the glass, but suddenly gooseberry, pear, and lingonberry arrive. The structure in the mouth is fat and concentrated. This wine will probably become great, but don't bet too heavily on it.

- 1999 P. MONCUIT 85, DEC 2003 (88)
(100% CH)
Very round and developed honey-ish fruit, bordering on honeysuckle. Super-focused and sweetly rich, yet still full of mineral. Fruit bomb that's not lacking in finesse.

- 1998 P. MONCUIT VIEILLES VIGNES 84, SEP 2003 (89)
(100% CH)
For the time being the nose is rather mute and subdued, with a few cheeky green notes of rhubarb, gooseberry, and grass. Otherwise, impressively well built with an oily texture and a unified, focused, concentrated taste. Store for many years to come.

- 1997 P. MONCUIT 84, OCT 2003 (87)
(100% CH)
Yet another excellent, compact wine from this resurrected producer. The fruit is honeyed and rather exotic, with notes of mango and papaya. I don't think I should exaggerate the importance of storage here, but why not purchase a few bottles and take a chance on long storage for a bottle produced in true Mesnil spirit.

- 1996 P. MONCUIT 92, SEP 2003 (94)
(100% CH)
Extraordinary nose of mandarin orange and orange blossom, together with vanilla pastries. Irresistible taste of nut toffee, mandarin orange, and tranquil, exclusive Burgundy. Razor-sharp acidity enveloped in an oily layer of fruit—thus never intrusive. Highly reminiscent of Peters Cuvée Spéciale from the same year. A real winner—Le Mesnil has got a new world-class player.

- 1995 P. MONCUIT 85, DEC 2003 (87)
(100% CH)
Exceedingly soft and pleasant. Creamy, minty aromas dominate over the exotic generosity, both in the nose and palate. It feels as if the wine is ripe and evolved, but there might still be a little acidic under the soft fruity layers that will enable it to develop beautifully into the future.

- 1990 P. MONCUIT 87, SEP 2003 (89)
(100% CH)
A brilliantly rich and fleshy Blanc de Blancs with honey notes and stone fruit. Powerful nose, velvety smooth, and richly long, impressive taste.

- 1989 P. MONCUIT 75, MAY 1994 (82)
(100% CH)
Here the shimmering green wine has a closed nose. The flavor is rich and full-bodied, but the aftertaste is short.

- 1988 P. MONCUIT 76, MAY 1994 (84)
(100% CH)
Bitingly acidic and hard, but a promising structure and young, unripe fruitiness.

- 1986 P. MONCUIT 83, JAN 1995 (84)
(100% CH)
Very enjoyable and creamy Blanc de Blancs in a classic style.

- 1982 P. MONCUIT 30, SEP 1992 (?)
(100% CH)

- 1981 P. MONCUIT 87, MAR 1992 (88)
(100% CH)
Definitely the most enjoyable Champagne from this firm I've tasted. An extremely multifaceted, flowery nose spread with citrus fruits and mint. The flavor is light, delicate, and uplifting.

- 1980 P. MONCUIT 85, MAY 1994 (85)
(100% CH)
A deep color. A mature Champagne that has not developed lingonberry aromas. Instead one notices the vintage's smoky style and the proper weight.

- 1964 P. MONCUIT 87, SEP 2003 (87)
(100% CH)
A big, mature Champagne with notes of honey, figs, chocolate-toffee, and dried fruit. Quickly dissipates in the glass, becoming completely flat. Powerful, fiery taste. Probably quite high alcohol content.

MONCUIT, ROBERT *** R-M
2, place de la Gare
51190 Le Mesnil-sur-Oger
03 26 57 52 71
Far less well known than Pierre Moncuit, but the Champagnes that I tasted were distinctly promising. Close to four stars!

- ROBERT MONCUIT BLANC DE BLANCS 77
(100% CH)

- 1987 ROBERT MONCUIT 80, FEB 1997 (84)
(100% CH)
A full-bodied, village-typical, rich Champagne, with notes of nutshell and pears. This wine resembles F. Billion.

- 1982 ROBERT MONCUIT 83, MAY 1999 (86)
(100% CH)
Mature, slightly rugged nose. The taste has potential for development and a good acidity at heart.

- 1976 ROBERT MONCUIT 94, OCT 2002 (94)
(100% CH)
Dear Robert has moved to Canada, as the high rate of French taxes became too much for him—pity for those of us who have tasted the best of his vintage wines. I'd been eyeing up this '76 in a jeroboam on the distinguished wine list of the restaurant Le Mesnil for a long time before I gathered enough people to take it on. Fresh, sound 1976s are always incredibly delicious and impressive with their butterscotchy, sweet, nut-toffee-scented style. Magnificently toasted and mineral-sated in village-typical style.

- 1973 ROBERT MONCUIT 90, MAY 1999 (91)
(100% CH)
Yet another wine that exhibits Le Mesnil's tremendous potential. I have rarely tasted a more refreshing '73. The wine relies entirely on its mineral character and clean, acidic elegance. It might appear too lean, if not for a pleasant creaminess enveloping the acidity like a silk cocoon. Classic walnut tone in the empty glass.

- 1970 ROBERT MONCUIT 90, JUN 2003 (90)
(100% CH)
Salon-like oxidative nose of hay, malt, oxidized apples, and old butter. Rich and meaty with lovely tastes of maturity. Few wines from 1970 can display such acidity. Rather developed color. Drink immiediately. Delightful in jeroboam.

MONTAUDON N-M

6, rue Ponsardin
51100 Reims
03 26 47 53 30
Production: 1,200,000

For more than a hundred years the Montaudon family has succeeded in keeping the firm in its own hands, and today it is run by Luc Montaudon. The firm's own vineyards lie in Aube; they are very happy with the grapes there, even though most of the grapes are bought in from Marne. The wines are uncomplicated and fruity with a spicy tone that has many supporters. Personally, I remain unimpressed.

• MONTAUDON BRUT "M"	53	
(50% PN, 25% PM, 25% CH)		
• MONTAUDON CLASSÉ	68	
(40% PN, 60% CH)		
• MONTAUDON BLANC DE BLANCS	38	
(100% CH)		
• MONTAUDON SEC	30	
(50% PN, 25% PM, 25% CH)		
• 1997 MONTAUDON	78, JUN 2003	(79)
(30% PN, 55% PM, 15% CH)		
• 1989 MONTAUDON	67, MAY 1996	(78)
(60% PN, 40% CH)		
• 1988 MONTAUDON	52, NOV 1993	(60)
(60% PN, 40% CH)		
• 1979 MONTAUDON	79, JUL 1995	(79)
(60% PN, 40% CH)		
• 1990 MONTAUDON ROSÉ	55, MAY 1996	(68)
(60% PN, 40% CH)		
• 1988 MONTAUDON ROSÉ	32, NOV 1993	
(65% PN, 35% CH)		

MONTEBELLO N-M

2, boulevard du Nord
51160 Aÿ
03 26 55 15 44
Production: 250,000

The Montebello Champagne house was founded in 1834 by the count of the same name in the magnificent Château de Mareuil. He was the son of one of Napoleon's best friends, Maréchal Lannes. The firm has long been owned by Ayala, and is nowhere near the class of its big brother. A couple of years ago they lost their membership of the Syndicat des Grandes Marques at last. I haven't tasted the company's Champagnes, and in fact I had never even seen one of their bottles before I found the old one you can read about here.

• 1964 MONTEBELLO	88, MAR 2002	(88)
(75% PN, 25% CH)		

A vigorous, chocolate-sated knockout that went well with ptarmigan and mushroom sauce. The wine exhibited a dark power combined with notes of iron, boiled vegetables, and wood. Unfortunately, the wine went quickly downhill in the glass.

MONTVILLERS N-M

17, rue de la Charte
51160 Aÿ
03 26 54 82 58
Production: 180,000

The importers Arvid Nordqvist and Bengt Frithiofsson took a liking to this property in Aÿ. I've never been there myself but deem the quality acceptable. The company is run by Monsieur Montgolfier and has a connection to Bollinger. They own no vineyards of their own and buy to suit their needs.

• MONTVILLERS BENGT FRITHIOFSSON COLLECTION SEC	70
(50% PN, 25% PM, 25% CH)	
• MONTVILLERS BENGT FRITHIOFSSON COLLECTION BRUT	73
(50% PN, 25% PM, 25% CH)	

MOREL, JEAN-PAUL R-M

14, rue Chanzy
51360 Verzenay
03 26 49 48 01
Production: 70,000

This grower runs the production at Landragin along with his own Champagne.

• J.-P. MOREL BRUT SELECTION	77
(80% PN, 20% CH)	
• J.-P. MOREL BLANC DE BLANCS DE VERZENAY	74
(100% CH)	
• J.-P. MOREL ROSÉ	72
(100% PN)	

MORIZET & FILS, G. R-M

19, rue du Moutier
51530 Cramant
03 26 57 50 92
Production: 60,000

Madame Morizet has more than ten hectares in Cramant that are planted with relatively young vines. The wines are fermented in steel tanks and are put through malolactic fermentation and filtration.

• G. MORIZET GRAND CRU BRUT	72
(100% CH)	

MOUTARD-DILIGENT N-M

rue des Ponts
10110 Buxeuil
03 25 38 50 73
Production: 400,000

The firm was founded in 1927 by François Diligent. Today it's run by his daughter and her husband, François Moutard—they have more than twenty-one hectares. As much as 75 percent of the production is exported. The house makes wines under two different labels: François Diligent and Moutard Père & Fils. The firm is one of the few that makes a Champagne from the almost extinct Arbanne grape.

• MOUTARD-DILIGENT TRADITION	55
(70% PN, 20% PM, 10% CH)	
• MOUTARD-DILIGENT EXTRA BRUT	60
(50% PN, 50% CH)	
• MOUTARD-DILIGENT GRANDE CUVÉE	62
(100% PN)	

- MOUTARD-DILIGENT GRANDE RÉSERVE   53
  (100% CH)
- MOUTARD-DILIGENT RÉSERVE   60
  (100% CH)
- MOUTARD-DILIGENT ARBANNE VIEILLES VIGNES   83
  (100% ARBANNE)

An extremely idiosyncratic wine that frightened a few tasters and fascinated others. The density and concentration are fantastic. The aromatic profile is, on the other hand, anything but classic. I found banana, white currants, oil, and litchi—almost like a Gewürztraminer in the nose. The taste was nearer to a big, dry Chenin Blanc from Loire. The mousse is coarse and indelicate, probably because the density is so high that the bubbles are unable to move about in the languid fluid. This wine has to be experienced in order to understand what I'm jabbering about.

- MOUTARD-DILIGENT ROSÉ   70
  (100% PN)
- 1985 MOUTARD-DILIGENT VIEUX MILLÉSIMÉ   58, OCT 2002 (58)
  (100% CH)
- 1983 MOUTARD-DILIGENT   83, OCT 1997 (83)
  (100% CH)

Lovely biscuity nose, medium-bodied, balanced flavor, and a rather short aftertaste.

- 1964 MOUTARD   89, DEC 2003 (89)
  (100% CH)

Very impressive! A wine from Aube that is still unbelievably fresh and enjoyable. The fruit is still youthful with notes that I compare to peach, gooseberry, and strawberry. Like a sort of summery fruit salad backed up by vanilla sugar and cream. No secondary aromas at all!

- MOUTARD-DILIGENT PRESTIGE   69
  (50% PN, 50% CH)
- MOUTARD-DILIGENT ROSÉ PRESTIGE   69
  (70% PN, 30% CH)

MOUTARDIER, JEAN N-M
route d'Orbais
51210 Le Breuil
03 26 59 21 09
Production: 180,000

Despite a long growing tradition in the Moutardier family, this house wasn't actually founded until 1920. Jean owns sixteen hectares in the Marne valley, which supplies 86 percent of his production needs. Englishman Jonathan Saxby is beginning to take over more and more of his father-in-law's workload, having given up a brilliant career in the British business world in order to study Champagne at the enology school in Avize. There are differing opinions about whether the Leuvrigny cooperative or Jean Moutardier produce the finest Meunier grapes outside of the *premier* and *grand cru* villages. Jacques Peters, cellar master at Veuve Clicquot, always uses Moutardier's Meunier grapes as his yardstick.

- JEAN MOUTARDIER BRUT   39
  (90% PM, 10% CH)
- JEAN MOUTARDIER SÉLECTION   72
  (50% PN, 50% CH)
- JEAN MOUTARDIER ROSÉ   42
  (100% PM)

MOUZON-LEROUX R-M
16, rue Basse des Carrieres
51380 Verzy
03 26 97 96 68
Production: 80,000

Established in 1938 by Roger and Cécile Mouzon. Today they own nine hectares. All the wines from Mouzon-Leroux are pure *grand cru* Champagnes from Verzy.

- MOUZON-LEROUX DEMI-SEC   53
  (70% PN, 30% CH)
- MOUZON-LEROUX GRANDE RÉSERVE   61
  (70% PN, 30% CH)
- MOUZON-LEROUX ROSÉ   69
  (100% PN)
- CUVÉE MOUZON-JUILLET   86
  (70% PN, 30% CH)

A pure '89 made in oak barrels. This *cuvée de prestige* is the best I've tasted from Verzy. It's heavy, smoky, and nutty, with impressive concentration and potential. The ugliest bottle in the history of wine!

MOUZON, JEAN-CLAUDE R-M
4, rue des Perthois
51380 Verzenay
03 26 49 48 11
Production: 11,000

Jean-Claude Mouzon owns 3.5 hectares in Verzenay and sells a great deal of his wine to Moët & Chandon.

- JEAN-CLAUDE MOUZON BRUT   68
  (68% PN, 7% PM, 25% CH)
- JEAN-CLAUDE MOUZON CUVÉE FLEURIE   83
  (100% CH)

A rarity—a Blanc de Blancs from Verzenay. A good, fresh Champagne with a flowery, perfumed nose of gooseberry and melon. Unexpectedly light flavor and a fruity nectar.

- JEAN-CLAUDE MOUZON RÉSERVE   73
  (68% PN, 7% PM, 25% CH)
- JEAN-CLAUDE MOUZON TRADITION   69
  (68% PN, 7% PM, 25% CH)
- JEAN-CLAUDE MOUZON ROSÉ   80
  (80% PN, 7% PM, 13% CH)

What a charmer! Relatively light color, an appetizing nose of mango, strawberry, leather, smoke, and stable. Sweet, free-and-easy rounded flavor with plenty of vigor and tones of passion fruit.

- JEAN-CLAUDE MOUZON GRAND CRU VERZENAY   79, JUL 1997 (85)
  (65% PN, 35% CH)

A pure '96. Surprisingly light and floral with citrus notes and a weak secondary tone of banana and flour. Otherwise delicious and difficult to put down.

MUMM *** N-M
29, rue du Champ de Mars
51100 Reims
03 26 49 59 69
Production: 8,000,000

Mumm is one of the very biggest Champagne houses. They have a particularly steady grip on the American market, which really loves Cordon Rouge. In 1827 the house was founded by three brothers,

Jacobus, Gottlieb, and Philipp Mumm, along with Friedrich Giesler. They set up P. A. Mumm, named after their father, Peter-Arnold. The Mumm family was already established in the Rhine valley, but wanted to try producing the sparkling French wine. World War I was particularly troublesome for Mumm, due to the German origins of the owners. Between the wars René Lalou became the man with the drive to restore the Mumm name, and after World War II the firm expanded enormously by pushing the export market hard.

From 1969 the company was for a long time owned by the Canadian concern, Seagram. In June 1999 it was acquired by the Hicks Muse Tate & Furst Investment Group, and then by Allied Domecq. Mumm owns 327 hectares with grapes of very high quality (average quality 95 percent), but three-quarters of the grapes are bought in from simpler vineyards. The nonvintage Champagne is constantly improving. Like many other great Champagne houses, Mumm made its foremost Champagnes in the 1950s. The '59 Rosé is magical, and the white '55 is a most delectable and vigorous wine.

- MUMM CORDON ROUGE   74
  (35% PN, 55% PM, 10% CH)
- MUMM GRAND CRU   85
  (58% PN, 42% CH)
  For only a tiny bit more money you get this nonvintage Champagne instead of Cordon Rouge. Production is minuscule, as the wine is only made with grapes from Verzenay, Bouzy, Aÿ, Avize, and Cramant. This is a superb drink with really high-class structure. Both bready and slightly toasted, with a clean, classic, balanced taste. Dry and long.
- MUMM CORDON VERT   49
  (50% PN, 25% PM, 25% CH)
- MUMM DEMI-SEC   50
  (35% PN, 55% PM, 10% CH)
- MUMM ROSÉ   56
  (60% PN, 18% PM, 22% CH)
- 1997 MUMM   79, SEP 2003 (82)
  (66% PN, 34% CH)
  A slightly shy champagne with the house's milky toffee style—almost like an extension of Cordon Rouge. The wine becomes more and more gamy in the glass and has a peppery finish. A big step-down in quality from the two brilliant previous vintages.
- 1996 MUMM   87, OCT 2003 (90)
  (63% PN, 37% CH)
  Delightfully voluptuous, uplifting Champagne, with Mumm's soft toffee tone handsomely restrained by a refreshing apple-scented fruitiness. Everything seems consciously "tightened up" by the increasingly more dexterous winemaker, Demarville.
- 1995 MUMM   85, OCT 2003 (86)
  (63% PN, 37% CH)
  For the moment slightly unripe and smelling of gooseberries. Its future is difficult to judge: some of it exhibits a soft, toffee-drenched fruitiness at the same time as the acidity tickles the tongue. Already good and harmonic despite its two paradoxical sides. Recently minty and delicious.
- 1990 MUMM   86, AUG 1999 (89)
  (54% PN, 46% CH)
  Developed, glorious aroma of fudge and vanilla. Soft, luxurious taste that is very difficult to spit out. A large portion of the aromatic spectrum is frankly reminiscent of a red Rioja.

- 1988 MUMM   80, JUL 1996 (87)
  (70% PN, 30% CH)
  A broad, developed, bready, Moët & Chandon-like, high-class nose. The flavor is more ordinary, with a rich fruity sweetness and fair balance. Nutty finish.
- 1985 MUMM   89, MAR 2003 (89)
  (70% PN, 30% CH)
  A lovely, charming wine that unabashedly opens up and refuses to hide in the—for the '85s—obligatory tunnel. Elements of baked goods, vanilla, and toffee, with apple overtones and exotic fruit. Warm and generous medium-bodied palate with an uplifting, smoky final twist.
- 1982 MUMM   85, JAN 2002 (85)
  (75% PN, 25% CH)
  Blunt, musky nose in this rich, full-bodied, food Champagne. Probably already at its peak.
- 1979 MUMM   92, JAN 2002 (92)
  (75% PN, 25% CH)
  A lovely, mature and well-structured wine, with a full body and tones of chocolate and nut aromas. A long aftertaste of veal *fond*. Actually a more powerful wine than the '79 René Lalou.
- 1976 MUMM   87, APR 2000 (87)
  (75% PN, 25% CH)
  Anybody looking for elegance and appetizing freshness in their Champagne shouldn't bother with this. Here we have an old-fashioned food Champagne with a robust character and steady backbone, strong enough to carry a heavy meat dish. A bit tired lately.
- 1975 MUMM   86, APR 2004 (86)
  (75% PN, 25% CH)
  A very good vintage for Mumm, as the large Pinot content has been given room to play around and all the building blocks have fallen into place. Getting tired fast, though.
- 1973 MUMM   93, DEC 2002 (93)
  (70% PN, 30% CH)
  Unfortunately, I've never tasted this delicious wine in a regular bottle. I say "unfortunately," because it might give the reader a more nuanced picture of the wine. The wine in magnum, which I've had the pleasure of tasting, is supremely pleasant, with a newness that is probably lacking in a regular bottle. The nose is agreeable, with a classic bready balance and a handsomely placed citrus note. Nicely balanced dosage and a velvety-smooth finish with agreeable sweetness.
- 1971 MUMM   75, JAN 2002 (>)
  (70% PN, 30% CH)
- 1969 MUMM   93, APR 2000 (93)
  (70% PN, 30% CH)
  Extremely butterscotchy, caramelized Champagne with buoyant acidity and plentiful, uplifting mousse as a counterweight. Medium-bodied, "difficult-to-spit," delicious taste of vanilla, baked goods, and milk chocolate. Fruity finish.
- 1966 MUMM   90, JAN 2002 (90)
  (70% PN, 30% CH)
  When this wine was poured its strong bouquet filled the room. The Champagne is very well preserved and exceptionally fragrant, but with a somewhat short, sweet aftertaste. A later shipment was much too tired—that's the way it goes with old Champagne.
- 1964 MUMM   93, AUG 2001 (93)
  (70% PN, 30% CH)

Absolutely pure and balanced, like so many '64s. A stylish nose of vanilla and hazelnuts. In the mouth the wine is compact and genuine, with tones of cream and roasted coffee beans.

- 1961 MUMM   94, JUL 2002 (94)
(70% PN, 30% CH)
Strong stylish wine, with lots of power and a dry, classic finish.

- 1959 MUMM   83, AUG 1995 (>)
(70% PN, 30% CH)
The '59 has in all likelihood seen its best days. Of course, it may still be enjoyable with its fat, oily toffee flavor and chocolate-filled nose, but the vitality is about to die and the wine is quickly lost in the glass.

- 1955 MUMM   95, JUN 1999 (95)
(70% PN, 30% CH)
Oh my, this was good! Alive and vital at the age of forty. The nose has a magnificent spectrum of coffee and honey; there's a medium-bodied fruity flavor and a beautiful long aftertaste of soft candy and popcorn.

- 1953 MUMM   80, JAN 2002 (>)
(70% PN, 30% CH)
A curious wine with an exemplary appearance, the nose of a dry, high-class sherry and a long but extremely dry flavor for such an old Champagne.

- 1949 MUMM   94, OCT 1997 (94)
(70% PN, 30% CH)
A voluptuous wine with a wonderful nose of vanilla and butterscotch. Good to look at and easy to drink.

- 1947 MUMM   89, JAN 2002 (89)
(70% PN, 30% CH)
Mumm made rather an insipid wine in this great year. Some sherry aromas have crept in, but the one-dimensional, meaty structure keeps the wine from drowning for a few more years.

- 1937 MUMM
(70% PN, 30% CH)

- 1929 MUMM   80, JUN 2000 (>)
(70% PN, 30% CH)
Slightly musty, sweaty, and cheesy scent, and a somewhat overripe taste of honey and milk chocolate. Clearly on its way down.

- 1928 MUMM
(70% PN, 30% CH)

- 1982 MUMM ROSÉ   49, JUL 1988 (68)
(70% PN, 30% CH)

- 1979 MUMM ROSÉ   84, OCT 2002 (84)
(70% PN, 30% CH)
Fine color and appearance. Big, developed, slightly gloomy bouquet—mushrooms, leather, and dried prunes are all present. The taste is ample and unfortunately slightly bitter. The acidity is good and the mousse is weak, but fine. A robust food Champagne.

- 1966 MUMM ROSÉ   80, JUN 2002 (80)
(75% PN, 25% CH)
A heavily aged rosé with an oxidative, slightly unclean nose dominated by Danish cheeses and sweaty feet. Sweet, uncomplicated, and butterscotchy, with a good taste of peppermint candy cane and raspberry cream.

- 1964 MUMM ROSÉ   92, MAY 1999 (92)
(75% PN, 25% CH)
Surprisingly austere and dry with impressive warmth and power.

A smoky base note is attractively braided with aromas reminiscent of bitter chocolate. Still has decent mousse.

- 1959 MUMM ROSÉ   96, MAY 1997 (96)
(72% PN, 28% CH)
What a sensational wine! The concentration is astounding. The Champagne is almost treacly and fat, with a nectar-sweet assembly of exotic fruit. The nose is hardly exceptional, but it is extremely satisfying, with dense fruit and smoky barrel complexity.

- 1955 MUMM ROSÉ   94, JUN 2003 (94)
(72% PN, 28% CH)
My gosh, what great wines Mumm made in the 1950s! Smoky and monumental with a lovely, intact butterscotchiness—this powerful Champagne still seduces the lucky few who get to taste it in the twenty-first century.

- MUMM DE CRAMANT   85
(100% CH)
Previously Crémant de Cramant. It's considered a connoisseur's wine for people who know about the fine print. Watery white color, weak floral nose, slightly brittle and short, but with a very refreshing spring-like palate. It has improved lately.

- 1990 CORDON ROUGE CUVÉE LIMITÉE   87, DEC 2001 (91)
(55% PN, 45% CH)
This has the same wine base as the 1990 Grand Cordon, but with a large amount of Chardonnay reserve wines from '94, '93, and '92 in the dosage. Yes, you read correctly. This practice is actually more common than one thinks. Cristal, for example, get a portion of their luxuriously creamy-toffee character in the same way. The grapes come from Avize, Cramant, Verzy, Verzenay, Aÿ, Avenay, and Bouzy. In other words, fantastic raw material. This is Mumm's own personal style with an overabundance of milk toffee, toffee, and yogurt. The flavor is very good, but too ingratiating and somewhat too short. Perhaps I'm overly petulant. Let yourself be seduced, and then take my words with a pinch of salt.

- 1990 GRAND CORDON   87, DEC 2000 (90)
(55% PN, 45% CH)
A very successful Champagne that, admittedly, has strains of Mumm's "carameliness," but which primarily relies on a classically balanced theme with fine acidity. Drink after 2005.

- 1985 GRAND CORDON   85, JAN 2003 (85)
(50% PN, 50% CH)
The firm's latest *cuvée de prestige* has an exceptional softness and decent concentration, but the aromas are far too like the sweet, vapid flavor in the company's basic nonvintage Champagne. The first time I tasted this wine blind my spontaneous comment was—a very refined version of Mumm Cordon Rouge.

- 1985 MUMM DE MUMM   75, DEC 2001 (75)
(50% PN, 50% CH)

- 1985 RENÉ LALOU   88, OCT 1998 (90)
(50% PN, 50% CH)
Mild aromas that resemble herbal tea meet the olfactory senses. The flavor is more concentrated and intertwined, with a medium to fleshy body.

- 1982 MUMM DE MUMM   86, JAN 2002 (86)
(50% PN, 50% CH)
Rounded, rich Champagne that lacks a little acidity and newness. Big smoky nose of heavy Pinot Noir. Pleasant aftertaste of butter toffee.

- 1982 RENÉ LALOU   89, NOV 1999 (89)
  (50% PN, 50% CH)
  This Champagne is recognizable by its rich, juicy fruit and
  melon-like aftertaste.
- 1979 RENÉ LALOU   93, SEP 2003 (93)
  (50% PN, 50% CH)
  Tremendously enjoyable at the beginning of the 1990s, the wine
  lacked the necessary concentration it needed to develop further.
  A weak toasty bouquet with elements of peach and violet. The
  peaches returned in the soft, fruity, medium-long flavor.
- 1976 RENÉ LALOU   88, OCT 2001 (88)
  (50% PN, 50% CH)
  Like the '75 this is relatively light and comes equipped with a
  perfect mousse. The nose is faint and closed. The wine's best sides
  are only shown in the mouth, where it achieves a perfect balance
  in the long flavor of crème brûlée and vanilla.
- 1975 RENÉ LALOU   86, JUL 2003 (86)
  (50% PN, 50% CH)
  Medium-deepish color; broad, open, but youthful bouquet of
  exotic fruit. After a while in the glass the nose becomes clumsy
  and house-typical. The flavor is full and young, with a hard, dry
  finish.
- 1971 RENÉ LALOU   93, FEB 2002 (93)
  (50% PN, 50% CH)
  I'm finally beginning to learn the style of this wine through the
  years. It turns out that the style is actually constant, with a fine
  smoky bouquet of burned sugar and crispbread mixed with peach
  and vanilla. No vintage shows this better than 1971. Elegant and
  delicious with great vitality.
- 1966 RENÉ LALOU   91, JAN 2003 (91)
  (50% PN, 50% CH)
  Decidedly sumptuous and concentrated to have come from this
  strict, elegant year. Fat, honey-saturated, toffee-drenched essence
  that should have been given a touch more mousse and tartness.
- 1964 RENÉ LALOU
  (50% PN, 50% CH)
- 1990 MUMM ROSÉ CUVÉE LIMITÉE   84, NOV 2001 (86)
  (70% PN, 30% CH)
  A rare Millennium wine presented in a clear bottle. Heavy,
  peppery style with a chewy resistance and gastronomic qualities.
  Dark red fruit and a somewhat acerbic finish. A lot like Clicquot
  Rosé.

NAPOLEON (A. PRIEUR) N-M

2, rue de Villers-aux-Bois
51130 Vertus
03 26 52 11 74
Production: 150,000
The firm was founded in 1825 by Jean-Louis Prieur and since
then has stayed within the family. They took the name
Napoleon in order to conquer the Russian market, which they
succeeded in doing. Today the firm is led by the very pleasant
and committed Vincent Prieur. Napoleon have no vineyards of
their own and are forced to buy in all of their grapes. Many
wine journalists praise the quality of Prieur's Champagnes,
but although I am loath to admit it I'm afraid I cannot join in
singing their praises. The Champagnes are dominated by an
untypical tone of ginger, which has proved to be easy to spot
at blind tastings.

- NAPOLEON TRADITION CARTE D'OR   56
  (56% PN, 44% CH)
- NAPOLEON CARTE VERTE   50
  (19% PN, 40% PM, 41% CH)
- NAPOLEON ROSÉ   48
  (24% PN, 76% CH)
- 1992 NAPOLEON   77, NOV 2003 (77)
  (60% PN, 40% CH)
- 1985 NAPOLEON   76, OCT 2001 (76)
  (60% PN, 40% CH)
- 1981 NAPOLEON   60, JUL 1990 (70)
  (60% PN, 40% CH)

OUDINOT N-M

12, rue Godard-Roger
51200 Épernay
03 26 59 50 10
Production: 1,500,000
The company was founded at the turn of the century by a grower
from Avize. Today the house-style is still based on high-class
Chardonnay grapes. In 1981 Oudinot and Jeanmaire became part
of the Trouillard group. The nonvintage Champagne is aged for
three years before being sold and they export slightly more than
they sell in France. I can't comment on the firm's house-style, but
the reports I have had describe them as well-made and slightly
neutral Champagnes. Winemaker: Denis Colombier.

- OUDINOT BLANC DE BLANCS   68
  (100% CH)
- 1999 OUDINOT   74, FEB 2004 (77)
- 1998 OUDINOT   73, FEB 2004 (75)
- OUDINOT BLANC DE NOIRS   78
  (100% PN)

PAILLARD, BRUNO **** N-M

avenue de Champagne
51100 Reims
03 26 36 20 22
Production: 300,000
Bruno Paillard is one of Champagne's most influential figures. His
impressive height and stylish appearance, combined with great
knowledge and a large dose of humility have given him places on
the boards of various organizations in Champagne. He started his
house in 1981 after having worked for many years as a broker in
the business. In order to get going he bought stores of wine from
Champagne houses threatened with bankruptcy, or from growers.
He is the first to admit that he didn't create the *cuvées* in the early
years of Bruno Paillard Champagne. The '83 is his first real effort,
and it marks a leap in quality.

    Bruno Paillard is determined to become one of the top
Champagne producers. He has 120 permanent contracts with wine
growers in thirty-two villages. He uses 15 percent oak in all his
Champagnes, except the rosés. He is also careful to have a large store
of old reserve wines in barrels for six months. Only the *cuvée* is used in
Paillard's Champagne—a measure he finances by using the second
pressing wines for his other labels. The Pinot grapes mostly come from
Bouzy, Mailly, and Verzenay, and the Chardonnay from Mesnil,
Vertus, Cuis, and Sézanne. Paillard, who also has a fondness for
Jaguars and art, has followed in Mouton-Rothschild's footsteps and
allows various artists to decorate his vintage labels each year. Paillard is

also one of the few who releases the disgorging date on all of his wines. In August 1994, Paillard and Chanoine had the majority of shares in Boizel, which was permitted to continue to run its own vinification. Also included in the group are: De Venoge, Abel Lepitre, Alexandre Bonnet, and Philipponnat. Laurent Guyot is the winemaker.

- PAILLARD PREMIÈRE CUVÉE   80
  (45% PN, 22% PM, 33% CH)
  Weak, reddish, copper tone. Hard, slightly reserved nose, with hints of newly baked bread and yeast. Young taste with both red and green apples. Storable. Certain similarities with Roederer Brut Premier. Better and creamier recently.
- PAILLARD CHARDONNAY RÉSERVE PRIVÉE   85
  (100% CH)
  Almost transparent color with a greenish tone; an incredibly sophisticated, flowery nose of acacia, yellow roses, and freesia. The flower theme returns in the light flavor and is enriched with vanilla and lime aromas. Reminds me of Deutz and Pol Roger.
- PAILLARD ROSÉ   74
  (85% PN, 15% CH)
- 1995 PAILLARD   85, APR 2004 (88)
  (45% PN, 19% PM, 36% CH)
  For the first time, Bruno has used Pinot Meunier in the vintage Champagne. This gives a soft, rather fleshy '95 that will hardly go down in wine history, but which must be considered finely crafted. Broad, big-house-style with a mature bready nose leaning towards Moët.
- 1989 PAILLARD   88, MAR 2003 (90)
  (65% PN, 35% CH)
  A very well made and intensely aromatic '89, heavily marked by bready, ripe Pinot Noir. I regard this as a vigorous Champagne that most likely comes into its own served with white meat, veal sweetbreads, or mushroom dishes.
- 1985 PAILLARD   91, APR 1995 (93)
  (45% PN, 55% CH)
  A wonderful wine with a deep golden color and Krug-like aromas. Nuts, honey, marzipan, and the hard crust of dark, wholewheat bread bread can all be easily distinguished in the broad and tight nose. Oily, deep, and very rich flavor of all the products of the bakery.
- 1979 PAILLARD   84, JAN 2003 (84)
  (40% PN, 60% CH)
  A thin '79 of purity and some elegance, but without concentration. Mature and fleshy today.
- 1976 PAILLARD   84, JUL 1990 (87)
  (40% PN, 60% CH)
  Surprisingly light wine considering the vintage. Light color, elegant nose of bakeries and honey. Stylish flavor that lacks length.
- 1973 PAILLARD   86, APR 1996 (86)
  (50% PN, 50% CH)
  Broad, aged, and toasty nose with elements of chocolate and dried fruit. The flavor is quite full with certain signs of age.
- 1969 PAILLARD   87, JAN 2003 (>)
  (60% PN, 40% CH)
  A Champagne in the English style, huge autolytic character and certain oxidative flavor. Buttery, broad, and compact.
- 1995 PAILLARD BLANC DE BLANCS   88, MAR 2004 (92)
  (100% CH)
  After many years' absence, Bruno's Chardonnay returns in big style. The grapes come from Chouilly and Cuis, and lend a pure

and fine mineral note. There's also a bouquet hint of mature Riesling that pulls toward petroleum. This exciting aromatic map is complemented with a delicious, fat, and nutty butter-toffee layer. Brilliant!

- 1983 PAILLARD BLANC DE BLANCS   92, JAN 2004 (92)
  (100% CH)
  A richer and more full-bodied wine than the nonvintage Blanc de Blancs, with a less refined bouquet. Slightly smoky nose and a strong citrus aroma in the long taste.
- 1990 BRUNO PAILLARD N. P. U.   88, MAR 2004 (88)
  (50% PN, 50% CH)
  Early on, good old Bruno decided to make a prestige Champagne in which no efforts would be spared to achieve the finest quality: only wine from the seven *grand cru* villages; aging in oak barrels from Bordeaux for nine months; the first pressing only and at least eight years in the bottle, together with the sediment, before disgorging. This was the recipe that would give this newly started house a seat in the front row. The wine is super-concentrated and impressively rich, with aromas that carry one to the house in Aÿ that works with similar methods. Today, a little finesse is lacking, in favor of the New Worldy richness of fruit. Considering the extraction, I am convinced that the wine will hold up for a long time to come and that the *terroir* character will eventually come forth through the almost impenetrable layers of fruit that dominate today. Personally, I would not be surprised if both Robert Parker and *Wine Spectator* give N. P. U. 100 points, while the puritans in Champagne will be quite critical of Bruno's new *cuvée de prestige*. At the moment the wine is developing a little coarsely.

PAILLARD, PIERRE *** R-M
2, rue du 20ème Siècle
51150 Bouzy
03 26 57 08 04
Production: 60,000
The firm was founded in 1946, and today this grand owner works with a large proportion of oak barrels for his Chardonnay. The average age of the vinestocks is twenty-three years, going up to forty years old for the vintage wines.

- PIERRE PAILLARD BRUT   68
  (60% PN, 40% CH)
- 1990 PIERRE PAILLARD   59, MAY 2003 (59)
  (40% PN, 60% CH)
- 1989 PIERRE PAILLARD   91, FEB 2003 (91)
  (40% PN, 60% CH)
  Sensational Champagne with its own style, as all Chardonnay comes from Bouzy and has been stored in new oak barrels! Big nose of lilies and pineapple. There is a lovely separated vanilla note around the tart, dry flavor—all of it becoming more integrated and sophisticated. A beautiful jewel.
- 1985 PIERRE PAILLARD   83, DEC 1999 (83)
  (50% PN, 50% CH)
  A classic Bouzy Champagne with a great almond nose and a powerful, dry, masculine flavor. Strangely enough, it hasn't aged well.
- 1973 PIERRE PAILLARD   86, APR 1996 (87)
  (50% PN, 50% CH)
  Tasted when recently disgorged without dosage. A nose of leather, and licorice. High alcohol content and good freshness.

- 1971 PIERRE PAILLARD   94, SEP 2003 (94)
(70% PN, 30% CH)

A lovely normally disgorged magnum that was asleep for many years. Now it's a perfect grower's Champagne. Youthful acacia notes are beautifully braided together with elements of fresh mushrooms and rainy wet autumn forest. Exciting elements of balsamic vinegar, bergamot, and curry further spice this elegant, slender wine. The finish—tasting of both lemon and toffee-ishly aged Sauternes—is an extra delight.

PALMER & CO. *** C-M

67, rue Jacquart
51100 Reims
03 26 07 35 07
Production: 300,000

In total, two million bottles. Palmer is an unusual creature—it is a cooperative in Reims. The original idea of a cooperative came up among some growers in Avize, who needed some Pinot grapes from Verzenay in order to create a competitive *cuvée*. This happened in 1947, but when the firm became too big in 1959, Palmer moved into Teofile Roederer's old cellars in Reims. Jean-Claude Colson and his right-hand man Roland Priem lead a modern and effective team that has access to grapes from forty *crus*. Colson's philosophy is to combine traditional methods with the latest advances made by science. The firm is very proud of its 8,000-kilo press from which they only use *cuvée* (first pressing) for Palmer. The wines are well aged after four years in the cellar and carefully tested in the company's modern laboratory. Palmer has an unusually large amount of older vintages for sale, which are disgorged to order. The wines that are made by Michel Davesne are a little too impersonal and clinical for my taste. Perhaps they would have more character if they weren't put through cold stabilization and double filtering.

- PALMER & CO. BRUT   76
(50% PN, 10% PM, 40% CH)
- PALMER & CO. ROSÉ RUBIS   60
(70% PN, 10% PM, 20% CH)
- 1995 PALMER & CO.   83, APR 2003 (84)
Toasted, bready, and modern, with a "playing to the galleries" richness and generosity. Soft and balanced and very good in an uncomplicated way. Feels already quite mature.
- 1982 PALMER & CO.   83, APR 2003 (83)
(60% PN, 40% CH)
A well-built wine with chocolate-saturated maturity and evolved, balanced taste. Unfortunately, a little neutral and uninteresting.
- 1980 PALMER & CO. D. T.   87, JUN 2001 (87)
(25% PN, 75% CH)
Absolutely one of the most delicious, joyous bottles I've drunk from Palmer. Sure, the vintage's thin, slightly watered-down character is present, but the wine is still so expressive and sunny with its enjoyable coffee and toasted bready taste that one is tempted to take the next gulp as soon as the Champagne has reached the throat. A little Dom Pérignon.
- 1979 PALMER & CO. D. T.   84, SEP 2001 (84)
(50% PN, 50% CH)
All alone, the Champagne feels too evolved and plum-laden. With food, on the other hand, the wine takes off considerably and is pulled into great shape. Raisiny notes, fruit compote, deep color, and fine mousse.

- 1976 PALMER & CO. D. T.   91, OCT 2001 (91)
(50% PN, 50% CH)
Big, fat, vanilla-packed '76 with deliciously voluptuous luxuriance. Toffee taste and good freshness—everything is in the right place. One of the firm's best Champagnes ever.
- 1961 PALMER & CO. D. T.   83, MAR 2001 (84)
(20% PN, 10% PM, 70% CH)
Fantastically unevolved and light considering the wine's respectable age. Light and fine with an exemplary "aperitif-look." Acacia bouquet of faint, cold, hard-to-define notes which reveal that the wine is newly disgorged. I expected the Champagne to bloom in the glass but it stayed shy and withdrawn. Short, lightly refreshing taste, like mineral water.
- 1996 PALMER & CO. BLANC DE BLANCS   85, NOV 2003 (88)
(100% CH)
A delightful Champagne with a light, nutty, bready bouquet. The wine combines fine richness with high acidity. Sweet lemons, oranges, pineapple, and vanilla are notes that pass by on the tasting highway. A high-class Palmer.
- 1995 PALMER & CO. BLANC DE BLANCS   82, NOV 2003 (83)
(100% CH)
Nowhere near the same buoyancy and beautifully toasted character that is present in the '96. Here, the main theme is soft, buttery, fat Chardonnay with hints of vanilla. Fine and pleasant without tickling. The suppleness of this wine is probably perfectly suited to flatfish with a creamy white wine sauce.
- 1985 PALMER & CO. BLANC DE BLANCS   49, MAY 1995 (55)
(100% CH)
- 1983 PALMER & CO. BLANC DE BLANCS   79, APR 2001 (79)
(100% CH)
- 1970 PALMER & CO. BLANC DE BLANCS   70, JUL 2001 (>)
(100% CH)
- 1975 PALMER & CO. BLANC DE NOIRS D. T.
(100% PN)
- 1973 PALMER & CO. BLANC DE NOIRS D. T.   90, JAN 2000 (90)
(100% PN)
Absolutely newly disgorged, with a new color that reveals none of the wine's true age. Idiosyncratically fascinating bouquet of crawfish juice, dill, and chocolate wafers. Refreshing, but at the same time powerfully vegetable-sated, with a smoky palate and a certain sweetness in the finish.
- AMAZONE DE PALMER   87
(50% PN, 50% CH)
A *grand cru* Champagne from two vintages, with deep color and lovely toasty aroma of wholewheat bread and coffee beans. The flavor is dominated by mature Avize-Chardonnay with an added weight from some first-class Pinot Noir.

PERNET, JEAN R-M
6, rue Breche d'Oger
51190 Le Mesnil-sur-Oger
03 26 57 54 24
Production: 85,000

Hugette Pernet started this firm in 1947; today it is run by
Frédéric and Christophe Pernet. The property is 17.5 hectares in
total.

• JEAN PERNET   66
  (100% CH)

PERRIER-JOUËT **** N-M
26, avenue de Champagne
51201 Épernay
03 26 53 38 00
Production: 3,000,000

This house was founded in 1811 by Pierre-Nicholas-Marie Perrier-
Jouët. Under the leadership of his son Charles, the company
became famous under its nickname P-J. In 1950 Mumm bought a
majority shareholding in the company and the house became part
of the Canadian Seagram Group. Today the house is owned by
Allied Domecq who, as soon as they took over, alarmingly dug up
large portions of the house's fine old vines in Cramant.

    Michel Budin, who led the firm up until the 1980s, was
a great admirer of Art Noveau and opened a Belle Epoque museum
in 1990, twenty years after launching the *cuvée de prestige* of the
same name. Jean-Marie Barillere is president today. Belle Epoque
has become a great success everywhere, and the Americans in
particular have fallen for the flower-bedecked bottle. The house
owns 108 hectares in seven villages, and the other 65 percent of
the grapes are bought in from forty villages. The most important
village is Cramant, where the firm owns twenty-nine hectares of
the very best slopes. Compared to other big houses, the heritage
has been kept well. The vines are very old and produce fantastic
grapes that can dominate an entire *cuvée*, even if small in
proportion to the total content, and the delicate house-style is
dependent on these Chardonnay grapes. Perrier-Jouët compete
with neighboring house Pol Roger for the number one spot in
Épernay. Both make fruity, medium-bodied Champagnes in a
broad, sophisticated style, but Pol Roger's wines are somewhat drier
and more Pinot influenced, while Perrier-Jouët's Champagnes,
which are made by Hervé Deschamps, often appear somewhat
more personal and toasted. The vintage wine is a classic, and both
the Belle Epoque wines are a great source of joy for the romantic
wine lover. The 1985 Belle Epoque Rosé was voted as the foremost
rosé of all time at the Millennium Tasting.

• PERRIER-JOUËT GRAND BRUT   78
  (35% PN, 40% PM, 25% CH)
• 1997 PERRIER-JOUËT   81, JUL 2002 (85)
  (33% PN, 33% PM, 34% CH)
  Fine, youthful, slightly weak nose of candy and vanilla. Fine
  plummy fruit. Young and undeveloped—I must admit that I
  don't quite recognize the house-style here.
• 1996 PERRIER-JOUËT   85, SEP 2003 (90)
  (33% PN, 33% PM, 34% CH)
  A brilliantly classic house-typical Champagne with a nose of
  newly baked bread and vanilla butter cookies. Fluffy and airy like
  a soufflé with a sweet lemon note. Rich and acidic, as it should
  be this outstanding year. Run and buy for your cellar!

• 1992 PERRIER-JOUËT   85, MAR 2002 (88)
  (35% PN, 30% PM, 35% CH)
  Developed, delicious '92 that is partly reminiscent of a Pommery
  from the same year. Round and mature, bready Champagne with
  fine strawberry notes as well as an almost smoky spiciness.
  Slightly short and a tad too "kind" in the mouth.
• 1990 PERRIER-JOUËT   87, FEB 1998 (93)
  (40% PN, 33% PM, 27% CH)
  Lovely as usual, with a developed fruity and toasty nose.
  Naturally a biscuit aroma and all the sweet richness we've come
  to expect.
• 1988 PERRIER-JOUËT   89, NOV 2003 (91)
  (40% PN, 33% PM, 27% CH)
  It took a few years to discover how good the normal vintage wine
  from Perrier-Jouët is. Nowadays I never miss a new vintage, as
  the wine is always well made and full of Chardonnay elegance.
  The '88 is still in its infancy, but you can just perceive the freshly
  baked bread, the ready-to-burst Chardonnay and the silky-
  smooth fruity taste. At the age of twelve there are more chocolate
  aromas than toasted ones.
• 1985 PERRIER-JOUËT   93, MAY 2001 (94)
  (40% PN, 30% PM, 30% CH)
  Hugely well-developed, flowery nose with hints of spun sugar,
  peppermint candy, popcorn, coffee beans, chocolate wafers,
  and raspberry vinegar. After this broadside of scent impressions
  it's lovely to sip the unified taste, where peach and milk toffee
  set the tone. A veritable bull's-eye! Extremely toasted in
  magnum.
• 1982 PERRIER-JOUËT   93, MAY 2000 (93)
  (60% PN, 40% CH)
  As good as the Belle Epoque of the same vintage. A fabulous
  toasty and buttery bouquet. A balanced, creamy taste with
  medium body.
• 1979 PERRIER-JOUËT   95, SEP 2001 (95)
  (60% PN, 40% CH)
  Disgorged in May 1986. This wonderful wine leads me to
  suspect that '79 Belle Epoque is even better than I had previously
  imagined. This vintage wine is delicious and house-typical, with a
  superbly clean and dainty toasted bouquet. The balance in the
  taste is perfect. A wine that invites large gulps.
• 1978 PERRIER-JOUËT
  (60% PN, 40% CH)
• 1976 PERRIER-JOUËT   94, JAN 2003 (94)
  (60% PN, 40% CH)
  Fully mature with heavy fruit and vanilla aromas. Fabulously rich
  and sweet. A wonderful glass of Champagne!
• 1975 PERRIER-JOUËT   88, SEP 2001 (88)
  (60% PN, 40% CH)
  The nose is reminiscent of candle wax and beeswax. Good, dry,
  crispy taste. Medium bodied and clearly elegant. The fruit is
  unfortunately a little thin, and the mousse dies quickly despite
  the fine, light color.
• 1969 PERRIER-JOUËT   93, JUN 2000 (93)
  (60% PN, 40% CH)
  Despite a weak mousse, this is an excellent wine with an aromatic
  spectrum reminiscent of a grand nutty Meursault. Also fascinating
  is seeing how well this developed and mature wine keeps in the
  glass. More serious and vinous than many other vintages of this
  invariably delicious Champagne.

- 1966 PERRIER-JOUËT   91, JUN 2002 (91)
(60% PN, 40% CH)
At this grand old age, this is a relaxed, laid-back, beautiful lady
with style and class—but lacking a spring in her step. Toffee-ish,
weakly effervescent, with a good homogeneous taste that carries
one's thoughts to Christmas goodies.

- 1964 PERRIER-JOUËT   94, JAN 2002 (94)
(60% PN, 40% CH)
Old Champagne with its aromas at their most lovely. Unusually
developed; could even be ten years older. "After Eights" and
toffee dominate both taste and nose. A medium-bodied taste
carried by a weak mousse and reasonable acidity; very long.
Drink soon.

- 1961 PERRIER-JOUËT   94, DEC 1998 (94)
(60% PN, 40% CH)
Wonderfully toasty and buttery with all the flowers of the garden
wrapped in an oily structure. The '61 has many years left on the
scene.

- 1959 PERRIER-JOUËT   94, MAR 2001 (94)
(60% PN, 40% CH)
A masculine, impressive wine with magnificent power and
authority. Toffee-ish and gamy with a nutty finish.

- 1955 PERRIER-JOUËT   93, JAN 2000 (93)
(60% PN, 40% CH)
Fantastically youthful and well-preserved Champagne, with a
pure and complex bouquet of smoky notes, hazelnuts, cellar, and
dark chocolate. The same aromas reappear in the dry and actually
slightly too-restrained taste. Pure of style and aesthetic, but I miss
sweetness and length in the aftertaste. I recognize this lack of
charm and approachability from Krug '55.

- 1953 PERRIER-JOUËT   93, APR 1994 (93)
(60% PN, 40% CH)
Incredibly one can detect the firm's style clearly in this aged wine.
A certain oxidation and weak mousse. But a great wine that has
probably been even greater. Rich, toffee-like and gracefully
scented in the mid-1990s. Very complex. A few years left.

- 1949 PERRIER-JOUËT
(60% PN, 40% CH)

- 1947 PERRIER-JOUËT
(60% PN, 40% CH)

- 1943 PERRIER-JOUËT   93, OCT 1997 (93)
(50% PN, 50% CH)
A majestic and powerful Champagne typical of the vintage.

- 1928 PERRIER-JOUËT   92, JAN 1999 (92)
(60% PN, 40% CH)
My first wine from the vintage to end all vintages. The
Champagne was just as majestic as I had hoped, but only for a
couple of minutes. After that the wine undergoes maderization
very rapidly, even though the heroic structure remains. The color
was quite golden, and the mousse was tangible in the mouth.
The great nose hinted of cream and marine creosote. The
aftertaste was amazingly long and rich, with veal stock and port
wine my immediate association.

- 1921 PERRIER-JOUËT   95, APR 1999 (95)
(60% PN, 40% CH)
A wonderful vintage of a wine that at the time was considered to
be the absolute top. Rich and chewy but with a weak mousse.

- 1911 PERRIER-JOUËT   90, JUN 2000 (90)
(60% PN, 40% CH)

Light color, nonexistent mousse, and youthful, slightly chilly
aromas. Distinct bouquet of vanilla ice cream and a creamy
young flavor that unexpectedly possesses a sherry finish.

- 1978 PERRIER-JOUËT ROSÉ   90, NOV 1999 (90)
(70% PN, 30% CH)
There is something slim and green about all '78s. Vitality and a
beautiful flowery, aromatic bouquet pardon a certain lack of
depth. Perrier-Jouët passes with distinction yet again.

- 1976 PERRIER-JOUËT ROSÉ   90, JUN 1997 (92)
(70% PN, 30% CH)
The wine was so pale that my friends doubted it was a rosé we
were drinking. The nose was typical for a rosé from the 1970s,
with a basic tone of rose hip, strawberries, and a slight sour tone
that separates them from their white opposite numbers. A well-
structured, balanced '76 that will develop.

- 1975 PERRIER-JOUËT ROSÉ   90, FEB 2003 (90)
(70% PN, 30% CH)
Rather light, slightly dull color. Still, good fruit and richness with
a nutty side note that gives class to the entirety. An unfortunately
simpler nose of smoke, nut, and leather.

- 1966 PERRIER-JOUËT ROSÉ   93, NOV 1999 (93)
(70% PN, 30% CH)
A juicy, round, and easily imbibed beauty with a romantic side
that is definitely present. The fruit is very rich and the vintage's
freshness has remained intact. Several others beside myself found
similarities between DRC's juicy-sweet and drinkable '82s.

- 1964 PERRIER-JOUËT ROSÉ
(70% PN, 30% CH)

- 1959 PERRIER-JOUËT ROSÉ
(70% PN, 30% CH)

- BLASON DE FRANCE   88
(36% PN, 34% PM, 30% CH)
Considerably cheaper than Belle Epoque and eventually better
value. Rich, mature character in a heavier, slightly beefier style than
the firm's other prestige Champagne. A lovely freshness just recently.

- BLASON DE FRANCE ROSÉ   84
(47% PN, 27% PM, 26% CH)
Young, tranquil nose of green apples. A considerably smaller wine
than Belle Epoque Rosé, but even here the orangey elements are
noticeable. The wine tastes best at the age of ten, when the
sweetness is completely integrated with the fruit and the leathery
notes haven't yet taken over.

- BLASON DE FRANCE ROSÉ NEW LABEL   86
(55% PN, 5% PM, 40% CH)
New label and somewhat changed grape composition but with
retained quality. The wine feels somewhat more ingratiating, with
sweeter attributes and notes of vanilla, caramel, and strawberry
cream. Is this because of age or is the style somewhat different?

- 1976 BLASON DE FRANCE   96, JUN 1999 (96)
(60% PN, 40% CH)
One of the vintage's best Champagnes. Sensationally seductive
and rich with finesse. The aroma is a sparkling explosion in life-
affirming light colors. The elegance is also utterly palpable to the
palate. To me, this masterpiece seems more like a '71 than an
alcohol-rich '76.

- 1975 BLASON DE FRANCE   95, JAN 2002 (95)
(60% PN, 40% CH)
What an exquisite wine! Because so many '75s lack charm and
smiling radiance, it proved enormously satisfying to encounter

the sweet intensity of this underrated prestige Champagne. There is always a freshness and buoyancy in Perrier-Jouët's wines, which here play second fiddle to butterscotchy, treacly aromas. The total experience can in some strange way be likened to drinking caramel sauce without all the senses becoming sated.

- 1973 BLASON DE FRANCE   93, MAY 2002 (93)
(60% PN, 40% CH)
The wine is very similar to the Belle Epoque from the same year, if somewhat less intense. The balance between the contrasts is of the highest order, and this delicate wine demands total attention if it is to deliver its full effect.

- 1969 BLASON DE FRANCE   93, JUN 1999 (93)
(60% PN, 40% CH)
Deeply aged color, but brisk, diminishing mousse. Big, chocolate-soaked scent with an undertone of Champagne cellar. Honey-soft with classic caramel finish.

- 1966 BLASON DE FRANCE   95, JUN 1999 (95)
(60% PN, 40% CH)
Fabulously well-balanced, fresh Champagne with enormous attack and rich citrus fruit. A hint of chanterelle mushrooms in the nose.

- 1964 BLASON DE FRANCE   75, JAN 2003 (75)
(60% PN, 40% CH)

- 1961 BLASON DE FRANCE   85, NOV 1999 (>)
(60% PN, 40% CH)
Fresh bottles might exist, but the two that I tasted were too old and marked by oxidation. The toffee tones and smooth, honeyed aftertaste still work well with duck liver.

- 1996 BELLE EPOQUE   88, OCT 2003 (93)
(45% PN, 5% PM, 50% CH)
Let me say first of all that it's terribly difficult to judge this wine's potential. I probably wouldn't be able to predict the character of this Champagne's development if I hadn't had the benefit of thoroughly scrutinizing earlier vintages of Belle Epoque. At present, the '96 is in no way lacking in charm to drink, which means that the wine is going to be consumed much too early. The acidity is explosive, though at the same time blanketed in an eiderdown quilt of mature, oily Chardonnay. The structure is exemplary and the nose is un-evolved and painfully shy as yet. In time, the vanilla tones will be reinforced; they will interplay with the other sweet notes, and with the beautiful floral taste.

- 1995 BELLE EPOQUE   89, APR 2003 (93)
(45% PN, 5% PM, 50% CH)
Refined, youthfully appealing Champagne with seductive floral quality, citrus tone, and a substantial dose of mineral. Spring-like and sensual, with a caressing softness and refreshingly long house-typical resonance. For those of you who like mature Champagne, my advice is unequivocal: wait!

- 1994 BELLE EPOQUE   84, JAN 2002 (89)
(45% PN, 5% PM, 50% CH)
Surely an excellent '94, but personally I have greater expectations than this for Belle Epoque. Fresh, very young, with a floral, almost acrid, pungent nose of elderberry, bird cherry, and hawthorn. Fresh, gooseberry palate that is finely rounded off in the mouth. Caressing vanilla finish.

- 1990 BELLE EPOQUE   93, MAY 2003 (95)
(45% PN, 5% PM, 50% CH)
Moderately closed but high-class Champagne with perfect balance and rich fruit. Yet completely without toasted aromas.

Perhaps they should have used a lower dosage? In the present medium-mature phase of the wine, the sweetness is a little too noticeable because the acidity in the '90s isn't all that high.

- 1989 BELLE EPOQUE   93, MAR 2003 (94)
(45% PN, 5% PM, 50% CH)
A magical wine whose super-elegant toasty form is so reminiscent of a fine Montrachet. The nose explodes in the glass with tones of flowers, fruit, and roasted coffee. The flavor is exotic and classic simultaneously, with an amazingly enjoyable toffee finish. Very rich and nutty at the moment.

- 1988 BELLE EPOQUE   90, NOV 2003 (93)
(45% PN, 5% PM, 50% CH)
The first few times I tasted Belle Epoque I thought the bottle was more beautiful than the contents. In recent years I've been converted. The wines always have a brilliant flowery elegance that they keep for many years. Added to the elegance is a nutty and roasted coffee aroma of true greatness. The '88 has all these qualities encapsulated in a youthful shell.

- 1985 BELLE EPOQUE   93, MAR 2001 (95)
(45% PN, 5% PM, 50% CH)
There doesn't exist a more elegant *cuvée* Champagne than this! The wine is full of young, subtle nuances. If you know, for example, how beautifully the '73 develops, you'll understand how enlarged these aromas become with age. Today, you are met by a scent reminiscent of a bouquet of flowers in spring, as well as a rich but restrained fruit aroma backed up by vanilla, coffee, and saffron. A real hit at the Millennium Tasting.

- 1983 BELLE EPOQUE   91, JUL 2000 (92)
(45% PN, 5% PM, 50% CH)
The nose is full of aromas that wrestle with each other without ever really reaching out. It is as if someone has placed a lid over the wine: if it were to be lifted off the wine would bloom in a lovely manner. The taste is light and Chardonnay-influenced with a clear vanilla aroma.

- 1982 BELLE EPOQUE   94, JAN 2002 (94)
(45% PN, 5% PM, 50% CH)
The nose is still weak, but ultra elegant. There's a "difficult-to-beat," finesse-rich taste with a velvety-smooth feeling and a delicious layer of vanilla and handsome fruit. A little too short and, as stated, a little too discreet in the nose—but what class!

- 1979 BELLE EPOQUE   95, MAY 2003 (95)
(45% PN, 5% PM, 50% CH)
The '79 has a nose like an entire coffee-roasting house. The taste is creamier, though, like coffee-flavored ice cream. Relatively light but wonderfully long and full of aromas.

- 1978 BELLE EPOQUE   93, JAN 2001 (93)
(45% PN, 5% PM, 50% CH)
One of this lightweight vintage's truly first-rate Champagnes. There is nothing here of the green immaturity and herbal basic character that usually denote the '78s. On the contrary, there are lots of richly toasted, nutty aromas, which this inimitable prestige Champagne always succeeds in producing.

- 1976 BELLE EPOQUE   93, JUL 2003 (93)
(45% PN, 5% PM, 50% CH)
Not really the elegance that we've become accustomed to. The vintage has put its fat imprint on this wine, and of course the result is very good. The color is dark and the wine does not keep very well in the glass. Otherwise, the vintage-typical aromas are delightful.

- 1975 BELLE EPOQUE   91, JAN 2003 (91)
(45% PN, 5% PM, 50% CH)
Slightly disappointing, considering the vintage, but it is in any
case a delightfully elegant Champagne with lively acidity, mousse,
and a rich fruit with exotic overtones.

- 1973 BELLE EPOQUE   95, MAY 2003 (95)
(45% PN, 5% PM, 50% CH)
Light orange with exceptional mousse. Fantastically delicate,
complex nose where the flower, fruit, and honey aromas fight for
ascendancy. A well-balanced, elegant taste. Light to medium-
bodied, with hints of peach, apricot, cotton candy, and
"*vaniljdrömmar*"—small, white, porous, vanilla-butter cookies
that melt in your mouth. Typical—and outstanding—house-
style. Unfortunately, there are a few tired bottles in circulation.

- 1971 BELLE EPOQUE   89, JUN 2001 (89)
(45% PN, 5% PM, 50% CH)
The bottle that I had chosen as the Midsummer Champagne
looked perfect but was slightly antiquated. I don't know if I had
bad luck, but it would not surprise me if most of the few
remaining bottles of this wine have seen better days. The mousse
was weak, the nose was like an old white Burgundy, and the taste
had hints of mocha; it was dominated by honey as well as
candied fruit. With more vitality the wine would have made it to
just over ninety points.

- 1966 BELLE EPOQUE   91, MAY 2001 (91)
(45% PN, 5% PM, 50% CH)
Unfortunately, a Champagne that has seen better days. Still, the
wine is enjoyable in its dignified, aristocratically quiet way. The
bubbles are few and minimal in size. The color is dark, but still
has a vigorous shine when rays of sun hit the glass. Lars
Torstenson, Johan Edström, Johan Lidby, Staffan Brännstam,
Mats Hanzon, and I were all fascinated with the weight and
authority the old lady retained, despite the fact that her
infirmities could no longer be hidden. The aromas are more
burned than toasted and the fruit is overshadowed by mushroom,
forest, and straw-like vegetal aromas.

- 1964 BELLE EPOQUE   96, MAR 2001 (96)
(45% PN, 5% PM, 50% CH)
This—today—rare debut vintage of Belle Epoque was made for
Duke Ellington's seventieth birthday. I'm extremely honored to
have the pleasure of drinking this fantastic wine now when it's at
its peak. Truth be told, the perfectly stored magnum of which I
partook at a large Perrier-Jouët tasting at Villa Källhagen was
almost too young. The wine needed considerable airing in order
to release its peacock tail. When the entire beauty of this wine
was exposed it reminded me of the '73, '79, and '90. I found it
highly satisfying to see that the basic recipe for this personal wine
is apparently still the same. The nose is toasted and elusively
floral. The taste is reminiscent of a 1964 Moët in magnum, with
its lightly smoky, fine peach note. Dry and steely finish.

- 1966 BLASON DE FRANCE ROSÉ   93, SEP 2003 (93)
(60% PN, 40% CH)
It's always just as delightful to find this type of rarity. An element
of bitterness, leather, and forest mushrooms suggests its age. Even
the amber-dashed color and the sparse, sedate bubbles remind
one how old the wine actually is. All the more pleasant to
discover that the fruit is completely vigorous. The wine both
smells and tastes like a big red Burgundy, with its notes of red
beets and almost overripe strawberries.

- 1997 BELLE EPOQUE ROSÉ   90, JUL 2002 (92)
(55% PN, 5% PM, 40% CH)
A very nice Champagne at much too high a price. Undeveloped
floral nose and a pleasant roundness with juicy red fruit. All
creamy Chardonnay comes from Cramant.

- 1995 BELLE EPOQUE ROSÉ   90, MAY 2001 (93)
(50% PN, 5% PM, 45% CH)
Richer and somewhat more mature than the spring-like white
variety of this vintage. Nicely seductive nose of tropical fruit and
mint chocolate. Finesse-rich palate with its typically lovely
aftertaste that simply *is* Belle Epoque Rosé.

- 1989 BELLE EPOQUE ROSÉ   92, MAR 2003 (94)
(50% PN, 5% PM, 45% CH)
Restrained, high class, buttery, and aristocratic. Crystal-like,
"white," dense, and focused prestige rosé with a fabulous echo
that is as soft as honey.

- 1988 BELLE EPOQUE ROSÉ   93, NOV 2003 (95)
(50% PN, 5% PM, 45% CH)
The nose has notes of petroleum like a great Riesling, but also a
classical biscuit tone, mineral, and dense fruit. Wonderful balance
and elegance, but wait a while into this new century before
loosening the cork.

- 1986 BELLE EPOQUE ROSÉ   89, MAY 1994 (93)
(50% PN, 5% PM, 45% CH)
Belle Epoque Rosé is one of the greatest rosé Champagnes. The
wine has a personal style and the '86 is no exception. Lovely
orange color. Broad, deep nose of mature, musty Pinot Noir,
with uplifting tones of fruit and caramel. Meaty, classic
strawberry fruit with hints of orange and coffee. Superb elegance.

- 1985 BELLE EPOQUE ROSÉ   94, MAY 2000 (95)
(50% PN, 20% PM, 30% CH)
Even more roasted coffee than with the white version. Exactly the
same inviting delicious caramel tone with an extra bonus for the
beautiful color and the exotic richness. Selected as the world's
best rosé Champagne in history at the Millennium Tasting.

- 1982 BELLE EPOQUE ROSÉ   95, JUN 2003 (96)
(50% PN, 5% PM, 45% CH)
Mature orange color; fine, tiny, prolonged bubbles. Incredibly
complex, elegant nose of fresh-ground coffee, roast chestnuts,
tangerine, and cocoa. Cristal-like and almost oak-toasted and
barrel-like in character. Wonderfully rich creamy orangey taste,
spiced with the same aromas as the nose. Delightful buttery
Chardonnay finish.

- 1979 BELLE EPOQUE ROSÉ   93, MAY 2003 (93)
(50% PN, 5% PM, 45% CH)
Just as delicate and seductive as it looks. Divine elegance, a light,
buttery toffee tone and a classically smooth, mature Pinot finish.

- 1973 BELLE EPOQUE CUVÉE ALINDA   93, APR 2003 (93)
Is this the same wine as the usual Belle Epoque? The price tag is a
completely different story and the two bottles that I tasted lacked
mousse, which the usual '73 does not. That's why it's difficult to
determine whether there is any difference between the wines.
Despite the lack of mousse, the wine is light, big, and lovely, with
a nose of honey, walnut, marzipan, and vanilla. The taste is
excellent with big, oily concentration.

PERRIER, JOSEPH **** N-M
69, avenue de Paris
51016 Châlons-en-Champagne
03 26 68 29 51
Production: 600,000

The only Champagne house of any consequence in Châlons-en-Champagne today. And it is perhaps due to its geographical location that Joseph Perrier is often forgotten when the finest Champagnes are discussed. Ever since the firm was started in 1825 it has maintained a low profile but is well known among wine experts. Today this house is owned by Laurent-Perrier.

      The methods of vinification are modern, apart from the use of 600-liter oak barrels for the reserve wines. Monsieur Fourmon and the winemaker Claude Dervin deny the use of cognac in the dosage, which is an allegation put forward in some wine books. The company's style is based on the excellent Pinot locations they have in their twenty hectares in Cumières, Damery, and Hautvillers. The wines are always fruity and soft, with a great deal of elegance. The '79 is one of my favorites and the '53 is magical!

- JOSEPH PERRIER BRUT   73
  (35% PN, 30% PM, 35% CH)
- JOSEPH PERRIER PÈRE & FILS (1830–1840)   87
  Unabashedly fresh 170-year-old! Weak but ever-present mousse and a beautiful, light-golden color with hints of orange and fine clarity. Strong bouquet of coffee, smoke, aged wood, and dried fruit. There's also a faint undertone of cheese, fish, and sludge. Highly reminiscent of the 1907 Heidsieck & Co. Good, lightly effervescent, sweet yet still-balanced taste, with a toffee-ish and a buttery side. Long, harmonious aftertaste of an older Tokay or an older German Auslese from, let's see, 1953. The oldest Champagne I've ever tasted!
- JOSEPH PERRIER ROYAL BLANC DE BLANCS   78
  (100% CH)
- JOSEPH PERRIER DEMI-SEC   50
  (35% PN, 30% PM, 35% CH)
- JOSEPH PERRIER ROSÉ   68
  (25% PN, 75% CH)
- 1996 CUVÉE ROYALE   87, AUG 2003 (93)
  (50% PN, 50% CH)
  Brilliant freshness and vigor. One of the '96s that can become classic in twenty years. No charmer at the moment, but exceedingly enjoyable with its freshness and underlying taste extracts.
- 1995 CUVÉE ROYALE   88, SEP 2003 (92)
  (50% PN, 50% CH)
  Personally, this is one of the best vintage wines Joseph Perrier has made since 1979. Already its decided class and elegance bring this Champagne into the sphere of aristocratic wines. The nose is, as yet, suppressed, but you can guess at the nascent greatness that's just around the corner. The taste is perfectly balanced and extremely long, with an aromatic impression akin to a young '79.
- 1990 CUVÉE ROYALE   87, NOV 1998 (91)
  (45% PN, 5% PM, 50% CH)
  Already clearly developed aromas in the nose. The house-style is recognizable, with its roasted, almost burned aroma combined with tea-like tones. To the palate there is a marked sea salt flavor, reminiscent of crispbread served with Swedish "Kalle's" caviar. All vintages of Cuvée Royale age with dignity, as should this tasty '90.

- 1989 CUVÉE ROYALE   84, JUL 1998 (88)
  (50% PN, 50% CH)
  The house has succeeded in creating a Champagne that perfectly reflects both the vintage and house-style. The wine is laid-back and charming, with a delightful tone of toffee.
- 1985 CUVÉE ROYALE   83, MAR 1999 (89)
  (50% PN, 50% CH)
  A generous and well-interlaced wine with a chewy taste similar to meat paté and a heavy, almost overripe fruity nose.
- 1982 CUVÉE ROYALE   88, NOV 2001 (88)
  (50% PN, 50% CH)
  A very rich and fruity wine with exotic elements and classic structure. Today, luxuriantly fat and completely evolved.
- 1979 CUVÉE ROYALE   94, JUL 2003 (94)
  (35% PN, 15% PM, 50% CH)
  Fantastically youthful, with a beautiful honey-floral nose and a sensual citrus flavor. I bought a case of this classic wine and certain bottles had already developed a toffee-flavored maturity.
- 1978 CUVÉE ROYALE   87, JAN 2000 (87)
  (50% PN, 50% CH)
  Pure and full of berries. Several tasters were irritated by a stony undertone that I found piquant. Somewhat short aftertaste.
- 1976 CUVÉE ROYALE   91, JAN 2003 (91)
  (50% PN, 50% CH)
  This wine always gives a clear reflection of the vintage. Anyone who values the '76s highly won't be disappointed by the extra fatness and butterscotch aroma in this Champagne. The '79 is more classic.
- 1975 CUVÉE ROYALE   92, DEC 2002 (92)
  (60% PN, 40% CH)
  I can't think of a better way to learn the character of different vintages than holding a vertical tasting of Joseph Perrier. The '75 is classically structured but a little less friendly than the other vintages of the 1970s.
- 1973 CUVÉE ROYALE   89, MAR 1996 (89)
  (50% PN, 50% CH)
  This tastes powerful and distinct. The aftertaste is warm, generous, and bready.
- 1971 CUVÉE ROYALE   93, JUL 2002 (93)
  (50% PN, 50% CH)
  Wonderful honeysuckle scent. Exotic yummy fruit taste with perfect balance and a new vanilla-like tone in the aftertaste.
- 1969 CUVÉE ROYALE   94, JUN 1999 (94)
  (50% PN, 50% CH)
  Unmatched elegance and grace. A noticeable honeysuckle tone, just like the '71, but it is backed up here by a slender lemon tone. Extremely long and oily Chardonnay taste with a fine residual sweetness and a citrus-fresh undertone.
- 1966 CUVÉE ROYALE
  (50% PN, 50% CH)
- 1964 CUVÉE ROYALE
  (50% PN, 50% CH)
- 1953 CUVÉE ROYALE   97, JUN 1999 (97)
  (50% PN, 50% CH)
  No wine can be this bright at this age! Fantastic foaming mousse and an almost tropical, nectar-like fruit sweetness. Ravishing! Without a doubt Joseph Perrier's best wine of all time.
- CENT CINQUANTENAIRE   90, MAY 2002 (90)
  (50% PN, 50% CH)

It took me a long time to find a bottle of this threatened species, which I finally did in England. The house-style is instantly recognizable, and the step up from the vintage wine is hardly noticeable. Just as with Grand Siècle, this *cuvée de prestige* is made from grapes from three vintages.

- 1990 JOSEPHINE   91, DEC 2003 (91)
(55% PN, 45% CH)
Very voluptuous and exotically rich Champagne full of delicious notes of maturity such as peach, apricot, chocolate, and almond, but unfortunately also overtones of leather, raisin, fig, and date. Good, but for how long will this rich and velvety smooth wine hold on?

- 1989 JOSEPHINE   92, JUL 2001 (92)
(50% PN, 50% CH)
Very similar to earlier vintages and actually suddenly completely mature. The balance is first class, as usual. One of Champagne's forgotten greats. A pleasant tone of honey, peppermint, candy cane, and treacle are present. Completely evolved now. Don't store.

- 1985 JOSEPHINE   91, JAN 1999 (93)
(55% PN, 45% CH)
Josephine is one of the new prestige *cuvées*. It's inspired by the Belle Epoque with its flower-adorned bottle, and the contents are just as romantic and sensual as the original. The new wine Josephine has joined the ranks of classic prestige *cuvées* straightaway. The '85 is much like the '82, although slightly less developed. The nose is full of sweet honey tones and Earl Grey-ish aromas, and the flavor can be compared to that of a juicy peach.

- 1982 JOSEPHINE   92, JAN 1999 (93)
(55% PN, 45% CH)
Closed in the glass, strangely enough, considering that the aromas are so sweet and ripe. Ten minutes later an explosion of coconut, bergamot oil, mint, and coffee. A sweet, long, and sensual flavor. An emotional Champagne that has held a lot of meaning for me.

- 1975 JOSEPH-PERRIER WEDDING CUVÉE   92, OCT 1999 (92)
(47% PN, 8% PM, 45% CH)
One of the many special Champagnes produced for the wedding of Lady Diana Spencer and Prince Charles in Britain. This magnum has a developed color and aroma. The taste is conversely stringent, dry, and indestructible. Not as charming as the '79, but more classic in its structure.

PERRION, THIERRY *** R-M

24, rue Chanzy
51360 Verzenay
03 26 49 89 80
Production: 6,000
Jessica Perrion is the only Swedish winemaker in Champagne, and one of the few winemakers who has been to my home in Sweden. Together with her husband Thierry, she runs this small firm in the *grand cru* village of Verzenay. With some artistic talent, Jessica designs the Champagne labels herself. Thierry and Jessica do everything themselves on this little property, and 75 percent of the grapes are sold to established Champagne houses. The quality goes up every year and I wait with excitement to see if they will vinify Verzenay's oldest vineyard in a separate *cuvée*. It remains to be seen whether or not Jessica can convince Thierry that a few hundred

bottles can be worth so much trouble. I succeeded in convincing *her*, at least, over a bottle of 1938 La Tâche.

- THIERRY PERRION TRADITION   69
(80% PN, 20% CH)
- THIERRY PERRION PRESTIGE (97/98)   81, FEB 2004 (85)
(90% PN, 10% CH)
The heaviest and most derivative Champagne so far from Perrion. Big, beefy nose of ripe fruit, freshly baked bread, spices, and sun-warmed skin. Fleshy taste with power and robust character, where plum, banana, and cherry are clear notes together with a gamy element.

- 1996 THIERRY PERRION   80, MAY 2003 (84)
(90% PN, 10% CH)
Fully packed with exotic, soft fruit. Rather sweet, with notes of kiwi, pear, tutti-frutti, and banana. Fleshy and surprisingly hard to put down; also low in acidity considering the vintage.

- 1952 THIERRY PERRION   94, DEC 2003 (94)
(100% CH)
I had this undisgorged bottle standing in my cellar for a few months before I—just in time for Christmas and a private dinner with Mats Hanzon's family—dared to disgorge it by myself. It proceeded brilliantly, as the cork wanted to get out all by itself. The color was incredibly beautiful and clear with a faint stream of microscopic bubbles. The nose was cold and refined with the same elegance as a sophisticated elderly lady. The creamy fresh taste exuded iron, flint, resin, tar, mushroom cream, as well as pure, buoyantly acidic apple aromas. Much less forceful than expected, but what elegance! Fifty years of age seems to be nothing for chalky Chardonnay from Trépail.

PERROT-BOULONNAIS R-M

51130 Vertus
A small grower in Vertus that only has access to Chardonnay.

- PERROT-BOULONNAIS BLANC DE BLANCS   68
(100% CH)

PERTOIS-LEBRUN *** R-M

28, rue de la Libération
51530 Cramant
03 26 57 54 25
Production: 80,000
This Cramant grower owns six hectares in the village and also makes charming Champagnes that are typical of the *cru*. The result would be even better with a lower dosage.

- PERTOIS-LEBRUN BLANC DE BLANCS   71
(100% CH)
- 1992 PERTOIS-LEBRUN   87, JAN 2003 (89)
(100% CH)
A sensational '92! This relatively unknown grower in Cramant goes from strength to strength. The '91 was already surprisingly good, and with the '92 (which was for most a very weak vintage) they have produced a lovely Champagne with a big, Burgundy-like aroma and a concentrated taste of the loveliest grapefruit juice.

- 1991 PERTOIS-LEBRUN   82, JAN 1999 (87)
(100% CH)
Fizzy, invigorating, fruity, and absolutely clean. Clear tones of grape and pineapple in both the scent and the taste. Buoyant, harmonic, and very satisfying '91.

• 1989 PERTOIS-LEBRUN   78, NOV 1994 (85)
(100% CH)

Here too the dosage is a little heavy-handed, which is a shame when the grapes themselves have such lovely sweet aromas.

PERTOIS-MORISET *** R-M

13, avenue de la République
51190 Le Mesnil-sur-Oger
03 26 57 52 14
Production: 100,000

Yet another grower in Le Mesnil to keep an eye on. Pertois-Moriset also owns vineyards in Pinot villages from which he makes three Blanc de Noirs. Other wines: Blanc de Noirs, Sélection, Vintage, Brut Rosé.

• PERTOIS-MORISET BLANC DE BLANCS   80
(100% CH)

Rich, developed Chardonnay aromas in both nose and flavor. The wine relies on its richness more than any finesse, which is unusual for Le Mesnil.

• 1988 PERTOIS-MORISET SPECIAL CLUB   86, MAY 1995 (92)
(100% CH)

A wonderfully rich wine with an almost perfumed, flowery Mesnil nose. Tight and creamy structure with a taste of mango and vanilla.

PERTOIS, DOMINIQUE R-M

13, avenue de la République
51190 Le Mesnil-sur-Oger
03 26 57 52 14
Production: 100,000

The grower has more than fifteen hectares planted with thirty-year-old vines in Mesnil, Oger, Avize, Cramant, and Pinot Noir in Sézanne. All Blanc de Blancs are blended from all of the villages.

• DOMINIQUE PERTOIS BLANC DE BLANCS   67
(100% CH)

Pale and vaguely flowery, with a light, pure flavor which makes one long for Pinot Noir.

PETERS, PIERRE **** R-M

26, rue des Lombards
51190 Le Mesnil-sur-Oger
03 26 57 50 32
Production: 150,000

The Peters family came originally from Luxembourg, before Pierre settled in Le Mesnil. The always smiling and tremendously skilful François Peters controls 17.5 hectares, twelve of which lie in the very best parts of Le Mesnil. For several years grapes from the old vines in Les Chétillons were included in the vintage wine, but nowadays they make a Cuvée Spéciale from grapes just from this unique location. The nectar-like '89 became Systembolaget's (the Swedish Wine Monopoly's) first Champagne from the "Champagne village of Champagne villages." The enthusiasm generated by this wine all over the world is huge—and that's before anyone has had a chance to taste a mature bottle. Mesnil's wines take a long time to mature, but Champagne from Peters offers from the start an accessible fruitiness that resembles tangerine and a large portion of butterscotch and nut aromas. With age they become majestic and deep as a well, full of coffee and walnut aromas and a fleeting, vibrant, exotic fruitiness. Pierre Peters is a

hidden treasure of Champagne—so far anyway—and the prices are laughable considering the quality of the wines.

• PIERRE PETERS CUVÉE DE RÉSERVE   80
(100% CH)

Sadly, the bottle variation is great. The quality is always high, but some mature examples rise above the rest with their toasty Mesnil character.

• PIERRE PETERS EXTRA BRUT   77
(100% CH)

• PIERRE PETERS PERLE DU MESNIL   80
(100% CH)

Weakly sparkling, citrus fresh, and easily drunk, but without any great complexity.

• 1997 PIERRE PETERS   83, APR 2003 (88)
(100% CH)

A producer that always makes fine, elegant Champagnes whatever the vintage. Mandarin orange, lemon, mineral, and a polished finesse of the highest class should make this wine really interesting to follow in the future.

• 1996 PIERRE PETERS   88, AUG 2003 (93)
(100% CH)

Classic, village-typical, and tartly undeveloped with refreshing tones of citrus and mineral. Naturally not as concentrated as the village's prestige wines made from grapes taken from old vines. The mandarin-orange tone developed handsomely during the winter of 2001.

• 1995 PIERRE PETERS   85, JUN 2001 (91)
(100% CH)

It is always a delight to put one's nose into a glass of Pierre Peters. Some tasters speak of cheeses and nuts, petroleum, and mandarins. This time I am content to say, "typical Peters."

• 1992 PIERRE PETERS   80, MAY 2000 (85)
(100% CH)

A very fruity Champagne. Clear aromas of pear and banana, which has over the last year developed a tone of mandarin and butterscotch. The wine is clean and light, even though somewhat too fragile and lean. Not my kind of Peters.

• 1991 PIERRE PETERS   80, JAN 2000 (85)
(100% CH)

The tangerine aromas are already there, but it lacks the structure needed to bring it up to the producer's normal standard.

• 1990 PIERRE PETERS   91, JUL 1998 (93)
(100% CH)

The '90 is a little bit special, with a personal style in which the yogurt-like, red-fruit nose is often confused with Pinot Noir. The structure is incredibly tight and focused. A great wine in the making.

• 1989 PIERRE PETERS   86, JUL 1995 (91)
(100% CH)

The '89, with grapes from Oger, Mesnil, Avize, and Chouilly. During 1995 the Champagne developed very quickly and is now large and bushy, filled with toasty tones. The flavor is somewhat loose, but it is creamy and packed with fruit.

• 1986 PIERRE PETERS   83, NOV 1994 (84)
(100% CH)

Juicy, mature, and chocolate scented. Drink within a couple of years.

• 1985 PIERRE PETERS   92, MAR 2003 (93)
(100% CH)

Perfectly clean and purebred, with tranquil, beautiful young tones fighting for control. Packed with mineral aromas and seductive notes. Dry and extremely potent.

- 1982 PIERRE PETERS   92, JUN 1997 (92)
(100% CH)
Honey-soft, buttery, and easily drunk.

- 1979 PIERRE PETERS   94, APR 1995 (95)
(100% CH)
An outstanding wine that shows how beautifully the village's Champagne ages. In a normal bottle the wine has a nutty nose, and from the magnum one is struck by a perfect aroma of butter-fried chanterelle mushrooms. The flavor is identical in both bottle sizes. The elegant, acidic flavor is wrapped in an oily envelope and displays aromas of beeswax, tobacco, coffee, and walnuts.

- 1973 PIERRE PETERS   96, JUN 1993 (96)
(100% CH)
Only Dom Pérignon can compete for the title of "Champagne of the vintage." The '73 produced by Peters is golden nectar, with a fabulous Montrachet-like bouquet. Petroleum, walnuts, melon, mango, autumn leaves, and coffee fill the room when the wine is poured. The flavor is oily and smooth as honey.

- 1997 PIERRE PETERS CUVÉE SPÉCIALE   85, AUG 2003 (90)
(100% CH)
Extremely vineyard-typical, with an exceptionally typical taste profile, strongly characterized by mineral and spicy notes. Fat and oiliness are missing this time. A part of the concentration will surely present itself with time, but a big vintage it is not.

- 1996 PIERRE PETERS CUVÉE SPÉCIALE   93, APR 2004 (96)
(100% CH)
It is fascinating to see how unchangeable this wine is. I felt immediately at home during a Mauritian sunset when the evening's first blind taster was poured in the velvety night. The wine is almost identical to my recollection of how the '90 had tasted at the same age. The old vines impart a sweet, caressing concentration, and the aromatic fingerprint is the same for all vintages. Incredibly charismatic and easily recognized. Later bottles have conveyed a meaner, tarter, and more youthful impression.

- 1995 PIERRE PETERS CUVÉE SPÉCIALE   92, NOV 2003 (94)
(100% CH)
Difficult to judge at first. The intensity in the apple-flavored aromas is astonishing, as well as the cracklingly fresh acidity. Put down in the cellar! If you have the opportunity, buy the wine in a few years' time, to gain a little extra needed autolytic character. Half a year later the subtle wine will have adopted beautiful aromas that remind one of a high-class, featherlight Montrachet made in a stainless-steel vat.

- 1994 PIERRE PETERS CUVÉE SPÉCIALE   78, DEC 1998 (85)
(100% CH)
Of course they only produce good wines from this exceptional vineyard, but the '94 must be considered an anomaly, or at least a mislabeled wine. Why not include these grapes in the normal vintage Champagne in such a weak vintage? The aroma is green, unripe, and vegetal. The taste is steely and flinty, without the so-characteristic mandarin-orange tone. Sure to be quite storable thanks to the formidable acidity.

- 1991 PIERRE PETERS CUVÉE SPÉCIALE   82, DEC 1998 (87)
(100% CH)

A very small number of bottles were produced of this vintage. Like the '94, this is a wine that one can do without. That is not to say that the Champagne is bad in any way. It is just that Cuvée Spéciale usually competes with Selosse "N" for first place among the grower Champagnes. Should be stored for quite a while if it is to reach its highest potential.

- 1990 PIERRE PETERS CUVÉE SPÉCIALE   94, JAN 2004 (95)
(100% CH)
A superbly concentrated Chardonnay wine that brings a smile to my lips as I take up my pen. The wine combines the muscular mandarin-orange aroma of the '89 with the stony stringency of the '88. Wonderful today; magical after 2010.

- 1989 PIERRE PETERS CUVÉE SPÉCIALE   95, MAR 2003 (95)
(100% CH)
This Vieilles Vignes Champagne from seventy-year-old vines in Les Chétillons has been part of the very elite since its very first vintage. The wine's rich mandarin-orange flavor leads many to expect a short life. In actual fact this exotically rich and toasty Champagne is full of life-sustaining acidity that lies in wait under the surface. A buttery nut-toffee taste dominates more and more. In a magnum an exciting note of strawberry yogurt has crept in.

- 1988 PIERRE PETERS CUVÉE SPÉCIALE   92, NOV 2003 (94)
(100% CH)
The '88 is not really as rich and fruity as the '89, but it still has an even more classic structure and fresher, more multifaceted floral nose, with hints of roasted coffee beans—especially in magnum, where the clarity far outshines what you find in a regular bottle.

- 1985 PIERRE PETERS CUVÉE SPÉCIALE   90, APR 1995 (96)
(100% CH)
The owner's own favorite wine. At the age of ten the acidity was still huge, and the flowery nose is extremely fine but somewhat closed. The flavor resembles a drier and more elegant version of the 1985 Roederer Cristal.

- 1978 PIERRE PETERS SPECIAL CLUB   91, APR 1997 (91)
(100% CH)
Incredibly elegant and refreshing Champagne with stringent acidity and broad toasty aromas, plus a delicious citrus flavor. One of the gems of this vintage.

- 1973 PIERRE PETERS SPECIAL CLUB   91, MAY 1996 (91)
(100% CH)
The old club bottle-shape has proved to be unsuitable for long aging. Compared to the ordinary 1973 Pierre Peters, this version is far more developed, with certain signs of oxidation. Both the nose and flavor are delightfully rich, but any finesse is subdued.

PETITJEAN, H. N-M

12, rue St Vincent
51150 Ambonnay
03 26 57 08 79
Production: 100,000

Petitjean was founded in 1846 but was of negligible importance until Henri Petitjean took over. In 1959 it was the turn of Michel Petitjean to take the helm, and the firm is still owned by the family today. Only 5 percent of the grapes come from the house's own vineyards in Ambonnay, and the remainder is bought in from seven high-ranking villages. In 1993 the firm launched something as tasteless as three different Pavarotti Champagnes that were accompanied by CDs. I have nothing against the concept of

Champagne and opera in itself, but as a commercial idea the union is rather more doubtful. Fortunately the Champagne is far from tasteless.

- 1985 BAL MASCHERA–FERNANDO PAVAROTTI 82, JAN 1994 (87)
(60% PN, 40% CH)
 Golden color, aristocratic toasty nose, and a creamy, long taste that reverberates at least as long as Pavarotti's high C.

PHILIPPART, MAURICE R-M
16, rue de Rilly
51500 Chigny-les-Roses
03 26 03 42 44
Production: 30,000
- MAURICE PHILIPPART BRUT 66
(10% PN, 80% PM, 10% CH)
- MAURICE PHILIPPART DEMI-SEC 30
(10% PN, 80% PM, 10% CH)
- MAURICE PHILIPPART ROSÉ 64
(20% PN, 80% PM)
- 1989 MAURICE PHILIPPART 79, JAN 1999 (79)
(10% PN, 80% PM, 10% CH)
- 1986 MAURICE PHILIPPART 75, OCT 1997 (75)
(10% PN, 80% PM, 10% CH)
- 1989 MAURICE PHILIPPART PRESTIGE 75, OCT 1997 (80)
(10% PN, 90% CH)

PHILIPPONNAT **** N-M
13, rue du Pont
51160 Mareuil-sur-Aÿ
03 26 56 93 00
Production: 500,000
The house was founded in 1910 by Pierre Philipponnat, and in 1935 he bought the jewel in the company's crown, the 5.5-hectare vineyard, Clos des Goisses. In 1987 Philipponnat became part of the Marie-Brizard group, and today the house is in Bruno Paillard's stable-block. They buy in 75 percent of the grapes from very highly ranked vineyards (97 percent, on average), with the remaining quarter coming from Mareuil-sur-Aÿ. Today the firm is run with a purposeful hand by the friendly and humble Charles Philipponnat. He manages the excellent grapes in a praiseworthy manner; the wines share his charm and personality. All of them are intensely fruity, with a characteristically youthful tone of gooseberry in the nose. Only the first pressing is used by Philipponnat, since they have Abel Lepitre as their second label.

 Clos des Goisses is consistently one of the world's foremost wines. They still use a small number of oak barrels, even if certain vintages, like the '89, are completely vinified in steel tanks. This Champagne is a real slow starter that should preferably be decanted if it's going to be drunk before its twentieth birthday. The unique slope beside the canal in Mareuil-sur-Aÿ is planted with 70 percent Pinot Noir and 30 percent Chardonnay. I recently held a complete vertical tasting of this personal wine. The Champagnes were amongst the most ravishing I've tasted. Most impressive was an invaluable magnum from 1955. In certain years a rare—though hardly exciting—still red variety is made from the batch. Even rarer, and definitely more exciting, are the 200 bottles of still Chardonnay that Philipponnat makes every year for their own use; in my opinion it is Champagne's foremost still white wine. The four stars are all totally thanks to Clos des Goisses.

- PHILIPPONNAT BRUT 75
(55% PN, 15% PM, 30% CH)
- LE REFLET 80
(50% PN, 50% CH)
Clos des Goisses's second wine, in principle. Those grapes that don't really meet the high standards are included instead in Le Reflet, together with Chardonnay from Côte des Blancs. The wine that's sold in 1995 is in reality a pure 1990. A lovely, generous young fruit that turns one's thoughts to gooseberries and Williams pears. The flavor, too, is strikingly fruity and easily drunk, and it will develop well for many years despite its immediate charm.
- PHILIPPONNAT CUVÉE 1522 85
(60% PN, 40% CH)
Something between a nonvintage Champagne and a prestige. The wine has a beautiful label depicting Aÿ as it looked in 1522. The wine itself is very good, with a base from 1996. The taste is full of honey and mint caramel. Rich and luxurious.
- PHILIPPONNAT ROSÉ 66
(55% PN, 10% PM, 35% CH)
- 1993 PHILIPPONNAT 82, DEC 2003 (84)
(65% PN, 35% CH)
Philipponnat has succeeded absolutely in making an unusually fleshy '93. The wine has a buttery, unexpected, fat structure that suggests good wine-craft—if you like the house's style, you should not be disappointed. There is a concentrated plump fruit and strong gamy tones. Personally, I'm not enamored of this wine's style; I prefer more elegant wines, or wines with even more distinct tastes—if you keep to the weightier school. The wine does keep well, though, because a portion of it has not been put through malolactic fermentation.
- 1991 PHILIPPONNAT 83, DEC 2003 (83)
(65% PN, 10% PM, 25% CH)
Initially, this was a rather bushy wine, with big, slightly coarse fruit and certain medicinal elements mixed with purple coneflower, rhubarb, and pineapple. Fleshy, but short. Now the wine is completely evolved and should be drunk immediately. Round, ample, and creamy, with notes of chocolate and leather.
- 1990 PHILIPPONNAT 85, DEC 2003 (85)
(65% PN, 35% CH)
For a long time the best regular vintage wine I have tasted from Philipponnat. The wine is full of almond flavor and spicy tones backed up by a Bollinger-like ripe apple taste. But it is aging too fast and has worsened recently.
- 1989 PHILIPPONNAT 80, AUG 1997 (83)
(65% PN, 35% CH)
A rich, mighty Champagne with tremendous maturity. Already one notices tones of mint chocolate and raisins. Most remarkable is an idiosyncratic tone of echinacea (purple coneflower).
- 1988 PHILIPPONNAT 70, OCT 1994 (75)
(65% PN, 35% CH)
- 1985 PHILIPPONNAT 87, APR 1996 (89)
(65% PN, 35% CH)
A very successful vintage for this firm. There's something lightweight and relaxed about this wine that attracts me. The nose is lightly toasted and very creamy, a feature that is repeated and expanded in the mouth.
- 1982 PHILIPPONNAT 85, DEC 2003 (85)
(65% PN, 35% CH)

A late-disgorged wine from Philipponnat's treasure-chest that had good elasticity and intact freshness. Otherwise the aromas were aged and oxidative. I suggest a little caution before buying; check how the wine has been stored. A food wine with a big personality and beefy aromas.

- 1976 PHILIPPONNAT   90, DEC 2003 (90)
(65% PN, 35% CH)
Stored in the house's cellar, this is a big wine that's still fruity. The nose is bready and heavy, like the aftertaste, but the medium palate is exotically fruity and full of sweet, delicious aromas. My favorite vintage of this wine!

- 1998 GRAND BLANC   84, OCT 2002 (88)
(100% CH)
Delightfully pure, floral, spring nose—like a young Chardonnay (without autolytic character) usually has. When aired, aromas of marzipan and hawthorn appear. Rich, delicious taste with hints of vanilla, biscuits, and pineapple

- 1996 GRAND BLANC   85, MAR 2004 (89)
(100% CH)
A thoroughbred wine with intensely whirling mousse and sparkling vitality. Rich notes of butter toffee and sweet citrus appear at the same time as the buoyant acidity. A delightful wine which magnificently represents the vintage.

- 1991 GRAND BLANC   85, OCT 2002 (87)
(100% CH)
A very successful Champagne in my opinion. Vigorous and tasteful, with a certain imprint of grapes from Mareuil-sur-Aÿ. The wine makes up for, in fullness and vigor, what it is missing in multifaceted richness.

- 1990 GRAND BLANC   82, OCT 2002 (>)
(100% CH)
When the wine turned up on the market I was impressed, but it has proven that it is necessary to subscribe to Charles Philipponnat's theory about lower dosage and a protective addition of sulfur in order to avoid oxidation. The wine is already over-oxidized and on its way down, despite its abundance of fruit.

- 1989 GRAND BLANC   92, SEP 2003 (93)
(100% CH)
A truly impressive Champagne, and one of the foremost Grands Blancs ever made. Big, powerful scent of honey and nut-toffee essence. Compact and syrupy, with identical palate and nose. Truly long and built-up in the same way as the outstanding '76.

- 1988 GRAND BLANC   78, OCT 2003 (>)
(100% CH)

- 1988 GRAND BLANC NON DOSÉ   65, OCT 2002 (>)
(100% CH)

- 1985 GRAND BLANC   88, OCT 2002 (88)
(100% CH)
Here, Grand Blanc displays its somewhat shyer and more discreet side. The Champagne is light and elegant with a faint, yet elegantly creamy nose. A faint waft of fine mushroom browned in butter emerges when aired.

- 1983 GRAND BLANC   83, OCT 2002 (83)
(100% CH)
Still unusually youthful, with an acacia nose and a fresh, acidic taste. There is a surprising lightness that combines with a slightly tropical aromatic spectrum.

- 1982 GRAND BLANC   81, OCT 2002 (81)
(100% CH)

Regardless of the vintage, this is a wine that never seduces me. Most of the bottles I have drunk have been at Royal Champagne—in other words, only a stone's throw from the producer—so one cannot complain about the freshness. The '82 is clean, evolved, and short.

- 1980 GRAND BLANC   89, OCT 2002 (89)
(100% CH)
Light, delicate, and deliciously toasted. A perfectly evolved, rather fragile, and quiet Champagne that would probably be described as thin and uninteresting in its youth. Today, it is really handsome and polished.

- 1976 GRAND BLANC   95, MAR 2003 (95)
(100% CH)
A wonderful newly disgorged Champagne from Philipponnat's treasure-chest. Low cellar temperature, prolonged contact with the yeast, and a high portion of ripe Chardonnay are considered the most important components to enable fine, small bubbles to develop. All these requirements are fulfilled here! One year after disgorging the wine was deep gold in color and the mousse altogether exceptional, with a continuous stream—and great quantity—of tiny bubbles. The nose is deliciously vintage-typical, reminiscent of Comtes de Champagne and Des Princes from the same year. However, the wine is not as fully concentrated and, furthermore, the aftertaste is shorter. The aromas in the bouquet and the fat, oily, sweet palate are dominated by vanilla, butter toffee, cinnamon bun, and lemon custard.

- 1974 GRAND BLANC   90, OCT 2002 (90)
(100% CH)
It's hardly probable that this odd vintage was particular in any way, either in youth or in middle age. Only now, with truly long, life-preserving and enriching yeast contact, have the wonderful acacia notes and luscious, luxuriant magnolia character developed. The taste is light and as pure as an alpine stream, with great beauty. See what long storage can bring about!

- 1991 PHILIPPONNAT SUBLIME RÉSERVE   81, MAY 2001 (81)
(100% CH)
What a delightful idea! It goes without saying that Chardonnay, with its lemony-fresh taste, is most suitable to meet the sweetness. Despite its thirty-five grams of sugar, this is an elegant and buttery wine with a refreshing and delicious finish. One of the best of its kind, well suited to both foie gras and fruitcake.

- 1991 CLOS DES GOISSES   89, JAN 2004 (92)
(70% PN, 30% CH)
Exciting nose of petroleum and Sauternes, together with dried fruit. A madly delicious '91 with a fleshiness that otherwise is completely lacking this year. Long, exotic, and relatively developed modern taste.

- 1990 CLOS DES GOISSES   92, NOV 2003 (96)
(70% PN, 30% CH)
It's hardly surprising that Clos des Goisses performed so well this brilliant year. There is an unreleased finesse here, built up of freshness and crispy acidity on top of a foundation of concentrated fruit. At the Millennium Tasting this idiosyncratic wine couldn't do itself justice. Big nose resembling a Sauternes.

- 1989 CLOS DES GOISSES   92, JAN 2002 (96)
(70% PN, 30% CH)
Intensively flowery, nearly perfumed scent of grass, gooseberry, and hawthorn. Very rich and quite concentrated. At the age of eleven years, notes of vanilla and honey are beginning to appear, suggesting that full maturity is just around the corner.

• 1988 CLOS DES GOISSES   89, NOV 2003 (94)
(70% PN, 30% CH)

I can never really understand how Clos des Goisses performs as a young wine. Experience shows that all vintages become powerhouses with great age. The '88 isn't at all as undeveloped and grassy as the '82 was at the same age. Instead, it is only medium bodied and delicate, with bready and toasted aromas as well as a fine crispy fruit. Certain bottles are actually medicinal and have a taste of gooseberry. What's going to happen?

• 1986 CLOS DES GOISSES   94, JUN 2001 (94)
(70% PN, 30% CH)

During a lunch at the company, Paul Couvreur really convinced me that certain Champagnes benefit by being decanted. An undecanted and a decanted glass of the '86 were amazingly dissimilar. The nose from the decanted glass resembled Bollinger R. D. and had a broad, smoky, nutty, classical young Pinot bouquet. The flavor was extremely concentrated and rich. A cannonade of hazelnuts and chocolate met my palate, and the aftertaste was aristocratic. The wine easily coped with its company, a steak in morel sauce. A great wine!

• 1985 CLOS DES GOISSES   94, MAR 2003 (96)
(70% PN, 30% CH)

Henrik Arve, my closest friend among wine-tasters, claims this is one of the greatest wines he has ever tasted in the middle-aged phase it is currently enjoying. I too am very impressed by the amazingly creamy fruit and the complex, intertwined, subtle spectrum of distinct Champagne aromas.

• 1983 CLOS DES GOISSES   94, APR 2003 (94)
(70% PN, 30% CH)

A fascinating wine where the nose hints at old Champagne while the flavor is still very young. The bouquet is rich in chocolate, smoky, and nutty. On the palate the attack is fresh and the fruit is youth itself. Long, long aftertaste.

• 1982 CLOS DES GOISSES   95, MAY 2003 (96)
(70% PN, 30% CH)

The first times I tasted the '82 I doubted the greatness of this vineyard's location, as the wine was floral and shy for so many years before unfolding its peacock tail of tastes. At a large horizontal tasting of the twenty best '82s, Clos des Goisses and Salon stood out as the least evolved wines. The long aftertaste was, however, prominent from the beginning. I'm already longing for the next bottle in order to see if it has begun to develop its lovely chocolate style.

• 1980 CLOS DES GOISSES   94, DEC 2003 (95)
(70% PN, 30% CH)

A truly handsome wine with swirling lightness and uplifting features. Coffee and hazelnut waft through the nose together with notes of snow and sea. Crispy, clean taste with high-octane mineral quality. Far from a typical Clos des Goisses, but what does that matter when the wine is still so seductive? Certain bottles taste like a somewhat fuller 1980 Dom Pérignon.

• 1979 CLOS DES GOISSES   95, JAN 2002 (95)
(70% PN, 30% CH)

What a brilliant wine! The nose is extremely broad, with a flowery, youthful element and a nutty, older, more serious style. As it warms up in the glass it is dominated by hazelnuts and honeysuckle. The flavor is as deep as the ocean floor and thrillingly invigorating. Certain bottles are unfortunately already overripe.

• 1978 CLOS DES GOISSES   94, DEC 1996 (94)
(70% PN, 30% CH)

Even in such a poor year this unique creation is excellent. Completely developed, with great fruitiness and overflowing with toasty aromas. Is there a better '78 outside Vosne-Romanée?

• 1976 CLOS DES GOISSES   95, MAR 2003 (95)
(70% PN, 30% CH)

This monster vineyard and monster year can only produce a monster wine, right? Of course, this is a fantastically rich, monumental wine with a gigantically big taste—but it's so rich it almost goes overboard and turns itself inside out. The nose is so strong, it's difficult to differentiate the nuances. I have to go away from the glass again and again in order to approach it carefully once more, and during the first instant formulate what I think. The taste is a homogeneous tidal wave of viscous sweets. I wonder if the wine will be less noisy in the future? One hundred points on the other side of the Atlantic, for sure, but I want more finesse to be completely satisfied.

• 1975 CLOS DES GOISSES   94, JUN 2001 (94)
(70% PN, 30% CH)

Clos des Goisses is the Champagne that has taken me the longest time to get to know. This wine is a kind of key, as all the mature and great elements are already quite obvious, while the young, sometimes odd aromas are still around. Slightly coarser than expected, despite maturity having set in.

• 1973 CLOS DES GOISSES   92, DEC 2003 (92)
(70% PN, 30% CH)

Unfortunately I haven't tried this wine directly from Philipponnat's own cellar. The only bottle that reached me was somewhat low in level and had only a streak of mousse left. Still very good with a nose of nuts, old Riesling, oil, and resin. Big, intensely chocolaty, fleshy taste. A real duck-liver wine!

• 1970 CLOS DES GOISSES
(70% PN, 30% CH)

• 1966 CLOS DES GOISSES   97, MAR 2003 (97)
(70% PN, 30% CH)

Disgorged in July 1998. It was extremely enlightening and instructive to compare the '66 and the '64 back-to-back. The '66 is certainly lighter and slimmer, but compensates with an unparalleled finesse and a fantastically euphoria-creating, toasted bouquet. Somewhat less impressive at the Millennium Tasting at Villa Pauli.

• 1964 CLOS DES GOISSES   96, MAR 2002 (97)
(70% PN, 30% CH)

Disgorged in July 1998. Actually slightly restrained in the nose, especially in comparison with the pleasant-smelling '66 that stood beside it. This is the downside of newly disgorged oldies. On the other hand, the wine profits from the date of disgorgement in its youthfully new and magnificently creamy taste. Extremely concentrated and resounding resonance.

• 1959 CLOS DES GOISSES   99, JAN 2003 (99)
(70% PN, 30% CH)

This bottle is among the greatest wines I've ever tasted. Even though Pinot Noir is the dominant grape, there are strong similarities with the '59 Salon. I tasted it blind beside five old *cuvée* Champagnes from major houses and it was so apparent that this was a mono-*cru*, with all the advantages that implies in terms of power, intensity, and personality. This is a creamy and youthful creation with an almost narcotically seductive nose.

The flavor is so very full and creamy with citrus tones. Once the wine has stood in the glass for a while, the special youthful grass and gooseberry nose appeared. A wine that is a long voyage in itself. Not as impressive if too recently disgorged.

- 1955 CLOS DES GOISSES   99, MAR 1999 (99)
  (70% PN, 30% CH)

A newly disgorged magnum filled with some of the most delicious nuances that my senses have experienced. Everything that was present in the '53 and the '52 was in this wine as well. The difference as I experienced it was that the '55 had a somewhat greater depth, and almost an extra dimension that evoked thoughts of religion and some sort of higher power. Anders Röttorp's favorite Champagne, bar none.

- 1953 CLOS DES GOISSES   98, MAR 1999 (98)
  (70% PN, 30% CH)

One of the absolutely last magnums left in the world. Naturally direct from the house and disgorged two months prior to my tasting. One is met directly by an unprecedented unique and fascinating aromatic spectrum, spanning such wildly distinct and unexpected aromas as cedar, resin, eucalyptus, grilled steak, grass, gooseberry, and gunpowder! After a time in the glass, all three wines from the 1950s resembled each other, with a fabulously euphoric perfumed scent that is much like passion fruit. The taste is perhaps the richest and most charming of the three in this unbeaten tasting trio.

- 1952 CLOS DES GOISSES   96, MAR 1999 (96)
  (70% PN, 30% CH)

Disgorged in July 1998. A magnificent wine where the character is somewhat softer and more buttery than in the other fifty or so vintages from the house. As usual, Clos des Goisses's special spicy tone—which reminds one of fresh ginger—is also found here; in addition the youthful fruit that borders on passion fruit. Other clearly discernible nuances are orange blossom, sandalwood, clove, eucalyptus, and duck pâté.

- 1951 CLOS DES GOISSES   90, MAR 2003 (90)
  (70% PN, 30% CH)

A bottle that comes directly from the house is, of course, in extra-good condition. The mousse was weak and the color beautifully golden, with dashes of old-age tones leaning toward amber. The nose was powerful, with hints of molasses and tar under the strong ground-covering of browned butter. There's still good sting in the mouth and an impressive fleshiness, but the oxidation is slowly beginning to change the spectrum of aromas into a Tokay.

- REFLET MILLÉNAIRE JUBILEUM   83, JUN 2000 (86)
  (50% PN, 50% CH)

Actually, the same wine as the regular Reflet, but before the Millennium the base wine happened to be even better than before. A creamy and lemony-fresh "mini-Clos des Goisses."

- 1990 CLOS DES GOISSES MILLÉNAIRE   93, MAR 2003 (96)
  (70% PN, 30% CH)

You can try this Millennium edition in magnum for around $550. The wine is identical to what you find in a regular bottle, only the dosage is somewhat higher, like the price!

PIERRON-LÉGLISE, J. R-M

8, rue Fort
51190 Oger
03 26 59 72 68

Production: 10,000
The grower works with Chardonnay from their five hectares in Oger and makes three *cuvées*. La Cuvée Fondateur is always a pure vintage from Les Barbettes.

- J. PIERRON-LÉGLISE EXTRA BRUT   74
  (100% CH)

PIPER-HEIDSIECK **** N-M
51, boulevard Henry-Vasnier
51100 Reims
03 26 84 43 00
Production: 5,000,000
All three Heidsieck houses originate from the same company, Heidsieck & Co., which was formed in 1785 by Florens-Louis Heidsieck. The Piper-Heidsieck branch was founded in 1834 by Christian Heidsieck. The house remained within the family right up until 1989, when it became part of Rémy-Cointreau. Daniel Thibault, up until his recent early death, made the *cuvées* at Charles Heidsieck and was even responsible for Piper-Hiedsieck; he was always careful to maintain the separate identity of the two houses. Piper doesn't own any vineyards themselves, buying in grapes from seventy villages. The wines are centrifuged, though they never used to be put through malolactic fermentation, which led to razor-sharp wines without extract. Today, Piper makes a softer and more easily accessible nonvintage Champagne. All Champagnes from the firm gain a great deal from cellaring, which Piper unfortunately neglects to tell its consumers about.

    The '55 and the '53 were both masterpieces, and old vintages of Florens-Louis are legendary, but during the 1970s, up until the middle of the 1990s, the house was the weakest of the Heidsieck troika. Today they are again making brilliant Champagnes, something proven very clearly with the fabulous '96. Their extremely lavish cellar tours are constructed in the best Hollywood style, something that should suit their best customers—the Americans—admirably. As I've mentioned before, it was a train ride around Piper's cellars that confirmed my fascination for Champagne. Thibault left a great void when he passed away in the spring of 2002. It's a big challenge for the new winemakers to continue on his successful path.

- HEIDSIECK BRUT   69
  (33% PN, 33% PM, 34% CH)
- PIPER-HEIDSIECK BRUT   80
  (55% PN, 30% PM, 15% CH)

I've wondered before why they don't use malolactic fermentation for such a thin wine. The acidity is exceedingly intrusive when extract is missing. Now I've got my answer: malolactic fermentation is encouraged and Piper has pulled this wine together considerably in recent years under Thibault as *chef de cave*. Certain mature bottles are deliciously toasted. Better than ever.

- PIPER-HEIDSIECK DEMI-SEC   26
  (55% PN, 30% PM, 15% CH)
- PIPER-HEIDSIECK ROSÉ   50
  (45% PN, 40% PM, 15% CH)
- 1996 PIPER-HEIDSIECK   88, MAR 2003 (92)
  (55% PN, 15% PM, 30% CH)

Through the years, Piper-Heidsieck have made some of the slowest-developing wines in all of Champagne. This time they've followed the new trend, and maybe even more followed Charles

Heidsieck's house-style. From the start, the wine is very generous, with chewy fruit, and a rich taste of nut toffee and roasted almonds. A really impressive wine that stood out at Wine International's gigantic tasting in September 2003. Brilliant acidity and bite.

- 1996 WAITROSE   88, OCT 2003 (92)
(55% PN, 15% PM, 30% CH)
Same wonderful wine as the 1996 Piper-Heidsieck, in different clothing.
- 1995 PIPER-HEIDSIECK   89, SEP 2003 (91)
(55% PN, 15% PM, 30% CH)
Truly a wine that's a perfect partner to most seafood delicacies. Super-fresh and pure, with a decided sharpness and promising young fruit. Fine generosity in the nose with bready notes, sea tones, and a fresh appley-ness. Balanced, youthful palate with all its bits and pieces in the right place. The wine has proven to be even better than I'd predicted. Deep, luxurious taste and better acidity than almost all the other '95s at Wine International's big Champagne tasting in September 2003.
- 1990 PIPER-HEIDSIECK   81, NOV 1999 (90)
(55% PN, 15% PM, 30% CH)
This is one of the less developed '90s. It is filled with razor-sharp apple tang and flowery, fresh fruit. Without question a classic storage Champagne that with time will develop toasted and deep aromas.
- 1989 PIPER-HEIDSIECK   75, FEB 1997 (87)
(55% PN, 15% PM, 30% CH)
Really stealing from the cradle with hard acidity that burns in the stomach, but don't be surprised if great complexity and fine, toasty aromas turn up and take over soon.
- 1988 BRUT SAUVAGE   76, JAN 2003 (85)
(70% PN, 30% CH)
A weak nose that is typical of the house, with discreet fruit and a cold, clear flavor with biting acidity and weak fruit. Just beginning to open up.
- 1985 BRUT SAUVAGE   75, JAN 1997 (82)
(70% PN, 30% CH)
The Champagne was heavy and bready in the nose. The flavor, on the other hand, is somewhat raw and sharp. A hint of rubber tones lowers the overall impression in what is otherwise a very full-bodied Champagne.
- 1985 PIPER-HEIDSIECK   80, MAY 1998 (85)
(55% PN, 15% PM, 30% CH)
This wine demands a customer with a good sense of smell! It's all there, but very weak. The flavor is light, soft, agreeable, and ultra-modern. If you look hard enough you'll find hints of orange, chocolate, lime, and licorice.
- 1982 BRUT SAUVAGE   77, JUN 1994 (84)
(70% PN, 30% CH)
Quite without dosage. What I call a "big-house-style", with broad and mixed tones, polished and pure. Tangerine, orange, and minerals dominate the acidic flavor.
- 1982 PIPER-HEIDSIECK   85, JAN 2003 (85)
(55% PN, 15% PM, 30% CH)
Unusually sweet and supple. Pleasant to drink, but unlikely to develop further. Less toasted than expected.
- 1979 BRUT SAUVAGE   88, MAY 1999 (88)
(70% PN, 30% CH)
Very dry Champagne that is aging nicely. Lovely cacao bouquet.

- 1976 PIPER-HEIDSIECK   84, OCT 1998 (90)
(60% PN, 10% PM, 30% CH)
This rich year should suit Piper's frail, acidic style perfectly. I was disappointed when the wine proved itself to be yet another loose and fat '76. Evolved and chocolate-laden, but devoid of charm.
- 1975 PIPER-HEIDSIECK   88, JAN 2001 (88)
(60% PN, 10% PM, 30% CH)
A big smoky nose with hints of breadiness. The flavor is fresh and light, with a pure, medium-long aftertaste of minerals.
- 1969 PIPER-HEIDSIECK
(65% PN, 35% CH)
- 1964 PIPER-HEIDSIECK   95, OCT 1998 (95)
(65% PN, 35% CH)
Fantastically fresh and well-balanced Champagne in the bloom of youth.
- 1961 PIPER-HEIDSIECK   91, MAR 1996 (91)
(65% PN, 35% CH)
Mineral and salt; sophisticated, bready Champagne.
- 1955 PIPER-HEIDSIECK   97, AUG 2001 (97)
(65% PN, 35% CH)
A magical, sensational Champagne. I opened it as an extra bottle one evening when we'd met to enjoy the legendary 1947 Krug. This wine was even better! Light and with a mousse that didn't look a day over ten years old. A superb nose of roasted coffee, bread, wood, nuts, honeysuckle, lily of the valley, and wet wool. Vigorous and fat flavor where lime and peaches have the upper hand. Remarkable balance!
- 1953 PIPER-HEIDSIECK   97, OCT 2001 (97)
(65% PN, 35% CH)
Piper-Heidsieck was fantastically good a few decades ago! I can't help but compare the '53 with the magical '55. Both these wines are "as deep as a well" and complex like few others. More than anything else, they combine an unreal, high acidity and freshness with a butterscotchiness and creaminess that is superb. The '55 is more toasted, but the '53 is even fatter, and rich in extract.
- 1952 PIPER-HEIDSIECK   95, JAN 2003 (95)
(65% PN, 35% CH)
There's something extra-special about Piper's wines from the 1950s. By so categorically avoiding malolactic fermentation, and because wines at that time were fermented in oak barrels, wine-lovers today enjoy a brilliantly fresh arsenal of complex old wines from Piper-Heidsieck. The '52 is, of course, beautifully toasted and similar to the other 1950s vintages, but perhaps somewhat lighter and, if possible, even fresher. Fine undertone of orange blossom, both in nose and palate.
- 1928 PIPER-HEIDSIECK   90, OCT 1997 (90)
(65% PN, 35% CH)
Almost without sparkle, but still an impressive Champagne. Deep old taste of tar, dried fruit, and leather. Only one half bottle tasted.
- 1982 PIPER-HEIDSIECK ROSÉ   87, AUG 2002 (87)
(75% PN, 25% CH)
Dark color, constant youthful mousse and a weighty, smoky, plum-like bouquet with a hint of red beet—an aroma common in red Burgundy. Fresh and vigorous with fine rip-and-tear. Hardly a masterpiece, but still a fine example of how good wines that haven't gone through malolactic fermentation can be, if you have the patience to wait.

- 1979 PIPER-HEIDSIECK ROSÉ   90, DEC 2002 (90)
(75% PN, 25% CH)
In many ways this wine is similar to Florens-Louis, with its idiosyncratic, super-intense combination of toasted and crispbread, which can only be achieved if malolactic fermentation is avoided. The taste also has notes of red wine and is somewhat less finely shaded than the firm's best white Champagnes.

- 1975 PIPER-HEIDSIECK ROSÉ   84, FEB 1996 (84)
(50% PN, 50% CH)
As with all older vintages from Piper, this wine retains a youthful freshness. This '75 is, however, too weak in the nose and limited in flavor to make me jump for joy.

- PIPER RARE   89
(35% PN, 65% CH)
This vintage-less prestige *cuvée*, with its deliciously toffee-ish, toasted style, will soon pass the ninety-point mark. Very similar to the beautiful '88, and perhaps it can become just as good with storage. Try to find out which vintages have been used in the blend you are drinking—I myself haven't succeeded in finding out. Only tasted on one occasion. A real Thibault-wine.

- 1988 PIPER RARE   93, NOV 2003 (93)
(35% PN, 65% CH)
At first very discreet on the nose; today an explosively fresh, toasty, enjoyable Champagne with creamy aromas. Sensational development. A great wine that is similar to Florens-Louis.

- 1985 PIPER RARE   73, MAR 1995 (85)
(35% PN, 65% CH)
Sour, full of minerals, and relatively thin, but with good development possibilities.

- 1979 PIPER RARE   84, JUN 2001 (85)
(35% PN, 65% CH)
A lightweight with a surprisingly low-key demeanor. You have to search hard for the mineral tones that are there, somewhere. Today, this wine is very similar to a fine Riesling from Weinbach in Alsace. Very idiosyncratic, "un-typical" Champagne.

- 1976 PIPER RARE   90, OCT 2003 (90)
(35% PN, 65% CH)
A masterpiece of elegance in this powerful year. A nose of sea and flowers, and a crispy, multifaceted flavor with minimal bubbles that burst against the palate like pellets of caviar. Unfortunately the wine is too light and fragile to make me fall head over heels.

- 1975 CUVÉE FLORENS-LOUIS   92, JUN 2003 (93)
(20% PN, 80% CH)
This *cuvée de prestige* disappeared from the market a long time ago, to be replaced by Piper Rare. To me the wine tasted a lot like its successor: light and elegant without any great depth. Still too young, but with impressive complexity.

- 1973 CUVÉE FLORENS-LOUIS   91, JAN 2002 (91)
(20% PN, 80% CH)
Somewhat richer than the '71, but with less outspoken elegance and length. I suppose that most would prefer the '73 above the '71 as it's been painted with a broader brush and clearer strokes. Personally I prefer the teasing refinement of the '71.

- 1971 CUVÉE FLORENS-LOUIS   94, MAY 2001 (94)
(20% PN, 80% CH)
Tasted blind at the Le Vigneron restaurant, I had no problems naming the year and the producer. The wine is light but very elegant, due to the lack of malolactic fermentation.

- 1969 CUVÉE FLORENS-LOUIS   95, OCT 2001 (96)
(20% PN, 80% CH)
It is evident that all of Piper's wines demand long storage. Previously I nearly always dismissed them as sour and uninteresting. Today Florens-Louis is one of the Champagnes I seek out most feverishly. The '69 is reminiscent of the unreal '66, but it actually seems as if it has another gear to go. The aroma is incredibly refined and the taste shares the sensual lime tone of Jacquesson's 1969.

- 1966 CUVÉE FLORENS-LOUIS   97, JUN 1999 (97)
(20% PN, 80% CH)
Despite a constant low level and some leaking bottles, the color is always fair and the mousse delightfully brisk. An amazing roasted scent with tones of tar, crispbread, and coffee. Fresh and balanced citrus taste with an exceptional length and finesse. A wine that is very easy to identify at blindfold tastings.

- 1964 CUVÉE FLORENS-LOUIS   91, FEB 2003 (91)
(20% PN, 80% CH)
Supposedly this wine is just as good as the '66 and the '69. It was thus unfortunate that my treasure came from a warm Milanese cellar that destroys Champagnes within a couple of years. Florens-Louis seems to be very nearly an indestructible wine for, despite the abuse and the total lack of effervescence, the wine was still rather light in color and fresh in its acidity. It seems that these are completely resistant to oxidation. Impressive!

- 1961 CUVÉE FLORENS-LOUIS   97, DEC 2003 (97)
(20% PN, 80% CH)
Yet again, the opportunity for an unforgettable experience from Florens-Louis. The wine has that indescribably intense, personal nose that I can trace in a split second. This time it was spiced with eucalyptus and mint leaves, but the foundation was identical to earlier vintages. Fresh, deep, gamy, nutty, apricot-sated, cigar-smelling, and full of jet fuel. These are all good descriptions, but oh-so-inadequate.

PLOYEZ-JACQUEMART *** N-M
8, rue Astoin
51500 Ludes
03 26 61 11 87
Production: 35,000
The house was founded in Ludes in 1930 by Marcel Ployez. After his death it was taken over by his widow until their son Gérard was old enough to take up the reins, which he continues to do to this day. Ployez-Jacquemart own 1.8 hectares in Mailly and Ludes but buy in 85 percent of their grapes from fine vineyards in the Marne Valley and Côte des Blancs. The famous *cuvée de prestige*, Liesse d'Harbonville, is fermented in oak barrels.

- PLOYEZ-JACQUEMART BRUT   60
(55% PN, 15% PM, 30% CH)

- PLOYEZ-JACQUEMART ROSÉ   64
(35% PN, 30% PM, 35% CH)

- 1995 PLOYEZ-JACQUEMART   83, JAN 2004 (85)
(50% PN, 50% CH)
A wine whose nose exudes Pinot Noir from Ludes and its surroundings; the flavor is characterized by creamy Chardonnay. The nose has notes of raisin, purple coneflower, and plum. The fresh taste has hints of cream, citrus, gooseberry, and a dash of Pinot-related raspberry aroma.

• 1989 PLOYEZ-JACQUEMART   84, NOV 2001 (84)
(50% PN, 50% CH)

There are many exciting local Champagnes to choose from at the restaurant Le Grand Cerf—all at good prices. This wine was superb with cod in cardamom sauce. The wine is made in a rich style reminiscent of several vineyards near Ludes.

• 1996 PLOYEZ-JACQUEMART BLANC DE BLANCS   79, NOV 2001 (84)
(100% CH)

With this much acidity, you need one year for Chardonnay from Montagne de Reims to really get going. If you store this lemon-fresh, fleshy wine for a few years, you might be in for something exciting.

• 1988 PLOYEZ-JACQUEMART BLANC DE BLANCS   68, APR 1993 (74)
(100% CH)

• 1990 CUVÉE LIESSE D'HARBONVILLE   88, FEB 2003 (89)
(100% CH)

Ployez-Jacquemart's *cuvée de prestige* is never a shrinking violet. Liesse d'Harbonville always takes a lot of space with its breadth, fleshiness, and richness. In comparison to the very best, there's a slight lack of aristocratic stature—but what does that matter when the mouth is full of tasty, generous, sweet tastes? Oak barrels make themselves known with the combined aromas of nuts, vanilla, and wood. The nuttiness became very apparent and enjoyable, together with different truffle creations, at the excellent Waterside Inn at Bray, about 45 minutes from London.

• 1985 CUVÉE LIESSE D'HARBONVILLE   84, MAY 1995 (88)
(100% CH)

A robust, vinous Blanc de Blancs with good depth and personality. The barrel character is perhaps a little too tangible in relation to the fruit.

POIROT R-M

2, rue Pernet
51130 Bergères-les-Vertus
03 26 52 02 26
Production: 15,000

Alain Poirot is the name of the current owner, the third generation in a company that has existed since 1920. The firm owns three hectares in Bergères-les-Vertus. Other wines: Blanc de Blancs, Vintage, Réserve, Demi-Sec.

• POIROT BRUT   62
(100% CH)

POL ROGER ***** N-M

1, rue Henri Lelarge
51206 Épernay
03 26 59 58 00
Production: 1,400,000

No other person means more to their house than Christian Pol-Roger does. The manner in which he welcomes wine-lovers in Champagne is beyond compare. Christian looks and acts like an English aristocrat, with a dry humor that wouldn't shame the late Sir Alec Guinness. His joyful lifestyle is as charming and effervescent as his Champagne. He loves his house, his hometown, and his Champagne, and he lets his friends share his delight. Together with Christian de Billy, he runs Winston Churchill's favorite house in the same spirit as his ancestors. Hubert de Billy stands by ready to take over.

The house was founded in 1849 by Pol Roger, who was succeeded by his sons, Maurice and Georges. At the turn of the

century the Roger family changed its name to Pol-Roger. Maurice was the mayor of Épernay during the week-long occupation of the town by the Germans in September, 1914. Despite German threats to shoot him and burn the town, he remained defiant and was later hailed as a town hero. He was voted honorary mayor for life.

England has always been the main export market for Pol Roger, and when the wartime prime minister Sir Winston Churchill died the wine's label was black-edged in memory. After a period of mourning, the 1975 Cuvée Sir Winston Churchill was launched, in magnums only. The wine is made in a style they believe Sir Winston would have appreciated. His favorite vintages were 1928, 1934, and 1947. Today the firm owns eighty-five hectares of vineyards, most of them close to Épernay: Mardeuil, Chouilly, Pierry, Moussy, Chavot, Cuis, Cramant, and Grauves. They meet 45 percent of the firm's needs, and the rest is taken from Pinot villages to give the wine backbone. Pol Roger's vinification is quite normal, which leads me to the concluson that the secret lies in the quality of the grapes and, above all, in the skill of James Coffinet in assembling the *cuvées*. The wines are medium bodied, with a lovely fruit balance and perfect dosage. The mousse is exemplary, with smaller bubbles than usual because of a cellar temperature half a degreee below the average. Pol Roger had more wines and more older wines in the Millennium Tasting than almost any other Champagne house, which is completely natural because Pol Roger's Champagnes have enormous class and are so long-lived. They are normally most famous for their Pinot-dominated *cuvées*, but at Villa Pauli they were rewarded for the best Blanc de Blancs ever made, with their powerful 1959—and my only 100-pointer is a Blanc de Blancs from Pol Roger. I love the entire range of the firm's products, from the regular nonvintage Champagne all the way to the Cuvée Sir Winston Churchill, and I guarantee you that every sound bottle you drink will impart a life-enhancing experience of pure joy.

• POL ROGER BRUT   80
(33% PN, 33% PM, 34% CH)

Some of the best bottles of nonvintage Champagne I have tasted have been well-stored Pol Roger. The ability to age with grace despite its Pinot Meunier content is the wine's best asset. After a bad patch they are back on track again.

• POL ROGER EXTRA DRY   80
(33% PN, 33% PM, 34% CH)

Reserved for the English market. Bubbly charm and delightful bready bottle maturity.

• POL ROGER DEMI-SEC   55
(33% PN, 33% PM, 34% CH)

• POL ROGER RICH   51
(33% PN, 33% PM, 34% CH)

• 1996 POL ROGER   89, DEC 2003 (93)
(60% PN, 40% CH)

An almost overripe nose with oxide notes and tons of bread, licorice, and chocolate—all appearing right from the start. Big and mellow like the '90, but not as classic as the '95, '85, and '88. We'll see where it goes. Maybe it will dry up and stop in its premature growth curve. The first time I was disappointed, but the next time I was impressed by the power and the dark, fine red-wine-like structure.

• 1995 POL ROGER   88, SEP 2003 (92)
(60% PN, 40% CH)

For the time being rather unevolved, with austere acidity, nascent breadiness, and layers of sweet fruit. My first reaction was that the wine was difficult to grasp; this somewhat slippery impression will most likely be removed in the near, harmonizing future. Fine future prospects.

- **1993 POL ROGER**   87, OCT 2001 (89)
(60% PN, 40% CH)

A wine that was surprisingly similar to the fruity and charming nonvintage Champagne when it was released on the market. In a very short time the character has gained depth—we are already dealing with a classic but as-yet light and rapidly maturing Pol Roger. To be drunk in great, refreshing gulps. Because the house-style is intact, it will surely mature handsomely. No great depth, but still a good piece of work.

- **1990 POL ROGER**   88, SEP 2003 (91)
(60% PN, 40% CH)

Pol Roger in a nutshell. Sophisticated and utterly charming. Fruity, creamy, balanced, and long.

- **1989 POL ROGER**   87, SEP 1999 (90)
(60% PN, 40% CH)

More generous than the '88, with a mighty nose of mature Pinot Noir and a bold, rich, and juicy flavor of mature Chardonnay. The house-style isn't lost, however, despite the rich vintage.

- **1988 POL ROGER**   88, APR 2004 (92)
(60% PN, 40% CH)

Pol Roger's vintage Champagne always ages well. It wouldn't surprise me if the '88 transformed dramatically after the year 2000. For a long time this was a tight, restrained Champagne with purity and a stunning dryness. Today there is a nascent maturity.

- **1986 POL ROGER**   85, FEB 1995 (89)
(60% PN, 40% CH)

Much more generous than the '88 even when launched, and very enjoyable today. The spectrum of aromas includes jasmine, orchids, caramel, and lemon. The taste is juicy and well balanced: refreshing, lemon-fresh, and lush.

- **1985 POL ROGER**   85, MAY 2002 (90)
(60% PN, 40% CH)

Classic vintage Champagne with a convincingly tight structure. Pure fruit dominates the biscuity aromas. Complex, medium-bodied taste with a long acidic aftertaste of green apples.

- **1983 POL ROGER**   86, OCT 1998 (86)
(60% PN, 40% CH)

The '83 should be viewed as a failure for Pol Roger, especially when you consider that, because no prestige *cuvées* were made this year, the best grapes have been used in this rather insignificant wine.

- **1982 POL ROGER**   90, JUL 2003 (90)
(60% PN, 40% CH)

The entire wine is typical of the vintage. Big nose of bread and rich fruit. Medium bodied and soft with vanilla aftertaste. The wine has developed a touch too rapidly these past few years for it to be a real long-term hope.

- **1979 POL ROGER**   94, JUN 2003 (94)
(60% PN, 40% CH)

Tasted newly disgorged and without dosage in Pol Roger's cellar in April 1995. Dosage and bottle maturity are really needed here! Lacking in generosity and pared down, with a slightly thin structure but pure aromas. Overripe in a regular bottle.

Beautifully floral and complex in a magnum, completely fantastic in a jeroboam. The best wine at wedding! The points are for the jeroboam, which isn't really fair for those of you who come across a regular bottle—be prepared for something under ninety points.

- **1976 POL ROGER**   92, DEC 2001 (92)
(60% PN, 40% CH)

The '76 is much fatter and more developed than the '75. The wine is extremely generous, with strong aromas of chocolate and coffee. The maturity is impressive and the sweetness rich. Hardly a great vintage but a very good Champagne.

- **1975 POL ROGER**   94, OCT 1998 (94)
(60% PN, 40% CH)

The '75 is a buttery, seductive, and lovable Champagne. The fruit is very rich and the nut aromas are almost woody. Rich, soft, and balanced.

- **1973 POL ROGER**   91, JUN 2003 (91)
(60% PN, 40% CH)

Voluptuous and homogeneous with its rich, chocolaty, mature style. When newly disgorged, it's full of mushroomy aromas.

- **1971 POL ROGER**   87, MAR 1997 (87)
(60% PN, 40% CH)

Pol Roger offers quite a powerful '71, with a big, muscular body and chocolate aromas. Low acidity, and on the way to losing its grip on what holds the building blocks together.

- **1969 POL ROGER**   92, OCT 1999 (92)
(60% PN, 40% CH)

Deep color with elements of red. Developed to the point of having already seen its best days. Big, full-bodied, oxidative taste; the familiar, stylish Pol Roger fruit invokes thoughts of apricot, orange, and peach.

- **1966 POL ROGER**   94, JUL 2003 (94)
(65% PN, 35% CH)

Tasted both newly disgorged and normally disgorged. Like all of Pol Roger's wines they gain from maturing in the bottle. That's when the freshly baked bread is revealed and the citrus fruits progress to a peach-like complexity. Very long, full taste of chocolate and marzipan.

- **1964 POL ROGER**   92, DEC 2001 (92)
(60% PN, 40% CH)

As if it was taken out of the instruction manual! A classic '64 with more weight than the elegant '66. The finish is really good. It has a creamy aroma and density that is seldom seen. Certain bottles are unfortunately showing signs of tiredness.

- **1962 POL ROGER**   94, DEC 1999 (94)
(65% PN, 35% CH)

Tasted only in a magnum. A classic Pol Roger that reveals more house-style than vintage character. Very buoyant and filled with creamy effervescence. The balance is perfect, as is the soft, honeyed fruit.

- **1961 POL ROGER**   94, APR 1995 (94)
(65% PN, 35% CH)

Great bottle variation, but always wonderfully creamy, soft, and peach-flavored, despite the dark, aged color. Much more charming than many tough '61s. Old Champagne, when it succeeds in combining the tones of old wood with apricot and peach aromas, is one of the most enjoyable things in the world. Certain bottles of Pol Roger '61 have reached even higher on the points scale.

• 1959 POL ROGER   97, NOV 2001 (97)
(60% PN, 40% CH)

The most powerful Pol Roger I have tasted. The wine is almost
fiery, and must be described as extremely robust. The aroma is
dark and exciting—like a novel by Umberto Eco. Both the aroma
and taste have tones of mushrooms and Champagne cellars from
first-class Pinot Noir. 1962 Bollinger seemed to be a lightweight
charmer in comparison with this monumental wine.

• 1955 POL ROGER   95, JUN 2003 (95)
(60% PN, 40% CH)

A wonderfully well-kept Champagne with toasty and nutty aromas.
The fruit is intense and exotic. The aftertaste is a little short.

• 1953 POL ROGER
(70% PN, 30% CH)

• 1952 POL ROGER   92, NOV 2001 (92)
(70% PN, 30% CH)

"Tom Stevenson's favorite Champagne! Incredibly light and well
maintained. Almost like a Champagne from the eighties," was
what I wrote in 1995. The wine has suddenly aged unexpectedly
fast and some of the finesse has disappeared. Despite this, the
wine is still good and interesting.

• 1949 POL ROGER   96, JUN 1999 (96)
(60% PN, 40% CH)

Quite wonderfully fresh and elegant. Somewhat lighter than
expected, but with a Krug-like depth and elegance that reminded
me of a '66. The nose is dominated by cotton candy, peach, and
exotic fruit.

• 1947 POL ROGER   96, MAY 1997 (96)
(70% PN, 30% CH)

Winston Churchill's favorite Champagne and "a Churchill of a
wine," according to Christian Pol-Roger. This '47 magnum was
planned as the highlight of a Pol Roger dinner in Stockholm in
1993. Imagine my disappointment when the US $500-magnum
had transformed into madeira and was poured away at once. Of
course Christian let me taste an enchanting bottle directly from
his cellar. Perfect!

• 1945 POL ROGER   94, JAN 1999 (94)
(70% PN, 30% CH)

The wine is just as splendid as it should be from this year of
peace. A colossal, Cognac-like bouquet with hints of walnut and
plum. The taste is superbly vital, like an elderly lady who has
aged with grace. A classic Pol Roger with a certain
understandable bottle variation.

• 1943 POL ROGER   86, MAR 1999 (>)
(70% PN, 30% CH)

This was the first time I have tasted from an "imperial pint."
The experience was made no less notable by the fact that it was
one of Churchill's war vintages. Unfortunately the bubbles had
disappeared and oxide tones were clearly evident, but the
structure and the toffee-like aromas were still very good. Pol
Roger certainly has more properly stored whole bottles left in the
cellar.

• 1942 POL ROGER   93, OCT 1998 (93)
(70% PN, 30% CH)

A seldom-seen war vintage that lacks the presence expected. On
the other hand this particular bottle got its second wind as a sort
of ultra-sophisticated soft drink. The aroma is weakly toasted with
dominant tones of kiwi and grapefruit. Exemplary "tingle" to the
bubbles, and the wine is fabulously good and easy to drink.

• 1934 POL ROGER   98, OCT 2001 (98)
(80% PN, 20% CH)

Disgorged in July 1998. We had just finished tasting our way
through ten vintages of Salon, and the tasting group was crying
for an encore. I hesitated as long as possible. How would we be
able to find a Champagne that was on a level with a 1949 Salon?
This well-stored Pol Roger became my choice, a choice that no
one around the table regretted. All twelve tasters held this magic
wine to be that evening's—and one of life's—foremost. Older
vintages of Pol Roger always have a special, almost luminous
glow. Perfect mousse and an extremely light color. The wine's
finesse is unmatched; it has an aristocratic stature, floral bouquet,
and beautifully roasted aromas. It is said that Champagne should
be cold, dry, and cost nothing. This bottle was certainly not free,
but both cold and dry, even if the finish, it goes without saying,
had that fabulous nougaty sweetness. An unforgettable
experience.

• 1928 POL ROGER
(70% PN, 30% CH)

• 1926 POL ROGER   94, AUG 1998 (94)
(80% PN, 20% CH)

An almost completely still honey nectar with thick, Sauternes-like
structure. A perfect finale to an historic evening.

• 1921 POL ROGER   97, JAN 2004 (97)
(80% PN, 20% CH)

Perhaps the most enjoyable of all of the Champagnes tasted at
the "century tasting" at Pol Roger in October 1998. The bottle
we tasted had just undergone *dégorgement* and was very elegant
and youthful. The entire wine exuded charm and buoyancy. The
fruit and the lightly toasted aromas resemble those found in the
'47 and the '75, but the butter-toffee aftertaste is even longer.

• 1914 POL ROGER   97, NOV 2000 (97)
(80% PN, 20% CH)

It's hard not to be influenced by the occasion when one is
drinking a 1914 Pol Roger together with the owner in Winston
Churchill's favorite room in the house. To then hear Christian
tell the fascinating story behind this wine was almost too much.
The greatest wine experience of my life! Remove the story and
the occasion from your thoughts and the wine is still no
disappointment. The bottles do apparently vary greatly, but the
one that I had the honor of tasting was perfect. The color was
deep and shining, like a golden pagoda. Weak but constant
mousse. Remarkably large, complex nose with loads of sweets,
honey, rum, chocolate, coffee, and treacle. The taste was chewy
and tremendously sweet, almost like an old Sauternes. This
would go well with duck liver. When Ulf Smedberg was thanked
for his fine work with the SAS Wine Club in Scandinavia,
Christian Pol-Roger took out one of his rare remaining magnum
bottles of this wine. Ninety-eight points in magnum!

• 1911 POL ROGER   97, JUN 1999 (97)
(80% PN, 20% CH)

Christian Pol-Roger has a talent for bringing out historical wines
when least expected. After a late dinner with one of Australia's
foremost Champagne experts, Christian brought out a magnum
of this divine wine. Imagine being able to swallow large gulps of
something so heavenly after an intense week of work involving
the constant spitting out of wonderful treats. The wine itself was
in perfect condition. The quality was on a par with the legendary
1914, but the style was different. This wine was both drier and

tighter, with a nutty, serious, everlasting taste. The depth of the flavor was comparable to the Mariana Trench. Considerably more tired and simple in a normal bottle.

- **1892 POL ROGER**   89, OCT 1998 (89)
(80% PN, 20% CH)

Pol Roger is one of the very few Champagne producers that still have bottles from the 1800s in their cellars. The 1892 vintage is a legendary and long-lived one; it was the finale in our "century tasting" in October 1998. Christian himself and members of the film team that followed the test considered this oldie to be one of the very best Champagnes in the test. Personally I was disturbed by the unmistakable madeira tone that had sneaked its way in.

Otherwise this is still a very big wine with fantastic concentration. The color was very deep and the bubbles were microscopic. The depth of flavor was enormous and the similarity to a fine old Cognac was very evident. Remarkably enough, once a bit of the madeira tone aired out of the glass it was replaced by an aroma which was reminiscent of burned chocolate candy.

- **1996 BLANC DE CHARDONNAY**   88, APR 2004 (94)
(100% CH)

Never before has there been such a large difference in development between this wine and the usual vintage wine. For the moment, this is a crystal-clear, little lime sweetie with its lovely acidity and superb finesse.

- **1995 BLANC DE CHARDONNAY**   88, JUL 2003 (93)
(100% CH)

Youthful, somewhat bound, storable Champagne. The wine is similar to the '88 of the same age. Exceedingly obvious, classic glass development. For the moment this austere wine is characterized by mineral and a suppressed layer of buttery Chardonnay just waiting to explode like a time-bomb with taste.

- **1993 BLANC DE CHARDONNAY**   85, JUN 2002 (90)
(100% CH)

There's nothing wrong with this, but shouldn't a *cuvée de prestige* from Pol Roger be something completely special? Maybe I'm wrong about this wine's future prospects, but when newly released on the market it was anonymous and impersonal. Now, it's already more classic and fleshier.

- **1990 BLANC DE CHARDONNAY**   96, JUL 2004 (96)
(100% CH)

As sound as a bell and crystal-clear, dry, and stately. Enjoy this classic Blanc de Blancs long into the next century. White flowers dominate the young, voluminous fragrance.

- **1988 BLANC DE CHARDONNAY**   95, NOV 2003 (96)
(100% CH)

This label is very consistent through the years. Already from the start, the '88 was charming, and distinguished with a faint note of citrus and a soft aftertaste. Delightfully complex bouquet, with a nutty tone and classic purity developed in the beginning of the twenty-first century; by 2003 the wine had broken all barriers. Now it's sensationally voluptuous and rich, with a Comtes-like exotic mint-toffee sweetness and layers of butter toffee and fat Chardonnay.

- **1986 BLANC DE CHARDONNAY**   80, APR 1995 (87)
(100% CH)

Pol Roger has, as we know, many fine Chardonnay *grand cru* vineyards. The style of their Blanc de Chardonnay is always broad, polished, and refined, but it perhaps lacks the depth and

concentration of the true greats. The '86 is slightly creamy, with a young, fresh, and flowery bouquet. Somewhat lighter than the vintage Champagne of the same year.

- **1985 BLANC DE CHARDONNAY**   88, NOV 2001 (90)
(100% CH)

Classical and typical of the house, with a lovely youthfulness. Parts of this wine are best when young. The fruit is bursting with vitality; under the surface lie weak tones of freshly ground coffee beans.

- **1982 BLANC DE CHARDONNAY**   95, MAR 2002 (95)
(100% CH)

A great favorite among journalists, but it had problems fully convincing me. The mineral tones were stony, almost earthy, disturbing the rich, buttery, and orange-like Chardonnay taste. Today it is ravishing and oily, like a great white Burgundy.

- **1979 BLANC DE CHARDONNAY**   87, DEC 1989 (91)
(100% CH)

It took ten years for the skeleton to get some meat on its bones. Only then did an elusive bouquet of lemon, hawthorn, and toasted bread, and a well-balanced buttery softness emerge. Perfect aperitif wine.

- **1975 BLANC DE CHARDONNAY**   95, JUN 2002 (95)
(100% CH)

Splendidly buoyant and grating in its acidity. The usual buttery and citrus-influenced style is accompanied here by the somewhat unexpected aromas of red fruits and berries. Tightly packed, straight-backed Champagne that was a delight to drink in front of the fireplace at the home of Christian and Danielle Pol-Roger.

- **1964 BLANC DE CHARDONNAY**   96, MAR 2002 (96)
(100% CH)

Grand, deep Champagne, rich in finesse, characterized by the village of Le Mesnil. Wonderful notes of walnut and browned butter. Immensely elegant!

- **1961 BLANC DE CHARDONNAY**   93, MAY 1999 (93)
(100% CH)

A classic and reliable super-bubbly, boasting the entire aromatic spectrum we have come to associate with this fantastic house. Somewhat less elegant than the '64 and less concentrated than the '59.

- **1959 BLANC DE CHARDONNAY**   96, JUN 1999 (96)
(100% CH)

Debut vintage for Pol Roger's Chardonnay Champagne. At thirty-nine years of age, it is still light in color with a lively mousse. Scent of tobacco, chocolate, and lime. The house-style and grape character are better recognized in the palate. Creamy, acidity, and well-balanced, with a very long, powerful, and somewhat harsh, tannin-rich finish. Declared the best Blanc de Blancs ever produced in the world during the Millennium Tasting.

- **1928 POL ROGER GRAUVES**   100, MAR 2003 (100)
(100% CH)

Disgorged in July 1998. Ridiculously young! I'd heard that this wine was supposed to be exceptionally lively and pale, but I would never have been close in my guesses if it hadn't been served in the last round at Villa Pauli in 1999, where there were only oldies. The nose was fabulously, beautifully braided, with notes of lime, linden, and lily of the valley. The taste was super-fresh, with a wonderful oily fruitiness that lasted for several minutes. My second bottle of this "out of this world" wine had the same date of disgorging, so it was with a certain hesitation that I dared wait five years before releasing the cork. The wine was enjoyed at one of the most magical dinners in the history of Swedish gastronomy, at the Pontus in the Green House restaurant in Stockholm, March 2003. That evening we drank a 1986 Selosse, three legendary vintages of Bollinger, two phenomenal Dom Pérignon Rosés, a '61 Comtes de Champagne, Ramonet, Lafite, Romanée-Conti, Richebourg, Romanée-Saint-Vivant and a 1947 Cheval Blanc. The '28 swept the floor! The nose was so intense that I was moved to tears. Its already phenomenal bouquet of aromas had expanded further, with exotic notes of coconut, papaya, and mint chocolate. Somehow, this wine—on the very day we opened it—stood at the apex of its life; it succeeded in uniting the '79 Krug Clos du Mesnil's acidic elegance with a '76 Comtes de Champagne's exoticism and a '38 Krug's mint notes. I must admit that—spoiled and pampered as I am—I didn't think that a wine could affect me so deeply as this wine did that evening. I am in love!

- 1996 POL ROGER ROSÉ   86, JAN 2004 (91)
(65% PN, 35% CH)
Lighter and shyer than the white vintage wine, with the house's lively, delightfully laid-back style intact. A superbly fresh and crackling rosé for future special occasions.

- 1995 POL ROGER ROSÉ   89, AUG 2003 (90)
(65% PN, 35% CH)
What a languorous bower wine! Meltingly soft, sensual, and floral, with a light, beautifully seductive color, creamy luxurious mousse, and a beautiful aromatic purity. The wine is strongly marked by its house-style, with all the smiling toffee charm that has made Pol Roger famous. It's as if they'd taken a prototype Pol Roger and poured in a pinch of strawberry essence along with the heaviest whipping cream you could find.

- 1993 POL ROGER ROSÉ   82, AUG 2001 (85)
(65% PN, 35% CH)
Are we witnessing the beginnings of a change of style? The wine is markedly lighter and shyer than before. Chalky, slightly bready, with a delicate, subtle fruit reminiscent of pears. Light, refreshing flavor and a somewhat skinny composition. Pleasantly harmonious finish, with youthful acidity and a distinct note of Granny Smith apples.

- 1990 POL ROGER ROSÉ   88, JUN 2002 (91)
(65% PN, 35% CH)
A magnificently structured and rich '90 with an unusually buttery deep-fruitiness. Here you will find all the red fruits gathered together in one glass. Delicious!

- 1988 POL ROGER ROSÉ   84, AUG 1998 (89)
(60% PN, 40% CH)
Very pure and delicate, with better structure than the '86 but without its sensual style.

- 1986 POL ROGER ROSÉ   87, MAR 2002 (89)
(65% PN, 35% CH)
After I had said that this wine tasted like Billecart-Salmon, Christian Pol-Roger revealed that it was James Coffinet's first Champagne for Pol Roger. He had earlier worked for Billecart. Fine, pale color; ultra-elegantly pure and fruity. Very weak hints of nut and raspberry.

- 1985 POL ROGER ROSÉ   83, SEP 1999 (83)
(65% PN, 35% CH)
Orange color and personal scent of lavender and meat. The taste is mature and soft with one-dimensional charm.

- 1982 POL ROGER ROSÉ   89, JUN 2002 (89)
(65% PN, 35% CH)
By no means an obvious rosé if you don't consider the color. The nose is heavy and complex with hints of diesel fumes, thorn bushes, and smoke. Aromas of woodlands are present in the full-bodied but vigorous taste.

- 1979 POL ROGER ROSÉ   89, JUL 1996 (89)
(75% PN, 25% CH)
A fine, salmon-pink rosé, with an abundance of ripe fruits and deliciously toasty aromas. Exellent acidity.

- 1973 POL ROGER ROSÉ   80, MAY 2000 (80)
(70% PN, 30% CH)
This wine has not aged gracefully. Hurry up and drink it if you have any bottles left in the cellar. The color is beautifully orange, but with a slightly dull surface. The mousse fades quickly in the glass and the wine breathes age. Grand, oxidative bouquet with elements of ripe banana peel, almond, and apple sauce. The flavor is extremely rich and demanding in all its potency. Flaccid tartness.

- 1959 POL ROGER ROSÉ
(80% PN, 20% CH)

- 1995 CUVÉE SIR WINSTON CHURCHILL   93, JAN 2004 (96)
Already big and creamy, with a well-organized structure and thundering weight. Not in any way "hard to get": it makes its mark immediately. A big wine packed with silky fruit, toffee, and chocolate right from the start. Buy all that you can find—you won't be disappointed.

- 1993 CUVÉE SIR WINSTON CHURCHILL   93, DEC 2003 (94)
Lighter than expected, with Chardonnay as the commander in the first phase of this wine. Pinot Noir makes up the main portion, and experience has shown that the wine changes dramatically four to five years after disgorging. Newly disgorged at the home of Christian Pol-Roger, the wine imparted floral notes of jasmine, acacia, and mimosa—even a strong element of green apples and gooseberry. Elegant and complex, with big muscles at rest. Wonderful Pinot character turned up in April 2002!

- 1990 CUVÉE SIR WINSTON CHURCHILL 94, MAY 2003 (95)
Fabulously creamy and nut-toffee-scented in the same style as P. R. '88. Winston is usually a slow starter, which is hardly the case with this vintage. Because the grape composition is secret, it is safe to speculate on the subject. Namely, it appears that the '90 contains slightly more Chardonnay than usual. To me this is a 1990 P. R.!

- 1988 CUVÉE SIR WINSTON CHURCHILL   92, NOV 2003 (95)
A very slow starter, with perfect balance and wonderful but understated aromas. Everything can be sensed under the blanket that covers this time bomb. Today a massive and multifaceted, youthful fruitiness dominates. In ten years' time this fruitiness will combine with the high acidity to carry Winston to unimaginable heights. Decanting is recommended for the impatient.

- 1988 CUVÉE SIR WINSTON CHURCHILL MILLENNIUM CUVÉE
                                        94, APR 2004 (97)
I think you can imagine how beautiful a jeroboam of Winston Churchill can look. If, moreover, it is decorated with an extra gold script stating that this bottle is number 728 of 1000, and the wine is lying in an incredibly sober, black wooden box lined with red silk—well, you will understand that I got goosebumps

when a good friend of mine opened just such a bottle on his fortieth birthday. All wines from Pol Roger are extremely good in magnum, and actually even better on the rare occasions you find a mature jeroboam. The floral acacia notes and the refined aroma of passion fruit and orange blossom are accentuated; at the same time the taste has an incomparable depth and a buoyancy. But I must admit that it was much too early to open this wine. You would probably have to wait ten more years before the nascent coffee notes and the dark, striking fruit have taken command.

- 1988 P. R.   96, NOV 2003 (97)
(50% PN, 50% CH)
Here Pol Roger has hit the nail on the head. The '88 is quite wonderful today, with its sensual bouquet and crystal-clear, balanced flavor. If you have the patience, then put a few bottles in your cellar and eventually you'll experience something even more magical. This, together with the 1975 vintage, is the best P. R. I've tasted.

- 1986 CUVÉE SIR WINSTON CHURCHILL   89, JUN 2001 (92)
Christian Pol-Roger refuses to reveal the grape content after making a promise to the Churchill family. However, I think my guess of 70 percent Pinot Noir and the rest Chardonnay is close to the truth. The wine is made mainly from the firm's own *grand cru* vineyards. This is the wine from Pol Roger that needs the longest storage. The '86 is hard and young, but has a great richness of extracts and a high concentration. As usual, better in a magnum.

- 1986 P. R.   87, MAY 1999 (87)
(50% PN, 50% CH)
For me, P. R. is as great a Champagne as Cuvée Sir Winston Chuchill. The '86 is just as light as the vintage usually is, with tons of citrus and mineral notes. For a long time the taste was floral and light with a long aftertaste of Chardonnay; today an element of asparagus has become disturbing.

- 1985 CUVÉE SIR WINSTON CHURCHILL   94, JUN 2001 (96)
The favorite Champagne among Swedish wine journalists. It combines magnificent richness of taste and concentration with an accessible, fruity style. Both the nose and taste create a silky-smooth impression, and a layer of toasty aromas spice the rich fruit. One of the greatest Winston Churchills ever made.

- 1985 P. R.   90, JAN 1994 (92)
(50% PN, 50% CH)
The '85 is a voluptuously, massive wine, more toasty and nutty than the Winston Churchill but slightly less concentrated. Tasting them together is always a great experience.

- 1982 CUVÉE SIR WINSTON CHURCHILL   93, MAR 2002 (93)
Like the ordinary '82, very typical for its year. That means that the wine is also a touch impersonal. This year the Winston Churchill was definitely lighter than P. R. Several times I've drunk them beside each other and always preferred the P. R. After several years of hesitation, the wine has finally begun to come around. Superb toasty aromas in magnum.

- 1982 P. R.   93, DEC 2001 (93)
(50% PN, 50% CH)
The '82 resembles Dom Pérignon in many ways. A little lighter than usual, and with a more toasty and exotic fruity style. The aftertaste contains many citrus aromas, and hints of mango and peach.

- 1979 CUVÉE SIR WINSTON CHURCHILL   94, JUN 2001 (94)
Only tasted once before in my career. My impression then was that the '79 was very elegant and well-balanced, full of bushy, developable fruit, but that it lacked the extra dimension that a prestige Champagne should have. Christian Pol-Roger supplied us with a magnum for the Millennium Tasting. The wine was rich and surprisingly aged. Bottle variation was marked. On Sweden's National Day in 2001, I held a Pol Roger tasting at the restaurant Gondolen, where the '79 was magnificently elegant and vintage-typical.

- 1979 P. R.   92, FEB 1990 (93)
(50% PN, 50% CH)
It's unbelievable that the Pinot content wasn't higher. The wine evinces a heavy, almost Bollinger-like robust character with masses of chocolaty and powerful, oily aftertaste. The '79 lacks a little elegance, but is a very impressive wine—a wine that I've hunted for high and low, since this was a Champagne that I believe I underestimated at the beginning of my career.

- 1975 CUVÉE SIR WINSTON CHURCHILL   96, JUN 2001 (97)
The first vintage of this *cuvée* was made in magnum only. Christian Pol-Roger was kind enough to allow me to taste a recently disgorged magnum of this classic. The nose wasn't fully developed, but the flavor was phenomenal. What depth! What length! An almost perfect Champagne, with dense fruit and toasty aromas.

- 1975 P. R.   96, JUN 2001 (96)
(50% PN, 50% CH)
Drunk on a warm July evening in 2001 on the Klum family's dock on Lake Mälaren. A magical evening and a magical wine. It completely overshadowed a 1985 La Mission Haut-Brion, which otherwise was perfect. Deep golden color, and fine, continuous small bubbles—as should be with a Pol Roger. Impressive, overwhelming bouquet of almond, marmalade, hay, dark chocolate, and honey. Robust structure with extremely deep intensity. A broad palate spectrum that strongly breathes Pinot Noir, yet leaves the mouth with a delightful breeze of distinguished, aristocratic Chardonnay.

- 1990 POL ROGER "2000"   88, NOV 2003 (92)
(60% PN, 40% CH)
Many were disappointed when they opened this magnum at the millennium, as the wine demands many years of storing. Those patient enough will be rewarded with a classic, fully packed, pure Pol Roger. Just recently, a magnum seemed a tad too sweet.

- 1947 POL ROGER WEDDING CUVÉE   93, OCT 2000 (93)
(70% PN, 30% CH)
Disgorged for the wedding in Britain in 1981 between Lady Diana Spencer and Prince Charles. I have so far tasted this wine on three occasions without really finding my way. The first time was a normally disgorged magnum that had been subjected to too much rough handling. The next time it was a painfully youthful, newly disgorged bottle at Pol Roger, and now a bottle that was drunk a little too late after an already late disgorging. Now I am waiting for a bottle with a touch of maturity, without the leathery, sherry-like oxidation that this wedding bottle has. Otherwise, the color and mousse were exceedingly vigorous, but it was not in totally perfect aromatic condition.

POMMERY **** N-M

5, place du Général Gouraud
51100 Reims
03 26 61 62 63
Production: 8,000,000

In 1856 Pommery & Greno was founded after having been known as Dubois-Gosset for the previous twenty years. The firm established a sales channel to the English as early as the nineteenth century, and were pioneers with their dry Champagne—quite without dosage. The Marquise de Polignac was one of the first owners, and one of her direct descendants, Prince Alain de Polignac, was for a long time the man in charge of assembling the *cuvées*. Prince Alain is a fascinating man who, better than any other winemaker, can describe the philosophy behind his winemaking art. In 1990, Pommery was one of those firms that ended up as part of the powerful Moët-Hennessy Group, and in 2002 Vranken took over. But the house-style remains intact, thanks to Thierry Gasco, who was trained by the prince. Pommery is among the firms that own the most land in the *grand cru* villages, but less well known is the fact that their locations within the area are not always the best. Besides Pommery's own grapes, 70 percent of their supply comes from throughout Champagne, and they are vinified in modern style.

Pommery is undoubtably a great name in historical terms. The house-style is made up of dry, restrained, pure Champagnes with young fruit and an unmistakable steeliness that takes many years to round off. The *cuvée de prestige*, Louise Pommery, doesn't fit that description, but instead is often too soft and polished to compete with the top wines of its competitors. During 1999, I have been amazed time and again by the greatness of the older vintages from Pommery. Only recently I bought a large number of bottles dating from 1911 to 1979, which have lain untouched since birth in the dark recesses of Champagne. Every bottle that I've opened has been fantastic. These bottles play a large part in the four stars that I have awarded this faithful-to-style and historically eminent house.

• POMMERY BRUT ROYAL 75
(35% PN, 35% PM, 30% CH)

• POMMERY BRUT ROYAL APANAGE 80
(45% PN, 20% PM, 35% CH)
A very clean and elegant nonvintage made from high-class grapes. The aroma is discreet and bready with an undertone of sun-dried sheets. The taste is well balanced, with a fine fruitiness reminiscent of kiwi and melon.

• POMMERY EXTRA BRUT 60
(35% PN, 35% PM, 30% CH)

• POMMERY POP 65
(100% CH)

• POMMERY BLANC DE BLANCS SUMMERTIME 84
(100% CH)
To sit together with the prince in one of the castle's most beautiful rooms, watching the first rays of summer sun filter through the curtains, and to be served this most uplifting Champagne, belongs among the most joyful of life's moments. Alain de Polignac has, with relatively simple grapes, really succeeded in concocting a perfect summery aperitif with floral bouquets and a taste that is as mild as a summer breeze. I would be surprised if the wine is improved in the cellar. Don't miss the chance to enjoy its youthfully elusive merits. Summertime is too short!

• POMMERY BLANC DE NOIRS WINTERTIME 87
(80% PN, 20% PM)
A completely new wine from Pommery that seems very promising. This seems to me to be a successful combination of the firm's stringent and apple-like house-style, and the mature, generous fullness of the Pinot grapes. The fruit, which borders upon currant, is backed up by smoky and bready tones. With age these wines take on a delightful, gun-smoky characteristic.

• 1980 LOUISE POMMERY ANNIVERSARY CUVÉE 85, APR 2000 (85)
(40% PN, 60% CH)
Intrinsically the same wine as the usual Louise, with a later disgorging and a somewhat different presentation. At twenty years of age this is still a very fresh and lively Champagne. The bouquet is fantastically similar to a Swedish waffle piled with strawberry jam and whipped cream. Slightly vegetal and peaked flavor, with strains of unripe grapes. Fine tartness and a beautiful creaminess.

• POMMERY ROSÉ 55
(70% PN, 30% CH)

• 1996 POMMERY 85, APR 2003 (90)
(50% PN, 50% CH)
Unexpectedly hard and green with unpolished acidity, a heavy apple-sauce-like aroma, but with a handsome mineral carpet under the surface. It's a little uncertain to predict the future of this wine, but history speaks for Pommery's capacity to furnish its wines with the ability to metamorphose. Delightful balance at the end of 2003.

• 1995 POMMERY 88, AUG 2003 (91)
(50% PN, 50% CH)
The wine felt fresher, more elegant, and more easily drunk than the 1989 Louise Pommery that we drank at the same time. Perhaps a little sweeter than usual, but absolutely the same uplifting mineral-fresh taste that we've grown accustomed to. More charming than usual.

• 1992 POMMERY 87, MAR 2000 (88)
(50% PN, 50% CH)
Few Champagne houses have such a constant house-style as Pommery. The '92 was charmingly direct when it was released. Its fine, classic bread tone plays in perfect harmony with a delicate fruit, and has developed quickly over just a few months. The wine relies primarily upon its voluptuous, toffee-like and toffee-saturated fruit, in combination with a fine depth created by mineral and smoky undertones. A somewhat short aftertaste. Certain bottles have already developed the gunpowder tone from Aÿ. A Champagne for early consumption.

• 1991 POMMERY 82, MAY 1999 (87)
(50% PN, 50% CH)
As usual, well-made, austere, dry, and clean as a whistle. Unfortunately the mousse is still a bit boisterous. Earlier vintages have shown that this is a temporary phenomenon. A certain bready quality has begun to be discernible.

• 1990 POMMERY 86, MAY 1999 (90)
(50% PN, 50% CH)
This label has been given the *grand cru* name for the first time. This really is a great year for Pommery. Steely, classical, closed but with a nose ripe for development, backed by undertones of butter and apple.

• 1989 POMMERY 93, MAY 2003 (93)
(50% PN, 50% CH)

As usual, steely, metallic, and hollow when young. Unlike the '88, however, there is a hint of toasted Chardonnay notes. Astonishingly fine growth curve, and even more lovely in magnum.

- 1988 POMMERY   60, AUG 1994 (75)
(50% PN, 50% CH)

- 1987 POMMERY   74, JAN 2002 (74)
(50% PN, 50% CH)

- 1985 POMMERY   85, JUN 1999 (88)
(50% PN, 50% CH)

More buttery and softer than other Pommery vintages. Open caramel nose with elements of peppermint candy cane and flowers.

- 1983 POMMERY   80, MAY 1991 (87)
(50% PN, 50% CH)

Surprisingly good and rich with Clicquot-like Pinot fruit and pepperiness. Bready flavor with good acidity.

- 1982 POMMERY   80, DEC 1998 (84)
(50% PN, 50% CH)

Fresh and apple-ish, but with Pommery's metallic hardness. Some lemon licorice and burned rubber had crept in around the age of ten.

- 1981 POMMERY   87, NOV 2001 (87)
(50% PN, 50% CH)

Completely mature and chocolaty. Decidedly less sophisticated than Flacon in magnum. Very rich bouquet of almond, chocolate, and honey. Clear palate of aged bottle with a fine plumpness despite the high acidity.

- 1980 POMMERY   85, JAN 2002 (85)
(50% PN, 50% CH)

One of the thinnest and lightest vintages made by Pommery. When young, this wine was extremely innocuous—today, this light wine has acquired a fine, floral bouquet and a minty complexity in the palate.

- 1979 POMMERY   92, FEB 2001 (92)
(50% PN, 50% CH)

A normally labelled magnum with a wonderfully complex, gunpowder-like and flowery bouquet. The body is a bit thin and the length could be better, but the clarity and finesse are irreproachable. Of course, more evolved in a bottle, with fine nuttiness and depth.

- 1978 POMMERY   88, MAY 2002 (88)
(50% PN, 50% CH)

An exciting and lively Champagne with a floral nose that carries one's thoughts to a high-class Riesling. Light and refreshing, without any great concentration in the flavor.

- 1976 POMMERY   87, DEC 2002 (87)
(50% PN, 50% CH)

Faint and restrained—albeit masculine—nose. Powerful, smoky flavor with low acidity. Overall a little clumsy.

- 1975 POMMERY   93, NOV 2001 (93)
(50% PN, 50% CH)

A glorious wine with deep, brilliant color and a nose that in many ways is similar to white Burgundy. Even the taste points in that direction, with a fleshiness and an abrasiveness you seldom find in Chardonnay from Champagne, but with an aromatic arsenal that I only associate with the white grape.

- 1973 POMMERY   93, JUN 2000 (93)
(50% PN, 50% CH)

What a bull's-eye! Apparently the vintage's fat style superbly suits Pommery's restrained disposition. Magnificently toasty bouquet and fat concentrated flavor that resounds in a honey-soft finish. Classic Champagne.

- 1969 POMMERY   94, MAY 2001 (94)
(50% PN, 50% CH)

A superb flowery and attractive wine with a broader nose than is usually the case with Pommery. In the mouth one finds toffee and smoky elements, and an elegant, crispy Chardonnay finish.

- 1966 POMMERY   87, JUN 1999 (>)
(50% PN, 50% CH)

Only one not completely perfect bottle tasted. Bottles that have been better kept should still provide very memorable experiences.

- 1964 POMMERY   80, MAR 1993 (>)
(50% PN, 50% CH)

I've tasted this wine twice, both times from magnums. One bottle was completely maderized, the other had a toasty bouquet and great richness—but even there the aftertaste was filled with sherry aromas.

- 1962 POMMERY   87, MAY 2001 (87)
(50% PN, 50% CH)

Big, powerfully rich Champagne with a fat, warm character. Chocolate and honey seem to be the clearest elements. Slightly loose in the flesh and a tad rustic. Excellent with duck liver and figs.

- 1961 POMMERY   91, DEC 1993 (91)
(50% PN, 50% CH)

Once again, a restrained nose. Dark bouquet of tar, tobacco, molasses, forest, and turpentine. A full-bodied flavor of wood, earth, and chocolate; long and very well built. A wine for macho-men.

- 1959 POMMERY   95, JAN 2000 (95)
(50% PN, 50% CH)

So elegant and beautiful! Well balanced and full of generous fruit. Made in the same style as Billecart-Salmon's now legendary 1959. Dry and stringent, it avoids the vintage's relative clumsiness.

- 1955 POMMERY   84, DEC 1991 (>)
(50% PN, 50% CH)

The bottle I tasted had a perfect level and let off a confident-sounding hissing sound. The color was also promising, but the Champagne had too small a nose and the flavor was too much like Tokay for it to reach brilliance. Not as good as the '53.

- 1953 POMMERY   93, JAN 2002 (93)
(50% PN, 50% CH)

The '53 has a dark amber color, but the mousse seems indestructible. The nose is weak, with tones of molasses, treacle, and burned sugar. The flavor is wonderfully rich, with a lovely, peach-like aroma and sweet, aged aftertaste.

- 1952 POMMERY   95, FEB 2003 (95)
(50% PN, 50% CH)

Lots of '52s are youthful and fresh, but very few are as delicate as Pommery's. The color is light and the microscopic bubbles stream around the glass like tiny pearls. The nose resembles a great white Burgundy from the 1970s, and the tight, restrained flavor with its elements of milk toffee is—to all intents and purposes—perfect.

- 1949 POMMERY   95, NOV 2000 (95)
(50% PN, 50% CH)

Weak mousse, only a slightly broad nose, but plenty of purity where elements of toffee, cream, cocoa, cola, and coffee can be distinguished. The flavor was one of the richest I've experienced.

Exceptionally fruity, with plums, mango, pastries, and an extremely sweet aftertaste of milk chocolate.

- 1947 POMMERY   92, APR 2001 (92)
(50% PN, 50% CH)
Just as with other, older vintages of Pommery, the flavor was more impressive than the nose. The cork was pulled with a corkscrew and the "pop" was weak. Deep amber color and almost invisible mousse. The nose contained gingerbread, dates, and dark chocolate. The flavor was nowhere near the lovely fruity sweetness of the '49, but had a massive wall of alcoholic power and character of raisins. No madeira tone.

- 1945 POMMERY
(50% PN, 50% CH)

- 1943 POMMERY   94, NOV 2001 (94)
(50% PN, 50% CH)
Insolently fresh and elegant, with a color that seemed to indicate the wine was only fifteen years old at the most. Brilliant evidence of how important it is that the oldest vintages be stored in the darkest cellars of Champagne. Three bottles were considerably older and flatter during a tasting at the Pontus in the Green House restaurant in Stockholm, Sweden.

- 1942 POMMERY
(50% PN, 50% CH)

- 1941 POMMERY   96, DEC 2001 (96)
(50% PN, 50% CH)
I bought a batch of older Pommery vintages that, ever since being released, had lain untouched in one of the Pommery family's cellars in Chigny-les-Roses. I must admit that I have rarely been so satisfied with quality as with these bottles. This unknown war vintage rendered a fabulously fresh and enjoyable wine that had the superb bouquet of a bakery's full range of goodies. Matchless finesse and unbelievable complexity considering the age.

- 1937 POMMERY   95, OCT 2000 (95)
(50% PN, 50% CH)
Fantastically well preserved as usual. Wonderful balance, toffee-like, but also relatively light and elegant with a grandiose, youthful mousse.

- 1934 POMMERY   95, MAY 2002 (95)
(50% PN, 50% CH)
Just as young as I'd expected. A fantastic wine with several layers and a youthful touch. A toasted, complex Champagne that brings good fortune.

- 1929 POMMERY   96, APR 2003 (96)
(50% PN, 50% CH)
Superb on all seven occasions I've had the pleasure of enjoying this deep, majestic Champagne.

- 1928 POMMERY   88, SEP 1997 (>)
(50% PN, 50% CH)
An incredibly concentrated wine that unfortunately has fared badly during storage. Faded rapidly in the glass. I have a jeroboam that looks brilliant—I'll get back to you on that one later!

- 1921 POMMERY   98, DEC 2003 (98)
(50% PN, 50% CH)
This was Pommery's own choice for the Millennium Tasting. I understand why! We were given two bottles for the tasting, but ten days before, one of the bottles began to leak profusely. There was only one thing to do: give in and drink it up that same evening.

My good friend Mattias Klum, master photographer and Champagne lover, was in any case going to come over for a little asparagus and Champagne, so it didn't feel that wrong when the slightly more than half-full bottle was uncorked. The wine was fantastic! An unmatched depth and a 1950s color uplifted by a fine mousse. The bouquet was heavy and grand with a strong imprint of Pinot Noir. The taste was very refreshing and balanced, with a creamy-buttery and youthful Chardonnay tone. Majestic!

- 1911 POMMERY   96, JUN 2002 (96)
(50% PN, 50% CH)
We opened this bottle thinking it was a 1934 Pommery Rosé. Imagine our surprise when we found the drink to be light yellow. The surprise was probably even greater when we took a look at the cork: 1911! All old Pommery vintages that have lain untouched in Champagne seem almost indestructible. Color, mousse, and vitality—all were like a Champagne from the '80s. The bouquet of these archetypal Champagnes is never huge, but very classical and deep, with aromas as dignified as old aristocrats. The mountain-stream-fresh, buoyant palate has an oily concentration, with notes of cigar, chanterelle, apricot, and burned leaves.

- 1964 POMMERY CUVÉE SPECIALE   93, MAR 2003 (93)
(100% CH)
Drunk during a gorgeously beautiful spring evening at Sofiero Castle in the province of Skåne (Scania), accompanied by a fabulous duck-liver creation. Even the wine was spring-like and enviously youthful. Lively mousse, shimering green color, and a faint, ever-floral bouquet that became increasingly nutty and honey-saturated in the glass. Crispy taste with an almost metallic mineral note and a short but ambitious finish.

- 1962 POMMERY AVIZE   88, JUN 2001 (88)
(100% CH)
Looking by chance a little closer at my box of Pommery '62s, I discovered that four of them were decorated with a minute "Avize" designation. The mousse was weak and the wine more mature than the usual vintage of this age. Big, abundant, oily structure, and aromas of aged butter just going rancid.

- 1961 POMMERY AVIZE   88, DEC 2002 (88)
(100% CH)
Perhaps a little hard and metallic, but a fascinatingly youthful and peevish Champagne with dry tastes and a certain smokiness. It lacks a little fruit, to be sure, but certainly tastes good.

- 1973 POMMERY ROSÉ   87, NOV 2002 (87)
(80% PN, 20% CH)
Mature, beefy, heavy red-wine-like Champagne, with notes of iron, leather, meat, and bouillon. Fleshy, forceful palate that I wouldn't hesitate serving with a big chunk of meat. Dry, slightly bitter finish.

- 1961 POMMERY ROSÉ   90, JUN 2001 (90)
(80% PN, 20% CH)
Refreshing mousse, dark cellar flavors, and irrepressible masculine vitality. This is a wine that placed high during a very comprehensive magnum tasting of Pommery on the Fjäderholm Islands outside of Stockholm. In my opinion the wine was verging on the unbalanced and demanding with all its passion and muscle-power. Tar, toffee, and tobacco were other discernible notes. A Champagne for mealtimes.

- 1959 POMMERY ROSÉ   94, NOV 2001 (94)
(80% PN, 20% CH)
A demanding but most impressive mealtime Champagne. The wine is as uncompromising as an English aristocrat. A Latour of

Champagnes; it puts its confidence in a magnificently classic structure—with all that that implies—instead of trusting in aromatic beauty.

- 1947 POMMERY ROSÉ   88, MAR 2000 (88)
(80% PN, 20% CH)
Unfortunately, only tasted in half bottles without mousse and with Tokay-like flavors. Undeniably a very great and concentrated wine that is probably fantastic in magnum.
- 1945 POMMERY ROSÉ   92, MAR 2000 (92)
(80% PN, 20% CH)
Not as refreshing as the '41; more characterized by old vintage tones in looks, bouquet, and flavor. The color is reminiscent of Tawny and the mousse is weak. Still, the wine held its own in the glass and the depth and richness was impressive. The wine was a perfect complement to reading a good book in a lounge chair in front of the fireplace.
- 1943 POMMERY ROSÉ
(80% PN, 20% CH)
- 1941 POMMERY ROSÉ   93, DEC 2001 (93)
(80% PN, 20% CH)
Not really as exciting as the white '41, but still a very fine and vigorous Champagne. The color is intensely red with youthful notes. The bouquet was characterized by cherry and a taste of fine Pinot, with a certain spicy juniper-berry bitterness in the finish.
- 1937 POMMERY ROSÉ   95, NOV 2000 (95)
(80% PN, 20% CH)
Weak mousse, orange color with shades of amber. Butterscotchy, sweet, and integrated. Krug-like depth and a potent, full-bodied Pinot made from a very low yield. The aftertaste, with the ultra-elegant note of nut toffee, carries my thoughts to Cristal. Actually, a little too young and undeveloped in magnum!
- 1934 POMMERY ROSÉ   97, JAN 2000 (97)
(80% PN, 20% CH)
Indescribably fine and youthful, despite the almost nonexistent mousse. Aromatically speaking, the wine resembles a Richebourg from DRC more than a Champagne. Rose water, truffles, orange peel, and raspberries are distinct associations we tasters got when we encountered this unique wine. Extremely "drinkable" essence. At my blind tasting, the group guessed that the vintage was a 1985. Do I need to say that the wine had lain untouched in Champagne for the whole of its more-than-sixty-year life?
- 1929 POMMERY ROSÉ   96, FEB 2001 (96)
(55% PN, 45% CH)
A legendary magnum that I enjoyed with various TV heads at Källhagen's eminent restaurant. The color was quite similar to the pale 1995 Billecart-Salmon Rosé that stood beside it. Pale and clear, leaning toward bronze and orange. The nose was seductively beautiful and multifaceted. Count Basey, a brothel, a summer's evening, and an Aston Martin were similes the TV people used to describe this sensual wine. Roast coffee and nut toffee sound trivial, but to me these are the most prominent notes. Mild palate and creamy butterscotch, youthfully bubbling over like a calf let out to pasture. More Chardonnay than usual.
- 1995 LOUISE POMMERY   87, OCT 2003 (91)
(40% PN, 60% CH)
Young and impatient, like a sprinter in the starting blocks. Fresh,

bubbling, recalcitrant Champagne rich in fruit, mineral, and acidity. Chardonnay has the upper hand for the moment.
- 1990 LOUISE POMMERY   89, MAY 2000 (93)
(40% PN, 60% CH)
A large and magnificent wine with many layers. The house-style is intact with an extra natural addition of sweet, exotic fruit that is so typical of the vintage. There is so much power here that I am convinced the wine will need to be served with food when it finally matures some time after 2010.
- 1989 LOUISE POMMERY   93, APR 2003 (95)
(30% PN, 70% CH)
Impressive and rich as can be. A real food Champagne with big, overloaded fruit and a powerful oxidative character of nut chocolate, raisin, fig, date, and honey. Dry, fine finish. The high points only pertain to a magnum, where a toasted refinement is fabulously beautiful.
- 1988 LOUISE POMMERY   87, JAN 2003 (87)
(40% PN, 60% CH)
This is the first vintage with the beautiful white label. Even the wine is beautiful and tasteful. The nose is already mature, with elements of cheese, milk toffee, and licorice. The taste, on the other hand, is considerably less developed, with a dry freshness and aromas of Avize Chardonnay. Some bottles are developing alarmingly fast.
- 1987 LOUISE POMMERY   91, APR 1999 (91)
(40% PN, 60% CH)
Pleasant nose of baked goods and chocolate. Originally I thought it was too hollow, with a much too thin and fruity taste for a prestige Champagne, but today it's become wonderfully refined and toasted.
- 1985 LOUISE POMMERY   90, NOV 2001 (92)
(40% PN, 60% CH)
The firm's *cuvée de prestige* is always made in a softer and more refined style than the vintage wine. The '85 has an exceptionally soft and luxuriant mousse. The nose is typical of Louise Pommery, with a cheesy, mature element combined with vanilla, fresh baked bread, and orange. A tremendously melting and easily drunk Champagne. Stylish, but perhaps a touch too carefully arranged.
- 1985 POMMERY FLACON D'EXCEPTION   83, JUN 2000 (87)
(50% PN, 50% CH)
Deep color; somewhat one dimensional with a heavy bouquet. Tasted beside the '83, this wine seems strongly influenced by Pinot Noir, despite the grape composition being the same. Full bodied and robust with a dry resonance. Plum, leather, and licorice aromas. Much more toasted in a methusalem bottle!
- 1983 POMMERY FLACON D'EXCEPTION   86, JUN 2000 (89)
(50% PN, 50% CH)
Greenish-yellow and strongly characterized by Chardonnay; a charming wine, with faint Dom Pérignon-like undertones. Just like the '81, the wine has profited from attaining an acacia-scented autolytic character several years before disgorging. Refreshing and uplifting on the palate.
- 1982 LOUISE POMMERY   91, MAR 2002 (91)
(40% PN, 60% CH)
Attractive both to look at and drink. Medium-bodied and very soft, with a charming big-house-style. Maximum seduction in magnum.
- 1981 LOUISE POMMERY   86, JAN 2001 (86)
(40% PN, 60% CH)

Most '81s in Champagne live on an exquisite flowery elegance. Louise Pommery, on the other hand, trusts its mature Aÿ Pinot, with plenty of cheese and charming chocolate aromas. The wine is medium bodied and has a relatively short aftertaste.

• 1981 POMMERY FLACON D'EXCEPTION   90, JUN 2000 (91)
(50% PN, 50% CH)
Oh, this was good! Wonderful bouquet of toasted bread, acacia, lilac, and hawthorn. Cleanly elegant, medium-bodied Chardonnay flavors. Slightly green and grassy, with a soft, sweet, fruity finish, despite the wine being completely dry.

• 1980 LOUISE POMMERY   85, APR 2001 (85)
(40% PN, 60% CH)
Very discreet when young. Far broader and larger as the years go by. The color is still very light, and the nose is expansive, like an '82 with polished and toasted bread tones. The toasted aromas return in the flavor, which is fat and finished.

• 1980 POMMERY FLACON D'EXCEPTION   90, OCT 2003 (90)
(50% PN, 50% CH)
This is a splendid example of how the use of a magnum can add to storage potential and, above all, how long contact with its yeast can increase a wine's complexity. A few years ago this was a peaked and boring Champagne. Today these well-cared-for magnums have developed a wonderful scent of magnolia. Lemon-fresh, perfumed elements are found, together with an oiliness that, when too concentrated, reminds one of plastic. For me, the previous sentence is an analysis of the scent of magnolias and equally a description of this Champagne's bouquet. Like many wines from 1978, the flavor is fresh, short, and pleasant, but also characterized by greenish tones betraying unripe grapes.

• 1979 LOUISE POMMERY   95, FEB 2002 (95)
(40% PN, 60% CH)
Prince Alain de Polignac was kind enough to send me two bottles of this debut vintage. It was disgorged in 1986 and since then has lain untouched in Pommery's cellar, until December 2001. The wine is a revelation, with the acacia notes that newly disgorged wines usually have. The color is light, the bubbles are tiny, and the bouquet is unbelievably rich in niceties. Besides the floral nuances, coffee, lemon peel, and Valhrona chocolate are apparent. Superbly balanced taste with great finesse.

• 1979 POMMERY FLACON D'EXCEPTION   94, FEB 2003 (94)
(50% PN, 50% CH)
Bottle variation is relatively large among wines that have lain for such a long time in contact with their yeast deposit. Yet my latest magnum was classically nutty, with a Krug-like depth. Certain bottles have been stingier in the nose and shorter in the aftertaste. I think the surest time to really enjoy this crystal-clear, late-disgorged Champagne is a few years after *dégorgement*, before the more stylish and sharper corners have been smoothed down too much to become a honey-soft and smoky impressive totality.

• 1992 LOUISE POMMERY ROSÉ   89, JUL 2002 (91)
(55% PN, 45% CH)
Yet again, a brilliant '92 from Pommery. This really is a house that does well even during weak years. The wine is soft and pleasant, with a beautiful color and aristocratic bearing. Nothing is exaggerated, but most of what you expect to find is there.

• 1990 LOUISE POMMERY ROSÉ   91, MAY 1999 (94)
(55% PN, 45% CH)

A wonderful wine, rich with finesse and exceedingly good. The mousse is soft as a peach. It isn't just the pale pink color that is reminiscent of Cristal Rosé. The entire wine's mineral-rich subtlety and butter-toffee-like scent and taste is cast in the same mold as the much-celebrated wine from the other side of Reims. Only the concentration of all of the greatness is a bit lower. The house-style was pretty clearly recognizable at the Millennium Tasting.

• 1989 LOUISE POMMERY ROSÉ   80, MAR 1997 (87)
(57% PN, 43% CH)
Chalky, cold, and hard, but with an underlying strength and a dry, elegant, fresh flavor with a hint of strawberry.

• 1988 LOUISE POMMERY ROSÉ   83, JAN 1999 (88)
(45% PN, 55% CH)
Weak and chalky scent with good purity. Dry, very crisp, and house-typical taste that lacks the wonderful creaminess of the '90. Store this one!

• 1982 LOUISE POMMERY ROSÉ   93, FEB 2002 (93)
(40% PN, 60% CH)
Now an incredibly delicious and sweet, pleasurable wine. Sweet and butterscotchy, elegant flavor, with tons of charm and audience-pleasing, vanilla-packed raspberry aroma. The somewhat more rustic and gamy, mature nose is backed up by handsome notes reminiscent of whipped cream and strawberries.

POYET, MICHEL R-C
9, imp. Richebout
51190 Le Mesnil-sur-Oger
03 26 57 97 41
This grower has joined the cooperative and no longer makes any wine of its own.

• MICHEL POYET   65
(100% CH)

PRÉVOST, JÉRÔME *** R-M
51390 Gueux
One of Anselme Selosse's disciples, who works with exactly the same methods—and partly together with Anselme in Avize. Prévost is an incredibly exciting newcomer who, for the moment, only works with Pinot Meunier.

• JÉRÔME PRÉVOST LIEUX DIETS EXTRA BRUT   87
(100% PM)
Selosse's disciple makes a sensational debut here with a wine that I tasted blind without knowing of its existence. My guess was Tarlant in Oeuilly: they work with grapes from the Marne Valley, avoid malolactic fermentation, and vinify wholly in small, new oak barrels. I also said that it could be Selosse, as certain notes are identical to what the great master does. Incredibly interesting to find that it's possible to vinify such a wine only using Pinot Meunier. It must be the first time it's been done from new oak barrels, which shows that it isn't so strange that Krug and José Michel make such big and storable wines with a high proportion of Pinot Meunier. I long to follow a vintage Champagne from Prévost into the future.

PRIN N-M
51190 Avize
03 26 53 54 56
Every time I'm in Avize, I get a guilty conscience that I haven't visited Prin.

- LE SIXIÈME SENS   83, OCT 2003 (84)
  (100% CH)

A *cuvée de prestige* from the house's best grapes, produced by slow pressure and by using the heart of the *cuvée* only. The grapes come from the following vintages: '98, '97, '96, and '95. The taste is developed and surprisingly coarse and rustic. Mineral and apple aromas are present, but also mature notes of honey and exotic fruit. The wine should be better and younger than it actually is, with its slightly oxidative character.

QUENARDEL R-M
Place de la Mairie
51360 Verzenay
03 26 49 40 63
Production: 45,000
Eight hectares planted mostly with black grapes in Montagne de Reims. His oldest vines are fifty-five years old and are included in the prestige wines. Modern vinification.

- QUENARDEL BRUT   50
  (100% PN)
- QUERNARDEL ROSÉ   69
  (100% PN)
- 1985 QUENARDEL   69, JUL 1991 (83)
  (100% PN)

Copper-colored and coarsely perfumed nose with elements of banana. The concentrated flavor lies in wait with a surprise. Iron and blood are definable tones in the aftertaste.

- 1991 QUENARDEL BLANC DE BLANCS   78, FEB 2003 (78)
  (100% CH)
- 1989 QUENARDEL SPECIAL CLUB   87, AUG 2001 (88)
  (70% PN, 30% CH)

In the last years, many Pinot champagnes from '89 have proven to be both very delicious and balanced. This brilliant wine has a warm, generous fruit together with the vintage's toffee notes, as well as a grape-typical spectrum of tastes. Sea notes are present, handsomely integrated with notes from the animal kingdom and an autumn forest. Fleshy and impressive.

QUENARDEL-ESQUERRÉ R-M
7, rue Werle
51360 Verzenay
03 26 49 41 81
Closed 10 years ago and the land was sold to the cooperative.

- 1979 QUENARDEL-ESQUERRÉ   84, AUG 2001 (84)
  (80% PN, 20% CH)

Fairly newly disgorged for the millennium, this champagne is still very young. The nose and palate exude ripe grapes and impart a sweet general impression. Notes of raisin, plum, and honey are backed up by a hint of mussel shell. Soft and good, if a tad simplistic.

- 1989 QUENARDEL-ESQUERRÉ PRESTIGE   80, MAR 2000 (83)
  (80% PN, 20% CH)

Milder than expected, with a thirst-quenching, light tropical fruit. Smoothly creamy and Chardonnay-like champagne with a somewhat sweet finish.

RAFFLIN, BERTRAND R-M
4, rue des Carrières
51500 Chigny-les-Roses
03 26 03 48 47
Production: 7,000
The grower has more than 2.5 hectares planted with all three grape types in Chigny and Ludes. Today the wines are made by Feuillatte and are part of the Chigny Cooperative.

- BERTRAND RAFFLIN BRUT   63
  (33% PN, 34% PM, 33% CH)
- BERTRAND RAFFLIN DEMI-SEC   38
  (33% PN, 34% PM, 33% CH)
- BERTRAND RAFFLIN SEC   48
  (33% PN, 34% PM, 33% CH)
- BERTRAND RAFFLIN ROSÉ   51
  (40% PN, 30% PM, 30% CH)
- BERTRAND RAFFLIN CUVÉE ST VINCENT   74
  (70% PN, 30% CH)

REDON, PASCAL R-M
2, rue de la Mairie
51380 Trépail
03 26 57 06 02
Production: 32,000
Pascal is rather new to the game, as he only started the property as recently as 1980. Today he has more than 4.3 hectares, dominated by Chardonnay.

- PASCAL REDON TRADITION   76
  (20% PN, 80% CH)
- PASCAL REDON CUVÉE HORDON   74
  (50% PN, 50% CH)
- PASCAL REDON BLANC DE BLANCS   60
  (100% CH)
- PASCAL REDON ROSÉ   82
  (20% PN, 80% CH)

Sensationally impressive, delicious rosé Champagne with a big creamy, luxurious character. Exotic and purebred all at the same time. Long and creamy.

RÉMY, ERNEST R-M
3, rue Aristide Briand
51500 Mailly
03 26 49 41 15
Only old bottles have crossed my path.

- 1964 ERNEST RÉMY
  (100% PN)
- 1953 ERNEST RÉMY   92, APR 2003 (92)
  (100% PN)

It is exceedingly unusual for me to run into really old Blanc de Noirs. This type of wine is not for guys without hair on their chests! Half the tasting group with whom I shared the wine distinctly disliked this truffle-scented, vegetal wine. The rest of us were fascinated by the Bordeaux-like bell-pepper notes and the slightly squalid parts that in many ways are similar to old red Burgundys. Very long taste of leather, mushroom, sewing-machine oil, and diesel.

RÉMY, G N-M
5, rue Longchamp
51700 Cerseuil
03 26 58 28 94
Unusual for a grower in Cerseuil to make Blanc de Blancs!
- G. RÉMY BLANC DE BLANCS   58
  (100% CH)

RENAUDIN, R. N-M
Domaine des Conardins
51530 Moussy
03 26 54 03 41
Production: 230,000
This is the firm that produces Taillevent (see "Buyer's Own Brand") and owns twenty-four hectares around Moussy and Pierry. Dominique Tellier began making kosher Champagne in 1990, and has since received a great deal of attention in the British wine press.
- RENAUDIN BRUT RÉSERVE   54
  (70% PM, 30% CH)
- RENAUDIN GRANDE RÉSERVE   57
  (25% PN, 20% PM, 55% CH)
- 1993 RENAUDIN CD   76, MAY 2001 (80)
  (5% PN, 15% PM, 80% CH)
  A special, decidedly spicy style with a hint of woodiness. Rich fruit and a certain bitterness in the finish.
- 1985 RENAUDIN CD   82, MAY 2001 (82)
  (5% PN, 15% PM, 80% CH)
  Rich oxidative style where the fruit is beginning to lean toward overripe apples and raisins. Fat taste with notes of dark chocolate and honey.
- 1996 RENAUDIN MILLENNIUM   82, DEC 2002 (84)
  (100% CH)
  An interesting Chardonnay wine that feels like a rustic variety of Jacquesson. Slightly earthy, gingerbread-influenced bouquet with a clear note of pear and a whiff of lemon. The same notes in the somewhat light palate, which is cut off rather short.

REVOLTÉ, ADAM R-M
58, rue de la Porte d'En-Bas
51160 Hautvillers
03 26 59 48 41
One of the few producers of Hautvillers Blanc de Blancs. Jean-Paul Adam is *chef de cave*. Other wines: Brut, Demi-Sec, Réserve, Rosé, Cuvée Prestige.
- ADAM REVOLTÉ BLANC DE BLANCS   66
  (100% CH)

RICCIUTI-RÉVOLTE R-M
18, rue du Lieutenant de Vaisseau Paris
51160 Avenay
03 26 52 30 27
Production: 20,000
Ricciuti-Révolte is probably the only American grower in Champagne. His grapes come from 3.5 hectares in Avenay and one hectare in Mareuil-sur-Aÿ, and he sells 25 percent of them to Mumm.
- RICCIUTI-RÉVOLTE BRUT   70
- RICCIUTI-RÉVOLTE BRUT ROSÉ   60

RIVIÈRE, FRANCK R-M
30, impasse de l'Ancienne Mairie
51530 Cramant
03 26 57 99 31
Production: 50,000
A new winemaker that neighbors say is better at playing the piano than making wine. Is this true? Vineyard size: six hectares. The grower uses a certain amount of oak barrels for his wines.
- FRANCK RIVIÈRE   58
  (100% CH)

ROBERT, ALAIN ** R-M**
25, avenue de la République
51190 Le Mesnil-sur-Oger
03 26 57 52 94
Production: 100,000
Alain Robert is one of Champagne's most unique winemakers, with control of vineyards in five Chardonnay villages. The grapes are picked by hand, the Mesnil grapes ferment in oak barrels, and the youngest nonvintage Champagne is nine years old. In May of 1995, they sold 1978 and 1979 as vintage Champagnes! All this is made possible by asking an awfully high price. Robert's prestige wine is in fact the second most expensive in Champagne after the Krug Collection. Unfortunately I haven't tasted his vintage wines, but the rich nonvintage examples are very good, if a trifle rustic. Other wines: Vintage.
- A. ROBERT BRUT   82
  (100% CH)
  A pure '85 with a rich, honeyed bouquet in a classic oxidative style. The power and maturity are superb, as is the long aftertaste of walnut and butter.
- A. ROBERT MESNIL SÉLECTION   80
  (100% CH)
  A pure '83. Broad, nutty, classically old-fashioned nose, with a buttery-rich, somewhat one-dimensional flavor.
- A. ROBERT SÉLECTION   73
  (100% CH)
- A. ROBERT VIEUX DOSÉ   90
  (100% CH)
  Made from thirty-year-old vines from the harvests in 1980 and 1982. Completely vinified in oak barrels and for sale ten years after being disgorged! A lovely, golden Champagne with green elements and a classic toasty, oaky nose. The wine is mature but holds up terrifically well in the glass.

ROBERT, ANDRÉ R-M
15, rue de l'Orme
51190 Le Mesnil-sur-Oger
03 26 57 59 41
Production: 40,000
The Robert family has been making wine for over 100 years, but today's company and cellar were created by André Robert in 1961, with his son Bertrand Robert, who now runs the firm. The vines on the company's nine hectares in Mesnil and Vertus average twenty-five years of age.
- ANDRÉ ROBERT ROSÉ   29
- 1996 ANDRÉ ROBERT   80, FEB 2002 (85)
  (100% CH)
  The company's only wine that is 100 percent Mesnil, something that is immediately noticeable. The wine represents a special,

slightly difficult style that some people hate. Jardin and Jacquart are leaders of this somewhat blunt, gamy, musty, and burned style. Some tasters spoke of rotten fish, others of burned rubber, and some went so far as to mention the stench from a drainpipe! For me, words like earth, forest, and boiled meat come to mind when I try to describe this wine.

ROCOURT, MICHEL R-M

1, rue Zalieu
51190 Le Mesnil-sur-Oger
03 26 57 94 99
Production: 40,000

Michel, former head of the vineyard at Henriot, now owns 5.5 hectares in Mesnil and Vertus and began business in 1975. The vines are twenty-nine years old. This grower releases his vintage Champagne at a remarkably mature age. The wines are vinified in modern fashion and are put through malolactic fermentation.

- M. ROCOURT ROSÉ DU MESNIL   62
  (100% CH)

- 1993 M. ROCOURT   82, MAR 2004 (83)
  (100% CH)
  Relatively expansive, slightly oxidative style with very good extract. Scent of quince, cider, and browned butter. Fleshy palate with hints of windfall fruit, stone, and leather.

- M. ROCOURT GRAND VINTAGE   85, MAR 2004 (85)
  (100% CH)
  Basically a pure '98 with older reserve wines. Very tranquil and creamily polished. Creamy taste with a handsomely sophisticated, fresh finish.

ROEDERER, LOUIS ***** N-M

21, boulevard Lundy
51100 Reims
03 26 40 42 11
Production: 2,600,000

Roederer did not get its present name until 1833, but was in existence as far back as 1760 under the name of Dubois Père & Fils. Louis Roederer was a hardworking man who succeeded in selling his Champagne in several important export markets. Roederer's real ace was, as with Clicquot, the Russian market. Tsar Alexander II wanted a more impressive label to show his guests, and in 1876 he made a special order for the first transparent Cristal bottles, which at that time actually were made of genuine crystal. The wine was stunningly sweet and gave Roederer had some problems with disposal after the Russian revolution, when the firm was stuck with unpaid invoices and stores full of sweet Champagne that no one else wanted. The company recovered in the 1930s, when Camille Olry-Roederer took the helm. She invested the money earned from sales in some exceptional vineyards: in Aÿ, Hautvillers, Cumières, Louvois, Verzy, Verzenay, Vertus, Avize, Cramant, Chouilly, and Le Mesnil. Roederer also owns several well-respected vineyards in other locations: Roederer Estate, Ramos Pinto, Haut-Beauséjour and Château de Pez. Today the firm is the most financially successful in the region, thanks largely to these vineyards, which supply Roederer with some 70 percent of its grapes. The house is now run by Jean-Claude Rouzaud and the wines are assembled by Michel Pansu, who works according to the same principles as those applied in past decades.

All the wines ferment separately, *cru* by *cru*, in small steel vats, while the reserve wines are stored in large oak barrels. This is said to give the company its special "vanilla touch." I'm not alone in wondering if certain wines for the prestige variety Cristal aren't stored in these barrels, as it is precisely in Cristal that one can sometimes discover a nutty, oily, and vanilla-tasting barrel-like character. Another explanation for this toffee-like note of maturity could be that they use a large portion of the best, older, oak-barrel-stored reserve wines in the dosage. Apart from this, up to 20 percent of the oak-aged reserve wine is used in the nonvintage Champagne Brut Premier. Roederer has no set recipe regarding malolactic fermentation; the personal qualities of the wine differ from case to case. Roederer is without doubt a brilliant Champagne house with an exceptional portfolio of wines. The nonvintage Champagne is brilliant. The rosé and Blanc de Blancs offer an aristocratic elegance typical of the house, and the vintage wine is always among the best. Cristal is today the most sought-after *cuvée de prestige*, and has perhaps the most appetizing appearance of any wine in the world. Cristal Rosé is not only the most expensive rosé Champagne—it is obviously the best. In my opinion, this house is one of the four best in all of Champagne.

- LOUIS ROEDERER BRUT PREMIER   82
  (62% PN, 8% PM, 30% CH)
  Invariably praised, nonvintage Champagne with a high proportion of reserve wines that had been stored in big oak barrels. Four years in the bottle before disgorging; only the first pressing is used. For several years, an appley, storable, and decently good nonvintage Champagne. Today, a Cristal-like Champagne with outstanding finesse.

- LOUIS ROEDERER EXTRA DRY   60
  (62% PN, 8% PM, 30% CH)

- LOUIS ROEDERER CARTE BLANCHE   55
  (62% PN, 8% PM, 30% CH)

- LOUIS ROEDERER GRAND VIN SEC   55
  (62% PN, 8% PM, 30% CH)

- LOUIS ROEDERER ROSÉ   86
  (70% PN, 30% CH)
  This wine, though no longer made, is still very enjoyable and delicious if you should be lucky enough to run into a bottle or two. Judging by the taste, the bottles I've encountered seem to date from the 1970s. This is therefore a very mature, chocolate-sated Champagne with a gorgeous honeyed, almond palate. The color is, of course, just as light as other rosé Champagnes from this house. Somewhat lower taste concentration than the vintage rosé.

- 1996 LOUIS ROEDERER   92, JUN 2003 (95)
  (66% PN, 34% CH)
  Exceptionally delicious already, and yet it would be sacrilege to consume this within the next few years. The wine has a plumpness and fleshy intensity that the other wines from Roederer lack for the moment. This vintage wine is like an impudent boy, grabbing what he wants without waiting. Wonderful taste of chocolate, caramel, and butterscotch apple.

- 1995 LOUIS ROEDERER   88, FEB 2003 (94)
  (66% PN, 34% CH)
  Classic, youthful Roederer with austere character and incredibly elegant apple tone. Layers of indescribable grapiness and ultra-sophisticated luxuriousness caress the tongue like a velvety carpet of music delivered by Pat Metheny.

- 1994 LOUIS ROEDERER   87, NOV 2000 (92)
(66% PN, 34% CH)
Though normally considered a rather dismal vintage, Roederer has succeeded in producing an entire flurry of superior-class vintage wines. What they all have in common is high acidity together with elegantly balanced fruit and a trace of Roederer's characteristic note of caramel and toffee.

- 1990 LOUIS ROEDERER   91, APR 2002 (94)
(66% PN, 34% CH)
Wonderful balance and refinement. Creamy and classically smoky with fine, resoundingly pure acidity.

- 1989 LOUIS ROEDERER   84, MAR 2002 (92)
(66% PN, 34% CH)
So classical and enjoyable at the same time. Both the nose and the flavor have clear elements of fudge and dark chocolate. The wine is made in a balanced and medium-bodied style with tons of authority and charm.

- 1988 LOUIS ROEDERER   92, NOV 2003 (93)
(66% PN, 34% CH)
This sterling wine began to find its way home in 2003. Big, magnificent nose of newly baked bread, red apples, and nuts. The taste is round and its outward form is big. A clear note of almond shows similarities to the '79. Should be at its peak between 2005 and 2010.

- 1986 LOUIS ROEDERER   85, MAR 1997 (87)
(66% PN, 34% CH)
Light and slender with a citrus-fresh breeze and tones of toffee. Somewhat lacking in concentration.

- 1985 LOUIS ROEDERER   91, MAR 2003 (93)
(66% PN, 34% CH)
A wonderful wine that conceals depths of beauty under the subdued surface. Pure, slightly buttery, classical build, and perfect balance. Drink after the year 2005.

- 1983 LOUIS ROEDERER   80, JUN 1989 (89)
(66% PN, 34% CH)
Only tasted in its youth. Then it was very fresh and Granny Smith-influenced. Crystal-clear acidity in a medium body. Promising!

- 1982 LOUIS ROEDERER   93, SEP 2001 (93)
(66% PN, 34% CH)
Crystal-clear house-style with polished, ultra-sophisticated character and uplifting freshness. Delightfully butterscotchy, and saturated with vanilla and sophisticated, fat fruit.

- 1981 LOUIS ROEDERER   84, DEC 1994 (84)
(66% PN, 34% CH)
The 1981 is usually dominated by an elegant fruit aroma, but here Roederer have instead produced a creamy and fat Champagne with plenty of toffee in the nose. Short aftertaste.

- 1979 LOUIS ROEDERER   93, JAN 2002 (93)
(66% PN, 34% CH)
This wine is perhaps the clearest example I can give of how Champagne ages best in magnums. In magnum, this '79 has an exotic nose of orchids and honeysuckle, along with several jars of roasted coffee. The taste is a sensual experience, with a richness reminiscent of hazelnut-filled milk chocolate. Long and classical. In the normal-sized bottles, the dosage seems a bit high and the wine exudes treacle, windfall fruit, almonds, and hazelnut.

- 1978 LOUIS ROEDERER   88, AUG 1996 (88)
(66% PN, 34% CH)
A rare vintage with great depth, delicious caramel flavor, and a soft afternote of honey.

- 1976 LOUIS ROEDERER   94, JAN 2003 (94)
(66% PN, 34% CH)
Roederer are apparently the firm to go for this year. This '76 achieves a rare richness and sophisticated fruit sweetness. Very much like the Cristal from the same vintage, but slightly richer chocolate aromas and less buttery Chardonnay taste. Long and united.

- 1975 LOUIS ROEDERER   91, JUL 1991 (93)
(66% PN, 34% CH)
The nose isn't as nice as the '76, but the acidity and the attack boast of a longer life. The nose played on a vegetable theme, accompanied by a weak but clear Gorgonzola tone. The Pinot Noir is more apparent here than in the '76, despite the fact that the grape proportions are identical.

- 1974 LOUIS ROEDERER   84, APR 2000 (84)
(66% PN, 34% CH)
Despite good company and a fabulous spring evening in the open country, I was not really enchanted by this much lauded '74. Roederer has, as is well known, an ability to conjure forth grand wines—even during weak years—but here both purity and length are missing. On the other hand, the wine is tolerably rich, with a mature bouquet of toffee and a fat taste of honey. In my opinion, the undertone of subterranean storeroom is somewhat disturbing.

- 1973 LOUIS ROEDERER   88, MAR 2002 (88)
(66% PN, 34% CH)
Ripe and almost devoid of mousse. Hardly one of Roederer's more memorable vintages.

- 1971 LOUIS ROEDERER   95, OCT 2000 (95)
(66% PN, 34% CH)
This wine reached its peak probably a few years ago, but it still bestows lots of pleasure with its oily richness and developed nut and leather aroma—though this only applies to regular bottles. In magnum, the wine is completely fantastic, with unbeatable stature and elegance. Can you believe there would be such a difference?!

- 1969 LOUIS ROEDERER   94, JUL 2001 (94)
(66% PN, 34% CH)
Well-groomed appearance and a big, powerful nose. I find the cellar note and mushroom aroma to be slightly too pronounced, to the point that they overshadow the fat caramel tones. The taste is exceedingly, impressively rich, balanced, and devastatingly delicious. What an aftertaste!

- 1967 LOUIS ROEDERER   89, DEC 2002 (89)
(66% PN, 34% CH)
Aged nose of leather and mushroom, with a faint sherry tone as well as a hint of tea. Lively and medium bodied; good acidity; and a classic finish à la Roederer with caramel tones.

- 1966 LOUIS ROEDERER   95, JUN 1999 (95)
(66% PN, 34% CH)
Even though this Champagne is nearly still, the color is light golden and youthful. A veritable bag of toffees, with soft, beautiful vanilla aroma and irresistible charm.

- 1964 LOUIS ROEDERER   93, JAN 2002 (93)
(66% PN, 34% CH)
Heavy, gamy, vegetal nose of butter-fried wild fowl, boiled vegetables, and tar. With lengthy airing there are more notes of

caramel and dried fruit. A powerful palate with less charm and a stricter character than normal. Perfect looks and vitality, as well as a long, slightly abrasive finish.

- 1962 LOUIS ROEDERER   95, MAY 2001 (95)
(66% PN, 34% CH)

My birth year continually increases in stature. I just hope that I will remain as vital and vibrant as the foremost Champagnes. This wine definitely belongs in that category. Intense, multi-layered, orange-blossom-like bouquet. Soft, harmonious flavor, laden with sweet richness and exotic fruit. Majestically dignified and distinguished exit, with scents of aged hardwood.

- 1961 LOUIS ROEDERER   88, JAN 1995 (>)
(66% PN, 34% CH)

It's rare to see a Champagne with such an effervescent mousse combined with a brown amber color. The broad nose is very similar to an old Tokay, with tones of prune, overripe apple, and rotten wood. A heavy Pinot taste, with sweet, toffee-like aromas. Not completely clean, however, and the aftertaste is a touch maderized.

- 1959 LOUIS ROEDERER   96, JAN 2000 (96)
(66% PN, 34% CH)

More a classic Roederer than a typical '59. Certainly there is strength and a suggestion of smoky aromas, but considerably more apparent is the house's balanced and creamy style. The cleanness is impressive, as well as the finesse created by the chalky mineral hints that border on goat cheese. Extremely close to ninety-seven points.

- 1955 LOUIS ROEDERER   95, OCT 2000 (95)
(66% PN, 34% CH)

A perfect mousse, Roederer's unmistakable toffee nose, and a nervous, acidic undertone in this wonderfully balanced, honeyed wine.

- 1949 LOUIS ROEDERER   97, FEB 2004 (97)
(66% PN, 34% CH)

One of the mot delicious Champagnes at the Millennium Tasting, with its essence of nectar-like, caramel-drenched tastes. Enchanting.

- 1947 LOUIS ROEDERER   97, OCT 2000 (97)
(66% PN, 34% CH)

Just as good as it sounds! The house-style gets the better of the vintage character. One of the lightest Pinot-dominated '47s I have tasted, but also one of the best. Harmony, balance, and charm are keywords when I attempt to describe this delicious Champagne.

- 1945 LOUIS ROEDERER   97, OCT 2001 (97)
(66% PN, 34% CH)

Greater volume and strength than usual. Incredibly impressive wine; one of the vintage's best.

- 1941 LOUIS ROEDERER   94, JAN 2003 (94)
(66% PN, 34% CH)

Deeply straw-colored yet still extremely lively. Soft, sweet attack evolves into a wonderfully clear, creamy, vigorous taste with a good, dry, very long aftertaste. Very high, uplifting acidity.

- 1928 LOUIS ROEDERER   96, OCT 2000 (96)
(70% PN, 30% CH)

I finally got the chance to see how great the '28s could be. Roederer's perfect Champagne has a colossal, irrepressible power combined with a toffee flavor so typical of the house. Superb acidity. Maderized at the Millennium Tasting.

- 1923 LOUIS ROEDERER   96, OCT 2003 (96)
(70% PN, 30% CH)

Big! Beautifully youthful eighty-year-old with an awfully grand bouquet. Tons of roasted coffee beans, popcorn, browned butter, and nectar-like fruit aromas. Balanced, fresh taste with a dry, chalky finish. A wealth of mineral notes are beautifully braided into layers of velvety-smooth nut caramel. Two bottles tasted with identical structure and aroma profile, despite the one being still and the other freshly bubbling.

- 1997 LOUIS ROEDERER BLANC DE BLANCS   92, AUG 2003 (94)
(100% CH)

This wine is impressively consistent from year to year. Cleaner and lighter than Cristal itself, but with more than a dash of its luxurious butter-caramel tone. White flower scents and green citrus notes exist in abundance, together with a pleasant fruity sweetness and a breeze of euphoria. Delightful!

- 1996 LOUIS ROEDERER BLANC DE BLANCS   90, JAN 2003 (95)
(100% CH)

There's always something ethereally, shimmeringly beautiful about this wine, no matter the vintage. Pure as an alpine spring through and through, this creation has razor-sharp acidity and a nascent faint creaminess all in house-typical luxury wrappings.

- 1995 LOUIS ROEDERER BLANC DE BLANCS   90, AUG 2003 (94)
(100% CH)

Unexpectedly muffled and stringent with an undeveloped, intrinsic greatness. High-class, faint nose in the same style as Pol Roger Blanc de Chardonnay. Stylish, young, refined taste of ruby grapefruit, lemon peel, and mineral.

- 1994 LOUIS ROEDERER BLANC DE BLANCS   88, NOV 2000 (92)
(100% CH)

They've done it again! The wine exudes Roederer through and through. Few companies, if any, have as consistent a house-style as the giant on Boulevard Lundy. This lemony-fresh wine, with its fine *grand cru* Chardonnay style, is softly blanketed in the most delicious butter caramel. This wine actually seems to be on a par with Cristal!

- 1993 LOUIS ROEDERER BLANC DE BLANCS   87, MAY 1999 (91)
(100% CH)

Almost transparent, like mineral water, with minimal perky bubbles. Refined and as-yet floral bouquet. Once more Roederer exhibits their greatness as a Champagne house.

- 1990 LOUIS ROEDERER BLANC DE BLANCS   95, MAY 2004 (95)
(100% CH)

Superbly delicious, sophisticated wine, with a juicy and easy-to-drink overall feel. The flavor is loving and romantic, with tones of vanilla buns and sweet lemon.

- 1989 LOUIS ROEDERER BLANC DE BLANCS   85, JUL 1997 (93)
(100% CH)

Really it's just a question of style as to which Roederer '89 you prefer. All of them share a sophisticated house-style. Personally, I have a weakness for this outstandingly fresh Blanc de Blancs which, in common with Cristal, has more malic acid than usual.

- 1983 LOUIS ROEDERER BLANC DE BLANCS   90, APR 1992 (92)
(100% CH)

Roederer's Blanc de Blancs are very rare. The '83 is a wonderful wine, with great similarities to the Cristal of the same vintage. The nose is powerful and elegant, with nuts, pastries, and sweet, creamy fruit. The wine has a softness and maturity that is so typical in high-class grapes. Long, classic aftertaste.

- 1971 LOUIS ROEDERER BLANC DE BLANCS 89, JUN 1988 (89)
(100% CH)
A weaker mousse than usual. Buttery and slim in a wonderful way. In 1988 the acidity was a little low, and the wine may well be on the way out.

- 1955 LOUIS ROEDERER BLANC DE BLANCS 96, JUN 1997 (96)
(100% CH)
Tasted alongside the ordinary '55, this has a deeper color and weaker mousse. If possible, the nose is even more delightful, filled with toffee aromas. The flavor is magically smooth and nectar-like. A minor masterpiece.

- 1996 LOUIS ROEDERER ROSÉ 89, OCT 2003 (93)
(70% PN, 30% CH)
This rosé takes the biscuit for paleness! I was served the wine blind and absolutely thought I'd gotten a young Blanc de Noirs in the glass before I felt the house-typical, ultra-elegant bouquet that can only come from Roederer. The entire wine is "white" in its aromas. For the moment, crispy Chardonnay actually dominates with its crackling freshness. When aired you catch a whiff of strawberry and whipped cream. Luxurious and handsome.

- 1995 LOUIS ROEDERER ROSÉ 94, JUN 2002 (95)
(70% PN, 30% CH)
I have no idea how many times I have been amazed by a new release from Roederer. This is surely one of the vintage's foremost Champagnes. How one can accomplish such a treacly and butter-toffee-soft wine as intensely fruity-fresh as this is beyond my comprehension. I hardly dare to imagine what Roederer's other '95s are like.

- 1994 LOUIS ROEDERER ROSÉ 87, NOV 2000 (92)
(70% PN, 30% CH)
Pale and delicate with a fine, discreet bouquet of elegant Pinot Noir. Almost creamy, despite the high acidity. In terms of quality, it is indistinguishable from the regular vintage Champagne.

- 1993 LOUIS ROEDERER ROSÉ 87, MAY 1999 (90)
(70% PN, 30% CH)
A paler rosé does not exist! I only mean in color, of course—the character is anything but pale. Creamy, mellow, sophisticated, with a breeze of strawberries. Brilliantly flavorful '93.

- 1991 LOUIS ROEDERER ROSÉ 84, OCT 1997 (88)
(75% PN, 25% CH)
It's surprising that a quality house should produce a '91. The wine hardly reaches Roederer's normal standard, but is very good considering its vintage.

- 1989 LOUIS ROEDERER ROSÉ 90, NOV 2003 (90)
(70% PN, 30% CH)
Floral, light, and full of rich, red fruit. Unfortunately too sweet, but still incredibly, luxuriously delicious. Nuttier and heavier—but hardly better—with more time. Drink soon.

- 1988 LOUIS ROEDERER ROSÉ 92, NOV 2001 (94)
(70% PN, 30% CH)
Roederer's rosé has a very good reputation. I myself was surprised to discover when I wrote my first book that I had only tried a few vintages of this fine wine. The '88 is a crystal-clear, stylish Champagne with purebred, vigorous Pinot aromas of plum and raspberry.

- 1976 LOUIS ROEDERER ROSÉ 90, MAR 2002 (90)
(70% PN, 30% CH)
Very substantial, smoky Champagne with a somewhat dried-up finish. Considerably sweeter fruit a few years ago. Today, full of dark, heavy aromas, suitable for serving with meat.

- 1971 LOUIS ROEDERER ROSÉ 92, OCT 2001 (92)
(70% PN, 30% CH)
This wine can probably perform even better than it did the one time I found a bottle. Despite a fine mousse and a young, pale color, a faint aroma of mold from the cellar it had been stored in had penetrated the cork. The aroma was weak and acceptable, and the wine was in all other ways brilliant in its typically upper-crust, Roederer way.

- 1966 LOUIS ROEDERER ROSÉ 94, JUL 1995 (94)
(70% PN, 30% CH)
This wine is proof that rosé Champagnes can be aged. Only the color reveals the wine's identity. The nose is divine, with a broad spectrum of sweet aromas typical of this vintage. The taste is very tight and elegant, with tones of nut, toffee, and honey.

- 1961 LOUIS ROEDERER ROSÉ 97, JUL 1999 (97)
(70% PN, 30% CH)
Enjoyed with nature photographers Mattias and Monika Klum, on a wonderfully clear Swedish summer night in the Uppland archipelago. Roederer never disappoints! This predecessor to Cristal Rosé is right at the top of its long curve of life. The color is crystal-clear and light with a salmon-pink undertone. The finesse is very apparent, despite the vintage's potential fire and glowing strength. The taste is initially dry but with an everlastingly sweet aftertaste that spreads out over the whole tongue. A wine that makes you wish you could offer it to all of your friends. I am convinced that my friends the nature photographers will pull out the memory of this magical Champagne the next time they eat their boiled canned beans in Borneo's rainforest.

- 1959 LOUIS ROEDERER ROSÉ 95, OCT 2000 (95)
(75% PN, 25% CH)
A magnum, where the cork wouldn't budge, that exhibited a wonderfully beautiful light-pink color. Strangely, the mousse was all but nonexistent. Still, the general impression was youthful and florally seductive. There is much here to remind one of Cristal Rosé. Vanilla ice cream with strawberry jam and whipped cream. If the mousse had remained intact the wine would surely have received higher points. On a later occasion: perfect mousse, magnificent smoky impression, and vintage-typical.

- 1953 LOUIS ROEDERER ROSÉ 94, APR 2003 (94)
(70% PN, 30% CH)
Very pale color. Vigorous form and homogeneous, irresistible taste. The nose is creamy with elements of raspberry and strawberry. The finish is powerful—characterized by its remarkable age in a totally satisfactory fashion.

- 1952 LOUIS ROEDERER ROSÉ 96, JUL 1996 (96)
(70% PN, 30% CH)
An incredible Champagne with amazing fruit, elegance, and breeding. The vitality is awesome, as is the length of the magical aftertaste of butter and wild raspberry.

- 1997 CRISTAL 92, APR 2004 (95)
(55% PN, 45% CH)
It's hardly surprising that Roederer, with its brilliant vineyards, has succeeded so well in 1997. Cristal, of course, is a star as usual, with layers of fat, oily tastes. Honey, vanilla, exotic fruit, and cakes sound trivial for a wine with this complexity and elegance—so let's just enjoy this delicious tidbit without analyzing its beauty to death.

- 1996 CRISTAL   93, JAN 2004 (97)
(55% PN, 45% CH)
It is, of course, insane to drink this wine this early. I quake at the thought of how much Cristal is going to be stolen from the cradle at nightclubs and fashionable restaurants in the rich parts of the world. I was almost ashamed when I—for professional reasons, of course—popped the cork. The entire register is certainly here already, but everything is so incredibly shy and subordinate to the high acidity. Buy all you can find and leave it forgotten for the time being in some dark corner of the basement. Having said that, certain bottles are already deliciously honeyed. Decanting is recommended at least up until 2004.

- 1995 CRISTAL   94, MAY 2003 (97)
(55% PN, 45% CH)
Considerably shyer and more discreet than the ecstatic rosé of the same vintage. Initially just a youthfully floral, tranquil nose that merges into expressive grape ripeness and buttery complexity. Perfectly balanced, purebred finesse on the palate, with crystal-clear aromas and a lively development and taste transformation in the mouth. An extremely femininely composed, classic Cristal, with handsome aromas of licorice, vanilla, apples, and butter toffee—and a fabulous finish.

- 1994 CRISTAL   89, JUN 2002 (93)
(55% PN, 45% CH)
A weak vintage and surely a disappointment to many, considering the name and the price tag. The wine is still incredibly discreet and unborn. Everything is delicate but super-elegant, and actually faithful to its extraction. Like a skeleton, if compared to—say—an '82 Cristal. Very promising, though.

- 1993 CRISTAL   90, JAN 2002 (93)
(55% PN, 45% CH)
Steely and hard, but with unmistakable Cristal tones. The fruit is rich with tones of caramel and Granny Smith. The taste and mousse are always luxuriously clear and well defined.

- 1990 CRISTAL   95, JAN 2003 (97)
(58% PN, 42% CH)
A classic Cristal that is sometimes more open and a bit fatter than the '89, but is mostly a bitingly acidity, unreleased wine. There is the same delightful aromatic spectrum, with Roederer's typical toffee tone and rich but varied fruit. Big bottle variation probably due to the partial avoidance of malolactic fermentation. Absolutely wonderful lately.

- 1989 CRISTAL   97, MAR 2003 (98)
(50% PN, 50% CH)
Many connoisseurs are probably disappointed in this as-yet young, tart wine. The nose is certainly discreet, but under the surface lurks a finesse and concentration rarely seen. Caramel, Granny Smith apples, and hazelnuts are the aromas that blossom if the wine is decanted. Similar to the '90. Simply fantastically multifaceted and wonderfully good at the beginning of the twenty-first century.

- 1988 CRISTAL   96, NOV 2003 (97)
(50% PN, 50% CH)
Roeder's Cristal belongs to the elite of prestige Champagnes. It combines Bollinger's and Krug's heavy, nutty, Pinot-inspired style, with Taittinger Comtes de Champagne's enjoyably exotic fruitiness and butter-caramel taste. The only comment I have is that the vintages can be rather uneven and that the dosage tends to be a little too high for my taste. The '88 is young and classic with a rich fruit, nascent nuttiness, and great depth. Even this wine has developed in an amazing way and is now a world-class experience.

- 1986 CRISTAL   87, DEC 2001 (87)
(50% PN, 50% CH)
To be honest, this is a very weak Cristal. It reached full maturity at the early age of eight and will last just a couple more years. Buttery, sweet, and easy to drink, but without freshness or concentration.

- 1985 CRISTAL   93, JAN 2003 (95)
(60% PN, 40% CH)
This wine is now in a dormant phase where the nose is slightly less luxuriant than in its youth. The 79 went through the same rest period at a corresponding age, then went on later to bloom in full splendor. The 1985 Cristal is otherwise just as delicious as it sounds—an aristocratic Champagne with a wonderfully long aftertaste of crème caramel.

- 1983 CRISTAL   92, NOV 2002 (92)
(60% PN, 40% CH)
For a long time I was impressed by this Champagne—but, rather early on, it began a downhill journey. Bottles that have been stored in private cellars are often rather tired and dark in color. Even bottles that come from Roederer have seen better days, despite the color being light and the mousse irreproachably beautiful. The aftertaste has a desiccating bitterness and the fruit has diminished in intensity. Now the wine is dominated by a tone of raw mushrooms, undergrowth, hazelnut, and Autumn Fire—not too bad, actually, but the wine is no longer a classic Cristal.

- 1982 CRISTAL   94, JUL 2003 (94)
(55% PN, 45% CH)
One of this vintage's really top wines. Luxuriously scented and creamy rich. Slightly high dosage, but devastatingly good with its overflow of vanilla, almonds, honey, white chocolate, and citrus aromas. Drink it soon! The last bottle I had at Georges Blanc was a bit tired.

- 1981 CRISTAL   94, DEC 2001 (94)
(60% PN, 40% CH)
Cristal has few superiors in this vintage. A classic, with pure buttery Chardonnay and wonderfully mature chocolate Pinot. Incredibly nutty bouquet.

- 1979 CRISTAL   96, NOV 2001 (96)
(60% PN, 40% CH)
For a long time this wine was undeveloped and young. At the age of twenty-two years, however, all its bits and pieces are in the right places. The nose is wonderful, with its elegance and peachy intensity. Now there are also delicious notes of roasted lobster shell and black truffles. The taste is superb, with an incredibly rich, exotic fruitiness. The height of elegance.

- 1978 CRISTAL   93, MAY 2001 (93)
(60% PN, 40% CH)
Perhaps a little thinner than usual, but it contains the entire range of aromas. The lovely nose includes elements of lilies, apricot, and nut chocolate.

- 1977 CRISTAL   93, JAN 1999 (93)
(60% PN, 40% CH)
Definitely the best wine of the vintage. Charming and refreshing, but with an elegant yet somewhat short aftertaste.

- 1976 CRISTAL   96, MAY 2001 (96)
(60% PN, 40% CH)

One of the most perfect Cristals I've ever experienced. It sums up everything the firm stands for in such a magically concentrated and buttery drink. The fruit is incredibly rich and the freshness is outstanding. This wine is wonderful and easily understood.

- 1975 CRISTAL   94, MAY 2001 (94)
(60% PN, 40% CH)
The '75 is impressive and intense, but it's a touch rough and has an exaggerated smoky character that stops it being a truly great Cristal. If asked to taste this blind, I'd probably say it was a '76 with its full, low-acidic, mature taste. The Pinot grapes are very dominant here.

- 1974 CRISTAL   91, JAN 1999 (91)
(60% PN, 40% CH)
Roederer never fails to make great wines, even in the most mediocre vintages. Creamy, nutty, and most delicious.

- 1973 CRISTAL   90, MAR 2003 (90)
(60% PN, 40% CH)
Owing to overproduction in the early 1970s, the '73 is a little lacking in concentration. The structure is relaxed and the unusually thin taste is dominated by an almond aroma.

- 1971 CRISTAL   97, OCT 2000 (97)
(60% PN, 40% CH)
Normally the '71s are super-elegant but slightly thin. Here the elegance is complete, but the body is well built and the richness of delicious nut-toffee and vanilla notes is effusive. A fantastic wine that is among the most voluptuous one can drink.

- 1970 CRISTAL   92, OCT 1999 (92)
(60% PN, 40% CH)
A quickly developed and typically aromatic Cristal. A bit smokier than normal, with a certain lack of finesse. Still one of the vintage's best Champagnes.

- 1969 CRISTAL   96, OCT 2002 (96)
(60% PN, 40% CH)
This is in fact more developed than the '66, which this wine otherwise so resembles. The color, mousse, and the explosive nose are perfect. The flavor is tremendously rich and fruity, with a luxurious, fat finish.

- 1967 CRISTAL   93, AUG 1999 (93)
(60% PN, 40% CH)
Incredibly good with all the classic Cristal aromas; the only weak point is an aftertaste that is too short and flat to reach the normal level. Definitely the best wine of the vintage.

- 1966 CRISTAL   97, OCT 2000 (97)
(60% PN, 40% CH)
It's hard to conceive of a wine being more enjoyable than this one. The fruit is incredibly dense and the style is unimpeachable. A classic Champagne that has everything and more. A little lighter and more elegant than the awesome '59.

- 1964 CRISTAL   98, JUN 1999 (98)
(60% PN, 40% CH)
There's something magical about Cristal. Every vintage from the 1960s is wonderful and stylish. I wonder if the '64 isn't the best of them all. Here we find all the usual points: the sweet toffee tone, the creaminess, and the amazing balanced fruit. The seductive flow is supported this time by a La Tâche-like Pinot depth, which is unmatched anywhere else.

- 1962 CRISTAL   97, MAR 2004 (97)
(60% PN, 40% CH)

To think that the year of my birth could produce such fantastic wines! A magnum with panache—the most delightful aromas, structure, and intellectual charm belong to a perfect world. So much sweet fruit, mint notes, and a silky feeling in the mouth—magnificent!

- 1959 CRISTAL   98, OCT 2000 (98)
(60% PN, 40% CH)
Majestic and irresistible. As usual Cristal manages to charm both the expert and the novice with its beautiful, exotic sweetness and creamy toffee flavor. This wine doesn't show us anything new or unexpected, but quite simply offers more of all the good things we find in these wines. Let me know if you find a wine that gives you more pleasure!

- 1955 CRISTAL   99, MAR 2002 (99)
(55% PN, 45% CH)
During an incomparable evening at the restaurant Pontus in the Green House, we succeeded in picking out three basically perfect Champagnes in different styles. A beautifully floral and acidly austere 1961 Salon was the first on the stage, before a Latour-like 1914 Bollinger blew away any memory of the Salon bottle. Last but not least was this perfect charmer. Simply the most perfect, caramel-sated *cuvée*.

- 1953 CRISTAL   94, DEC 2001 (94)
(60% PN, 40% CH)
A monumental wine that has been even better. If Roederer have any bottles left in their cellar then they're probably as close to perfection as you can get. The only two examples I've tasted had a faint Madeira tone but still reached ninety-four points.

- 1949 CRISTAL   98, OCT 2000 (98)
(60% PN, 40% CH)
Wonderfully good! This is both one of my favorite Champagnes and one of my favorite vintages. Naturally the result is bound to be brilliant if you, like me, manage to find a well-kept bottle. The epitome of elegance!

- 1995 CRISTAL ROSÉ   94, JUN 2003 (97)
(70% PN, 30% CH)
An incomparably beautiful Champagne of brilliant attributes—the wine literally radiates aristocratic elegance and seductive charm. The color borders on white Champagne and the nose has the same unsurpassed complexity as earlier vintages of this magnificent creation.

- 1990 CRISTAL ROSÉ   94, MAY 2003 (97)
(70% PN, 30% CH)
Cristal Rosé '90 can't be anything but wonderful. This is a very young and as-yet discreet Champagne with a peerless balance and finesse. The '89 will be preferable a few years hence, but the time will come when the '90 might pass it by.

- 1989 CRISTAL ROSÉ   95, DEC 2003 (97)
(70% PN, 30% CH)
Somewhat less elegant than the '88, but with a sparklingly colorful knockout fruit and generous softness. Without doubt one of this vintage's absolutely foremost Champagnes.

- 1988 CRISTAL ROSÉ   97, NOV 2003 (98)
(70% PN, 30% CH)
Potentially the best rosé I've tasted. There is a finesse and crystal-clear elegance that makes me happy. This rosé reminds me very much of the white '89, with its perfect balance, crackling acidity, and irresistible aromatic purity. A wonderful gift from the Royal Ballet's premier dancer, Brendan Collins.

Best "Party Champagne" ever produced, according to the Millennium Tasting.

- 1985 CRISTAL ROSÉ   94, JUN 1999 (96)
(70% PN, 30% CH)

What a wine! The price may well be considered ludicrous, but the elegance is inimitable, and after a few years in the cellar the honey and toffee tones will break out in full bloom. Undeniably one of the very best rosé Champagnes available.

- 1983 CRISTAL ROSÉ   90, JAN 1997 (94)
(70% PN, 30% CH)

A light and young creation with a classic Cristal flavor. However, I should note that the rosé of this vintage is both drier and more acidic than its white cousin. The long aftertaste is superb, with sackfuls of Granny Smith aromas.

- 1982 CRISTAL ROSÉ   97, JAN 2003 (97)
(70% PN, 30% CH)

Magnificent as always. Powerful and rich with a distinctive tone of toffee in both fragrance and taste. A sparklingly colorful firework display of the exquisitely fruity aromas mixed with elegant notes of mineral. Excellent!

- 1981 CRISTAL ROSÉ   95, MAR 2002 (95)
(70% PN, 30% CH)

Cristal Rosé is one of the Champagne world's gems. The '81 has a very light color and behaves more as if it were a white Champagne than a rosé. Only a very faint strawberry tone distinguishes it from its white sibling. An entrancing bouquet of honey, hazelnuts, and milk chocolate. Fantastically balanced and well oiled, with an aftertaste of white Toblerone.

- 1976 CRISTAL ROSÉ   97, DEC 2002 (97)
(60% PN, 40% CH)

As brilliant as one could expect. Hardly a hint of red—more like a slightly aged, orange tone. Super-elegant, crystal-clear nose of honey and tart, dried fruits. Fat, magnificent, sweet, and concentrated essence with beautiful underlying freshness. Yet another milestone in the Champagne world.

- 1990 CRISTAL "2000"   94, JAN 2001 (97)
(49% PN, 51% CH)

They only produced 2,000 of these much-lauded and frightfully expensive Methuselahs for the millennium. I am very grateful that an anonymous friend of mine thought that I should taste this treasure together with him and a few close friends. There is no doubt about it: this wine rises above the usual Cristal from 1990. The wine, strangely enough, is more developed and accessible, despite the size of the bottle. I believe this is because the grapes used for these giant bottles were even sweeter and more mature, from old vines. The bouquet is very smoky with a—for the time being—marked dominance of Aÿ. The palate resembles the smoothest essence of Chardonnay that it is possible to create. A world-class wine that few have the privilege of tasting, and even fewer will have the privilege of drinking completely evolved in ten to twenty years.

ROEDERER, THÉOPHILE N-M

20, rue Andrieux
51100 Reims
03 26 40 19 00
Production: 150,000

This house was founded on March 22, 1864, by Léon Bousiques and Théophile Roederer in Reims. The house was bought up by the older brother, Louis Roederer, as early as 1907. Having no vineyards of its own, the house buys in all its grapes from different cooperatives in the surrounding area. The wines are made and stored separately from Louis Roederer, but the winemaking team is the same, so don't be surprised if you find certain similarities with the well-known giant on Boulevard Lundy.

- THÉOPHILE ROEDERER BRUT   60
(46% PN, 20% PM, 34% CH)
- 1997 THÉOPHILE ROEDERER   68, SEP 2003 (69)
(66% PN, 34% CH)

ROUALT-CROCHET R-M

51530 Dizy

This firm no longer exists, and I have failed to find anyone in Dizy with this name who could help me discover any more about it.

- 1966 ROUALT-CROCHET   84, OCT 2003 (84)
(70% PN, 15% PM, 15% CH)

A wine that invited much discussion during a tasting in Gothenburg. Sweet ketchup, pickled relish, and simple lemon-juice concentrate were all extremely distinct associations when someone opened our eyes to them. White Rhône wine, violets, and gingerbread dough were notes that I found first. Extremely lively, strange, and idiosyncratic—I don't really know what to think. A fun wine, in any case.

- 1956 ROUALT-CROCHET   83, APR 2003 (83)
(70% PN, 15% PM, 15% CH)

This strange grower's wine from Dizy went through a metamorphosis in the glass. After an hour the harmony and the butterscotchy complexity had appeared. Initially this strongly effervescent liquid both tasted and smelled like a dusty sofa!

ROUSSEAUX, GILLES R-M

15, place Chanzy
51360 Verzenay
03 26 49 40 78
Production: 40,000

Considerably better than the slightly more famous Jacques Rousseaux from the same village.

- G. ROUSSEAUX GRANDE RÉSERVE   76
(90% PN, 10% CH)

ROUSSEAUX, JACQUES R-M

17, rue Mailly
51360 Verzenay
03 26 49 81 81
Production: 35,000

This grower's wines are not as good as those produced by his neighbor Gilles from his dark Pinot Noir grapes.

- J. ROUSSEAUX RÉSERVE   55
(70% PN, 30% CH)
- J. ROUSSEAUX ROSÉ   59
(90% PN, 10% CH)

RUFFIN, YVES ET FILS R-M

6, boulevard Jules Ferry
51160 Avenay Val d'Or
03 26 52 32 49
One of Avenay's more famous growers.
• YVES RUFFIN BRUT

RUINART **** N-M

4, rue des Crayères
51100 Reims
03 26 77 51 51
Production: 2,000,000
Dom Thierry Ruinart, a priest from Reims who was a good friend
of Dom Pérignon, passed on enough knowledge to his nephew,
Nicolas Ruinart, to enable him to form the first Champagne house
in 1729. It is therefore quite logical that Ruinart should belong to
the Moët-Hennessy Group. The company soon became successful
in widely different export markets, and was a popular place to visit
due to its deep, exceptionally beautiful chalk cellars, which are now
classified as a historical monument. Deep down in these cellars
several of Sweden's best wine sommeliers have competed in the
Trophée Ruinart. The company president holds over fifteen hectares
in Sillery and Brimont, which provide only 20 percent of their
grape needs. The other 80 percent is bought in from 200 villages.
Ruinart's wines often have a strong toasty character, combined with
fine purity and good richness of minerals. The prestige wine Dom
Ruinart is absolutely of the highest class with a very elegant style.
The '79 is the world's second-best Blanc de Blancs, according to the
jury of the Millennium Tasting. Even Dom Ruinart Rosé can be
brilliant with its typical Pinot character, which is present despite the
wine containing 80 percent Chardonnay. The toasted, slightly
Charles Heidsieck-like and Dom Pérignon-like Champagnes are
today made by Jean Philippe Moulin.

• "R" DE RUINART   74
(48% PN, 5% PM, 47% CH)

• RUINART BLANC DE BLANCS   81
(100% CH)
The wine is very young, but at the same time made in a rather
sweet, soft, and exotically rounded personal style. The nose has
young notes similar to Riesling and Sauvignon Blanc, and the
taste borders on acacia, pineapple, and banana. A fun wine made
from *premier cru* grapes. Unfortunately, there is a weak, intrusive
suggestion of filtration—but I seem to be the only one who
senses it.

• RUINART ROSÉ   51
(40% PN, 10% PM, 50% CH)

• 1996 RUINART   89, JAN 2004 (93)
(51% PN, 49% CH)
A handsome, typical Ruinart style appears with clarity. Already
toasted and impressive, with good length and superb acidity.
Probably the most striking vintage that has been made by
Ruinart! Oh, there are so many wonderful '96s you can buy now!

• 1995 RUINART   87, NOV 2003 (88)
(58% PN, 42% CH)
Promisingly fine-tuned and tart Champagne, with an underlying
smokiness and good length. The wine probably needs a few years
in the cellar before the mellowness and toasted notes will appear.
The dosage feels more apparent than usual.

• 1992 RUINART   83, MAR 1999 (85)
(58% PN, 42% CH)
Rich, bready, house-typical taste with a somewhat green finish. A
caramel tone in the middle register indicates a higher dosage than
normal. A well-made and charming Champagne.

• 1990 RUINART   87, DEC 2000 (90)
(59% PN, 41% CH)
As so often, a fine toasty tone in the nose, but here it's backed up
by a clear, deep Pinot aroma. The flavor is quite full, with a Moët
& Chandon-like keynote. The reliability of this vintage is
confirmed once again.

• 1988 RUINART   84, OCT 2003 (84)
(50% PN, 50% CH)
Like the '88 Moët with its developed mushroom paste and citrus
style. Mighty, Pinot Meunier-inspired nose, but the taste isn't so
good, unclear and earthy as it is.

• 1985 RUINART   73, APR 1993 (84)
(50% PN, 50% CH)
Steely hard style all the way through; maybe some good
developmental possibilities.

• 1982 RUINART   74, APR 1993 (83)
(50% PN, 50% CH)
Once again steely, appley, and hard. Probably quite different now.

• 1981 RUINART   82, NOV 1995 (82)
(50% PN, 50% CH)
A quite powerful '81, full of depth and flavor. Bready and
chocolaty keynotes.

• 1966 RUINART   80, OCT 2002 (80)
(70% PN, 30% CH)
Fine color and good mousse. The wine has managed to escape
exaggerated oxidation, but feels too flat and thin to be a '66.
Have Ruinart made any big vintage Champagnes that hold up
over time? I'm still looking.

• 1959 RUINART   65, APR 2000 (65)
(70% PN, 30% CH)

• 1955 RUINART
(70% PN, 30% CH)

• 1947 RUINART   87, MAR 1997 (87)
(70% PN, 30% CH)
Lively and light with a faint nose of tar and crème brûlée. Lots of
fruit at first, but it is quickly replaced by darker aromas of wood,
tar, and cigars. Dry finish.

• 1945 RUINART   90, APR 2000 (90)
(70% PN, 30% CH)
Finally a Ruinart that has aged beautifully. Weak mousse.
Marzipan, hyacinth, and caramel bouquet. Fine tartness; brisk
palate. Good fruit that makes one think of mandarins and
apricots. Sweet, butterscotchy finish.

• 1961 RUINART ROSÉ   78, JAN 2000 (78)
(80% PN, 20% CH)

• 1955 RUINART ROSÉ   70, FEB 1999 (70)
(100% PN)

• L'EXCLUSIVE RUINART   87, JAN 1999 (94)
(100% CH)
Here I am making an exception to my rule about not giving out
potential points to nonvintage Champagnes. I am doing this
partly because this Champagne will only exist in a single
edition, and partly because the wine so obviously requires

storage. This millennium-magnum's appearance and presentation is to say the least spectacular. Those who drank this very expensive bubbly on that magical New Year's Eve were probably disappointed by its youthful and undeveloped taste. The concept was that several vintages of Dom Ruinart would be blended together to create a super-*cuvée*.

The wines included were: 10 percent 1985, 10 percent 1986, 15 percent 1988, 40 percent 1990, and 25 percent 1993. Tasted side by side with '88 and '90 Dom Ruinart it seemed bound and unready. The elegance and clarity are, however, unmistakable.

- 1993 DOM RUINART   90, OCT 2003 (92) (100% CH)

Light, pure as a mountain stream, fine-limbed, chalky Champagne with interesting nuances that lend the kind of elegance one can only find in a French wine. The lightest edition I've tasted of this prestige Champagne. Improves both in complexity and concentration with storage, something unique for fine Champagne. Sixty-five percent of the grapes come from Côte des Blancs and 35 percent from Montagne de Reims.

- 1990 DOM RUINART   92, MAR 2003 (94) (100% CH)

It is always difficult to confidently predict the future development potential of a newly evolved Champagne. So far this has none of the seductive roasted aromas of the '88, but it has instead an exemplary cleanness and a bitingly fresh and sweet taste of exotic fruit. Gorgeous nose of nut toffee develops when the wine is left out for a while.

- 1988 DOM RUINART   95, MAR 2004 (96) (100% CH)

Already surprisingly developed and generous, with a massive tropical richness of mango and oranges. There is also a delightful attack and sophisticated, multifaceted, long aftertaste to follow into the twenty-first century. A superb Dom Ruinart! Of course, very toasted, in the same style as Dom Pérignon, but as a Blanc de Blancs. Certain bottles are surprisingly undeveloped.

- 1986 DOM RUINART   84, SEP 1998 (89) (100% CH)

Weak currant tones backed up by roasted chestnuts and a discreet element of acacia honey. The flavor is still very young and aggressive, but the attack is promising. An unusually storable '86 that shouldn't be consumed before the year 2005.

- 1985 DOM RUINART   80, NOV 1992 (86) (100% CH)

Here we have the remarkable tone of blackcurrants easily discernible in the nose. Several professional wine tasters thought this was a Sauvignon Blanc at a large SAS tasting in 1992. However, I recognized the style from earlier Dom Ruinarts. Even though the blackcurrant character was a bit too dominant, this is a tasty wine that might surprise in the future.

- 1983 DOM RUINART   90, JAN 1994 (92) (100% CH)

Gorgeous green/yellow color and a prolonged, fast mousse. Broad, smoky, enormously toasty nose that is exquisite, although slightly over-dimensioned. The mature, currant-like fruit is noticed first in the soft aftertaste.

- 1982 DOM RUINART   94, DEC 2002 (94) (100% CH)

Incredible how beautiful and classic this once so coarse and unbalanced wine has become. Oily and sublime, with vintage-typical maturity and well-balanced freshness. Similar today to the wonderful '79.

- 1981 DOM RUINART   92, NOV 1999 (93) (100% CH)

Supremely delicious, discreetly toasted, and beautifully flowery—like the Cuvée Baccarat of the same vintage. The mousse is exemplary; the color is gloriously brilliant and sparklingly emerald. The wine is lighter than usual, which allows room for a greater elegance than other vintages have. The fruit is dominated by white currant and raspberry.

- 1979 DOM RUINART   97, FEB 2004 (97) (100% CH)

This gorgeous vintage seldom disappoints. Ruinart's '79 is very personal, with its classic toasted keynote. The nose is outstandingly floral, with an exceedingly fine-tuned spectrum of nature's most beautiful nuances. The fruit is aromatically very similar to fresh beef tomatoes and redcurrants. The acidity is lovely and the length grandiose. The best Dom Ruinart that I've tasted, and the second-best Blanc de Blancs ever made in the world, according to the jury at the Millennium Tasting.

- 1978 DOM RUINART   92, SEP 2001 (92) (100% CH)

A great, overpowered wine with a unique nose of overripe oranges and yeast. Massive round flavor of ripe fruit, low acidity.

- 1976 DOM RUINART   90, DEC 1996 (90) (100% CH)

Extremely green color. A touch miserly on the nose, but a concentrated, exotic fruit flavor with a soft, fine aftertone.

- 1975 DOM RUINART   70, AUG 1989 (70) (100% CH)

- 1973 DOM RUINART   94, APR 2001 (94) (100% CH)

Fresh looks and a complex bouquet where almond, brioche, and spices dominate. Medium-bodied, fresh taste, with perfect balance and generous citrus fruit. Supple aftertaste. On the whole a very drinkable Champagne for all tastes.

- 1971 DOM RUINART   95, SEP 2003 (95) (100% CH)

This is great stuff! A bold bouquet of toasted bread and overripe lemons. A full, intense flavor with the same aromas. Delightfully elegant and flowery; seductive and with acacia notes in certain bottles.

- 1969 DOM RUINART   93, MAY 2000 (93) (100% CH)

Ochre yellow nuances in a basic lime-green color. Extremely active and youthful. A decadent, cold nose of sea, oyster shell, and rubber. On the palate the impressions are more classical and tasting of lime. Fleshy, fat, and long.

- 1966 DOM RUINART   95, JAN 2004 (95) (100% CH)

A languid essence with a fine mousse and delightfully sweet aromas. Vanilla, treacle, licorice, and butter toffee are easy to identify. A true duck-liver wine for those of us who love Chardonnay when it has matured. Dom Ruinart is almost always a genuine winner.

- 1964 DOM RUINART   96, FEB 2001 (96)
(100% CH)
Almost glutinous in its fat, concentrated form. Slightly reminiscent of a '76 Des Princes with its broad, minty, and butter-caramel tasting charm. Sweet citrus, vanilla, and pastry-like flavors caress the palate. Extremely voluptuous, luxurious Champagne in very good condition.

- 1961 DOM RUINART   93, JAN 2003 (93)
(100% CH)
Still very fresh, with lovely active acidity. The nose suggests leather, vanilla, and clean sheets. The flavor is slightly short but very refreshing and sophisticated, lemony-fresh.

- 1955 RUINART BARON PHILIPPE DE ROTHSCHILD   90, JAN 1999 (90)
(50% PN, 50% CH)
The old baron always wanted to drink his own Champagne before continuing on to his great wines from Bordeaux. The Champagne houses understand that it is a great honor to be allowed to produce the baron's Champagnes. Up until the beginning of the 1980s, Henriot made the Champagne that carried Baron Rothschild's name. In the 1940s and 1950s the task had obviously fallen to Ruinart. Chocolate-sated bouquet, delicate color, fine mousse, dry, exquisite initial taste and an aged, medium-bodied finish.

- 1949 RUINART BARON PHILIPPE DE ROTHSCHILD
(50% PN, 50% CH)

- 1945 RUINART BARON PHILIPPE DE ROTHSCHILD
(50% PN, 50% CH)

- 1943 RUINART BARON PHILIPPE DE ROTHSCHILD
(50% PN, 50% CH)

- 1990 DOM RUINART ROSÉ   94, AUG 2003 (95)
(15% PN, 85% CH)
They've gone and done it again! Just as good as the '88, which was the best rosé Champagne Ruinart had ever made when it was launched. Fantastic, Burgundy-inspired nose. White or red, one then wonders? Well, actually a bit of both. Here you'll find the wonderfully erotic, moldering and truffle-like aromas that are present in red wines from Vosne-Romanée, and at the same time the buttery, roasted-coffee aromas that make you think of oaky Puligny-Montrachet.

- 1988 DOM RUINART ROSÉ   94, JAN 2004 (94)
(15% PN, 85% CH)
A sensational super-wine! Probably also the best Dom Ruinart Rosé to be made so far. The Champagne is gorgeously scented, reminding one of a Dom Pérignon Rosé. Beautiful pale orange, mature, flashing color. Deliciously soft-scent spectrum, with sun-ripened, packed fruit and coffee notes in the best Burgundy style. Soft, harmonious, and caressingly tingly in the mouth. Sophisticated big-house style. The red wine comes from Verzy and Verzenay. Completely evolved—actually, there's a bit of a hurry to drink it up.

- 1986 DOM RUINART ROSÉ   91, NOV 2002 (91)
(20% PN, 80% CH)
The color has elements of orange. The nose is pleasant, with notes of maturity and an indefinable berry note—that's why it's surprising that for such a long time the taste was so young: rich in minerals and austere acidity. Today it is a fully mature wine, with a big nose of sensual red Burgundy.

- 1985 DOM RUINART ROSÉ   80, NOV 1993 (84)
(10% PN, 90% CH)
Fine salmon color, aggressive mousse, vinous style with tones of tobacco and leather. Powerful taste of bitter chocolate and tobacco, but a touch short for it to be completely satisfying.

- 1982 DOM RUINART ROSÉ   75, MAY 1998 (78)
(20% PN, 80% CH)

- 1981 DOM RUINART ROSÉ   86, NOV 1998 (89)
(20% PN, 80% CH)
A certain development potential remains. Clean, delicate, bready, with a touch of Burgundy-like personality. A bit on the light side.

- 1979 DOM RUINART ROSÉ   89, APR 2001 (89)
(20% PN, 80% CH)
Deep orange color. Strong nose of bouillon, strawberries, and bread. Full and rich fruity flavor. An atypical '79—very reminiscent of the '76 but lacking its powerful fruity richness.

- 1978 DOM RUINART ROSÉ   93, SEP 1999 (93)
(20% PN, 80% CH)
An exceptionally fine '78 that is Pål Allan's favorite rosé. The nose is high-class and toasted, and the taste is long, fresh, and exceedingly exotic.

- 1976 DOM RUINART ROSÉ   93, NOV 2000 (93)
(20% PN, 80% CH)
Splendid! The nose is like a mature, top-class red Burgundy. The strong bouquet is followed by a sweet ice-cream-like round and mild raspberry flavor. Mature.

- 1971 DOM RUINART ROSÉ   90, OCT 2000 (90)
(20% PN, 80% CH)
Deep orange color; weak, slow mousse. Intense bouquet of Cognac, Cointreau, leather, and marmalade. Concentrated fullness in the palate, fluffy taste of cherry preserves. Can be used in place of dessert. The oxidative tones became intrusive after fifteen minutes in the glass.

- 1973 DOM RUINART ANNIVERSARY CUVÉE   94, FEB 1999 (94)
(100% CH)
Only 5,000 bottles were made of this exemplary Blanc de Blancs. It is entirely possible that this is exactly the same wine as the '73 Dom Ruinart, but the bottles of Anniversary that I have tasted have been extremely consistent in their style. The toasty aromas are downplayed to the advantage of the wonderful perfume of English butterscotch and lemon. Utterly elegant.

RUTAT, RENÉ R-M
27, avenue du Général du Gaulle
51130 Vertus
03 26 52 23 03
Production: 50,000
This six-hectare property was founded in 1965 by René Rutat and is run today by Michel Rutat.

- RUTAT BLANC DE BLANCS   70
(100% CH)

- 1990 RUTAT   78, FEB 1999 (82)
(100% CH)
Large open bouquet of saffron and red-colored fruits. The taste is full bodied and tolerably square, with a fat, slightly rustic flavor.

SACOTTE N-M

13, rue de la Verriere Magenta
15200 Épernay
03 26 55 31 90

This company was founded in 1887 by Léon Sacotte, the father-in-law of Gaston Burtin, who ran it until he started his own, highly successful Champagne house (Marne & Champagne). Sacotte make simple, low-price Champagne that is popular in England. Today owned by Vranken.

- SACOTTE CARTE RUBIS BRUT   39
  (30% PN, 40% PM, 30% CH)
- SACOTTE BLANC DE BLANCS   49
  (100% CH)
- 1976 SACOTTE   92, MAY 1999 (92)
  (100% CH)
  This grower in Avize was completely unknown to me until Claude, the inimitable cook at the restaurant in Le Mesnil, popped the cork on this wonderful, aromatically sweet '76. Vintage-typical like few others. Aromas of toffee, crème brûlée, smoke, candied fruit—all literally explode in the glass and mouth. Deliciously clean caramel finish.

SACY, LOUIS DE N-M

6, rue de Verzenay
51380 Verzy
03 26 97 91 13
Production: 240,000

When you arrive in the beautiful village of Verzy, the overall impression is somewhat marred by a block of concrete on a wall displaying the giant letters, SACY. The contrast between the ancient Faux de Verzy and this modern complex is pronounced, to say the least. Sacy is a fast-growing house that owns twenty hectares of land in five highly ranked villages. Only a small amount of Chardonnay is bought in to satisfy the company's grape needs. The Sacy family has a background in wine going back as far as the seventeenth century, but only received house status in 1968. Today the firm goes in for constant new investment, which has yet to show results in the quality of the product.

- LOUIS DE SACY TRADITION   52
  (70% PN, 10% PM, 20% CH)
- LOUIS DE SACY GRAND CRU   78
  (70% PN, 10% PM, 20% CH)
- LOUIS DE SACY ROSÉ   67
  (90% PN, 10% PM)
- 1989 LOUIS DE SACY   65, SEP 2003 (65)
  (30% PN, 30% PM, 40% CH)
- 1983 LOUIS DE SACY   70, MAY 1994 (>)
  (30% PN, 30% PM, 40% CH)
- 1996 GRAND SOIR   83, MAR 2004 (84)
  (50% PN, 10% PM, 40% CH)
  The wine has fermented in old barrels and taken on a strongly oxidative character. Lots of fruit and acidity, yet I'm still doubtful if this wine will hold up satisfactorily. The company's wines have a tendency to oxidize quickly.

SAINT CHAMANT R-M

31, rue des Bergers
51530 Chouilly
03 26 55 40 67

I have not succeeded in finding any young wines from this grower, who has been impossible to reach during my work on this book.

- 1961 SAINT CHAMANT   80, JUL 2001 (80)
  (100% CH)
  An exceedingly powerful wine that needs several people to share the bottle, and one that must be accompanied by a hefty serving of duck liver. I was terribly fond of this type of Champagne earlier in my career; today I have a little difficulty with this downright English taste. This Champagne has simply seen better days—it's become a dessert wine and has taken on a big, homogeneous, toffee-orange liqueur character. The mousse disappeared in a few seconds; but don't come and say that the wine tastes like sherry or Madeira, despite the fact that its looks tend to suggest it might do so.

SALMON, MICHEL R-M

21, rue Capit Chesnais
51170 Chaumuzy
03 26 61 81 38
Production: 60,000

Moulin Touchais, the famous château in the Loire Valley, has a case of Michel Salmon's Champagne in its cellar. I hope they haven't confused it with Billecart-Salmon!

- MICHEL SALMON BRUT SÉLECTION   55
  (100% PM)
- MICHEL SALMON PRESTIGE   58
  (100% PM)

SALON ***** N-M

5, rue de la Brèche d'Oger
51190 Le Mesnil-sur-Oger
03 26 57 51 65
Production: 50,000

Salon is the most sought-after Champagne among connoisseurs. This magnificent wine is so rare that only a few people have had the chance to taste the quintessence of Le Mesnil. In 1867 a perfectionist by the name of Aimé Salon was born. He grew up in Champagne and dreamed of creating the perfect Champagne at an early age. After a short period as a teacher he became a successful fur trader, which gave him the capital he needed to buy two small vineyards covering a total of one hectare in Le Mesnil. He made his first Champagne in 1911 and formed a Champagne house in 1914. As early as 1920, Salon became the house wine at the legendary Parisian restaurant, Maxim's.

Salon was the first commercial Blanc de Blancs, and a mono-*cru* besides. It's quite remarkable that the fame and praise heaped upon the firm has continued through the years, as the big names see Salon's philosophy as a direct antithesis of theirs. In principle Salon is a grower's Champagne, in the sense that the wine contains only one kind of grape from just one *cru*. Salon may well be the best "grower" of all, but the success of Selosse, Peters, Diebolt, and Charlemagne shows that they are all on the right course after all. When even the masters of the blend—Krug—made a mono-*cru* Champagne from Le Mesnil, it became harder for the major companies to sing the praises of blending in such a dogmatic fashion.

After Aimé died in 1943, the firm stayed within the family until 1963, when Besserat de Bellefon took over the show. In 1989 Salon was bought by Laurent-Perrier, and today the firm is run by the infinitely charming and pleasant Didier Depond, who once worked for Laurent-Perrier. Recently the oak barrels have been thrown out, but that hardly affects the flavor, as the Le Mesnil Chardonnay grapes take up the most nutty and toasty aromas you can imagine, without even having seen an oak cask. Salon's two plots in the village are always the ones where the leaves come out first, which shows that the microclimate there is exceptional. The average age of the vines is around fifty years old, and the other 75 percent of the grapes needed are chosen each year from the best growers in the village.

Salon demands longer storage than any other Champagne. The wines do not go through malolactic fermentation and have a razor-sharp acidity in their youth, which carries the wine to unparalleled heights through the years. A mature Salon expresses a gigantically broad aromatic spectrum, and has a Burgundy-like vinosity. The stringency is maintained throughout the wine's life, and as Salon has almost no dosage, the wine never becomes an exotic charmer like Taittinger Comtes de Champagne, but it is unmatched in terms of class and purity. Salon is only made in exceptionally good years, and in other years the grapes go to make up Delamotte. Since 1921 the following vintages have been produced: 1921, '25, '28, '34, '37, '43, '45, '46, '47, '48, '49, '51, '52, '53, '55, '59, '61, '64, '66, '69, '71, '73, '76, '79, '82, '83, '85, '88, '90, and 1995. Salon is without any doubt a five-star producer.

- 1995 SALON   92, NOV 2003 (95)
(100% CH)
Tasting these wines without dosage and newly disgorged, before they have come onto the market, is almost like being subjected to barrel sample. I might change my mind about this wine because it will most likely go through a metamorphosis in coming years. At the age of six and a half, this is a refreshing, mountain-stream-pure experience, with sharp apple acidity and bone-dry, almost stony mineral character. Such complexity takes many years to build up. Directly after adding the dosage the wine quickly became more accessible. At the end of 2003 this seems to be a creamy, elegant, and very charming Champagne in modern style. We'll have to wait a long time before the baby fat dries up and the nutty and autumn-scented complexity takes over.

- 1990 SALON   94, DEC 2003 (97)
(100% CH)
At the age of five the '90 still felt like a barrel sample! Clear as a bell and appley, with Chablis-like aromas and grandiose young fruit. Today it is decidedly more developed, but at the same time in a slightly boring phase, where the aromas of dried hay and malt dominate over the finesse and fruit.

- 1988 SALON   94, NOV 2003 (96)
(100% CH)
Without a doubt, this is the vintage's least developed Champagne. The nose hints at nut and chocolate, but the taste is mercilessly hard at the moment. A big wine in six to ten years'

time. Strangely enough, it seems that the wine is more mature and accessible in magnum.

- 1985 SALON   94, JAN 2003 (97)
(100% CH)
Some, including Salon itself, claim that the '85 is less developed than the '88. I claim the opposite, and question the decision to launch the vintages in reverse order. The phase the wine was in, just when the next vintage was about to be launched, was perhaps not terribly exciting, but already there was a range of mature tones in the form of licorice and a slight smokiness. At the start of the century's last year (1999) the peacock's tail had begun to unfold in all its glory. Having said that, it is a wine that I totally misjudged at the Millennium Tasting.

- 1983 SALON   93, DEC 2003 (93)
(100% CH)
The aromas are a touch clearer than in the '82. The nose is spicy and flowery with a sweet, honeyed depth. The flavor is creamy, with citrus aromas and a powerful aftertaste of walnuts and melted butter. Lately I've become worried about the development of this wine, as certain bottles are already showing signs of oxidation. Great bottle variation; hardly a wine to recommend.

- 1982 SALON   96, AUG 2003 (96)
(100% CH)
It took a few years before the '82 really found itself. Now it is wonderfully harmonious, if a little uneven from bottle to bottle. A classic Salon with brilliant acidity and an exceptionally dry aftertaste of lanolin and butter.

- 1979 SALON   96, JUN 2003 (96)
(100% CH)
Incredibly hard and closed for many years, before it opened up a classically walnut-scented depth at the age of fourteen. The flavor is still restrained, dry, and full of malic acid. The mineral-rich aftertaste is textbook stuff.

- 1976 SALON   96, MAR 2004 (96)
(100% CH)
A quite wonderful toasty Mesnil bouquet, with elements of coconut, coffee, and autumn leaves. Outstandingly rich—almost fat. Hardly one of the most elegant Champagnes to have come from this house, but it is one of the best wines of this vintage.

- 1973 SALON   88, FEB 1994 (>)
(100% CH)
A perfect level, color, and mousse, but somewhat overripe and with a hint of maderization. Rich fruit and nut aromas, although still a disappointment.

- 1971 SALON   93, DEC 2002 (93)
(100% CH)
Great bottle variation. Certain bottles contain cider-like apple tones and are on their way out. Others are very fresh but slightly thin.

- 1969 SALON   97, JUN 2003 (97)
(100% CH)
The photographer and illustrator on my first book, Pelle Bergentz, joined that project after having tasted this heavenly wine. The color was light, clear, and bright, and all the flowers of the garden were present in the almost narcotically seductive bouquet. The toasty tones were there already, albeit muffled. The

flavor is a fresh and life-enhancing experience. A well-balanced masterpiece from the very top drawer.

- 1966 SALON   96, JUN 2001 (97)
(100% CH)

Recently disgorged. Lighter than the '83 and insanely beautiful, with its intensively brilliant sparkling green color. Youthful, ultra-sophisticated, flinty, lightly toasted, and magnolia-scented. Surprisingly light and flighty Salon, with a fragile, delicate, and refined taste that in spite of its light-as-a-butterfly construction rings true and endlessly long on the palate.

- 1964 SALON   97, DEC 2000 (97)
(100% CH)

Not as sensual as the 1964 Comtes de Champagne, but just as good in a more restrained and younger style. Light, lime-green color and prolonged, minimal bubbles. A strict nose that needs airing for it to open up the inner depths of Salon's typical aromas. Exquisitely balanced with an intense attack and acidity. Salon in a nutshell!

- 1961 SALON   98, MAR 2002 (98)
(100% CH)

A magnum tasted in England that was exceedingly light and bound in the nose during the entire welcoming toast. This wine stood out as one of the least memorable from a dinner of grand wines selected from all over the world. After the dinner, our host went out to the kitchen and brought back the half-full magnum. By now it was the best of them all! In other words, it took this forty-three-year-old three hours to open up its refined taste spectrum of all the most sensual things one can think of. An ultra-elegant and relatively light vintage for Salon.

- 1959 SALON   97, JUN 1999 (98)
(100% CH)

As light as a Champagne from the 1980s. At first a very closed nose that wanted a quarter of an hour in the glass before it developed a momentous depth of autumn leaves, walnuts, chocolate, smoke, and jasmine aromas. The flavor softened with time, but was extremely concentrated and hard. The power is beaten only by the Bollinger Vieilles Vignes Françaises. Not the most charming Salon vintage, but one of the best I've tasted. The thought-provoking depth, combined with the wine's dazzling youth, make 1959 Salon one of the greatest wine experiences I have ever had. And it can develop even further!

- 1955 SALON   98, JUN 1999 (98)
(100% CH)

Somewhere between the '53 and '47 in terms of style. Superbly classical, toasty, and nutty, with a strong feel of woodlands. Acidic, amazingly long flavor with tones of walnut and lemon.

- 1953 SALON   98, OCT 1995 (98)
(100% CH)

This is an incredible and wonderful wine that has united youthful vigor and majestic maturity in an unsurpassable manner. The fresh nose is borne up by aromas that transport you straight into some deep, autumnal forest. The vinosity and mineral richness give the eternal flavor perfect balance.

- 1951 SALON   93, JAN 1999 (93)
(100% CH)

A distinctly odd vintage that I've only found at the restaurant, Le Vigneron. The freshness is almost laughable. The color is once again like a Champagne from the 1980s, and the nose is flowery

with faint nutty tones. The flavor is sensational, with all its acidity and youthfulness. Naturally it's not as rich in extracts as the classic vintages.

- 1949 SALON   97, NOV 1999 (97)
(100% CH)

The color reminds one of a middle-aged Sauternes. A fabulous caramelized scent that is quite typical of the vintage. Palate and tongue are subjected to a heavenly caress. The rich, exotic fruitiness initially hides the fact that the wine still has incredible acidity. There is a wonderful aroma of porcini mushrooms that runs straight through the experience.

- 1948 SALON   93, DEC 1999 (93)
(100% CH)

It is certainly very impressive that a wine can be so youthful and fresh after having passed the fifty-year mark. I still don't feel that the wine has enough extract and fruit to be considered one of the really big ones. *Terroir* character is present, along with a whip-cracking acidity; but the wine might benefit from a couple more years of storage after disgorging, and I believe that a dash of sugar wouldn't harm this razor-sharp wine.

- 1947 SALON   98, MAY 1997 (98)
(100% CH)

A legend that costs a fortune and is actually worth its price. The nose is remarkable, with tones of hay, caramel, walnut, cognac, and browned butter. However, clearest of all is a tone of crème brûlée. The flavor is tremendously full and rich, with an accelerating, smoky aftertaste.

- 1946 SALON   92, OCT 1998 (92)
(100% CH)

A somewhat light color, with a barely visible mousse. The scent resembles a marc de Champagne, with a rough tone of hay, plum, and raisin. Personal and interesting, but not very exciting. The taste is top class, thanks to its mouth-numbing acidity and characteristic Salon flavor. The wine was almost unchanged the next morning, which says it all about a Salon's length of life.

SAVÈS, CAMILLE **** R-M
4, rue de Condé
51150 Bouzy
03 26 57 00 33
Production: 60,000

Definitely one of the highlights of Bouzy. The Savès—father and son—are among Champagne's most passionate winemakers. The wines are stored in the cellar for at least five years and the yield is very low. Malolactic fermentation is avoided, the reserve wines are stored in small oak barrels, and only the *cuvée* is good enough for them. Their vines have an average age of twenty-five.

- C. SAVÈS BRUT   77
(75% PN, 25% CH)
- C. SAVÈS CUVÉE DE RÉSERVE   79
(40% PN, 60% CH)
- C. SAVÈS ROSÉ   76
(75% PN, 25% CH)
- 1996 C. SAVÈS   88, NOV 2003 (91)
(75% PN, 25% CH)

In this wine Savès introduces a really sweet, plump, fruit-bomb, with all the allure of excess and abundance. It would be difficult to guess the vintage at a blind tasting, because the wine is so soft and the acidity plays such a—to say the least—subordinate roll. Savès probably harvested later than their neighbors, and have consequently produced a super-rich, mature wine, full of juicy fruit.

- 1995 C. SAVÈS   85, JAN 2002 (88)
  (75% PN, 25% CH)
  A pure, beautiful champagne where freshness, elegance, and balance are honorable epithets—something that might seem strange considering its origin. Savès have, nevertheless, made a name for themselves in Bouzy as the epitome of elegance.
- 1994 C. SAVÈS   80, DEC 1998 (82)
  (75% PN, 25% CH)
  Very lively, soft, and refreshingly exotic and fruity. Hardly typical for Bouzy, though, with its invigorating taste of passion fruit.
- 1988 C. SAVÈS   89, SEP 1997 (92)
  (75% PN, 25% CH)
  Surprisingly light color and small bubbles for Pinot Noir. An expansive nose of hazelnut and cocoa, with a wave of marzipan and thick, dark fruit. The malic acidity supports the rich flavor and leads on to a classic finish.
- 1959 C. SAVÈS   94, APR 1995 (94)
  (80% PN, 20% CH)
  It was very exciting to taste two '59s from Bouzy on the same day. Paul Bara's example was a normally disgorged half bottle, and Savès's a recently disgorged full-size bottle. The difference was apparent, despite a better mousse and freshness in Savès's wine, I preferred the amazingly concentrated nectar from Paul Bara. Both had an alcohol level of 13 percent and a deep golden color. Savès's '59 had a nose of forest, fresh mushrooms, boiled vegetables, and smoked meat. The flavor was broad, with big, sweet plums and a deep aftertaste of Finnish tar pastilles. The wine resembles an old red Burgundy.

SCHMITTE, BERNARD *** R-M
12, ruelle des Jutées
51190 Le Mesnil-sur-Oger
03 26 57 54 14
Unfortunately, dear Bernard Schmitte no longer sells any vintage Champagne. If you find his eminent nonvintage Champagne from Le Mesnil, it will contain wine from 1996 or older. He has retired and hasn't really decided yet if anyone will take over after him, or if the big houses will get his grapes.

- B. SCHMITTE BLANC DE BLANCS   81
  (100% CH)
  A richly seductive wine, with a strong honey and caramel nose. The flavor is full of exotic fruits and almond aromas. The Champagne possesses a concentration that is a result of the old vines from which the grower harvests his grapes.

SECONDÉ PRÉVOTEAU R-M
51150 Ambonnay
This house has really frustrated me over the years. For many years I tried to arrange a visit to the property, but the names of the owners have changed, as has the address. Those Champagnes I have managed to locate have been very good. André Secondé's family has always sold grapes to Louis Roederer, and the Russian tsar's rosé Champagne was colored by still red wine from Secondé's great slopes in Ambonnay. The firm's Ambonnay rouge is one of the best in the region. The company owns twelve

hectares in Ambonnay, Bouzy, and Louvois, but for the moment they lie fallow. Other wines: Blanc de Blancs, Fleuron de France.

- PRINCESSES DE FRANCE   70
  (88% PN, 12% CH)
- PRINCESSES DE FRANCE ROSÉ   76
  (88% PN, 12% CH)

SECONDÉ, FRANÇOIS *** R-M
6, rue des Galipes
51500 Sillery
03 26 49 16 67
Production: 30,000
François Secondé is the uncrowned king of Sillery. From his four hectares he makes first-class wines with a wonderful *cru* character.

- FRANÇOIS SECONDÉ BRUT   73
  (80% PN, 20% CH)
- FRANÇOIS SECONDÉ INTEGRAL   79
  (80% PN, 20% CH)
- FRANÇOIS SECONDÉ DEMI-SEC   50
  (80% PN, 20% CH)
- FRANÇOIS SECONDÉ ROSÉ   81
  (80% PN, 20% CH)
  What a pleasant surprise! Personal and classic simultaneously. A deep, thought-provoking nose, with aromas of truffles, leather, blackberry, and caramel. A smooth, creamy, elegant flavor in which a tone of strawberry in the finish provides sensual satisfaction.
- 1997 FRANÇOIS SECONDÉ BLANC DE BLANCS   83, AUG 2003 (86)
  (100% CH)
  What juicy, dense, and delightfully personal Champagne! There's a difficult-to-describe, sunny taste of ripe, yellow fruit that I have occasionally found in Dom Ruinart—which in fact uses exactly the same Sillery Chardonnay grapes as Secondé. Luxuriant and almost oily, with a weighty, serious, vinous as well as soft finish. This is a wine that should definitely be tasted by those who want to recognize all the many faces of this district.
- 1995 FRANÇOIS SECONDÉ BLANC DE BLANCS   83, NOV 2000 (87)
  (100% CH)
  Obtrusive toasty nose that leans toward smoky. Heavy and oily with great richness and concentration. Nice, lucid expression of grapes and soil.
- 1992 FRANÇOIS SECONDÉ BLANC DE BLANCS   80, MAR 1996 (83)
  (100% CH)
  An exciting wine where the village character provides fullness and leather aromas and the grapes contribute with an exotic fruitiness.

SECONDÉ, JEAN-PIERRE R-M
14, rue Carnot
51500 Mailly
03 26 49 44 57
Production: 60,000
This grower has vineyards in Mailly, Sillery, and Verzenay. The vines average thirty years of age and the dosage is stored in oak barrels! The five *cuvées* are strongly influenced by Pinot Noir.

- JEAN-PIERRE SECONDÉ BRUT   78
  (80% PN, 20% CH)

SELOSSE, JACQUES ***** R-M

22, rue Ernest Vallé
51190 Avize
03 26 57 53 56
Production: 40,000

I've mentioned the name of Anselme Selosse on several occasions earlier in this book, partly because he's my favorite grower, and partly because he's the most original winemaker in all of Champagne. The charismatic Anselme is influenced by his time at the Lycée Viticole in Beaune, where he studied together with several famous winemakers from Burgundy. Anselme was determined to attempt to make a great Champagne using Burgundy methods. His father Jacques already owned some of the best strips of land in the Côte des Blancs, full of old vines, so Anselme did have some excellent basic materials to work with. Today Anselme owns four hectares in Avize, one in Oger, one in Cramant, and one in Aÿ. The land in Aÿ is right next to Bollinger's Côte aux Enfants; Anselme has made an oak-fermented Blanc de Noirs from these grapes. All of Selosse's thirty-five Chardonnay locations are vinified separately in small Burgundy barrels bought in from Domaine Leflaive in Puligny-Montrachet.

Anselme, the perfectionist, does almost everything himself. The old vines—average age thirty-eight years old—are pruned to the maximum in order to minimize the yield. The grapes are harvested later than most and are individually picked. After the pressing, the juice is tapped into 225-liter *barriques* (10 percent new barrels), where it stays for a year. Once a week Anselme lifts up the sediment with a steel rod in order to further enrich the wine, in a traditional Burgundy process called "*bâtonnage.*" Selosse categorically rejects malolactic fermentation, which means his rich wines have a bite that is unbeatable. The wines are then stored up to eight years in the bottle before being disgorged. Just as with Krug, all Selosse's well-kept wines need at least six months' bottle age after being disgorged in order for them to be accessible. The dosage is always very low, and only fruit sugar is used to maintain the wine's natural balance.

Selosse's wines have given Champagne a new dimension, with their unique, vinous, Chardonnay style. The forty-five year old from Avize has swiftly become Champagne's cult grower number one, after having been chosen as France's top winemaker in all categories by the magazine *Gault Millau* in 1994. Despite this fame, his wines cost nothing compared with Petrus, Romanée-Conti, or Krug Clos du Mesnil.

- J. SELOSSE EXTRA BRUT — 89
(100% CH)
My own house Champagne! Disgorged after five years in the cellar and without any dosage, this wine demands one more year in the bottle to round off that sharp malic acidity. Loads of peaches, mango, and nutty barrel tones. No one knows how good this wine can become, but between ten and fifteen years after disgorging should be a perfect period of storage. An exceptional nonvintage Champagne.

- J. SELOSSE TRADITION — 85
(100% CH)
Selosse's youngest Champagne needs a few months after being disgorged for it to develop those Selosse aromas that are so hard to describe. Undoubtedly a great Champagne which with time will both taste and smell of Brazil nuts.

- J. SELOSSE VERSION INITIALE — 83
(100% CH)
The same wine as Tradition with a new name. As refreshing as an Arctic sea breeze. Oaky and potent, with pear, apple, and oriental spice aromas.

- J. SELOSSE BRUT ORIGINALE — 87
(100% CH)
The same wine as Extra Brut with a new name. As yet, a little too young, but with an enormous integral power and fantastic acidity. Too oaky for some.

- J. SELOSSE VIEUX RÉSERVE — 83
(100% CH)
Old reserve wines from relatively unsuccessful vintages, according to Anselme. Mature, oxidative, soft style with a broad spectrum of tastes, from exotic fruit to mature cheeses.

- J. SELOSSE SUBSTANCE — 93
(100% CH)
A new name for the Solera wine from Selosse. First Origine, then Substance—why not just call it Solera? There is, of course, a certain difference, because the wine changes slightly from year to year, depending on the youngest and most recent vintage used as an addition. The wine is still somewhat oakier and younger, but has a very clean and pure tart base to stand on. It would be wonderful to have a tasting with all of the different Solera blends made by Amselme, ever since the '87 was poured into the steel tank in which all the wines are mixed.

- J. SELOSSE ORIGINE — 93
(100% CH)
A new invention from the genius of Avize. A wine made according to the Solera principle, where the oldest wine is from 1987. Fresh acidity is mixed with an oxidative character in a Krug-like way. The wine's beautiful nose of coconut and meringue is best appreciated when decanted.

- J. SELOSSE ROSÉ — 84
(10% PN, 90% CH)
Powerful and full in Selosse's unmistakable style. The Champagne has high acidity and wonderful length. The nose has a hint of strawberry aroma and spices.

- 1995 J. SELOSSE — 89, OCT 2003 (93)
(100% CH)
Anselme was kind enough to let me taste this wine almost two years after it had come on to the market, which perhaps doesn't do the wine justice. Newly disgorged and devoid of dosage, the wine was closed tight as a mussel for a long time before it slowly began to show its signature—that unmistakable and indescribable Selosse aroma. Otherwise the wine feels, paradoxically enough, rather soft and less powerful than earlier vintages. Only time will tell what this wine's real spirit looks like.

- 1993 J. SELOSSE — 89, MAR 2002 (93)
(100% CH)
In 1993 Selosse produced, of course, only a small number of bottles. Careful winemaking at all stages rewards the fantastic Anselme with one of this vintage's best Champagnes. The style is austere and youthful, without too strong an oaky barrel imprint. Fine mineral tone and an almost clinically clean pure bouquet. Acidic and multifaceted.

- 1992 J. SELOSSE — 90, OCT 2003 (92)
(100% CH)

Exaggeratedly oaky and heavy at first. If one has the patience to let the wine breathe in the glass—or, better still, decant it—a buttery, Cramant-like spectrum will shine. Soft and impressively rich. He's done it again!

- 1990 J. SELOSSE   95, FEB 2004 (96)
  (100% CH)
  One size smaller than Cuvée "N," but still a fantastic and classic Selosse. The development of maturity varies greatly in individual bottles right now. Wait a few years for the nutty tones and syrupy fatty fruit to come to the fore.

- 1989 J. SELOSSE   94, MAR 2003 (95)
  (100% CH)
  The Swedish State Wine Monopoly bought almost half the production of this wine. They got a very great wine that is still a little bound, but the richness of extract and acidity will keep it alive long into the twenty-first century.

- 1988 J. SELOSSE   96, NOV 2003 (96)
  (100% CH)
  Higher acidity than in the '89 and with a much less developed style. Stylish and rich in mineral, and recently absolutely fantastic with its idiosyncratic, lightly narcotic nose—just like the '86 had a few years ago. More beautiful nose but less concentrated than "N."

- 1986 J. SELOSSE   97, APR 2003 (97)
  (100% CH)
  The wine that gave Anselme the title of "Winemaker of the Year in France 1994." A majestic wine with outstanding personality. The nose is like a smorgasbord—it contains everything and is unlike anything else: sesame oil, oriental spices, and a particularly acidic fruity tone. The flavor is amazing, with a tropical wealth—and supported by the freshest attack I've ever felt in a Champagne. The fact is that Selosse succeeded in making a wine with 35 percent higher acidity than the '85 (eleven grams!). Need I add that the aftertaste is phenomenally long?

- 1985 J. SELOSSE   89, MAY 1995 (91)
  (100% CH)
  Selosse is one of the few producers to have made a better Champagne in 1986 than the previous year. This has caused the '85 to be neglected, but the nose is buttery and spicy, with Selosse's unmistakable exotic wealth and nut aromas. Slightly square and full-bodied taste with good length.

- 1983 J. SELOSSE   86, OCT 1992 (87)
  (100% CH)
  Plenty of the "Avize apple" and ripe pears in the nose. Woody, fat, full flavor with a rather rough finish where bananas and cinnamon leave their fingerprints. Not a great Selosse.

- 1982 J. SELOSSE   94, MAR 1993 (95)
  (100% CH)
  One of the greatest '82s. A very rich Blanc de Blancs that closely resembles Comtes de Champagne from the same vintage. The nose is like a fruit firework display, with butter and vanilla as added extras. The same exotic fruitiness meets the palate, and the aftertaste is bettered only by Krug this year.

- 1981 J. SELOSSE   87, DEC 1995 (87)
  (100% CH)
  Well-developed style with evident flavors of hazelnuts and vanilla. Probably even better today—like most '81s.

- 1979 J. SELOSSE   94, MAY 1994 (95)
  (100% CH)
  Basically somewhat lighter than the '82, but with deeper mature tones in the nose. Brioche and duck liver are hinted at, together with the creamy fruit. Long, delicate aftertaste of hazelnut.

- 1976 J. SELOSSE   70, MAY 1992 (>)
  (100% CH)

- 1975 J. SELOSSE   93, APR 1995 (93)
  (100% CH)
  The last year in which the good Jacques was the winemaker. I've never encountered such a scent of truffles in a wine before. Rich, autolytic flavor that resembles the 1975 Jacquesson D. T., which also comes from Avize.

- 1995 J. SELOSSE CONTRASTE   93, SEP 2002 (95)
  (100% PN)
  Pure Aÿ-Pinot, made the Selosse way, is a gorgeous recipe. If you can imagine a blend of Selosse "N" and Bollinger Vieilles Vignes, you would be close to the aromatic, structural reality of this wine. Dense and powerful, with honey-sated fruit and an oaky spiciness, as fitting for this wizard of a winemaker. It's very exciting to find leather, dried fruit, honey, sesame oil, and ruby grapefruit all in the same wine.

- 1990 J. SELOSSE "N"   94, JAN 2002 (97)
  (100% CH)
  A monstrous powerhouse with a high alcoholic content and Burgundy-like depth. It definitely needs maturing in order to round off the oakiness. Best without dosage. Selosse is almost impossible to miss at a blindfolded test. The nose has become very big and complex of late.

- 1989 J. SELOSSE "N"   96, FEB 2003 (97)
  (100% CH)
  Since 1988 Anselme separates out a tiny portion of his wine from his two best locations in Avize, which are planted with very old vines. In deference to the extreme concentration of the wine, Anselme uses 85 percent new oak barrels! Despite all that, the wine feels balanced. Naturally this Burgundy copy requires long storage, but it is already highly impressive, with its rich, velvet-smooth fruit and majestic aftertaste.

- 1988 J. SELOSSE "N"   96, NOV 2003 (97)
  (100% CH)
  A wine that seemed salty and a little straggling in its youth. Today the wine has gone through a complete metamorphosis: the concentration is equal to a Bollinger Vieilles Vignes and the taste is enormous. Selosse perfume is present but still needs a few years to reach full strength.

- 1987 J. SELOSSE ORIGINE   88, JUL 1997 (90)
  (100% CH)
  The first Champagne to be wholly vinified in new oak barrels—a practice that, as you know, many others have now adopted. After decanting, the oak was integrated and the wine became much like a white Burgundy. Broad aroma of peaches, wood, vanilla, and butterscotch.

SENEZ, CRISTIAN N-M

6, Grande Rue
10360 Fontette
03 25 29 60 62
Production: 350,000

Cristian Senez was a cheesemaker, lumberjack, and a gravedigger before he became a grower in 1955. This makes me think of the Monty Python TV show! After many years as a grower, Cristian Senez decided in 1985 to become a *négociant* (house) with a license to buy grapes. He sells his Champagnes under his own name and as Cuvée Angélique. The firm exports 30 percent of its product and uses modern vinification methods. Today Frédérick Roger owns thirty-two hectares.

- CUVÉE ANGÉLIQUE   44
  (52% PN, 48% CH)
- 1995 SENEZ GRANDE RÉSERVE   70, DEC 2002 (71)
  (60% PN, 10% PM, 30% CH)
- 1995 SENEZ MILLÉSIME   51, NOV 2002 (55)
  (30% PN, 70% CH)
- 1994 SENEZ GRANDE RÉSERVE   56, NOV 2002 (56)
  (60% PN, 10% PM, 30% CH)
- 1993 SENEZ GRANDE RÉSERVE   60, MAR 2004 (60)
  (60% PN, 10% PM, 30% CH)
- 1990 SENEZ GRANDE RÉSERVE   71, MAR 2004 (71)
  (75% PN, 25% CH)
- 1988 SENEZ MILLÉSIME   59, MAY 1995 (64)
  (30% PN, 70% CH)
- 1973 SENEZ MILLÉSIME   83, MAY 1995 (83)
  (50% PN, 50% CH)
  A very successful vintage for the company, and one that they still sell. A dark, developed color and a one-dimensional wine that does possess a lovely rich chocolate aroma in both nose and flavor.
- 1988 SENEZ ROSÉ   43, APR 1995 (43)
  (82% PN, 18% CH)
- 1985 SENEZ ROSÉ   68, OCT 2000 (68)
  (80% PN, 20% CH)

SEVERIN-DOUBLET R-M

10, rue des Falloises
51130 Vertus
03 26 52 10 57
Production: 50,000

The property in Vertus has one of the best names in Côte des Blancs, but the reputation comes chiefly from their vintage Champagnes, which aren't commercially available.

- SEVERIN-DOUBLET BLANC DE BLANCS   70
  (100% CH)

SIMON-SELOSSE R-M

20, rue d'Oger
51190 Avize
03 26 57 52 40
Production: 20,000

Jacques Selosse's sister runs this property across from the wine school in Avize. Given the fame of her relative, my expectations were high when I tasted their *cuvée de prestige*. In contrast to Jacques Selosse's wines, these are fermented in steel tanks and are put through malolactic fermentation.

- SIMON-SELOSSE EXTRA BRUT   60
  (100% CH)
- SIMON-SELOSSE BLANC DE BLANCS   60
  (100% CH)
- 1990 SIMON-SELOSSE CUVÉE PRESTIGE   70, APR 1995 (73)
  (100% CH)

SOUSA, DE **** R-M

12, place Léon-Bourgeoise
51190 Avize
03 26 57 53 29
Production: 55,000

This company was founded in 1986. Erick de Sousa owns six hectares in Avize, Cramant, and Oger, where the average age of the vines is thirty-five years old. Erick is very goal-oriented and has surely taken a peek at the success of Selosse, imitating them in many ways in terms of work in the vineyard and the process of vinification itself. Since 1995, oak barrels from Chablis have been used for all wines from the fifty-year-old stocks, of which 15 percent are new oak. The wines are never chaptalized and every plot is vinified separately. This company already has a very good reputation, despite having been on the Champagne scene for only a short time.

- DE SOUSA TRADITION   66
  (25% PN, 25% PM, 50% CH)
- DE SOUSA RÉSERVE   82
  (100% CH)
  Fine, nutty, concentrated nonvintage Champagne with good fleshiness and more than respectable length. Somewhat more mature than the blended nonvintage wine.
- DE SOUSA BLANC DE BLANCS   75
- DE SOUSA CUVÉE DES CAUDALIES   89
  (100% CH)
  Completely made in oak barrels and from vines that are more than fifty years old. Very fine Champagne with undertones similar to white Burgundy or Chablis. Good freshness and elegance with a handsome, mild oak note enveloped in a fine vanilla aroma. It just gets better and better each time I taste the wine—one of the absolutely best nonvintage Champagnes.
  (100% CH)
- 1999 DE SOUSA VIEILLES VIGNES   83, OCT 2003 (88)
  (100% CH)
  Actually, distinctly poorer than the grower's fantastic nonvintage Champagne. Unexpectedly tropical and atypical for the moment, with aromas of pineapple, grapefruit, and spices dominating this young wine. Given the raw material Sousa has access to, this wine will, of course, become much better in a few years.
- 1996 DE SOUSA VIEILLES VIGNES   84, APR 2003 (90)
  (100% CH)

This wine has not been through malolactic fermentation or filtration. De Sousa has sensibly peeked at his neighbor, Selosse, and made a wine completely vinified in oak barrels from vines that are all more than fifty years old. At the moment, the wine feels a little too hard and bound with an ignominiously short aftertaste—time and patience are needed.

- 1993 DE SOUSA   81, MAY 1998 (87)
  (100% CH)
  Clean with velvety fruit and a clear saffron tone. A good '93 for the cellar.
- 1993 DE SOUSA VIEILLES VIGNES   85, MAR 2003 (88)
  (100% CH)
  A lively wine with an elegant golden color containing hints of green. Fruity nose with fine elements of lilies and gardenia. There is also a luscious butteriness, both in the austere, mineral-laden taste and in the beautiful, refined bouquet.
- 1992 DE SOUSA   80, MAY 1998 (84)
  (100% CH)
  Shorter and thinner than the '93, but with clean, classic tones of Chardonnay.
- 1990 DE SOUSA   85, APR 1990 (91)
  (100% CH)
  Young, closed nose, but an open, oily, rich flavor of butter and strawberry.
- 1989 DE SOUSA   86, MAY 1998 (88)
  (100% CH)
  Creamy and buttery, but less explosive than usual. Somewhat short, though delightfully aromatic and soft.
- 1988 DE SOUSA   80, JUL 1995 (86)
  (100% CH)
  More developed but somewhat smaller dimensions than the '90.
- 1982 DE SOUSA   88, MAY 1998 (88)
  (100% CH)
  Exciting scent of roses and truffles. A developed, medium-bodied Champagne that is unfortunately somewhat short.
- 1981 DE SOUSA   88, MAY 1998 (88)
  (100% CH)
  Wonderful, complex scent. Somewhat mint-like and bare with an herbal finish.
- 1995 DE SOUSA CUVÉE 2000   91, MAY 2003 (93)
  (100% CH)
  Very much like the Selosse "N" in scent. It has spicy oak and a clear Avize character with a nutty base. The fruit is extremely concentrated and soft. With time the wine almost became like a beautifully barrel-fermented Chablis. Only 2,000 bottles were made of this wonderful Champagne.
- 1990 DE SOUSA CUVÉE 2000   83, NOV 1999 (91)
  (100% CH)
  A horribly ugly bottle containing a very potent wine. Because the wine lacks dosage and is newly disgorged, it is rather unattractive now. Store until at least 2005.

SOUTIRAN-PELLETIER N-M

12, rue St Vincent
51150 Ambonnay
03 26 57 07 87
Production: 105,000

Also known as Veuve Victorine Mongardien. Today Alain Soutiran makes the wines while his daughter Valérie runs the tiny house with steely determination. It is one of those companies that would rather be situated on the Côte des Blancs. They praise the Chardonnay grapes without having any great ability to grow them. If you want to get to know Soutiran's wines, go to their shop in the middle of the village, called La Palette de Baccus.

- ANGÉLINE GODEL BRUT   61
  (50% PN, 10% PM, 40% CH)
- SOUTIRAN-PELLETIER ROSÉ   48
  (15% PN, 85% CH)
- 1989 CUVÉE VICTORINE   70, JAN 1995 (76)
  (50% PN, 50% CH)
- 1985 CUVÉE VICTORINE   76, SEP 1994 (78)
  (50% PN, 50% CH)

STEPHANE & FILS R-M

1, place Berry
51480 Boursault
03 26 58 40 81
Production: 18,000

Founded in 1907 by Auguste Foin. Today, a very small property planted with old vines of all three grape types. Vines average fifty years old; these are probably the oldest I've encountered in Champagne. Vineyard size: 6.5 hectares. Michel Foin is the manager today.

- STEPHANE CARTE BLANCHE   55
  (50% PN, 50% PM)
- STEPHANE GRANDE RÉSERVE   63
  (50% PN, 50% PM)
- 1995 STEPHANE DIONYSOS   84, MAR 2002 (87)
  (33% PN, 33% PM, 34% CH)
  Prestige wine from vines that are more than fifty years of age. Elegant as well as concentrated and vinous. Refreshing and promising. The wine is reminiscent of Alfred Gratien, which is logical considering the grape composition. Resoundingly pure finish.

SUGOT-FENEUIL **** R-M

40, impasse de la Maire
51530 Cramant
03 26 57 53 54
Production: 100,000

This masterly grower in Cramant owns seven hectares in Bergères-les-Vertus, Chouilly, Oiry, and above all Cramant. Only Chardonnay grapes are used in the vintage wine. Robert Sugot is the fourth generation of winemakers in the family, and Sugot-Feneuil's Champagnes, so wonderfully typical of the village, are some of my absolute favorites. The Special Club is made from three excellent locations called Les Beurons, Biennes, and Mont-Aigu, with thirty-year-old vines. Sugot only produces 8,000 bottles of the Special Club, so it is a question of sharpening your elbows when a new vintage is released.

- SUGOT-FENEUIL CARTE PERLE   75
  (100% CH)
- SUGOT-FENEUIL BLANC DE BLANCS   82
  (100% CH)
- 1990 SUGOT-FENEUIL   88, NOV 2003 (88)
  (100% CH)
  More oxidative and slightly thinner than Special Club. Good,
  appley fruit and fine rustic taste.
- 1988 SUGOT-FENEUIL   88, NOV 2003 (88)
  (100% CH)
  Big bottle variation. Sometimes fairly oxidative with hints of
  windfall fruit and leather, other times fresher with good mineral
  and citrus character. Always an agreeable, creamy, medium
  palate.
- 1985 SUGOT-FENEUIL   92, JUN 1999 (94)
  (100% CH)
  The beautiful Chardonnay comes to life in this crisp and lively
  Champagne. Small, delicate bubbles dance on the palate, leaving
  refreshing flavors of lime and lemon. Refreshing with a
  wonderful expression of fruit.
- 1979 SUGOT-FENEUIL   94, APR 1995 (95)
  (100% CH)
  M. Sugot's favorite vintage, and it's easy to understand why. The
  wine has a young, greenish color and a euphoric nose of
  chocolate, nuts, coffee, lily of the valley, and white Toblerone. A
  nutty flavor with lovely depth for the aesthete and layers of fruit
  for the romantic.
- 1990 SUGOT-FENEUIL SPECIAL CLUB   92, JUL 2003 (93)
  (100% CH)
  Very much like Bonnaire's *cuvée de prestige*. Lots of rich, exotic
  fruit and saffron to add to the normal buttery characteristics.
- 1988 SUGOT-FENEUIL SPECIAL CLUB   93, NOV 2003 (93)
  (100% CH)
  One of the creamiest and most butter-toffee-scented
  Champagnes that can be found in Cramant today. Similar to a
  1982 Bonnaire in its richness. Certain bottles are too oxidized.
- 1987 SUGOT-FENEUIL SPECIAL CLUB   87, JUL 1997 (>)
  (100% CH)
  Already on its way downhill, but the wine still gives us sybarites a
  good excuse to enjoy ourselves.
- 1986 SUGOT-FENEUIL SPECIAL CLUB   88, SEP 1997 (88)
  (100% CH)
  A fast-matured wine that is a pleasure to enjoy today. Open nose
  of honey nectar and butterscotch, and a soft, creamy, focused
  flavor of peaches and fudge.
- 1985 SUGOT-FENEUIL SPECIAL CLUB   91, JAN 2003 (91)
  (100% CH)
  For several years an austere classic with a multifaceted floral nose
  and a slightly toasted, balanced taste with overtones of lemon.
  Today, a little too chocolaty and massively mature.
- 1983 SUGOT-FENEUIL SPECIAL CLUB   87, JAN 1996 (88)
  (100% CH)
  A bit shy and reserved, with crystal-clear acidity and fine aromas.
  Nice lemony finish.

TAITTINGER **** N-M
9, place St. Nicaise
51100 Reims
03 26 85 45 35
Production: 4,700,000

The house of Forneaux, as Taittinger's predecessor was called, was
among the first Champagne houses when founded in 1734. The
company's financial upturn came when the Taittinger family
bought it in 1936. Pierre Taittinger purchased a palace called La
Marquetterie and built up an impressive arsenal of vineyards.
Today's owner, Claude Taittinger, took over in 1960, and the
company now has 256 hectares in twenty-six villages, which
supply some 45 percent of its grape needs. Experiments with
small numbers of new oak barrels began in 1988 with the
prestige wine Comtes de Champagne; otherwise all the wines are
fermented in large steel tanks and put through malolactic
fermentation.

    The firm is well known for its efforts to support major
projects outside the local region. For example, the company owns
one hotel chain, two wine companies in the Loire Valley, and one
wine company in California. The artist-designed Collection
bottles have become a huge success in sales terms, in spite of the
exorbitant prices that will soon become even dearer. The
nonvintage Champagne was a touch uneven earlier, but it often
reflects the soft, flowery house-style well. The vintage wine is a
real charmer, which sadly lacks storage potential. The real star is
the Comtes de Champagne, an exemplary Blanc de Blancs from
Cramant, Avize, Oger, Le Mesnil, Chouilly, and old vines in
Pierry. The Champagne is the best in its style, with its soft, exotic,
and creamy taste. I imagine that the Comtes de Champagne is
the Champagne most appreciated by the broadest public. It
contains no difficult aromas, but instead an abundance of
charmingly sweet and soft tastes in an elegant and luxurious style.
In any case, it contains an aromatic spectrum that is exciting
enough for even the most fastidious expert to fall head over heels
for its beauty. Even Comtes de Champagne Rosé can be a treat if
you have patience. This Champagne—made by contact with
Pinot Noir grapeskins from Ambonnay and Bouzy—can appear
sweet and clumsy when young, but it usually develops magically.
Gentle Maurice Morlot is the man responsible for how these
wines taste and the wonderful Pierre-Emmanuel Taittinger is
responsible for the running of the company. Very close to five
stars!

- TAITTINGER BRUT   77
  (42% PN, 20% PM, 38% CH)
- TAITTINGER PRÉLUDE GRANDS CRUS   86
  (50% PN, 50% CH)
  Only *grand cru* from the first pressing. Grapes from Avize,
  Le Mesnil, Bouzy, and Ambonnay. Slightly bound in the nose
  with young, beautiful, withdrawn aromas. Subtle, very
  thirst-quenching taste in a fine, creamy, bubbling apparel,
  with aromas of peach, flowers, and passion fruit. Pure, fine,
  resounding note with several taste layers, vanilla being
  the most tangible.
- TAITTINGER PRESTIGE ROSÉ   62
  (70% PN, 30% CH)
- 1998 TAITTINGER   86, APR 2004 (90)
  (60% PN, 40% CH)

It feels a little too early to release fine vintage Champagne after just four and a half years. The wine is certainly charming and floral with creaminess and uplifting, elastic fruit—still, I would recommend waiting to buy the wine until you're sure you'll get a later disgorging and a richer, bready, autolytic character as well.

• 1996 TAITTINGER   89, SEP 2003 (92)
(60% PN, 40% CH)
I'd expected much more from this '96 initially. The problem is, the two bottles I managed to taste recently suffered from being newly disgorged and recently transported. I wouldn't be surprised if this vegetal, acid-rich wine suddenly changes. I have tried some since, and that's exactly what has happened—the creaminess has already presented itself. At the age of seven the Chardonnay shines the brightest and the nose has acquired a Dom Pérignon-like toasted shimmer.

• 1995 TAITTINGER   88, NOV 2003 (91)
(60% PN, 40% CH)
Relatively bound nose with an exciting underlying richness. Soft, relatively sweet flavor that fills the palate with enjoyable tingling. A classic Taittinger!

• 1992 TAITTINGER   85, SEP 2003 (85)
(60% PN, 40% CH)
Tasted alongside the Stevenson-praised Nyetimber from England, this wine seemed like a giant. Viewed from a Champagne perspective it is at best normal and house-typical. Fine, soft, melting mousse and creamy, slightly sweet fruit. Showing full maturity now.

• 1991 TAITTINGER   82, MAR 1999 (85)
(60% PN, 40% CH)
A soft, house-typical Champagne with a big dollop of happiness and charm. Aromas of vanilla and butterscotch.

• 1990 TAITTINGER   84, MAY 1997 (90)
(60% PN, 40% CH)
A faintly cheesy nose that is quickly blown away until it becomes a subdued but fruity and chocolate-laced bouquet. First and foremost it's the full flavor that impresses me. The '90 is packed with fruit and bold, biscuity layers. A perfect dosage and balance.

• 1988 TAITTINGER   83, APR 1994 (83)
(60% PN, 40% CH)
Taittinger's vintage Champagnes are made for early consumption and so rarely reach the heights of their most famous competitors. The '88 is good, sure, but does it have any more to give? Bushy, ingratiating, generous, sweet, and saffron-scented.

• 1986 TAITTINGER   88, APR 2000 (88)
(60% PN, 40% CH)
Completely mature, stately Champagne with fine soft mousse and a rounded, somewhat short taste. Fleshier than expected, with a rich aroma of windfall fruit and heavy Pinot Noir. A few points better as a magnum.

• 1985 TAITTINGER   90, SEP 2003 (90)
(60% PN, 40% CH)
Early developed and ingratiating, like most of the vintages of this wine. The delicate mousse forms beautiful pearl necklaces in the glass. The nose is broad and exotic, with vanilla and saffron leading the field. The taste is sensual with its fruit sweetness and long, chewy fullness.

• 1983 TAITTINGER   87, JAN 2003 (87)
(60% PN, 40% CH)

Almost identical to the Taittinger Collection, but much cheaper. Broad, Pinot-dominated nose; fleshy, impersonal, and completely mature.

• 1982 TAITTINGER   87, DEC 2001 (87)
(60% PN, 40% CH)
This wine caused me to doubt whether Collection and Millesimé are the same wine. The 1982 Collection has always impressed me, whereas this wine has had similar aromas without the grandiose structure of Collection. It was with relief and pride that I—the first journalist to be told—discovered that Collection was not the same wine as the usual vintage Champagne. Grape composition is the same, it is true, but the selection and the blending are more refined in Collection. Thanks for solving one of the most difficult mysteries in the world of Champagne.

• 1980 TAITTINGER   81, JUL 1991 (>)
(60% PN, 40% CH)
Bready, mushroom aromas without fruit in the bouquet. However, the taste is fine, with sweet, plum-like fruit. The wine is rich and tasty, but flabby and loosely hung.

• 1979 TAITTINGER   88, JAN 2002 (88)
(60% PN, 40% CH)
Like a lollipop with its immediately ingratiating, softly exotic fruitiness. Seductively delicious.

• 1976 TAITTINGER   92, FEB 1999 (92)
(60% PN, 40% CH)
I have often voiced my opinion that the vintage Champagnes from Taittinger do not age especially gracefully. It is, however, not surprising that the house's '76 will be good for several decades to come. The vintage's high alcohol content and abundance of rich extracts compensate for the relatively low acidity. The aroma bears a certain resemblance to the heavenly Comtes de Champagne from the same year, but has less elegance and a more noticeable chocolate aroma. The fruit is juicy and crisp at the same time. The aftertaste is buttery and long. The mousse is exemplary.

• 1971 TAITTINGER   90, NOV 2000 (90)
(60% PN, 40% CH)
Tired in a regular bottle; impressively nutty and deliciously mature in magnum. The house-style is well suited to this year's elegance.

• 1970 TAITTINGER
(60% PN, 40% CH)

• 1966 TAITTINGER   94, FEB 2003 (94)
(60% PN, 40% CH)
Utterly, brilliantly delicious and impressive! Deep tea-colored with fine small bubbles and a ravishingly butterscotchy nose. A well-balanced, soft, and still creamy palate that has great grace and vitality. A really big, wonderful old Taittinger that should be seen as the perfect representative of the house-style they are aiming for.

• 1964 TAITTINGER   94, NOV 2003 (94)
(60% PN, 40% CH)
Big, powerful Champagne with the dignity of old age. Dark notes of treacle, dark-roasted coffee, bitter chocolate, and wood. Powerful taste with the warmth and authority of this great vintage. A very rich, gorgeous Champagne with sweet, toffee-ish finish. Only tasted in magnum, it should be noted.

- 1961 TAITTINGER
(60% PN, 40% CH)

- 1959 TAITTINGER   94, JAN 2003 (94)
(60% PN, 40% CH)

A wine worthy of the vintage. A muscular structure that isn't disturbed in the least by the acidity's influence in the glass. The wall of tastes is as compact and impenetrable as a knight's castle; tons of chocolate and toffee have been draped around the strong frame. Very good and impressive, to say the least.

- 1961 TAITTINGER ROSÉ   94, MAY 1998 (94)
(100% PN)

Tasted at a blind test at the restaurant Le Vigneron. My guess was 1964 Taittinger Rosé, which shows that the style of the firm keeps constant. Like the '59 with the same Pinot-weight, but it has a delicious, rich fruit and an exemplary mousse. Probably the precursor to the Comtes Rosé with 100 percent Pinot Noir.

- 1959 TAITTINGER ROSÉ   84, JUL 1997 (>)
(100% PN)

I have to admit that the existence of this wine was a complete surprise to me until it turned up in a store in Paris. Probably a precursor to Comtes Rosé and made entirely from Pinot Noir. Still a very powerful wine with a deep color. Unfortunately, too affected by oxidation to completely shine.

- 1995 COMTES DE CHAMPAGNE   93, APR 2004 (96)
(100% CH)

Fantastically delicious and ultra-sophisticated. The balance has found its footing from the start. Floral, fruity, buttery, perfumed, honey-soft, refreshing, stony, elegant, crisp, toffee-drenched, nutty. It doesn't matter which positive adjectives one uses. All you seek shall be yours!

- 1994 COMTES DE CHAMPAGNE   89, APR 2003 (92)
(100% CH)

Cradle-snatching! Crystal-clear and citrus-fresh with a chalky, Chablis-like style. Fantastically intense and at the same time smooth mousse. Only available as a magnum.

- 1993 COMTES DE CHAMPAGNE   90, JAN 2003 (93)
(100% CH)

It's a great pity that the foremost '93s have been forced out so early because of the millennium. Never before have I tasted such an ascetic, bound Comtes de Champagne. For a long time the nose was exceedingly weak and youthful, with elements of grass and flint. The taste was keenly fresh and dry, with Chablis-like aromas of lime and mineral. As if by a stroke of magic, a dramatic change took place during the spring of 2000—suddenly the wine became oily and incomparably buttery, with the famous nut-caramel note extremely prominent in both nose and palate.

- 1992 TAITTINGER COLLECTION MATTA   85, APR 2004 (87)
(60% PN, 40% CH)

Creamy and good with a crisp acidity. Almost identical to the vintage wine. Charming, well-made, and house-typical.

- 1990 COMTES DE CHAMPAGNE   94, MAR 2004 (95)
(100% CH)

In magnum it is young with a clean, dry taste. The scent is almost identical to a Les Clos from Dauvissat. Even the taste breathes of mineral and unmistakable class. In a regular bottle a riper and sweeter Comtes appears, with a long, fat, and toasted oaky aftertaste.

- 1990 TAITTINGER COLLECTION CORNEILLE   93, APR 2004 (94)
(60% PN, 40% CH)

Sensationally good of late. Brendan Collins opened the most memorable bottle in his beautiful garden. My spontaneous guess was a developed bottle of 1990 Cristal. Fantastically rich, buttery, and nutty, with a concentration and class rarely seen.

- 1989 COMTES DE CHAMPAGNE   93, APR 2003 (93)
(100% CH)

A charmer with nice, intact acidity. Incredibly beautiful pearl-necklace mousse. Classically creamy and rich, with a distinct note of oak. Long, sweet aftertaste of butter toffee.

- 1988 COMTES DE CHAMPAGNE   96, NOV 2003 (97)
(100% CH)

As with so many '88s, almost hard in its stringency when it was introduced. At the turn of the millennium, there was a nutty weight and veils of mint aromas that were waiting to burst out in full bloom. At the end of 2003 it happened—the wine became even oilier, mintier, and fleshier than I'd understood. Wonderfully good and completely in line with the best vintages of the 1970s.

- 1988 TAITTINGER COLLECTION IMAÏ   89, APR 2004 (91)
(55% PN, 45% CH)

I've always thought it strange that I like Collection so much better than Vintage, when they claim it's the same wine. I learned in May 2001, to my great joy, what I've always suspected: Collection is another wine altogether! Greater autolytic character, of course, but also a greater finesse and complexity. Fine, classic, big-house Champagne with bready, chocolaty character. More austere and younger than the '90.

- 1986 COMTES DE CHAMPAGNE   93, JUN 2003 (93)
(100% CH)

Comtes de Champagne is one of my favorite Champagnes. Creamier and more easily drunk Champagnes just don't exist! The '86 is made in that style, but it's not counted as one of the great vintages. It is creamy with a long finish of almond and honey. Dosage a touch high.

- 1986 TAITTINGER COLLECTION HARTUNG   93, APR 2004 (93)
(60% PN, 40% CH)

Outrageously expensive artist-decorated bottles—with a gaudy plastic casing, according to some. The '86 is a house-typical, mature, voluptuous wine that has developed sensationally well. At a blind tasting the amazing Champagne collector Kennet Liberg wanted to prove to me how wrong I was with my earlier dismissal of this wine. He succeeded! Today the wine is nutty, creamy, sensual, and very rich.

- 1985 COMTES DE CHAMPAGNE   95, AUG 2003 (96)
(100% CH)

A brilliant, deep yellow revelation with an astoundingly beautiful mousse. The '85 is a dense and refined wine with an incredible, nuanced, medium-broad nose. Red apples, mint, coconut, vanilla, treacle, and butter are obvious participants. Classic Blanc de Blancs structure with an uplifting citrus taste. Dry initially, but with an exemplary sweet, tropical aftertaste.

- 1985 TAITTINGER COLLECTION LICHTENSTEIN   90, APR 2004 (93)
(60% PN, 40% CH)

Tasted alongside the ordinary '85, this Collection felt even more rich in finesse, complex, and elegant, due perhaps to its greater autolytic character and finer selection of grapes. Still young.

- 1983 COMTES DE CHAMPAGNE   93, JUN 2002 (93)
(100% CH)
I misjudged the '83 in its youth. It went on to mature rapidly in 1993 and 1994, and suddenly its bouquet and taste were huge. A tidal wave of sweet tones meets the palate, embedded in an oily, silk-smooth structure. A long aftertaste of almond and vanilla.

- 1983 TAITTINGER COLLECTION DA SILVA   87, APR 2004 (87)
(60% PN, 40% CH)
Designed by Da Silva and similar to an '83 Vintage. Fleshy, well-made, but slightly impersonal Champagne. Initally very good but now slightly dreary in the nose—but still with an elastic taste.

- 1982 COMTES DE CHAMPAGNE   94, MAR 2003 (94)
(100% CH)
Comtes on top form! Overwhelming, rich, romantic, and euphoric Champagne. Bubbling mousse with that unique pearl-necklace formation. The generous buttery nose includes tons of exotic ripe fruit, red apples, coconut, and a nutty complexity. The sweetness is tangible in the juicy taste. Creamy, fat, full bodied, buttery, and wonderfully long. The wine melts in the mouth like ice cream and runs down the throat like nectar.

- 1982 TAITTINGER COLLECTION MASSON   94, APR 2004 (94)
(60% PN, 40% CH)
The bottle is designed by the artist André Masson, and the wine is made in a Cristal-like style. High-class, aristocratic Champagne with overflowing fruit. The concentrated taste is perfectly balanced and has a lovely finish that brings to mind English butterscotch.

- 1981 COMTES DE CHAMPAGNE   94, JAN 2000 (94)
(100% CH)
Light and slightly closed at first. The pearl necklaces that the mousse formed are among the most beautiful I have seen in a Champagne glass. The nose is feminine and unusually discreet. Flowery, with tones of newly washed sheets that have been hung to dry outdoors. The acidity is pure although the dimensions are a bit smaller than usual. All the exotic fruits are there, but to a lesser degree than usual. Lovely recently.

- 1981 TAITTINGER COLLECTION ARMAN   89, APR 2004 (89)
(60% PN, 40% CH)
Arman's design of a surrealistically golden string instrument against a black background is my favorite of the Collection bottles, even if the contents are nothing to rave about. Admittedly delicate and refined, but without the expected concentration—maybe it's presented itself now? I wouldn't be surprised, considering how often Taittinger and the vintage have positively surprised me. Yes! The wine is completely different now with an exciting, smoky, and tar-saturated nose and flavor. Extremely interesting and still vigorous.

- 1979 COMTES DE CHAMPAGNE   97, MAY 2003 (97)
(100% CH)
Relatively light vintage for the company. Unmistakable style, with refreshing, creamy, citrus and butter-toffee notes. Extremely easy to drink and terrifically enjoyable. A wonderful perfume of white flowers and crystal-clear nut taste. Sensational improvement in quality at the end of the previous century. Michel Dovaz's favorite at the Millennium Tasting.

- 1978 TAITTINGER COLLECTION VASARELI   93, APR 2004 (93)
(60% PN, 40% CH)
This is the first, most expensive, and most sought after of the collector bottles. Just like the '81, Taittinger never released a regular vintage in 1978. It is obvious that they wanted to make a fine and concentrated wine for their debut. The fruit is exotic and surprisingly rich, and the mousse is exemplary as usual. One of the foremost Champagnes of the vintage. The price is an outrage, even considering Vasareli's beautiful golden bottle.

- 1976 COMTES DE CHAMPAGNE   98, NOV 2003 (98)
(100% CH)
This '76 was one of the Champagnes that sparked my obsession with the area and its wines. Never before have I tasted anything so exotic, fruity, and enjoyable. It still holds up very well, even if the character has changed a little. An enormous nose and taste of sweet lemons have now replaced the butteriness. These can be found in many mature Champagnes, but never as clearly as in the Comtes de Champagne '76. A classic milestone, and absolutely one of the ten Champagnes I would pick out for someone who doubts that Champagne can be really good and big. A champion in its class!

- 1975 COMTES DE CHAMPAGNE   94, AUG 2003 (96)
(100% CH)
An unusually austere version of this prestige *cuvée*. Creamy nose and slightly pared down, long and mineral-rich in taste. Clear note of coconut in the empty glass. Lovely long aftertaste of lemon. Still developable.

- 1973 COMTES DE CHAMPAGNE   95, MAY 2001 (95)
(100% CH)
This '73 should in all likelihood begin to withdraw from its peak now. In the late eighties it was fully mature, with a dark color and an almost overripe Sauternes nose. Colossally powerful, like a dessert. Who could fail to be impressed by this bounteous Champagne? Some bottles recently have been fabulously exotic and concentrated.

- 1971 COMTES DE CHAMPAGNE   96, JAN 2003 (96)
(100% CH)
Simply a fabulous Champagne, with an elegance difficult to beat and a perfect combination of floweriness and fruitiness. It's truly amazing that one can make such a light, ethereally floating and feminine wine so rich and concentrated.

- 1970 COMTES DE CHAMPAGNE   85, SEP 2003 (85)
(100% CH)
Definitely a very good Champagne that was at its peak between the ages of ten and fifteen. However, the acidity wasn't high enough to keep the wine alive for a longer period. When Comtes de Champagne gets too old it develops its very own oxidative tones. The sweetness becomes huge and the structure is very fat. A Manzanilla-like tone disturbs the whole.

- 1969 COMTES DE CHAMPAGNE   97, MAY 2001 (97)
(100% CH)
It's actually rare for this ever-brilliant prestige Champagne to combine subtle lemony-fresh acidity with such a coconut fatty richness, as is the case here. Juicy and nectar-ish, with tons of caramel notes and an appetizing, ascending aftertaste of newly picked Mediterranean lemons.

- 1966 COMTES DE CHAMPAGNE   94, NOV 2003 (94)
(100% CH)
Most of the bottles of the '66 are on their way down, but you can still find vigorous, slightly laid-back examples that have the charm of old age. Massive strawberry taffy aroma.

- 1964 COMTES DE CHAMPAGNE   96, JUN 2002 (96)
(100% CH)

Comtes at its best, with its lively, deep yellow appearance. Full bodied, fat, oily, and creamy. Packed with aromas from dried fruits, magnificently rich and smooth—with the same softness and sweetness in the long aftertaste.

- 1961 COMTES DE CHAMPAGNE   96, MAR 2003 (96)
(100% CH)

Compact, mature, and creamy, with chocolate and truffle aromas. Uniform buttery taste. An amazing Comtes with a wonderful mint tone and a concentrated, glycerol-rich fruit that is unreal. I've drunk the wine more than ten times since and only run into one bad bottle.

- 1959 COMTES DE CHAMPAGNE   97, JAN 2002 (97)
(100% CH)

Accompanied by a reverent silence, the torn cork was pulled out with a corkscrew—not a trace of a "pop." The wine was completely still but clear yellow, like middle-aged Burgundy. Ravishing depth and regal bouquet, with the vintage's dark and powerful attributes. Under the heaviest aromas I could just make out the typical minty, exotically delicious notes that are Comtes' signature. Just imagine if the massive, petroleum-like taste had been offset by a tiny bit of mousse?—two weeks later my wish was granted. A magnificent bottle with finesse, buttery maturity, and a cannonade of tastes completely satisfied me. The mousse was downright youthful.

- 1953 COMTES DE CHAMPAGNE
(100% CH)

- 1952 COMTES DE CHAMPAGNE   97, JUN 2004 (97)
(100% CH)

Oh, oh, oh! What an experience to drink this first vintage of Comtes, or Blanc de Blancs, as Sean Connery does in one of the early Bond movies. Even though the wine didn't come directly from the producer, and despite the mousse being almost nonexistent, it was wonderful. The color was very deep, and many probably expected a maderized nose, but there was nothing of the sort. The basic character was highly influenced by wood, varnish, and forest aromas, all handsomely braided into a really fat, toffee costume. After a while, I even noticed the light overtones of mint, flowers, and lemon. A world-class experience!

- 1996 COMTES DE CHAMPAGNE ROSÉ   91, APR 2004 (94)
They are *gorgeous*, these Comtes! The new, fruity and more Chardonnay-propelled style—introduced when the '95 entered the market—is a great triumph. It feels terribly luxurious and delicious to sip this wine. The aromas are creamy and refreshing, with notes of raspberry ice cream, and the feeling on the palate is silky and caressing. It's difficult not to be in a good mood when treated to such a wine. Note also the exceptional quality of the mousse.

- 1995 COMTES DE CHAMPAGNE ROSÉ   90, AUG 2003 (93)
(70% PN, 30% CH)

A change of style for this Champagne. Previous vintages have—by the house's own admission—been considered slightly too removed from Taittinger's characteristically charming, smiling, and easily drunk style. The wine has required lengthy storage, and lived more on its weight and vitality than on refinement. The pink Comtes has therefore been eased into a style reminiscent of Billecart-Salmon, Roederer, and Pol Roger.

- 1993 COMTES DE CHAMPAGNE ROSÉ   85, FEB 1998 (92)
(100% PN)

I really wonder why this famous and expensive Champagne is sold as a baby. The color is salmon-pink and the taste is soft and creamy as usual. Cherries and apple peel are very noticeable, which proves how immature the wine is.

- 1991 COMTES DE CHAMPAGNE ROSÉ   87, FEB 1998 (89)
(100% PN)

I haven't seen a trace of pink Comtes 1988, '89, or '90, and then suddenly along come '91 and '93. I don't get it! Both these wines are unexpectedly characterized by new oak barrels.

- 1986 COMTES DE CHAMPAGNE ROSÉ   92, MAR 2003 (92)
(100% PN)

Tasted every day for two weeks. Always from a magnum. Unfortunately it seems that Taittinger has some cork problems here: a third of the bottles were corked. The healthy bottles were fantastically lush and Burgundy-like. The aroma contained truffles, autumn leaves, leather, overripe strawberries, cabbage, and red beets. The taste was homogeneously rich and sweet. A shining example of grape character.

- 1985 COMTES DE CHAMPAGNE ROSÉ   91, OCT 2003 (92)
(100% PN)

As opposed to the white version of Comtes de Champagne, the rosé contains only Pinot grapes. Bouzy is usually the dominant village, and so it is in the '85. Broad, full-bodied, and robust rosé with good, raspberry-like fruitiness. The color is always deep. Today like a mature Burgundy.

- 1983 COMTES DE CHAMPAGNE ROSÉ   94, AUG 2002 (94)
(100% PN)

It's always a wonderful, romantic journey to sit with a pink Comtes in private. In the glass the wine changes, always inviting new sensations. The color is deep with hints of orange. The mousse is lively and the red fruit notes are mixed up with gooseberry, sabayone, mint taffy, and leather. Juicy and voluptuously grandiose Champagne.

- 1981 COMTES DE CHAMPAGNE ROSÉ   82, AUG 1989 (90)
(100% PN)

The Taittinger rosés always take a long time to mature. The '81 had only begun to enter its mature period at the age of nine. Huge, well structured, vinous, and compact.

- 1979 COMTES DE CHAMPAGNE ROSÉ   97, JUL 2001 (97)
(100% PN)

What fantastically enjoyable wine! This must be the best and most romantic, seductive drink to come out of the cellars at Reims. The nose is erotic with its sea notes and balsamic, spicy style. The supple, caressing sensation in the mouth can only be compared to an angel's kiss. It's so good and sensual that I chose it as the Champagne to celebrate my and my dear Sara's engagement.

- 1976 COMTES DE CHAMPAGNE ROSÉ   94, JAN 2002 (94)
(100% PN)

Fat and sweet with a wonderful concentration. Hardly classic, but with a wonderful explosion of tastes. The nose is completely distinct, with notes of juniper, thyme, pine needle, Sweet Gale, and an intractable strength. The color is unusually dark and the flavor is similar to red Bordeaux.

- 1973 COMTES DE CHAMPAGNE ROSÉ   94, JUL 2001 (94)
(100% PN)

When my fiancée tasted this Champagne blind in a Sardinian sunset, she was convinced it was a white, aged Champagne. The color was actually a lot like an amber-colored bubbly from the fifties. The mousse was weak, but fine. The nose was exemplary, with exciting elements of cranberry, gooseberry, mushrooms, and honey. The best thing about the wine, however, was the taste. Today the '73 is purest nectar. The sweet ripe fruit taste contains tones of apricot, peach, mango, passion fruit—and an entrancing aftertaste of acacia honey.

- 1971 COMTES DE CHAMPAGNE ROSÉ 98, MAR 2000 (98)
  (100% PN)
  Light orange-yellow, like a Cristal Rosé. Extreme finesse straight through. Just as irresistibly beautiful as a wood spirit, playfully running across a flowery midsummer's meadow. With a joyful smile, this Champagne opens its arms to the chosen few who find her. The best rosé I have come across.

- 1970 COMTES DE CHAMPAGNE ROSÉ 91, JUN 1997 (93)
  (100% PN)
  The nose may not be generous, but this is compensated for by a delightful, concentrated, nectar-like flavor. The fruit tones resemble blood orange, grapefruit, and mango.

- 1969 COMTES DE CHAMPAGNE ROSÉ 96, JAN 2003 (96)
  (100% PN)
  Once again completely fantastic! DRC-like, with bubbling charm and buoyancy. Sweet candied fruit, caramel-drenched strawberries, newly picked raspberries, and the gorgeously buttery-creamy richness where butter-toffee notes border on coconut. All of this in a medium-sized outer coat, backed up by fresh young acidity.

- 1966 COMTES DE CHAMPAGNE ROSÉ 90, FEB 2001 (>)
  (100% PN)
  Strongly reminds me of an aged red burgundy. Here are elements of truffle, leather, plum, and red beet. The Champagne keeps its dignity, but the freshness is gone.

- TAITTINGER MILLENNIUM 90, MAY 2003 (93)
  (50% PN, 50% CH)
  Full marks to Taittinger for not asking an insane amount of money for their Millennium Champagne. A handsome magnum with *grand cru* from 1995 and especially 1996. The grapes come from Avize, Oger, Mesnil, Ambonnay, Bouzy, and Mailly in equal amounts. For the moment the wine is very young and the mousse is exaggeratedly intrusive. The wine is very potent and developable, like many other millennium bubblies. Already one year after the turn of the century the wine has stabilized and become exceedingly charming. Toasted and delicious, with a Moët-like charm. Difficult to spit out.

TARLANT *** R-M
51480 Oeuilly
03 26 58 30 60
Production: 100,000
A family property consisting of thirteen hectares in Oeuilly, Celles les Condé, and Boursault. Unusually, they use new oak barrels from the Vosges for their vintage wines and prestige Champagne, Cuvée Louis. Today Jean-Mary Tarlant runs this company, which has a history of viticulture dating back to 1687. There is also a little boarding house and a wine museum on the property.

- TARLANT BRUT ZÉRO 73
  (33% PN, 34% PM, 33% CH)
- TARLANT RÉSERVE 58
  (33% PN, 34% PM, 33% CH)
- TARLANT TRADITION 62
  (50% PN, 20% PM, 30% CH)
- TARLANT DEMI-SEC 58
  (33% PN, 34% PM, 33% CH)
- TARLANT ROSÉ 53
  (20% PN, 80% CH)
- 1995 TARLANT 86, SEP 2003 (88)
  (40% PN, 60% CH)
  This is truly a serious producer that seems to be getting better and better. They appear to have full control over their oak barrels and let the wood tones integrate with a fresher as well as richer fruit than before. The '95 is brilliant in a modern, fruit-dominated way. A little like a successful garage wine from Saint-Emilion.
- 1995 TARLANT ROSÉ 80, DEC 2003 (80)
  (20% PN, 80% CH)
  Unfortunately, this powerful Champagne showed that it couldn't take airing in the glass—so is completely mature at the age of eight. Otherwise the wine was impressive when newly poured, with a sturdy fruit, generous oaky notes, and a marmalade-like concentration. I miss a little finesse.
- 1988 TARLANT 77, JUL 1995 (81)
  (40% PN, 60% CH)
  Open, pleasant nose of honey and marzipan. Rich, rounded flavor with the same aromas as in the nose.
- CUVÉE LOUIS 83
  (50% PN, 50% CH)
  One of two Champagnes completely vinified in new oak casks. The chief reason for the balance of the wine is that it is only in contact with the oak for three weeks. Another explanation is that the malolactic fermentation is avoided and that the oak from the Vosges gives a mild oak tone. Only a few thousand bottles of this unique wine from thirty-year-old vines are produced. The nose is broad, smoky, and influenced by the barrel. Full-bodied and muscular, this Champagne is definitely suitable for drinking with white meat.
- 1996 TARLANT CUVÉE PRESTIGE 86, SEP 2003 (90)
  Tough acidity and a crispy, pure flavor. Cleaner than the '95 and very promising with its fresh style.
- 1995 TARLANT CUVÉE PRESTIGE 86, SEP 2003 (88)
  I don't know what difference there is between this wine and the usual vintage wine. My tasting notes and points were strikingly similar when I tasted this wine in London together with my British colleagues at Wine International. Very good and enjoyable already.

TASSIN, EMMANUEL R-M
13, Grande Rue
10110 Celles-sur-Ource
03 25 38 59 44
Production: 15,000
The firm was started by Emmanuel Tassin as recently as 1988. Like many others in Aube, Pinot Noir now accounts for 85 percent of production from the 3.5 hectares.

- E. TASSIN CUVÉE DE RÉSERVE   40
  (80% PN, 20% CH)

TELMONT, J. DE * N-M**
1, avenue de Champagne
51480 Damery
03 26 58 40 33
Production: 1,500,000
Henri Lhopital began selling Champagne in 1920 but first achieved house status in 1952, and his family still runs the company. In 1989 they carried out major renovations, such as building a luxurious reception room. The Monsieur Lhopital of today reminds one of Gérard Depardieu, but produces far better wines than the great actor does in Anjou. The company own twenty-eight hectares in Cumières, Damery, Romery, and Fleury, but buy in most of their grapes.

- TELMONT GRANDE RÉSERVE   68
  (34% PN, 35% PM, 31% CH)
- TELMONT ROSÉ   65
  (100% PN)
- 1999 TELMONT   75, DEC 2003 (79)
  (35% PN, 34% PM, 31% CH)
- 1997 TELMONT   69, OCT 2002 (71)
  (35% PN, 34% PM, 31% CH)
- 1988 TELMONT   82, APR 1995 (85)
  (35% PN, 34% PM, 31% CH)
  A very personal Champagne dominated by a nose of lilac and a round, soft peach flavor. Already quite a mature Champagne, with acidity a touch low.
- 1999 TELMONT BLANC DE BLANCS   82, MAR 2004 (84)
  (100% CH)
  Broad, sensual, and buttery, and already with a distinct element of nutty caramel. There is no pressing reason to store this charming bundle of muscles for too long.
- 1996 TELMONT BLANC DE BLANCS   82, JUL 2002 (84)
  (100% CH)
  Summery-fresh, floral Champagne, with a lot of sweet overtones. Dried pineapple and papaya can be picked up in the relatively light taste. Mild and pleasant, with an unexpectedly low acidity.
- 1988 TELMONT BLANC DE BLANCS   73, APR 1995 (76)
  (100% CH)
- 1997 GRAND COURONNEMENT   86, MAR 2004 (88)
  (100% CH)
  A very good, reliable *cuvée de prestige* with Comtes-like overtones. Mint, coconut, cream, kiwi, gooseberry, pineapple, parsnip, and vanilla make up the distinct and subtle parts of this symphony. Elegant, sophisticated, very bright and first-rate.

- 1995 GRAND COURONNEMENT   88, MAY 2003 (91)
  (100% CH)
  A fantastically, beautifully perfumed and expressively scented Champagne. An exotic variety of Pol Roger Blanc de Chardonnay, or a close relative of Amour de Deutz. A truly first-rate Champagne to follow on its path through life.
- 1993 GRAND COURONNEMENT   85, JAN 2003 (86)
  (100% CH)
  A really delightful '93, full of smiling charm and accommodating softness and maturity. The scent imparts expectations of a soft melon ice-cream-like flavor—these are met by the melting, creamy experience on the palate. Lightly tropical and refreshingly enjoyable. Somewhat short.
- 1993 TELMONT CONSÉCRATION   85, MAR 2004 (88)
  (100% CH)
  Pure *grand cru* in oak barrels. Despite the oak, this is a floral, elusive Champagne with notes of kiwi, pineapple, and mango. Good acidity and a fine, pure taste with a dash of vanilla in the finish.
- 1990 GRAND COURONNEMENT   89, SEP 2003 (90)
  (100% CH)
  A really big, powerful '90, full of evolved, almost American exotic fruitiness. The alcohol is high and the wine feels sturdy and stable. Almond, honey, saffron, and hay are other associations from our tasting group.
- 1983 GRAND COURONNEMENT   83, JUN 1995 (83)
  (10% PN, 90% CH)
  A gamy, musty scent that puts a lot of people off. On the other hand, the taste is oily and concentrated.

TESTULAT, COLLECTIVE N-M
23, rue Léger Bertin
51200 Épernay
03 26 54 10 65
Production: 350,000
This low-profile house was founded in 1862 and still works using traditional methods.

- TESTULAT CARTE D'OR   70
  (50% PN, 50% PM)
- TESTULAT BLANC DE BLANCS   74
  (100% CH)
- TESTULAT BLANC DE NOIRS   75
  (100% PN)

THIBAUT, GUY R-M
7, rue des Perthois
51360 Verzenay
03 26 49 41 95
Production: 15,000
Claude and Gérard Thibaut own 1.7 hectares in this wonderful *grand cru* village. Although the production is small, the quality is high. Other wines: Réserve, Demi-Sec.

- GUY THIBAUT BRUT   63
  (80% PN, 20% CH)

THIÉNOT *** N-M
14, rue des Moissons
51100 Reims
03 26 47 41 25
Production: 600,000

Thiénot is a relatively new house that was formed as late as 1980. Most of the grapes are bought in from reasonably good areas. The founder, Alain Thiénot, is still at the helm. In 1994 he bought Marie Stuart, and Laurent Fedou is winemaker for both houses. M. Thienot is very hospitable and charming, as is his attractive wife.

• THIENOT BRUT	60
(45% PN, 25% PM, 30% CH)	
• 1995 THIENOT GRANDE CUVÉE	85, OCT 2003 (88)
(40% PN, 60% CH)	

A wine that gains a lot from being aired properly. After a while the yeasty, plump aromas appear—reminiscent of a '82 Dom Pérignon at the same age. Structurally a very fine wine that waits a while before flirting with the public.

• 1990 THIENOT GRANDE CUVÉE	85, JAN 2003 (87)
(60% PN, 10% PM, 30% CH)	

Handsomely unified, focused *cuvée de prestige*; it still lacks that something special to really get close to the true masters. Good balance and rich, bready, fruity character, with an undertone of chocolate.

• 1988 THIENOT GRANDE CUVÉE	88, JAN 2002 (90)
(60% PN, 10% PM, 30% CH)	

The first vintage using new oak barrels. Broad, powerful, chocolate-laden, bready bouquet. Rich, harmonious fleshy taste and fine roundness. Thienot's best wine so far.

• 1985 THIENOT GRANDE CUVÉE	85, MAY 1996 (88)
(60% PN, 10% PM, 30% CH)	

The first vintage that Alain Thienot was satisfied with—and I can understand why. The '85 is very sophisticated and worthy of its prestige label. The wine has brilliant balance between mature Pinot aromas and refreshing, top-class Chardonnay in a medium-bodied style.

TIXIER, GUY R-M
12, rue Jobert
51500 Chigny-les-Roses
03 26 03 42 51
Production: 30,000

Guy Tixier founded his company in 1960, and the current owner is Olivier Tixier. With the help of the cooperatives in Chigny and Chouilly, they vinify Champagne made from grapes from five hectares in Chigny.

• GUY TIXIER SÉLECTION	76
(60% PN, 40% CH)	
• GUY TIXIER CUVÉE RÉSERVE	58
(40% PN, 40% PM, 20% CH)	
• GUY TIXIER ROSÉ	62
(50% PN, 20% PM, 30% CH)	

TIXIER, PAUL R-M
8, rue Jobert
51500 Chigny-les-Roses
03 26 03 42 45
Production: 23,000

This grower has five hectares in Chigny-les-Roses and the vines average twenty-five years old.

• PAUL TIXIER BRUT	37
(20% PN, 60% PM, 20% CH)	
• PAUL TIXIER GRANDE ANNÉE	40
(20% PN, 60% PM, 20% CH)	
• PAUL TIXIER DEMI-SEC	27
(20% PN, 60% PM, 20% CH)	

TORNAY, BERNARD *** R-M
Chemin Petit Haut
51150 Bouzy
03 26 57 08 58
Production: 100,000

Bernard Tornay has run this company ever since it started in 1950. He is definitely one of Bouzy's best growers. The entire wine production is housed in his normal-sized house situated on the edge of the village. The ten-hectare vineyard is not situated in Bouzy's best belt, but the yield is low and, best of all, his wines are stored longer than anyone else's in the village. The style is made up of uncompromising food Champagnes of smoky complexity and hazelnut aromas.

• BERNARD TORNAY CARTE D'OR	74
(70% PN, 30% CH)	
• BERNARD TORNAY CUVÉE BELLE DAMES	88
(70% PN, 30% CH)	

The *cuvée de prestige* is a blend of three vintages, aged together with the yeast for at least eight years. Clumsy compared to a Blanc de Blancs, but wonderful together with breast of pheasant in morel sauce.

• 1989 BERNARD TORNAY	90, JUL 2001 (90)
(70% PN, 30% CH)	

What a gorgeous Champagne! Certainly there are a few difficult gamy, cheesy notes in the nose that repel many, but any kid would love the flavor. My six-year-old daughter Stella and a few of her friends were in complete agreement—the wine smelled the worst and tasted by far the best of the five kinds that I had put out that evening. Even we adults were enchanted by the candy-like sweet, intense fruit taste of the wine. Enormous concentration.

• 1988 BERNARD TORNAY	91, AUG 2001 (91)
(70% PN, 30% CH)	

Yet again, Tornay convinces with their rich, fruity-sweet, mature, luscious Champagnes. A gigantically broad, saturated, sweet bouquet of cloudberries, honeysuckle, and dark fudge. Fleshy and treacle-like long taste, with honey leading a brace of more-or-less sweet fruit tastes.

• 1981 BERNARD TORNAY	80, SEP 1992 (82)
(70% PN, 30% CH)	

This vintage was sold in 1992 (eleven years old). The broad nose was majestic, while the flavor couldn't quite hold up its end. The spectrum of aromas included honey, almond, leather, and plum.

TRIBAUT R-M

21, rue St Vincent
51480 Romery
03 26 58 64 21

I don't know if it's just bad luck, but of the four bottles of Tribaut that I've tasted, three were corked! Two were bought in the U.S.A. and the others in France.

- TRIBAUT CARTE BLANCHE
  (33% PN, 33% PM, 34% CH)

TRIOLET N-M

22, rue Pressoirs
51260 Bethon
03 26 80 48 24
Production: 45,000

The grower owns nine hectares in Bethon, Montgenost, and Villenauxe-la-Grande. Triolet is one of the winemakers with the best reputation in Sézanne. Other wines: Vintage.

- TRIOLET BRUT   67
  (10% PN, 10% PM, 80% CH)
- TRIOLET SÉLECTION   69
  (100% CH)

TRITANT, ALFRED R-M

23, rue de Tours
51150 Bouzy
03 26 57 01 16
Production: 30,000

This producer started his business in 1930 in Bouzy and still uses traditional methods. He now owns 3.5 hectares in Bouzy.

- A. TRITANT GRAND CRU BRUT   68
  (60% PN, 40% CH)
- 1989 A. TRITANT   82, SEP 1997 (85)
  (60% PN, 40% CH)
  A powerful Champagne with notes of fish and bread in the nose and mushrooms and figs on the palate.

TROUILLARD N-M

2, avenue Foch
51208 Épernay
03 26 55 37 55
Production: 250,000

A house that is better known for its change in ownership than its Champagne. The Trouillard Group is better known than Trouillard itself. The company is currently run by Bertrand Trouillard. Other wines: Vintage, Rosé.

- TROUILLARD CUVÉE DIAMANT   55
  (60% PN, 40% CH)
- TROUILLARD SÉLECTION   57
  (40% PN, 30% PM, 30% CH)
- TROUILLARD BLANC DE BLANCS   70
  (100% CH)
- 1988 TROUILLARD CUVÉE FONDATEUR   80, APR 1996 (85)
  (100% CH)
  A good, pure Blanc de Blancs at a very reasonable price. Even a certain finesse about it.
- 1966 TROUILLARD DIAMANT   87, FEB 2000 (87)
  (50% PN, 50% CH)

Vintage-typical, and initially a handsomely roasted Champagne. Unfortunately, it quickly wanes in the glass, which brings down the points to under ninety. The taste is becoming more and more gamy and demanding.

TURGY, MICHEL *** R-M

17, rue d'Orme
51190 Le Mesnil-sur-Oger
03 26 57 53 43
Production: 60,000

When you travel around the growers in Le Mesnil there is one name, besides Salon, that always turns up. Old vintages from Turgy are regarded by several growers to be the best wines ever made in the village. After Michel's recent death the sale of vintage wine was blocked, and this means that the nonvintage Champagne also contains wine that would normally be classed as a vintage. The blend on sale in 1995, for example, was based on 1988's harvest and contained very old reserve wines! As Le Mesnil wines have such longevity, Turgy, together with Guy Charlemagne, usually offer one of the very best nonvintage Champagnes (if you discount Krug Grand Cuvée from this category).

- MICHEL TURGY SÉLECTION   82
  (100% CH)
  I've drunk purer nonvintage Champagnes, but hardly any more enjoyable. The honeyed nose is very broad. The flavor is filled with mint chocolate and has a complex aftertaste of old reserve wines. Unfortunately a bit younger lately.

VALLOIS, GUY *** R-M

2, rue de l'Egalité
51530 Cuis
03 26 51 78 99
Production: 60,000

Unfortunately, I've never visited this well-known grower in Cuis—but his relationship with Diebolt-Vallois in Cramant is promising, as are the wines I've run into. If you're lucky, today you can taste some of the grower's older vintages at Jacques Diebolt's home.

- GUY VALLOIS BLANC DE BLANCS   77
  (100% CH)
- 1985 GUY VALLOIS NON DOSÉ   90, DEC 2003 (91)
  (100% CH)
  A brilliantly deep Champagne with paradoxical lightness and finesse. Both the nose and the palate exude cream and sophisticated fruit, with hints of passion fruit. The delightful aftertaste of strawberries with whipped cream awakens my longing for summer.
- 1982 GUY VALLOIS NON DOSÉ   80, DEC 2003 (80)
  (100% CH)
  Fine color, acidity, structure, and mousse—but the praise ends there. Oxidative aromas of malt, tea, licorice, earth, and raisin. However, I must point out that many people who have bought supplies of this wine, including Jacques Diebolt, are decidedly more captivated than I am.
- 1979 GUY VALLOIS NON DOSÉ   90, DEC 2003 (90)
  (100% CH)
  One of four older vintages that Guy left behind undisgorged. On the two occasions I've tasted the wine so far, it performed in two

completely different ways. The first time, elegance and floweriness were in focus and the points were a fair bit over ninety. The second time, the Champagne lacked charm and was a little clumsy, with certain coarse notes of maturity despite a medium-deep color and good mousse. I find the whole trilogy—'85, '79, and '76—fascinating, because the wines are still undisgorged and really give the taster the chance to see how individual bottles develop after such lengthy contact with the yeast sediment.

- 1976 GUY VALLOIS NON DOSÉ   93, DEC 2003 (93)
  (100% CH)

A pure Chardonnay from Cuis. Walnut and butter melting in a frying pan. Salon-like and dry, with the same nose and palate. Unfortunately, an oxidized tone has worked its way into the aftertaste in certain bottles, showing clear similarities to a 1983 Salon. The best bottles and all the magnums that reach 94.5 points are light and lively, with a nice, crème-brûlée sweetness despite the wine being undosed. The floral bouquet has notes of spring flowers, candy, and vanilla. Even the taste is seductive, with delightful fruit and balance.

- 1973 GUY VALLOIS NON DOSÉ   94, DEC 2003 (94)
  (100% CH)

What depth! A pure Cuis wine, newly disgorged and without dosage. Unfortunately there are very few bottles remaining—but those who get to taste this rare wine will be in for a powerful experience, where notes of forest mushrooms, mocha, cacao, nuts, and tart fruit operate in a lovely symbiosis. The wine has a rare attack and explosive intensity, actually slightly reminiscent of well-preserved bottles of Salon and Diebolt from the 1950s and 1960s.

VARLOT-LENFANT R-M

1, rue de la Mairie
51380 Trépail
03 26 57 05 03
Production: 30,000
This well-cared-for property is dominated by Chardonnay.

- VARLOT-LENFANT BRUT   49
  (20% PN, 80% CH)
- 1992 VARLOT-LENFANT L'EDEN   48, APR 2002 (48)
  (20% PN, 80% CH)

VAUGENCY, HENRY DE R-M

1, rue Avize
51190 Oger
03 26 57 50 89
Production: 50,000
This grower has more than eight hectares in Oger and environs.

- HENRY DE VAUGENCY CARTE NOIR   49
  (100% CH)

VAUTIER, JOËL R-M

36, Grande Rue
51360 Beaumont-sur-Vesle
03 26 03 95 59
Production: 40,000
One of the few growers I've found in the *grand cru* village of Beaumont-sur-Vesle.

- J. VAUTIER GRANDE RESERVE   69
  (70% PN, 30% CH)

VAUTRAIN-PAULET R-M

195, rue du Colonel Fabien
51530 Dizy
03 26 55 24 16
Production: 60,000
A neighbor of Jacquesson, Vautrain-Paulet is run by Arnaud Vautrain and owns eight hectares in Dizy and Aÿ. Other wines: Blanc de Blancs and Grand Réserve.

- VAUTRAIN-PAULET CARTE BLANCHE   60
  (50% PN, 20% PM, 30% CH)

VAZART-COQUART R-M

7, rue Dom Pérignon
51530 Chouilly
03 26 55 40 04
Production: 100,000
The Vazart-Coquart father and son are extremely proud about what they achieve, and the firm has many fans. The winemakers are innovative and ready to experiment with their own ideas. The family is often arranging exciting tastings, serving the same wines but with varying bottle sizes, different sugar content, or date of disgorging. Vazart-Coquart use plenty of old reserve wines in their Champagnes. They have also released a Champagne called Foie Gras (goose liver) which contains wines from around ten old vintages and which should suit the fat delicacy admirably. Despite these laudable ideas, I'm not so impressed by the company's Champagnes. There is always an excess of clumsy almond aromas and a dosage that is often too high—something with which they themselves agree, strangely enough. They appear to have disregarded their own ideals in favor of an anticipated demand from the public.

- VAZART-COQUART GRAND BOUQUET   62
  (100% CH)
- VAZART-COQUART CUVÉE FOIE GRAS   74
  (100% CH)
- VAZART-COQUART ROSÉ   59
  (10% PN, 90% CH)
- 1989 VAZART-COQUART GRAND BOUQUET   75, DEC 1996 (77)
  (100% CH)
- 1988 VAZART-COQUART   75, AUG 1993 (76)
  (100% CH)
- 1982 VAZART-COQUART   76, JUL 1993 (76)
  (100% CH)

VAZART, LUCIEN C-M

2, rue d'Avize
51530 Chouilly
03 26 55 61 15
Production: 50,000

The village of Chouilly is packed with producers called Vazart or Legras. Lucien is one of the more well known. As with R. & L. Legras, the almond aroma so typical of the village is avoided in favor of a purer, more classic Chardonnay style.

- LUCIEN VAZART PRIVATE CUVÉE   75
  (100% CH)
  Almost colorless and with fast, minimal bubbles. Perfectly pure, pale, young, steely nose with excellent character from the soil. The flavor exhibits a broad spectrum of faint, delicate nuances. A perfect aperitif Champagne.

VENOGE, DE **** N-M

46, avenue de Champagne
51200 Épernay
03 26 53 34 34
Production: 1,700,000

Along with the Germans who founded Champagne houses, there is one Swiss, Marc-Henri de Venoge. He started work in Mareuil-sur-Aÿ in 1837, but soon moved to Épernay. Throughout the twentieth century the house has belonged to the most important producers in Champagne. Half of the firm's produce is exported to the German-speaking countries and to Great Britain. Ninety percent of the grapes are bought in and vinified in modern steel vats. Today the house is run by the extremely capable young vinophile, Gilles de la Bassetière. Previously, the winemaker Eric Lebel, who today does the same job at Krug, assembled the wines. Now, this job is carried out by Isabelle Tellier. The company's style is rather difficult to grasp, as it ranges from Blanc de Blancs to Blanc de Noirs. If you want to find a common denominator it might be the gunsmoke note that is strong in all the wines, except the ones that contain only Chardonnay. The nonvintage Champagne is the house's best buy, together with the lovely Des Princes. It is that creamy, butter-toffee tasting *cuvée de prestige* Des Princes that is one of my latest and most important discoveries in the hunt for gems among Champagnes. This house produced two wines among the twelve best ever, according to the jury at the Millennium Tasting. Truly impressive!

- DE VENOGE BRUT CORDON BLEU   79
  (50% PN, 25% PM, 25% CH)

- DE VENOGE CUVÉE PARADIS   70
  (70% PN, 30% CH)

- DE VENOGE EXTRA QUALITY   90
  (1958-based) A wine that can only turn up at a tasting with the boys from De Venoge. Not a pure Blanc de Blancs, but with a clear predominance of Chardonnay. The dosage is a tad too generous, but otherwise this is a buttery and still extremely vigorous Champagne.

- DE VENOGE BLANC DE BLANCS   60
  (100% CH)

- DE VENOGE BLANC DE NOIRS   78
  (80% PN, 20% PM)

- DE VENOGE DEMI-SEC   50
  (50% PN, 25% PM, 25% CH)

- DE VENOGE PRINCES ROSÉ   75
  (40% PN, 50% PM, 10% CH)

- 1995 DE VENOGE   85, SEP 2003 (88)
  (70% PN, 10% PM, 20% CH)
  Undeveloped, but with an expansive bouquet. Incredibly flavorful and jam-packed with fruit. Young acidity and good length. It will be most interesting to follow this wine's development.

- 1991 DE VENOGE   80, OCT 2001 (82)
  (70% PN, 10% PM, 20% CH)
  Strongly influenced by Pinot Noir with a scent of chocolate, leather, and red fruit. Rather fat structure and slightly languid tartness. Perhaps I am mistaken about the future prospects for this rather uninteresting wine.

- 1990 DE VENOGE   89, OCT 2003 (89)
  (51% PN, 34% PM, 15% CH)
  Wonderfully house-typical, smoky '90. Fine acidity and stock of sweet, sun-ripened fruit as well. This is one of the company's best vintage Champagnes ever. Unfortunately, somewhat tired, the last few times I've tasted the wine.

- 1989 DE VENOGE   85, AUG 1999 (88)
  (51% PN, 34% PM, 15% CH)
  A deep, beautiful color with a snow-white mousse. A broad, mature Pinot nose with clear tones of chocolate and toffee. A balanced, buttery flavor with big, rich fruit.

- 1988 DE VENOGE   90, OCT 2001 (90)
  (60% PN, 20% PM, 20% CH)
  A wine that's developed wonderfully in recent years. Always a charmer today with its coffee aroma and nutty depth. Perfectly balanced, with more taste of Chardonnay than is true in reality.

- 1987 DE VENOGE   84, NOV 2001 (84)
  (70% PN, 10% PM, 20% CH)
  A really nice wine from this weak vintage, with a very fine nose of cakes and newly baked bread. Light to medium-bodied taste without greater complexity. A wine that gives temporary pleasure and leaves you with no food for thought—just like an American comedy.

- 1986 DE VENOGE   86, AUG 1999 (86)
  (51% PN, 34% PM, 15% CH)
  Developed and toasty nose with elements of chocolate. Something of a one-track, mature flavor with low acidity and respectable fruit—as well as being very toasted and smoky. A wine that is very easy to appreciate.

- 1985 DE VENOGE   85, AUG 1999 (88)
  (51% PN, 34% PM, 15% CH)
  This is a delightful Champagne that is far too cheap. It has heaps of classic Champagne character, where notes of chocolate, fresh-baked bread, and honey are clearly discernible. A wine I would like to have in my cellar.

- 1983 DE VENOGE   70, MAY 2001 (70)
  (70% PN, 10% PM, 20% CH)

- 1983 DE VENOGE BRUT ZERO   84, NOV 2001 (84)
  (70% PN, 10% PM, 20% CH)
  A wine that will be sold newly disgorged at the age of twenty. Considerably more fresh in this form than when newly disgorged. The nose is oxidative with forest aromas and plum. The taste is soft but still pure. Don't store!

- 1982 DE VENOGE   88, SEP 2003 (88)
  (51% PN, 34% PM, 15% CH)

Highly developed nose, packed with coffee aromas. Sadly the aftertaste is a bit short, but otherwise a very nutty and pleasant Champagne at a modest price.

- 1979 DE VENOGE   90, DEC 1995 (90)

(51% PN, 34% PM, 15% CH)

Toasty, nutty, and bready are the usual judgements on the 79s. They are admirably apt here. Now fully mature.

- 1976 DE VENOGE   87, MAY 2003 (87)

(51% PN, 34% PM, 15% CH)

Powerful and rich in alcohol, as it should be with layers of sweet, almost burned fruit. One-dimensional and merciless in its insensitive, "bulldozer" way. Still, impressive and very good. I'm sure that the wine will get even higher points from less style-conscious wine-lovers than myself.

- 1975 DE VENOGE   82, MAY 2001 (82)

(51% PN, 34% PM, 15% CH)

A little coarse and overripe today. It tastes better than it smells. In the nose slightly squalid notes of oxidation disturb me, even if cacao and iron can be discerned. The taste is one-track and rustic, with good pull and fleshiness.

- 1973 DE VENOGE   86, OCT 2000 (86)

(50% PN, 25% PM, 25% CH)

Recently bought back by De Venoge at a French auction. Very developed and mature with a rather one-dimensional expression. A goose-liver wine with big butterscotchiness and sweet toffee aromas. Of course, not of the same class as Des Princes.

- 1971 DE VENOGE   91, JAN 1999 (91)

(51% PN, 34% PM, 15% CH)

Enormous scent as from an entire hedgerow of honeysuckle. Powerful, malt-like and honey-soft taste, with a hint of rough, oxidative finish, which pulls down the points total somewhat. The aroma is heavenly!

- 1970 DE VENOGE BRUT ZERO   85, DEC 2003 (85)

(40% PN, 10% PM, 50% CH)

Unusually youthful '70 with good structure, fresh acidity and burned, smoky aromas of wood and leather. Oily and predictable, slightly one-dimensional. Severe and tasty. Newly disgorged in the house's cellar.

- 1961 DE VENOGE   96, JUN 1999 (96)

Unfortunately not even the management knows which grapes went into this wine. It seems that Chardonnay dominates to a high degree. A seldom-seen Champagne that perfectly combines the richness of the vintage with an elegance that very few have had the chance to experience.

- 1937 DE VENOGE   93, MAY 2001 (93)

(51% PN, 34% PM, 15% CH)

It hasn't happened very often that I've had the pleasure of sharing a bottle from my own cellar with the head of a Champagne house. Gilles and Aymeric from De Venoge appreciated—as I did—this almost completely still, chocolate-tasting Champagne. Despite its old-age aromas, it held up well in the glass. We were all surprised that the house hadn't written anything about an anniversary on the label, as the firm was founded in 1837. Their surprise was even greater when I brought out a magnum of this, which was as young as Champagne from the 1970s. How strange the world of Champagne can be!

- 1995 DE VENOGE BLANC DE BLANCS   79, MAR 2003 (81)

(100% CH)

An 80 percent *grand cru* that has unfortunately been blended with 20 percent Sezanne, which has made the wine more approachable and wimpy. Good grape character and rather fleshy style. I found unfortunate floury notes at Wine International's big autumn tasting in 2003.

- 1990 DE VENOGE BLANC DE BLANCS   80, FEB 1997 (85)

(100% CH)

Smoky and tough, with tones of tar and forest. The fruit flavor is generous, though, with hints of apricot.

- 1983 DE VENOGE BLANC DE BLANCS   87, APR 2001 (87)

(100% CH)

Perfectly youthful, refined nose of citrus, sea breeze, and brioche. Light, bordering on thin, youthfully fresh taste with impressive acidity and mineral character.

- 1979 DE VENOGE BLANC DE BLANCS   83, APR 2001 (83)

(100% CH)

Surprisingly heavy, old bouquet. Surely there must exist bottles with better elasticity and grape character. This bottle was satisfactory and chocolate-saturated, but probably at the end of its life.

- 1978 DE VENOGE CRAMANT BLANC DE BLANCS   93, MAY 2003 (93)

(100% CH)

In De Venoge's cellar there's still a considerable stock of this forgotten, never-released looker in magnum. What a beautiful, early summer nose of lily of the valley and rain-wet beech forest! Floweriness is typical for this somewhat anemic vintage that always exhibits youth and green, slightly immature tones. Classically pure, elegant taste that is devoid of—for the vintage—the typically hollow medium-palate. Pure, beautiful, and homogeneous!

- 1995 DE VENOGE BLANC DE NOIRS   92, FEB 2004 (92)

(100% PN)

Sensational! I have never before encountered a dry Champagne that resembles a Sauternes as much as this. Besides this unexpected tone, the wine is fabulously luxurious and packed with corpulent, sweet fruit. Already smoky and extremely easily drunk. I must admit that I have never succeeded in spitting out this Champagne, even though it is my rule never to drink when working.

- 1990 DE VENOGE BLANC DE NOIRS   82, JAN 1997 (88)

(80% PN, 20% PM)

Sophisticated and smooth big-house style. Full bodied and polished in balanced fashion. Quite unlike any Blanc de Noirs from a grower. None of the typical Pinot character, despite the grape content.

- 1982 DE VENOGE ROSÉ   87, MAR 1999 (87)

(100% PN)

A classic, vintage-typical rosé with a minty undertone and rich creamy fruit.

- 1979 DE VENOGE ROSÉ   88, MAY 2000 (88)

(100% PN)

Dark red, brisk appearance, with a grand bouquet that transports me southward to Côte de Beaune's pale, sweet, ingratiating red wines. Excellent Pinot Noir, even in its smooth strawberry and cinnamony palate. An interesting wine with big personality.

- 1977 DE VENOGE ROSÉ   83, DEC 1999 (83)

(100% PN)

I tasted this unusual vintage, together with Gilles, at Bubble Lounge in New York, and we agreed that the wine was fresh and youthful but hardly exciting, with its nose of tea and light fruit.

- **1976 DE VENOGE ROSÉ**   85, MAY 2001 (85)
(80% PN, 20% CH)
I drank a handsome magnum in perfect condition and must say that I was more impressed by the nose than by the taste. In the mouth the wine tastes a little thin and short, with a fine mousse and discreet buttery character. The nose is Burgundy-like and bound with gamy, vegetal aromas. Actually, the wine's scent is highly reminiscent of a strongly reduced chicken or vegetable stock.

- **1973 DE VENOGE ROSÉ NON DOSÉ**   90, NOV 2002 (90)
(80% PN, 20% CH)
Magnificently Burgundian! Dark as an aged Musigny and concentrated as few others. It was no shock putting my nose into the glass, because the wine smells as it looks. If it hadn't been for the bubbles, I'm convinced that even tasters more skillful than me would have guessed a red *grand cru* from Côte de Nuits. Impressive sweetness considering that I tasted this magnum one minute after disgorging—that is to say completely without sugar. Somewhat less impressive during our tour in Scandinavia. The wine appeared to fare poorly with traveling.

- **1983 DE VENOGE 20 ANS**   84, MAR 2004 (84)
(70% PN, 10% PM, 20% CH)
Identical to Brut Zero, which I've tasted directly in the cellar, but now out on the market in limited numbers. A wonderful concept, whereby Gilles wants to show different wines at the perfect age of twenty years. We await with excitement the newly disgorged and unsweetened '85, which will appear in the year 2005.

- **1995 DES PRINCES**   81, AUG 1999 (88)
(50% PN, 50% CH)
Unfortunately, they've abandoned the concept of using pure Chardonnay in Des Princes, and blended in Pinot Noir in order to appeal to a greater audience when the wine is released into the market. This is certainly still very good Champagne, but not as distinctive and superb as its predecessor has proven itself to be. Luckily, the next Des Princes will be divided into two versions— Blanc de Blancs and a Blanc de Noirs.

- **1993 DES PRINCES**   88, MAR 2003 (91)
(100% CH)
Luckily, I know how these wines usually develop. Otherwise I would probably be thoroughly disappointed in this modest wine. Chalky and slightly citrus scented, with fine acidity and an underlying predestined fatness, which I long for.

- **1992 DES PRINCES**   82, JAN 1999 (87)
(100% CH)
Decent concentration considering the vintage. Lovely toasted aroma with a refined, soft, citrus taste. I have almost always stayed on the low side when considering the potential points for Des Princes. It is possible that the '92 will develop in the same manner as previous vintages of this wonderful Champagne, but the herblike, grassy tone that this vintage possesses makes me think otherwise.

- **1990 DES PRINCES**   87, JAN 1999 (92)
(100% CH)
Brilliant, shining bright, with ultra-fine bubbles. Also a faint, subtle nose that reveals the truth: this is a multi-*cru*. A smooth

mousse and flavor, which is similar to the Deutz Blanc de Blancs from the same vintage.

- **1989 DES PRINCES**   90, JAN 1999 (92)
(100% CH)
An extremely refined Champagne with a glimmering green hue. A glorious nose of lime, lily of the valley, mint, and toasted bread. Multifaceted, crystal-clear flavor with aristocratic elegance.

- **1985 DES PRINCES**   92, DEC 2003 (93)
(100% CH)
A slowly developing wine that, in the beginning, I didn't believe in. It seems I was wrong, as the wine today has an oily structure and a fine concentration of tastes. It's becoming more and more similar to the big vintages of this wine.

- **1983 DES PRINCES**   92, MAR 2004 (92)
(100% CH)
Lightly toasted, nutty, weak mint tone. Creamily concentrated, high-class '83 that is now completely mature, with an oiliness that is so typical of this wine, whatever the vintage.

- **1982 DES PRINCES**   94, MAY 2003 (94)
(100% CH)
Very strange scent of spruce forest, turpentine, and hawthorn. There is, however, an element of lemon and toasted bread. Luscious and light with a long, nutty finish. Today, completely harmonious, with a vintage-typical butter-toffee note and a wonderful balance.

- **1979 DES PRINCES**   97, JUL 2003 (97)
(100% CH)
The young wine-lovers that run De Venoge today claimed forcefully that the '79 was often even better than the heavenly and chewable '76. When we tasted them together in January 1999, the '76 just won. At the Millennium Tasting the order was reversed. This is a perfect Blanc de Blancs that has everything one believes Comtes de Champagne should have.

- **1979 DES PRINCES NON DOSÉ**   92, OCT 2000 (94)
(100% CH)
An excellent example of what bottle aging and a temperate dosage can do to increase quality. Certainly the wine is very beautiful and pure with a euphoric bouquet, but it seems almost hard and stingy compared to the normally disgorged wine. Tasted in the cellar of De Venoge, disgorged on the spot.

- **1976 DES PRINCES**   97, OCT 2000 (97)
(100% CH)
So unbelievably rich and concentrated that it takes one's breath away. "Almost like an American Chardonnay in its over-explicitness," remarked one taster. I myself am completely seduced by this romantic, Comtes-like aromatic spectrum. It is clear to me now that Des Princes is one of the Champagnes that I have most underestimated. Magnificent every time!

- **1973 DES PRINCES**   91, JAN 2000 (91)
(100% CH)
I found saffron, honey, mint, and raspberry candy in this easy-to-drink wine. Hardly a classic, but very round and enjoyable. As usual it makes you think of Comtes de Champagne.

- **1973 DES PRINCES NON DOSÉ**   89, OCT 2000 (91)
(100% CH)
Totally unlike the normally disgorged commercial variety of the same wine. Gamy and vegetal, with notes of asparagus, artichoke, and green bell pepper, which here slightly dominate over desires of the flesh.

- 1971 DES PRINCES
(100% CH)
- 1966 DES PRINCES   94, JUN 2002 (94)
(100% CH)

Chalkier and smokier than earlier vintages, with an abrasive and harsh element. However, it opens in the glass and shows its class with an exceptional length.

- 1964 DES PRINCES   96, APR 1999 (96)
(100% CH)

Oh, what an enormous bouquet! I have never before experienced such butterscotch in a wine. Rich, "scrumptious" taste along the same theme. Very slight mousse.

- 1961 DES PRINCES   97, AUG 1999 (97)
(100% CH)

What a fabulous Champagne! I had the great honor to drink the house's last bottle. This is also the first vintage of Des Princes. Actually, the wine is without vintage, but it is a typical '61. The wine combines, in a unique way, an unbelievable buttery quality with a nutty depth.

VERGNON, J.-L. R-M

1, Grande Rue
51190 Le Mesnil-sur-Oger
03 26 57 53 86
Production: 40,000

No malolactic fermentation for the vintage wine, which comes from forty-year-old vines. Sadly the company is going downhill.

- J.-L. VERGNON EXTRA BRUT   73
(100% CH)
- J.-L. VERGNON BLANC DE BLANCS   66
(100% CH)
- 1998 J.-L. VERGNON   85, FEB 2004 (88)
(100% CH)

Wonderfully floral, beautifully perfumed nose with pure *terroir* character. Acidity, crystal-clear taste where everything is clearly defined. Lime fresh and stony with a strong spine.

- 1995 J.-L. VERGNON   85, JUL 2003 (88)
(100% CH)

Big, luxurious, citrus-influenced Chardonnay with soft but still-fresh acidity. An exceedingly pleasant, sought-after Blanc de Blancs. It seems like the company is back on track.

- 1988 J.-L. VERGNON   84, NOV 2003 (85)
(100% CH)

In the beginning somewhat unclean bouquet that fortunately disappears when aired. The wine has a village-typical style, but was still a relative disappointment in its youth. Much more fun and homogeneous at the age of fifteen.

- 1987 J.-L. VERGNON   86, JAN 1996 (87)
(100% CH)

Delightful, sensational wine, with a distinctive, perfumed nose, and a classically pure, chalky flavor. The dominant fruit aroma is kiwi and melon.

- 1986 J.-L. VERGNON   76, MAY 1992 (76)
(100% CH)
- 1982 J.-L. VERGNON   70, JUL 1990 (77)
(100% CH)

VESSELLE, ALAIN R-M

8, rue de Louvois
51150 Bouzy
03 26 57 00 88
Production: 130,000

The Vesselle family has worked the soil of Bouzy since 1885. Alain went his own way in 1958 and today's owner Eloi Vesselle works mainly with his Bouzy *rouge*.

- ALAIN VESSELLE BRUT TRADITION   60
(66% PN, 34% CH)
- ALAIN VESSELLE CUVÉE ST ELOI   77
(50% PN, 50% CH)
- ALAIN VESSELLE ROSÉ   77
(55% PN, 45% CH)
- 1993 ALAIN VESSELLE   79, FEB 1999 (83)
(50% PN, 50% CH)

Surprisingly buttery aroma. In the mouth the wine behaves more as expected, with the freshness of the vintage playing nicely against the background of Bouzy's weighty presence and mineral flavor.

VESSELLE, GEORGES *** R-M

16, rue de Postes
51150 Bouzy
03 26 57 00 15
Production: 145,000

The best of the "weasels," as they are called in Swedish wine circles. The good Georges had previously worked for Mumm and had time to become the mayor of Bouzy. He owns 17.5 hectares in Bouzy and Ambonnay and makes some of the best red wines in the area. His Champagnes are nothing to sniff at either.

- GEORGES VESSELLE BRUT   80
(90% PN, 10% CH)

A ten-year-old half bottle of this Champagne is among the nicest nonvintage Champagnes I've tasted. Chocolaty and rich as a dessert. Recently disgorged full-size bottles are naturally less generous and developed, but they contain a mighty fruit that is ready to burst into full bloom.

- GEORGES VESSELLE ROSÉ   75
(90% PN, 10% CH)
- 1998 GEORGES VESSELLE   82, FEB 2004 (87)
(90% PN, 10% CH)

No malolactic fermentation imparts a nose of hard, tough acidity and a matchbook's striking surface. Good structure, but you've got to store this wine for a very long time!

- 1996 GEORGES VESSELLE   82, NOV 2001 (88)
(90% PN, 10% CH)

Powerful fruit, acidity, and structure. Not at all finished or polished; yet another wine for the cellar.

- 1996 GEORGES VESSELLE BRUT ZERO   81, NOV 2001 (87)
(90% PN, 10% CH)

The same wine without dosage. Somewhat cleaner and fresher. Much shorter in the aftertaste.

- 1995 GEORGES VESSELLE   84, AUG 2002 (88)
(90% PN, 10% CH)

Creamy as well as deep. I am really fond of this powerful Pinot Champagne. There is a chocolate-sated richness and an underlying mineral tone that is impressive. The aftertaste has elements of both red and yellow fruits and berries.

• 1995 GEORGES VESSELLE BRUT ZERO   86, JAN 2003 (88)
(90% PN, 10% CH)

Delightfully developed nose of almond, chocolate, penny-bun mushroom, and newly baked country bread. Fleshy, gunpowder-splashed palate with good sharpness and a tough, dry finish.

• 1991 GEORGES VESSELLE   78, NOV 1998 (84)
(90% PN, 10% CH)

Deep golden-red color; big, plum-like aroma with a metallic undertone. Soft, rounded Pinot taste, but with a tendency toward iron and blood. Future possibilities hard to judge.

• 1989 GEORGES VESSELLE   84, APR 1997 (88)
(90% PN, 10% CH)

More developed and broader than the '88, but lacking its restrained mineral finesse. Honey and chocolate are already the dominant aromas.

• 1988 GEORGES VESSELLE   81, FEB 1995 (89)
(90% PN, 10% CH)

This is how a Pinot Champagne should be built. Deep golden color; tight, young, creamy nose with elements of olive and iron. Powerful, acidic, and masculine flavor with good length.

• 1988 GEORGES VESSELLE BRUT ZERO   82, JUL 1997 (89)
(90% PN, 10% CH)

The same Champagne without any dosage.

• 1985 GEORGES VESSELLE   87, MAR 2000 (92)
(90% PN, 10% CH)

He sure can do it, good old Georges. Handsome and purebred, with a beautiful combination of *terroir* and grape character. Full bodied and elegant. Masterful craftsmanship.

• CUVÉE JULINE   89
(90% PN, 10% CH)

This *cuvée de prestige* is the village's most expensive, but hardly its best. I've previously drunk a few dreary, perfumed bottles of this wine. Now, they've finally put together the honeyed, nectar-like drink that they had intended to produce all along.

VESSELLE, JEAN R-M

2, place J. B. Barnaut
51150 Bouzy
03 26 57 01 55
Production: 70,000

Jean Vesselle is the family member who makes the least wine, and he also makes the youngest, most unpredictable Champagnes. The family is very hospitable and enthusiastic, but the problem seems to be that they have a limited area to cultivate and vines that are too young.

• JEAN VESSELLE BRUT   75
(100% PN)

• JEAN VESSELLE EXTRA BRUT   69
(80% PN, 20% CH)

• JEAN VESSELLE OEIL DE PERDRIX   49
(100% PN)

• JEAN VESSELLE DEMI-SEC   50
(80% PN, 20% CH)

• JEAN VESSELLE SEC   59
(80% PN, 20% CH)

• JEAN VESSELLE ROSÉ   30
(100% PN)

• 1985 JEAN VESSELLE   67, DEC 1992 (71)
(100% PN)

• 1992 JEAN VESSELLE PRESTIGE   84, FEB 1999 (86)
(70% PN, 30% CH)

Well, this was both delicious and unexpected! Jean Vesselle has hardly impressed me before, but here they have succeeded in producing a glorious Champagne in a year when few performed memorably. Even the aromatic spectrum is surprising. The fragrance literally roars with gunpowder smoke, like an old Champagne from Aÿ. There are also many similarities to Dom Pérignon from the same year. All of the toasted and balsamic aromas are even stronger in the grower-produced wine. However, the fruit is richer and more elegant in Dom Pérignon.

VESSELLE, MAURICE *** R-M

2, rue Yvonnet
51150 Bouzy
03 26 57 00 81
Production: 40,000

The business was started in 1955 and includes 8.3 hectares in Bouzy and Tours-sur-Marne. There are plenty of producers who make Bouzy *rouge*, but Didier Vesselle is one of the few to make a Bouzy *blanc*.

• MAURICE VESSELLE BRUT   68
(80% PN, 20% CH)

• MAURICE VESSELLE RÉSERVE   70
(80% PN, 20% CH)

• MAURICE VESSELLE ROSÉ   75
(100% PN)

• 1989 MAURICE VESSELLE   85, JAN 1999 (90)
(80% PN, 20% CH)

To say the least, a sensational deep and creamy '89 in magnum. Despite drinking it as New Year's bubbly amid firecracker smoke and sub-zero temperatures, it was very rich in taste and first-rate, with its Bollinger-like style.

• 1988 MAURICE VESSELLE   80, FEB 1999 (81)
(85% PN, 15% CH)

Considering how good the '89 is, I was disappointed in this—a rich and expressive but somewhat limp wine. Those who like honey, licorice, and oxidized apples will get their fill here. A big question mark over the wine's storability.

• 1985 MAURICE VESSELLE   80, NOV 1998 (83)
(80% PN, 20% CH)

Soft and well-made *grand cru* in a surprisingly elegant style. Clear breadiness and mineral character discernible beneath the outer layer.

VEUVE CLICQUOT **** N-M

1, place des Droits de l'Homme
51100 Reims
03 26 89 54 40
Production: 10,000,000

In Sweden, no Champagne is as well known as the "Gula Änkan," the Yellow Widow. The house was founded in 1772 by Philippe Clicquot. His son, François, married Nicole-Barbe Ponsardin, who took over the company at the age of twenty-seven when she found herself a widow. By her side was Comte Edouard Werlé and the firm's *chef de caves*, Antoine Müller. Together with Müller she developed "*remuage*" using "*pupitres.*" One Heinrich Bohne then helped to take the Russian market by storm. Throughout the nineteenth century and right up to the 1970s, Clicquot was reckoned as one of the top four or five Champagne companies, a position that was lost when the decision was made to increase sales by several hundred percent.

At first the company merged with Canard-Duchêne, but today it is a part of the powerful Louis Vuitton Moët Hennessy (LVMH) group. The 284 hectares owned by Clicquot in twenty-two villages are enough for around three of the almost ten million bottles produced each year. The most important *crus* for La Grande Dame and the vintage wine are Ambonnay, Bouzy, Avize, Cramant, Le Mesnil, Oger, and Verzenay. Since 1962 modern vinification techniques and stainless-steel tanks have been used. If you find old, well-kept vintages they'll be very like Bollinger and Krug. Despite the factory scale, the house has managed to keep its Pinot-based classic style, where dough, bread, and pepper are clear elements. Jacques Peters, who is brother to François Peters in Le Mesnil and an equally gifted winemaker, should get the credit for Clicquot's quality today. The rich and powerful La Grande Dame is a wonderful Champagne, but the vintage wine often gives best value for money. A classic house that is one of the greatest!

- VEUVE CLICQUOT BRUT   79
  (56% PN, 16% PM, 28% CH)
- VEUVE CLICQUOT DEMI-SEC   55
  (56% PN, 16% PM, 28% CH)
- VEUVE CLICQUOT SEC   55
  (56% PN, 16% PM, 28% CH)
- 1996 VEUVE CLICQUOT   90, JAN 2004 (93)
  (59% PN, 8% PM, 33% CH)
  As expected, a big Clicquot with young juicy, sweet, almost exotic fruit, rich breadiness, and big muscles. The acidity is in no way intrusive, keeping instead under the sweet fruit—but it does guarantee a long life, and is noticeable in the finish. Most likely enjoyable in all phases of its life. For the moment, however, fine creamy Chardonnay is in the driver's seat.
- 1995 VEUVE CLICQUOT   90, MAR 2003 (93)
  (67% PN, 33% CH)
  A totally brilliant wine, already with tons of sublime charm and enormous potential. The fruit is rich and balanced with a fantastically creamy mousse. Enviable length and a classic nascent biscuity nuttiness.
- 1991 VEUVE CLICQUOT   80, SEP 1999 (85)
  (62% PN, 5% PM, 33% CH)
  A well-made wine with a very pleasurable scent of strawberry yoghurt, an aroma one often finds in red Burgundy from Mongeard Mugneret for example. Classic Clicquot taste that grabs

the attention, lacking only a little something in the middle register.
- 1990 VEUVE CLICQUOT   90, DEC 2003 (93)
  (56% PN, 11% PM, 33% CH)
  Deliciously tight, and drier than the charming La Grande Dame. A fine, complex scent of newly baked bread and clean sheets. An elegant, fresh, and promising taste that so far—mostly—is characterized by Chardonnay.
- 1989 VEUVE CLICQUOT   88, MAR 2003 (89)
  (67% PN, 33% CH)
  The '89 is somewhat fruitier than usual, with distinct elements of mature Chardonnay, even if the classic breadiness is present in the background. Very interesting to taste against the '88, which surprisingly is very much like the '89. Perhaps there's a slightly greater roundness and fleshiness in the '89, and the '88 definitely has more nuances of taste and, above all, better length.
- 1988 VEUVE CLICQUOT   92, JAN 2004 (93)
  (67% PN, 33% CH)
  The vintage wine from Clicquot is always a sure bet with a bready, yeasty, peppery nose and rich autolytic taste. The '88 is no exception. A gorgeously rich '88 that has a very fascinating aftertaste. Big, nutty depth and wonderful fruit tones reminiscent of orange and mandarin.
- 1985 VEUVE CLICQUOT   85, JAN 1995 (90)
  (67% PN, 33% CH)
  For many years a bargain wine at the Swedish State Monopoly. More house-typical and classic than La Grande Dame of the same year. Broad, mature, peppery, and bready Clicquot nose. The full-bodied flavor is along the same lines, too.
- 1983 VEUVE CLICQUOT   77, MAR 1992 (85)
  (62% PN, 5% PM, 33% CH)
  Bready and bushy Clicquot nose with a peppery flavor and undeveloped aftertaste.
- 1982 VEUVE CLICQUOT   94, DEC 2002 (94)
  (62% PN, 5% PM, 33% CH)
  This is the company's best wine from 1982, as La Grande Dame wasn't made this year. The Champagne has a fine, well-built body and a mature, fully packed fruitiness. Wonderful in magnum with a delicious aroma of oatcakes.
- 1980 VEUVE CLICQUOT   83, FEB 1988 (87)
  (67% PN, 33% CH)
  One of the first Champagnes I ever bought. Extremely restrained and mineral-rich for an '80. Pure fruit and long, stony aftertaste.
- 1979 VEUVE CLICQUOT   94, OCT 2003 (94)
  (67% PN, 33% CH)
  Very well preserved and youthful with aromas of chocolate, nut, cellar, and newly baked bread. Excellent attack and a pure fruity taste with length. A personal favorite that I love serving my guests.
- 1978 VEUVE CLICQUOT   80, JAN 1988 (82)
  (62% PN, 5% PM, 33% CH)
  Mature and smoky Champagne that demands food. One-dimensional and robust.
- 1976 VEUVE CLICQUOT   93, OCT 2003 (93)
  (67% PN, 33% CH)
  If the rosé of 1976 was clumsy, the white '76 was far more successful. Warm, open, generous nose of new-baked bread and classically mature Clicquot flavor.
- 1973 VEUVE CLICQUOT   92, DEC 2002 (92)
  (67% PN, 33% CH)

The flesh is looser than in the '75, but with just as much chocolaty richness. An old-fashioned dark and woody aftertaste feels very piquant.

- 1970 VEUVE CLICQUOT   92, SEP 1999 (92)
(67% PN, 33% CH)
Wonderfully good served with fowl on my thirty-seventh birthday. The forgotten vintage of 1970 provided good, rich Pinot Noir, with superb length, and Veuve Clicquot was one of the best that year.
- 1969 VEUVE CLICQUOT   93, FEB 2003 (93)
(67% PN, 33% CH)
Meaty nose; dry, long, nutty flavor and nice acidity.
- 1966 VEUVE CLICQUOT   95, JAN 2003 (95)
(67% PN, 33% CH)
Not as massive as the '64, but with an aristocratic stature and freshness that is of the highest class. A textbook Clicquot.
- 1964 VEUVE CLICQUOT   94, AUG 2003 (94)
(67% PN, 33% CH)
Heavy and vinous, with the vintage's typical mint-chocolate aroma, along with a fat, long aftertaste with layers of vanilla. One of the vintage's most full-bodied Champagnes.
- 1962 VEUVE CLICQUOT   96, JAN 2004 (96)
(67% PN, 33% CH)
Astonishingly concentrated as well as distinctive, like a Florens-Louis, with notes of jet-fuel, popcorn, railway track, and volatile sensations. I'm convinced that the wine has not been through malolactic fermentation, as these tones only appear with wines that have been through that process. Young mousse and beautiful color with hints of orange. A really great wine, and one of the vintage's real big shots.
- 1961 VEUVE CLICQUOT   96, JUN 2002 (96)
(67% PN, 33% CH)
The color indicates great age but the mousse is exemplary, as is the nutty and complex flavor. For some, the bouquet is perhaps a tad too vegetal and characterized by tar aromas—personally, I'm very enthusiastic. One of the greatest Clicquots I've ever tasted.
- 1959 VEUVE CLICQUOT   94, NOV 2003 (94)
(67% PN, 33% CH)
Not quite as monumental as the '61, but meaty, broad, and well structured. The fruit and the acidity are more obvious than in most other '59s. The nose is nutty, with elements of mushroom and bread. The everlasting flavor is focused and fruity.
- 1955 VEUVE CLICQUOT   99, JAN 2004 (99)
(67% PN, 33% CH)
Champagne that belongs in the world of the divine. The nose is heavenly, with so many tiny nuances that I could fill an entire page. Strongest is a cold freshness with aromas of newly roasted coffee beans. The best Clicquot of all time!
- 1953 VEUVE CLICQUOT   96, DEC 2000 (96)
(67% PN, 33% CH)
Maderized on three occasions, so '53 Clicquot is definitely not a sure thing. The four well-kept examples I have drunk were wonderful. The wine had a richness and concentration you seldom find in today's Champagne. The mousse is often very weak, but the oily wine has a Burgundy-like bouquet and a honeyed flavor. Large bottle variation.
- 1949 VEUVE CLICQUOT   95, MAR 1996 (95)
(67% PN, 33% CH)

Wonderfully sublime with layers of delicious tastes and a fabulous finish. The wine could be twenty years younger—so don't be surprised if you miss the age at a blind tasting.

- 1947 VEUVE CLICQUOT   89, JUN 2002 (89)
(67% PN, 33% CH)
Unfortunately a tad aged to be "complete," but a gigantic wine with monumental dimensions. Bouquet like a grand Cognac and fiery, aged, massive, chewable, long taste, with a sherry-like resounding note. Supposed to be one of the best Champagnes the house has ever made.
- 1945 VEUVE CLICQUOT   96, DEC 2000 (96)
(67% PN, 33% CH)
One of the top '45s. A young, many-layered nose with a feminine form. Extravagantly long, fresh, and deep, very concentrated flavor.
- 1943 VEUVE CLICQUOT
(67% PN, 33% CH)
- 1942 VEUVE CLICQUOT
(67% PN, 33% CH)
- 1937 VEUVE CLICQUOT   94, FEB 1996 (94)
(67% PN, 33% CH)
A very deep color and a weak but appreciable mousse. Incredibly concentrated, fat, fruity flavor with a long, impressive aftertaste of honey.
- 1934 VEUVE CLICQUOT   93, MAY 2003 (93)
(67% PN, 33% CH)
Vigorous and refreshing, with a cellar tone that disturbed my co-tasters. Lighter than expected, with a refreshingly mineral note and pure hazelnut aroma, together with butterscotch and dried fruit.
- 1929 VEUVE CLICQUOT   95, OCT 2003 (95)
(67% PN, 33% CH)
It's always wonderfully grand to be there when really old Champagne still crackles with *joie de vivre* and vitality. This fully packed '29 shows no signs of impending mortality. The wine radiates authority and charm, with its richly sweet palate of peach, nougat, and digestive biscuit. Sit back and enjoy.
- 1928 VEUVE CLICQUOT   95, AUG 1995 (95)
(67% PN, 33% CH)
A hardly visible mousse but a surprisingly light appearance. A bouquet full of finesses like butterscotch and roses. A magnificent flavor of damp wood and bitter chocolate. Holds well in the glass.
- 1923 VEUVE CLICQUOT   91, NOV 2000 (91)
(67% PN, 33% CH)
Majestically grand appearance, but a tad heavy, and slightly earthy and bitter in its full-bodied flavors. Smoky and rich in tannin. Fine mousse and respectable fruit.
- 1919 VEUVE CLICQUOT   95, JUN 1997 (95)
(67% PN, 33% CH)
What a superb, lively vintage! The nose is more developed than the flavor. It reveals dark chocolate, plum, and orange, while the mouth enjoys two layers of flavor: one incredibly fresh and acidic, and the other extremely buttery and rounded. A hugely long, citrus-influenced aftertaste.
- 1904 VEUVE CLICQUOT   91, JUL 2004 (91)
(67% PN, 33% CH)
I know that Veuve Clicquot still have a few undisgorged bottles of this wine in their cellar. They intend to drink it—the oldest

wine they have—in 2004, when an elderly winemaker, like the wine, turns 100 years old. A bottle that had been carelessly treated for the past ninety-nine years was, despite this, in the pink of health, and very butterscotchy with a hint of mousse.

- 1996 VEUVE CLICQUOT RICH RÉSERVE   83, JAN 2004 (85)
(59% PN, 8% PM, 33% CH)
Yet again, Clicquot has proven that they are the undisputed masters of sweet Champagne. The '96 is, in my opinion, the best Rich Réserve yet created, and probably one of the foremost sweet Champagnes ever made. The naturally high acidity latent in this vintage's profile makes the added sugar hardly noticeable. The wine is fresh and grandiose through and through, carrying other dishes besides desserts. I bet that fat salmon dishes, herring, duck liver, and goose liver would purr like cats in the company of this Champagne. I was very satisfied with my combination of Rich Réserve and goat cheese, Parmesan, and fig confit.

- 1995 VEUVE CLICQUOT RICH RÉSERVE   82, FEB 2004 (83)
(68% PN, 32% CH)
Yet another successful dessert bubbly from the Widow. The question is—would this wine gain anything through storage? The tone of nut toffee and the soft creaminess are already there. The fruit is rich and juicy.

- 1993 VEUVE CLICQUOT RICH RÉSERVE   81, JAN 2003 (82)
(68% PN, 32% CH)
Refreshing, medium-bodied, sweet Champagne, without the great torso that earlier vintages of this wine have had. So far, the wine pins its hopes on a certain amount of floral aromas, refreshing tartness, and a pleasant aftertaste of candied fruits.

- 1991 VEUVE CLICQUOT RICH RÉSERVE   70, SEP 1999 (75)
(68% PN, 32% CH)

- 1990 VEUVE CLICQUOT RICH RÉSERVE   80, AUG 1999 (83)
(56% PN, 11% PM, 33% CH)
The best sweet Champagne I have tasted. Wonderful base wine that is honey-soft, but somewhat one-tracked with the sugar. A marvellous wine for serving with sweet-and-sour sauces—for example, gravlax with mustard sauce.

- 1989 VEUVE CLICQUOT RICH RÉSERVE   79, DEC 2003 (80)
(68% PN, 32% CH)
Of course these sweet vintage Champagnes are best suited to dessert, but they can also carry slightly unexpected dishes like herring, gravlax, and duck liver.

- 1988 VEUVE CLICQUOT RICH RÉSERVE   83, DEC 2003 (83)
(68% PN, 32% CH)
Sweet vintage Champagne! Fleshy and bready with autolytic character. Soft, rich taste. A well-made wine that has developed very nicely.

- 1996 VEUVE CLICQUOT ROSÉ   84, OCT 2003 (90)
(65% PN, 7% PM, 28% CH)
Today this wine needs decanting. I think that most buyers drink this wine much too early. There is a certain similarity to old, big, gamy, cigar-smelling vintages of this slowly developing wine. The acidity is tough and there's a hint of tannin, but also a pleasant, currant-scented fruit and pure, integrated clarity. Fine with truffle dishes and light meat. Don't be afraid to wait for twenty years to pop the cork, if you have the patience.

- 1995 VEUVE CLICQUOT ROSÉ   85, JUL 2002 (89)
(64% PN, 8% PM, 28% CH)
Like so many beautiful '95s, harmonious right from the first. The red wine is integrated, and the entire wine is airy and palatable, with notes of cherry, raspberry, and vanilla ice cream.

- 1993 VEUVE CLICQUOT ROSÉ   73, SEP 1999 (83)
(73% PN, 27% CH)
For the moment the added red wine is trying to make contact with the surrounding wine. At present, the bitterness is clear in the finish and the entire wine is unbalanced. Be patient with these food Champagnes.

- 1990 VEUVE CLICQUOT ROSÉ   88, AUG 1999 (92)
(56% PN, 11% PM, 33% CH)
A charming and accessible mint-scented rosé with massive creamy fruit and outstanding potential. Very reminiscent of Pol Roger's rosé from 1990.

- 1989 VEUVE CLICQUOT ROSÉ   88, MAY 2003 (90)
(73% PN, 27% CH)
Like the '73 already matured! Magnificently deep and thought-provoking Pinot character. My thoughts spin around in an autumn forest with all of its moist and ripe scents. Big rosé with a long, smoky finish.

- 1988 VEUVE CLICQUOT ROSÉ   82, MAY 1997 (86)
(73% PN, 27% CH)
A typical rosé from Clicquot with good balance and a faint element of strawberry. Otherwise the nose is broad and bready and the flavor is smooth and delicate with a sweet finish.

- 1985 VEUVE CLICQUOT ROSÉ   88, OCT 2003 (88)
(64% PN, 8% PM, 28% CH)
The color is medium-deep with hints of copper and bronze. The nose is peculiar, with earthy aromas similar to hyacinth and geranium. The taste is abrupt, continuing along the same theme, combined with a peppery aftertaste. I should add that the wine has become creamier with age.

- 1983 VEUVE CLICQUOT ROSÉ   68, SEP 1992 (>)
(73% PN, 27% CH)

- 1979 VEUVE CLICQUOT ROSÉ   86, NOV 2001 (86)
(73% PN, 27% CH)
If the wine's fruit is sufficient, the '79 will last long. Toasty and nutty, with barrel-like aromas and full Pinot flavor.

- 1978 VEUVE CLICQUOT ROSÉ   85, MAY 2001 (85)
(73% PN, 27% CH)
Sensual, successful '78. Biscuits and perfumed tones blended with mature cheeses and strawberry aroma. Soft, creamy, and somewhat one-dimensional, medium-long flavor.

- 1976 VEUVE CLICQUOT ROSÉ   68, DEC 1997 (71)
(73% PN, 27% CH)

- 1975 VEUVE CLICQUOT ROSÉ   91, FEB 2004 (91)
(73% PN, 27% CH)
A substantial, full-bodied rosé where the nose fills the room with its notes of marzipan and leather. The mousse is on its last legs, but there's nothing wrong with its power and authority. Bring on the truffles and sweetbreads!

- 1973 VEUVE CLICQUOT ROSÉ   88, AUG 1998 (92)
(73% PN, 27% CH)

Only tasted from magnum. Very youthful Champagne with a wonderful Pinot character. Full bodied and concentrated, with tones of iron and boiled vegetables.

- 1970 VEUVE CLICQUOT ROSÉ   90, JAN 2003 (90)
(73% PN, 27% CH)

A very concentrated, fleshy wine with Burgundian grape character. Dark, red fruit against vegetal elements. Fiery and long, with somewhat low acidity. Tar and leather in the aftertaste.

- 1969 VEUVE CLICQUOT ROSÉ   92, SEP 1998 (92)
(73% PN, 27% CH)

Very rich and solid with a deep, beautiful color and a good mousse. A bread-like scent and a fine taste that makes you think of ripe cherries. A small minus for the cellar tone that has sneaked into it during the maturation process.

- 1959 VEUVE CLICQUOT ROSÉ   94, JUN 1999 (94)
(75% PN, 25% CH)

This Champagne is reputed to be the best rosé that Clicquot has ever produced. I first drank it during an unforgettable lunch with Christian Maille and Jacques Peters, where it ended up in the shadow of the senselessly good white '55. In spite of that, this is a fantastically massive, chewable, smoky rosé of the highest class. The tasting group at Villa Pauli was deeply split when it came to this wine.

- 1932 VEUVE CLICQUOT ROSÉ
(75% PN, 25% CH)

- 1928 VEUVE CLICQUOT ROSÉ   90, DEC 2000 (90)
(73% PN, 27% CH)

Unfortunately no bubbles left and fraught with cloudy particles. Grand, expansive, sweet taste with a very high flavor concentration. Truly grand if stored properly.

- 1996 LA GRANDE DAME   93, JUL 2004 (97)
(64% PN, 36% CH)

A surprisingly tranquil, high-octane, elegant La Grande Dame that will probably develop into one of the greatest vintages of this wine ever made. The balance is extraordinary and the wine has a silky appearance, devoid of both sharp edges and an exaggeratedly chocolaty, muscular body. Hints of hazelnut and white chocolate are present, but for the moment handsome fruit and fine mineral notes from Oger and Le Mesnil dominate. A uniquely long aftertaste that should convince doubters that something big is happening here.

- 1995 LA GRANDE DAME   94, JAN 2004 (95)
(62% PN, 38% CH)

It's difficult making a wine more enjoyable than this at the young age of six years. This wine stood out extremely clearly during a prestigious tasting with all the great houses' most recent *cuvées de prestige*, in Paris in December 2001. There's an unbeatable concentration and roundness that in young years sweeps the board with its competitors. The wine is packed with sweets and warm, exclusive richness. The viscosity and the fat, buttery style is so delicious that it's impossible to intellectualize away the greatness of this wine. Let yourself be swept away!

- 1993 LA GRANDE DAME   90, OCT 2003 (92)
(62% PN, 38% CH)

Sensational and luxuriant. What a rigorous grape selection Clicquot must have made: achieving such pressure in a Pinot-dominated '93 is truly impressive. Fine notes of brioche and chocolate creams.

- 1990 LA GRANDE DAME   93, DEC 2003 (95)
(61% PN, 39% CH)

The '90s give a very soft and sweet impression. Experience shows that these wines, despite their immediate charm, have good potential. The strong scent of newly baked saffron bread is almost like a parody. There is also a fantastic attack and a rich, accelerating taste of exotic fruits, vanilla, and lemon chiffon pie. Honestly, I have missed the chocolate-flavored Champagne that went into the curvy bottle that was available until 1985. Peters and his eight-man-strong team have really put the pieces together. It's a wonderful wine!

- 1989 LA GRANDE DAME   91, APR 2003 (93)
(62% PN, 38% CH)

Developed, chocolaty, and full of honey. A touch richer than the '88, but hardly as good as the saffron-scented, exotic '90. Full of generous fruit that is still youthful and compressed.

- 1988 LA GRANDE DAME   95, NOV 2003 (95)
(62% PN, 38% CH)

The new bottle has also meant a change in style. The Champagne is now even more toasted and feels lighter, less majestic, but with a honeyed aftertaste. The wine is showing beautifully now, but appears to be completely mature already.

- 1985 LA GRANDE DAME (NEW BOTTLE)   92, DEC 2002 (93)
(62% PN, 38% CH)

This wine is slightly lighter and less complex than the blend that was made in the old curvy bottle with the lady on the label. The nut and chocolate tones are somewhat less distinct in this slightly younger wine decorated with an orange label.

- 1985 LA GRANDE DAME (OLD BOTTLE)   95, MAY 2003 (95)
(62% PN, 38% CH)

This was the year when Clicquot changed bottles. Those sold in the new bottle are reminiscent of Dom Pérignon, while the older, more curvaceous bottle contains a wine more typical of the house, with deep chocolate tones. I doubt that the disgorging is the only reason for this.

- 1983 LA GRANDE DAME   90, FEB 1998 (91)
(62% PN, 38% CH)

Heavy, powerful and old-fashioned, but with an earthy secondary note that has crept into the chocolate-laden, rich totality. The latest bottles I've tasted have displayed a younger, fresher side than previously. That's how strange the growth curve can be sometimes.

- 1979 LA GRANDE DAME   96, JAN 2004 (96)
(62% PN, 38% CH)

This rich, Pinot-dominated Champagne is a classic. At the age of eight, appley and fresh, elegant and long. At ten it had developed Bollinger-like richness and weight. Flowing with chocolate, honey, nuts, cheese, Champagne cellar and huge fruit of mature red apples. Very consistent through the years. A real diamond.

- 1978 LA GRANDE DAME   93, MAY 2003 (93)
(62% PN, 38% CH)

Clicquot succeeded in making an effusively rich, honey-scented, chocolate-laden La Grande Dame, even for this rather weak year. Probably the most ample Champagne I've come across from 1978.

- 1976 LA GRANDE DAME   97, NOV 2003 (97)
(62% PN, 38% CH)

Many years went by before I ran into this fantastic wine. This grandiose Champagne is still very fresh, light, and lively, with a colossal fruity richness and sweet concentration. You don't have to be Einstein to notice the similarities to the lovely '79, with its notes of exotic fruit, juicy red apples, honey, and white chocolate. The '76 is less nutty and actually even more chracterized by French bakery and dark chocolate in the nose. In conclusion, you may describe the difference thus: the '79 has more finesse and the '76 is even more concentrated.

- 1975 LA GRANDE DAME   97, AUG 1999 (97) (62% PN, 38% CH)

The wine of this vintage! Dark, but brilliant and full of vigor. What dimensions! The nose is of an entire bakery full of pastries: dark and light chocolate and nougat are all easily definable tones. Bigger, softer, fruitier, and longer than the famous 1975 Bollinger R. D.

- 1973 LA GRANDE DAME   94, MAY 2003 (94) (62% PN, 38% CH)

My, oh my, it *is* delightful running into old, almost extinct celebrities. At that time, the bottle had the curvaceous forms that were abandoned with the '85, but the label was disagreeably dull and greenish-yellow instead of its magnificent black and gold successor. The wine itself is still elastic, with a dominating note of hazelnut both in the nose and palate. The vintage's mature character is pronounced, as is the similarity to the regular vintage wine of the same year. With a little more intact fruit the points would be even higher. A truly impressive, nutty pastry.

- 1969 LA GRANDE DAME   94, JAN 2003 (94) (62% PN, 38% CH)

Tarter and thinner than other vintages, with an ascetic purity far from the chocolate-saturated charm that the noble lady often possesses. Still, I'm captivated by the pleasant hazelnut tone and the attack that grabs the tongue for a long, long time. A handsome wine in classic, pared-down style.

- 1966 LA GRANDE DAME   94, MAR 2004 (94) (62% PN, 38% CH)

Lively mousse, with a somewhat lighter image than usual and a dry twist at the finish. Fine notes of coffee, apricots, and nougat play beautifully with the acidity.

- 1962 LA GRANDE DAME   95, APR 2000 (95) (62% PN, 38% CH)

The first, and today very rare vintage of Clicquot's prestige Champagne. Originally it was made as a strictly limited one-time thing. The first commercial vintage didn't appear until 1969. My bottle was purchased in Italy and had been stored a tad too warmly. Despite the unkind treatment and the rushed development, this is still a fantastic Champagne. Barely discernible mousse in this amber-colored drink.
The scent is mature, like a '53, with notes of mint chocolate, resin, treacle, and butterscotch. A colleague of mine thought the scent reminded him of his old boathouse on days when the summer sun bakes its sides. I know exactly what he means. The wood scent is even in the taste, backed up by a decidedly sweet chocolate tone. Incredibly fat, with unlimited layers of taste.

- 1990 LA GRANDE DAME ROSÉ   92, DEC 2001 (94) (62% PN, 38% CH)

I'm not sure if my prophecy will come true—that this wine will be even better than the first vintage of 1988. Slightly richer and creamier, with exceptional volume and authority. Layer upon layer of intense, young fruit.

- 1989 LA GRANDE DAME ROSÉ   93, AUG 2003 (94) (62% PN, 38% CH)

A wonderful Champagne that is both house-typical and worthy of its prestige label. Here we're dealing with a grand, magnificent wine full of majestic, slightly mushroomy, gamy Pinot Noir, backed up by a blood-orange-dominated rich fruitiness and a velvety-smooth seductive sensation on the tongue. A perfect wine for romantic, late-summer evenings in the sunset. • 1988 LA GRANDE DAME ROSÉ   93, NOV 2003 (93) (62% PN, 38% CH)

An extraordinary debut vintage! The house-style is easily recognized with its fleshy, chocolate-laden Pinot Noir. Also present is a sublime, aristocratic depth that pushes this newcomer right up into the elite series. The wine went into a peculiar, dry, smoky phase for a short period, only to finally find itself at the end of 2003. Then the wine acquired hints of orange, and the nose and palate suddenly exhibited that classic, toffee-ish nuttiness and notes of coffee that certain top rosés can get. Reminiscent of an '88 Billecart Elisabeth Rosé.

- 1989 CLICQUOT TRILENNIUM CUVÉE   82, NOV 1998 (89) (67% PN, 33% CH)

Tasted blind in Malmö with the legendary wine-collector Nils Sternby and a winemaker from Veuve Clicquot. None of us guessed that it was a Clicquot! The wine is said to be the same as the regular vintage Champagne but with a lower dosage, later disgorgement, and only available in magnum. We all thought that the wine seemed more like an '88 with its astringency and mineral-rich taste. Store this one!

- 1975 VEUVE CLICQUOT WEDDING CUVÉE   94, MAY 2003 (94) (67% PN, 33% CH)

Oh Clicquot, what a year 1975 was for you! Wonderfully well-kept, vibrant wine with generous toasty and nutty tones that are similar to Bollinger in style. Superbly mature brioche flavor and fresh fruit.

- 1970 CLICQUOT JUBILÉE   93, APR 2001 (93) (67% PN, 33% CH)

Yet another *cuvée* made for the British queen Elizabeth II's Silver Jubilee in 1977. Fresher, more elegant and a younger impression than the smokier, more masculine feeling that the normally labelled wine from the same vintage gives. Classic Clicquot notes—with all that these imply—evoking bready associations. Fat structure and fine mousse.

VEUVE FOURNY * R-M**

5, rue du Mesnil
51130 Vertus
03 26 52 16 30
Production: 70,000

Since 1955, the Fourny family has made its own Champagne. Today, Monique and Charles Fourny make delicious Champagnes from their 6.5 hectares. Organic farming, old vines, and oak barrels are the keys to their quick success.

• FOURNY GRANDE RÉSERVE   78
(20% PN, 80% CH)

• FOURNY BLANC DE BLANCS   64
(100% CH)

• FOURNY ROSÉ   71
(40% PN, 60% CH)

• 1996 FOURNY   88, MAR 2004 (90)
(100% CH)

This grower goes from strength to strength. A superbly compact, creamy, modern, impressive wine with big-house elegance, in the style of Henriot. Rich, pure fruit, eggnog aroma, and honey, as well as a delicious finish of vanilla.

• 1989 FOURNY   84, DEC 1998 (86)
(100% CH)

A big and full-bodied '89 where the fruit is very mature and massively concentrated. Long aftertaste of caramel and vanilla.

• 1996 FOURNY CLOS NOTRE DAME   84, JAN 2004 (90)
(100% CH)

An exciting *cuvée de prestige* from fifty-year-old vines and 100 percent old oak barrels. There isn't much oak character or "marmaladiness" here, rather a powerful, almost stony mineral character and a dry, austere, uniformly classic sensation on the tongue. The vintage's tough acidity isn't noticed either; instead they are handsomely camouflaged by the rich, appley fruit. The wine becomes more complex when aired, and to say that the wine is promising is an understatement.

• FOURNY CUVÉE "R"   91
(15% PN, 15% PM, 70% CH)

A wonderful prestige *cuvée* that was made to honor the founder, Roger Fourny. Organic handling of the old stocks, low yield, no filtration, local natural yeast, 50 percent old reserve wines, and everything in old barrels. Still, there is a Selosse-like spectrum of aromas: butter pears, dwarf bananas, sesame seeds, and new barrels in a deliciously buttery outer layer.

VEUVE LANAUD R-M

3, place Léon-Bourgeois
51190 Avize
03 26 57 99 19
Production: 160,000

This little Champagne house was founded seventy years ago by Henry Léopold Tabourin. The firm's largest export market is Belgium. The wines are sold under three labels: Veuve Lanaud, Ed Gauthier, and Charles Montherland.

• VEUVE LANAUD BLANC DE BLANCS   66
(100% CH)

VÉZIEN, MARCEL R-M

68, Grande Rue
10110 Celles-sur-Ource
03 25 38 50 22
Production: 150,000

Marcel Vézien is mayor of Celles-sur-Ource and makes heavy, Pinot-influenced Champagne.

• MARCEL VÉZIEN BRUT   55
(80% PN, 20% CH)

VILMART ** R-M**

4, rue de la République
51500 Rilly-la-Montagne
03 26 03 40 01
Production: 100,000

Vilmart has quickly established cult status, only topped among growers by J. Selosse. The firm was started in 1890 in Rilly and is now run by René and Laurent Champs. The grapes are of mere *premier cru* level, but the vinification is exceptional. Vilmart is one of the few growers that cultivate their grapes organically and have most of the grape juice ferment in large oak barrels (*foudres*) and the rest— ninety barrels in total—in small one-, two- and three-year-old barrels from Allier. All the wines lie in the barrel for ten months and are enriched through *bâtonnage*. The perfectly pure Champagnes that Vilmart produce from Rilly-la-Montague and Villers-Allerand all have a high, fine acidity due to the avoidance of malolactic fermentation. Since young Laurent took over from his father in 1991, the company has become one of the true gems with the perfect wine, Coeur de Cuvée, as its most brilliant star. The wine was the best made in Champagne during the "off-years" of '91, '92, '93, and '97. Hunt like a demon for the scarce 5,000 bottles that were made of this gem!

• GRANDE RÉSERVE   76
(70% PN, 30% CH)

• GRAND CELLIER   82
(30% PN, 70% CH)

I found a lot of oaky, heavy aromas in earlier versions of this wine. Today, Vilmart has found their way with this Chablis-like, romantically floral, first-class, nonvintage Champagne. The taste is pure and elegant. The grapes come from thirty-year-old vines.

• CUVÉE RUBIS ROSÉ   70
(90% PN, 10% CH)

• 1998 GRAND CELLIER D'OR   87, DEC 2003 (91)
(20% PN, 80% CH)

The regular vintage wine ferments and is stored in a blend of small and large barrels, as well as steel tanks. Tasted beside the Coeur de Cuvée, this wine feels slightly light and common, but if you sit for a time and delve down into the hidden chambers of this wine, you will discover great complexity, with a good balance between all its most important parts. There is a fine acidity and a spicy side, with notes of brioche, almond, and vanilla, as well as a concentrated chocolaty richness that will become even clearer if you have patience and keep your hands off it for a few years.

• 1997 GRAND CELLIER D'OR   85, FEB 2003 (88)
(30% PN, 70% CH)

An intense, distinctive wine with notes of Sauternes, glue, banana, sandalwood, and dark, slightly burned caramel. Richly mature, spicy taste; generous, exotic fruit is finely integrated with oak barrel character.

- 1993 GRAND CELLIER D'OR   90, DEC 2003 (90)
(30% PN, 70% CH)

On first contact with this wine I recoiled away from its fishy, gamy, unruly, protesting aromas. At the age of ten the wine has become fully mature and harmonious. The fruit is rich and exotic, handsomely backed up by elastic acidity and supple oak aromas.

- 1992 CRÉATION   78, DEC 2003 (78)
(20% PN, 80% CH)

- 1992 GRAND CELLIER D'OR   83, OCT 1999 (87)
(30% PN, 70% CH)

Finely structured and compact '92 with notes of barrel, vanilla, fresh spices, and melon. The finesse and elegance could be stronger. This is balanced by a wealth of exotic fruit that carries one's thoughts beyond France. I can understand why Americans love Vilmart.

- 1991 GRAND CELLIER D'OR   83, OCT 1999 (87)
(30% PN, 70% CH)

Oaky and fruity in "New World Style." Fine, idiosyncratic Champagne strongly imprinted by distinctive winemaking.

- 1989 GRAND CELLIER D'OR   81, APR 1995 (85)
(30% PN, 70% CH)

In the glass one is met by heavy, smoky, slightly stale aromas. The flavor is a lot better, with the exotic passion fruits leading on to a pure and long finish.

- 1979 GRAND CELLIER D'OR   76, APR 2001 (76)
(30% PN, 70% CH)

- 1997 COEUR DE CUVÉE   96, DEC 2003 (96)
(20% PN, 80% CH)

The company's most exclusive wine, as you know. The grapes are selectively picked from fifty-year-old vines and only the essence of the *cuvée* is used in these Chardonnay-dominated super-Champagnes. The wine is then stored for ten months in small 225-liter barrels before it winds up in its beautiful bottle. This time the harvest was unusually large, so there are 5,000 bottles for us Champagne nuts to share. The wine itself is incredibly concentrated and is basically identical to big white Burgundies from Lafon or Ramonet. To get a ninety-five-point experience directly, you should decant the Champagne, which will then shout out its gorgeous spectrum of nuts, toasted bread, lemon, new barrels, buttery dense creaminess, and deep oily exoticism. The wine is incredibly rich, with layers of coconut-y fruit and juicy vanilla aroma. Has anyone else done this well in this mediocre year?

- 1996 COEUR DE CUVÉE   88, JUL 2003 (94)
(20% PN, 80% CH)

I must admit that I'd expected more of this wine. For the moment, the wine is slightly bound with fishy keynotes. When aired, more harmony and complexity as well as sweet tones arise. Gamy, rather wild, rambunctious taste with impressive acidity. A very exciting wine going through a slightly strange phase. It's probably better than I deduced from my first bottle. Store for a really long time if you—unlike the grower himself—have any bottles left in your cellar.

- 1993 COEUR DE CUVÉE   94, NOV 2001 (94)
(20% PN, 80% CH)

A real turbo-wine that knocks all your senses for a loop. Certainly the oak character is massive, and the similarities with fruit-propelled American Parkerized monsters are striking. Still, you can't help but be impressed by one of the most massive Champagnes the world has ever seen. A cannonade of sweet spices and fruits is braided into the oak aroma. The wine feels sweet and almost tropical, with its tastes of coconut, banana, mango, and pineapple essence. The super-fresh acidity contrasts nicely with the richness of fruit. Of course, the wine will stand long storage, but I don't believe the wine will ever be more impressive than it is now, when newly launched.

- 1992 COEUR DE CUVÉE   96, DEC 2003 (96)
(20% PN, 80% CH)

Eleven years old, this magnum was released into the market in a limited edition. The wine is mature and elastic in a perfect, balanced way. In my wildest dreams, I couldn't imagine that it was possible to make such wonderfully good Champagne this year. The wine caresses with a velvety structure and oily fruit. The length and the heavy cream-caramel tone are irresistible. The most elegant wine Vilmart has ever created.

- 1991 COEUR DE CUVÉE   93, DEC 2003 (93)
(20% PN, 80% CH)

Laurent Champs has—even in this bad year—succeeded exceptionaly well. In a magnum this wine is still youthful, with an impressive, toasted, gamy bouquet. In a regular bottle maturity is complete, and both bottle sizes present a buttery, dense, extremely rich wine. It's emerged that Vilmart Coeur de Cuvée has consistently been Champagne's best wine in secondary years.

- 1990 COEUR DE CUVÉE   93, DEC 2003 (93)
(20% PN, 80% CH)

Oaky and dry with chewable density. Full of rich, mature oriental fruit on the palate. A real winner that Tom Stevenson has praised to the skies. The father's last vintage—and somewhat coarser than with Laurent Champs at the helm. One of the wines that placed worst at the Millennium Tasting, though it had murderous competition.

- 1989 COEUR DE CUVÉE   88, APR 1995 (93)
(30% PN, 70% CH)

A wonderfully elegant wine that resembles 1985 Gosset Grand Millésime with its multifaceted nose and crystal-clear flavor. One of the few '89s that have enough acidity to age well.

- 1997 GRAND CELLIER RUBIS ROSÉ   94, DEC 2003 (96)
(60% PN, 40% CH)

This is the first time I have met this rare wine. Only 2,000 bottles were made for our world. Not the oldest vines, but still traditional handling in small oak barrels for ten months, and Pinot dominates in this special *cuvée*. The color is light orange and pink. The mousse is exemplary. The nose is deep and complex with notes reminiscent of red Burgundy: petroleum, ripe cherries, strawberries, vanilla, and spices. Yes, the taste is fleshy and long, but still lighter, sweeter, creamier, and less woody than the scent hints at. Yet again, another great wine from Vilmart!

VISNEAUX, PATRICK R-M

4, rue Rommes
51160 Champillon
03 26 59 47 83
Production: 8,000

One of the smallest wine houses I've succeeded in finding that makes and sells its own Champagne.

- PATRICK VISNEAUX BRUT   75
  (70% PM, 30% CH)
- 1998 PATRICK VISNEAUX   82, MAY 2003 (85)
  Elasticity and fleshiness in nice harmony. Crackling juiciness leaning toward apple. Rounded, pleasant finish and an unusually big portion of elegance from a grower hailing from the Marne Valley.

VOIRIN-JUMEL R-M

555, rue Libération
51530 Cramant
03 26 57 55 82
Production: 60,000

Actually the only example I've found in Cramant where the wines are coarse and the property mismanaged.

- VOIRIN-JUMEL BLANC DE BLANCS   60
  (100% CH)
- 1994 VOIRIN-JUMEL   20, FEB 1999 (>)
  (100% CH)
- 1993 VOIRIN-JUMEL   50, JAN 1999 (>)
  (100% CH)
- 1990 VOIRIN-JUMEL   75, FEB 1997 (80)
  (100% CH)
  This is a very rich and chocolaty wine, with a fat structure and pompous expression. I do miss some of Cramant's purity.
- 1982 VOIRIN-JUMEL   60, APR 1996 (60)
  (100% CH)

VOLLEREAUX N-M

rue Léon-Bourgeois
51530 Pierry
03 26 54 03 05
Production: 400,000

The company owns forty hectares in the Marne valley and makes low-price Champagnes for the French market. Only 20 percent is exported.

- VOLLEREAUX BRUT   53
  (33% PN, 33% PM, 34% CH)
- VOLLEREAUX BLANC DE BLANCS   60
  (100% CH)
- VOLLEREAUX ROSÉ   35
  (100% PN)
- 1989 VOLLEREAUX   65, AUG 1995 (78)
  (50% PN, 10% PM, 40% CH)
- 1975 VOLLEREAUX   83, JUL 1995 (84)
  (30% PN, 30% PM, 40% CH)
  Unashamedly fresh and young twenty-year-old with beautiful green/yellow color and a youthful nose of lemon peel, hay, and popcorn. A sparkling mousse and a light lime, crispy finish.

- 1994 VOLLEREAUX BLANC DE BLANCS   68, MAR 1999 (70)
  (100% CH)
- 1991 VOLLEREAUX BLANC DE BLANCS   65, MAR 1999 (69)
  (100% CH)
- 1993 CUVÉE MARGUERITE   70, MAR 1997 (84)
  (25% PN, 75% CH)
  A very young, fresh Champagne where the subdued nose has a flowery side, and the promising flavor is jam-packed with uplifting acidity.

VRANKEN N-M

42, avenue de Champagne
51200 Épernay
03 26 53 33 20
Production: 1,800,000

Paul-Francois Vranken from Belgium is one of the smartest businessmen in Champagne, having built up a small empire from virtually nothing. He owns Vranken, Demoiselle, Charles Lafitte, Sacotte, Barancourt and—since 1996—Heidsieck & Monopole. In 1976 Vranken decided to create a brand that bore his own name. He also produces *cava* in Spain and has businesses in his old homeland, Belgium. Apart from Champagne, he also has a passion for port, and consequently owns three different port-wine producers: Quinta do Convento, Sao Pedro, and Quinta do Paco. What a guy!

- VRANKEN BRUT   60
  (33% PN, 33% PM, 34% CH)
- 1975 VRANKEN   93, OCT 2000 (93)
  (10% PN, 90% CH)
  Vranken's first own-vintage wine is truly sensational. The developed, soft nose is similar to a '64, with its notes of nut, marzipan, duck liver, gunsmoke, and brioche. Soft, nutty, subtle, and exceedingly charming.

WAFFLART, GUY R-M

6, rue Saint Caprais
51390 Bouilly
03 26 49 21 01
Production: 80,000

This grower uses all three grape types in its *cuvées*. They have more than six hectares in Bouilly and the surrounding area. The wines are put through malolactic fermentation and their prestige *cuvées* ferment in oak barrels.

- GUY WAFFLART RÉSERVE   48
  (100% PM)
- GUY WAFFLART ROSÉ   45
  (100% PM)

WANNER-BOUGE R-M

177, rue du 8 Mai 1945
51530 Cramant
03 26 57 52 35
Production: 250,000

The firm was founded in 1870. Jacques Wanner produces slightly thin but elegant Champagnes from his seven hectares in Cramant, Oiry, and Chouilly.

- WANNER-BOUGE GRANDE RÉSERVE   58
  (20% PN, 20% PM, 60% CH)
- WANNER-BOUGE BLANC DE BLANCS   68
  (100% CH)
- 1990 WANNER-BOUGE   69, JUL 1995 (80)
  (100% CH)
  Closed and surprisingly thin, but with village-typical creamy
  aromas.

WARIS-LARMANDIER R-M

608, remparts du Nord
51190 Avize
03 26 57 79 05
Production: 8,000
Vincent Waris started the company in 1984, and his production
comes from three hectares in Avize, Cramant, and Chouilly.
- WARIS-LARMANDIER BLANC DE BLANCS   70
  (100% CH)

WARRIS ET CHENAYER R-M

1, rue Pasteur
51190 Avize
03 26 57 50 88
Production: 80,000
Vincent Waris founded this company in 1894; his minimal
production comes from three hectares in Avize, Cramant, and
Chouilly. Owned by Delbeck. Other wines: Super Imperator, Rosé,
Vintage, and Cuvée Etrusque.
- WARRIS ET CHENAYER BLANC DE BLANCS   68
  (100% CH)

TAITTINGER COLLECTION MASSON
1982

TAITTINGER COLLECTION DA SILVA
1983

DOM RUINART BLANC DE BLANCS
1988

BOLLINGER VIEILLES VIGNES FRANÇAISES
1990

SALON LE MESNIL
1985

LOUISE POMMERY ROSÉ
1990

MOËT ET CHANDON DOM PÉRIGNON
1961

MOËT ET CHANDON BRUT IMPÉRIAL
1921

MUMM CORDON ROUGE
1955

RENÉ LALOU
1979

BOLLINGER BRUT
1964

BOLLINGER GRANDE ANNÉE
1990

BOLLINGER RD
1969

BOLLINGER VIEILLES VIGNES FRANÇAISES
1970

DAMPIERRE PRESTIGE
1985

PIPER HEIDSIECK FLORENS LOUIS
1966

GASTON CHIQUET BLANC DE BLANCS D'AŸ
1970

GASTON CHIQUET BLANC DE BLANCS D'AŸ
1982

The best Champagnes

These lists reflect an evaluation based solely on a given wine's number of inherent maximum-potential points.

The wine's quality today is not taken into account. Deciding on the comparative ranking of the producers in each group is left to the reader.

THE 100 BEST CHAMPAGNES

1	1928 Pol Roger Grauves	100
2	1938 Krug	99
3	1955 Clos des Goisses	99
4	1979 Krug Clos du Mesnil	99
5	1988 Krug Clos du Mesnil	99
6	1982 Krug Clos du Mesnil	99
7	1996 Bollinger Vieilles Vignes	99
8	1959 Billecart-Salmon N.F.	99
9	1955 Billecart-Salmon N.F.	99
10	1955 Cristal	99
11	1959 Henriot	99
12	1955 Clicquot	99
13	1985 Krug Clos du Mesnil	99
14	1959 Clos des Goisses	99
15	1945 Bollinger	99
16	1952 Gosset	99
17	1938 Krug Collection	98
18	1947 Salon	98
19	1934 Pol Roger	98
20	1953 Salon	98
21	1961 Billecart-Salmon N.F.	98
22	1964 Dom Pérignon	98
23	1928 Krug Collection	98
24	1989 Krug Clos du Mesnil	98
25	1959 Cristal	98
26	1990 Krug Clos du Mesnil	98
27	1953 Clos des Goisses	98
28	1949 Cristal	98
29	1949 Krug Collection	98
30	1966 Billecart-Salmon B. de B.	98
31	1966 Krug	98
32	1990 Bollinger Vieilles Vignes	98
33	1985 Bollinger Vieilles Vignes	98
34	1966 Krug Collection	98
35	1964 Diamant Bleu	98
36	1961 Krug Collection	98
37	1969 Jacquesson D.T.	98
38	1970 Bollinger Vieilles Vignes	98
39	1955 Gratien	98
40	1955 Salon	98
41	1988 Cristal Rosé	98
42	1961 Krug	98
43	1964 Cristal	98
44	1982 Krug	98
45	1976 Comtes de Champagne	98
46	1914 Bollinger	98
47	1988 Krug	98
48	1971 Comtes de Champ. Rosé	98
49	1959 Salon	98
50	1921 Moët & Chandon	98
51	1921 Pommery	98
52	1959 Krug Collection	98
53	1961 Dom Pérignon	98
54	1976 Des Princes	98
55	1961 Salon	98
56	1989 Bollinger Vieilles Vignes	98
57	1989 Cristal	98
58	1959 Ed Bonville	98
59	1914 Pol Roger	97
60	1966 Cristal	97
61	1961 Roederer Rosé	97
62	1959 Krug	97
63	1929 Bollinger	97
64	1911 Pol Roger	97
65	1966 Florens-Louis	97
66	1921 José Michel	97
67	1979 Krug Collection	97
68	1959 Bollinger	97
69	1959 Pol Roger	97
70	1966 Bollinger	97
71	1979 Krug	97
72	1976 La Grande Dame	97
73	1976 Cristal Rosé	97
74	1975 Winston Churchill	97
75	Grand Siècle (75/73/70)	97
76	1955 Krug	97
77	1961 Des Princes	97
78	1949 Salon	97
79	1979 Des Princes	97
80	1947 Launois	97
81	1990 Selosse "N"	97
82	1981 Krug Clos du Mesnil	97
83	1966 Salon	97
84	1949 Roederer	97
85	1949 Krug	97
86	1971 Cristal	97
87	1986 Selosse	97
88	1988 Pol Roger P.R.	97
89	1996 Cristal	97
90	1964 Clos des Goisses	97
91	1966 Launois	97
92	1979 Dom Ruinart	97
93	1990 Cristal "2000"	97
94	1914 Moët & Chandon	97
95	1947 Roederer	97
96	1921 Pol Roger	97
97	1964 Salon	97
98	1979 Launois Special Club	97
99	1990 Cristal Rosé	97
100	1988 Dom Pérignon Rosé	97

THE BEST CHAMPAGNES IN EACH CATEGORY

NON-VINTAGE CHAMPAGNES FROM ALL CATEGORIES

1	Moët & Chandon Les Sarments d'Aÿ	90
2	De Sousa Caudalies	89
3	Selosse Extra Brut	89
4	Selosse Originale	87
5	Jérome Prévôst	87
6	Chèvres Pierreuses	86
7	Clos des Champions	85
8	Henriot Blanc de Blancs	85
9	Selosse Tradition	85
10	Moët Le Vigne de Saran	84

NON-VINTAGE CHAMPAGNES FROM THE CHAMPAGNE HOUSES

1	Gosset Grande Réserve	83
2	Henriot Souverain Brut	83
3	Bollinger Special Cuvée	82
4	Roederer Brut Premier	82
5	Jacquesson Perfection	81
6	Deutz Brut Classic	80
7	Pol Roger Brut	80
8	Billecart-Salmon Brut	80
9	Gosset Brut Excellence	80
10	Veuve Clicquot Brut	79

DATED NON-VINTAGE CHAMPAGNES

1	Grand Siècle (75/73/70)	97
2	Grand Siècle (55/53/52)	96
3	Grand Siècle (76/75/73)	96
4	Grand Siècle (96/95/93)	96
5	Grand Siècle (90/88/85)	95
6	Grand Siècle (79/78/76)	95
7	L'Exclusive Ruinart	94
8	Clos du Moulin (85/83/82)	94
9	Grand Siècle (85/82/81)	93
10	Reserve Charlie Mis en Cave 90	93

DEMI-SEC (MEDIUM DRY)

1	1996 Veuve Clicquot Rich	85
2	Billecart 150 Anniversary Cuvée	85
3	Selosse Excuisse	84
4	1990 Veuve Clicquot Rich	83
5	1988 Veuve Clicquot Rich	83
6	1995 Veuve Clicquot Rich	83
7	1990 Delamotte	83
8	1991 Philipponnat Sublime	81
9	1993 Veuve Clicquot Rich	82
10	1989 Veuve Clicquot Rich	80

NON-VINTAGE ROSÉS

1	Krug Rosé	95
2	P. Laurain Rosé	89
3	Gosset Grand Rosé	88
4	Fliniaux Rosé	88
5	Collery Rosé	88
6	Billecart-Salmon Rosé	86
7	B. Hatté Rosé	84
8	A. Clouet Rosé	84
9	Selosse Rosé	84
10	P. Bara Rosé	84

PRESTIGE NON-VINTAGE CHAMPAGNES

1	Krug Private Cuvée	96
2	Krug Grande Cuvée	96
3	Charles Heidsieck Cuvée 140	95
4	L'Exclusive Ruinart	94
5	Grand Siècle	93
6	Reserve Charlie	93
7	Selosse Origine	93
8	Selosse Substance	93
9	Taittinger Millennium	93
10	Clouet Cuvée 1911	93

VINTAGE ROSÉS

1	1988 Cristal Rosé	98
2	1971 Comtes de Champ. Rosé	98
3	1976 Cristal Rosé	97
4	1961 Roederer Rosé	97
5	1990 Cristal Rosé	97
6	1988 Dom Pérignon Rosé	97
7	1985 William Deutz Rosé	97
8	1989 Cristal Rosé	97
9	1979 Comtes de Champ. Rosé	97
10	1985 Dom Pérignon Rosé	97
11	1988 William Deutz Rosé	97
12	1995 Cristal Rosé	97
13	1934 Pommery Rosé	97
14	1982 Cristal Rosé	97
15	1996 William Deutz Rosé	96
16	1985 Cristal Rosé	96
17	1990 William Deutz Rosé	96
18	1982 William Deutz Rosé	96
19	1952 Roederer Rosé	96
20	1966 Dom Pérignon Rosé	96
21	1962 Dom Pérignon Rosé	96
22	1959 Mumm Rosé	96
23	1929 Pommery Rosé	96
24	1990 Dom Pérignon Rosé	96
25	1969 Comtes de Champ. Rosé	96
26	1997 Vilmart Cellier Rubis	96
27	1969 Dom Pérignon Rosé	96
28	1982 Belle Epoque Rosé	96
29	1959 Dom Pérignon Rosé	96
30	1985 Belle Epoque Rosé	95
31	1990 Dom Ruinart Rosé	95
32	1995 Signature Rosé	95
33	1988 Belle Epoque Rosé	95
34	1990 Signature Rosé	95
35	1981 Cristal Rosé	95
36	1937 Pommery Rosé	95
37	1971 Dom Pérignon Rosé	95
38	1973 Dom Pérignon Rosé	95
39	1975 Bollinger Rosé	95
40	1988 Billecart Elisabeth	95

COTEAUX CHAMPENOIS, WHITE

1	1992 Clos des Goisses Blanc	89
2	Moët & Chandon Saran	80

COTEAUX CHAMPENOIS, RED

1	1953 A. Clouet Bouzy Rouge	90
2	1946 A. Clouet Bouzy Rouge	90
3	1990 Gatinois Aÿ Rouge	86
4	1996 Gosset-Brabant Aÿ Rouge	86
5	1995 Gosset-Brabant Aÿ Rouge	85
6	1996 Gatinois Aÿ Rouge	85
7	1976 R.H. Coutier Ambonnay Rouge	85
8	1976 Secondé-Prevoteau Ambonnay Rouge	84
9	1993 Gatinois Aÿ Rouge	84
10	1990 René Geoffroy Cumières Rouge	83

THE BEST CHAMPAGNES FROM 2000 TO 1892

2000

1	Leglapart Apôtre	91
2	Leglapart Artiste	90

1999

1	Diebolt Fleur de Passion	96
2	Mesnillésime	94
3	Launois Special Club	91

1998

1	Diebolt Fleur de Passion	95
2	Gosset Grand Millésimé Rosé	94
3	Egly-Ouriet	93
4	Bonnaire Prestige	92
5	Vilmart Grand Cellier d'Or	91
6	André Clouet	91
7	Philippe Gonet Special Club	91
8	Taittinger	90

1997

1	Vilmart Coeur de Cuvée	96
2	Vilmart Grand Cellier Rubis	96
3	Roederer Blanc de Blancs	94
4	Diebolt Fleur de Passion	94
5	Billecart-Salmon Blanc de Blancs	93
6	Bonnaire Sois Bois	93
7	Billecart-Salmon N.F.	92
8	Belle Epoque Rosé	92
9	Billecart-Salmon Elisabeth Rosé	91
10	Amour de Deutz	91

1996

1	Bollinger Vieilles Vignes	99
2	Cristal	97
3	Jacquesson Blanc de Noirs Aÿ	97
4	Bollinger Grande Année	96
5	William Deutz Rosé	96
6	Dom Pérignon	96
7	Diebolt Fleur de Passion	96
8	Peters Cuvée Spéciale	96
9	Roederer Blanc de Blancs	95
10	Roederer	95

1995

1	Cristal Rosé	97
2	Cristal	97
3	Bollinger Grande Année	96
4	Comtes de Champagne	96
5	Cuvée Sir Winston Churchill	96
6	Dom Pérignon	95
7	La Grande Dame	95
8	Billecart-Salmon Blanc de Blancs	95
9	Diebolt Fleur de Passion	95
10	Signature Rosé	95

1994

1	Cristal	93
2	Comtes de Champagne	92
3	Roederer Blanc de Blancs	92
4	Launois Special Club	92
5	Roederer Rosé	92
6	Roederer	92
7	Belle Epoque	89
8	Bonnaire Sois Bois	89
9	André Clouet	88
10	Lanson	88

1993

1	Cuvée Sir Winston Churchill	94
2	Vilmart Coeur de Cuvée	94
3	Dom Pérignon Rosé	94
4	Cristal	93
5	Selosse	93
6	Dom Pérignon	93
7	Signature	93
8	Comtes de Champagne	93
9	La Grande Dame	92
10	Dom Ruinart	92

1992

1	Bollinger Vieilles Vignes	97
2	Vilmart Coeur de Cuvée	96
3	Selosse	92
4	Bollinger Grande Année	92
5	Dom Pérignon	90
6	Dom Pérignon Rosé	90
7	Pommery	89
8	Pertois-Lebrun	89
9	Gatinois	88
10	Perrier-Jouët	88

1991

1	Vilmart Coeur de Cuvée	93
2	Clos des Goisses	92
3	Elisabeth Salmon Rosé	90
4	Billecart N.F.	89
5	Bonnaire	89
6	Comtes de Champagne Rosé	89
7	A. Gratien	89
8	Roederer Rosé	88
9	Gatinois	87

1990
1 Krug Clos du Mesnil 98
2 Bollinger Vieilles Vignes 98
3 Selosse "N" 97
4 Cristal "2000" 97
5 Cristal Rosé 97
6 Salon 97
7 Cristal 97
8 William Deutz Rosé 96
9 Billecart-Salmon Blanc de Blancs 96
10 Dom Pérignon Rosé 96

1989
1 Krug Clos du Mesnil 98
2 Bollinger Vieilles Vignes 98
3 Cristal 98
4 Selosse "N" 97
5 Krug 97
6 Clos des Goisses 96
7 Selosse 95
8 Pierre Peters Cuvée Spéciale 95
9 Comtes de Champagne 94
10 Belle Epoque Rosé 94

1988
1 Krug Clos du Mesnil 98
2 Krug 98
3 Cristal Rosé 98
4 Pol Roger P.R. 97
5 Dom Pérignon Rosé 97
6 William Deutz Rosé 97
7 Cristal 97
8 Bollinger Vieilles Vignes 97
9 Selosse Cuvée "N" 97
10 Comtes de Champagne 97

1987
1 Louise Pommery 91
2 Selosse Origine 90
3 Bonnaire 88

1986
1 Selosse 97
2 Krug Clos du Mesnil 96
3 Clos des Goisses 94
4 Bollinger Vieilles Vignes 94
5 Dom Pérignon Rosé 94
6 Comtes de Champagne 93
7 Bonnaire Special Club 93
8 Belle Epoque Rosé 93
9 Winston Churchill 92
10 Comtes de Champ. Rosé 92

1985
1 Krug Clos du Mesnil 99
2 Bollinger Vieilles Vignes 98
3 William Deutz Rosé 97
4 Dom Pérignon Rosé 97
5 Salon 97
6 Cristal Rosé 96
7 Comtes de Champagne 96
8 Winston Churchill 96
9 Clos des Goisses 96
10 Peters Cuvée Spéciale 96

1983
1 Krug Clos du Mesnil 96
2 Billecart-Salmon Blanc de Blancs 94
3 Cristal Rosé 94
4 Champagne Charlie 94
5 Clos des Goisses 94
6 Gratien 94
7 Diebolt 94
8 Comtes de Champ. Rosé 94

9 Salon 93
10 Bonnaire Special Club 93

1982
1 Krug Clos du Mesnil 99
2 Krug 98
3 Cristal Rosé 97
4 William Deutz Rosé 96
5 Salon 96
6 Bollinger Vieilles Vignes 96
7 Belle Epoque Rosé 96
8 Clos des Goisses 96
9 Selosse 95
10 Billecart-Salmon Grande Cuvée 95

1981
1 Krug Clos du Mesnil 97
2 Bollinger Vieilles Vignes 97
3 Krug 96
4 Cristal Rosé 95
5 Launois Special Club 95
6 Bonnaire Special Club 95
7 Comtes de Champagne 94
8 Cristal 94
9 Charles Heidsieck Blanc de Blancs 94
10 Dom Ruinart 93

1980
1 Krug Clos du Mesnil 97
2 Bollinger Vieilles Vignes 95
3 Clos des Goisses 95
4 Dom Pérignon Rosé 92
5 Dom Pérignon Oenoteque 92
6 Leclerc-Briant Cuvée Liberté 92
7 Dom Pérignon 91
8 Audoin de Dampierre 91
9 Orpale 91
10 Pommery Flacon d'Exception 90

1979
1 Krug Clos du Mesnil 99
2 Krug Collection 97
3 Krug 97
4 Des Princes 97
5 Dom Ruinart 97
6 Launois Special Club 97
7 Comtes de Champagne Rosé 97
8 Comtes de Champagne 97
9 La Grande Dame 96
10 Salon 96

1978
1 Clos des Goisses 94
2 La Grande Dame 93
3 Dom Pérignon Oenoteque 93
4 Cristal 93
5 Billecart N.F. 93
6 Belle Epoque 93
7 Dom Ruinart Rosé 93
8 Dom Pérignon 93
9 De Venoge Cramant 93
10 Gosset 91

1977
1 Cristal 93

1976
1 Comtes de Champagne 98
2 Des Princes 98
3 La Grande Dame 97
4 Cristal Rosé 97
5 Enchanteleurs 97
6 Billecart-Salmon N.F. 96
7 Cristal 96
8 Dom Pérignon Oenoteque 96

9 Baccarat 96
10 Salon 96

1975
1 Winston Churchill 97
2 La Grande Dame 97
3 Deutz Aÿ 96
4 Bollinger Vieilles Vignes 96
5 Comtes de Champagne 96
6 P.R. 96
7 Bonnaire 96
8 Diamant Bleu 95
9 Bollinger R.D. 95
10 Pol Roger Blanc de Chardonnay 95

1974
1 Cristal 91
2 Billecart-Salmon Rosé 91
3 Philipponnat Grand Blanc 90

1973
1 Dom Pérignon Oenoteque 96
2 Dom Pérignon 96
3 Pierre Peters 96
4 Belle Epoque 95
5 Comtes de Champagne 95
6 Krug Collection 95
7 Krug 95
8 Dom Pérignon Rosé 95
9 Billecart-Salmon Blanc de Blancs 94
10 Dom Ruinart 94

1971
1 Comtes de Champagne Rosé 98
2 Cristal 97
3 Krug Collection 96
4 Krug 96
5 Comtes de Champagne 96
6 Castellane Blanc de Blancs 96
7 Bollinger Chouilly Reserve 96
8 Dom Pérignon Rosé 95
9 Roederer 95
10 Dom Ruinart 95

1970
1 Bollinger Vieilles Vignes 98
2 Gratien 94
3 Bollinger R.D. Année Rare 94
4 Bollinger R.D. 94
5 Gosset 94
6 Veuve Clicquot Jubilée 93
7 Bollinger 93
8 Comtes de Champagne Rosé 93
9 Veuve Clicquot 92
10 Cristal 92

1969
1 Jacquesson D.T. 98
2 Salon 97
3 Comtes de Champagne 97
4 Bollinger Vieilles Vignes 96
5 Cristal 96
6 Florens Louis 96
7 Dom Pérignon 96
8 Dom Pérignon Rosé 96
9 Bollinger R.D. 96
10 Bollinger 95

1967
1 Cristal 93

1966
1 Billecart-Salmon Blanc de Blancs 98
2 Krug 98
3 Krug Collection 98
4 Cristal 97

5 Florens Louis		97
6 Bollinger		97
7 Salon		97
8 Launois		97
9 Clos des Goisses		97
10 Dom Pérignon		96
1965		
1 José Michel		93
1964		
1 Dom Pérignon		98
2 Diamant Bleu		98
3 Cristal		98
4 Salon		97
5 Clos des Goisses		97
6 Des Princes		96
7 Pol Roger Blanc de Blancs		96
8 Launois		96
9 Belle Epoque		96
10 Comtes de Champagne		96
1962		
1 Cristal		97
2 Dom Pérignon Oenoteque		96
3 Diamant Bleu		96
4 Dom Pérignon Rosé		96
5 Veuve Clicquot		96
6 Bollinger		95
7 La Grande Dame		95
8 Krug Collection		95
9 Krug		95
10 Roederer		95
1961		
1 Billecart-Salmon N.F.		98
2 Krug Collection		98
3 Krug		98
4 Dom Pérignon		98
5 Salon		98
6 Roederer Rosé		97
7 Florens-Louis		97
8 Des Princes		97
9 Diebolt		97
10 Comtes de Champagne		96
1959		
1 Billecart-Salmon N.F.		99
2 Henriot		99
3 Clos des Goisses		99
4 Cristal		98
5 Salon		98
6 Krug Collection		98
7 Ed Bonville		98
8 Krug		97
9 Bollinger		97
10 Pol Roger		97
1958		
1 Guiborat		94
1955		
1 Clos des Goisses		99
2 Billecart-Salmon N.F.		99
3 Cristal		99
4 Clicquot		98
5 Gratien		98
6 Salon		98
7 Piper-Heidsieck		97
8 Krug		97
9 Henriot		97
10 Piper-Heidsieck		96
1954		
1 Henriot		96
1953		

1 Salon		98
2 Clos des Goisses		98
3 Diebolt		97
4 Joseph Perrier		97
5 Piper-Heidsieck		97
6 Krug		96
7 Clicquot		96
8 Moët & Chandon		95
9 Cristal		94
10 Bollinger		94
1952		
1 Gosset		99
2 Roederer Rosé		96
3 Clos des Goisses		96
4 Pommery		95
5 Dom Pérignon		95
6 Heidsieck & Monopole		95
7 José Michel		94
8 Pol Roger		93
9 Jacquesson Perfection		93
10 Krug Collection		92
1951		
1 Salon		93
1949		
1 Cristal		98
2 Krug Collection		98
3 Salon		97
4 Roederer		97
5 Krug		96
6 Pol Roger		96
7 Clicquot		95
8 Pommery		95
9 Charles Heidsieck		94
10 Mumm		94
1948		
1 Salon		93
1947		
1 Salon		98
2 Launois		97
3 Roederer		97
4 Pol Roger		96
5 Krug		94
6 Moët & Chandon		94
7 Pol Roger Wedding Cuvée		93
8 Pommery		92
1945		
1 Bollinger		99
2 Roederer		97
3 Clicquot		96
4 Pol Roger		94
5 Delbeck		94
6 Boizel		94
7 Pommery Rosé		92
1944		
1 Mailly		91
1943		
1 José Michel		96
2 Krug		95
3 Irroy		94
4 Moët Coronation Cuvée		94
5 Dom Pérignon		94
6 Pommery		94
7 Perrier-Jouët		93
1942		
1 Pol Roger		92
2 Victor Clicquot		91
1941		
1 Pommery		96

2 Charles Heidsieck		94
3 Roederer		94
4 Pommery Rosé		93
5 Mercier		93
1938		
1 Krug		99
2 Krug Collection		98
1937		
1 Krug		95
2 Pommery		95
3 Pommery Rosé		95
4 Clicquot		94
1934		
1 Pol Roger		98
2 Pommery Rosé		97
3 Pommery		95
4 Clicquot		91
1929		
1 Bollinger		97
2 Pommery Rosé		96
3 Pommery		96
4 Heidsieck & Monopole		95
5 Veuve Clicquot		95
1928		
1 Pol Roger Grauves		100
2 Krug Collection		98
3 Bollinger		97
4 Roederer		96
5 Moët & Chandon		96
6 Jacquesson Perfection		95
7 Irroy		95
8 Clicquot		95
1926		
1 Krug		95
2 Pol Roger		94
1923		
1 Roederer		96
2 Clicquot		91
1921		
1 Moët & Chandon		98
2 Pommery		98
3 José Michel		97
4 Pol Roger		97
5 Heidsieck & Monopole		96
6 Lanson		96
7 Perrier-Jouët		95
1919		
1 Clicquot		95
2 Heidsieck & Co.		94
1915		
1 De Castellane		93
1914		
1 Bollinger		98
2 Pol Roger		97
3 Moët & Chandon		97
1911		
1 Pol Roger		97
2 Pommery		96
3 Moët & Chandon		95
4 Perrier-Jouët		90
1907		
1 Heidsieck & Co.		89
1904		
1 Moët & Chandon		94
1892		
1 Pol Roger		89
2 Lanson		87

THE BEST CHAMPAGNES BY DECADE

THE 1990s
1	1996 Bollinger Vieilles Vignes	99
2	1990 Krug Clos du Mesnil	98
3	1990 Bollinger Vieilles Vignes	98
4	1990 Selosse "N"	97
5	1996 Cristal	97
6	1990 Cristal "2000"	97
7	1990 Cristal Rosé	97
8	1995 Cristal Rosé	97
9	1992 Bollinger Vieilles Vignes	97
10	1995 Cristal	97

THE 1980s
1	1988 Krug Clos du Mesnil	99
2	1982 Krug Clos du Mesnil	99
3	1985 Krug Clos du Mesnil	99
4	1989 Krug Clos du Mesnil	98
5	1985 Bollinger Vieilles Vignes	98
6	1988 Cristal Rosé	98
7	1982 Krug	98
8	1988 Krug	98
9	1989 Bollinger Vieilles Vignes	98
10	1989 Cristal	98

THE 1970s
1	1979 Krug Clos du Mesnil	99
2	1970 Bollinger Vieilles Vignes	98
3	1976 Comtes de Champagne	98
4	1971 Comtes de Champ. Rosé	98
5	1976 Des Princes	98
6	1979 Krug Collection	97
7	1979 Krug	97
8	1976 La Grande Dame	97
9	1976 Cristal Rosé	97
10	1975 Cuvée Sir Winston Churchill	97

THE 1960s
1	1961 Billecart-Salmon N.F.	98
2	1964 Dom Pérignon	98
3	1966 Billecart-Salmon B. de B.	98
4	1966 Krug	98
5	1966 Krug Collection	98
6	1964 Diamant Bleu	98
7	1961 Krug Collection	98
8	1969 Jacquesson D.T.	98
9	1961 Krug	98
10	1964 Cristal	98

THE 1950s
1	1955 Clos des Goisses	99
2	1959 Billecart-Salmon N.F.	99
3	1955 Billecart-Salmon N.F.	99
4	1955 Cristal	99
5	1959 Henriot	99
6	1959 Clos des Goisses	99
7	1955 Clicquot	99
8	1952 Gosset	99
9	1953 Salon	98
10	1959 Cristal	98

THE 1940s
1	1945 Bollinger	99
2	1947 Salon	98
3	1949 Cristal	98
4	1949 Krug Collection	98
5	1949 Salon	97
6	1947 Launois	97
7	1949 Roederer	97
8	1949 Krug	97
9	1947 Roederer	97
10	1945 Roederer	97

THE 1930s
1	1938 Krug	99
2	1938 Krug Collection	98
3	1934 Pol Roger	98
4	1934 Pommery Rosé	97
5	1937 Krug	95
6	1937 Pommery	95
7	1937 Pommery Rosé	95
8	1937 Veuve Clicquot	94
9	1937 De Venoge	93
10	1934 Veuve Clicquot	91

THE 1920s
1	1928 Pol Roger Grauves	100
2	1928 Krug Collection	98
3	1921 Moët & Chandon	98
4	1921 Pommery	98
5	1929 Bollinger	97
6	1921 José Michel	97
7	1921 Pol Roger	97
8	1928 Bollinger	97
9	1929 Pommery Rosé	96
10	1923 Roederer	96

THE 1910s
1	1914 Bollinger	98
2	1914 Pol Roger	97
3	1911 Pol Roger	97
4	1914 Moët & Chandon	97
5	1911 Pommery	96
6	1919 Clicquot	95
7	1911 Moët & Chandon	95
8	1919 Heidsieck & Co.	94
9	1904 Moët & Chandon	94
10	1915 De Castellane	93

MY FAVORITE CHAMPAGNES

THE PRODUCERS
Billecart-Salmon
Bollinger
Guy Charlemagne
Deutz
Diebolt-Vallois
Gosset
Charles Heidsieck
Henriot
Jacquesson
Krug
Moët & Chandon
Perrier-Jouët
Pierre Peters
Pol Roger
Roederer
Salon
Selosse
Taittinger
Veuve Clicquot
Vilmart

MY FAVORITE CHAMPAGNES SINCE 1980
Billecart Grande Cuvée
Billecart N.F.
Belle Epoque
Belle Epoque Rosé
Bollinger Grande Année
Bollinger Vieilles Vignes
Charlemagne Mesnillésime
Clicquot La Grande Dame
Cuvée William Deutz Rosé
Diebolt Fleur de Passion
Dom Pérignon
Dom Pérignon Rosé
Dom Ruinart
Jacquesson Signature
Jacquesson Signature Rosé
Krug Clos du Mesnil
Krug Vintage/Collection
Philipponnat Clos des Goisses
Pierre Peters Cuvée Spéciale
Pol Roger Winston Churchill
Pol Roger P.R.

Roederer Blanc de Blancs
Roederer Cristal
Roederer Cristal Rosé
Salon
Selosse "N"
Selosse Vintage
Taittinger Comtes de Champagne
Taittinger Comtes de Champagne Rosé
Vilmart Coeur de Cuvée

THE BEST CHAMPAGNES TO HAVE RECENTLY HAD THEIR SEDIMENT REMOVED, BY ORDER OF EXCELLENCE
1	1928 Pol Roger Grauves	100
2	1955 Clos des Goisses	99
3	1959 Henriot	99
4	1955 Clicquot	99
5	1934 Pol Roger	98
6	1953 Clos des Goisses	98
7	1969 Jacquesson D.T.	98
8	1959 Ed Bonville	98
9	1921 Moët & Chandon	98

10	1921 Pommery	98
11	1959 Clos des Goisses	97
12	1914 Moët & Chandon	97
13	1966 Salon	97
14	1964 Clos des Goisses	97
15	1921 Pol Roger	97
16	1959 Salon	97
17	1966 Clos des Goisses	97
18	1953 Diebolt	97
19	1976 Enchanteleurs	97
20	1961 Diebolt	97
21	1959 Lanson	96
22	1964 Dom Pérignon	96
23	1975 Deutz d'Aÿ	96
24	1969 Bollinger R.D.	96
25	1964 Bollinger R.D.	96
26	1947 Pol Roger	96
27	1985 Clos des Goisses	96
28	1952 Clos des Goisses	96
29	1976 Dom Pérignon	96
30	1976 Henriot	96
31	1954 Henriot	96
32	1928 Moët & Chandon	96
33	1961 Lanson	96
34	1961 De Venoge	96
35	1966 Dom Pérignon	95
36	1975 Bollinger R.D.	95
37	1976 L-P Millesimé Rare	95
38	1973 Dom Pérignon	95
39	1976 Salon	95
40	1964 Lilbert	95
41	1979 Clos des Goisses	95
42	1980 Clos des Goisses	95
43	1964 Moët & Chandon	95
44	1959 Laurent-Perrier Rosé	94
45	1979 Des Princes	94
46	1985 Bollinger R.D.	94
47	1970 Bollinger R.D.	94
48	1990 Bollinger R.D.	94
49	1964 Alfred Gratien	94
50	1975 Clos des Goisses	94

MY PERSONAL RATING OF THE VILLAGES

CHARDONNAY
GRAND CRU 100%
1 Le Mesnil
2 Cramant
3 Avize
4 Oger
5 Chouilly
6 Grauves

PREMIER CRU 95%
7 Cuis
8 Vertus
9 Aÿ

PREMIER CRU 93%
10 Oiry
11 Bergères-les-Vertus
12 Ambonnay
13 Verzenay
14 Bouzy
15 Rilly-la-Montagne
16 Sillery
17 Villers-Marmery

PREMIER CRU 90%
18 Chigny-les-Roses
19 Dizy
20 Mareuil-sur-Aÿ
21 Verzy
22 Louvois
23 Cumières
24 Mailly

85%
All other villages classified *grand cru*
or *premier cru.*

80%
All remaining villages.

PINOT NOIR
GRAND CRU 100%
1 Aÿ
2 Verzenay
3 Ambonnay
4 Mareuil-sur-Aÿ
5 Bouzy
6 Verzy
7 Cumières

PREMIER CRU 95%
8 Mailly
9 Sillery
10 Dizy
11 Louvois

PREMIER CRU 90%
12 Tours-sur-Marne
13 Trépail
14 Chigny-les-Roses
15 Champillon
16 Hautvillers
17 Damery
18 Ludes
19 Villers-Marmery
20 Mutigny
21 Tauxières
22 Bisseuil
23 Beaumont-sur-Vesle

85%
All other villages classified *grand cru*
or *premier cru.*

80%
All remaining villages.

THE LARGEST CHAMPAGNE-PRODUCING CONGLOMERATES

1 **LVMH**
Moët, Clicquot, Mercier, Ruinart,
Canard-Duchêne
63.4 million bottles annually.

2 **Marne & Champagne**
Besserat, Lanson, Marne, Burtin, Massé
22.7 million bottles annually.

3 **Rémy-Cointreau**
Piper-Heidsieck, Charles Heidsieck,
Bonnet
15.6 million bottles annually.

4 **Allied-Domecq**
Mumm, Perrier-Jouët
12.2 million bottles annually.

5 **Vranken Monopole**
Vranken, Lafitte, Demoiselle,
Heidsieck & Monopole, Barancourt,
Collin, Charbaut, Germain,
Pommery, Sacotte
11.3 million bottles annually.

6 **Laurent-Perrier**
Laurent-Perrier, De Castellane,
Salon, Delamotte, Lemoine
10.7 million bottles annually.

7 **Duval-Leroy**
Duval-Leroy, various other makes
7.5 million bottles annually.

8 **Martel**
Mansard-Baillet, Martel,
de Noiron m. fl
7.3 million bottles annually.

9 **BCC**
Bruno Paillard, Chanoine, Philipponnat,
De Venoge, Abel Lepitre, Boizel,
Alexandre Bonnet
6.9 million bottles annually.

10 **Taittinger**
Taittinger, Irroy
5.6 million bottles annually.

FRENCH GOVERNMENT REGULATIONS AND STATISTICS

Strict inspection procedures are carried out at every stage in the Champagne-production process. These procedures must conform to French government regulations established for the field.

A few examples:

• All new plantings and re-plantings are strictly limited to a legally defined geographical region containing 34,000 hectares (84,000 acres). This legislation was enacted in 1927. The cultivated portion of this area covers 30,396 hectares (75,000 acres), or 2.6% of all French vineyards.

• Only three varieties of grape can be planted: Chardonnay, Pinot Noir and Pinot Meunier. Rarer varieties, such as Petit Meslier, Gamay, Pinot Blanc, and Arbanne may be used in blends but not planted.

• By contrast with most of the other wine-producing regions of France, in all villages eligible for the Champagne appellation plantings must be made on specific plots of land located within clearly defined areas in each commune. Requests to plant in new areas are subject to approval by the European Union.

• The distance between the rows of rooted vines must not be greater than 1.5 meters (4.88 feet), and that between each rooted vine from .9 to 1.5 meters (2.93 to 4.88 feet). The total of these distances must not be greater than 2.5 meters (8.13 feet).

• Only four methods of tying the vines to stakes or other supports are authorized. The maximum height of the buds is calculated from ground-level upwards. Height also depends on the method used. For the Chablis and Guyot techniques, height is .6 meter (1.95 feet). For the Marne and Cordon Royal methods it is .5 meter (1.63 feet). The Chablis and Cordon Royal methods are the only modern ones authorized for rootstock planted in areas classified *grand cru* and *premier cru*. The Marne method is used only for Pinot Meunier grapes.

• Only a carefully specified quantity of grapes may be harvested each year on each plot of land authorized to carry the Champagne appellation.

• A minimum and maximum alcohol content is established each year.

• All of these wines must be produced entirely in the region. Furthermore, they must not be aged with the addition of grape juice or wine from other regions.

• Champagne must remain in contact with the sediments for at least 15 months.

• A champagne cork must measure 48 mm (1.87 in.) in length and 31 mm (1.21 in.) in diameter.

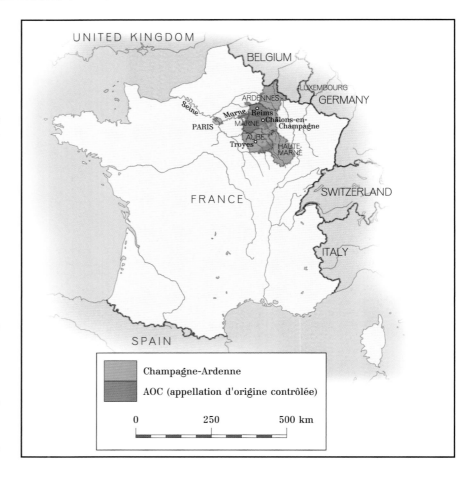

Champagne-Ardenne

AOC (appellation d'origine contrôlée)

0   250   500 km

Number of producers
5,091 grower-producers (G-P)
48 production cooperatives (P-C)
280 dealer-producers (D-P)

Average yield
In 2000, the average yield at harvest was 12,576 kg/hectare (1,110 pounds/acre).

Area under cultivation
The total area under cultivation of 30,396 hectares (75,110 acres) is divided as follows:
22,461 hectares (55,500 acres) in La Marne
2,033 hectares (5,024 acres) in L'Aisne
5,862 hectares (14,490 acres) in L'Aube
20 hectares (49 acres) in Haute Marne

Stock
As of 31 July 2000, producers had 1,023,000,000 bottles stored in their cellars.

Sales
A total of 253 bottles was sold in 2000, broken down as follows:
66.4% sold by champagne producers.
33.6% sold by dealer-producers and cooperatives
149 million bottles sold in France (59.1%)
104 million bottles exported (40.9%)

CONTACT INFORMATION

*Telephone numbers of producers,
listed by city and village*

AILLEVILLE
Jacquot, Michel   03 25 27 06 66

ALLEMANT
Remy, Bernard   03 26 80 60 34

AMBONNAY
Batonnet-Gautier   03 26 57 80 13
Beaufort, Alain   03 26 57 08 65
Beaufort, André   03 26 57 01 51
Beaufort, Claude   03 26 57 01 32
Beaufort, Jacques   03 26 57 01 50
Beaufort, J.-M.   03 26 57 02 59
Beaufort-Dupont   03 26 57 08 90
Bernard, Brémont   03 26 51 01 65
Billiot, Henri   03 26 57 00 14
Billiot, Marcel   03 26 57 01 04
Coop. Vinicole d'Ambonnay
                         03 26 57 01 46
Coutier, René-Henri   03 26 57 02 55
Croizy, Roger   03 26 57 01 52
Demière, Serge   03 26 57 07 79
Dethune, Paul   03 26 57 01 88
Egly-Ouriet   03 26 57 00 70
Fauvet, Claude   03 26 57 00 39
Foureur, Robert   03 26 57 02 68
Gaston Warin   03 26 57 01 29
Gauthier, Roger   03 26 57 01 94
Georges, Simon   03 26 57 00 59
Houry, Thierry   03 26 57 82 96
Hubert Père & Fils   03 26 57 08 11
Huguet, Michel   03 26 57 01 45
Hulin, J.   03 26 57 01 97
Ledru, Michel   03 26 57 00 71
Marguet-Bonnerave   03 26 57 09 98
Millot, C.   03 26 57 07 25
Minelle, François   03 26 57 02 14
Moreau, Jean   03 26 57 09 07
Moreau, Michel   03 26 57 81 51
Payelle, Gérard   03 26 57 02 57
Pérard, J.-P.   03 26 57 00 96
Petit, T.H.   03 26 57 01 13
Petitjean, H.   03 26 57 08 79
Pierlot, Serge   03 26 57 01 11
Remy, Claude   03 26 57 00 01
Rodez, Eric   03 26 57 04 93
Rodez, Michel   03 26 57 00 27
Soutiran-Pelletier   03 26 57 07 87
Varlot, Jean   03 26 57 00 65

ARCIS-SUR-AUBE
Bourgeois & Fils   03 25 37 80 47

ARCONVILLE
Gaucher, Bernard   03 25 27 87 31

AVENAY
Anceau   03 26 52 62 08
Augustin, Jean-Paul   03 26 52 31 20
Billiard, Pierre-Alain   03 26 52 32 76
Brunet, Stephane   03 26 52 34 13

Coop. d'Avenay Val d'Or 03 26 52 31 24
Justine, Paul   03 26 52 32 58
Marniquet, Francois   03 26 52 32 36
Morlet, Pierre   03 26 52 32 32
Pagin, Gabriel   03 26 52 31 03
Picart-Thiout   03 26 52 31 71
Remion, Jean-Paul   03 26 52 31 05
Renault-Allart   03 26 52 31 14
Ricciuti-Révolte   03 26 52 30 27
Saintot, Roger   03 26 52 32 67
Saintot, William   03 26 59 09 04
Vatel-Fouquy, William   03 26 52 30 09

AVIREY-LINGEY
Chardin, Roland   03 25 29 33 90
Goussard, Delagneau   03 25 29 10 41
Goussard, Didier & Dauphin
                         03 25 29 30 03
Hennequière   03 25 29 85 32
Marin, Christian & Fils 03 25 29 32 55
Mathieu, Serge   03 25 29 32 58
Pescheux, Père & Fils   03 25 29 30 79
Pidansat, Germain   03 25 29 36 04

AVIZE
Agrapart   03 26 57 51 38
Assailly-Leclaire   03 26 57 51 20
Berthelot, Christian   03 26 57 58 99
Bonville, Franck   03 26 57 52 30
Bricout   03 26 53 30 00
Callot & Fils   03 26 57 51 57
Chapier-Chabonat   03 26 57 51 67
Clément, Thomas   03 26 57 94 85
Coop. des Anciens de la Viticulture
d'Avize   03 26 57 79 79
Coop. Union Champagne
                         03 26 57 94 22
Delbeck   03 26 53 30 00
Deregard-Massing   03 26 57 52 92
Dubois, Gérard   03 26 57 58 60
Dubois, Hervé   03 26 57 52 45
Fallet, Michel   03 26 57 51 97
Gaspard, Francoise   03 26 57 50 97
Ghys, Michel   03 26 57 51 05
Gonet, Michel   03 26 57 50 56
Lanaud, Veuve   03 26 57 99 19
Le Brun-Servenay   03 26 57 52 75
Leclaire, Philippe   03 26 57 79 48
Leclaire-Gaspard   03 26 57 55 66
Paveau   03 26 57 93 87
Perriere   03 26 57 40 30
Petit & Fils   03 26 57 51 63
Petit, Hubert   03 26 57 57 86
Pierson-Whitaker   03 26 57 77 04
Prin   03 26 53 54 55
Schlessler, Patrick   03 26 57 94 29
Selosse, Jacques   03 26 57 53 56
Simon-Selosse   03 26 57 52 40
Sousa, De   03 26 57 53 29
Varnier-Fanniere   03 26 57 58 39
Waris-Larmandier   03 26 57 79 05
Warris & Chenayer   03 26 57 50 88

AŸ
Ayala   03 26 55 15 44
Besserat, Christian   03 26 55 20 72
Bollinger   03 26 53 33 66
Brun, Ed.   03 26 55 20 11
Brun, René   03 26 55 21 24

Collery   03 26 54 01 20
Collet, Raoul   03 26 55 15 88
Dauby, Guy   03 26 54 96 49
Deutz   03 26 55 15 11
Driant, E.   03 26 54 27 16
Fliniaux, Régis   03 26 55 21 04
Fliniaux, Richard   03 26 55 14 97
Gabriel Collin   03 26 55 49 04
Gatinois   03 26 55 14 26
Giraud, Henri   03 26 55 18 55
Godmé, Serge   03 26 55 43 93
Gosset   03 26 56 99 56
Gosset-Brabant   03 26 55 17 42
Goutorbe, H.   03 26 55 21 70
Hamm, E.   03 26 55 44 19
Henin, Pascal   03 26 54 61 50
Husson   03 26 55 43 05
Ivernel   03 26 55 21 10
Juget-Brunet   03 26 55 20 67
Lallier, James   03 26 55 32 87
Laurain, Pierre   03 26 55 18 90
Leboeuf, Pierre   03 26 55 21 58
Luc, Eric   03 26 51 67 22
Massing, Julien   03 26 55 20 37
Méric, De   03 26 55 20 72
Montebello   03 26 55 15 44
Montvillers   03 26 54 82 58
Pol Roger, Jean   03 26 54 68 66
Roger, André   03 26 55 20 61
Vatel   03 26 55 44 05

BAGNEUX-LA-FOSSE
Beaujean, Michel   03 25 29 37 44
Bertrand, Paul Marie   03 25 29 30 58
Fontaine, Gérard   03 25 29 31 87
Fournier, Eric   03 25 29 91 66
Josselin, Jean-Michel   03 25 29 99 71
Ménetrier, Philippe   03 25 29 39 69
Prignot, Christian   03 25 29 11 15
Rousseau, Pierre   03 25 29 35 00
Walczak, Bernard   03 25 29 31 69
Walczak, Christophe   03 25 29 10 55

BALNOT-SUR-LAIGNES
Coop. de Balnot-sur-Laignes
                         03 25 29 35 15
Gremillet, J.M.   03 25 29 37 91

BAROVILLE
Baere, Hervé de & fils   03 25 27 07 15
Barfontarc, G. de   03 25 27 07 09
Fourrier, Etienne   03 25 27 15 75
Fourrier, Philippe   03 25 27 13 44
Harvengt, Didier   03 25 27 06 50
Maillet, Jean   03 25 27 07 21
Raclot, Marinette   03 25 27 27 14
Urbain, Père & Fils   03 25 27 00 36
Vincent, B.   03 25 27 08 36

BAR-SUR-AUBE
Mougin, Laurent   03 25 27 31 98

BAR-SUR-SEINE
Chassenay, D'Arce   03 25 38 30 70
Devaux, A.   03 25 38 30 65
Gravure   03 25 29 94 94
Noellat   03 25 38 39 40
Viardot Frères   03 25 29 39 21

BASLIEUX-SOUS-CHÂTILLON
Billard-Girardin, J.-P. 03 26 58 11 46
Chevillet, Joël   03 26 59 15 28
Franck, Pascal   03 26 51 89 80
Liébart-Régnier   03 26 58 11 60
Pascal-Delette   03 26 58 11 35
Pascal-Poudras, Claude   03 26 58 11 54
Régnier, Jean-Pierre   03 26 58 11 70
Remi, Guy   03 26 58 11 29
Rigot Francois, Pierre   03 26 58 11 44
Rouillère, Hervé   03 26 58 15 26
Taillet   03 26 58 11 42
Vizeneux, Roland   03 26 58 15 33

BASSUET
Chaure, André   03 26 73 93 16
Chauré, Jean-Louis   03 26 73 91 55
Coop. Bassuet   03 26 74 18 90
L'hoste   03 26 73 94 43
Lonclas, Bernard   03 26 73 98 20
Ortillon-Beaulieu   03 26 73 95 19

BAYE
Barré, Marc   03 26 52 81 70
Collin, Daniel   03 26 52 80 50
Jacques, Yves   03 26 52 80 77
Moret, Odil   03 26 52 81 65

BEAUMONT-SUR-VESLE
Portier, Virgile   03 26 03 90 15
Vautier, Maurice   03 26 03 90 63
Vautier, Pierre   03 26 03 90 62

BEAUNAY
Gaunel-Jacquet, Michel   03 26 59 30 92
Jacquesson, Michel   03 26 59 34 94
Moreau, Alain   03 26 59 33 35
Thuillier

BELVAL-SOUS-CHÂTILLON
Bérat, Daniel   03 26 58 14 46
Chabroulet, Christian   03 26 58 11 72
Faivre, Robert   03 26 58 13 19
Follet Ramillon, Joël   03 26 58 11 68

BERGÈRES
Prieur, Claude   03 25 27 44 01
Rigolet, Jean   03 25 27 43 77

BERGÈRES-LES-VERTUS
Adnot, Christian   03 26 52 18 34
Batteux-Busson   03 26 52 02 22
Champion, Denis   03 26 52 02 13
Coop. "le Mont Aime"   03 26 52 02 15
Cottray, Lionel   03 26 52 00 95
Jacopin, Y.   03 26 52 26 25
Lefèvre, Alain   03 26 52 24 07
Malin, Henri   03 26 52 26 51
Milliat, Serge   03 26 52 20 42
Perrot, Roger   03 26 52 12 26
Poirot   03 26 52 02 26
Vallet-Gadret, R.   03 26 81 25 33
Vallois   03 26 52 23 71

BERGÈRES-SOUS-MONTMIRAIL
Champion, Daniel   03 26 81 22 93
Crochet-Rivière   03 26 81 26 85

BERRU
Coop. Berru	03 26 03 22 68
Dufrene, Jacques	03 26 03 22 48
Florent, Thierry	03 26 03 22 82
Fourmet, Héry	03 26 03 20 15
Guillaume, Guy	03 26 03 20 56
Philippe, Jean-Pierre	03 26 03 21 90
Picard, Jacques	03 26 03 22 46
Rémi, Adam	03 26 03 26 66

BETHON
Coop. U.V.C.B.	03 26 80 48 61
Jarry, André	03 26 80 48 04
Jarry, J.-P	03 26 80 47 55
Laurent, Paul	03 26 81 91 11
Le Brun de Neuville	03 26 80 48 43
Petit, Guy	03 26 80 48 31
Triolet	03 26 80 48 24
Vandier, André	03 26 80 48 17

BILLY-LE-GRAND
Bocart, Jean-Claude	03 26 67 95 67
Collard, Pascal	03 26 67 98 93
Earl de Mont	03 26 70 91 53
Lapie, Jean	03 26 66 01 45
Lapie, Roger	03 26 65 57 83
Lapie Wiart	03 26 67 97 15
Lapie-Longe	03 26 67 99 13
Oudea, Robert	03 26 67 96 31
Picard, Francis	03 26 67 95 54

BINSON & ORQUIGNY
Coutelas, Francis	03 26 58 04 73
Dissaux-Brochot, J.-C.	03 26 58 05 63
Dissaux-Verdoolaeghe	03 26 58 03 57
Gilmaire, Etienne	03 26 58 33 24
Godinat, Gérard	03 26 58 33 23
Landat, Marcel	03 26 58 00 67
Moussé, Jean-Luc	03 26 58 08 91
Moutte, J.-L.	03 26 58 04 75
Rigot, Jean-Marie	03 26 58 33 38

BISSEUIL
Bauchet	03 26 58 92 12
Bonanfant	03 26 58 96 23
Chochina	03 26 58 91 01
Clos-Babot	03 26 58 92 12
Hémard	03 26 58 96 60
Jorquera	03 26 58 90 07

BLIGNY
Binon, Thierry	03 25 27 42 91
Château de Bligny	03 25 27 40 11
Demilly, Gérard	03 25 27 44 81
Gauthrin, Laurent	03 25 27 45 83
Laval	03 25 27 40 16
Montaux, J.-C.	03 25 27 40 25

BOUILLY
Mériguet-Leclabart	03 26 49 20 77
Wafflart, Guy	03 26 49 21 01

BOULT-SUR-SUIPPE
Petit-Perseval	03 26 03 31 97

BOUQUIGNY
Cheutin, Serge	03 26 52 72 19
Leconte, Aimé	03 26 52 70 23
Leconte, Xavier	03 26 52 73 59

Pottin, Bernard	03 26 52 71 33
Raymond, Joël	03 26 52 70 89

BOURGOGNE
Guillaume, Hervé	03 26 97 24 61

BOURSAULT
Bérat, Jacques	03 26 58 42 45
Bouchez-Benard	03 26 58 41 81
Château de Boursault	03 26 58 42 21
Dagonet, Lucien	03 26 58 41 29
Diouy, Raymond	03 26 58 47 18
Foin Moigneau	03 26 58 61 03
Gilbert	03 26 58 47 17
Joliet-Rodier	03 26 58 40 05
Lemaire Rasselet	03 26 58 44 85
Lete, Jean	03 26 58 45 87
Rousseau, Philippe	03 26 58 62 29
Stephane & Fils	03 26 58 40 81

BOUVANCOURT
de Vreese-Fauvet	03 26 48 51 89

BOUZY
Bandock-Mangin	03 26 57 09 09
Bara, Paul	03 26 57 00 50
Barancourt	03 26 53 33 40
Barnaut, E.	03 26 57 01 54
Beaufort, Herbert	03 26 57 01 34
Bernard, Ledru	03 26 57 00 04
Brice	03 26 52 06 60
Clouet, André	03 26 57 00 82
Clouet, Paul	03 26 57 07 31
Dauvergne, Hubert	03 26 57 00 56
Hulin, Pierre	03 26 57 01 37
Lahaye, Serge	03 26 57 00 38
Lallement, René	03 26 57 00 68
Lefèvre, Jean	03 26 57 06 58
Martin, Louis	03 26 57 01 27
Paillard, Pierre	03 26 57 08 04
Pléner, J.F.	03 26 57 00 21
Rémy, E.	03 26 57 08 98
Rémy, Galichet	03 26 57 02 94
Savès, Camille	03 26 57 00 33
Tornay, Bernard	03 26 57 08 58
Tritant, Alfred	03 26 57 01 16
Vesselle, Alain	03 26 57 00 88
Vesselle, Georges	03 26 57 00 15
Vesselle, Jean	03 26 57 01 55
Vesselle, Maurice	03 26 57 00 81

BROUILLET
Ariston	03 26 97 47 02
Ariston Fils	03 26 97 43 46
Gérin	03 26 97 46 31

BROYES
Collin, Olivier	03 26 80 54 47
Jacopé, Yves	03 26 80 70 72
Petit-Bollot, André	03 26 80 56 30
Petit-Lemoine	03 26 81 85 50
Rousseaux, Jean-Jacques	03 26 80 56 70
Vinot, Gérard	03 26 80 56 32

BRUGNY-VAUDANCOURT
Bourdelat, Edmond	03 26 59 97 95
Didier, J.	03 26 59 97 89
Filaine, Thierry	03 26 57 58 65
Fresne, Gabriel	03 26 59 98 09
Oudart, Etienne	03 26 59 98 01

BUXEUIL
Albin, D'Aube	03 25 38 50 29
Couche, Père & Fils	03 25 38 53 96
Diligent, André	03 25 38 51 78
Diligent, Pierre	03 25 38 51 79
Gruet, Claude	03 25 38 54 94
Leblond-Lenoir, Noël	03 25 38 53 33
Leblond-Lenoir, Pascal	03 25 38 54 04
Lenoir, C & R.	03 25 38 50 72
Moutard-Diligent	03 25 38 50 73

CELLES-SUR-OURCE
Arnoult, Jean	03 25 38 56 49
Baroni, Jacqueline	03 25 38 52 44
Bouchard, Jean-Claude	03 25 38 55 62
Bouchard, Jean-Pierre	03 25 38 55 73
Brocard, Michel	03 25 38 51 43
Brocard, Pierre	03 25 38 55 05
Carreau, Jean-Luc	03 25 38 54 51
Cheurlin, Arnaud de	03 25 38 53 90
Cheurlin, Daniel	03 25 38 51 34
Cheurlin, Richard	03 25 38 55 04
Cheurlin-Dangin	03 25 38 50 26
Dangin, Paul & Fils	03 25 38 50 27
Delot, Maurice	03 25 38 50 12
Fays, André	03 25 38 51 47
Fays, Philippe	03 25 38 51 47
Fumey-Tassin	03 25 38 56 90
Furdyna, Michel	03 25 38 54 20
Gautherot	03 25 38 50 03
Gerbais, Pierre	03 25 38 51 29
Gyejacquot, Daniel	03 25 38 51 46
Gyejacquot, Michel	03 25 38 56 07
Huguenot, Benoit	03 25 38 54 49
Langry, Didier	03 25 38 57 37
Laurent	03 25 38 50 10
Laurent, Jean	03 25 38 56 02
Legrand, Eric	03 25 38 55 07
Legrand, Frères	03 25 38 57 14
Lozey, Philippe de	03 25 38 34 22
Maître, Eric	03 25 38 58 69
Patour, Michel	03 25 38 51 32
Pilloud, Gérard	03 25 38 53 03
Sandrin, Jean	03 25 38 52 42
Sandrin, Jean	03 25 38 57 04
Simon, Monique	03 25 38 54 08
Tassin, Benoit	03 25 38 52 27
Tassin, Bernard	03 25 38 50 19
Tassin, Emmanuel	03 25 38 59 44
Tassin, Jeannine	03 25 38 53 22
Vézien, Marcel	03 25 38 50 22

CERSEUIL
Baillet, Denis	03 26 52 71 05
Comte de Lantage	03 26 51 11 39
Debargue	03 26 52 71 65
Dehours, S.A.	03 26 52 71 75
Delovin, Chayoux	03 26 52 71 87
Liébart, Didier	03 26 52 72 09
Mansard, Joel	03 26 52 72 80
Marx, Denis	03 26 52 71 96
Mathelin	03 26 52 73 58
Piot & Fils	03 26 52 71 37
Remy, G.	03 26 58 28 54
Tournant	03 26 52 72 58

CHÂLONS-EN-CHAMPAGNE
Brun, Albert le	03 26 68 18 68
Perrier, Joseph	03 26 68 29 51

Société Champenoise d'exploitation vinicole	03 26 68 18 68

CHAMBRÉCY
Lallement-Pelletier	03 26 61 88 52
Lerouge, Alain	03 26 61 80 64

CHAMERY
Bertrand, Gilbert	03 26 97 64 57
Bonnet, Roger	03 26 97 64 48
Bonnet-Ponson	03 26 97 65 40
Coop. de Chamery	03 26 97 64 67
Delespierre, Michel	03 26 97 65 02
Dravigny	03 26 97 65 46
Feneuil, Daniel	03 26 97 62 35
Grimet-Lagauche	03 26 97 65 69
Guerlet	03 26 97 64 06
Labbé, Michel	03 26 97 65 89
Lallement, Claude	03 26 97 64 04
Laurent-Vasseur	03 26 97 65 72
Maillart, Henri	03 26 97 63 27
Maletrez	03 26 97 63 92
Michel, André	03 26 97 64 66
Parmantier, Gérard	03 26 97 63 15
Perseval, Gérard	03 26 97 62 14
Perseval-Deleplanque	03 26 97 64 70
Perseval-Foubert	03 26 97 66 17
Perseval-Harteel	03 26 97 64 88
Philippe Hanon	03 26 97 65 60
Rigaut, Daniel	03 26 97 64 08
Rigaut, Etienne	03 26 97 65 54
Robaille, Michel	03 26 97 63 47
Viard	03 26 97 65 24

CHAMPIGNOL-LEZ-MONDE
Dumont, R.& fils	03 25 27 45 95

CHAMPILLON
Aquarelle	03 26 59 46 71
Autreau de Champillon	03 26 59 46 00
Beguin, Roland	03 26 59 47 04
Boucher, Gilles	03 26 59 48 17
Cuinet	03 26 59 47 87
Devavry, Bertrand	03 26 59 46 21
Gelin, Fernand	03 26 59 46 26
Josseaux, Georges	03 26 59 46 70
Lamotte, René	03 26 59 46 62
Méa, Jean-Loup	03 26 59 47 50
Remy, Claude	03 26 59 46 34
Roualet, André	03 26 59 46 45
Roulet, René	03 26 59 46 55
Visneaux, Patrick	03 26 59 47 83

CHAMPLAT & BOUJACOURT
Grandin, Thierry	03 26 58 11 71

CHAMPVOISY
Lequart-Laurent	03 26 58 97 48

CHANGY
Pierre-Mougeot	03 26 73 42 16

CHANNES
Brigandat, Pierre	03 25 29 36 20
Coquard	03 25 29 31 30
Guilleminot, Michel	03 25 29 37 77
Philipaux, Pierre	03 25 29 35 57

CHARLY-SUR-MARNE
Baron Albert — 03 23 82 02 65

CHÂTEAU-THIERRY
Coop. Pannier — 03 23 69 51 30

CHÂTILLON-SUR-MARNE
Benard, Philippe — 03 26 58 09 63
Cazé Thibault — 03 26 58 36 87
Charlier, Jackie — 03 26 58 35 18
Charlot — 03 26 58 34 72
Coop. "La Grappe" — 03 26 58 34 54
Coop. de Châtillon — 03 26 58 35 33
Fournaise, Daniel — 03 26 58 06 44
Heucq — 03 26 58 10 08
Meunier — 03 26 58 30 52
Perrin — 03 26 58 34 31
Perrin, André — 03 26 58 06 98
Philippe, Roland — 03 26 58 34 41
Plekhoff, Henri — 03 26 58 34 77
Plekhoff, Hervé — 03 26 58 34 34
Plekhoff, Yves — 03 26 58 34 49

CHAUMUZY
Gillery, Lucien — 03 26 61 83 84
Herbelet-Augé — 03 26 61 83 60
Leclercq, Denis — 03 26 61 87 81
Salmon, Michel — 03 26 61 81 38

CHAVOT
Coop. de Chavot — 03 26 54 31 89
Demarest, Charles — 03 26 55 24 55
Desbordes, Roger — 03 26 54 31 94
Ingeniére — 03 26 55 63 08
Jacquesson, René — 03 26 54 32 13
Lagache-Lecourt — 03 26 54 86 79
Laherte, Roland — 03 26 54 31 91
Lebeau, Robert — 03 26 54 32 52
Leblond, Lucien — 03 26 54 32 56
Lequien, Max — 03 26 54 32 28
Pernet, Jean — 03 26 57 54 24
Pothelet — 03 26 54 32 81
Prin — 03 26 54 32 74
Selosse, Jackie — 03 26 54 32 25
Tissier, André — 03 26 54 32 16
Tissier, Diogene — 03 26 54 32 47

CHENAY
Dampierre, Comte Audoin de
— 03 26 03 11 13

CHIGNY-LES-ROSES
Barbelet-Leroux — 03 26 03 43 00
Broggini, Jacky — 03 26 03 44 77
Cattier — 03 26 03 42 11
Coop. de Chigny-les-Roses
— 03 26 03 44 30
Cossy, Michel — 03 26 03 44 28
Duchesne, Geneviève — 03 26 03 42 76
Dumangin, Guy — 03 26 03 46 25
Dumangin, Jacky — 03 26 03 46 34
Dumangin, Jean — 03 26 03 42 17
Dumangin-Rafflin — 03 26 03 48 21
Dumenil — 03 26 03 44 48
Gardet — 03 26 03 42 03
Gounel-Lassalle — 03 26 03 43 05
Lassalle, J. — 03 26 03 42 19
Lassalle, Maurice — 03 26 03 42 20
Lassalle-Hanin — 03 26 03 40 96

Lepitre, Francois — 03 26 03 42 05
Leroux, Fred — 03 26 03 42 35
Leroux, Hilaire — 03 26 03 42 01
Mayot, Alain — 03 26 03 48 39
Mazet, Pascal — 03 26 03 41 13
Menu, Gilles — 03 26 03 43 35
Perthois Gerlier — 03 26 03 48 20
Philippart, Maurice — 03 26 03 42 44
Rafflin, Bertrand — 03 26 03 48 47
Rafflin, Michel — 03 26 03 48 23
Thoumy, Michel — 03 26 03 44 58
Thoumy, Robert — 03 26 03 44 58
Tixier, Guy — 03 26 03 42 51
Tixier, Paul — 03 26 03 42 45

CHOUILLY
Banchet-Legras — 03 26 55 41 53
Broquet-Melbeck — 03 26 54 06 82
Champion, Roland — 03 26 55 40 30
Coop. Feuillatte, Nicolas — 03 26 59 55 50
Farigoul — 03 26 55 40 21
Gauthier pere & fils — 03 26 55 40 02
Genet, Claude — 03 26 54 50 38
Genet, Michel — 03 26 55 40 51
Gue, C. — 03 26 54 50 32
Hostomme — 03 26 55 40 79
Legras & Haas — 03 26 54 92 90
Legras, David — 03 26 54 97 77
Legras, R. & L. — 03 26 54 50 79
Legras-Noël — 03 26 55 41 71
Moineaux, Marcel — 03 26 55 40 99
Pouillard, Michel — 03 26 54 58 58
Simart, Bruno — 03 26 55 40 53
Simart, Dominique — 03 26 54 50 65
Simonnet, Guy — 03 26 55 40 29
Vazart, Lucien — 03 26 55 61 15
Vazart-Coquart — 03 26 55 40 04
Voirin-Desmoulins — 03 26 54 50 30
Vol, Michel — 03 26 55 41 10

COIZARD-JOCHES
Guyard, Gérard — 03 26 59 31 62

COLOMBÉ-LA-FOSSE
Courtillier, Roger — 03 25 27 11 35
Cudel, Philippe — 03 25 27 24 51
Gallois, Frédéric — 03 25 27 83 72
Viot, Elisabeth — 03 25 27 02 07

COLOMBÉ-LE-SEC
Boulachin, Claude — 03 25 27 22 10
Boulachin, Hubert — 03 25 27 35 35
Breuzon, Bernard — 03 25 27 02 06
Christophe — 03 25 27 18 38
Coop. Charles Clement — 03 25 92 50 70
Cornevin, André — 03 25 27 24 44
Dosne, René — 03 25 27 02 14
Paradis, C.F. — 03 25 27 02 12
Renet, Jean-Guy — 03 25 27 18 26

CONGY
Breton — 03 26 59 31 03
Collard-Greffier — 03 26 59 35 60
Desbrosse, Robert — 03 26 59 31 08
Girost, Jean-Claude — 03 26 59 32 30
Lambert-Bérat, J.-F. — 03 26 59 31 37
Moussy, Maurice — 03 26 59 31 29

CORMICY
Baudvin, Michel — 03 26 61 31 20
Boulard-Bauquaire — 03 26 61 30 79
Cantoni, Serge — 03 26 61 31 58
Didier, Francois — 03 26 61 32 90
Lecrocq, Philippe — 03 26 61 30 10

CORMOYEUX
Baudin-Pierrot, J.-P. — 03 26 58 64 03
Bochet-Lemoine — 03 26 58 64 11
Boude-Pongnot, Claude — 03 26 58 64 37
Dessaint, Alain — 03 26 58 64 51
Faniel — 03 26 51 68 19
Mondet, Daniel — 03 26 58 64 15

COULOMMES-LA-MONTAGNE
Lepitre, Christian — 03 26 49 20 34
Lepitre, Jean-Claude — 03 26 49 78 20
Massonnot, Jean-Marie — 03 26 49 76 74
Ponson — 03 26 49 20 17

COURJEONNET
Bression — 03 26 59 31 51

COURMAS
Alexandre, Yves — 03 26 49 20 78
Bourgeois, J.-B. — 03 26 49 21 79
Minard, P. — 03 26 49 20 67

COURTERON
Cottet-Dubreuil — 03 25 38 23 24
Deguise, Maurice — 03 25 38 23 39
Dubreuil Frères — 03 25 38 20 94
Fleury — 03 25 38 20 28
Mannoury, E.M. — 03 25 29 67 45
Réaut, Noirot — 03 25 38 23 10
Schreiber — 03 25 38 22 95

COUVIGNON
Aurélien — 03 25 27 40 94

CRAMANT
Bertin — 03 26 57 93 38
Bonnaire — 03 26 57 50 85
Bonningre-Durant — 03 26 57 59 99
Brun, William — 03 26 57 91 32
Collard, Pol — 03 26 57 93 55
Coop. de Cramant — 03 26 57 50 72
Courtois-Camus — 03 26 57 91 18
Crépaux, J.-F. — 03 26 57 50 61
Crépaux, J.-N. — 03 26 57 56 38
Diebolt-Vallois — 03 26 57 54 92
Guiborat — 03 26 57 54 08
Huret-Colas — 03 26 57 54 44
Lancelot-Pienne — 03 26 57 55 74
Lancelot-Royer — 03 26 57 51 41
Lancelot-Wanner — 03 26 57 58 95
Larmandier — 03 26 57 52 19
Lebrun, Paul — 03 26 57 54 88
Lesage, Guy — 03 26 57 95 58
Lilbert — 03 26 57 50 16
Mallol — 03 26 57 96 14
Morizet & Fils, G. — 03 26 57 50 92
Pertois-Lebrun — 03 26 57 54 25
Petitjean, C. — 03 26 57 51 19
Populos-Cazenave — 03 26 57 54 53
Richomme — 03 26 57 52 93
Simon, Michel — 03 26 57 57 37
Sugot-Feneuil — 03 26 57 53 54

Vignier-Lebrun — 03 26 57 54 88
Voirin-Jumel — 03 26 57 55 82
Wanner-Bouge — 03 26 57 52 35

CUCHERY
Bonningre, Denis — 03 26 58 12 54
Brugneau, Didier — 03 26 57 69 13
Charbonnier, Gilbert — 03 26 58 12 04
Chaumuzart-Gé, J.-P. — 03 26 58 12 92
Levasseur, Albert — 03 26 58 35 43
Mancier, Claude — 03 26 58 12 79
Moreau-Billard — 03 26 58 14 55
Poissinet-Ascas, J.-P. — 03 26 58 12 93
Quenot, Claude — 03 26 58 11 20
Rémy, Christian — 03 26 58 14 00

CUIS
Coop. de Blémond — 03 26 59 78 30
Gilbert, Yves — 03 26 59 78 20
Gimonnet, Jean — 03 26 59 78 39
Gimonnet, Pierre — 03 26 59 78 70
Grellet — 03 26 59 79 69
Le Brun & fils — 03 26 59 78 51
Michel, Paul — 03 26 59 79 77
Richard, Julien — 03 26 59 78 69
Robert, Daniel — 03 26 59 78 77
Vallois, Jean-Claude — 03.26 51 78 99

CUISLES
Fresne, Emilien — 03 26 58 10 54
Heucq, Roger — 03 26 58 10 50
Lécurieux, Jean — 03 26 58 10 61
Moussé, Jean-Marc — 03 26 58 10 80
Orban, Lucien — 03 26 58 10 51
Schreiner, Jean-Pierre — 03 26 58 10 33

CUMIÈRES
Bertrand, Pierre — 03 26 55 24 41
Blosseville-Maniquet — 03 26 55 25 47
Boutet — 03 26 55 32 94
Delabaye, Jeannine — 03 26 51 63 81
Dominique Denois — 03 26 55 42 45
Etienne, Jean-Marie — 03 26 51 66 62
Gaillot, Madeleine — 03 26 55 24 80
Gaillot, Philippe — 03 26 55 66 12
Geoffroy, René — 03 26 55 32 31
Itasse, André — 03 26 54 84 51
Laval, Alain — 03 26 51 61 83
Maitre, Geoffroy — 03 26 55 29 87
Mignon, Yves — 03 26 55 31 21
Pain — 03 26 55 60 75
Plateau, Roger — 03 26 55 28 61
Poittevin — 03 26 51 69 86
Poittevin, Ludolf — 03 26 55 26 03
Sanchez-Guédard — 03 26 51 66 39
Suisse, Alain — 03 26 55 30 56
Vadin-Plateau — 03 26 55 23 36

DAMERY
Billiard, Jacky — 03 26 58 43 18
Billiard, Jean — 03 26 58 42 58
Caillez, Daniel — 03 26 58 46 02
Caillez, Grosjean — 03 26 58 42 02
Caillez-Lemaire — 03 26 58 41 85
Casters, Louis — 03 26 58 43 02
Casters, Vincent — 03 26 58 41 50
Codan-Remy — 03 26 58 47 97
Fanel-Filaine — 03 26 58 62 67
Gonet, Paul — 03 26 58 42 67

Goutorbe, André 03 26 58 43 47
Goutorbe-Boillot 03 26 58 40 92
Goyot, Roland 03 26 58 46 55
Guistel 03 26 59 48 46
Haton, Jean-Noël 03 26 58 40 45
Haton, Philippe 03 26 58 41 11
Jeeper 03 26 58 41 23
Lefebvre, Joseph 03 26 58 42 76
Lemaire, Eric 03 26 58 64 47
Lemaire, Michel 03 26 58 41 47
Lemaire, Raoul 03 26 58 41 89
Lenoble, A.R. 03 26 58 42 60
Lété, A. 03 26 58 44 50
Lète, Pierre 03 26 58 41 37
Michel, Henry 03 26 58 45 10
Moinier, Dominique 03 26 58 63 84
Namur, Bernard 03 26 58 41 18
Namur, J.C. 03 26 58 40 57
Niziolek, Guy 03 26 58 61 96
Pajon, Claude 03 26 58 46 18
Papleux, Dominique 03 26 58 47 43
Pertuiset-Haton 03 26 58 42 13
Prévoteau, Yannick 03 26 58 41 65
Prévoteau-Perrier 03 26 58 41 56
Telmont, J. de 03 26 58 40 33
Tissier-Lemaire 03 26 58 41 31

DIZY
Bernard, Alain 03 26 55 24 78
Bernard, J.-L. 03 26 51 23 34
Berthelot, Paul 03 26 55 23 83
Bourdelois, Raymon 03 26 55 23 34
Charbonnier 03 26 51 55 60
Chiquet, Gaston 03 26 55 22 02
Jacquesson & Fils 03 26 55 68 11
Lagrange 03 26 55 22 02
Leclère Gérard 03 26 55 23 09
Léfuvée, Paul 03 26 55 46 82
Tarillon, Francis 03 26 55 33 93
Tarillon, Jean 03 26 55 33 68
Vautrain-Paulet 03 26 55 24 16

DORMANS
Accariés, Jil 03 26 58 85 59
Bruneaux, Michel 03 26 58 81 95
Bruneaux, Thomas 03 26 58 82 89
Coche, Joël 03 26 58 80 02
Descotes-Loyaux 03 26 58 51 24
Dubois, Roland 03 26 58 26 14
Dubois-Lentendu, Th. 03 26 58 85 48
Le Brun-Le Gouive 03 26 58 25 00

ÉCUEIL
Allouchery, Alain 03 26 49 77 48
Allouchery, Daniel 03 26 49 71 61
Allouchery, Jean-Pierre 03 26 49 74 19
Allouchery-Bailly 03 26 49 77 48
Allouchery-Perseval 03 26 49 74 61
Baillet, Jean-Marie 03 26 49 77 65
Bernardon, Marie-Rose 03 26 49 77 66
Brochet, Jean-Louis 03 26 49 74 23
Brochet-Dolet, Claude 03 26 49 26 22
Brochet-Hervieux 03 26 49 74 10
Brochet-Prévost, Alain 03 26 49 77 44
Brugnon, Alain 03 26 49 25 95
Brugnon, Marc 03 26 49 77 59
Coop. d'Écueil 03 26 49 77 09
Godbillon, Marie-F. 03 26 49 77 12
Lacourte, Jean-Guy 03 26 49 74 75

Leclère-Brochet, T. 03 26 49 77 56
Maillart, Michel 03 26 49 77 89
Piontillart, Jean-Louis 03 26 49 77 24
Piontillart, Philippe 03 26 49 74 95
Savart, Daniel 03 26 49 77 07
Varry, Michelle 03 26 49 77 34
Vely, Yves 03 26 49 74 52

ENGENTE
Gauthier, André 03 25 27 10 33

ÉPERNAY
Achille Princier 03 26 54 04 06
Bauget-Jouette 03 26 54 44 05
Beaumet 03 26 59 50 10
Besserat de Bellefon 03 26 78 50 50
Boizel 03 26 55 21 51
Bonnaire, Richard 03 26 55 01 43
Boyer, L.F. 03 26 51 07 07
Caltonn 03 26 55 27 37
Castellane, De 03 26 51 19 19
Castelnau, De 03 26 51 63 09
Cazanove, De 03 26 59 57 40
Charbaut 03 26 54 37 55
Collective Testulat 03 26 54 10 65
Collot, Daniel 03 26 54 12 69
Contet 03 26 51 06 33
Coop. Esterlin 03 26 59 71 52
Coquillette, Christian 03 26 54 38 09
Delabarre 03 26 54 78 57
Demoiselle 03 26 53 33 20
Desmoulins, A. 03 26 54 24 24
Duval-Pretrot 03 26 58 45 26
Ellner, Charles 03 26 55 60 25
Gratien, Alfred 03 26 54 38 20
Heidsieck & Monopole 03 26 59 50 50
Jacquinot 03 26 54 36 81
Jacquot 03 26 54 10 17
Janisson, Baradon 03 26 54 45 85
Jeanmaire 03 26 59 50 10
Leclaire Thiefaine 03 26 55 34 98
Leclerc-Briant 03 26 54 45 33
Lefevre, Didier 03 26 54 57 16
Lionel, Charlot 03 26 54 22 58
Mansard-Baillet 03 26 54 18 55
Marne & Champagne 03 26 78 50 50
Marquis de la Fayette 03 26 51 00 90
Martel & Cie, G.H. 03 26 51 06 33
Mercier 03 26 51 22 00
Merillod 03 26 54 46 43
Mignon & Pierrel 03 26 51 93 39
Mignon, Charles 03 26 58 33 33
Moët & Chandon 03 26 51 20 00
Oudinot 03 26 59 50 10
Perrier-Jouët 03 26 53 38 00
Picault, Michel 03 26 54 12 61
Pierlot, Jules 03 26 54 45 52
Pol Roger 03 26 59 58 00
Ragouillaux-Mangin, M. 03 26 54 13 14
Rapeneau 03 26 51 06 33
Regent 03 26 54 46 21
Sacotte 03 26 55 31 90
Sulcova, Gonet 03 26 54 37 63
Trouillard 03 26 55 37 55
Venoge, De 03 26 55 34 34

ÉTOGES
Aimé, Lucas 03 26 59 35 99
Bression-Salmon 03 26 59 34 51

Buffry, Pierre 03 26 59 34 85
Grongnet 03 26 59 30 50
Les Hautes Caves 03 26 59 35 90
Ruffin & Fils 03 26 59 30 14
Verrier, Francis 03 26 59 32 42

ETRÉCHY
Courty-Bonnet, Claude 03 26 52 20 19

FEREBRIANGES
Bergère 03 26 59 30 23
Duvat, Alberic 03 26 59 35 69
Duvat, Xavier 03 26 59 35 69
Joudart, Jean-Marie 03 26 59 30 68
Joudart, Vincent 03 26 59 36 08
Leroux, Pascal 03 26 57 67 11
Pernet, Marcel 03 26 59 30 58
Vautrelle, Francis 03 26 59 30 71

FESTIGNY
Berthelot-Piot 03 26 58 08 42
Boonen-Meunier 03 26 58 36 83
Callot, Gérard 03 26 58 32 58
Danteny Lebond 03 26 58 00 97
Fournier, Thierry 03 26 58 04 23
Gaston, Perrin 03 26 58 32 66
Gaudinat, Jean-Pierre 03 26 58 32 89
Hygiène 03 26 51 68 48
Lelarge Ducroco, André 03 26 58 32 75
Loriot, Michel 03 26 58 33 44
Loriot Pagel, Joseph 03 26 58 33 53
Munoz-Bruneau 03 26 58 32 63
Trudon, Noël 03 26 58 00 38
Vely-Chartier Fils 03 26 58 00 49
Vergeat-Besnard & Fils 03 26 58 32 94

FLEURY-LA-RIVIÈRE
Bouché, Jean-Pierre 03 26 58 43 19
Bouché, Michel 03 26 58 47 20
Bouzy, Bernard 03 26 58 42 88
Charpentier, Michel 03 26 58 40 02
David-Heucq 03 26 58 47 19
Delaunois, Gaston 03 26 59 49 86
Delaunoy, Sylvain 03 26 58 48 33
Demière, Gout 03 26 58 47 82
Demière, Jack 03 26 58 43 36
Hatté, Thomas 03 26 58 43 70
Lallement, Daniel 03 26 58 40 13
Lecourt, Fabrice 03 26 58 63 49
Marc, Olivier 03 26 58 42 46
Marc, Patrice 03 26 58 46 88
Maumy-Chapier 03 26 58 44 38
Monnard, Jean-Pol 03 26 58 60 44
Pommelet, Christophe 03 26 58 62 34
Rouyer, Philippe 03 26 58 44 29
Sibeaux, Michel 03 26 58 46 95
Vauthier, Henri 03 26 58 42 71

FONTAINE
Gaupillat, Gérard 03 25 27 28 67

FONTETTE
Jurvilliers, Doussot 03 25 29 68 60
Lhuillier, René 03 25 29 61 80
Ludinard-Robert 03 25 29 65 43
Ribault, Jacques 03 25 29 66 16
Senez, Christian 03 25 29 60 62

FRESNE-LES-REIMS
Guerlet-Marchois 03 26 97 15 07

GIVRY-LES-LOISY
Gérard-Denis, Bernard 03 26 59 33 61

GRAUVES
Coop. Royal Coteau 03 26 59 71 12
Courty-Leroy, José 03 26 59 76 37
Domi, Pierre 03 26 59 71 03
Driant-Valentin, Jacques 03 26 59 72 26
Gaspard, Bertrand 03 26 59 72 46
Gaspard-Bayet 03 26 59 75 41
Godard & Fils 03 26 59 71 19
Mathieu-Princet 03 26 59 71 31
Populus, Bernard 03 26 59 71 34
Ruelle, Lagedamont 03 26 59 72 35

GYÉ-SUR-SEINE
Barbichon, Robert 03 25 38 22 90
Bartnicki, Père & Fils 03 25 38 24 53
Beauny, Jean 03 25 38 20 25
Cheurlin 03 25 38 20 27
Cousin, Claude 03 25 38 21 67
Demets, Marie 03 25 38 23 30
Février, Jean-Marie 03 25 38 23 93
Hérard & Fluteau 03 25 38 20 02
Hutinel, Michel 03 25 38 22 80
Josselin, Jean & Fils 03 25 38 21 48
Préaut, Guy 03 25 38 21 55

HAUTVILLERS
Bliard, Jean
Bosser, J.-P. 03 26 59 41 56
Boyer, Martin 03 26 59 42 66
Descotes, André 03 26 59 40 61
Gobillard, Hervé 03 26 59 45 66
Gobillard, J.M. 03 26 51 00 24
Gobillard, Pierre 03 26 59 40 67
L'Altavilloise 03 26 59 40 18
Lemaire, Fernand 03 26 59 40 44
Locret-Lauchaud 03 26 59 40 20
Lopez-Martin 03 26 59 42 17
Martin, Henri 03 26 59 41 95
Nicaise, Louis 03 26 59 40 21
Patigny, Jean-Pierre 03 26 59 40 36
Tribaut, G. 03 26 59 40 57

HERMONVILLE
Batillot-Dupont, Josette 03 26 61 52 53
Hazart-Frères 03 26 61 55 08
Minière, Gérard 03 26 61 50 82

HOURGES
Lefebvre, Jean 03 26 48 53 33

IGNY-COMBLIZY
Lourdeaux, Laurent 03 26 58 33 80

JANVRY
Beauchamp, Michel 03 26 03 64 53
Blin, Armand 03 26 03 64 15
Ch. de L'Auche 03 26 03 63 40
Coop. de Germigny-Janvry-Rosnay
03 26 03 63 40
Delagarde, Paul 03 26 03 63 45
Lamblot, René 03 26 03 63 11
Ponsart-Delagarde 03 26 03 64 23

JONCHERY-SUR-VESLE

Cornu-Jancart	03 26 48 52 72
Gandon, Jean-Marie	03 26 48 52 67

JOUY-LES-REIMS

Aubry & Fils	03 26 49 20 07
Aubry, Jean & Fils	03 26 49 20 12
Coop. Rurale & Vinicole	03 26 49 20 20
Cossy, Francis	03 26 49 75 56
Crinque Bonnet	03 26 49 20 58
Dautreville, J.-F.	03 26 49 75 08
Perserval, Bernard	03 26 49 21 80
Perseval, J.-J.	03 26 49 21 25
Perseval, Julien	03 26 49 78 42
Tual, J.-P.	03 26 49 21 27

LA NEUVILLE-AUX-LARRIS

Billy-Briffoteaux	03 26 58 14 49
Boulard, Raymond	03 26 58 12 08
Claisse, Simone	03 26 58 12 29
Coop. l'Entraide	03 26 58 12 18
Devillers, Père & Fils	03 26 58 13 44
Ruelle, Mimin	03 26 58 14 57
Savoye, Gérard	03 26 58 14 23

LANDREVILLE

Chaussin-Vetraino	03 25 38 52 61
Dufour, Jacques	03 25 38 52 23
Dufour, Robert	03 25 29 66 19
Isaac	03 25 38 53 05
Jolly, Jean	03 25 38 56 63
Jolly, René	03 25 38 50 91
Lardoux, Daniel	03 25 38 52 87
Royer, Père & Fils	03 25 38 52 16
Virey	03 25 38 56 00

LE BREUIL

Bernard, Marie	03 26 59 24 94
Charpentier-Sertelet, R.	03 26 59 22 07
Debret, Guy	03 26 59 21 28
Dépit, Didier	03 26 59 24 04
Dépit, Jean	03 26 59 21 22
Dépit, Roger	03 26 59 22 29
Mignon, Anne-Marie	03 26 59 25 20
Mignon, Philippe	03 26 59 24 99
Mignon, Pierre	03 26 59 22 03
Moutardier, Jean	03 26 59 21 09
Sendron Destouches	03 26 59 21 04

LE MESNIL-SUR-OGER

Bardy, Père & Fils	03 26 57 57 59
Billion, F.	03 26 57 51 34
Bliard-Moriset	03 26 57 53 42
Cazals, Claude	03 26 57 52 26
Charlemagne, Guy	03 26 57 52 98
Charlemagne, Robert	03 26 57 51 02
Chrochet, Jean Pierre	03 26 57 55 24
Coop. Le Mesnil	03 26 57 53 23
Delamotte	03 26 57 51 65
Gonet, François	03 26 57 53 71
Gonet, Philippe	03 26 57 53 47
Jacquart, André	03 26 57 52 29
Jardin, René	03 26 57 50 26
Launois, Leon	03 26 57 50 28
Launois, Père & Fils	03 26 57 50 15
Lebis, A.	03 26 03 61 65
Lorin, Michel	03 26 57 54 13
Moncuit, Pierre	03 26 57 52 65
Moncuit, Robert	03 26 57 52 71

Moncuit-Bigex, Alain	03 26 57 95 65
Moussy-Mary, J.	03 26 57 94 46
Pattin, J.-B.	03 26 57 92 30
Pernet, Jean	03 26 57 54 24
Pertois, Bernard	03 26 57 53 18
Pertois, Dominique	03 26 57 52 14
Pertois-Moriset	03 26 57 52 14
Peters, Pierre	03 26 57 50 32
Poyet, Michel	03 26 57 97 41
Robert, Alain	03 26 57 52 94
Robert, André	03 26 57 59 41
Rocourt, Michel	03 26 57 94 99
Salon	03 26 57 51 65
Schmitte, Bernard	03 26 57 54 14
Solor-Descotes	03 26 57 50 86
Turgy, Michel	03 26 57 53 43
Vergnon, J.-L.	03 26 57 53 86

LES MESNEAUX

Bougy Moriset	03 26 36 22 35
Féry Bourgeois	03 26 36 22 77
Jacquinet & Fils	03 26 36 25 25
Jacquinet, Michel	03 26 36 23 04
Leroy-Bertin, Maurice	03 26 36 23 60
Michaut Lionel	03 26 36 33 41
Trousset, Jackie	03 26 36 22 95

LES RICEYS

Augé-Dascier	03 25 29 31 83
Batisse, André	03 25 29 35 38
Bauser, André	03 25 29 31 54
Bauser, René	03 25 29 32 92
Bonnet, Alexandre	03 25 29 30 93
Cheriot, Guy	03 25 29 35 38
Clergeot, Michel	03 25 29 36 68
Coop. des Riceys	03 25 29 33 29
Dechannes, Roland	03 25 29 32 63
Defrance, Jacques	03 25 29 32 20
Defrance,Terebenec	03 25 29 17 85
Despret, Jean	03 25 29 36 75
Forez, Guy de	03 25 29 98 73
Foureur, Père & Fils	03 25 29 88 72
Gaetan, Pehu	03 25 29 39 25
Gallimard	03 25 29 32 44
Horiot Père & Fils	03 25 29 32 21
Horiot, Serge	03 25 29 32 16
Jardin	03 25 29 38 46
Lamoreaux, Daniel	03 25 29 33 41
Lamoureux, Guy	03 25 29 34 39
Lamoureux, J.-J.	03 25 29 11 55
Lamoureux, Jean-Pierre	03 25 29 34 39
Lamoureux-Plivard	03 25 29 30 75
Laurenti Père & Fils	03 25 29 32 32
Leducq, Didier	03 25 29 36 21
Marchand, J.P.	03 25 29 35 85
Marquis de Pomereuil	03 25 29 32 24
Morize, Père & Fils	03 25 29 30 02
Noirot, Michel	03 25 29 38 46
Sonnet, Alain	03 25 29 38 00
Sonnet, Jacques	03 25 29 37 64
Walczak, Joseph	03 25 29 31 57
Vallet-Gadret, R.	03 25 29 32 31

LEUVRIGNY

Boudin, M.	03 26 58 31 74
Brateau, Michel	03 26 58 31 20
Brateau-Moreaux	03 26 58 00 99
Cave Coop. de Leuvrigny	
	03 26 58 30 75

Cornet Marie	03 26 58 03 66
Laberthe-Bonnand	03 26 58 03 76
Lasnier, F.	03 26 58 31 88
Mangin	03 26 58 01 18
Rodier, A.	03 26 58 39 52
Rodier, C.	03 26 58 30 03
Vignot, Philippe	03 26 58 05 45

LIGNOL-LE-CHÂTEAU

Mehlinger & Fils	

LOCHES-SUR-OURCE

Amyot, Robert	03 25 29 63 19
Dautel-Cadot, René	03 25 29 61 12
Doussot, Alain	03 25 29 67 92
Poinson, Frères	03 25 29 66 18
Tassin	03 25 29 67 15

LOUVOIS

Beautrait, Yves	03 26 57 03 38
Boever, André	03 26 57 03 43
Boever, Pierre	03 26 57 04 06
Bunel, Eric	03 26 57 03 06
Chassey, Guy de	03 26 57 04 45
Cuvelier Pierson	03 26 57 00 75
Faye, Serge	03 26 57 81 66
Henin, Jean-Noël	03 26 57 03 71
Marquis, Friand	03 26 57 03 71
Méa, Guy	03 26 57 03 42

LUDES

Bérèche & Fils	03 26 61 13 28
Blondel, Thierry	03 26 03 43 92
Canard-Duchêne	03 26 61 10 96
Coop. de Ludes	03 26 61 10 63
Coquillard, Brixon	03 26 61 11 89
Doré, Gérard	03 26 61 10 04
Emery, Régis	03 26 61 13 54
Forget-Brimont	03 26 61 10 45
Forget-Chauvet	03 26 61 11 73
Forget-Chemin	03 26 61 12 17
Forget-Favereaux, J.-P.	03 26 61 13 34
Forget-Menu	03 26 61 13 03
Francois, Jean-Claude	03 26 61 12 97
Gaidoz-Forget	03 26 61 13 03
Georgeton-Rafflin	03 26 61 13 14
Huré	03 26 61 11 20
Janisson, Francis	03 26 61 13 23
Jullien-Diot J.P.	03 26 61 12 58
Lallement, Denis	03 26 61 10 24
Menu, Gilles	03 26 61 10 77
Monmarthe & Fils	03 26 61 10 99
Ployez-Jacquemart	03 26 61 11 87
Quartresols, Jean	03 26 61 10 57
Quatresols-Gauthier	03 26 61 10 13
Quatresols-Jamein	03 26 61 10 22
Quenardel, J.-H.	03 26 61 10 52
Raffin, Serge	03 26 61 12 84
Sohet, René	03 26 61 12 94

MAILLY

Barbier, A.M.	03 26 49 41 34
Coop. les Clos	03 26 49 41 47
Coop. Mailly Grand Cru	03 26 49 41 10
Decotte Auge, Eric	03 26 49 80 64
Gentil, Bernard	03 26 49 43 33
Remy, Ernest	03 26 49 41 15
Rémy, Frères	06 85 70 39 57
Roguet, Lucien	03 26 49 41 36

Secondé, J.-P.	03 26 49 44 57

MANCY

Desbordes, José	03 26 59 71 79
Domi-Moreau, M.	03 26 59 72 72
Girardin, Bernard	03 26 59 71 65
Pernet-Lebrun	03 26 59 71 63

MARDEUIL

Albert, Eric	03 26 51 61 66
Barbier, Charles	03 26 51 58 38
Bénard, Gérard	03 26 55 55 21
Blaise-Lourdez & Fils	03 26 55 30 59
Cadel, Guy	03 26 55 24 59
Charlot-Tanneux	03 26 51 93 92
Coop. Vinicole de Mardeuil	
	03 26 55 29 40
Fourny, A.	03 26 51 57 99
Gaillard, Girot	03 26 51 64 59
Gaillot, Albert	03 26 51 58 39
Gaillot, Michel	03 26 51 58 84
Gamet, Francois	03 26 55 25 46
Garnier, Marcel	03 26 51 58 25
Guiborat & Fils	03 26 51 75 60
Guiborat, Daniel	03 26 51 64 39
Guiborat, M.	03 26 54 27 48
Guichon, L. Albert	03 26 55 32 63
Leclère, Emelie	03 26 55 24 45
Lenique	03 26 55 23 27
Lenique, André	03 26 55 07 82
Lioté, Joannes	03 26 55 32 02
Père, L. Albert	03 26 55 24 98
Plancon, Franck	03 26 55 60 16
Pol Briaux	03 26 51 55 76
Tanneux, Jacques	03 26 55 24 57

MAREUIL LE PORT

Guay-Leblond, Gilles	03 26 58 32 98
Lecart-Bousselet, Daniel	03 26 58 30 11

MAREUIL-SUR-AŸ

Bénard, Roland	03 26 50 60 36
Bénard-Pitois	03 26 50 60 28
Billecart-Salmon	03 26 52 60 22
Bouvet, Guy	03 26 52 62 44
Charbaut, Guy	03 26 52 60 59
Danteny, André	03 26 52 60 30
Danteny-Mangin	03 26 52 60 30
Hébrart, Marc	03 26 52 60 75
Ledru, Gilbert	03 26 52 61 56
Lepitre, Abel	03 26 56 93 11
Lheureux, Saintot	03 26 52 60 68
Niceron, Hervé	03 26 52 60 06
Philipponnat	03 26 56 93 00
Pouillon, James	03 26 52 60 08
Thiébert	03 26 57 86 80

MARFAUX

Lionel-Benoit	03 26 61 82 74
Macquart, Denis	03 26 61 82 78
Moreau, Fabrice	03 26 61 84 25
Pavot-Ballassi	03 26 61 84 63

MERFY

Chartogne-Taillet	03 26 03 10 17
Lemoine, Thierry	03 26 03 10 27
Lemoine-Billet	03 26 03 01 96

MERREY-SUR-ARCE

Cligny, Gérard 03 25 29 99 80
Jacob Père & Fils 03 25 29 83 74
Porte, Jean-Claude 03 25 29 89 09

MEURVILLE

Perron-Beauvineau 03 25 27 40 56
Tapprest, Gilles 03 25 27 38 61
Tapprest, Guy 03 25 27 41 28

MONTGENOST

Cocteaux, Michel 03 26 80 49 09
Copinet, Jacques 03 25 80 49 14
Thiebault, Hubert 03 26 80 47 26

MONTGUEUX

Beaugrand 03 25 79 85 11
Beliard-Lassaigne 03 25 74 83 04
Corniot, Jean 03 25 74 84 37
Corniot, Régis 03 25 79 05 22
Doué, Didier 03 25 79 44 33
Doué, Etienne 03 25 74 84 41
Guerinot, Jean 03 25 74 84 76
Henin, Francois 03 25 74 96 94
Lassaigne, Gérard 03 25 74 84 88
Lassaigne, Jacques 03 25 74 84 83
Lassaigne, Olivier 03 25 74 84 75
Lassaigne-Berlot 03 25 74 84 60

MONTHELON

Brest, Gill 03 26 59 73 21
Chopin, Julien 03 26 59 70 46
Coop. Monthelon 03 26 59 70 04
Dérouillat, Franquet 03 26 59 76 54
Franquet, Christian 03 26 59 70 44
Frezier, Denis 03 26 59 70 16
Guichon, Michel 03 26 59 70 56
Hazard, Robert 03 26 59 70 57
Marchand, A. 03 26 59 70 63
Marchand Rivierre, B. 03 26 59 70 55
Mont, Hauban du 03 26 59 70 27
Moussé, Claude 03 26 59 70 65
Muller, Guy 03 26 59 70 24
Pienne, Alain 03 26 59 70 54
Pienne, Michel 03 26 59 70 94
Pienne, Sylvain 03 26 59 76 31
Robert, Philippe 03 26 59 74 37

MONTIGNY-SOUS-CHÂTILLON

Billet-Quencez 03 26 58 36 23
Conart-Rioblanc 03 26 58 35 64
Lacroix 03 26 58 35 17
Pierlot 03 26 58 09 22
Plinguier, Potel 03 26 58 36 28

MOUSSY

Crété, Pertois 03 26 54 03 63
Crete, Roland 03 26 54 03 61
Michel, Guy 03 26 54 03 17
Michel, Jean 03 26 54 03 33
Michel, José 03 26 54 04 69
Michel, R. 03 26 54 05 52
Renaudin, R. 03 26 54 03 41
Thiercelin 03 26 54 02 69
Wirth 03 26 54 04 71

MUTIGNY

Humbert, Serge 03 26 52 31 02
Thibaut, Raymond 03 26 52 32 92

NEUVILLE-SUR-SEINE

Charasse, Lucette 03 25 38 21 40
Clérambault 03 25 38 38 60
Deline-Mannoury 03 25 38 21 80
Guyot, Bernard 03 25 38 20 69
Herard, Paul 03 25 38 20 14
Prié, Philippe 03 25 38 21 51

NOË-LES-MALLETS

Brison, Louise 03 25 29 66 62
Drouilly, Jean-Francois 03 25 29 75 32
Thevenin, Claude 03 25 29 61 84
Veuve Doussot 03 25 29 60 61

NOGENT-L'ABBESSE

Beaudouin, Roger 03 26 03 22 78
Fiévet, Ghislain 03 26 03 21 28
Fossé, Laurent 03 26 03 26 63
Huet, Christian 03 26 03 21 89
Maquin, Dominique 03 26 03 28 71
Mouchel, Guy 03 26 03 22 91
Remy, Christine 03 26 88 78 15
Warnet, Patrick 03 26 03 21 55

ŒUILLY

Lemarie, Philippe 03 26 58 30 82
Littière, Alain 03 26 58 01 32
Mortier, Gilles 03 26 58 08 48
Rasselet 03 26 58 30 26
Tarlant 03 26 58 30 60

OGER

Bonnet, F. 03 26 57 52 43
Bonville, A. 03 26 57 53 88
Bonville, Ed 03 26 57 53 19
Chapuy 03 26 57 51 30
Chinchilla 03 26 57 52 61
Coop. Les Côteaux Champ. 03 26 57 53 37
Coop.Les Grappes d'Or 03 26 57 55 79
Desautels-Roinard 03 26 57 53 75
Descotes-Lemaire 03 26 57 53 61
Dzieciuck, Bernard 03 26 57 50 49
Fierfort, G. 03 26 57 55 13
Milan, Jean 03 26 57 50 09
Vaugency, Henry de 03 26 57 50 89

OIRY

Lang-Biémont 03 26 55 43 43
Malard, Jean-Louis 03 26 55 20 59
Martin, Christophe 03 26 57 67 30

OLIZY

Bétouzet, Luc 03 26 58 10 38
Coop. Olizy 03 26 58 10 76
Leveau-Berat 03 26 58 10 31
Mimin, Gilbert 03 26 58 10 63
Rigaut, Jean 03 26 58 10 74
Vincent, Lucien 03 26 58 10 71

PARGNY-LES-REIMS

Cossy, Pascal 03 26 49 21 05
Jackowiak, Denis 03 26 49 20 25
Leguay-Truchon 03 26 49 78 46
Leloir, Gérard 03 26 49 21 38

PASSY GRIGNY

Caillot, Maurice 03 26 52 94 86
Caillot, Renée 03 26 52 90 27
Cez, Pascal 03 26 52 95 56

Cez, Robert 03 26 52 90 66
Coop. Passy Grigny 03 26 52 92 65
Houlle, Marc 03 26 52 90 04
Legendre, J.-C. 03 26 52 90 68
Lequart, Claude 03 26 52 90 29
Liébart, Christian 03 26 52 90 08
Pelletier, Jean-Jacques 03 26 52 90 36
Pelletier, Jean-Michel 03 26 52 65 86
Robion, Chantal 03 26 52 01 67
Robion, Jacky 03 26 52 92 88
Rocourt, Alain 03 26 52 92 15
Thevenet, Lucien 03 26 52 90 63
Thévenet-Delouvin, X. 03 26 52 91 64

PÉVY

Degenne-Squelart 03 26 48 23 52
Hautbois, Jean-Pol 03 26 48 20 98
Vaquette-Driguet 03 26 48 23 23

PIERRY

Bagnost & Fils 03 26 54 04 22
Billiard, G. 03 26 54 02 96
Bouché Père & Fils 03 26 54 12 44
Broggini, J. & D. 03 26 54 01 96
Canteneur 03 26 54 03 20
Coop. d'Astrée, Vincent 03 26 54 03 23
Gobillard, Paul 03 26 54 05 11
Lagache, Gilbert 03 26 54 03 12
Lenique, Michel 03 26 54 03 65
Mandois, H. 03 26 54 03 18
Michel, Guy 03 26 54 67 12
Michel, J.B. 03 26 55 10 54
Picart, Robert 03 26 54 57 87
Pothelet, Paul 03 26 54 02 88
Séléque, Richard 03 26 54 02 55
Vollereaux 03 26 54 03 05

POLISY

Brosolette, Francois 03 25 38 57 17
Moutard, René 03 25 38 52 37

PORT À BINSON

Cordoin-Didierlaurent 03 26 58 09 24
Harlin 03 26 58 34 38
Lecart, René 03 26 58 30 08
Rigot, Gilles 03 26 58 03 45
Sombert-Lecart 03 26 58 38 22

POUILLON

Bourdaire-Massonnot, D. 03 26 03 17 92
Cuillier-Blin, Patrick 03 26 03 18 74
Debrosse, Dominique 03 26 03 00 83
Doury, Philippe 03 26 03 12 49
Massonnot, Philippe 03 26 03 12 15
Milet-Govin, Eric 03 26 03 18 26
Simon, Georges 03 26 03 16 29

POURCY

Meunier-Benoit 03 26 59 43 53

PROUILLY

Couvreur, Alain 03 26 48 58 95
Fauvet-Courleux 03 26 48 24 78
Malingre, Pierre 03 26 48 55 74
Malingre-Truchon 03 26 48 58 85
Waquelin-Fauvet, André 03 26 48 58 38

REIMS

Abelé 03 26 87 79 80

Balahu de Noiron 03 26 54 45 53
Billiard 03 26 77 50 10
Bonnet, Ferdinand 03 26 84 44 15
Bur, Paul 03 26 07 34 10
Chanoine 03 26 36 61 60
Chaudron 03 26 66 44 88
Goulet, George 03 26 66 44 88
Heidsieck, Charles 03 26 84 43 50
Henriot 03 26 89 53 00
Irroy 03 26 88 37 27
Jacquart 03 26 07 88 40
Krug 03 26 84 44 20
Lanson 03 26 78 50 50
Marie-Stuart 03 26 47 92 26
Massé 03 26 47 61 31
Médot 03 26 47 46 15
Montaudon 03 26 47 53 30
Mumm 03 26 49 59 69
Paillard, Bruno 03 26 36 20 22
Paillard, Rémy 03 26 40 07 06
Palmer 03 26 07 35 07
Piper-Heidsieck 03 26 84 43 00
Pommery 03 26 61 62 63
Roederer, Louis 03 26 40 42 11
Ruinart 03 26 77 51 51
Taittinger 03 26 85 45 35
Thiénot 03 26 47 41 25
Veuve Clicquot 03 26 89 54 40

REUIL

Alliot, Vincent 03 26 58 01 02
Biliard, Arnaud 03 26 58 66 60
Bondon-Mouton 03 26 58 38 87
Braux, Frédérick 03 26 58 32 47
Clément, Gérard 03 26 58 05 71
Clément, James 03 26 58 00 08
Collard, Michel 03 26 58 32 29
Dourdon-Viellard 03 26 58 06 38
Kremer, Jacques 03 26 58 67 00
Lagache, Jean 03 26 58 32 07
Leveau, Gérard 03 26 58 01 80
Léveque-Poudras 03 26 58 32 02
Marquette, Jacques 03 26 58 37 68
Nanet-Garitan 03 26 58 00 79
Pernet, John 03 26 51 09 00
Pessenet, Daniel 03 26 58 04 76
Pessenet, Jean-Jacques 03 26 58 03 43
Pessenet-Hegenberger 03 26 58 38 87
Poudras, Michel 03 26 58 01 71
Vollereaux, Christian 03 26 57 68 50

RILLY-LA-MONTAGNE

Adam, Daniel 03 26 03 40 77
Allemandou, Claude 03 26 03 40 40
Beurton, J.-M. 03 26 03 46 27
Binet 03 26 03 49 18
Bouxin, Michel 03 26 03 40 35
Chauveet, Marc 03 26 03 42 71
Chauvet, Henri 03 26 03 42 54
Chauvet, Robert 03 26 03 44 14
Couvreur, Jaques 03 26 03 40 05
Couvreur, Yves 03 26 03 47 04
Couvreur-Deglaire 03 26 03 44 54
Couvreur-Fondeur 03 26 03 41 14
Delaunois, André 03 26 03 42 87
Delaunois, Daniel 03 26 03 48 85
Delaunois, Pere & Fils 03 26 03 40 53
Didier, Herbert 03 26 03 41 53
Dumont, Daniel 03 26 03 40 67

Fagot, Francois 03 26 03 42 56
Fagot, Joseph 03 26 03 40 60
Fagot, Michel 03 26 03 40 03
Garnotel, Adam 03 26 03 40 22
Germain, H. 03 26 03 49 18
Guiardel, Louis 03 26 03 42 55
Jeangout-Fagot 03 26 03 40 63
Lacour 03 26 03 45 13
Lemoine 03 26 03 40 25
Lepitre, Veuve Maurice 03 26 03 40 27
Manceaux, Maurice 03 26 03 42 57
Manceaux, Roger 03 26 03 42 57
Martial-Couvreur, Ch. 03 26 03 48 07
Morizet, Tièche 03 26 03 43 19
Pacque, Claude 03 26 03 41 62
Paques & Fils 03 26 03 42 53
Paulet, Hubert 03 26 03 40 68
Philbert Père & Fils 03 26 03 42 58
Pouillon-Chayoux 03 26 03 47 46
Regnault, Jean 03 26 03 40 18
Vilmart 03 26 03 40 01
Vilmart, Franck 03 26 03 41 57

ROMERY
Charpentier, Pierre 03 26 58 46 70
Sacret 03 26 57 04 07
Tribaut 03 26 58 64 21

ROUVRES-LES-VIGNES
Chrétien, Jean-Guy 03 25 92 03 17
Falmet, Marcel 03 25 92 00 99
Legout, Philippe 03 25 92 04 69

SACY
Chemin, Jean-Luc 03 26 49 22 42
Coop. de Sacy 03 26 49 22 90
Degenne, Damien 03 26 49 75 92
Degesne-Ronseaux 03 26 49 22 33
Goulin-Roualet 03 26 49 22 77
Grill, J.-C. 03 26 49 23 04
Hervieux-Dumez 03 26 49 23 86
Mimin-Prévost 03 26 49 78 65
Mobillion 03 26 49 27 01
Perseval-Dumez 03 26 49 22 79
Ponsart-Brochet 03 26 49 75 85
Poret, Jany 03 26 49 22 45
Prévost-Hannoteaux 03 26 49 78 65
Rigaut-Poret 03 26 49 22 22
Robert, Denis 03 26 49 22 65
Valentin, J.-L. 03 26 49 22 51
Wafflart, J. 03 26 49 22 32
Wafflart-Briet 03 26 49 22 41

SAINT-EUPHRAISE
Chemin, Roger 03 26 49 27 08
Chemin-Marchal 03 26 49 20 99
Delong, Guy 03 26 49 20 86
Lallement, Yves 03 26 49 21 08
Marly, Yves 03 26 49 20 91
Moreau-Couillet 03 26 49 21 69

SAINT-MARTIN-D'ABLOIS
Cez, Jean 03 26 59 93 54
Coop. St-Martin-d'Ablois 03 26 59 34 39
Desmoulins 03 26 59 93 10
Didier-Ducos 03 26 59 93 94
Didier-Niceron 03 26 59 90 25
Huot, L. 03 26 59 92 81
Jamart 03 26 59 92 78

Joffre-Desmoulins 03 26 59 99 11
Lalouelle, Jean-Pierre 03 26 59 92 20
Ouy, Champillon 03 26 59 93 77
Rigolot, Lucien 03 26 59 95 52
de Villepin 03 26 59 92 74

SARCY
Ballassi-Descotes 03 26 61 86 75
Bouchet-Mézières 03 26 61 86 33
Camus-Laluc 03 26 61 86 09
Couvreur, Gérard 03 26 61 86 49
Jobart, Abeel 03 26 61 86 63

SAULCHERY
Figuet, Bernard 03 23 70 16 32

SAULCY
Geoffroy, James 03 25 27 09 98
Huguenin, Richard 03 25 27 21 10
Parisot, Claude 03 25 27 12 04

SEPT-SAULX
Lefévre-Chauffert 03 26 03 90 27

SERMIERS
Coop. Sermiers 03 26 97 62 09
Lacuisse Frères 03 26 97 64 97
Rat-Winkler, Jean 03 26 97 62 94
Thuillier, Robert 03 26 97 62 20

SERZY-ET-PRIN
Bailly, Alain 03 26 97 41 58
Delozanne, Chemin 03 26 97 43 77
Delozanne, Yves 03 26 97 40 18
Delozanne-Gaudin, M. 03 26 97 42 51
Housset, Bernard 03 26 97 45 53
Jumeau Delozanne 03 26 97 46 61
Rogier 03 26 97 42 84

SÉZANNE
Debruyne-Leherle 03 26 42 03 66
Dugay, Maurice 03 26 80 60 73
Pinard, Pierre 03 26 80 58 81

SILLERY
Fresnet-Baudot 03 26 49 11 74
Langlais-Decotte 03 26 49 41 64
Secondé, Francois 03 26 49 16 67

TAISSY
Barthelemy 03 26 05 02 43
Brochet, Oliver 03 26 05 78 67
Gondé-Rousseaux 03 26 82 22 41

TAUXIÈRES
Clément, Nicolas 03 26 57 83 13
Cochut 03 26 57 03 25
Coop. de Louvois & Tauxières
03 26 57 03 22
Lhopital-Yannick 03 26 57 04 56
Louvet, Yves 03 26 57 03 27
Mahé, F. 03 26 57 03 76
Richard, J.J. 03 26 57 83 07

TORVILLIERS
Jaillant-Badelet 03 25 79 16 97

TOURS-SUR-MARNE
Charles-Lafitte 03 26 59 50 50

Charlin, C. 03 26 51 88 95
Chauvet 03 26 58 92 37
Delporte, Yves 03 26 58 91 26
Faucheron-Gavroy 03 26 52 10 08
Glorieux 03 26 58 91 45
Lahaye, Joël 03 26 58 96 70
Lamiable 03 26 58 92 69
Laurent-Perrier 03 26 58 91 22
Rousseau-Lefevre 03 26 58 95 30

TRÉPAIL
Beaufort, Claude 03 26 57 05 63
Carré, Claude 03 26 57 06 04
Carré, Guébels 03 26 57 05 02
Carré-Herbin 03 26 57 05 74
Coop. Trépail 03 26 57 05 12
Dupont, J.-C. 03 26 57 05 59
Fredestel 03 26 57 06 19
Gabriel, Pierre 03 26 57 05 46
Guébels, Gilbert 03 26 57 05 58
Guébels, Guy 03 26 57 05 65
Maiziières, Georges 03 26 57 05 04
Mercier-Offret 03 26 57 82 06
Petiau, Gilbert 03 26 57 05 48

TRESLON
Bergeronneau, Frank 03 26 97 43 12
Lagille, Bernard 03 26 97 43 99

TRIGNY
Blin, Joannesse 03 26 03 18 82
Blin, R. 03 26 03 10 97
Forest, A. 03 26 03 14 33
Goulard Gérard, J.-L. 03 26 03 18 78
Guillemart, Michel 03 26 03 01 69
Malot, J.C. 03 26 03 11 81
Rogé, Jean-Claude 03 26 03 16 39

TROIS-PUITS
Baillette, Jean 03 26 82 37 14
Baillette, Pierre 03 26 82 09 41
Larnaudie-Gadret 03 26 82 37 50
Larnaudie-Hirault 03 26 85 47 14

TROISSY
Bracquemart-Patrel 03 26 52 70 55
Charpentier, André 03 26 52 70 68
Charpentier, Didier 03 26 52 74 05
Charpentier, Yvan 03 26 52 74 71
Coop. Troissy 03 26 52 70 14
Jacquesson, Gilbert 03 26 52 70 69
Jobert, Bernard 03 26 52 70 52
Leconte, Agnus 03 26 52 70 24
Lourdeaux, Jean-Louis 03 26 52 72 36
Masse-Liébart 03 26 52 70 17
Mathelin, Didier 03 26 52 71 66
Mathelin, Hervé 03 26 52 70 25
Moreau, Yves 03 26 52 70 35
Moreaux, Patrick 03 26 52 70 16
Orban, Charles 03 26 52 70 05
Vieillard, Raymond 03 26 52 70 90
Visse 03 26 52 70 08

UNCHAIR
Chalmet 03 26 48 20 35
Chereau-Lamblot 03 26 48 52 14
Potié-Lamblot 03 26 48 52 55

URVILLE
Billette, Daniel 03 25 27 40 09
Coop. d'Urville 03 25 26 40 14
Drappier 03 25 27 40 15
Labbé, Bernadette 03 25 27 46 80
Perrin, Daniel 03 25 27 40 36

VANDEUIL
Fournaise-Dubois 03 26 48 28 95
Morel, Yves 03 26 48 52 39

VANDIÈRES
Ardinat, José 03 26 58 36 07
Coop. Vinicole l'Union 03 26 58 68 68
Delabarre 03 26 58 02 65
Delouvin, Bertrand 03 26 58 07 96
Delouvin, Gérard 03 26 58 04 17
Delouvin-Bagnost 03 26 58 03 91
Faust, Serge 03 26 58 02 12
Leriche-Tournant 03 26 58 01 19
Liébart, André 03 26 58 06 66
Nowack, Bertrand 03 26 58 02 69
Plekhoff, André 03 26 58 07 81
Salomon, Denis 03 26 58 05 77
Tournant-Salomon 03 26 58 02 53

VAUDEMANGE
Beaufort, William 03 26 67 97 12
Bourgeois, Alain 03 26 52 16 94
Charpentier, Paul 03 26 52 23 57
Coop. Vaudemange 03 26 69 10 98
Coop. Vaudemanges 03 26 67 98 84
Francart, Philippe 03 26 67 99 06
Hautem, Philippe 03 26 67 97 03
Lapie, Didier 03 26 67 95 20
Machet, Pascal 03 26 67 96 10
Moncuit-Valentin 03 26 67 96 03
Moreaux, Guy 03 26 52 25 84
Perrot, Pascal 03 26 52 12 96
Rochet-Bocart, Jacques 03 26 67 99 15

VENTEUIL
Autréau-Lasnot 03 26 58 49 35
Boulard Mignon 03 26 58 60 79
Boyer-Rouillère 03 26 58 60 31
Coop. de Venteuil 03 26 58 48 46
Coutelas-Rahir 03 26 58 48 60
Degardin-Bouché 03 26 58 60 37
Déhu-Lechevalier 03 26 58 48 19
Demay-Déhu 03 26 58 49 21
Drot, Francois 03 26 58 48 69
Dubois, Claude 03 26 58 48 37
Grumier, Andry 03 26 58 49 33
Grumier, Maurice 03 26 58 48 10
Guerre, Michel 03 26 58 62 72
Hennequin 03 26 58 60 46
Launay, J.-F. 03 26 58 48 54
Liébart & Fils 03 26 58 48 09
Marniquet, J.-P. 03 26 58 48 99
Marx-Barbier 03 26 58 48 39
Marx-Coutelas 03 26 58 63 64
Mignon, Gérard 03 26 58 49 57
Mignon, Thierry 03 26 58 61 62
Mignon Père & Fils 03 26 58 48 90
Moutte, L. & J.B. 03 26 58 49 06
Petit Mignon, James 03 26 58 49 58
Potel-Prieux 03 26 58 48 59
Prévoteau, Gérard 03 26 58 49 09

VERNEUIL

Bouby-Legouge 03 26 52 90 11
Coop. Verneuil 03 26 52 93 17
Copin 03 26 52 92 47
Godard, Laurent 03 26 52 93 76
Legouge-Copin 03 26 52 96 89
Léveque, Paul 03 26 52 93 90
Léveque-Boulard 03 26 58 08 60
Lheureux 03 26 52 91 27
Piot, J.-F. 03 26 52 94 52

VERT-TOULON

Francois-Charlot, Louis 03 26 52 21 61
Lefevre, Jean-Claude 03 26 52 15 17
Leherle, Raymond 03 26 52 26 94
Mathieu, Claude 03 26 52 02 08
Prat, Alain 03 26 52 12 16
Ravillion, Henri 03 26 52 10 95

VERTUS

Bonnet 03 26 52 22 46
Bouché, René 03 26 52 23 95
Boulonnais, J.-P. 03 26 52 23 41
Burgeois-Boulonnais 03 26 52 26 73
Colin 03 26 58 86 32
Coop. Henri Augustin 03 26 52 13 41
Coop. de Vertus 03 26 52 14 53
Coop. La Vigneronne 03 26 52 20 31
Doquet, Jean-Claude 03 26 52 14 68
Doublet-Hadot 03 26 52 26 96
Douquet-Jeanmaire 03 26 52 16 50
Doyard, Robert 03 26 52 14 74
Doyard-Mahé 03 26 52 23 85
Duval-Leroy 03 26 52 10 75
Faucheret, Guy 03 26 52 18 13
Férat, Pascal 03 26 52 25 22
Férat, Pierre 03 26 52 15 30
Fourny, Veuve 03 26 52 16 30
Geoffroy 03 26 52 28 69
Goerg, Paul 03 26 52 15 31
Gonet, Philippe 03 26 59 44 50
Guyot, Pierre 03 26 52 10 79
Jacopin, Guy 03 26 52 20 30
Larmandier, Guy 03 26 52 12 41
Larmandier-Bernier 03 26 52 13 24
Napoleon (A. Prieur) 03 26 52 11 74
Pernet & Pernet 03 26 52 22 57
Person, T.D. 03 26 59 98 23
Pesnel-Haumont 03 26 52 13 15
Pougeoise, Charles 03 26 52 26 63
Pougeoise, Georges 03 26 52 26 85
Pougeoise-Kint, Patrick 03 26 52 27 83
Rouge, Michel 03 26 52 15 68
Rutat, René 03 26 52 14 79
Severin-Doublet 03 26 52 10 57
Thomas, Frédéric 03 26 52 12 85
Viard-Rogué 03 26 52 16 76
Weynand 03 26 52 25 74

VERZENAY

Arnould, Michel 03 26 49 40 06
Arnould-Ralle 03 26 49 40 12
Bernard, André 03 26 49 40 28
Bovière, Denis 03 26 49 43 40
Bovière-Perinet 03 26 49 80 96
Busin, Christian 03 26 49 40 94
Busin-Beaufort, Jacques 03 26 49 40 36

Cappelle-Charpentier 03 26 49 81 01
Carlini, Jean-Yves de 03 26 49 43 91
Chardonnet-Decotte, P. 03 26 49 44 84
Coop. de Verzenay 03 26 49 40 26
Desautez 03 26 49 40 59
Floquet-Gelot 03 26 49 42 92
Foureur 03 26 49 45 20
Francinet 03 26 49 40 86
Godmé, Hugues 03 26 49 48 70
Godmé Père & Fils 03 26 49 41 88
Hatté, Bernard 03 26 49 40 90
Hatté, Ludvic 03 26 49 43 94
Henriet, Marc 03 26 49 41 79
Henriet, Michel 03 26 49 40 42
Hevry-Quenardel 03 26 49 44 52
Janisson, Manuel 03 26 49 40 19
Lallement 03 26 49 43 52
Landragin 03 26 49 48 01
Lefèvre, Henri 03 26 49 40 18
Morel, Jean-Paul 03 26 49 48 01
Mouzon, Jean-Claude 03 26 49 48 11
Namur, J.-M. 03 26 49 40 56
Penet, J.-M. 03 26 49 40 71
Périnet, Pierre 03 26 49 40 68
Pithois, Michel 03 26 49 41 77
Quenardel 03 26 49 40 63
Rousseaux, G. 03 26 49 40 78
Rousseaux, Vincent 03 26 49 43 66
Rousseaux-Batteux, Denis 03 26 49 81 81
Rousseaux-Fresnet, J.-B. 03 26 49 45 66
Rousseaux-Pecourt 03 26 49 42 73
Thibaut, Guy 03 26 08 41 30
Vignon, Michel 03 26 49 80 39

VERZY

Burlot-Nahé 03 26 97 91 71
Coop. de Verzy 03 26 97 98 04
Cuperly 03 26 70 23 90
Deville, J.-P. 03 26 97 93 50
Deville, Pierre 03 26 97 91 75
Faucheron, J.-M. 03 26 97 96 53
Fresnet-Juillet 03 26 97 93 40
Hanotin, J. 03 26 97 93 63
Hurier, Alain 03 26 97 93 60
Hurier-Jouette 03 26 97 90 87
Lallement, Alain 03 26 97 92 32
Lallement, Juillet 03 26 97 91 09
Lallement, Pierre 03 26 97 91 09
Lallement-Deville 03 26 97 95 90
Lardennois 03 26 97 91 23
Lefèvre, Etienne 03 26 97 96 99
Lepreux, J.-P. 03 26 97 95 52
Mouzon-Leroux 03 26 97 96 68
Penet-Chardonnet 03 26 97 94 73
Renoir-Bouy 03 26 97 90 55
Roze, Jean 03 26 97 90 90
Sabatier-Loquard, Viguie 03 26 97 98 07
Sacy, Louis de 03 26 97 91 13
Thill, Fernand 03 26 97 92 29

VILLEDOMMANGE

Bardoux 03 26 49 25 35
Bergeroneaux 03 26 49 24 18
Bergeronneau-Marion, F. 03 26 49 75 26
Camus, Daniel 03 26 49 25 29
Chardonnet, René 03 26 49 25 21
Charlier, Jaques 03 26 49 25 19

Charlier, Laurent 03 26 49 26 47
Cl. de la Chapelle 03 26 49 25 33
Coop. V.D.C. 03 26 49 26 76
Coop. Villedommange 03 26 49 75 10
Devilliers, Pascal 03 26 49 26 08
Ducret, Fresne 03 26 49 24 60
Froux, Guy 03 26 49 25 14
Jacquinet, Olivier 03 26 49 21 04
Leboeuf 03 26 49 24 39
Poret, Denis 03 26 49 25 23
Serurrier, J.-M. 03 26 49 24 10
Veuve Bardoux 03 26 49 24 05
Villart, Henry 03 26 49 25 03

VILLERS-ALLERAND

Prévot, Claude 03 26 97 66 85
Prévot, René 03 26 97 61 16
Stroebel Frères 03 26 97 60 12
Stroebel, Marcel 03 26 97 60 40

VILLERS-MARMERY

Adnet, Pascal 03 26 97 93 46
Boutillez, Gérard 03 26 97 95 87
Boutillez-Guer 03 26 97 91 38
Brassart, Emelie 03 26 97 90 23
Coop. de Villers-Marmery 03 26 97 91 51
Delabarre, Alain 03 26 97 92 96
Henriet-Bazin 03 26 97 96 81
Lejeune 03 26 97 93 98
Loncle 03 26 97 91 73
Lustig, Roger 03 26 97 91 03
Malot, Sadi 03 26 97 90 48
Margaine 03 26 97 92 13
Remy, Jean 03 26 97 94 32
Simonet, Jackie 03 26 97 92 41
Urbany-Cheminon 03 26 97 93 41

VILLERS-SOUS-CHÂTILLON

Allait, Claude 03 26 58 33 29
Boutillier-Bauchet, René 03 26 58 02 37
Charpentier, J. 03 26 58 05 78
Château de Villers 03 26 58 33 01
Chevalier-Girot, Jackie 03 26 58 06 46
Chopin, Ouy 03 26 58 05 24
Clouet, Bérnard 03 26 58 01 13
Collard-Chardelle 03 26 58 00 50
Coop. Villers-sous-Châtillon
 03 26 58 33 26
Coutelas, David 03 26 59 07 57
Coutelas, Hubert 03 26 58 06 57
Guérin, José 03 26 58 00 76
Guérin, Luc 03 26 58 36 27
Hubert Père & Fils 03 26 58 33 11
Lemarie-Tournant 03 26 58 36 79
Loriot, Eric 03 26 58 36 26
Loriot, Roger 03 26 58 33 42
Loriot, Xavier 03 26 58 08 28
Marle, Alain 03 26 58 07 03
Ohl-Thevenet, J.-L. 03 26 52 19 33
Robert-Allait 03 26 58 37 23
Rosseau, Bernard 03 26 58 33 20
Trujillo-Poittevin 03 26 58 36 70

VILLE-SUR-ARCE

Barbe, Régis 03 25 38 78 47
Coessens, Alain 03 25 38 77 07

Coop. Chassenay d'Arce 03 25 38 30 10
Feries, Jean-Marie 03 25 38 74 13
Féviés, J-N. 03 25 38 76 49
Fèvre 03 25 38 76 63
Massin, Dominique 03 25 38 74 97
Massin, Rémy & Fils 03 25 38 74 09
Massin, Thierry 03 25 38 74 01
Massin, Yvon 03 25 38 75 20
Penot, Claude 03 25 38 76 46
Thévenin, Philippe 03 25 38 78 04
Thévenin, Raymond 03 25 38 75 21

VILLEVENARD

Barnier, David 03 26 52 82 84
Barnier, Roger 03 26 52 82 77
Coop. Villevenard 03 26 52 81 66
Michel, André 03 26 58 97 22
Niquet-Michault, Jacky 03 26 52 82 34
Piètrement-Renard 03 26 52 83 03
Rihn, Jacky 03 26 52 82 62
Thomas, Jean-Pierre 03 26 52 82 56

VILLIERS-AUX-NOEUDS

Germain-Brochet 03 26 36 32 66
Leroy 03 26 36 27 68

VINAY

Arrois, René 03 26 59 90 12
Closquinet, Roger 03 26 59 90 73
Coop. P. Decarrier 03 26 59 90 09
Filaine, Eric 03 26 59 90 13
Franquet, Hervé 03 26 59 90 74
Guinard, Jean 03 26 59 91 29
Lecomte Père & Fils 03 26 59 90 79
Lorrette 03 26 59 08 53
Mignon, Pierre 03 26 59 90 58
Thomas, Christophe 03 26 59 96 20

VINCELLES

Beaufrère, Jean-Francois 03 26 58 23 94
Blin, H. 03 26 58 20 04
Durdon, Jacki 03 26 58 24 26
Hu, Christian 03 26 58 85 16
Sévilland, Nicholas 03 26 58 23 88

VINDEY

Depoivre, Bernard 03 26 80 56 34
Depoivre, Michel 03 26 80 50 20
Depoivre, Yves 03 26 80 67 72
Doyard, Bernard 03 26 80 67 49
Gonet, Michel 03 26 80 50 03

VITRY-EN-PERTHOIS

Chevalier, Dominique 03 26 73 76 90
Gérardin, Hugues 03 26 74 62 05
Munier-Chevalier 03 26 74 62 45

VIVIERS-SUR-ARTAUT

Arnaud, Nicolas 03 25 38 51 09

GLOSSARY

Alcohol: in this context, the ethyl alcohol produced during fermentation.

Aldehyde: chemical produced during oxidation of the alcohol in wine that has a significant effect on the wine's bouquet.

AOC: *Appellation d'Origine Contrôlée*, an official guarantee of the origin and quality of French wine.

Ash, black: a dark, energy-rich soil used as fertilizer in the region.

Autolysis: the process by which yeast cells are broken down by enzymes. For Champagne, this is a crucial biochemical reaction that produces the wine's distinctive bouquet.

Balance: the relationship of various components in a wine to one another. A good wine is well balanced.

Barrique: large wooden barrel or cask.

Batonnage: the process of stirring the wine during *élévage* (the maturing of wine after fermentation and before bottling) to keep the sediment in suspension, increasing aromatic quality and roundness.

Batch: a large quantity of unbottled wine that can be either a blend or an unblended first pressing.

Blanc de Blancs: a white wine made from white grapes.

Blanc de Noirs: a white wine made from dark grapes.

Body: major characteristic of wine with a high alcoholic content and significant depth.

Cava: a sparkling Spanish wine.

Chalk, Belemni *(Quadrata Belemnita):* a soil particularly suited for the production of champagne.

Chaptalization: the addition of sugar to grape juice before fermentation in order to enhance the alcohol content.

Chef de cave: the cellar master, whose profession requires a masterly knowledge of the composition of blends and successful vintages, is responsible for deciding how long to let the champagne age.

Clamp: the wire fastener holding a champagne cork in place.

Clarification: a process during which certain particles are separated from the wine. This is done using a filter or by adding a substance that will carry the particles to the bottom of the fermentation vat.

Cleansing: clarification of the grape juice.

Cliffs: geographical characteristic of the Champagne region.

Clone: a plant derived asexually from a single parent plant and replicating its genetic make-up exactly.

Clos: an enclosed vineyard.

Comité Interprofessionnel du Vin de Champagne **(C.I.V.C.):** the Champagne trade association.

Cru: geographical origin of the grapes.

Cuvée: (a) grape juice that is unfermented or in the process of fermenting; (b) the blend of wines in a given champagne.

Cut, second: a third pressing, now prohibited.

Dealer-producer: firm producing and marketing Champagne.

Demi-muid: a wooden cask containing 600 liters.

Denominazione di Origine Controllata e Garantita **(D.O.C.G.):** Italian guaranteed-quality label carried by the best local wines.

Disgorging: procedure used to expel sediment deposits from bottle necks by plunging the top of the bottle into a brine bath of –68°F (–20°C) and then popping off the temporary stopper to remove the frozen deposits. Labels stamped with RD show that a bottle has been *récemment dégorgé* (recently disgorged).

Dosage: Sugar added to a sparkling wine after it has been disgorged.

Effervescence: bubbles and froth formed by wines containing carbonic acid.

Enology: the study of wine.

Épinette: a type of pruning shears used to harvest grapes.

Ester: a fragrant, mellow substance generated during the fermentation and aging of wine.

Extraction: elimination of sediment.

Fermentation, malolactic: process of fermentation which converts pure malic acid into lactic acid.

Filtration: elimination of fermentation and other particles prior to bottling.

Foudre: a large oak cask.

Foule, en: an old method of tying grape vines to a stake or support.

Grand Cru: the highest classification, applied to only 17 out of 324 villages in the region; a *grand cru* village ranks 100% on the scale of vintages.

Grower-producers (G.-P.): growers marketing their own champagne.

Jeroboam: a bottle holding the equivalent of four standard-sized bottles. Also called double magnum. Contains three liters.

Length: taste remaining in the mouth after wine has been swallowed, or tasted and then discarded. A great wine will always have significant, long-lasting length.

Liqueur, extender: yeast-and-sugar added to wine prior to the second fermentation in the bottle.

Liqueur, sweetener: sugar additive.

Maceration: process of steeping during which the grape must extracts the pigment of the tannin from grape skins.

Maderized: characteristic of wine that has aged for too long, resulting in a dark reddish color and a bouquet of sherry, overripe apples, raisins, and plum.

Marque Auxiliaire **(M.A.):** Subsidiary designation, house-brand of wholesale wine-dealer.

Mines, chalk: Gallo-Roman chalk mines used as cellars in the Champagne region.

Mono-*cru:* wine originating in only one village.

Must: grape juice that is unfermented or in the process of fermenting

Négoce: (wine) dealership

Premier *cru:* villages ranked immediately below *grand cru*, 90% to 99% on the scale of vintages. Grapes grown in these 41 villages are generally considered as occupying second place in terms of quality.

Production-cooperatives: cooperatives producing Champagne under their own label.

Racking: the process of clarifying the wine before rebottling it (also known as riddling).

Racks: large wooden shelves on which bottles of Champagne are placed during the racking process, during which they are tipped periodically in order to work sediment deposits toward the cork.

Reserve wines: aged wines used to give undated Champagnes a more mature taste.

Residue: all components remaining in wine after the evaporation of water and alcohol.

Slats, on: bottles laid horizontally on slats during cellar-aging.

Spheres, turning: a method developed by Moët & Chandon to simplify the turning of Champagne bottles using yeast kneaded into spherical shapes and covered with seaweed.

S.R.: sediment (recently) removed.

Stopper, Champagne: specially designed stoppers commonly used when storing opened Champagne bottles for future use. Available models are adapted for various types of Champagne: Brut Absolu, Brut Intégral, Brut Non Dosé, Brut Zéro, unsweetened.

Streak (*also* **teardrop):** traces of liquid adhering to the sides of the glass and indicating a high glycerol, sugar, or alcohol content.

Sulfiting: treating the wine with sulfite in order to protect it from oxidation, or to arrest fermentation.

Tasting, blind: comparison of wines by tasters who have not been told which wine each glass contains.

Tasting, semi-blind: comparison of wines by tasters who have been told which wines are involved, but do not know the order in which they will be presented.

Terroir: the multifaceted growing environment of a particular vineyard, including the soil composition, microclimate, altitude, and local weather.

Turner: person responsible for "turning," as described below.

Turning: shifting the position of bottles at various stages in the champagne-production process in order to collect the sediment at one end prior to removal.

Upending: stage in the production of Champagne during which the bottles are stored vertically, neck downwards, in order to collect sediment at the cork end prior to removal.

Umami: Japanese word meaning subtle and fragrant, considered by some experts to constitute a fifth basic-bouquet category.

Vinification: the process during which the vintner converts grapes into wine.

Vitis vinifera: the genus of grape suitable for wine-making.

ACKNOWLEDGMENTS

Richard Juhlin extends his warmest thanks to the many people who have lent their help and support to his passion for Champagne. The list would be too long if everyone were to be named. Nevertheless, he particularly wishes to thank his family for being so understanding, especially Sara, and his father Erik Juhlin, who has constantly and unconditionally provided his help.

A big thank you to Flammarion, Lennart, and Bodil who, in their different ways, have contributed to the final version of this book, to both the illustrations and the text.

Thanks equally to Pål Allan, the international photographer, and to all the members of the Champagne Club and the T.J.C.C.

In addition, Richard Juhlin wishes to thank Les Champagnes de Vigneron and all the Champagne producers. Without their support and interest, Richard would never have dared embark on this colossal project.

The editors wish to thank Loréa Albistur, Felicity Bodenstein, Diane Gaudin, and Jean Tiffon for their help in the making of this book.

They also thank Bodil Tammisto, Christophe Luciani, and Caroline Parisot for their valuable assistance and their availability.

THE CHAMPAGNE CLUB

If you wish to read more and discover all the tasting notes—even those for wines with less than 80 points—and if you would like to receive updates about the way in which these wines are aging, you can become a member of Richard Juhlin's Champagne Club. You can meet other people who share your passion and you can participate in various Champagne-related activities.

The website address is www.champagneclub.com

Samples can be sent to:

Richard Juhlin
Stenbitsvägen 12
181 30 Lidingö
Sweden

Translated from the Swedish and French by Ingrid Booz Morejohn, Josephine Bacon, and David Radzinowicz

Copyediting: Penny Isaac

Typesetting: Claude-Olivier Four

Proofreading: Penny Isaac and Slade Smith

Color separation: Penez Éditions, Lille

Distributed in North America by Rizzoli International Publications, Inc.

Simultaneously published in French as *4000 Champagnes*
© Éditions Flammarion, 2004
English-language edition
© Éditions Flammarion, 2004

All photographs reproduced in this book are by Pål Allan with the exception of page 30 © Veuve Clicquot.

Maps © Stig Söderlind, Stockholm

05 06 4 3 2

FC0470-05-XI
ISBN-13: 9782080304704
ISBN-10: 2-0803-0470-4
Dépôt légal: 11/2004

Printed in Italy by Errestampa